CIVIL PROCEEDINGS

THE SUPREME COURT

The Queen's Anniversary Prizes for Higher and Further Education recognise the contribution of universities and colleges to the social, economic, cultural and intellectual life of the nation.

In 1994, the inaugural year of the competition, The Queen's University of Belfast was awarded a prize for the work of Servicing the Legal System.

The prize citation for SLS reads:

> *"This is an outstanding service to overcome the special problems of distributing knowledge about new law inside a small jurisdiction. It is an international exemplar."*

The Servicing The Legal System Programme

This programme was inaugurated in August 1980 in the Faculty of Law at Queen's University, Belfast to promote the publication of commentaries on various aspects of the law and legal system of Northern Ireland. Generous financial and other support for the programme has been provided by the Northern Ireland Court Service, the Inn of Court of Northern Ireland, the Bar Council of Northern Ireland, the Law Society of Northern Ireland and Queen's University. Details of other SLS publications may be obtained from the SLS Office, School of Law, The Queen's University of Belfast, Belfast BT7 1NN.

Civil Proceedings
The Supreme Court

B.J.A.C.Valentine, LL.B.
of the Inn of Court, Northern Ireland
Barrister-at-Law

SLS Legal Publications (NI)
1997

First published 1997 by SLS Legal Publications (NI), School of Law, Queen's University, Belfast BT7 1NN.

ISBN 0 85389 707 7

Typeset by SLS Legal Publications (NI)
Printed by MPG Books Ltd, Bodmin, Cornwall

DEDICATION

To Grace Valentine born 9 March 1995

Books by the same author

County Court Procedure in Northern Ireland (SLS 1985) with consultant editor T.F.Glass

Criminal Procedure in Northern Ireland (SLS 1989) with consultant editor A.R.Hart

'PACE' Supplement to Criminal Procedure in Northern Ireland (SLS 1990)

Booklet of Criminal Offences in Northern Ireland (1988, 1992, 1997)

Cricket's Dawn that Died: The Australians in England 1938 (1991)

PREFACE

The genesis of this book was to some extent fortuitous. I intended at first to write a second edition of *County Court Procedure in Northern Ireland* but postponed commencement of work on it because there was expected to be a thorough revision of the County Court Rules. As time passed and that revision seemed still to be distant, I commenced work on a book on High Court procedure. This work snowballed and it is now intended to be the major treatise on the principles of civil procedure and evidence. I now envisage that the second edition of the County Court work will be a much smaller companion, which will be published after the revision of the County Court Rules has been properly completed.

The object of this book is to expound the civil procedure and laws of civil evidence in the Supreme Court in Northern Ireland, with particular reference to the ordinary writ action in the Queen's Bench and Chancery Divisions. It includes special sections on the law and practice of judicial review and *habeas corpus*, and it deals fully with appeals to the Court of Appeal. The laws of evidence in civil proceedings are dealt with fully. There is full discussion on the law of damages in personal injury cases. Enforcement of judgments and contempt of court are also featured.

The following are excluded, or rather discussed only in outline terms or peripherally: admiralty, matrimonial, probate proceedings, care of patients and minors, criminal proceedings (other than in judicial review and *habeas corpus*), insolvency and company law procedure, internal practice in the Enforcement of Judgments Office, remittal and removal and appeals from the county court.

Special statutory jurisdictions of the High Court and Court of Appeal are not central to this work, though the general principles of statutory applications and appeals are discussed in Chapter 18, and Appendix One contains what is intended to be as nearly as possible an exhaustive list of statutes under which the Court has special jurisdiction.

Being a book on procedure, general principles of substantive law are not investigated, except in relation to the increasingly important topic of judicial review, where the absence of any major text on the principles and scope of judicial review in Northern Ireland has led me to state the law as well as the procedure.

The book is aimed at all those who need a full working knowledge of procedural law and evidence. Most of those will have some degree of knowledge of the terminology and principles, but for others I have given a glossary of common words and expressions. Those new to procedure might also look at the table of Basic Steps in Appendix Three. It is also interesting to note that there are several books like the White Book which deal with civil procedure in the form of annotated commentaries on Rules (such a book has recently been published in the Republic of Ireland) but that there is very little in the way of text book treatment of Supreme Court and civil procedure in England or elsewhere, and it is possible that this book may be of some assistance to practitioners in other countries where the English form of civil procedure is basically followed.

As the Supreme Court practice in Northern Ireland is closely modelled on that of England and Wales, readers who want to use this book to its full advantage should have access to the a recent edition of the 'White Book' There are numerous references to paragraphs of the latest (1997) edition of the White Book. Sometimes references are to previous editions of the White Book, for one of two reasons: (1) some useful passages in previous editions of the White Book have been omitted from later editions for reasons of space; (2) some rules in the Northern Ireland Rules of the Supreme Court are based on the original forms of English rules which have in recent years been revised. I therefore suggest that the reader should use this Book in conjunction with the latest White Book, as well as the 1979 or earlier edition thereof, and leading English text books on civil practice, drafting, evidence, damages and judicial review. It is also advisable to have to hand the 'Red Book' containing an up-to-date version of the NI Rules of the Supreme Court, and Volume 31 of Halsbury's *Statutes of England* (1994 re-issue) which contains the Judicature (Northern Ireland) Act 1978.

I have tried throughout the book to use Irish and Northern Ireland case law precedents as authorities and illustrations of the propositions and principles stated in the text. Special attention is also given to cases from the Republic of Ireland, Scotland and Commonwealth Countries, where their law is sufficiently similar to allow comparison. If comparatively lesser attention is given to English cases that is only because of the ready availability of English case law digests and text books. Even so, the importance of England as a source of jurisprudence is such that there are probably more English case citations than from any other country.

Any authority is quoted only for what it is worth and no warranty is given that it should or must be applied in our courts. In referring to the content of cases, statutes and rules, there is inevitably some condensation, so that exact quotes are rarely given; so the reader should always check the exact wording of the source to determine the way in which it resolves any issue in question. My own personal views are of course worth little or nothing and are sparsely given. My main object is to state the basic tenets and to point the reader in the direction of the materials from which he or she may find a view of the law on a particular point as it arises in practice.

The sad state of law reporting in Northern Ireland means that there is no such thing as a reported Northern Ireland decision subsequent to 1993, a situation which is about to be rectified. Many important decisions have been given by our courts in recent years (some would say too many) and for the text of the judgment I can only refer the reader to its name and date and suggest that he or she embark on a search for it in the Bar Library or elsewhere. The *Bulletin of Northern Ireland Law* provides the only proper attempt to publish an up-to-date record by summarising the judgments of the Northern Ireland courts within a few months of their creation.

We all welcome the belated resumption of publication of judgments so that the wisdom of our judges is spread among lawyers here and abroad. The *Northern Ireland Law Reports* for 1992 has been published recently and its citations are incorporated in the text. The 1993 volume has now appeared, but too late for inclusion in the text. Readers will therefore bear in mind, that any citation from [1993] NIJB (the 'Blue Books') may now be cited in [1993] NI. It is possible that by the time this Book is published more volumes will have appeared, and that publication of the Blue Books will have resumed, starting from 1994.

In the interests of space and simplicity I have followed a policy of quoting only one (the best) citation for a case. This means the Official Law Report (QB, AC, Fam etc.) where a case is reported there. Otherwise, the Weekly Law Reports and All England Reports are of equal rank. Many practitioners prefer to operate from the All England Law Reports and of course virtually every case cited in the Law Reports or the Weekly Law Reports appears in the All England. In citing decisions in very recent years I have stated the level of court involved, and readers may bear in mind that a recent case may be the subject of a pending appeal

The book is published on materials available to me on 31 June 1997, so that it is hoped that it includes all relevant statute and case law published by that date. It is increasingly common nowadays for statutes to be passed into law but left to be brought into force by a future Commencement Order. There are several instances of statutes passed which are not yet in force and which, at the time of writing have not been given a commencement date. In such cases I have stated the law as it stands at the moment and followed it by a statement if the law as it will be when the new statute comes into force. Where a statutory provision is not yet in force the text makes that clear and where there are substantial passages of law not yet in force, square brackets are used to emphasise the fact. The most important of these new 'statutes in waiting' is the Social Security (Recovery of Benefits) (NI) Order, which deals with recoupment of benefits paid to a plaintiff from damages awarded against the tortfeasor. Other important statutory changes pending are in the law of defamation and in the rights of charges and partition of land.

There is a proposed reform of the law of civil evidence, which will virtually abolish the rule against hearsay in civil cases. A special section is devoted to that proposal, tied by references to the appropriate paragraphs of the main text. As proposals for Northern Ireland Orders-in-Council are published with a view to receiving comments from the public, it is likely that the proposed order will be passed a considerable time ahead and come into force several months after that and it may differ slightly in its drafting from the proposed Order.

I must thank several people for their assistance, beginning with the staff of SLS, in particular Mrs Michelle Madden, Secretary, and Mrs Sara Gamble, Publications Editor, who handled every stage of the publication and ferreted out the little errors, inconsistencies, ambiguities in content and discrepancies in style which the author tends to overlook. Thanks are due also to Mr Justice Kerr, Mr Jack Burton of the Crown Office, Master Robert

Ellison, Master Basil Glass, Master Robert Millar and Master Christopher Napier. Above all I must express my appreciation to Master John Wilson, the senior master in Queen's Bench business, who read through the entire text of the book and made comments and suggestions, both major and minor, which have ensured, I hope, that the book is free of any substantial misconceptions. Of course the responsibility for the content of the work and therefore for any errors remains solely my own.

Barry Valentine
August 1997

STOP PRESS

- *Connelly* v *RTZ Corp* [1996] QB 361(CA) is reversed on appeal, 'The Times' 4 August 1997 (HL). The availability of legal aid or other financial assistance in the forum chosen by the plaintiff is relevant in deciding whether the action should be stayed for a more appropriate forum (para.11.175).
- SR 1997/265 adds a new Order 118, which provides for application by originating motion to the High Court for the quashing of a tainted acquittal under the Criminal Procedure and Investigations Act 1996 s.54, in force on 30 June 1997 (Appendix One para.4-a).
- The Court Funds Rules (NI) 1979 are amended by SR 1997/286. the chief effects are (1) to enable money to be paid out of court to a payee by cheque or by 'BACS'; (2) money lodged in court (on or after 21 July 1997) under Order 22 rule 1 is not accepted within the 21-day time limit, it is placed on deposit and thus starts to carry interest; (3) the rules as to placing court funds on deposit are changed and rule 54 is repealed. (para.11.171).
- Article 5(1)(2) of the Protection from Harassment (NI) Order 1997 is in force on 17 June 1997. This provides for harassment to be an actionable wrong, but the part of the Article which enables the Court to issue a warrant of arrest on breach thereof is not yet in force (paras.9.16, 14.86).

TABLE OF CONTENTS

Preface		vii
Table of Cases		xvii
Table of Statutes, Rules and Other Enactments.		lxv
Proposed Civil Evidence (NI) Order		lxxxix
Abbreviations		xcix
Glossary of Terms		ci
CHAPTER 1	**THE SUPREME COURT**	1
	Courts, Judges and Officers	1
	Definitions and Interpretation	4
	Rules of Procedure	7
	Territorial Jurisdiction	8
	Rules of Law and Equity	10
	Which Division?	11
	Court Funds	12
	Court Documents and Fees	12
	Irregularities	13
	Time Limits	15
CHAPTER 2	**STEPS BEFORE PROCEEDINGS**	19
	Generally	19
	Other Steps in Particular Cases	22
	Early Negotiations	23
	Instructing Counsel	24
	Steps by Defendant	24
CHAPTER 3	**SETTING UP THE LITIGATION**	27
	CHOOSING THE COURT	27
	PARTIES	27
	Private Individuals	28
	Private Bodies of Persons	31
	Public Bodies	34
	JOINDER OF CAUSES OF ACTION	35
	JOINDER OF PARTIES	37
	Consolidation, Hearing Together etc.	38
	Representation of Estates and Trusts	40
	LEGAL REPRESENTATION	42
	Legal Aid	46
CHAPTER 4	**TIME FOR SUING**	51
	Accrual of Cause of Action	51
	Limitation Period	51
CHAPTER 5	**INVOKING THE LEGAL PROCESS**	57
	STEPS BEFORE ACTION	57
	COMMENCING PROCEEDINGS	58

Writ of Summons 59
Debt or Liquidated Demand 61

CHAPTER 6 **SERVICE OF DOCUMENTS** 65
SERVICE OF ORIGINATING PROCESS 65
Service of Writ of Summons 65
Service of Other Originating Process 68
Setting aside Service 68
Service where Defendant is outside Northern Ireland 68
SERVICE OF DOCUMENTS GENERALLY 72
Proof of Service 75

CHAPTER 7 **APPEARANCE** 77
DEFENDANT'S OPTIONS 77
Appearance 77
STAY OF PROCEEDINGS FOR ARBITRATION 80

CHAPTER 8 **JUDGMENT IN DEFAULT** 85
Setting aside Judgment 89

CHAPTER 9 **PLEADINGS** 91
FUNCTION AND FORM OF PLEADINGS 91
STATEMENT OF CLAIM 94
DEFENCE 97
Tender before Action 102
Cross-claims: Counterclaim and Set-off 103
Counterclaim against Plaintiff and Another 107
REPLY AND SUBSEQUENT PLEADINGS 108
JUDGMENT IN DEFAULT OF PLEADING 109
CLOSE OF PLEADINGS 110
STRIKING OUT PLEADINGS 110
IRISH CASES ON PLEADING 110
FURTHER PARTICULARS 112
FORMAL ADMISSIONS 116

CHAPTER 10 **THIRD-PARTY PROCEEDINGS** 119
THIRD-PARTY RELIEF 119
Order 16 rule 1(1)(a): "Indemnity" 119
Order 16 rule 1(1)(a): "Contribution" 121
Other Relief 123
THIRD-PARTY PROCEDURE 123
Third-Party Notice against Existing Party 127
Fourth etc. Party Notice 128
INTERPLEADER SUMMONS 128

CHAPTER 11 **INTERLOCUTORY PROCEEDINGS** 129
GENERAL 129
Evidence by Affidavit 135
AMENDMENT 136
Amendment as to Parties 140
Time Problems on Amendments 142
CHANGE OF PARTIES: ORDER TO CARRY ON 145
SUMMARY JUDGMENT 148

INTERIM PAYMENTS 152
SECURITY FOR COSTS 153
INJUNCTIONS 155
Urgent Cases 158
Mareva Injunction 159
INSPECTION AND PRESERVATION OF PROPERTY 160
DISCLOSURE OF EVIDENCE 163
Discovery by Disclosure of Documents 163
Interrogatories 172
Discovery as a Primary Remedy 175
Disclosure of Names of Partners 178
Disclosure of Medical and Expert Evidence 178
REMITTAL TO COUNTY COURT 180
REMOVAL FROM COUNTY COURT 181
PAYMENT INTO COURT 181
'Lodgments' 181
Offers Analogous to Lodgments 187
Other Provisions for Money in Court 187
STAY OF PROCEEDINGS 189
STRIKING OUT PLEADINGS AND PROCEEDINGS 192
DISMISSAL FOR WANT OF PROSECUTION 194

CHAPTER 12 **WITHDRAWALS, COMPROMISES AND FIXING THE TRIAL** 201
DISCONTINUANCE 201
SETTLEMENTS 202
'Minor Settlements' 206
Structured Settlements 209
SETTING DOWN FOR TRIAL 211
Fixing a Date 212

CHAPTER 13 **EVIDENCE** 215
PREPARING THE EVIDENCE FOR TRIAL 215
Procuring the Evidence 215
RECEIVABILITY OF EVIDENCE 219
Burden of Proof 222
ADDUCTION OF EVIDENCE 226
Competence and Compellability 228
Privilege 229
ORAL WITNESSES 237
Examination-in-Chief 238
Cross-Examination 241
Re-Examination 245
Role of the Judge and Jury 245
ADMISSIBILITY OF EVIDENCE 246
Opinion Evidence 247
Foreign Law 249
Estoppel 250
Estoppel *per rem judicatem* 251
'BEST EVIDENCE' RULES 255
Hearsay 255
Exceptions to the Rule against Hearsay 256
Extrinsic Evidence of a Documented Transaction 263

	Proving a Document	264
	Statutory Provisions as to Documentary Evidence	268
	Real Evidence	270
	Exhibits	271
CHAPTER 14	**THE TRIAL**	273
	Sitting in Private	273
	Jury Trial	274
	Mode of Trial: Splitting into Issues	277
	The Trial of an Action	279
	Contested Trial	281
	REMEDIES: DAMAGES	291
	Damages in Personal Injury Cases	292
	Fatal Injuries	304
	Damages by Periodical Payments	306
	Contributory Negligence	307
	Provisional Damages	308
	Interim Award	309
	Interest	309
	OTHER REMEDIES	310
	Remedies against the Crown	315
CHAPTER 15	**THE JUDGMENT**	317
	Finality of Judgment	319
	Interest on Judgments	322
	PROCEEDINGS UNDER OR AFTER JUDGMENT	323
CHAPTER 16	**ENFORCEMENT AND PENAL PROVISIONS**	325
	ENFORCEMENT OF JUDGMENTS	325
	Reciprocal Enforcement of Judgments	330
	Application to the EJ Office	332
	Other Methods of Enforcing a Money Judgment	335
	Committal Powers on Money Judgment	336
	Non-Monetary Judgments	339
	Effect of Party being in Contempt	345
	Other Forms of Civil Contempt	345
	CONTEMPT GENERALLY	346
	Civil Contempt	347
	Criminal Contempt	347
	Dealing with Contempt	350
	Appeal	352
CHAPTER 17	**COSTS**	355
	GENERAL PRINCIPLES	355
	Discretion over Costs	355
	PARTICULAR CASES WHERE ISSUES AS TO COSTS ARISE	362
	Costs of Default or Summary Judgment	362
	Costs where Relief within County Court Jurisdiction	363
	Costs where Separate Issues Disputed	369
	Costs where Contributory Negligence	369
	Costs where Multiple Parties	371
	Costs in Particular Cases	373
	Costs of Misconduct, Neglect	376

Costs against a Solicitor 376
Costs of Interlocutory Proceedings and Adjournments 377
Costs of Appeals and Removed Proceedings 378
SOLICITOR AND OWN CLIENT COSTS 379
LEGAL AID 383
TAXATION OF COSTS 389
How Costs are Taxed 391
Payment of Costs 401

CHAPTER 18 **SPECIAL TYPES OF PROCEEDINGS** 403
EXTENT OF HIGH COURT JURISDICTION UNDER STATUTE 403
Exclusions of Jurisdiction 403
Applications and Appeals to the High Court 403
MODE OF PROCEEDING 406
Originating Summons 406
Originating Motion 408
Petitions 409
QUEEN'S BENCH DIVISION 409
Admiralty 410
Defamation Actions 410
Commercial and Accounting Actions 413
Actions relating to Goods and Chattels 416
Actions relating to Land 416
FAMILY DIVISION 420
Matrimonial Causes 420
Probate 421
Jurisdiction over Minors 422
Jurisdiction over Mental Patients 422
CHANCERY DIVISION 423
Proceedings re Sale of Property 426
Administration of Estates; Execution of Trusts 427
Married Women's Property Act 1882 430
Mortgages and Charges 430
Partition 435
Partnerships 436
Personal Insolvency 436
Companies 437

CHAPTER 19 **CROWN SIDE** 439
BAIL 439
JUDICIAL REVIEW 440
The Scope of Judicial Review 440
Grounds for Judicial Review 450
The 'Judicial or Administrative' Dichotomy 459
Void or Voidable 463
Discretion to refuse Judicial Review 465
Procedure in Civil Causes 467
Application for leave 468
The originating motion 473
Matters arising pending the hearing 474
The hearing of the motion 476
Remedies 479
Costs 482

Appeal 482
In a Criminal Cause or Matter 483
HABEAS CORPUS 486
Habeas Corpus ad subjiciendum 486
Other Forms of *Habeas Corpus* 490

CHAPTER 20 **APPEALS** 491
APPEALS TO COURT OF APPEAL 491
Restrictions on Appeal 492
Procedure for Appeal to Court of Appeal 496
Interlocutory Powers 501
Presenting the Case for Appeal 504
The Hearing of the Appeal 507
Particular Types of Appeal 520
APPEAL TO HOUSE OF LORDS 521
REFERENCE TO EUROPEAN COURT OF JUSTICE 524

APPENDIX ONE
STATUTORY JURISDICTIONS OF THE HIGH COURT AND COURT OF APPEAL 525

APPENDIX TWO
HIGH COURT PLEADINGS AND OTHER PRECEDENTS 541
1-7. Pleadings 542
8-9. Other Precedents 559
10. Judicial Review 564

APPENDIX THREE
TABLE OF BASIC STEPS IN A HIGH COURT ACTION (QUEEN'S BENCH DIVISION) 577

APPENDIX FOUR
ERRORS IN 'RED BOOK' AND IN RULES OF THE SUPREME COURT 581

Index 585

TABLE OF CASES

For a list of abbreviations of legal reports, see Osborne's Law Dictionary. For a list of Irish reports, see Surrency 'Legal Research in the Law of Northern Ireland' (1964) 15 NILQ 77. [11.09,175 means paras. 11.09 and 11.175]

Abbey National *v* Grugan (Ch D, NI) 7 March 1997 .... 8.17, 11.07, 16.69
Abbey National *v* Key Surveyors [1996] 3 All ER 184 .... 13.93
Abbey National *v* McCann, CA, NI, 13 June 1997 .... 9.36, 11.69
Abbott *v* Woodroffe (1855) 1 Ir Jur NS 50 .... 9.87
Abrahamson *v* Law Society [1996] 1 IR 403 .... 19.34,78
Abse *v* Smith [1986] QB 536 .... 3.54
Abu Dhabi Helicopters *v* International Aeradio [1986] 1 WLR 312 .... 6.02
Acheson *v* Henry (1871) IR 5 CL 496 .... 11.124
Ackbar *v* CF Green [1975] QB 582 .... 4.06
Adair Smith Motors *v* Nissan Motor [1993] 11 NIJB 18 .... 11.01,175
Adams *v* Kyle (1908) 42 ILTR 22 .... 8.13
Adams *v* London Coach [1921] 1 KB 495 .... 17.11
Adamson *v* Connaughton (1893) 27 ILTR 114 .... 18.25
Addison *v* Addison [1960] 1 WLR 1088 .... 20.24
Advocate (Lord) *v* RW Forsyth, 1990 SLT 458 .... 19.20
Aectra Refining *v* Exmar NV [1994] 1 WLR 1634 .... 7.16
Aegis Blaze, The [1986] 1 Lloyds R 203 .... 13.41
Aero Zipp *v* YKK [1978] 2 CMLR 88 .... 11.187
Agitrex *v* O'Driscoll [1995] 2 ILRM 23 .... 17.77
Agnew *v* McDowell (1884) 14 LR Ir 445 .... 14.86
Ahmed *v* Government of Saudi Arabia [1996] ICR 25 .... 3.20
Aiden Shipping *v* Interbulk [1986] AC 965 .... 17.03,61
Ainsworth *v* Criminal Justice Commission (1992) 175 CLR 564 .... 19.07
Airbus Industrie *v* Patel, *The Times*, 12 Aug 1996 .... 11.177
Aitkin *v* Pressdram, *The Times*, 21 May 1997 .... 14.04
Albany Home Loans *v* Massey [1997] 2 All ER 609 .... 18.72
Alberta *v* Stearns Catalytic (1991) 81 DLR 4th 347 .... 13.42
Alcock *v* South Yorkshire Police [1992] 1 AC 310 .... 14.62
Aldam *v* Brown [1890] WN 116 .... 12.10
Aletesmesh Rein *v* Union of India (1989) 15 Comm LB 1178 (India) 19.13
Alexander *v* Anderson [1933] NI 158 .... 13.29, 14.30
Alexander (Jonathan) *v* Proctor [1996] 1 WLR 518 .... 17.59
Allardyce *v* Carnlough Construction [1975] 6 NIJB 1.34
Allen *v* O'Callaghan (1876) 10 ILTR 131 .... 5.00
Allen *v* Quigley (1878) 12 ILTR 46 .... 5.08
Allen *v* Redland Tile [1973] NI 75 .... 11.188,195
Allen *v* Sir Alfred McAlpine [1968] 2 QB 229 .... 11.190
Allen, *in re* [1987] 6 NIJB 94 .... 19.36,44,45
Allied Irish Bank *v* Ernst & Whinney [1993] 1 IR 375 .... 11.136
Allied Irish Bank *v* Hughes, *The Times* 4 Nov 1994 .... 12.09
Allied Irish Bank *v* McAllister [1993] 5 NIJB 82 .... 18.73
Allied Irish Bank *v* McWilliams [1982] NI 156 .... 16.33, 18.70
Allison (Kenneth) Ltd *v* Limehouse [1992] 2 AC 105 .... 6.03,05,21
Allsop *v* Allsop (1980) 11 Fam Law 18 .... 12.10
Alltrans Express *v* CVA Holdings [1984] 1 WLR 394 .... 17.04, 20.08
Almack *v* Moore (1878) 2 LR Ir 90 .... 3.08,09
Alsop Wilkinson *v* Neary [1996] 1 WLR 1221 .... 17.56
American Cyanamid *v* Ethicon [1975] AC 396 .... 11.63
American Tobacco *v* Guest [1892] 1 Ch 630 .... 17.19

Amon *v* Bobbett (1889) 22 QBD 543 ....17.25
Anderson *v* Belfast Corp [1943] NI 34 ....14.43
Anderson *v* Hyde (CA, NI, 23 Feb 1996) [1996] 3 BNIL 6 *The Times*, 2 May 1996 (NI) 17.55
Anderson *v* Londonderry & Enniskillen Rly (1855) 4 Ir Ch R 254 ....18.75
Andrew *v* City of Glasgow DC, 1996 SLT 814 ....19.24
Andrews *v* Dunn [1960] NI 181 ....10.20
Andrews *v* NIR [1992] NI 1 ....13.39
Anglin, *in re* (QBD, NI) 29 Aug 1996; [1996] 9 BNIL 63 ....19.35
Anisminic *v* Foreign Compensation Commission [1969] 2 AC 147 ....19.16,41
Annesley *v* Annesley (1913) 47 ILTR 207 ....16.60
Anonymous decision of Pennefather B, cited in Copinger p.41 ....3.27
Antcliffe *v* Gloucester Health Authority [1992] 1 WLR 1044 ....11.188
Anton Piller *v* Manufacturing Processes [1976] Ch 55 ....11.86
Antrim Land *v* Stewart [1904] 2 IR 357 ....18.72
Antrim Newtown *v* DOE [1989] NI 26 ....7.15, 18.02
Aquaculture *v* NZ Green Mussel Co [1992] LRC (Comm) 692; [1990] 3 NZLR 299 ....14.92
Arab Monetary Fund *v* Hashim (No 2) [1990] 1 All ER 673 ....9.91
Arab Monetary Fund *v* Hashim (No 7) [1993] 1 WLR 1014 ....13.34
Archdale *v* Anderson (1888) 21 LR Ir 527 ....15.18
Archdall *v* Supple (1841) 3 Ir LR 287 ....11.58
Archdeacin (Doe de) *v* Thrustout (1843) 5 Ir LR 591 ....7.06
Ards BC *v* Northern Bank [1994] 10 BNIL 34 ....9.96, 20.41
Aries *v* Bradley (1917) 51 ILTR 215 ....9.20
Arkins *v* Armstrong (1869) IR 3 CL 373 ....17.28
Armour *v* Bate [1891] 2 QB 233 ....14.20
Armstrong *v* Dickson [1911] 1 IR 435 ....18.59,72
Armstrong *v* Garrity [1993] 10 NIJB 6 ....14.62
Arndt *v* Smith (1995) 126 DLR 4th 705 ....4.06
Arnold *v* National Westminster Bank [1991] 2 AC 93 ....13.104
Arranging Debtor, *in re an* [1965] NI 24 ....11.09
Arthur *v* Arthur (1879) 3 LR Ir 1 ....9.52
Ash *v* Buxted Poultry, *The Times* 29 Nov 1989 ....13.154
Ashmore *v* British Coal [1990] 2 QB 338 ....3.39
Ashphalt & Public Works *v* Indemnity Guarantee[1969] 1 QB 465 ....10.25
Aspell *v* O'Brien [1993] 3 IR 516 ....17.104
Associated Bulk Carriers *v* Koch Shipping [1978] 2 All ER 254 ....11.49
Associated Provincial Picture Houses *v* Wednesbury Corp [1948] 1 KB 223 ....19.37
Association of General Practitioners *v* Minister of Health [1995] 1 IR 382 ....19.34
Astro Exito *v* Southland Enterprise (No 2) [1983] 2 AC 787 ....16.59
Atkins *v* Thompson [1922] 2 IR 102 ....6.17
Atkinson *v* Stewart [1954] NI 146 ....9.75
Atkinson, *re* (1908) 42 ILTR 226 ....12.09
Atlanta *v* Bundesamt [1996] All ER (EC) 31 ....19.12
Atlas Maritime *v* Avalon (No 2) [1991] 1 WLR 633 ....20.10
A-G (McGarry) *v* Sligo CC [1991] 1 IR 99 ....17.107
A-G (Northern Territory) *v* Kearney (1985) 158 CLR 500 ....13.42
A-G (Northern Territory) *v* Maurice (1986) 161 CLR 475 ....13.41
A-G (UK) *v* Heinemann [1988] LRC (Const) 1007; 165 CLR 30 ....19.19
A-G for UK *v* Wellington Newspapers [1988] 1 NZLR 129 ....19.19
A-G *v* Alick [1993] 3 LRC 535 (Hong Kong) 19.91
A-G *v* Associated Newspapers [1994] 2 AC 238 ....16.72
A-G *v* Connolly [1947] IR 213 ....16.78
A-G *v* Equiticorp Industries [1995] 2 NZLR 135 ....13.13
A-G *v* McIlwaine [1939] IR 437 ....11.19
A-G *v* Mines [1943] NI 66 ....16.24
A-G *v* O'Leary [1926] IR 445 ....13.15
A-G *v* O'Sullivan [1930] IR 552 ....13.35

A-G *v* Ross [1909] 2 IR 246 .... 20.61
A-G *v* Times Newspapers [1992] 1 AC 191 .... 16.47
A-G, *in re* an application by the [1965] NI 67 .... 19.55
AB *v* John Wyeth, *The Times* 14 May 1991, 2 Med LR 341 .... 9.18
Auckland Casino *v* Casino Control [1995] 1 NZLR 142 .... 19.50
Auckland RA *v* Mutual Rental Cars [1987] 2 NZLR 647 .... 13.17
Austin *v* Hart [1983] 2 AC 641 .... 3.06
Austin Rover *v* Crouch [1986] 1 WLR 1102 .... 6.02
Austintel, *ex parte* [1997] 1 WLR 616 .... 20.11,14
Australasian Meat Employees *v* Mudginberri Station Pty [1987] LRC (Crim) 587; (1986) 161 CLR 98 .... 16.56
Australian Consolidated *v* Morgan (1965) 112 CLR 483 .... 16.65
Autodesk *v* Dyason (No 2) (1993) 173 CLR 330 .... 20.77
Aviagents *v* Balstravest [1966] 1 WLR 150 .... 20.60
Aylward *v* Jones (1884) 18 ILTR 111 .... 13.139

B *v* John Wyeth [1992] 1 WLR 168 .... 9.17, 11.144, 13.41
B, *in re* [1946] NI 1 .... 19.101
B and B *v* An Bord Uchtála [1997] 1 ILRM 15 .... 19.07
Bacal *v* Modern Engineering [1980] 2 All ER 655 .... 11.24
Bagot *v* Bagot (1878) 1 LR Ir 308; (1880) 5 LR Ir 72 .... 13.156
Bailie *v* Cruikshank [1995] 6 BNIL 79 .... 11.08
Bailie *v* Inglis [1926] NI 53 .... 11.95, 15.12
Baillie, *in re* [1995] 7 BNIL 82 .... 19.57
Bains *v* Yorkshire Insurance (1963) 38 DLR 2d 417 .... 13.116
Baird *v* Thompson (1884) 14 LR Ir 497 .... 11.40, 16.04
Baird, *in re* [1989] NI 57 .... 18.03
Bakht *v* Medical Council [1990] 1 IR 515 .... 20.69
Balkanbank *v* Taher (No 2) [1995] 1 WLR 1067 .... 11.01, 18.12
Ballasty *v* Army & Navy (1916) 50 ILTR 114 .... 7.17
Ballyjamesduff Loan Society *v* Tierney (1907) 41 ILTR 187 .... 20.60
Balogh *v* St Albans Crown Ct [1975] QB 73 .... 16.67
Baly *v* Barrett [1988] NI 368 .... 6.07
Bangor Flagship Developments, *in re* (Taxing Master, NI) 4 March 1993 .... 17.105
Bank of America Nat Trust *v* Christmas [1994] 1 All ER 401 .... 1.30
Bank of Ireland *v* Lyons [1981] IR 295 .... 17.11
Bank of Ireland *v* Ryan (1895) 29 ILTR 101 .... 9.06
Bank of Scotland *v* IMRO, 1989 SLT 432 .... 19.19
Bankamerica *v* Nock [1988] AC 1002 .... 17.51, 20.08,09
Bannon *v* Craigavon DC [1984] NI 387 .... 11.185,193
Banque Commerciale *v* Akhil Holdings [1990] LRC (Comm) 702;169 CLR 279 .... 14.19
Banque Keyser *v* Skandia (No 2) [1988] 2 All ER 880 .... 17.49
Barbour *v* Rutherford [1925] NI 187 .... 10.31
Barclays Bank *v* Bemister [1989] 1 WLR 128 .... 1.21
Barclays Bank *v* Fairclough Building [1995] QB 214 .... 14.74
Barclays Bank *v* Hahn [1989] 1 WLR 506 .... 6.02
Barclays Bank *v* Piper, *The Times*, 31 May 1995 (CA) 11.46
Barker *v* Hempstead (1889) 23 QBD 8 .... 17.28
Barnardo *v* Ford [1892] AC 326 .... 19.104
Barnett *v* Lucas (1872) IR 6 CL 247 .... 3.28
Barr *v* SHSSB [1986] 10 NIJB 1 .... 11.21
Barrett *v* WJ Lenehan [1981] ILRM 207 .... 3.48
Barron *v* Ryan (1907) 41 ILTR 39 .... 16.24
Barry *v* Buckley [1981] IR 306 .... 11.174
Barry *v* Griffin (1906) 40 ILTR 10 .... 17.75
Barry *v* Fitzpatrick [1996] 1 ILRM 513 .... 19.50
Bastow *v* Bradshaw (1881) 8 LR Ir 30 .... 9.26
Battersby, *re* (1892) 31 LR Ir 73 .... 16.50

Battle *v* Irish Art [1968] IR 252 .... 3.54
Baxter Laboratories *v* Cutter Ltd (1984) 2 DLR 4th 621 .... 16.49
Baxter *v* Harland & Wolfe [*sic*] [1990] NI 147 .... 4.06
Beamish *v* Beamish (1876) IR 10 Eq 413 .... 6.28
Beaufort *v* Ledwith [1894] 2 IR 16 .... 9.12
Beaumont *v* Figgis [1945] IR 78 .... 14.91, 17.31
Beaumont *v* Senior [1903] 1 KB 282 .... 17.48
Beckett *v* Attwood (1881) 18 Ch D 54 .... 20.02
Beddoe, *Re* [1893] 1 Ch 547 .... 17.56, 20.08
Beggs, *in re* [1944] NI 121 .... 15.09, 19.100
Beggs *v* Beggs (Taxing Master, NI) 11 May 1994 .... 18.47
Begley *v* Keays (1920) 54 ILTR 40 .... 9.20
Behan *v* Medical Council [1993] 3 IR 523 .... 9.87
Behan *v* Tickell (1886) 20 ILTR 23 .... 11.124
Beirne *v* Commissioner of Garda Siochána [1993] ILRM 1 .... 19.06
Belfast CC *v* Valuation Commr [1915] 2 IR 319 .... 20.19
Belfast Corp *v* Daly [1963] NI 78 .... 19.09
Belfast Corp *v* OD Cars [1960] AC 490; [1960] NI 60 .... 13.17,153
Belfast Empire, *in re* [1963] IR 41 .... 11.169
Belfast Telegraph *v* Blunden [1995] 10 BNIL 48 .... 16.27,32
Bell (George) *v* Nethercott [1988] NI 299 .... 11.59
Bell *v* Bell [1995] 9 BNIL 58 .... 16.17
Bell *v* McPhilpin (1891) 25 ILTR 23 .... 11.98,102
Bell *v* NIHE [1990] NI 119 .... 11.135
Bell *v* Northern Constitution [1943] NI 108 .... 18.19
Bell *v* Quinn [1982] 8 NIJB 17.33
Bell (R) & Co *v* DOE [1982] NI 322 .... 13.96
Bellew (Lord) *v* Markey (1878) 2 LR Ir 185, affd (1879) 4 LR Ir 747 .... 11.46
Belville Holdings *v* Revenue Commrs [1994] 1 ILRM 29 .... 15.12
Benburb Meats, *in re* (Taxing Office, NI) 29 June 1995 .... 17.108
Benson *v* NIRTB [1942] AC 520 (NI) 20.60
Benson *v* Sec of State [1976] NI 36 .... 11.39
Beoco *v* Alfa Laval [1995] QB 137 .... 9.14, 11.18,23
Bermingham *v* Colleran (1892) 26 ILT 698 .... 11.28
Berriello *v* Felixstowe Dock & Rly [1989] 1 WLR 695 .... 14.63
Best *v* Wellcome Foundation [1993] 3 IR 421 .... 13.92
Best *v* Wellcome Foundation [1996] 1 ILRM 34 .... 17.97,101,105,107
Best *v* Woods (1905) 39 ILTR 44 .... 11.15
Beta Construction *v* Channel 4 [1990] 2 All ER 1012 .... 14.04
Bettaney *v* Five Towns (1971) 115 SJ 710 .... 11.150
Bettinson *v* Bettinson [1965] Ch 465 .... 11.174
Bevan *v* Gillows (1906) 40 ILTR 251 .... 6.17
BICC *v* Burndy Corp [1985] Ch 232 .... 9.36
Bickerstaff *v* ATGWU (QBD, NI) 15 Jan 1965 .... 17.39
Bignell, *in re* (CA, NI) 21 March 1997 .... 19.39,63
Binnie *v* Rederij Theodoro BV, 1993 SC 71 .... 13.29
Birch *v* Harland & Wolff [1991] NI 90 .... 4.00, 14.51,61, 17.36,37,38
Birch *v* Pirtill [1936] IR 122 .... 11.58
Bird *v* Keep [1918] 2 KB 692 .... 13.132
Bird Moyer, *in re* (1964) 98 ILTR 202 .... 6.24
Birkett *v* James [1978] AC 297 .... 11.186,189
Birmingham Citizens *v* Caunt [1962] Ch 883 .... 18.73
Birse Construction *v* Haistie [1996] 2 All ER 1 .... 10.09
Black *v* Baxter (QBD, NI) January 1996 .... 17.35,38
Black *v* Harland & Wolff [1977] 2 NIJB 17.96,105
Black *v* McCabe [1964] NI 1 .... 13.111, 14.74
Black *v* Sangster (1834) 1 CM & R 521 (149 ER 1186) 11.22
Black, *in re* [1993] 2 NIJB 63 .... 19.47,59,69,91

Blackall *v* Grehan [1995] 3 IR 208 ... 19.11
Blackburne *v* Gernon (1899) 33 ILTR 119 ... 19.48
Blackwood *v* Gregg (1831) Hayes 277 ... 13.14,117
Blair *v* Crawford [1906] 1 IR 578 ... 11.174, 12.13
Blair *v* Lochaber DC, 1995 SLT 407 ... 19.05
Blair, *in re* [1985] NI 68 ... 19.37
Blake *v* Appleyard (1878) 3 Ex D 195 ... 17.25
Blanchfield *v* Murphy (1913) 47 ILTR 24 ... 20.68
Blatcher *v* Heaysman [1960] 1 WLR 663 ... 17.87
Blizard *v* Mulloy (1887) 21 ILTR 11 ... 3.30, 5.12
Blount *v* O'Connor (1886) 17 LR Ir 620 ... 16.10
Blumberg *v* McCormick [1915] 2 IR 402 ... 11.54, 20.43
BMWE *v* Canadian Pacific (1996) 136 DLR 4th 289 ... 11.62
Boddington *v* British Transport Police, *The Times*, 23 July 1996 ... 19.09
Boocock *v* Hilton International [1993] 1 WLR 1065 ... 1.30, 6.05
Boss Group *v* Boss France SA, *The Times* 15 April 1996 ... 1.14
Bourke *v* CIE [1967] IR 319 ... 12.17
Bowen *v* Barlow (1875) IR 9 CL 55 ... 11.56
Bowes *v* Judge Devally [1995] 1 IR 315 ... 19.23
Bowes *v* MIB [1989] IR 225 ... 16.17
Bowles *v* Stewart (1803) 1 Sch & L 209 ... 13.24,42
Bowman *v* Harland & Wolff [1991] NI 300 ... 4.06
Bowring(CT) *v* Corsi Partners [1994] 2 LLoyds R 567 ... 11.56
Bowskill *v* Dawson [1954] 1 QB 288 ... 13.127
Boyd *v* Antrim CC [1941] NI 127 ... 20.73
Boyd *v* Dooley (1881) 15 ILTR 4 ... 10.20
Boyd *v* Ellison (Taxing Office NI) preliminary ruling 1994 ... 17.102,106
Boyd *v* Ellison (Taxing Office NI) 22 Feb 1995 ... 17.98,103
Boyd *v* Ellison (QBD, NI) 29 June 1995 ... 17.102,103
Boyd *v* Lee Guinness [1963] NI 49 ... 6.16
Boyd *v* Sinnamon [1974] June NIJB ... 11.185,188,191,195,196
Boyle *v* An Post [1992] 2 IR 437 ... 11.68
BP Exploration *v* Hunt (No 2) [1983] 2 AC 352 ... 14.78
Brabazon *v* Brabazon (1883) 17 ILTR 9 ... 8.15
Bradford *v* DOE [1986] NI 41 ... 7.11
Bradley *v* Clayton (1890) 26 LR Ir 405 ... 11.127
Bradley *v* Eagle Star [1989] AC 957 ... 16.13
Bradshaw *v* McMullan (1922) 56 ILTR 93 ... 17.27
Bradshaw *v* McMullan [1920] 2 IR 412 ... 13.107
Brady *v* Chief Constable [1988] NI 32 ... 11.181, 13.102
Brady *v* Deignan (1950) 84 ILTR 38 ... 10.33
Brady *v* Macdonald [1931] NI 157 ... 3.35
Braithwaite *v* Anley [1990] NI 63 ... 11.185,188,189,194,196
Brankenbank Lodge *v* Peart, *The Times* 26 July 1996 ... 17.04
Brasserie du Pêcheur *v* Germany [1996] QB 404 ... 19.88
Braun *v* Johnston (1901) 35 ILTR 55 ... 11.174
Braybrook, *in re* [1916] WN 74 ... 3.37
Breathnach *v* Ireland (No 2) [1993] 2 IR 448 ... 11.181, 13.110
Bredin *v* Corcoran (1861) 12 ICLR App 9 ... 12.03
Breen *v* Cooper (1870) 4 ILT 65 ... 11.174
Brennan *v* Gale [1949] NI 178 ... 14.71
Brennan *v* Lockyer [1932] IR 101 ... 6.17
Brennan *v* Minister of Finance (1962) 96 ILTR 54 ... 14.42
Brennan *v* Minister of Justice [1995] 1 IR 612 ... 19.16,40,50
Breslin, *in re* [1987] NI 1 ... 19.65
Bridge Shipping *v* Grand Shipping [1992] LRC (Comm) 730; 173 CLR 231 ... 11.34
Bridge Wholesale *v* Shores [1994] 2 NZLR 222 ... 1.31
Brien *v* Sullivan (1884) 14 LR Ir 391 ... 16.03

Briggs *v* Mulvenna [1969] NI 1 ....9.77
Bristol & West Building Soc *v* Ellis, *The Times*, 2 May 1996 ....18.73
Bristow *v* Millar (1854) 6 Ir Jur OS 285 ....18.57
British Association of Glass Bottle Manufacturers *v* Nettlefold [1912] AC 709....11.108
British Coal *v* Dennis Rye [1988] 3 All ER 816 ....13.41
British Columbia (Milk Board) *v* Grisnich (1995) 126 DLR 4th 191 ....19.24
British Egg Marketing *v* Gillespie [1969] NI 139 ....6.24
British and Commonwealth Holdings *v* Quadrex [1989] QB 842 ....11.55
British Legal *v* Sheffield [1911] 1 IR 69....9.79,84
British Lighting *v* Simpritol Lighting (1912) 46 ILTR 37 ....11.191
British Medical Association *v* Greater Glasgow Health Board [1989] AC 1211 ....3.22
British Oxygen *v* Min of Technology [1971] AC 610 ....19.26
British Road Services *v* Crutchley [1967] 1 WLR 835 ....20.30
British Waterways *v* Norman, *The Times*, 11 Nov 1993 ....17.11
Broderick, *in re* [1986] 6 NIJB 36 ....9.27, 12.11
Brookes *v* Harris [1995] 1 WLR 918 ....17.87
Brooksbank *v* Rawsthorne [1951] 2 All ER 413 ....20.77
Brown *v* Belfast Corp [1955] NI 213....9.20
Brown *v* Donegal CC [1980] IR 132 ....13.153
Brown *v* E & M Rly (1889) 22 QBD 391 ....13.15
Brown *v* Executive Committee of Edinburgh District Labour Party 1995 SLT 985 .....19.04
Brown *v* Hamilton [1994] 1 BNIL 21 ....11.147, 17.33
Brown *v* Hamilton DC, 1983 SC (HL) 1....19.08
Brown *v* Pollen (Taxing Master, NI) 20 March 1991....17.105
Brown Bros *v* Ballantine Bros (1878) 12 ILTR 70....7.04
Browne *v* An Bord Pleanála [1991] 2 IR 209 ....19.50
Browne *v* Dundalk UDC [1993] 2 IR 512 ....19.08
Bruce *v* Brophy [1906] 1 IR 611 ....18.72
Bruce *v* Legal Aid Board [1992] 3 All ER 321 ....3.57, 17.01
Bruce *v* Pascoe (1940) 74 ILTR 14 (NI) 16.16
Brunker *v* North (1880) 15 ILTR 10....10.26
Brunskill *v* Powell (1850) 19 LJ Ex 362....3.27
Bryce *v* British Railways, 1996 SLT 1378....13.69
BTK *v* Greater Edmonton Development Corp (1992) 95 DLR 4th 573 ....11.98
Buchanan *v* Brook Walker [1988] NI 116 ....1.14, 11.175
Buck *v* Bawone (1976) 135 CLR 110....19.23
Buckland *v* Palmer [1984] 1 WLR 1109....3.28, 11.183, 12.11
Buckley *v* Crawford [1893] 1 QB 105 ....16.64
Buckley *v* Daly [1990] 8 NIJB 28 ....19.05
Buckley *v* Healy [1965] IR 618 ....17.26,31
Buckley *v* Irish Industrial Benefit Society (1888) 22 LR Ir 579 ....17.04
Bula Ltd *v* Crowley [1991] 1 IR 220 ....11.104
Bula Ltd *v* Crowley [1994] 1 ILRM 495 ....13.42
Bula Ltd *v* Tara Mines (No 1) [1987] IR 85 ....11.78
Bula Ltd *v* Tara Mines (No 5) [1994] 1 IR 487....11.93,102,106,111, 13.43
Bunyan *v* Bunyan [1916] 1 IR 70 ....18.72
Burgess *v* Stafford Hotel [1990] 1 WLR 1215 ....20.06
Burke *v* Beatty [1928] IR 91 ....17.61, 20.72
Burke *v* Central TV [1994] 2 ILRM 161....9.79, 11.114, 13.53
Burke *v* O'Callaghan (1865) 17 ICLR 42 ....15.09
Burke *v* Patterson [1986] NI 1....3.22, 11.64,66
Burns *v* Boland (QB, NI) 15 March 1968 ....11.164, 17.47,89
Burns, *in re* [1985] NI 279 ....19.14
Burris *v* Azadani [1995] 1 WLR 1372....11.68, 14.86
Burt *v* Governor-General [1992] 3 NZLR 672 ....19.13
Busby *v* Cooper, *The Times*, 15 April 1996 ....11.31
Busch *v* Stevens [1963] 1 QB 1 ....11.22
Bush *v* Air Canada (1992) 87 DLR 4th 248 ....14.58

Bush *v* Curran (1858) 9 ICLR App 28 .... 11.23
Butcher *v* Dowlen [1981] RTR 24; [1981] 1 Lloyds R 310 .... 9.91
Butera *v* DPP (1987) 164 CLR 181 .... 13.157
Butler *v* DOE [1992] 7 NIJB 12 .... 11.33
Butterly *v* Cuming [1898] 1 IR 196 .... 16.51
Buttes Gas *v* Hammer Gas (No 3) [1982] AC 888 .... 19.19
Byers *v* Byers [1927] IR 184 .... 14.21
Byrne *v* Fox [1938] IR 683 .... 17.65
Byrne *v* Londonderry Tram Co [1902] 2 IR 457 .... 13.22
Byrne *v* McDonnell [1996] 1 ILRM 543 .... 19.81
Byrne *v* Somers (1928) 62 ILTR 152 .... 8.17
Bywater *v* Dunne (1882) 10 LR Ir 380 .... 9.26, 14.20

C *v* C [1973] 1 WLR 568 .... 11.128
C (a Minor) *v* Hackney LBC [1996] 1 WLR 789 .... 13.102
C (Hearsay Evidence: Contempt), *in re* [1993] 4 All ER 690 .... 13.13
Cairns *v* Whelan (1828) 1 Hud & Br 552 .... 3.27
Caldbeck *v* Boon (1873) IR 7 CL 32 .... 10.17, 13.42
Calvin *v* Carr [1980] AC 574 .... 19.51
Cambridge Street Properties *v* City of Glasgow Licensing Board, 1995 SLT 913 .... 20.09
Camdex International *v* Bank of Zambia [1996] 3 All ER 431 .... 3.19
Cameron *v* Orr 1995 SLT 589 .... 16.67
Campbell (Donald) *v* Pollak [1927] AC 732 .... 20.08
Campbell College *v* Commrs of Valuation [1964] NI 107 (HL) 13.109
Campbell International *v* Van Aart [1992] 2 IR 305 .... 1.14
Campbell *v* McFarland [1972] NI 31 .... 10.07, 16.16
Campbell (J.C.) *v* Davidson (Ch D, NI) 27 Sept 1967, 18 NILQ 461 .... 17.04
Canada (A-G) *v* Mossop (1993) 100 DLR 4th 658; [1994] 2 LRC 436 .... 19.50
Canada Trust *v* Stolzenberg, *The Times*, 1 May 1997 .... 1.14
Cannon *v* Fallon (1918) 52 ILTR 34 .... 6.19, 10.19
Carey *v* Cuthbert (1872) IR 6 Eq 599 .... 13.41
Carey *v* Grispi (1858) 9 ICLR 25 .... 16.24
Carey *v* Ryan [1982] IR 179 .... 11.27,151
Cargill *v* Bower (1879) 10 Ch D 502 .... 9.14
Carlingford Harbour *v* Everard [1985] NI 50 .... 6.16
Carlisle *v* Belfast Board of Guardians (1881) 15 ILTR 49 .... 11.193
Carlisle *v* Chief Constable [1988] NI 307 .... 3.22
Carlisle, *in re* [1950] NI 105 .... 13.136
Carlton, Atkinson and Sloan *v* AIB [1977] NI 158 .... 10.33
Carltona *v* Works Commrs [1943] 2 All ER 560 .... 19.26
Carna Foods *v* Eagle Star [1995] 1 IR 526 .... 19.05
Carnie *v* Esanda Finance Corp (1995) 69 ALJR 206 .... 3.37
Carr *v* Poots [1995] 6 BNIL 80 .... 17.40,85,97,98,102,105,108
Carroll *v* Masterson (1905) 39 ILTR 211 .... 11.176
Carroll *v* Tighe (1906) 40 ILTR 150 .... 17.24
Carroll, *in re* [1988] NI 152 .... 19.06
Carruth *v* Carruth (Taxing Master, NI) 7 Nov 1995 .... 17.85,105
Carson *v* Crozier (1917) 51 ILTR 38 .... 6.18
Casey *v* Dept of Education (QBD, NI) 16 Oct 1996 .... 19.25
Casey *v* Parson (1868) IR 2 CL 677 .... 8.14
Cassidy *v* Foley [1904] 2 IR 427 .... 3.42
Cassidy *v* Sullivan (1878) 1 LR Ir 313 .... 17.57
Casson *v* O'Brien (1842) Arm Mac & Og 263 .... 14.35
Castanho *v* Brown & Root [1981] AC 557 .... 11.176
Caulfield *v* Bell (1959) 93 ILTR 108 .... 9.73
Cave *v* Torre (1886) 54 LT 515 .... 9.85
Cavendish *v* Dublin Corp [1974] IR 171 .... 13.24
CCSU *v* Minister for Civil Service [1985] AC 374 .... 19.07,22,34,37,41

Central Electricity *v* Bata Shoe [1983] 1 AC 105 .... 15.16, 20.71,72
Century Insurance *v* Falloon [1971] NI 234 .... 13.42
Century Insurance *v* Larkin [1910] 1 IR 91 .... 16.49
Chaggar *v* Chaggar [1997] 1 All ER 104 .... 17.89
Chamberlain *v* Boodle [1982] 1 WLR 1443 .... 17.80
Chamberlain *v* Deputy Commr of Taxation (1988) 164 CLR 502........ 3.30
Chambers *v* DOE [1985] NI 181 .... 19.09
Chambers, *in re* (1832) Alc & Nap 183 .... 13.08
Chan, *in re* [1987] NI 13 .... 19.19,31
Chan-Sing-Chuk *v* Innovisions Ltd [1992] LRC (Com) 609 .... 11.19
Chance *v* Tanti (1901) 35 ILTR 126........ 3.52
Chandless *v* Nicholson [1942] 2 KB 321 .... 15.14
Channel Tunnel Group *v* Balfour Beatty [1993] AC 334........ 7.21, 11.62,175
Chappell *v* Cooper [1980] 1 WLR 958 .... 6.07
Charrington & Co *v* Camp [1902] 1 Ch 386 .... 11.83
Chatsworth Investments *v* Amoco [1968] Ch 665 .... 10.16
Cheeseman *v* Bowaters Ltd [1971] 1 WLR 1773 .... 11.161, 14.42
Chell Engineering *v* Unit Tool [1950] 1 All ER 378 .... 17.43
Cheltenham & Gloucester *v* Booker, *The Times*, 20 Nov 1996........ 18.73
Cheltenham & Gloucester *v* Krausz [1997] 1 All ER 21 .... 18.73
Cheltenham & Gloucester *v* Norgan [1996] 1 All ER 449 (CA) 18.73
Chemical Bank *v* McCormack [1983] ILRM 350 .... 11.132
Chief Adjudication Officer *v* Foster [1992] QB 31; [1993] AC 754 .... 19.09,63
Chief Constable, *in re* [1983] 3 NIJB 19.47
Chiltern DC *v* Keane [1985] 1 WLR 619 .... 16.53,55,80
Cholmeley's School (Warden of) *v* Sewell [1893] 2 QB 254 .... 9.43
Christie *v* Odeon Ltd (1957) 91 ILTR 25 .... 14.38
Christie's Curator *v* Kirkwood 1996 SLT 1299 .... 20.57
Chrulew *v* Borm-Reed [1992] 1 WLR 176 .... 17.107
Chui *v* Min of Immigration [1994] 2 NZLR 541; [1994] 1 LRC 433 .... 19.26
Church's Trustee *v* Hibbard [1902] 2 Ch 784 .... 16.45
Church and General Insurance *v* Moore [1996] 1 ILRM 202........ 9.83, 16.60
Chute *v* McGillicuddy (1833) Hay & Jon 172 .... 16.68
CILFIT *v* Italian Minister of Health [1982] ECR 3415 .... 14.16
City of Glasgow Friendly Society *v* Gilpin [1970] Dec NIJB 17.04
Claibourne Industries *v* National Bank (1989) 59 DLR 4th 533 .... 11.128
Clanricarde *v* Ryder [1898] 1 IR 98........ 1.20, 14.20
Clare CC *v* Mahon [1995] 3 IR 193........ 13.104,109
Clare CC *v* Wilson [1913] 2 IR 89 .... 6.16
Clark *v* Urquhart [1930] AC 28; [1930] NI 4 .... 3.27, 11.157
Clarke *v* Brown [1986] 2 NIJB 1 .... 13.88
Clarke *v* Chief Constable [1978] 3 NIJB 14.53,59,61
Clarke *v* Clarke [1899] WN 130 .... 11.128
Clarke *v* Dublin Steam (1891) 25 ILTR 21........ 8.13
Clarke *v* Harper [1938] NI 162........ 6.16
Clarke *v* Judge Hogan [1995] 1 IR 310 .... 19.44
Clarke *v* McLaughlin & Harvey [1978] 2 NIJB........ 3.33, 10.01, 15.03, 17.49
Clarke *v* Midland Great Western Rly [1895] 2 IR 294........ 3.29
Clarke *v* Stow (Taxing Office NI) 14 June 1995........ 17.105,107
Clayton *v* Renton (1867) LR 4 Eq 158 .... 18.62
Clear *v* Thermal Ltd [1969] IR 133 .... 12.14
Cleland *v* Neill [1951] NI 61 .... 11.124, 18.22
Clifford, *in re* [1921] 2 AC 570 (Ir) 19.83,92,108
Clinton *v* Chief Constable [1991] 2 NIJB 53 .... 9.80,86,87,91
Clinton *v* Kell [1993] 10 NIJB 52 .... 19.82
Cloake, *re* (1892) 61 LJ Ch 69 .... 11.03
Clokey *v* London & NW Rly [1905] 2 IR 251 .... 5.05
Close, *in re* [1972] NI 27 .... 19.99

Co-operative Retail *v* Sec of State [1980] 1 WLR 271 .... 20.63
Co.Meath Education Committee *v* Joyce [1994] 2 ILRM 210 .... 19.09
Coca Cola *v* Concentrate Manufacturing [1990] NI 77 .... 11.01
Cockle *v* Treacy [1896] 2 IR 267 .... 11.50, 20.08
Coen *v* Employers Liability Assurance [1962] IR 314 .... 7.17
Coenen *v* Payne [1974] 1 WLR 984 .... 14.12
Cohen *v* Downham (1904) 5 NIJR 32 .... 11.159
Cole *v* Dawson (1882) 16 ILTR 96 .... 17.75
Coleman *v* Coleman (1898) 32 ILTR 66 .... 13.04
Coleman, *in re* [1988] NI 205 .... 1.02, 19.75,91
Colgan, *in re* (QBD, NI) undated 1996 .... 19.39,86
Colgan *v* Rice (1903) 37 ILTR 57 .... 11.160, 20.57
Colhoun *v* McNamee (1901) 1 NIJR 275 .... 17.104
Colledge *v* Bass Mitchells [1988] 1 All ER 536 .... 14.63
Collier *v* Creighton [1996] 2 NZLR 257 (PC) 4.04
Collings *v* Wade [1903] 1 IR 89 .... 3.33, 10.28, 11.38
Colmey *v* Pinewood Developments [1995] 1 ILRM 331 .... 14.95
Colton *v* McCaughey [1969] 3 All ER 1460 .... 17.25,28
Colville *v* Bowman (1904) 38 ILTR 75 .... 20.58
Colville *v* Hall (1865) 10 Ir Jur NS 261 .... 17.76
Comet Products *v* Hawkex Plastics [1971] 2 QB 67 .... 13.44, 16.54
Commission for New Towns *v* Cooper (GB) [1995] Ch 259 .... 14.93
Commissioners Decision No 1/92(CRS) [1993] 1 BNIL 95 .... 14.66
Commissioners Decision No 2/92(CRS) [1993] 4 BNIL 118 .... 14.66
Commr for Railways *v* Murphy (1967) 41 ALJR 77 .... 13.154
Commr of Taxation *v* Myer Emporium (1986) 160 CLR 220 .... 20.33
Commrs of State Revenue *v* Royal Insurance [1994] 4 LRC 511 .... 19.27,88
Compania Anonima *v* Barnett (1904) 4 NIJR 187 .... 11.98
Compania Naviera Vascongada *v* Hall (1906) 40 ILTR 114 .... 9.49
Compania Naveria Vascongada *v* R & H Hall (No 1) (1906) 40 ILTR 245 .... 9.76
Compania Naviera Vascongada *v* R & H Hall (No 2) (1906) 40 ILTR 246 .... 11.95
Computer Machinery *v* Drescher [1983] 1 WLR 1379 .... 13.43, 17.05
Concrete Constructions *v* Plumbers and Gasfitters (1988) 14 Comm LB 1266 (Aus) 14.89
Conlin *v* Patterson [1915] 1 IR 169 .... 19.97
Conlon *v* Carlow CC [1912] 2 IR 535 .... 1.17
Conlon *v* Times Newspapers [1995] 2 ILRM 76 .... 11.179
Connelly *v* RTZ Corp [1996] QB 361 .... 11.175
Connolly *v* Crozier (1924) 58 ILTR 171 .... 11.158
Connolly *v* Huddleston [1952] NI 21 .... 17.42
Connolly *v* Morrow [1979] 6 NIJB 14.32,61, 20.41
Connor *v* Kelly [1957] Ir Jur Rep 41 .... 11.180
Conroy *v* Connolly (1943) 77 ILTR 15 .... 17.104
Considine *v* Morony (1842) 5 Ir LR 485 .... 12.03
Conway *v* Hannaway [1988] NI 269 .... 4.06
Conway *v* Rimmer [1968] AC 910 .... 13.46
Conway *v* Smith [1950] Ir Jur Rep 3 .... 9.28
Conyers *v* Dorgan (1881) 15 ILTR 121 .... 11.80
Cook (No 2) , *in re* [1986] NI 283 .... 16.47,53,56,57, 19.82
Cook *v* Swinfen [1967] 1 WLR 457 .... 11.163
Cooke *v* Head (No 2) [1974] 1 WLR 972 .... 17.87
Cooke *v* Reynolds [1942] NI 97 .... 10.10
Cooney *v* Wilson [1913] 2 IR 402 .... 6.16
Cooper *v* MIB [1985] QB 575 .... 10.07
Cooper *v* Miller (1994) 113 DLR 4th 1 .... 14.63
Cooper *v* Phibbs (1865) 17 Ir Ch R 73; LR 2 HL 149 .... 13.23
Cooper *v* Scott-Farnell [1969] 1 WLR 120 .... 6.24
Cooper, *in re* [1991] NI 257 .... 19.25
Copeland, *in re* [1990] NI 301 .... 11.13, 19.101

Corbett *v* Barking Health Authority [1991] 2 QB 408 ... 14.72
Corby DC *v* Holst [1985] 1 WLR 427 ... 11.167
Cork CC *v* Whillock [1993] 1 IR 231 ... 1.33
Cornwall *v* Saurin (1886) 17 LR Ir 595 ... 20.74
Corry (James P) *v* Clarke [1967] NI 62 ... 20.50
Cory *v* Cory [1923] 1 Ch 90 ... 11.95
Cosgrave, *in re* [1937] IR 292 ... 17.76
Costellow *v* Somerset CC [1993] 1 WLR 256 ... 1.33,35, 11.194
Cox (Peter) *v* Thirwell (1981) 125 SJ 481 ... 17.22
Cox *v* Dublin Distillery [1917] 1 IR 203 ... 3.39, 13.105
Cox *v* Electricity Board (No 2) [1943] IR 231 ... 11.20, 15.22
Coyle *v* Hannan [1974] NI 160 ... 9.88
CR *v* An Bord Uchtála [1993] 3 IR 535 ... 19.26, 19.51
Craig *v* Boyd [1901] 2 IR 645 ... 9.47, 17.01,104, 18.48
Craig *v* Kanssen [1943] KB 256 ... 1.28
Craig *v* South Australia (1995) 69 ALJR 873 ... 19.43,45
Crampsie *v* Unit Construction (CA, NI) 29 June 1966 ... 13.68, 14.38,40
Crane *v* Wallis [1915] 2 IR 411 ... 8.00
Crawford *v* Donnelly (1889) 23 LR Ir 511 ... 11.26
Crawford *v* James [1988] 8 NIJB 19 ... 2.11, 3.36, 9.47,51, 11.147, 13.111
Crawford *v* Vance [1908] 2 IR 521 ... 9.79, 20.57
Crawford, *in re* [1995] 2 BNIL 60 ... 19.37,41,92
Crazy Prices *v* Hewitt [1980] NI 150 ... 11.63
Crean *v* McMillan [1922] 2 IR 105 ... 17.39,42,44
Creed *v* Creed [1913] 1 IR 48 ... 11.19
Creed *v* Scott [1976] RTR 485 ... 13.114
Creeney, *in re* [1988] NI 167 ... 15.12
Cresswell *v* Ministry of Defence (Taxing Master, NI) 28 Sept 1993 ... 17.103
Crest Homes *v* Marks [1987] AC 829 ... 11.117
Cretazzo *v* Lombardi (1975) 13 SASR 4; [1976] Aust Law Dig p.91 ... 17.32
Croft *v* Crofts (1854) 6 Ir Jur OS 249 ... 13.33
Croft, *in re* (QBD, NI) 29 Jan 1997 ... 19.34,38
Cronin *v* Paul (1881) 15 ILTR 121 ... 13.33
Crossey, *in re* [1975] NI 1 ... 16.28
Crothers *v* Crothers (1901) 35 ILTR 179 ... 12.10
Crymble *v* Russell (CA, NI) 23 May 1968 ... 13.13,119
CSI *v* Archway [1980] 1 WLR 1069 ... 9.46
Cuddy *v* McMahon (1893) 27 ILTR 101 ... 3.31
Culbert *v* Belfast Co-op (CA NI) 6 June 1966, 17 NILQ 442 ... 9.08
Cullen *v* Chief Constable [1996] 6 BNIL 76 ... 14.12, 20.52
Cullen *v* Clein [1970] IR 146 ... 10.28
Cullen *v* Moran (1856) 2 Ir Jur NS 28 ... 5.11
Cullen *v* Toft (1903) 37 ILTR 65 ... 10.26
Cullen, *in re* [1987] 5 NIJB 102 ... 15.01, 19.54,69
Cummins *v* Hall [1933] IR 419 ... 13.151
Cummins *v* Murray [1906] 2 IR 509 ... 17.53
Cunningham *v* Milk Marketing Board [1990] 11 NIJB 33 ... 20.52
Curran *v* Micheals (1880) 14 ILTR 30 ... 11.180
Curran *v* NICHA [1987] NI 80 ... 14.12
Curran, *in re* [1985] NI 261 ... 19.24
Curreen *v* Walsh (1838) 1 Ir Eq R 200 ... 11.05
Curry *v* Rea [1937] NI 1 ... 13.148, 17.74
Curry *v* Tevlin (1876) IR 10 CL 458 ... 3.42
Curtis *v* Armstrong [1897] 2 IR 327 ... 17.41
Customs & Excise *v* JH Corbitt [1981] AC 22 ... 20.62
Cutts *v* Head [1984] Ch 290 ... 11.167, 13.43, 17.08

D *v* Northern HSSB [1993] 5 BNIL 92 (Taxing Master) ... 17.98

Dabelstein *v* Hildebrandt, 1996 (3) SA 42 .... 11.86
Dagnell *v* Freedman [1993] 1 WLR 388 .... 6.07
Dairy Disposal *v* Lixnaw Creamery[1937] IR 592 .... 13.23
Dale *v* British Coal [1992] 1 WLR 964 .... 11.00
Dallas, *in re* [1997] 3 BNIL 76 .... 19.06
Dalton *v* Ringwood (1906) 40 ILTR 52 .... 20.27,60
Daly *v* Daly (1882) 9 LR Ir 383 .... 3.09
Daly *v* ITGWU [1926] IR 118 .... 9.79
Danchevsky *v* Danchevsky [1975] Fam 17 .... 16.55
Danvaern Production *v* Schuhfabriken Otterbeck [1995] CLY 699 (ECJ) 9.37
Danvers *v* Danvers (1974) 118 SJ 168 .... 17.88,89
Darley, *in re*, QBD, NI, 16 June 1997 .... 1.35, 19.53
Dass *v* Masih [1968] 2 All ER 226 .... 13.126
Davey *v* Chief Constable [1988] NI 139 .... 14.52
Davidson *v* North Down Quarries [1988] NI 214 .... 3.28
Davies *v* Bentick [1893] 1 QB 185 .... 9.92
Davies *v* Dublin & Drogheda Rly (1872) 6 ILTR 128 .... 11.124
Davies *v* Elsby [1961] 1 WLR 170 .... 11.31
Davies *v* Powell Duffryn [1942] AC 601 .... 20.68
Davies *v* Taylor (No 2) [1974] AC 225 .... 17.11
Davin *v* MacCormack [1932] IR 681 .... 11.27
Davis *v* Northern Ireland Carriers [1979] NI 19 .... 1.29,33,35, 20.24
Davy *v* Spelthorne BC [1984] AC 262 .... 19.88
Davy International *v* Tazzyman, *The Times*, 9 May 1997 .... 16.49
Davy-Chiesman *v* Davy-Chiesman [1984] Fam 48 .... 17.64
Dawson *v* DJ Hamill (No 2) [1991] 1 IR 213 .... 19.81
Dawson *v* McClelland [1899] 2 IR 486 .... 3.33
Dawson *v* Thomson (1837) 5 Law Rec NS 199 .... 17.65
de Freyne *v* Fitzgibbon (1904) 4 NIJR 253 .... 20.63
de Vos *v* Baxter [1987] 11 NIJB 103 .... 11.63,68
Dean *v* Dean [1987] 1 FLR 517 .... 16.54,65
Dean *v* Gallagher [1995] 4 BNIL 95 .... 13.12,14,16
Debtor's Summons, *in re* a [1929] IR 139 .... 3.16, 7.06
Debtor, *in re a* [1993] Ch 286 .... 17.77
Debtor, *in re a* [1997] 2 WLR 57 .... 16.40
Deery *v* Frazer (QBD, NI) 6 Dec 1996 .... 11.190
Deighan *v* Sunday Newspapers [1985] NI 9 .... 11.57
Deighan *v* Sunday Newspapers [1987] NI 105 .... 13.94,100,104,14.12
Delaney *v* Delaney [1996] QB 387 .... 16.83
Delmas *v* Vancouver Stock Exchange (1996) 130 DLR 4th 461 .... 19.51
Deman, *in re* (QBD, NI) 19 Jan 1996 .... 19.05
Dempsey *v* Min of Justice [1994] 1 ILRM 401 .... 19.34
Dempsey *v* Scribbans [1944] Ir Jur R 17 .... 20.73
Denis *v* Gorman (1879) 4 LR Ir 356 .... 12.03
Dennis *v* Best (1878) 12 ILTR 152 .... 12.09
DOE *v* George [1982] NI 357 .... 19.09
DOE *v* Leeburn [1990] NI 135 .... 13.96, 18.43
DOE *v* Thompson [1991] 11 NIJB 56 .... 19.09
DHSS *v* Derry Construction [1980] NI 187 .... 11.186,187,188,190,193
Dept of Social Security *v* Butler [1995] 1 WLR 1528 (CA) 11.62, 18.00
Dept of Transport *v* Chris Smaller [1989] AC 1197 .... 11.188
Derby & Co *v* Weldon [1990] Ch 48,65 .... 11.74
Derby & Co *v* Weldon (No 8) [1991] 1 WLR 73 .... 13.41
Derby & Co *v* Weldon (No 9), *The Times*, 9 Nov 1990 .... 18.30
Derham *v* Doyle [1914] 2 IR 135 .... 16.24
Derry Construction *v* DHSS [1980] NI 187 .... 11.08
Desart *v* Townsend (1888) 22 LR Ir 389 .... 11.49
Devenny *v* DOE (L'derry Rec Ct) 9 Oct 1985 [1985] 9 BNIL 127 .... 13.132

Devine *v* Carson [1929] NI 26 .... 20.41
Devine, *in re* [1990] 9 NIJB 96 .... 19.24
Devitt *v* Minister of Education [1989] ILRM 639 .... 19.34
Devlin *v* NIHE [1982] NI 377 .... 13.96
Devlin, *in re* [1995] 9 BNIL 28 .... 1.16
Devonsher *v* Ryall (1877) IR 11 Eq 460 .... 11.180
Devonshire *v* Foot [1900] 2 IR 211 .... 19.83
Devrajan *v* DJ Ballagh [1993] 3 IR 377 .... 1.14, 19.25
Dews *v* NCB [1988] AC 1 .... 14.58
Dexter *v* Courtaulds [1984] 1 WLR 372 .... 9.13
Dhand *v* McCrabbe (1962) 96 ILTR 196 .... 20.27,32
Dickson *v* Blackstaff Weaving [1989] NI 197 .... 3.13, 13.96, 16.13
Dietz *v* Lennig Chemicals [1969] 1 AC 170 .... 12.10,14
Dillane *v* Sullivan (1843) Ir Cir Rep 855 .... 1.23
Dillon *v* Dunnes Stores [1966] IR 397 .... 11.176
Dillon *v* Lynch (No 2) (1961) 95 ILTR 189 .... 20.76
Dinnon *v* Aubrey (1833) 1 Law Rec NS 38 .... 7.05
Director of Buildings *v* Shun Fung Ironworks [1995] 2 AC 111 .... 11.149
Diven *v* Belfast Corp [1969] NI 34 .... 14.44
Dixon Stores *v* Thomas Television [1993] 1 All ER 349 .... 13.43
Dixon *v* Forster [1952] NI 24 .... 3.22
Dobbs *v* Carr (1915) 49 ILTR 243 .... 9.72
Dobler *v* Walsh [1950] NI 150 .... 11.56
Doherty *v* MOD [1979] 6 NIJB 14.42, 20.58
Doherty *v* MOD [1991] 1 NIJB 68 .... 1.30, 11.03, 13.48,58, 14.03
Doherty, *in re* [1988] NI 14 .... 19.23,42,43,45,48
Doherty, *in re* [1996] 2 BNIL 77 .... 19.38,92
Dolan *v* AOTC (1993) 19 Comm LB 1366 (Aus) 13.45
Donaghey *v* Donaghey (1899) 33 ILTR 97 .... 6.04
Donaldson *v* Chief Constable [1989] 1 NIJB 63 .... 14.12
Donaldson *v* Chief Constable [1989] 7 NIJB 21 .... 14.12
Donaldson *v* EHSSB (Taxing Master NI) 4 Sept 1996 .... 17.98a
Donaldson *v* EHSSB (Taxing Master NI) 17 Dec 1996 .... 17.85,107
Donegan *v* Fitzgerald (1903) 37 ILTR 35 .... 12.02
Donnan *v* Creaney [1995] 10 BNIL 26 .... 15.01
Donnelly *v* Coyne [1901] 2 IR 7 .... 11.149, 17.28
Donnelly *v* Gray [1970] Oct NIJB 11.07,195
Donnelly *v* Hackett [1988] 6 NIJB 6 .... 9.20, 14.58,71
Donnelly *v* McCoy [1995] 9 BNIL 20 .... 14.68
Donnelly *v* NHSSB [1993] 10 NIJB 31 (QBD) 17.83,108
Donnelly *v* Verschoyle [1919] 2 IR 101 .... 17.27,30,38
Donnelly, *in re* [1988] 8 NIJB 26 .... 19.34
Donoghue *v* Burke [1960] IR 314 .... 20.68
Donovan *v* Todd, Burns & Co [1908] 2 IR 100 .... 11.98
Dooley *v* Murdock Harwood (QBD, NI) 4 June 1996 .... 11.147, 17.24
Doone *v* McPartland [1987] NI 119 .... 4.06, 11.133
Doran *v* Power [1995] 2 IR 402 .... 18.17
Doran *v* Thompson [1978] IR 223 .... 2.01, 13.96
Douglas *v* Ewing (1856) 6 ICLR 395; 3 Ir Jur NS 174 .... 20.57
Dowd *v* Kerry CC [1970] IR 27 .... 11.188, 20.43
Dowie *v* Melvin [1973] NI 60 .... 13.28
Dowling *v* Dowling (1860) 10 ICLR 236 .... 13.14
Dowling *v* Great Southern Rly [1943] Ir Jur R 7 .... 14.58
Downey *v* Murray [1988] NI 600 .... 11.135, 13.41
Doyle *v* Commonwealth (1985) 156 CLR 510 .... 16.53,55
Doyle *v* Doris [1993] 6 NIJB 1 .... 16.17
Doyle *v* Doyle (1974) 52 DLR 3d 143 .... 6.11
Doyle *v* Gaffney (1923) 57 ILTR 156 .... 11.159

Doyle *v* Patterson [1934] IR 116 .... 7.07
DPP *v* Hutchinson [1990] 2 AC 783 .... 19.09,81
Drayne *v* Chiko Foods (Taxing Master, NI) 31 Jan 1991 .... 17.107
Drummond & Co *v* Lamb [1992] 1 WLR 163 .... 3.57
Dubai Bank *v* Galadari [1990] Ch 98 .... 13.40
Dubai Bank *v* Galadari (No 2) [1990] 2 All ER 738 .... 11.112
Dubai Bank *v* Galadari (No 7) [1992] 1 WLR 106 .... 13.40
Dublin Corp *v* Bray Commrs [1900] 2 IR 88 .... 13.132
Dudley *v* An Taoiseach [1994] 2 ILRM 321 .... 19.13
Duff *v* Devlin [1924] 1 IR 56 (NI) 18.59,72
Duffy *v* McLaron [1985] NI 285 .... 12.14
Duffy *v* MOD [1979] NI 120 .... 11.08, 13.10
Duffy *v* News Group [1992] 2 IR 369 .... 3.36
Duffy, *in re* [1991] 7 NIJB 62 .... 19.23,92
Duke of Buccleuch [1892] P 201 .... 11.20,24
Duncan *v* Mackin [1985] 10 NIJB 1 .... 1.20, 18.40
Dunlop Rubber *v* Dunlop [1921] 1 AC 367 .... 6.16
Dunn *v* Shanks [1932] NI 66 .... 13.96
Dunne *v* Clancy (1880) 6 LR Ir 395 .... 9.23
Dunne *v* Johnson (1901) 2 NIJR 23 .... 11.107
Dunne, *in re* (1880) 5 LR Ir 76 .... 20.02
Dunne, *in re* [1907] 1 IR 202 .... 18.66
Dunnes Stores *v* Deramore Lamont [1996] 9 BNIL 68 .... 11.122
Dunning *v* United Liverpool Hospitals [1973] 1 WLR 586 .... 11.134
Durity *v* JLSC [1996] 2 LRC 451 .... 19.95
Duxbury *v* Barlow [1901] 2 KB 23 .... 17.28

Eagil Trust *v* Pigott-Brown [1985] 3 All ER 119 .... 14.42
Eagle Star *v* Provincial Insurance [1994] 1 AC 130 (PC) 10.08
Eogan *v* University College Dublin [1996] 1 IR 390 .... 19.06
Ealing LBC *v* El Issac [1980] 1 WLR 932 .... 15.15
East Cork Foods *v* O'Dwyer Steel [1978] IR 103 .... 20.72
Eastwood *v* Channel 5 [1992] NI 183 .... 11.34,35
Eastwood *v* Channel 5 [1992] 2 NIJB 45 .... 11.123, 18.22
Eastwood *v* Channel 5 [1992] 2 NIJB 53 .... 14.25,18.24
Eastwood *v* Channel 5 [1992] 2 NIJB 58 .... 13.71
Eastwood *v* News Group [1992] 2 NIJB 1 .... 18.24
EB Tractors, *in re* [1986] NI 165 .... 13.20
Edgill *v* Cullen [1932] IR 734 .... 11.125
Edinburgh Life *v* Y [1911] 1 IR 306 .... 13.15
Edison & Swan *v* Holland (1889) 41 Ch D 28 .... 20.37
Edmunds *v* Lloyd Italico [1986] 1 WLR 492 .... 5.12, 14.79
Edwards, *in re* [1982] Ch 30 .... 20.64
EEL, *in re* [1938] NI 56 .... 19.101
Egleso *v* Stokes (1826) Batty 213 .... 5.05
Elgindata (No 2), *Re* [1992] 1 WLR 1207 .... 17.39
El Capistrano *v* ATO [1989] 1 WLR 471 .... 16.54
Electronic Sales *v* Sec of State [1979] NI 151 .... 17.105
Ellis *v* Ballycassidy Sawmills (Taxing Master, NI) 18 Sept 1991 .... 17.105
Elwyn Ltd *v* Master of High Court [1989] IR 14 .... 19.11
Ely *v* Dargan [1967] IR 89 .... 11.149
Ely *v* Moule (1851) 5 Exch 918 (155 ER 401) 16.02
EMI *v* Pandit [1975] 1 WLR 302 .... 11.109
Emerald Stainless Steel *v* South Side Distribution 1982 SC 61 .... 13.94
Enfield LBC *v* Mahoney [1983] 1 WLR 749 .... 16.55
English *v* Murphy (1941) 75 ILTR 128 .... 16.24
Equiticorp Industries *v* The Crown (No 3) [1996] 3 NZLR 690 .... 14.82
Erebus Royal Commission, *in re* [1983] NZLR 663 (PC) 19.32

Errington *v* Wilson 1995 SLT 1193 ....19.41
Esdaile *v* Paine (1889) 40 Ch D 520, [1891] AC 210 ....20.24
Eshelby *v* Federated Bank [1932] 1 KB 254 ....11.30
Eshywilligan, *in re* Lands at [1992] 3 NIJB 79 ....4.07
Esso *v* Southport Corp [1956] AC 218....................9.02
Esso Petroleum *v* Milton [1997] 2 All ER 593....................9.36,43
Evans *v* Bartlam [1937] AC 473....................8.17, 11.08
Evans Constructions *v* Charrington [1983] QB 810 ....11.34
Evans *v* Davies [1893] 2 Ch 216 ....11.82
Evans *v* Evans (1883) LJ Ch 304....................18.77
Evans *v* Figgis (1849) 11 Ir LR 587 ....11.22
Evans *v* Keane [1908] 2 IR 629 ....9.51
Ewing, *ex parte* (No 2) [1994] 1 WLR 1553 ....5.02

Factortame *v* Sec of State for Transport see R *v* Secretary of State for Transport
Fahy *v* Pullen (1968) 102 ILTR 81 ....9.77, 20.08
Fair Employment Commission, *in re* [1990] 10 NIJB 38 ....19.35
Fairfold Properties *v* Exmouth Docks (No 2) [1993] Ch 196 ....17.75
Faley *v* O'Mahony [1929] IR 1 ....16.43
Falgat Constructions Pty, *re* (1996) 70 ALJR 609....................3.50
Fallon *v* An Bord Pleanála [1992] 2 IR 380 ....20.35
Fancourt *v* Mercantile Credits (1983) 154 CLR 87....................6.24
Farden *v* Richter (1889) 23 QBD 124....................8.13
Fares *v* Wiley [1994] 1 ILRM 465 ....11.57,58
Farrell *v* Reilly (1955) 89 ILTR 7 ....18.63
Farrell *v* Sec of State [1980]1 WLR 172; [1980] NI 55 (HL) 9.00,02,71,
....................11.21, 20.48
Farren, *in re* [1990] 6 NIJB 72 ....19.26
Feehan *v* Mandeville (1890) 26 LR Ir 391 ....11.198
Felix *v* Shiva [1983] QB 82 ....1.12
Felton *v* Callis [1969] 1 QB 200 ....11.76
Fergus Syndicate *v* Hewitt (1944) 78 ILTR 14....................9.36
Ferguson *v* Davies [1997] 1 All ER 315 ....9.27
Ferguson *v* Ferguson [1920] 1 IR 81 ....11.172
Ferguson *v* Rapid Metal [1972] June (Pt II) NIJB 20.50,55
Ferguson *v* Taggart (1893) 27 ILTR 134 ....1.35, 9.59
Fermanagh CC *v* Parker [1932] NI 153 ....18.00
Ferndale Films *v* Granada TV [1993] 3 IR 362 ....1.14
Ferrall *v* Curran [1899] 2 IR 470 ....11.44
Ferris *v* O'Kean [1907] 1 IR 223 ....17.55
Ferryhaugh *v* Farrell (1875) IR 9 CL 422 ....11.28
FF *v* CF [1987] ILRM 1....................18.77
Ffrench Mullen *v* Murphy (1911) 45 ILTR 210....................10.20
Field *v* Catherwood [1931] NI 150....................9.78
Fielding *v* Rigby [1993] 1 WLR 1355 ....11.41
Finch *v* Telegraph Construction [1949] 1 All ER 452 ....17.36
Findlater *v* Tuohy (1885) 16 LR Ir 474 ....16.10
Finlay, *in re* [1983] 9 NIJB 19.41
Finucane *v* Yorkshire TV [1997] 2 BNIL 105....................18.22
First National Commercial Bank *v* Anglin [1996] 1 IR 75 ....11.49
Firth Finance *v* McNarry [1987] NI 125....................3.44
Firth *v* John Mowlem [1978] 3 All ER 331....................7.11
Fisher *v* Moynagh (1912) 46 ILTR 187 ....10.24
Fitzgerald *v* Kenny [1994] 2 ILRM 8 ....20.43
Fitzgerald *v* Lane [1989] AC 329 ....14.74
Fitzgerald *v* Williams [1996] QB 657....................11.58
Fitzgerald, *in re* [1925] 1 IR 39 ....11.130
Fitzpatrick *v* Independent Newspapers [1988] IR 132 ....1.12

Flanagan *v* BP [1926] IR 51 .... 9.20
Flanagan *v* Fahy [1918] 2 IR 361 .... 13.78
Fleming *v* Hargreaves [1976] 1 NZLR 123 .... 18.77
Fletcher *v* Manitoba Insurance (1990) 74 DLR 4th 637 .... 17.08
Fletcher, *re* , *The Times* 12 June 1984 .... 1.02
Flynn & McMorrow, *in re* [1951] Ir Jur Rep 1 .... 17.75
Fogarty *v* O'Donoghue [1926] IR 531 .... 17.55, 20.75
Foley *v* Coffey (1909) 43 ILTR 13 .... 9.32
Foley *v* Daly [1938] Ir Jur R 5 .... 17.67
Fookes *v* Slaytor [1978] 1 WLR 1293 .... 8.11, 14.74
Ford *v* Servotomic [1977] CLY 1216 .... 9.51
Forde *v* McEldowney [1970] NI 11(HL) 19.09
Forest Lake, The [1968] P 270 .... 14.22
Forrest *v* Carte [1897] 2 IR 314 .... 17.43
Forster *v* Donovan (1980) 114 ILTR 104 .... 10.12
Forward *v* Hendricks [1997] 2 All ER 395 .... 4.06
Forward *v* West Sussex CC [1995] 4 All ER 207 .... 6.02, 20.43
Foster *v* Edwards (1879) 48 LJQB 767 .... 11.08
Foto-Frost *v* Hauptzollamt L①beck-Ost [1987] ECR 4199 .... 14.17, 19.12
Fox *v* Drake (1886) 20 ILTR 6 .... 8.18
Fox *v* Star Newspaper [1900] AC 19 .... 14.20,46
Fox, *in re* [1987] 1 NIJB 12 .... 19.105,108
Francovich *v* Italian Republic [1993] 2 CMLR 66 .... 19.88
Franklin *v* Franklin [1915] WN 342 .... 3.40
Franklin *v* Walker (1870) IR 4 CL 236 .... 11.180
Fraser *v* Buckle [1996] 1 IR 1 .... 3.19
Freedman *v* Opdeheyde [1945] Ir Jur R 22 .... 6.17
Friends' Provident *v* Hillier Parker May & Rowden [1997] QB 85 .... 10.09
Friis *v* Paramount Bagwash (No 2) [1940] 2 KB 654 .... 17.65
Fry *v* Johnson (1856) 6 Ir Ch R 56 .... 18.57
Fullam *v* Associated Newspapers [1955-6] Ir Jur R 45 .... 13.114
Fuller *v* Dublin CC [1976] IR 20 .... 11.26
Funston *v* Funston (QB Mat, NI) 18 June 1965; 16 NILQ 418 .... 13.28, 14.33
Furey *v* Conception Bay RC School (1993) 104 DLR 4th 455 .... 19.34
Fury *v* Smith (1822) 1 Hud & Br 735 .... 13.151
Fusco *v* O'Dea [1994] 2 ILRM 389 .... 11.135

G *v* Caledonian Newspapers 1995 SLT 559 .... 11.01
G *v* DPP [1994] 1 IR 374 .... 19.56
Gailey *v* Hurley (1901) 2 NIJR 30 .... 8.17
Gairloch, The SS[1899] 2 IR 1 .... 20.65
Gale *v* Superdrug Stores [1996] 3 All ER 468 .... 9.96
Gallaher *v* Brand [1987] 2 NIJB 54 .... 17.98
Gallagher *v* Revenue Commrs (No 2) [1995] 1 IR 55 .... 19.40,41
Gallagher *v* Sloan [1983] NI 78 .... 12.09, 15.22
Gallagher *v* Young [1939] NI 146 .... 11.151
Galvin *v* Graham-Twomey [1994] 2 ILRM 315 .... 11.96
Gannon *v* British & Irish Steam Packet [1993] 2 IR 359 .... 1.14
Garbett *v* Cooper (No 2) [1936] NI 64 .... 17.75
Garcin *v* Amerindo Advisors [1991] 1 WLR 1140 .... 13.34
Gardiner *v* Irish Land Comm (1976) 110 ILTR 21 .... 13.147
Gardiner *v* Mathewson (1854) 6 Ir Jur OS 147 .... 3.29
Gardner *v* Brooke [1897] 2 IR 6 .... 10.14
Garner *v* Foote (1903) 3 NIJR 110 .... 12.01
Garratt (Henry) *v* Ewing [1991] 4 All ER 891 .... 5.02
Gaskins *v* British Aluminium [1976] QB 524 .... 11.158
Gaynor *v* Gaynor [1901] 1 IR 217 .... 18.70
Geary, *in re* [1939] NI 152 .... 3.19, 18.64

Gee *v* BBC, *The Times* 26 Nov 1984 .... 14.09
Geffen *v* Goodman Estate (1991) 81 DLR 4th 211 .... 13.42
Geogas SA *v* Trammo Gas [1991] 1 WLR 776 .... 20.07,12,15
George *v* Camarthenshire CC (1975) 119 SJ 407 .... 11.188
Geraghty *v* Minister of Local Government [1975] IR 300 .... 13.38
Gerrard *v* Beggan (1857) 2 Ir Jur NS 311 .... 16.24
Gervais, *in re* [1903] 1 IR 172 .... 10.14
Gestion Complexe *v* Canada (1995) 125 DLR 4th 559 .... 19.06
Gethings *v* Cloney (1914) 48 ILTR 55 .... 3.48
Giannarelli *v* Wraith (1991) 171 CLR 592 .... 17.107
Giant's Causeway *v* A-G (1905) 5 NIJR 301 .... 13.121
Gibson *v* British Rail, 1995 SLT 953 .... 14.39
Giese *v* Williston (1963) 37 DLR 2d 447 .... 19.40
Gilbert *v* Endean (1878) 9 Ch D 259 .... 16.45
Giles *v* Thompson [1994] 1 AC 142 .... 3.19
Gillen, *in re* [1988] NI 40 .... 19.99,101
Gillen, *in re* [1990] 2 NIJB 47 .... 19.14
Gillespie *v* Anglo-Irish Beef [1994] 4 BNIL 68 .... 10.22, 11.95
Gillespie *v* Reid (1894) 28 ILTR 140 .... 16.40
Gillick *v* West Norfolk Health Authority [1986] AC 112 .... 19.07
Gilliland, *in re* [1940] NI 125 .... 13.121
Gilmurray *v* Corr [1978] NI 99 .... 14.86
Gilroy *v* McLoughlin [1988] IR 44 .... 13.104,111
Gilsenan *v* McGovern (1892) 30 LR Ir 300 .... 5.12, 17.77
Gilson *v* Bennett [1920] 1 IR 75 .... 20.32
Gingles *v* Magill [1926] NI 234 .... 18.77
Glass *v* McManus (High Ct, NI) 7 June 1996 [1996] 5 BNIL 75 .... 18.77
Glor Na nGael, *in re* [1991] NI 117 .... 19.71
Glover *v* BLN Ltd [1973] IR 388 .... 19.05
Goldman *v* Hesper [1988] 1 WLR 1238 .... 17.107
Goldstone *v* Williams [1899] 1 Ch 47 .... 13.41
Gomba Holdings *v* Minories Finance [1993] Ch 171 .... 17.95
Good *v* Aherne (1842) 2 Leg Rep 386 .... 13.54
Good *v* Jagoe (1881) 15 ILTR 50 .... 9.46
Goodbody *v* Gallaher (1885) 16 LR Ir 336 .... 9.34
Goodchild *v* Duncan [1895] 2 IR 393 .... 11.49
Goodman International *v* Hamilton (No 3) [1993] 3 IR 320 .... 13.46
Goodman *v* Whyte (1949) 83 ILTR 159 .... 11.151
Goodwin *v* UK, *The Times*, 28 March 1996 (EHCR) 13.53
Gordon *v* Craddock [1964] 1 QB 503 .... 11.54
Gordon *v* East Kilbride Dev Corp 1995 SLT 62 .... 13.43
Gordon *v* Gordon [1951] IR 301 .... 12.05
Gordon *v* Kirwan (1889) 24 LR Ir 245 .... 11.174
Gore-Booth *v* Gore-Booth (1962) 96 ILTR 32 .... 16.56
Gort *v* Rowney (1886) 17 QBD 625 .... 17.47
Gould *v* Vaggelas (1984) 157 CLR 215 .... 17.51
Govern *v* Rowland (1858) 7 ICLR 619 .... 15.09
Grace *v* Finnucane (1842) Arm Mac & Og 365 .... 14.27
Graffin *v* Famac Network (CA, NI) 24 Jan 1997 .... 20.79
Graham *v* Bogle [1924] 1 IR 68 (NI) 13.40
Graham *v* Dodds [1983] NI 22 .... 14.71
Graham *v* Dublin, Wicklow & Wexford Rly (1895) 29 ILTR 134 .... 20.57
Graham *v* E & A Dunlop [1977] 1 NIJB 9.70, 14.39
Graham *v* Hugh Burns [1978] 3 NIJB 14.30
Graham *v* McPherson [1991] NI 1 .... 3.24, 10.06,08
Graham *v* Ulsterbus [1993] 3 NIJB 102 .... 13.56
Grainger Building *v* McCreedy [1990] NI 126 .... 13.96
Gray *v* Boyd, 1996 SLT 60 .... 9.24

Great Atlantic *v* Home Insurance [1981] 1 WLR 529 .... 13.41
Greaves *v* Wm Barker [1995] CLY 3900 .... 5.00
Grech *v* Minister for Immigration (1993) 19 Comm LB 40 (Aus) 19.14,32
Green *v* Rozen [1955] 2 All ER 797 .... 12.09
Green (R & H) *v* BRB [1985] 1 WLR 570 .... 4.03
Greencore Group *v* Murphy [1996] 1 ILRM 210 .... 13.43
Greene *v* Boyle [1937] Ir Jur Rep 3 (NI) 14.44
Greene *v* Governor of Mountjoy [1995] 3 IR 541 .... 19.23
Greene *v* Mooney (1901) 1 NIJR 215 .... 6.10
Gregan *v* Rafter [1940] Ir Jur R 80 .... 17.15
Gregg *v* Fraser [1906] 2 IR 545 .... 7.20
Grehan *v* Medical Inc [1986] IR 528 .... 6.16
Grennan *v* DJ Kirby [1994] 2 ILRM 199 .... 19.48
Gresham Hotel *v* Manning (1867) IR 1 CL 125 .... 13.115
Greville *v* Hayes [1894] 2 IR 20 .... 10.20
Greyhound Australia *v* Deluxe Coachlines (1988) 14 Comm LB 106 (Aus) 13.04,05
Gribben, *in re* [1987] NI 129 .... 19.31,43
Gribbon, *in re* [1990] 6 NIJB 15 .... 19.06
Griebart *v* Morris [1920] 1 KB 659 .... 11.125
Grierdon *v* Brereton (1794) Ir Term R 281 .... 14.30
Griffiths *v* Patterson (1888) 22 LR Ir 656 .... 17.25,27,41
Grimes *v* Connell [1920] 2 IR 61 .... 11.197
Grimes *v* Owners of SS Bangor Bay [1948] IR 350 .... 17.31
Grimley *v* Henry [1981] 1 NIJB 14.39,44
Grogan, *in re* [1988] 8 NIJB 87 .... 19.31
Grogan, *in re* [1993] 10 NIJB 18 .... 19.19,26
Grosvenor Chemical *v* Greenfield [1909] 1 IR 32 .... 9.82
Group 4 Securitas *v* McIldowney (Ch D, NI) 13 Feb 1997 .... 11.75,86,194
Grovit *v* Doctor [1997] 1 WLR 640 .... 11.181,186
Guardians of Belfast Union *v* Belfast Corp (1909) 43 ILTR 247 .... 11.24, 20.02
Guardians of Sligo *v* Miller (1903) 3 NIJR 203 .... 17.24
Guardians of South Dublin *v* Jones (1883) 12 LR Ir 358 .... 20.74
Guinness Peat *v* Fitzroy Robinson [1987] 1 WLR 1027 .... 11.117
Gundry *v* Sainsbury [1910] 1 KB 645 .... 17.11
Gupta *v* Comer [1991] 1 QB 629 .... 17.62
Gupta *v* Gupta's Trustee, 1994 SC 74 .... 19.08
Gwenzi *v* Cebekhula 1996 (1) SA 525 .... 11.176

H (a bankrupt), *in re* (1936) 70 ILTR 199 .... 16.64
H (Minors) (No 2), *in re* [1992] 2 AC 303 .... 17.90
H (Minors) (Sexual Abuse: Standard of Proof), *in re* [1996] AC 563 .... 13.20
H *v* DPP [1994] 2 ILRM 285 .... 19.14
Hafner, *re*; Olhausen *v* Powderley (1940) 74 ILTR 126 .... 11.19
Haggan *v* Porter [1975] 7 NIJB 9.77, 11.20
Haig *v* McMahon [1901] 2 IR 350 .... 1.29
Haiti (Republic of) *v* Duvalier [1990] 1 QB 202 .... 6.13
Hales *v* Kerr [1908] 2 KB 601 .... 13.15
Hamilton *v* Colhoun [1906] 2 IR 104 .... 17.104
Hamilton, *in re* (1840) 1 Cr & D CC 624 .... 13.149
Hammond *v* Hammond (1874) IR 8 Eq 322 .... 12.09
Hanak *v* Green [1958] 2 QB 9 .... 17.43
Hanbury *v* Jones (1863) 9 Ir Jur NS 5 .... 8.15
Hanbury *v* Upper Inny Drainage Board (1883) 12 LR Ir 217 .... 10.26
Hancock Shipping *v* Kawasaki [1992] 1 WLR 1025 .... 11.34
Handbridge Ltd *v* British Aerospace [1993] 3 IR 342 .... 1.14
Hanley *v* Randles (No 2) [1960] Ir Jur R 67 .... 11.149
Hanlon *v* Law Society [1981] AC 124 .... 17.87
Hanna *v* Chief Constable [1986] NI 103 .... 13.20,69,84

Hannay *v* Graham (1883) 12 LR Ir 413 ....11.180
Hannays *v* Baldeosingh [1992] 1 WLR 395 ....20.53
Hanrahan *v* Merck, Sharp [1988] ILRM 629 ....20.69
Haoucher *v* Minister for Immigration (1990) 169 CLR 648; [1991] LRC (Const) 819 ...19.34
Harbord *v* Monk (1878) 38 LT 411 ....9.91
Hardie Rubber *v* General Tire (1973) 129 CLR 521 ....13.10
Hardy, *in re* [1988] 12 NIJB 66 ....11.116
Hardy, *in re* [1989] 2 NIJB 81 ....19.92
Harkness *v* Bell [1967] 2 QB 729....1.30
Harley Development *v* Commr of Inland Revenue [1996] 1 WLR 727 ....19.51
Harper *v* Associated British Foods [1991] NI 244 .... 11.146, 14.52
Harper *v* Gray [1985] 1 WLR 1196 ....10.28
Harpur *v* Buchanan [1919] 1 IR 1 ....18.72
Harrison *v* Ennis [1967] IR 286 ....11.162
Harrison *v* Liverpool Corp [1943] 2 All ER 449 ....13.89
Harrison *v* Tew [1990] 2 AC 523 ....17.77
Hart *v* Carswell [1973] NI 154....4.04
Hartley *v* Saunders (1962) 33 DLR 2d 638 ....11.128
Harvey *v* Derrick [1995] 1 NZLR 314 ....19.49
Harvey *v* Smith-Wood [1964] 2 QB 171 ....13.63
Hassall *v* Sec of State [1995] 1 WLR 812 .... 14.68,68g
Hastings *v* Henry (1912) 46 ILTR 308 ....16.74,80
Hatton *v* Harris [1892] AC 547 (Ir) 15.13
Haughey *v* Prendiville (Ch D, NI) 17 Dec 1996.... 11.117, 13.53
Haughey *v* Sunday Newspapers [1989] 5 NIJB 102 ....14.04
Haughey, *in re* [1986] 16 NIJB 17 ....19.06
Haulage Services *v* Larne Harbour [1987] 5 NIJB 1 ....11.26
Hawes *v* Chief Constable of Avon, *The Times* 20 May 1993 ....20.18
Hawkesley *v* Fewtrell [1954] 1 QB 228 ....14.44
Hay *v* London Brick (1981) [1989] 2 Lloyds Rep 7 ....11.31
Hay *v* O'Grady [1992] 1 IR 210 ....20.65
Hayes *v* Shell Ltd (Ch D, NI) 16 Nov 1995 ....11.68
Healy *v* Nolan (1946) 80 ILTR 78....9.16,72
Heany *v* Malocca [1958] IR 111 ....11.57
Hearn *v* Downes (1920) 54 ILTR 50 ....11.101
Heaton's Transport *v* TGWU [1973] AC 15 ....16.50
Hedley *v* Sparrow [1964] NI 72....3.35
Heffernan *v* Atkin (1913) 47 ILTR 245 ....6.00
Hegarty *v* Henry [1990] 7 BNIL 61 ....13.33
Hempston *v* Humphreys (1867) IR 1 CL 271 ....16.68
Henderson *v* Henry Jenkins [1970] AC 282 ....13.29
Hennessey *v* Rohmann [1877] WN 14; 36 LT 51 ....11.86
Hennessy *v* Keating (1907) 41 ILTR 203 ....20.35
Hennessy *v* Lavery [1903] 1 IR 87 ....11.96
Hennessy *v* Quinn [1968] IR 274....10.26
Henry *v* Geoprosco [1976] QB 726....7.09
Henty *v* Beckett [1914] 2 IR 206 ....11.110
Herbinson *v* O'Neill [1985] 3 NIJB 84 ....11.142
Hermon *v* Yorkshire TV [1992] NI 27.... 9.86, 11.110, 18.22
Herd *v* Clyde Helicopters, 1997 SLT 672....17.90
Herskind *v* Hall [1908] 2 IR 99 ....11.98
Hesketh *v* Ford Motor Co (Taxing Master, NI) 11 May 1995 ....17.35
Hession *v* Jones [1914] 2 KB 421 ....20.77
Hewson *v* Cleeve [1904] 2 IR 536....9.02,93
Hibernian Bank *v* McArdle (1932) 66 ILTR 28 ....15.06
Hibernian Stock *v* Fottrell (1884) 13 LR Ir 335 ....11.41
Hickey *v* DOE [1992] 1 NIJB 54 ....4.06, 11.35
Hickey *v* Hickey (1881) 15 ILTR 41....9.38

Hickey *v* Kelly [1929] IR 628 .... 16.44
Hickman *v* Foley (1905) 39 ILTR 21 .... 10.26
Hicks *v* South Yorkshire Chief Constable [1992] 2 All ER 65 .... 14.70
Higgins *v* Dorries [1965] Qd R 389; [1965] Aust Law Digest 281 .... 3.35
Higgins *v* Patterson [1971] IR 111 .... 14.31
Hildige *v* O'Farrell (1881) 8 LR Ir 158 .... 11.179
Hill *v* Chief Constable [1990] 1 WLR 946 .... 14.04
Hill *v* Deakin (1974) 118 SJ 389 .... 12.10
Hill *v* Maunsell-Eyre [1944] IR 499 .... 18.72
Hilton *v* Lancashire Dynamo [1964] 2 All ER 769 .... 13.126
Hines *v* Birkbeck College (No 2) [1992] Ch 33 .... 13.106
Ho Ming-sai *v* Director of Immigration [1994] 1 LRC 409 (Hong Kong) 19.56
Hoban *v* McPherson (1905) 39 ILTR 15 .... 11.180
Hobbs *v* Marlowe [1978] AC 16 .... 17.04
Hockey *v* Yelland (1984) 157 CLR 124 .... 19.16,41,45
Hodgson *v* Hart DC [1986] 1 WLR 317 .... 6.02
Hodgson *v* Trapp [1989] AC 807 .... 14.59,71
Hoecheong Products *v* Cargill Ltd [1995] 1 WLR 404 .... 20.52
Hogan, *in re* [1986] 5 NIJB 81 .... 19.56,79
Hogan (No 2)), *in re* [1986] 9 NIJB 45 .... 16.48,49,57
Hogan *v* Bayer Products (1950) 84 ILTR 145 .... 11.97, 13.52
Hogan *v* Davis Estates [1942] IR 370 .... 13.115
Hogan *v* Hogan [1924] 2 IR 12 .... 11.05
Hogan *v* Jones [1994] 1 ILRM 512 .... 11.190,191
Hogg *v* Belfast Corp [1919] 2 IR 305 .... 7.16
Holden *v* Holden [1968] NI 7 .... 13.20
Holgate-Mohammed *v* Duke [1984] AC 437 .... 19.14
Hollingsworth *v* Humphry, *The Independent*, 21 Dec 1987; [1988] CLY 2931 .... 12.09
Hollis *v* Burton [1892] 3 Ch 226 .... 11.18
Holloway *v* Belenos (No 2) [1988] IR 494 .... 1.12
Holmes, *in re* [1934] IR 693 .... 13.121
Holtby *v* Hodgson (1889) 24 QBD 103 .... 15.06
Hone, *in re* [1987] NI 160 .... 19.92
Hongkong Bank *v* Wheeler Holdings (1993) 100 DLR 4th 40 .... 14.95
Hood-Barrs *v* Crossman [1897] AC 172 .... 20.72
Hoole *v* Earnshaw (1878) 39 LT 409 .... 5.08
Hooton *v* Dalby [1907] 2 KB 18 .... 11.125
Hope (The) (1883) 8 PD 144 .... 12.05
Hoppe *v* Titman [1996] 1 WLR 841 .... 9.51, 11.157
Hopson *v* R [1994] 2 LRC 741 (PC) 13.113
Horan, *in re* [1964] IR 263 .... 17.77
Horner *v* Min of Development [1971] March NIJB 13.96, 20.39
Hot Holdings *v* Creasy (1996) 70 ALJR 286 .... 19.07
Houlihan *v* O'Sullivan (1930) 64 ILTR 178 .... 9.08,93
House of Spring *v* Waite [1991] 1 QB 241 .... 13.102
Houston *v* Corry [1972] April NIJB 11.188,191
Howard *v* Commr of Works [1994] 2 ILRM 301 .... 11.07, 15.11
Howard *v* Howard (1892) 30 LR Ir 340 .... 11.36,44,58, 18.34
Howard *v* Howard (1893) 32 LR Ir 454 .... 1.29
Howden *v* Ulster Bank [1924] 1 IR 117 (NI) 13.135
Huddleston *v* Control Risks [1987] 1 WLR 701 .... 11.88
Hudson *v* Dublin Corp [1931] IR 264 .... 17.26
Hudson *v* Elmbridge BC [1991] 1 WLR 880 .... 11.157
Hudson *v* Lindsay (1880) 6 LR Ir 420 n.1 .... 20.14,28
Hughes *v* European Components [1990] 2 NIJB 29 .... 20.80
Hughes *v* Hughes [1990] NI 295 .... 1.35,37, 11.192,198
Hughes *v* Hughes [1997] 1 BNIL 47 .... 18.75
Hughes *v* Justin [1894] 1 QB 667 .... 17.22

Hughes *v* Law [1988] 12 NIJB 30 ..... 13.39
Hughes *v* Liverpool CC, *The Times*, 30 March 1988 ..... 14.33
Hughes *v* O'Rourke [1986] ILRM 538 ..... 11.20
Hughes *v* West (1884) 13 LR Ir 224 ..... 11.41
Hughes, *in re* [1986] NI 13 ..... 19.91
Hull & County Bank, *in re* (1880) 13 Ch D 261 ..... 20.05,08
Hultquist *v* Universal Pattern [1960] 2 QB 467 ..... 11.162
Humberclyde Finance *v* McFarland [1997] 3 BNIL 108 ..... 20.35
Hummerstone *v* Leary [1921] 2 KB 664 ..... 14.31
Humphries, *in re* [1989] 12 NIJB 1 ..... 11.42
Hungerfords *v* Walker [1989] LRC (Comm) 397; 171 CLR 125 ..... 14.80
Hunt *v* Egan (1842) 1 Leg Rep 174 ..... 6.21
Hunt *v* RM Douglas [1990] 1 AC 398 ..... 15.16, 17.111
Hunt *v* Severs [1994] 2 AC 350 ..... 14.55,63
Hunt *v* Worsfold [1896] 2 Ch 224 ..... 3.26, 18.76
Hunter *v* Butler, *The Times*, 28 Dec 1995 ..... 14.58,71
Hunter *v* Chief Constable [1982] AC 529 ..... 11.181, 13.110
Hunter *v* Gray [1970] NI 1 ..... 13.154
Hunter *v* Hannay (1892) 26 ILTR 129 ..... 11.00
Hunter, *in re* [1989] 1 NIJB 86 ..... 19.50
Hurst Ltd *v* Brown (Taxing Master, NI) 1 April 1993 ..... 17.103
Hussain *v* Hussain [1986] Fam 134 ..... 16.64
Hutch *v* Dublin Corporation [1993] 3 IR 551 ..... 13.28
Hutchinson *v* Minister of Justice [1993] ILRM 602 ..... 19.13
Hytec Information *v* Coventry CC, *The Times*, 31 Dec 1996 ..... 1.37

Iberian Trust *v* Founders Trust [1932] 2 KB 87 ..... 16.49,53,57
IG Farbenindustrie, *re* [1944] Ch 41 ..... 11.27
Imperial Tobacco *v* McAllister (No 1) (1916) 50 ILTR 156 ..... 11.46
Imperial Tobacco *v* McAllister (No 2) (1916) 50 ILTR 157 ..... 11.53
Impex Transport *v* Thames Ltd [1981] 1 WLR 1548 ..... 9.46
Incorporated Law Society *v* Carroll [1995] 3 IR 145 ..... 3.23
Independent Newspapers *v* Irish Press (1938) 72 ILTR 11 ..... 13.10
Inland Revenue *v* Church Commrs [1975] 1 WLR 251 ..... 20.85
International Bank *v* Insurance Corp [1989] IR 453 ..... 6.16
International Bulk Shipping *v* Minerals Trading Corp [1996] 1 All ER 1017 ..... 11.34
Ipswich BC *v* Fisons [1990] Ch 709 ..... 20.12
Iran Navubat, The [1990] 1 WLR 1115 ..... 8.13, 20.14
Irish Agric Soc *v* St Enda's Co-Op [1924] 2 IR 41 ..... 6.22
Irish Agric Soc *v* McCowan (1913) 47 ILTR 20 ..... 11.108
Irish Bonding *v* Belfast Securities (Ch D, NI) 23 Dec 1965; (1966) 17 NILQ 288 ..... 16.54
Irish Commercial *v* Plunkett [1987] ILRM 504 ..... 11.07
Irish Land Commission *v* Ryan [1900] 2 IR 565 ..... 13.104
Irish Life *v* Dublin Land [1989] IR 253 ..... 13.20
Irish Peoples Assurance *v* City of Dublin Assurance [1928] IR 204 ..... 9.79
Irish Press *v* Ingersoll Ltd [1995] 2 ILRM 270 ..... 3.36
Irtelli *v* Squatriti [1993] QB 83 ..... 16.85
Irvine *v* Freeland [1967] NI 146 ..... 11.141
Irvine *v* O'Hare [1987] 2 NIJB 79 ..... 14.39, 20.65
Irving *v* Askew (1870) LR 5 QB 208 ..... 15.10
Irwin *v* Brown [1993] 6 NIJB 18 ..... 20.43
Irwin *v* Donaghy (QBD, NI) 15 Dec 1995 ..... 11.135
Isaacs *v* Robertson [1985] AC 97 (PC) 1.30, 16.50
Islam *v* Askar, *The Times* 20 Oct 1994 ..... 12.09
Ismail *v* Rickards Butler [1996] QB 711 ..... 3.50
Israelson *v* Dawson [1933] 1 KB 301 ..... 16.12
Istel (AT & T) *v* Tully [1993] AC 45 ..... 13.44
ITC *v* Video Exchange [1982] Ch 431 ..... 13.50

J McL, *in re* [1986] NI 397 .... 19.43,52
J– *v* Henry (1890) 24 ILT 70 .... 7.05
Jacks (Wm) & Co *v* Chemquip [1991] LRC (Comm) 814 .... 3.48
Jackson *v* Anglo-American Oil [1923] 2 KB 601 .... 17.40
Jackson *v* John Dickinson [1952] 1 All ER 104 .... 11.57
Jackson *v* McKelvey (1884) 18 ILTR 88 .... 8.17
Jackson *v* Mirror Group, *The Times* 29 March 1994 .... 11.142
Jackson *v* Sterling Industries (1987) 162 CLR 612 .... 11.77
Jackson *v* Wine (1905) 39 ILTR 12 .... 9.79,87
Jaggard *v* Sawyer [1995] 2 All ER 189 .... 14.91
Jamaican Rly *v* Colonial Bank [1905] 1 Ch 677 .... 11.26
Jaman Estate *v* Hussain (1995) 126 DLR 4th 567 .... 4.04
James *v* Radnor CC [1890) 6 TLR 240 .... 9.87
Jamison, *in re* (QBD, NI) 14 Oct 1996 .... 19.31,51
Janov *v* Morris [1981] 1 WLR 1389 .... 11.182
Jeffs *v* Dickson [1958] NI 12 .... 9.88
Jelson Estates *v* Harvey [1983] 1 WLR 1401 .... 16.82
Jenkins *v* Livesey [1985] AC 424 .... 15.11
Jennings *v* Kelly [1940] NI 47; [1940] AC 206 .... 19.90, 20.88
Jervis *v* Harris [1996] Ch 195 .... 5.12
Jocelyn *v* Webb (1854) 6 Ir Jur OS 306 .... 13.10
John *v* Mirror Group [1996] 2 All ER 35 .... 18.24
Johnson *v* Gilpins Ltd [1989] NI 294 .... 13.128, 20.24
Johnson *v* Reed [1992] 1 All ER 169 .... 17.98
Johnson *v* Ribbins [1977 1 WLR 1458 .... 10.26
Johnson *v* Sandiford (1897) 31 ILT 392 .... 16.41
Johnston *v* Cliftonville FAC [1984] NI 9 .... 18.12
Johnston *v* Mohan [1978] NI 126 .... 4.06, 6.07
Johnston *v* Moore [1965] NI 128 .... 16.47
Jones *v* Bravender (1902) 36 ILTR 59 .... 9.63
Jones *v* Horne (1852) 4 Ir Jur OS 203 .... 9.37, 16.24
Jones *v* Quinn (1878) 2 LR Ir 516 .... 9.23
Jones *v* Vans Collins [1996] 1 WLR 1580 .... 5.02
Jones, *in re* [1996] 9 BNIL 84 .... 19.56
Jordan, *in re* See R *v* Governor of Crumlin Rd 19.24
Jordan, *in re* [1996] 7 BNIL 15 .... 14.03
Joseph Lynch Land Co *v* Lynch [1995] 1 NZLR 37 .... 13.103
Joyce *v* Joyce [1978] 1 WLR 1170 .... 11.191
Joynt *v* McCabe [1899] 1 IR 104 .... 12.09
Joynt *v* Mecredy (1899) 33 ILTR 175 .... 17.22
JPD *v* MG [1991] 1 IR 47 .... 13.156
Judge *v* McBrien [1971] March NIJB 20.58
Julian *v* Goodbody (1943) 77 ILTR 160 .... 3.43, 18.65
Jureidini *v* National British [1915] AC 499 .... 7.17

Kajala *v* Noble (1982) 75 Cr Ap R 149 .... 13.157
Kamouh *v* AEI [1980] QB 199 .... 3.04
Kane, *in re* [1943] Ir Jur R 30 .... 18.25
Kane *v* Munster & Leinster Assurance (1926) 60 ILTR 56 .... 9.33
Karshe *v* Uganda Transport [1967] EA 774 .... 9.51
Kavanagh *v* Coalisland Pipe [1983] 3 NIJB 4.06
Kavanagh *v* Government of Ireland [1996] 1 ILRM 133 .... 19.14
Kavanagh *v* Kilmurray [1945] Ir Jur R 61 .... 17.36
Keane *v* Ryan (1942) 76 ILTR 69 .... 9.58
Kearney *v* A-G (1916) 50 ILTR 85 .... 17.75
Kearon *v* Dublin Port and Docks Board (1906) 40 ILTR 74 .... 16.08
Keary Developments *v* Tarmac [1995] 3 All ER 534 .... 11.60

Keates *v* Woodward [1902] 1 KB 532 .... 17.31
Keefe *v* McCue (1840) 2 Cr & Dix CC 69 .... 11.179
Keen *v* Towler (1924) 41 TLR 86 .... 17.47
Keenahan *v* Gannon [1894] 1 IR 412 .... 20.19
Keenan, *in re* [1972] 1 QB 533 .... 19.100
Keenan *v* Shield Insurance [1988] IR 89 .... 20.41
Kehoe *v* Agar (1930) 64 ILTR 86 .... 16.59
Kei Brick & Tile Co *v* AM Construction 1996 (1) SA 150 .... 9.27
Kelly *v* Anglo-American Oil (1907) 41 ILTR 243 .... 11.159
Kelly *v* Bastable, *The Times*, 15 Nov 1996 .... 4.06
Kelly *v* Colhoun (1899) 33 ILTR 33 .... 13.45
Kelly *v* Cruise Catering [1994] 2 ILRM 394 .... 6.16
Kelly *v* Falls (1867) 1 ILT 702 .... 11.174
Kelly *v* Farrans [1954] NI 41 .... 14.74
Kelly *v* Hennessy [1995] 3 IR 253 .... 14.62
Kelly *v* Kelly (1874) IR 8 Eq 497 .... 16.45
Kelly *v* Larkin [1910] 2 IR 550 .... 3.40
Kelly *v* London Transport [1982] 1 WLR 1055 .... 17.90
Kelly *v* Marley Tile (1977) 122 SJ 17 .... 11.193
Kelly *v* McCurdy [1965] NI 124 .... 10.32
Kelly *v* Rafferty [1948] NI 187 .... 11.26
Kelly *v* Rice (1904) 38 ILTR 193 .... 15.18
Kennane *v* Mackey (1889) 24 LR Ir 495 .... 9.21
Kennedy *v* Connick (1912) 46 ILTR 67 .... 16.41
Kennedy *v* Healy [1897] 2 IR 258 .... 17.34,39,104
Kennedy *v* Merchant Warehousing [1924] 2 IR 85 .... 15.03
Kennedy *v* Midland Oil (1976) 110 ILTR 26 .... 9.75,91
Kennedy *v* Smith (CA, NI) 9 Feb 1968 .... 14.42
Kennett *v* Brown [1988] 1 WLR 582 .... 11.35
Kenning *v* Eve Construction [1989] 1 WLR 1189 .... 9.17, 11.144, 18.30
Kenny *v* Kelly [1988] IR 457 .... 19.34
Kenny *v* Kenealy [1895] 2 IR 544 .... 13.28
Keogh *v* Incorporated Dental Hospital [1910] 2 IR 166 .... 9.79,87
Keohane *v* Byrne [1935] NI 63 .... 13.141
Kerr, *in re* (QDB, NI) 31 July 1996 .... 19.53
Kerry CC *v* Gun Browne [1948] IR 399 .... 13.24
Kerry CC *v* Liverpool Salvage (1904) 38 ILTR 7.(CA) 13.41
Kerry CC *v* Liverpool Salvage [1905] 2 IR 38 (QBD) 13.41
Ketchum *v* Group Public Relations [1996] 4 All ER 314 .... 20.33
Ketteman *v* Hansel Properties [1987] AC 189 .... 11.31
Keyes *v* Sec of State [1979] 4 NIJB 13.72
Keymer *v* Reddy [1912] 1 KB 215 .... 7.09
Khan *v* Armaguard Ltd [1994] 1 WLR 1204 .... 13.85, 18.31
Khan *v* Gollecha [1980] 1 WLR 1482 .... 13.104,107
Khanna *v* Lovell White [1995] 1 WLR 121 .... 13.05
Kidd *v* Kidd (1884) 18 ILTR 5 .... 9.41
Kildare CC *v* Keogh [1971] IR 330 .... 13.104
Kilgariff *v* McGrane (1881) 8 LR Ir 354 .... 8.13, 9.12
Killiney UDC *v* Kirkwood [1917] 2 IR 614 .... 6.16
King *v* Armstrong (1868) IR 2 CL 495 .... 9.91
King *v* King [1941] Ir Jur R 29(NI) 11.15
King *v* T & W Farmiloe [1953] 1 All ER 614 .... 3.60
Kingdom Yacht Co *v* Wilson (1892) 26 ILTR 130 .... 13.03
Kingston *v* Irish Dunlop [1969] IR 233 .... 14.95
Kinkead *v* Hagan [1982] NI 412 .... 4.06, 6.07
Kirklees BC *v* Wickes Supplies [1993] AC 227 .... 11.69
Kirkpatrick *v* Watson [1943] Ir Jur R 4 (NI) 20.41
Kirkwood Hacket *v* Tierney [1952] IR 185 .... 9.26, 14.38

Kirton *v* Augustus Ltd [1996] 9 CLM 75 .... 14.18
Kitson *v* Black [1976] 1 NIJB 20.65
Kleinwort Benson *v* Glasgow CC [1996] QB 57 (ECJ) 14.16
Kleinwort Benson *v* Glasgow CC [1996] QB 678 .... 1.14
KM *v* DPP [1994] 1 IR 514 .... 19.83
Knight *v* Lambeth LBC [1995] CLY 3969 .... 17.84
Kok Hoong *v* Leong Mines [1964] AC 993 .... 13.104,105
Kondor *v* Honeywell (1970) 104 ILT 220 .... 6.17
Krakauer *v* Katz [1954] 1 WLR 278 .... 11.08
KSK Enterprises *v* An Bord Pleanála [1994] 2 ILRM 1 .... 11.05
Kumari *v* Jalal [1996] 4 All ER 65 .... 16.54
Kutchera *v* Buckingham Holdings [1988] IR 61 .... 6.16, 14.88
Kuwait Airways *v* Iraqi Airways (No 2) [1994] 1 WLR 985 .... 17.111, 20.71
Kuwait Airways *v* Iraqi Airways [1995] 1 WLR 1147 .... 3.20, 6.21

L (Police Investigation: Privilege), *in re* [1997] AC 16 .... 13.42
L'Amie *v* Wilson [1907] 2 IR 130 .... 11.132
Lacey *v* Harrison [1993] PIQR P10; [1993] CLY 3295 .... 11.142
Lacey *v* Kendal (1883) 17 ILTR 112 .... 9.69
Ladd *v* Marshall [1954] 1 WLR 1489 .... 19.90, 20.42
Laffey *v* McCloskey [1986] 1 NIJB 9 .... 13.25
Laing *v* Channel Reprographics etc. [1989] CLY 2942-2945 .... 17.18
Laing (John) *v* Dastur [1987] 1 WLR 686 .... 5.11
Lake *v* Lake [1955] P 336 .... 20.05
Lamb *v* Keeping (1914) 111 LT 527 .... 17.27
Lambton *v* Parkinson (1887) 35 WR 545 .... 12.01
Land and Property, *re* [1991] 1 WLR 601 .... 20.08
Land Registration Act 1970 and McNeill, *in re*, (Ch D, NI) 10 Jan 1996 .... 13.106
Lands at Eshywilligan, *in re* [1992] 3 NIJB 79 .... 4.07
Lane *v* Esdaile [1891] AC 210 .... 19.62,65,95, 20.12,15
Lane *v* Lane (1854) 4 ICLR 268 .... 11.149
Lane *v* Willis [1972] 1 WLR 326 .... 11.139,142
Langdale *v* Danby [1982] 1 WLR 1123 .... 11.54, 20.42
Lange, *in re* (QBD, NI) 17 May 1965 .... 19.99,100
Lanigan *v* Chief Constable [1991] NI 42 .... 11.116, 13.47
Lanigan-O'Keefe *v* Irish American Oil (1930) 64 ILTR 135 .... 9.77
Larkin *v* Groeger [1990] 1 IR 461 .... 17.110
Lart, *re* [1896] 2 Ch 788 .... 18.57
Lau Biv *v* A-G [1982] CLY 2486 .... 9.91
Lavelle *v* Robinson [1964] NI 17 .... 17.36,37, 20.08
Lavery *v* MOD [1984] NI 99 .... 14.52
Lavery, *in re* [1994] 6 BNIL 2 .... 19.39
Law *v* Bayley (1905) 5 NIJR 297 .... 11.49
Lawder *v* Lawder (1855) 5 ICLR 27 .... 13.63
Lawler *v* Kelly (1899) 33 ILTR 38 .... 20.05
Lawless *v* Bus Éireann [1994] 1 IR 474 .... 13.102,111
Lazard Bros *v* Banque de Moscou [1932] 1 KB 617 .... 7.05
Leahy *v* Corboy [1969] IR 148 .... 13.20
Leahy *v* Tobin (1887) 19 LR Ir 433 .... 11.38
Leather *v* Kirby [1965] 1 WLR 1489 .... 16.02
Leavis *v* Leavis [1921] P 299 .... 16.37
Ledwith *v* Ross [1910] 1 IR 151 .... 17.04
Lee *v* Hayes (1865) 17 ICLR 394 .... 9.06
Lee *v* South West Thames HA [1985] 1 WLR 845 .... 11.135
Lee *v* Walker [1985] QB 1191 .... 16.55
Leech *v* Gov of Parkhurst [1988] AC 533 .... 19.15
Legal Aid Board *v* Russell [1991] 2 AC 317 .... 11.155, 15.15, 17.111
Leitch *v* Abbott (1886) 31 Ch D 374 .... 9.90

Lenaghan *v* Ayrshire & Arran Health Board, 1994 SC 365 ..... 14.60
Lennon *v* Clifford [1993] ILRM 77 ..... 19.43
Lennon *v* Ganly [1981] ILRM 84 ..... 11.64
Lennon *v* Meegan [1905] 2 IR 189 ..... 13.109
Leonard (Cyril) *v* Simo Securities [1972] 1 WLR 80 ..... 9.90
Leonard *v* Scofield [1936] IR 715 ..... 11.56
Leppington *v* Belfast Corp (CA, NI) 18 March 1969, 20 NILQ 308 ..... 20.47
Les Fils Dreyfus *v* Clarke [1958] 1 WLR 300 ..... 11.54
Letang *v* Cooper [1965] 1 QB 232 ..... 3.25
Lett *v* Lett [1906] 1 IR 618 ..... 11.177
Levene *v* Roxhan [1970] 1 WLR 1322 ..... 18.24
Lewin *v* Trimming (1888) 21 QBD 230 ..... 17.25
Lewis *v* Daily Telegraph (No 2) [1964] 2 QB 601 ..... 3.50
Lewis *v* Lewis [1991] 1 WLR 235 ..... 16.49
Lewis *v* Ogden (1984) 153 CLR 682 ..... 16.67
Liff *v* Peasley [1980] 1 WLR 781 ..... 11.31
Ligate *v* Abick (1996) 134 DLR 4th 539 ..... 14.59
Limavady BC, *in re* [1993] 5 NIJB 43 ..... 20.79
Lindsay *v* Mid Western Health Board [1993] 2 IR 147 ..... 13.29
Linnett *v* Coles [1987] QB 555 ..... 19.100
Linotype-Hell *v* Baker [1992] 4 All ER 887 ..... 20.33
Linton *v* MOD [1983] NI 51(HL) 20.42,43
Lissenden *v* Bosch [1940] AC 412 ..... 20.39
Littauer *v* Steggles Palmer [1986] 1 WLR 287 ..... 17.83
Livingstone *v* MOD [1984] NI 356 ..... 9.71, 11.21, 20.41,48
Loane *v* Rush (QBD, NI) 31 March 1969; *sub nom* Loan *v* Rush, 20 NILQ 324 ..... 8.13
Lobb *v* Phoenix Assurance [1988] 1 NZLR 285 ..... 20.09
Locke, *in re* [1988] 4 NIJB 18 ..... 19.06
Lockheed-Arabia *v* Owen [1993] QB 806 ..... 13.140
Lockley *v* National Blood [1992] 1 WLR 492 ..... 17.89
Logan *v* Cahoon (QBD, NI) 19 Jan 1996 ..... 14.63
Logan *v* O'Donnell [1925] 2 IR 211 ..... 14.43
Logan, *in re* [1975] 1 NIJB 13.136
Logue *v* British Thompson-Houston [1956] NI 179 ..... 9.73
Lombank *v* Kennedy [1961] NI 192 ..... 5.12
London Bank *v* Newnes (1900) 16 TLR 433 ..... 9.89
London Car Co *v* Kelly (1886) 18 LR Ir 43 ..... 11.197
London College of Science Ltd *v* Islington LBC, *The Times* 23 July 1996 ..... 3.15
Lonrho, *in re* [1990] 2 AC 154 ..... 16.76
Lonrho *v* Fayed [1992] 1 AC 448 ..... 11.179
Lonrho *v* Fayed (No 4) [1994] QB 775 ..... 16.64
Lonrho *v* Shell [1982] AC 173 ..... 9.16
Loose *v* Williamson [1978] 1 WLR 639 ..... 11.131
Lord Advocate *v* RW Forsyth, 1990 SLT 458 ..... 19.20
Loughery *v* Swan (1889) 23 ILTR 54 ..... 15.12
Loughnan *v* O'Sullivan [1922] 1 IR 103, 160 ..... 9.36
Loughrey *v* Maguire [1897] 2 IR 140 ..... 9.43
Loveday *v* Renton (No 2) [1992] 3 All ER 184 ..... 17.98,102
Loveland *v* Ejector (1839) 2 Ir LR 240 ..... 1.28
Lowry *v* Buchanan [1982] NI 243 ..... 14.29,30
Lutton *v* Ulster Rly (1875) 9 ILTR 171 ..... 3.47
Lyle, *in re* [1987] 7 NIJB 24 ..... 11.12,63,73, 19.05
Lynch *v* Egan (1901) 35 ILTR 74 ..... 12.03
Lynch *v* MOD [1983] NI 216 ..... 13.28,116
Lynch Land Co *v* Lynch [1995] 1 NZLR 37 ..... 13.103
Lynn *v* Brand [1959] NI 140 ..... 3.36
Lynott *v* Greene (1862) 7 Ir Jur NS 278 ..... 6.00
Lyons *v* Eagle Star [1939] NI 189 ..... 7.17

Lysaght *v* Mullen (1898) 32 ILTR 65 .... 11.108

M, *in re* [1976] 8 NIJB.......... 18.02
M and M *v* An Bord Uchtála [1977] IR 287.......... 9.26
M *v* Home Office [1994] 1 AC 377..........3.22, 11.66, 14.99, 16.46,76, 19.12,69,70,84
M *v* P [1993] Fam 167 .... 16.80,85
M, *re* (1878) 1 LR Ir 188 .... 16.44
Mackey, *in re* [1971] Nov-Dec NIJB 19.14
Mackie *v* Wilde [1995] 1 ILRM 468.......... 3.48
Macklin *v* Graecen [1983] IR 61 .... 13.134
Macrete *v* GRE [1988] NI 332 ....6.16, 11.175
Macton, *in re* (1988) 43 DLR 4th 391 .... 18.02
Madden, *in re* [1991] NI 14 .... 19.14,92
Madden & Finnucane *v* Causeway Health Trust (QBD, NI) 14 March 1997.......... 11.130
Magauran *v* Dargan [1983] ILRM 7 .... 17.107
Magee *v* Grant (High Ct, NI) 27 May 1968 .... 9.16
Magill *v* Magill [1914] 2 IR 533 .... 8.11
Magill *v* MOD [1987] NI 194.......... 9.02
Magowan *v* Magowan [1921] 2 IR 314 .... 15.11
Magrath *v* Browne (1842) Arm Mac & Og 133 .... 13.35
Magrath *v* Moffett (1901) 1 NIJR 176 .... 20.57
Maguire *v* Duffy (1938) 72 ILTR 132 .... 17.97
Maguire *v* PJ Lagan [1976] NI 49 ....13.158, 20.56,58
Maguire, *in re* [1993] 9 NIJB 60 .... 19.15
Maher, *in re* [1910] 1 IR 167 .... 13.135
Maher, *in re* [1986] 16 NIJB 1 .... 19.06
Maher *v* Hibernian Development (1906) 36 ILTR 212 .... 11.180
Maher *v* Judge O'Donnell [1995] 3 IR 530 .... 19.31
Mahon *v* Burke [1991] 2 IR 495..........3.06, 13.102
Mahon *v* Mahon (1903) 3 NIJR 253 .... 20.28
Mahon *v* Sharma [1990] NI 106.......... 9.16
Mahony *v* J.Kruschich (1985) 156 CLR 522 .... 10.09
Mahony, *in re* [1909] 1 IR 133 .... 18.77
Maidment *v* Maxwell [1938] NI 158 .... 11.163
Mailey, *in re* [1980] NI 102 .... 19.40
Mainwaring *v* Goldbeck Investments [1997] 1 All ER 467.......... 17.59
Malec *v* JC Hutton Ltd (1990) 169 CLR 638 .... 14.75
Malevez *v* Knox [1977] 1 NZLR 463 .... 16.64
Mallett *v* McGonagle [1970] AC 166; [1969] NI 91 ....14.71, 20.68
Malone *v* Brown Thomas [1995] 1 ILRM 369 .... 20.35
Malone *v* GNR [1931] IR 1 .... 3.39
Malone *v* Spellessey (1842) Ir Circ Rep 504 .... 13.65
Malone, *in re* [1986] 9 NIJB 74 .... 19.05
Malone, *in re* [1988] NI 67 .... 19.79,87
Maltby *v* MOD, QBD, NI, 2 May 1997.......... 14.72
Man (Sugar) (E.D. & F.) *v* Haryanto, *The Times* 9 Aug 1996 .... 16.24
Manchester Breweries *v* Coombs (1901) 82 LT 347 .... 13.15
Manders *v* Kildare CC (1909) 43 ILTR 9 .... 1.27
Manley *v* Law Society [1981] 1 WLR 335 .... 17.76
Manning *v* Moriarty (1883) 12 LR Ir 372 .... 11.46
Manning *v* Shackleton [1994] 2 IR 397 .... 19.33
Mannix *v* Pluck [1975] IR 169 ....13.15,116
Maple Ridge District *v* BC Assessors (1991) 84 DLR 4th 512 .... 15.01
Mapp *v* Gilhooley [1991] 2 IR 253 .... 13.56
Maracle *v* Travellers' Indemnity Co (1991) 80 DLR 4th 652 .... 2.01
Mareva Compania *v* International Bulkcarriers (1975)[1980] 1 All ER 213 .... 11.74
Marinari *v* Lloyds Bank [1996] QB 217 .... 1.14
Mark *v* Flexibox [1988] NI 58 .... 13.39

Marriott *v* Chamberlain (1886) 17 QBD 154 ... 11.123, 18.22
Marsden *v* Marsden [1972] Fam 280 ... 3.48, 12.10
Marshall *v* Inter-Oceanic (1885) 1 TLR 394 ... 9.91
Marshall *v* LPTB [1936] 3 All ER 83 ... 5.07
Marshall, *in re* [1996] 10 BNIL 72 ... 19.14
Martin *v* Brady (1934) 68 ILTR 136 ... 9.43
Martin *v* Doherty (1880) 6 LR Ir 195 ... 13.149
Martin *v* McTaggart [1906] 2 IR 120 ... 9.74
Martin *v* Williams (1869) IR 3 CL 5 ... 6.10
Martin *v* Wilson [1913] 1 IR 470 ... 17.55
Martin, *in re* (1879) 3 LR Ir 255 ... 15.11
Martin, *in re* [1990] NI 73 ... 11.02, 14.02
Masokanye *v* Additional Magistrate 1994 2 SA 308 ... 13.45
Masterson *v* Scallan [1927] IR 453 ... 11.46
Matheson *v* Wilson (1928) 62 ILTR 49 ... 11.09
Mathew *v* TM Sutton [1994] 1 WLR 1455 ... 14.79,82
Mathews, *re* [1905] 2 Ch 460 ... 11.25, 12.12
Matthews *v* Ulster Tin Box [1970] Feb NIJB ... 12.15, 17.103
Matua Finance *v* Equiticorp Industries [1993] 3 NZLR 650 ... 13.42
Mawhinney *v* NIHE [1982] NI 302 ... 9.01, 11.21,19.09
Mayer *v* Harte [1960] 1 WLR 770 ... 17.51
McAdoo *v* Wilson [1981] 4 NIJB ... 14.74
McAfee *v* Gilliland [1979] NI 97 ... 1.11
McAleenan, *in re* [1985] NI 496 ... 19.82,100
McAllister *v* NI Office [1988] NI 606 ... 3.21, 16.35
McAllister *v* Wilson [1955] NI 208 ... 11.05,194,196
McAnuff *v* Taylor (QBD, NI) 5 June 1964 ... 17.104
McArdle *v* Gaughran [1903] 1 IR 106 ... 14.82
McAvoy *v* Goodyear [1971] NI 185 ... 11.97,101
McAvoy *v* Goodyear [1972] NI 217; [1973] March-April NIJB ... 13.68
McAvoy *v* Goodyear [1973] March-April NIJB ... 13.80, 14.10, 20.36,68
McBride *v* Stitt [1944] NI 7 ... 13.29,118
McC, *in re* [1985] AC 528 ... 19.49
McCabe *v* Bank of Ireland (1889) 14 App Cas 413(Ir) ... 12.03
McCabe *v* Joynt [1901] 2 IR 115 ... 11.173
McCabe, *in re* (QDB, NI) 20 Sept 1994 ... 19.57
McCaffery *v* Datta [1997] 2 All ER 586 ... 11.165, 14.67,68d
McCallum *v* G.Madill [1965] NI 187 ... 14.63
McCallum *v* Westbridge [1971] CLY 9360 ... 17.89
McCance *v* Newall Installations, 1996 SLT 1133 ... 17.102
McCann *v* Belfast Corp [1952] NI 49 ... 11.156
McCann *v* Kane [1971] June NIJB ... 14.29
McCann *v* Mullan [1984] NI 186 ... 19.49
McCann, *in re* [1992] 7 NIJB 60 ... 19.37
McCann, *in re* [1992] 9 NIJB 1 ... 19.24
McCann, *in re* [1997] 1 BNIL 61 ... 3.58
McCartan *v* Finnegan [1994] 2 BNIL 67 ... 13.17
McCartan *v* Hulton (1922) 56 ILTR 152 ... 6.17, 11.14,15
McCarthy *v* ATGW (Ch D, NI) 31 Jan 1966 ... 17.04
McCarthy *v* Fitzgerald [1909] 2 IR 445 ... 20.57
McCarthy *v* Hastings [1933] NI 100 ... 13.153, 20.76
McCarthy *v* O'Flynn [1979] IR 127 ... 11.99
McCarthy *v* Roche (1876) 10 ILTR 141 ... 8.09
McCartney *v* Sunday Newspapers [1988] 13 NIJB 48 ... 18.24
McCartney *v* Sunday Newspapers [1988] NI 565 ... 13.15, 18.24
McCartney, *in re* [1986] 13 NIJB 46, [1987] 11 NIJB 94 ... 13.22, 19.15
McCaughey *v* Sec of State [1975] NI 133 ... 14.78
McCaughey *v* Stringer [1914] 1 IR 73 ... 15.12

McCauley, *in re* [1992] 4 NIJB 1 .... 19.47,81
McClaren *v* Home Office [1990] ICR 824 .... 19.04
McClatchey *v* Reilly [1960] NI 118 .... 11.122
McClellan *v* PR of Love [1976] NI 126 .... 3.44
McClelland *v* Quirey (1898) 32 ILTR 128 .... 1.17
McClements *v* Larkin [1991] 1 BNIL 82 .... 17.105
McClure *v* McClure [1951] IR 137 .... 16.49
McClurg *v* DOE [1990] NI 112 .... 13.137
McCluskey *v* Colas [1994] 4 BNIL 69 .... 11.189
McColgan, *in re* [1986] NI 370 .... 19.43
McCombe *v* Simmons (1879) 4 LR Ir 527 .... 11.174, 17.66
McConnell *v* Lombard & Ulster [1982] NI 203 .... 3.33, 13.99,102,105
McConnell *v* McConnell (1880) 5 LR Ir 474 .... 18.62
McConnell *v* McConnell (1980) 10 Fam Law 214 .... 14.88, 16.63, 20.05
McConnell, *in re* [1956] NI 151 .... 20.46,70
McCooey *v* Breen [1980] 2 NIJB 5.04, 20.39
McCotter, *in re* [1970] April NIJB 13.110
McCreedy Ltd *v* SE & LB, Taxing Office NI, June 1991 .... 17.107
McCroary *v* McKendry [1981] NI 71 .... 13.46
McCrory *v* DOE [1977] 5 NIJB 13.96
McCullough *v* BBC (QBD, NI) 8 March 1996 .... 9.65
McCullough *v* Munn [1908] 2 IR 194 .... 13.140,152
McCurdy *v* McFall (1902) 36 ILTR 52 .... 3.25
McCurry *v* DOE [1988] 6 NIJB 1 .... 17.108
McDaniel *v* Hughes (1910) 44 ILTR 187 .... 6.22
McDermott *v* Dept of Agriculture [1984] 2 NIJB 14.95
McDermott *v* Derry Construction [1976] 8 NIJB 13.15
MacDonald *v* Sec of State, 1994 SC 234 .... 14.99
MacDonald *v* Sec of State for Scotland (No 2) 1996 SLT 575 .... 19.09
McDonnell *v* Douglas(QBD, NI) 30 Jan 1996 .... 14.62
McDonnell *v* King [1943] IR 1 .... 11.164
McDonnell *v* McDonnell (1886) 17 LR Ir 582 .... 18.57
McDonnell *v* McMahon (1889) 23 LR Ir 283 .... 17.57, 20.08
McDonnell *v* Woodhouse, *The Times*, 25 May 1995 .... 17.08
McDowell *v* McKibbin [1988] NI 172 .... 9.16
McDowell *v* Strannix [1951] NI 57 .... 11.139
McElduff, *in re* [1972] NI 1 .... 19.100
McElhill *v* McElhill (1938) 72 ILTR 14 .... 11.172
McElhinney *v* Williams [1995] 3 IR 382 .... 3.20
McEntaggart *v* Byrne (1896) 30 ILTR 165 .... 11.62
McEntire *v* Sun Fire Office (1895) 29 ILTR 103 .... 12.12
McEvoy *v* James Calder (1921) 55 ILTR 121 (HL) 20.56
McFall *v* McCredy [1957] NI 73 .... 3.36
McFarland, *in re* [1987] NI 246 .... 19.51
McFarlane *v* McFarlane [1972] NI 59 .... 18.70
McFarlane, *in re* [1991] 6 NIJB 42 .... 19.15,34
McGarvey *v* McGarvey (Taxing Master, NI) June 1995 .... 17.85
McGimpsey *v* O'Hare [1959] NI 98 .... 20.01
McGlinchey, *in re* [1987] 3 NIJB 1 .... 19.20,50,91
McGowan *v* Hamilton [1903] 2 IR 311 .... 17.48
McGrane *v* Behan (1972) 106 ILT 218 .... 8.12
McGrath *v* Munster & Leinster [1959] IR 313 .... 14.91
McGrath *v* Taylor [1936] NI 158 .... 18.00
McGreene *v* Hibernian Taxi (No 2) [1931] IR 377 .... 20.57
McGregor (John G.) *v* Grampian RC 1991 SC (HL) 1 .... 15.00, 20..88
McGrillen *v* Cullen [1991] NI 54 .... 19.49
McGrory *v* DOE [1977] 5 NIJB 13.96, 17.04
McGucken *v* Kennedy [1928] NI 54 .... 17.51

McGucken *v* McGucken [1991] NI 33 ....17.89
McGucken *v* McGucken [1990] NI 1 ....13.108,109
McGuigan *v* MOD [1982] 19 NIJB 14.59
McGuigan, *in re* [1994] 6 BNIL 1 ....19.71
McGuiness *v* Dunn [1986] NI 81....9.51, 11.147
McGuiness *v* Kellogg Co [1988] 1 WLR 913 ....13.85
McHale *v* Johnston (1935) 69 ILTR 256 ....17.59
McHenry *v* McHenry [1896] 1 IR 60 ....11.57
McHugh *v* McGoldrick [1921] 2 IR 163 ....20.39
McHugh *v* Phoenix Laundry [1966] IR 60 ....17.58
McIlhatton *v* Wallace [1972] NI 50....6.01
McIlveen *v* Charlesworth [1973] NI 216 ....14.29,30, 20.59,65,76
McIlwraith *v* Judge Fawsitt [1990] 1 IR 343 ....19.89
McInally *v* Clackmannan DC, 1993 SC 314 ....17.89
McInerny *v* DOE [1984] NI 1 ....4.00
McIntyre *v* Lewis [1991] 1 IR 121 ....14.44
McIntyre *v* NIHE [1995] 7 BNIL 60....3.61, 7.18
McIvor *v* SHSSB [1978] 1 WLR 757 (NI) 11.136
McKay *v* Hutchins (1991) 17 Comm LB 845 (Aus) 13.127
McKay *v* McClure [1960] NI 34....9.77
McKay *v* McKay [1988] NI 611 ....13.42
McKay *v* McNally (1879) 4 LR Ir 438 ....13.148
McKee *v* Alexander Greer [1974] NI 60 ....14.33,42, 20.40,58,68,73
McKee *v* Beaverbrook Newspapers (QBD, NI) 28 Feb 1963 ....9.79
McKee *v* McMahon (1935) 69 ILTR 180 (NI) 7.20
McKee, *in re* [1990] 11 NIJB 1 ....19.71
McKee, *in re* [1993] 8 NIJB 88 ....19.34,37,92
McKenna, *in re* *See* R *v* Chief Constable *ex p* McKenna....
McKenna *v* Best Travel [1995] 1 IR 577 ....11.101, 16.12
McKenna *v* Commr of An Garda Siochána [1993] 3 IR 543 ....11.68
McKernan *v* HM Prison Governor [1983] NI 83 ....20.43
McKerr, *in re* [1993] 5 NIJB 18 ....13.62, 19.40
McKibbin *v* McClelland [1894] 2 IR 654....1.31
McKieran, *in re* [1985] NI 385....19.15
McKinlay *v* Mackey [1895] 1 IR 302....3.03, 18.56,66
McKinley *v* Montgomery [1993] 11 NIJB 1 ....3.18
McKinney, *in re*: See R *v* Belfast Magistrate *ex p* McKinney....
McKnight *v* Armagh CC [1922] 2 IR 137 ....20.41
McKnight *v* McLaughlin [1963] NI 34....9.74
McL, *in re* [1986] NI 397 ....19.43,52
McLarnon *v* Carrickfergus UDC [1904] 2 IR 44 ....17.75
McLaughlan *v* Brown (1878) 12 ILT 89 ....16.41
McLaughlin *v* Latchman [1938] Ir Jur Rep 85 ....9.28
McLaughlin *v* NIHE [1986] NI 379 ....17.104
McLaughlin, *in re* [1989] 8 NIJB 83 ....3.58
McLaughlin, *in re* [1990] 6 NIJB 41 ....19.19
McLean, goods of [1950] IR 180 ....13.24
McLoughlin *v* Alexander (1910) 44 ILTR 253....9.82
McLoughlin *v* Life Assoc of Scotland (1915) 49 ILTR 166....6.17
McM *v* Manager of Trinity House [1995] 1 IR 595 ....19.26
McMahon *v* Donaldson [1969] NI 145 ....11.162, 14.74, 17.40,98,102
McMahon *v* Thompson (1878) 13 ILTR 92 ....9.23
McMenamin *v* A-G [1985] 2 NZLR 274 ....19.48
MacMillan Bloedel *v* Simpson (1996) 137 DLR 4th 633....3.04, 16.47
McMullan *v* Wallace [1977] NI 1....6.20, 11.193,195,196,199
McMullen *v* Harland & Wolff [1985] NI 1 ....11.123
McNally, *in re* *See* R *v* Belfast Recorder *ex p* McNally
MacNaughton *v* Murphy [1961] Ir Jur R 41 ....9.77

McNeill, *in re*, (Ch D, NI) 10 Jan 1996 .... 13.106
McNicholl *v* Neely [1983] NI 43 .... 3.09,15, 15.12, 17.15,58
McParland *v* John Tinnelly [1982] NI 110 .... 8.11, 14.50
McPherson *v* Fox [1941] NI 163 .... 16.16
McQuaid *v* Sec of State [1976] 9 NIJB 14.83
McQueen *v* Glasgow Garden Festival 1995 SLT 211 .... 13.29
McQuillan, *in re* [1939] NI 164 .... 18.63
McSheffrey *v* Lanagan (1887) 20 LR Ir 528 .... 17.30
McSorley *v* Governor of Mountjoy [1996] 2 ILRM 331 .... 19.100
McSorley *v* Chief Constable [1993] 2 NIJB 73 .... 13.62
McTear *v* Scottish Legal Aid Board, 1997 SLT 108 .... 3.58
McWatters *v* Belfast E & LB (QBD, NI) 1 Feb 1996 .... 17.89
McWatters *v* Maxwell [1932] NI 176 .... 9.70
McWilliams *v* Gilbert (1913) 47 ILTR 297 .... 6.16
Mechanical & General *v* Austin [1935] AC 346 .... 20.67
Medway Oil *v* Continental Contractors [1929] AC 88 .... 17.39,42,44
Meehan *v* Enniskilllen Meat Packers [1975] 6 NIJB 9.16
Meekatharra Ltd, *in re* [1995] 6 BNIL 105 .... 19.06,19.27
Megaleasing *v* Barrett [1992] 1 IR 219 .... 20.33
Megarrity *v* Ryan [1982] AC 81 .... 17.90
Mehaffey *v* Mehaffey [1905] 2 IR 292 .... 8.16
Meng Ching Hai *v* A-G [1992] LRC (Const) 840 (Hong Kong) 19.76
Meng Leong *v* Jip Hong Trading [1985] AC 511 .... 20.39
Mephistopholes Debt Collection *v* Lotay [1994] 1 WLR 1064 .... 3.15
Mercantile Group *v* Aiyela [1994] QB 366 .... 11.75,131
Mercedes Benz AG *v* Leiduck [1996] 1 AC 284 .... 6.16, 11.75
Mercer *v* Mercer [1924] 2 IR 50(NI) 20.57
Mercury Communications *v* DG of Tele-Communications [1996] 1 WLR 48 .... 19.08
Mercury Ltd *v* Electricity Corp [1994] 1 WLR 521 (PC) 19.06,08
Merrigan *v* Clark [1939] Ir Jur R 63 .... 11.176
Merriman *v* Greenmills Food [1997] 1 ILRM 15 .... 13.29
Metalloy Supplies *v* MA (UK), *The Times*, 12 Dec 1996 .... 17.55
Metcalfe *v* Chief Constable [1991] NI 237 .... 11.34
Metroinvest *v* Commercial Union [1985] 1 WLR 513 .... 1.30
Michel S *v* Fonds National des Handicapés [1973] ECR 457 .... 14.17
Midhurst (The) *v* The Lake Atlin [1972] 2 Lloyds Rep 489 .... 11.193
Midland Rly Co, *in re* (1904) 38 ILTR 52 .... 13.14, 14.11
Midwood *v* Kelly (1901) 1 NIJR 199 .... 11.80
Millar *v* Harper (1888) 38 Ch D 110 .... 9.90
Millar *v* Peebles (CA, NI) 23 Oct 1995 .... 14.12, 20.62
Millen *v* Brown [1984] NI 328 .... 11.20,24,27, 20.02
Miller *v* Hatrick [1907] 1 IR 82 .... 18.60
Miller, *in re* [1912] 3 KB 1 .... 16.38
Millican *v* Tucker [1980] 1 WLR 640 .... 17.39,43
Millington *v* CIE (1974) 108 ILTR 61 .... 13.29
Millwall, The [1905] P 155 .... 20.02
Milor S.r.l. *v* British Airways [1996] QB 702 .... 11.175
Minister of Development *v* Law [1970] June NIJB 13.84, 18.02, 20.39
Minister of Education *v* Letterkenny Technical College [1995] 1 ILRM 438 .... 19.06,50
Minister of Foreign Affairs *v* Vehicles and Supplies Ltd [1991] 1 WLR 551 .... 19.69
Minister of Home Affairs, *in re* [1972] May NIJB 19.57
Minister of Immigration *v* Teoh [1995] 1 LRC 1 (Aus) 1.16, 19.34
Minister of Justice *v* Wang Zhu Jie [1993] 1 IR 426 .... 20.09
Ministry of Defence, *in re* [1994] 7 BNIL 9 .... 13.48, 14.02,03
Mitchell *v* Chief Constable [1992] NI 35 .... 11.181
Mitchell *v* Darley Dale Colliery (1884) Cab & Ell 214 .... 11.93,106
Mitchell *v* DOE [1996] 3 BNIL 15 .... 14.68
Mitchell *v* Harris [1967] 2 QB 703 .... 11.34

Mitchell *v* HAT (No 3) 1993 SLT 1199 .... 11.55
Mitchell *v* Smyth [1894] 2 IR 351 .... 16.67
Mitchell, *in re* [1992] 8 NIJB 10 .... 17.85,98,108
MM, *in re* [1933] IR 299 .... 16.80
Moan *v* Moan [1984] 3 NIJB 20.67
Moane *v* Reilly [1984] NI 269........ 4.06, 14.12
Moffat *v* RW Archer (1962) 96 ILTR 21 .... 13.69,84
Molony *v* Molony (1888) 21 LR Ir 91 .... 18.25
Monaghan *v* Chief Constable [1988] NI 316 .... 13.46
Monck *v* Smythe [1895] 1 IR 200........ 9.60
Moncrieff *v* Johnston (1902) 36 ILTR 61 .... 11.95
Montgomery *v* Bellew (1903) 37 ILTR 241 .... 11.176
Montgomery *v* Montgomery (1856) 6 ICLR 522........ 3.32, 11.25
Moody *v* Godstone RDC [1966] 2 All ER 696........ 6.24
Moore, *in re* [1996] 6 BNIL 40 .... 19.41
Moore *v* Adair (CA, NI) 9 Feb 1996........ 11.187,188,190
Moore *v* A-G [1929] IR 544 .... 20.02,35
Moore *v* A-G (No 2) [1930] IR 471 .... 16.47
Moore *v* Alwill (1882) 8 LR Ir 245 .... 11.22
Moore *v* Harland & Wolff [1991] NI 188 .... 4.06
Moore *v* Hughes (1906) 40 ILTR 139 .... 11.173
Moore *v* McGlynn [1894] 1 IR 74 .... 9.82
Moore *v* O'Donnell (1856) 6 ICLR 46 .... 15.09
Moore *v* Southern Counties [1889] WN 156 .... 12.01
Moran *v* O'Farrell (1883) 17 ILTR 63 .... 11.95
Morel Bros *v* Westmoreland [1904] AC 11........ 8.10, 13.99
Morelli *v* DOE [1976] NI 159 .... 17.04
Morelli, *in re* [1968] IR 11 .... 17.53
Morgan *v* Kelly (1897) 31 ILT 546 .... 17.59
Morris, *in re,* (QBD, NI) 29 Nov 1996........ 19.06
Morris, *in re,* CA, NI, 30 April 1997........ 19.89
Morris (B.O.) *v* Perrott [1945] 1 All ER 567 .... 15.03
Morris *v* Power Supermarkets [1990] 1 IR 296 .... 18.02,05
Morris *v* Roe (1836) 1 M & W 207 (150 ER 408) 11.130
Morris *v* Wallis (QBD, NI) 4 Feb 1997........ 17.25
Morrisey *v* Kelly (1972) 106 ILTR 9 .... 11.188
Morrison *v* AVX [1990] 1 BNIL 81 .... 13.07
Morrison *v* Barton, 1994 SC 100........ 20.73
Morrison *v* MIB [1987] NI 204 .... 12.13, 16.17
Morrison *v* Pankratz (1995) 122 DLR 4th 352 .... 14.68
Morrison, *in re* [1991] NI 70 .... 19.35,45
Morrow *v* McAdam [1978] NI 82; [1978] 3 NIJB 13.88, 20.76
Morrow, *in re* [1987] 3 NIJB 16 .... 16.56
Mortgage Corp *v* Sandoes, *The Times*, 27 Dec 1996........ 1.35
Moss *v* Chin (1994) 120 DLR 4th 406 .... 12.10
Mossman *v* Motherwell (1842) Ir Cir R 668 .... 14.30
Motor & General *v* Pavy [1994] 1 WLR 462 .... 16.16
Mountcashel's Estate [1920] 1 IR 1 .... 13.104
MPD *v* MD [1981] ILRM 179........ 1.33
Mulgrew *v* O'Brien [1953] NI 10 .... 11.179,180, 12.03, 13.108
Mulholland *v* McCrea [1961] NI 135 .... 14.72
Mulholland *v* McParland (1908) 42 ILTR 2 .... 17.105
Mulholland *v* Mitchell [1971] AC 666 .... 20.43
Mullen *v* Dublin United Tramways (1907) 41 ILTR 236 .... 13.39
Mullen *v* Quinnsworth [1990] 1 IR 59........ 9.06, 13.29
Mullen *v* Smith (1933) 67 ILTR 103 .... 18.58
Muller Staub *v* McBride (1922) [1925] NI 7 .... 13.23
Muller *v* Linsley & Mortimer, *The Times* 8 Dec 1994 .... 13.43

Mulligan *v* Mulligan [1934] NI 9 .... 17.51
Mullins *v* Howell [1879) 11 Ch D 763 .... 11.07
Mulvenna, *in re* [1985] 13 NIJB 76 .... 19.15
Munchie Foods *v* Eagle Star [1993] 9 NIJB 69 .... 11.60, 20.62
Munster & Leinster Bank *v* Mackey [1917] 1 IR 49 .... 11.41
Murdanaigum *v* Henderson, 1996 SLT 1297 .... 16.67
Murphy d. Wray *v* Morrison (1829) 2 Hud & Br 406 .... 13.149
Murphy *v* AIB [1994] 2 ILRM 221 .... 14.82
Murphy *v* Crean [1915] 1 IR 111 .... 9.28
Murphy *v* Culhane [1977] QB 94 .... 14.74
Murphy *v* Duffy [1996] 10 BNIL 73 .... 17.97,103,105
Murphy *v* Greene [1990] 2 IR 566 .... 5.02
Murphy *v* Hennessy [1984] IR 378 .... 11.177
Murphy *v* J.O'Donoghue [1996] 1 IR 123 .... 10.21, 11.120
Murphy *v* Kearns (1924) 58 ILTR 29 .... 8.07, 17.16
Murphy *v* Kirwan [1993] 3 IR 501 .... 13.42
Murphy *v* Logan (1859) 10 ICLR 87 .... 9.20
Murphy *v* MOD [1991] 2 IR 161 .... 20.42
Murphy *v* O'Shea (1944) 78 ILTR 151 .... 18.00
Murphy *v* Turf Club [1989] IR 171 .... 19.05
Murphy *v* Walsh (1923) 57 ILTR 129 .... 11.95
Murphy *v* Willcocks [1911] 1 IR 402 .... 16.48
Murphy *v* Young & Co [1997] 1 All ER 518 .... 17.03
Murphy, *in re* [1991] 5 NIJB 88 .... 19.14,27
Murphy, *in re* [1991] 7 NIJB 97 .... 3.61, 14.21, 17.88,89, 19.47,81
Murray, *in re* [1997] 3 BNIL 106 .... 14.03, 19.27
Murray *v* Conlan [1984] 8 NIJB 2.11
Murray *v* Doherty [1986] NI 136 .... 14.52,56
Murray *v* Finkle (1914) 48 ILTR 178 .... 6.16,17
Murray *v* Hibernian Dance Club, *The Times*, 12 Aug 1996 .... 11.34
Murray *v* Northern Whig (1912) 46 ILTR 77 .... 11.126
Murray *v* O'Riordan (1915) 49 ILTR 186 .... 17.27
Murray *v* Sheriffs of Dublin (1842) Arm Mac & Og 130 .... 13.54
Murray *v* Times Newspapers [1995] 3 IR 244 .... 1.14
Murtagh *v* St Emer's [1991] 1 IR 482 .... 19.06
MV 'Turquoise Bleu' [1995] 3 IR 437 .... 11.176
Myers *v* Phelan (1890) 26 LR Ir 218 .... 11.164, 17.28,30
Myers *v* Sherick [1974] 1 WLR 31 .... 10.15,16
Myers *v* Willis (1907) 41 ILTR 229 .... 5.12

Nabney *v* Belfast Co-op (1933) 67 ILTR 211 (NI) 9.40
Nadreph *v* Wilmett [1978] 1 WLR 1537 .... 9.36
Naish, *re* [1895] 1 IR 266 .... 20.39
Napier *v* Hunter [1993] AC 713 .... 3.19, 10.05
National and Provincial Building Society *v* Chambers [1996] 6 BNIL 76 .... 17.57
National and Provincial Building Society *v* Graham [1997] 2 BNIL 76 .... 17.57
National and Provincial Building Society *v* Lynd [1996] 9 BNIL 69 .... 18.73
National and Provincial Building Society *v* Slane (Ch D, NI) 28 July 1995 .... 18.73
National and Provincial Building Society *v* Williamson [1996] 9 BNIL 70 .... 18.73
National Bank *v* Cullen [1894] 2 IR 683 .... 16.26
National Bank *v* Hunter [1948] Ir Jur Rep 33 .... 8.06
National Benzole *v* Gooch [1961] 1 WLR 1489 .... 20.34
National Insurance *v* Whirlybird Holdings [1994] 2 NZLR 513 .... 13.41
National Irish Bank *v* Graham [1994] 1 IR 215 .... 16.80
National Trust *v* Shields (Ch D, NI) 6 June 1995 .... 14.91
National Westminster Bank *v* Daniel [1993] 1 WLR 1453 .... 11.49
National Westminster Bank *v* Kitch [1996] 1 WLR 1316 .... 18.72
National Westminster Bank *v* Powney [1991] Ch 339 .... 16.40

Naylor *v* Preston Area Health Authority [1987] 1 WLR 958 .... 11.145
Needham *v* Needham (1842) 1 Hare 633 (66 ER 1183); affd 12 LJ Ch 378 .... 16.48
Neil *v* Silcock (1904) 38 ILTR 5 .... 13.10
Neill *v* Corbett [1992] NI 251 .... 11.08,189,194
Neill *v* North Antrim Mag Ct [1992] 1 WLR 1220 (NI) 19.28,46,47
Neill *v* Short Bros [1971] NI 73 .... 20.57
Neilly *v* Moypark Ltd, (QBD, NI) 20 Oct 1995 .... 11.97,136
Newell *v* Bowden [1976] 4 NIJB 13.29
Newfoundland Telephone Co *v* Board of Public Utilities (1992) 89 DLR 4th 289 .... 19.41
Newman *v* Caffelle (1900) 34 ILTR 108n* 17.61
Newry Salt Works *v* MacDonnell [1903] 2 IR 454 .... 3.33
New Zealand Maori Council *v* A-G [1996] 3 NZLR 140 .... 19.13
Ng Chun Pui *v* Lee Chuen Tat [1988] RTR 298 .... 13.29
Nicholson *v* Armstrong (QBD, NI) 2 May 1996 .... 11.180
Nicolls *v* Corr [1909] 2 IR 655 .... 17.26
Niedner Ltd *v* Lloyds Bank (1990) 72 DLR 4th 147 .... 13.15
Nimmo (William) & Co *v* Russell Construction (No 2), 1997 SLT 122 .... 17.39
Nisbet *v* Marley Roof Tile, 1988 SC 29 .... 11.55
Nixon *v* Loundes [1909] 2 IR 1 .... 8.16, 11.178
Noble *v* NI Electricity [1955] NI 193 .... 9.73
Nolan *v* Irish Land Comm [1981] IR 23 .... 19.31
Nolan *v* Listowel UDC [1966] IR 56 .... 10.20
Nolan *v* Marquis of Drogheda (1892) 31 LR Ir 84 .... 11.41
Norbrook Laboratories, *in re* [1992] 10 NIJB 36 .... 19.24
Norglen *v* Reed Rains [1996] 1 All ER 945 .... 11.44
North Down BC, *in re* [1986] NI 304 .... 19.31
North Down Hotels *v* Province-wide Filling Stations [1993] 10 NIJB 60 .... 13.96
North West Water *v* Binnie [1990] 3 All ER 547 .... 11.181
Northern Bank *v* Adams (Ch D, NI) 1 Feb 1996 .... 18.72,77
Northern Bank *v* Beattie [1982] 18 NIJB 18.77
Northern Bank *v* Charlton [1979] IR 149 .... 20.65
Northern Bank *v* Haggerty [1995] 5 BNIL 64 .... 16.33, 18.78
Northern Bank *v* Jeffers [1996] 10 BNIL 67 .... 8.13, 12.10, 13.135, 16.03, 18.73
Northern Banking *v* Devlin [1924] 1 IR 90 (NI) 18.75
Northern Banking *v* Carpenter [1931] IR 268 .... 13.61
NIES, *in re* [1987] NI 271 .... 19.75
NIHE *v* Fox [1981] 9 NIJB 5.07, 11.64, 18.43
NIHE *v* Magee (Ch D, NI) 9 Nov 1995 .... 18.45
NIHE *v* McAuley [1974] NI 233 .... 18.45
NIHE *v* Wimpey [1989] NI 395 .... 11.185,188,190,191
Northern Ireland Rlys *v* Tweed [1982] 15 NIJB 20.65
Norwest Refrigeration *v* Bain Davies (1984) 157 CLR 149 .... 17.51
Norwich Building Society *v* Steed [1991] 1 WLR 449 .... 20.24
Norwich Pharmacal *v* Commrs of Customs [1974] AC 133 .... 11.131
Nowlan *v* Gibson (1849) 12 Ir LR 5 .... 13.95
NPO *v* Cornhill Insurance [1956] NI 157 .... 7.13,18
Nugent *v* Keady UDC (1912) 46 ILTR 221 .... 3.29
NUPE, *in re* [1988] NI 255 .... 19.31,34
NV Amsterdamsche Lucifersfabrieken *v* H & H [1940] 1 All ER 587 .... 17.43

O *v* M [1977] IR 33 .... 1.12
O, *in re* [1991] 2 QB 520 .... 19.91
O'Boyle *v* A-G [1929] IR 558 .... 19.100
O'Brien *v* Bord na Mona [1983] IR 255 .... 19.40
O'Brien *v* Fleming [1946] IR 236 .... 17.80
O'Brien *v* Freeman's Journal (1907) 41 ILTR 35 .... 9.79
O'Brien *v* Ireland [1995] 1 IR 568 .... 11.116
O'Callaghan *v* O'Sullivan [1925] 1 IR 90 .... 13.94

Ó Cathain, *in re* (QBD, NI) undated 1996 .... 19.50
O'Connell *v* Hanlon (1898) 32 ILTR 95 .... 5.08
O'Connell *v* Peckin (1913) 47 ILTR 80 .... 17.50
O'Connor *v* Anderson (1880) 14 ILTR 14 .... 9.52
O'Connor *v* Commercial General [1996] 1 IR 68 .... 6.18
O'Connor *v* McManus [1969] NI 243 .... 11.141
O'Connor *v* O'Connor, Taxing Office NI, 1995 .... 17.85,107
O'Connor, *in re* [1991] NI 77 .... 19.26,34
O'Daly *v* Gulf Oil [1983] ILRM 163 .... 6.16
O'Doherty *v* Gallagher [1995] 9 BNIL 44 .... 13.69,83
O'Donnell *v* Hegarty [1941] IR 538 .... 13.110
O'Donnell *v* O'Donnell (1852) 3 ICLR 29 .... 16.68
O'Donnell *v* O'Donnell (1937) 71 ILTR 148 .... 16.80
O'Donnell *v* O'Sullivan (1913) 47 ILTR 253 .... 12.12
O'Donnell *v* Walsh [1943] Ir Jur Rep 55 .... 9.87
O'Driscoll *v* Irish Shell [1968] IR 215 .... 9.94, 17.66
O'Dwyer, *in re* (CA, NI) 19 Dec 1996 .... 19.33
O'Fearail *v* McManus [1994] 2 ILRM 81 .... 3.50
O'Flynn *v* Bord Gais [1982] ILRM 324 .... 7.16
O'Flynn *v* Mid-Western Health Board [1991] 2 IR 223 .... 19.57
O'Gorman *v* Harding (1884) 18 ILTR 93 .... 3.36
O'Grady *v* Synan [1900] 2 IR 602 .... 19.78
O'Hanlon *v* ESB [1969] IR 75 .... 14.38
O'Hare *v* Ireland (1921) 55 ILTR 119 .... 9.82
O'Hare, *in re* [1989] NI 77 .... 19.15
O'Kane *v* Higgins (1901) 1 NIJR 276 .... 14.45, 15.03
O'Kane *v* Mullan [1925] NI 1 .... 13.153
O'Kean, *in re* [1907] 1 IR 223 .... 11.170
O'Keefe *v* Todd-Burns (1931) 65 ILTR 71 .... 1.35
O'Keeffe *v* An Bord Pleanala [1993] 1 IR 39 .... 19.33
O'Keeffe *v* Ferris [1993] 3 IR 165 .... 11.176
O'Keeffe *v* Walsh [1903] 2 IR 681 .... 3.25,31,33, 13.16
O'Leary *v* Clerke (1893) 27 ILTR 123 .... 14.21
O'Leary *v* Law Integrity [1912] 1 IR 479 .... 6.16
O'Leary *v* Min of Industry [1966] IR 676 .... 13.46
O'Leary *v* O'Dea [1922] 1 IR 8 .... 15.11
O'Loughlin, *in re* [1985] NI 421 .... 1.29, 19.47
O'Mahony *v* Horgan [1995] 2 IR 411 .... 11.75
O'Mara *v* Dodd [1912] 2 IR 55 .... 6.16
O'Meara *v* Barry [1895] 2 IR 454 .... 17.104
O'Neill *v* DHSS (No 2) [1986] NI 290 .... 1.17, 3.22,14.30,91
O'Neill *v* Finn (1972) 106 ILTR 77 .... 9.74
O'Neill *v* Iarnród Éireann [1991] ILRM 129 .... 19.05,58,62
O'Neill *v* McErlean (1896) 30 ILTR 162 .... 16.53
O'Neill *v* Nicholson [1996] 4 BNIL 77 .... 17.62
O'Neill *v* O'Neill (1879) 4 LR Ir 218 .... 9.24
O'Neill *v* Ryanair (No 2) [1992] 1 IR 160 .... 3.36, 11.149
O'Neill *v* St Brigid's Well [1895] 2 IR 442 .... 6.01
O'Neill, *in re* [1967] NI 129 .... 15.18, 18.72
O'Neill, *in re* [1990] 3 NIJB 1 .... 19.50
O'Neill, *in re* (QBD, NI) 20 March 1995 .... 19.39,57
O'Rafferty *v* Rickard (1920) 54 ILTR 195 .... 11.25
O'Reilly *v* CIE [1973] IR 278 .... 11.186,188,191
O'Reilly *v* Granville [1971] IR 90 .... 9.31
O'Reilly *v* Mackman [1983] 2 AC 237 .... 19.08,79
O'Reilly *v* McCall [1910] 2 IR 42 (HL) 20.57,76
O'Reilly *v* Moroney [1992] 2 IR 145 .... 5.02
O'Reilly *v* O'Reilly (1899) 33 ILTR 17 .... 8.02

O'Reilly, *in re* [1995] 6 BNIL 97 .... 11.39,40, 16.05
O'Rorke *v* Healy (1903) 37 ILTR 69 .... 3.31
O'Rourke *v* Miller (1985) 156 CLR 342 .... 19.41
O'Shea *v* Cork RDC [1914] 1 IR 16 .... 3.33
O'Sullivan *v* Dwyer (No 2) [1973] IR 81 .... 20.71
O'Sullivan *v* Herdmans [1986] NI 214 .... 11.100, 13.40
O'Sullivan *v* Herdmans [1987] 1 WLR 1047 .... 11.136
O'Sullivan *v* Herdmans (No 2) [1988] 1 WLR 1373 .... 17.91
O'Toole *v* Haughton (1924) 58 ILTR 160 .... 3.36
O'Toole *v* Heavey [1993] 2 IR 544 .... 14.31
Oakacre *v* Claire Cleaners [1982] Ch 197 .... 4.00
Oaklee Housing Association, *in re* [1994] 6 BNIL 46 .... 9.87, 11.97, 19.47
Oaks *v* Carroll (1926) 60 ILTR 117 .... 9.74
Ocean Software *v* Kay [1992] QB 583 .... 20.01,11,52
Odum *v* Hartley (1881) 15 ILTR 31 .... 9.43
Official Solicitor and Briggs *v* Brett [1996] 8 BNIL 22 .... 14.71, 15.08
Ogle *v* Mills [1931] NI 26 .... 17.110
Ogwr BC *v* Knight, *The Times* 13 Jan 1994 .... 20.34,77
Olhausen *v* Powderley (1940) 74 ILTR 126 .... 11.19
Oliver, *in re* [1995] 6 BNIL 69 .... 3.58, 19.33
Ollett *v* Bristol Aerojet [1979] 1 WLR 1197 .... 18.32
Onslow *v* Inland Revenue (1890) 25 QBD 465 .... 15.00, 20.88
Orchard *v* SE Electricity [1987] QB 565 .... 3.61
Orion Properties *v* du Cane [1962] 1 WLR 1085 .... 20.33
Ormond (Marquis of) *v* Burke (1854) 6 Ir Jur OS 112 .... 18.34
Ormond *v* Ireland [1988] ILRM 490 .... 17.98
Ormsby *v* Good [1895] 1 IR 103 .... 18.49
Orr Ewing, *re* (1883) 22 Ch D 456; 9 App Cas 34 .... 7.07
Orr *v* Oneida [1972] June NIJB (Pt II) 9.75,92
Osborne *v* British Coal 1996 SLT 736 .... 18.00
Osborne *v* Snook [1953] 1 All ER 332 .... 11.19
Osborne *v* Sullivan [1965] NZLR 1095 .... 13.40
Oscar *v* Chief Constable [1992] NI 290 .... 9.11
Oscar *v* Chief Constable (Taxing Office NI) 21 June 1995 .... 17.103
Owen *v* Grimsby Transport [1992] PIQR Q27; *The Times*, 14 Feb 1991 .... 9.17
Owen *v* Pugh [1995] 3 All ER 345 .... 11.193
Owen *v* Tate [1976] QB 402 .... 10.03
Owens Bank *v* Bracco [1994] QB 509(ECJ) 16.22

Padfield *v* Min of Agriculture [1968] AC 997 .... 19.24
Page *v* Smith [1996] 1 AC 155 .... 14.62
Palmer *v* Bateman [1908] 2 IR 393 .... 13.29
Palmer *v* Durnford [1992] QB 483 .... 11.181
Palmer, *in re* [1994] Ch 316 .... 1.31
Panayiotou *v* Sony Music [1994] Ch 142 .... 13.10
Parker(Harry) Ltd *v* Mason [1940] 2 KB 590 .... 13.13
Parker-Tweedale *v* Dunbar Bank [1991] Ch 26 .... 17.57
Parkes *v* Knowles [1957] 3 All ER 600 .... 17.29
Parry *v* Cleaver [1970] AC 1 .... 14.63
Patel *v* Comptroller of Customs [1966] AC 356 .... 13.113
Patel *v* Smith [1987] 1 WLR 853 .... 11.64
Paterson *v* Chadwick [1974] 1 WLR 890 .... 11.133
Paterson *v* Wellington Kindergarten [1966] NZLR 468 .... 5.12, 8.13
Patten *v* Burke Publishing [1991] 2 All ER 821 .... 8.02
Patterson *v* Donnell [1954] NI 96 .... 9.77
Pavilion Restaurant *v* Dominion Breweries [1987] 2 NZLR 644 .... 18.28
Paxton *v* Baird [1893] 1 QB 139 .... 7.08
Payne *v* Harrison [1961] 2 QB 403 .... 20.57,66

PB, *in re* [1986] NI 88 .... 13.32
Peclar *v* Johnstone (1919) 53 ILTR 31 .... 9.23
Peddie *v* Kyle [1900] 2 IR 265 .... 3.31
Pedlow, *in re* (QBD Bankruptcy, NI) 4 Oct 1965; 17 NILQ 163 .... 15.11
Peete, *re* [1952] 2 All ER 599 .... 13.137
Pembroke *v* Warren [1896] 1 IR 76 .... 11.37, 17.55
Penman *v* Parker [1986] 1 WLR 882 .... 3.55
Pennefather *v* Tobin (1884) 18 ILTR 54 .... 15.01
Penny *v* Penny [1996] 1 WLR 1204 .... 11.56
People *v* Taylor [1974] IR 97 .... 13.64
Pereira *v* Beanlands [1996] 3 All ER 528 .... 11.120
Perry, *in re* [1996] 5 BNIL 37 .... 19.05,25
Persse, *in re* [1912] 1 IR 18 .... 11.172
Petaling Tin *v* Lee Kian Chan [1994] 4 LRC 180 (Malaysia) 19.07,86
Peterson *v* Bannon (1994) 107 DLR 4th 616 .... 9.24
Petrunic *v* Barnes (1990) 16 Comm LB 764 (Vic) 17.104
Petticrew *v* Chief Constable [1988] NI 192 .... 20.41
Phillip *v* DPP [1992] 1 AC 545 .... 19.99
Phillips, *in re* (QBD, NI) 18 Jan 1995 (CA, NI) 12 Feb 1996 .... 19.04,05,79
Phillips *v* Taunton and Somerset NHT, *The Times* 15 Aug 1996 .... 1.35
Philpot *v* Philpot (1908) 42 ILTR 165 .... 20.24
Phipps *v* Orthodox Unit Trust [1958] 1 QB 314 .... 9.88
Phonographic Performance *v* Cody [1994] 2 ILRM 241 .... 9.26, 13.33
Pickwick *v* Multiple Sound [1972] 3 All ER 384 .... 11.12
Pidduck *v* Eastern Scottish Omnibuses [1990] 1 WLR 993 .... 14.71,72
Pigs Marketing Board *v* Redmond [1978] NI 73 .... 1.27, 14.16, 19.47
Piller (Anton) *v* Manufacturing Processes [1976] Ch 55 .... 11.86
Pillman *v* Goodbody (1909) 43 ILTR 32 .... 8.13
Pine Valley *v* Minister of Environment [1987] IR 23 .... 19.88
Pinson *v* Lloyds Bank [1941] 2 KB 72 .... 9.91
Pioneer Concrete *v* NEMGIA [1985] 2 All ER 395 .... 16.13
Pirrie *v* York Street Flax Spinning [1894] 1 IR 417 .... 20.39
Pitt *v* Bolger [1996] 1 IR 108 .... 11.58
Pittalis *v* Grant [1989] QB 605 .... 20.40
Pittalis *v* Sherefettin [1986] QB 868 .... 15.10
Pitts *v* Hunt [1991] 1 QB 24 .... 14.74
PJ Holdings *v* Gilroy [1985] 12 NIJB 39; [1986] 3 NIJB 100 .... 16.56,58
Pocklington Foods *v* Alberta (1995) 123 DLR 4th 141 .... 11.07
Poh, *in re* [1983] 1 WLR 2 .... 19.62
Police Association, *in re* [1990] NI 258 .... 19.06,34,50
Pollock *v* Sec of State for Scotland, 1993 SLT 1173 .... 19.41
Pontin *v* Wood [1962] 1 QB 594 .... 11.31
Poole *v* O'Sullivan [1993] 1 IR 484 .... 1.31
Poole *v* Stewart (1903) 37 ILTR 74 .... 8.13
Pople *v* Evans [1969] 2 Ch 255 .... 11.198
Porter *v* Kirtlan [1917] 2 IR 138 .... 17.73
Porter *v* Scott [1979] NI 6 .... 13.41
Portion Foods *v* Min of Agriculture [1981] ILRM 161 .... 14.16
Portrush UDC *v* Mairs [1937] NI 52 .... 20.35
Potter *v* Carlisle [1939] NI 114 .... 14.39
Potts *v* Plunkett (1858) 9 ICLR 290 .... 11.180
Powell *v* Heffernan (1879) 4 LR Ir 703 .... 11.97
Powell *v* McGlynn [1902] 2 IR 154 .... 13.116
Power *v* Dublin United Tramway [1926] IR 302 .... 13.122, 14.44
Power *v* Lorimer (Taxing Master, NI) 4 March 1993 .... 17.98,102
Presentaciones Musicales *v* Secunda [1994] Ch 271 .... 3.48, 4.01, 5.04
Price, *in re* [1986] NI 390 .... 19.40
Pringle *v* Ireland [1994] 1 ILRM 467 .... 11.181

Prior *v* Johnston (1893) 27 ILTR 108 ....16.49
Proctor *v* Peebles [1941] 2 All ER 80 ....13.89
Propend Finance *v* Sing, *The Times* 2 May 1997....3.20
Provincial Bill Posting *v* Low Moor Iron [1909] 2 KB 344 ....9.48
Public Service Board *v* Osmond [1987] LRC (Const) 681; (1986) 159 CLR 656 ....19.33.
Public Works *v* AF Hastings [1972] June NIJB (Part I) 17.43
Pujolas *v* Heaps (1938) 72 ILTR 96 ....9.28
Purcell *v* Trigell [1971] 1 QB 358 ....11.07
Morris *v* Wallis (QBD, NI) 4 Feb 1997....11.188
Purse *v* Purse [1981] Fam 143 ....11.39
PW *v* CIE [1967] IR 137....9.93
Pyke *v* National Westminster Bank, *The Times* 10 Dec 1977; [1977] CLY 2310 ....16.60

Quain *v* Fitzgerald (1889) 19 ILTR 58 ....8.13
Quennell v Maltby [1979] 1 All ER 568....18.72
QUB *v* McLaughlin [1982] 9 NIJB 20.39
Quigley *v* Burke [1996] 1 ILRM 469....11.100
Quigley *v* Chief Constable [1983] NI 238 ....19.99,101
Quigley, *in re* [1983] NI 245 ....19.104,105
Quigley, *in re* [1997] 3 BNIL 40 ....19.27,89,91
Quinn *v* Hession (1879) 4 LR Ir 35 ....9.39
Quinn *v* McKinlay [1902] 2 IR 315 ....17.27
Quinn *v* Sec of State [1977] 2 NIJB 13.24
Quinn, *in re* [1987] NI 325 ....19.43
Quinn, *in re* [1988] 2 NIJB 10 ....19.15,41,45,50
Quinn, *in re* [1996] 10 BNIL 36....3.21
Quirk *v* Fitzgerald (1879) 13 ILTR 64....9.23
Quirke *v* Bord Luthchleas na h'Eireann [1988] IR 83 ....19.05

R *v* Advertising Standards Authority, *ex p* Vernons [1992] 1 WLR 1289 ....19.69
R *v* Andrews [1987] AC 281 ....13.114
R *v* Aylesbury Vale DC, *ex p* Chaplin, *The Times* 23 July 1996....19.33
R *v* Barnet LBC *ex p* Shah [1983] 2 AC 309 ....19.24
R v BBC *ex p* Referendum Party, *The Times* 29 April 1997....19.06
R *v* Bedwellty JJ *ex p* Williams [1997] AC 225....19.43,46
R *v* Belfast Magistrate *ex p* McKinney [1992] NI 63 ....19.47,81
R *v* Belfast Recorder *ex p* McNally [1992] NI 217 ....19.02,16,43,45,49
R *v* Bolton JJ *ex p* Graeme (1986) 150 JP 190 ....19.95
R *v* Bolton JJ *ex p* Scally [1991] 1 QB 537 ....19.36
R *v* British Coal Corp, *ex p* Vardy [1993] ICR 720 ....19.04,05
R *v* Burke (1859) 4 Ir Jur NS 11 ....13.72
R *v* Camden LBC *ex p* Martin, [1997] 1 All ER 307....19.60
R *v* Central Criminal Ct *ex p* Francis [1989] AC 346 ....13.42
R *v* Chief Constable *ex p* McKenna [1992] NI 116 ....19.02,14,23,50,51,69,92
R *v* Chief Constable of West Midlands *ex p* Wiley [1995] 1 AC 274 ....13.47
R *v* Christie [1914] AC 545 ....13.119
R *v* Clarke [1985] 2 NZLR 212 ....19.91
R *v* Coll (1889) 24 LR Ir 522 ....13.78
R *v* Commr of Police *ex p* Bennett [1995] QB 313 ....19.20
R *v* Consolidated Fastfrate Transport [1995] 4 LRC 549 (Canada) 11.75
R *v* Criminal Injuries Compensation Board, *ex p* Cook 1996] 1 WLR 1037....19.35
R *v* Cripps, *ex p* Muldoon [1984] QB 686 ....15.13
R *v* Darcy (1826) Batty 247 ....13.134
R *v* Department of Environment [1992] NI 278 ....19.45
R *v* Deputy Governor of Parkhurst, *ex p* Hague [1992] 1 AC 58 ....19.99
R *v* Derby Magistrates' Court, *ex p* B [1996] 1 AC 487....13.76
R *v* Devereux (1838) Cr & D ANC 157 ....16.63
R *v* Director of SFO, *ex p* Smith [1993] AC 1 ....19.91

R *v* Disciplinary Committee of the Jockey Club, *ex p* Aga Khan [1993] 2 All ER 853 .. 19.05
R *v* Dodson [1984] 1 WLR 971 .... 13.157
R *v* Effik [1995] 1 AC 309 .... 13.51
R *v* Ewing [1983] QB 1039 .... 13.140
R *v* Foxford [1974] NI 181 .... 13.77
R *v* Freeman's Journal [1902] 2 IR 82 .... 16.57
R *v* Gardner (1794) Ir Term Rep 285 .... 16.67
R *v* Governor of Crumlin Rd *ex p* Jordan [1992] NI 148 .... 19.24
R *v* Governor of Spring Hill, *ex p* Sohi [1988] 1 WLR 596 .... 19.100
R *v* Greenwich LBC, *ex p* Lovelace (No 2) [1992] QB 155 .... 17.90
R *v* Halpin [1975] QB 907 .... 13.132
R *v* Harrow Crown Ct, *ex p* Dave [1994] 1 WLR 98 .... 19.33,36
R *v* Hendon JJ, *ex p* DPP [1994] QB 167 .... 19.48
R *v* Henley Revising Barrister [1912] 3 KB 518 .... 19.07,82
R *v* Hereford Mag Ct *ex p* Rowlands [1997] 2 WLR 854 .... 19.51
R *v* Higher Education Council, *ex p* IDS [1994] 1 WLR 242 .... 19.33
R *v* HM Attorney-General *ex p* Devine [1992] 1 WLR 262 .... 19.24
R *v* Horseferry Road Mag Ct *ex p* Bennett [1995] COD 321 .... 13.34
R *v* Horseferry Road Mag Ct *ex p* Pearson [1976] 2 All ER 264 .... 19.27
R *v* Horsham DC *ex p* Wenman [1995] 1 WLR 680 .... 19.52,68
R *v* Hull University Visitors, *ex p* Page [1993] AC 682 .... 19.05,16,,43
R *v* Immigration Appeal Tribunal, *ex p* Hassesin [1987] 1 All ER 74 .... 19.27
R *v* Industrial Injuries Commr *ex p* AEU [1966] 2 QB 21 .... 19.64
R *v* Institute of Chartered Accountants *ex p* Andreou (1996)
8 Admin LR 557; [1997] 1 CLM 13 .... 19.66
R *v* IRC, *ex p* Nat Fed of Self-employed [1982] AC 617 .... 19.56
R *v* IRC, *ex p* Preston [1985] AC 835 .... 19.34,38
R *v* Islington LBC *ex p* Rixon, *The Times*, 17 April 1996 .... 19.27
R *v* Judge Fraser Harrison *ex p* Law Society[1955] 1 QB 287 .... 17.87
R *v* Kearley [1992] 2 AC 228 .... 13.113
R *v* Kensington & Chelsea LBC, *ex p* Hammell [1989] QB 518 .... 19.70
R *v* Knightsbridge Crown Court, *ex p* ISC [1982] QB 304 .... 19.45
R *v* Lancashire CC, *ex p* Huddleston [1986] 2 All ER 941 .... 19.68,71
R *v* Lanigan [1987] NI 367 .... 13.88
R *v* Legal Aid Board *ex p* Hughes (1992) 24 HLR 698 .... 3.58
R *v* Legal Aid Board, *ex p* Bruce [1992] 1 WLR 694 .... 3.57, 17.101
R *v* Legal Aid Board, *ex p* Donn & Co [1996] 3 All ER 1 .... 19.05
R *v* Leicester City JJ, *ex p* Barrow [1991] 2 QB 260 .... 3.46
R *v* Leipert (1997) 143 DLR 4th 38 .... 13.46
R *v* Leroy (1987) 13 Comm LB 69 .... 13.113
R *v* Liverpool CC, *ex p* Muldoon [1996] 1 WLR 1103 .... 19.66
R *v* London QS, *ex p* Rossi [1956] 1 QB 682 .... 6.24
R *v* Lord Chancellor's Dept, *ex p* Nangle [1992] 1 All ER 897 .... 19.04
R *v* McClafferty(No 2) [1976] 6 NIJB 13.76
R *v* McGlinchey [1985] NI 435 .... 13.153
R *v* McGrath [1989] 4 BNIL 37 .... 13.76
R *v* McNeill [1987] 10 NIJB 41 .... 16.67
R *v* Meehan [1981] 1 NIJB 13.155
R *v* Miller [1983] 1 WLR 1056 .... 17.11
R *v* Minister of Agriculture *ex p* Anastasiou [1994] COD 329 .... 19.75
R *v* Ministry of Defence, *ex p* Smith [1996] QB 517 .... 19.37
R *v* Monopolies Commission, *ex p* Argyll Group [1986] 1 WLR 763 .... 19.62
R *v* Montgomery [1995] 2 All ER 28 .... 16.81
R *v* Murphy [1990] NI 306 .... 13.157
R *v* Murphy [1993] 4 NIJB 42 .... 13.116
R *v* NCB *ex p* NUM [1986] ICR 791 .... 19.05
R *v* Newcastle-under-Lyme JJ *ex p* Massey [1994] 1 WLR 1684 .... 19.53,89
R *v* Newham LBC *ex p* Dada [1996] QB 507 .... 19.23

R *v* Northavon DC *ex p* Palmer, *The Times* 1 Aug 1995 .... 19.88
R *v* Panel on Take-overs *ex p* Datafin [1987] QB 815 .... 19.04,06
R *v* Pieterson [1995] 1 WLR 293 .... 13.113
R *v* Pollution Inspectorate, *ex p* Greenpeace [1994] 1 WLR 570 .... 19.69
R *v* Rasool, *The Times,* 17 Feb 1997 .... 13.51
R *v* Reading Crown Ct, *ex p* Hutchinson [1988] QB 384 .... 19.09
R *v* Rent Officer, *ex p* Muldoon [1996] 3 All ER 498; *sub nom* R *v* Liverpool CC [1996] 1 WLR 1103 .... 19.66
R *v* Roberts (1732) 2 Str 937 (93 ER 953) 19.67
R *v* Sec of State for Employment, *ex p* EOC [1995] 1 AC 1 .... 19.06,07,56
R *v* Sec of State for Environment, *ex p* Hackney LBC [1983] 1 WLR 524; [1984] 1 WLR 592 .... 19.78,90
R *v* Sec of State for Environment, *ex p* Kirkstall Valley Ltd [1996] 3 All ER 304 .... 19.41
R *v* Sec of State for Environment, *ex p* RSPB [1995] CLY 2162 .... 19.70
R *v* Sec of State for Environment, *ex p* Tower Hamlets LBC [1993] QB 632 .... 19.07
R *v* Sec of State for Foreign Affairs, *ex p* World Development Movement [1995] 1 WLR 386 .... 19.56
R *v* Sec of State for Health, *ex p* US Tobacco [1992] QB 353 .... 19.34
R *v* Sec of State for Home Dept ex p Fayed [1997] 1 All ER 228 .... 19.16,33,41
R *v* Sec of State for Home Dept, *ex p* Al-Mehdawi [1990] 1 AC 876 .... 19.36
R *v* Sec of State for Home Dept, *ex p* Begum [1990] COD 107 .... 19.60
R *v* Sec of State for Home Dept, *ex p* Brind [1991] 1 AC 696 .... 19.37
R *v* Sec of State for Home Dept, *ex p* Dew [1987] 1 WLR 881 .... 19.79
R *v* Sec of State for Home Dept, *ex p* Fire Brigades Union [1995] 2 AC 513 .... 19.13
R *v* Sec of State for Home Dept, *ex p* Gardian, *The Times* 1 April 1996 .... 20.31
R *v* Sec of State for Home Dept, *ex p* Hargreaves [1997] 1 All ER 397 .... 19.26,34
R *v* Sec of State for Home Dept, *ex p* Khawaja [1984] AC 74 .... 13.20, 19.23,77
R *v* Sec of State for Home Dept, *ex p* Momin Ali [1984] 1 WLR 663 .... 19.90
R *v* Sec of State for Home Dept, *ex p* Muboyayi [1992] QB 244 .... 19.63,69,100
R *v* Sec of State for Home Dept, *ex p* Read [1989] AC 1014 .... 19.92
R *v* Sec of State for Home Dept, *ex p* Turkoglu [1988] QB 398 .... 19.62,73
R *v* Sec of State for Home Dept, *ex p* Wynne [1992] QB 406; [1993] 1 WLR 115 .... 13.09
R *v* Sec of State for Trade and Industry, *ex p* Lonrho [1989] 1 WLR 525 .... 19.33
R *v* Sec of State for Transport *ex p* Factortame (No 2) [1991] 1 AC 603 .. 11.66, 19.12,70,84
R *v* Shumiatcher (1967) 64 DLR 2d 24 .... 16.67
R *v* Solicitor-General *ex p* Taylor, *The Times,* 14 Aug 1995 .... 19.13
R *v* South Ribble Stip Mag *ex p* Cochrane, *The Times,* 24 June 1996 .... 13.61
R *v* Special Educational Needs Tribunal *ex p* South Glamorgan CC, *The Times,* 12 Dec 1995 .... 19.65
R *v* Staffordshire CC, *ex p* Ashworth, *The Times* 18 Oct 1996 .... 19.78
R *v* Stubbs [1982] 1 WLR 509 .... 13.74,79
R *v* Trafford BC, *ex p* Colonel Food [1990] COD 351 .... 19.89
R *v* Wandsworth Cty Ct, *ex p* Wandsworth LBC [1975] 1 WLR 1314 ...... 16.29, 18.42,45,72
R *v* Wareham Mag Ct, *ex p* Seldon [1988] 1 WLR 825 .... 19.57
R *v* West London Licensing JJ, *ex p* Davis, *The Times,* 16 March 1994 .... 19.07
R *v* Westminster CC, *ex p* Ermakov [1996] 2 All ER 302 .... 19.35
R *v* Wicks, [1997] 2 All ER 801 .... 19.09, 19.48
R (A-G) *v* Belfast JJ [1981] NI 208 .... 19.36,81
R (A-G) *v* County Court Judge for Co Down [1967] NI 171 .... 19.23
R (Baines) *v* Industrial Ct [1970] NI 197 .... 19.23
R (Bobbett) *v* Meath JJ (1917) 51 ILTR 182 .... 19.46
R (Bryson) *v* Lisnaskea Guardians [1918] 2 IR 258 .... 19.44
R (Burns) *v* Tyrone CC Judge [1961] NI 167 .... 19.36,76
R (Butler) *v* Navan UDC [1926] IR 466 .... 19.05
R (Cahill) *v* Dublin JJ [1920] 2 IR 230 .... 19.31
R (Campbell College) *v* Dept of Education [1982] NI 125 .... 19.50
R (Campbell College) *v* Judge Hanna (CA, NI) 29 March 1963 .... 19.45
R (Carl) *v* Tyrone JJ [1917] 2 IR 437 .... 1.23
R (Childers) *v* Adjutant-General [1923] 1 IR 5 .... 19.100

R (Cross) *v* Co Tyrone JJ (1908) 42 ILTR 112 .... 19.54
R (Curry) *v* National Insurance Commr [1974] NI 102 .... 11.00, 19.90
R (Darcy) *v* Co Carlow JJ [1916] 2 IR 313 .... 19.46
R (DHSS) *v* Armagh Supplementary Benefit Appeal Tribunal [1980] 9 NIJB 19.45
R (DHSS) *v* National Insurance Commrs [1980] 8 NIJB 19.50,81
R (Diamond & Fleming) *v* Warnock [1946] NI 171........ 19.56
R (Doris) *v* Min of Health [1954] NI 79 .... 19.06
R (Flanigan) *v* Armagh JJ (1922) 56 ILTR 46........ 19.16
R (Fleming) *v* Londonderry JJ (1908) 42 ILTR 205 .... 19.81
R (Greenaway) *v* Armagh JJ [1924] 2 IR 55 .... 19.23
R (Hade) *v* Carlow JJ [1912] 2 IR 382 .... 14.02
R (Hanna) *v* Minister of Health [1966] NI 52 .... 19.46
R (IUDWC) *v* Rathmines UDC [1928] IR 260 .... 19.82
R (Johnstone) *v* O'Sullivan [1923] 2 IR 13 .... 19.100,108
R (Kelly) *v* Maguire [1923] 2 IR 58 .... 19.05
R (Kildare CC) *v* Commr of Valuation [1901] 2 IR 215 .... 19.50
R (King) *v* Judge Hanna (CA, NI) 29 June 1962 .... 19.45,90
R (Lee) *v* Fermanagh JJ (1936) 70 ILTR 132 (NI) 19.76
R (Magee) *v* Down JJ [1935] NI 51 .... 19.23
R (Martin) *v* Mahony [1910] 2 IR 695 .... 19.41,46
R (McCann) *v* Belfast JJ [1978] NI 153 .... 19.97,104
R (McCreesh) *v* Armagh CC Judge [1978] NI 164 .... 19.45
R (McGrath) *v* Clare JJ [1905] 2 IR 510 .... 19.25
R (McPherson) *v* Min of Education (1973)[1980] NI 115 .... 19.06,50
R (McSwiggan) *v* Co Londonderry JJ [1905] 2 IR 318 .... 19.44,48,50
R (Miller) *v* Monaghan JJ (1906) 40 ILTR 51 .... 19.51
R (O'Brien) *v* Governor of Military Camp [1924] 1 IR 32 .... 19.100
R (O'Hanlon) *v* Governor of Belfast Prison (1922) 56 ILTR 170 .... 19.99
R (Proctor) *v* Hutton [1978] NI 139 .... 19.46
R (SBC) *v* Belfast SB Appeal Trib [1980] 6 NIJB 19.16
R (Sec of State) *v* Recorder of Belfast [1973] NI 112 .... 19.57
R (Shields) *v* Down JJ [1970] NI 173 .... 1.27
R (Smyth) *v* Co Antrim Coroner [1980] NI 123 .... 19.35
R (Westropp) *v* Clare RDC [1904] 2 IR 569 .... 19.82
R, *in re* [1995] 1 WLR 184 .... 20.08
Racal, *re* [1981] AC 374 .... 15.09, 19.41,43,64, 20.01
Racz *v* Home Office [1994] 2 AC 45 .... 14.05
Rafidain Bank *v* Agom Sugar [1987] 1 WLR 1606 .... 11.119
Rahman, *in re* [1997] 1 All ER 796 .... 19.23
Rainey Bros *v* Kearney [1990] NI 18 .... 18.38
Rainey *v* Weatherup [1997] 2 BNIL 50........ 18.78
Rainsford *v* Eager (1852] 3 ICLR 120........ 5.14
Rainsford *v* Limerick Corp [1995] 2 ILRM 561 .... 11.190,191
Rajah *v* College of Surgeons [1994] 1 IR 384 .... 19.05,33
Raleigh *v* Goschen [1898] 1 Ch 73 .... 11.26
Ralston Purina *v* Thompson View Fur Farms (1985) 12 DLR 4th 228 .... 14.44
Ramsey *v* Mullan [1974] June NIJB 9.02
Rantzen *v* Mirror Group [1994] QB 670 .... 18.24, 20.68
Rath *v* CS Lawrence [1991] 1 WLR 399 .... 11.189
Rath *v* McMullan [1916] 1 IR 349 .... 17.74
Ratych *v* Bloomer (1990) 69 DLR 4th 25 .... 14.63
Rea, *in re* (No 2) (1879) 4 LR Ir 345 .... 16.67
Read's Trustee *v* Smith [1951] Ch 439........ 9.35
Reddy *v* Dublin Corp [1941] IR 255 .... 3.31
Redmond *v* Ireland [1992] 2 IR 362 .... 20.33
Redpath *v* Belfast and Co Down Rly [1947] NI 167 .... 14.63
Reekie *v* Messervey (1989) 59 DLR 4th 481; 66 DLR 4th 765 .... 14.60
Reen *v* Jeffers (1939) 73 ILTR 100 .... 17.105

Regalbourne *v* East Lindsey DC, *The Times*, 16 March 1993 ..... 1.35, 20.07
Regent Oil *v* JT Leavesley [1966] 1 WLR 1210 ..... 11.07
Registrar General *v* Chirwa [1994] 1 LRC 146 (Zimbabwe) 13.102
Reid *v* Edinburgh Accoustics 1995 SLT 982 ..... 17.64
Reid *v* Howard (1995) 69 ALJR 863 ..... 13.44
Reid *v* Millar [1928] NI 151 ..... 13.24
Reilly *v* Moore [1935] NI 196 ..... 9.16
Reilly *v* Valley Dyeworks [1973] Oct NIJB 11.20
Renton Gibbs *v* Neville [1900] 2 QB 181 ..... 9.41
Republic of Haiti *v* Duvalier [1990] 1 QB 202 ..... 6.13
Republic of India *v* India Steamship [1993] AC 410 ..... 13.101, 16.21
Republic *v* High Court [1988] LRC (Const) 610 (Ghana) 19.85
Revenue Commrs *v* Bradley [1943] IR 16 ..... 20.41
Revere Trust *v* Wellington Handkerchief [1931] NI 55 ..... 17.04
Reybran Business *v* Governors of Sullivan Upper [1996] 3 BNIL 75 ..... 9.32
Reynolds *v* Enfield Cycle Co (1903) 3 NIJR 205 ..... 17.24
Rhodes, *re* [1987] CLY 3116 ..... 1.30
Rice *v* Toombes [1971] IR 38 ..... 17.29
Rice, *in re* [1994] 4 BNIL 67 ..... 11.09, 19.11
Richards *v* Gogarty (1870) IR 4 CL 300 ..... 13.121
Richardson *v* Richardson (1910) 44 ILTR 196 ..... 20.35
Richardson, *re* [1933] WN 90 ..... 9.38
Rickards *v* Rickards [1990] Fam 194 ..... 20.07
Rinder *v* Deacon (1866) 11 Ir Jur NS 414 ..... 8.14
Rio Tinto Zinc *v* Westinghouse Electric [1978] AC 547 ..... 13.44
Roberts *v* Burns Philp (1987) 13 Comm LB 1310 (NSW) 13.127
Roberts *v* Oppenheim (1884) 26 Ch D 724 ..... 11.104,112,119
Robertson *v* Banham & Co [1997] 1 All ER 79 ..... 6.02
Robinson *v* Chambers [1946] NI 38 ..... 11.122
Robinson *v* Woodroffe (1870) 4 ILT 181 ..... 8.13
Rocco *v* Tradex [1984] 1 WLR 742 ..... 15.15
Roche *v* DJ Martin [1993] ILRM 651 ..... 19.46
Roche *v* Meyler [1896] 2 IR 35 ..... 9.79
Roche *v* Roche (1892) 29 LR Ir 339 ..... 17.75
Roche *v* Sherrington [1982] 1 WLR 599 ..... 1.28
Rochfort *v* Sedley (1861) 12 ICLR App 4 ..... 13.143
Roebuck *v* Mungovin [1994] 2 AC 224 ..... 11.190
Rogers *v* Creswell (1900) 34 ILTR 173 ..... 6.28
Rohan *v* Bord na Mona [1990] 2 IR 425 ..... 4.04
Rolph *v* Zolan [1993] 4 All ER 202 ..... 6.02
Ronson Products *v* Ronson Furniture [1966] Ch 603 ..... 16.64
Rooney, *in re* (CA, NI) 12 Sept 1995 ..... 19.71
Rooney and McParland *v* Carlin [1981] NI 138 ..... 14.93
Rooney *v* Conway [1982] 5 NIJB 13.127
Ross *v* Blakes Motors [1951] 2 All ER 689 ..... 9.90
Ross *v* Eason [1911] 2 IR 459 ..... 6.16
Ross *v* Tower Upholstery [1962] NI 3 ..... 11.139,142, 20.62
Rosse *v* Sylvester (1893) 27 ILTR 109 ..... 20.73
Roussell Uclaf *v* Pharmaceutical Management [1997] 1 NZLR 650 ..... 19.76
Routledge *v* McKay [1954] 1 WLR 615 ..... 20.61
Rover International *v* Cannon Films [1987] 1 WLR 1597 ..... 13.126,129
Rowan Hamilton, *re* [1927] NI 132 ..... 20.60
Rowley *v* Liverpool CC, *The Times* 26 Oct 1989 ..... 11.97
Rowntree, *in re* [1991] 11 NIJB 67 ..... 19.31
Roy *v* Kensington FPC [1992] 1 AC 624 ..... 19.08,88
Royal Bank *v* Nolan (1958) 92 ILTR 60 ..... 6.10, 8.16
Royal Bank *v* O'Rourke [1962] IR 159 ..... 13.106
Royal Trust *v* Dunne (1992) 86 DLR 4th 491 ..... 6.00

RT *v* VP [1990] 1 IR 545 .... 13.88
Rush & Tomkins *v* GLC [1989] AC 1280 .... 13.43
Rushbrooke *v* O'Sullivan [1926] IR 500 .... 13.38
Russell *v* Cox [1983] NZLR 654 .... 14.18
Russell *v* Northern Bank Development [1989] 5 NIJB 1 .... 14.88
Russell *v* Waterford & Limerick Rly (1885) 16 LR Ir 314 .... 3.28,30
Russell Bros *v* Breen (QBD, NI) 14 March 1997 .... 7.16
Russell, *in re* [1990] NI 188 .... 19.15,76,86
Russell, *in re* [1996] 9 BNIL 33 .... 19.97
Ryan *v* Fraser (1884) 16 LR Ir 253 .... 17.27
Ryan *v* Ring (1890) 25 LR Ir 184 .... 13.121
Ryan *v* Shee (1845) 8 Ir LR 268 .... 15.13
Ryan, *re* (1916) 50 ILTR 11 .... 18.25,58

S (Hospital Patient: Court's Jurisidiction), *in re* [1996] Fam 1 .... 14.95
S *v* Special Needs Tribunal [1996] 1 All ER 171 .... 18.02
Sabre Leasing *v* Copeland 1993 SLT 1099 .... 9.28
Safeway Stores *v* National Appeal Panel, 1996 SLT 235 .... 19.35
Salmon *v* Belfast Alhambra (1903) 37 ILTR 72 .... 11.57
Sampson *v* O'Donnell (1880) 6 LR Ir 471 .... 9.09
Samuel, *re* [1945] Ch 364 .... 20.34
Samuels *v* Linzi Dresses [1981] QB 115 .... 1.37, 11.198
Sanders *v* Hamilton (1907) 96 LT 679 .... 3.30
Sanderson *v* Cunningham [1919] 2 IR 234 .... 6.16
Sandes *v* Dublin United Tramways (1883) 12 LR Ir 206, 424 .... 3.33
Sandford *v* Porter [1912] 2 IR 551 .... 20.58
Sankey *v* Alexander (1874) IR 8 Eq 241 .... 13.38
Saunders *v* Jones (1877) 7 Ch D 437 .... 11.18
Savage, *in re* [1991] NI 103 .... 3.22, 11.49, 13.23, 19.17,65
Savill *v* Southend HA [1995] 1 WLR 1254 .... 1.35, 11.08
Savings Bank *v* Gasco BV [1988] Ch 423 .... 16.54
S-C, *re* (Mental Patient: Habeas Corpus) [1996] 1 All ER 532; 2 WLR 146 (CA). 19.100
Scampton *v* Colhoun [1959] NI 106 .... 9.09,16
Scarson *v* Maguire (1953) 87 ILTR 200 .... 20.19
Schawel *v* Reade [1913] 2 IR 64 (HL) 14.44, 20.67
Scherer *v* Counting Instruments [1986] 1 WLR 615 .... 17.05, 20.08
Schofield *v* Church Army [1986] 1 WLR 1328 .... 16.03
Scofish International *v* MV Anton Lopatin [1995] 3 IR 503 .... 9.42
Scotland *v* Commr of Metropolitan Police, *The Times*, 30 Jan 1996 (CA) 14.58
Scotsburn Co-op *v* WT Goodwin (1985) 16 DLR 4th 161 .... 20.88
Scott's Tyre *v* Northern Wheeleries [1899] 2 IR 34 .... 17.27
Scott *v* McDade (1898) 32 ILTR 89 .... 17.27
Scott *v* Pollock [1976] NI 1 .... 20.69
Scottish Widows *v* Blennerhassett [1912] AC 281 (Ir) 20.01,83
Scullion *v* Chief Constable [1989] 6 NIJB 1 .... 14.52
Scullion, *in re* See R *v* Department of Envoronment
Scully *v* Boland [1962] IR 58 .... 10.12
SE Asia Fire *v* Non-metallic Union [1981] AC 363 .... 19.16
Sea Insurance *v* Carr [1901] 1 QB 7 .... 18.28
Seaconsar *v* Bank Markazi [1994] 1 AC 438 .... 6.17
Seagate Technology *v* Goh an Kim [1996] 1 LRC 724 .... 3.19
Seamar Holdings *v* Kupe Group [1995] 2 NZLR 274 .... 11.115, 20.09
Secretary of State for Education *v* Tameside MBC [1977] AC 1014 .... 19.23
Secretary of State for NI, *in re* [1991] NI 64 .... 1.29,18.02, 19.83
Secretary of State for War *v* Booth [1901] 2 IR 692 .... 13.121
Securicor *v* Anglia Building Soc [1992] 7 NIJB 34 .... 13.27,117
Seddon's Pneumatic Tyre *v* Sweeny (1895) 29 ILTR 96 .... 9.47, 11.193
Selective Trimming, *in re* (Taxing Master, NI) 2 Feb 1994 .... 17.98

Selective Trimming, *in re* [1992] 3 BNIL 113 ....18.81
Sennar, The [1985] 1 WLR 490 ....13.106
Serge Caudron *v* Air Zaire [1986] ILRM 10 ....9.14, 11.01
Shaddock (L.) *v* Parramatta CC (1983) 151 CLR 590 ....15.13
Shanley *v* Casey [1967] IR 338 ....17.58
Sharpe (P & F) *v* Dublin City Manager [1989] IR 701 ....19.37
Sharples *v* Eason [1911] 2 IR 436 ....6.17
Shaw *v* Sloan [1982] NI 393 ....13.102,111
Shearer, *in re* [1993] 2 NIJB 12 ....19.34,57
Sheehy *v* Dorman (1824) 2 Fox & Sm 238 ....11.174
Sheehy *v* Freeman's Journal (1892) 26 ILTR 47 ....16.74
Sheerin *v* MOD [1993] 10 NIJB 89 ....4.06
Sheldon *v* Brown Bayleys [1953] 2 QB 393 ....7.07
Shell Pensions *v* Pell Frischmann [1986] 2 All ER 911 ....18.29
Shell-Mex *v* Manchester Garages [1971] 1 All ER 841 ....11.45
Shellew, In goods of (1949) 83 ILTR 190 ....13.132
Shelswell-White *v* O'Connor (1961) 95 ILTR 113 ....6.22
Sheppard *v* McAllister (1988) 40 DLR 4th 233 ....14.72
Sherrard *v* Jacob [1965] NI 151 ....13.17
Sherratt *v* Bromley [1985] QB 1038 ....11.151
Shetland Line *v* Sec of State for Scotland, 1996 SLT 653 ....19.29,38
Shevill *v* Presse Alliance [1996] AC 959 ....1.14
Shipsey *v* British Steam [1936] IR 65 ....6.16
Shocked v Goldschmidt, *The Times,* 4 Nov 1994 ....14.18
Short *v* Lamb [1925] 1 IR 135 ....9.82,87, 18.25
Showlag *v* Mansour [1995] 1 AC 431 ....13.100
Shtun *v* Zaljejska [1996] 3 All ER 411 ....11.188
Siebe Gorman *v* Pneupac [1982] 1 WLR 185 ....1.33, 12.10, 15.14
Simmonds *v* Cronin (1910) 44 ILTR 47 ....8.07, 17.16
Simpson *v* Crowle [1921] 3 KB 243 ....20.60
Simpson *v* Harland & Wolff [1988] NI 432 ....14.61
Simpson *v* Law Society [1987] AC 861 ....17.87
Simpson, *in re* [1984] 1 NZLR 738 Simpson, *re* [1936] P 40 ....13.121,11.41
Singapore Amateur Athletics Assoc. *v* Haron bin Mundir [1994] 3 LRC 563 (Singapore) 19.05
Singh *v* Sec of State for Home Dept, 1993 SC (HL) 1 ....6.25
Sinnott *v* Quinnsworth [1984] ILRM 523 ....10.03,12
Sion *v* Hampstead HA, *The Times*, 10 June 1994 ....11.34
Sivret *v* New Brunswick Power Corp (1995) 121 DLR 4th 274 ....3.09
Skeate *v* Slaters [1914] 2 KB 429 ....13.84
Sloan *v* McGaffin (1895) 29 ILTR 118 ....14.21
Smalley, *in re* [1985] AC 622 ....20.86
Smith Ltd *v* Middleton [1986] 1 WLR 598 ....20.08
Smith *v* Campbell (1895) 29 ILTR 97 ....17.39
Smith *v* Delacherois (1865) 10 Ir Jur NS 357 ....11.23
Smith *v* Huey [1993] 8 NIJB 49 ....14.62
Smith *v* Linskills [1996] 1 WLR 763 ....11.181
Smith *v* Manchester Corporation (1974) 17 KIR 1 ....14.60
Smith *v* Molloy [1905) 39 ILTR 221 ....16.47
Smith *v* Nissan Motor [1993] 11 NIJB 18 ....11.01,175
Smith *v* Springer [1987] 3 All ER 252 ....5.00, 17.18
Smith *v* UMB Chrysler 1978 SC (HL) 1 ....10.02
Smith *v* Williams [1922] 1 KB 158 ....11.39
Smithwick *v* Boland (1905) 5 NIJR 269 ....17.48
Smoker *v* London Fire Authority [1991] 2 AC 502 ....14.63
Smurfit Paribas *v* AAB [1990] 1 IR 469 ....13.38
Smurthwaite *v* Hannay [1894] AC 494 ....3.25
Smyth *v* Byrne (1913) 47 ILTR 279 ....11.41

Smyth *v* Cunningham(1901) 1 NIJR 87 .... 6.28
Smyth *v* Dempsey, [1995] 9 BNIL 23 .... 13.89
Smyth *v* Dolan (1913) 47 ILTR 287 .... 6.04
Smyth *v* Smyth (Taxing Master, NI) 11 May 1994 .... 3.59
Smyth's Trusts (1904) 40 ILTR 70 .... 11.172
Snell *v* Unity Finance [1964] 2 QB 203 .... 20.41
Société Aerospatiale *v* Lee Kui Jak [1987] AC 871 .... 11.177
Sokha *v* Sec of State for Home Dept, 1992 SLT 1049 .... 19.21
Solicitor, *re a* (1919) 53 ILTR 51 .... 16.62
Somers *v* Erskine (No 2) [1944] IR 368 .... 13.21,121
Somers *v* Good [1941] IR 345 .... 11.113
South Hams DC *v* Shough, *The Times*, 8 Dec 1992 .... 18.44
Southern HSSB *v* Lemon [1995] 6 BNIL 60 .... 19.24,31
Spalding *v* Gamage [1914] 2 Ch 405 .... 17.48
Spanier *v* Marchant [1878] WN 214 .... 20.49
Sparks *v* Holland [1977] 1 WLR 143 .... 11.174
Spence *v* Parkes [1900] 2 IR 619 .... 18.57
Spence, *in re* [1993] 4 NIJB 97 .... 19.39
Spencer *v* Hayes [1894] 2 IR 14 .... 17.25
Spiliada *v* Cansulex [1987] AC 460 .... 11.175
Spratt *v* Doherty [1983] NI 136 .... 19.91
Sproule *v* Bogle [1949] NI 134 .... 14.74
SS Gairloch, The [1899] 2 IR 1 .... 20.65
Stacey *v* O'Callaghan [1958] IR 320 .... 8.06, 9.12
Stafford, *in re* [1990] 5 BNIL 1 .... 19.50
Stanley *v* Hart [1932] IR 649 .... 1.28
Stanley *v* Saddique [1992] QB 1 .... 14.72
Staples *v* Young [1908] 1 IR 135 .... 13.148
Starkey *v* Railway Exec [1951] 2 All ER 902 .... 17.36
Starr *v* NCB [1977] 1 WLR 63 .... 11.139
State (A-G) *v* Judge Connelly [1948] IR 176 .... 19.82
State (Batchelor) *v* DJ Ó Floinn [1958] IR 155 .... 19.14
State (Browne) *v* Feran [1967] IR 147 .... 19.44
State (Colquhoun) *v* D'Arcy [1936] IR 641 .... 19.05
State (Creedon) *v* Criminal Injuries Compensation Tribunal [1988] IR 51 .... 19.33
State (Cronin) *v* Western Circuit Judge [1937] IR 34 .... 19.43
State (Cussen) *v* Brennan [1981] IR 181 .... 19.50
State (Davidson) *v* Farrell [1960] IR 438 .... 19.44
State (DPP) *v* Walsh [1981] IR 412 .... 16.71a
State (Gallagher Shatter) *v* de Valera [1991] 2 IR 198 .... 17.101
State (Holland) *v* Kelly [1977] IR 193 .... 19.23
State (Hunt) *v* Midland Circuit Judge [1934] IR 196 .... 3.41
State (Keegan) *v* Stardust Compensation Tribunal [1986] IR 642 .... 19.37
State (McFadden) *v* Governor of Mountjoy (No 2) [1981] ILRM 120 .... 19.106
State (Nevin) *v* Tormey [1976] IR 1 .... 19.23
State (O'Duffy) *v* Bennett [1935] IR 70 .... 19.16
State (Quinn) *v* Mangan [1945] IR 532 .... 19.81
State (Roche) *v* Delap [1980] IR 170 .... 19.51
State (Wood) *v* West Cork Board [1936] IR 401 .... 19.81
State Bank *v* Heinrich (1991) 17 Comm LB 465 .... 11.99
Staunton *v* Counihan (1958) 92 ILTR 32 .... 11.132
Staunton *v* Durkan [1996] 2 ILRM 509 .... 17.104
Steel *v* Slocock (1926) 60 ILTR 100 .... 17.75
Steele *v* Gilliland [1928] NI 19 .... 20.56
Steele *v* GNR (1890) 26 LR Ir 96 .... 3.06,45, 11.25, 14.73
Steele *v* Tiernan (1889) 23 LR Ir 583 .... 1.12
Stephenson *v* Garnett [1898] 1 QB 677 .... 11.181
Stephenson, *in re* [1987] 4 NIJB 79 .... 19.31

Sterling Realty *v* Manning [1964] NZLR 1017 ....20.39
Sterling *v* Cohen [1987] NI 409.... 4.03, 10.10,18, 11.187,188,199
Sterman *v* E & W Moore [1970] 1 QB 596....5.07, 11.31
Sterritt, *in re* [1980] NI 234 .... 13.03,07, 19.40
Stevens *v* Simons, *The Times*, 20 Nov 1987 ....13.89
Stevenson *v* Midlothian DC 1983 SC (HL) 51 ....11.57
Stevenson *v* National Bank [1987] 2 NZLR 331 ....10.16
Stevenson *v* Sweeney 1995 SLT 29 ....14.57,59
Stevenson, *in re* [1984] NI 373 ....19.45,75
Stewart *v* Bowen [1975] NI 10 ....10.18
Stewart *v* Ellis [1974] Jan NIJB 10.18
Stewart *v* Kilkenny (1911) 45 ILTR 154 ....17.104
Stewart *v* Ratner Safe Co (1907) 41 ILTR 74 ....11.96
Stewart, *in re* (QBD, NI) 12 Jan 1996....13.22
Storer *v* Wright [1981] QB 336 ....17.85
Storey *v* Storey [1961] P 63 ....14.30
Stott *v* West Yorkshire Road Car Co [1971] 2 QB 651 ....10.23
Stoughton *v* Crosbie (1843) 5 Ir Eq R 451 ....13.84
Strathclyde RC *v* Gallagher, 1995 SLT 747 ....20.88
Stuart (Carl) *v* Biotrace [1993] ILRM 633....1.14
Stuart, In goods of [1944] Ir Jur R 62 ....13.151
Stubbings *v* Webb [1993] AC 498....4.06
Suffolk Estate *v* McQuillan (1932) 66 ILTR 78 (NI)....12.01
Sullivan *v* Orpen [1909] 1 IR 47 ....18.62
Sumner *v* Sumner [1935] NI 173 ....11.97
Sumner *v* Sumner [1936] Ir Jur Rep 29 (NI) 9.28
Sun Fat Chan *v* Osseous [1992] 1 IR 425 ....11.180,182
Sunday Newspapers *v* Deighan [1989] 3 NIJB 51 ....11.46, 16.21
Supply of Ready Mixed Concrete (No 2), *re* [1995] 1 AC 456 ....16.57
Sutherland *v* Gustar [1994] Ch 305....3.15, 20.02
Swan *v* Doak (1856) 6 Ir Ch R 55 ....18.57
Swansea CC *v* Glass [1992] QB 844 ....4.00
Swanzy *v* Southwell (1869) 3 ILT 118 ....11.124, 20.73
Sweeney *v* DJ Brophy [1993] 2 IR 202 ....19.48
Sweeney *v* Duggan [1991] 2 IR 274 ....4.06
Sybron Corp *v* Barclays Bank [1985] Ch 299 ....13.06
Symons, *re* (1886) 54 LT 501 ....18.57
Symphony Group *v* Hodgson [1994] QB 179 ....17.03

Taaffe *v* Fitzsimmons [1894] 1 IR 63 ....16.44
Taher Meats *v* State Co [1991] 1 IR 443 ....6.16
Tait *v* Beggs [1905] 2 IR 525 ....13.117
Talbot *v* Berkshire CC [1994] QB 290 .... 2.11, 10.15, 13.108
Talwar *v* Chief Constable [1994] 2 BNIL 92 ....11.58
Tan Cheong Poh *v* Teo Ah Keow (1995) 21 Comm LB 1131 ....14.59
Tang Man Sit *v* Capacious Investments [1996] 1 AC 514 (PC) 9.14, 14.45,96
Tannian *v* Synnott (1903) 37 ILT 275 ....13.52
Tansey *v* Sec. of State [1981] NI 193....18.02
Tarr, *in re* [1995] 2 BNIL 59 .... 19.51a,81,92
Tata Cellular *v* Union of India [1996] 1 LRC 342....19.06
Tate *v* Minister of Social Welfare [1995] 1 IR 421 ....19.88
Tassan Din *v* Banco Ambrosiano [1991] 1 IR 569 ....15.11
Taylor *v* Anderton [1995] 1 WLR 447 ....13.47
Taylor *v* Chief Constable of Cheshire [1986] 1 WLR 1479 ....13.157
Taylor *v* Clemson (1842) 2 QB 978 (114 ER 378) 19.44
Tedcastle *v* Robertson [1929] IR 597....6.16
Terry *v* Gould (No 2) (1924) 69 SJ 212 ....17.47
Thames Investment *v* Benjamin [1984] 1 WLR 1381 ....11.174

Thames Valley Electricity *v* NZFP [1994] 2 NZLR 641 .... 19.38
Theodore *v* Australian Postal Commission (1989) 15 Comm LB 66 .... 11.100
Theodoropoulas *v* Theodoropoulas [1964] P 311 .... 13.43
Thew (R & T) *v* Reeves (No 1) [1982] QB 172.......... 3.58
Thoday *v* Thoday [1964] P 181 .... 9.51
Thomas *v* Bunn [1991] 1 AC 362 .... 14.78, 15.16
Thomas *v* Commr. of Police [1997] 1 All ER 747 .... 13.74
Thomas *v* Hammond-Lawrence [1986] 1 WLR 456.......... 11.03
Thompson *v* Commr of Police [1997] 2 All ER 762 .... 14.52
Thompson *v* DOE [1986] NI 196 .... 17.98
Thompson *v* Kennedy (1794) Ir Term R 253 .... 20.73
Thompson *v* Reynolds [1926] NI 131 .... 14.39
Thompson *v* Wynne (1867) IR 1 CL 600 .... 11.122
Thompson *v* YMCA [1986] NI 183 .... 17.90
Thompson, *in re* [1993] 10 NIJB 25 .... 19.33 ,39
Thomson *v* Brown [1981] 1 WLR 747 .... 4.06
Thornton *v* McTaggart (1910) 44 ILTR 119 .... 17.38
Thorpe *v* Alexander Fork Lift [1975] 1 WLR 1459 .... 11.187
Three Rivers DC *v* Bank of England [1996] QB 292.......... 3.19
Thwaite *v* Thwaite [1982] Fam 1 .... 12.10, 15.11,22
Tilcon *v* Land Investments [1987] 1 WLR 46 .... 11.19
Tingay *v* Harris [1967] 2 QB 327 .... 11.150
Tobin *v* Hourihane (1946) 80 ILTR 60 .... 17.48
Tod-Heatley *v* Barnard [1890] WN 130 .... 20.34
Tolstoy-Miloslavsky *v* Aldington [1996] 1 WLR 736 .... 17.61
Tomkins *v* Greene (1880) 6 LR Ir 474 .... 11.198
Toole, In goods of [1913] 2 IR 188 .... 11.12
Toomey *v* Murphy [1897] 2 IR 601 .... 5.12
Topglass, *in re* [1996] 2 BNIL 8 .... 18.81
Topping *v* Warne Products [1986] 9 NIJB 14 .... 11.64
Tormey *v* Tormey (1894) 28 ILTR 48 .... 11.174
Tottenham *v* Foley [1909] 2 IR 500 .... 11.46
Tower Tea *v* Doheny (1908) 42 ILTR 22 .... 13.06
Towers *v* Morley [1992] 1 WLR 511 .... 7.07
Trainor, *in re* [1997] 1 BNIL 33 .... 19.57,81
Trainor *v* McKee [1988] NI 556 .... 12.11, 13.107,111
Treacy *v* Ryan (1878) 2 LR Ir 130 .... 20.32
Treanor *v* Loughran [1989] NI 135 .... 9.16
Triple A Investments *v* Adams Bros (1986) 23 DLR 4th 587 .... 13.154
TSB *v* Chabra [1992] 1 WLR 231 .... 11.26
Tubman *v* Johnston [1981] NI 53 .... 18.78
Tubridy *v* Finnegan [1983] NI 340.......... 6.07
Tucker, *in re* (QBD, NI) 25 Aug 1995 .... 19.35
Tucker *v* Oldbury UDC [1912] 2 KB 317 .... 13.122
Tudor Accumulator *v* China Mutual [1930] WN 200 .... 11.78
Tumelty *v* MOD [1988] 3 NIJB 51 .... 14.74
Turner *v* Fenton [1982] 1 WLR 52.......... 7.18
Turner *v* Plasplugs [1996] 2 All ER 939 .... 3.59
Turkington *v* St Oswald [1996] 6 BNIL 79 .... 11.175
Turkington *v* The Telegraph [1996] 6 BNIL 105 .... 18.24
Twigg *v* Mason (1916) 50 ILTR 173 (HL) 3.40

Udall *v* Capri Lighting [1988] QB 907 .... 16.62
UDT *v* Patterson [1973] NI 142.......... 8.06
Ulster Bank *v* Chambers [1979] NI 1 .... 15.22, 16.26,31
Ulster Bank *v* Min of Finance [1923] 2 IR 173 (NI) 13.16
Ulster Banking *v* McKinney (1879) 4 LR Ir 51 .... 1.27
Ulster Chemists *v* Hemsborough [1957] NI 185 .... 20.65

Ulsterbus *v* Donnelly [1982] 13 NIJB 14.52
Umfreville *v* Johnson (1875) LR 10 Ch App 580 .... 17.47
Union Bank *v* Lelakis [1996] 4 All ER 305 .... 6.19
United Meat *v* Nordsteine Allgemeine [1996] 2 ILRM 260 .... 6.17
United Tobacco *v* Goncalves, 1996 (1) SA 209 .... 13.127
United Telephone *v* Dale (1884) 25 Ch D 778 .... 16.49
Unsworth *v* Southern [1996] 2 CLM 222 .... 14.68
Upmann *v* Forester (1883) 24 Ch D 231 .... 17.19
US Government *v* Bowe [1990] 1 AC 501 .... 19.91

Valentine *v* Valentine (1893) 31 LR Ir 488 .... 17.04
Van Gervan *v* Fenton (1992) 175 CLR 327 .... 14.55
van Oppen, *in re* [1953] WN 51 .... 18.64
Vandeleur *v* Glynn [1905] 1 IR 483 .... 13.24
Venter *v* Scottish LA Board 1993 SLT 147 .... 3.62
Ventouris *v* Mountain [1991] 1 WLR 607 .... 11.116, 13.40
Ventouris *v* Mountain (No 2) [1992] 1 WLR 887 .... 13.126
Vernon *v* Bosley [1994] PIQR P337 .... 13.14, 20.61
Vernon *v* Bosley [1995] 2 FCR 78 .... 13.54
Vernon *v* Bosley (No 1) [1997] 1 All ER 577 .... 13.88
Vernon *v* Bosley (No 2) [1997] 1 All ER 614 .... 3.02, 11.93,106,111, 13.42, 20.77
Villiers *v* Villiers [1994] 2 All ER 149 .... 16.83
Volkes *v* EHSSB [1990] NI 388 .... 7.07,11
Voluntary Purchasing *v* Insurco [1995] 2 ILRM 145 .... 11.12

Waddell *v* Norton [1966] NI 85 .... 6.16,17
Walker *v* BMW [1990] 6 NIJB 1 .... 1.14, 11.175
Walker *v* Turpin [1994] 1 WLR 196 .... 11.150
Walkley *v* Precision Forgings [1979] 1 WLR 606 .... 4.06, 6.07
Wall *v* Radford [1991] 2 All ER 741 .... 13.111
Wallace *v* Mulhall [1979] 7 NIJB 17.102
Wallace Smith Trust Co *v* Delloitte Haskins & Sells [1996] 4 All ER 403 .... 11.116
Wallersteiner *v* Moir [1974] 1 WLR 991 .... 11.185
Walsh and Gallagher, *in re* (QB, Bankruptcy), 11 Jan 1968 .... 11.09
Walsh *v* Curry [1955] NI 112 .... 9.00, 14.39
Walsh *v* Fitzgerald (1884) 18 ILTR 54 .... 12.03
Walsh *v* George Kemp [1938] 2 All ER 266 .... 20.45
Walsh *v* MOD [1985] NI 62 .... 14.52
Walsh *v* Walsh (1866) 17 ICLR 195 .... 17.30
Ward *v* Freeman (1851) 2 ICLR 460 .... 9.16
Ward *v* Guiness Mahon & Co [1996] 4 All ER 112 .... 17.47a
Ward *v* Macdonald's Restaurants (1987) 39 DLR 4th 469 .... 20.65
Ward *v* Ward [1980] 1 WLR 4 .... 15.20
Warden of Cholmeley's School *v* Sewell [1893] 2 QB 254 .... 9.43
Warner *v* Sampson [1959] 1 QB 297 .... 9.23, 11.22
Warnock *v* Harland & Wolff [1976] NI 156 .... 17.33, 20.74
Warnock *v* Mann [1896] 2 IR 630 .... 11.199
Warren *v* T Kilroe [1988] 1 WLR 516 .... 20.14
Warren *v* Warren [1996] 4 All ER 664 .... 13.51
Wasson *v* Chief Constable [1987] NI 420 .... 9.81
Waterford Corp *v* Newport (1846) 11 Ir LR 359 .... 18.00
Waterhouse *v* Barker [1924] 2 KB 759 .... 11.132
Waters *v* Cruikshank [1967] IR 378 .... 13.22
Watkins *v* Olafson (1989) 61 DLR 4th 577 .... 12.25, 14.59
Watson *v* Cammell Laird [1959] 2 All ER 757 .... 13.40
Watson *v* Cooper (1851) 3 Ir Jur OS 156 .... 11.22
Watson *v* Holliday (1882) 20 Ch D 780 .... 17.55
Watson *v* Knilans (1874) 8 ILTR 157 .... 3.11

Watson *v* Panton (1907) 41 ILTR 40 .... 1.31
Watts *v* Morrow [1991] 1 WLR 1421 .... 14.78
Waugh *v* BRB [1980] AC 521 .... 13.39
Waung *v* Subbotovsky (1969) 43 ALJR 372 .... 13.126
WEA Records *v* Visions Channel 4 [1983] 1 WLR 721 .... 19.64, 20.01,11
Weatherall, *in re* [1984] 19 NIJB 19.43,94,100
Webster *v* Auckland Harbour Board [1987] 2 NZLR 129 .... 19.06
Webster *v* Southwark LBC [1983] QB 698 .... 16.47
Weeks *v* Chief Constable [1997] 3 BNIL 105 .... 11.181
Weir, *in re* [1988] NI 338 .... 11.09, 15.11, 19.11,91
Weldon *v* Home Office [1992] 1 AC 58 .... 19.99
Wells *v* McGregor (1908) 42 ILTR 86 .... 8.14
Wells *v* NI Office [1993] 5 NIJB 61 .... 19.06,67
Wells *v* Wells [1997] 1 All ER 673 .... 14.57,59
Wells, *in re* [1962] 1 WLR 397, 874 .... 18.25
Wellworth FW, *in re* [1996] 6 BNIL 1 .... 19.71
Wellworth FW, *in re* (No 2), (QBD, NI) 28 June 1996; [1996] 8 BNIL 131 .... 19.27,34
Welsh Development Agency *v* Redpath Dorman Long [1994] 1 WLR 1409 ... 10.29, 11.33,35
Welsh *v* Hall (1841) 9 M & W 14 (152 ER 7) 1.28
Wenlock *v* River Dee (1887) 19 QBD 155 .... 18.25
Wentworth *v* Woollahra Council (1982) 149 CLR 672 .... 14.91
West *v* Morgan (1988) 44 DLR 4th 381 .... 11.156
West *v* Sec of State for Scotland 1992 SC 385 .... 19.04
West *v* Versil, *The Times* 31 Aug 1996 .... 14.59
Western HSSB, *in re* [1988] 5 NIJB 20 .... 20.79,81
Westmeath *v* Coyne [1896] 2 IR 436 .... 16.11
Weston *v* Central Criminal Court Administrator [1977] QB 32 .... 16.67
Whaley (Geo) *v* DOE [1983] 3 NIJB 19.08
Wheeler *v* John Jeffrey [1921] 2 IR 395 .... 6.16
Wheeler *v* Leicester CC [1985] AC 1054 .... 19.38
Wheeler *v* Somerfield [1966] 2 QB 94 .... 20.08
Whelan *v* Dixon [1963) 97 ILTR 195 .... 16.16
Whelan *v* Kelly (1884) 14 LR Ir 387 .... 5.12
Whelan, *in re* [1990] NI 348 .... 19.40,92
White *v* Brunton [1984] QB 570 .... 11.00, 20.10,14
White *v* DOE [1988] 5 NIJB 1 .... 20.65
White *v* Garvin (1933) 67 ILTR 105 .... 13.29
White *v* Spendlove [1942] IR 224 .... 14.20,46
White *v* Warnock (1947) 81 ILTR 35 (HL) 19.100,104
Whitehouse Hotels *v* Lido Savoy (1974) 48 ALJR 406 .... 20.22
Whitehouse *v* Jordan [1980] 1 All ER 650 affd [1981] 1 WLR 246 .... 9.17, 11.144, 18.30
Whitmore *v* O'Reilly [1906] 2 IR 357 .... 17.38
Whitton *v* Hanlon (1885) 16 LR Ir 137 .... 9.43
Whytte *v* Ticehurst [1986] Fam 64 .... 11.39
Wightman *v* Mullan [1977] 3 NIJB 20.58
Wilander *v* Tobin, *The Times*, 8 April 1996 .... 19.05
Wilcox *v* McDonnell (1913) 47 ILTR 169 .... 11.158, 12.03
Wiley *v* Smith [1894] 1 IR 153 .... 10.27
Wiley *v* Spanjer (1933) 67 ILTR 69 .... 6.17
Willis *v* Redbridge HA [1996] 3 All ER 114 .... 17.95
Wilkinson *v* Banking Corp [1948] 1 KB 721 .... 7.07
Wilkinson *v* Kenny [1993] 1 WLR 963 .... 20.08
Wilkinson *v* McCann (1900) 1 NIJR 14 .... 9.82
Williams (C.O.) *v* Blackman [1990] LRC (Const) 70 (Barbados SC) 1.30
Williams, (C.O.) *v* Blackman [1995] 1 WLR 102 (PC) 19.12
Williamson *v* DOE, Taxing Office NI, 1995 .... 17.98,107
Williamson *v* Rover Cycle [1901] 2 IR 615 .... 13.24
Willowgreen *v* Smithers [1994] 1 WLR 832 .... 6.24

Wilson *v* Imrie Engineering, 1993 SLT 235 .... 14.36
Wilson *v* Casey (1952) 86 ILTR 34 .... 17.77
Wilson *v* Liquid Packaging [1979] NI 165 .... 13.40,41
Wilson *v* Marshall (1868) IR 2 CL 356 .... 5.14
Wilson *v* United Counties Bank [1920] AC 102 .... 11.42
Wilson, *in re* [1983] 10 NIJB 19.47,61,82,94
Wilson, *in re* [1989] NI 415 .... 19.57
Wimpress *v* Scott [1985] 6 BNIL 99 .... 9.51, 11.177
Winchester Cigarette Machinery *v* Payne, *The Times*, 19 Oct 1993 .... 18.29
Winder *v* Glover (1909) 43 ILTR 259 .... 11.124
Wislang, *in re* [1984] NI 63 .... 19.05,50
Witten *v* Lombard Australia [1969] Australian Law Digest, p.296 .... 13.126
Wynn *v* NSW Insurance Corp (1996) 70 ALJR 147 .... 14.58
Wong *v* Minister of Justice [1994] 1 IR 223 .... 16.73
Wood *v* Cousins [1993] 6 NIJB 41 .... 16.17
Wood *v* Gahlings, *The Times*, 29 Nov 1996 .... 20.59,77
Wood *v* Perry (1849) 3 Ex 442 (154 ER 918) 3.27
Woods, Application of [1970] IR 154 .... 19.106
Woods *v* McCann (1901) 35 ILTR 210 .... 3.07
Wookey *v* Wookey [1991] Fam 121 .... 14.88
Working Men's Mutual, *re* (1882) 21 Ch D 831 .... 16.68
Workman *v* Belfast Harbour Commrs [1899] 2 IR 234 .... 7.18
Wraith *v* Wraith [1997] 2 All ER 526 .... 17.88,89
Wright *v* Jess [1987] 1 WLR 1076 .... 16.55
Wynn *v* NSW Ins Corp (1996) 70 ALJR 147 .... 14.58

X Ltd *v* Morgan-Grampian [1991] 1 AC 1 .... 16.60
X (Minors) *v* Bedfordshire CC [1995] 2 AC 633 .... 9.16, 19.09

Yates *v* Yates [1954] 1 WLR 564 .... 20.63
Yianni *v* Yianni [1966] 1 WLR 120 .... 13.05, 16.54
Yonge *v* Toynbee [1910] 1 KB 215 .... 7.05
Yorkshire Electricity *v* West Yorkshire CC [1980] CLY 2193 .... 20.05
Yorkshire RHA *v* Fairclough Builders [1996] 1 WLR 210 .... 11.36
Young *v* Mead [1917] 2 IR 258 .... 17.110
Young *v* O'Neill [1995] 3 BNIL 105 .... 11.133
Young *v* Pharmaceutical Society [1994] 2 ILRM 262 .... 19.12
Young *v* Power (1862) 7 Ir Jur NS 388 .... 16.62

Zanussi *v* Anglo-Venezuelan Development, *The Times*, 18 April 1996 .... 17.02
Zierenberg *v* Labouchère [1893] 2 QB 183 .... 9.90
Zuliana *v* Veira [1994] 3 LRC 705 (PC) 17.77
Zurich Insurance *v* Shield Insurance [1988] IR 174 .... 10.08

TABLE OF STATUTES, RULES AND OTHER ENACTMENTS

6-02,21 *means* 6-02, 6-21

ACTS OF THE IRISH PARLIAMENT (TO 1800)

1695 **7 Will 3**
Statute of Frauds Act, c.12 9.31
Sunday Observance Act, c.17
s.7 6.02,21, 16.81

1697 **9 Will 3**
Clandestine Mortgages Act, c.11 18.76

1707 **6 Ann**
Administration of Justice Act, c.10
s.12 9.31

1737 **11 Geo 2**
Administration of Justice (Language) Act, c.6 1.23, 14.01

1781 **21 & 22 Geo 3**
Habeas Corpus Act, c.11
s.1 19.104
s.4 19.104
s.5 19.106
s.15 19.106
Crown Debts Act, c.20
s.4 16.07
s.23 8.09, 14.81

ACTS OF THE PARLIAMENT OF THE UNITED KINGDOM

1297 **25 Edw 1**
Magna Carta, c.29 1.16

1320s **2 Edw 2**
Perogativa Regis, c.11 & 12 18.52

1804 **44 Geo 3**
Habeas Corpus Act, c.102 19.109

1806 **46 Geo 3**
Witnesses Act, c.37 13.44

1816 **56 Geo 3**
Habeas Corpus Act, c.100
ss.1, 2 19.104
s.3 19.104,105

1819 **60 Geo 3 & 1 Geo 4**
Criminal Libel Act, c.8
s.1 18.24

1828 **9 Geo 4**
Statute of Frauds Amendment Act, c.14 9.31

1832 **2 & 3 Will 4**
Prescription Act, c.71 9.82

1843 **6 & 7 Vic**
Libel Act, c.96
s.1 18.20
s.2 18.19

1844 **7 & 8 Vic**
Marriages (Ireland) Act, c.81
s.32 13.23
ss.68-71 13.153

1845 **8 & 9 Vic**
Libel Act, c.75
s.2 18.19
Evidence Act, c.113
s.1 13.153
s.2 13.153

1849 **12 & 13 Vic**
House of Lords Costs Taxation Act, c.78 17.02, 20.89

1851 **14 & 15 Vic**
Fines (Ireland) Act, c.90 16.56
Evidence Act, c.99
s.7 13.153
s.9 13.153
s.13 13.153
s.14 13.153

1856 **19 & 20 Vic**
Mercantile Law Amendment Act, c.97
s5 10.05

1859 **22& 23 Vic**
British Law Ascertainment Act, c.63 13.94

1860 **23 & 24 Vic**
Landlord and Tenant Law Amendment (Ireland) Act, c.154 ("Deasy's Act")
s.23 13.153
ss.45-6 18.39
s.48 9.43
s.52 18.34
ss.58, 65, 66 18.38
ss.63, 69 11.169
s.64 11.169, 18.38
s.75 11.56, 18.38
ss.76, 77 18.38

1863 **26 & 27 Vic**
Registration of Marriages (Ireland) Act, c.90
ss.11, 17-19 13.153

1864 **27 & 28 Vic**
Naval Prize Act, c.25
ss.3-4 18.17

1865 **28 & 29 Vic**
Criminal Procedure Act, c.18
s.3 13.64
ss.4, 5 13.76
s.6 13.74
s.7 13.145
s.8 13.140

Year	Statute	Para
1868	**31 & 32 Vic**	
	Documentary Evidence Act, c.3	13.153
	Partition Act, c.40	
	ss.3, 4, 9	18.77
	Promissory Oaths Act, c.72	
	s.4	1.16
1869	**32 & 33 Vic**	
	Newspapers, Printers and Reading Room Repeal Act, c.24	
	Sch.2	11.130, 18.22
1871	**34 & 35 Vic**	
	Prevention of Crimes Act, c.112	
	s.18	13.26,74,153
1872	**35 & 36 Vic**	
	County Boundaries (Ireland) Act, c.48	13.153
1874	**37 & 38 Vic**	
	Vendor and Purchaser Act, c.78	
	s.2	13.153
1875	**38 & 39 Vic**	
	Public Records (Ireland) Act 1867 Amendment Act, c.59	
	s.10	13.153
1876	**39 & 40 Vic**	
	Partition Act, c.17	
	ss.3, 7	18.77
	s.4	11.169
	Parochial Records Act, c.58	13.153
	Appellate Jurisdiction Act, c.59	20.89
1877	**40 & 41 Vic**	
	Supreme Court of Judicature (Ireland) Act, c.57	1.12
	s.27(3)	9.52, 10.31
	s.27(5)	11.173
	s.52	20.08
1878	**41 & 2 Vic**	
	Petty Sessions Clerks and Fines (Ireland) Act, c.69	
	s.8	14.07
1879	**42 & 43 Vic**	
	Registration of Births, Deaths and Marriages (Army) Act, c.8	13.153
	Bankers' Books Evidence Act, c.11	
	ss.3-5	13.133
	s.6	13.36,51
	s.7	11.132
1881	**44 & 45 Vic**	
	Conveyancing Act, c.41	
	s.5	15.18
	s.14(2)	18.40
	s.19	18.59,72
	s.69	11.169, 18.40
	Newspaper Libel and Registration Act, c.60	
	s.15	13.153
1882	**45 & 46 Vic**	
	Documentary Evidence Act, c.9	13.153
	Bills of Exchange Act, c.61	
	ss.48-50	5.01
	s.57	8.09, 14.81
	Married Women's Property Act, c.75	
	s.17	18.70
1887	**50 & 51 Vic**	
	Land Law (Ireland) Act, c.33	
	s.30	18.41
1888	**51 & 52 Vic**	
	Law of Libel Amendment Act, c.64	
	s.5	3.36, 18.21
1889	**52 & 53 Vic**	
	Commissioner for Oaths Act, c.10	
	s.6	11.13
	Interpretation Act, c.63	
	s.3	1.31
	s.18	1.10
	s.26	6.24
1890	**53 & 54 Vic**	
	Partnership Act, c.39	
	ss.1, 4, 5-12, 14	3.15
	s.15	13.117
	s.23(1)(2)	16.09
	s.35	18.79
1891	**54 & 55 Vic**	
	Stamp Act, c.39	
	s.14	13.147, 20.61
	Slander of Women Act, c.51	17.10
1892	**55 & 56 Vic**	
	Colonial Probates Act, c.6	3.42
	Foreign Marriage Act, c.23	
	ss.16-18	13.153
1894	**57 & 58 Vic**	
	Notice of Accidents Act, c.28	
	s.3(4)	17.93
1895	**58 & 59 Vic**	
	Documentary Evidence Act, c.9	13.153
	Mortgagees Legal Costs Act, c.25	17.55
1896	**59 & 60 Vic**	
	Life Assurance Companies (Payment into Court) Act, c.8	11.169
	Land Law (Ireland) Act, c.47	
	s.16	18.41
1898	**61 & 62 Vic**	
	Prison Act, c.41	
	s.11	13.09
1907	**7 Edw 7**	
	Evidence (Colonial Statutes) Act, c.16	13.94
1915	**5 & 6 Geo 5**	
	Prize Courts Act, c.57	18.17
1916	**6 & 7 Geo 5**	
	Naval Prize (Procedure) Act, c.2	18.17
	Finance Act, c.24	
	s.66	11.171
1920	**10 &11 Geo 5**	
	Maintenance Orders (Facilities for Enforcement) Act, c.33	18.47
	Government of Ireland Act, c.67	
	s.41	1.03
	Administration of Justice Act, c.81	
	s.9	16.22
	s.9(5)	16.21
	s.10	16.18
1927	**17 & 18 Geo**	
	Colonial Probates (Protected States and Mandated Territories) Act, c.43	3.42
1932	**22 & 23 Geo 5**	
	Northern Ireland (Miscellaneous Provisions) Act, c.11	
	s.9(3)	18.35,61

Year	Enactment	Para
1933	**23 & 24 Geo 5**	
	Foreign Judgments (Reciprocal Enforcement) Act, c.13	
	s.2	16.22
	s.6	16.21
	s.8	13.100
	s.10	16.18
1939	**2 & 3 Geo 6**	
	Prize Act, c.65	18.17
1940	**3 & 4 Geo 6**	
	Evidence and Powers of Attorney Act, c.28	13.153
1946	**9 & 10 Geo 6**	
	Statutory Instruments Act, c.36	
	s.5	1.10
1947	**10 & 11 Geo 6**	
	Crown Proceedings Act, c.44 (as adapted for NI by SI 1981/233)	
	s.4(1)	10.00
	s.4(2)	14.74
	ss.13-33	3.21
	s.13	3.21
	s.14	5.13, 18.26, 20.20
	s.16	10.33, 16.36
	s.17	3.21
	s.17(4)	11.28
	s.17(5)	11.43
	s.18	6.01,23
	s.19	3.21
	s.20(2)(c)	17.10,24
	s.21	14.99
	s.21(1)(b)	18.37
	s.21A	17.09
	s.22	16.07, 20.00
	s.23	3.21, 14.99
	s.24(1)	15.15
	s.24(3)	14.78
	s.25	16.07
	s.26(1)(2)	16.07
	s.26(2A)	16.40
	s.26(2B)	16.44
	s.27	16.35
	s.27(3)	16.57
	s.28	11.95,122,126, 13.48
	ss.29-30	18.17
	s.32	11.39
	s.35(2)(a)	6.12
	s.35(2)(b)	5.10
	s.35(2)(c)	8.04
	s.35(2)(d)	11.45
	s.35(2)(f)	13.10
	s.35(2)(g)	9.44
	s.38	3.21, 14.99, 19.12,86,103
	s.40(2)(3)	3.22
	s.40(5)	19.82
1949	**12, 13 & 14 Geo 6**	
	Ireland Act, c.41	
	s.2	1.10, 13.126
	s.3	1.10, 13.94
1950	**14 Geo 6**	
	Arbitration Act, c.27	
	ss.35-42	16.23
	s.37	7.22
	Maintenance Orders Act, c.37	
	ss.16-25	18.47
1951	**14 & 15 Geo 6**	
	Reserve and Auxiliary Forces (Protection of Civil Interests) Act, c.65	
	s.2	16.04
1955	**3 & 4 Eliz 2**	

Year	Enactment	Para
	Army Act, c.18	
	s.151A	16.08
	Air Force Act, c.19	
	s.151A	16.08
1956	**4 & 5 Eliz 2**	
	Administration of Justice Act, c.46	
	Sch.1	18.17
1957	**5& 6 Eliz 2**	
	Naval Discipline Act, c.53	
	s.128E	16.08
1958	**6 & 7 Eliz 2**	
	Maintenance Orders Act, c.39	
	ss.2, 2A, 5	18.47
1960	**8 & 9 Eliz 2**	
	Administration of Justice Act, c.65	
	s.12	14.03, 16.74
	s.14(1)	19.102
	s.14(2)	19.106
1961	**9 & 10 Eliz 2**	
	Criminal Justice Act, c.39	
	s.29	13.09
1963	Oaths and Evidence (Overseas Authorities and Countries) Act, c.27	
	s.5	13.153
1964	Diplomatic Privileges Act, c.81	3.20, 13.51
	Sch.1 Art.32	9.45
	Sch.1 Arts.31, 37	13.36
1965	Nuclear Installations Act, c.57	6.16
1966	Arbitration (International Investment Disputes) Act, c.41	16.23
1967	Parliamentary Commissioner Act, c.13	19.51
	s.5	1.04
	s.11	13.36,51
1968	Consular Relations Act, c.18	3.20, 13.51
	Sch.1 Art.32	9.45
	Sch.1 Arts.44, 58	13.36
	International Organisations Act, c.48	3.20, 13.51
1969	Post Office Act, c.49	
	s.30(5)	5.02
	Administration of Justice Act, c.58	
	ss.12-16	20.85
	s.20	11.55
	s.21	11.87
1970	Taxes Management Act, c.9	
	s.69	14.81
	s.70	13.153
	s.75	11.83
	s.86-92	8.09, 14.81
	Administration of Justice Act, c.31	
	s.31	11.134,136
	s.32(1)	11.135,136
	s.32(2)	11.89
	s.33(2)	11.89
	s.35	11.87, 89,136
	s.36	18.73
1971	Administration of Estates Act, c.25	
	ss.2-4	3.42
	Powers of Attorney Act, c.27	
	s.3	13.153
1972	Maintenance Orders (Reciprocal Enforcement) Act, c.18	18.47
	European Communities Act, c.68	
	s.3	13.94

Year	Statute	Para
1973	Administration of Justice Act, c.15	
	s.8	18.73
	Northern Ireland Constitution Act, c.36	
	ss.7-11, 35	3.21
	ss.17, 18	19.39
	s.19	9.16, 19.39
1974	Northern Ireland Act, c.28	
	Sch.1	3.21, 13.153
	Consumer Credit Act, c.39	
	s.139	7.12
	Friendly Societies Act, c.46	
	s.103	3.14
1975	Arbitration Act, c.3	7.14
	ss.3-6	16.23
	Evidence (Proceedings in Other Jurisdictions) Act, c.34	13.31
	Litigants in Person (Costs and Expenses) Act, c.47	17.59
	Policyholders Protection Act, c.75	10.06
1976	Fair Employment (Northern Ireland) Act, c.25	
	s.52	13.51
	Congenital Disabilities (Civil Liability) Act, c.26	3.10
1977	Tort (Interference with Goods) Act, c.32	
	s.3	14.83
	s.4	11.78
	s.5	11.157, 14.83
	s.8	9.29, 18.33
	s.11(1)	14.74
	s.11(3)	9.23
	s.13	11.169
	Unfair Contract Terms Act, c.50	
	s.4	10.02
1978	Oaths Act, c.19	11.13, 13.56
	Judicature (Northern Ireland) Act, c.23 *See separate table*	
	Interpretation Act, c.30	
	s.5	1.31
	ss.6, 8, 11, 17, 22-3	1.10
	s.7	6.24
	s.24	1.11
	Sch.1	1.10,31
	Sch.2 para.4(2)	1.10
	State Immunity Act, c.33	3.20
	s.2(6)	9.45
	s.12	8.04
	s.13	14.86, 16.08
	Civil Liability (Contribution) Act, c.47	
	s.1(1)	10.09
	s.1(2)(3)	10.10
	s.1(4)(5)(6)	10.11
	s.2	10.12
	s.2(3)	10.09
	s.3	3.33, 8.10, 9.36, 13.102
	s.4	17.10
	s.5	10.00
	s.6	3.33, 10.09
	s.7(3)	10.09
1979	Estate Agents Act, c.38	
	s.16	10.06
	Sale of Goods Act, c.54	
	s.52	14.84
1980	Criminal Appeal (Northern Ireland) Act, c.47	
	s.17	19.01
	s.28	17.93
1981	International Organisations Act, c.9	3.20
	Contempt of Court Act, c.49	
	s.2	16.73
	ss.3-5	16.74
	s.4	14.03, 16.73
	s.6	16.74
	s.7	16.74
	s.8	16.72
	s.9	14.01, 16.72
	s.10	13.53
	s.11	14.03, 16.73
	s.13 (as modified in Sch.4)	16.67
	ss.14, 16	16.83
	Sch.1	16.73
	Sch.4	16.67
	Supreme Court Act, c.54	
	s.18	20.08
	ss.33-34	11.136
	s.132	13.153
1982	Civil Aviation Act, c.16	
	s.91	18.17
	Oil and Gas (Enterprise) Act, c.23	
	s.23	1.15
	Civil Jurisdiction and Judgments Act, c.27	
	ss.4, 6	16.22
	s.11	13.153
	s.12	16.19
	s.16(1)(a)	19.19
	s.18	16.19,22
	s.18(8)	16.21
	s.19	13.100
	s.24	11.01
	s.25	11.01,70
	s.26	18.17
	s.30	1.13
	s.31	13.100
	s.32	13.100, 16.21
	s.34	16.21
	ss.41-46	1.14,15
	s.49	11.175
	Sch.1 Art.1	19.19
	Sch.1 Arts.2, 3, 5, 6, 8-15, 16, 17, 18-19, 20, 52	1.14
	Sch.1 Art.6	1.14, 9.39, 10.00,19
	Sch.1 Art.10	10.06
	Sch.1 Art.16	1.14, 16.20, 18.81
	Sch.1 Art.18	7.07
	Sch.1 Art.20	8.06, 11.174
	Sch.1 Arts.21-3	11.176
	Sch.1 Art.24	11.01
	Sch.1 Arts.26-30	13.100
	Sch.1 Arts.31-49	16.19
	Sch.1 Arts.31-32, 36-37, 40, 41	16.22
	Sch.4	1.15
	Sch.4 Art.6	9.39, 10.09,19
	Sch.4 Art.16	16.20, 18.81
	Sch.4 Art.18	7.07
	Sch.4 Art.20	8.06, 11.174
	Sch.4 Art.24	11.01
	Sch.5 para.4	19.19
	Sch.6	16.19,22
	Sch.7	16.19,22
	Sch.8	19.19
	Northern Ireland Act, c.38	
	Sch.2 para.7	1.11
	Administration of Justice Act, c.53	

s.1 14.61
s.2 14.55
s.5 14.54
s.23 18.50
s.42 11.171
Sch.6 3.06
Sch.6 para.9 14.70
Sch.6 para.10 14.75
1984 Data Protection Act, c.35
s.21 11.130
Repatriation of Prisoners Act, c.47 19.92
1985 Enduring Powers of Attorney Act, c.29
s.7 13.153
Interception of Communications Act, c.56
s.9 13.51
Child Abduction and Custody Act, c.60
s.20 11.176
Sch.1 art.16 11.176
Administration of Justice Act, c.61
s.64 11.138
1986 Family Law Act, c.55
s.22 11.176
ss.44-54 13.100
Financial Services Act, c.60 6.16, 18.53
1987 Recognition of Trusts Act, c.14 3.40
Banking Act, c.22 6.16, 11.169
Consumer Protection Act, c.43
s.41 9.16
1988 Income and Corporation Taxes Act, c.1
s.328 11.171
s.329 14.79
s.329AA 12.25, 14.73a
Consumer Arbitration Agreements Act, c.21 7.14
Copyright, Designs and Patents Act, c.48
s.280 13.51
1989 Fair Employment (Northern Ireland) Act, c.32
s.19 13.51
1990 Contracts (Applicable Law) Act, c.36 14.16
Courts and Legal Services Act, c.41
s.8 20.69
1991 Civil Jurisdiction and Judgments Act, c.12 1.14,16.19
Foreign Corporations Act, c.44 3.13
1992 Social Security Administration Act, c.5
s.101 14.66
Social Security Contributions and Benefits (Northern Ireland) Act, c.7 6.16, 14.66
Social Security Administration (Northern Ireland) Act, c.8
ss.77-89 14.66
ss.77(1), 77(5), 78-79, 82-83, 86, 91-92, 98 14.67
s.79 11.152, 14.67
s.82 11.55, 14.75
s.84 12.22, 14.73a
s.89 11.152,157
s.89(5) 11.166
s.90(1) 2.13
ss.93, 94 14.68
s.99 14.66
s.112 13.153
Social Security Consequential Provisions (Northern Ireland) Act, c.9
Sch.4 para.11 14.66
Taxation of Chargeable Gains Act, c.12
s.61 11.171
Friendly Societies Act, c.40
ss.5-8 3.14
Tribunals and Inquiries Act, c.53
s.10 19.30
ss.11, 13, Sch.1 18.08
s.12 19.18
Civil Service (Management Functions) Act, c.61 19.26
1994 Intelligence Services Act, c.13
s.9 19.16
Vehicle Excise and Registration Act, c.22
s.52 13.153
Value Added Tax Act, c.23
s.25 17.100
Trade Marks Act, c.26
s.87 13.51
Criminal Justice and Public Order Act, c.33
s.53 17.93
Deregulation and Contracting Out Act, c.40
ss.69-79 19.26
1995 Merchant Shipping Act, c.21
s.163 10.06
s.165 16.14
ss.166, 177 18.17
s.175 16.14
s.286 13.133
Sch.4 10.06, 16.14
Criminal Appeal Act, c.35
s.12(7) 19.01
Civil Evidence Act, c.38
s.10 14.53
1996 Northern Ireland (Emergency Provisions) Act, c.22
s.3 19.02
s.47 19.92
Arbitration Act, c.23
ss.2-6 7.15
s.7 7.17
s.9 7.15,16,17,20
s.10 7.15, 10.33
s.11 7.15, 18.17
s.13 7.22
s.30 7.17
s.43 13.03
s.49(4) 8.09, 14.81
ss.59-65 7.22
s.66 7.15,22
s.70(7) 11.169
s.82(2) 7.16
s.84 7.14
ss.85, 86 7.14,18
s.87 7.14,15
ss.89-91 7.19
s.94 7.23, 18.00
ss.99-105 7.22, 16.23

Criminal Procedure and Investigations Act, c.25
s.18(9) 13.86
s.54 19.48
Defamation Act, c.31
ss.1, 13, 14, 15 18.21
ss.2-4 18.20
s.3(8)(a) 10.11
s.7 18.24
ss.8-10 18.22a
Damages Act, c.48
s.1 14.59
s.2(1) 12.17,25, 14.73a
s.2(2) 11.55
s.3 14.76
ss.4-5 12.22,23
s.6 12.23
1997 Social Security (Recovery of (Benefits) Act, c.27
ss.26,27 14.68b
Crime (Sentences) Act, c.43
Sch.1 para.3 13.09
Police Act, c.50
s.112 13.74

ACTS OF THE PARLIAMENT OF NORTHERN IRELAND (1921 to 1972)

1921 **12 Geo 5**
Ministries of Northern Ireland Act, c.6
s.2 3.21
s.3 13.17,153
1923 **13 & 14 Geo 5**
Public Records Act, c.20
s.6 13.153
1930 **20 & 21 Geo 5**
Third Parties (Rights against Insurers) Act, c.19 16.13
1937 **1 Edw 8 & 1 Geo 6**
Arbitration Act, c.8 7.14
Law Reform (Miscellaneous Provisions) Act, c.9
s.14 3.06, 11.39, 14.70,71
1939 **2 & 3 Geo 6**
Evidence Act, c.12
s.1 13.63,120
s.1(1)(4)(5) 13.126
s.1(2)(3)(5) 13.127
s.2(1) 13.127
s.3 13.146
s.4 13.144
s.7 13.127
1945 Criminal Justice Act, c.15
s.29 14.01
1947 Frustrated Contracts Act, c.2 14.78
1948 Law Reform (Miscellaneous Provisions) Act, c.23
s.2 14.74
s.3(1)(1A)(3) 14.66
s.3(4) 14.54
1953 Prison Act, c.18
s.16 13.09
s.38 19.92
1954 Administration of Justice Act, c.9
ss.13, 16 1.03
Interpretation Act, c.33
ss.1, 29, 33 38, 40, 43 , 45 1.11
s.20(4) 9.16
s.21 1.12
s.22 17.70, 18.03
s.24(1) 6.25
s.24(2) 6.26
s.25 1.27
s.37 1.11, 13.44
s.39 1.31-32
s.46(2) 17.01,88
1955 Defamation Act, c.11
ss.5, 6, 9(1), 10 18.21
s.11 10.02, 18.21
s.12 13.16, 18.21
s.13 3.36, 18.21
Administration of Estates Act, c.24
s.1(2) 18.50
s.3 3.42
s.43 18.63
1958 Trustee Act, c.23
s.31(1) 16.10
s.31(2) 10.04, 17.55
s.40 3.40, 11.04, 18.65
ss.56, 57, 61 11.04
s.43(1)(f), 50, 51 16.59
s.47 15.18
s.48 18.60,77
s.59 3.40, 14.45, 18.65
s.62 10.04
s.63 11.169, 18.63
1963 Recorded Delivery Service Act, c.5 6.25
1964 Law Reform (Husband and Wife) Act, c.23
s.3 18.70
s.3(7) 15.20
ss.4-5 3.19
Charities Act, c.33
s.6 18.66
s.8 11.172
s.9 17.93
1965 Factories Act, c.20
s.166 13.24,153
1966 Matrimonial Causes (Reports) Act, c.29 14.03
Maintenance and Affiliation Orders Act, c.35
ss.9-16 16.25, 18.47
Hire Purchase Act, c.42
s.63 13.24
1967 Administration of Estates (Small Payments) Act, c.5 11.172
1968 Costs in Criminal Cases Act, c.10
s.4A 17.110
Children and Young Persons Act, c.34
s.71 13.74
s.72 16.83
s.173 13.153
1969 Theft Act, c.16
s.29 13.44
1970 Police Act, c.9
s.14 3.24, 12.12, 16.08
Land Registration Act, c.18
s.5 18.61
s.9 15.11

Year	Enactment	Paragraph
	s.11	13.23,153
	s.64	13.153
	Sch.1 para.11	13.153
	Sch.7 Pt I para.1(2)	18.78
	Sch.7 Pt I para.5	18.75
	Registration of Deeds Act, c.25	
	ss.1(6), 6	13.153
	s.3	16.00
	Equal Pay Act, c.32	
	s.2(3)	11.182, 14.15
1971	Administration of Estates Act, c.31	3.42
	Civil Evidence Act, c.36	
	s.1(1)(3)	13.128
	s.1(2)	13.120,129
	s.2	13.130
	s.3(1)	13.129
	s.3(2)	13.128
	s.3(3)	13.129
	s.3(4)	13.120,129
	s.4	13.129
	s.6	13.128
	ss.7, 8	13.25
	s.9	13.25, 18.24
	s.10	13.44
1972	Local Government Act, c.9	
	s.82D	19.56
	ss.94, 120, 124	13.153
	s.116	3.24
	s.121	11.130

MEASURES OF THE NORTHERN IRELAND ASSEMBLY AND ORDERS IN COUNCIL TREATED AS SUCH (1972 TO DATE)

Year	Enactment	Paragraph
1972	Employers' Liability (Defective Equipment and Compulsory Insurance Order, SI 963 (NI 6)	
	Art.5	10.06
1975	Administration of Justice Order, SI 816 (NI 7)	
	Art.6	19.18
1976	Solicitors Order, SI 582 (NI 12)	18.54
	Art.3	17.73
	Art.19	16.70, 17.10
	Art.19(2)(b)	17.73
	Art.25	17.10
	Art.25(1)(3)	17.73
	Art.38	11.200
	Arts.44(3)	3.49
	Art.51A	3.49, 17.63
	Art.51B	17.83
	Art.63	10.04,06
	Art.64	17.80
	Art.64(2)	17.11
	Art.65	17.80
	Art.65(3)	17.11, 17.95
	Art.65(4)	17.11
	Art.66	17.80
	Art.67	17.80
	Art.68	3.52, 17.80
	Art.69	3.52, 17.74
	Art69(2)	3.50
	Art.70	17.78
	Art.71	17.81
	Art.71A	17.11,81
	Art.71C	11.115, 17.77
	Art.71D	17.77
	Art.71E	5.01, 17.77
	Art.71F	17.77
	Art.71F(2)(a)	17.93
	Art.71G	17.77
	Art.71H	17.75
	Art.78	11.13
	Sch.1	3.47
	Births and Deaths Registration Order, SI 1041 (NI 14)	
	Arts.38-41	13.153
	Sex Discrimination Order, SI 1042 (NI 15)	
	Art.61	13.51
1977	Criminal Damage Order, SI 426 (NI 4)	
	Art.11	13.44
	Criminal Damage (Compensation) Order, SI 1247 (NI 14)	
	ss.10(1)(c), 17	14.65
	Family Law Reform Order, SI 1250 (NI 17)	
	Arts.8,9,11	13.156
	Art.14	13.24
	Fatal Accidents Order, SI 1251 (NI 18)	
	Art.2	3.06, 14.71
	Art.3A	14.71
	Art.4	3.06, 14.73
	Art.4(4)	9.20
	Art.5(1)(1A)(3) (3A)	14.72
	Art.5(4)	14.71
	Art.5(5)	11.150
	Art.6	14.72
	Art.7	14.72
	Rates Order, SI 2157 (NI 28)	
	Art.48	13.153
1978	Property Order, SI 459 (NI 4)	
	Art.6	14.15
	Health and Safety at Work Order, SI 1039 (NI 9)	
	Art.43	9.16
	Matrimonial Causes Order, SI 1045 (NI 15)	18.47
	Art.5	4.00
	Arts.38, 48, 53	18.47
	Art.55	18.70
	Sch.1	11.176
	Rent Order, SI 1050 (NI 20)	
	Arts.13-14	18.41
	Art.69(3)	17.10
	Theft Order, SI 1047 (NI 23)	
	Art.7(2)	13.44
	Rehabilitation of Offenders Order, SI 1908 (NI 27)	
	Art.5	13.25,74
	Art.8	13.25,74
	Art.9	18.24
1979	Inheritance (Provision for Family and Dependants) Order, SI 924 (NI 8)	11.39, 18.69
	Art.23	13.121
	Statutory Rules Order, SI 1573 (NI 12)	1.12
	Administration of Estates Order, SI 1575 (NI 14)	
	Arts.3-11	18.50
	Art.5	3.43, 18.50,65

Year	Provision	Paragraph
	Art.6	3.43, 18.49
	Art.8	18.50
	Art.18	18.50
	Art.21	15.08
	Art.25	13.153
	Art.35	18.63
	Art.40	16.10
	Art.42	3.44
	Building Regulations Order, SI 1709 (NI 16)	
	Art.20	9.16
	Perjury Order, SI 1714 (NI 19)	
	Art.3	13.57
	Art.13	13.81
1980	County Courts Order, SI 397 (NI 3)	17.31
	Arts.2(2), 28(1), 45(1)	19.43
	Art.12	18.34
	Art.37	16.24
	Art.45A	17.31
	Arts.57, 59	13.153
1981	Road Traffic Order, SI 154 (NI 1)	
	Art.90, 92	10.07
	Arts.96	2.04
	Art.98	16.15,16,17
	Art.98A	2.04, 16.15,16,17
	Art.98A(4)	11.27, 16.15
	Art.99	2.12, 14.54
	Art.190	13.153
	Art.207	13.24
	Judgments Enforcement Order, SI 226 (NI 6)	
	Art.4	16.25
	Art.11	10.33, 16.25
	Art.13(1)(f)	16.03, 18.73
	Art.14	16.03
	Art.15	16.30
	Art.16	16.27
	Art.17	16.26
	Art.17(4)	16.04,09
	Art.17(5)	16.04
	Art.22	16.26
	Arts.27-29	16.30
	Art.44	16.36
	Art.46	16.33
	Art.52	16.33, 18.72
	Art.53	16.29,52
	Art.56	16.29,36
	Art.57	16.29
	Art.57(2)	14.83
	Arts.62-65	16.34
	Art.69	16.12
	Art.84(4)	11.174
	Arts.88(3A), 90(3A)	18.53
	Arts.95-96	16.32
	Art.96A	16.06
	Art.96A-105, 107	16.25
	Art.98	16.06
	Art.98(b)	16.42
	Arts.99, 102, 105	18.47
	Art.103	16.42
	Art.106	16.40
	Art.107(1)(2)	16.40
	Art.107(3)	16.42
	Art.107(4)(5)	16.41
	Art.108	16.41
	Art.109	16.43
	Art.110	16.43
	Art.111	16.39,48,58
	Art.113	16.57
	Art.114	16.30
	Art.115	16.44
	Art.116(3)	16.03,43
	Art.117	16.00
	Art.125	16.43,45
	Art.126	16.28
	Art.127	15.15
	Art.128	16.28
	Art.139	16.30,59
	Art.140	16.26,31
	Legal Aid, Advice and Assistance Order, SI 228 (NI 18)	
	Arts.3-8	3.57, 17.92
	Art.10	3.58
	Art.10(3)	3.62
	Art.10(5B)(5C)	3.58
	Art.10(6)	17.84
	Art.11(1)(b)	17.83
	Art.11(1)(d)	17.86
	Art.11(1)(e)	17.88
	Art.12(4)	17.86
	Art.12(5)	12.12, 17.87
	Art.12(6)	17.87
	Art.12(7)	17.87,110
	Art.13	17.85
	Art.13(1)(2)	17.83
	Art.13(3)(b)	17.85
	Art.14	3.58
	Art.16	17.90
	Art.16(5)	17.91
	Art.17(4)(6)	17.90
	Art.24	3.61, 13.51,74
	Art.26	17.87
	Sch.1	3.58
	Sch.2	17.83, 88
	Sch.2 para.4	17.85
	Magistrates' Courts Order, SI 1625 (NI 26)	
	Arts.5-6	19.49,88
	Art.145A	19.49,88
	Art.148	19.01
	Art.159	19.80
1983	Dogs Order, SI 764 (NI 8)	
	Art.53	9.16
	Housing Order, SI 1118 (NI 15)	
	Arts.24-47	18.41
	Art.46(3)	17.10
1984	Fire Services Order, SI 1821 (NI 11)	
	Art.44A	9.16
	Family Law (Miscellaneous Provisions) Order, SI 1984 (NI 14)	
	Part II (Arts.3-14)	18.46
	Art.4	18.41
	Art.12	18.74
	Art.16	18.70
1985	Foreign Limitation Periods Order, SI 754 (NI 5)	4.08
	Credit Unions Order, SI 1205 (NI 12)	
	Art5	3.14
1986	Mental Health Order, SI 595 (NI 4)	
	Art.3	3.11
	Arts.44-45	16.83
	Arts.97-109	3.11
	Arts.97-118	18.52
	Art.133	5.02, 11.04
	Companies Order, SI 1032 (NI 6)	
	Art.38(7)	3.13, 11.43
	Arts. 121A, 295, 431, 640A, 641	3.13
	Art.602	3.13, 11.43
	Arts.644A,645,673	6.01

Art.658 13.153
Art.658(5) 13.04
Art.674 11.56,60
Business Names Order, SI 1033 (NI 7)
Arts.6-7 3.15
1987 Enduring Powers of Attorney Order, SI 1627 (NI 16) 18.52
Limitation (Amendment) Order, SI 1629 (NI 17)
Art.5 4.04
Consumer Protection Order, SI 2049 (NI 20)
Art.7 4.03
Adoption Order, SI 2203 (NI 22)
Arts.12-32, 50-57 18.51a
Art.40 14.71
Art.63 13.153
1988 Criminal Injuries (Compensation) Order, SI 793 (NI 4)
Arts.6(2), 18 14.65
Minors' Contracts Order, SI 930 (NI 9) 12.13
Criminal Justice (Serious Fraud) Order, SI 1846 (NI 16)
Art.3(3) 19.16
1989 Matrimonial and Family Proceedings Order, SI 677 (NI 4)
Part IV (Arts.16-30) 18.47
Part V (Arts.31-40) 18.47
Sch.1 18.47
Limitation Order, SI 1339 (NI 11) 9.31
Art.2(2) 4.02, 16.40
Arts.2(3), 4-19, 21-23, 29-32, 34, 36, 37, 40, 42- 45 4.03
Arts.7, 9, 50 4.05
Arts.8(3), 26, 27, 33, 35, 38-39, 41 4.07
Art.13 4.03, 10.18
Art.16(1) 4.03, 16.40
Art.16(2) 4.03, 15.16
Arts.48, 51-6, 57-58, 62-66, 71 4.04
Art.50 4.06, 6.07
Art.72 7.18
Art.73 4.09, 9.41, 10.18,29
Art.73(1)(2)(8) 9.55
Art.73(2) 9.46, 11.33,34
Art.73(4)(a) 10.29, 11.34
Art.73(5) 11.34
Art.73(6) 3.42, 11.34
Art.73(7) 10.32, 11.35
Art.74 3.21
Sch.2 4.02, 11.32
Police and Criminal Evidence Order, SI 1341 (NI 12) 19.91
Art.26 16.47
Solicitors (Amendment) Order, SI 1343 (NI 14) 3.47
Insolvency Order, SI 2405 (NI 19) 18.80
Art.21(1) 16.38
Arts.102-3 5.13
Art.103 5.13, 16.28,38
Art.106 11.43
Art.110 3.13, 11.43
Art.142 5.02
Arts.228, 279 11.42
Arts.241, 242 5.13, 16.38
Art.242(1)(b) 16.28
Art.245 (as modified) 18.62,65
Art.258 3.05, 11.42
Art.287 3.05
Art.309 18.77
Art.371 15.11
Sch.3 3.05
1990 Licensing Order, SI 594 (NI 6)
Arts.42-43 13.153
Companies (No 2) Order, SI 1504 (NI 10)
Art.75 3.13
1991 Access to Personal Files and Medical Reports Order, SI 1707 (NI 14)
Arts.3-14 11.130
1992 Industrial Relations Order, SI 807 (NI 5)
Arts.3-4 3.18
1993 Access to Health Records Order, SI 1250 (NI 4) 11.130
Roads Order, SI , 3160 (NI 15)
Art.8 9.16
1994 Statutory Sick Pay Order, SI 766 (NI 5) 14.66,68c
Civil Service (Management Functions) Order, SI 1894 (NI 9) 19.26
Wills and Administration Proceedings Order, SI 1899 (NI 13)
Arts.25-29 13.136, 18.50
Art.32 18.68
Art.33 18.13,54
Art.34 18.48
Art.35 18.68
Criminal Justice Order, SI 2795 (NI 15)
Art.17 14.64
1995 Children Order, SI 755 (NI 2)
Arts.8-16 18.51
Art.60 3.10
Art.168, 170(1) 14.02
Art.169(1) 13.56
Art.169(3)(4) 13.35,56
Art.169(5)(6) 13.32
Art.170(2) 14.03
Art.171 13.44
Art.173 18.51
Children's Evidence Order, SI 757 (NI 3)
Art.4(4) 19.16
Trade Union and Labour Relations Order, SI 1980 (NI 12)
Art.29 11.67, 14.86
Art.93(5) 17.11
Art.99(1) 11.73
Art.99(2) 11.64
Art.120 11.67, 14.86
Art.122(3) 17.11
Art.123 11.67, 14.86
Police (Amendment) Order, SI 2993 (NI 17)
Art.30 13.47
Road Traffic Order, SI 2994 (NI 18)
Art.51(6) 13.28
Street Works Order, SI 3210 (NI 19)
Art.37 10.04
Art.42 9.16
1996 Business Tenancies Order, SI 725 (NI 5)
Art.5 18.41

Year	Legislation	Paragraph
	Juries Order, SI 1141 (NI 6)	
	Arts.3-7, 16, 17, 29	14.06
	Arts.8-11, 16(2), 26	14.07
	Art.16(4)	14.44
	Arts.12-14, 18, 27	14.08
	Arts.12(3), 19-20, 22-24, 28	14.09
	Art.29	14.44
	Commissioner for Complaints Order, SI 1297 (NI 7)	
	Art.16	19.51
	Art.21	13.36,51
	Ombudsman Order, SI 1298 (NI 8)	19.51
	Art.19	13.36,51
	Proceeds of Crime Order, SI 1299 (NI 9)	
	Sch.2 para.6	13.86
	Road Traffic Offenders Order, SI 1320 (NI 10)	
	Art.45(5)	19.69
	Deregulation and Contracting Out Order, SI 1632 (NI 11)	
	Art.11-16	19.26
1997	Property Order, SI 1183 (NI 12)	
	Art.38	18.41
	Art.48	16.33, 18.78
	Art.49	18.77
	Art.50	18.72
	Protection from Harassment Order, SI 1180 (NI 9)	
	Art.5	9.16, 14.86, 16.46
	Social Security (Recovery of Benefits Order, SI 1183 (NI 12)	
	Art.3	14.68b,72
	Art.4	14.68a
	Art.5, 6, 7	14.68c
	Art.8, 9, 10	14.68d
	Arts.12, 13, 14, 15	14.68f
	Art.17	14.68d
	Art.18	11.152,157,165,14.54,61
	Art.19	14.68d
	Art.20	14.73a,75
	Art.20(1)(2)(3)	11.55
	Art.20(3)(4)(5)	12.22
	Art. 21	14.68b
	Art.22	14.68f
	Arts.23, 24	14.68d
	Art.25	2.13, 14.68c
	Art.27	14.68b
	Sch.1	14.68b,72
	Sch.2	14.68c

SUBORDINATE LEGISLATION

STATUTORY RULES AND ORDERS (UK) (TO 1948) AND STATUTORY INSTRUMENTS (UK) (FROM 1949 TO DATE)

Year	Legislation	Paragraph
1905	Rules of the Supreme Court (Ireland) SR 439	1.12
	Ord.9 r.22	6.05
	Ord.19 r.21	9.28
	Ord.20 r.7	9.10,22
	Ord.21 r.10	9.24
	Ord.22 r.6	11.156
	Ord.31 r.15	11.119
	Ord.37 rr.36-9	13.124
	Ord.39	20.56
	Ord.55 r.4	18.63
	Ord.58 r.10	20.14
	Ord.58 r.14	20.53
	Ord.58 r.18	20.14
	Ord.65 r.4	17.27
	Ord.65 r.65(41)(42)	17.24,27
1936	Rules of the Supreme Court (Northern Ireland) SR 70 (p.2559)	1.12
	Ord.27 r.1	11.194
	Ord.37 rr.36-39	13.124
1938	Aircraft (Wreck and Salvage) Order, SR 136 (amended SI 1964/489)	18.17
1965	Rules of the Supreme Court, SI 1776 [Eng/Wales]	
	Ord.28 r.9	18.12
	Ord.38 rr.35-44	18.29
	Ord.59 r.4(3)	20.17
	Ord. 70	13.31
	Ord.71 rr.37-38	16.19
1972	European Communities (Enforcement of Community Judgments) Order, SI 1590	16.22
1978	European Communities (Service of Lawyers) Order, SI 1910	3.54
1979	Reserve and Auxiliary Forces (Protection of Civil Interests) (Northern Ireland) Order, SI 291	16.04
1981	Crown Proceedings (Northern Ireland) Order , SI 233	3.21
1985	Commonwealth Countries and Republic of Ireland (Immunities and Privileges) Order, SI 1983	3.20
1987	Civil Jurisdiction (Offshore Activities) Order, SI 2197	1.15
1993	Civil Jurisdiction and Judgments (Authentic Instruments and Court Settlements) Order, SI 604	16.22
1994	Rules of the Court of Session , SI 1443 [Scotland]	
	Ch.62, rr.37,38	16.19
	Ch.66	13.31
	Parental Orders (Human Fertilisation and Embryology) Regulations, SI 2767	18.46
	Unfair Terms in Consumer Contracts Regulations, SI 3159	7.19
1996	Arbitration Act 1996 (Commencement No 1) Order, SI 3146	7.14
	High Court and County Court (Allocation of Proceedings) Order, SI 3215	7.16,22

1997 Civil Jurisidiction and Judgments Act 1982 (Interim Relief) Order, SI 302 11.01,70

STATUTORY RULES AND ORDERS (NI) (1921 TO DATE)

1925 Public Records Order-in - Council, no.170 (p.275) 13.153
1965 Legal Aid (General) Regulations, no. 217 3.58
rr.3, 4, 5, 7, 10 3.58
r.4(7) 17.88
r.6 3.62
rr.9, 12, 13, 16 3.60
r.11 3.59
rr.12(3) 3.61
r.13(1) 17.88
r.13(4) 17.87
r.14(1) 17.88
r.14(3) 17.87
r.15 3.61,62
r.15(8) 17.85
r.15(14A) 3.63
r.15(16) 17.83
r.16(6)(7) 17.88
r.17(1)(2)(3)(4)(5) 17.87
r.17(2) 17.87
r.17(8)(9) 17.87
r.18 17.88
r.18(2) 17.89
r.19 17.83
r.21 12.12, 17.83
r.21(5) 17.21,83,85,88
r.21(6) 17.88
r.21(7) 17.85
r.23 17.85
r.24 17.85
r.25 17.85
r.26 17.87
Legal Aid (Costs of Successful Unassisted Parties) Regulations, no. 235 17.90
rr.2, 3 17.90
rr.4-5, 11-14 17.91
1971 Registration of Pending Actions Regulations, no. 86 16.00
1973 Registration (Births, Still-births and Deaths) Regulations, no. 373 13.153
1974 Legal Aid (General) (Amendment) Regulations, no. 126 17.82
1975 Employers' Liability (Compulsory Insurance) General Regulations, no. 231 10.06
1977 Solicitors Remuneration Order, no. 252 17.78
Solicitors Remuneration (Land Registry) Order, no. 253 17.78
1978 Blood Test (Evidence of Paternity) Regulations, no. 379 13.156
1979 Court Funds Rules, no. 105 1.05
rr.7-17, 19, 20, 21, 24, 25, 29-36 11.171
r.11 11.163
rr.16, 41, 42, 55 11.172
r.18 . 11.149
rr.20, 30 11.169
r.28 11.50,148,151
rr.37-50 11.172
r.39 15.08
r.42 11.38
r.43(1) 11.155
r.43(2) 9.32, 11.156,157,158
r.54 11.160
rr.56-7 11.171
1980 Rules of the Supreme Court, no. 346
See separate section
1981 Judgment Enforcement Rules, no. 147
r.5 16.26
r.5(1)(b) 16.04
r.5(1)(c) 16.02
r.5(1)(f) 16.04
r.5(1)(g) 16.04,10
r.5(1)(h) 16.26, 18.45
r.5A 16.22
rr.6-11 16.26
r.27 16.03
r.35 16.29
rr.103-105 16.03
r.103(6) 18.45
Matrimonial Causes Rules, no. 184 18.47
Legal Aid (Assessment of Resources) Regulations, no.189 3.58
Matrimonial Causes (Costs) Rules, no. 196 (amended 1989/217) 18.47
County Court Rules, no. 225
Ord.15 r.2(2) 11.119
Ord.22 r.11 11.147
Ord.55 r.14(3)(4) 17.35
Ord.55 r.19 17.35
Legal Advice and Assistance Regulations, no. 366 3.57
1984 Magistrates' Courts Rules, no. 225
r.20 13.153
1985 Judgment Enforcement (Recovery of Admitted Debts) Rules, no. 78 16.32
1986 Judgments Enforcement (1981 Order) (Application to Non-money Foreign Judgments) Order, no. 360 16.22
1989 Vehicle and Driving Records (Evidence) Regulations, no. 32 13.153
Motor Vehicles (Compulsory Insurance) Regulations, no. 84 16.15
Rules of the Supreme Court (NI) (Amendment No 6) Rules, no. 343(containing Ord.84 (Adoption)) 18.51
1990 Social Security (Recoupment) Regulations, no. 85 (amended 1990/282, 1991/204, 1992/6,

1992/ 201, 1993/233, 1994/103) 2.13, 14.66
Blood Test (Evidence of Paternity) (Amendment) Regulations, no. 212 13.156
1991 Insolvency Rules, no. 364 18.80
1993 Motor Vehicles (Compulsory Insurance) Regulations, no. 57 10.08
County Courts (Financial Limits) Order, no. 282 16.40, 17.31,80
1994 Motor Vehicles (Third Party Risks) Regulations, no. 46 10.07
Access to Health Records (Steps to Secure Compliance and Complaints Procedures) Regulations, no. 158 11.130
Access to Health Records (Control of Access) Regulations, no. 159 11.130
Land Registration Rules, no. 424
r.85 15.19, 16.02
r.91 16.00
r.127 13.153
1995 Prison and Young Offenders Centre Rules, no. 8
r.50 11.80
rr.107-109 16.83
Road Traffic Accidents (Payments for Treatment) Order, no. 139 2.12, 14.54
Insolvent Partnerships, no. 255 18.79
1996 Supreme Court Fees Order, no. 100 1.24
Judgment Enforcement Fees Order, no. 101 16.25
Supreme Court (Non-Contentious Probate) Fees Order, no. 104 1.24, 18.50
Family Proceedings Fees Order, no. 105 1.24,18.47
Juries Regulations, no. 269 14.06,07
Children (Allocation of Proceedings) Order, no. 300 18.51
Children (Admissibility of Hearsay Evidence) Order, no. 301 13.32
Family Proceedings Rules, no. 322 18.47
rr.1.4, 2 18.47
r.2.29 . 11.176
rr.2.40-2.45 13.133
r.4 18.51
r.7.2 11.61
r.8 16.06,25
Administration of Insolvent Estates of Deceased Persons Order, no. 365 18.62,65
Unfair Arbitration Agreements (Specified Amounts) Order, no. 598 7.19

OTHER ENACTMENTS

Brief and Negotiation Fees:
Queen's Bench Personal Injury Actions (Bar Council NI) 1 Feb 1996 [1996] 1 BNIL 69 17.96,103
Brussels Convention on Jurisdiction and Enforcement of Judgments in Civil and Commercial Matters, 27 Sept 1968 1.14, 16.19
Code of Conduct for the Bar of Northern Ireland (8.11.1990)
para 12 2.09
para 15 3.61
para.14 13.35
para.18 3.55, 9.04
para.20 11.144
para.22 1.06
para.6 12.05
para.8 9.06, 11.12,106,117, 13.54,66,68,71, 14.41
paras. 11, 22 3.55
Euratom Treaty 14.16
European Coal and Steel Treaty 14.16
European Community Directive, 15 March 1976, no 76/308/EC 6.16
European Convention on Human Rights 1950 1.16, 13.53
Hague Conference Convention on the Law Applicable to Trusts and their Recognition (1984) 3.40
Hague Convention on Service Abroad of Judicial and Extra-judicial Documents in Civil and Commercial Matters, 15 Nov 1965 (Cmnd 3986) 6.18,23
Lugano Convention on Jurisdiction and Enforcement of Judgments in Civil and Commercial Matters 1988 1.14, 16.19
Note for Guidance on Reference by National Courts for Preliminary Rulings (Court of Justice of the European Communities) [1996] 9 BNIL 43 14.17
Treaty of the European Community 1957 (amended Treaty of European Union)
Art.48 19.39
Art.177 14.16, 19.47
'Uninsured Drivers Agreement' between Dept of the Environment (NI) and the Motor Insurers' Bureau, 20 Dec 1989 2.04, 16.17

OTHER COUNTRIES
Republic of Ireland
Jurisdiction of Courts and Enforcement of Judgments (European Communities) Act 1988 (No.3), Sch.5 Pt I 1.14
Rules of the Superior Courts 1986 (SI no.15) as amended SI 1989 no.14

Ord.39 rr.39-44 13.31
Ord.42A 16.19

PRACTICE DIRECTIONS ETC.

[In Chronological Order]

Chancery (Proof of Service) 18 Jan. 1968 6.28
Chancery (Orders by consent) 23 Oct 1973 12.09
Supreme Court (citation of authorities) [1981] 3 BNIL 79 14.24
Queen's Bench , 6 May 1981 11.06
Lord Chief Justice [1982] 9 BNIL 90 17.03,58
Office of Care and Protection [1982] 7 BNIL 87 18.51
Queen's Bench 1983 [1983] 5 BNIL 96 11.06
Queen's Bench 1984 No 1 [1984] 1 BNIL 99 11.48
Supreme Court 1987 [1987] 4 BNIL 93 1.06
Queen's Bench 1987 [1987] 8 BNIL 83 13.91, 14.23
QB and Appeals 1987 [1987] 9 BNIL 73 20.47
Chancery 1987 No 1 [1987] 9 BNIL 70 11.04,15, 18.54
Chancery 1987 No 2 [1987] 9 BNIL 70 11.15
Chancery 1987 No 3 [1987] 9 BNIL 71 11.15
QB and Appeals 1988 [1988] 7 BNIL 102 13.139
Taxing Office Consolidation 11 April 1988 (Anderson p.163 (amended [1990] 6 BNIL 64 (Anderson p.183) (corrected [1989] 4 BNIL 78; [1989] 7 BNIL 133) 17.77, 100,102,107
Taxing Office 1988 No 1 [1988] 3 BNIL 110 17.107
Taxing Office 1988 No 2 [1988] 3 BNIL 113 17.107
Taxing Office 1988 No 5 [1988] 9 BNIL 70 17.107
Chancery 1989 No 1[1989] 2 BNIL 83 11.73
Chancery 1989 No 2 [1989] 3 BNIL 82 8.12, 11.49
Taxing Office 1989 No 1 [1989] 1 BNIL 119 17.107
Taxing Office 1989 No 2 [1989] 1 BNIL 119 17.107
Queen's Bench 1990 [1990] 8 BNIL 46 11.08
Queen's Bench [1990] 8 BNIL 47 12.30
Queen's Bench [1990] 8 BNIL 48 13.09
Chancery 1990 No 1 [1990] 3 BNIL 98 18.13,54,69
Taxing Office 1990 No 1 [1990] 3 BNIL 101 17.107
Taxing Office 1990 No 2 [1990] 6 BNIL 63 17.54
Taxing Office 1990 No 4 [1990] 7 BNIL 95 17.106,107
QB and Appeals 1991 [1991] 7 BNIL 139 11.94
Chancery 1991 No 1[1991] 1 BNIL 81 11.08
Taxing Office 1991 No 1 [1991] 3 BNIL 96 17.100
Taxing Office No 3 [1991] 10 BNIL 54 17.93
QB and Appeals [1992] 3 BNIL 112 12.26
Family (Matrimonial) 1992 [1992] 3 BNIL 111 18.47
Queen's Bench [1994] 10 BNIL 84 11.06
Chancery 1994 No 1[1994] 7 BNIL 84 12.26,31
Chancery 1994 No 2 [1994] 10 BNIL 83 18.71
Chancery No 1 1995 [1995] 4 BNIL 91 18.54
Taxing Office 1996 No 1 [1996] 1 BNIL 70 17.103
Taxing Office 1996 No 2 [1996] 4 BNIL 76 17.85,107
Chancery 1997 No 4 [1997] 5 BNIL 11.14, 12.31, 13.33,59, 14.23,24a
Chancery 1997 No 5 [1997] 5 BNIL 4.42, 15.01
Chancery 1997 No 6 [1997] 5 BNIL 14.24

House of Lords

(in White Book (1997) Vol. 2, Part 16)
Civil (January 1996) 20.89,90
Criminal (March 1995) 20.92
Directions for the Taxation of Bills of Costs in the House of Lords (1993) 20.89
Practice Direction (Civil Procedure: Stay of Execution) [1996] 10 CLM 58 20.91

Practice Notes etc.

Practice Note (Bankruptcy and Companies Office and Chancery Office) 1985 [1985] 8 BNIL 61 11.15
Practice Note by Taxing Master, 21 April 1986 17.66
Taxing Master's Practice Notes 1988 [1988] 3 BNIL 112 (amended [1988] 4 BNIL 90) 17.107
Taxing Office General Order [1988] 4 BNIL 89 17.85
Lord Chancellor's Direction [1990] 3 BNIL 100 1.06
Announcement of High Court Judges, through Carswell J, March 1993 17.33,34
Chancery Note No 1[1995] 3 BNIL 106 . 11.06, 18.54
'Memorandum to the Profession' (Taxing Office) 4 September 1996 17.98a

English Practice Directions

"Solicitors: Rights of Audience"

[1986] 1 WLR 545 3.54
VAT on Costs [1994] 1 WLR 431 17.100
Commercial Court [1994] 4 All ER 52 11.74,86

JUDICATURE (NORTHERN IRELAND) ACT 1978 (c.23)

[*For completeness, every section and its subject-matter is listed here, including those which are not referred to in the text*]

Part I: The Supreme Court
s.1 Supreme Court 1.01
s.2 High Court 1.01
s.3 Court of Appeal 1.01
s.4 Crown Court
s.5 High Court Divisions 1.01
s.5(4) 1.01, 1.20
s.6 Judges assisting others 1.01
ss.7 -8 Temporary Judges 1.01
s.9 Qualifications 1.01
s.10 Precedence
s.11 Absence of Lord Chief Justice 1.01
ss.12 -14 Appointment etc.
s15 Judge not disqualified as rate or taxpayer
Part II: The High Court
s.16 General Jurisdiction 1.02
s.17 Assignment of judges
Supervisory jurisdiction
ss.18--25 19.03
s.18 Judicial Review application
s.18(2)(a) 19.55
s.18(2)(b) 19.58
s.18(2)(c)(d) 19.68
s.18(3)(4) 19.79
s.18(5) 19.44,48,80
s.18(6) 19.68,90
s.19 Stay and interim relief 19.69
s.20 Damages 19.88
s.21 Remittal power on *certiorari* 19.81
s.22 Ouster clauses 19.18
s.23 Declaratory judgment 14.95
s.24 Injunction re public office 14.86, 19.85
s.25 Sentence on *certiorari* 19.97
s.25(4) 19.01,72,96
Other matters
s.26 Wardship 18.51
s.29 Transfer of proceedings affecting minor or patient 3.10, 18.51,52
s.30 Admiralty 18.17
s.31 Remittal and removal to or from county court 11.146,147
s.32 Vexatious litigant 5.02, 11.174
s.33 Order to execute instrument 16.59
s.33A Interest on debt or damages 8.09, 14.78, 17.31
s.33A(2)(3) 14.79
Part III: Court of Appeal and House of Lords
Court of Appeal
s.34 General Jurisdiction 1.02
s.34(2)(a) 19.64
s.35 Appeals from High Court
s.35(1) 19.73,107, 20.03
s.35(2)(a)(b)(c)(d)(e)(h)(i) 20.07
s.35(2)(a) 19.95,98
s.35(2)(c) 11.54
s.35(2)(f) 20.08
s.35(2)(g) 20.10
s.35(2)(g)(iv) 18.17,47
s.35(2)(g)(vi) 19.90
s.35(2)(i) 20.85
s.35(3) 11.54, 20.10
s.35(4) 20.10
s.35(5) 20.04
s.35(6) 18.06, 20.04
ss.36-38 20.78
s.36 Composition of Court 20.46,70
s.37 Single judge 20.31
s.37(2) 20.16
s.38 Powers on appeal
s.38(1) 20.52
s.38(1)(e) 20.65
s.38(1)(f) 20.80
s.38(1)(g) 17.69
s.38(1)(h) 20.35
s.38(2) 20.37
s.38(2)(a) 20.53
s.38(2)(b) 20.19,53
s.38(3)(4) 20.70
s.38(4) 20.77
House of Lords
s.41 Criminal cause 19.95,98,107, 20.84,87
s.42 Civil cause 19.107, 20.88
s.43 Saving for civil appeal from High Court
Particular appeals
s.44 Appeals in contempt proceedings 16.84
s.44(3) 16.85
s.45 Appeals in *Habeas Corpus* 19.107
Part IV The Crown Court
ss.46-53
Part V Practice, procedure and trials
s.54 Supreme Court Rules Committee 1.12
s.55 Rules of Court 1.12
s.55(2)(cc) 14.14, 18.27
s.56 Publication of Rules 1.12
s.57 Vacations 1.03
s.58 Sittings 1.03, 14.01
s.58(3) 14.01
s.59 (1)(4) Costs: Discretion of Court 17.02
s.59(2) 17.23, 17.45
s.59(3) 18.01
s.60 Taxation of costs 17.02
s.60(1) 17.02,93
s.60(2) 17.02,109
s.61 Trial with assessors 14.13, 20.48
s.62 Trial with and without jury 14.50
s.62(1)(2) 14.04
s.62(3)(4) 14.05
s.62(5) 14.12, 18.12
s.64 Jury in civil trial 14.09
s.65 Rules as to juries 14.08
s.66 Affidavits taken abroad 11.13
s.67 *Subpoena* in Great Britain 13.03
s.67(2) 18.48
Part VI Departments and Officers
ss.68-77 1.04
s.68 Supreme Court Departments
s.69 Northern Ireland Court Service 1.04
ss.70 -72 Statutory officers
s.73 Restrictions on practice 1.04
s.74 Deputising officers 1.04
s.75 Official Solicitor 3.53
s.76 Property held by officers

Part VII Funds in Court
ss.77-85 1.05, 11.171
s.77 Accountant-General
s.78 Accounts
s.79 Bank account
s.80 Payment in and transfer of money in court
s.81 Investment 12.17
s.82 Court Funds Rules
s.84 Statutory deposits
s.85 Making good default
Part VIII Rules of Law
s.86 Law and equity; power to stay 1.17
s.86(2) 9.52, 12.09
s.86(3) 11.173
s.86(4) 11.177
s.87 Assignment of chose in action 5.01, 10.34, 11.169
s.88 Stipulations in contracts at to time etc. 9.33
s.89 Merger of estates
s.90 Equitable waste
s.91 Sale, injunction, receiver
s.91(1)(a) 11.82, 15.18,20
s.91(1)(b) 11.62
s.91(1)(c) 11.82
s.91(2) 11.62
s.91(3) 11.67, 14.85
s.91(4) 11.74
s.92 Damages in lieu 14.91
s.93 Power of mortgagor in possession
s.94 Relief from ejectment 11.169, 15.11, 18.40
s.94A Privilege in intellectual property cases 11.85,86, 13.44
Part IX: Inferior courts
s.97 Civil jurisdiction of magistrates and district judges
ss.98-100 Amendments of County Courts and Magistrates' Courts Acts
s.102 Supplementary
Part X: Miscellaneous
s.103 Justices of the peace
s.104 Under-sheriffs
s.105 Solicitor as officer of Supreme Court 3.47
s.106 Rights of audience 3.54
s.107 Barrister/solicitor qualifications
s.108 Election courts
s.109 Regulations for enrolment etc. of documents in Supreme Court
s.110 Court Bonds 1.26
s.111 Lost negotiable instrument
s.112 Oaths and affidavits 11.13
s.112(3) 13.10
s.113 Appointment of conveyancing counsel 11.84
s.114 Foreign law, proof of 13.22,94
s.115 Seals of Supreme Court 1.23, 13.153
s.116 Court fees 1.24
s.117 Functions of Lord Chancellor
s.117A Judges' allowances
s.118 Application of Act to Crown
s.119 Rules etc. under the Act
s.120 Interpretation 1.07, 17.01,25, 20.03
s.121 Financial
s.122 Amendments and repeals
s.123 Short title and commencement
Sch.1 Appeal to House of Lords in criminal matters 20.84
Sch.1 para.4 19.107
Sch.2 Departments
Sch.3 Statutory officers
Sch.4 Superannuation
Sch.5 Amendments
Sch.6 Transitional Provisions 1.12
Sch.7 Repeals

SUPREME COURT (NORTHERN IRELAND) 1980

(S.R & O. 1980 no.346 as amended 1-07, 1-12)

[*For completeness, every Order and its subject-matter is listed here, including those which are not referred to in the text*]

ORDER 1
Part I Citation, application, interpretation and Forms
r.1 Introductory
r.2 18.47
r.2(3) 19.93
r.3 1.08
r.4 1.12
r.5 18.37
r.6 1.01
r.7 References to Treasury
r.8 1.27
r.9 1.25
Part II A: Distribution among Divisions of the High Court
r.10 18.53
r.11 1.19, 18.16
r.11(h) 17.93
r.12 18.46
r.12A (1)(3) 1.20
r.12A(2) 11.03
Part II B: Assignment of Business to Departments
r.13 1.05
r.13(b) 20.13
r.14 1.05
r.15 1.05
r.16 1.05, 18.46
r.17 1.05, 18.46
r.18 1.05, 17.93
ORDER 2
Effect on Non-compliance
r.1(1)(2) 1.28,30, 11.17, 15.11, 20.22
r.1(3) 5.04
r.2 1.28
ORDER 3
Time
r.1 1.31
r.2 1.31
r.2(5) 20.26
r.3 1.31
r.4 1.31, 20.20
r.5 1.33, 11.194, 15.05, 20.21

r.6(1) 11.199
r.6(2) 11.193,195
r.6(3) 11.195
ORDER 4
Transfer and Consolidation of Proceedings
r.1(1) 1.21
r.1(2) 1.20
r.2 18.62
r.3 1.01
r.4 1.21
r.5 3.35,39
ORDER 5
Mode of beginning proceedings in High Court
r.1 5.03
r.2 5.03
r.3 5.03, 18.05
r.4(1) 5.03
r.4(2) 5.03, 18.10
r.5 5.03, 18.14,15
r.6 3.45
ORDER 6
Writ of Summons
r.1 Form of writ
r.2(a) 5.07
r.2(b) 5.08
r.2(c) 5.10, 18.34
r.2(d) 5.10, 18.33
rr.2A, 2B, 2C 5.09
r.3 5.10
r.4 5.04, 05, 7.00
r.4(4) 11.174
r.5 5.06
r.6(1) 6.13
r.6(2)(3) 5.05
r.6(4)(5)(6) 5.06
r.7 6.07
ORDER 7
Originating Summons
rr.1-7 18.10
r.5 18.11
ORDER 8
Originating and other motions
r.1 Application of Order 8
r.2 11.05, 18.14
r.3 18.14
r.3(1)(2)(6) 1105
r.4 11.01,05
r.5 11.05, 18.14
ORDER 9
Petitions
rr.1-5 18.15
ORDER 10
Service of originating process
r.1(1)(2)(4)(5)(7) 6.00
r.1(3) 6.02,28
r.1(5) 7.03
r.2 6.14
r.3 6.14
r.4 6.00, 04, 05, 18.34
r.5 6.09, 18.09,11
ORDER 11
Service out of the jurisdiction
r.1(1) 6.15, 11.75
r.1(1)(*l*) 18.48
r.1(1)(m) 16.21
r.1(2) 6.13
r.1(3) 7.03
r.3, 5, 6, 7, 8 6.18
r.4 6.17
r.9 6.19, 18.09
r.9(4) 11.05, 16.49, 20.25
ORDER 12
Entry of appearance to writ or originating summons
rr.1-6 7.03
r.1(2) 3.45
r.6(2) 9.21
r.7 7.09
r.8 7.10
r.8A 6.08, 7.00
r.9 18.11
ORDER 13
Default of appearance in writ action
r.1 8.01
r.2 8.01
r.3 8.01
r.4 8.01
r.5 8.01
r.6 8.02
r.7(1)(3)(4)(5) 8.00
r.7(2) 6.20, 11.05
r.7(3)(5) 6.05
r.7A 8.04
r.7B 8.04
r.8 8.13
ORDER 14
Summary Judgment
r.1(1) 11.45-47
r.1(2) 11.45
r.2 11.46
r.3(1) 11.48
r.3(2)(3) 11.50
r.4 11.48
r.5 11.45
r.6 11.52
r.7 11.50, 51
r.8 11.47,50
r.9 11.50
r.10 11.50, 18.40
r.11 11.53
ORDER 15
Joinder of causes of action, counterclaims, joinder of parties, change of parties, representative parties
r.1 3.25, 14.73
r.2(1) 9.38
r.2(2) 3.25
r.2(3) 9.39,47
r.2(4) 14.48
r.3(1) 9.52
r.3(2)(3) 9.54
r.3(4) 12.12
r.4(1) 3.31
r.4(2) 3.32, 11.25, 18.48
r.5(1) 3.26,31
r.5(2) 9.42
r.6(1)(2) 11.24,28,44
r.6(2) 9.56, 10.21, 16.05
r.6(3) 11.27
r.6(4) 11.25
r.6(5) 11.33
r.6(5)(b) 11.34
r.6(6) 11.34
r.7 11.36-44, 16.05, 20.38
r.8 11.29
r.8(1) 11.22,24
r.8(3)(4) 11.36
r.8(4) 11.26,29
r.9 11.41
r.10 11.27
r.11 3.23

r.12 3.18,37, 16.04
r.13 3.38, 18.65
r.14 3.40, 18.65
r.15 3.43, 18.65
r.16 3.44
r.17 18.33
r.18 3.03, 18.56
ORDER 16
Third-party proceedings etc.
r.1(1) 10.19
r.1(1)(a) 10.01,09
r.1(1)(b) 10.15
r.1(1)(c) 10.16
r.1(2) 10.19
r.1(3) 10.19
r.2 10.19
r.3 10.19
r.3(4) 10.19, 10.23
r.4 10.20,21
r.5 10.23
r.6 10.23
r.7 10.24
r.7(2) 16.04
r.8 10.28
r.8(6) 10.30
r.9 10.32
r.10 10.13, 11.168, 17.08
r.11 10.23
r.12 10.00
r.13 16.15
ORDER 17
Interpleader
rr.1-8 10.33
r.4 11.174
ORDER 18
Pleadings
r.1 9.09
r.2 9.21
r.2(2) 11.52
r.3 9.57
r.4 9.60
r.5 9.04
r.6 9.04
r.7 9.06
r.8(1) 9.06,25,26,57
r.8(2) 9.29
r.8(3)(4) 9.13
r.9 9.06
r.10 9.58
r.11 9.06
r.12 19.88
r.12(1) 9.07
r.12(2) 9.12
r.12(3)(6) 9.83
r.12(4) 9.07,86
r.12(5) 9.84
r.12(7) 9.93
r.13 . 9.06
r.13(1)(2) 9.23
r.13(3)(4) 9.24
r.14 9.57
r.15(1) 9.14
r.15(2) 9.10
r.15(3) 9.09
r.16 9.32
r.17 9.37
r.18(a) 9.39
r.18(b) 9.57
r.19 11.178
r.20 9.66
r.21 9.05
r.22 18.17
r.23(1)(2)(3) 13.26, 18.24
r.23(4) 13.74
ORDER 19
Default of pleadings
r.1 9.62, 11.194
rr.2-7 9.63
r.7 8.02
r.8 9.64
r.9 9.65
ORDER 20
Amendment
r.1 11.16
r.2 7.11, 11.18
r.3 11.16
r.4 11.16
r.5(1) 11.18
r.5(2) 11.33
r.5(3) 11.34
r.5(4) 3.42, 4.01, 11.19,34
r.5(5) 11.34
r.6 11.18
r.7 11.18
r.8 11.18
r.9 11.22
r.10 11.16,22
r.11 15.12
r.12 11.17
ORDER 21
Withdrawal and discontinuance
r.1 7.11, 12.00
r.2 12.00
r.2(4) 12.07
r.3 12.01
r.4 12.03
r.5 11.174, 12.03
r.6 11.06
ORDER 22
Payment into and out of court
r.1 17.46, 18.19, 20.50
r.1(1) 11.149
r.1(2) 11.150
r.1(2A) 11.152
r.1(3) 11.151
r.1(4)(5)(6) 11.150
r.1(7) 11.152
r.2 11.150,166
r.3(1) 11.155, 18.18
r.3(2) 11.157
r.3(3) 11.157,166
r.3(4) 11.151,156
r.4(1) 9.32, 11.156
r.4(2)(3) 11.157
r.4(3) 11.156
r.5 11.158,160
r.6 11.154,166
r.7 11.160
r.8(1) 11.172
r.8(2) 9.32, 11.50,151
r.9 11.172
r.10 11.172
r.11 2.12
r.12 11.154,171
ORDER 23
Security for costs
r.1 11.56
r.2 11.56
r.3 11.56
ORDER 24
Discovery and inspection of documents
r.1 11.92

r.2(1) 10.23, 11.92
r.2(2)(3)(4) 11.92
r.2(5)(6) 11.94
r.2(7) 11.94
r.3 11.95, 19.71
r.4 11.96
r.5 11.102
r.6 11.95,103
r.7 11.110
r.8 11.136
r.8(6) 11.134
r.9 11.97,110,136
r.10 11.103,112
r.11 11.91,112
r.12 11.112
r.13 11.114
r.14 11.115
r.15(1) 11.116
r.15(2) 11.104,115
r.16 11.114
r.17 11.117
r.18 11.115
r.19 11.120
r.20 11.118

ORDER 25

Medical evidence
r.1 11.143
r.2 9.17, 11.143
r.3 11.140,143
r.4 11.143,149
r.5 11.140,143
r.6 11.143
r.7 11.143
r.8 . 11.143
r.9(1) 11.144
r.9(2) 11.145
r.10 11.143
r.11 11.144

ORDER 26

Interrogatories
r.1 11.122
r.2 11.126
r.3 . 11.122
r.4 . 11.122
r.5(1) . 11.126
r.5(2)(3) 11.127
r.6 11.127
r.7 11.128
r.8 11.129

ORDER 27

Formal admissions
r.1 9.95, 13.143
r.2 9.97
r.3 9.96
r.4 . 9.98, 13.143
r.4(1)(2)(3) 11.105
r.4(3) 13.11,149
r.5 (1)(2)(3) 9.98, 13.11,143
r.5(4) 13.11,150

ORDER 28

Originating summons procedure
r.1 18.10
r.1A 18.11
r.2 18.11
r.3(1)(2)(3) (5) 18.11
r.3(4) 18.12
r.4 18.12
r.5 18.12
r.6. 18.11
r.7 18.12
r.8 18.12
r.9 18.12
r.10 18.12
r.11 18.12

ORDER 29

Part I: Interlocutory injunctions, interim detention etc. of property
r.1(1) 11.62
r.1(2) 11.62,73
r.1(3) 11.73
r.1A 18.53
r.2 11.78
r.2(3) 11.81
r.3 11.78
r.4 11.78
r.5 11.78,82
r.6 11.65,85
r.7 11.81
r.8 11.69,85
r.9 11.87,89
r.10 11.81

Part II: Interim payments
rr.11-17 11.55
r.18 11.150
r.19 11.55
r.20 19.70

ORDER 30

Receivers
rr.1-8 11.83, 15.21
r.6 11.169

ORDER 31

Part I: Sale etc. of land by Court
rr.1-4 18.55
r.2(d) 11.169

Part II: Conveyancing Counsel
rr.5-6 11.84, 15.18

ORDER 32

Proceedings in chambers
r.1 11.02
r.2 11.02,03, 18.12
r.3(1) 11.03
r.3(2) 11.12
r.4 11.06
r.5 1.33, 11.05
r.6 11.06
r.7 11.06, 18.12
r.8 11.12
r.9 11.06, 13.03
r.10 20.89
r.11(1) 11.04, 18.54, 19.54
r.11(1)(a) 19.94
r.11(1)(b) 19.101
r.11(1)(c) 17.108
r.11(1)(d) 5.02
r.11(1)(e) 18.65
r.11(1)(f) 11.62
r.11(1)(g) 12.13
r.11(2) 12.19, 18.52
r.11(3) 18.12
r.12 11.06, 19.54
r.12A 4.06
r.13 11.06,08, 18.12,44
r.14 11.06
r.15 11.06
r.16 11.06
r.17 11.02, 14.02,45
r.18 11.06,14

ORDER 33

Place and mode of trial; splitting issues
r.1 14.01
r.2 14.01

r.3 14.12
r.4(1)(2)(4)(5)(6) 14.04
r.4(1)(3) 12.27
r.4(5)(6) 14.05
r.5 14.13
r.6 14.12
ORDER 34
Setting down for trial in writ action
r.1 12.26
r.2 12.26
r.3 12.26
r.4 12.26
r.4(3) 12.28
r.4(4) 20.59
r.4(6) 12.26
r.5 12.32
r.6. 12.32
r.7(1) 12.26
r.7(2) 12.07
r.7(3) 11.155
r.8 11.38
ORDER 35
Proceedings at trial
r.1 14.18
r.2 14.18, 20.64
r.3 14.21
r.4 14.25
r.4(3)(4) 14.37
r.4(4) 14.34
r.5 13.154
r.6. 11.40, 14.45
r.7 15.00
r.8 13.158, 15.00
r.9 13.158, 15.00
r.10 13.158
ORDER 36
Trial before master or referee
rr.1-5 14.14, 18.27
ORDER 37
Part I: Assessment of Damages after Judgment
r.1 8.11, 11.50, 14.50
r.2 8.11, 14.50
r.3 8.11, 14.49
r.4 8.11
r.4(1)(a) 14.49
r.4(1)(b)(2) 14.49
r.5 8.11, 14.50,83
r.6 4.00, 14.51
Part II: Provisional damages for personal injuries
rr.7-10 14.75
ORDER 38
Evidence
Part I: Adduction of evidence
r.1 13.30
r.1A 13.85,89,131,142, 18.32
r.1B 13.89, 18.32
r.2 13.33
r.2(3) 11.13,15, 18.02,09, 19.76
r.3 13.34
r.3A 13.85, 17.105
r.4 13.33,34,85
r.5 13.94
r.6 14.14,50
r.7 13.10
r.8 13.151,153
r.9 3.40
r.10 15.17
r.11 11.06, 13.05, 13.34
Part II: Writ of *subpoena*
r.12 13.03
r.13 13.04
r.14 13.04
r.15 13.06
r.16 13.06
r.17 13.03
Part III: Duty record and computer evidence (1971 Act)
rr.18-19, 21-24, 26, 27-28 13.130
r.18(3) 14.14,50
rr19, 20 13.129
r.22 13.129
r.23 13.129
rr.24-29 13.129
ORDER 39
Evidence by deposition
r.1 13.10
rr.2, 3, 3A 13.10
r.4-14 13.10
r.15 13.31,124
ORDER 40
Court Expert
rr.1-6 13.93
r.6 13.89
ORDER 41
Affidavits
rr.1, 2, 3 11.15
r.4 11.15
r.5 11.14
r.6. 11.14
r.7 11.15
r.8 11.13
r.9 11.15
r.10 11.15
r.11 11.14
r.12 11.06,13, 17.106
r.13 11.13
r.14 11.15
ORDER 42
Judgments
r.1 15.01
r.2 15.01
r.3 15.02
r.4 15.05, 16.48, 19.82
r.5 15.05, 16.48, 19.82
r.6 14.83
r.7(1) 8.00, 9.63
r.7(2) 8.06
r.8 15.06
r.9 15.15
r.9(3) 16.27
r.10 15.06, 16.25
ORDER 43
Accounts and Inquiries
rr.1-8 18.25
r.9 guardian of minor
ORDER 44
Proceedings under Chancery Judgments and orders
rr.1-2 18.57
r.3 18.58
rr.4-8 18.58
rr.9-10 18.67
rr.11-12 18.58
ORDER 45
Enforcement of Judgments
r.1 interpretation
r.2 16.39
r.3 16.52
r.4 16.48, 19.82,83

r.5 16.49
r.5(3) 16.57
r.5(5) 15.05
r.6. 16.59, 19.82
r.7 16.02,47
r.8 16.02
r.9 16.03

ORDER 46
Leave to enforce Judgment
r.1 16.04

ORDER 47
Sequestration
r.1 16.58

ORDER 48
Examination of party liable on non-monetary Judgment
rr.1-2 16.51

Order 49 none made

ORDER 50
Stop order on funds in court
r.1 16.34

Order 51 none made

ORDER 52
Committal for contempt
r.1(1) 16.76
r.1(2) (6) 16.78
r.1(3) 16.53,76
r.1(4) 16.76
r.1(5) 16.81
r.2 16.79
r.2(1) 16.53
r.3 16.79
r.4 16.53
r.5 16.54,79
r.6 16.77
r.7 16.67,77
r.8 16.79
r.8(1)(2)(4) 16.54
r.9 16.81
r.10 16.81
r.11 16.81

ORDER 53
Judicial review
r.1 19.79
r.2 19.97
r.3(1)(2)(4) 19.54
r.3(1) 19.55
r.3(3) 19.54,94
r.3(4) 19.57
r.3(5) 19.56
r.3(6) 19.58
r.3(7) 19.51,59,81
r.3(8)(10) 19.60
r.3(9) 19.61
r.3(11) 19.94
r.3(12) 19.60
r.3(13) 19.69
r.4 19.57
r.5. 19.66
r.5(1)(6) 19.68
r.5(7) 19.75
r.5(8) 19.63,75,95
r.6(1) 19.66
r.6(2)(3) 19.75
r.6(4) 19.68
r.7 19.79,88
r.8(1) 19.74,76,94,96
r.8(2) 19.74
r.8(3) 19.96
r.9(1) 19.75
r.9(2)(3)(4) 19.81
r.9(5) 19.79
r.10 20.10
r.10(a) 19.62
r.10(b) 19.90
r.11 19.85

ORDER 54
Habeas corpus
r.1 19.101
r.2 19.101
r.3 19.104
r.4(1) 19.101,104
r.4(2) 19.102
r.5 19.104
r.6 19.104
r.7(1) 19.104
r.7(2) 19.105
r.8 19.105
r.9 13.09
r.10 Forms
r.11 19.102

ORDER 55
Part I: Appeal to High Court from county court
rr.1-12A 18.02
Part II: appeals, references and applications to High Court under statute
rr.13-18 18.02
r.19(1) 18.04
r.19(2) Land Registry
r.20 5.03, 18.05
r.21 18.03
r.22 18.03,04

ORDER 56
Appeal to High Court by case stated
rr.1-5 18.07

ORDER 57
Crown Side proceedings
rr.1-5 19.00

ORDER 58
Appeal to judge in chambers from master etc.; appeal from judge in chambers
r.1 11.08,54, 19.60
r.2(b) 14.50
rr.2-3 11.10, 14.14, 18.27, 20.03
r.4 20.03
r.5 10.33

ORDER 59
Appeals and applications for new trial to Court of Appeal
r.1 . 20.13,78
r.2 . 20.13,50,56
General procedure
r.3(1) 20.50
r.3(1)(2) 20.18
r.3(3) 20.36
r.3(4) 20.20
r.3(5) 20.30
r.4(1) 20.20
r.4(2) 20.20
r.4(3) 20.20,85
r.5(1) 20.26
r.5(2) 20.26,44
r.6(1) 20.06,29
r.6(2) 20.36
r.6(3)(4) 20.29
r.7 20.36
r.8(1)(2)(a) 20.37
r.8(2)(b) 20.53
r.9 20.44
r.10(1) 20.53
r.10(2) 20.42

r.10(3) 20.65
r.10(4) 20.19
r.10(5) 20.35
r.10(6) 20.53
r.10(7)(8) 20.53
r.11(1) 20.50,55,56
r.11(2) 20.58
r.11(3) 20.59
r.11(4) 20.69
r.11(5) 13.167, 20.61
r.12 20.50
r.13(1) 20.33
r.13(2) 15.16, 20.33,71
r.14(1) 20.31
r.14(2) 20.14,21
r.14(3) 19.62, 20.11,14
r.14(4) 20.14,31
r.15 20.14,21
Particular appeals
r.16 20.04
r.17 Patents
r.18 16.84

ORDER 60
Appeal to Court of Appeal from Restrictive Practices Court
rr.1-4

ORDER 61
Appeal to Court of Appeal by case stated
rr.1, 2, 7 20.79
r.3 20.80
r.4 20.79,81
rr.5-6 case stated in county court appeal
r.8 20.80
rr.9-10 VAT Tribunal appeals
rr.11-12 Immigration appeals

ORDER 62
Costs
Part I: Interpretation and application of Order
r.1 17.01
r.1(3) 17.53
r.2 17.01
Part II: Entitlement to costs
r.3(1)(2)(3) 17.02
r.3(4) 17.12,94
r.3(5) 17.14,66
r.4(1) Pension appeals
r.4(2) Representation of People
r.4(3) 18.48
r.5. 17.06
r.5(2) 1.28, 17.22
r.5(3) 12.00
r.5(4) 11.155
r.5(4)(6) 11.157
r.5(5) 18.18
r.5(6) 11.166
r.6. 17.07
r.6(2) 17.54
r.6(3) . 18.81
r.6(3)(4) 18.58
r.6(5) 11.16
r.6(6) 1.33
r.6(7) 9.97
r.6(8) 9.98, 11.105, 13.143
r.6(9) 11.89,136
r.7 17.12,94
r.7(2) 11.83
r.7(3) 5.08, 8.01, 17.16
r.7(4) 17.12
r.7(5) 18.58
r.7(6)(7) 9.97,98, 11.105
r.8(1)(2)(3)(8) 17.13,65,94
r.8(4) 17.69
r.8(4)(6) 17.70
r.8(5)(6)(7) 17.71
r.9(a) 11.168
r.9(b) 10.13, 11.160
r.10 9.24, 17.60
r.10A 13.30, 17.60
r.11 17.62,85
r.11(7) 17.61
Part III: Taxation and assessment of costs
rr.12-35 17.77
r.12 17.95
r.12(3) 17.12
r.13 17.12
r.14 17.54
r.15 17.78
r.16 12.18, 17.79
r.17(1)(3) 17.97
r.17(2) 17.78
r.17(3) 8.01, 11.51, 17.16
r.17(4)(5)(6) 17.23
r.17(5)(6) 17.34
r.17(7) 17.35
r.17(8) 17.24
r.17(9) 11.84
r.18 17.59
Part IV: Powers of Taxing Master
rr.19-28 17.106
r.19 17.93
r.22 17.107
r.22(2)(3) 17.78
r.23 17.110
r.24 18.25
r.25 11.06,84
r.26 17.53
r.27 17.107
r.28 17.106,107
Part V: Taxation procedure
rr.29-30 17.107
r.29(1) 11.155
r.29(2) 17.77
r.31 17.107
r.32 17.107
r.32A 17.96,107
Part VI: Review of taxation
r.33-34 17.108
r.35 17.108
Appendix 1: allowance of certain costs
paras.1-4 17.107
para.4(2) 13.93
Appendix 2: Criteria for taxation
Pts I & II 17.78,97
Pt I para.1(2) 17.98
Pt I para.2 17.102
Pt I para.3 13.90, 17.105
Pt II 17.98
Appendix 3: Fixed costs
Pts I, II & III 17.21
Pt I 17.99
Pt I col (a) 5.08
Pt I col (b) 8.01, 17.16
Pt I col (c) 11.51
Pt II 8.01, 11.51, 17.17,99
Order 63 none made

ORDER 64
Sittings, vacations and Office hours
rr.1-5 1.06
r.4(1) 11.01, 16.54, 19.54,74
r.4(2) 14.01, 19.75

ORDER 65
Service of documents
r.1 6.21
r.2 6.21
r.3 6.01
r.3(1) 6.21
r.4 6.04,22, 16.49
r.5 6.20, 20. 25
r.6 6.23
r.7 6.23
r.8 6.28
r.9 6.20, 8.06, 11.05, 11.199
ORDER 66
Documents for use in court, printing, copies and inspection
rr.1-5 1.25
r.2(5) 1.08
ORDER 67
Appointment, discharge or change of solicitor
rr.1, 2, 3, 4, 5 3.50,51
r.5(4) 3.51,60
r.6 6.20
Order 68 none made
ORDER 69
Service of process for foreign court
rr.1-4 6.23
ORDER 70
Taking evidence for foreign court
rr.1-6 13.31
ORDER 71
Reciprocal Enforcement of Judgments
Part I. Commonwealth and other countries (1920 and 1933 Acts)
rr.1-10 16.22
r.11 16.18
Part II. Judgment of European Community
rr.13-21 . 16.22
Part III. European countries and Great Britain (Civil Jurisdiction and Judgments Acts)
rr.22-31 16.22
rr.32 , 33(3), 34(5) 16.19
rr.33-35 16.22
ORDER 72
Commercial actions
rr.1-8 18.28
r.2(2) 1.01
r.3 5.03, 18.28
r.5 11.04, 18.28
r.9(1)(2) 18.29
r.9(3(4)(7) 18.30
r.9(5) 18.31
r.9(6) 18.32
ORDER 73
Arbitration proceedings
Pt. I (rr.1-22) 7.22
r.6 7.16
Pt II (rr.23-27) 7.14
Pt.III (rr.28-32) 7.22
ORDER 74 revoked
ORDER 75
Admiralty proceedings
rr.1-43 18.17
ORDER 76
Contentious Probate
rr.1-15 18.48
r.14 3.43, 18.49
r.15 9.42, 18.48
ORDER 77
Proceedings by or against the Crown
r.1 Interpretation
r.2 5.10
r.3 6.01,12,20,23
r.4 9.44
r.5(1) 11.45, 18.60
r.5(2) 11.46
r.6 5.13, 18.26
r.6(7) 20.20
r.7 11.26
r.8(1) 8.04
r.8(2) 10.23
r.9 10.19,32
r.10 10.33
r.11(1) 11.92
r.11(2) 11.95,102,104, 13.48
r.11(3) 11.98
r.12 3.21, 14.01
r.13(1) 13.31
r.13(2) 13.10
r.14 16.07
r.15 16.35
r.16 5.02
r.17(1) 11.28
r.17(2) 18.17
ORDER 78
Remittal to and removal from the county court
rr.1-10 11.146,147
r.9 11.147
ORDER 79
Bail applications
rr.1-13 . 19.01
ORDER 80
Disability (patients and minors)
r.1 Definitions
r.2 3.07,45
r.3 3.07
r.3(2)(4)(6) 3.11
r.4 3.07, 8.05
r.4(1)(b) 9.54
r.4(2) 10.23
r.4(3) 18.11,14,15
r.4(4) 18.57
r.5 11.36
r.6 3.08, 9.63
r.7 11.90
r.8 3.08, 12.13,20
r.9 12.13,20
r.10 3.08, 12.20, 15.08
r.11 . 15.08
r.12(1) 11.156
r.12(2) 12.20
r.13 3.08, 6.01,21
r.13(4) 13.06, 16.49,53
r.14 3.08, 12.17, 18.51
ORDER 81
Partners and sole traders
rr.1, 7 3.16
r.2 3.16, 11.137
r.3 6.01,28
r.4 7.04
r.5 16.04,09
r.5(1) 7.04
r.6. 16.04
r.8 3.17, 6.01
ORDER 82
Defamation actions
r.1 drafting
r.2 5.10, 18.18

r.3 9.57,60, 18.18
r.4(1) 18.18
r.4(2) 18.19
r.5. 18.19
r.6. 11.123, 18.22
r.7 18.20
r.8 18.20
ORDER 83
Consumer Credit Act 1974
rr.1-4 7.12
r.3 8.04
ORDER 84
Adoption (SR 1989/343 - not printed in *Red Book*) 18.51a
ORDER 84A
Parental Rights orders
ORDER 85
Actions for administration of, or relating to, an estate
r.1 Interpretation
r.2 18.63
r.2(3)(b) 11.169
r.3 3.43, 18.65
r.3(3) 18.67
r.4 18.65
r.5(1) 18.63
r.5(2) 18.66
r.6. 18.55
ORDER 86
Chancery actions for specific performance etc.: summary Judgment
rr.1-7 18.60
ORDER 87
Debenture holders' actions
rr.1-6 18.81
ORDER 88
Mortgage and charge actions
r.1 18.71
r.2 5.13, 18.34,53,72
r.3 18.71
r.4 18.11,71
r.5 18.71,74
r.5A 16.33, 18.71,74
r.6 18.71
r.7 18.72
ORDER 89
Wards of Court and patients: co-ordination of jurisdiction
rr.1-9 3.10,12, 18.51,52
r.6 3.07, 5.05,10
ORDER 90
Part I. General
rr.1-2 Interpretation; assignment to Family Division
Part II. Wardship and guardianship of minors
rr.3-5 18.51
Part III. Child Abduction and Custody Act 1985
rr.10-25
Part IV. Registration of UK custody orders (Family Law Act 1986)
rr.26-35
ORDER 91
Revenue proceedings in Chancery Division
ORDER 92
Funds in court under various statutes: Chancery Division
rr.1,2,3A,4 11.169
r.3 War Damage Act
r.5 11.172
ORDER 93
Applications and appeals under various statutes assigned to Chancery Division
ORDER 94
Appeals under specific statutes to High Court and Court of Appeal by case stated
r.1 18.08
r.2 20.81
r.3 18.08, 20.81
ORDER 95
Bills of Sale Acts and Industrial and Provident Societies Act
ORDER 96
Access to health records
rr.1-3 11.130
ORDER 97
Non-contentious probate
rr.1- 63 18.50
r.39 3.42
rr.50, 54 18.50
r.51 18.50,65
ORDER 98
Declarations as to marriage and legitimacy (Matrimonial and Family Proceedings (NI) Order 1989)
r.1 Definitions
rr.2- 3A Legitimacy declarations
rr.4- 5 Overseas adoptions
rr.6-18 General
ORDER 99
Inheritance (Provision for Family and Dependants) Order
rr.1-10 18.69
ORDER 100
Trade Marks Act
ORDER 101
Appeals from Pension Appeals Tribunal
ORDER 102
Companies
rr.1-15 18.81
ORDER 103
Declarations under Elected Authorities (NI) Act 1989
ORDER 104
Patents, Registered Designs etc.
ORDER 105
Maintenance orders
Part I. Interpretation
Part II. Registration under 1920 Act
r.2 18.47
Part III. Registration under 1950 and 1958 Acts
rr.3-9 18.47
Part IV. Registration under 1966 Act
rr.10-15 18.47
Part V. Enforcement under 1972 Act
rr.16-23 18.47
Part VI. Attachment of earnings orders
rr.24-34 18.47
ORDER 106
Supervision of solicitors
r.1 Interpretation
r.2 11.125, 17.75,80,81
r.2A 17.77
r.2B 17.80
rr.3-5 17.77
rr.5-16 3.47
ORDER 107
Part I. Interpretation
Part II. Commissioners for Oaths
rr.2-8 11.13

Part III. Notaries Public
rr.9-17
ORDER 108
Court Bonds
rr.1-4 1.26, 11.56
ORDER 109
Care and protection of mental patients
rr.1-79 18.52
r.3 3.11
ORDER 109A
Enduring powers of attorney
rr.1-18 18.52
ORDER 110
The Official Solicitor
rr.1-2 3.53
ORDER 111
Committal of recalcitrant judgment debtor (Judgments Enforcement (NI) Order 1981, Art.107)
r.1 Interpretation
rr.2-4 16.41
r.5 16.41
rr.6- 8 16.42
rr.9-12 16.43
ORDER 112
Blood and DNA tests to determine paternity
rr.1-6 13.156
r.4 11.26
ORDER 113
Summary proceedings for possession of land against "squatters"
rr.1-5 18.43
rr.6-7 18.44
r.6(3) 18.45
ORDER 114
Reference to European Court
rr.1-6 14.17, 20.93
r.6 14.17, 20.10
ORDER 115
Family Law (Misc Provs) (NI) Order 1984 Part II (spouse's charge on matrimonial home)
ORDER 116
Confiscation, restraint orders and forfeiture of proceeds of crime and terrorism
ORDER 117
Appeal under Criminal Appeal (NI) Act 1980: assessment of appellant's legal aid costs

---

APPENDIX A
General Forms in Supreme Court proceedings
1 5.07
2 5.07
3 . 18.48
4, 5 6.18
6, 7, 8 18.10
9 18.43
10 18.11
11 18.14
12 7.03
13 7.03
14-15 9.54
19A 2.04
20 11.150
21 11.155
22 11.102
22, 23 11.95
24, 25 13.03
27 11.03
28 11.03
28A 11.136
29-32 8.00
29-33 15.01
33 18.45
34-35 12.26
59-60 19.104
61-62 19.109
APPENDIX B
Admiralty Forms
APPENDIX C
Non-contentious Probate Forms
APPENDIX D
Patient's Affairs
APPENDIX E
Enduring Powers of Attorney Forms
APPENDIX H
Parental Order Forms

A PROPOSED 'CIVIL EVIDENCE (NI) ORDER'

Background to the legislation

A proposal for a draft Civil Evidence (NI) Order has been published. It repeals the hearsay provision of the Evidence Act (NI) 1939 and the Civil Evidence Act (NI) 1971. It implements (with some changes) the Report of the Law Reform Advisory Committee for Northern Ireland on Hearsay Evidence in Civil Proceedings (LRAC No 3 1996), and is substantially the same as the Civil Evidence Act 1995 (applying in England/Wales),[1] and similar to the Civil Evidence (Scotland) Act 1988. Its main provision is that, by Article 3, evidence is not to be excluded in civil proceedings on the ground of it being hearsay, including multiple hearsay. It greatly expands the statutory law of Northern Ireland which at present generally allows only first-hand documentary hearsay by a person disinterested (1939 Act) and duty record multiple documentary hearsay (1971 Act). Its provisions are noted here by way of supplementary commentary to the appropriate paragraph of the main text. Some rules will have to be made in the RSC to implement and modify it. Subject to transitional provisions of the Commencement Order, the proposed Order will apply only in proceedings commenced after the date of its coming into force as appointed by the Secretary of State.

Affidavit evidence

11.14 Under the existing Order 41 rule 5, hearsay is not admissible in an affidavit used at the trial of an action but is admissible in an affidavit in interlocutory and certain other proceedings provided that the deponent states the source thereof. It is submitted that the rule is inconsistent with Article 3 of the proposed Order, and will have to be amended.

Preparatory steps before trial

13.11 The Civil Evidence Act 1971 requirement to give notice of intention to adduce 'duty record hearsay' is repealed. But where a party intends to adduce to a statement of hearsay in any form, admissible under the proposed Order, it will be prudent to give notice to the other parties of intention to do so. It will be prudent to serve a copy or record of the statement on those parties and invite them to state in advance whether they have any objection to the statement being adduced without the maker being called, and to inform them of any good reason why the maker should not or cannot be called to testify. To do so may help to enhance the credibility of the statement, and avoid any penalty in costs. On the other hand, the other party on receipt of such notice should respond with any objection to the use of the statement and give notice that he intends to seek

---

1 The main sources of comment on the English Act are by Ockelton in *Current Law Statutes* and Keane's *Modern law of Evidence* (1996). The English Act came into force in January 1997 and the author has not yet seen any reported decision under it.

leave of the court to cross-examine the maker of the statement. The LRAC (NI) Report (No 3 1996) (5.8.4) takes this view.

Discretion to exclude evidence

13.13 Where evidence is admissible under the proposed Order there is no discretion to exclude it, even in a jury trial, save under those specific provisions of the Order where leave of the Court is required to adduce a statement.

Reputation and opinion evidence

13.17 It may be that the common law rules as to admissibility of reputation evidence and opinion evidence on family pedigree to prove the truth of the facts opined survives after the proposed Order. However the common law restrictions on pedigree evidence do not apply to evidence which is also admissible under the proposed Order (as the Evidence Act (NI) 1939, s.7(b) is repealed and not re-enacted.)

Witness refreshing memory

13.62 A document used by a witness to 'refresh memory' does not become evidence of the truth of the matters stated in it unless-

(1) the Court gives leave under Article 7(2)(a);

(2) to rebut a suggestion that his evidence is fabricated (Art.7(2)(b)); or

(3) opposing counsel cross-examines him out of parts of the document not used by him to refresh his memory (Art.7(5)).

Attacking own witness

13.63-13.64 Counsel calling a witness can adduce in evidence any previous statement by him by leave of Court, under Article 7(2) of the proposed Order. Subject to provision of the RSC, a statement put to a hostile witness by counsel who called him cannot be admissible under the proposed Order but if it is admitted under section 3 of the Criminal Procedure Act 1865 it is evidence of the matters stated in it (Art.7(3)(a)(4)).

Cross-examination as to consistency

13.76 In cross-examination by opposing counsel a statement previously made by the witness is not admissible under the proposed Order (subject to RSC) save in accordance with the Criminal Procedure Act 1865 (ss.4 and 5); but if so admitted the statement is evidence of the matters stated in it (Art.7(3(b)(c)(4)).

Foreign law

13.94 Statutes of British Dominions must continue to be proved under the Evidence (Colonial Statutes) Act 1907 (Art.12(3)(d)).

Application of and definitions in the proposed Order

13.113 The proposed Order applies to any civil proceedings[2] before a court or tribunal in which the strict rules of evidence apply[3] (Art.2(3)). For the purposes

---

[2] Including an application to commit for civil contempt: *Savings Bank* v *Gasco BV* [1988] Ch 423.

of the Order hearsay is defined as a statement, made otherwise than by a person giving oral evidence in the instant proceedings, which is tendered as evidence of the matters stated, and includes hearsay of whatever degree (i.e. second-hand, third-hand etc. hearsay) (Art.3(2)). 'Oral evidence' includes evidence by writing or signs of a person with defective speech or hearing. A 'statement' is any representation of fact or opinion, however made. The 'original statement' in relation to hearsay, means the underlying statement of fact by a person with personal knowledge of that fact, or of opinion by a person holding that opinion. A 'document' is anything in which any information is recorded. A 'copy' of a document is anything onto which information recorded in a document has been copied by any means, directly or indirectly (Art.2(2)).

Restricted definition of hearsay

13.113a The definition of hearsay for the purposes of the proposed Order is not exactly the same as the definition of hearsay as developed by the common law in the line of cases culminating in *R* v *Kearley*.[4] The proposed Order confines hearsay to a "representation of fact or opinion, however made" tendered as evidence of the matters stated. This includes any assertive conduct, such as nodding, making signs, facial expressions or gestures. Ockelton takes the view that the definition excludes certain conduct from which an inference is sought to be drawn, and which is hearsay at common law of the *Kearley* type. For example, the conduct of the policeman in examining car tyres and letting the car drive on, tendered to show that the tyres were safe; the sea captain who examined the whole of the ship and then set sail, tendered to show that the ship was seaworthy; the placing by numerous orders by persons to X for drugs, tendered to show that X was a drug dealer; the refusal of hotel guests to stay in a particular room, tendered to show that the light in that room was inadequate. It seems that the admissibility of hearsay of this type continues to be governed by the common law and the proposed Order will not affect it.

Admissibility of hearsay

13.113b "In civil proceedings evidence shall not be excluded on the ground that it is hearsay" (Art.3(1)) but subject to certain 'safeguards' set out in Articles 4-6. "Nothing in this Order affects the exclusion of evidence on grounds other than that it is hearsay" including exclusion of evidence on failure to comply with a rule or order of the Court (Art.12(1)). In effect all hearsay is now admissible however many intermediaries there are between the person with the personal knowledge and the person or document who furnishes the hearsay to the court; and it makes no difference whether the hearsay is oral or written. Thus an admission by one defender can be used by the pursuer (plaintiff) as evidence against another defender.[5]

---

[3] Presumably this means, in the Supreme Court any proceedings, including interlocutory applications, in which factual evidence is adduced, except for (a) statutory appeals from administrative bodies and tribunals; and (b) management of the affairs of patients, child care and wardship proceedings. The LRAC Report draft Order specifically excluded child care proceedings.

[4] [1992] 2 AC 228.

[5] M & I Instrument Engineers v Varsada, 1991 SLT 106, at 109K.

13.113c It is implicit, though not explicit, in the proposed Order that it must be shown or inferred that: (a) the maker of the first statement was purportedly speaking with personal knowledge of the fact stated (as opposed to having made it up as a piece of fiction, dreamt it or discerned it though psychic powers); or (b) the maker of the first statement was speaking of an opinion held by him where that opinion would be admissible if stated by him as testimony in court (see paras.13.17 and 13.88). This is implicit from the definition of "original statement" in Article 2(2),[6] and from the fact that a statement by a person of which he had no personal knowledge or of a non-expert opinion would be inadmissible on grounds of irrelevance. It is also implicit that it must be proved or inferred that there is a direct chain of reportage from the maker of the original statement to the witness or document by whom the statement is adduced to the Court. There is no express requirement in the proposed Order as to the identification of the maker of the statement or of any intermediary reporter. It is submitted that it is implicit that there must be some evidence of the identity of the maker and the intermediaries (if any), by name, occupation or some other description. Thus a witness cannot testify: "I heard somebody say that the defendant was driving too fast"; but can say: "I heard a tall man in a grey coat standing at the corner of the junction between X and Y Street say that the defendant was driving too fast". However, in the case of hearsay in a record compiled in the course of a duty by an employee or official ('duty record hearsay') where the maker of the statement might be any unknown employee or member of the public, the maker may not be identifiable in any way.

Proof of documentary hearsay

13.113d If the content of the hearsay statement has been written down by the maker or any reporter of it, it is submitted that the hearsay must be proved by production of the document containing it or of a copy thereof (Art.8); and can be proved by oral evidence only on the same terms as secondary evidence is admissible at common law (paras.13.148-13.152).

Common law exceptions to rule against hearsay

13.113e "All common law rules providing for exceptions to the rule against hearsay in civil proceedings are superseded by this Order" (Art.3(2)). However by Article 3(4)(5), "nothing in this Order affects the admissibility of evidence admissible apart from this Article" and the safeguards in Articles 4-6 do not apply to such evidence, even though it may be admissible also under this Article. The drafting here is not entirely clear. Article 3 means either-

(1) that the common law rules for admission of hearsay are repealed and that only statutory provisions (save those repealed by the Order) for admission of hearsay continue in force without regard to the safeguards in the Order; or

(2) that the Order supplements and renders unnecessary the common law rules, but that hearsay admissible under statute and common law remains admissible without regard to the safeguards in the Order.

---

[6] Though that phrase is used in the Order only in the context of weight to be attached to hearsay in Art. 5(3)(b).

The LRAC (NI) (No 3 1996) clearly advocated the first of the above propositions, and in its recommended draft, Article 3(4) read: "Nothing in this Order affects the admissibility of *hearsay* evidence which, apart from this Article, is admissible *under any statutory provision ...*" The fact that the proposed Order omits these italicised words lends credence to the argument that the legislator intends to preserve the common law exceptions. It is to be hoped that this matter will be resolved by an amendment to the Order before it becomes law.

Cross-examination of the maker of the statement

13.113f The RSC may provide that where party adduces hearsay evidence of a statement made by a person, any other party may seek leave of the Court to call the maker of the statement and cross-examine him as if the maker had been called by the adducing party; and the Court, on granting leave, may adjourn the proceedings, on terms as to costs or otherwise, for the maker to be called or for the other party to investigate the statement or the maker's credibility (Art.4). *Semble,* Article 4 only deals with the maker of the original statement and it does not confer power to call and cross-examine any intermediate reporter such as the compiler of the record containing the statement. Note that the adducing party can put the statement in evidence without having to explain the absence of the maker as a witness and without having to give prior notice; but these matters go to weight of the statement. Also the Court can exercise its discretion to order or disallow costs against the adducing party if he has unreasonably failed to call the maker or give prior notice; or against the other party if he has unreasonably or unnecessarily sought an adjournment. If it is shown that the maker is unknown, untraced, dead or now incapable of testifying, the Court should refuse leave to cross-examine. If the maker is beyond the seas or unfit to come to court, the Court may grant leave to cross-examine through a live television link, or by a deposition taken before an examiner. *Quaere,* the failure of the maker to attend for cross-examination does not allow the Court to exclude the statement, though obviously it greatly affects its weight. The LRAC (NI) Report (5.8.1) thought that it is unlikely save in the most unusual circumstances that the Court will give any weight to a statement where the maker is unwilling to testify. It also says (5.9.1): "[The Court] will no doubt be slow to allow an adjournment where the opposing party could have anticipated the hearsay evidence, and even slower where he had notice that it would be called and failed to take steps to require the witness to be brought or to investigate the statement. Conversely, if the Court takes the view that the adducing party is trying to avoid having a witness called or is keeping him out of the way, it may decline to adjourn the case and may simply place no weight on the hearsay statement."

Weight of hearsay

13.113g In estimating the weight (i.e. the cogency) of the hearsay statement, the Court must have regard to any circumstances from which inferences as to its reliability may be drawn; and to the fact that the adducing party did or did not give notice, and sufficient notice, to the other party(ies) of intention to adduce the hearsay (Art.5(1)(2)). The Court may also have regard to whether: (a) it was reasonable and practicable to call the maker as a witness; (b) the original statement was made contemporaneously with the event stated; (c) it is multiple hearsay (i.e. the more intermediaries, the more unreliable the report of the original statement is likely to be); (d) any person involved (the maker or any intermediary) had a motive to conceal or misrepresent; (e) the original statement was an edited account or made in collaboration with another person or for a particular purpose (e.g. a statement made or recorded for an important reason or under a duty, rather than casually, is more reliable; a statement taken by a solicitor for the litigation may have less weight); (f) the circumstances of the adduction of the hearsay suggests an attempt to prevent proper evaluation of its weight (Art.5(3)). The Court can attach no weight to it, especially if the maker is unfit or unwilling to attend.[7] On the other hand the Court may treat the statement as true even where the maker has subsequently retracted it.[8]

Hearsay of incompetent persons

13.113h Hearsay is not admissible under the proposed Order if it is shown that the maker of the statement or the person proving the statement was at that time incompetent as a witness, that is, could not give evidence on oath or, as a child, was not capable of giving unsworn testimony (see para.13.35) (Art.6(1)(2)). This means that if any person making or reporting the statement did so when mentally incompetent or too young, it is not admissible under the proposed Order. Also if the maker or reporter was speaking when bound by a privilege vested in another (e.g. a solicitor speaking of confidential information passing between him and his client).

Credibility of maker or reporter

13.114i Where the maker of the original statement or any reporter of it is not called as a witness, then evidence can be adduced (under Art.6(3)) -

(a) which would be admissible to attack that person's credibility as a witness (see para.13.71);

(b) with leave of the Court, which could be put to that person in cross-examination of him relating to his credibility but which could not be adduced as evidence-in-chief to contradict his answers (see paras.13.71-13.76);[9]

(c) which proves that he has made a statement inconsistent with the statement now adduced, where it would be admissible to prove that he has contradicted himself (see paras.13.63 and 13.76); such statement is admissible as evidence of the matters stated in it;

---

7 *TSB* v *James Mills*, 1992 SLT 519.

8 *K* v *Kennedy*, 1993 SLT 1283.

9 "In considering whether to grant leave to adduce such evidence, we would expect the Court to take into account any risk of unfairness to the cross-examining party which might result from his inability to impeach the credibility of the maker of the statement (either by calling the maker of the statement or otherwise), any risk of unfairness to the maker of the statement which might arise from his inability to rebut the evidence by reason of his absence from the trial, the importance of the evidence to the Court's assessment of the reliability of the maker of the hearsay statement, and the need to avoid undue prolongation of the proceedings": LRAC (NI) Report (5.10.6).

(d-1) which would be admissible to support his credibility (see paras.13.15; 13.78);

(d-2) with leave of the Court, which proves that he has made a statement consistent with the statement now adduced, where it would be admissible to prove to support his credibility (see para.13.78); such statement is admissible as evidence of the matters stated in it.

Common law exceptions

13.114 *Res gestae,* if proved by evidence admissible under the existing law, *may* continue to be admissible apart from the proposed Order, and certainly is so if the *res gestae* is outside the definition of hearsay in the proposed Order (see para.13.113a), in which case the safeguards in Articles 4-6 are not applicable.

13.116 An admission by a party, if proved by evidence admissible under the existing law, *may* continue to be admissible against him without regard to the safeguards in the proposed Order.

13.119 A statement made in the presence of a party or witness, if proved by evidence admissible under the existing law, *may* continue to be admissible against him without regard to the safeguards in the proposed Order.

Previous consistent statement of a witness (self-corroboration)

13.120 A statement made previously by a party or witness, if admissible under the existing common law, continues to be admissible apart from the proposed Order, where it is not adduced in proof of the truth of the matters stated in it. A statement cannot be admitted under the 1939 and 1971 Acts as the relevant provisions thereof are repealed.[10] The common law rule against self-corroboration or 'narrative hearsay' is revoked by Article 3 of the proposed Order, but is made subject to the conditions in Article 7. A statement made by a person called as a witness is admissible as hearsay (i.e. to prove the truth of the matters stated in it) (Art.7(1)); but if the party calling the witness wants to adduce the statement, it is admissible only: (a) by leave of the Court, or (b) to rebut a suggestion that his evidence is fabricated (Art.7(2)); or if he has used it to refresh his memory and opposing counsel has cross-examined him out of parts of the document not used by him (see para.13.62) (Art.7(5)). Such a statement is not admissible under the Order in cross-examination by counsel calling him when declared a hostile witness save as stated in para.13.64 (Art.7(3)(a)). A previous oral or written statement put to a witness in cross-examination by opposing counsel is not admissible save as stated in para.13.76 (Art.7(3)(b)(c)). Any statement admissible under Article 7(2) or under the provisions of Article 7(3) is admissible as evidence of the matters stated in it (Art.7(4)) and is subject to the safeguards in Articles 4-6. The restrictions of admissibility of corroborative hearsay by a person called as a witness are to preserve the discretion of the Court to prevent unnecessary evidence being adduced in an attempt to make the witness look more credible. The situations in which leave is likely to be given are likely to be those where, due to lapse of

---

[10] 1939 Act ss.1-2; 1971 Act ss.1-6.

time or otherwise, the witness cannot give a full and accurate recollection of the events. In such case counsel calling him may seek leave to put in evidence a statement made by him at a time closer to the events.[11]

Further common law exceptions

13.121 A statement made by a person now deceased, if proved by evidence admissible under the existing law, *may* continue to be admissible as hearsay without regard to the safeguards in the proposed Order. But the Inheritance (Provision for Family and Dependants) (NI) Order 1979, Article 23, is repealed.

13.123 Testimony given in previous proceedings between the same parties or their privies on the same issues *may* continue to be admissible against a party without regard to the safeguards in the proposed Order.

Statutory provisions as to documentary hearsay

13.125-13.130 The Evidence Act (NI) 1939 (ss.1-2) and the Civil Evidence Act (NI) 1971 (ss.1-6) are repealed.

13.131 A medical report or map, diagram, photograph etc., continues to be admissible under Order 38 rule 1A, without regard to the safeguards in the proposed Order.

13.132-13.133 Hearsay admissible under statutes continues to be admissible apart from the proposed Order. Hearsay admissible under the common law rules may continue to be admissible apart from the proposed Order.

Proof of contents of documents

13.139 Where a statement in a document is admissible as evidence in civil proceedings, it may be proved by production of it or a copy thereof, authenticated in such manner as the Court may approve (Art.8(1)). It is submitted that this provision is laid out in such a way[12] as to mean that the authentication "in such manner as the court may approve" applies to both proof of the document and proof of a copy of it. Ockelton suggests that Article 8 does not apply so that the common law requirements of proving it remain, where the document itself is material as the operative transaction (e.g. a deed, will, written contract).

Proof of business or public records

13.139a A document which is shown to form part of the records of a business or public authority may be received in evidence without further proof; and it can be so shown by production of a certificate purportedly signed by a responsible officer of the authority (Art.9). The absence of an entry in the records of such authority may be proved by affidavit of an officer (Art.9(4)). The Court may direct that all or any part of this Article shall not apply to particular documents or records or classes thereof (Art.9(6)). 'Business' includes any regular activity whether or not for profit, by a corporate or

---

[11] See for instance *Morris v Stratford-on Avon RDC* [1973] 1 WLR 1059; decided under the English Civil Evidence Act 1968.

[12] Like the English Act, but unlike the recommended draft of the LRAC (NI) Report (No.3 1996).

incorporated body or an individual. 'Public authority' includes any public or statutory undertaking, UK or NI Government department, or person holding office under the Crown (Art.9(5)). Note that Article 9 applies to proof of a document either where its contents are adduced as admissible hearsay or where the document itself is admissible as an operative transaction.

Proof of document by copy

13.148-13.152 Where a statement contained in a document is admissible as evidence in civil proceedings, it may be proved by production of a copy of it or its material part authenticated in such manner as the court may approve; it does not matter whether the document itself is still in existence, and the copy produced can be a copy of a copy at any number of removes from the original (Art.8). A copy means anything onto which the information recorded in the document has been copied by whatever means, directly or indirectly (Art.2(2)). Obviously this covers photo-copies, computer print-outs and carbon copies,[13] but does it include exact reproductions of the contents made through human agency? This provision of the proposed Order abolishes the common law rule against 'secondary evidence' of the contents of a document, but only in relation to copies. Other forms of secondary evidence, such as the oral evidence of a person who has read the document, summaries and recitals of its contents in drafts and other documents, and circumstantial evidence, are still subject to the common law rules restricting secondary evidence. Also, it seems that Article 8 does not apply so that the common law restrictions on proof by a copy in lieu of the original remain, where the document itself is material as the operative transaction (e.g. a deed, will, written contract).

Statutory provisions as to documentary evidence

13.153 All statutory provisions listed here relating to admissibility and proof of documentary evidence are unaffected by the proposed Order (Arts.3(4) and 12(2)). Government proclamations, orders etc. must continue to be proved by HMSO copies under the Documentary Evidence Acts; and registers and certificates of foreign authorities must continue to be proved under the Oaths and Evidence (Overseas Authorities and Countries) Act 1963 (Art.12(3)).

Damages in personal injuries cases: financial loss

14-53 The Civil Evidence Act 1995, s.10 (Ogden actuarial tables) is replaced without amendment by the proposed Order, Art.10.

[13] And probably electronically restored facsimiles of an original by restoring the imprint of a page on the page underneath it ("ESDA" tests).

ABBREVIATIONS

For abbreviations of case citations see Osborne's Law Dictionary; *for such abbreviations in Irish law reports up to 1964, see Surrency 'Research in the Law of Northern Ireland' 15 NILQ 77*

Aldous & Alder	*Applications for Judicial Review* (Butterworths 2nd ed. 1993)
Anderson	*Legal Costs in Northern Ireland* (SLS 1993)
App	Appendix
Art(s).	Article(s) (of an Order or Convention)
Bar Handbook	Code of Conduct of the Bar of Northern Ireland (1990)
CA	Court of Appeal
Ch D	Chancery Division
CF Rules	Court Funds Rules (NI) 1979
Contempt Act	Contempt of Court Act 1981
Copinger	*Law and Practice of the County Courts in Ireland* (Dublin 1858)
Court Funds Rules	Court Funds Rules (NI) 1979
Cross	Cross and Tapper *on Evidence* (Butterworths, 8th ed. 1995)
Crown Proceedings Act	Crown Proceedings Act 1947, as adapted for NI by SI 1981/233
CRU	Compensation Recovery Unit (see para. 14.66)
Daniell	*Chancery Practice* (1914)
Deasy's Act	Landlord and Tenant Law Amendment (Ireland) Act 1860
DC	Divisional Court of the High Court
EC	European Community
ECJ	European Court of Justice
EJ Office	Enforcement of Judgments Office
ex p	*ex parte*
Fam D	Family Division
FP Rules	Family Proceedings Rules (NI) 1996
Halsbury's *Statutes*	Halsbury's *Statutes of England and Wales (4th ed)*
Halsbury's *SIs*	Halsbury's *Statutory Instruments*
H Ct	High Court
HL	House of Lords
Huband	*Juries in Ireland* (revised ed. 1911)
Hunter	*Northern Ireland Personal Insolvency* (SLS 1992)
ICLMD	*Irish Current Law Monthly Digest*
JE Order	Judgments Enforcement (NI) Order 1981
JE Rules	Judgments Enforcement Rules (NI) 1981
JR	*JR (Judicial Review)* ed. Fordham (Wiley, Quarterly from March 1996)
Jackson	*NI Supplement to Cross on Evidence* (SLS 1983)
Judicature Act	Judicature (Northern Ireland) Act 1978
LA	Legal Aid
LA Digest	Legal Aid: a Practical Digest (Law Society NI, 1994)

LA Order	Legal Aid, Advice and Assistance (NI) Order 1981
LA Gen Regs	Legal Aid (General) Regulations (NI) SR 1965/217
LCJ	Lord Chief Justice
Lewis	*Judicial Remedies in Public Law* (Sweet & Maxwell 1992 + Supplement 1994)
Lowry	*Procedure at Nisi Prius*, privately circulated notes by Sir Robert Lowry, LCJ, 1970s
LRC	Law Reports of the Commonwealth (1980 to date)
Odgers	*High Court Pleading and Practice* (Sweet & Maxwell, 23rd ed. 1991)
Order 00	Order 00 of the Rules of the Supreme Court
Ord.	Order (of the RSC)
Ord.00 r.0	Order 00 rule 0 (of the RSC)
O'Hare & Hill	*Civil Litigation* (Oyez 1988)
Osborne	*County Courts in Ireland (Equity and Probate)* (2nd ed., by AB Babington, 1910)
para.1.01	paragraph number 1.01 of the text of this work
Phipson	*On Evidence* (14th ed. 1990)
PD	Probate Division
PR	personal representative
QBD	Queen's Bench Division
r(r).	rule(s)
Red Book	Loose bound updated edition of the RSC (NI)
RSC	Rules of the Supreme Court (NI) (1980)
s(s).	section(s)
SC	Supreme Court *or as a case citation* Session Cases
Sch.	Schedule
SI	Statutory Instrument (UK)
SR	Statutory Rule and Order (NI)
Supperstone & Goudie	*Judicial Review* (Butterworths 1992)
Valentine (& Glass)	*County Court Procedure in Northern Ireland* (SLS 1985)
Valentine (& Hart)	*Criminal Procedure in Northern Ireland* (SLS 1989)
Wade & Forsyth	*Administrative Law* (7th ed. 1994)
White Book	The (English) *Supreme Court Practice,* now published every two years
Wylie	*The Judicature Acts (Ireland) and Rules of the Supreme Court 1905* (Dublin 1906)

GLOSSARY OF TERMS

[This Glossary is intended for those who have no substantial knowledge of civil procedure]

ACCOUNTANT-GENERAL Court Officer who controls investment of money paid into court

ACTION proceeding in the High Court by a plaintiff against a defendant commenced by writ or originating summons, called a "cause" in the Rules of the Supreme Court

ADMISSION a concession by one party which narrows the issues in dispute

AFFIDAVIT a statement of facts in connection with proceedings sworn on oath before a Commissioner for Oaths

AMENDMENT alteration or correction of a writ or pleading

'ANTON PILLER' ORDER order for inspection or seizure of articles or documents made by a court *ex parte* and in secret so as to prevent the opponent from having forewarning

APPEARANCE notification by defendant or his solicitor that he is considering whether to defend the action, and providing an address for service. It operates to prevent a judgment in default of appearance

BESPEAK obtain from a court office a court order or other court document made in particular proceedings, on payment of a fee per page

CENTRAL OFFICE rooms in Law Courts where process and judgments are issued in Queen's Bench proceedings

CHAMBERS court sitting in private, so that public have no right to enter

CLOSE OF PLEADING point at which all pleadings have been deemed to be served, preparatory to setting down for trial

COMMITTAL imprisonment for contempt of court

CONSOLIDATION merging two actions so as to become one for all purposes

CONTEMPT (a) scandalising courts or prejudicing justice in proceedings; (b) misbehaviour in face of court; (c) failure of witness to obey subpoena; (d) failure of party to comply with court order

CONTRIBUTION liability of one wrongdoer to pay a portion of the loss sustained by the claimant

CONTRIBUTORY NEGLIGENCE fault by the victim of a tort which was partly responsible for his injury and which can effect a reduction in his damages

COSTS expenses and profit charges incurred by a solicitor for a party in relation to court proceedings; expenses and notional profit charges of a personal litigant

COUNTERCLAIM claim made by a defendant in the nature of a cross-action

COURT OF APPEAL court of usually three Lord Justices, hearing appeals from High Court

DAMAGES monetary compensation

DEBT claim for ascertainable sum of money due in contract or quasi-contract

DECLARATION judgment in favour of a plaintiff declaring his rights

DEFAMATION libel or slander

DEFAULT failure by a defendant to take a procedural step (e.g. enter appearance or deliver defence) which may result in judgment against him; failure by plaintiff to take procedural step (e.g. deliver statement of claim or set action down for trial) which may result in dismissal of action

DEFENCE pleading by defendant in response to statement of claim, replying to the allegations therein and raising any new fact in defence
DEFENDANT person sued
DEPONENT person who makes an affidavit
DISABILITY incapacity to control proceedings by or against one, due to age (under 18) or mental deficiency
DISCONTINUANCE unilateral abandonment of a claim
DISCOVERY disclosure by one party to an opponent of existence of all documents in his possession relevant to the proceedings, with an indication of those documents which the opponent will be allowed to inspect
ENFORCEMENT OF JUDGMENTS OFFICE Separate judicial establishment which exercises exclusively all powers of enforcement of court orders, except committal for contempt
EXHIBIT document or article referred to in affidavit or produced by witness in court
EX PARTE APPLICATION request to court to make an order against a party without prior notice to him, usually obtained by lodging "docket" which Master considers without oral hearing
FATAL ACCIDENT CLAIM action, usually by personal representative, on behalf of dependants of deceased against the tortfeasor who caused the death
FIRM unincorporated business partnership; using the firm name in the title of an action has the effect of joining all partners
FURTHER AND BETTER PARTICULARS request for more details of some matter relating to the statement of claim, defence or reply
GENERAL DAMAGES compensation for a loss or injury which cannot be quantified, e.g. personal pain, loss of amenity or loss of future earnings
GREEN FORM LEGAL AID Law Society scheme for remunerating a solicitor for work done before proceedings commence
GUARDIAN *ad litem* adult person who controls proceedings on behalf of a defendant under disability
HABEAS CORPUS "you may have the body": a writ commanding any person to produce to the High Court a person who is alleged to be unlawfully detained
HIGH COURT Queen's Bench Division, Chancery Division, Family Division: judges and masters thereof
INDEMNITY claim by a wrongdoer that his liability to monetary compensation should be wholly satisfied by another person
INJUNCTION order of court that a party must do or not do an act
INTERLOCUTORY ORDER order made in an action otherwise than at the conclusion of the trial thereof
INTERROGATORIES questions asked by one party to be answered in writing by the other party on oath
ISSUE OF PROCESS the procedure whereby a writ or other document is made effective by being sealed at the Central Office
JUDGMENT verdict and order of the court upon the trial of an action
JUDICIAL REVIEW power of the High Court to quash or vary the decision or refusal to decide by an inferior court or by an administrative body acting in the public law area
LAW REFORM ACT CLAIM action by personal representative of deceased for damages to be paid into his estate
LIMITATION period of time between accrual of cause of action and issue of writ. If statutory time limit is exceeded it raises a defence against the action
"LODGMENT" colloquial term for payment into court by a defendant of a sum to satisfy the plaintiff's monetary claim. It is without admission of liability and if not accepted, is kept secret from the trial judge

"MAREVA" INJUNCTION order requiring defendant to preserve his assets so that they will be available to satisfy any judgment obtained by the plaintiff
MASTER a court officer who hears most interlocutory proceedings in the QBD
MASTER (TAXING OFFICE) officer who taxes costs
MATTER proceeding in the High Court other than a cause or action
MOTION originating or interlocutory application on notice, heard by judge in open court
NEXT FRIEND adult who controls proceedings on behalf of a plaintiff under disability
ORIGINATING SUMMONS process commencing certain types of action, usually used because directed by statute or because there is no factual dispute
PARTICULARS sub-paragraphs in a pleading in which aspects of an allegation, e.g. of negligence, breach of contract, fraud, are itemised
PERSONAL INJURIES physical or mental suffering and impairment caused by defendant's wrong
PLAINTIFF person suing in an action
PLEADINGS formal statement of party's case, not on oath, which restricts the evidence that he can adduce at the trial: statement of claim, defence and/or counterclaim, reply and/or defence to counterclaim
PRIVILEGE the right of a party or witness at his option not to disclose confidential facts or documents on grounds of legal professional privilege, public interest or self-incrimination
PROCEEDINGS any cause or matter
PROCESS any writ, summons, notice of motion
PROSECUTION, WANT OF failure by plaintiff to deliver statement of claim, set down for trial or otherwise proceed with his action, for which defendant may apply to dismiss action
PROVISIONAL LIST list issued by Lists Office of actions which have been set down for trial and which will be given a date for trial at the next call-over
"RED BOOK" Rules of Supreme Court (NI) in loose leaf updated form
REMITTAL transfer of proceedings by High Court to county court
REMOVAL transfer ordered by High Court of proceedings in county court to High Court
REPLY pleading by plaintiff to Defence, joining issue, raising new facts or pleading Defence to Counterclaim
REPRESENTATIVE PARTY party ordered by Court to represent, and bind, other persons with identical interest in the dispute
SECURITY FOR COSTS court order that plaintiff pay money into court to be available to satisfy any judgment for cost obtained by the defendant
SET-OFF a cause of action pleaded by a defendant which operates a defence to the plaintiff's claim
SETTING DOWN entry of action by plaintiff so that date for trial may be fixed
SETTLEMENT contractual agreement reached between parties as to the disposal of proceedings. If the plaintiff is under disability it does not bind him unless approved by the Court
STATEMENT OF CLAIM pleading by plaintiff endorsed on writ or after defendant's appearance, stating facts material to the cause of action and to the relief sought
STAY order of Court preventing further prosecution of an action
STRIKING OUT deleting a pleading or proceeding from the record
SUBPOENA AD TESTIFICANDUM a command to a witness to attend to give evidence
SUBPOENA DUCES TECUM a command to a person to attend and produce to the court a document or thing

SUMMARY JUDGMENT (Order 14) judgment granted to plaintiff on affidavit evidence on ground that there is no prospect of a real defence to the claim
SUMMONS a command to a party to appear at the hearing of an interlocutory application in chambers
SUPREME COURT High Court and Court of Appeal
TAXATION the measuring of a proper sum for costs payable by one party to another or by a client to his solicitor
THIRD-PARTY NOTICE a process issued by a defendant against another person, whether or not a party, claiming indemnity, contribution or other relief related to the plaintiff's claim
TRIAL the hearing of an action resulting in final verdict and judgment (subject to appeal)
UNDERTAKING a promise by a party or solicitor given to a Court, enforceable by committal
WEEKLY LIST list showing the actions listed for hearing on each day of the following week
"WHITE BOOK" the English Rules, similar to "Red Book" but with annotations
WRIT process which commences most actions in High Court upon its issue; it may be general, i.e. containing only a concise general statement of the claim, or indorsed with a full statement of claim

CHAPTER ONE

THE SUPREME COURT

1.00 This book concerns civil procedure in Northern Ireland. The bulk of civil litigation is under the jurisdiction of the High Court or the county court. The High Court, though now operating under the Judicature (NI) Act 1978, inherits under section 16 of that Act the jurisdictions of the Court of King's/Queen's Bench, Court of Chancery, and Ecclesiastical courts which existed until the last century.[1] The High Court is unique in one very important sense: its substantive jurisdiction is not confined by statute. Every other court or tribunal in the country, including the Court of Appeal, can make a decision or order on a substantive issue only by reference to some statutory provision which confers on it the power to do so, though the Court of Appeal is said to have inherent jurisdiction over some ancillary or procedural matters. If a High Court judge had to ask himself under what statutory power he was acting, half of his work would be gone. The High Court's inherent jurisdiction is both substantive and procedural: comprising its power to resolve disputes and liabilities at common law or equity; and its power to set aside proceedings and orders, and prevent abuses of court process.

COURTS, JUDGES AND OFFICES

1.01 The Judicature (NI) Act 1978, Part I (ss.1-15) sets up the *Supreme Court*, consisting of the Court of Appeal, High Court, and the Crown Court. The latter's jurisdiction is exclusively criminal. The High Court has three Divisions: the Chancery, the Queen's Bench, and the Family Divisions. "Without prejudice to any statutory provision relating to or affecting the distribution of business, all jurisdiction vested in the High Court belongs to all the Divisions alike" (s.5(4)). The Supreme Court judiciary consists of: (a) the Lord Chief Justice, who is presiding judge of both the Court of Appeal and the High Court; (b) three Lord Justices of the Court of Appeal; and (c) not more than seven *puisne* judges (Mr Justice ...) of the High Court. One of the High Court judges is assigned to the Family Division, one to the Chancery Division and the rest to the Queen's Bench Division. One of the Queen's Bench judges is nominated Commercial Judge (RSC, Ord.72 r.2(2)). Any judge can sit in a Division to which he is not assigned (s.6). By arrangement with the Lord Chief Justice or the judge to whom a case is pending or assigned, any other judge may hear it or an application in it (Ord.4 r.3). Any Lord Justice, on request of the LCJ, or High Court judge (or by request of the Lord Chancellor any county court judge, Law Lord who has practised at the Northern Ireland Bar, or retired Supreme Court judge) may sit in any Division of the High Court. If the LCJ is unavailable, his functions are performed by the senior Lord Justice (Judicature

---

[1] For a history of the Supreme Court in Northern Ireland see: Newark 'Notes on Irish Legal History' (1947) 7 NILQ 121; Lord MacDermott 'Law and Practice in Northern Ireland' (1953) 10 NILQ 47, at 69-73; 'Another Look at the Supreme Court' (1970) 21 NILQ 254; Osborough 'Law in Ireland' (1972) 23 NILQ 48; MacLean etc. 'Developments since 1921' 23 NILQ 82.

Act, s.11; RSC, Ord.1 r.6).The Lord Chancellor may appoint any member of the Bar of at least ten years' practice to sit as a temporary High Court judge. Any serving High Court judge may sit in the Court of Appeal on a civil cause or matter upon request of the LCJ.

1.02 Section 16 states that the *High Court* is a superior court of record which has any jurisdiction conferred by the Judicature Act and any subsequent statutory provision, and any existing jurisdiction of the Court or any Division or officer thereof "in pursuance of any statutory provision, prerogative, law or custom, and also all ministerial or other powers, duties and authorities incident to any and every part of the jurisdiction so vested." Save as otherwise provided by statutory provision, its jurisdiction "shall be exercised by a single judge" (s.16(5)). Where by mistake a Divisional Court of two or more judges exercises a jurisdiction which was historically exercised by such court, its order is not void.[2] By section 34 the *Court of Appeal* is a superior court of record which inherits its existing jurisdiction, the jurisdiction of the former Court of Criminal Appeal, and any jurisdiction conferred by the Act and any subsequent statutory provision. Its substantive jurisdiction is exercised by a court of two or three judges (see Chapter 20). The jurisdiction of the *House of Lords* is dealt with in sections 41-43 (see para. 20.83).

1.03 The Supreme Court inherits the jurisdiction of the Irish Supreme Court under section 41 of the Government of Ireland Act 1920. The High Court and Court of Appeal are continuing courts, with rules providing for hearings during vacation (Judicature Act, s.57). Both sit in the Royal Courts of Justice, Chichester Street, Belfast, or elsewhere as directed by the Lord Chancellor (s.58).[3] The High Court often sits at Crumlin Road, Belfast for the hearing of bail applications.

1.04 Part VI (ss.68-77) of the Judicature Act deals with departments of the Supreme Court, the Northern Ireland Court Service, statutory officers, and the Official Solicitor. The main Departments, offices and officers relevant to the Supreme Court are as follows-

Lord Chief Justice's Office	Principal Secretary Legal Secretary
Central Office	Master (Queen's Bench and Appeals) Master (High Court)
Chancery Office	Master (Chancery)
Bankruptcy & Companies Office	Master (Bankruptcy)
Probate and Matrimonial Office	Master (Probate and Matrimonial) District Judge [probate functions only]
Office of Care and Protection	Master (Care and Protection)

2 *In re Coleman* [1988] NI 205, at 209; but see *contra: Re Fletcher*, 'The Times' 12 June 1984.

3 Where suitable accommodation is not available, the judge may direct or adjourn the sitting to a convenient place: Administration of Justice Act (NI) 1954, s.13. That section does not apply to or affect the Royal Courts of Justice: *ibid.* s.16.

Taxing Office	Master (Taxing Office) *
Official Solicitor's Office	Official Solicitor
Enforcement of Judgments Office *	Master (Enforcement of Judgments) *
Court Funds Office	Accountant-General

* The Enforcement of Judgments Office is not part of the Supreme Court but is part of the Court Service under the Lord Chancellor. Traditionally one person occupies the two offices of Master (Taxing Office) and Master (Enforcement of Judgments).

Save for the Official Solicitor acting as such, none of the above may practise as a barrister or solicitor (s.73). The Lord Chancellor may appoint deputy and additional officers (s.74(1)). Any statutory officer may perform the functions of another if the latter is unavailable or his post is vacant (s.74(3)). The courts and Enforcement of Judgments Office staffs are members of the Northern Ireland Court Service appointed by the Lord Chancellor (s.69). The Court Service is subject to investigation by the 'ombudsman' under section 5 of the Parliamentary Commissioner Act 1967.

1.05 The Central Office deals with all Queen's Bench and Court of Appeal business (from any Division), and all business transacted there before 1980 (Ord.1 r.13). It consists of-

- the Writ Office, where writs, summons and *subpoenas* are issued, appearances entered, and notices filed
- the Judgments Office, where judgments are entered and drawn up, and matters relating to Admiralty are handled
- the Crown Office (part of the Judgments Office) which deals with Crown Side business, bail, *habeas corpus* and judicial review (see para.19.00), contempt of Queen's Bench orders, and criminal contempt
- the Appeals and Lists Office, which deals with listing of cases, appeals to the High Court or Court of Appeal, and cases stated.

The other Supreme Court Offices deal with business as follows, under Order 1 rules 14-18 respectively-

Rule 14 - the Chancery Office with Chancery business, except rule 15 business

Rule 15 - the Bankruptcy and Companies Office with insolvency, bankruptcy and company and winding-up matters

Rule 16 - the Probate and Matrimonial Office with all Family Division business, except rule 17 business

Rule 17 - the Office of Care and Protection with wardship, adoption, guardianship and abduction of minors, and mental patients

Rule 18 - the Taxing Office with taxation of costs of proceedings in the High Court, Court of Appeal and Crown Court, before an arbitrator or umpire or statutory body, costs between solicitor and client, other costs as provided by statute, and remuneration in insolvency.

The Accountant-General holds an account at the Bank of Ireland and maintains and invests funds in court in accordance with the Judicature Act (ss.77-85) and the Court Funds Rules (NI) 1979.[4]

1.06 The High Court and Court of Appeal sit for three terms each year from September to June (Michaelmas, Hilary and Trinity) (Ord.64 r.1). A court can be a Court of one or more judges, a judge in chambers or a master (see para.1.08). A vacation judge sits as required between terms and no order by him can be altered without consent, save by a divisional court of two or more judges or the Court of Appeal (Ord.64 rr.2,3). Urgent applications can be heard in vacation by him, by a court of two judges or the Court of Appeal, as may be necessary; a party to a cause or matter may apply by summons to a judge for an order for it to be tried or heard during vacation (Ord.64 r.4). In a civil cause, the judge and counsel do not robe in vacation sittings save on a trial of an action or contested matrimonial cause (Bar Handbook 22-01). Courts normally sit from 10.30am to 1.00pm and 2.00pm to 4.15.[5] Court offices are open all working days throughout the year save as directed by the Lord Chancellor (Ord.64 r.5). Office hours are 10.00am to 4.30pm.[6]

DEFINITIONS AND INTERPRETATION

In the Judicature Act and Rules of the Supreme Court

1.07 Section 120 applies to words used in the Judicature Act and the Rules of the Supreme Court.[7] The important definitions are as follows-

"action" means a civil proceeding commenced by writ or in such other manner as may be prescribed by rules of court, except a criminal proceeding by or in the name of the Crown

"cause" includes any action, suit or other original proceeding between a plaintiff and defendant and any criminal proceeding by or in the name of the Crown

"costs" includes fees, charges, disbursements, expenses or remuneration

"defendant" includes any person served with a writ of summons or process or served with notice of or entitled to attend any proceedings

"judgment" includes order, decision and decree

"jurisdiction" includes power and authority

"lower deciding authority" includes any inferior court or other tribunal and any authority exercising judicial or quasi-judicial functions

"matter" includes every proceeding in court not in a cause

"party" includes every person served with notice of or attending any proceeding, although not named on the record

"plaintiff" includes every person asking any relief (other than as counterclaiming defendant) against any other person by any form of proceeding

---

4 SR 1979/105 amended SR1997/166.

5 Practice Direction [1987] 4 BNIL 93.

6 Lord Chancellor's Direction [1990] 3 BNIL 100.

7 SR 1980/346.

"pleading" includes petition or summons, the statement in writing of the claim or demand of a party and of the defence or reply of a party to a claim or demand made against him[8]

"Royal Courts of Justice" is the building at Chichester Street, Belfast

"statutory provision" means any provision of a statute or instrument made under a statute (by whatsoever Parliament passed or by whomever made) for the time being in force in Northern Ireland.

In the Rules of the Supreme Court only

1.08 Other definitions for the purposes of the RSC are provided in Order 1 rule 3 -

"action for personal injuries" means an action in which there is a claim for damages in respect of personal injuries (including disease or impairment of physical or mental condition) to the plaintiff or any other person, or in respect of a person's death (see further para.4.06 and para.11.133)

"appropriate office" means the office where proceedings are pending

"Cause Book" means the book or other record [i.e. computer files] kept in the Supreme Court Offices in which the number and other details of a cause or matter are entered

"the Court" means, subject to specific provisions, the High Court or any one or more judges in court or in chambers, or any master[9]

"FAX" means electronic transmission of a facsimile copy

"Long Vacation" means the summer vacation

"master" means a master other than the Taxing Master

"originating summons" means any summons not in a pending cause or matter

"pleading" does not include a writ, petition or summons, but includes a Statement of Claim endorsed on a writ

"vacation" means the intervals between terms (Christmas, Easter and Summer)

"writ" means a writ of summons.

A "notice" under the Rules must be written but can be given orally by leave of the Court (Ord.66 r.2(5)).

As will be seen below, the Judicature Act is also governed by the Interpretation Act 1889 and partially by the Interpretation Act 1978. The RSC are governed also by the Interpretation Acts 1889 and 1978 to the same extent, and possibly also by the Interpretation Act (NI) 1954.

Definitions in general statute law

1.09 There are for Northern Ireland two sources of legislation. One is the supreme authority, the UK Parliament. The other is the former NI Parliament and NI Assembly, and the Privy Council which makes Orders in Council designed to rank as such Acts and Measures. The legislation of the former is interpreted in accordance with the Interpretation Acts 1889 and 1978; the latter

---

8 Note the narrower definition in the RSC only, *infra*.

9 In any other statute "court" means one or more judges sitting in open court and "judge" means a judge in chambers: White Book (1997) Vol. 2 [4604].

in accordance with the Interpretation Act (NI) 1954. The statutory provisions by which this scheme of interpretation is brought about are extremely complex and are explained below as simply as possible.

'UK Legislation'

1.10 The Interpretation Act 1978 applies to what may be termed 'UK legislation', that is Acts of the United Kingdom Parliament[10] and subordinate legislation thereunder (ss.22-3 thereof). It does not apply to what may be called 'NI legislation', nor to Statutory Instruments subject to annulment by Parliament under section 5 of the Statutory Instruments Act 1946.[11]

Definitions in the 1978 Act

Where a UK enactment repeals and re-enacts, with or without modification, an enactment, references to the latter are taken to be to the former and all rules and proceedings made under the latter continue as if made under the former (s.17). Words used in subordinate legislation and rules have the same meaning as in the parent statute (s.11).

> The "United Kingdom" means Great Britain (England/Wales and Scotland) and Northern Ireland (Sch.1). "The British Islands" means the United Kingdom, Channel Islands and Isle of Man (Sch.1),[12] and in UK Acts up to 1978 it also includes the Republic of Ireland (Sch.2 para.4(2)). For the purpose of any law, the Republic of Ireland is not a "foreign country" and words such as "foreigner" and "alien" are construed accordingly.[13] In Acts passed up to 2 June 1949, "HM Dominions" includes the Republic of Ireland.[14]
>
> Singular means plural, masculine means feminine and *vice versa* (s.6). Distance is as the crow flies (s.8).
>
> "High Court" and "Supreme Court" mean in relation to Northern Ireland the High Court and the Supreme Court respectively of Northern Ireland (Sch.1). "The Secretary of State" means any of Her Majesty's principal Secretary of State [of cabinet rank] (Sch.1)

'NI Legislation'

1.11 The Interpretation Act 1978 does not apply to what may be called 'NI legislation', save that the definitions in Schedule 1 thereto of "Tax Acts" etc. apply to NI Orders in Council (s.24 thereof). The Interpretation Act (NI) 1954[15] applies only to "enactments" which is defined by section 1 of that Act to be Acts of the NI Parliament and subordinate legislation thereunder. The 1954

---

[10] In relation to Acts passed before 1 January 1979 most of its provisions except Sch.1 apply: see Sch.2. Such Acts continue to be governed by the Interpretation Act 1889. These include the Judicature (NI) Act 1978. The only significant difference is that in pre-1979 statutes, masculine includes feminine but **not** *vice versa.*

[11] Which includes the RSC (NI) 1980; but words in the RSC have the same meaning as in the parent Judicature Act: Interpretation Act 1978, s.11.

[12] "British Islands" is so defined also in the Interpretation Act 1889, s.18.

[13] Ireland Act 1949, s.2.

[14] Ireland Act 1949, s.3.

[15] For a commentary on the 1954 Act, see Leitch and Donaldson (1955) 11 NILQ 66, (1965) 16 NILQ 215.

Act in effect applies to all 'NI legislation', which may be defined to mean Acts of the Northern Ireland Parliament and subordinate legislation thereunder, Measures of the Northern Ireland Assembly and Orders in Council which rank as such Acts and Measures, and subordinate legislation thereunder;[16] and Orders in Council made on reserved matters for Northern Ireland.[17] Where the 1954 Act refers to "statutory provision" it means legislation by or under Acts of any Parliament (s.1 thereof). In NI legislation, "enactment" means any statute of the UK or NI Parliament; the narrower definition of the word in section 1 of the 1954 Act is for the purposes of that Act only.[18]

Definitions in the 1954 Act

Where an enactment repeals and re-enacts, with or without modification, an enactment, all rules and proceedings made under the latter continue as if made under the former (s.29). Words used in subordinate legislation and rules have the same meaning as in the parent statute (s.33).

> "The British Islands" means the United Kingdom, Channel Islands and Isle of Man, and it also includes the Republic of Ireland (s.43).
>
> Singular means plural, masculine means feminine and *vice versa* (s.37). In enactments after 1954 "shall" is imperative and "may" is permissive and empowering (s.38). Distance is as the crow flies (s.40). In post-1954 enactments, "land" includes hereditament, estate in land and water, buildings and other structures; "estate in land" includes legal or equitable interest, easement, right, charge lien, encumbrance etc. (s.45). "The Secretary of State" means any of Her Majesty's principal Secretary of State [of cabinet rank] (s.43(1)).

RULES OF PROCEDURE

1.12 Section 54 of the Judicature Act sets up the Supreme Court Rules Committee which makes rules for pleading, practice and procedure and other matters set out in section 55.[19] If a statute gives the Rules Committee power to make rules to exercise a new power, the Court has no jurisdiction to exercise that power until, and only to the extent that, the rules allow.[20] If NI legislation confers or extends jurisdiction of the Court, the Committee may make rules of procedure.[21] If a statute confers jurisdiction and enables rules of procedure to be made, the Court can exercise the jurisdiction before rules are made;[22] and in the absence of rules, the Court should apply, as appropriate, Order 55 rules 13-22 (for appeals, applications and references to the High Court), Order 56 (for appeals by case stated to the High Court), Order 59 (for appeals to the Court of Appeal), or Order 61 (for appeals by case stated to the Court of Appeal).

---

16 Because these Measures and Orders in Council all expressly state that they are governed the 1954 Act.

17 Northern Ireland Act 1982, Sch.2 para.7.

18 *McAfee* v *Gilliland* [1979] NI 97.

19 It has been held by the Irish High Court that those words give power to make rules for discovery against a non-party: *Holloway* v *Belenos (No 2)* [1988] IR 494; *Fitzpatrick* v *Independent Newspapers* [1988] IR 132.

20 *Felix* v *Shiva* [1983] QB 82.

21 Interpretation Act (NI) 1954, s.21.

22 *Steele* v *Tiernan* (1889) 23 LR Ir 583; *O* v *M* [1977] IR 33.

Procedure in the Supreme Court is governed by the Rules of the Supreme Court (NI) 1980[23] (the "RSC") made under section 55 of the Judicature Act.[24] The RSC are Statutory Rules and Orders for the purpose of the Statutory Rules (NI) Order 1979 and are subject to annulment by resolution of either House of Parliament (s.56). They were exempted from publication in the annual volume of Statutory Rules and Orders, but all amendments since 1980 are published therein. The RSC are published by HMSO in a loose-bound red-covered Book, commonly called "The Red Book", in which pages incorporating all amendments as they occur are published for insertion. Pre-1978 Rules made under Acts relating to the Supreme Court continue in force subject to amendment or revocation by the Rules Committee (Sch.6). All forms and methods of civil and criminal procedure and practice operating in 1978 may continue to be used in so far as not inconsistent with the Judicature Act or rules thereunder (Sch.6). Any reference in the RSC to things done under a rule includes things done under the rule's predecessor; and any reference to a statutory provision includes that provision as amended, extended etc. (Ord.1 r.4).

TERRITORIAL JURISDICTION

1.13 The territorial jurisdiction of the Court is limited by restrictions on service of process outside Northern Ireland (see para.6.11); and by the Civil Jurisdiction and Judgments Act 1982. By section 30 of the 1982 Act, no court has jurisdiction to entertain proceedings chiefly concerned with a question of title to or the right of possession of immovable property situate outside Northern Ireland.

1.14 The 1982 Act imports into law, as Schedule 1 thereto, the Brussels Convention 1968 which has now been signed and ratified by all European Community countries.[25] It applies to civil and commercial matters other than the status of persons, matrimonial property, wills, succession, bankruptcy, winding up, social security and arbitration. If the defendant is domiciled[26] in a Convention State, he must be sued in that State (Sch.1, Art.2), or in another Convention State which has a connection with the dispute (in the case of

---

23 SR 1980/346.

24 In Ireland the original Rules, made under the Supreme Court of Judicature (Ir) Act 1877 were revised and consolidated several times until the 1905 Rules, which are the subject of the last edition of Wylie's *Judicature Acts*. In Northern Ireland, the Rules were consolidated in the 1936 Revision which introduced numerous changes in detail (as described in (1936-37) 1 NILQ 42, 84, 127, 177) and which like the previous versions were modelled on the English Rules of 1883 as amended. Between 1962 and 1965 a major overhaul of the English Rules was effected, and the 1980 version of the Rules, which operates in Northern Ireland to-day, is closely modelled on the English 1965 Rules.

25 The Civil Jurisdiction and Judgments Act 1991 ratifies the Lugano Convention 1988. That Convention, which adopts and incorporates the Brussels Convention, has been signed by all EFTA countries and ratified so far by the United Kingdom, Sweden and Switzerland.

26 As defined by the law of the State: Art.52. The 1982 Act (ss.41-46) defines domicile for the purpose of deciding whether a person is domiciled in the United Kingdom. A human person is domiciled where he is resident in circumstances which indicate a substantial connection; a corporate person is domiciled where it has its registered office or its central management and control. Note that under the Jurisdiction of Courts and Enforcement of Judgments (European Communities) Act 1988 (Republic of Ireland), Sch.5 Pt.I, a human person is domiciled in the Republic if he is "ordinarily resident" there.

contract that State where the obligation in question is to be performed[27] or in the case of tort or delict, where the harmful event occurred)[28] (Art.5). It is for the plaintiff to prove clearly that he can sue in a State which is not the defendant's domicile.[29] If there are co-defendants the plaintiff may sue in the State where any one of them is domiciled, and third-party proceedings may be brought before the court of the State seised of the original claim, unless the proceedings were initiated solely to enable a foreigner to be made amenable to that State (Art.6).[30] A counterclaim arising out of the same contract or facts as the claim may be raised in the State where the claim is brought (Art.6). If the plaintiff sues as an insurance policy holder or a consumer, he may sue in the State of his own domicile (Arts.8-15). Regardless of domicile, certain cases, for example, rights *in rem* or tenancies of land, must be brought in the State with a particular connection (Art.16). Subject to Articles 12-16, action must be brought in a State to which the parties, either or both of whom are domiciled in a Convention State, have agreed in writing to give exclusive jurisdiction (Art.17).[31] Save for Article 16, which the Court must apply of its own motion, the Court has jurisdiction in any case if the defendant enters an appearance which does not contest the jurisdiction (Arts.18-19).[32] If the defendant does not enter an appearance, the Court shall of its own motion apply the Convention (Art.20). If the defendant is domiciled in a Convention State, the Court does not have jurisdiction merely because he is served with a writ whilst temporarily present in Northern Ireland, nor because he has property here (Art.3). The 1982 Act provides for the jurisdiction of a court in Northern Ireland to grant interim relief in cases where the Convention does or may apply (see para.11.01). Since the High Court as a superior court has jurisdiction to inquire into the existence of its own substantive jurisdiction, it can compel evidence relevant to its jurisdiction (e.g. *subpoena* documents relevant to the issue of the defendant's domicile).[33]

1.15 The above jurisdictional rules apply in modified form (under Sch 4 to the 1982 Act) if the defendant is domiciled in a part of the United Kingdom, or if a part of the United Kingdom has exclusive jurisdiction under Article 16 or 17 of Schedule 1. Sections 41-46 of the 1982 Act define domicile for the

---

27 See *Stuart (Carl)* v *Biotrace* [1993] ILRM 633; *Hanbridge Ltd* v *British Aerospace* [1993] 3 IR 342; *Ferndale Films* v *Granada TV* [1993] 3 IR 362. It includes a void contract: *Kleinwort Benson* v *Glasgow Corp* [1996] QB 678 (CA); and a contract the existence of which is disputed by the plaintiff: *Boss Group* v *Boss France SA*, 'The Times' 15 April 1996 (CA).

28 Which means both where the harmful act was done and where the damage first occurred: *Marinari* v *Lloyds Bank* [1996] QB 217 (ECJ). Whether the harmful event occurred in NI is to be determined as a matter of NI law: *Shevill* v *Presse Alliance* [1996] AC 959 (HL). If sued in the state where the defendant is domiciled the plaintiff can recover for his damage suffered anywhere, but if sued in a state where the harmful act or damage occurred, he is confined to the damage suffered in that state: *Murray* v *Times Newspapers* [1995] 3 IR 244 (Egan J).

29 *Handbridge Ltd* v *British Aerospace* [1993] 3 IR 342.

30 See *Gannon* v *British & Irish Steam Packet* [1993] 2 IR 359.

31 See *Buchanan* v *Brook Walker* [1988] NI 116; *Walker* v *BMW* [1990] 6 NIJB 1.

32 See *Campbell International* v *Van Aart* [1992] 2 IR 305; *Devrajan* v *DJ Ballagh* [1993] 3 IR 377.

33 *Canada Trust* v *Stolzenberg*, 'The Times' 1 May 1997 (CA).

purpose of deciding whether a person is domiciled in the United Kingdom or a part of the United Kingdom. A human person is domiciled where he is resident in circumstances which indicate a substantial connection; a corporate person is domiciled where it has its registered office or its central management and control.

The NI High Court has jurisdiction in civil law over conduct mentioned in section 23(2) of the Oil and Gas (Enterprise) Act 1982 in the 'Northern Irish' sea area as delineated in the Civil Jurisdiction (Offshore Activities) Order, SI 1987/2197).

RULES OF LAW AND EQUITY

1.16 Every judge appointed to any court in Northern Ireland takes the judicial oath under section 4 of the Promissory Oaths Act 1868 swearing that he "... will do right to all manner of people after the laws and usages of this realm, without fear or favour, affection or ill-will". These words are the basis of the operation of the rule of law. Unlike most other countries in the world there is no constitutional framework guiding the operation of the courts. A judge must seek to apply the settled rules and doctrines of law and equity, evolved from case law precedents, and the legislation made by and under the Parliament of the United Kingdom. The European Convention on Human Rights has no direct effect and can be used only as an aid to interpreting internal law.[34] The nearest approach to a general constitutional law is Magna Carta 1297, which states at c.29. "To no man will we sell, deny or defer right or justice".[35]

1.17 Every civil court continues to administer common law and equity with the rules of equity prevailing, and to give effect to all equitable estates, rights, remedies, counterclaims and defences, and duties and liabilities, and subject thereto to all legal claims, estates, rights etc. created at common law or by custom or statute, and shall ensure that all matters in dispute in a cause or matter may be completely and finally determined (Judicature Act, s.86(1)(2)). The Court cannot, even by consent, grant relief wholly unconnected to any claim pleaded.[36] Any Division of the High Court can grant any legal or equitable remedy or allow any legal or equitable defence;[37] but must always bear in mind the difference between law and equity. If a common law claim is proved, then subject to any legal or equitable defence, the common law remedy (debt, damages or ejectment) follows as a right. Any equitable remedy is discretionary: if the cause of action proved is equitable,[38] only the discretionary remedies (injunction, specific performance, damages in lieu etc.) are available.[39] Another distinction exists in property rights: a common law right is *in rem* and

---

[34] *In re Devlin* [1995] 9 BNIL 28 (Kerr J). It can be argued from *Minister of Immigration* v *Teoh* [1995] 3 LRC 1 (HC Aus) that an obligation placed on the government by an international treaty or convention, which has not been enacted by statute, creates a legitimate epectation that the obligation will be honoured unless persons affected are given an opportunity to make representations.

[35] See Samuels 'Magna Carta as Living Law' (1969) 20 NILQ 49.

[36] *McClelland* v *Quirey* (1898) 32 ILTR 128.

[37] See for example *Conlon* v *Carlow CC* [1912] 2 IR 535.

[38] E.g. breach of confidence: *O'Neill* v *DHSS (No 2)* [1986] NI 290.

[39] But see para.14.92.

binds all the world; equitable rights are *in personam* and do not bind a *bona fide* purchaser for value. As to suing on equitable rights, see para.3.40. No pending proceedings in the Supreme Court can be stayed by prohibition or injunction, but any court on equitable grounds may stay any proceedings or the execution of its process (s.86(3)(4)).

WHICH DIVISION?

1.18 The High Court has inherited the inherent civil jurisdiction of the pre-1877 superior courts. Any civil proceeding, however small in nature, can be brought in the High Court, save where by statute a special jurisdiction is created in some other tribunal, such as licensing applications, criminal injury appeals in the county court and claims for unfair dismissal in the Industrial Tribunal. The plaintiff may choose in which Division of the High Court to sue, though Order 1 assigns certain proceedings to each Division. Claims for damages for personal injury are invariably brought in the Queen's Bench Division. Other claims for debt or damages are almost invariably brought there, more rarely in the Chancery Division.

1.19 Order 1 rule 11 assigns to the Queen's Bench Division-

(a) all proceedings civil or criminal within its jurisdiction at the coming into force of the 1980 Rules

(b) Admiralty jurisdiction

(c) Judgment Enforcement (NI) Order 1981 (Arts.107-110), save in respect of orders made in matrimonial proceedings

(d) *habeas corpus*

(e) judicial review

(f) proceedings assigned by statute

(g) and (h) appeals relating to legal aid costs in criminal proceedings in the Crown Court and on appeal therefrom.

Proceedings assigned to the Chancery Division are listed at para.18.53; and to the Family Division at para.18.46.

1.20 All jurisdiction of the High Court vests in each Division (Judicature Act, s.5(4)). Assignment of a cause or matter to a Division does not mean that it must be allocated to that Division (Ord.1 r.12A(3)) nor that it must be transferred to that Division (Ord.4 r.1(2)). Proceeding in the wrong Division is not fatal and the case may be allowed to proceed there.[40] It cannot be dismissed.[41] It has been the policy since 1877 to avoid multiplicity of proceedings in the High Court. The RSC are not designed to prevent a plaintiff from joining in one action a Queen's Bench claim and a Chancery claim which are related. Order 1 rule 12A(1) allows a person commencing any proceedings in the High Court to allocate them to whatever Division he thinks fit by naming the Division on the originating process, subject to transfer under Order 4; and

---

40 *Duncan* v *Mackin* [1985] 10 NIJB 1, at 7.
41 *Clanricarde* v *Ryder* [1898] 1 IR 98.

requires all interlocutory applications to be made in the Division to which allocated or transferred.

Transfer between Divisions

1.21 Proceedings may be transferred at any stage to another Division by order of the Court of the Division in which pending (Ord.4 r.1(1)); whether or not any party applies or consents, provided that the parties are allowed to be heard (Ord.4 r.4). Transfer would be ordered where there is a connected action pending in the other Division, or the subject-matter of the proceedings is better dealt with in the other Division. The chance to have a speedier trial is not *per se* a good ground.[42]

COURT FUNDS

1.22 The powers of the Court and the procedure for dealing with money paid into court is dealt with at para.11.171.

COURT DOCUMENTS AND FEES

1.23 As a court of record the Supreme Court keeps a record of proceedings before it, which is conclusive evidence of what it states.[43] All writs, orders etc. bearing a seal of the Supreme Court are admissible in all courts in the United Kingdom (Judicature Act, s.115). All writs, pleadings etc. must be in English.[44] The authentification of a judgment covers everything stated on its face.[45] The general rule is that orders are final in the proceedings in which given (see para.15.09).

1.24 Certain formal documents in connection with litigation in the Supreme Court, such as writs and originating processes, notices of motion and summonses, setting down for trial, notices of appeal etc., require payment of a fee.[46] The former system whereby the litigant had to purchase and affix a revenue stamp has gone. Now he must pay in cash and the Court official in issuing the document endorses a receipt on it. The Lord Chancellor may in a particular case remit or reduce the fee. If court fees are unpaid, the Official Solicitor may apply to the Court for an order that the solicitor do pay the fees personally (Ord.62 r.11(7)).

1.25 Where rules require a document to be lodged or served on the Court, this is normally done by taking it to the appropriate Court Office and handing it to an official. However, directions can be given for any business to be conducted by post (Ord.1 r.9). Where rules require a notice to be given, it cannot be given orally save by leave of the Court (Ord.66 r.2(5)). Documents must be legibly printed or written on durable A4 size paper with a left hand margin ("judicature paper"); photocopies, but not carbon copies are acceptable

---

42 *Barclays Bank* v *Bemister* [1989] 1 WLR 128.

43 *R (Carl)* v *Tyrone JJ* [1917] 2 IR 437.

44 Administration of Justice (Language) Act (Ir) 1737.

45 *Dillane* v *Sullivan* (1843) Ir Cir Rep 855.

46 Under the Supreme Court Fees Order (NI) SR 1996/100 amended SR 1997/175; or the Orders for matrimonial causes, SR 1996/105 amended SR 1997/177; or non-contentious probate, SR 1996/104 amended SR 1997/176. These Orders are made under the Judicature Act, s.116.

(Ord.66 rr.1-2). A party preparing a document for use in the Supreme Court must, on request and on payment of the proper charges, provide a copy for any other party indorsed with his name (Ord.66 rr.3-4). A person (whether a party to proceedings or not) is entitled to search for and take a copy of any writ, other originating process, judgment given in court and by leave any other document, in the Central, Chancery or Bankruptcy and Companies Offices (Ord.66 r.5). A party to proceedings has a right to search for and take copies of any affidavit or document filed in those proceedings. A non-party needs leave to see documents and orders made in chambers. Pleadings are not public knowledge, except a Statement of Claim endorsed on a writ.

Court bonds

1.26 Court bonds, which are sometimes ordered to be given as security for costs, are dealt with in the Judicature Act (s.110), and Order 108.

Use of forms

1.27 "The Forms in the Appendices shall be used where applicable with such variations as the circumstances of the particular case may require" (Ord.1 r.8). Any deviation from a form prescribed by rules can be cured by amendment.[47] "Where a form is prescribed or specified by any enactment [i.e. NI legislation], deviations therefrom not materially affecting the substance nor calculated to mislead, shall not invalidate the form used" (Interpretation Act (NI) 1954, s.25). This section probably only refers to printed forms;[48] and "only in the case where the proceedings have been initiated by means of a proper machinery but there is a defect or deviation in the content of the document used".[49] A form should not be followed in so far as it conflicts with statutory procedure.[50] It is also the practice to adapt and use the many procedural forms of the English Supreme Court, set out in the White Book (1997) Vol. 2, in cases where there is no form provided in the RSC. Practitioners also consider the precedents in the 'Blue Atkin', Chitty & Jacob's *Queen's Bench Forms* and Daniell's *Chancery Forms* (1932).

IRREGULARITIES

1.28 "Where in beginning or purporting to begin any proceedings or at any stage in the course or in connection with any proceedings, there has been, by reason of anything done or left undone, a failure to comply with the requirements of these Rules, whether in respect of time, place, manner, form or content or in any other respect, the failure shall be treated as an irregularity and shall not nullify the proceedings, any step taken in the proceedings, or any document, judgment or order therein" (Ord.2 r.1(1)). The Court may set aside wholly or in part the proceedings or any step or judgment or order on ground of such failure, or deal with the proceedings by amendment or otherwise (Ord.2 r.1(2)). An application to set aside for irregularity a step or proceeding or any judgment or order shall not be allowed unless made within a reasonable time

---

47 *Manders* v *Kildare CC* (1909) 43 ILTR 9.

48 *Pigs Marketing Board* v *Redmond* [1978] NI 73; not to deviations which constitute an error of procedure: *ibid.*

49 *Per* Gibson J, *R (Shields)* v *Down JJ* [1970] NI 173, at 181.

50 *Ulster Banking* v *McKinney* (1879) 4 LR Ir 51.

and before taking a fresh step; and is made by summons or motion stating the grounds of objection (Ord.2 r.2). Failure to state the ground is not fatal, but the applicant may be refused his costs.[51] If the summons is dismissed the applicant pays the costs automatically (Ord.62 r.5(2)). Order 2 rule 2 does not apply to an application to set aside for an irregularity which amounts to a nullity,[52] nor to an application to amend,[53] nor, *semble*, to an objection as to substance.[54]

1.29 Order 2 applies only to the RSC and to rules which are expressed to form part of the RSC;[55] but in *Howard* v *Howard*,[56] Palles CB thought that where justice requires, any court may waive a rule of court unless to do so is contrary to statute. There is only an irregularity if a rule or the *cursus curiae* has not been observed.[57]

1.30 Order 2 rule 1 is capable of curing any breach of those rules however great, except possibly where it is a breach of natural justice, or where it would validate an act by a party done beyond the limit of the power set by the rules. For example, it would not validate an order made by a master which Order 32 bars him from making. A purported order made by an official which under rules only a judge can make cannot be validated.[58] The rule can be used to cure a defect in service on a company under the Companies (NI) Order 1986.[59] However it cannot cure an amendment which contravenes Order 20 rule 5 and the Limitation (NI) Order 1989 as to the limitation period (para.11.30).[60] In *Doherty* v *MOD*[61] the Court of Appeal, hearing an appeal from an order made irregularly in that it was not heard on summons on motion, waived the defect and heard the appeal, but directed that the proper summons should be issued for the purpose of the appeal hearing. In *CO Williams* v *Blackman*[62] an applicant applied successfully for leave to sue and was given costs of the application; in holding that leave to sue was unnecessary, the Court treated the granting of leave as irregularity to be cured under Order 2 rule 1 and set aside the order for costs. An irregular proceeding cannot be regarded as valid until the Court has dealt with it under Order 2 rule 1.[63] An irregular court order is effective until set aside, at least in the sense that it must be obeyed.[64]

---

51 *Loveland* v *Ejector* (1839) 2 Ir LR 240; *Stanley* v *Hart* [1932] IR 649.
52 *Craig* v *Kanssen* [1943] KB 256 (order made in default against unserved defendant).
53 *Welsh* v *Hall* (1841) 9 M & W 14 (152 ER 7).
54 *Roche* v *Sherrington* [1982] 1 WLR 599, at 611BC.
55 *Davis* v *Northern Ireland Carriers* [1979] NI 19; *In re O'Loughlin* [1985] NI 421; but see the apparently contrary decision in *Re Secretary of State's Application* [1991] NI 64.
56 (1893) 32 LR Ir 454, at 474.
57 *Haig* v *McMahon* [1901] 2 IR 350.
58 *Re Rhodes* [1987] CLY 3116 (CA); *sed contra*: *Harkness* v *Bell* [1967] 2 QB 729.
59 *Boocock* v *Hilton International* [1993] 1 WLR 1065.
60 *Bank of America Nat Trust* v *Christmas* [1994] 1 All ER 401.
61 [1991] 1 NIJB 68, at 75-6.
62 [1990] LRC (Const) 70 (Barbados SC), appealed on other points [1995] 1 WLR 102 (PC).
63 *Metroinvest* v *Commercial Union* [1985] 1 WLR 513.
64 *Isaacs* v *Robertson* [1985] AC 97 (PC).

TIME LIMITS

1.31 "Month" means a calendar month, in statute or rules[65] and in any order or document in proceedings (Ord.3 r.1). Order 3 rule 2 applies to times fixed by the RSC or by judgments and orders. If an act is to be done within X days after or from a date, that date is excluded. If an act is to be done or within or not less than X days before a date, that date is excluded. If the act is to be done X clear days before or after a date, the period excludes both the day of the act and the date. (See further the White Book (1997) 3/2.) A time limit of seven days or less excludes Saturday, Sunday and bank holidays (Ord.3 r.2(5)). The time limit for doing an act at a court office, if it expires on a day when the office is closed and cannot therefore be done, is extended to the next day that the office is open (Ord.3 r.4)[66] and if the act is done on the latter day, any further time limit runs from the latter date.[67] Time for any act is extended where it is impossible to do the act on the last day.[68] Unless otherwise directed the Long Vacation is excluded in time limits set by the RSC or by an order for serving, filing or amending a pleading (Ord.3 r.3). Sunday is a *dies non juridicus*, except for urgent injunctions, and process cannot be served (see para.6.21). An act or event is subject to enquiry as to the time of day when it happened, but not a judicial act which is deemed to take place at the start of the day; so if a party dies on the same day as judgment is given, the death is deemed to occur after the judgment; but that ancient rule was criticised and questioned in *In re Palmer*.[69] Where a statute allows act X to be done "within 21 days after event Y", act X cannot be done *before* event Y.[70]

1.32 The Interpretation Act (NI) 1954 (s.39) applies to time limits under NI legislation. Time limits in UK legislation, the Judicature Act and in the RSC are governed by the Interpretation Acts 1889 and 1978.

Alteration of time limits

1.33 The High Court and Court of Appeal "may, on such terms as it thinks just, by order extend or abridge the period within which a person is required or authorised by these Rules, or by any judgment, order or direction, to do any act in any proceedings", and may extend time on application made after the expiry of the period; the time limit for serving, filing or amending a pleading or other document may be extended by written consent without an order (Ord.3 r.5). Application is by summons which may be served up to the day before the hearing thereof (Ord.32 r.5). There is no rule that the applicant must show good reason for the delay.[71] He must bear the costs of the application unless otherwise ordered (Ord.62 r.6(6)). Order 3 rule 5 does not apply to time limits

---

[65] Interpretation Acts 1889, s.3; 1978, s.5, Sch.1; Interpretation (NI) Act 1954, s.39.
[66] *Aliter* for time limits set by statute: *Watson* v *Paxton* (1907) 41 ILTR 40; where however the acting party may be able to rely on the doctrine *lex non cogit ad impossibilia*.
[67] *McKibbin* v *McClelland* [1894] 2 IR 654.
[68] *Poole* v *O'Sullivan* [1993] 1 IR 484; e.g. the Office is closed or is not accepting post on a particular day; or the performance is illegal.
[69] [1994] Ch 316 (CA).
[70] *Bridge Wholesale* v *Shores* [1994] 2 NZLR 222.
[71] *Costellow* v *Somerset CC* [1993] 1 WLR 256.

fixed by statute,[72] nor by rules which are not expressed to be read as part of the RSC. A statutory time limit can be extended only under statutory power.[73] Where the Court is given power to dispense with a time limit, the Court must exercise a discretion.[74] The Court has inherent power to vary time limits set by its own orders, even orders made by consent unless the consent order expressly precludes it.[75]

1.34 Abridgement of time is usually give on consent or in cases of urgency, for example to shorten notice of motion, as in *Allardyce* v *Carnlough Construction*.[76]

1.35 Application for extension of time should be made on notice.[77] It can be sought after the expiry and after the late act has been done. The considerations for extending time are set out in *Davis* v *Northern Ireland Carriers*-[78]

(1) an application made before expiry of the time will be more favourably received, if the reason is good;
(2) if the time has expired, the extent of the default;
(3) the effect on the respondent and whether he can be compensated in costs;
(4) whether there has already been a hearing on the merits or refusal of an extension would deny it;
(5) whether there is a point of substance which will not be heard if refused;
(6) whether there is a point of general, not merely particular importance;
(7) the rules are there to be observed.

The English Court of Appeal has made the following additional loose guidelines: (a) the Court should look at all the circumstances and good reason for the default is not always required; (b) extension which will cause a postponement of the date of trial is a last resort; (c) the parties should try to agree a new timetable and the Court will accept it if it does not delay the trial date; (d) if not agreed, the parties should seek the Court's directions promptly; (e) no favour is shown to a party who seeks to take tactical advantage from the opponent's default.[79] Extension of time for a procedural step such as serving a Statement of Claim will usually be granted in the absence of prejudice;[80] with

---

72 A statutory time limit can be extended only by express power in the statute: *Cork CC* v *Whillock* [1993] 1 IR 231. But it seems that the RSC can substitute a time limit set by statute relating to proceedings in the Supreme Court, and if so, the new time limit is extendable under Ord.3 r.5.

73 In *MPD* v *MD* [1981] ILRM 179, at 184, Carroll J suggested that any time limit can be waived by consent of the parties but this is not thought to be the law in Northern Ireland.

74 *Davis* v *Northern Ireland Carriers* [1979] NI 19, at 20A.

75 *Siebe Gorman* v *Pneupac* [1982] 1 WLR 185.

76 [1975] 6 NIJB.

77 *Ferguson* v *Taggart* (1893) 27 ILTR 134.

78 [1979] NI 19.

79 *Mortgage Corp* v *Sandoes*, 'The Times', 27 December 1996; applied in *In re Darley*, QBD, NI (Girvan J) 16 June 1997.

80 *Costellow* v *Somerset CC* [1993] 1 WLR 256; but see *Hughes* v *Hughes* [1990] NI 295, and *Phillips* v *Taunton and Somerset NHT*, 'The Times' 15 August 1996 (CA).

the exceptions of the time for serving a writ, for appealing, for lodging money in court under Order 22; and for taking a step by an applicant for committal for contempt. In appeals from an inferior tribunal, excuse for delay must normally be shown before the time for appeal will be extended.[81] "Micawber-like" applications, for example to extend time for appeal indefinitely in the hope that some ground of appeal will come to light, will be refused.[82]

1.36 In practice, most acts to be done under the RSC, such as delivery of pleadings, setting down for trial etc., are often done by the parties out of time without any formal order or written consent for extension.[83] The step is irregular but will be treated as valid under Order 2 unless the other party specifically applies to set it aside. The main exceptions to this practice are: (a) service of the writ; (b) lodgments under Order 22, which are generally only taken into account if made within the time set by the RSC or extended by the Court; (c) appeals to a judge or to the Court of Appeal, where a formal consent or order extending time should be given at some stage; and (d) contempt proceedings, where procedures must be strictly observed.

1.37 Where a party is in default of some step under the RSC, the Court may make an "unless" order, that unless within X days of service of the order (or unless by X date) he does act Y, the action shall be dismissed, or the defence struck out and judgment entered. Even after the expiry of the time limit, the time limit for compliance can be extended.[84] An 'unless' order is an order of last resort so that non-compliance should normally lead to striking out, unless it was beyond the party's control.[85] Explanation for the default is usually but not automatically required.[86]

---

81 *Regalbourne* v *East Lindsey DC*, 'The Times', 16 March 1993, approved in *Savill* v *Southend HA* [1995] 1 WLR 1254 (CA).

82 *O'Keefe* v *Todd-Burns* (1931) 65 ILTR 71.

83 However the RSC caters for the situation where there has been no proceeding had between the parties for at least a year, or two years (see para.11.195, para.11.199).

84 *Samuels* v *Linzi Dresses* [1981] QB 115.

85 *Hytec Information* v *Coventry CC*, 'The Times' 31 December 1996 (CA).

86 *Hughes* v *Hughes* [1990] NI 295.

CHAPTER TWO

STEPS BEFORE PROCEEDINGS

2.00 This chapter is written in the form of advices to the solicitor as to how to handle a new case from the moment when the client first approaches him or her, to the commencement of proceedings.

GENERALLY

2.01 *When a client(prospective claimant) first comes to a solicitor's office*

(1) Speak to him briefly to ascertain the nature of his claim. The most important thing at this stage is to find out the date when his cause of action arose so that it can be seen whether there is any urgency for limitation purposes. If the cause of complaint involves an issue of public law or relates to the conduct or decision of a public or statutory body, then treat the matter as one of great urgency, as any application for leave for judicial review must be made 'promptly', within days rather than weeks.

(2) Find out whether he may have insurance cover in respect of the loss of which he is complaining (e.g. house insurance, comprehensive motor insurance); and if so, ensure that he reports immediately to the insurer, and make direct contact with the insurer yourself.

(3) If it appears that he has suffered personal injury or damage to property as a result of criminal conduct, ensure that the incident has been reported, or will be reported at once, to the police and consider whether to give notice of intention to apply for compensation from the Northern Ireland Office.

(4) Arrange an appointment, asking him to bring with him any documents which he has relating to his claim, and as to his income and capital.

(5) Open a file on the case. For the purposes of an ultimate taxation of costs, solicitor (and counsel) must keep a contemporaneous written record of dates and times of all steps taken in the proceedings and date all documents prepared or received.

First appointment

(6) The main questions are: what is his cause of action, what type of injury, loss or damage has he suffered, who appears to be liable, and what form of proceedings in what court should be taken.

(7) Work out the date of expiry of the limitation period and write it prominently on the front of the file.

(8) Take a statement from the client covering all the matters which he knows about or believes, and not confined to matters in his own personal

knowledge; then let him read it over to check that it is a correct record of the interview and sign it.

(9) If it appears that he may be eligible for legal aid, arrange for him to fill in legal aid application forms, including a statement of the facts. Explain to him what prospects he has in litigation, the likely time span and his liability for costs.

(10) Ask him to start the process of checking for witnesses and of collecting and identifying all documents relevant to the case.

The opening shots

(11) Next, write a solicitor's letter to the proposed defendant. This letter should specify the nature of the claim, the time and the place, but should not be too specific about the facts or the legal cause of action. For example-

> We are instructed by our client AB, that on X date at Y place he suffered injury/loss/damage to his property and it appears that you are liable for the same. Unless we receive a satisfactory offer of compensation within 28 days of receipt of this letter, we intend to issue proceedings without further notice.

(12) If you know the identity of the defendant's insurance company and/or of a solicitor already instructed to act for him, send a copy of the letter to them. In other cases advise the defendant to pass the letter on to his insurance company.

(13) Where appropriate, put the defendant on notice that the plaintiff will seek to inspect documents, or machinery etc., so that the defendant will be aware of the need to preserve them.

(14) If there is more than one potential defendant, a *Bullock* letter should be written to all of them.

> We have been instructed by our client AB to bring proceedings in the High Court in respect of his/her injuries in a road accident at (place) on (date). We intend to institute proceedings against both you and X (other defendant) for negligence which caused the personal injury, loss and damage to our client. It is our contention that one or both of you is liable for this. Accordingly, unless within 14 days you undertake to accept full, complete and sole liability for all the plaintiff's damages, we shall commence an action against both you and X and the contents of this letter will be put before the Court on the issue of costs. A similar letter has been sent to X.

(15) Apply as soon as possible for legal aid, having filled in the application form with details of the client's disposable income and capital and a summary of his cause of action. At first the Legal Aid authority may grant a civil aid certificate limited to obtaining counsel's opinion on liability or quantum, or an expert report or medical report. Legal aid must be applied for separately in respect of each client and each separate action, even if they are connected.

Gathering the evidence

(16) Collect evidence of special damages and obtain a medical report on the plaintiff's injuries. This must be done before counsel is asked to draft proceedings as such information is necessary to decide whether to sue in the High Court or a county court.

(17) Be wary of asking a specialist medical expert for a report too soon, before he can give any definite opinion about the injuries: a premature report is an unnecessary expense.

(18) If the client has unsightly wounds, bruises, swelling etc., arrange for good colour photographs of them as they may have disappeared by the time of the trial.

Preparing to commence litigation

(19) Brief counsel with a summary of the case and all available documents.

(20) Ensure that the client consents to proceedings being taken on his behalf.

(21) If he is under 18 years of age, the written consent of his parent or other person as "next friend" must be filed in the High Court office along with a certificate of the solicitor that the plaintiff is a minor (Ord.80 r.3).

(22) Consider whether it will be necessary to bring proceedings for an injunction or other interlocutory order at an early stage in the action. An injunction can even be sought *ex parte* before proceedings commence.

(23) Consider, especially in a medical negligence case, whether to apply by originating summons for discovery from the proposed defendant before action (see para. 11.134).

(24) If the defendant is not to be found in Northern Ireland, consider whether it is necessary to apply *ex parte* for leave to issue and serve a writ outside the jurisdiction. If the defendant is domiciled outside Northern Ireland, consider whether the courts in Northern Ireland have jurisdiction to hear a claim.

- Do not get 'bogged down' in correspondence in an attempt to settle the case. Set a time for yourself, after which you will issue a writ.[1]

Personal injuries action

2.01a If the claim is in respect of an accident, illness or disease, information to be prescribed by regulations about the accident, illness or disease must be given to the the DHSS (CRU) if the claimant receives or claims a listed benefit

---

1 See *Doran* v *Thompson* [1978] IR 223, where the defendant's insurance company wrote that it was investigating the accident and asked for a medical examination; the plaintiff's solicitor expected an admission of liability and let the limitation period expire; it was held that the defendant was not estopped from denying liability and could plead the limitation defence. Even an admission of liability before action does not estop the defendant from pleading a limitation defence: *Maracle* v *Travellers' Indemnity Co* (1991) 80 DLR 4th 652 (SC, Canada)

paid for it (incapacity benefit, jobseeker's allowance, sickness benefit, unemployment benefit, attendance allowance, mobility allowance etc.) (see para. 14.68a).

OTHER STEPS IN PARTICULAR CASES

Employer's liability action

2.02 In a factory or other employment injury case, the following steps in particular should be considered -

(1) Ask the defendant for inspection of the machine and for copies of the accident report book. There is a statutory procedure for obtaining pre-action inspection (para. 11.87) and discovery (para. 11.134).

(2) Write to the Factory Inspectorate of the Department of Economic Development for a copy of the Inspector's report.

(3) Retain the services of a civil engineer to make a report. In Northern Ireland there are few experts in specialist areas, so that a general expert will be used, or in a major case a specialist from elsewhere may have to be retained.

(4) Check the status of the employer: is it an individual trader, a partnership, a limited company?

(5) Find out the name of the defendant's insurance company and write to it.

Road traffic accident action

2.03 In a road traffic accident case, consider the following steps -

(1) View the *locus* of the accident and take a sketch and photographs.

(2) Inspect and take photographs of the vehicles.

(3) Serve notice of the action on the defendant's insurer

(4) Check if the car owner is comprehensively insured, and if so, ensure that the car owner has claimed on the insurance for damage to his vehicle; take instruction from the insurer as to claiming that loss in the name of the insured

(5) Seek a report from the police.

Notice to insurer

2.04 In a road accident case it is essential to serve a notice on the defendant's insurer under Article 98A(1)(a) of the Road Traffic (NI) Order 1981, before or within seven days after the commencement of the action. Such notice, which is in Form 19A, will make a judgment against the defendant enforceable directly against his insurer. The claimant has a right to demand the insurance details of the person claimed against and failure to respond is an offence (Art.96). Under the Road Traffic Order the insurer may be liable to the plaintiff even where he can repudiate liability to indemnify the defendant; and even where the insurer can resist liability to the plaintiff, it generally waives it because of the Motor Insurers' Bureau ("MIB") agreement. The MIB is a non-statutory body set up and funded by the Insurance Companies in agreement with the Government, which satisfies claims for damages by persons injured by uninsured or untraced drivers. In non-road accident cases, it is prudent also to notify the defendant's insurer of the claim.

Police report in road accidents

2.05 Find out whether the police were contacted in relation to the accident: there is a duty under the Road Traffic Order on persons involved as driver or owner of a vehicle to report any accident on a public place in which injury or damage to property occurs, and to give particulars of the driving, ownership and insurance of the vehicles. A police constable who responds to the report of an accident has no statutory duty to investigate, but will do so: (a) if death has resulted (reporting it to the coroner); (b) if there is evidence of an offence such as careless driving, defective tyres, no insurance etc.; (c) to record the event for statistical purposes. The constable's main concern is to look for breaches of the criminal law: he does not act at any stage with a view to civil proceedings. If the accident is minor, he will merely note the names and addresses and insurance particulars of the parties. In a more serious accident where there is suspicion of an offence, he takes measurements at the scene, takes statements, notes the damage and injuries and the weather conditions. He puts these into a complete report on the accident which is considered by senior police (and in some cases the Director of Public Prosecutions). At this stage as solicitor for a party you may on request receive the names and addresses of the drivers and the name of the investigating constable, but no more. Once the police investigation is closed, either by decision not to prosecute or by the conclusion of a criminal prosecution and any appeal, you can write to the Subdivisional Commander for the area where the accident happened for a copy of the police report, on payment of the standard fee.[2] You then receive the complete police report excepting the police summary and comments on criminal liability. If the police took photographs they can be obtained at a cost.[2] If the police "authorised officer" examined any vehicle for defects, his report can be sought.[2]

Other police involvement

2.06 In other matters investigated by the police, such as assaults, a police report containing only names and addresses can be obtained after any criminal proceedings.[2]

2.07 A police officer acting as such will not attend court to testify in a civil action unless a *subpoena* has been served on him. If subpoenaed, he may consent to being interviewed before the trial, for which a fee is payable to the RUC.[2]

EARLY NEGOTIATIONS

2.08 At this early stage before proceedings are issued and major items of costs incurred, the parties may explore the chance of a settlement. A meeting,

---

[2] The current rate is £50 plus £2 per page after 24 pages; £15 per photograph; £2 per page for the authorised officer's report; £2 per page for other reports; no charge for supplying brief particulars on verbal request; £84 for an interview. The complete list is set out in *The Writ* (Law Society of NI, Issue No 72 Sept 1996) p.19.

telephone call or exchange of letters between the plaintiff's solicitor and the defence insurance company's claims manager or solicitor may effect it. Counsel may be involved for either or both parties. The solicitor has no ostensible authority, so that any settlement is ineffective unless within the express authority of the parties. Costs will usually be settled by referring to the Belfast Solicitors' Scale. A solicitor should be cautious about settling a large case without instructing counsel and without waiting for a firm prognosis about the injuries. If he settles at an unfair value, he may have to face an action by his client for negligent advice.

INSTRUCTING COUNSEL

2.09 Except in ordinary debt cases, junior counsel should always be instructed before proceedings commence. He should be asked to advise on whether and where to sue and to draft the writ or other originating process. The solicitor should gather together all relevant information, legal aid certificate, medical and other reports, full statement and instructions from the client, statements from witnesses, and documentation about special damage and loss. Preface the brief with "Instructions to Counsel", containing a summary of the facts, issues and problems as you see them, and stating what you want counsel to do- "draft proceedings", "advise on liability" etc. Send him copies (never originals) of all relevant documents. Save in exceptional cases, counsel must be sent full type-written instructions.[3] If the case appears to be one of public law involving judicial review, send papers to counsel as soon as possible, and select a counsel who will be able to deal with the case expeditiously.

2.10 Counsel should do what is asked of him and advise generally. If asked for an opinion it should be in direct simple language (using the first person), addressed to "instructing solicitor", and referring to the client as "Querist". If citing statute or case law, he should ensure that his opinion as to the law is clearly stated, not buried in the research.

STEPS BY DEFENDANT

2.11 You may be consulted by a client who has received a letter of claim or a writ or other process. Ensure that he brings to consultation the letter or writ, in order to see the nature of the claim and the name of the claimant's solicitor. If the writ has not yet been served, write to the claimant's solicitor indicating your involvement, and, with the client's authority, state that you are authorised to accept service of the writ on his behalf. If not insured, the client may be eligible for legal aid. Full legal aid for court representation can be applied for after the proceedings have commenced. Investigate from your client whether he is insured in respect of the liability claimed, and contact his insurer. The solicitor for the defendant will in many cases receive his instructions from an insurance company, which has by virtue of the policy a right to conduct the action on behalf of the defendant. However, as far as the court and the law is concerned the defence solicitor is acting for the defendant and has a duty to act

---

[3] Bar Handbook 12-01.

reasonably in the interests of both him and the insurer.[4] For instance, it is prudent to ask the defendant whether he has suffered any damage himself, and find out whether he wishes to instruct you to counterclaim. In a road accident case it is desirable that the insured driver/owner should be represented by the same solicitor in defending and in pursuing his own claim unless there is a conflict of interest between him and the insurer.[5]

2.12 In a road accident case the defendant or his insurer is liable under Article 99 of the Road Traffic (NI) Order 1981 to pay a sum not exceeding [currently £2949] for the hospital expenses. He must within seven days after the claim for the injuries is made, give notice to all parties in the action that he has paid or will pay under Article 99 (Ord.22 r.11).

2.13 If the claim against him relates to any accident, injury or disease, the defendant must within 14 days after receipt of the claim notify the 'CRU' of the DHSS (para. 14.66) of details of the claimant.[6] [*to be replaced by*: If the claim against him relates to any accident, injury or disease, the defendant must give prescribed information about the claimant to the 'CRU' of the DHSS (para.14.68a) in a manner and time presribed by regulations.[7]]

---

4 See *Murray* v *Conlan* [1984] 8 NIJB.

5 *Crawford* v *James* [1988] 8 NIJB 19. See also *Talbot* v *Berkshire CC* [1994] QB 290, at 298. There the defendant's solicitor issued a third-party notice for contribution but made no claim for the defendant's own injuries. The defendant was thereby estopped from suing for his own injuries and the solicitor was guilty of negligence.

6 Social Security Administration (NI) Act 1992, s. 90(1); and Regulations SR 1990/85, reg.8.

7 Social Security (Recovery of Benefits (NI) Order 1997, Art.25.

CHAPTER THREE

SETTING UP THE LITIGATION

CHOOSING THE COURT

3.00 A person deciding to initiate legal proceedings must decide first whether they are criminal in nature; if so, proceedings begin by complaint to a Justice of the Peace for proceedings in a magistrates' court. If civil in nature, then subject to statute, proceedings can be commenced in the High Court. If the claim is within the jurisdiction of the county court it should be brought there. Some civil claims (such as rate demands, small ejectments and domestic proceedings) should be brought in the magistrates' court. County courts, the Lands Tribunal, industrial tribunals, the Coroner's Court and others have exclusive jurisdiction over specific types of proceedings under statute. The High Court itself and the Court of Appeal also have exclusive jurisdiction under various statutes.[1]

3.01 If proceedings are to be brought in the High Court, the further choice must be made as to which Division: Queen's Bench, Chancery or Family, a question which is discussed at para. 1.18.

PARTIES

Position and duties of parties

3.02 Every proceeding in a court must be brought by the appropriate person(s) as plaintiff, applicant or complainant, and in nearly all cases, against an appropriate person(s) as defendant or respondent. In actions the parties are called *plaintiff* and *defendant*. In the long-running *Vernon v Bosley* saga,[2] the Court of Appeal has used the experience of that case to articulate the duties of litigants and their counsel in an extended fashion. The plaintiff sued for nervous shock and recovered substantial damages from Sedley J after a lengthy trial, on the basis of expert psychiatric reports that he had a major and lasting mental illness. The Court of Appeal affirmed the award for the illness and was about to enter its judgment when the defendant applied for the appeal to be re-opened. Defence lawyers received an anonymous letter containing reports which the plaintiff had used in a contest over custody of his children in the Family Court, reports which showed that he had made a substantial recovery from his mental problems. The plaintiff and his counsel knew of these reports before the trial at first instance commenced. Stuart-Smith and Thorpe LJJ held that a litigant in civil proceedings has a duty of good faith as follows: he need not reveal facts

---

[1] For a list of statutory jurisdictions of the county court, see the author's *County Court Procedure in NI* (SLS 1985) Appendix B. (A new edition of that work is pending.) For statutory jurisdiction of the High Court see Appendix One of this book.

[2] *Vernon v Bosley (No 2)* [1997] 1 All ER 614.

which are unhelpful to his case, but he must not mislead the Court by stating as fact something which he knows or believes to be untrue, and if he has put forward a fact *bona fide* to the Court or his opponent and he later finds that that fact is or has become untrue, his duty is to disclose the change of circumstances. This latter duty continues up to the conclusion of the proceedings, including any appeal proceedings. Counsel must advise the litigant to comply with this duty and must cease to act if the litigant does not; or even (*per* Thorpe LJ) disclose the facts to the opponent. Evans LJ agreed broadly that that there should be a disclosure, but only up the end of the evidence, and in the present case disagreed that the change of prognosis was so radical as to require disclosure.

3.03 In a straightforward action the conduct of the proceedings, that is the discretion as to how and whether to prosecute the proceedings, rests on the plaintiff. However, the Court may give conduct of proceedings to any person (Ord.15 r.18). The need for this usually arises in proceedings under a Chancery judgment (see para. 18.56) and in consolidated actions (see para. 3.35). Generally conduct is given to a plaintiff, or in proceedings for sale of property to the holder of the legal title. Conduct may be refused or removed from a party who has delayed unreasonably. This rule includes proceedings not yet commenced but which are directed in the course of existing proceedings.[3]

PRIVATE INDIVIDUALS

3.04 *Unknown or untraced.* If a person has disappeared and cannot be declared dead, the law of Northern Ireland makes no provision for representing his rights and liabilities, nor does it recognise the title of a person under foreign law.[4] His interests can be represented: (a) by power of attorney executed before disappearance; (b) by the Official Solicitor; (c) in a representative action (Ord.15 r.12); (d) by representation order in administration suit (Ord.15 r.13); (e) by payment of money awarded to him into court. If an injunction or other order is sought against a person of unknown name, such as a squatter, writs and orders can be issued against "John Doe" and served on him in that name, with liberty for either party to apply to substitute the real name. Where an order is sought against a group of agitators, they can be issued against "John Doe, Jane Doe and persons unknown".[5]

3.05 *Bankrupt.* The Insolvency (NI) Order 1989 provides that in litigation concerning property, only the trustee, with the sanction of the creditors' committee or of the Insolvency Court, can sue or defend on behalf of a person declared bankrupt (Arts.258, 287, Sch.3). Leave of the Court is necessary to sue an undischarged bankrupt (Art.258).

3.06 *Action after death.* Where a person in whom a cause of action has vested dies (whether the death arises out of the cause of action or independently), the cause of action surviving,[6] his personal representative may

---

[3] *McKinlay* v *Mackey* [1895] 1 IR 302, at 306.

[4] *Kamouh* v *AEI* [1980] QB 199.

[5] *MacMillan Bloedel* v *Simpson* (1996) 137 DLR 4th 633 (SC, Canada).

[6] See further para. 11.39.

sue on behalf of the estate under section 14 of the Law Reform (Miscellaneous Provisions) Act (NI) 1937. If the death arises out of the event, an action may be brought[7] under the Fatal Accidents (NI) Order 1977[8] for the benefit of those relatives of the deceased specified in Article 2. The claim is brought by or in the name of the personal representative, but if there is none or if he has not sued within six months of the death, a dependant may sue (1977 Order, Art.4(1)(2)). Premature action by the dependant is irregular but not void unless the personal representative has already sued.[9] One action may be brought in respect of the same subject of complaint (Art.4(3)). If the personal representative sues, the Court will not allow the dependants to join as co-plaintiffs.[10] If the victim received compensation by judgment or settlement before his death, there is no cause of action surviving for the dependants,[11] but an award of provisional damages is no bar to a fatal accident action (para. 14.76).

Party under disability

Minors (aged under 18)

3.07 A minor conducts proceedings under the dominion of an adult (usually his parent or guardian). Such adult is called a "next friend" if the minor is suing or claiming; or a "guardian *ad litem*" if defending, counterclaiming or intervening or appearing as noticed party in proceedings under a judgment. Any act to be done by a party under the RSC is to be done by the next friend/guardian; and must be done through a solicitor (Ord.80 r.2). The next friend/guardian is appointed without a court order by lodging the written consent and a certificate of the party's solicitor in the office and he is entitled to act unless and until the Court by order appoints someone else (Ord.80 r.3). The party cannot enter an appearance or appear at any hearing until such appointment. If a minor plaintiff sues without a next friend, the defendant should apply under Order 12 rule 8 to set aside the writ, or to stay the action. In an action, no further proceeding can be taken against a minor defendant[12] who is in default of appearance, until a guardian *ad litem* has been appointed on application of the plaintiff. In proceedings by originating process in which no appearance is required, or in proceedings under a Chancery judgment, the Court may appoint a guardian at the hearing (Ord.80 r.4). If a nominee of the plaintiff is appointed guardian, the plaintiff pays his costs and adds them to the costs payable by the defendant.[13] If any party is a ward of court, that must be stated on the writ or originating process; and if a minor becomes a ward, the party acting on his behalf must have the proceedings amended accordingly (Ord.89 r.6).

3.08 Any document to be served personally, and any originating process, must be served not on the minor but on his parent, guardian or person with

---

7 Usually it is joined in the same action with a Law Reform Act claim.
8 As extensively amended by the Administration of Justice Act 1982, Sch. 6.
9 *Austin* v *Hart* [1983] 2 AC 641.
10 *Steele* v *GNR* (1890) 26 LR Ir 96.
11 *Mahon* v *Burke* [1991] 2 IR 495.
12 Including a defendant to a counterclaim, or third party.
13 *Woods* v *McCann* (1901) 35 ILTR 210.

whom he resides, but an order requiring him to do or not to do an act, a notice of motion for committal, and a *subpoena*, must be served on the minor (Ord.80 r.13). In his pleading, failure to deal with an allegation is not treated as an admission (Ord.80 r.6). Any money recovered for a minor by settlement is not binding and must be approved by a judge (Ord.80 r.8). Any money recovered must be dealt with under directions of the Court (Ord.80 r.10), and if paid into court the Court may appoint a guardian of his estate. When the minor reaches the age of 18 a note should be filed in the Office and notice given to the other parties: thereupon he assumes full control over the proceedings, and may adopt or repudiate the proceedings on his behalf.[14]

3.09 The *next friend* is *dominus litis* on procedural decisions in the action. He can choose and sack the solicitor;[15] and the action cannot be compromised without his authority. Any compromise, undertaking not to appeal or abandonment of appeal must also be approved by the Court. If he dies a new next friend can be appointed *ex parte*.[16] If he has an adverse interest or acts contrary to the interests of the minor, for example by refusing a good offer of compromise, he can be removed. He must undertake to be liable for costs, with a right of indemnity from the minor's estate if he acts *bona fide* and reasonably.[17]

The guardian *ad litem* is not personally liable for costs unless he acts negligently or improperly.

3.10 Order 89, made under section 29 of the Judicature Act, provides that where a cause or matter affecting a minor comes before a judge (the "seised judge") he may make the minor a ward of court and transfer the matter to the judge assigned to such matters or refer the question to the assigned judge, or dispose of the question himself (Ord.89 r.3) and he furnishes a report to the Office of Care and Protection (Ord.89 r.4). If the seised judge makes a wardship order or an order affecting a ward, a copy of the order is transmitted to the Office of Care and Protection (Ord.89 r.7).

The Congenital Disabilities (Civil Liability) Act 1976 deals with the rights of a child born disabled.

In child care proceedings a child (defined as a person not over 18 years) must be represented by a guardian *ad litem*, or directly by a solicitor.[18]

Patients

3.11 A "patient" is a person suffering or apparently suffering from a mental disorder as defined by Article 3 of the Mental Health (NI) Order 1986. He is a person under disability and the rules and procedures relating to minors apply,

---

[14] White Book (1997) 80/2/12; *Almack* v *Moore* (1878) 2 LR Ir 90. Current practice seems to be to for an *ex parte* order to be made by a master amending the title of the action.

[15] *Almack* v *Moore* (1878) 2 LR Ir 90.

[16] *Daly* v *Daly* (1882) 9 LR Ir 383. Where the minor has disappeared without trace (falling off a bridge into a river) but cannot yet be presumed dead, the next friend can agree a settlement and the Court can approve it, taking into account that the minor is probably dead: *Sivret* v *New Brunswick Power Corp* (1995) 121 DLR 4th 274 (CA, New Brunswick).

[17] *McNicholl* v *Neely* [1983] NI 43, at 49H.

[18] Children (NI) Order 1995, Art.60.

with the following modifications. It is the duty of a Health Board, private hospital or nursing home management, or the Mental Health Commission to notify the Office of Care and Protection[19] of any person whose affairs need to be taken over (Art.107). Such person can be made a patient by the High Court taking control of his property and affairs (through the Office of Care and Protection) under Articles 97-109; and it may give directions and authorisations for the conduct of legal proceedings for the patient (Art.99(1)(i)). Any person authorised under the 1986 Order (usually a controller appointed by the High Court under Art.101) is entitled to be the next friend/guardian, and is appointed by lodging his written consent and a sealed copy of the authorisation in the office. If not so authorised the person is appointed by lodging his written consent and a certificate of the patient's solicitor (Ord.80 r.3(2)(6)). If a party is not made a patient under those provisions, a next friend/guardian can only act if there is substantial evidence of incapacity.[20] A plaintiff who disputes his incapacity can apply to have himself struck out from the action. If he recovers his health he should apply for an order discharging the next friend/guardian. Service of documents is in the same way as for a minor, the person to be served being the authorised person or person with whom he resides. If any party is a patient whose affairs are under the control of the Court, that fact must be stated on the writ or originating process; and if a person becomes such a patient, the party acting on his behalf must have the proceedings amended accordingly (Ord.89 r.6). Where a party in pending proceedings becomes such a patient, application must be made to the Court to appoint a next friend/guardian (Ord.80 r.3(4)).

3.12 Order 89 provides that where a cause or matter affecting a patient comes before a judge (the 'seised judge') he may refer the question to the assigned judge, or dispose of the question himself (Ord.89 r.3) and he furnishes a report to the Office of Care and Protection (Ord.89 r.4). If the seised judge makes an order which affects a patient or brings a person within the jurisdiction of the Office of Care and Protection a copy of the order is transmitted to the Office (Ord.89 r.7).

PRIVATE BODIES OF PERSONS

Companies

3.13 A body incorporated under the Companies (NI) Order 1986, previous Companies Acts or similar legislation in foreign countries[21] or by special Act or charter is a corporate legal person. Any company must register in the Companies Registry if it is incorporated in Northern Ireland (Art.295) or if it has a place of business in Northern Ireland (Art.641 if incorporated in Great Britain or Gibraltar; Art.640A if incorporated elsewhere). A change of name of a company does not make proceedings defective (Art.38(7)). A shareholder is not debarred from recovering damages against the company (Art.121A). The

---

[19] Within 14 days: Ord.109 r.3.

[20] *Watson* v *Knilans* (1874) 8 ILTR 157.

[21] A foreign corporation can sue or be sued if its continued existence is recognized by the law of the country of incorporation. Recognition of company registered in an unrecognized state: see Foreign Corporations Act 1991.

Dept of Economic Development can in certain circumstances bring proceedings in the name of a company (Art.431). A dissolved company cannot sue or be sued,[22] but on application of the liquidator or a person interested within two years[23] of the dissolution, the High Court may declare the dissolution void (Art.602). Leave of the winding-up court is necessary to bring or continue an action against a company in liquidation.[24] As to service of documents on a company, see para. 6.01.

3.14 A registered credit union is a corporate body under the Credit Unions (NI) Order 1985 (Art.5). A friendly society may be incorporated under the Friendly Societies Act 1992 (ss.5-8). An unincorporated friendly society may sue or be sued in the name of its trustees under the Friendly Societies Act 1974 (s.103).[25]

Firms

3.15 A firm is "persons who have entered into partnership with one another" (Partnership Act 1890, s.4). 'Partnership' is the relation between persons carrying on business in common with a view to profit (s.1).[26] It is not a legal person. Firms, companies and individuals who trade under a label which does not consist of their names, must state full names and an address for service on all letters, invoices, orders etc.; and an action to enforce a business contract concluded during non-compliance must be dismissed if it has prevented the defendant from pursuing a claim under the contract or caused him financial loss, unless the Court is satisfied that it is just to allow the action.[27] Partners are jointly liable for each other's acts in the business, and their estates are severally liable (1890 Act ss.5-12). A person holding himself out as a partner is liable to anyone who gives credit on faith thereof (s.14).

3.16 Persons[28] who were partners when a cause of action accrued, carrying on business within Northern Ireland may sue or be sued in the name of the firm (Ord.81 r.1). If the plaintiff or defendant is a firm name, the opposing party may serve notice requiring a statement of the names and addresses of all the partners, and in default the Court may so order; thereafter the action continues as if those names appeared on the writ (Ord.81 r.2). The rest of Order 81 provides for service on a firm, appearance by the partners, enforcement of judgment, and actions between partners. Order 81 applies also to actions by originating summons (Ord.81 r.7). Order 81 only applies if the firm name is used alone in the title of the action, as where it says "Steptoe and Son"; but if it

---

22 *Dickson* v *Blackstaff Weaving* [1989] NI 197.

23 The time limit was increased to 12 years by the Insolvency (NI) Order 1989, Sch.9 Pt.I para.19; but the Companies (No 2) (NI) Order 1990, Art.75 restored the two year limit, stating that the limit does not apply in personal injury/death cases.

24 Insolvency (NI) Order 1989, Art.110.

25 Extended to Northern Ireland by the 1992 Act.

26 Authorities in the English Court of Appeal conflict as to whether partners can act independently in proceedings: see *Sutherland* v *Gustar* [1994] Ch 305 (3 judges); *Mephistopheles Debt Collection* v *Lotay* [1994] 1 WLR 1064 (2 judges).

27 Business Names (NI) Order 1986, Arts.6 and 7. The Order applies to a person or body "carrying on business", and that can include an educational establishment: *London College of Science Ltd* v *Islington LBC*, 'The Times' 23 July 1996 (CA).

28 Human: *In re a debtor* [1929] IR 139.

says "Harold Steptoe and Albert Steptoe, t/a Steptoe and Son" that simply makes the two men co-parties in the normal way. Most practitioners overlook this point.

Individual trader

3.17 Order 81 applies also to an action against (but not by) an individual carrying on business in a name other than his own *whether or not he is within Northern Ireland*[29] (Ord.81 r.8).

Other Associations

3.18 A non-proprietary *member's club* is not a legal person and cannot be a party in its own name, but a named member can represent the others under Order 15 rule 12. A member of the club cannot sue a club representative.[30] A *proprietary club* may sue or be sued as a trust or as a firm. A *commercial club* is a firm. *Trusts* are usually represented by the trustees (see para. 3.40). *Trade Unions* and *Employers' Associations* can sue and be sued under the Industrial Relations (NI) Order 1992 (Arts.3 and 4).

Suing on the right of another

3.19 As to suing by trustee or beneficiary to enforce equitable rights see para. 3.40. By the Law Reform (Husband and Wife) Act (NI) 1964, a life or endowment insurance policy for the benefit of a spouse or child of the holder is a trust in their favour (s.4) and a contract for the benefit of a spouse or child is directly enforceable by them (s.5). The principle of subrogation[31] has never been recognised by English common law countries. Some cases are created by statute.[32] Equity has developed the doctrine in the case of indemnity: a person who pays under an indemnity is subrogated to the rights of the indemnitee and can sue in his name or enforce an equitable lien over any money received by the indemnitee.[33] In respect of a debt incurred by the personal representative in administering the estate, the creditor is subrogated to the personal representative's right of indemnity from the estate and may thus claim the debt against the estate;[34] so also, *semble*, a creditor of a trustee.

Subject to the above principles, the law generally regards the assignment of the fruits of a cause of action and any action solely for the benefit of another as maintenance and champerty and contrary to public policy;[35] except the *bona fide* assignment of a debt or other chose in action.[36] An assignee, legal or equitable, of a chose in action can sue in his own name to enforce it; and in the

---

29 The White Book (1997) 81/9/4 continues to say that the writ cannot be served on him abroad, but that ignores the amendment introduced as shown by the italicised words after the Civil Jurisdiction and Judgments Act 1982.

30 *McKinley* v *Montgomery* [1993] 11 NIJB 1 (CA).

31 That if X owes money to Y and Y owes money to Z, Z can step into the shoes of Y and sue X

32 E.g. the Third Parties (Rights against Insurers) Act (NI) 1930 (para. 16.13); Mercantile Law Amendment Act 1856, s.5 (para. 10.05).

33 See *Napier* v *Hunter* [1993] AC 713; *Seagate Technology* v *Goh Han Kim* [1996] 1 LRC 724, at 742-3 (Singapore).

34 *In re Geary* [1939] NI 152.

35 See *Giles* v *Thompson* [1994] 1 AC 142; *Fraser* v *Buckle* [1996] 1 IR 1 (SC).

36 *Camdex International* v *Bank of Zambia* [1996] 3 All ER 431 (CA).

case of an equitable assignment, each has title to sue on it but the court will normally require the other to be made a party.[37]

PUBLIC BODIES

3.20 A recognised foreign government can sue except on its penal, revenue or political laws, but it cannot generally be sued unless it submits to the jurisdiction.[38] Diplomats, consuls, their staff and families have some immunity from suit.[39]

3.21 Northern Ireland Ministries (now called Departments) are corporate bodies.[40] NI Departments and UK Departments are branches of the Crown with no distinction.[41] In law, all of Her Majesty's Secretaries of State are as one person, so that any one can exercise all the powers of the others.[42] The Crown Solicitor can act for Ministers and Departments of the United Kingdom Government and, so far as permitted by the Attorney-General, for executive authorities in Northern Ireland.[43] The Crown can sue and be sued in accordance with the Crown Proceedings Act 1947.[44] In the Act, "civil proceedings" by or against the Crown includes proceedings in the High Court or county court for recovery of a fine or penalty, and in Parts III and IV (ss.24-33) any proceedings in which the Crown, an officer, a Department or the Attorney-General is a party, excluding judicial review (s.38). For the purposes of Parts II-IV (ss.13-33) of the Act 'relator' actions are excluded (ss.23,38). For the purposes of Part II (ss.13-23) proceedings relating to Northern Ireland charities and the Land Registry are excluded (s.23). All civil proceedings in the High Court by or against the Crown are to be had under rules of court (s.13).[45] The Department of Finance and Personnel publishes an HMSO list of authorised government departments with the name and address of their solicitors, and civil proceedings by or against the Crown may be issued by or against the appropriate Department or the Attorney-General (s.17). If proceedings are brought against the Attorney-General or a Department, application may be

---

[37] *Three Rivers DC* v *Bank of England* [1996] QB 292 (CA).

[38] State Immunity Act 1978; exceptions include commercial contracts, employment, injury, damage, land, where the matter arises in the United Kingdom. See *Ahmed* v *Government of Saudi Arabia* [1996] ICR 25 (CA). The Act extends to bodies exercising the broad functions of government such as police: *Propend Finance* v *Sing*, 'The Times' 2 May 1997 (CA). In the Republic of Ireland immunity is governed still by common law: as to the immunity of the UK Government for tort committed by a soldier on the south side of the border, see *McElhinney* v *Williams* [1995] 3 IR 382 (SC).

[39] See *Kuwait Airways* v *Iraqi Airways* [1995] 1 WLR 1147. And see the Diplomatic Privileges Act 1964; Consular Relations Act 1968; International Organisations Acts 1968 and 1981; Commonwealth Countries and Republic of Ireland (Immunities and Privileges) Order 1985 (SI 1985/1983); White Book (1997) Vol. 2 [4656].

[40] Ministries of Northern Ireland Act (NI) 1921, s.2; Northern Ireland Act 1974, Sch.1.

[41] *McAllister* v *NI Office* [1988] NI 606, at 609-10.

[42] *In re Quinn* [1996] 10 BNIL 36 (Kerr J).

[43] Northern Ireland Constitution Act 1973, s.35. As to executive functions in Northern Ireland: see the Northern Ireland Constitution Act 1973, ss.7-11 and the Northern Ireland Act 1974, Sch.1 para..2.

[44] As applied to Northern Ireland by SI 1981/233.

[45] Order 77 provides several modifications of the RSC in civil proceedings to which the Crown is a party, which are noted at the appropriate parts of this book.

made to substitute the proper party (see para. 11.28). The Crown is bound by the Limitation (NI) Order 1989 save in suing for the recovery of taxes and duties and statutory forfeiture (Art.74 thereof). Civil proceedings by or against the Crown are tried at the Royal Courts of Justice, Belfast unless the Court otherwise directs or the Crown consents.[46]

3.22 'The Crown' includes a body which is an agent of the Crown;[47] it is such if so described by statute or if it exercises governmental functions.[48] An electoral officer is an agent of the Crown,[49] and the Chief Constable of the RUC.[50] But for the purposes of proceedings to which the 1947 Act applies, 'the Crown' has a narrower meaning of a Government Department and the Attorney-General.[51] The Crown is liable for tort only in the capacity of United Kingdom or Northern Ireland Government, as to which the certificate of a Secretary of State is conclusive.[52] As before 1947, an individual Crown servant can be sued for a tort committed by him (White Book (1997), 77/1/1); and a government minister or official sued for acts done by him is liable like any citizen.[53]

3.23 The Attorney-General can sue to enforce the rights of the public, to restrain interference with a public right, to compel performance of a public duty, or to abate a public nuisance. He may do so in a '*relator action*', entitled "Attorney-General (at the relation of AB)", where AB is a private citizen who desires to enforce the civil or criminal law without necessarily having a legal interest.[54] Before the action is commenced the citizen must through his solicitor file in the office a written authorisation (Ord.15 r.11). A relator action is not covered by sections 13 to 40 of the Crown Proceedings Act.

3.24 A local authority is a corporation aggregate; a council may prosecute or defend to protect or promote the interests of itself, the inhabitants or the district, by section 116 of the Local Government Act (NI) 1972.[55] State schools are legally part of the area Education and Library Board. State hospitals are part of the area Health and Social Services Board. The Chief Constable is liable for torts committed by police, under the Police Act (NI) 1970 (s.14).[56]

JOINDER OF CAUSES OF ACTION

3.25 One action may join any cause of action between the plaintiff and the defendant acting in the same capacity, or the capacity of personal representative if the personal claim is with reference to the estate (Ord.15 r.1). Any other

---

46 Crown Proceedings Act, s.19; Ord.77 r.12.
47 *British Medical Association* v *Greater Glasgow Health Board* [1989] AC 1211.
48 See *Dixon* v *Forster* [1952] NI 24; *O'Neill* v *DHSS (No 2)* [1986] NI 290.
49 *Burke* v *Patterson* [1986] NI 1, at 6.
50 *Carlisle* v *Chief Constable* [1988] NI 307.
51 *British Medical Association* v *Greater Glasgow Health Board* [1989] AC 1211.
52 Crown Proceedings Act, s.40(2)(3); *In re Savage* [1991] NI 103.
53 *M* v *Home Office* [1994] 1 AC 377.
54 See *Incorporated Law Society* v *Carroll* [1995] 3 IR 145 (SC).
55 See White Book (1997) 15/11/5.
56 Vicarious liability of the Chief Constable, see *Graham* v *McPherson* [1991] NI 1.

claim may be joined by leave obtained *ex parte* on affidavit before commencement of the action. The same rule applies to joinder of counterclaims (Ord.15 r.2(2)). The rule applies to joinder of causes of action by or against one party, or parties jointly.[57] An alternative cause of action can be joined against the defendant, even if inconsistent.[58] A "cause of action" in this context means the combination of such facts which entitle the plaintiff to a judgment,[59] not the legal label of trespass, nuisance etc.[60] Each cause of action should be stated in separate paragraphs in the indorsement.

3.26 If the writ joins causes of action improperly without leave, the defendant waives the irregularity by taking any step to defend the action other than appearing.[61] Whether joinder is proper or not, he may apply at any time for separate trials or other order if the joinder may cause embarrassment, delay or other inconvenience (Ord.15 r.5(1)).

Splitting a cause of action

3.27 "A claimant ... must prove and recover damages arising from one and the same cause of action, once and for all".[62] That applies to recovery by judgment, compromise or acceptance of a lodgment. Where there are several items in a tradesman's bill as part of a course of dealing, the plaintiff cannot sue separately on each even though strictly there are separate contracts.[63] The same is true for items of piece-work.[64] Items from different courses of dealing do not have to be sued for together merely because the plaintiff entered them in one book and put them on one account which he sent to the defendant.[65] Where the plaintiff lent a sum to the defendant and lent another sum four months later, Pennefather B held that he could sue separately for each.[66]

3.28 If a comprehensively insured motor vehicle driver/owner has recovered his £50 excess from the other driver, a second action in his name by his insurer is an abuse of court.[67] A plaintiff can sue separately in respect of an accident for damage to his property and injury to his person.[68] A personal representative can sue separately for damage to the deceased's property and for fatal accident damages.[69] A person cannot sue separately for damage caused by the carrier to different goods in one consignment.[70]

---

57 *Smurthwaite* v *Hannay* [1894] AC 494. Joinder of causes of action by or against different parties must come within Ord.15 r.4.
58 *McCurdy* v *McFall* (1902) 36 ILTR 52.
59 *Letang* v *Cooper* [1965] 1 QB 232.
60 *O'Keeffe* v *Walsh* [1903] 2 IR 681, at 718.
61 *Hunt* v *Worsfold* [1896] 2 Ch 224.
62 *Clark* v *Urquhart* [1930] AC 28, at 54 (NI), *per* Lord Sumner. Where the wrong is committed or damage suffered in more than one Brussels Convention State or part of the United Kingdom, separate actions can be brought in each: see para. 1.14.
63 *Wood* v *Perry* (1849) 3 Ex 442 (154 ER 918).
64 *Cairns* v *Whelan* (1828) 1 Hud & Br 552.
65 *Brunskill* v *Powell* (1850) 19 LJ Ex 362.
66 Anonymous decision cited in Copinger p.41.
67 *Buckland* v *Palmer* [1984] 1 WLR 1109.
68 *Davidson* v *North Down Quarries* [1988] NI 214.
69 *Barnett* v *Lucas* (1872) IR 6 CL 247.
70 *Russell* v *Waterford & Limerick Rly* (1885) 16 LR Ir 314.

3.29 In *Clarke* v *Midland Great Western Rly*,[71] the plaintiff had recovered damages for interference with the flow of his stream due to the defendant's trespass; then without further trespass the flow later deteriorated: it was held that he could sue for further damages. Although trespass is actionable *per se*, the trespasser continues to be liable as long as the effect of his trespass remains operative. Walker C said (at p.318): "Let us see .. whether we can find not only fresh damage but a continuance of the cause of damage". On the other hand, in *Nugent* v *Keady UDC*,[72] an action for interference with easement of support, damages were assessed once and for all. In *Gardiner* v *Mathewson*[73] the plaintiff obtained judgment against the seller for the price of a cow which was warranted sound but had a fatal disease; later four other cows owned by the plaintiff died from the disease contracted from the seller's cow; Monaghan CJ dismissed a fresh action as being founded on the same cause of action.

3.30 If a plaintiff sues for part of his cause of action[70] or recovers too small a sum,[74] a second action on that cause can be dismissed on the basis of *res judicata*. The proper course is to have the first judgment set aside and then sue afresh,[75] or to have the judgment amended (see para. 8.14).

JOINDER OF PARTIES

3.31 Persons may be joined as plaintiffs or defendants in one action if there is some common issue of law or fact; and if all relief claimed in the action whether joint, several or alternative arises from the same transaction or series of transactions;[76] and otherwise only by leave (Ord.15 r.4(1)). If joinder is improper the Court may: (a) strike out the action;[77] (b) strike out a party; (c) allow the action to continue as constituted; or (d) put the plaintiff(s) on election as to which claim will continue.[78] Even if joinder is within the rule, separa.te trials may be ordered if the joinder may cause embarrassment, inconvenience or delay (Ord.15 r.5(1)). Order 15 rule 4 may be subject to the old rule in Chancery cases that all persons interested in the subject-matter (other than beneficiaries represented by the trustee) may be joined as plaintiffs or defendants (see para. 3.33).

Plaintiffs

3.32 A person can only be a plaintiff by his consent, and if not he should apply to be struck out.[79] Except in a probate action,[80] all persons jointly entitled must, save by statute or leave, be joined as plaintiffs, and any who refuses must

---

71 [1895] 2 IR 294.
72 (1912) 46 ILTR 221.
73 (1854) 6 Ir Jur OS 147.
74 *Sanders* v *Hamilton* (1907) 96 LT 679; *Blizard* v *Mulloy* (1887) 21 ILTR 11.
75 *Chamberlain* v *Deputy Commr of Taxation* (1988) 164 CLR 502 (HC of Aus).
76 I.e. the right or liability is connected in substance, though it may have separate elements: *Peddie* v *Kyle* [1900] 2 IR 265; *O'Keefe* v *Walsh* [1903] 2 IR 681; *O'Rorke* v *Healy* (1903) 37 ILTR 69.
77 *Reddy* v *Dublin Corp* [1941] IR 255.
78 *Cuddy* v *McMahon* (1893) 27 ILTR 101.
79 *Montgomery* v *Montgomery* (1856) 6 ICLR 522.
80 Where the right to cite persons jointly entitled exists.

be made a defendant, in which case he is entitled to an indemnity for costs from the plaintiff (Ord.15 r.4(2)). Plaintiffs joined in one action must make a case which does not conflict with each other and must have the same solicitor,[81] save in exceptional circumstances.

Defendants

3.33 In common law actions in contract or tort, the plaintiff can choose to sue any one defendant and does not have to sue all who are liable. Judgment against one person who is liable for debt or damage does not bar pursuit against any other person jointly (or severally) liable, by virtue of section 3 of the Civil Liability (Contribution) Act 1978.[82] Judgment against one person liable in the alternative bars pursuit of the other.[83] If the plaintiff recovers judgment against two defendants jointly liable for damage, the proper order is that each defendant is liable for the total damages and costs, with right of contribution *inter se*.[84] Due to section 6 of the 1978 Act, the right of contribution *inter se* arises between them whether liable in tort, breach of contract, breach of trust etc. In *Collings* v *Wade*,[85] the defendants A and B were found jointly liable; A paid the whole judgment to the plaintiff; seven years later B died and life insurance money was payable to his estate; A was granted an order to revive the proceedings against the executor for contribution. No person should be made a defendant against whom no relief is claimed,[86] nor should he be joined solely for discovery or costs, unless he is liable on the cause of action.[87] In Chancery actions, the practice is that any person who has or claims an interest in the subject-matter may be joined as a defendant; a beneficiary suing a trustee should join all living trustees.[88] If the plaintiff is in doubt as to who is liable he can join defendants as liable in the alternative, usually preceded by a '*Bullock* letter' (para. 2.01, point 14). The benefit of this is seen in the law on submission of no case to answer (para. 14.31) and in costs (para. 17.51).

Misjoinder of parties

3.34 Misjoinder of parties is not fatal in any proceedings (see para. 11.24). Objection to misjoinder may be taken at any stage up to the trial (White Book (1997) 15/4/11).

CONSOLIDATION, HEARING TOGETHER ETC.

3.35 Proceedings pending in one Division may be ordered to be consolidated or to be heard together or consecutively, or one stayed till the determination of the other under Order 4 rule 5(1) if: (a) a common legal or factual question

---

81 So also, *semble*, defendants joining in the same Defence and/or Counterclaim.
82 Though s.4 restricts the right to costs if the claim is for damages: see para. 17.10.
83 *McConnell* v *Lombard & Ulster* [1982] NI 203.
84 *Dawson* v *McClelland* [1899] 2 IR 486; *Newry Salt Works* v *MacDonnell* [1903] 2 IR 454 (debt case; liability for costs); *Clarke* v *McLaughlin & Harvey* [1978] 2 NIJB.
85 [1903] 1 IR 89.
86 *Sandes* v *Dublin United Tramways* (1883) 12 LR Ir 206, reversed on other ground: *ibid.* p.424.
87 *O'Shea* v *Cork RDC* [1914] 1 IR 16, at 22 (*obiter*) (but see para. 11.131).
88 *O'Keeffe* v *Walsh* [1903] 2 IR 681, at 686-9, 708-9, 713-5. The same principles apply equally where a Chancery-type action is brought in another Division.

arises; (b) the claims arise out of the same transaction(s); or (c) it is desirable for some other reason. Even if only heard together, the Court may treat the parties as party to both for the purpose of awarding costs (Ord.4 r.5(2)). By ordering only a hearing together, the Court thereby allows the plaintiffs to retain separate solicitors,[89] and also allows a person to remain as defendant in one action and plaintiff in the other. In a consolidated action, the evidence of witnesses is admissible for and against every party. If actions are only heard together, the evidence must be separated in the judge's mind, because for example the testimony of one defendant is not admissible against the other.[90] In consolidated actions there is only one judgment. In actions heard together there are separate judgments.

3.36 Actions can be consolidated only if there is an important common question, as where they arise from substantially the same transaction,[91] or from one road accident;[92] and not merely because the witnesses are the same.[93] In *Crawford* v *James*,[94] where a motor cyclist sued for his injuries against the driver and owner of the car, and the car owner sued separately for damage to the car against the cyclist, it was held proper to consolidate the actions and order that the car owner be represented by the same solicitor and counsel, there being no conflict of interest between him and his insurer. In a road accident case there is no point in consolidating or hearing together if liability is agreed.[95] The saving of costs and inconvenience is balanced against the risk of confusion or miscarriage of justice.[96] Where one plaintiff sues several persons separately in respect of substantially the same libel, slander or malicious falsehood, the actions can be consolidated.[97] Actions can be consolidated or heard together on one issue (e.g. liability) and be kept separate for assessment of damages. Proceedings of a different type (e.g. a ordinary action and an application under a statute) cannot be consolidated, though they may be heard together.[98]

Representative and "test" actions

3.37 Where numerous[99] persons have the same interest in proceedings, the proceedings may be brought by or against one as representative of all; and during proceedings the plaintiff may apply for a person to be representative defendant; judgment binds the represented persons[100] though it cannot be enforced against them without leave (Ord.15 r.12). The rule should be

---

89 *Brady* v *Macdonald* [1931] NI 157.
90 Cf. *Hedley* v *Sparrow* [1964] NI 72; and see *Higgins* v *Dorries* [1965] Qd R 389; [1965] Aust Law Digest 281.
91 *O'Toole* v *Haughton* (1924) 58 ILTR 160.
92 *McFall* v *McCredy* [1957] NI 73 (tried together).
93 *O'Gorman* v *Harding* (1884) 18 ILTR 93.
94 [1988] 8 NIJB 19.
95 *Lynn* v *Brand* [1959] NI 140.
96 *Duffy* v *News Group* [1992] 2 IR 369.
97 Law of Libel Amendment Act 1888, s.5; Defamation Act (NI) 1955, s.13
98 *O'Neill* v *Ryanair (No 2)* [1992]1 IR 160; though it was done in *Irish Press* v *Ingersoll Ltd* [1995] 2 ILRM 270.
99 Five is not numerous unless the subject-matter is small or the other persons consent: *Re Braybrook* [1916] WN 74.
100 *Carnie* v *Esanda Finance Corp* (1995) 69 ALJR 206 (HC of Aus).

interpreted liberally: persons may have the same interest even if their claims arise under a separate transactions or tort; and provided that it is clear whether any person is a member of the class it is not necessary to know the names of all persons in the class.[100] The persons are not bound if they show fraud or collusion or that the case was not fairly contested.[101]

3.38 In proceedings concerning a deceased's estate, trust property or construction of an instrument, the Court may appoint a person to represent any persons or class of persons who have or may have a present or future interest, where they cannot be ascertained or traced or where it is otherwise expedient, and they are bound by any judgment or approved compromise (Ord.15 r.13).

3.39 Instead of consolidating or hearing all the actions together, Order 4 rule 5 enables the Court to hear one as a "test action" and stay the others pending its resolution. Save by their consent the parties in the stayed actions are not bound by any finding in the test action, unless there is a relationship of privity which attracts the operation of *res judicata*.[102] The only coercive power of the Court is to stay the other actions;[103] but if the selected action fails, the continuation of the other actions may be struck out as an abuse of process.[104]

REPRESENTATION OF ESTATES AND TRUSTS

3.40 Trustees and personal representatives represent the beneficiaries (Ord.15 r.14).[105] A beneficiary is bound by any judgment unless the trustees have acted in a way impeachable under trust law. A beneficiary should be a party: (a) if he has a separate interest; (b) if he is an accounting party; (c) if the litigation is between the trustees or between the estate and a person who is or claims to be a beneficiary; or (d) if trustees and beneficiaries claim under different instruments. A beneficiary can sue in the name of the trustee against an outsider, upon offering an indemnity to the trustee.[106] A proper *cestui qui trust* can sue to enforce the trust against an outsider without prior demand on the trustee.[107] Proof of consent of a trustee to act is by verified signature (Ord.38 r.9). The general rule is that all living trustees must be joined. If one refuses to sue he should be made a defendant. So also all personal representatives who have taken out a grant of probate or letters of administration. Where a trustee, constructive trustee or personal representative who is sued as such cannot be found despite diligent search for service on him, the Court may hear the case in his absence.[108]

---

[101] White Book (1997) 15/12/14.

[102] *Cox* v *Dublin Distillery* [1917] 1 IR 203.

[103] *Malone* v *GNR* [1931] IR 1.

[104] *Ashmore* v *British Coal* [1990] 2 QB 338.

[105] The Recognition of Trusts Act 1987 provides for the recognition of trusts created under the law of Great Britain, certain colonies, and states which are parties to the Hague Conference of 1984.

[106] *Twigg* v *Mason* (1916) 50 ILTR 173 (HL, *per* Lord Wrenbury).

[107] *Kelly* v *Larkin* [1910] 2 IR 550 (Div Ct); *contra*: White Book (1997) 15/14/4, citing *Franklin* v *Franklin* [1915] WN 342, an *ex tempore* judgment.

[108] Trustee Act (NI) 1958, s.59. The Court may appoint a new trustee under s.40.

3.41 An 'executor *de son tort*', who is someone who performs functions of a personal representative without having been so appointed, is liable for the liabilities of the estate up to the value of assets actually received by him; and to that extent a judgment can be executed *de bonis propriis*.[109]

3.42 Generally an estate cannot be represented in Northern Ireland unless a grant is taken out here. However, Great Britain grants are recognised without resealing.[110] Grants in HM Dominions may be recognised resealing under Order 97 rule 39.[111] An executor can sue before a grant of probate, though the action may be stayed till it is granted.[112] An administrator cannot sue before a grant of letters of administration, except for an urgent injunction or receiver to preserve the estate.[113] If he sues without title and the limitation period expires after the proceedings started, the action can be cured by amendment.[114] All property of an intestate vests in the Probate Judge (i.e. the Family Judge) until a grant of administration is taken out.[115]

3.43 Where the unrepresented estate of a deceased is interested in proceedings, the Court may proceed in the absence of, or may appoint a person to represent the estate; and any judgment binds the estate (Ord.15 r.15). An administration suit is not properly constituted unless a personal representative representing the estate is a party.[116] In actions for administration of an estate or execution of a trust, all trustee/personal representatives must be parties, and beneficiaries and claimants need not be (Ord.85 r.3). The High Court can appoint an administrator of an estate where it is necessary or expedient, limited as the Court thinks fit, under the Administration of Estates (NI) Order 1979 (Art.5). This power might be used when there are proceedings in the High Court concerning the unrepresented estate. If there is a pending probate action, the High Court can appoint an administrator *pendente lite* under Article 6 of the 1979 Order and Order 76 rule 14.

3.44 An action purportedly commenced *by* a dead human being is a nullity, but not an action *against* a dead human, by virtue of rules made under the Administration of Estates (NI) Order 1979 (Art.42). Where a claimant wishes to sue but the person liable has died with no grant of representation for his estate, he may sue his estate. A plaintiff may have purportedly sued a defendant who was dead when the writ was issued. The plaintiff must, whilst the writ remains valid for service, apply to the Court (*ex parte* if there is no other defendant) for an order appointing a person, or the actual personal representative, to represent the estate in the action; before doing so the Court may require notice to be served on the deceased's insurer or other person

---

[109] *State (Hunt)* v *Midland Circuit Judge* [1934] IR 196, at 216.

[110] Administration of Estates Act 1971, ss.2, 4 (a UK Act).

[111] As provided by Statutory Instrument under the Colonial Probates Acts 1892 and 1927, amended by the Administration of Estates Act (NI) 1971.

[112] *Curry* v *Tevlin* (1876) IR 10 CL 458.

[113] *Cassidy* v *Foley* [1904] 2 IR 427.

[114] Limitation (NI) Order 1989, Art.73(6); Ord.20 r.5(4).

[115] Administration of Estates Act (NI) 1955, s.3.

[116] *Julian* v *Goodbody* (1943) 77 ILTR 160; White Book (1997) 15/14/13.

interested (Ord.15 r.16). The plaintiff should tell the Court of any person willing to act, state whether the deceased was insured and exhibit any correspondence with the insurer or a beneficiary of the estate; he should try to agree with the solicitor for the insurer a name to be submitted, without delaying the progress of the action.[117] A person must consent to being appointed. As a last resort a nominee of the plaintiff will be appointed, or judgment given against the estate without a personal representative under Order 15 rule 16(7).[118]

LEGAL REPRESENTATION

3.45 In general any person may carry on or defend proceedings in person or through a solicitor, but a corporate body must do so through a solicitor (Ord.5 r.6; Ord.12 r.1(2)), unless the Court in exceptional circumstances allows a director to represent the company.[119] So must the next friend/guardian *ad litem* of a party under disability (Ord.80 r.2). An unincorporated body or club can appear by its secretary or trustee.[120]

A person who is not a party can be represented by counsel holding a "watching brief" without any leave of the Court needed, and the judge will listen to any necessary submissions by the counsel.[121]

3.46 A party can address the court as his own advocate (unless he has solicitor or counsel retained to speak for him). In the High Court this is very rare except in certain types of proceeding, such as contempt hearings. A litigant in person can have a friend present to advise *sotta voce* and take notes, without leave of the court but subject to such restriction as the court may impose in the interests of justice and orderly proceeding.[122] He is entitled to costs (see para. 17.59).

3.47 A solicitor is an officer of the Supreme Court.[123] The professional supervision of solicitors by the Law Society and its Tribunal is dealt with by the Solicitors (NI) Order 1976,[124] particularly Schedule 1, under the overall jurisdiction of the High Court (Ord.106 rr.5-15) and of the Lord Chief Justice (Ord.106 r.16). Subject to statute, the Supreme Court has inherent jurisdiction over a solicitor: (a) to strike him off the roll; (b) to order compensation for misconduct; (c) to enforce his undertaking; (d) to order delivery up of money or documents.[125] Only one solicitor can appear for a party.[126] An unqualified solicitor who acts in a case is guilty of contempt (Art.19).

---

[117] *McClellan* v *PR of Love* [1976] NI 126.
[118] *Firth Finance* v *McNarry* [1987] NI 125.
[119] White Book (1997) 5/6/2; e.g., its assets are frozen by a *Mareva* injunction.
[120] White Book (1997) 5/6/1.
[121] *Steele* v *GNR* (1890) 26 LR Ir 96.
[122] *R* v *Leicester City JJ, ex p Barrow* [1991] 2 QB 260.
[123] Judicature Act, s.105.
[124] As amended by the Solicitors (Amendment) (NI) Order 1989.
[125] White Book (1997) Vol. 2 [3871].
[126] *Lutton* v *Ulster Rly* (1875) 9 ILTR 171.

3.48 A solicitor who appears for a party in legal proceedings is assumed to act with his authority unless the contrary is shown. Whether a solicitor has actual authority to sue or appear for a party is a matter of fact; there is no rule that the authority must be in writing.[127] If it is proved that a solicitor does not in fact have authority for the named plaintiff, the action will be stayed pending inquiry and then struck out,[128] unless the action is subsequently ratified by him.[129] If a solicitor sues or appears without authority or on behalf of a dead or non-existent party, he is personally liable for costs.[130] Where a party appears through a solicitor that solicitor is deemed to represent him until the final conclusion of the proceedings in the Supreme Court, unless action is taken under Order 67. The solicitor is employed by an express or implied contract of retainer, and, in a common law action of damages at least, it is deemed to be for the whole action. He cannot discharge himself except on good grounds and on notice to the client. After proceedings commence, a solicitor on record for a party (by having issued a writ, entered an appearance or otherwise) has implied authority to accept service of documents, to make formal or informal admissions or to conclude a compromise, if it is reasonable, *bona fide* and not contrary to express instructions, and he has implied authority to receive money for the client who is not under disability.[131] He has ostensible authority to bind the client against the other party by a compromise, even if it is unreasonable or contrary to express instruction or subsequently repudiated. Such compromise is not binding if it purports to be agreed by the party personally,[132] or if it involves matters not connected to the subject of the litigation.[133] If a court order has been made on a compromise reached contrary to express instructions, it can be set aside if the client gives notice of application to do so before the order is perfected.[134] As a matter of prudence a solicitor should never conclude a compromise outside the written authority of the client.

3.49 If a Supreme Court or county court judge or a resident magistrate reports a prima facie case of misconduct of a solicitor to the Law Society, the Society must bring a complaint before the Solicitors' Disciplinary Tribunal under the Solicitors (NI) Order 1976 (Art.44(3)). The Tribunal may take remedial action where a solicitor is found to have rendered inadequate services (Art.51A).

3.50 A party may change his solicitor by filing a notice of change in the office and serving a copy of it on every other party and on the former solicitor (Ord.67 r.1). Where a party in person appoints a solicitor he must file a notice and serve a copy on the other party (Ord.67 r.2). Where a party removes his solicitor to act in person he must file a notice, which must include an address for service, and serve a copy on the other party and the former solicitor (Ord.67

---

[127] *Mackie* v *Wilde* [1995] 1 ILRM 468.

[128] *Wm Jacks & Co* v *Chemquip* [1991] LRC (Comm) 814 (Malaysia, SC).

[129] *Presentaciones Musicales* v *Secunda* [1994] Ch 271.

[130] White Book (1997) Vol. 2 [3874].

[131] White Book (1997) Vol. 2 [3881] and [4614].

[132] *Gethings* v *Cloney* (1914) 48 ILTR 55.

[133] *Barrett* v *WJ Lenehan* [1981] ILRM 207.

[134] *Marsden* v *Marsden* [1972] Fam 280.

r.3). The discharged solicitor has a lien for his costs on documents, and until they are paid he cannot be compelled to give them up to the client or new solicitor. The Court Office should refuse a notice from one of several plaintiffs.[135] If a solicitor has died, disappeared or ceased to practise and no notice is given under the above rules, any other party may apply to the Court by summons (or to the Court of Appeal by motion) on affidavit served on the unrepresented party, for an order declaring that the solicitor has ceased to act; and such order must be entered in the office and served on every other party (Ord.67 r.4). If a solicitor has ceased to act for a party and that party has not given notice thereof under the rules, that solicitor may apply for an order in the same way as under rule 4, in common parlance "to come off record" (Ord.67 r.5); the court has a discretion but will normally make the order where the solicitor has in fact ceased to act, rightly or wrongly.[136] In *O'Fearail* v *McManus*,[137] the solicitor retained by the defendant's insurer applied to come off record because the insurer had repudiated its liability to indemnify the defendant; it was held that in its discretion the court should grant the application, whether or not the insurer's repudiation was proper, rather than force him to continue to represent the defendant; costs were awarded against the insurer. A solicitor who discharges himself can be compelled to hand over documents to the new solicitor on the latter's undertaking to preserve his lien for costs.[138] A solicitor can discharge himself on good ground, such as the client's failure to give instructions; or the client's failure to pay a reasonable sum on account for costs (1976 Order, Art.69(2)). If he has no good ground he loses his right to a fee and the Court may refuse to let him come off record.

3.51 An order under Order 67 rules 4 or 5 "shall not affect the rights of the solicitor and the party for whom he acted as between themselves". If a party's legal aid certificate is revoked or discharged, then on determination of his retainer under the Legal Aid (General) Regulations (NI) 1965, regulation 13(2) (see para. 3.60), the party is deemed to be acting in person until a notice under rule 2 is given (Ord.67 r.5(4)). Whenever a solicitor comes or is taken off the record under any part of rules 4 or 5, his client is now acting in person, and his address for service is deemed to be his last known address.[139]

3.52 A solicitor in contentious business may take security from the client for his costs; and has good cause to withdraw on reasonable notice if the client does not comply with a request for a reasonable sum on account; and on application for an order declaring that the solicitor has ceased to act, the Court may determine the reasonableness (Solicitors (NI) Order 1976, Art.69). Refusal of the client to accept the solicitor's judgment on the conduct of the case is

---

[135] *Lewis* v *Daily Telegraph (No 2)* [1964] 2 QB 601, at 619-20.

[136] *Re Falgat Constructions Pty* (1996) 70 ALJR 609 (HC of Aus).

[137] [1994] 2 ILRM 81 (SC).

[138] If the client sues the former solicitor for return of the papers, the court can order their return upon payment into court of the claimed costs: *Ismail* v *Rickards Butler* [1996] QB 711 (Moore-Bick J).

[139] Or in the case of a corporation, its registered or principal office. Of course a corporation cannot continue to prosecute or defend until a new solicitor is appointed under Ord.67.

good cause.[140] If the solicitor dies, is dismissed or withdraws before completing the agreed work under a contentious business agreement, the Court may enforce it or set it aside and may direct the taxation of the work already done (Art.68). The topic of costs is dealt with at para. 17.72.

3.53 The *Official Solicitor* acts in accordance with the Judicature Act and any direction of the Lord Chancellor (s.75 thereof). He assists the LCJ or any court, and performs the duties formerly done by the General Solicitor and duties analogous to those of the Official Solicitor in England (Ord.110). His costs must be taxed and paid from such fund or by such parties as the court directs (Ord.110 r.2).

Rights of audience

3.54 A litigant in person can address the court (as advocate as well as witness) in any proceedings in the Supreme Court. A solicitor retained by a party cannot address the court, and must instruct counsel to do so, except: (a) in arrangements, receivership, bankruptcy or winding up; (b) in matters heard in chambers or adjourned from chambers to court; (c) in a matter in which instructed counsel is unable to appear; (d) in any other case by leave of the court if he has not had reasonable opportunity to instruct counsel adequately (Judicature Act, s.106(1)(2)).[141] In proceedings before a master or other statutory officer, the solicitor, and by leave an experienced solicitor's clerk, have right of audience (s.106(3)). Section 106(4) contains a saving for the inherent power of the Court or a judge to grant audience to any person. In *Battle* v *Irish Art*,[142] an application by a director to represent a company was refused. A person entitled to practise as advocate, barrister, solicitor etc. in a European Union Country can act in proceedings if he acts with and in conjunction with a local lawyer, and may do so through legal aid.[143]

3.55 Counsel must be a member of the Bar practising in Northern Ireland and a member of the Inn of Court. The professional duties of barristers are set out in *The Code of Conduct for the Bar of Northern Ireland* (1990) (the 'Bar Handbook'); and as to his duties to avoid misrepresenting the facts to the Court, see para. 3.02 of this book. It is contrary to Bar etiquette to appear on instructions directly from a lay client. Senior counsel (a QC) can appear without a junior counsel but should not do so if he considers a junior to be necessary for the conduct of the case (Bar Handbook 18-03; 18-06). Senior counsel is instructed in the majority of High Court actions and very rarely without a junior. Senior counsel appears very rarely in interlocutory proceedings before a master. He does not draft pleadings. He should approve pleadings in which fraud is alleged. In court or chambers counsel wears wig

---

140 *Chance* v *Tanti* (1901) 35 ILTR 126.

141 After it was held in *Abse* v *Smith* [1986] QB 536 that a solicitor should be allowed audience in open court in exceptional circumstances, the English Supreme Court issued a Practice Direction "Solicitors: Rights of Audience" [1986] 1 WLR 545, that he should be allowed audience in formal or unopposed proceedings.

142 [1968] IR 252.

143 European Communities (Service of Lawyers) Order 1978 (SI 1978/1910) as amended (See Halsbury's *Statutory Instruments*, Vol. 19).

and gown, except in civil proceedings (other than trials) during the Summer Vacation (22-01). Counsel should always be attended in court before a judge by his solicitor or a member of his staff (11-10). If for any reason he is not attended, he must so state to the judge and seek direction as to whether to proceed unattended. Counsel has implied and ostensible authority over the conduct of the proceedings, to make admissions and to compromise, in the same way as a solicitor (White Book (1997) Vol. 2 [4613]). Presumably he has no authority to accept service of documents outside court precincts[144] or to receive money for his client.

LEGAL AID

3.56 Since 1965, there has been a statutory scheme for payment out of public funds of the legal costs of litigants, on a means-tested basis, administered by the Law Society, now under the control of the Lord Chancellor. The governing statute is now the Legal Aid, Advice and Assistance (NI) Order 1981 (hereinafter called the "LA Order").

'Green Form' advice and assistance

3.57 Under the scheme operating under Articles 3 to 8 of the LA Order and the Legal Advice and Assistance Regulations (NI) 1981,[145] the client fills in a green form and the solicitor can give advice and assistance, charging the Legal Aid Fund up to a prescribed figure [£88], but this does not allow for representation in civil matters in the High Court (Legal Advice and Assistance Regs, reg.17, Sch.3), save in child care proceedings as provided in regulations to be made under the LA Order (Art.5(4A)). It can be used to gather information prior to commencement of the action. Costs in excess of that limit can be charged only with the prior approval of the Legal Aid Committee.[146] The Legal Aid Committee has issued a General Authority (June 1992) for certain steps to be taken though they may bring the expenditure over the limit: for example in a personal injuries case, to get a medical consultant's report; in a road traffic case, to get a police report. The solicitor cannot charge the fees of a non-legal expert for advice on a special area of law.[147]

Legal aid

3.58 Full legal aid is governed by the LA Order and the Legal Aid (General) Regulations (NI) 1965 (the "LA Gen Regs").[148] If the client appears to be eligible for legal aid, the solicitor should advise him of his right and request his consent to apply to the Legal Aid Authority before taking any other step, unless the situation is urgent. A certificate cannot operate and cannot be amended to pay for costs incurred before it is granted.[149] It is available for any proceedings

---

144 He has authority to accept service of a document in court if neiher solicitor nor client are present: *Penman* v *Parker* [1986] 1 WLR 882.

145 SR 1981/366.

146 *Drummond & Co* v *Lamb* [1992] 1 WLR 163 (HL).

147 *R* v *Legal Aid Board, ex p Bruce* [1992] 1 WLR 694; sub nom. *Bruce* v *Legal Aid Board* [1992] 3 All ER 321.

148 SR 1965/217 as amended by several subsequent SRs, most notably SR 1974/126.

149 *R & T Thew* v *Reeves (No 1)* [1982] QB 172.

in the High Court, Court of Appeal and House of Lords, except those wholly or partly relating to defamation, recovery of an admitted debt, relator actions, election petitions (LA Order, Sch.1). In child care proceedings, legal aid must be granted to the child and the parent (Art.10(5B)(5C)). Legal aid will only be granted for contentious proceedings. It is not given for non-contentious proceedings, such as applying for a grant of probate, unless necessary for the prosecution of contentious proceedings.[150] It is not granted to a defendant until proceedings have been issued against him.[151] Application is made to a certifying committee,[152] or for appeals from the High Court, to a Legal Aid Committee (LA Gen Regs, reg.3). Refusal by the certifying committee can be appealed to the Legal Aid Committee, before which the client may put in a written statement and the client and/or his solicitor or counsel may appear (reg.10). The Secretary of the appropriate committee may approve the application or refer it to the committee (reg.5(5)). The applicant must be within the limits of disposable income and capital[153] and must show reasonable grounds for taking, defending or being a party to proceedings and legal aid may be refused if it appears unreasonable (Art.10), if the proceedings offer trivial advantage or are of simple nature (reg.5(6)), or on other grounds stated in regulation 7.[154] Thus the appropriate committee has a wide discretion to refuse legal aid even where the applicant's claim or defence is reasonable.[155] It must consider and assess the cost to the public purse, the benefit of the litigation to the client, and the chance of success.[156] Thus it may refuse on the ground that the benefit of the litigation to the client is not enough to warrant the costs to the public purse, but in doing so should take into account whether the client has a high prospect of success and of recovering costs from the other party and thus causing no net loss to the Legal Aid Fund.[157] Refusal of legal aid can be challenged by judicial review, on grounds, for example, of error of law or *Wednesbury* unreasonableness,[155] but not on ground of failure to state reasons unless the likely reason for refusal

---

150 LA Practical Digest, II 6.8.

151 LA Practical Digest, II 6.9.

152 Usually called an "adjudicator".

153 As defined by the LA Order, Art.14 and the assessment of resources regulations SR 1981/189 as amended. The limits are set out in SRs which are usually revised in April of each year. The current limits are around £7,500 annual disposable income, and £7,000 disposable capital. Between certain limits, the applicant is liable for a contribution to the Fund. The limits are more generous in personal injury/death claims.

154 E.g. that the applicant is resident outside the United Kingdom or the subject-matter arose outside Northern Ireland.

155 *In re McLaughlin* [1989] 8 NIJB 83, at 95; where on judicial review the refusal by the certifying committee and on appeal the LA Committee was upheld even though leave of the High Court had been given in a judicial review application to challenge the Sinn Fein media ban. Contrast *R* v *Legal Aid Board ex p Hughes* (1992) 24 HLR 698, which held that the test for grounds for the High Court in granting leave for judicial review was substantially the same as the test for the LA Authority in granting legal aid, though each body makes its own judgment on the facts known to it.

156 *McTear v Scottish Legal Aid Board*, 1997 SLT 108.

157 *In re McCann* (1994) [1997] 1 BNIL 61 (Kerr J)

is indiscernible.[158] If the client is under a disability, the next friend/guardian *ad litem* must undertake to be liable to the LA Fund (reg.4). However it is the minor's means only which are assessed, not the means of the parent. There is provision for taking into account other persons' means where the applicant is litigating in a representative, fiduciary or official capacity or on behalf of numerous other persons with the same interest, or on a shared right, or is a member of a body which may fund him (reg.5(9)-(13)).

3.59 Every certificate must state exactly what step or steps are authorised by it: for example, "to prosecute an action for damages in the High Court [or in the county court]". If a step is taken outside that certificate and outside the scope of an prior authorisation of the Legal Aid authority, the likely result is that the costs thereof will not be allowed, and the costs of such a proceedings may be enforced against the client personally (see paras. 17.83-17.88). When steps authorised by the certificate have been performed it is spent, and the client thereupon ceases to be a legally assisted party.[159] A certificate with a blank space authorises no step at all, and the solicitor must have it properly amended by the Legal Aid authority *before* taking any step.[160] An initial certificate may be granted limited to obtaining counsel's opinion, an expert report, or pre-action discovery. In urgent cases, such as seeking an *ex parte* injunction, judicial review or High Court non-scheduled bail the committee may issue an Emergency Certificate; if a full Certificate is later given it operates retrospectively from the date of the Emergency Certificate; but if the Emergency Certificate is revoked the client is deemed never to have been legally aided (LA Gen Regs, reg.11). An Emergency Certificate is granted if: (a) in the interests of justice; (b) there is not enough time to apply for an ordinary certificate; and (c) there is no unreasonable delay in applying. In extreme urgency it can be sought by telephone.

3.60 Before a client accepts an offer by the appropriate committee, it is prudent to explain his liability, if any, for contribution and operation of the statutory charge whereby any money or property recovered for him is subject to payment of costs not recovered from the other party. Notice that a party is legally-aided (and of its amendment, suspension, discharge or revocation) must be served on the other party (reg.16)[161] and filed in the Court Office as part of the papers for the trial judge on setting down for trial. The Court cannot amend the certificate, even for clerical error, but the Legal Aid Committee can amend, extend or restrict it (reg.9). A certificate can be suspended if the client fails to pay instalments of his contribution or if a representation is received from any person as to a change in the client's means (reg.12(1A); and the LA Fund is not liable to the client's solicitor for any costs incurred during the period of suspension save as authorised by the LA Committee (reg.12(1C)). A certificate can be discharged on the grounds set out in regulation 12(2)(3), for example, on

---

158 *In re Oliver* [1995] 6 BNIL 69 (Carswell LJ).

159 *Turner* v *Plasplugs* [1996] 2 All ER 939 (CA).

160 *Smyth* v *Smyth*, Taxing Office, NI (Master Napier) 11 May 1994.

161 Failure to do so does not affect the client's status as legally aided: *King* v *T & W Farmiloe* [1953] 1 All ER 614.

client's request; for arrears of contribution; client dead or bankrupt; solicitor cannot get instructions; on a re-determination of his means; or on information showing that he no longer has reasonable grounds for litigating. On application of the Law Society or of the other party, the Court may revoke or discharge the certificate for lack of frankness by the client (reg.12(7)). On revocation or discharge the solicitor's retainer is determined (reg.13(2)). Discharge of a certificate does not affect the client's right to payment of his costs to date. Revocation is retrospective in that the client is deemed never to have been legally aided (reg. 13(1)), and the LA Fund will pay the solicitor's costs to date but may recover them from the client. The party is thence deemed to be acting in person until a notice of appointment of a solicitor is served (Ord.67 r.5(4)).

3.61 Information given to the committee or Law Society for the purpose of legal aid must not be disclosed for purposes other than the LA Authority's functions, save by consent of the client, or if the information was furnished by someone else, that person (LA Order, Art.24). For the avoidance of doubt, Article 24(5) declares that information given by the client to his solicitor or counsel is not information given to the LA Authority. Solicitor and counsel must give information as required on the progress of the action to the committee; and must make a report within three months of its conclusion (LA Gen Regs, reg.15(14)(14A)). The solicitor must disclose information to the committee without being bound by professional privilege (reg.15(15)). He should tell if the client refuses a reasonable compromise.[162] He may discharge himself, so reporting to the committee, if the client failed to give frank information under the regulations or requires undue expense (reg.15(9)(10)). Counsel should have regard to the regulations if the interests of the client conflict with those of the Fund.[163] The committee may transfer the legal aid to another solicitor and a certificate to that effect is admissible on an application by the new solicitor under Order 67 (see para. 3.50) (reg.15(12)). Any person may report to the committee any information which affects the propriety of legal aid and in doing so an opposite party can breach 'without prejudice' privilege (reg.12(3)). Subject to the legislation, legal aid does not affect the relationship and privileges of the client with his solicitor and counsel, nor the rights and liabilities of the other party, nor the exercise of a discretion by the Court (Art.10(6)).[164] Note that the legal advisers of the legally aided party have no duty of care towards the opposing party.[165]

3.62 One certificate can relate to one or more claims or any step or part of proceedings, but it can only cover one action, cause or matter, and any other proceedings arising out of it, including a notice of appeal (LA Gen Regs, reg.6). One certificate cannot cover both hearing at first instance and an appeal, except an interlocutory appeal (*ibid*). However a new statement of resources is

---

[162] Nicholson (1966) 17 NILQ 175, at 179.

[163] Bar Handbook, 15-01.

[164] In *In re Murphy* [1991] 7 NIJB 97, at 103, where counsel asked for an adjournment on the non-appearance of his client, it was held proper to take into account that he was legally aided and thus not subject to any effective sanction in costs. But see *McIntyre* v *NIHE* [1995] 7 BNIL 60 (para. 7.18).

[165] *Orchard* v *SE Electricity* [1987] QB 565. The LA Practical Digest is wrong on this point.

not required. If the client is the party appealing, an opinion on the merits of appeal from counsel is required. The certificate covers all work reasonably necessary within the scope of the certificate, and no more. It covers the solicitor named, and where necessary counsel instructed by him (LA Order, Art.10(3)). Prior authority of the LA Committee is required under the existing certificate to add a party, bring an interlocutory appeal, instruct more than one counsel, or plead an unconnected cross-claim (reg. 15(3)). The LA Committee may authorise employment of two or more counsel (reg.15(4)). The LA Committee can issue written general authorities to obtain an expert or other report and transcript of court proceedings, and approval is necessary for any extra or unusual expenditure (reg.15(5)(6)(7)). When asked to approve unusual expenditure the LA Committee should have regard to the likely expense of the proposed step, its importance to the proceedings, and whether there is any better alternative step.[166] In personal injury actions the LA Committee has given general authority for two medical witnesses in High Court actions, and in injury and damage actions, for an engineer.[167]

3.63 Within three months after the conclusion of the litigation, a report on its conduct should be made to the LA Committee (reg.15(14A)).

Effect of legal aid on costs

3.64 A legally aided party is in a special position as regards costs. This topic is discussed at para. 17.82.

---

[166] *Venter* v *Scottish LA Board*, 1993 SLT 147 (1st Div).
[167] LA Practical Digest, II Chap.8.

CHAPTER FOUR

TIME FOR SUING

ACCRUAL OF CAUSE OF ACTION

4.00 A plaintiff can only sue in respect of a cause of action which has accrued before the commencement of proceedings.[1] Thus he must already have title to sue and must sue on a claim on which liability has matured,[2] though he may rely on symptoms and events up to judgment in assessment of the damages or other appropriate remedy. He can sue for specific performance before any actionable damage has occurred.[3] In a continuing cause of action, damages are assessed down to the date of judgment (Ord.37 r.6). This must be distinguished from a 'recurrent' cause of action, such as the tort of an employer in providing unsafe conditions of work: there the plaintiff recovers damages for symptoms and losses which are attributable to the tortious conduct up to the date of the issue of the writ.[4] In a debt claim, save as otherwise provided by agreement, it is not essential to demand payment of the money due before suing.[5] A divorce petition cannot be presented before two years of marriage.[6]

4.01 If the limitation period has expired since proceedings commenced, an amendment to alter the capacity in which a party sues may be allowed even if the new capacity has been acquired since commencement of proceedings (Ord.20 r.5(4)). Where a solicitor sues without the authority of the plaintiff the action can be ratified by the plaintiff even though the limitation period has since expired.[7]

LIMITATION PERIOD

4.02 The Limitation (NI) Order 1989 (the '1989 Order') governs all civil proceedings commenced since 3 October 1989; generally speaking it applies to all causes of action which were not statute-barred on 11 April 1982 (see further Sch.2). The time provisions of the Interpretation Act (NI) 1954 apply. It provides for a time limit in which an action must be brought. Article 2(2) of the 1989 Order defines 'action' as including "any proceeding (other than crimiinal proceedings) in a court established by law". It does not apply to a cause of action for which a specific time limit is otherwise set (e.g. the Carriage by Air Act 1961).

---

[1] A defendant's counterclaim must relate to a cause of action which accrued before delivery of his Defence and Counterclaim

[2] A cause of action in negligence for damage to property or economic loss accrues when the actionable damage or loss occurs: *McInerny* v *DOE* [1984] NI 1.

[3] *Oakacre* v *Claire Cleaners* [1982] Ch 197.

[4] *Birch* v *Harland & Wolff* [1991] NI 90, at 100.

[5] *Swansea CC* v *Glass* [1992] QB 844.

[6] Matrimonial Causes (NI) Order 1978, Art.5.

[7] *Presentaciones Musicales* v *Secunda* [1994] Ch 271.

Time limits

4.03 The time limits set by the 1989 Order for expiry of the limitation period are (from date of accrual of cause of action unless otherwise stated)-

One year	• libel, slander, malicious falsehood etc. arising since 4 September 1996 (Art.6(2))
Two years	• claim for contribution, from date of judgment for damages at first instance or payment or agreement to pay the liability for which contribution now sought (Art.13)
Three years	• personal injury claims, and claims for injury or damage from defective products under the Consumer Protection (NI) Order 1987, from date of accrual or from date of knowledge of, *inter alia*, the seriousness of the injury, its cause and the identity of the person liable (Arts.7-8) • fatal accident claims, from date of death or date of knowledge (Arts.9-10) • libel and slander arising before 4 September 1996 (Art.6(2))
Six years	• damages for non-personal injury negligence, i.e. six years from accrual, or three years from knowledge and title to sue, but not more than 15 years after the negligent conduct (Arts.11-12) • tort claims (Art.6) • personal injury claims arising from statutory tort of harassment (Art.7(1A))
Six years	• contract, quasi-contract, debt (from date of demand in writing unless date fixed) and money recoverable under statute (Arts.4-5) • on a judgment, from it becoming enforceable (Art.16(1)) • on arrears of interest on judgment debt (Art.16(2)) • rent charges (Art.29); rent (Art.30); annuity charged on personalty (Art.31) • mortgage interest (Art.37) • breach of trust (Art.42) • interest on legacy (Art.44(2))
Six years	• on claims for indemnity, from the date when the ascertainment of the extent of the liability for which indemnity is sought (*R & H Green* v *BRB* [1985] 1 WLR 570; *Sterling* v *Cohen* [1987] NI 409, at 415)
Ten years long stop	• damage from defective products from "the relevant time", i.e. the time the product was supplied (1989 Order, Art.8; Consumer Protection (NI) Order 1987, Art.7)
Twelve years	• contract under seal (1989 Order, Art.15) • recovery of land (Art.21) • mortgagee's sale (Art.32) • mortgagor's redemption (Art.34) • recovery of money charged on land or personalty (Art.36) • personal rights over land (Art.40) • share of personal estate (Art.44(1))
Special provisions	• action for account (Art.14) • conversion of chattels (Arts.17-18) • future interest in land (Arts.22-3)
Equitable time limits	• specific performance, injunction (Art.19)
No period	• recovery of trust property from trustee, fraudulent breach of trust (Art.43) • fraud by personal representative (Art.45)

A personal representative is not a trustee for limitation purposes (Arts.2(3), 45(1)).

Extension of period

4.04 If on the date when the cause of action accrued, the plaintiff was under disability (a minor or mental patient): time starts when he becomes *sui juris* or dies (Art 48). This applies where the mental disability arises from the accident on which the action is brought.[8] It does not apply to a claim of a child as dependant under the Fatal Accidents (NI) Order 1977, which must be brought within three years under Articles 9-10 of the 1989 Order.[9]

Time (if not yet expired) starts afresh -

(1) If the right of the claimant is acknowledged (in writing and signed) in recovery of land and mortgage actions (Arts.52-56); in debt and mortgage debt cases (Art.57)[10] or in claims for share of an estate (Art.58).

(2) If part payment is made of a debt, mortgage debt, share of an estate (Arts.62-66).

(3) A fresh cause of action accrues to a new owner in claims for negligence for latent damage to property (Limitation (Amendment) (NI) Order 1987, Art.5).

(4) If the defendant is sued for fraud,[11] or has concealed the plaintiff's rights, or the action is for relief from mistake, time runs from the date of discovery (1989 Order, Art.71).

(5) In libel, slander, malicious falsehood etc. arising since 4 September 1996, the court may disapply the time limit if it appears equitable to do so (Art.51, as substituted 1996). In libel and slander arising before 4 September 1996, by leave of the High Court an action may be brought up to one year after discovery of the facts (Art.51, original form).

4.05 In personal injury and fatal accident cases, the time limit begins to run from the date of the cause of action or from the date of the claimant's knowledge of his right (Arts.7, 9). Date of knowledge is defined by Article 11.

4.06 In personal injury and fatal accident cases, the time limit can be overridden by the Court if it appears equitable to do so (Art.50)[12] usually on application to a judge as preliminary issue before or at the trial; or by summons of the plaintiff before the master (Ord.32 r.12A). A decision under Article 50

---

8 *Rohan* v *Bord na Mona* [1990] 2 IR 425.

9 Cf. *Jaman Estate* v *Hussain* (1995) 126 DLR 4th 567 (Manitoba CA).

10 See *Hart* v *Carswell* [1973] NI 15.

11 Including equitable fraud, such as breach of fiduciary duty: *Collier* v *Creighton* [1996] 2 NZLR 257 (PC).

12 See *Thompson* v *Brown* [1981] 1 WLR 744 (HL); *Conway* v *Hannaway* [1988] NI 269; *Kinkead* v *Hagan* [1982] NI 412; *Kavanagh* v *Coalisland Pipe* [1983] 3 NIJB; *Baxter* v *Harland & Wolfe* [sic][1990] NI 147; *Moore* v *Harland & Wolff* [1991] NI 188; *Hickey* v *DOE* [1992] 1 NIJB 54; *Sheerin* v *MOD* [1993] 10 NIJB 89; *Kelly* v *Bastable*, 'The Times', 15 November 1996 (CA). Art.50 does not allow waiver of time limits in a claim where the cause of action arose up to 31 December 1952 or between 1 January 1955 and 31 December 1958: see *Bowman* v *Harland & Wolff* [1991] NI 300, at 329-30.

should never be made *ex parte*.[13] It should be heard by a judge in those rare cases where there is conflicting oral evidence to be heard.[14] Article 50 does not allow the waiver of time for a second action when a first was commenced within time, save in exceptional circumstances.[15] These provisions do not apply to an action against a solicitor for negligence in pursuing a personal injury claim, as it is not "for damages in respect of personal injuries".[16] Where the personal injury is based on an intentional trespass to the person, the time limit is six years with no extension.[17]

Effect of the Limitation Order

4.07 Generally the Limitation Order bars a right of action by making it unenforceable if pleaded by the defendant; thus in a High Court action the plaintiff's claim fails only if the limitation issue is mentioned in the Defence. To prevent the pointless pursuit of the action to trial, the defendant may apply by summons to have the action struck out or stayed where he intends to plead an unanswerable limitation defence (see para. 11.174). However, in damage from defective products, recovery of land, mortgagee's sale and right to repayment, mortgagor's redemption, personal right over land, the expiry also operates to extinguish the title (Arts. 8(3), 26-27, 33, 35, 38-9, 41); and in these cases the Court must give effect to the limitation defence even if not pleaded as such. The title does not expire if an ejectment action is commenced within the period.[18]

4.08 Where a foreign law applies to the cause of action, the limitation time limit under the foreign law is applied by the Foreign Limitation Periods (NI) Order 1985.

4.09 The material date for counting back the limitation period is the date on which the legal proceedings commence, that is the date of issue of the writ or other originating process. Where a new claim is made in pending proceedings, Article 73 of the 1989 Order categorises them into -

(1) a new claim brought between existing parties adding or substituting a new cause of action;

(2) a claim by an added or substituted party;

(3) by an existing party against a non-party by joining him as defendant to a claim already made by the existing party;

---

13 *Johnston* v *Mohan* [1978] NI 126, at 135C.

14 *Moane* v *Reilly* [1984] NI 269, at 274-5.

15 *Walkley* v *Precision Forgings* [1979] 1 WLR 606; *Kinkead* v *Hagan* [1982] NI 412 (first writ not served because defendant breached his promise to collect it); *Forward* v *Hendricks* [1997] 2 All ER 395 (CA).

16 *Doone* v *McPartland* [1987] NI 119. See also *Ackbar* v *CF Green* [1975] QB 582, and the conflicting decision of *Sweeney* v *Duggan* [1991] 2 IR 274. See also *Arndt* v *Smith* (1995) 126 DLR 4th 705 (Brit Col CA).

17 *Stubbings* v *Webb* [1993] AC 498. This decision may have to reversed by legislation because of Human Rights Court proceedings.

18 *In re Lands at Eshywilligan* [1992] 3 NIJB 79.

(4) an original set-off or counterclaim by an existing party who has not previously made any claim in the action; and

(5) any other new claim brought by an existing party against a non-party, called "third-party proceedings".

Types (1) (2) (3) and (4) are deemed to be back-dated to the start of the pending action. Types (1)(2)(3) can be disallowed if the back-dating is liable to defeat a limitation defence. Type (5) is deemed to start when it is first raised.

CHAPTER FIVE

INVOKING THE LEGAL PROCESS

STEPS BEFORE ACTION

Solicitor's letter

5.00 It is an almost invariable practice that a solicitor acting for a person making a claim in contentious litigation should send a letter before action to the proposed defendant. It states briefly the nature of the complaint, the remedy sought, and that the plaintiff will issue proceedings within a specified time unless the defendant makes a satisfactory offer of settlement. A very concise and accurate reference to the cause of action is essential, as the contents of the letter can be used against the plaintiff in evidence.[1] Save by contractual agreement, the claimant has no right to the costs of the letter nor to any legal costs, unless proceedings are later issued, when they can be included as part of taxed costs. Therefore a letter demanding payment of a debt should demand only the debt due, not costs.[2] If the debtor tenders the debt in full, the plaintiff who refuses it and sues for the purpose of recovering the debt and costs will be met with a defence of tender. A plaintiff who receives the debt in full and sues for recovery of his costs will be met with the defence of accord and satisfaction. In a claim for unliquidated damages or other relief, the plaintiff should claim some reasonable costs, and if the defendant offers a satisfactory settlement but without costs, the plaintiff can refuse it and sue.[3] An action can be stayed as an abuse of process if the plaintiff sues without waiting for a reply, but only if the defendant, or his insurer, can show that they were deprived of sufficient details of the claim to make a fair offer in settlement.[4]

Other steps

5.01 In particular cases, certain steps are legally required before suing, for example-

(1) notice of dishonour when suing on a bill of exchange (Bills of Exchange Act 1882, ss.48-50);
(2) notice of assignment of a chose in action (Judicature Act, s.87);
(3) notice of proceedings to the road accident insurer (para. 2.04);
(4) a demand for return of goods may be necessary before suing for their detention;
(5) consent of next friend for action by a person under disability (para.3.07);

---

[1] For precedents see para. 2.01.

[2] See the Note in (1942) 5 NILQ 60, and *Allen* v *O'Callaghan* (1876) 10 ILTR 131.

[3] *Smith* v *Springer* [1987] 3 All ER 252.

[4] *Greaves* v *William Barker* [1995] CLY 3900 (Eng Cty Ct, quoting several county court decisions).

(6) notice before solicitor sues his client on a bill of costs (Solicitors (NI) Order 1976, Art.71E).

In urgent cases, an *ex parte* application for an interim injunction can be made to a judge under section 91 of the Judicature Act.

Leave to issue proceedings

5.02 Leading instances where leave to issue proceedings is required are-

(1) Where a defendant cannot be served in Northern Ireland and is domiciled outside a Convention State (see para. 6.15).

(2) The liquidator of a company being wound up by the Court needs leave of the Court or the liquidation committee to sue in the name of the company.[5]

(3) Against any individual person for an act done purportedly under the Mental Health (NI) Order 1986 (Art.133 thereof) by application to a judge not a master (Ord.32 r.11(1)(m)).[6]

(4) Where the plaintiff has been declared a vexatious litigant under section 32 of the Judicature Act, leave for him to institute legal proceedings[7] must be sought from the High Court; a judge not a master (Ord.32 r.11(1)(d)).[8]

(5) To sue the Post Office for a lost or damaged postal packet by a person suing in the name of the sender or addressee.[9]

COMMENCING PROCEEDINGS

5.03 Subject to statute or rules, proceedings may be begun by writ or originating summons, or where specified, by originating motion or petition (Ord.5 rr.1,4(1),5). Proceedings with a claim for tort (other than trespass to land), fraud, damages for personal injuries or death or damage to property, or for infringement of patent *must* be begun by writ (Ord.5 r.2). Actions for breach of contract, or recovery of land, and most actions for common law or equitable remedies are usually brought by writ. Proceedings by originating application under a statute *must* be begun by originating summons, save as otherwise stated in statute or rules (Ord.5 r.3).[10] Proceedings concerning interpretation of a statute or document or a question of law, or in which no substantial dispute of fact is likely, *may* be begun by originating summons (Ord.5 r.4(2)). In any cause in the Queen's Bench Division relating to a business or commercial transaction, the plaintiff's solicitor may request it to be

---

[5] Insolvency (NI) Order 1989, Art.142.

[6] See *Murphy* v *Greene* [1990] 2 IR 566; *O'Reilly* v *Moroney* [1992] 2 IR 145.

[7] Or to appeal from one court to a higher court: *Henry Garratt* v *Ewing* [1991] 4 All ER 891.

[8] Unlike s.32, the equivalent English provision of the 1981 Act specifically states that no appeal lies from refusal of leave: see *Ex parte Ewing (No 2)* [1994] 1 WLR 1553. *Quaere* therefore, whether appeal lies from the refusal of leave. The proposed defendant has no *locus standi* to apply to set aside leave: *Jones* v *Vans Colina* [1996] 1 WLR 1580 (CA).

[9] Post Office Act 1969, s.30(5); Ord.77 r.16. The rule refers to the statutory provision which was repealed and replaced by the 1969 Act.

[10] But Ord.55 r.20 states that any such application may be begun by originating motion.

put in the Commercial List (Ord.72 r.3). All originating processes attract a Court fee (currently £150 in most cases).

5.04 A writ issued without authority of the plaintiff is irregular, not void, and can be retrospectively ratified by him.[11] The defendant may require the solicitor in whose name the writ was issued to declare in writing that the writ was issued with his authority, and if not may apply to stay the action (Ord.6 r.4(2)(3)). A proceeding shall not be wholly set aside on the ground that the wrong originating process was used (Ord.2 r.1(3)). The defendant waives any objection by contesting on the merits.[12] If an action is wrongly begun by originating summons it can be ordered to be continued as if by writ. An action wrongly begun by writ can be ordered to be set down without pleadings.

WRIT OF SUMMONS

5.05 Most actions are commenced by writ of summons, which is issued out of the Central Office (for Queen's Bench), Chancery Office (for Chancery) or Probate and Matrimonial Office (for Probate) (Ord.6 r.6(2)(3)). Every writ is headed with the Division, the year and writ number and title of the action ("Between X plaintiff and Y Defendant"). Parties' full names should be stated if known, rather than merely initials.[13] Judgment can only be given against the defendant of the name and address stated in the writ, and is only enforceable against the person so identified, so any mistake or change of name or address must be corrected in the title of the proceedings by amendment. A writ which falsely states a defendant's address in Northern Ireland if he actually resides abroad will be struck out.[14] The writ must state the address of the plaintiff and the address of his solicitor within Northern Ireland, which is an address for service of documents on him; if unrepresented, the writ must state his own address and an address for service inside Northern Ireland (Ord.6 r.4(1)). If the plaintiff is a minor or mental patient, the writ must state the name of the next friend. If any party is a ward of court or a patient whose affairs are under the control of the court that must be stated on the indorsement of the writ (Ord.89 r.6(1)).

5.06 The writ is taken to the appropriate Office; it is there stamped and sealed with the date of issue, which is the date for limitation purposes; the writ number is assigned to it and entered in the heading; the Office takes one copy (Ord.6 r.6(4)(6)); and hands back the original writ. A concurrent writ, marked "concurrent" (Ord.6 r.4(5)), may be issued at any time while the writ is valid (Ord.6 r.5). It can be issued for any reason, usually where there are two or more defendants to be served, or where the original has been lost. A writ or concurrent writ to be served outside Northern Ireland cannot be issued unless either leave has been granted under Order 11, or it complies with Order 6 rule 6 (see para. 6.13).

---

[11] *Presentaciones Musicales* v *Secunda* [1994] Ch 271(CA).
[12] *McCooey* v *Breen* [1980] 2 NIJB.
[13] *Egleso* v *Stokes* (1826) Batty 213.
[14] *Clokey* v *London & NW Rly* [1905] 2 IR 251.

5.07 The writ may be either 'generally indorsed' (in Form 1) with a concise statement of the nature of the claim or[15] the relief or remedy required (Ord.6 r.2(a)); or 'specially indorsed' (in Form 2) with a full Statement of Claim. The words 'general' and 'special' in this context were found in the RSC before 1980, and although not in the current RSC are still commonly used by practitioners. The general form is usual in claims for damages, the latter in claims for debt or liquidated demand. The special is desirable if there appears to be no defence to the action, as it will facilitate an early application for summary judgment under Order 14. In a generally indorsed writ it is not essential to state the cause of action expressly if it is implicit,[16] but highly desirable.[17] If it fails to reveal a cause of action, the plaintiff will have to have it amended, which will be granted even if the limitation period has expired unless the defendant is surprised.[17] It is not enough to state "damages for negligence" without adding "in the driving of a motor vehicle/in the employment of the plaintiff/etc.".[18] A writ for a debt must obviously claim an exact sum, but a writ for unliquidated damages need not quantify any total monetary claim.

5.08 Whichever is used, a writ for a debt or liquidated demand alone must be indorsed with the sum claimed and a statement of the costs as fixed by Order 62 Appendix 3, Part I column (a), to be paid if the defendant pays the sum claimed within the time limit for appearance (14 days, or longer if the defendant is to be served outside Northern Ireland) (Ord.6 r.2(b)). Thus in a non-debt case, the paragraph in the writ referring to 14-day costs should be crossed out. In a debt case, if the defendant does pay the 14-day costs in accordance with the indorsement (or if the plaintiff accepts as if so paid) the defendant can still require the costs to be taxed (Ord.62 r.7(3)). If the plaintiff enters judgment in default for the indorsed costs he cannot have them taxed (*ibid*). If the plaintiff accepts the indorsed costs paid after 14 days as if paid within time, he can claim no further costs.[19] If an amended writ is re-served on the defendant he does not have a further 14 days to pay[20] unless, *semble*, the amendment is as to the amount of the debt. The omission or error as to the sum due in a 14-day costs indorsement is a mere irregularity which the defendant waives by appearing.[21]

5.09 A writ must state a claim for interest, with particulars of how it is due, the rate, the starting date, the amount due at the date of the writ, and a claim for "further interest at the same rate from the date of issue of the writ till judgment or sooner payment"-

(1) in a debt claim (Ord.6 r.2A);

(2) if interest is claimed under contractual right (Ord.6 r.2B); and

(3) if interest is claimed under the Bill of Exchange Act 1882 (Ord.6 r.2C).

---

15 In practice this means "and".
16 *NIHE* v *Fox* [1981] 9 NIJB at 7-8.
17 *Sterman* v *E & W Moore* [1970] 1 QB 596. See further para. 11.31.
18 *Marshall* v *LPTB* [1936] 3 All ER 83, at 90.
19 *Hoole* v *Earnshaw* (1878) 39 LT 409.
20 *O'Connell* v *Hanlon* (1898) 32 ILTR 95, where the amendment was to correct a defect.
21 *Allen* v *Quigley* (1878) 12 ILTR 46.

Generally speaking a writ for an unliquidated claim need not mention interest, unless the Statement of Claim is indorsed on it.

5.10 A writ for libel must give particulars sufficient to identify the publication (Ord.82 r.2). A writ for recovery of land must state if it is a dwelling house and whether the Rent (NI) Order 1978 applies to it (Ord.6 r.2(c)). A writ for recovery of goods must state their value (Ord.6 r.2(d)). A writ against the Crown must state the circumstances of the liability and the Crown Department/officer liable; if not, the defendant may give notice before the time for appearance requiring such information; the plaintiff may resist the request by applying to the Court for a decision that the information is unnecessary; and the time limit for appearance is extended (Ord.77 r.2).[22] If proceedings affect or join as a party a ward of court or patient, the writ or originating process must so state (Ord.89 r.6). If the plaintiff or defendant is joined in a representative capacity (executor, trustee etc.) the writ must state that capacity (Ord.6 r.3).

DEBT OR LIQUIDATED DEMAND

5.11 "A liquidated demand is in the nature of a debt, i.e. a specific sum of money due and payable under or by virtue of a contract. Its amount must be either already ascertained or capable of being ascertained as a mere matter of arithmetic."[23] The amount, even if a definite sum is claimed, must be unliquidated damages if the assessment requires non-calculable investigation or qualitative estimate;[24] or the liability does not arise from an express or implied promise to pay (e.g. the costs of repair of a car damaged in a road accident).[25]

5.12 A claim for expense and loss on breach of contract is unliquidated. If the contract provides a measure for damages to be paid upon breach of the contract, the sum is liquidated if it is a genuine and reasonable pre-estimate of damage. If not a reasonable pre-estimate, it is a penalty and not recoverable.[26] A claim for a fixed sum to be paid under the contract on a certain event, such as agreed termination, is liquidated, even if it is penal.[27] Thus, where a lease provides that upon breach of covenant to repair the landlord may give notice to repair and on non-compliance with the notice may perform the repair work himself and recover the costs and expenses thereof on demand, a claim for them is a debt due rather than damages for breach of contract; it is a sum payable under the contract on the event of the landlord having performed and demanded in the costs of repairs, albeit preceded by a breach of contract.[28] A claim by an assignee of a debt is liquidated. A claim pleaded as a debt which depends upon proof of fraud is in substance unliquidated.[29] A claim in *quantum meruit* is liquidated;[30] unless the sum is claimed after adjustment for extras and

---

[22] Made under the Crown Proceedings Act, s.35(2)(b).
[23] White Book (1997) 6/2/4.
[24] *Cullen* v *Moran* (1856) 2 Ir Jur NS 28.
[25] *John Laing* v *Dastur* [1987] 1 WLR 686.
[26] The use of the word 'penalty' is not conclusive: *Toomey* v *Murphy* [1897] 2 IR 601.
[27] *Lombank* v *Kennedy* [1961] NI 192.
[28] *Jervis* v *Harris* [1996] Ch 195.
[29] *Blizard* v *Mulloy* (1887) 21 ILTR 11.
[30] *Whelan* v *Kelly* (1884) 14 LR Ir 387.

deductions which are not measured or valued.[31] A solicitor's bill of costs is liquidated though subject to taxation.[32] A claim for a specific sum paid on a consideration which has failed is liquidated. A specific sum claimed as money received by the defendant to the use of the plaintiff is liquidated. If a price is payable by instalments each is a liquidated demand.[33] A claim for money due under an insurance policy is deemed to be unliquidated.[34] A debt claim and judgment on it can be expressed in foreign currency.

Methods of pursuing a debt claim

5.13 An action for a debt can always be brought in the High Court, usually in the Queen's Bench Division.[35] A claim for money secured under a mortgage or charge on real or leasehold property should be brought in the Chancery Division (Ord.88 r.2), unless the creditor chooses merely to sue for the debt without relying on the security (see para. 18.72, para.5). If the debt due is £15,000 or less, the plaintiff should consider suing by civil bill in the county court; if £3,000 or less (public debts only) the 'admitted debt procedure' of the Enforcement of Judgments Office (see para. 16.32). If there is reason to believe that the debtor may be insolvent, he may have recourse to a 'statutory demand' which if not paid within three weeks constitutes an act of bankruptcy, or (in the case of a company debtor) grounds for winding up.[36] The Crown may apply summarily for money due on excise duty, stamp duty, VAT, or tax under a NI statute.[37] If the action is against the debtor or surety on a consumer credit agreement, the defendant can, by serving a notice under section 139(1) of the Consumer Credit Act 1974, have the agreement reopened as being extortionate, and the Court can act under sections 137-140 to relieve the defendant of unreasonable liability (see Ord. 83).

5.14 A claim in debt often arises from an 'account stated', which can be pleaded as a cause of action without having to state how each debt in the account was incurred. There are two types of account stated-

(1) an account stated proper, where the plaintiff has delivered to the defendant an account of money due and the defendant has acknowledged orally or in writing or even possibly by silence. This is prima facie evidence of the indebtedness.[38] The pleading should state the nature of the debts, the date and amount of the account stated, and the manner of its acknowledgement. Alternatively the plaintiff can plead the individual debts.

(2) a settled account, where the parties with mutual debts have struck an agreed balance. This is a new contract which discharges the previous debts

---

[31] *Paterson* v *Wellington Kindergarten* [1966] NZLR 468.
[32] *Gilsenan* v *McGovern* (1892) 30 LR Ir 300.
[33] *Myers* v *Willis* (1907) 41 ILTR 229.
[34] *Edmunds* v *Lloyd Italico* [1986] 1 WLR 492, at 493H.
[35] Usually by 'specially indorsed' writ. As to pleading particulars of the claim, see para. 9.12.
[36] Insolvency (NI) Order 1989, Arts.241-2 and 102-3, respectively. See Hunter *Northern Ireland Personal Insolvency* (SLS 1992) Chap.6.
[37] Crown Proceedings Act, s.14; by originating motion or summons: Ord.77 r.6.
[38] *Wilson* v *Marshall* (1868) IR 2 CL 356. An 'I.O.U.' is mere evidence of the debt: *Rainsford* v *Eager* (1852] 3 ICLR 120.

and it must be pleaded as such. If the plaintiff tries to sue on the prior debts, the defendant can plead the settled account as a defence.

CHAPTER SIX

SERVICE OF DOCUMENTS

SERVICE OF ORIGINATING PROCESS

SERVICE OF WRIT OF SUMMONS

6.00 A writ may be served in Northern Ireland by the plaintiff or his agents by one of the following methods. The copy served must bear the seal of the Supreme Court Office (Ord. 10 r.1(7)).

Generally

A writ for service on a defendant within the jurisidiction may be served -

(1) by personal service on the defendant (Ord.65 r.2) (see para. 6.21). This is expressed by Order 10 rule 1(1) to be the obligatory method of service but is subject to the other methods which are available in most cases.

(2) by sending a copy by ordinary pre-paid first class post (not recorded delivery) to the defendant at his usual or last known address (Ord.10 r.1(2)(a)).

(3) by inserting a copy in the letter box in a sealed envelope addressed to the defendant (Ord.10 r.1(2)(b)).

Service of a writ may also be effected-

(1) by a solicitor who returns the original indorsed with a statement that he accepts service on behalf of the defendant (Ord.10 r.1(4)). The writ is deemed served on date of indorsement. This is good service even if the defendant is outside Northern Ireland.[1] If in fact the solicitor is not authorised, all proceedings are irregular.[2]

(2) by an unserved defendant entering an unconditional appearance. The writ is deemed served on date of appearance (Ord.10 r.1(5)).

(3) in action for recovery of land, either as above or by delivery at the defendant's residence to his spouse, relative or employee aged over 16 years, even if the defendant is outside Northern Ireland (Ord.10 r.4).

On particular parties

6.01 A writ is to be served in the following cases-

(1) on a *minor*: by service on his parent/guardian or person with whom he resides (Ord.80 r.13);

(2) on a *patient*: on the person authorised under the Mental Health (NI) Order 1986 or the person with whom he resides (Ord.80 r.13);

---

[1] *Heffernan* v *Atkin* (1913) 47 ILTR 245.

[2] *Lynott* v *Greene* (1862) 7 Ir Jur NS 278; *Royal Trust* v *Dunne* (1992) 86 DLR 4th 491.

(3) on the *Crown*: by ordinary post to, or by leaving with an employee or agent of, the solicitor for the department or the Crown Solicitor (Crown Proceedings Act, s.18; Ord.77 r.3);

(4) on a *company*: only by leaving it at or by post[3] to its registered office as stated in the Companies Register.[4] If there is no registered office the writ can be served under Order 65 rule 3.[5] If the company is being wound up it should be served on the liquidator;[6]

(5) on a *foreign company*: by delivery or post[3] to the name and address in Northern Ireland registered in the Companies Register, or at any place of business in Northern Ireland under Order 65 rule 3, if that person is absent or no name is registered;[7]

(6) on a *corporation*: by personal service on clerk, secretary etc. or by posting it to or leaving it at its registered or principal office (Ord.65 r.3);

(7) on a *partnership* sued in the name of a firm: on any partner, or on a manager at the principal place of business in Northern Ireland (with a notice that he is served in that capacity), or by ordinary first class post to that place. This is good service on the firm unless it has to the plaintiff's knowledge been dissolved before the action commenced (Ord.81 r.3);

(8) on an *individual trader* using a firm name: on him or on a manager at or by post to the place of business in Northern Ireland (Ord.81 r.8).

6.02 A writ served by post or by insertion in the letter box is presumed to have arrived on the seventh day (including weekend) after doing so;[8] an affidavit of service must depose that the letter will come to his knowledge within seven days, and if posted that it has not been returned undelivered (Ord.10 r.1(3)).[9] The presumption of service is rebuttable by evidence on behalf of either plaintiff or defendant that the writ arrived earlier or later than the presumed date or not at all.[10] If the writ is posted on a Sunday, service in so far as it is deemed to take place on the following Sunday is void,[11] so that the plaintiff would have to argue that it is deemed to be served on the Monday eight days after posting. If the plaintiff sent a copy of the writ "for information only", it is not service.[12] The correct destination is the defendant's usual (i.e. current)

---

3 Paradoxically this must be registered or recorded delivery post: see Ord.10 r.1(6) and para. 6.25.

4 Companies (NI) Order 1986, Art.673 If a change of address has been notified to the Companies Registrar service at the old address is bad, even if it is proved that the writ was forwarded to the new address: *McIlhatton* v *Wallace* [1972] NI 50 (*sed quaere*, see the cases at para. 6.02).

5 *O'Neill* v *St Brigid's Well* [1895] 2 IR 442.

6 White Book (1997) 65/3/7.

7 Companies (NI) Order 1986, Arts.644A and 645.

8 I.e., a writ posted on Wednesday is deemed served on the following Wednesday.

9 This does not apply to service on a company, which is presumed to arrive in the ordinary course of post.

10 *Hodgson* v *Hart DC* [1986] 1 WLR 317.

11 Sunday Observance Act (Ir) 1695, s.7; see para. 6.21.

12 *Abu Dhabi Helicopters* v *International Aeradio* [1986] 1 WLR 312; but see para. 7.07.

address or his last known address (see para. 6.25). In serving a defendant at his 'usual or last known address', and in serving a partner as service on a firm, the writ may be served at his residence or place of business.[13] A letter posted to the wrong address is validly served once it is forwarded and delivered to the right address and comes to the defendant's knowledge,[14] but service under Order 10 rule 1 by posting or insertion in the letter box is void if the defendant proves either that the letter containing the writ did not come to his notice until after the seventh day or that it did not come to his notice at all, even if the letter was not returned undelivered.[15] *Semble*, service by post or insertion in the letter box is invalid if the (human) defendant is outside Northern Ireland at the time.[16]

6.03 A writ must be served in accordance with one of the methods stated above, unless the parties agree a different form.[17] It can be served at any time of the day but not on a Sunday.[11] It cannot be served by FAX.

6.04 The Court may order substituted service of a writ or other originating process (Ord.65 r.4); and in an action for recovery of land, by affixing a copy on the land (Ord.10 r.4). If the defendant is outside Northern Ireland, substituted service can be ordered if he left for the purpose of avoiding the litigation;[18] or has left since the issue of the writ,[19] or if the writ is for service outside the jurisdiction.

6.05 The RSC in Ireland/Northern Ireland from 1877 up to 1980 contained a rule (Wylie, Ord.9 r.22)[20] enabling the Court to declare the service actually effected sufficient There is no such general provision in the current RSC.[21] The Court of Appeal in *Boocock* v *Hilton International*[22] held that irregular service could be validated and deemed good by invoking Order 2 rule 1. Where a writ served by ordinary first class post is returned by post undelivered after the plaintiff has entered judgment in default, the Court may, on *ex parte* application by the plaintiff, set aside the judgment or may direct that service be treated as good (Ord.13 r.7(3)(5)).

6.06 Particulars of the way in which the writ is served should be kept by the plaintiff's solicitor in case an affidavit of service proves necessary.

Duration of writ for service

6.07 A writ or concurrent writ is valid for service for 12 months beginning with date of the issue of the original. However if it has not been served, the Court may extend the time limit, and it is resealed then with the period of

---

13 *Robertson* v *Banham & Co* [1997] 1 All ER 79.

14 *Barclays Bank* v *Hahn* [1989] 1 WLR 506 (HL); *Austin Rover* v *Crouch* [1986] 1 WLR 1102.

15 *Forward* v *West Sussex CC* [1995] 4 All ER 207 (CA); leave to appeal refused by House of Lords [1996] 1 WLR 438.

16 See *Barclays Bank* v *Hahn* [1989] 1 WLR 506. Contrast the position in the county court: *Rolph* v *Zolan* [1993] 4 All ER 202.

17 *Kenneth Allison Ltd* v *Limehouse* [1992] 2 AC 105 (HL).

18 *Donaghey* v *Donaghey* (1899) 33 ILTR 97.

19 *Smyth* v *Dolan* (1913) 47 ILTR 287.

20 See also Wylie, p.217.

21 Except in an action for recovery of land: Ord.10 r.4(2)(b).

22 [1993] 1 WLR 1065; but see *Kenneth Allison Ltd* v *Limehouse* [1992] 2 AC at 126G

extension stated (Ord.6 r.7). Extension will be granted only for good cause, for example that the defendant cannot be traced, or that the defendant has prevaricated by offering to negotiate. If good cause is shown, the Court then considers the balance of convenience, and if the limitation period has expired, requires exceptional circumstances.[23] Extension of time is applied for *ex parte*. *Ex parte* application is inappropriate in a case where the limitation period has now expired in a personal injury action and the crucial issue is whether the Court should disapply the limitation period under Article 50 of the Limitation (NI) Order 1989 (see para. 4.06).[24] In such case the Court should adjourn the application so that the plaintiff can issue a fresh writ, serve it and apply on notice to the defendant under Article 50.[25] However, such a strategy would seem to be rendered futile by subsequent case law[26] which says that in a second action the limitation period should be disapplied only if the first has been dropped because of the representation or misconduct of the defendant.

6.08 The defendant may serve a notice requiring the plaintiff within 14 days either to serve the writ or discontinue the action and if not, the defendant may apply by summons for dismissal of the action or other order (Ord.12 r.8A).

SERVICE OF OTHER ORIGINATING PROCESS

6.09 Broadly the same provisions apply to service of an originating summons or motion, and petition (Ord.10 r.5).

SETTING ASIDE SERVICE

6.10 Defective or non-service of the writ is waived by the defendant entering an unconditional appearance. To set aside service he should apply before appearance or on entering a conditional appearance. It is the defendant, not the person wrongly served, who has *locus standi* to apply, except possibly where the defendant cannot be contacted.[27] Service can be set aside if the affidavit of service is shown to be inaccurate.[28]

SERVICE WHERE DEFENDANT IS OUTSIDE NORTHERN IRELAND

6.11 Subject to statute and the RSC, a writ cannot be served outside Northern Ireland, but if a foreign defendant happens to be in the province,[29] he can be served here, unless: (a) the Northern Ireland Court is deprived of

---

[23] *Dagnell* v *Freedman* [1993] 1 WLR 388 (HL); *Baly* v *Barrett* [1988] NI 368 (HL); *Tubridy* v *Finnegan* [1983] NI 340.

[24] And extension should not be given on that ground: *Chappell* v *Cooper* [1980] 1 WLR 958.

[25] So held by Murray J in *Johnston* v *Mohan* [1978] NI 126. This decision seems to introduce unnecessary complexity and artificiality in procedure. Surely it would be easier for the Court to consider granting the extension *ex parte*, and if so, the defendant could apply to set the *ex parte* order aside by motion on notice, at which the Court could then have regard to Art.50.

[26] *Walkley* v *Precision Forgings* [1979] 1 WLR 606; *Kinkead* v *Hagan* [1982] NI 412; and *Tubridy* v *Finnegan*.

[27] *Royal Bank* v *Nolan* (1958) 92 ILTR 60, but see *Greene* v *Mooney* (1901) 1 NIJR 215, where the applicant was the defendant's wife on whom substituted service had been ordered.

[28] *Martin* v *Williams* (1869) IR 3 CL 5.

[29] Even if brought involuntarily: *Doyle* v *Doyle* (1974) 52 DLR 3d 143 (in police custody); or casually passing through.

jurisdiction by the Civil Jurisdiction and Judgments Acts; or (b) he has been induced by fraud to come here for the purpose of serving the writ.

6.12 The Crown Proceedings Act (s.35(2)(a)) requires rules to provide for service of a writ or notice thereof in proceedings by the Crown against a person not resident in the United Kingdom; but no specific rules have been made apart from ground (*n*) (below, para. 6.16). The rules set out below relating to service outside the jurisdiction do not apply to process *against* the Crown (Ord.77 r.3).

Service without leave

6.13 A writ for service outside Northern Ireland cannot be issued without leave of the Court unless-

- the Court has jurisdiction under the Civil Jurisdiction and Judgments Act 1982, and no proceedings on the same cause are pending in Great Britain or any Brussels Convention territory, such facts to be indorsed on the writ; or
- the Court has jurisdiction under another statute (Ord.6 r.6(1); Ord.11 r.1(2)).[30]

As Order 11 rule 1(2) points out, the application of the 1982 Act is attracted only if: (a) the defendant is domiciled in Great Britain or a Brussels Convention territory, (b) proceedings are within Article 16 of the said Convention, concerning rights *in rem* over land etc. situate in such places, or (c) the parties, one of whom is domiciled in such place, have agreed in writing that the courts of such place shall have exclusive jurisdiction.

6.14 If the action relates to a contract made in Northern Ireland with an agent in Northern Ireland, the plaintiff may seek leave on *ex parte* application to serve the writ on the agent, sending a copy to the defendant at his address outside Northern Ireland (Ord.10 r.2). If the High Court has jurisdiction to hear an action under a contract which provides for service on the defendant at a specified place, then service under it is good, though if the place is outside Northern Ireland Order 11 rule 1 must be complied with (Ord.10 r.3). If the defendant is a partnership or a individual trader sued in the name of a firm carrying on business in Northern Ireland, Order 81 enables a writ to be served at its place of business even if a partner or that trader is outside Northern Ireland.

Service with leave

6.15 Service outside Northern Ireland is permissible by leave under Order 11 rule 1(1) in an action begun by writ. The rule is much less important now because of the Civil Jurisdiction and Judgments Acts 1982 and 1991, but it is still important where the defendant is domiciled in North or South America, Asia, Africa, a Commonwealth country or anywhere outside the European Community and 'EFTA', or where the subject-matter is outside the Acts. The grounds are discussed in the White Book and Wylie (notes to Ord.11 in both books), and are stated here together with a reference to post-1905 Irish cases.

---

[30] See *Republic of Haiti* v *Duvalier* [1990] 1 QB 202.

6.16 Service on a defendant outside the jurisdiction is permissible by leave of the Court if -

(a) he is domiciled in Northern Ireland (as defined by ss.41-6 of the 1982 Act)

(b) an injunction is sought for him to do or not to do an act in Northern Ireland (*Dunlop Rubber* v *Dunlop* [1921] 1 AC 367; *Taher Meats* v *State Co* [1991] 1 IR 443)

(c) he is a necessary or proper party to a claim against a duly served defendant (*Ross* v *Eason* [1911] 2 IR 459; *Cooney* v *Wilson* [1913] 2 IR 402; *McWilliams* v *Gilbert* (1913) 47 ILTR 297; *Boyd* v *Lee Guinness* [1963] NI 49; *Waddell* v *Norton* [1966] NI 85; *Macrete* v *GRE* [1988] NI 332; *International Bank* v *Insurance Corp* [1989] IR 453)

(d) the claim relates to a contract or the breach of a contract which was made in Northern Ireland (*Wheeler* v *John Jeffrey* [1921] 2 IR 395; *Clare CC* v *Wilson* [1913] 2 IR 89; *Murray* v *Finkle* (1914) 48 ILTR 178; *Tedcastle* v *Robertson* [1929] IR 597; *Sanderson* v *Cunningham* [1919] 2 IR 234; *O'Leary* v *Law Integrity* [1912] 1 IR 479; *Taher Meats* v *State Co* [1991] 1 IR 443; *Kelly* v *Cruise Catering* [1994] 2 ILRM 394); or through an agent in Northern Ireland; or is governed by Northern Ireland law (*Clarke* v *Harper* [1938] NI 162; *Kutchera* v *Buckingham* [1988] IR 61); or has a term conferring jurisdiction on the Northern Ireland High Court. See generally *Shipsey* v *British Steam* [1936] IR 65; *O'Leary* v *Law Integrity*

(e) the claim relates to a breach committed in Northern Ireland of a contract (*O'Mara* v *Dodd* [1912] 2 IR 55; *Clare CC* v *Wilson* [1913] 2 IR 89)

(f) the claim relates to a tort if the damage was sustained or resulted from an act in Northern Ireland (*O'Daly* v *Gulf Oil* [1983] ILRM 163; *Grehan* v *Medical Inc* [1986] IR 528) (wording different in these cases)

(g) the whole subject-matter is land situate in Northern Ireland (*Clare CC* v *Wilson* [1913] 2 IR 89; *Killiney UDC* v *Kirkwood* [1917] 2 IR 614; *Carlingford Harbour* v *Everard* [1985] NI 50)

(h) the claim relates to an act, deed, liability affecting land in Northern Ireland

(i) the claim relates to a debt secured on immoveable property in Northern Ireland, or rights of security in moveable property in Northern Ireland

(j) he is a trustee of a written trust which ought to be executed in Northern Ireland

(k) the claim relates to administration of estate of person who died domiciled in Northern Ireland

(l) in a probate action

(m) in an action to enforce a judgment or arbitration award

(n) in a claim by the Inland Revenue against defendant not domiciled in Great Britain

(o) in a claim under the Nuclear Installations Act, or a claim for Social Security Act contributions

(p) in a claim for sum under Directive 76/308/EEC (re financing of Agricultural Guidance; agricultural levies and duties; and VAT)
(q) in a claim under the Financial Services Act 1986 or Banking Act 1987
(r) in a claim against him as constructive trustee who is liable for acts committed in Northern Ireland.

The above grounds refer to the substantive claims for relief in the action. A claim for a procedural or interim remedy such as a *Mareva* injunction cannot be the basis for leave to serve outside Northern Ireland.[31]

6.17 An application for leave to issue and serve outside Northern Ireland is made *ex parte* to the master on affidavit of the grounds and deposing to a cause of action and where the defendant is to be found (Ord.11 r.4(1)).[32] Leave is granted only if it is shown that it is a proper case for service, and if for service in Great Britain, the Court has regard to the comparative ease of pursuing a remedy there;[33] the order must state a time limit for appearance (Ord.11 r.4). The plaintiff must show a good arguable case that the alleged cause of action is within Order 11 rule 1 and then show a serious issue to be tried for the existence of the cause of action.[34] In a doubtful case, the Court gave leave but stayed the action for a month to enable the defendant to apply to set aside the leave.[35] Leave may be given limiting the claim to those causes of action to which the rule applies.[36] Leave may be refused if the action could be brought in the county court.[37] If after obtaining leave under ground (c) the plaintiff discontinues against the local defendant, the Court may stay the action as an abuse of process.[38] The defendant can apply to set aside the service on him without entering an unconditional appearance, and the Court should do so if it appears that on the facts deposed to in the plaintiff's affidavit, the granting of leave was wrong; the fact that the High Court has jurisdiction under the Brussels or other convention is irrelevant, as the plaintiff can invoke the Convention by issuing a writ indorsed to that effect.[39]

Mode of service of writ outside Northern Ireland

6.18 Order 11 rules 3, 5-8 deal with the mode of service of a writ outside Northern Ireland, both where leave is required and where it is not.[40] The writ is in Form 4 and it is served if the defendant is in Great Britain. If he is outside

---

31 *Mercedes Benz* v *Leiduck* [1996] 1 AC 284 (PC).

32 The plaintiff has a duty of *uberrimae fides*: see *Brennan* v *Lockyer* [1932] IR 101; *Freedman* v *Opdeheyde* [1945] Ir Jur Rep 22; *Waddell* v *Norton* [1966] NI 85. Defective affidavit: *McCartan* v *Hulton* (1922) 56 ILTR 152 (failure to state source of hearsay). The application must show which ground under Ord 11 r.1 is relied on: *Kondor* v *Honeywell* (1970) 104 ILT 220.

33 See *Murray* v *Finkle* (1914) 48 ILTR 178.

34 *Seaconsar* v *Bank Markazi* [1994] 1 AC 438.

35 *McLoughlin* v *Life Assoc of Scotland* (1915) 49 ILTR 166.

36 *Bevan* v *Gillows* (1906) 40 ILTR 251; *Atkins* v *Thompson* [1922] 2 IR 102.

37 *Wiley* v *Spanjer* (1933) 67 ILTR 69.

38 *Sharples* v *Eason* [1911] 2 IR 436.

39 *United Meat* v *Nordsteine Allgemeine* [1996] 2 ILRM 260 (Carroll J).

40 As to substituted service, see *Carson* v *Crozier* (1917) 51 ILTR 38, and the White Book (1997) 65/4/11.

Great Britain, notice of the writ (in Form 5) is served;[41] it must state a time limit for appearance in accordance with Order 11 rule 1(3). The Brussels Convention on Civil Jurisdiction appended to the 1982 Act should not be confused with the Conventions for service of documents mentioned in Order 11 rules 5-8.

Service of other process

6.19 Service of other originating processes outside Northern Ireland is provided for by Order 11 rule 9. An application to serve a third-party notice is made *ex parte*.[42] Any summons, notice or order issued in pending proceedings[43] may be served outside Northern Ireland by leave, or without leave in proceedings where the originating process could be served without leave (Ord.11 r.9(4)).

SERVICE OF DOCUMENTS GENERALLY

Service in Supreme Court proceedings

6.20 Order 65 rule 5 deals with service on a party of notices, summonses and other documents which are not originating processes. Save where a rule requires personal service, they may be served as follows-

(1) by leaving it or by post (or between solicitors only, by FAX and following letter) to the proper address for service or if none to the office of his solicitor or his own usual or last known address (or if a corporation, its registered or principal office); or

(2) if the address for service or the writing paper of the party or his solicitor has a document exchange box number, by leaving it at that exchange (addressed to the box number) or at an exchange which transmits daily to it.

This does not apply to the Crown, which is served by posting to or leaving the document with an employee of the departmental or Crown solicitor (Ord.77 r.3). If a solicitor is on record, by issuing a writ or entering an appearance or otherwise, service on him is good service until the conclusion of the proceedings unless a notice is filed and served under Order 67; and where the solicitor has been taken off the record under Order 67 or the party's legal aid certificate is revoked or discharged, his last known address (or if a corporation, its registered or principal office) is the place for service (Ord.67 r.6). The fact of service must be proved on balance of probability.[44] If a party is in default of appearance[45] or has no address for service, service may be dispensed with, unless the rules require personal service or the document is an originating

41 In which case service of the writ itself is bad and will be set aside: *O'Connor* v *Commercial General* [1996] 1 IR 68 (Morris J).

42 *Cannon* v *Fallon* (1918) 52 ILTR 34.

43 Including an order made after final judgment in aid of enforcement: *Union Bank* v *Lelakis* [1996] 4 All ER 305 (CA).

44 *McMullan* v *Wallace* [1977] NI at 6G, 9F.

45 As to which the Court may decide to satisfy itself: Ord.13 r.7(2).

process (Ord.65 r.9). This rule does not apply against the Crown (Ord.77 r.3(3)).

6.21 *Personal service.* This is effected by leaving a copy with the person served (Ord.65 r.2) or in personal service on a body corporate not provided for by statute, by leaving a copy with the mayor, clerk, secretary, or other officer[46] (Ord.65 r.3(1)). No document need be personally served unless a rule or a court order so requires (Ord.65 r.1). Personal service is never necessary on the Crown (Ord.77 r.3). Personal service on a minor is on his parent/guardian or person with whom he resides; personal service on a patient is on the person authorised under the Mental Health (NI) Order 1986 or person with whom he resides; but a *subpoena* or injunctive order must be served personally on the minor or patient (Ord.80 r.13). The server must satisfy himself of the identity of the person to be served and then personally hand the copy to him, showing him or telling him what the document is. In *Hunt* v *Egan*[47] showing the document to the servee through a window and leaving it on the window sill was held good. Handing it an authorised agent of X is not personal service on X.[48] Service can be effected at any time of day, but service of a writ, process, warrant, order, judgment, or decree on a Sunday is void to all intents and purposes.[49] Therefore, where the last day for service expires on a Sunday, the time limit may be extended to Monday, by virtue of the doctrine *lex non cogit as impossibilia.*

6.22 *Substituted service.* This can be ordered of an originating process or of any document which is required by the RSC to be served personally, by application *ex parte* on affidavit showing that service in prescribed manner is impracticable for any reason (Ord.65 r.4), for example that the defendant is evading service; or that a process server refuses to enter the defendant's area for lack of security.[50] Where a document is to be served on a husband and wife or two co-habitees, there being a risk that one will intercept mail, the Court should order substituted service by post only if personal service is impossible and if absolutely certain that the form of service will ensure notification to both parties.[51] It cannot be ordered on a dead person or defunct company. The Court may order service by advertisement, or on a friend or relative, former solicitor,[52] insurance company or the Motor Insurers' Bureau. Once service so ordered is performed it constitutes effective service unless set aside. If not performed, the order must be discharged before any other form of substituted service can be ordered.[53]

6.23 A document, other than originating process, served after 4pm on Tuesday is deemed to be served on Wednesday; if after noon on Saturday, then the next Monday (Ord.65 r.7). A document is served on the Crown in

---

46 Of similar standing: *Kuwait Airways* v *Iraqi Airways* [1995] 1 WLR 1147 (HL).
47 (1842) 1 Leg Rep 174; but see White Book (1997) 65/2/1.
48 *Kenneth Allison Ltd* v *Limehouse* [1992] 2 AC 105.
49 Sunday Observance Act (Ir) 1695, s.7.
50 *Irish Agric Society* v *St Enda's Co-Op* [1924] 2 IR 41.
51 *Abbey National* v *Grugan*, Ch D, NI (Girvan J) 7 March 1997.
52 *Shelswell-White* v *O'Connor* (1961) 95 ILTR 113.
53 *McDaniel* v *Hughes* (1910) 44 ILTR 187.

accordance with section 18 of the Crown Proceedings Act (Ord.77 r.3).[54] As to service of documents on the Court, see para. 1.25. As to service of a process for proceedings in a foreign country, under the Hague Convention 1965 or otherwise, see Order 69. Defective or non-service is waived by appearing in the proceedings or by making or appearing in any application in the proceedings (other than to set aside service).

Service under statute

6.24 Where UK legislation[55] requires service by post, it means service by ordinary pre-paid post (Interpretation Act 1978, s.7);[56] and on proof of posting there is a conclusive presumption that it was delivered, and a rebuttable presumption that it arrived in the ordinary course of post. This means that where the statutory provision prescribing service does not stipulate service at a particular time, then mere posting is conclusive evidence of service; it is only when the provision makes time of service material that evidence is admissible to show that the document was not received at the proper time or at all; time of service is not material merely because it is a step which must precede some further step at an indefinite time in the future.[57] So where the statute requires service within X days of an event or X days before an event, or notice is to be given of a hearing on a specified day,[58] or even within a reasonable time or "in due course",[59] posting is not good service if the letter is returned undelivered. Where originating process is served on a company by registered post and returned undelivered, the plaintiff cannot treat the time limited for appearance as having started to run.[60] If it is posted addressed to the proper address, service is good even if the person served was not at home.[61] Curiously, the 1978 Act does not state the address to which the document is to be posted: on an absurd literal construction, the letter could be addressed to any place at all. The servee's address must be a place where he has had some continuing presence.[62]

6.25 Where NI legislation[63] requires service by post, it means pre-paid registered or recorded delivery post to his usual or last known place of abode or business. There is also a conclusive presumption that it was delivered and a rebuttable presumption that it arrived in the ordinary course of post.[64] The case law under the 1978 Act (above) applies. A letter is properly "addressed to the last known place of abode or business" if it is posted to the postal address from which the servee collects his mail; such place need not be physically located at

---

54 Including service on a minister or head of department in proceedings to which the Crown is not a party: Ord.65 r.6.
55 As defined at para. 1.10.
56 Identical to its predecessor, Interpretation Act 1889, s.26. Recorded delivery service is also valid if not returned undelivered.
57 *Moody* v *Godstone RDC* [1966] 2 All ER 696, at 701.
58 *British Egg Marketing* v *Gillespie* [1969] NI 139.
59 *R* v *London QS, ex p Rossi* [1956] 1 QB 682.
60 *In re Bird Moyer* (1964) 98 ILTR 202.
61 *Cooper* v *Scott-Farnell* [1969] 1 WLR 120.
62 *Willowgreen* v *Smithers* [1994] 1 WLR 832; a decision under a county court rule which also does not state what address.
63 As defined at para. 1.10.
64 Interpretation Act (NI) 1954, s.24(1); Recorded Delivery Services Act (NI) 1963.

the place of abode.[65] Service at the last known abode is good even if the server knows that the servee has left it.[66]

6.26 Where NI legislation[67] does not prescribe a mode of service, it may be done personally, or by registered/recorded delivery post, or by leaving it at the usual or last known abode with a person over 16 years; on a body or corporation by post or delivery to a clerk etc. at the registered or principal office; on unoccupied premises by affixing to a conspicuous part.[68]

6.27 These statutes do not mean that personal service is bad (White Book (1997) 65/5/4). Defective or non-service is waived by appearing in the proceedings or by making or appearing in any application in the proceedings (other than to set aside service).

PROOF OF SERVICE

6.28 Where required, service is usually proved by affidavit of the server, stating by whom, how and where and the day and date served (Ord.65 r.8).[69] The place of service must be stated.[70] The server should indorse details of service on the original at the time of service and so swear in his affidavit. The affidavit must state the identity of the person served. The best evidence of identity is that the person resembles a photograph which is proved in court to be of the person;[71] but the server's averment that the person served stated his identity is normally sufficient. The affidavit of service of originating process by post or leaving it in the letter box must state the belief that it will come to the defendant's knowledge in seven days and state that it has not been returned undelivered (Ord.10 r.1(3)(b)).[72] In urgent cases service can be proved by oral evidence. In *Smyth* v *Cunningham*[73] the process server indorsed service on the writ but died before making an affidavit; the judge gave leave to enter judgment in default in ten days, on notice by post to the defendant.

---

[65] *Fancourt* v *Mercantile Credits* (1983) 154 CLR 87, at 93-5.
[66] *Singh* v *Sec of State for Home Dept*, 1993 SC (HL) 1.
[67] As defined at para. 1.10.
[68] Interpretation Act (NI) 1954, s.24(2).
[69] As to proof of service in the Chancery Division, see Practice Direction 18 January 1968.
[70] *Rogers* v *Creswell* (1900) 34 ILTR 173.
[71] *Beamish* v *Beamish* (1876) IR 10 Eq 413.
[72] If served on a firm by post, see Ord.81 r.3(2)(b).
[73] (1901) 1 NIJR 87.

CHAPTER SEVEN

APPEARANCE

DEFENDANT'S OPTIONS

7.00 If the defendant believes that a writ has been issued against him but that it has not yet been served on him, he may serve a notice on the plaintiff requiring him to serve the writ or discontinue (Ord.12 r.8A) or may simply enter a *gratis* appearance under Order 10 rule 1. The defendant may require the solicitor in whose name the writ was issued to declare in writing that the writ was issued with his authority, and if not may apply to stay the action (Ord.6 r.4(2)(3)). If the defendant believes that a writ has been issued without the authority of the person named as plaintiff, he may apply to strike out the action.

7.01 If the defendant sees that he has no defence to the claim made in the writ and is liable for the whole amount or other relief claimed on the writ he should offer to pay the amount claimed or the relief sought, with, in an action for a debt or for recovery of land, the 14-day costs indorsed on the writ. If he cannot yet do so, he may take no step; this allows the plaintiff to proceed to judgment in default, and the defendant will be liable for a smaller sum in costs than if he enters an appearance and delivers a Defence.

7.02 If the defendant believes that the action is beyond the Court's jurisdiction or defective in the issue or service of the writ, he should apply to set aside the proceedings, entering only a conditional appearance. If the defendant contemplates a defence on the merits, as to liability and/or quantum, he should enter an ordinary appearance, and will normally do so in a claim for unliquidated damages.

APPEARANCE

7-03 The defendant should enter an appearance[1] (by handing or posting a memorandum of appearance and two copies to the appropriate Office) within 14 days[2] after service of the writ, though he may enter a late appearance at any time before judgment is entered against him (Ord.12 rr.1-6). An appearance after judgment requires leave (Ord.12 r.6). The memorandum, in Form 12, must state an address (the solicitor's address if he acts) which is an address for service. If the address is not genuine the plaintiff can apply to set aside the appearance (Ord.12 r.3(4)). Order 12 rule 4 provides for entering the appearance in the court records and for posting one copy to the plaintiff at his address for service. A company can appear only through a solicitor (Ord.12 r.1(2)). A party under disability must appear by a guardian *ad litem* (Ord.80

---

1 The English RSC were revised in 1979, replacing "appearance" with "acknowledgement of service" which does not waive objection to the writ.

2 A longer time is allowed if the writ was served outside Northern Ireland: see Ord.11 r.1(3).

rr.3-4). In an action removed from the county court, the defendant must enter an appearance in Form 13. An appearance can be entered at any time after the issue of the writ, and if the writ has not yet been served or improperly served, it is deemed to be served on the date when the appearance is entered (Ord.10 r.1(5)).

7.04 If the defendant is sued as a firm name, an appearance must be entered by the partners (not a manager) in their own names or the individual trader in his own name; the action then continues in the firm name; a person can state on his appearance that he denies being a partner at the material time (Ord.81 r.4). An appearance in the name of the firm is a mere irregularity curable by amendment.[3] If a person was served as a partner he must enter an appearance denying such, otherwise he is liable to execution of any judgment against the firm (Ord.81 r.5(1)).

7.05 Only the defendant or a solicitor for him can enter an appearance, though any authorised person may lodge the documents. An appearance for a dead, defunct or non-existent person is void and all proceedings thereon will be set aside by the Court of its own motion.[4] An appearance by a solicitor entered without the defendant's authority is contempt by him and either party may apply to vacate the appearance with costs against the solicitor even if innocent of blame.[5] Judgment thereon should be set aside with costs against the solicitor.[6] Where by mistake a solicitor for one defendant entered an appearance for both, it was amended.[7]

7.06 If wrongly named in the writ, the appearance should appear in that name adding "who is properly known as ....", and the plaintiff should later have the writ amended. An appearance in the wrong name alone is irregular,[8] but not void.[9]

Effect of appearance

7.07 An unconditional appearance waives defects in the issue and formal contents of the writ or in the indorsement for costs;[10] and in the service of the writ or non-service. It waives service of an expired writ;[11] or improper service outside Northern Ireland.[12] It appears that a defendant who enters an unconditional appearance to an unserved writ is estopped from disputing that he has been served[13] and is deemed to have been served on the date of his appearance. It is a submission to the procedural jurisdiction; but it does not

---

3 *Brown Bros* v *Ballantine Bros* (1878) 12 ILTR 70.

4 *Lazard Bros* v *Banque de Moscou* [1932] 1 KB 617, at 624.

5 *Yonge* v *Toynbee* [1910] 1 KB 215.

6 Even if innocent: *Dinnon* v *Aubrey* (1833) 1 Law Rec NS 38.

7 *J--* v *Henry* (1890) 24 ILT 70.

8 *In re Debtor's Summons* [1929] IR 139.

9 *Doe de Archdeacin* v *Thrustout* (1843) 5 Ir LR 591.

10 *Doyle* v *Patterson* [1934] IR 116.

11 *Sheldon* v *Brown Bayleys* [1953] 2 QB 393.

12 *Re Orr Ewing* (1883) 22 Ch D 456, at 463-4; *affd.* 9 App Cas 34.

13 Unlike England where Ord.10 r.1(5) is differently worded (see *Towers* v *Morley* [1992] 1WLR 511).

waive a substantive defence that the Court is deprived of jurisdiction to hear the action by statute;[14] nor an objection to the substance of the claim on the writ (e.g. that it discloses no cause of action or omits required particulars). Appearance by a defendant domiciled in Great Britain or a Brussels Convention State is a submission to the jurisdiction unless entered to contest the jurisdiction.[15] An "appearance without prejudice" is an unconditional appearance.[16]

7.08 An unqualified appearance is to every capacity in which the defendant is sued. An appearance stands to the writ as it may later be amended,[17] but if an amendment adds a defendant he must appear.

Conditional appearance

7.09 A defendant who wishes to dispute the Court's jurisdiction or the validity of the issue or service of the writ should apply to set aside the writ without appearing, or seek leave to enter a conditional appearance under Order 12 rule 7. Application is made *ex parte* to a master and the defendant must show a *bona fide* desire or ground for setting aside the writ or service. The appearance stands as an unconditional appearance unless the Court otherwise orders or the defendant applies within the time limited for serving a Defence under Order 12 rule 8 to set aside the writ or service. The time limit can be extended.[18] A conditional appearance ranks as an ordinary appearance for all purposes save that the defendant may make such application. It bars judgment in default; but is not *per se* a submission to the jurisdiction of the Court.[19]

Application to set aside

7.10 Before entering an appearance, or after entering a conditional appearance within the time limited for serving a Defence, the defendant may apply to set aside the writ or service or to declare service ineffective (Ord.12 r.8) on summons stating the defect and on affidavit of the facts.

Withdrawal or amendment

7.11 Only by leave of the Court in its discretion, an appearance can be amended (Ord.20 r.2), for example in order to enter a conditional appearance.[20] By leave an appearance can be withdrawn (Ord.21 r.1) as where the defence solicitor was unaware that the writ was served out of time.[21] In *Volkes* v *EHSSB*[16] leave was given to withdraw an appearance and substitute a conditional appearance, because the defence solicitor evinced an intention throughout to repudiate service of the writ and merely erred by misunderstanding the procedure.

---

14 *Wilkinson* v *Banking Corp* [1948] 1 KB 721.

15 Civil Jurisdiction and Judgments Act 1982, Sch.1 Art.18 and Sch.4 Art.18. The exclusive jurisdiction of the state where land is situate in actions on rights *in rem* cannot be so waived.

16 *Volkes* v *EHSSB* [1990] NI 388.

17 *Paxton* v *Baird* [1893] 1 QB 139.

18 Cf. *Keymer* v *Reddy* [1912] 1 KB 215, at 221.

19 *Henry* v *Geoprosco* [1976] QB 726 (*semble*).

20 *Firth* v *John Mowlem* [1978] 3 All ER 331.

21 *Bradford* v *DOE* [1986] NI 41.

Consumer credit

7.12 If the action is brought against the debtor or surety on a consumer credit agreement the defendant may serve notice under section 139(1)(b) of the Consumer Credit Act 1974 that it should be re-opened as being extortionate, by filing and serving on every other party a notice, as well or instead of entry of appearance, and thereafter judgment in default cannot be entered without leave (Ord.83).

7.13 No text allocated.

STAY OF PROCEEDINGS FOR ARBITRATION

7.14 Any persons who deal with each other may agree that an actual or potential dispute between them be referred to an arbitrator, referee, umpire etc.: that is a 'submission to arbitration'. The Arbitration Act 1996 applies to arbitral proceedings commenced on or after 31 January 1997, subject to the transitional provisions of a commencement order (s.84). Sections 85-87, which make special provision for domestic arbitration agreements, are not yet in force. It repeals the old law, namely, the Arbitration Act (NI) 1937 and the Consumer Arbitration Act 1988 (which Acts apply to a domestic agreement) or the Arbitration Act 1975 (non-domestic). RSC Order 73, which regulates the procedure under the Arbitration Acts, has been replaced by a new Order 73 (by SR 1997/70). The old law applies to: (a) arbitral proceedings commenced before 31 January 1997, and (b) applications in court proceedings relating to arbitration where either the application or the arbitral proceedings commenced before that date.[22] Part II (rr.23-27) of the new Order 73 governs proceedings under the old law.

7.15 The Arbitration Act 1996 applies to arbitrations of which the 'seat' as designated by the parties or arbitral body is in England/Wales or Northern Ireland (ss.2-3) but sections 9-11 and 66 apply regardless of the seat. Those and certain other sections apply notwithstanding an agreement to the contrary (s.4). The Act applies to an 'arbitration agreement', defined as an agreement in writing to submit to arbitration present or future disputes (whether contractual or not) (ss.5-6). An agreement in writing which does not contain an arbitration clause but which refers to a written form of arbitration clause or to a document containing an arbitration clause is an arbitration agreement if the reference is such as to make that clause part of the agreement (s.6(2)). A contractual clause that the decision of an arbitrator (or any person) on a point of law is final and binding, is void as being an ouster of the jurisdiction of the courts.[23] [In a domestic arbitration agreement a clause precluding challenge to the court on a point of law is effective only if entered into after the arbitral proceedings have commenced (s.87) - date of commencement not yet published].

---

22 Arbitration Act (Commencement No 1) Order 1996 (SI 1996/3146); and the preamble to the new RSC, Order 73.

23 *Antrim Newtown* v *DOE* [1989] NI 26.

7.16 If legal proceedings are commenced in a court (whether by way of claim or counterclaim)[24] against a party to an 'arbitration agreement' on a matter agreed to be referred,[25] he may apply to that court for a stay of the proceedings so far as they concern that matter (s.9(1)). The application must be made in the court in which the proceedings are pending.[26] "Party" includes a person claiming through or under a party to the agreement (s.82(2)). The applicant for a stay cannot apply before taking the appropriate procedural step (if any) to acknowledge the proceedings nor after taking any step to answer the substantive claim (s.9((3)). A 'step' is a proceeding at court which incurs costs.[27] Delivery of a Defence or filing an affidavit showing a defence to resist summary judgment under Order 14 are steps to answer the substantive claim.[28] The applicant must serve notice of the application in Form 8A on every other party to the court proceedings at his address for service or last known abode; the Court may stay the court proceedings pending determination of the issue whether there is a valid arbitration agreement and whether it covers the dispute in the proceedings (Ord.73 r.6).

7.17 The court must grant a stay unless satisfied that the arbitration agreement is null and void, inoperative or incapable of being performed (s.9(4)). Unless otherwise agreed the arbitration agreement is a distinctive part of any overall agreement of which it forms part and is not rendered ineffective by reason that the overall agreement is invalid, non-existent or has become ineffective (s.7) and the arbitral tribunal is able to rule on its own jurisdiction as to whether there is a valid arbitration agreement and as to the matters covered by it, subject to the rights of appeal under the Act (s.30). The following cases may still be good law (though only where the applicant has disclaimed the arbitration clause itself): he cannot apply if he has disclaimed the contract as void;[29] or as avoided;[30] but can apply if he has repudiated liability under the terms of the agreement.[31]

7.18 [In the case of a domestic arbitration agreement only,[32] the court may refuse a stay if satisfied that there are other sufficient grounds for waiving the arbitration clause, e.g. that the applicant for the stay is or was at any material time not ready and willing to do all things necessary for the proper conduct of the arbitration or of any agreed prior dispute resolution procedure (s.86). In *NPO* v *Cornhill Insurance*[25] the defendant did not agree a proper venue until after the action started. A stay may be refused if the plaintiff is unable to bear

---

24 If the defendant pleads a set-off which is connected to the plaintiff's claim, the Court will not stay the set-off under s.9: *Aectra Refining* v *Exmar NV* [1994] 1 WLR 1634 (CA).

25 *NPO* v *Cornhill Insurance* [1956] NI 157.

26 High Court and County Court (Allocation of Proceedings) Order 1996 (SI 1996/3215).

27 *O'Flynn* v *Bord Gais* [1982] ILRM 324.

28 *Russell Bros* v *Breen*, QBD, NI (Pringle J) 14 March 1997.

29 *Coen* v *Employers Liability Assurance* [1962] IR 314.

30 *Ballasty* v *Army & Navy* (1916) 50 ILTR 114; *Jureidini* v *National British* [1915] AC 499. Both these cases involved a *Scott* v *Avery* clause.

31 *Lyons* v *Eagle Star* [1939] NI 189 (also a *Scott* v *Avery* clause); White Book (1995) Vol.2 [5707]. This passage is accidentally omitted in the 1997 edition.

32 I.e. an agreement in which: (a) neither party is a national or habitual resident of a state outside the UK or a corporate body incorporated or centrally controlled in such state; and (b) the seat of the arbitration (if any) is in the UK: s.85.

arbitration costs because of the defendant's acts;[33] or if the root of the dispute concerns a point of law;[34] or where the dispute involves a charge of fraud, constructive fraud[35] or professional incompetence against the plaintiff.[36]] Note that section 86 is not yet in force. The repeal of the equivalent provisions of the 1937 Act is in force, so that the discretion of the Court to refuse a stay under the 1937 Act is in abeyance for the time being.

7.19 Section 89 says: "The following sections [ss.90-91] extend the application of the Unfair Terms in Consumer Contracts Regulations 1994 (SI 1994/3159) in relation to a term which constitutes an arbitration agreement." The Regulations apply where the consumer is a legal person as well as a human person (s.90). Such a term is unfair so far as it relates to a monetary claim which does not exceed an amount specified [currently £3,000][37] (s.91).

7.20 Though it forms grounds for a stay, the submission to arbitration is not a defence to an action, unless the arbitration award is made a condition precedent to suing.[38] If the court refuses a stay under section 9, a *Scott* v *Avery* arbitration clause (i.e. that an arbitration award is a condition precedent to any court proceedings on the matter submitted to arbitration) is no defence (s.9(5)). However, it seems that may remain a defence if no application for a stay is made.

7.21 Apart from the above statutes, the Court has inherent power to stay an action brought in breach of an agreement to resolve disputes by a particular method, whether by arbitrator, foreign court or otherwise.[39]

Arbitration proceedings generally

7.22 Under the new law, the Arbitration Act 1996 and RSC, Order 73 Part I (rr.1-22) govern procedure and provide for appeal and review of the arbitrator's proceedings and award by the High Court. The Lord Chancellor may by order allocate jurisdiction between the High Court and county court under the Act (s.105). He has done so by the High Court and County Court (Allocation of Proceedings) Order (SI 1996/3215) which seems to apply to Northern Ireland as well as England/Wales, and in effect allocates all jurisdiction in Northern Ireland to the High Court.[40] Applications which may be made are listed in Appendix One of this book. The award itself can be sued for as a debt; and a domestic award (and foreign awards in Geneva Convention States) can be enforced as a judgment by leave of the court under section 66

---

33 But the Court cannot refuse to stay because the plaintiff can only litigate in a court for which legal aid is available; Art.10(6) of the Legal Aid Order (para. 3.61) forbids such consideration: *McIntyre* v *NIHE* [1995] 7 BNIL 60 (Carswell LJ).

34 *Hogg* v *Belfast Corp* [1919] 2 IR 305, *per* Madden J at 312.

35 *Workman* v *Belfast Harbour Commrs* [1899] 2 IR 234.

36 *Turner* v *Fenton* [1982] 1 WLR 52.

37 SR 1996/598

38 *Gregg* v *Fraser* [1906] 2 IR 545 (the '*Scott* v *Avery*' clause). The clause must be clear and effective: *McKee* v *McMahon* (1935) 69 ILTR 180 (NI).

39 *Channel Tunnel Group* v *Balfour Beatty* [1993] AC 334.

40 Save that application under section 9 for a stay must be brought in the court before which the legal proceedings are pending, and proceedings under ss 66 and 101(2) (enforcement of award) may be brought in either court.

(1950 Act, s.37; 1996 Act, s.99). An award in a New York Convention State may be enforced by leave of the court (1996 Act, s.101). The procedure for enforcement of awards is now governed by RSC Order 73 Part III (rr.28-32). The Limitation (NI) Orders 1987 and 1989 apply to arbitrations (s.13). As to costs, see sections 59-65.

Statutory arbitration

7.23 Part I if the 1996 Act (i.e. those provisions which apply to a non-domestic arbitration) apply also to an arbitration under a statutory provision (s.94). Therefore where a statute or subordinate legislation of the UK or NI Parliaments provides that a dispute shall be dealt with by arbitration, any action on that dispute must be stayed on application of the defendant under section 9(4).

Arbitration by order of court

7.24 Reference of dispute to an arbitrator by the Court can be ordered under Order 36 (see para. 14.14).

CHAPTER EIGHT

JUDGMENT IN DEFAULT

8.00 At any time after the expiry of time for appearance (in effect not sooner than the morning post has been opened on the 15th day after the deemed date of service), the plaintiff may enter judgment in default of appearance under Order 13, by going to the appropriate Office with the following documents as required by Order 13 rule 7(1) and Order 42 rule 7(1) -

(1) the original writ

(2) an affidavit of service, or the indorsement of acceptance of service by a solicitor on the original writ. If served by post this affidavit is in Form HC/115.[1] If after the judgment the copy writ is returned undelivered the plaintiff must request judgment to be set aside or apply for directions (Ord.13 r.7(3)(4)(5))

(3) two draft judgments in one of Forms 29-32

(4) in a debt case, an affidavit in Form HC/119 of the amount now due, crediting any payment since the writ was issued, and quantifying the interest up to the current date

(5) in an action for recovery of land, a certificate of the solicitor or affidavit that the claim is not mortgage-related, and not relating to a dwelling house

(6) in an action for recovery of land for non-payment of rent, a certificate of the solicitor or affidavit that it does not include agricultural land, and an affidavit that one year's rent was due

8.01 On checking that no appearance has been entered the officer will grant -

(1) *in a debt/liquidated demand claim*: final judgment "for a sum not exceeding the amount claimed", (i.e. the amount due at the issue of the writ crediting payments since then) (Ord.13 r.1), with interest to date under section 33A of the Judicature Act or otherwise; and with scale costs under Order 62 Appendix 3 Part I column (b) if at least £600 is awarded unless the Court otherwise orders[2] (Ord.62 r.17(3)). A final judgment for debt may include interest due as of right, or interest up to the statutory rate (currently 8% p.a.) under section 33A down to the date of judgment, provided that interest has been claimed on the writ. If the plaintiff enters judgment for the amount of the "14-day costs" indorsement on the writ (i.e. Ord.62 App.3 Part I col.(a)), he cannot have his costs taxed (Ord.62 r.7(3))

---

1 Proof of service is essential: *Crane* v *Wallis* [1915] 2 IR 411. 'HC' forms are those used and so described in Central Office usage, and are not to be found in the RSC.

2 I.e. a judge or a master, not the official granting judgment.

(2) *in a damages claim*: interlocutory judgment for damages to be assessed (Ord.13 r.2)

(3) *in a claim for detention of goods*: interlocutory judgment for return of the goods or their value; or only for their value; or the plaintiff may elect to apply by summons on affidavit for judgment for specific return (Ord.13 r.3)

(4) *in a claim for recovery of land*: final judgment for possession; with scale costs under Order 62 Appendix 3 Part II. If the requisite documents are not filed, the plaintiff may apply by summons for leave to enter judgment (Ord.13 r.4)

(5) *in a claim mixing any of the above types of claim (and no other type)*: the appropriate judgment in respect of each (Ord.13 r.5)

8.02 If the writ includes a claim for another remedy such as an injunction, specific performance or declaration, the plaintiff cannot enter judgment.[3] He should serve his Statement of Claim under Order 13 rule 6, and apply for judgment under Order 19 rule 7. A motion for judgment carries a court fee of £40. If the Statement of Claim was indorsed on the writ, he may apply directly under Order 19 rule 7. No evidence is admissible: the facts are taken as those alleged in the Statement of Claim. However, if the defendant is under disability, the facts must be proved by affidavit or other evidence. The plaintiff is confined to the final relief prayed for in the Statement of Claim.[4] The Court is reluctant to give a declaration without a full trial.[5] If the defendant satisfies the plaintiff's claim, the plaintiff may apply by summons for judgment for costs (Ord.13 r.6(2)).

8.03 Proceeding for judgment in default under Order 13 rules 1-5 does not prevent the plaintiff from seeking at any stage an interlocutory remedy, such as a *Mareva* injunction. He should ask the judge to order that the *Mareva* should continue in force after judgment until satisfaction of the claim.

8.04 Leave of court is required to enter judgment in default -

(1) against the Crown (Ord.77 r.8(1));[6]

(2) against a foreign state (Ord.13 r.7A) on proof of compliance with section 12 of the State Immunity Act 1978;

(3) in an action on a consumer credit agreement where the debtor or surety has served a notice to re-open (Ord.83 r.3);

(4) in a mortgage action (Ord.88 r.6) (see para. 18.71); or

(5) where the writ was duly served outside Northern Ireland without leave, or served in Northern Ireland on a defendant domiciled in a Great Britain or a Convention territory (Ord.13 r.7B).

---

3 Alternatively he may waive such remedy and enter judgment under rules 1 to 5 as appropriate: White Book (1997) 13/6/1.

4 *O'Reilly* v *O'Reilly* (1899) 33 ILTR 17.

5 Unless justice demands it: *Patten* v *Burke Publishing* [1991] 2 All ER 821.

6 Made under s. 35(2)(c) of the Crown Proceedings Act.

In cases (1), (2) and (4), the summons applying for leave must be served on the defendant even though he is in default of appearance. In case (5) the application is *ex parte* on affidavit stating the grounds on which the Court has jurisdiction.

8.05 A defendant sued as personal representative admits by his failure to defend that the estate has assets to satisfy the judgment and judgment will be against him '*de bonis testatoris et si non de bonis propriis*'.[7]

If a defendant under disability has not had an appearance entered for him, the plaintiff cannot proceed until he has applied to the Court for the appointment of a guardian ad litem, supported by evidence that the defendant is under disability, that the proposed guardian is willing, proper and disinterested, that the writ was duly served and that notice of this application has been served on the defendant (Ord.80 r.4).

8.06 The Office enters judgment only if the proper documents in proper order are produced (Ord.42 r.7(2)) and without regard to any substantive defence, such as expiry of the limitation period, even if it appears on the face of the writ. In *National Bank* v *Hunter*[8] judgment was allowed against a consul-general despite his right to claim diplomatic privilege. But matters affecting the right to judgment and procedural regularity must be considered. In *Stacey* v *O'Callaghan*[9] the court officer properly refused judgment where the particulars of debt were insufficient under the rules. In *UDT* v *Patterson*[10] the officer referred to a judge to direct whether the claim was a penalty, and counsel for the Attorney-General was brought in as *amicus curiae*. If the defendant is domiciled in a Brussels Convention State or Great Britain, the issue of the Court's jurisdiction must be considered.[11] If more than a year has elapsed since service of the writ and no other proceeding had, judgment can be given without one month's prior notice of intention to proceed, as the notice does not have to be served on a party in default of appearance (Ord.65 r.9).

8.07 Judgment follows the writ. Judgment should be given for the amount due at the date of issue (not service) of the writ, with appropriate costs thereon, deducting any subsequent payments by the defendant.[12] If sued in a firm name, judgment is against the firm.

8.08 If the plaintiff wants to enter judgment for more than the sum claimed in the writ, he must have it amended and re-served. If judgment is entered for less than is due, the plaintiff must have it amended or set aside; he cannot sue for the balance (see para. 3.30). If judgment is entered for more than is actually due at the date of judgment, it is irregular and must be amended under the slip rule or set aside.[13]

---

7 White Book (1997) 13/1/8.
8 [1948] Ir Jur Rep 33.
9 [1958] IR 320.
10 [1973] NI 142.
11 Civil Jurisdiction and Judgments Act 1982, Sch.1 Art.20; Sch.4 Art.20.
12 White Book (1997) 13/6/3; *Simmonds* v *Cronin* (1910) 44 ILTR 47; *Murphy* v *Kearns* (1924) 58 ILTR 29.
13 White Book (1997) 13/1/12.

8.09 In entering final judgment for a debt the Office can add interest claimed in the writ, in any of the following cases: (a) under section 33A of the Judicature Act; (b) as agreed under contract by express or implied term or by commercial custom or a course of dealing;[14] (c) in an action on a negotiable instrument to which the Bill of Exchange Act 1882 applies (including a promissory note, cheque or banker's draft) both interest and the expenses of noting and protesting the bill are deemed to be liquidated (s.57 thereof); (d) under statute.[15] As to costs, see further para. 17.21.

8.10 Judgment in default does not bar further pursuit to judgment against a co-defendant;[16] but does bar where the defendants are liable in the alternative only.[17] Judgment in default creates a limited estoppel *per rem judicatem* (see para. 13.105).

A party may requisition a copy of a judgment in Form HC/124.

Assessment of damages after judgment in default

8.11 After obtaining interlocutory judgment for damages, the plaintiff obtains an appointment for hearing to assess damages by a master under Order 37 (see para. 14.50), notice of which must be served in Form HC/123 on the defendant and such service proved. Alternatively he may apply for assessment by a judge on a Friday morning by notice of motion (Ord.37 r.4). The latter is especially advisable in a serious personal injury case. If the action is proceeding against co-defendants, damages will be assessed at the trial (Ord.37 r.3). At the hearing no deduction can be made for contributory negligence.[18] The Court may direct that damages be assessed by trial before a judge (Ord.37 r.4(1)(b)). If judgment in default of appearance or defence is given against one defendant, damages are to be assessed at the trial of the action against the other defendant (Ord.37 r.3). Apart from that, and save as otherwise provided by the judgment, damages are assessed by a master (Ord.37 r.1). The claimant obtains an appointment and serves seven days' notice of it on the party liable under Order 65 rule 5 even if he is in default of appearance. The master tries the issue in accordance with Order 35 and witnesses can be compelled by *subpoena*. The provisions as to evidence in Order 38 rules 1-5,18-29 apply. Order 37 is subject to section 62 of the Judicature Act, so that where it so dictates, the assessment of damages must be by judge and jury.[19] Where damages are assessed by a master in the Queen's Bench Division he enters final judgment for the amount; in the Chancery Division he makes an order for payment (Ord.37 r.2). Order 37 rules 1-4 apply also to judgments for the value of goods to be assessed (Ord.37 r.5). An assessment of damages by the Queen's Bench master, under Order 37 or otherwise, is appealable to the Court of Appeal (Ord.58 r.2).

---

14 *McCarthy* v *Roche* (1876) 10 ILTR 141.

15 E.g. Arbitration Act 1996, s.49(4) (interest on award); Crown Debts Act (Ir) 1781, s.23 (12% on overheld public monies); Taxes Management Act 1970, ss.86-92 (on arrears of taxes).

16 Civil Liability (Contribution) Act 1978, s.3.

17 *Morel Bros* v *Westmoreland* [1904] AC 11.

18 *Fookes* v *Slaytor* [1978] 1 WLR 1293.

19 *McParland* v *John Tinnelly* [1982] NI 110; cf.*Magill* v *Magill* [1914] 2 IR 533.

Motion for judgment

8.12 Either at the wish of the plaintiff or because Order 19 rule 7 requires it, the plaintiff may serve the Statement of Claim and apply to the Court for judgment.[20] In *McGrane* v *Behan,*[21] where counsel appeared for the defendant and asked for an adjournment but did not appear at the adjourned hearing, the Court held proof of service to be unnecessary.

SETTING ASIDE JUDGMENT

The grounds

8.13 Any judgment under Order 13 may be set aside or varied by the Court on such terms as it thinks fit (Ord.13 r.8). The defendant may show some irregularity in the obtaining of the judgment, such as failure to serve the writ properly, or at least some mistake or surprise.[22] He may rebut the presumption of due service by post by showing that the writ did not arrive at his proper address. Otherwise it is an almost[23] inflexible rule that the defendant must show by affidavit some defence to the claim,[24] and if successful he will usually be ordered to pay costs thrown away, and may be ordered to pay money into court.[25] If the defendant shows a defence on the merits as to part of the sum claimed, the Court may set it aside in part and affirm judgment for the undisputed amount.[26] A regularly obtained judgment cannot be set aside if extrinsic evidence shows that it arose as part of a contractual compromise between the parties.[27]

8.14 If judgment is obtained irregularly the defendant is entitled to have it set aside if he applies within a reasonable time, without any conditions save that he may have to undertake not to sue for damage caused by the judgment.[28] But if the defect is formal, the judgment may be cured by virtue of Order 2 rule 1 or Order 20 rule 11. Judgment entered for more than was actually due at the date of judgment[29] is bad and will be set aside; but if done by *bona fide* mistake[30] the

---

20 As to motions in the Chancery Division, see the Practice Direction [1989] 3 BNIL 82.

21 (1972) 106 ILT 218.

22 Examples of irregular judgment: writ not served properly, even if defendant knew of it: *Adams* v *Kyle* (1908) 42 ILTR 22; defendant outside jurisdiction on date of service: *Poole* v *Stewart* (1903) 37 ILTR 74; defendant under disability and no guardian appointed: *Pillman* v *Goodbody* (1909) 43 ILTR 32; final judgment given for sum not truly a liquidated demand: *Paterson* v *Wellington Kindergarten* [1966] NZLR 468; judgment entered too soon, before expiry of time for apppearance: *Kilgarriff* v *McGrane* (1881) 8 LR Ir 354; or entered too late, at the same time as or after the appearance has been entered: *Robinson* v *Woodroffe* (1870) 4 ILT 181.

23 *Quain* v *Fitzgerald* (1889) 19 ILTR 58.

24 White Book (1997) 13/9/5.

25 *Farden* v *Richter* (1889) 23 QBD 124; *Clarke* v *Dublin Steam* (1891) 25 ILTR 21; *Loane* v *Rush*, QBD, NI, 31 March 1969; 20 NILQ 324.

26 *The Iran Navubat* [1990] 1 WLR 1115 *(obiter)*.

27 *Northern Bank* v *Jeffers,* Ch D, NI (Girvan J), 5 December 1996; [1996] 10 BNIL 67.

28 *Wells* v *McGregor* (1908) 42 ILTR 86.

29 Or for too much costs: *Casey* v *Parson* (1868) IR 2 CL 677.

30 E.g. plaintiff's solicitor entered judgment before plaintiff had a chance to inform him of payment.

plaintiff may apply to have the judgment amended.[31] Such application may be granted *ex parte* if the defendant consents or if the application is made before the defendant is aware of the judgment.[32]

8.15 Judgment may also be set aside for fraud of the plaintiff or his witness; or where he has deliberately stuck to the letter of the rules and failed to take an obvious step to inform the defendant of the action,[33] or entered judgment whilst his offer of compromise is still open;[34] or where through some misfortune not the fault of the plaintiff the defendant is taken by surprise, such as a breakdown in the post.

The application

8.16 The defendant, that is the person against whom the judgment was entered, should apply, rather than the person wrongly served, except possibly where the defendant cannot be contacted.[35] The Court can allow a non-party to apply to set aside judgment if he can show a direct interest, either with leave of the defendant or on making him co-respondent to the application. Thus intervention can be made by the defendant's insurer who is liable under Article 98 of the Road Traffic (NI) Order 1981; the next-of-kin where the defendant personal representative colluded in a judgment;[36] and a creditor where the judgment is collusive and a fraud on creditors.[37] The Court may set aside judgment of its own motion where it is given against a dead or defunct defendant.

8.17 The applicant should apply promptly after becoming aware of the judgment, which may be after steps to enforce it have been taken. Delay is not a fatal bar. A defendant does not necessarily waive his right to apply by asking for time to pay;[38] nor by paying under protest[39] nor by co-operating in enforcement.[40] A judgment will not be set aside where a third party who has acted on faith of the order will be prejudiced by setting it aside, until that party has been given an opportunity to be heard by the Court.[41] A properly obtained judgment was not set aside where the defendant had involved a third person in the subject-matter to the possible prejudice of the plaintiff.[42]

8.18 It is not the practice of the Enforcement of Judgments Office to suspend execution of a judgment merely because there is a pending application to set it aside. In setting aside the judgment the Court may set aside any execution thereon, but should not set aside a sale to a *bona fide* purchaser.[43]

---

31 *Rinder* v *Deacon* (1866) 11 Ir Jur NS 414.
32 White Book (1997) 13/1/13.
33 *Brabazon* v *Brabazon* (1883) 17 ILTR 9.
34 *Hanbury* v *Jones* (1863) 9 Ir Jur NS 5, *per* Lefroy CJ.
35 *Royal Bank* v *Nolan* (1958) 92 ILTR 60.
36 *Mehaffey* v *Mehaffey* [1905] 2 IR 292.
37 *Nixon* v *Loundes* [1909] 2 IR 1.
38 *Evans* v *Bartlam* [1937] AC 473.
39 *Gailey* v *Hurley* (1901) 2 NIJR 30.
40 *Byrne* v *Somers* (1928) 62 ILTR 152.
41 *Abbey National* v *Grugan*, Ch D, NI (Girvan J) 7 March 1997.
42 *Jackson* v *McKelvey* (1884) 18 ILTR 88.
43 *Fox* v *Drake* (1886) 20 ILTR 6.

CHAPTER NINE

PLEADINGS

FUNCTION AND FORM OF PLEADINGS

9.00 Pleadings consist of the Statement of Claim (whether indorsed on the writ or not), the Defence and/or Counterclaim, the Reply and/or Defence to Counterclaim, any subsequent pleading (rare), the Replies to a Notice for Particulars, and any formal admission. The function of pleadings is to ensure that each party and the court of trial knows what material facts each party is alleging or disputing and so to define and limit the disputed issues on the record. "The primary purpose of pleadings ... is to define the issues and thereby inform the parties in advance of the case they have to meet and take steps to deal with it": so said Lord Edmund-Davies in *Farrell* v *Sec of State for Defence.*[1] In that case the plaintiff was shot by soldiers who were tackling an armed robbery. The Statement of Claim pleaded assault and negligence by the soldiers. The Court of Appeal directed a verdict for the plaintiff on the ground of negligence of the Army authorities in planning the operation. Viscount Dilhorne said (at p.82G): "If in the Statement of Claim such allegations had been put forward, the defence would have been notified of the fact that evidence might be required to meet them and the trial would then have taken a very different course". So where the plaintiff in a road accident case pleads that the defendant drove negligently, he cannot recover judgment on the basis that the defendant's vehicle was negligently overloaded.[2]

9.01 In *Mawhinney* v *NIHE*,[3] Hutton J distinguished *Farrell* in allowing the plaintiff to raise an issue not pleaded by him. Against his claim of a prima facie tortious act, the Defence pleaded authorisation given by the Department of Environment under statute. The plaintiff was allowed to assert the invalidity of the authorisation. In other words some laxity is allowed to the plaintiff on matters which he should have pleaded in rebuttal of a defence either by anticipation in the Statement of Claim or by way of Reply.

9.02 A pleading differs from oral and affidavit evidence in that: (a) it is not on oath; (b) it is formally binding on the party; and (c) its content is capable of being amended. A party is bound by the scope of his pleading in adducing evidence.[4] Often the questioning and argument of counsel at the trial is allowed some latitude by the judge, but that does not *per se* broaden the issues beyond those joined in the pleadings, unless the judge allows an amendment.[5] Such

---

1 [1980] NI 55, at 84E (HL).

2 *Walsh* v *Curry* [1955] NI 112.

3 [1982] NI 303.

4 *Esso* v *Southport Corp.* [1956] AC 218.

5 *Farrell* v *Sec of State* at 85A.

amendment should be applied for.[6] The defendant cannot object on appeal to departure at the trial from the injuries pleaded if he did not object at the trial.[7] A party cannot object that he is surprised by evidence under a very vague or wide pleading, because he could have sought particulars of it.[8]

9.03 A pleading must state material facts (*facta probanda,* the facts to be proved) rather than evidence (*facta probantia,* the facts proving them). It must state facts rather than law. Recourse may be had to English precedents in books such as *Bullen and Leake*, ("Blue") *Atkin's Court Forms* and *Odgers on Pleading and Practice*, but they should be treated with some caution because the material facts may differ because of divergence in the law from England, and because traditional practice has created some peculiarities in Northern Ireland pleading, which will be noted in this Chapter. In any case it is always better to draft the pleading out of one's own head first and then check the precedents for omissions and extra ideas. A set of common precedents in Queen's Bench proceedings is given in Appendix Two of this Book.

9.04 A pleading is headed like the writ, describes itself and states its date of service; it is set out in numbered paragraphs, and is indorsed with the solicitor's (or personal litigant's) address, and is signed by whoever drafted it (Ord.18 r.6). It is usually drafted by junior counsel. If senior counsel drafts a pleading, he should do so along with the junior, unless no junior is instructed.[9] A Statement of Claim states the date on which the writ was issued. The time limits for pleading in Order 18 are rarely adhered to in practice and strictly enforced. A pleading may be served during the Long Vacation, though the time limits do not run (Ord.18 r.5). Pleadings are served between the parties and, except in the Commercial List, do not have to be lodged in the Office.

Trial without pleadings

9.05 In any action begun by writ, save one for defamation, malicious prosecution, false imprisonment or alleging fraud, any party may apply by summons for an order for trial without (further) pleadings (Ord.18 r.21). This might be done where the only issues in dispute are made manifestly clear by the writ, correspondence between the parties or an agreed statement of facts. Under the rule the Court may direct or settle a statement of facts.

Drafting of pleadings

9.06 Golden rules of pleading.

(1) Plead in fairly short paragraphs, in ordinary language.

(2) Call the parties "the plaintiff" etc., not by name.

(3) Plead in summary form the material facts which as plaintiff you need to prove to obtain the desired judgment, or which as defendant you need to prove or dispute (Ord.18 r.7(1)) with all necessary identifying names, places, dates etc.

---

6 *Magill* v *MOD* [1987] NI 194, at 202.

7 *Ramsey* v *Mullan* [1974] June NIJB (CA, *per* Jones LJ).

8 *Hewson* v *Cleeve* [1904] 2 IR 536.

9 Bar Handbook 18-07.

(4) Do not anticipate by pleading a fact which is only relevant if the issue is raised by the opponent (e.g. a defence of limitation or Statute of Frauds) though it is proper to plead acknowledgement of a statute-barred debt or extension of the limitation period.

(5) Do not plead a fact on which you do not have the burden of proof, unless the opponent has already traversed it (Ord.18 r.7(3)). A plaintiff in defamation need not aver that the words are untrue.

(6) The existence of an act or event which is a condition precedent to your cause of action or defence is implied and need not be pleaded (Ord.18 r.7(4)), but in suing on a 'bouncing' cheque, notice of dishonour should be pleaded.[10]

(7) In pleading a response to a claim or defence, plead specifically any matter such as limitation, illegality, performance, release, or fraud, which defeats that claim or defence or which may take the opponent by surprise, or which raises a factual issue not arising from previous pleadings (Ord.18 r.8(1)).

(8) Plead any material matter arising before or after the action commenced (Ord.18 r.9) but a plaintiff cannot plead a cause of action which accrued only after issue of the writ (see paras. 4.00-01).

(9) Where a document or conversation is material, plead only its effect and the material words in it (Ord.18 r.7(2)). If a document is referred to it is treated as incorporated in the pleading.[11]

(10) As plaintiff plead particulars of and quantify special damage.

(11) As plaintiff do not plead general allegations or quantifications of general damages, but plead specific facts which affect quantum, by giving particulars of injuries, specific employment prospect or hobby which is affected.

(12) Plead every final relief or remedy which may be sought.

(13) Plead specifically to every fact alleged by the opponent's last pleading, save where joinder of issue is permitted (Ord.18 r.13).

(14) Be careful about pleading fraud, ensuring that there is a credible case for it (Bar Handbook 8-24(iii)). The allegation should be approved by senior counsel if instructed.

(15) Omit any prejudicial or scandalous matter which will not be admissible in evidence.

(16) Do not plead an allegation unsupported by your instructions (Bar Handbook 8-24).

(17) If in doubt, put it in.

---

[10] *Bank of Ireland* v *Ryan* (1895) 29 ILTR 101.

[11] *Lee* v *Hayes* (1865) 17 ICLR 394.

(18) It is permissible to plead inconsistent allegations or denials in the alternative, but co-plaintiffs, and co-defendants who join in one Defence and/or Counterclaim, cannot conflict *inter se*.

(19) If you find a defect or omission, get it amended as soon as possible.

(20) Do not plead evidence, except in certain cases. A conviction or finding of adultery in the United Kingdom, admissible under the Civil Evidence Act, has to be pleaded (see para. 13.26). It is permissible to plead a doctrine of evidence or presumption, such as *res ipsa loquitur*, or breach of the Highway Code. It is not essential to plead *res ipsa loquitur* expressly provided that the facts from which it arises are stated.[12] Medical evidence must be served with the Statement of Claim.

(21) Do not plead law, but you may identify and raise a point of law (Ord.18 r.11) or a doctrine of law such as *volenti non fit iniuria,* and *ex turpi causa non oritur actio*. The law of any state outside Northern Ireland must be pleaded as a fact. If breach of statutory duty is alleged the statutory provision must be named.

(22) If a statutory provision is relied on the relevant section, paragraph etc. of it must be pleaded (Ord.18 r.7(5)).

9.07 Particulars of every claim or defence or other matter must be given, including of negligence, breach of statutory duty, breach of trust, misrepresentation, fraud, fault etc. and of condition of mind, malice or intention (Ord.18 r.12(1)). Particulars of how a party knows a fact do not have to be pleaded, but the opponent can seek an order to give such particulars (Ord.18 r.12(4)) (see para. 9.86).

9.08 It is important to get the details in the pleading right, even though it can later be amended, because errors give a bad impression and may affect the credibility of the party's case. In *Culbert* v *Belfast Co-op*,[13] Lord MacDermott LCJ, in the context of a Statement of Claim in a negligence case, stressed the need for a party's lawyers to investigate the facts carefully at an early stage, because failure to do so leads to unnecessarily wide, elaborate and prolix particulars in pleadings. A pleading which omits required particulars is not void. It can be cured by amendment, or by reply to a notice for particulars, or by the fact that the defendant has delayed in objecting until the trial and is not misled or surprised.[14]

STATEMENT OF CLAIM

9.09 The plaintiff should deliver to each defendant a Statement of Claim indorsed on the writ, served with the writ, or served at any time until six weeks after the appearance (Ord.18 r.1). In theory at least, at any time after the expiry of the time limit, the defendant can apply for dismissal of the action (Ord.19 r.1) (see para. 11.194). A late Statement of Claim is valid and regular if served

---

[12] *Mullen* v *Quinnsworth* [1990] 1 IR 59, at 63.

[13] CA, NI, 6 June 1966, at 7-9, noted at 17 NILQ 442. McVeigh and Curran LJ concurred in the remarks.

[14] *Houlihan* v *O'Sullivan* (1930) 64 ILTR 178.

at any time before the defendant applies to dismiss the action for want of prosecution.[15] Its function is to set down the facts which the plaintiff intends to prove to establish his right to judgment. It is headed with the title of the action; and the date on which the writ was issued (Ord.18 r.15(3)). The body of it starts by referring to the relationship between the parties, then the facts on which the cause of action is based, with particulars of the breach of duty, then particulars of the loss and damage, including any special damages and in a personal injuries case, particulars of the injuries, then the relief or remedy claimed. The date and place of all material events must be stated.

9.10 It may alter, modify or extend the claim in the writ, but must be confined to allegations in respect of the cause of action mentioned on the writ or facts comprised in that cause of action (Ord.18 r.15(2)). It cannot allege breach of statutory duty where the writ only mentions negligence.[16] If fraud is alleged it should be approved by senior counsel. As stated in the old Rules (Wylie Ord.20 r.7) separate claims, in the sense of separate sets of facts giving rise to a claim for relief, should be pleaded separately and distinctly.

9.11 The plaintiff generally should not plead facts relevant only to rebut an anticipated defence. In some cases it is proper practice to do so, especially where the facts alleged in the claim reveal an apparent defence. The plaintiff should plead facts relevant to take the case out of the limitation period, though of course that does not relieve the defendant of the obligation to plead the limitation defence. In an action for false imprisonment against the police, the plaintiff should anticipate that a defence of lawful arrest and detention will be pleaded and should in the Statement of Claim plead facts in rebuttal.[17]

9.12 A Statement of Claim for a debt or liquidated demand is usually indorsed on the writ. It need not state in simple debt cases the express cause of action (the original contract) but it must state the date of the original transaction and certainly the date on which the money became payable.[18] If particulars of debt, expenses etc. exceed three folios[19] they should be set out in a separa.tely served document referred to in the pleading (Ord.18 r.12(2)). If not served with the pleading, the pleading must state the date when it was delivered.[20]

9.13 A claim for interest, whether generally under section 33A of the Judicature Act or otherwise, must be pleaded (Ord.18 r.8(4)). If a special rate of interest is claimed facts justifying it must be pleaded.[21] Exemplary damages and provisional damages must be claimed, and the facts supporting them (Ord.18 r.8(3)).

---

15 *Sampson* v *O'Donnell* (1880) 6 LR Ir 471.

16 *Scampton* v *Colhoun* [1959] NI 106.

17 *Oscar* v *Chief Constable* [1992] NI 290, at 314.

18 *Beaufort* v *Ledwith* [1894] 2 IR 16; or, in a claim based on *quantum meruit*, the dates on or between which the services were given: *Kilgariff* v *McGrane* (1881) 8 LR Ir 354.

19 A folio is defined by the English RSC as 72 words.

20 *Stacey* v *O'Callaghan* [1958] IR 320.

21 *Dexter* v *Courtaulds* [1984] 1 WLR 372.

9.14 The specific relief or remedy claimed (except costs) must be stated (Ord.18 r.15(1)) but only the substantive final relief, not any interlocutory order which may be applied for.[22] Relief can be claimed in the alternative on one cause of action, and the plaintiff need not elect between them until judgment is being awarded to him.[23] At the trial any relief not claimed but consistent with the relief claimed can be awarded.[24] The case of *Beoco* v *Alfa Laval*[25] illustrates the vital need for the plaintiff to plead an alternative or 'fall-back' cause of action. There the plaintiff bought a heater from X which was found to be defective, was repaired by Y, and later exploded causing damage to property. In suing X he pleaded a claim for damages for loss caused by the explosion. During the trial it became clear that the explosion was caused by Y's defective repairs rather than the original defect. The plaintiff should have pleaded in the alternative against X a claim for the cost of repairing the defect.

Negligence and injury claims

9.15 In giving particulars of negligence, there are certain standard phrases which are normally used, such as "failing to warn the plaintiff," but in each individual case it is essential to comb through the evidence for particular items of act or omission which can be alleged.

9.16 In giving particulars of breach of statutory duty, the nature of the breach should be stated as well as the section, article, rule or paragraph. It is a duty separate and distinct from negligence.[26] Creation of criminal liability by NI legislation does not *per* se affect any civil liability.[27]

(As to when statutory duty is actionable see *Ward* v *Freeman* (1851) 2 ICLR 460, at 499; *Reilly* v *Moore* [1935] NI 196 (Shops Act holiday pay); *Magee* v *Grant*, High Ct, NI, 27 May 1968, at 6-7; *Lonrho* v *Shell* [1982] AC 173; *McDowell* v *McKibbin* [1988] NI 172 (Rent Acts duty of repair); *Mahon* v *Sharma* [1990] NI 106 (Planning Acts); *Treanor* v *Loughran* [1989] NI 135 (Dogs Order); *Meehan* v *Enniskilllen Meat Packers* [1975] 6 NIJB (slaughterhouses); *Healy* v *Nolan* (1946) 80 ILTR 78 (Road Traffic Act safety provisions not actionable); *X (Minors)* v *Bedfordshire CC* [1995] 2 AC 633; Health and Safety at Work (NI) Order 1978 Art.43; Consumer Protection Act 1987, s.42 (unsafe consumer goods); Building Regulations (NI) Order 1979, Art.20 (*not yet in force*!); Street Works (NI) Order 1995, Art.42 (*not yet in force)*; Roads (NI) Order 1993, Art.8; Dogs (NI) Order 1983, Art.53; Fire Services (NI) Order 1984, Art.44A; Northern Ireland Constitution Act 1973, s.19 (discrimination by public authority); Protection from Harassment (NI) Order 1997, Art.5 (*not yet in force*) (see Stop Press p.x) and other specific statutes.)

9.17 In a personal injury claim the first paragraph should state the plaintiff's date of birth and occupation. In an action for personal injuries or death (except

---

[22] *Serge Caudron* v *Air Zaire* [1986] ILRM 10.
[23] *Tang Man Sit* v *Capacious Investments* [1996] 1 AC 514 (PC).
[24] *Cargill* v *Bower* (1879) 10 Ch D 502, at 508.
[25] [1995] QB 137 (CA).
[26] *Scampton* v *Colhoun* [1959] NI 106.
[27] Interpretation Act (NI) 1954, s.20(4).

a contested medical negligence case) "medical evidence substantiating all the personal injuries alleged in the Statement of Claim" must be served with the Statement of Claim (Ord.25 r.2). The whole report, including an accompanying note, must be served.[28] An expert report should be written by the expert, not settled by counsel, and its content should not be coloured by the interests of the litigation.[29] On request the plaintiff must disclose the full medical history sent to the doctor on which his medical opinion was based.[30] Order 25 requires further medical reports which the plaintiff will rely on to be served; but it is not essential to make consequential amendment of the particulars of injuries.[31]

9.18 It is not enough to refer to the medical reports; particulars of the injuries must be stated in the body of the pleading.[32] In Northern Ireland the practice has been to give particulars of injuries in the traditional manner with no reference in the body of the pleading to the reports.

9.19 In pleading special damage (such as expenses incurred to date, loss of earnings to date, property lost or damaged) particulars and values should be given. Plead that loss of earnings continues and claim the benefit of any relevant wage increases. General damages should not be pleaded, but the plaintiff should plead the heads of general damage and the facts affecting them, particular hobbies affected, particular career prospect which has been lost; and a claim for aggravated or exemplary damages and provisional damages.

9.20 In a *fatal accidents claim*, the plaintiff must deliver to the defendant or his solicitor full particulars of the persons for whom the action is brought and the nature of the claim.[33] Failure to do so does not render the action defective; the defendant can serve a notice for particulars.[34] The defendant is entitled to particulars of the fatal injuries;[35] of the dependants and extent of the dependency of each;[36] of the financial loss and loss of services to the family;[37] but not of the deceased's actual monetary contributions to each dependant;[38] nor of other persons who contributed to the maintenance of the dependants.[39]

DEFENCE

9.21 The defendant should serve a Defence within 21 days after delivery of the Statement of Claim, 21 days after his appearance or 12 days after leave to defend under Order 14, whichever is the latest (Ord.18 r.2).[40] But a late

---

28 Cf. *Kenning* v *Eve Construction* [1989] 1 WLR 1189.

29 *Whitehouse* v *Jordan* [1980] 1 All ER 650, at 655f (CA), *affd.*[1981] 1 WLR 246 (HL).

30 *B* v *John Wyeth* [1992] 1 WLR 168.

31 *Owen* v *Grimsby Transport* [1992] PIQR Q27, at Q37; 'The Times', 14 February 1991.

32 *AB* v *John Wyeth*, 'The Times' 14 May 1991, 2 Med LR 341, at 344 col.1 (*obiter*).

33 Fatal Accidents (NI) Order 1977, Art.4(4).

34 *Murphy* v *Logan* (1859) 10 ICLR 87.

35 *Flanagan* v *BP* [1926] IR 51.

36 *Aries* v *Bradley* (1917) 51 ILTR 215.

37 *Donnelly* v *Hackett* [1988] 6 NIJB 6.

38 *Begley* v *Keays* (1920) 54 ILTR 40.

39 *Brown* v *Belfast Corp.* [1955] NI 213.

40 If his appearance was entered out of time, "he shall not, unless the Court otherwise orders, be entitled to serve a Defence or do any other thing later than if he had appeared within that time": Ord.12 r.6(2). *Semble,* this provision is only relevant if the Statement of Claim

Defence is valid and regular if served at any time before judgment is entered.[41] The defendant may withdraw his Defence or part of it at any time (para. 12.00).

9.22 It must deal with each allegation in the Statement of Claim, stating those which are denied or not admitted, and pleading any new fact on which a defence is based. If there is more than one cause of action or more than one plaintiff, the Defence must make it clear what defences are pleaded against which cause or plaintiff. The Defence must plead any cross-claim by the defendant against the plaintiff by way of Counterclaim and/or Set-off. As stated in the old Rules (Wylie Ord.20 r.7), separate defences and counterclaims must be separately and distinctly pleaded.

Traverses

9.23 "Any allegation of fact made by a [plaintiff] in his pleading is deemed to be admitted by the [defendant] unless it is traversed ... in his pleading" (Ord.18 r.13(1)), unless the latter is a party under disability (Ord.80 r.6). "The defendant does not admit" and "the defendant denies" have the same effect, and a denial can be express or by necessary implication (see Ord.18 r.13(2)).[42] The defence should avoid pregnant denials, and make clear which element if any of the allegation is not denied. "A denial must not be so framed that two or more different facts would justify it" (Wylie p.387).[43] It should end with a catch-all denial, as follows: "Save as otherwise stated herein, the defendant denies each and every allegation of fact contained in the Statement of Claim as if the same were set forth and specifically traversed *seriatim*." This is accepted as sufficient for minor allegations;[44] but is not enough on its own.[45] In *Jones* v *Quinn*[46] Fitzgerald B said that a general denial "cannot be done in any case in which specific traverse of each material fact averred in the Statement of Claim in the terms of the respective averments would not be admissible". Denial of the plaintiff's claim to title to goods does not amount to an act of conversion.[47]

9.24 Every allegation in a claim or counterclaim is deemed to be admitted unless specifically dealt with,[48] save that an allegation of damage and its amount is deemed to be traversed unless admitted (Ord.18 r.13(3)(4)). A denial cannot be treated as an implied admission merely because the Defence shows a

---

was endorsed on the writ, because otherwise the time limit for serving the Defence has no connection with the date of appearance.

41 *Kennane* v *Mackey* (1889) 24 LR Ir 495 (action for recovery of land).

42 But the White Book (1997) 18/13/5, suggests that a mere non-admission may not allow the defendant to adduce contrary evidence.

43 A pregnant or insufficient denial is not necessarily an admission sufficient to entitle the plaintiff to judgment: *McMahon* v *Thompson* (1878) 13 ILTR 92. The proper course is to seek further particulars of the denial or to apply to have the pleading set aside or amended as embarrassing.

44 *Warner* v *Sampson* [1959] 1 QB 297.

45 *Quirk* v *Fitzgerald* (1879) 13 ILTR 64. Even a plea that "the statements in para.graph .. of the Statement of Claim are denied" is not enough: *Dunne* v *Clancy* (1880) 6 LR Ir 395. A catch-all denial was held to be a sufficient traverse in *Peclar* v *Johnstone* (1919) 53 ILTR 31, but the decision is probably wrong. Ord.18 r.13(3) says that a general denial or non-admission of an allegation is not a sufficient traverse.

46 (1878) 2 LR Ir 516.

47 Tort (Interference with Goods) Act 1977, s.11(3).

48 Unless the defendant is under disability (para. 3.08).

lack of candour.[49] If the plaintiff has pleaded a conviction, it must be specifically answered, by denying its existence, denying its relevance or alleging it to be erroneous. There is no need to deny the damages but the defendant must deal with causation of damage; and Order 18 rule 8(1), *infra,* requires him to plead an allegation that the plaintiff has failed to mitigate his loss.[50] There is no need to deny an allegation not pleaded, but there is nothing wrong in traversing a fact which is implied in the Statement of Claim.[51] The old RSC (Wylie Ord.21 r.10) said that an unwarranted denial or non-admission of facts in a Defence could result in a special order for the extra costs thereby occasioned, and this practice can be continued by invoking Order 62 rule 10.

Other defences

9.25 In pleading a response to a claim, the defendant must plead specifically any matter such as illegality, release, fraud etc., which defeats that claim or which may take the opponent by surprise, or which raises a factual issue not arising from previous pleadings (Ord.18 r.8(1)). Apart from admissions/denials, the defence may raise: (a) an objection on a point of law; (b) confession and avoidance (contributory negligence, *ex turpi causa non oritur actio*, *volenti non fit iniuria*, statutory authority, inevitable accident, act of God etc.); (c) a special defence (set-off, tender before action, limitation period, Statute of Frauds).

9.26 Confession and avoidance includes equitable defences;[52] *bona fide* purchase for value; *res judicata*;[53] estoppel; fraud.[54] A personal representative must plead *plene administravit* if the estate has insufficient assets, otherwise he will be liable for the judgment out of his own property. A defence of act of God or inevitable accident must be pleaded, without thereby assuming the burden of proof (Ord.18 r.8(1)). Inevitable accident is a defence which must be pleaded to a strict liability claim such as trespass, but in a claim for negligence it is covered by a denial of negligence.[55] It is permissible for a denial and a confession-and-avoidance to cohabit in the same Defence. This is normally effected by pleading: "If (which is denied) ..., then ...". The defendant can plead and rely on inconsistent defences.[56] Indeed it is the duty of defence counsel to plead every reasonable "fall-back" defence. In a defamation action, the defendant may make an offer of amends at any time up to the service of his Defence, and if he relies on such offer as a defence he must do so to the exclusion of all other defences (para. 18.20).

---

49 *Gray* v *Boyd*, 1996 SLT 60 (2nd Div).
50 *Peterson* v *Bannon* (1994) 107 DLR 4th 616 (CA, BC).
51 *O'Neill* v *O'Neill* (1879) 4 LR Ir 218.
52 In opposing the granting of a discretionary remedy, the defendant can raise the issue of delay without having pleaded it: *M and M* v *An Bord Uchtála* [1977] IR 287 (SC, *per* Henchy J only).
53 *Bywater* v *Dunne* (1882) 10 LR Ir 380.
54 *Bastow* v *Bradshaw* (1881) 8 LR Ir 30.
55 White Book (up to 1995 ed.) 18/12/15.
56 *Kirkwood Hacket* v *Tierney* [1952] IR 185 (denial of slander and claim of privilege); *Phonographic Performance* v *Cody* [1994] 2 ILRM 241 (denial of copyright infringement and assertion that amount claimed is unreasonable).

Defence of satisfaction

9.27 When the defendant claims to have satisfied the plaintiff's claim, whether in contract or tort, the position is as follows.[57]

(1) If the claim is for *debt or liquidated demand*, he can plead-

(a) *payment*: that he has paid the full amount claimed before issue of the writ.

(b) *accord and satisfaction*: that he has paid sum less than the amount claimed which has been accepted by the plaintiff. Acceptance may be express or it may be implied by the failure of the plaintiff for some time after receipt to reject it or protest that it is insufficient. Payment of a sum less than that claimed cannot, even if accepted, amount to a defence if the payment was not declared to be in full settlement.[58] Where payment is made "in full settlement", acceptance "without prejudice" is ambiguous but if the creditor adds that he looks forward to proposals for paying the rest of the debt, there is clearly no acceptance in full settlement.[59] Agreement as to acceptance of the lesser sum is not enough in itself. In order to succeed the debtor must show consideration (e.g. that he has paid before the due date for payment). If the creditor has not yet performed all of the service for which the debt is claimed, waiver of performance can be consideration. If the debtor has a *bona fide* dispute as to his liability for the entire debt or a *bona fide* cross-claim against the creditor, the waiver thereof is good consideration. Payment in cash or by cheque is not consideration, even if the cheque is drawn on the account of a third person, but payment directly by a third person of a lesser sum in full settlement is binding if accepted.[59] Where the debtor has paid a sum "in full settlement" which he states to be that which he admits to be due, it is no accord and satisfaction, either because there is no consideration or because the non-response of the plaintiff to such a payment is not implied acceptance.[60] Both the accord (agreement) and the satisfaction (consideration) must be pleaded in the Defence.

(c) promissory estoppel: in the absence of consideration the defendant might plead that the plaintiff accepted the sum in full satisfaction and the defendant acted on faith thereof to his detriment.

(d) *tender*: that he offered a sum to the plaintiff, whether the amount claimed or a different sum, which the plaintiff refused, which sum he then pays into court on being sued (see below para. 9.32).

(2) If the plaintiff's claim is for *unliquidated damages*, whether for breach of contract or for tort, no payment or tender by the defendant can be a defence

---

[57] See any standard text on the law of contract, such as *Chitty on Contracts* (27th ed. 1994) Vol.1, Chap. 22.

[58] *Kei Brick & Tile Co* v *AM Construction*, 1996 (1) SA 150 (E Cape Div).

[59] *In re Broderick* [1986] 6 NIJB 36 (Carswell J).

[60] *Ferguson* v *Davies* [1997] 1 All ER 315 (CA).

because there is no fixed sum to satisfy the claim. The defendant can plead *accord and satisfaction*: that the defendant has paid a sum in full satisfaction of the claim and the plaintiff has so accepted it expressly or impliedly. If a reasonable sum is rejected, the defendant's proper course is to make a 'lodgment' on being sued (para. 11.148).

(3) In respect of a claim for *non-monetary relief*, the defendant can plead performance as a defence to any claim for injunction or specific performance, though he may still be liable for damages for the period before performance. If performance is impossible because of rejection by the plaintiff, he should, on being sued, make a *Calderbank* offer by open letter (para. 11.167).

9.28 As stated in the old RSC (Wylie Ord.19 r.21) a bare denial of a contract or agreement is a denial of the fact of agreement[61] and of the facts from which agreement may be inferred, but is not a denial of the contract's legality or sufficiency under the Statutes of Frauds 1695 and 1828, or otherwise. The defendant can raise illegality of a contract, as should the Court itself, without having pleaded it.[62] So also he can contend that the contract is contrary to public policy;[63] or illegal under the Gaming Acts.[64] But it is good practice to plead such defences expressly.

9.29 In an action for interference with goods, the Defence may plead that a third person has better title (*jus tertii*).[65] If sued for recovery of land the defendant must plead every ground of defence and not merely plead possession (Ord.18 r.8(2)). If a debtor or surety sued on a consumer credit agreement desires to re-open the transaction under section 139 of the Consumer Credit Act 1974, he must give notice under Order 83 rule 2 rather than plead it in his Defence.

9.30 An objection on point of law ('demurrer') is optional; if raised it usually leads to the point of law being tried as a preliminary issue.

Special defences

9.31 The following are special statutory pleas.

(1) In an action for debt, a plea of payment (Administration of Justice Act (Ir) 1707, s.12).

(2) A plea that under the Statute of Frauds Act (Ir) 1695, a contract for guarantee of a debt or for sale of land is unenforceable if not in writing.

(3) A plea under the Limitation (NI) Order 1989 that the right of action is barred.

---

61 Thus denial of a contract puts the pursuer [plaintiff] to proof of all the elements which constitute agreement: *Sabre Leasing* v *Copeland*, 1993 SLT 1099 (1st Div).

62 *Murphy* v *Crean* [1915] 1 IR 111; *Conway* v *Smith* [1950] Ir Jur Rep 3.

63 *Sumner* v *Sumner* [1936] Ir Jur Rep 29 (NI).

64 *Pujolas* v *Heaps* (1938) 72 ILTR 96 (Circuit Ct); *McLaughlin* v *Latchman* [1938] Ir Jur Rep 85 (denial of indebtedness in betting transaction, held sufficient).

65 Tort (Interference with Goods) Act 1977, s.8.

(4) Set-off of a mutual debt or related cross-claim (para. 9.36).

Pleas (2), (3) and (4) must be pleaded even if the facts in the Statement of Claim reveal the defence;[66] except the 12 year limitation period in an action concerning title to land (Wylie p.384).

TENDER BEFORE ACTION

9.32 This is a defence against a liquidated demand only, and not on an ejectment for non-payment of rent.[67] The defendant must plead it and pay into court under Order 22 "the amount alleged to have been tendered" (Ord.18 r.16), giving notice of payment in to the plaintiff (White Book (1997) 18/16/1). If the plaintiff accepts it, the money can be paid out only in accordance with an order of court which will deal with costs (Ord.22 r.4(1); CF Rules r.43(2)(ii)) awarding them to the defendant if the previous tender is proved and possibly also ordering the defence costs to be paid first out of the money in court. It is not kept secret from the trial court. In his pleading the defendant may state that money paid into court under Order 14 is to be treated as payment under Order 18 rule 16 (Ord.22 r.8). It is arguable[68] that the Defence can plead tender where the money has been or will be paid into court as a 'lodgment' under Order 22 rule 1, because both elements of the defence are present: tender before action and payment into court.

9.33 Under the defence of tender the defendant must prove a tender of a sum at least as great as was justly due (without costs) before the issue of the writ, in cash, or by cheque unless the plaintiff objected to cheque, made by the defendant or his privy to the plaintiff or his privy. The offer must have been explicit and unconditional and there must have been actual production of the money. Tender under protest is good but tender subject to a stamped receipt or to acceptance as full settlement is bad. The tender must be available at all times, so the defence fails if the plaintiff later requested the money tendered. *Semble*, if a date for payment was agreed and expressly made of the essence by the parties, under section 88 of the Judicature Act, tender after that date is bad. If the debt carries contractual or statutory interest as of right, the amount tendered must include interest to date. If the defendant informs the plaintiff that he intended to offer the money and the plaintiff forestalls the tender by saying he will not accept it, the defendant may plead the defence of 'Tender Excused' and pay the sum into court.[69]

9.34 In High Court actions tender after issue of the writ is no defence. In *Goodbody* v *Gallaher*,[70] the plaintiff pleaded a tender after action brought of a sum plus costs, which the plaintiff agreed; the defendant paid into court: it was held a good defence, not as tender but as contract.

---

66 *O'Reilly* v *Granville* [1971] IR 90. In so far as it goes on to say that a defendant can be added as a party without regard to the limitation period, this case is no longer authoritative by reason of Art. 73 of the Limitation (NI) Order 1989.

67 *Foley* v *Coffey* (1909) 43 ILTR 13.

68 Notwithstanding the contrary *obiter dicta* of Judge Hart in *Reybran Business* v *Governors of Sullivan Upper* [1996] 3 BNIL 75.

69 *Kane* v *Munster & Leinster Assurance* (1926) 60 ILTR 56 (Circuit Ct).

70 (1885) 16 LR Ir 336.

9.35 If the plaintiff proceeds to trial and recovers no more than the sum tendered, the defendant gets judgment with full costs. Subject to any order of the Court as to payment of the defendant's costs out of the money in court, the money found due is paid out to the plaintiff in full satisfaction. If the plaintiff recovers more than the amount tendered the position depends on whether it was a tender in respect of a whole indivisible debt. If so, the plaintiff gets judgment for the whole debt with full costs and the sum in court is paid out in partial satisfaction. If there were several divisible debts, the plaintiff gets judgment for the excess only with costs thereon, and the money in court is paid out in partial satisfaction.[71]

CROSS-CLAIMS: COUNTERCLAIM OR SET-OFF

Set-off

9.36 A set-off is a monetary cross-claim which operates as a defence. There are three categories-

(1) in a claim for debt, any cross-claim for a debt due between the parties in the same capacity. Debts due to a deceased when alive cannot be set off against a debt due by the personal representative from his estate, and *vice versa*. A defendant sued on a joint debt cannot set off a debt owed to him alone.[72] A defendant sued on a sole debt cannot set off a debt owed jointly to him and another person.[73] *Semble*, since the Civil Liability (Contribution) Act 1978 (s.3), a defendant sued on a sole debt can set off a debt owed jointly by the plaintiff and another (adding the other as a party if he wishes). A defendant sued by an assignee of a debt can set off a debt due by the assignor provided the latter debt became due before notice of the assignment. So also a defendant can set off against a trustee a debt due by a *cestui qui trust*.[74]

(2) a cross-claim for debt or damages which is connected with the same or a close transaction from which the claim arises, so related that it would be unjust to disregard it.[75] The plaintiff's claim may be for debt or damages, or for specific performance based on a monetary claim.[76] 'Transaction' must be taken to mean some form of contractual or other personal relationship between the parties: so a defendant driver sued for damages in a road accident counterclaims for his own damage rather than pleads it as a set off.

(3) a deduction from a head of plaintiff's damage of a related benefit accruing to the plaintiff as a result of the defendant's wrongful conduct.[77]

9.37 A set-off (except presumably of type 3) must be a cause of action accrued before issue of the writ.[78] It is submitted that a set-off necessarily

---

71 See *Read's Trustee* v *Smith* [1951] Ch 439.
72 *Fergus Syndicate* v *Hewitt* (1944) 78 ILTR 14.
73 *Loughnan* v *O'Sullivan* [1922] 1 IR 103.
74 *Abbey National* v *McCann*, CA, NI, 13 June 1997 (Carswell LJ at p.26).
75 *Esso Petroleum* v *Milton* [1997] 2 All ER 593.
76 *BICC* v *Burndy Corp* [1985] Ch 232.
77 *Nadreph* v *Wilmett* [1978] 1 WLR 1537. This case concerned the merits and did not discuss the pleading point. It may be that it is not so much a defence of set-off as a matter in reduction of the plaintiff's damages. In any event, it would seem that it should be pleaded in the Defence.

connotes an admission of liability on the claim: if the defendant disputes that he owes anything at all to the plaintiff, his own claim must be regarded as a full counterclaim. It may be pleaded as a defence of set-off and alternatively as a counterclaim (Ord.18 r.17). A set-off does not survive the disposal of the claim. If the plaintiff is domiciled in a Brussels Convention State, the jurisdiction to hear a set-off, being a pure defence, is a matter for the internal law.[79]

Counterclaim

9.38 A counterclaim is any other cross-claim on a cause of action accruing at any time before it is pleaded (Ord.15 r.2(1)) and it is treated as a separate claim brought in the plaintiff's action. The parties need not be in the same capacity.[80] By virtue of the Civil Liability (Contribution) Act 1978, the defendant can counterclaim with or without joining a person jointly liable, but cannot counterclaim alone if another person is jointly entitled on the counterclaim.

9.39 A counterclaim may be for debt, damages or any relief, and may be entirely unconnected to the claim, factually, legally and in the relief claimed.[81] If the plaintiff is domiciled in Great Britain or a Brussels Convention State, the counterclaim must arise from the same contract or facts.[82] It must be pleaded by way of addition to the Defence. The rules for Statements of Claim apply, and it must state the specific relief or remedy (Ord.18 r.18(a)). A full counterclaim survives even if the plaintiff's claim is stayed or disposed of (Ord.15 r.2(3)).

Pleading the cross-claim

9.40 In deciding whether a cross-claim is a set-off or a full counterclaim the Court looks to substance rather than the formal pleading.[83] It should be pleaded in the Defence in separate paragraphs under the heading "Counterclaim" or "Set-off and Counterclaim". If the cross-claim is a defence alternative to the denial of the plaintiff's claim, it is normal to use the formula: "If (which is denied) ..." If the cross-claim is founded on some facts which have been pleaded by way of defence, the Set-off/Counterclaim should incorporate those facts by the words: "The defendant repeats the allegations made in paragraph .. of the Defence herein".

9.41 A set-off or counterclaim can be pleaded by the plaintiff in his reply, but it will be struck out unless it is connected to the defendant's claim and is in substance a set-off,[84] and is liable to be struck out under the Limitation (NI) Order 1989 (Art.73) if the limitation period has expired before the service of the Reply.

---

78 *Jones* v *Horne* (1852) 4 Ir Jur OS 203. See previous page.

79 Because the Brussels Convention, 1982 Act Sch.1 Art.6 (para. 9.39), applies only to a counterclaim claiming a separate judgment in the action: *Danvaern Production* v *Schuhfabriken Otterbeck* [1995] CLY 699 (ECJ).

80 *Re Richardson* [1933] WN 90 (CA), *sed contra: Hickey* v *Hickey* (1881) 15 ILTR 41.

81 *Quinn* v *Hession* (1879) 4 LR Ir 35.

82 Civil Jurisdiction and Judgments Act, Sch.1 Art.6 and Sch.4 Art.6.

83 *Nabney* v *Belfast Co-op* (1933) 67 ILTR 211 (NI).

84 *Kidd* v *Kidd* (1884) 18 ILTR 5; *Renton Gibbs* v *Neville* [1900] 2 QB 181.

9.42 The defendant may withdraw his counterclaim or any claim therein within 21 days after service of the Reply (para.12.00). Any party against whom a counterclaim is made may apply for it to be struck out or tried separately if it appears that it ought for any reason to be disposed of by separate action[85] (Ord.15 r.5(2)). If the defendant counterclaims for grant or revocation of representation of an estate, unless the plaintiff has it struck out, the whole action must be transferred to the Family Division (Ord.76 r.15).

Restrictions on cross-claims

9.43 In an action on a cheque or bill of exchange a set-off is not usually allowed.[86] In an ejectment for non-payment of rent a set-off of a connected debt will be allowed;[87] and a counterclaim for damages is rarely allowed.[88] In ejectment on title a counterclaim is allowed only against a claim for *mesne* profits;[89] but a cross-claim for relief against forfeiture is allowed.[90] "All claims and demands by any landlord against his tenant in respect of rent shall be subject to a deduction or set-off in respect of all just debts due by the landlord to the tenant" (Deasy's Act s.48). This may allow a counterclaim, but not a set-off, for damages.[91]

9.44 A set-off/counterclaim cannot be pleaded against the Crown in an action for taxes, duties or penalties; nor can a set-off/counterclaim relating to such taxes etc. be made in other proceedings by the Crown (Ord.77 r.4(1)). Leave of the Court, sought by summons, is necessary for a counterclaim or set-off by or against the Crown if the cross-claims relate to different Government departments or if the Attorney-General sues or is sued (Ord.77 r.4(2)). This rule is made pursuant to section 35(2)(g) of the Crown Proceedings Act.

9.45 A foreign state can be subject to a counterclaim only if it is arises out of the state's claim.[92] A diplomat is subject only to a counterclaim directly connected with his claim.[93]

Effect of cross-claim

9.46 A set-off or counterclaim against the plaintiff is deemed for limitation purposes to have commenced back on the date when the plaintiff's action began; it cannot be prohibited under Article 73 of the Limitation (NI) Order 1989 unless the defendant has already made a claim in the action (Art.73(2)). A cross-claim by a plaintiff against the defendant is liable to be disallowed under

---

85 Possible grounds are that the counterclaim is prejudicial to the plaintiff's claim, or will delay it, or is wholly unconnected, or is connected in such a way as will cause confusion. A counterclaim for libel, however close its connection to the claim, is liable to be struck out because the party accused of libel should not lose the right of defending before a jury: *Scofish International* v *MV Anton Lopatin* [1995] 3 IR 503.

86 Because commercial efficacy requires such payment to be treated as if in cash: see *Esso Petroleum* v *Milton* [1997] 2 All ER 593.

87 *Whitton* v *Hanlon* (1885) 16 LR Ir 137.

88 *Loughrey* v *Maguire* [1897] 2 IR 140.

89 *Odum* v *Hartley* (1881) 15 ILTR 31.

90 Warden of Cholmeley's School v Sewell [1893] 2 QB 254.

91 *Martin* v *Brady* (1934) 68 ILTR 136.

92 State Immunity Act 1978, s.2(6).

93 Diplomatic Privileges Act 1964, Sch.1 Art.32; Consular Relations Act 1968, Sch.1 Art.45.

Article 73. For other procedural purposes a cross-claim commences only when it is served.[94] A late cross-claim can be raised by leave, even after final judgment but not after judgment has been satisfied.[95] *Semble*, a counterclaim cannot be allowed to be pleaded on appeal.[96]

9.47 A full *counterclaim* is treated so far as just as an independent action.[97] It may be proceeded with where the claim fails, or is settled, discontinued or otherwise dismissed (Ord.15 r.2(3)).[98] If both are tried the judge will give judgment on each, or may give judgment for the balance only. Where an action is brought for damages in a road accident, the defendant's cross-claim for his own injury/damage should never be treated as a set-off and the Court should never give judgment for the balance of one over the other, because of the involvement of insurance.[99]

9.48 A *set-off* is a defence, which goes to reduce or extinguish the claim. It does not survive if the claim fails. At the trial the plaintiff recovers judgment for the balance only. If the amounts be equal the defendant gets judgment. In the case of an equitable set-off at least, the judge may in the interests of justice give judgment on each claim.[100]

9.49 If the cross-claim, having all the qualities of a set-off, exceeds the value of the claim (an 'overtopping set-off'), it is best regarded as a set-off up to the value of the claim and a counterclaim for the excess.[101] For example if the plaintiff proves a debt of £50,000 and the defendant proves a debt of £80,000, the judge should dismiss the action and grant judgment to the defendant for £30,000.

9.50 A counterclaim or set-off cannot be allowed beyond the amount of the claim where the plaintiff claims as assignee and the defendant cross-claims for a liability of the assignor.

As to *judgment* on claim and cross-claim, see para. 14.48; and as to *costs*, see paras. 17.41-45.

Cross-claims by separate action

9.51 It is the policy under the Judicature Act that a defendant be encouraged to counterclaim rather than bring a separa.te action. However he is free to do the latter. Failure to raise a counterclaim or set-off in one action does not create any estoppel preventing the defendant in that action from suing separa.tely.[102] Indeed if a defendant is sued in the county court, a cross-claim which exceeds the county court limit should be brought by separa.te action in the High Court.

---

94 *Impex Transport* v *Thames Ltd* [1981] 1 WLR 1548.

95 *CSI* v *Archway* [1980] 1 WLR 1069.

96 *Good* v *Jagoe* (1881) 15 ILTR 50 (civil bill appeal).

97 Though costs of it are part of the 'costs of the action': *Craig* v *Boyd* [1901] 2 IR 645.

98 And *Seddon's Pneumatic Tyre* v *Sweeny* (1895) 29 ILTR 96.

99 See *Crawford* v *James* [1988] 8 NIJB 19, at 23-4.

100 *Provincial Bill Posting* v *Low Moor Iron* [1909] 2 KB 344 (plaintiff in liquidation).

101 See *Compania Naviera Vascongada* v *Hall* (1906) 40 ILTR 114.

102 *Ford* v *Servotomic* [1977] CLY 1216 (Cty Ct), applying *Thoday* v *Thoday* [1964] P 181; *Karshe* v *Uganda Transport* [1967] EA 774 (in *Annnual Survey of Commonwealth Law* (1968) p.743); *Hoppe* v *Titman* [1996] 1 WLR 841 (CA). But see para. 13.108.

The High Court should not stay the county court action;[103] but in its discretion may remove the county court action and consolidate it as a counterclaim in the High Court.[104] Where cross-actions are brought in the High Court they are separa.te for procedural purposes, though they may be heard together or consolidated. In *Evans* v *Keane*,[105] cross-actions in the High Court were brought for torts arising out of one incident; the Court stayed the second action thus inducing the party who issued the later writ to counterclaim in the first action.

COUNTERCLAIM AGAINST PLAINTIFF AND ANOTHER

9.52 If the counterclaiming defendant alleges that any other person "is liable to him along with the plaintiff in respect of the subject-matter of the counterclaim, or claims against such other person any relief relating to or connected with the original subject-matter" he may join him as 'defendant to the counterclaim' (Ord.15 r.3(1)). The counterclaim must claim some relief against the plaintiff,[106] as well as against the added party. The counterclaim must be connected with, or the relief sought must relate to, the plaintiff's claim.[107] The liability of the plaintiff and the defendant to counterclaim can be joint or purely in the alternative.[108] *Semble*, the counterclaim under Order 15 rule 3 cannot be regarded as a mere set-off.

9.53 The person's name is added to the title in the Counterclaim and the defendant serves a copy of it on him, and if not already a party he becomes a party with the same rights as if duly sued. This means that he can counterclaim against the defendant or issue a third-party notice.[109]

9.54 If the person is already a party to the action the counterclaim must be served on him within the time limited for service of the Defence (Ord.15 r.3(3)). If the person is not already a party, the defendant must issue it out of the Office like a writ (indorsed with directions as to entry of appearance in Form 14) and serve it and the writ and all pleadings already served on the new person, who becomes a party from the date of such service (Ord.15 r.3(2)).[110] The added party must enter an appearance in Form 15 (Ord.15 r.3(4)) and may suffer judgment in default under Order 13 if he does not appear. If he is under disability, he must appear in the proceedings through a guardian *ad litem*, and if not, the defendant must apply for the appointment of a guardian *ad litem* (Ord.80 r.4(1)(b)).

9.55 If the person joined as defendant to the counterclaim is not already a party, and, if the limitation period on the counterclaim has expired since the

---

103 *Wimpress* v *Scott* [1985] 6 BNIL 99.

104 See *McGuiness* v *Dunn* [1986] NI 81, at 86F; *Crawford* v *James* [1988] 8 NIJB 19.

105 [1908] 2 IR 629.

106 *Arthur* v *Arthur* (1879) 3 LR Ir 1.

107 Supreme Court of Judicature (Ir) Act 1877, s.27(3) (which continues by virtue of s.86(2) of the Judicature Act 1978); *O'Connor* v *Anderson* (1880) 14 ILTR 14.

108 White Book (1997) 15/3/1.

109 White Book (1997) 15/3/5.

110 If the new person is outside Northern Ireland Ord.10 r.3 and Ord.11 apply.

plaintiff's writ was issued, then Article 73 of the Limitation (NI) Order 1989 comes into play. It is submitted[111] that the claim against the added party is "third-party proceedings" under Article 73(8).[112] If so, the person added as defendant to the counterclaim can plead any time limit which expired after the issue of the writ and before the counterclaim was made (Art.73(1)(a)). However, the original plaintiff cannot plead such a defence because the counterclaim against him is deemed to have commenced on the issue of the writ (Art.73(1)(b)) and he cannot have it struck out under Article 73(2).

Counterclaim by defendant and another

9.56 Order 15 rule 3 does not allow a non-party to be added to join as claimant on a counterclaim with the defendant; but the Court under Order 15 rule 6(2) can add such person as defendant. Indeed if the defendant counterclaims on a cause which he enjoys jointly only with another person, the plaintiff can require that person to be added.

REPLY AND SUBSEQUENT PLEADINGS

9.57 In many cases the plaintiff (and defendant to a counterclaim) will deliver a Reply, within 21 days after the Defence on him (Ord.18 r.3). The Reply serves to respond to any new fact alleged in the Defence and to act as a Defence to any allegation in the Counterclaim and/or Set-off. He must reply to a Counterclaim (Ord.18 r.3(2)). Failure to reply to the Set-off/Counterclaim acts as an admission of the allegations in it, but otherwise the plaintiff is taken to deny any facts alleged in the Defence by "joining issue" with it, and there is an implied joinder of issue if no Reply is served; there can be no joinder of issue, express or implied, on a Counterclaim, so the plaintiff must plead to it as if it were a Statement of Claim (Ord.18 r.14). A Defence to Counterclaim must be included in the Reply (Ord.18 r.3(3)) and it must be pleaded like a Defence (Ord.18 r.18(b)). Apart from the case of a set-off/counterclaim, the plaintiff is obliged to serve a Reply where in a defamation action the defendant pleads fair comment or privilege (Ord.82 r.3(3)). In a defamation action, if the Defence pleads an offer of amends as a defence, the plaintiff may reply that the defendant knew or had reason to believe that the statement referred to him and was both false and defamatory (para. 18.20). A simple Reply usually joins issue with the defendant upon his Defence, save for admitting specified facts and save as the Defence consists of admissions (see Ord.18 r.14(4)). A Reply should plead performance, waiver, fraud, limitation, etc. which defeats the defence or counterclaim, or any new fact which might surprise the defendant or raises an issue of fact not arising from previous pleadings (Ord.18 r.8(1)).

9.58 The plaintiff in his Reply cannot depart from the Statement of Claim by making a new inconsistent or alternative case, save by amending his

---

[111] In opposition to the White Book (1997) 15/3/6.

[112] I.e. proceedings brought in the course of the action by the defendant to the action against a person not previously a party to the action, other than by joining the person as defendant to a claim already made in the original action by the defendant.

pleadings (Ord.18 r.10);[113] but he can make an alternative response to the allegations in the Defence, usually using the "If (which is denied) ..." phrase. The Reply should always contain the paragraph: "Save as the same consists of admissions, the plaintiff joins issue with the defendant upon his Defence".

9.59 Because failure to serve a Reply constitutes an automatic joinder of issue, and leads automatically to the close of pleadings, it is arguable that a Reply served out of time is irregular. In *Ferguson* v *Taggart*,[114] the plaintiff applied for extension of time *ex parte*, and Holmes J directed notice to the defendant.

Subsequent pleadings

9.60 After the Reply can come the Rejoinder etc., but these are only by leave of Court (Ord.18 r.4), and are now virtually unknown. Leave must be sought by summons, not *ex parte*.[115] If the defendant has counterclaimed for defamation, and the plaintiff has pleaded fair comment or privilege in the Reply, the defendant relying on express malice has to plead that by Rejoinder (Ord.82 r.3(3)(4)).

JUDGMENT IN DEFAULT OF PLEADING

9.61 The time limits for service of pleadings are never adhered to strictly, and a pleading served late will usually be accepted unless there has been inordinate delay. If the time limit has expired the opponent normally waits for a period then writes requesting the pleading to be served. If this does not produce a response within a reasonable time, then the powers under Order 19 will be invoked. Order 19 also comes into operation when the Court has ordered a pleading to be struck out for procedural default or abuse of process.

Default of Statement of Claim

9.62 If the plaintiff has failed to serve the Statement of Claim on him within the time, the defendant may apply for a dismissal of the action (Ord.19 r.1). See para. 11.194.

Default of Defence

9.63 At any time after the time for delivery of the Defence has expired, the plaintiff may seek final or interlocutory judgment in default (Ord.19 rr.2-7). The practice is the same as for default of appearance under Order 13 rules 1-6 (see Chap. 8) except that the Statement of Claim has already been served and instead of an affidavit of service of the writ, the plaintiff produces to the Office a certificate of no Defence served (Ord.42 r.7(1)). If more than a year has elapsed the plaintiff must serve one month's notice of intention to proceed, under Order 3 rule 6. [116] Failure to serve a Defence for a defendant under disability is not an admission of the plaintiff's case (Ord.80 r.6), so judgment cannot be entered against him.

---

[113] And *Keane* v *Ryan* (1942) 76 ILTR 69.

[114] (1893) 27 ILTR 134.

[115] *Monck* v *Smythe* [1895] 1 IR 200.

[116] *Jones* v *Bravender* (1902) 36 ILTR 59.

9.64 The defendant can enter judgment under Order 19 in default of service of the Defence to Counterclaim (Ord.19 r.8).

9.65 Any judgment in default of pleading can be set aside or varied (Ord.19 r.9). Judgment in default of Defence should be set aside if in the interests of justice, which usually means that the defendant must depose to a defence on the merits which shows that there is a real triable issue, and the Court will set side the judgment without further adjudging the chances that the defence will succeed.[117]

CLOSE OF PLEADINGS

9.66 'Close of pleadings' is an event which is deemed to occur 21 days after the service of the Defence or of the Reply/Defence to Counterclaim, whichever is the later; and even though a request or order for further particulars has not yet been answered (Ord. 18 r.20).

STRIKING OUT PLEADINGS

9.67 A pleading may be struck out if it discloses no reasonable cause of action or defence, or is scandalous or vexatious or is an abuse of process (Ord.18 r.19). See para. 11.178.

IRISH CASES ON PLEADING

9.68 Odgers is the leading text expounding English case law on pleading. Wylie pp.361-415 lists the Irish case law up to 1905. The following notes concentrate on cases since 1905. Bear in mind that all except Northern Ireland cases after 1980 are decided under the old RSC.

Actions for damages

9.69 The material facts are: (a) the facts showing liability, wrongful act and causation, (b) the type of damage (in practice now not quantified), and (c) special damage (*Lacey* v *Kendal* (1883) 17 ILTR 112).

Negligence and personal injury actions

9.70 "The plaintiff will rely on any other acts or omissions of the defendant constituting negligence [etc.] as may be given in evidence or otherwise appear at the trial" is bad pleading. In *McWatters* v *Maxwell* [1932] NI 176 the Court amended it to: "The plaintiff will rely in proof of the negligence [etc.] alleged on such facts as are in the knowledge of the defendant (her servants and agents) but not of the plaintiff, and appear from the evidence of the defendant and her witnesses at the trial." Such paragraph is habitually added after the particulars of negligence etc. in Northern Irish pleadings. See also *Graham* v *Dunlop* [1977] 1 NIJB (para. 14.39).

---

[117] *McCullough* v *BBC*, QBD, NI (Girvan J) 8 March 1996. In that case the defendant succeeded in a second application to set aside judgment having failed to deliver a Defence after a first judgment in default.

9.71 In an action for injuries caused by shooting by a soldier on operational duties, a claim of negligence by the soldier does not allow evidence of negligent planning of the operation by the Army authorities (*Farrell* v *Sec of State for Defence*, para. 9.00). If the claim pleads assault, (i.e. intentional shooting) the Defence must plead any defence of justification (*Livingstone* v *MOD* [1984] NI 356, at 362A).

9.72 In *Dobbs* v *Carr* (1915) 49 ILTR 243, where the plaintiff alleged that the defendant damaged his vehicle in breach of the Construction and Use Regulations under the Road Traffic Acts; he conceded the right to particulars of the regulations breached. Note however that such regulations are not strictly material as they are not actionable (*Healy* v *Nolan* (1946) 80 ILTR 78).

9.73 In accident at work claims, the defendant is entitled to particulars of failure to provide a safe system of work, and of the way in which equipment was unsafe or inadequate (*Caulfield* v *Bell* (1959) 93 ILTR 108; *Noble* v *NI Electricity* [1955] NI 193). If the claim alleges negligence by servants or agents, he is entitled to the names and negligent conduct of each of them; but not to particulars of failure to provide supervision (*Logue* v *British Thompson-Houston* [1956] NI 179).

9.74 A defendant who traverses negligence can adduce evidence at the trial of mechanical defect, or fault of another (*McKnight* v *McLaughlin* [1963] NI 34). As to mechanical defect this case may be no longer authoritative because of the terms of Order 18 rule 8, but it is submitted still that a defendant can adduce evidence of fault of another without pleading it. Blaming another is evidentially relevant but not a material fact on the dispute between plaintiff and defendant. Under a plea of no defect, the supplier of a vehicle cannot adduce a case that he took all reasonable precautions (*O'Neill* v *Finn* (1972) 106 ILTR 77). The plaintiff is entitled to particulars of a plea of sole negligence or inevitable accident (*Oaks* v *Carroll* (1926) 60 ILTR 117). The plaintiff is entitled to particulars of a plea of contributory negligence and inevitable accident (*Martin* v *McTaggart* [1906] 2 IR 120).

9.75 No reduction of damages for contributory negligence can be made unless it has been pleaded, and the plaintiff is entitled to particulars of it (*Atkinson* v *Stewart* [1954] NI 146), and see *Orr* v *Oneida* [1972] June NIJB Pt II; *Kennedy* v *Midland Oil* (1976) 110 ILTR 26.

Damages

9.76 See Wylie p.377-8. Particulars of the cause of damage were ordered in *Compania Naveria Vascongada* v *R & H Hall (No 1)* (1906) 40 ILTR 245.

9.77 *Injuries.* In answering a Notice for Particulars the plaintiff pleaded pain in right arm and "chronic discomfort and pain"; held wide enough to cover evidence of pain in left arm (*Fahy* v *Pullen* (1968) 102 ILTR 81). Pleading "irregular menstrual cycle and dysmenorrhoea" does not cover evidence of pain on sexual intercourse (*Haggan* v *Porter* [1975] 7 NIJB). Particulars of "impairment of general health" need not be given (*Lanigan-O'Keefe* v *Irish American Oil* (1930) 64 ILTR 135). If the defence representatives have already examined the plaintiff medically, particulars of visible deformity need not be given, unless the defence doctor says that he cannot find it (*Patterson* v

Donnell [1954] NI 96). Pleading "weakness in back" allows evidence of unbalancing of muscles and resultant tilt of the back to one side (*MacNaughton* v *Murphy* [1961] Ir Jur R 41). Osteo-arthritis must be pleaded (*McKay* v *McClure* [1960] NI 34), but not necessarily the possibility thereof (*Briggs* v *Mulvenna* [1969] NI 1).

9.78 *Special damages.* Medical etc. expenses, items and dates of lost profits, were ordered in *Field* v *Catherwood* [1931] NI 150. Loss of earnings: see paras. 9.19 and 9.88.

Fatal Accidents, see para. 9.20.

Other actions

9.79 *Defamation.* Particulars ordered of when, where and to whom published (*British Legal* v *Sheffield* [1911] 1 IR 69; *Irish Peoples Assurance* v *City of Dublin Assurance* [1928] IR 204), but not if the nature of the publication is clear, e.g. in a newspaper (*Keogh* v *Incorporated Dental Hospital* [1910] 2 IR 166), and not of persons present (*Jackson* v *Wine* (1905) 39 ILTR 12). See also *Roche* v *Meyler* [1896] 2 IR 35 (slander of title). As to pleading the so called 'rolled-up plea', see *McKee* v *Beaverbrook Newspapers*, QBD, NI, 28 February 1963; *Burke* v *Central TV* [1994] 2 ILRM 161, and privilege, see *O'Brien* v *Freeman's Journal* (1907) 41 ILTR 35. A plea of 'no libel' traverses all innuendoes pleaded (*Daly* v *ITGWU* [1926] IR 118). *Crawford* v *Vance* [1908] 2 IR 521 gives a set of pleadings.

9.80 *False Imprisonment.* On a defence of justification of arrest, particulars were ordered of the grounds on which the arresting constable suspected the plaintiff, but not of the grounds on which another officer instructed him to arrest (*Clinton* v *Chief Constable* [1991] 2 NIJB 53).

9.81 *Trespass.* Contributory negligence is a possible defence to action for trespass to person (*Wasson* v *Chief Constable* [1987] NI 420).

9.82 *Sale of Goods.* See *Wilkinson* v *McCann* (1900) 1 NIJR 14.

Trade mark. See *Grosvenor Chemical* v *Greenfield* [1909] 1 IR 32.

Ejectment. See Wylie p.370-1; pp.411-5; *O'Hare* v *Ireland* (1921) 55 ILTR 119. Prescription Act 1832 s.5.

Specific Performance. See *McLoughlin* v *Alexander* (1910) 44 ILTR 253.

Trusts. See *Moore* v *McGlynn* [1894] 1 IR 74.

Action for an account. See Wylie p.375-6; *Short* v *Lamb* [1925] 1 IR 135.

FURTHER PARTICULARS

Notice for further and better particulars

9.83 A party may by Notice request further and better particulars of the other party's pleading. Enclosed with an open letter, the Notice requires the opponent to give the particulars within X days. If the other party fails to give the particulars sufficiently or at all, the party should send an open letter demanding a proper reply within X days and if it is still not complied with, he may apply on affidavit exhibiting the correspondence, under Order 18 rule

12(3), for an order, on such terms as the Court thinks just, for "particulars of any claim defence or other matter stated in his pleading ... or a statement of the nature of the case on which he relies", and for particulars of an assertion that a person had knowledge or notice. Save for sufficient reason shown a party may not be ordered to give particulars unless he has been first asked for them by letter (Ord.18 r.12(6)). The order can provide that the action be dismissed or the defence struck out, if the respondent does not comply within a stated time.[118]

9.84 A defendant cannot require particulars before serving his Defence, unless he can show that it is necessary for the drafting of the Defence.[119] Save for special reason, an order for particulars should not be made before service of the Defence (Ord.18 r.12(5)).

9.85 The Notice can ask about material facts, not law or evidence, but it may ask the opponent to identity a point of law raised by him, the statutory duty breached, or about foreign law. Particulars will not be ordered of an immaterial allegation.[120] A useful test to apply in deciding whether a point asked for in the Notice is proper, is to ask: would the point be proper if the respondent had himself inserted it in his own pleading? A Notice designed only to elicit the evidence or names of witnesses will not be allowed, but it is no objection to a Notice that the reply will reveal evidence incidentally. A Notice cannot ask for particulars of evidence, unless evidence has been pleaded as a material fact (e.g. an admission as acknowledgement of an account stated).

9.86 A Notice can ask for the facts relied on to prove an allegation that a person had knowledge or notice of something, where the knowledge or absence of it is a material fact (Ord.18 r.12(4); White Book (1997) 18/12/12). In *Clinton* v *Chief Constable*,[121] on a false imprisonment claim, the Defence pleaded reasonable suspicion of terrorism as justification for the arrest; it was held that the defendant must give particulars of the grounds for the suspicion held by the arresting police officer (but not of the officer who briefed him) subject to public interest immunity in protecting police intelligence sources. In defamation, particulars of the defendant's state of mind will be refused as immaterial, save in relation to a claim for exemplary damages and to rebut a defence in mitigation that reasonable care was taken[122] and presumably where a defence of qualified privilege is raised.

9.87 A plaintiff cannot ask the defendant for particulars of a simple denial or traverse, unless it is a 'pregnant negative' or the plaintiff is not fully aware of the broad outline of the Defence case.[123] A Notice should not ask for particulars of how the opponent will deal with a matter which the applicant has the burden of proving.[124] So a plaintiff will not be required to give particulars of

---

118 See *Church and General Insurance* v *Moore* [1996] 1 ILRM 202 (SC).

119 See *British Legal* v *Sheffield* [1911] 1 IR 69.

120 *Cave* v *Torre* (1886) 54 LT 515.

121 [1991] 2 NIJB 53.

122 *Hermon* v *Yorkshire TV* [1992] NI 27 (a case concerning relevance for discovery).

123 *Behan* v *Medical Council* [1993] 3 IR 523.

124 *James* v *Radnor* CC [1890) 6 TLR 240; *Clinton* v *Chief Constable* [1991] 2 NIJB 53, at 59-60.

his rebuttal of a defence.[125] A party need not give particulars of matters which are not relied on as part of his own case.[126] A Notice cannot ask about matters which are within the applicant's knowledge, save in special circumstances where the matters are an essential part of the respondent's pleading.[127] The plaintiff can be ordered to give particulars of items which he has in his pleading credited to the defendant.[128] In an action claiming the taking of accounts, no particulars are ordered.[129]

9.88 Under the old RSC (up to 1980), under which particulars could be ordered of "matters stated in" a pleading, where the plaintiff claiming loss of earnings stated his gross wages at the date of the accident, it was held that the defendant was entitled to particulars of his tax and other deductions, but not of his wages for two years prior to that, unless the plaintiff has referred to his work record or the history is necessary to show his actual pre-accident earnings.[130] In *Phipps* v *Orthodox Unit Trust*,[131] the plaintiff sued for wrongful dismissal claiming arrears of remuneration and damages for the wrongful dismissal; the defendant sought particulars of all the plaintiff's income from the year of the dismissal onwards, with the amounts of tax assessments and tax allowances. The Court held that he was entitled to those particulars as they were material to the actual loss which the plaintiff suffered by the dismissal and on which he was claiming.

9.89 A Notice cannot ask for particulars of general damage or the amount claimed therefor,[132] except for particulars of the injuries etc. In a personal injury claim it is normal to ask and answer the plaintiff's national insurance number, and the name of his G.P. and doctors who treated him. In a claim involving damage to property or other loss, the plaintiff will be asked whether he is registered for VAT.

The obligation to reply

9.90 A party is obliged to reply and cannot insist on waiting till he has been afforded discovery of documents or interrogatories. In *Cyril Leonard* v *Simo Securities*[133] the Court of Appeal looked with disfavour on an order that the defendant in a wrongful dismissal action should give particulars as best he could before discovery of the grounds justifying dismissal. In special cases the

---

125 *O'Donnell* v *Walsh* [1943] Ir Jur Rep 55 (Circuit Ct).

126 *In re Oaklee Housing Association* [1994] 6 BNIL 46.

127 *Jackson* v *Wine* (1905) 39 ILTR 12; *Keogh* v *Incorporated Dental Hospital* [1910] 2 IR 166. The White Book (1997) 18/12/21, adds after quoting *Keogh*: "But this objection is misconceived: each party is entitled to know the outline of the case that his adversary is going to make against him and to bind him down to a definite story." Odgers, p.192, says the same. Neither book cites an authority.

128 *Abbott* v *Woodroffe* (1855) 1 Ir Jur NS 50.

129 *Short* v *Lamb* [1925] 1 IR 135.

130 *Coyle* v *Hannan* [1974] NI 160, as where the employment was sporadic: *Jeffs* v *Dickson* [1958] NI 12.

131 [1958] 1 QB 314.

132 *London Bank* v *Newnes* (1900) 16 TLR 433.

133 [1972] 1 WLR 80.

Court may direct the applicant to give discovery before the respondent has to reply to the Notice, as where the circumstances are such that the facts are within the knowledge of the applicant and not the respondent;[134] or where the applicant is alleging fraud;[135] or where the applicant has concealed facts or has a fiduciary duty to the respondent;[136] or is otherwise accountable to him.[137]

9.91 If the respondent says that he cannot, or cannot without great difficulty or expense, give the particulars sought, the Court often orders him to give the best replies he can presently give with liberty to supplement them by further reply after discovery,[138] but once an order has been made for particulars the respondent must either comply with it or appeal.[139] The Court may excuse the respondent if he genuinely cannot give in exact detail all the particulars sought.[140] If he can give no particulars of his claim or defence, his pleading may be ordered to be struck out as speculative.[141] Replies cannot be used as an opportunity to fill in gaps in the pleadings, so the particulars given must be consistent with the pleading.[142] A party can refuse to reply on the ground of privilege.[143]

9.92 If the Notice for Particulars has not been replied to at all, or not answered sufficiently, application should be made well before the trial for an order for further particulars, or an order that the Replies be struck out. The power to order particulars is discretionary and may be refused, for example, on grounds of delay. The Court may order the Replies to be given in a particular form, such as a map or diagram. In *Orr* v *Oneida*,[144] respondent's counsel gave the full replies orally in court, and Jones J simply directed the Replies to be recited in the Court's order. In ordering the particulars, the Court may peremptorily, or by subsequent order, direct that the respondent's pleading be struck out, and that judgment be then entered against him, in default of compliance.[145]

Effect of the Replies

9.93 The Replies should incorporate, before each reply, the corresponding item of the request or order for particulars (Ord.18 r.12(7)), a provision usually ignored in practice. The Replies are, like pleadings, not on oath but are formally binding within the scope of the question asked. Thus a Reply to a Notice asking for particulars of injuries binds the plaintiff as to evidence at the trial of injuries, but not as to evidence of damage to clothing, loss of earnings,

---

134 *Millar* v *Harper* (1888) 38 Ch D 110, at 112; *Ross* v *Blakes Motors* [1951] 2 All ER 689.

135 *Leitch* v *Abbott* (1886) 31 Ch D 374, at 379.

136 *Zierenberg* v *Labouchère* [1893] 2 QB 183.

137 *Arab Monetary Fund* v *Hashim (No 2)* [1990] 1 All ER 673.

138 *Marshall* v *Inter-Oceanic* (1885) 1 TLR 394.

139 *Harbord* v *Monk* (1878) 38 LT 411.

140 *King* v *Armstrong* (1868) IR 2 CL 495.

141 *Butcher* v *Dowlen* [1981] 1 Lloyds R 310; *Kennedy* v *Midland Oil* (1976) 110 ILTR 26.

142 *Pinson* v *Lloyds Bank* [1941] 2 KB 72, at 75.

143 *Lau Biv* v *AG* [1982] CLY 2486; *Clinton* v *Chief Constable* [1991] 2 NIJB 53 (*obiter*).

144 [1972] June NIJB Pt II.

145 *Davies* v *Bentick* [1893] 1 QB 185; and see para. 16.60.

or loss of hobbies etc. Failure to require specific particulars is a waiver of the right to the particulars, and the evidence at the trial may extend to anything consistent with the vague facts pleaded;[146] though a party may ask for an adjournment if genuinely surprised at the case made at the trial.[147] A party who elects not to seek further particulars of a matter alleged in the opponent's pleading waives the right to such particulars.[148] If a notice for particulars has not been answered, and no order of the Court is sought, then no objection can be made to the evidence at the trial on the matter.[149] An objection to the sufficiency of particulars should be made as soon as possible.

9.94 The party is under a continuing obligation to give particulars. If having given particulars of injuries, the plaintiff is found to have further injury, he should seek leave of the Court[150] to give particulars of it by way of further Reply[151] or by amendment of the Replies.

FORMAL ADMISSIONS

9.95 One other way in which the issues raised by the pleadings can be limited is by formal admission in writing under Order 27 rule 1 of the whole or any part of the opponent's case. This has not merely evidential effect; it means that for the purpose of the action the fact admitted is deemed to be true as against the admitting party and evidence of that fact becomes both unnecessary and irrelevant: it is not a fact in issue. A party under disability can, through his next friend/guardian, make such admission. The solicitor on record for a party has ostensible authority to make an admission. The admission must be clear and unambiguous. If not in writing it can be made formally by oral statement of a party or his counsel in open court. The admission may be one of primary or inferred fact, or of a legal conclusion arising from facts; for example, that the defendant admits that he is liable to the plaintiff. An admission of negligence is not an admission of liability as it does not concede causation of the damage.

9.96 The Court can give leave to withdraw an admission, refusing only if the grounds for withdrawal are outweighed by actual evidence of likely prejudice to the other party.[152] If given on a mistaken view of the law, leave to withdraw will be given unless the opponent has acted to his detriment on faith of the admission.[153] The admission is binding only between parties between whom there is an issue on the matter admitted. If not expressly limited to the trial only, a formal admission is binding on appeal or at a new trial, but not in a separate action. A party may apply at any time for such judgment as he appears entitled to on the admissions made by his opponent in his pleadings or otherwise (Ord.27 r.3).

---

146 *PW* v *CIE* [1967] IR 137.
147 *Hewson* v *Cleeve* [1904] 2 IR 536, at 559, 564.
148 *Hewson* v *Cleeve* [1904] 2 IR 536.
149 *Houlihan* v *O'Sullivan* (1930) 64 ILTR 178.
150 White Book (1997) 18/12/22.
151 *O'Driscoll* v *Irish Shell* [1968] IR 215.
152 *Gale* v *Superdrug Stores* [1996] 3 All ER 468 (CA).
153 *Ards BC* v *Northern Bank* [1994] 10 BNIL 34.

'Notice to admit'

9.97 A formal admission, for the purpose of the present cause or matter only, can be sought from the other party by 'notice to admit facts' served within 21 days after the setting down for trial (Ord.27 r.2). If the party responds by admitting the fact it is a formal admission of the fact. If he refuses or fails to do so, the other party may wish to secure the admission by interrogatory under Order 26; and may seek to prove the fact by evidence at the trial. The costs of proving the fact and the costs thrown away will fall on the party who failed to admit it, unless otherwise ordered (Ord.62 r.6(7)), and if not legally aided he may suffer those costs to be assessed by the Court and payable forthwith (Ord.62 r.7(6)(7)).

'Notice to admit documents'

9.98 A party may admit formally that a document is authentic, so that the document can be put in evidence against him without being proved. If a notice to admit authenticity is served on him within 21 days after setting down, he is deemed to admit authenticity unless he serves notice denying authenticity (Ord.27 r.5). If he does serve notice of non-admission, he bears the costs of proving the document and costs thrown away, unless otherwise ordered (Ord.62 r.6(8)), and if not legally aided he may suffer those costs to be assessed by the Court and payable forthwith (Ord.62 r.7(6)(7)). Order 27 rule 4 provides that documents given in discovery stand as if a notice to admit has been given in respect of them.

CHAPTER TEN

THIRD-PARTY PROCEEDINGS

10.00 A defendant in an action after appearance may issue a third-party notice, containing a claim against a non-party (Ord.16 r.1). A third-party notice can be issued against a person domiciled in a Brussels Convention State or in Great Britain, unless the plaintiff's action was brought in order to enable that.[1] A plaintiff can issue third-party proceedings in respect of a counterclaim (Ord.16 r.12). The grounds are set out in Order 16 rule 1(1). They are indemnity, contribution[2] and other relief connected with the claim. In England until 1929 and Northern Ireland until 1966 the RSC allowed a third-party notice for indemnity or contribution only.

THIRD-PARTY RELIEF

ORDER16 RULE 1(1)(A): "INDEMNITY"

10.01 A defendant may join a third party for indemnity where he claims a right by reason of their relationship to be re-imbursed for his liability to the plaintiff, for example an insured joining his insurer, a guarantor joining the principal debtor. It does not matter whether the plaintiff's claim is for debt or damages. Where an indemnity provision, contractual or statutory, contains a proviso that it does not apply where the parties are independently at fault, their liability is apportioned under the principles of contribution.[3]

10.02 *Contract.* A right of indemnity may arise expressly or impliedly under contract, whenever made. It is construed *contra proferentem.*[4] It must satisfy the test of reasonableness if the indemnitor is in the position of a consumer.[5] A contractual indemnity for libel is lawful unless the publisher knows that it is defamatory and does not believe reasonably in a defence.[6]

10.03 *Rule of law.* Indemnity may arise under a rule of law or equity; in favour of a personal representative, receiver or any fiduciary. An agent has indemnity for liability incurred for acts under the scope of his authority.[7] A right of indemnity lies for a person who acts at the request of another, and also

---

1 Civil Jurisdiction and Judgments Act 1982, Sch.1 Art.6; Sch.4 Art.6.

2 The law relating to indemnity and contribution applies by and against the Crown: Crown Proceedings Act, s.4(1); Civil Liability (Contribution) Act 1978, s.5.

3 *Clarke* v *McLaughlin & Harvey* [1978] 2 NIJB at 7.

4 *Smith* v *UMB Chrysler* 1978 SC (HL) 1 (no indemnity for negligence unless expressly mentioned).

5 Unfair Contract Terms Act 1977, s.4.

6 Defamation Act (NI) 1955, s.11.

7 Though not necessarily for negligent driving: *Sinnott* v *Quinnsworth* [1984] ILRM 523.

a person who acts for the benefit of another without his permission, if it was necessary to do so and it is just to ask for indemnity.[8]

10.04 *Statute.* The Law Society indemnifies a solicitor (Solicitors (NI) Order 1976, Art.63). A trustee has a right to his expenses (Trustee Act (NI) 1958, s.31(2)). A court may order a beneficiary to indemnify a trustee for breach of trust (Trustee Act, s.62). A street works undertaker is liable to indemnify the Department of the Environment for the costs of making suitable diversionary route.[9]

10.05 A person who pays under an indemnity is subrogated to the rights of the indemnitee and can sue in his name and has an equitable lien on money received by the indemnitee.[10] A person who has agreed to stand as surety for the debt is subrogated to the rights of the creditor and can sue in the name of the creditor against the debtor or any co-debtor or co-surety.[11]

Insurance

10.06 One important instance of the contractual right of indemnity is insurance, under a contract ('policy') whereby the insurer agrees to indemnify the insured in respect of any liability incurred by him to another person (called in the policy a 'third party').[12] If the defendant insured wishes to enforce his right of indemnity under the policy, he can serve a third-party notice for indemnity against the insurer. Any rule that this is improper has long gone, especially since the virtual abolition of jury trial.[13] Regardless of domicile in a Brussels Convention State, the insurer may be joined as a third party to a claim brought by the injured victim in a Northern Ireland court.[14] Protection for claims against an insurer who has become insolvent is dealt with in the Policy Holders' Protection Act 1975.

10.07 The Road Traffic (NI) Order 1981 (Art.90) makes it an offence to use or permit the use of a motor vehicle on a road without a policy of insurance which complies with Article 92 and the Regulations (SR 1994/46). The policy must insure specified persons and their personal representatives for non-contractual liability of the insured for death, bodily injury or damage to the property[15] of any person caused by such use. "Any person" does not include the driver or owner of that vehicle.[16] The insurance does not have to cover liability

---

8 *Owen* v *Tate* [1976] QB 402.

9 Street Works (NI) Order 1995, Art.37.

10 *Napier* v *Hunter* [1993] AC 713. See para. 3.19.

11 Mercantile Law Amendment Act 1856, s.5.

12 Several statutes require such insurance: e.g. the Employers' Liability (Defective Equipment and Compulsory Insurance) (NI) Order 1972, Art.5 and Regulations (NI), SR 1975/231; the Estate Agents Act 1979, s.16; Merchant Shipping Act 1995, s.163, Sch.4; and regulations under the Solicitors (NI) Order 1976, Art.63.

13 See *Graham* v *McPherson* [1991] NI 1.

14 Civil Jurisdiction and Judgments Act 1982, Sch.1 Art.10. Note that this is not repeated in the intra-UK provision (Sch.4).

15 As amended by SR 1989/84.

16 *Cooper* v *MIB* [1985] QB 575.

for contribution to a joint tortfeasor.[17] The injured person can enforce a judgment against the insurer direct under Article 98 (see para. 16.15).

10.08 *Priority of indemnities.* As to the precedence of overlapping rights of indemnity for liability to road accident victims, see *Graham* v *McPherson* [1991] NI 1 (driver's employer and driver's insurer); *Zurich Insurance* v *Shield Insurance* [1988] IR 174 (employer's motor insurer and employer's employment liability insurer); and *Eagle Star* v *Provincial Insurance* [1994] 1 AC 130 (PC) (driver's insurer and car owner's insurer). See also Article 92 of the Road Traffic Order (as amended by SR 1993/57).

ORDER 16 RULE 1(1)(A): "CONTRIBUTION"

10.09 A defendant may join a third party for contribution where he claims that by virtue of their common liability to the plaintiff, the third party should contribute to the plaintiff's award. For example a driver in an accident sued by a passenger joins another driver as joint tortfeasor. "Any person liable in respect of any damage suffered by another person may recover contribution from any other person liable in respect of the same damage (whether jointly with him or otherwise)" (Civil Liability (Contribution) Act 1978, s.1(1)). The Act applies to liability for damages[18] and restitution in quasi-contract,[19] but not debt, which is still governed by common law (see para. 10.14). Provided that both are responsible for the same damage to the same claimant,[20] and that the claimant could recover damages against both, it matters not whether they are liable in tort, contract, breach of trust or otherwise (s.6(1)). The right of contribution under that Act supersedes any other right to recover contribution, subject to any express contractual provision regulating contribution and to any express or implied right of indemnity (s.7(3)). The third party's contribution must not exceed the damages of the plaintiff as limited by any statute or agreement or as reduced by deduction for the plaintiff's contributory fault (s.2(3)).

10.10 The third party is liable notwithstanding that he has ceased to be liable for the damage since it occurred, unless he has ceased to be liable by reason of expiry of a limitation period which extinguished the right to claim against him (s.1(3)). Judgment against the defendant, payment of the plaintiff's claim or release by the plaintiff, do not bar him from claiming contribution (s.1(2)). For limitation purposes time starts to run on the defendant's claim against the third party from the time when the defendant is found liable or agrees to pay the plaintiff.[21] It is proper for the defendant to issue the third-party notice whilst still denying his own liability to the plaintiff.[22]

---

17 *Campbell* v *MacFarland* [1972] NI 31.

18 Including fatal cases: s.6(2).

19 *Friends' Provident* v *Hillier Parker May & Rowden* [1997] QB 85 (CA).

20 *Birse Construction* v *Haistie* [1996] 2 All ER 1 (CA). If the original accident is exacerbated by negligent medical treatment which was a foreseeable risk from the consequences of the injury, the doctor is a joint tortfeasor with the defendant who caused the accident for damages for the exacerbation: *Mahony* v *J.Kruschich* (1985) 156 CLR 522.

21 *Sterling* v *Cohen* [1987] NI 409.

22 *Cooke* v *Reynolds* [1942] NI 97.

10.11 In seeking contribution the defendant has to prove that the third party is or was liable to the plaintiff, but he does not have to prove that he himself is or was liable to the plaintiff. It is enough to show that he has made or agreed to make payment under a *bona fide* settlement, compromise or an accepted lodgment, assuming that the factual allegations of the plaintiff would make him liable (s.1(4)). In defamation this includes compensation paid under an offer of amends.[23] A prior judgment between the defendant and third party on the issue of fault contributory to the plaintiff's damage constitutes a *res judicata* between them. A prior judgment between the plaintiff and the third party does not constitute *res judicata* for or against the defendant, but section 1(5) makes a judgment in the United Kingdom conclusive as to any issue determined *against* the plaintiff in favour of the third party. Section 1(6) deals with the case where the liability of the defendant and/or third party may be governed by a foreign law: he is liable for the plaintiff's damage if a Northern Ireland court would find him liable applying either local law or the foreign law as dictated by the rules of conflicts of law.

10.12 By section 2, the defendant recovers from the third party such amount of contribution as is just and equitable having regard to the extent of his responsibility for the plaintiff's damage. It is possible for the Court to find both liable for the damage and yet assess contribution at 0 per cent (exempting the third party from contribution) or 100 per cent (contribution amounting to indemnity). If it does so the Court is saying that the responsibility of one party arises in law wholly from the fault of the other. It might give judgment for 100 per cent if the third party was negligent while acting as agent or employee of the defendant,[24] where the third party was principal who directed the wrongful act, or where the article which caused the injury was in the sole actual control of the third party;[25] or where the defendant took all reasonable steps to give advice to the third party which if heeded would have obviated the risk.[26] In such cases the plaintiff will recover against the defendant, who recovers 100 per cent against the third party. However, if the Court finds the third party to be solely liable in law, it must dismiss the plaintiff's claim, unless the third party is added as a defendant.

Contribution between co-defendants. See Order 16 rule 8(6) (para. 10.30).

10.13 Where a party (usually a third party or co-defendant) stands liable to contribute to any debt or damages, he may after appearance make a written offer to contribute a specified percentage share to the money which may be awarded to the plaintiff (Ord.16 r.10). If not accepted, the offer can be made known to the trial judge only after he has given his verdict on liability and quantum, and he must take it into account in his discretion as to costs (Ord.62 r.9(a)).

---

23 Defamation Act 1996, s.3(8)(a).
24 *Sinnott* v *Quinnsworth* [1984] ILRM 523.
25 *Scully* v *Boland* [1962] IR 58.
26 *Forster* v *Donovan* (1980) 114 ILTR 104.

Debt cases

10.14 The 1978 Act does not apply to actions where the plaintiff sues on a debt or liquidated demand. Co-debtors liable for the same debt have a common law liability to contribute in a fixed equal share. If two persons are jointly and severally liable for a debt, the plaintiff can sue each for the whole sum with a right of contribution *inter se* for one half: each is principal debtor for one half and surety for half.[27] The limitation period starts to run against one debtor only when the co-debtor pays off the debt.[28]

OTHER RELIEF

Order 16 rule 1(1)(b): Any remedy relating to or connected with subject-matter of the action and substantially the same as some remedy claimed by the plaintiff

10.15 Where the defendant has a claim against a third party connected with his liability to the plaintiff, he may join him to have the two claims adjudicated in the same action. A seller sued for breach of contract in selling defective goods, may join the distributor for breach of contract in selling those goods to him. Both the writ and the third-party notice claim the same relief, that is damages. The subject-matter, the goods, is the same. It is not essential to show that the issues in dispute are similar.[29] A defendant driver sued by an injured victim can and should claim by third-party notice for his own injuries as well as for contribution against the other blameworthy driver.[30]

Order 16 rule 1(1)(c): A question or issue relating to or connected with subject-matter of the action and which should be determined not only between plaintiff and defendant but also between either or both of them and the third party

10.16 If the defendant is sued for specific performance of a contract for sale of land which he is seeking to buy from a third party, he can claim specific performance against the third party under rule (1)(b); but if he wants rescission and/or damages he must rely on rule (1)(c).[31] Here also it is not necessary to show that the issues in dispute are similar.[29] Under this rule a defendant sued as guarantor on a debt was allowed to claim in negligence against the receiver of the principal debtor.[32]

THIRD-PARTY PROCEDURE

10.17 The defendant has a cause of action against the third party which, if it is within the purview of Order 16 rule 1, he can raise by third-party notice. He is also free to sue on it by a separate action, and the substantive law on his right

---

27 *In re Gervais* [1903] 1 IR 172. Thus each co-debtor defendant is subrogated to the rights of the plaintiff creditor to enforce the debt: see para. 10.05.

28 *Gardner* v *Brooke* [1897] 2 IR 6.

29 *Myers* v *Sherick* [1974] 1 WLR 31; but joinder can be disallowed if the issues are too dissimilar.

30 *Talbot* v *Berkshire CC* [1994] QB 290.

31 See *Chatsworth Investments* v *Amoco* [1968] Ch 665.

32 *Stevenson* v *National Bank* [1987] 2 NZLR 331.

to contribution, indemnity or other relief is the same. However once the injured party has issued a writ against him, it is obviously more convenient to make use of Order 16, and if he allows judgment against him without involving the person liable to indemnify him and then sues that person, he may recover only the amount of the award without the costs paid to the injured party.[33]

Issue of notice

10.18 For limitation purposes a third-party notice against a person who is not already a party is deemed to be a separate action commenced when the third-party proceedings are commenced.[34] In a third-party notice for contribution or indemnity this will not cause a problem because the limitation period does not start to run until the defendant's liability to the plaintiff is established.[35] The defendant can issue a notice against two or more third parties, who stand in relation to each other as co-defendants to the notice.[36]

10.19 The defendant must first enter an appearance to the writ. No leave is necessary if the defendant issues a third-party notice before Defence (Ord.16 r.1(2)), but thereafter he must apply *ex parte* for leave on affidavit (Ord.16 r.2) and the order of leave may state a time limit for issue (Ord 16 r.3(1)). Leave can be given at any time, even after the trial has started and, *semble*, even after judgment. In an action by originating summons, leave is always necessary. Leave is always necessary to issue a notice against the Crown, to be sought by summons served on the plaintiff and the Crown, satisfying the Court that the Crown has sufficient information as to its liability (Ord.77 r.9). The notice must state the nature of the claim against the third party and the grounds thereof or the question or issue to be determined (Ord.16 r.1(1)). The notice is issued like a writ, and served like a writ under Order 10 (Ord.16 r.3(4)). It can be issued for service outside the jurisdiction but leave to serve may be necessary in accordance with Order 11, obtained *ex parte*.[37] If the third party is domiciled in a Brussels Convention State or Great Britain, it can be served without leave.[38] From the service of the notice, the person becomes a party (Ord.16 r.1(3)). With the third-party notice the defendant must serve a copy of the writ and any pleadings (Ord.16 r.3(2)).

Interlocutory progress

10.20 After the third party enters an appearance under Order 12, the defendant applies under Order 16 rule 4 for directions by summons served on all parties (or if on written consent, *ex parte*); if he fails to do so the third party may apply. The Court may strike out the third-party notice as irregular, vexatious, scandalous, embarrassing etc. It may strike it out or order it or be tried separately, where the issues are too complex or not sufficiently connected

---

[33] *Caldbeck* v *Boon* (1873) IR 7 CL 32.

[34] Limitation (NI) Order 1989, Art.73; i.e. when the third-party notice is issued out of the appropriate Office: White Book (1997) 16/3/5.

[35] Limitation Order, Art.13; *Sterling* v *George Cohen* [1987] NI 409.

[36] *Stewart* v *Bowen* [1975] NI 10; fully reported *sub nom Stewart* v *Ellis* [1974] Jan NIJB.

[37] *Cannon* v *Fallon* (1918) 52 ILTR 34.

[38] Civil Jurisdiction and Judgments Act 1982, Sch.1 Art.6; Sch.4 Art.6.

to the plaintiff's claim, or all the points involved cannot be finally settled;[39] or where the issues have already been decided against the defendant in favour of the third party in another action.[40] The notice may be dismissed if the defendant does not show that there is a question fit to be tried;[41] or at least a case against the third party in the event of the plaintiff's disputed claim being successful.[42] In *Boyd* v *Dooley*,[43] Palles CB said that the Court could direct the defendant to make a formal admission on the plaintiff's claim or "to put in any pleas we think necessary". Of course the Chief Baron did not mean that in the absolute sense, rather that the Court can exact the admission or plea as a condition for allowing the third-party notice to proceed.

10.21 The Court may direct the manner in which the third-party issues be tried and/or allow the third party to defend against the plaintiff's claim; direct the extent to which the third party will be bound by judgment on the plaintiff's claim; grant judgment to the defendant; or dismiss the claim against the third party (Ord.16 r.4), or add the third party as a defendant (Ord.15 r.6(2)). The usual direction is for the defendant to serve a Statement of Claim, the third party to serve a Defence, the third party to have leave to defend against the plaintiff's claim and the third party issues to be tried at or immediately after the trial of the plaintiff's action as the trial judge shall direct.[44] Any direction may be later varied or rescinded (Ord.16 r.4(5)).

10.22 Note that the plaintiff cannot get judgment against the third party until the latter is added as a defendant, but the third party can plead and give evidence of any matter which goes to defeat the plaintiff's claim against the defendant. In the absence of an order joining the third party as a defendant, discovery cannot be had between plaintiff and third party, and they cannot be ordered to give particulars to each other: so held by Carswell LJ in *Gillespie* v *Anglo-Irish Beef*.[45] The third party can counterclaim against the defendant and issue a fourth party notice against any other person. He cannot counterclaim against the plaintiff unless he is made a defendant.

10.23 The defendant can discontinue the third party proceedings under Order 21 (Ord.16 r.3(4)). Proceedings on a third party notice may at any stage be set aside (Ord.16 r.6). Order 16 rule 5 deals with default of appearance and default in delivery of pleadings directed. If the third party is in default he is deemed to admit the claim against him and the defendant may enter judgment against him.[46] If either defendant or third party defaults in serving any ordered pleading,

---

39 *Ffrench Mullen* v *Murphy* (1911) 45 ILTR 210.

40 *Nolan* v *Listowel UDC* [1966] IR 56.

41 *Greville* v *Hayes* [1894] 2 IR 20 (old rule said: "fit to be tried").

42 *Andrews* v *Dunn* [1960] NI 181, at 182 line 20; but an affidavit is not now necessary.

43 (1881) 15 ILTR 4.

44 The importance of third-party directions is illustrated by *Murphy* v *J. O'Donoghue* [1996] 1 IR 123 (SC): defendant X had issued a third-party notice against defendant Y but failed to seek third-party directions; X secured an order for discovery against Y; but non-compliance with that order could not lead to striking out of Y's Defence because there was no Defence.

45 [1994] 4 BNIL 68. The White Book (1997) 16/1/23 states a contrary view, but the 1997 edition quotes *Gillespie* and concedes that Carswell LJ's is probably right.

46 Leave of the Court is necessary unless the claim is for contribution or indemnity and the defendant has satisfied the plaintiff's judgment.

the other may apply by summons for judgment. A judgment in default may be set aside or varied. If the third party in default of appearance is under disability, the defendant must apply for appointment of a guardian *ad litem* (Ord.80 r.4(2)). Leave is necessary for judgment in default against the Crown (Ord.77 r.8(2)). Unless directed, there is no automatic discovery (Ord.24 r.2(1)). Third-party proceedings can proceed to be determined after the plaintiff's claim has been satisfied (Ord.16 r.11).[47] Equally the third-party proceedings can be struck out, for abuse of process, want of prosecution etc., while the plaintiff's claim continues.

Trial and judgment

10.24 The normal directions at the trial are that the plaintiff, defendant and third party present their cases in that order; the third party may cross-examine the plaintiff's witnesses and adduce evidence against him so far as the plaintiff's allegations affect him; judgments between all parties to be given at the end. In some cases, as where he agrees liability to indemnify the defendant, the third party may be allowed to defend jointly with the defendant, or alone. If the plaintiff's action is tried by jury the Court can direct the third-party issues to be tried by judge alone.[48] At the trial of the action or by application, the defendant may seek judgment against the third party or *vice versa*; the defendant cannot without leave enforce judgment for contribution or indemnity until he has satisfied the plaintiff's award (Ord.16 r.7). Save as provided by statute where the third party is the insurer, the plaintiff has no right to enforce his judgment directly against the third party. *Semble*, he can seek a garnishee order from the Enforcement of Judgments Office to attach the judgment debt owed by the third party.

10.25 The third party can appeal against judgment for the defendant, and against the plaintiff insofar as he is bound by the plaintiff's judgment, but otherwise he needs leave of the Court to appeal against the plaintiff.[49]

Costs

10.26 The Court has a discretion as to who should pay the costs of all parties.[50] If the plaintiff loses the general practice is to award costs of the third party against the defendant;[51] even if the plaintiff is legally aided.[52] If the third party's joinder was a proper response to the plaintiff's claim, the Court may order the plaintiff to pay to the defendant his own costs and the costs payable to the third (and fourth etc.) party.[53] In a proper case the plaintiff may be ordered to pay costs directly to the third (and fourth etc.) party.[54] The third party should normally bear his own costs where the plaintiff discontinues.[55] A third party's

---

47 And *Stott* v *West Yorkshire Road Car Co* [1971] 2 QB 651.
48 Cf. *Fisher* v *Moynagh* (1912) 46 ILTR 187.
49 *Ashphalt & Public Works* v *Indemnity Guarantee* [1969] 1 QB 465.
50 See the White Book (1997) 16/7/4; 62/B/143.
51 *Hennessy* v *Quinn* [1968] IR 274.
52 *Johnson* v *Ribbins* [1977] 1 WLR 1458.
53 Cf. *Brunker* v *North* (1880) 15 ILTR 10.
54 *Hanbury* v *Upper Inny Drainage Board* (1883) 12 LR Ir 217.
55 *Cullen* v *Toft* (1903) 37 ILTR 65.

duty to indemnify does not mean that he must pay the costs of the defence where the defendant cannot recover costs from the plaintiff, unless so agreed.[56] If the plaintiff wins, the costs of the third-party proceedings usually follow the event. If the defendant wins against the third party he will get not only his own costs but also the costs payable to the plaintiff. A third party who is substantially the real defendant may be ordered to pay costs direct to the plaintiff.

10.27 Costs between the parties are usually on the "standard basis" taxation; but if the defendant who is liable to the plaintiff recovers against the third party on right of indemnity, the Court should order the defendant's costs to be taxed on the "indemnity basis".[57]

THIRD-PARTY NOTICE AGAINST EXISTING PARTY

10.28 A defendant can issue a third-party notice at any time after his appearance against an existing party, including a co-defendant or one co-plaintiff, unless the claim could be made by way of counterclaim (Ord.16 r.8). A third-party notice is of necessity based on a cause of action by the defendant, so it would seem that his claim against a plaintiff should always be by way of counterclaim.[58] He need not serve the pleadings with the notice, and the existing party need not enter an appearance if he has already appeared in the action. Directions by the Court are not necessary if the notice claims only contribution or indemnity. A notice between co-defendants creates a *lis* which can continue after the plaintiff's claim has been disposed of.[59]

10.29 For limitation purposes the third-party notice is deemed to have commenced back on the date when the plaintiff issued his writ.[60] Therefore the third-party notice must be struck out if the limitation period would have expired since the issue of the writ, unless arises out of substantially the same facts as the plaintiff's claim and is thus saved by Article 73(4)(a) of the Limitation (NI) Order 1989.[61] Of course in the case of a notice for contribution or indemnity, the limitation period does not start to run until liability to the plaintiff is established.

10.30 If defendants are sued as tortfeasors for the same damage, no notice need be served by one on the other but if one intends to rely for contribution or indemnity on some fact not pleaded by the plaintiff or on some contractual right, he must give particulars in writing (Ord.16 r.8(6)). As a result of the Civil Liability (Contribution) Act 1978, this declaratory provision (not expressly stated in the English RSC) should be read as covering any case in which the defendants are sued in respect of the same damage, whether in tort, breach of contract, breach of trust or otherwise.

---

56 *Hickman* v *Foley* (1905) 39 ILTR 21.

57 White Book (1997) 62/B/144; *Wiley* v *Smith* [1894] 1 IR 153 (case of separate action for indemnity).

58 See *Cullen* v *Clein* [1970] IR 146.

59 *Harper* v *Gray* [1985] 1 WLR 1196; *Collings* v *Wade* [1903] 1 IR 89.

60 Limitation (NI) Order 1989, Art.73.

61 *Welsh Development Agency* v *Redpath Dorman* [1994] 1 WLR 1409.

10.31 Where a defendant in his Defence makes a claim against a co-defendant and serves a copy of the Defence on the co-defendant, this was held to be a notice of claim against him under section 27(3) of the Supreme Court of Judicature (Ir) Act 1877.[62]

FOURTH ETC. PARTY NOTICE

10.32 A third party can issue a fourth-party notice against any person whether an existing party or not, including the plaintiff; and the fourth party can issue a fifth-party notice and so on. Leave is necessary unless the notice is issued within 28 days after service of the notice on him (Ord.16 r.9), and always, against the Crown (Ord.77 r.9). This chain of notices usually happens where the plaintiff sues the retailer for defective goods, and notices are issued through the chain of sellers up to the manufacturer.[63] The Court can order the defendant to pay the costs of fourth and subsequent parties;[64] just as it can order the plaintiff to pay the costs of third and subsequent parties. Article 73(7) of the Limitation (NI) Order 1989 puts the fourth-party notice in the same position as a third-party notice for limitation purposes.

INTERPLEADER SUMMONS

10.33 If a person liable for a debt or for any money or goods is sued or expects to be sued by competing claimants, he may apply for interpleader, by originating summons or by summons in the pending action; and the Court may direct the trial of the competing claims (Ord.17). It does not apply where the claim is for unliquidated damages. The Crown may interplead, under the Crown Proceedings Act, section 16 and Order 77 rule 10. The competing claims must relate to the same property and it must appear that only one can succeed.[65] The interpleader jurisdiction is not affected by Article 11 of the Judgments Enforcement (NI) Order 1981 as it does not relate to enforcement of judgments.[66] A summary determination under Order 17 is final unless leave to appeal is given by the judge or the Court of Appeal; but a decision upon trial is appealable without leave within 21 days (Ord.58 r.5). Where the interpleader relief is granted, the Court may direct the issue between the claimants to be determined under an arbitration agreement made between them.[67]

10.34 A debtor who has had notice of a disputed assignment of a chose in action may call upon the claimants to interplead under section 87 of the Judicature Act.

---

[62] *Barbour* v *Rutherford* [1925] NI 187; possibly continued by virtue of s.86(2) of the Judicature Act 1978.

[63] Under the common law, since there is no duty in negligence to prevent economic loss, the retailer has no direct cause of action against the manufacturer.

[64] *Kelly* v *McCurdy* [1965] NI 124.

[65] *Brady* v *Deignan* (1950) 84 ILTR 38.

[66] *Carlton Atkinson and Sloan* v *AIB* [1977] NI 158.

[67] Arbitration Act 1996, s.10.

CHAPTER ELEVEN

INTERLOCUTORY PROCEEDINGS

GENERAL

Definition of interlocutory proceeding

11.00 An order is only final if made on an application which must determine the action however it is decided. Thus an order is interlocutory if the application has been or could have been decided in such a way that the action continues.[1] Yet in *Hunter* v *Hannay*[2] judgment on motion for a new trial was held to be final; and in *Dale* v *British Coal*[3] the decision of a court to disapply the limitation period was held to be final. The White Book (1979 ed., 59/4/2; 1988 ed., 59/1/26) and Wylie (p.794) give examples of orders which have been held to be interlocutory: an order dismissing an action for want of prosecution; an order for Order 14 summary judgment; judgment in default; an order granting, confirming or setting aside judgment in default; an order for the working out of the rights of parties (e.g. a partition order directing accounts and inquiries). A decision as to liability tried as a preliminary issue is final. Some rules specify whether an order is deemed to be interlocutory, for the purpose of right of appeal.

Mode of application

11.01 Interlocutory relief can be sought at any time. If required to be heard promptly or immediately, during vacation, it is heard by the vacation judge (Ord.64 r.4(1)). A notice of motion may be served with the writ or at any time after service of the writ (Ord.8 r.4). Interlocutory relief should not usually be claimed in the writ or pleadings, and cannot be used as a ground for service outside the jurisdiction.[4] It can be granted where the issue is the Court's jurisdiction to hear the action.[5] Interlocutory relief can be granted even though a Great Britain or Brussels Convention State court has jurisdiction.[6] It can be granted for the purposes of proceedings which have been or are to be commenced in such court,[7] even if the claim in those proceedings is not a cause

---

1 *R (Curry)* v *National Insurance Commrs* [1974] NI 102; *White* v *Brunton* [1984] QB 570 (the *'Salaman* v *Warner'* test, [1891] 1 QB 734).

2 (1892) 26 ILTR 129, not following *Salaman* v *Warner*.

3 [1992] 1 WLR 964.

4 *Serge Cauldron* v *Air Zaire* [1986] ILRM 10.

5 Civil Jurisdiction and Judgments Act 1982, s.24.

6 *Ibid,* Sch.1 Art.24 and Sch.4 Art.24.

7 *Ibid.* s.25; as where the contract between the parties confers exclusive jurisdiction on the other state: *Coca Cola* v *Concentrate* [1990] NI 77; *Adair Smith Motors* v *Nissan Motor* [1993] 11 NIJB 18 (Carswell J: reversed by the CA on another point). If begun by originating summons, the application is subject to any counterclaim: *Balkanbank* v *Taher (No 2)* [1995] 1 WLR 1067.

of action recognised in our law.[8] It can now also be granted in relation to proceedings outside the scope of the Convention and in states other than Convention states.[9]

11.02 A judge may hear any proceedings in chambers in so far as statute or rules authorise or direct it (Ord.32 r.1). An application must be heard in chambers: (a) if statute or rules direct it to be in chambers or by summons; (b) if the Court directs it; or (c) if it is interlocutory and not authorised to be by motion[10] (Ord.32 r.2). In any judgment or order made in court a judge may direct proceedings in chambers (Ord.32 r.17). Where the RSC require an application to be made "by notice", it is by way of motion and must be heard in open court unless the Court otherwise directs in exceptional circumstances.[11]

11.03 Every application, unless made orally at the hearing of proceedings, must be made either by motion or summons: so a request to the Lists Office to list an application for hearing is irregular.[12] Every application made in chambers must be by summons (Ord.32 r.3(1). All interlocutory proceedings must be had in the Division in which the cause or matter is pending (Ord.1 r.12A(2). Thus a Queen's Bench master, sitting as such, cannot hear an application in a Chancery case,[13] though one master or other statutory officer can act in place of another where necessary (para. 1.04). An interlocutory application, if not made *ex parte*, is brought either by notice of motion in Form 27 or by summons in Form 28, according to the rule moved under, and issued out of the appropriate Office with a £40 stamp. A summons is for hearing in chambers (Ord.32 r.2).

11.04 Any application in chambers, whether by summons or *ex parte*, can be heard by a master, save for those excepted proceedings listed in Order 32 rule 11. The excepted proceedings are: matters relating to criminal proceedings or liberty of the subject; review of taxation of costs; leave to a vexatious litigant to sue; approval of transactions under inherent jurisdiction; granting of an injunction save on terms agreed; approval of settlements for minors and patients; charities; applications under sections 40,56,57 and 61 of the Trustee Act (NI) 1958, or Article 133(2) of the Mental Health (NI) Order 1986; and anything reserved by the Lord Chief Justice or Chancery Judge. In proceedings listed in the Commercial List, the Commercial Judge hears interlocutory applications unless he otherwise directs (Ord.72 r.5). As to listing before the judge of applications in the Chancery Division, see the Practice Direction [1987] 9 BNIL 70. As a matter of practice, masters will decline to hear

---

8 *G* v *Caledonian Newspapers*, 1995 SLT 559.

9 SI 1997/302.

10 Application for an injunction or application made in court at the trial may be made in open court: Ord.32 r.2.

11 *Re Martin* [1990] NI 73 (bail application).

12 *Doherty* v *MOD* [1991] 1 NIJB 68, at 75-8; though in that case, the opponent having been notified and attending, the defect was waived. But see *Thomas* v *Hammond-Lawrence* [1986] 1 WLR 456.

13 *Re Cloake* (1892) 61 LJ Ch 69.

interlocutory matters related to applications which have been or are being dealt with by a judge.

11.05 The notice or summons must state the nature of the claim or the order or remedy sought (Ord.8 r.3(2);[14] and preferably the rule moved under. Both a notice of motion (Ord.8 r.3(6)) and a summons (Ord.32 r.4(1)) are issued upon being sealed in the Office. Both notice of motion (Ord.8 r.2(2)) and summons (Ord.32 r.5) must be served at least two clear days before the return day.[15] The grounding affidavit and other documents should be served with it.[16] A notice of motion must be served "on the parties affected thereby". A summons is served "on every other party", that is every party to the summons, not to the action.[17] There is no need to serve a party who is in default of appearance, subject to specific exceptions (Ord.65 r.9). Service is governed by Order 65 (see para. 6.20). A summons or notice may be served outside Northern Ireland in the same way as a writ (Ord.11 r.9(4)). In urgent cases time can be abridged under Order 3 rule 5 or by leave.[18] A motion is issued by sealing at the appropriate Office (Ord.8 r.3(6)). It may be served in an action along with the writ (Ord.8 r.4). If an application is made affecting a party who has not entered an appearance, the Court may require to be satisfied that the party is in default of appearance (Ord.13 r.7(2)). The motion or summons can be amended by leave, which has retrospective effect.[19] A motion may be brought *ex parte* if delay might cause irrepara.ble or serious mischief: and any order so made may be set aside (Ord.8 r.2(1)). In *KSK Enterprises* v *An Bord Pleanála,*[20] the Irish Supreme Court held that an *ex parte* motion is "made" when it is moved in court;[21] a motion on notice is "made" when it is filed in the Office and served on all parties. Hearing of a motion may be adjourned (Ord.8 r.5).

11.06 Most interlocutory applications in the *Queen's Bench Division* are brought by summons. A summons is issued on being sealed at the Office, and cannot be amended thereafter without leave (Ord.32 r.4). Along with the summons is filed the grounding affidavit and an attested copy and copies of exhibits.[22] The summons must be accompanied by a copy of the writ or other originating process, as amended to date.[23] Any replying affidavit by the respondent must be filed with an attested copy and copy exhibits.[22] The hearing can be adjourned to a date or *sine die* (Ord.32 r.6). Most are heard by a master at the 10am Friday court; settlements and agreed first adjournments can be mentioned to the master up to 2pm on Thursday.[24] In recent years the masters

---

14 *Curreen* v *Walsh* (1838) 1 Ir Eq R 200.

15 A summons can be issued for hearing "on a date to be fixed".

16 *Hogan* v *Hogan* [1924] 2 IR 12.

17 White Book (1997) 32/1-6/13.

18 If leave for short notice of motion is given the notice must so state: Ord.8 r.3(1).

19 *McAllister* v *Wilson* [1955] NI 208.

20 [1994] 2 ILRM 1.

21 In Northern Ireland, most *ex parte* applications are made to a master simply by lodging a 'docket', without a court hearing. Presumably it is made when it is lodged.

22 Practice Direction [1983] 5 BNIL 96.

23 Practice Direction [1994] 10 BNIL 84.

24 Practice Direction, Queen's Bench , 6 May 1981.

have sat on Thursday afternoons as well. Evidence is invariably by affidavit, though a party can call oral evidence. In the *Chancery Division*, the master sits at regular times in mornings and afternoons throughout the week and most interlocutory summonses are heard in the afternoon appointments. Short applications can be listed at 11am and heard first.[25]

A *subpoena* for a witness can be issued only with leave (Ord.32 r.9). A master can summon a party to attend before him, require production of a document, examine a party or witness, or on request of a party summon a witness to attend (Ord.32 r.14), and may administer the oath (Ord.41 r.12)). The Court may at any stage in any proceedings order a person to attend and produce a document, subject to his claim of privilege (Ord.38 r.11).[26] The Court can seek expert assistance (Ord.32 r.15). The fee of the expert is fixed by the Taxing Master (Ord.62 r.25). Original documents must be used if available, and copies made only if the Court directs copies to be used (Ord.32 r.18). The parties are usually represented by junior counsel, though solicitors also have right of audience in chambers. The master can refer a matter to a judge, who may hear it or refer it back (Ord.32 r.12). The hearing may be adjourned by a judge from chambers into court and back (Ord.32 rr.13,16). A summons can be heard in the absence of a party; but the Court can re-hear it before the order is perfected, or a dismissed summons may be restored if the applicant did not appear (Ord.32 r.7). In awarding costs the master can certify for counsel's fee (Ord.62 App.2). A summons cannot be withdrawn without leave (Ord.21 r.6).

Orders

11.07 The Court may grant or dismiss the application or make any appropriate interlocutory order or direction. The Court may make "no order" on an application, with costs in the cause or no order as to costs, where the respondent has been at fault,[27] or may strike out with costs to the applicant where the respondent has granted the relief sought in the summons since its issue. An order, decision or direction is a judgment for the purpose of Order 42, and it can be altered at any time before it is drawn up and signed, as to which see para. 15.01. The Court has inherent power to set aside or vary any interlocutory order;[28] even if made by consent.[29] However the White Book (1997) 20/11/8 and 32/1-6/21, doubts whether interlocutory orders are any more reviewable than final orders. It may be that injunctions are in a special position.[30] The power to set aside or vary an interlocutory injunction can be

---

[25] Practice Direction [1995] 3 BNIL 106

[26] Note that a civil court cannot call a witness without the consent of a party (see para. 13.83).

[27] *Donnelly* v *Gray* [1970] Oct NIJB at 6.

[28] *Regent Oil* v *JT Leavesley* [1966] 1 WLR 1210 (interim injunction, discharged by reason of recent case law).

[29] *Mullins* v *Howell* [1879) 11 Ch D 763; *Irish Commercial* v *Plunkett* [1987] ILRM 504, quoting *Purcell* v *Trigell* [1971] 1 QB 358, at 363-4, where Lord Denning MR (only) thought that there is a larger discretion to reverse on appeal an interlocutory consent order.

[30] Bean on *Injunctions* (6th ed. 1994) says at pp. 37, 104, that an 'interim injunction' is a temporary order, and that an 'interlocutory injunction' is always expressed to be "until trial or further order", and that either type can be discharged by further order.

exercised only on an application made in the proceedings in which it was given.[31] Some rules (e.g. Ord.14 r.11 and Ord.24 r.16) expressly allow an order to be varied or revoked. No estoppel *per rem judicatem* arises from an order granting or refusing interlocutory relief, but a new application for the same relief which has been refused will be struck out as an abuse of process unless new grounds are shown.[32] If an order is made against a party who does not appear that party can apply to have it set aside either for irregularity of service (in which case it should be normally set aside as of right) or on deposing to an arguable defence or the relief claimed.[33]

Appeals and reviews

11.08 Either party may appeal from the master's judgment, order or decision to a judge in chambers; unless the Court otherwise orders, the appellant must issue a notice to attend the appeal within five days after the order and serve it on the parties to the proceeding at least two clear days before the date for hearing (Ord.58 r.1). A fee of £50 is payable. The five-day limit is of course extendable under Order 3 rule 5, but there must be some material for exercising the discretion to do so, however short the delay.[34] The appellant must lodge one appeal book, comprising the notice of appeal,[35] summons, affidavits and exhibits, and the master's order, at least two days before the date fixed for hearing.[36] It will not be listed until the appeal book is lodged. Save as directed by the Court, the appeal does not stay the proceedings (Ord.58 r.1(4)). The restrictions on appeal from an order as to costs or on consent in section 35 of the Judicature Act do not apply to an appeal from a master to a judge.[37] The appeal is a complete rehearing, though the appellant usually begins; new evidence may be adduced; the judge exercises his own discretion *de novo*.[38] In *Bailie* v *Cruikshank*[39] McCollum J said that although the judge has a full discretion to allow new evidence, he should be reluctant to do so unless it is shown that its admission is in the interests of justice and that there is good reason for not having adduced it before the master; and he should also consider whether it has been disclosed to the other party as soon as possible. The judge can direct or adjourn the hearing into open court and back (Ord.32 r.13).

11.09 Where the relevant rule allows the judge to "review, vary or rescind" the order of an officer, the appellant has an onus to show that the officer was wrong;[40] but it gives a wide discretion and new evidence is admissible.[41]

---

31 *Howard* v *Commr of Works* [1994] 2 ILRM 301.

32 *Pocklington Foods* v *Alberta* (1995) 123 DLR 4th 141.

33 *Abbey National* v *Grugan*, Ch D, NI (Girvan J) 7 March 1997.

34 *Savill* v *Southend HA* [1995] 1 WLR 1254 (CA).

35 In the Form in the White Book (1997) Vol. 2 Part 2B, PF110.

36 Practice Direction [1990] 8 BNIL 46 (QBD); [1991] 1 BNIL 81 (Ch Div).

37 *Foster* v *Edwards* (1879) 48 LJQB 767; White Book (1997) Vol. 2 [4606].

38 *Evans* v *Bartlam* [1937] AC 473; *Duffy* v *MOD* [1979] NI 120; *Derry Construction* v *DHSS* [1980] NI 187; though he may derive some assistance from reading the master's written judgment: *Neill* v *Corbett* [1992] NI 251, at 252j.

39 [1995] 6 BNIL 79, following *Krakauer* v *Katz* [1954] 1 WLR 278.

40 *In re Walsh and Gallagher*, QB (Bankruptcy), 11 January 1968 (Lowry J).

41 *In re Arranging Debtor* [1965] NI 24.

Apart from the express provisions of the RSC, the High Court has inherent power to review any decision by a master or officer under rules of court or under any function delegated to him by the Court, and judicial review does not lie.[42]

11.10 *Appeal to Court of Appeal.* Appeal from the Judge's interlocutory decision (whether original or on appeal from a master) lies to the Court of Appeal by leave (see para. 20.10). A decision by a master on a reference under Order 36 rule 1 (Chancery or QBD only), or on an assessment of damages (QBD only), must be appealed directly to the Court of Appeal (Ord.58 rr.2-3).

Ex parte applications

11.11 An application is made *ex parte* where the Court is asked to make an order without service of a notice or summons on the person against whom it is sought. An interlocutory order can be made on *ex parte* motion in any of the following instances: (a) a case of extreme urgency (e.g. an injunction to restrain a neighbour from cutting down the plaintiff's tree); (b) where prior notice of the order would lead the respondent to frustrate its purpose;[43] (c) by convention; (d) where statute or rules authorise or direct it.[44] In effect, because of Order 65 rule 9, subject to specific exceptions, interlocutory applications against a party who is in default of appearance or has given no address for service, can be made *ex parte*. Applications before commencement of proceedings are usually made *ex parte* (see paras. 5.01-5.02). For urgent applications, the Law Society can be asked to grant an emergency civil aid certificate (see para. 3.59).

11.12 The applicant has a duty to make full and fair disclosure of relevant facts known to him.[45] Counsel must make full disclosure of matters of fact and law.[46] An *ex parte* order is sought by *ex parte* docket in Form HCF 13, and is determined by the judge or master without a court hearing. Since 1996, the *ex parte* docket for a master carries a fee of £20. An *ex parte* injunction application requires a hearing before a judge, and the fee is £45. Costs are usually made "costs in the cause" or reserved for the *inter partes* hearing. If the respondent knows of the application he can appear and can be awarded costs.[47] The Court can direct the application to be made by summons (Ord.32 r.3(2)). An *ex parte* order will be refused if the applicant has delayed without excuse.[48] The applicant can appeal against refusal as with any interlocutory order, but the respondent should apply to set it aside rather than appeal. Any order made *ex parte* is liable to be set aside (Ord.32 r.8),[49] by the Court itself or on

---

[42] *Matheson* v *Wilson* (1928) 62 ILTR 49; *In re Weir* [1988] NI 338, at 351-3; *In re Rice* [1994] 4 BNIL 67; and see para. 19.11.

[43] E.g. an *Anton Piller* order (see para. 11.86).

[44] E.g. leave to issue and serve outside Northern Ireland (Ord.11) renewal of writ (Ord.6), applications for leave to sue, applications which do not involve any other person.

[45] *In goods of Toole* [1913] 2 IR 188.

[46] Bar Handbook 8-03.

[47] *Pickwick* v *Multiple Sound* [1972] 3 All ER 384.

[48] *In re Lyle* [1987] 7 NIJB 24, at 39.

[49] Also by inherent jurisdiction apart from the rule: *Voluntary Purchasing* v *Insurco* [1995] 2 ILRM 145.

application of a party. On such application the Court has the advantage of hearing both parties and can freely review the order.[50] As to appeal to the Court of Appeal, see Order 59 rule 14 (para. 20.11).

EVIDENCE BY AFFIDAVIT

11.13 In interlocutory proceedings, evidence is almost always adduced by affidavit. It is admissible on any application by motion or summons, though a party may apply for an order that the deponent attend for cross-examination (Ord.38 r.2(3)). An affidavit may be sworn before any Commissioner for Oaths (appointed under Order 107) or any court officer appointed by the Lord Chancellor or a judge; an affidavit may be sworn outside Northern Ireland before any person there authorised, and if authorised otherwise than by foreign law judicial notice is taken of his seal or signature (Judicature Act, s.112). Every practising solicitor in Northern Ireland has the powers conferred by any enactment on a Commissioner for Oaths (Solicitors (NI) Order 1976, Art.78). It may be sworn before a master or clerk (Ord.41 r.12). It must not be sworn before a solicitor or agent of the solicitor's firm appearing for the party in the action or any person who is interested in the proceedings (Solicitors Order, Art.78; Ord.41 r.8). An affidavit sworn in Great Britain, Republic of Ireland or any part of the Commonwealth is admissible without formal proof of seal or signature (Judicature Act, s.66; Ord.41 r.13). A British ambassador, consul or embassy official abroad may take oaths (Commissioner for Oaths Act 1889, s.6). The deponent swears, under the Oaths Act 1978, and signs the affidavit in the presence of the commissioner who signs the *jurat* attesting to the oath and signature. The *jurat* states the date and place (Judicature Act, s.112(6)). The deponent is liable in perjury for any statement which he knows to be false, but a person who supplies false information to the deponent is not guilty of perjury.[51]

11.14 An affidavit is sworn by a person who is best able to bear witness to the facts stated in it. Often this will be the party's solicitor. Usually counsel or the solicitor drafts it on instructions from the witness, who swears the affidavit. It must state his residence or place of business, and occupation. It begins: "I, Jo Bloggs, aged 21 years and upward, make oath and say [*or* solemnly declare and affirm] that- ...." Then comes a series of factual statements in numbered paragraphs made in the first person. The first paragraph states the deponent's role: "I am the plaintiff in the above action"; or "I am the solicitor for the defendant in the above action and am authorised to make this affidavit on his behalf." Then it states the relevant facts simply and directly and may deal with any anticipated allegations of the opponent. In interlocutory and certain other proceedings it may contain hearsay, provided the source is given, or the basis for knowing or believing a fact;[52] otherwise it may contain only such facts as the deponent can prove of his own knowledge (Ord.41 r.5). If a proposition of law is stated, it should state: "I am advised by my solicitor and believe that ...." If a document is relied on it should be mentioned by wording such as: "I beg leave to refer to [description of document] on which marked 'JB 1' I have put

---

[50] White Book (1997) 32/1-6/25.

[51] *In re Copeland* [1990] NI 301.

[52] See *McCartan* v *Hulton* (1922) 56 ILTR 152.

my initials at the time of swearing hereof"; and is exhibited by a photocopy annexed to the affidavit. A document referred to must be exhibited, not annexed, and identified by a certificate of the commissioner (Ord.42 r.11). The original of the document should not be annexed but it should be brought to court (Ord.32 r.18). The penultimate paragraph usually states: "Save as herein appears, I depose to the foregoing facts of my own personal knowledge". It concludes with a request for the order or remedy which the party seeks from the Court. At its foot is the deponent's signature and the *jurat*, and the name of the party on whose behalf the affidavit is filed. In Chancery proceedings, the solicitor who procures an affidavit must ensure that the affidavit is properly sworn.[53] The Court can strike out any scandalous, irrelevant or oppressive matter (Ord.41r.6), such as unwarranted references to offers of settlement.

11.15 The formal requirements of an affidavit are set out in Order 41 rules 1-3. Any alterations must be initialled (Ord.41 r.7). It is filed in the appropriate Office stating on whose behalf it is filed (Ord.41 r.9),[54] and a copy served on the other party (Ord.41 r.14(1)). It may be filed with the writ or originating process (Ord.41 r.1(9)). Having filed it, the party obtains an office copy for use in court proceedings (Ord.41 r.10(3)). It carries a court fee of £5 plus £2 per exhibit. A party intending to use an affidavit already filed for a previous proceeding must give notice of intention to use it (Ord.41 r.14(2)), usually by referring to it in a newly filed affidavit. An original affidavit can be used before it is filed (Ord.41 r.10), and a copy must be served on the other parties (Ord.41 r.14(3)). A party may apply for an order that the deponent attend for cross-examination (Ord.38 r.2(3)); this is very rare in interlocutory proceedings, though occasionally done in judicial review and contempt proceedings, and cross-examination is never ordered on an affidavit of discovery, or the affidavit of names of partners in a firm. At a hearing, counsel for the party using the affidavit reads it out or by leave of the court summarises its contents. An affidavit with a formal irregularity can be used with leave (Ord.41 r.4). Defects in the *jurat* should be waived only if there is no reason to suspect the *bona fides* of the application.[55] A defect in the content of an affidavit can be corrected by a supplemental affidavit or by oral evidence. As to the filing of affidavits and use of exhibits in the Chancery Division, see the Practice Directions [1987] 9 BNIL 70,71.

AMENDMENT

Amendment without leave

11.16 The writ may be amended once without leave up to the close of pleading, by having it re-sealed with an indorsement that it has been amended, and served; after the writ has been served on each defendant, an amendment

---

[53] Practice Direction 1997 No 4 (Ch D) [1997] 5 BNIL.

[54] Loose paged affidavits will not be accepted in the Chancery and Bankruptcy & Companies Offices: Practice Note [1985] 8 BNIL 61.

[55] *King* v *King* [1941] Ir Jur R 29(NI). Defects which were not waived include: hearsay statement without naming the source: *McCartan* v *Hulton* (1922) 56 ILTR 152; omission of the deponent's signature and place of swearing: *Best* v *Woods* (1905) 39 ILTR 44.

cannot be made without leave if it adds or removes a party or cause of action, or alters a party's capacity (Ord.20 r.1). A pleading may be amended once without leave at any time up to close of pleading, by re-service as amended, in which case the opponent can amend the responding pleading served by him (Ord.20 r.3). A Statement of Claim indorsed on the writ is amended under rule 3, not rule 1. The amendment can be inserted into the original document, or if there is no room to do so legibly, the document must be redrafted (Ord.20 r.10(1)). The changed or added words are underlined in red, any further amendment in green, then blue etc., and any deleted words should remain legible with a line across them in the same colour. The document is indorsed with the date and order or rule under which it is amended (Ord.20 r.10(2)). Costs of amendment without leave are borne by the amending party unless otherwise ordered (Ord.62 r.6(5)). The opponent can apply to the Court within 14 days of the service of the amended pleading for an order disallowing the amendment: the Court must strike out the amendment if it would not have been permitted under Order 20 rule 5 (Ord.20 r.4).

11.17 If there is a very minor defect in a pleading, such as an omission of a purely formal part, or an obvious mis-spelling, applying for amendment may be a waste of costs: a party may simply leave the pleading as it is, and ask the trial judge to waive the defect under Order 2 rule 1. If an amendment of substance is necessary which is fairly unimportant and needs only a small change in the wording, the party may also save costs by writing an open letter to the other party stating an intention to apply orally for amendment at the trial. The latter can scarcely object to a legitimate amendment of which he has had ample notice. Where a party decides not to prove an allegation of fact which he has pleaded, or to abandon a form of relief (such as an injunction) which he has claimed, he can do so without any amendment of his pleadings; but it may be prudent to give notice of the decision as the opponent may incur costs in preparing to dispute it. If a claimant wishes to abandon a claim, he should do so by notice under Order 21 rather than by amendment.

Any pleading may be amended on written consent of the other party, except for an alteration of parties on a counterclaim (Ord.20 r.12).

Amendment by leave

11.18 A writ, originating summons or motion, petition or pleading may be allowed to be amended by leave at any time (Ord.20 rr.5(1), 6, 7). It will generally be allowed in order to raise or clarify the real issues in the case or to correct a defect or error, provided that it is *bona fide* and there is no injustice to the other party which cannot be compensated in costs.[56] Any document other than a judgment or order may be amended at any stage to correct an error or get to the real question in controversy (Ord.20 r.8). An appearance can be amended by the defendant only by leave (Ord.20 r.2). An amendment may be to cure a purely formal defect, or to make a change of substance, however major. Only pleadings, notices and formal documents can be amended; that is, summonses, notices of motion, particulars, interrogatories.[57] Generally a pleading can be

---

[56] *Beoco* v *Alfa Laval* [1995] QB 137.

[57] White Book (1997) 20/5-8/30.

amended only on the application of the party who drafted it. The opponent cannot force him to alter the case which he chooses to make. The opponent can apply to have it set aside or a passage struck out or amended for scandal, embarrassment etc., and can have it expanded by requiring further particulars. The Court itself should not force a party to amend unless that it the only way to raise the real issue or remove a defect.[58] Where appropriate the Court can state that it will strike out a pleading unless the party agrees to amend it. Documents which constitute evidence, such as the body of an affidavit or the text of an expert report, cannot be amended. If a party wishes to alter the text of these he should get the author of it to draft and serve a supplemental affidavit or report.[59]

11.19 Formal defects can be amended, even the use of the wrong originating procedure.[60] An amendment may introduce a new case, but not a case which is unarguable,[61] and not at a late stage to change the character of the action.[62] Adding an allegation of fraud should be allowed only with caution, and only if grounds are shown.[63] If when the writ was issued the plaintiff had not an accrued cause of action or no title to sue, it cannot be amended to accord with title subsequently acquired.[64] There is one exception to this: an amendment can be made to alter the plaintiff's capacity even though he acquired that capacity after issue of proceedings, provided that the limitation period has expired since the issue of proceedings (Ord.20 r.5(4)).

11.20 Amendment can be done at any time, by interlocutory application, or at the hearing of any application in the action, or at the start or even during the trial. Delay or negligence is no objection to a *bona fide* amendment necessary in the interests of justice unless the opponent is prejudiced in a way not compensateable in costs. If the opponent is surprised by an amendment made at the trial he should be offered an adjournment and awarded costs thrown away.[65] A plaintiff should apply for the specific amendment before his opening speech.[65] He should apply at the conclusion of his case if the need appears during his evidence. An amendment during or at the end of the evidence in the trial should be allowed only if it enables the pleadings to conform to the issues actually contested.[66] Amendment can be made after judgment, as long as something

---

[58] White Book (1997) 20/5-8/3.

[59] The White Book says that answers to interrogatories can be amended, quoting *Hollis* v *Burton* [1892] 3 Ch 226, and *Saunders* v *Jones* (1877) 7 Ch D 437, at 412. The latter is very much *obiter,* and the former is really a case of seeking to withdraw an admission contained in the Defence. It is submitted therefore that answers to interrogatories are evidence, and cannot be amended.

[60] *Osborne* v *Snook* [1953] 1 All ER 332.

[61] *Chan-Sing-Chuk* v *Innovisions Ltd* [1992] LRC (Com) 609 (Hong Kong CA).

[62] *AG* v *McIlwaine* [1939] IR 437, where an amendment to add an alternative claim of a different nature was allowed on appeal only on special terms as to adjournment and costs.

[63] *Re Hafner; Olhausen* v *Powderley* (1940) 74 ILTR 126.

[64] *Tilcon* v *Land Investments* [1987] 1 WLR 46; *Creed* v *Creed* [1913] 1 IR 48.

[65] *Haggan* v *Porter* [1975] 7 NIJB.

[66] *Reilly* v *Valley Dyeworks* [1973] Oct NIJB at 3.

remains to be done in the action,[67] or if the time limit for appeal has not expired or appeal is pending,[68] or where statutory procedure for enforcement against the defendant's insurer is pending.[69] Such amendment, for example to alter the name of a party, may require a consequential amendment of the judgment. The Statement of Claim should not be amended in such a way as may lead to further judgment while the original still stands.[70] Amendment can be made on appeal (see para. 20.41).

11.21 In a surprisingly large number of contested cases, the running of the evidence or the legal argument reveals a need to make significant changes to the pleadings of one or both parties. It is vital that the amendment should be made so that the pleadings reflect the issues in dispute. The House of Lords emphasised this in *Farrell* v *Sec of State*,[71] as did the Court of Appeal in *Livingstone* v *MOD*.[72] But in *Mawhinney* v *NIHE*[73] Hutton J allowed the plaintiff to raise a point not pleaded in rebuttal of the Defence without amendment, the defendant being not surprised. In *Barr* v *SHSSB*,[74] on the twenty-second day of a complex medical negligence case, the cross-examination of a defence witness raised an unpleaded allegation. The judge invited the plaintiff to apply to amend and granted it on condition that each party could call additional evidence on the point.

11.22 The Court may amend itself or may give leave to amend. If the latter the party must execute the amendment within 14 days or as specified by the Court; otherwise the leave to amend lapses (Ord.20 r.9). An application for and an order of amendment should specify the exact change in wording. However the Court may give leave to amend in a specific way, or for a specific purpose, or generally,[75] in which case the party has the option of proceeding without amending.[76] "Leave to amend generally" entitles the party to vary his mode of proceeding;[77] but not in a way which the Court would have specifically refused.[78] The amendment can be inserted into the original document, or if there is no room to do so legibly, the document must be redrafted (Ord.20 r.10(1)). The changed or added words are underlined in red, any further amendment in green, then blue etc., and any deleted words should remain legible with a line across them in the same colour. The document is indorsed with the date and order or rule under which amended (Ord.20 r.10(2)). An amendment is retrospective: the pleading is to be read as if it always stood in its new form.[79]

---

67 *Duke of Buccleuch* [1892] P 201, at 211-2, especially *per* Fry LJ.
68 *Millen* v *Brown* [1984] NI 328, at 335E, 338F.
69 *Ibid.* at 335D; but see *Hughes* v *O'Rourke* [1986] ILRM 538.
70 *Cox* v *Electricity Board (No 2)* [1943] IR 231.
71 [1980]1 WLR 172.
72 [1984] NI 356.
73 [1982] NI 303.
74 [1986] 10 NIJB 1, at 95-7.
75 *Evans* v *Figgis* (1849) 11 Ir LR 587.
76 *Black* v *Sangster* (1834) 1 CM & R 521 (149 ER 1186).
77 *Watson* v *Cooper* (1851) 3 Ir Jur OS 156.
78 *Busch* v *Stevens* [1963] 1 QB 1.
79 *Warner* v *Sampson* [1959] 1 QB 297, at 321.

That rule of retrospection does not necessarily hold good where the amendment adds or deletes a party, nor where it affects a lodgment under Order 22. Where an amendment adds a new party, the writ must be amended accordingly (Ord.15 r.8(1)). If an amendment is to add a cause of action, both the Statement of Claim and the writ must be amended.[80]

11.23 Usually amendment is allowed only on condition that the applicant shall pay the costs of the application and other costs properly incurred by the opponent.[81] Such condition may not be imposed where the opponent refused a fair offer of costs in return for his consent;[82] or the error to be amended has not misled or prejudiced him;[83] or the amendment is necessitated by his own amendment.

AMENDMENT AS TO PARTIES

11.24 Apart from the methods of bringing in a new party,[84] an addition, substitution or deletion of a party can be effected by amendment. No proceedings are defeated by misjoinder or non-joinder of a party and the Court may determine the issues affecting the parties before it; but the Court may at any stage, even after final judgment, strike out any person who is not a proper or necessary party, or add a person who ought to be a party or whose presence is necessary for determination of all matters in dispute, *or between whom and any party there is an issue arising out of or connected with the relief claimed*[85] (Ord.15 r.6). A non-party can be added as plaintiff or defendant or an existing party can be joined in a new capacity.[86] Instead of ordering an amendment as to parties the Court can choose to proceed on the existing issues and parties, especially if the non-party can be brought in by other procedure such as third-party notice. An objection to misjoinder should be made as soon as possible and is too late after judgment. Otherwise an amendment as to parties can be made at any time: before or at the trial; after judgment;[87] until execution or pending appeal;[88] by the appellate court;[89] or after dismissal of an action.[90] An amendment pursuant to an order under Order 15 rule 6 must be made within 14 days or such other period as is specified, by amending the writ and endorsing the order and the date of amendment (Ord.15 r.8(1)).

---

80 *Moore* v *Alwill* (1882) 8 LR Ir 245.

81 In *Beoco* v *Alfa Laval* [1995] QB 137, a plaintiff given leave to make a major amendment of his case during the trial was ordered to pay all defence costs to date.

82 *Smith* v *Delacherois* (1865) 10 Ir Jur NS 357.

83 *Bush* v *Curran* (1858) 9 ICLR App 28 (clerical error of which opponent was aware but kept quiet).

84 E.g. counterclaim against plaintiff and another; third-party notice.

85 In reading the authorities it should be noted that the words in italics were added in England in 1971 and in Northern Ireland in 1980.

86 E.g. the plaintiff applying to have third party made a defendant.

87 *Duke of Buccleuch* [1892] P 201.

88 *Millen* v *Brown* [1984] NI 328.

89 *Guardians of Belfast Union* v *Belfast Corp* (1909) 43 ILTR 247.

90 *Bacal* v *Modern Engineering* [1980] 2 All ER 655, at 662d.

11.25 *Plaintiffs.* If there is doubt about the plaintiff's title to sue either alone or at all, a new plaintiff can be added. However, where the action is commenced in the name of a non-existent plaintiff, it cannot be cured by adding a valid plaintiff.[91] A person added as plaintiff must consent in writing (Ord.15 r.6(4)), unless he is in the position of a trustee.[92] The consent of the existing plaintiff is not essential. The defendant can insist that a person jointly entitled on the plaintiff's claim be added as plaintiff, or failing his consent as co-defendant (Ord.15 r.4(2)). In a fatal accident claim by the personal representative, the Court refused to add a dependant as plaintiff.[93] A plaintiff can be struck out if non-existent, incompetent to sue or not having authorised the action. If co-plaintiffs disagree or one withdraws or compromises, he should be struck out and added as defendant.[94]

11.26 *Defendants.* An application by the plaintiff to add or substitute a defendant will usually be given subject to paying costs thrown away. It may be refused if it will change the character of the action,[95] unless the new defendant is alleged to be liable in the alternative.[96] A defendant can be added on defence application, for example as co-claimant on a counterclaim, even if the plaintiff objects and seeks no relief against him;[97] but not if the addition would force the plaintiff to make a different and inconsistent case.[98] Where necessary for the determination of the issues, a defendant can be added though there is no cause of action against him.[99] The Commissioners of Inland Revenue cannot be made a party without their consent unless their presence is necessary (Ord.77 r.7). Under the Civil Liability (Contribution) Act 1978 the defendant has no right to have added as co-defendant a person jointly and/or severally liable. A new defendant does not become a party until the writ is served on him (Ord.15 r.8(4)), and *semble*, the amended writ should be served on the existing defendant in the same way as any non-originating process.[100] A defendant can have himself struck out, with costs, if he is improperly joined or if he is irrelevant to the issues raised or relief claimed.[101] As to when a defendant should be added after the expiry of the limitation period, see para. 11.34. If an application is made for the taking of a blood or DNA sample from a person, the Court may direct that person to be added as a party (Ord.112 r.4).

---

91 *O'Rafferty* v *Rickard* (1920) 54 ILTR 195 (action in firm name by a sole trader). Surely in that case the use of the firm name could have been regarded as a mere misnomer.

92 *Montgomery* v *Montgomery* (1856) 6 ICLR 522.

93 *Steele* v *GNR* (1890) 26 LR Ir 96.

94 *Re Mathews* [1905] 2 Ch 460.

95 *Raleigh* v *Goschen* [1898] 1 Ch 73, at 81.

96 *Crawford* v *Donnelly* (1889) 23 LR Ir 511.

97 Subject to the applicant paying the plaintiff's costs of the application in any event: *Haulage Services* v *Larne Harbour* [1987] 5 NIJB 1 (where a defendant against whom the plaintiff had discontinued was added again on application of co-defendant).

98 *Kelly* v *Rafferty* [1948] NI 187.

99 *TSB* v *Chabra* [1992] 1 WLR 231.

100 Cf. *Jamaican Rly* v *Colonial Bank* [1905] 1 Ch 677.

101 *Fuller* v *Dublin CC* [1976] IR 20.

11.27 *Intervener.* A non-party may intervene to apply to be joined as a party. A person applying to be added as a party should show his interest by affidavit (Ord.15 r.6(3)). In an action for recovery of land, a person in possession may apply to be added as defendant (Ord.15 r.10), but a person with an interest not in possession has no right to be added.[102] In *Carey* v *Ryan*[103] the insurer of the defendant was allowed to intervene in order to apply for withdrawal of money paid into court. A person with only a commercial interest in the dispute cannot intervene.[104] The following persons have a right to intervene: (a) a member of a class who objects to representation by the plaintiff; (b) a person whose property or financial rights are directly affected by the action or against whose property judgment may be enforced (e.g. the MIB or an insurer liable by statute to satisfy the judgment),[105] (c) a motor vehicle insurer upon whom notice of the action has been served;[106] and (d) the Attorney-General in litigation affecting the Crown, or revenue or public policy.

11.28 *Substitution.* Where a party's name has changed or been misdescribed, amendment can be made under Order 20, because the identity of the party has not changed,[107] so also an amendment as to capacity.[108] Thus where the correct party is joined but there is an error in naming the party, the title of the proceedings can be amended under Order 20 rule 5, and this does not constitute a change of parties. If the wrong person has been joined, whether or not the error is as to nominal or real identity, amendment must be by way of substitution under Order 15 rule 6; but the real or nominal nature of the change of identity has a bearing if limitation problems arise (see para. 11.34). If the Attorney-General or a Government department is sued, he/it may apply by summons for substitution of him or another Department as defendant (Crown Proceedings Act, s.17(4); Ord.77 r.17(1)).

11.29 A person added or substituted does not become a party until the writ is amended and, if a defendant, served on him (Ord.15 r.8(4)). A person added as defendant must be served with the amended writ and all pleadings and he must enter an appearance (Ord.15 r.8(2)(2A)(3)).

TIME PROBLEMS ON AMENDMENTS

11.30 A plaintiff cannot raise a cause of action arising since the issue of the writ;[109] subject to Order 20 rule 5(4) (para. 11.34).

11.31 An amendment to an already pleaded cause of action between existing parties can be made even though the limitation period has expired since the

---

[102] *Davin* v *MacCormack* [1932] IR 681.
[103] [1982] IR 179.
[104] *Re IG Farbenindustrie* [1944] Ch 41.
[105] *Millen* v *Brown* [1984] NI 328, at 331H-333B.
[106] Road Traffic (NI) Order 1981, Art.98A(4).
[107] *Ferryhaugh* v *Farrell* (1875) IR 9 CL 422.
[108] *Bermingham* v *Colleran* (1892) 26 ILT 698.
[109] *Eshelby* v *Federated Bank* [1932] 1 KB 254, 423.

issue of the writ and relates back to the commencement of the action.[110] An amendment altering the date on which the cause of action allegedly occurred is not to make a new cause of action.[111] If the writ fails to reveal a cause of action, the plaintiff will have to have it amended, which will be granted even if the limitation period has expired unless the defendant is surprised.[112] An amendment which merely changes the name of a party without in any way changing the identity of that party can be made regardless of the limitation period.[113]

11.32 If an amendment is effected in a pending action which adds or substitutes a new cause of action, it is treated as a separate action and is deemed to have commenced back on the date when the pending action commenced: see Article 73 of the Limitation (NI) Order 1989 (the 'relation back' principle).[114] An amendment which joins a non-party as defendant to a claim already made in the action by the amending party is saved by Article 73 'relation back'. Otherwise an amendment which makes a new claim by a party against a non-party is called "third-party proceedings" and is not saved by 'relation back'; there is no restriction on the Court's power to allow such amendment (Art 73(2)), but the added party can plead the limitation period if it expired before he was added.

11.33 If an amendment seeks to make a new claim which will by saved by 'relation back', then the power to allow the amendment is prohibited by Article 73(2) of the Limitation (NI) Order 1989, save in the circumstances set out in Article 73, Order 15 rule 6(5) and Order 20 rule 5(2). Under Article 73(2) the new claim is deemed to be made when the amendment is effected pursuant to the leave of the court, not on the date when the summons for leave was issued.[115] The Court is of course only bound by the restrictions in Article 73(2) if the limitation period has expired after the date of the issue of the writ and before the date when the application to amend is made. Thus in *Butler* v *DOE*,[116] a personal injuries action in which the plaintiff's knowledge of his cause of action was less than three years ago, the limitation period was unexpired under Article 7, and Article 73 was irrelevant. Therefore the Court before deciding about leave to amend can try as a preliminary issue the date of knowledge.[117] Equally it is irrelevant if the limitation period on the new claim had already expired when the action commenced: amendment can be allowed but will be futile if the limitation period is pleaded against it.

---

110 This proposition is implicit from the common law authorities, *Ketteman* v *Hansel Properties* [1987] AC 189; *Liff* v *Peasley* [1980] 1 WLR 781; *Pontin* v *Wood* [1962] 1 QB 594.; and is left undisturbed by Art.73 of the Limitation (NI) Order 1989.

111 *Hay* v *London Brick* (1981) [1989] 2 Lloyds Rep 7.

112 *Sterman* v *E & W Moore* [1970] 1 QB 596.

113 *Davies* v *Elsby* [1961] 1 WLR 170.

114 The common law position still applies to any action which was commenced before 1 December 1982: Limitation (NI) Order 1989, Sch.2 para. 7.

115 *Welsh Development Agency* v *Redpath Dorman Long* [1994] 1 WLR 1409, at 1421 (CA).

116 [1992] 7 NIJB 12.

117 *Busby* v *Cooper*, 'The Times', 15 April 1996 (CA), a decision under the similar provision for extension of time in non-personal injury negligence.

11.34 A 'relation back'-type new claim can be allowed only in the following circumstances-

(1) A claim by way of set-off or counterclaim by a party who has made no claim previously in the action is allowed (Art 73(2)).
(2) A new claim for damages for personal injuries, or under the Fatal Accidents Order, or for damages arising from defective goods under the Consumer Protection Order may be allowed if it appears equitable to disapply the limitation period under Article 50 of the Limitation (NI) Order 1989 (see Art.73(2) and Ord.16 r.6(5)(b)).
(3) An amendment adding or substituting a new cause of action may be allowed if just to do so[118] and if it arises out of (substantially) the same facts as are at issue on a claim already made in the action (Art.73(4)(a); Ord.20 r.5(5)). A claim for malicious prosecution was added in an action for false imprisonment because the facts supporting it were already pleaded, in *Metcalfe* v *Chief Constable*.[119] On the same basis slander was added in an action for libel in *Eastwood* v *Channel 5*.[120] This can be done where the facts as originally pleaded do not disclose a cause of action.[121]
(4) A person can be added or substituted as a party if the period was unexpired when proceedings commenced and his addition is necessary to the maintenance by or against an existing party of a claim already made in the action (Art.73(5)(b)). It is necessary if and only if (a) the plaintiff's claim for an equitable interest in property may be defeated if a person in whom it is vested is not added; (b) the person is entitled with the plaintiff jointly only; (c) the action is a 'relator' in which the Attorney-General should be the plaintiff; (d) the plaintiff is a shareholder enforcing a right of the company to be added; or (e) the person is liable with the defendant jointly only and the claim might be unenforceable (Ord.15 r.6(6)). This rule does not apply where the plaintiff was dead, defunct or non-existent as a legal person when the writ was issued.[122]
(5) A person can be substituted if just to do so[118] and it arises from a genuine mistake[123] in naming the party which was not misleading as to substantive identity (Art.73(5)(a); Ord.20 r.5(3)). This applies where the mistake arises by naming the wrong party, not where it arises from thinking that the wrong person should be the party.[124]

---

118 The claimant bears the burden of persuasion that it is just to do so: *Hancock Shipping* v *Kawasaki* [1992] 1 WLR 1025, at 1030C.

119 [1991] NI 237.

120 [1992] NI 183.

121 *Sim* v *Hampstead HA*, 'The Times', 10 June 1994 (CA).

122 *International Bulk Shipping* v *Minerals Trading Corp* [1996] 1 All ER 1017 (CA).

123 Including a blameworthy mistake: *Mitchell* v *Harris* [1967] 2 QB 703.

124 *Evans Constructions* v *Charrington* [1983] QB 810; *Bridge Shipping* v *Grand Shipping* [1992] LRC (Com) 730; 173 CLR 231 (HC of Aus); *Murray* v *Hibernian Dance Club*, 'The Times', 12 August 1996 (CA) (substituting named members for name of members' club).

(6) An amendment to alter the capacity in which a claimant sues can be allowed if just to do so[118] and even if he acquired that capacity after the proceedings commenced (Art.73(6); Ord.20 r.5(4)).

11.35 The same principles apply to a new claim made in third-party proceedings as in an original action (Art.73(7)). If the Court has wrongly allowed a new claim which should have been disallowed under Article 73, then so long as the order stands, the limitation defence cannot be pleaded against the new claim.[125]

CHANGE OF PARTIES: ORDER TO CARRY ON

11.36 Death or bankruptcy does not abate an action if the cause of action survives; if the interest or liability of a party is transmitted, assigned or devolved to another, the Court may order his substitution, on an *ex parte* application;[126] the applicant must ensure that the order is noted in the cause book and serve the order on every party and, if the substituted party is a defendant the writ and pleadings: the party[127] may apply to discharge the order within 14 days (Ord.15 r.7). The substituted party does not become a party until this is done; if the party is a defendant he must enter an appearance (Ord.15 r.8(3)(4)). The rule does not apply to a mere change of name or status (e.g. woman marrying, minor reaching adulthood). If a plaintiff is added his consent in writing must be produced. If the substituted party is already a party in the proceedings on the other side of the record, the order is deemed to include a provision that he cease to be a party on that side of the record (Ord.15 r.7(3)). Expiry of the limitation period since the action commenced is of no relevance and there is no restriction on substituting a person on whom the interest devolves.[128]

11.37 The original writ and proceedings already had in the action are not amended, but all subsequent proceedings are titled: "Between [the original parties] and between [the new parties] by the original writ and by an order

---

125 *Eastwood* v *Channel 5* [1992] NI 183, at 186e. *In Hickey* v *DOE* [1992] 1 NIJB 54, a defendant having been added by order of a master, the judge subsequently granted an application by him to be struck out, though no order was made expressly setting aside the master's order. In *Kennett* v *Brown* [1988] 1 WLR 582 the new claim was made not by order of amendment but by third-party notice against a co-defendant, and it was suggested that the limitation period can still be pleaded in the Defence against the new claim; but this case was overruled by a three-judge Court of Appeal in *Welsh Development Agency* v *Redpath Dorman Long* [1994] 1 WLR 1409. It held that a new claim by a plaintiff must be disallowed and a defendant's notice against a co-defendant must be struck out if it is not proper, because the 'relation back' doctrine will prevent the co-defendant from pleading a limitation defence. The authority of *Hickey* must also be treated as doubtful. (It should be noted that a defendant's notice for contribution or indemnity should cause no limitation problems anyway, as the cause of action does not accrue until liability to the plaintiff is established.)

126 Or on notice in a difficult case: *Howard* v *Howard* (1892) 30 LR Ir 340.

127 Or if under disability his next friend/guardian *ad litem*: Ord.80 r.5.

128 *Yorkshire RHA* v *Fairclough Builders* [1996] 1 WLR 210 (CA).

under Order 15 rule 7 dated the .. day of .. 19...." The new party steps into the shoes of the old; he is liable or entitled to the whole costs of the action.[129]

11.38 If, after an action has been set down for trial, an abatement, transmission etc. takes place, the plaintiff's solicitor must so certify to the listing office; an abated action will be struck out after a year (Ord.34 r.8). An order under Order 15 rule 7 can be made after judgment.[130] Where there has been a change of parties since an order or decree, any person claiming payment of money in court standing to the credit of the action must give notice to the Accountant-General stating his interest, verified by affidavit.[131]

Death

11.39 The rule at common law was: *actio personalis moritur cum persona.*[132] Now under section 14 of the Law Reform (Miscellaneous Provisions) Act (NI) 1937, all causes of action by or against a person survive on death to or against his estate (even if damage arose at or after the death), except actions for defamation. [133] Damages recoverable for the estate do not include exemplary damages or damages for loss of earnings after death, and are assessed without reference to any loss (except funeral expenses) or any gain caused by the death (s.14(2)). A dependant's right to damages for bereavement dies with him (s.14(1A)).

11.40 Order 15 rule 7 does not apply to a death before the action commenced, before issue of the writ. No abatement occurs if the death is after verdict and before judgment (Ord.35 r.6), even in defamation. And no abatement occurs of rights under an interim judgment.[134] An order can be made under Order 15 rule 7 at any time, even after judgment. As to death pending appeal see para. 20.38. No abatement can occur if a party remains in whom the right or liability continues. So where one of two plaintiffs jointly entitled dies, the action continues and no order under Order 15 rule 7 is necessary.[135] *Semble*, if a trustee dies his replacement should always be added as a party.

---

[129] *Pembroke* v *Warren* [1896] 1 IR 76, at 142.

[130] *Collings* v *Wade* [1903] 1 IR 89 (to enforce judgment); *Leahy* v *Tobin* (1887) 19 LR Ir 433 (to appeal).

[131] Court Funds Rules (NI) 1979, r.42.

[132] An action or application based on a statutory right is not an *actio personalis* and does not abate on death: *Benson* v *Sec of State* [1976] NI 36 (expressly overruled by statute in relation to criminal injury compensation: see Greer *Compensation for Criminal Injury* (SLS 1990) pp.201-2); and Ord.15 r.7 is applied to all such proceedings: *Smith* v *Williams* [1922] 1 KB 158. A divorce petition abates on death, but not all ancillary proceedings: *Purse* v *Purse* [1981] Fam 143. A claim under the Inheritance (Provision for Family and Dependants) (NI) Order 1979 abates on death of the claimant: *Whytte* v *Ticehurst* [1986] Fam 64; but not the right to payment under an interim order made before death: *In re O'Reilly* [1995] 6 BNIL 97.

[133] No abatement of proceedings by or against the Crown occurs by reason of the demise of the Crown: Crown Proceedings Act, s.32.

[134] *In re O'Reilly* [1995] 6 BNIL 97.

[135] *Baird* v *Thompson* (1884) 14 LR Ir 497.

11.41 If the plaintiff dies his personal representative applies if he has a grant valid in Northern Ireland. In *Hughes* v *West*,[136] the plaintiff died just before the trial, and his executor was given an order to carry on upon undertaking to take out and produce a grant of probate. The personal representative should apply before any further step in the action is taken, but failure to do so is a mere irregularity.[137] If the defendant dies, the personal representative or the plaintiff or co-defendant can apply. In *Munster & Leinster Bank* v *Mackey*,[138] a non-party (prior incumbrancer in a mortgagee's action) had himself added as plaintiff under Order 15 rule 6. If there is no personal representative of the defendant, a nominee of the applicant can be appointed.[139] In *Hibernian Stock* v *Fottrell*,[140] the Court ordered the action to continue in the absence of a personal representative; but the White Book (1997) 15/7/9 says that a personal representative must be added. A limited administrator can be appointed by the Probate Court.[141] Where on the death of a party no order has been made under Order 15 rule 7, the defendant or his personal representative, as the case may be, may apply for the action to be struck out unless it is proceeded with in a specified time (Ord.15 r.9)[142] or may apply under Order 15 rule 7.

Other events

11.42 *Bankruptcy.* If the plaintiff becomes bankrupt his cause of action vests in the trustee in bankruptcy, except claims relating to personal injury or character.[143] Upon appointment of the trustee the bankrupt's property is automatically vested in him, under the Insolvency (NI) Order 1989 (Art.279). Where the claim vests in the trustee he should apply to be made plaintiff under Order 15 rule 7 and if he fails to do so the defendant may apply to stay the action. Once a defendant has had bankruptcy proceedings commenced against him, the court hearing the action or the bankruptcy court may stay the action (Art.258), and will usually do so if the action is in respect of a provable debt (which includes tort damages claims). If not stayed the plaintiff or the trustee should apply under Order 15 rule 7 for the latter to be made defendant. Once an interim order of voluntary arrangement has been applied for, the Court can stay an action against the debtor (Art.228).[144]

11.43 *Corporate Bodies etc.* In Crown proceedings no abatement occurs by reason of the change of Attorney-General or of persons in a UK Department.[145]

---

136 (1884) 13 LR Ir 224.

137 *Fielding* v *Rigby* [1993] 1 WLR 1355 (writ served after death of plaintiff).

138 [1917] 1 IR 49.

139 *Re Simpson* [1936] P 40.

140 (1884) 13 LR Ir 335 (where one of several trustees sued for breach of trust died).

141 *Smyth* v *Byrne* (1913) 47 ILTR 279.

142 It was held in *Nolan* v *Marquis of Drogheda* (1892) 31 LR Ir 84, that the ancestor of Ord.15 r.9 did not apply to death pending appeal, so that when the defendant/respondent died after notice of appeal, his personal representative should apply under Ord.15 r.7 to be substituted as a party and have the appeal listed for hearing.

143 *Wilson* v *United Counties Bank* [1920] AC 102.

144 See Hunter on *Personal Insolvency*, paras. 28.13-28.25; Chap.19 (provable debt) and Chap.26 (arrangement); and *In re Humphries* [1989] 12 NIJB 1.

145 Crown Proceedings Act, s.17(5).

A change of name of a company does not make proceedings defective.[146] Winding-up proceedings against a company do not require a change in the title of an action by or against the company, as the liquidator acts in the name of the company; proceedings against the company may be stayed under the Insolvency (NI) Order 1989 (Art.106). When a winding-up order is made or a provisional liquidator appointed, no proceedings against the company or its property may be commenced or continued without leave of the High Court (Art.110). If the liquidator proceeds on a claim by the company the defendant can apply for security for costs (see para. 11.60). Once a company has been dissolved any action by or against it is dead, even if the companies court declares the dissolution void under Article 602 of the Companies (NI) Order 1986.[147]

11.44 *Assignment.* In cases of assignment, transmission or devolution, Order 15 rule 7 applies only where the interest of the party is passed to another.[148] Where a life tenant dies or a lease expires, the reversioner should apply under Order 15 rule 6.[149] So also in actions for recovery of land because the issue therein is possession, not interest.[149]

SUMMARY JUDGMENT

11.45 Where the plaintiff believes that there is no defence to his claim or any of his claims or part of a claim he may apply for summary judgment under Order 14 rule 1(1). It is usually invoked in debt cases, but it extends to all actions begun by writ, excluding claims based on fraud, defamation, malicious prosecution or false imprisonment, Family Division actions and Admiralty actions *in rem* (Ord.14 r.1(2)).[150] For Chancery actions relating to sale or lease of land, the summary judgment procedure is in Order 86 (see para. 18.67). A form of summary judgment for limited relief will be available in defamation (see para. 18.22a). Summary judgment for ejectment against squatters is provided by Order 113 (see para. 18.50). Summary judgment cannot be obtained against the Crown (Ord.77 r.5(1)).[151] Application can be made for summary judgment for an injunction, which must be heard by a judge in chambers.[152] A defendant may apply for an Order 14 judgment on his counterclaim after having served his counterclaim, and the rules apply *mutatis mutandis* (Ord.14 r.5).

Application for summary judgment

11.46 Summary judgment can be applied for at any time after the defendant has entered an appearance and the plaintiff has served his Statement of Claim (Ord.14 r.1(1)). Application can be made after close of pleadings,[153] even after

---

146 Companies (NI) Order 1986, Art.38(7).

147 White Book (1997) 15/7/14.

148 As in *Norglen* v *Reed Rains* [1996] 1 All ER 945 (CA).

149 *Ferrall* v *Curran* [1899] 2 IR 470; *Howard* v *Howard* (1892) 30 LR Ir 340.

150 Fraud is not excluded in England.

151 Made under the Crown Proceedings Act, s.35(2(d).

152 *Shell-Mex* v *Manchester Garages* [1971] 1 All ER 841, at 843a.

153 *Tottenham* v *Foley* [1909] 2 IR 500.

setting down for trial,[154] though the plaintiff may be penalised in costs for his delay. It is by summons to be heard by the master ten clear days after service, supported by affidavit of facts which prove the claim, which may include hearsay, and declaring a belief that there is no defence (Ord.14 r.2). In an ejectment for non-payment of rent, it must depose whether the land is agricultural or pastoral. It may be sufficient to refer to and verify the Statement of Claim,[155] which must itself show all the material facts of the cause of action. Correspondence which shows that the defendant has admitted the claim or failed to dispute it may be exhibited. In relation to the claim for which judgment is sought, the whole cause of action and the absence of defence thereto must be verified.[156] It may be enough to state that the deponent is "advised and believes" that there is no defence.[157] Failure to depose to all the necessary facts is not fatal, provided the omissions are cured by supplemental affidavit.[158] If the Crown is applying, the affidavit must be by its solicitor or an authorised officer, and it need only state a belief that the applicant is entitled to relief and there is no defence (Ord.77 r.5(2)).

11.47 The plaintiff may seek judgment in respect of part only of a claim (Ord.14 r.1(1)), or against one only of several defendants, and he may reserve the right to proceed with the rest of the claim, and against the other defendants (Ord.14 r.8), unless they are liable in the alternative (see para. 3.33).

11.48 If the defendant does not appear at the hearing, the plaintiff may argue for judgment, on proof of service of the Order 14 summons. The defendant may serve an affidavit disclosing his defence on the merits at least three clear days before the return day, and if not he should bear the costs of an adjournment.[159] He must not only depose to the existence of a defence or triable issue, but also what it is, particularising his response to the allegations of the plaintiff and his points of defence. The plaintiff may then serve a replying affidavit. The defendant may resist the summons either by showing that summary judgment is not proper, or that the application or evidence grounding it is irregular or deficient. He may show by affidavit (which may include hearsay) or otherwise "that there is an issue or question ... to be tried, or that there ought for some other reason to be a trial ..." (Ord.14 rr.3(1),4). The Court may require him to produce a document or be examined on oath (Ord.14 r.4(4)).

11.49 The defendant need only raise a reasonable doubt about the plaintiff's entitlement to judgment; assuming all facts in his favour (Wylie p.264), or that serious questions of fact or law are involved.[160] Obviously an Order 14 hearing

---

[154] *Sunday Newspapers* v *Deighan* [1989] 3 NIJB 51, at 58.

[155] White Book (1997) 14/2/5.

[156] *Lord Bellew* v *Markey* (1878) 2 LR Ir 185, affd. (1879) 4 LR Ir 747.

[157] *Manning* v *Moriarty* (1883) 12 LR Ir 372.

[158] *Masterson* v *Scallan* [1927] IR 453; *Barclays Bank* v *Piper*, 'The Times', 31 May 1995 (CA); *contra*: *Imperial Tobacco* v *McAllister* (No 1) (1916) 50 ILTR 156, where the motion on the defective affidavit had been dismissed.

[159] Practice Direction [1984] 1 BNIL 99. As to applications in the Chancery Division, see the Practice Direction [1989] 3 BNIL 82.

[160] *Goodchild* v *Duncan* [1895] 2 IR 393.

is rarely an appropriate forum for resolving issues of fact, but if the result of the action depends on an issue of pure law, even if complex or highly debatable, it should be fully investigated and determined under Order 14.[161] In *National Westminster* v *Daniel*[162] the Court of Appeal has laid down the test for unconditional leave to defend: is the evidence to which the defendant deposes credible and on the facts raised thereby, is there a fair or reasonable probability of him having a real or *bona fide* defence? Lodgment of the sum claimed in court does not give a right to leave to defend.[163] Inability to pay is no ground.[164] A Defence already served can be taken into account, but may not be enough on its own without the defence or triable issue being deposed to. In a damages claim if the defendant shows a triable issue as to quantum, judgment can be given for damages to be assessed but judgment cannot be given for any specific sum, except possibly on a distinct and quantifiable element of damage for which liability is indisputable.[165] An application for interim damages is more appropriate.

Order

11.50 The orders which the Court may make include-

(1) dismiss the summons with costs if the claim is not within Order 14 or if it appears that the plaintiff knew of the defendant's contention which warranted unconditional leave to defend (Ord.14 r.7).

(2) grant unconditional leave to defend if the defendant shows an issue or question to be tried, that is, a good defence or a set-off, or counterclaim which is connected to the subject of the claim.

(3) grant unconditional leave if there ought for some other reason to be a trial, as where the defendant shows some prospect that he may be able to raise a defence, or the plaintiff's case should be put to the proof, or the case is sufficiently complex or important to warrant a full trial.

(4) grant judgment on the claim but with a stay of enforcement pending trial of a counterclaim (Ord.14 r.3(2)). No stay will be given if the counterclaim is wholly separate or foreign to the claim, or if the plaintiff is suing on a dishonoured cheque or direct debit (see para.9.43).

(5) if the defence appears to be shadowy, improbable or incredible, grant leave to defend conditional upon terms as to security (e.g. the defendant paying money into court of an amount not too far beyond his means) with costs in the cause; or conditional upon payment of interim damages; or on terms as to time or mode of trial. A defendant who pays into court may by notice to the plaintiff appropriate it as (part of) a lodgment in satisfaction of the claim under Order 22 or as money paid in under a plea of tender

---

161 *Re Savage* [1991] NI 103, at 107.

162 [1993] 1 WLR 1453; applied in *First National Commercial Bank v Anglin* [1996] 1 IR 75 (SC).

163 *Law* v *Bayley* (1905) 5 NIJR 297.

164 *Desart* v *Townsend* (1888) 22 LR Ir 389.

165 *Associated Bulk Carriers* v *Koch Shipping* [1978] 2 All ER 254.

(Ord.22 r.8). He does so by notice in Form 2 of the Court Funds Rules 1979 (r.28 thereof).[166]

(6) grant judgment on the summons with costs. If there is a claim for damages which cannot be simply assessed, judgment will be for damages to be assessed under Order 37.[167] If the claim is for the return of goods the Court may order specific restitution in the same way as a trial court (Ord.14 r.9). If judgment is given for recovery of land for forfeiture for non-payment of rent, the tenant may apply for relief against forfeiture (Ord.14 r.10). If the plaintiff obtains judgment on one claim or part of a claim he may proceed with the rest of his claim or other claims against any defendant (Ord.14 r.8).

(7) if leave to defend is given for a defence, set-off or counterclaim which answers only part of the plaintiff's claim, give judgment for the balance of the latter over the former. If the amount remaining in dispute is within the county court jurisdiction, it is arguable that the Court can remit the action.

(8) in an ejectment by a superior landlord for non-payment of rent in agricultural land, certify that the non-payment is due to the default of a tenant (Ord.14 r.3(3)).

(9) in an action against a personal representative who shows a defence of *plene administravit*, give costs to the defendant and judgment to the plaintiff with costs against assets *quando acciderint*.[168]

11.51 *Costs.* If judgment is given either absolutely or in default of payment into court, it will carry costs. If the summons is dismissed, then costs are awarded to the defendant and may be ordered to be paid forthwith unless the plaintiff is legally aided (Ord.14 r.7).[169] Otherwise the normal order will be for costs in the cause. Unless the Court otherwise orders, summary judgment *for a debt* carries scale costs under Order 62 Appendix 3 Part I column (c), if at least £600 is awarded; for recovery of land scale costs under Order 62 Appendix 3 Part II; and the plaintiff will recover full High Court costs under Order 62 Appendix 3, even if the judgment is within the county court limit (Ord.62 r.17(3)). In a large or complex case, the Court may disapply rule 17(3) and order the plaintiff's costs to be taxed. If either party is legally aided, the judgment must direct his costs to be taxed under Schedule 2 to the Legal Aid Order (para. 17.21)

11.52 If leave to defend is given, or judgment stayed pending trial of a counterclaim, the Court must give directions as to the further conduct of the action (Ord.14 r.6(1)), as to the time limit for delivery of pleadings, or that the affidavit do stand as a pleading, discovery or an early trial. With consent of the

---

166 The Court Funds Rules 1979, r.28(2), says: "On receipt of notice of appropriation, payment shall be made by the Accountant-General to the plaintiff in satisfaction of his claim ...."; but presumably it must be a pre-requisite to payment out that it is authorised by acceptance by the plaintiff under the RSC, or by an order of court.

167 But see *Associated Bulk Carriers, supra*.

168 *Cockle* v *Treacy* [1896] 2 IR 267; White Book (1997) 14/3-4/19.

169 This rule is stated to be without prejudice to Ord.62 r.4(1). This must be taken as a reference to r.8(1)(2)(3) of the new Order 62 substituted in 1988.

parties the Court may direct trial by a master (Ord.14 r.6(2)). Unless otherwise directed, the defendant has 21 days to deliver his Defence (Ord.18 r.2(2)).

Finality of order

11.53 Any *judgment* against an absent party may be set aside or varied (Ord.14 r.11). Otherwise, once an application under Order 14 has been dealt with, a new application in the same action cannot be heard, unless it was dismissed for procedural reasons.[170]

11.54 Either party may appeal to a judge in chambers within five days (Ord.58 r.1). The appeal is a complete rehearing and further evidence may be allowed in his discretion. If the judge does not give unconditional leave to defend, the defendant may appeal as of right to the Court of Appeal, because it is deemed to be not interlocutory (Judicature Act, s.35(3)). If he gives unconditional leave, no party can appeal to the Court of Appeal (s.35(2)(c)).[171] If the judge gives conditional leave to defend either party may appeal as of right.[172] If the judge dismisses the Order 14 application, the plaintiff may appeal with leave of the judge or Court of Appeal (it being an interlocutory) but leave to appeal is not necessary if the judge dismissed on ground of no jurisdiction.[173] The Court of Appeal will freely review the judge's refusal of leave to defend, but will less readily review the granting of conditional leave. It decides on the facts now existing.[174] As it constitutes a hearing on the merits, on an appeal against the *granting* of summary judgment new evidence is admissible only on special grounds.[175]

INTERIM PAYMENTS

11.55 The plaintiff or counterclaiming defendant in any proceedings may apply for an interim payment of damages, debt or other sum which he may recover (Ord.29 rr.11-17).[176] He can do so at any time after the time for appearance by ten-day summons, on affidavit verifying special damages and medical reports etc. In an action for damages an interim award may be made, if (a) the defendant admits liability; (b) judgment for damages to be assessed has been given; or (c) the Court is satisfied that the plaintiff would get judgment for substantial damages. The award must not exceed a reasonable proportion of the net damages which are likely to be recovered in the action. The award is not confined to the actual loss suffered to date.[177] The burden of

---

170 White Book (1997) 14/1/6; *contra: Imperial Tobacco* v *McAllister* (no 2) (1916) 50 ILTR 157.

171 He can in England since 1981.

172 *Gordon* v *Craddock* [1964] 1 QB 503; because giving conditional leave is deemed synonymous with refusing unconditional leave within s.35(3).

173 *Les Fils Dreyfus* v *Clarke* [1958] 1 WLR 300, at 303.

174 *Blumberg* v *McCormick* [1915] 2 IR 402.

175 *Langdale* v *Danby* [1982] 1 WLR 1123 (HL).

176 Made under the Administration of Justice Act 1969, s.20.

177 *Nisbet* v *Marley Roof Tile,* 1988 SC 29.

proof on the plaintiff is not quite as high as in an Order 14 application.[178] In a personal injuries case an award will be made only if the defendant is insured, is a public authority or has enough means. The award is payable, by lump sum or instalments, to the plaintiff unless the Court orders it to be paid into court. In a personal injury or death case, the court may, with consent of the parties, order the award to take the form wholly or partly of periodical payments.[179] In granting or refusing the application the court may give directions and may order an early trial. The interim award must be kept secret from the trial judge until verdict on quantum and liability (Ord.29 r.17). In giving final judgment or order or in granting leave to discontinue the action or at any stage, the Court may deal with the interim payment, and may order repayment by the plaintiff, order the payment to be varied or discharged, or order payment by another defendant (Ord.29 r.19). Where both defendants A and B have made an interim payment, and the plaintiff has recovered final judgment against A and discontinued against B, the Court can order A to repay B.[180]

Semble, the defendant must deduct the CRU benefits certified to date when making the interim payment, and on paying the damages finally awarded should deduct the CRU benefits certified to date minus the amount already deducted.[181] [*to be replaced by*: Regulations under the Social Security (Recovery of Benefits) (NI) Order 1997 (Art.20(1)(2)(3)) will provide for the deduction of CRU benefits in personal injury cases].

SECURITY FOR COSTS

11.56 The defendant may apply for security for costs, where he believes that he may win the action or be awarded costs, but that it may be difficult to recover those costs from the plaintiff. However such application can only[182] be made where the plaintiff-

(1) is ordinarily resident outside Northern Ireland (Ord.23 r.1(1));
(2) is a nominal plaintiff (not suing in a representative capacity) who may not be able to pay costs (Ord.23 r.1(1));
(3) has deliberately misstated or changed his address (Ord.23 r.1(1)(2)); or
(4) is a limited company which appears to be unable to pay the costs (Companies (NI) Order 1986, Art.674).

The rule can be invoked against any party who is in the position of a plaintiff (Ord.23 r.1(3))[183] in the action or in a separate proceeding under the title of the action.[184] A plaintiff can apply for security for costs against a defendant who raises a counterclaim which is more than a set-off; or a defendant in possession

---

[178] *British and Commonwealth Holdings* v *Quadrex* [1989] QB 842, so that it can be granted where conditional leave to defend is given.
[179] Damages Act 1996, s.2(2).
[180] *Mitchell* v *HAT (No 3)*, 1993 SLT 1199.
[181] White Book (1997) 29/11/5; Social Security Administration (NI) Act 1992, s.82.
[182] Subject to any statutory provision: Ord.23 r.3.
[183] *Leonard* v *Scofield* [1936]] IR 715; *CT Bowring* v *Corsi Partners* [1994] 2 Lloyds R 567.
[184] *Penny* v *Penny* [1996] 1 WLR 1204 (CA).

defending an ejectment on behalf of another;[185] or a defendant in an ejectment for overholding;[186] or a defendant in a probate action who enters a *caveat* without having been cited;[187] but not against a defendant who claims interlocutory relief.[188] It can be ordered as security for costs yet to be incurred, not for costs already incurred in proceedings which are complete.[184] Security is to be given in such manner, time and on such terms as the Court directs (Ord.23 r.2), usually by payment into court, sometimes by bond under Order 108.

11.57 The Court has a discretion whether to order security. Save as stated above, bankruptcy or poverty is not a ground for ordering security.[189] Poverty is a neutral factor,[190] and even weighs against security if impoverishment was caused by the defendant's wrongdoing.[191] Security can be ordered against a legally aided plaintiff, but not on that ground, though the amount of the security should have regard to the plaintiff's restricted liability for costs personally.[192] If ordered on application of one defendant, no extra security should be ordered for a co-defendant.[193] The Court should make a conservative estimate of the defence costs that would be allowed on *inter partes* taxation, then deduct for the possibility of disposal without trial: an order for security can be varied in amount, as where the first estimate now appears to be erroneous.[194]

11.58 *Residence outside Northern Ireland.* "Ordinary residence" is a question of fact, and is not the same as domicile or long term residence; it means residence voluntarily adopted for a settled purpose as part of the ordered way of life for the time being.[195] Residence in Northern Ireland is temporary if there is a risk of leaving in the event of losing the action.[196] A foreign address on the writ is prima facie evidence of foreign residence.[197] If the plaintiff has taken up permanent residence in Northern Ireland since the writ was issued, security will be refused, or discharged.[196] The applicant must always show grounds for exercising the discretion to order security.[198] If he shows a prima facie defence he has a prima facie right to security.[199] Security will not be given on the ground

---

185 *Bowen* v *Barlow* (1875) IR 9 CL 55.

186 Deasy's Act, s.75; by recognisance and sureties.

187 *Dobler* v *Walsh* [1950] NI 150.

188 *CT Bowring* v *Corsi Partners* [1994] 2 Lloyds R 567 (CA), where the defendant was seeking an inquiry as to damages on the plaintiff's undertaking given for an interlocutory injunction.

189 *Salmon* v *Belfast Alhambra* (1903) 37 ILTR 72.

190 *Heany* v *Malocca* [1958] IR 111.

191 *Fares* v *Wiley* [1994] 1 ILRM 465.

192 *Jackson* v *John Dickinson* [1952] 1 All ER 104; *Stevenson* v *Midlothian* DC 1983 SC (HL) 51.

193 *McHenry* v *McHenry* [1896] 1 IR 60.

194 *Deighan* v *Sunday Newspapers* [1985] NI 9.

195 *Talwar* v *Chief Constable* [1994] 2 BNIL 92.

196 *Howard* v *Howard* (1892) 30 LR Ir 340.

197 *Archdall v Supple* (1841) 3 Ir LR 287.

198 *Birch* v *Pirtill* [1936] IR 122.

199 *Fares* v *Wiley* [1994] 1 ILRM 465.

of residence in Great Britain. At least in the absence of cogent evidence of difficulty in enforcement, security cannot be ordered on the grounds of being a national or resident of a European Union State.[200]

11.59 *Nominal plaintiff.* In *George Bell* v *Nethercott*[201] a counterclaiming defendant was ordered to give security where he had agreed to pay over 90 per cent of any money recovered on the claim to his assignee in bankruptcy.

11.60 *Insolvent company.* The decision is in the Court's unfettered discretion and may be refused if the plaintiff's impecuniosity may be caused by the defendant's alleged wrong,[202] or if security will probably stifle a valid claim.[203] Unlike the equivalent English section, Article 674 of the Companies (NI) Order 1986 is silent as to whether it applies only to a company registered in Northern Ireland. In *Munchie Foods*[202] it was treated as applicable where the plaintiff was registered in England.

11.61 In a matrimonial cause security may be ordered against the husband if the wife has no separate estate (FP Rules, r.7.2). An appellant can be ordered to give security for costs of an appeal, as to which see para. 20.35.

INJUNCTIONS

11.62 At any stage of the proceedings the Court may grant a mandatory or other injunction where it appears just and convenient for any proceedings before it, on any terms and conditions; and in urgent cases it may grant it before proceedings commence, on condition that the proceedings be commenced (Judicature Act, s.91(1)(*b*)(2)). A section 91 order cannot be granted in isolation: it must be incidental to and dependent on an enforceable legal right or cause of action.[204] Any party may apply before or after trial and whether or not an injunction is claimed in his writ or pleadings (Ord.29 r.1(1)). Usually the applicant is the plaintiff or a defendant who has pleaded a claim. The defendant who has not made any claim for relief can apply if he has an interest in preserving the subject-matter or the status quo.[205] Application may be by summons or motion, or *ex parte* in urgent cases (Ord.29 r.1(2)). Application for an interlocutory injunction is brought by summons in the Queen's Bench Division, by notice of motion in the Chancery Division on at least two clear

---

[200] *Fitzgerald* v *Williams* [1996] QB 657 (CA). It can be ordered against a resident of the Isle of Man who is not a national of the UK or any EC State: *Pitt* v *Bolger* [1996] 1 IR 108 (Keane J).

[201] [1988] NI 299.

[202] *Munchie Foods* v *Eagle Star* [1993] 9 NIJB 69.

[203] *Keary Developments* v *Tarmac* [1995] 3 All ER 534.

[204] Including a cause of action which has been or may be stayed because of an agreement to refer disputes to an arbitrator or foreign court: *Channel Tunnel Group* v *Balfour Beatty* [1993] AC 334, at 360-6; but excluding a claim which by statute is within the exclusive jurisdiction of an inferior court or tribunal: *Department of Social Security* v *Butler* [1995] 1 WLR 1528 (*contra: BMWE* v *Canadian Pacific* (1996) 136 DLR 4th 289 (SCC).

[205] *McEntaggart* v *Byrne* (1896) 30 ILTR 165 (injunction to restrain plaintiff from objecting to renewal of liquor licence).

days' notice. It must be heard by a judge (Ord.32 r.11(1)(f)).[206] The plaintiff serves with the summons an affidavit, which may contain hearsay (Ord.41 r.5). If the defendant does not appear the application may proceed on proof of service (Ord.32 r.7).

11.63 Principles on application for an interlocutory prohibitory injunction are stated in *American Cyanamid* v *Ethicon*.[207] The plaintiff must show a serious question to be tried in the action, that his claim is not frivolous, not necessarily a prima facie case.[208] He must have *locus standi*, in that the right injured or threatened must be vested in him.[209] The judge decides whether it is just to grant the injunction for the purpose of preserving or restoring the status quo as it was before the alleged wrong was committed,[210] so that the trial court can deal effectively with the merits. It is not for the purpose of enforcing the plaintiff's rights. The injunction may be refused if the plaintiff's rights can be compensated by damages which the defendant can pay, unless the plaintiff's undertaking in damages will compensate for any injustice to the defendant. If these tests do not decide the issue, the judge considers the balance of convenience, and if that is equal, favours preserving the status quo. The plaintiff's case and the likely defence may both be considered.[208]

11.64 These principles are modified in the following cases. If the plaintiff has delayed inordinately or held his hand until the eleventh hour, the injunction may be refused.[211] The injunction can be granted though it substantially satisfies the plaintiff's claim, especially where there appears to be no contest;[212] but not if it would decide the case and the facts are disputed.[213] If there is no arguable defence, balance of convenience is unimportant. A landowner has a right to an injunction to stop trespass unless the defendant shows an arguable case for justification.[214] If the issue in dispute is one of law only, the judge can disregard the *Cynamid* principles and decide on general equitable principles.[215] The Court must have regard to the likelihood of a successful defence that the acts are lawful in furtherance of a trade dispute.[216] Though it may be granted to restrain a breach of confidence an interlocutory order will not be allowed to restrain a libel which the defendant intends *bona fide* to justify at the trial.

11.65 The Court has an equitable discretion to refuse an injunction. It may order an early trial (Ord.29 r.6). The plaintiff may accept an undertaking in lieu by the defendant, which is enforceable like a court order.

---

206 A master may grant an injunction on terms agreed between the parties.
207 [1975] AC 396.
208 *Crazy Prices v Hewitt* [1980] NI 150.
209 *In re Lyle* [1987] 7 NIJB 24, at 41.
210 *de Vos* v *Baxter* [1987] 11 NIJB 103.
211 *Lennon* v *Ganly* [1981] ILRM 84.
212 *NIHE* v *Fox* [1981] 9 NIJB at 6-7.
213 *Burke* v *Patterson* [1986] NI 1, at 4F.
214 *Patel* v *Smith* [1987] 1 WLR 853.
215 *Topping* v *Warne Products* [1986] 9 NIJB 14, at 22-3.
216 Trade Union and Labour Relations (NI) Order 1995, Art.99(2).

11.66 Neither an injunction nor an interlocutory declaration in lieu can be given against the Crown.[217] However an injunction can be given against a minister or official personally liable.[218] In the exceptional circumstances where a plaintiff or applicant for judicial review shows a good prima facie case that the national law is incompatible with EC law, the Court is required to grant interim injunction against the Crown to stay implementation of the law.[219]

Types of order

11.67 *Prohibitory* (negative) injunction is the more usual type of order: that a person do not do, or stop doing something. On application by a person affected, the High Court can restrain unlawful industrial action,[220] and on application of a trade union member, the High Court can restrain industrial action without a ballot.[221] *Mandatory* (positive) injunction, is an order to do an act or undo the damage of a past act. The Court cannot compel an employee to work.[222] *Quia timet* injunction is an order to do or not to do an act in order to prevent damage which has not yet occurred. An injunction may be granted against a threatened or apprehended trespass or waste whether or not the defendant is in possession or claims title or right.[223]

11.68 As long as it relates to the protection of a legal right, the injunction is not confined to restraining unlawful acts; it can restrain a lawful act if necessary, for example to order a defendant who is harassing or molesting the plaintiff to stay out of an area.[224] A stronger case and more cogent need is to be shown if the order sought is a mandatory one,[225] though it can be given, even a mandatory *quia timet*, and is more readily given if the act to be done is simple and cheap;[226] or if the case is clear, or if the defendant is trying to steal a march;[227] or if, though mandatory in form, it is in substance operating to preserve the status quo.[228]

11.69 In granting *or refusing* an injunction, the Court may give directions as to further proceeding (Ord.29 r.8). The order may be interlocutory, to last until the trial, or interim, to last for a limited period, and should be expressed to be in force "until judgment or further order" or until a certain day. If refusing an injunction, the judge may grant a limited injunction to preserve the status quo pending appeal. An injunction will not be granted unless the plaintiff gives an undertaking to pay damages to the defendant in the event of his claim failing or

---

217 *Burke* v *Patterson* [1986] NI 1, at 6C.

218 *M* v *Home Office* [1994] 1 AC 377.

219 *R* v *Sec of State for Transport (No 2), ex p Factortame* [1991] 1 AC 603 (ECJ and HL).

220 Trade Union and Labour Relations (NI) Order 1995, Art.120.

221 *Ibid.* Art.29.

222 *Ibid.* Art.123.

223 Judicature Act, s.91(3).

224 *Burris* v *Azadani* [1995] 1 WLR 1373 (CA); a power to be expressly given by statute: see para.14.86.

225 *Hayes* v *Shell Ltd*, Ch D, NI (Pringle J) 16 November 1995.

226 *de Vos* v *Baxter* [1987] 11 NIJB 103.

227 *Boyle* v *An Post* [1992] 2 IR 437, at 440.

228 *McKenna* v *Commr of An Garda Siochána* [1993] 3 IR 543.

the injunction proving unnecessary. If the injunction is later discharged, whether by consent or by order of the Court, then save in special circumstances, the Court will use its discretion to enforce the undertaking, by ordering the plaintiff to pay damages for all such loss caused to the defendant by the injunction which is a proximate or natural consequence or of which the plaintiff had particular knowledge.[229] The undertaking need not be required if the injunction is in substance final. The Crown or other public or local authority may be excused from an undertaking if it is enforcing the law.[230] Costs are often made costs in the cause, but reserved for further order in the event of the action not being pursued.

11.70 Proceedings for an injunction alone can be brought in aid of a suit in Great Britain or a Brussels Convention territory under the Civil Jurisdiction and Judgments Act 1982 (s.25); or in aid of a suit to which the Convention does not apply and a suit in a country other than a Convention State.[231]

11.71 *Enforcement of injunctions.* Service of the order on the respondent is required to make it enforceable by committal (Ord.45 rr..4-6). Notice of motion for committal is provided for in Order 52 rules 4-5 (para. 16.53).

11.72 *Undertaking in lieu of injunction.* Often the defendant offers an undertaking in lieu of an injunction and if satisfactory it may be accepted, and should be in writing or signed, or recorded in the books of the Court. The terms of the undertaking must be as specific as a court order would be. The undertaking is enforceable like an injunction. The undertaking cannot be varied by the Court, but it can be discharged or the defendant can be relieved of compliance. A party cannot appeal against an undertaking.

URGENT CASES

11.73 Application may be made on shorter than two days notice,[232] or *ex parte* (see further para. 11.11). According to Order 29 rule 1(2) only a plaintiff can apply *ex parte* on grounds of urgency. The applicant must show that notice would cause an injustice either because of urgency or because of the need for surprise, and that the damage to the respondent is either compensatable or is outweighed by the injustice to the applicant. If urgent, a plaintiff may even apply before the commencement of his action, in which case an order provides for the issue of proceedings (Ord.29 r.1(3)). As to *ex parte* applications in the Chancery Division, see the Practice Direction [1989] 2 BNIL 83. If an application is brought to prevent action in furtherance of a trade dispute, all reasonable steps must be taken to give notice of the *ex parte* application.[233]

---

229 *Abbey National* v *McCann*, CA, NI, 13 June 1997 (Carswell LJ at pp.29-33).

230 *Kirklees BC* v *Wickes Supplies* [1993] AC 227.

231 SI 1997/302.

232 See *In re Lyle* [1987] 7 NIJB 24, at 40-1.

233 Trade Union and Labour Relations (NI) Order 1995, Art.99(1).

MAREVA INJUNCTION

11.74 A host of cases starting with *Mareva Compania* v *International Bulkcarriers*[234] establish the power of the Court to prevent the defendant from removing or disposing of his assets to make judgment for damages unenforceable. Until then it had always been understood that such an order could only relate to assets which were the subject of or connected to the action. It can be granted in relation to (present or future) assets within Northern Ireland whether or not the defendant is domiciled or present in Northern Ireland (Judicature Act, s.91(4)). It can restrain him from dealing with his assets anywhere in the world.[235] It can be granted at any time, *ex parte* before the writ is issued, pending trial or judgment, or after judgment until the judgment is enforced. The authorities are discussed in detail in the White Book (1997) 29/1/20. A form of order is set out in the English Practice Direction, White Book (1997) Supplement, para. 974/3, Annexes 2 and 3.

11.75 The plaintiff must show a good arguable case for an existing cause of action claiming some monetary remedy, show evidence from which it is likely that the defendant has assets which he may remove or conceal, and must make a full and frank disclosure of all relevant facts. There must be evidence of a risk that the defendant will deal with assets for the purpose of depriving the plaintiff.[236] An undertaking in damages will be required. He should submit a draft of the order desired. The order may provide for the allowance of the defendant's living, business or legal expenses. The Court in granting the draconian remedy of a *Mareva* injunction may impose strict time limits on the further prosecution of the action.[237] Other persons, such as the defendant's wife, solicitor or bank, as soon as they have notice of the injunction, are liable in criminal contempt to preserve the assets of the defendant in their possession. A *Mareva* injunction can be granted before or after judgment and it can be made against a person who has been joined as a party solely because he has assets of the wrongdoer.[238] The order has effect only *in personam*; it does not give the plaintiff any priority over creditors.[236] It should be remembered that a *Mareva* cannot be a substantive remedy; it must relate to a cause of action to be sued upon in Northern Ireland or elsewhere. Under the statutes mentioned in Appendix One (para. 4-c) the High Court can make restraint and charging orders in the nature of *Mareva* to preserve assets of an accused person to be available for a criminal court upon convicting him to confiscate the proceeds of his crime. There may also be power for a civil court to grant a *Mareva* injunction against an accused person to preserve his assets to be available for a criminal court to impose a fine upon him.[239] Desire for a *Mareva* to freeze

---

[234] (1975)[1980] 1 All ER 213.

[235] *Derby & Co* v *Weldon* [1990] Ch 48,65.

[236] *O'Mahony v Horgan* [1995] 2 IR 411 (SC).

[237] *Group 4 Securitas* v *McIldowney*, Ch D, NI (Girvan J) 13 February 1997. The action was dismissed though the summons to dismiss was issued only two weeks after the due date for service of the Statement of Claim.

[238] *Mercantile Group* v *Aiyela* [1994] QB 366, at 375-6.

[239] *R* v *Consolidated Fastfrate Transport* [1994] 4 LRC 549 (Ont, CA).

assets here cannot by itself be a ground for seeking leave to issue a writ for service outside the jurisdiction under Order 11 rule 1.[240]

11.76 Though the statutory power under the Debtors (Ir) Act 1872 has been repealed, the High Court still has inherent power to order a writ of arrest *ne exeat regno*, where the plaintiff sues on an equitable remedy, where there is evidence that the defendant intends to leave Northern Ireland and that his prolonged absence would prejudice the plaintiff in proving his claim, as where he intends calling the defendant as witness or obtaining discovery.[241]

11.77 Section 91 of the Judicature Act gives a general power of the High Court to order sale of any property[242] so that the Court might for *Mareva* purposes order sale of an asset of the defendant. In respect of assets proved to exist, the Court may order the defendant to deliver those assets to a named person or into court.[243]

INSPECTION AND PRESERVATION OF PROPERTY

Interlocutory application

11.78 The rules discussed herein have a dual purpose: (a) in preserving property which is the subject of the dispute so that the winning party will be able to recover it or its value intact; and (b) in making property available for inspection to afford evidence relevant to the dispute. On application by summons by any party, the Court may order detention, preservation or taking of samples of, or experimenting with any property which is the subject of the proceedings or as to which a question may arise; or inspection of such property in possession of a party; or delivery up of goods under section 4 of the Tort (Interference with Goods) Act 1977; and may make an ancillary order authorising entry on the lands of a party (Ord.29 rr.2-5). The right to inspection is not dependent on the strength of the applicant's case.[244] In these rules, "property" means physical property, not a process.[245] Order 29 can be used for inspection of a document, but only where the physical nature of the document (e.g. whether it is a forgery) is at issue. Inspection of its contents is only available under the statutes and rules relating to discovery of documents.

11.79 The Court has power to order blood tests in proceedings where paternity is at issue (see para. 13.156). There is a general power to order accounts and inquiries in any proceedings (see para. 14.14).

11.80 An order under Order 29 rules 2-5 can only be made against a party to the proceedings, so its effect will be subject to the consent of a person in whose possession the property is.[246] Inspections have been ordered to allow the

---

[240] *Mercedes Benz AG* v *Leiduck* [1996] 1 AC 284 (PC).

[241] See *Felton* v *Callis* [1969] 1 QB 200; White Book (1997) 45/1/37.

[242] A power not in the English Act.

[243] *Jackson* v *Sterling Industries* (1987) 162 CLR 612, at 625-6.

[244] *Bula Ltd* v *Tara Mines* (No 1) [1987] IR 85.

[245] *Tudor Accumulator* v *China Mutual* [1930] WN 200.

[246] See White Book (1997) 29/2-3/4.

plaintiff to identify the articles claimed to be his;[247] and of a farm to measure its acreage.[248] A person is not allowed to view a prison or Young Offenders' Centre or take photos etc., save as provided by statute or directed by the Secretary of State.[249]

11.81 The Court may order to be paid into court a specific fund in dispute (Ord.29 r.2(3)). If the real or personal property which is the subject of proceedings is more than enough to answer all claims, the Court may allow income from it to be paid to, or part of the property itself to be transferred to any parties interested in it (Ord.29 r.10). If the defendant to a claim for personal property asserts a lien for unpaid money (as unpaid seller, carrier or storekeeper for instance) the Court may order the property to be surrendered to the claimant if he pays into court the amount of money asserted (Ord.29 r.7).

11.82 The Court may, where just and convenient for the purpose of proceedings before it, order the sale of any property[250] or appoint a receiver, on any terms and conditions under the Judicature Act (s.91(1)(a)(c)); and may order sale of any personal property[251] which is perishable (Ord.29 r.5). There is a specific power of sale of land in the Chancery Division (see para. 18.55).

11.83 Order 30 deals with the appointment and duties of a receiver. A receiver will be appointed on interlocutory application on the same principles as to balance of convenience etc. as an interlocutory mandatory injunction.[252] Application may be made by summons or motion, and may be joined with an ancillary application for an injunction. Pending the making of an order of receiver the Court can grant an immediate *ex parte* injunction to restrain a party beneficially entitled from disposing of the property. A copy of the order appointing the receiver is served on all parties. The receiver's costs are allowable without taxation (Ord.62 r.7(2)). His function is to preserve any property or commercial business so as to maintain it and its profit or yield. He will be given possession if necessary.[253] A receiver is liable for tax.[254]

11.84 The Court may refer to conveyancing counsel[255] the investigation of title of property with a view to investment in it or sale of it, or any matter relating to the drafting of a conveyance or instrument, and any dispute over his opinion may be referred to the judge (Ord.31 rr.5-6). His fee is fixed by the Taxing Master (Ord.62 r.25). Costs incurred by the parties in having their own draft settled by counsel as well will be disallowed (Ord.62 r.17(9)).

11.85 On an application for an injunction or order under Order 29 the Court may give directions as to further proceedings (Ord.29 r.8). The Court may

---

247 *Midwood* v *Kelly* (1901) 1 NIJR 199.

248 *Conyers* v *Dorgan* (1881) 15 ILTR 121.

249 Prison and Young Offenders' Centre Rules (NI) 1995 (SR 1995/8), r.50.

250 Including land. Oddly, this general power of sale of property in the Judicature Act has no equivalent in the English Act or the 1877 Irish Act.

251 Including shares: *Evans* v *Davies* [1893] 2 Ch 216.

252 O'Hare & Hill pp.329-30.

253 *Charrington & Co* v *Camp* [1902] 1 Ch 386.

254 Taxes Management Act 1970, s.75.

255 Appointed under s.113 of the Judicature Act.

direct an early trial (Ord.29 r.6). The respondent can oppose an order under Order 29 on the grounds that it might incriminate him.[256]

Ex parte orders

11.86 An order can be made *ex parte* in an emergency.[257] If there is a real possibility that the defendant will destroy documents or things prejudicial to his defence, or publish material in which the plaintiff has a right of confidence, the plaintiff may apply *ex parte* for an '*Anton Piller'* order authorising him or his solicitor or other responsible agent, to seize the items without advance notice to the defendant.[258] It can be made for a preservative or evidential purpose. It may also be made for the purpose of securing documents and items which will help the plaintiff to trace assets for the purpose of enforcing a judgment.[259] The plaintiff must make full and frank disclosure and give a cross-undertaking in damages. He should lodge a draft of the order desired. The Court in granting such a draconian remedy may impose strict time limits on the further prosecution of the action.[260] An order can be made after the trial in aid of execution. An order will not be made, and the respondent can resist it, if it will incriminate him as to a criminal offence.[261] An *Anton Piller* order is not a search warrant; it cannot be executed by force, but if the order is so worded as to command the defendant to allow the search, the defendant's refusal to allow inspection is contempt and may lead the Court to infer that he has something to hide.

Pre-action inspection, detention etc.

11.87 On application of any person, in anticipation of *any type of proceedings*, the High Court may order inspection, photographing, taking samples, experimenting, preservation, custody and detention of land, chattel or other corporeal property which may become the subject of or as to which a question may arise in subsequent proceedings in the Court, under the Administration of Justice Act 1969 (s.21). Note that the respondent does not have to be a likely party to the subsequent proceedings. The section is binding against the Crown in proceedings involving a claim for personal injury or death (Administration of Justice Act 1970, s.35). An order cannot be made if injurious to the public interest (1970 Act, s.35(3)). Application is by originating summons (bearing a court fee of £30) on affidavit; the order may be made conditional on security; it must be refused if an order would reveal a secret invention not at issue and would not be made in pending proceedings (Ord.29 r.9).

---

256 Through such privilege is abrogated in passing off actions: Judicature Act, s. 94A.

257 *Hennessey* v *Rohmann* (1879) 36 LT 51.

258 *Anton Piller* v *Manufacturing Processes* [1976] Ch 55. See further White Book (1997) 29/2-3/6. Form of order White Book (1997) Supplement, para. 974/3, Annex 1.

259 *Dabelstein v Hildebrandt*, 1996 (3) SA 42.

260 *Group 4 Securitas* v *McIldowney*, Ch D, NI (Girvan J) 13 February 1997. The action was dismissed though the summons to dismiss was issued only two weeks after the due date for service of the Statement of Claim.

261 Though such privilege is abrogated in passing off actions: Judicature Act, s.94A.

11.88 This provision can be used for inspection of a document, but only where the physical nature of the document (e.g. whether it is a forgery) is at issue. Inspection of its contents is only available under the statutes and rules relating to discovery of documents.[262]

Inspection, detention etc. against non-party

11.89 On application of a party to proceedings involving a claim for personal injuries or death, the Court may order inspection, preservation, sampling etc. of any property which is not owned or possessed by a party, under the Administration of Justice Act 1970 (s.32(2)). The section binds the Crown (s.35). An order cannot be made if injurious to the public interest (s.35). Application is by summons on affidavit served personally on the respondent and every party; the order may be made conditional on security; it must be refused if an order would reveal a secret invention not at issue and would not be made against the respondent as a party (Ord.29 r.9). Order 62 rule 6(9) is obviously intended to confer a right on the respondent to costs unless otherwise ordered, as required by section 33(2), but there is a defect in its drafting.

DISCLOSURE OF EVIDENCE

11.90 As a general principle the parties in civil proceedings have no obligation to reveal the evidence in their possession or which they intend to use at the trial. Orders 24 and 26 form the major exception by allowing 'discovery'. The word 'discovery' which comes from the Court of Chancery, means strictly the process whereby one party discloses by list the existence of relevant documents. It is colloquially used to mean both the disclosure and the inspection of those documents. 'Discovery of facts' by interrogatories is the disclosure of statements of fact by answer to questions. Those Orders apply to a person under disability and his next friend/guardian *ad litem* (Ord.80 r.7). The Court has power to order blood tests in proceedings where paternity is at issue (see para. 13.156). There is a general power to order accounts and inquiries in any proceedings (see para. 14.14).

DISCOVERY BY DISCLOSURE OF DOCUMENTS

11.91 A party may by notice require inspection of a document referred to in his opponent's pleadings (Ord.24 r.11).

Automatic discovery in writ actions

11.92 Within 14 days after close of pleadings between them in an action begun by writ, each party is obliged, save as otherwise agreed, to send to the other a list (not on oath) of documents which are or have been in his possession, custody or power relating to matters in question between them (Ord.24 rr.1,2(1)). This automatic discovery does not apply in third-party proceedings; nor against the defendant to actions/counterclaims for recovery of a penalty (Ord.24 r.2(3)(4)), nor in proceedings in which the Crown is a party (Ord.77 r.11(1)). In an action/counterclaim where liability is admitted or where it arises from "an accident on land due to a collision or apprehended collision involving

---

[262] *Huddleston* v *Control Risks* [1987] 1 WLR 701.

a vehicle", discovery is limited to the issue of special damage (Ord.24 r.2(2)(4)).

11.93 Automatic discovery is a continuing duty, so that further disclosure must be made of documents as they come to a party: so says the White Book (1997) 24/1/2, citing *Mitchell* v *Darley Dale Colliery.*[263] However, at least in relation to discovery under a court order (there being no automatic discovery under the Irish RSC) the concept of continuing duty of discovery of documents created after the original list was rejected by Murphy J and the Supreme Court in *Bula Ltd* v *Tara Mines (No 5),*[264] pointing out that *Mitchell* v *Darley Dale* does not go that far. However, the English Court of Appeal has re-affirmed that discovery is a continuing duty, considering that to be implied in spirit in *Mitchell* v *Darley Dale,* and the duty continues though the close of evidence at the trial up to the very conclusion of the proceedings.[265]

11.94 A party may require his opponent to verify the list on oath (Ord.24 r.2(7)). If a party fails to give automatic discovery, the opponent should write an open letter seeking compliance within a specified time, then apply by summons under Order 24 rule 19 or Order 24 rule 3 without affidavit.[266] By summons within 14 days of close of pleadings, any party may apply for the restricting or waiving of discovery in so far as discovery is not necessary for disposal of the action or saving costs (Ord.24 r.2(5)(6)).

Applications for discovery

11.95 In any proceedings the Court may order discovery by a party to any other party, on oath or not, relating to any matter in question in the proceedings (Ord.24 r.3).[267] A 'party' can include a claimant in proceedings under a Chancery decree.[268] It cannot be ordered against a non-party. A person cannot be sued or joined as a party merely for discovery.[269] An action brought by a nominal plaintiff can be stayed until the real claimant gives discovery.[270] Discovery under the order is in Form 22, and if on oath with a verifying affidavit in Form 23. Subject to rules the Crown can be required to give discovery and inspection, saving the immunity for public interest; and the rules

---

263 (1884) Cab & Ell 215. There Hawkins J said that if after giving discovery a party finds a document which was not disclosed because it has been "forgotten, or overlooked, or supposed not to exist" , he must disclose it by supplementary affidavit or by notice.

264 [1994] 1 IR 487.

265 *Vernon* v *Bosley* (No 2) [1997] 1 All ER 614 (CA). Evans LJ, dissenting, held that there is no continuing duty, save in so far as the Court can order further discovery and can order discovery of documents not yet acquired.

266 Practice Direction, Master (QBD), [1991] 7 BNIL 139.

267 Under traditional Irish practice in the Queen's Bench Division, after an open letter requesting discovery has been unsuccessful and after service of pleadings, this was applied for ex parte on affidavit exhibiting correspondence and stating the issues between the parties: Moran v O'Farrell (1883) 17 ILTR 63; Wylie p.494; with appeal *ex parte*: *Murphy* v *Walsh* (1923) 57 ILTR 129. It seems that this practice has now fallen into disuse, even in cases where automatic discovery is excluded.

268 *Moncrieff* v *Johnston* (1902) 36 ILTR 61.

269 *Bailie* v *Inglis* [1926] NI 53, but see para. 11.131.

270 *Compania Naviera Vascongada* v *R & H Hall* (No 2) (1906) 40 ILTR 246.

provide for the Crown to refuse to disclose the existence of a document.[271] Discovery is available only between parties who are on opposite sides of the record or between whom there is some issue raised or a right to be adjusted. Thus there can be no discovery between the plaintiff and a third party unless the latter is added as a defendant.[272] A defendant to a claim or counterclaim is entitled on request to a free copy of the list served by a co-defendant on the plaintiff (Ord.24 r.6). Discovery must relate to a question in the action, but, under Order 24 rule 3, if the parties to the discovery are on the opposite side of the record it need not be a question between them.[273] Thus the defendant can seek from the plaintiff a document which supports his claim against a third party.

11.96 Documents are only discoverable which are relevant to the issues raised on the pleadings. For that reason a party will not normally be granted discovery before he has delivered his pleading. Discovery can be applied for at any time but will rarely be granted to a party who has not yet delivered his pleading. It may be granted after judgment.[274] In *Galvin* v *Graham-Twomey*[275] O'Flaherty J refused discovery (under the special procedure for discovery against a non-party, para. 11.135) of the document containing the alleged libel, as it was sought to enable the plaintiff to plead his cause of action. However in *Stewart* v *Ratner Safe Co*[276] the plaintiff was granted discovery before Statement of Claim where he had lost his copy of the contract sued upon. The Court may order an issue to be determined before discovery (Ord.24 r.4).

11.97 Discovery under Order 24 rule 3 will be refused or deferred if the Court is of the opinion that it is not necessary at that stage for disposing fairly of the action or saving costs (Ord.24 r.9). Thus it may be refused if there is no reasonable prospect of it being useful; or if it seems likely that there are no relevant documents;[277] or it would assist the applicant to make a case of fraud in which he was complicit.[278] It may be restricted so as to prevent disclosure of secrets.[279] The burden of persuasion is on the party resisting discovery, rather than the burden of proof; and McCollum J has taken the view that the effect of Order 24 rule 9 is there must be some material before the Court which shows that discovery is likely to be of some value for fairly disposing or saving costs.[280] The Court decides on pleadings and available information; it does not require evidence as to what documents actually exist. General discovery will be

---

271 Crown Proceedings Act, s.28(2); Ord.77 r.11(2). The Court directs what officer of the Crown shall make the affidavit: Ord.77 r.11(3).

272 *Gillespie* v *Anglo-Irish Beef* [1994] 4 BNIL 68. In a claim involving personal injuries or death, the plaintiff or third party can seek discovery against each other under the Administration of Justice Act 1970: see para. 11.135.

273 *Cory* v *Cory* [1923] 1 Ch 90.

274 *Hennessy* v *Lavery* [1903] 1 IR 87.

275 [1994] 2 ILRM 315.

276 (1907) 41 ILTR 74.

277 *Powell* v *Heffernan* (1879) 4 LR Ir 703.

278 *Sumner* v *Sumner* [1935] NI 173.

279 *Hogan* v *Bayer Products* (1950) 84 ILTR 145.

280 *Neilly* v *Moypark Ltd*, QBD, NI, 20 October 1995, at pp.6-7.

refused if it is too wide or oppressive or if it is for documents concerned with evidence or credit of witnesses, though that is often an incidental result..[281] Discovery is not given of evidence of similar fact instances, at least not of unproven allegations, unless of statistical value.[282] In an action for injuries against an employer, discovery was allowed of the earnings of comparative workers in the same employment.[283] Discovery is not ordered against the defendant in a road accident unless there is some special issue.[284]

11.98 The Court usually orders the discovery to be given by the respondent personally; or by his solicitor; or local agent.[285] If ordered by affidavit against the Crown, the order directs what officer (Ord.77 r.11(3)). If the respondent is a corporation, the order is for discovery by the secretary if known, or by the "secretary or other proper officer".[286] An order against a plaintiff firm suing in the firm name need not state who shall give discovery.[287] In ordering discovery the Court cannot make a peremptory order that the action/defence be struck out in default of compliance: a further order must be made after the default under Order 24 rule 19.[288]

11.99 '*Document*' includes written things on paper and any material from which evidence or information can be perceived such as computer software, microfiches, tape recordings and X-rays.[289]

11.100 '*Possession custody or power*'. The respondent must disclose documents which are or have been in his possession or ownership, whether sole or joint with others, and in his mere physical custody. He must disclose documents which he has a right to control, or which he has an enforceable right to inspect,[290] but not documents of which he has a right to copies without access to the original.[291] He must disclose documents which he holds as servant or

---

281 *McAvoy* v *Goodyear* [1971] NI 185. In that case the plaintiff, claiming for dermatitis against his employer, sought discovery of all the defendant's records relating to instances of dermatitis of any of its 4,000 employees at the factory. Lowry J held that such discovery would be too burdensome, and that the further one gets away from the plaintiff's job, the less easy it is to see its relevance; he confined discovery to the department of the factory in which the plaintiff and others worked.

282 *In re Oaklee Housing Assoc*. [1994] 6 BNIL 46.

283 *Rowley v Liverpool CC*, 'The Times' 26 October 1989.

284 White Book (1997) 24/2/6.

285 *Donovan* v *Todd, Burns & Co* [1908] 2 IR 100.

286 *Compania Anonima* v *Barnett* (1904) 4 NIJR 187. An employed solicitor is not to be regarded as a proper officer because much of the information known to him will be privileged: *BTK* v *Greater Edmonton Development Corp* (1992) 95 DLR 4th 573 (CA, Ont).

287 *Herskind v Hall* [1908] 2 IR 99.

288 *Bell* v *McPhilpin* (1891) 25 ILTR 23.

289 *McCarthy* v *O'Flynn* [1979] IR 127; *State Bank* v *Heinrich* (1991) 17 Comm LB 465 (SC, S Aus).

290 But not documents which he has a right to see under Freedom of Information legislation: *Theodore* v *Australian Postal Commission* (1989) 15 Comm LB 66 (SC Vic).

291 *O'Sullivan* v *Herdmans* [1986] NI 214, at 219D.

agent. This includes documents which are held by a person as his agent or employee.[292]

11.101 *'Relating to any matter in question'* means relating to an issue which is in dispute in the pleadings,[293] including liability and quantum of damages, but not the subject-matter of the action *per se*. It covers any document which is likely to contain information which may help a party to establish his case or damage his opponent's case, and is not limited to documents admissible in evidence.[294] Unfortunately there is no power to order discovery of the identity of his insurer or other person liable to indemnify him, and the defendant cannot be compelled to disclose that information even if the plaintiff has a direct right against the insurer by statute.[295]

Giving discovery

11.102 A party cannot refuse to give discovery on grounds of privilege. He claims the privilege in his list.[296] A claim that a document is privileged does not absolve him from disclosing its existence.[297] In claiming public interest immunity, the Crown may be justified in not disclosing the existence of a document (Ord.77 r.11(2)). Whether automatic or under order, discovery is by way of list, in Form 22, enumerating the documents with a short description of each or of a bundle of documents of similar nature (Ord.24 r.5). The list is divided as follows-

- *Schedule 1 Part 1*: documents in his possession which he is willing to disclose;
- *Schedule 1 Part 2*: documents in his possession which he objects to disclosing (describing the type of document or class and stating the ground of privilege, without having to identify each);
- *Schedule 2*: documents which are no longer in his possession. Copies of these in his possession should be listed in Schedule 1.

11.103 The list is served with a notice stating a time and place for inspection (Ord.24 r.10). In practice the solicitor usually sends photocopies of all Schedule 1 Part 1 documents. The list is oppressive if it is prolix or includes irrelevant documents. The discovering party is deemed to admit the relevance of any document he includes. A co-defendant is entitled to receive a copy of the list of documents given by a defendant to the plaintiff (Ord.24 r.6).

11.104 For Schedule 1 Part 2 documents he must state a valid ground of objection, one which normally falls within a head of privilege (see para. 13.37) or other ground such as irrelevance or claim of lien. He can only claim a privilege if he is the person in whom it is vested or if he has a right to claim it or is bound by a privilege vested in another. It is not necessary to identify each

---

292 *Quigley* v *Burke* [1996] 1 ILRM 469.
293 *Hearn* v *Downes* (1920) 54 ILTR 50.
294 *McAvoy* v *Goodyear* [1971] NI 185.
295 *McKenna* v *Best Travel* [1995] 1 IR 577 (Murphy J).
296 *Bell* v *McPhilpin* (1891) 25 ILTR 23.
297 *Bula Ltd* v *Tara Mines* (No 5) [1994] 1 IR 487, at 490-1 (Murphy J), approved at 495 (SC).

individual document.[298] It is sufficient to specify the class of documents and the ground of privilege. Except where necessary under public interest privilege, privilege does not enable a party to hide the existence of a document, though he need only give the barest description of it. If it is in the opinion of a Minister injurious to the public interest, the Crown need not disclose the existence of a document (Ord.77 r.11(2)). The ground of objection is conclusive unless stated on a non-existent ground or he has clearly misstated the nature and effect of the document.[299] The Court may inspect a document to determine the validity of the objection (Ord.24 r.15(2)).

11.105 A party giving discovery must decide three things in relation to each document or part of a document: (a) is it within his possession, custody or power; (b) is it relevant to the issue pleaded; (c) is there a ground for objecting to inspection of it? He must list a document even if it will not be admissible in evidence at the trial. If a one document contains irrelevant or privileged passages (e.g. employers' medical records referring to several persons as well as the plaintiff) those passages can be masked for the purposes of inspection. He should both disclose and allow inspection of any document which he intends to adduce in evidence at the trial. A list of discovery is deemed to include an implied notice to admit authenticity. Therefore a party on whom a list of documents is served is deemed to admit that the documents are authentic (though not that they are admissible) unless he denies it in his pleading or serves notice to the contrary after inspection (Ord.27 r.4(1)(2)); in which case he bears the costs of proving and the costs thrown away, unless otherwise ordered (Ord.62 r.6(8)), and if not legally aided he may suffer those costs to be assessed by the Court and payable forthwith (Ord.62 r.7(6)). The party receiving discovery can give secondary evidence of any document which the list states to be in the possession custody or power of the party giving discovery, without having to serve a notice to produce (Ord.27 r.4(3)).

Further discovery

11.106 It is the duty of a party who, after making an affidavit of discovery, finds a document which his opponent has a right to inspect, but which was not disclosed, to inform his opponent of it by supplementary affidavit or by notice.[300] If counsel becomes aware of a document which should have been disclosed, he must advise its disclosure and should return his brief if the advice is not taken.[301] In *Bula Ltd* v *Tara Mines (No 5)*[302] Murphy J, disagreeing with the White Book (1997) 24/1/2, confined that duty to documents overlooked which were in the party's possession at the time of giving the original discovery; but in *Vernon* v *Bosley (No 2)*[303] the English Court of Appeal has held that the duty extends to documents which have been created or acquired after the original discovery.

---

298 Unlike the Irish practice, see *Bula Ltd* v *Crowley* [1991] 1 IR 220.

299 *Roberts* v *Oppenheim* (1884) 26 Ch D 724.

300 *Mitchell* v *Darley Dale Colliery* (1884) Cab & Ell 214.

301 Bar Handbook 8-19.

302 [1994] 1 IR 487, at 493.

303 [1997] 1 All ER 614.

11.107 The assertion on oath that the deponent has discovered all relevant documents cannot be contradicted by replying affidavit.[304] If the applicant suspects that the list is not full and accurate, he has four possible remedies-

(1) to apply for discovery of a specific document or class under Order 24 rule 7 below;
(2) apply for inspection under Order 24 rule 12(2)(3) below;
(3) in the case of Schedule 1 Part 2 listed documents, ask the Court to inspect under Order 24 rule 15(2); or
(4) apply for 'further and better discovery'.

11.108 Further and better discovery may be given if the discovery given appears to be incomplete from a defect on its face or from the contents of the documents listed in it;[305] or from an admission by the respondent by letter or otherwise; [306] or where the deponent appears by omitting certain documents to have misconceived the nature of the case which he must make.[306] It will not be granted on mere suspicion that a document is in his possession.[307]

11.109 In exceptional circumstances, the Court may grant *ex parte* an order allowing the applicant to enter the respondent's premises to inspect documents.[308]

11.110 Whether or not discovery has already been given, a party may apply, on affidavit, for an order that the opponent state whether he has a specific document or class of documents, or has had it and what became of it (Ord.24 r.7).[309] The affidavit must depose to a belief in and show a prima facie case for possession etc. and relevance.[310] An order will be refused or deferred if the Court is of the opinion that it is not necessary for disposing fairly of the cause or saving costs (Ord.24 r.9). The respondent can comply by making an affidavit that he does not have the document or that he objects to production. The applicant can seek inspection under Order 24 rule 11.

11.111 A discovering party is not obliged to give further and better discovery of documents coming into existence after he has given his list of discovery. He may be ordered to give discovery under Order 24 rule 7 of a specific document created subsequently if (a) the document sought is specified; (b) there is proof of a special reason for its not being covered by privilege (documents created during proceedings being likely to be privileged); (c) the applicant cannot get a copy of it from another source; (d) the applicant shows that it has a specific relevance to the proceedings; (these conditions being not exhaustive).[311]

---

304 *Dunne* v *Johnson* (1901) 2 NIJR 23.

305 *Irish Agric* v *McCowan* (1913) 47 ILTR 20.

306 *British Association of Glass Bottle Manufacturers* v *Nettlefold* [1912] AC 709.

307 *Lysaght* v *Mullen* (1898) 32 ILTR 65.

308 *EMI* v *Pandit* [1975] 1 WLR 302.

309 Under Irish traditional practice application for discovery of a specific document could be made *ex parte: Henty* v *Beckett* [1914] 2 IR 206. This practice is now in disuse.

310 *Hermon* v *Yorkshire TV* [1992] NI 27.

311 *Bula Ltd* v *Tara Mines* (No 5) [1994] 1 IR 487, at 497-8 (SC). But see *Vernon* v *Bosley* (No 2) [1997] 1 All ER 614 (CA), para. 11.106.

Inspection of documents

11.112 A party can inspect the listed documents at the time and place specified in the discovery list (Ord.24 r.10). Also, a party may serve a notice requiring inspection of any document referred to[312] in the other party's pleadings or affidavits, whether discovery has been given or not (Ord.24 r.11), whether or not it has been claimed to be privileged,[313] and whether or not it is in the latter's possession, custody or power.[314] If the other party fails to allow inspection of his discovered documents, or fails to allow inspection under rule 10, or objects to inspection or offers an unreasonable time or place, the Court may order production to the party seeking inspection (Ord.24 r.12(1)). A party wishing to see a relevant document in the possession custody or power of the other party can apply, on affidavit deposing to that belief, for an order for inspection (Ord.24 r.12(2)(3)).

11.113 Grounds for the respondent objecting to inspection of a document are: (a) privilege; (b) that it is no longer in his possession, custody or power; (c) the right of possession arises in an office in which capacity he is not a party to the present litigation;[315] (d) irrelevance (which ground cannot be relied on if he has mentioned it in is pleading or affidavit); (e) that inspection not necessary to dispose of the proceedings or save costs; (f) a lien against the applicant.

11.114 A party entitled to inspect may elect to receive copies of discoverable documents rather than inspect the originals at a specified time and place. He can serve a notice to that effect undertaking to pay the cost (Ord.24 r.13). Where inspection of business books is sought the Court may order copies of the relevant parts, verified on oath, to be supplied (Ord.24 r.16). Nowadays the normal practice is for the discovering party to send, along with (or even instead of) his list of documents, photocopies of all documents which he does not object to producing. If there is any suspicion about tampering with the copies, or if (as often happens) the photocopy is 'cropped' or too feint to read, then the inspecting party should insist on inspecting the original. If it is suspected that the original is tampered with, or is a forgery, then inspection should be sought not under Order 24 but under Order 29 rule 2. In *Burke* v *Central TV*,[316] Finlay CJ rejected the suggestion that in exceptional circumstances disclosure might be limited to the applicant's lawyers, as such limitation would interfere with the lawyers' duty to represent their client.

11.115 The Court may at any stage order production to itself of any document in the possession, custody or power of a party relating to any matter in question (Ord.24 r.14), and may inspect a document in order to determine the validity of a claim of privilege or other objection to inspection (Ord.24 r.15(2)).[317] A summons for a rule 14 order should request the respondent to bring the

---

312 I.e. mentioned directly as a document: *Dubai Bank* v *Galaderi* (No 2) [1990] 2 All ER 738.

313 *Roberts* v *Oppenheim* (1884) 26 Ch D 724.

314 *Dubai Bank* v *Galaderi* (No 2) [1990] 2 All ER 738.

315 *Somers* v *Good* [1941] IR 345.

316 [1994] 2 ILRM 161, at 176; which case accords with *McIvor* v *SHSSB*, para. 11.136.

317 See *Seamar Holdings* v *Kupe Group* [1995] 2 NZLR 274 (CA).

document to the hearing of the summons. The party possessing the document can apply where he is in doubt as to his objection. The Court can make such orders of its own motion, as where it wishes to investigate an issue such as jurisdiction, illegality of contract, or public interest privilege. Discovery and inspection under Order 24 are subject to any rule of law preventing disclosure which would be injurious to the public interest (Ord.24 r.18). Note also that a judge in chambers has power to order the delivery up of any documents in the possession, custody or power of a solicitor.[318]

11.116 An order for production to a party or to the Court will be ordered only if it appears necessary either for disposal fairly of the proceedings or for saving costs (Ord.24 r.15(1)).[319] It is interesting to note that the onus has shifted: discovery is granted unless shown to be unnecessary (Ord.24 r.9) but inspection is refused unless shown to be necessary. Since there is an automatic right to inspect documents listed in discovery, one would have thought that Order 24 rule 15 can only apply where inspection is sought of a document not listed in discovery, or to which an objection to production has been stated. However, in *Ventouris* v *Mountain*,[320] the Court of Appeal said that an order for inspection is not automatic even in cases where a document has been listed as discoverable and not privileged. If a valid ground of public interest immunity is raised, the applicant bears the initial burden of showing that the document is not only relevant to the issues in the action but also likely to help to support his case.[321] Only after that can the Court consider the balance of the interests of justice against the public interest and decide whether to order production to the Court or to the applicant. If shown that the document is relevant and may be necessary (e.g. where it is statement about the material event in the action made soon after it) the Court should examine the document before refusing inspection.[322] The fact that a document may help the applicant's counsel to cross-examine the respondent's witnesses as to consistency does not make inspection necessary.[321]

Effect of discovery

11.117 Once a document has been inspected it is too late to claim privilege for it, unless procured by fraud or it is obvious to the opponent that privilege has been waived by mistake.[323] Counsel should refuse to make use of a document improperly obtained or inadvertently disclosed.[324] There is an implied duty of confidence that a party seeing the contents of a document disclosed under Order 24 will use the information only for the purposes of the action, which can be enforced by suing for breach of confidence.[325] In so far as the document is read

---

318 Solicitors (NI) Order 1976, Art.71C; under Ord.106 r.2.

319 A rule overlooked in *In re Hardy* [1988] 12 NIJB 66, at 71-2.

320 [1991] 1 WLR 607, at 622D and 623A.

321 *Lanigan* v *Chief Constable* [1991] NI 42.

322 *Wallace Smith Trust Co* v *Delloitte Haskins & Sells* [1996] 4 All ER 403 (CA). But the Court is not bound to inspect in all cases where valid public interest privilege is claimed: *O'Brien* v *Ireland* [1995] 1 IR 568.

323 *Guinness Peat* v *Fitzroy Robinson* [1987] 1 WLR 1027.

324 Bar Handbook 8-16.

325 *Haughey* v *Prendiville*, Ch D, NI (Sheil J), 17 December 1996.

or mentioned in open court it loses its confidentiality, unless the Court otherwise orders for special reason (Ord.24 r.17). The Court may relax the duty of confidence in exceptional circumstances.[326]

11.118 Any order under Order 24 may be revoked or varied by the Court at or before the trial (Ord.24 r.20).

Failure to comply

11.119 The old RSC (Wylie Ord.31 r.15) and the County Court Rules (NI) 1980 (Ord.15 r.2(2)) explicitly state that a party who has failed to comply with a notice to produce cannot put the document in evidence unless he satisfies the judge of a cause or excuse for not producing it. Privilege was not a good cause.[327] Though that rule has now gone, it is still the usual practice for the trial judge not to allow a party to rely on a document which he has not produced for inspection under Order 24.[328]

11.120 Any party who fails to comply with the rules or any order of the Court is liable to have his action dismissed or his defence struck out (Ord.24 r.19(1)). This power should be invoked either if the party is personally in deliberate default, or if it is necessary and if the applicant cannot have a fair trial because of the default.[329] Usually the Court will make an 'unless' order: that the action/defence stand as struck out if compliance is not made within a stated time. A party who fails to comply with a court order is liable to committal, on proof only that the court order was served on his solicitor, and a solicitor who fails to tell his client of the service of a court order is liable to committal (Ord.24 r.19(2)(3)(4)).

INTERROGATORIES

11.121 Order 26 provides for a form of 'discovery' of facts by way of interrogatories in any cause or matter: questions delivered in writing by one party to the other, to be answered on oath in writing. Where appropriate, the serving party should first serve a notice to admit a fact and serve the interrogatory if no admission is made.

11.122 A party may serve interrogatories once or twice without leave (Ord.26 rr.1(1),3(1)). In proceedings by or against the Crown the Crown may be required to answer interrogatories, saving the immunity for public interest.[330] Leave is always necessary for interrogatories against the Crown (Ord.26 r.3(3)). The interrogatory must relate to a matter in question between the parties, and it must be necessary for disposing fairly of the proceedings or for saving costs; so it is not proper merely because it would be permissible in oral cross-examination (Ord.26 r.1). The party served can apply for them to be varied or withdrawn (Ord.26 r.3(2)). Instead of or as well as serving directly, the interrogating party may apply for an order giving leave to serve

---

[326] *Crest Homes* v *Marks* [1987] AC 829.

[327] *Roberts* v *Oppenheim* (1884) 26 Ch D 724, at 732, 734-5.

[328] *Rafidain Bank* v *Agom Sugar* [1987] 1 WLR 1606, at 1612G, per Nourse LJ obiter.

[329] *Murphy* v *J.O'Donoghue Ltd* [1996] 1 IR 123 (SC); *Pereira* v *Beanlands* [1996] 3 All ER 528 (Ch D).

[330] Crown Proceedings Act, s.28.

interrogatories relating to any matter in question between them (Ord.26 r.1(2)), by a summons exhibiting the proposed questions (Ord.26 r.4(1)). An affidavit is not necessary.[331] A request for interrogatories sought when the action is ready for trial may be struck out if the respondent is prejudiced.[332] The Court will consider any offer by the respondent to give particulars or make admissions or produce documents (Ord.26 r.4(2)); so that an order for interrogatories to be answered may be refused as premature if made before the respondent has replied to a notice for particulars and given discovery.[333] Though interrogatories have been answered the Court can give leave to serve a further set.[334]

11.123 The interrogatory must be directed to facts which are relevant to prove or disprove the material issues in the case, must be capable of definite factual answer not opinion, and must be on a matter within the interrogated party's knowledge. It must relate to the liability of the defendant, not of someone else. It can relate to the issue of whether the court should extend or waive the limitation period, interrogating as to the date and source of the plaintiff's knowledge.[335] It can and should relate to the primary facts which are relevant to the material facts, rather than to inferred facts; and not to conjecture, opinion or law, nor to pure evidence like names of or credibility of witnesses.[336] In defamation, the defendant can be asked as to the sources of information which he published,[337] but not where he has pleaded the defences of fair comment or privilege (Ord.82 r.6).

11.124 An interrogatory is not necessary if it is directed to a fact which can be proved by a person who will be called at the trial as a witness anyway; nor if directed to a fact which is clearly disputed *bona fide*. It may relate to matters within the applicant's own knowledge, even if the burden of proof lies on him, as it may facilitate the proof of his case.[338] It may not ask about documents if the respondent has already given sufficient discovery; nor about the contents of a document,[338] except a document which the respondent has lost or parted with.[339] 'Fishing' is not allowed but the plaintiff may interrogate for the purpose of finding whether he has a good cause of action;[340] for example whether the defendant did or authorised the tort.[341] A question is permissible though it may criminate the respondent: he can claim privilege in his answer. If it is clearly designed to criminate and to shame the respondent if he claims privilege, it may

---

331 *Robinson* v *Chambers* [1946] NI 38.
332 *McClatchey* v *Reilly* [1960] NI 118.
333 *Dunnes Stores* v *Deramore Lamont* [1996] 9 BNIL 68 (Carswell LJ).
334 *Thompson* v *Wynne* (1867) IR 1 CL 600.
335 *McMullen* v *Harland & Wolff* [1985] NI 1.
336 *See Eastwood* v *Channel 5* [1992] 2 NIJB 45.
337 *Marriott* v *Chamberlain* (1886) 17 QBD 154.
338 *Cleland* v *Neill* [1951] NI 61.
339 *Davies* v *Dublin & Drogheda Rly* (1872) 6 ILTR 128.
340 *Acheson* v *Henry* (1871) IR 5 CL 496.
341 *Winder* v *Glover* (1909) 43 ILTR 259.

be disallowed.[342] It must not be prolix, unclear, scandalous, abusive, irrelevant or designed to intimidate the respondent into compromise.[343]

11.125 Interrogatories are sometimes allowed in road accident cases; for instance, where the applicant cannot remember because of his injuries.[344] The plaintiff cannot ask the defendant: "If your car did not hit the plaintiff, whose car did?"[345] In *Edgill* v *Cullen*[346] the following questions were allowed: is the defendant the owner of vehicle X; if yes, was vehicle X at a specified place at a specified time; was the defendant driving, and if not, who was the driver? The following were disallowed: was the driver a servant or agent of the owner; did vehicle X collide with the plaintiff?

11.126 The served interrogatories must state a time of at least 28 days for the answers, and if served on more than one party, on a body or on the Crown must state what officer or member is to be served (Ord.26 r.2(1); Crown Proceedings Act, s.28). The editor or reporter is not an officer or member of a publishing company.[347] The answer must be on affidavit (Ord.26 r.2(2)). If the respondent objects on ground of privilege he may so state in his answer (Ord.26 r.5(1)). He cannot object on ground of scandal or irrelevance. He answers clearly and unambiguously, or by "don't know"; or by saying that his source of knowledge is a privileged communication. He must answer on all information known to him, including hearsay, and on what appears from documents in his or his agents' possession or power. An officer answering for a corporation must inquire amongst other employees and agents. On the principle of *Vernon* v *Bosley (No 2)* (para. 3.02), it would appear that a party who has answered an interrogatory has a continuing duty up to the conclusion of the proceedings to tell the interrogating party where an answer, believed to be true when given, is now known to be false by reason of subsequent discoveries or change of circumstances.

11.127 If he answers insufficiently, the interrogator may ask for further particulars or seek an order of the Court for further answer by affidavit or oral examination (Ord.26 r.5(2)(3)). The test is sufficiency, not truth. A claim of privilege is conclusive unless shown by the rest of the answers or documents referred to, to be unfounded; or there is no reasonable ground for it.[348] If the party served fails to answer or to give a further answer the Court may make an appropriate order, and may dismiss his action or strike out his defence; a party who fails to comply with a court order is liable to committal, on proof only that the court order was served on his solicitor; and a solicitor who fails to tell his client of the service of a court order is liable to committal (Ord.26 r.6).

---

342 *Behan* v *Tickell* (1886) 20 ILTR 23.

343 *Swansey* v *Southwell* (1869) 3 ILT 118.

344 *Griebart* v *Morris* [1920] 1 KB 659.

345 Cf. *Hooton* v *Dalby* [1907] 2 KB 18, at 20 (remarks by way of analogy in a seduction case).

346 [1932] IR 734.

347 *Murray* v *Northern Whig* (1912) 46 ILTR 77.

348 *Bradley* v *Clayton* (1890) 26 LR Ir 405.

11.128 Statements made on oath in an answer to an interrogatory can be used in evidence against him, but are not formally binding admissions by him,[349] though obviously a party who tries to resile from an admission made on oath does so at his peril. Being on oath, it is submitted that an answer cannot be amended, and if a party finds that his answer is defective or factually incorrect, he should serve a further answer.[350] A party may put in evidence only some or parts of the answers but the Court can direct the whole to be put in (Ord.26 r.7). An answer expressed to be derived from information from others is evidence against the answering party unless he makes it clear that he disclaims any reliance on the truth of the information.[351] A party who puts in an answer adopts it as part of his case, but as with any other evidence may call conflicting evidence. In *C* v *C* [352] Latey J thought that an admission in one defendant's answer was evidence against a co-defendant, but there is Canadian authority to the contrary which is to be preferred.[353] Where a person who has answered interrogatories is called as a witness, his answers can be put to him in cross-examination.

11.129 Any order in relation to interrogatories can be revoked or varied by the Court at or before trial (Ord.26 r.8).

DISCOVERY AS A PRIMARY REMEDY

11.130 Discovery of documents and interrogatories under the RSC are not in themselves primary remedies. A party cannot bring an action or other proceeding for that purpose alone, except where the law confers that right as a substantive remedy.[354] Any person has a right, subject to qualification, to see private data stored in automatic form (such as computer records) relating to him (Data Protection Act 1984, s.21), and to manually held records of his medical treatment (Access to Health Records (NI) Order 1993).[355] Part III (Arts.6-14) of the Access to Personal Files and Medical Reports (NI) Order 1991 gives a right to see a medical report made on him since 25 December 1991 at the request of an insurance company or employer. Part II (Arts.3-5) of that Order, [*not yet in force*] gives a person a right to see manually held records about his Housing Executive tenancy and HSSB health and welfare records. An elector or ratepayer can inspect the minutes of a local council meeting.[356] A

---

[349] In *Clarke* v *Clarke* [1899] WN 130, Kekewich J remarked that an admission in an interrogatory was useful in limiting the issues to be tried. Presumably he was speaking of its practical rather than formal effect.

[350] See further para. 11.18.

[351] *Claibourne Industries* v *National Bank* (1989) 59 DLR 4th 533, at 543-5 (CA, Ont).

[352] [1973] 1 WLR 568.

[353] *Hartley* v *Saunders* (1962) 33 DLR 2d 638.

[354] See *Morris* v *Roe* (1836) 1 M & W 207 (150 ER 408); *In re Fitzgerald* [1925] 1 IR 39; White Book (1997) 24/1/6.

[355] Except information as to surrogate parenting: SR 1994/159. For procedure by originating summons, see SR 1994/158 and Order 96. The 1993 Order (and *semble*, the 1984 Act) applies fully where the person seeks the records for the purpose of a pending or proposed personal injury action by him: *Madden & Finnucane* v *Causeway Health Trust*, QBD, NI (Pringle J) 14 March 1997.

[356] Local Government Act (NI) 1972, s.121.

person can "file a bill" in any court for discovery of the name of the printer or publisher of any newspaper in order to claim for damages for defamation in that newspaper.[357] A beneficiary has a right to see accounts and documents held by his trustee.[358]

Joinder for discovery

11.131 A plaintiff can sue, or join as defendant, a person who has got 'mixed up' in the tortious conduct of others, whether knowingly or not, and without personal liability, for the purpose of obtaining discovery or interrogatories against him in order to reveal the real wrongdoer;[359] or a person who holds assets of the wrongdoer.[360]

Bankers' books

11.132 Under section 7 of the Bankers Books Evidence Act 1879 a party may apply for inspection and copies of entries in the books of a bank, Post Office or Building Society. The order may be made *ex parte*, but if inspection is sought of the bank account of a non-party notice should be given to the bank and to the person, and affidavit evidence must show that the entries are relevant to an issue and will be evidence for the applicant at the trial.[361] The person can oppose the order on grounds of irrelevance, or that the entries would be privileged in his own possession.[362] An order can be made under the Act for inspection of books held abroad.[363] Costs are in the Court's discretion and may be ordered against the bank if caused by its delay or default. The order is enforceable against the bank as if it were a party. The order must be served three days before compliance is due, unless otherwise ordered (s.7).

'Administration of Justice Act' discovery

11.133 The Administration of Justice Act 1970 confers on the High Court important powers beyond ordinary *inter partes* discovery. It is confined to proceedings on a "claim in respect of personal injuries or death". This has been interpreted widely, including a claim against a solicitor for negligence in the conduct of a personal injury claim.[364]

11.134 *Pre-action discovery (s.31).* On application of a person who appears likely to be a party to proceedings in which a claim in respect of personal injuries or death is made, the Court may order a person who appears likely to be a party to such proceedings and to be likely to have (had) relevant

---

357 Newspapers, Printers and Reading Room Repeals Act 1869, Sch.2. Presumably it would now be done by originating summons.

358 Wylie's *Irish Land Law* (2nd ed. 1986) paras. 10.051-10.052.

359 *Norwich Pharmacal* v *Commrs of Customs* [1974] AC 133; *Loose* v *Williamson* [1978] 1 WLR 639.

360 *Mercantile Group* v *Aiyela* [1994] QB 366, at 374-5.

361 *L'Amie* v *Wilson* [1907] 2 IR 130. *Staunton* v *Counihan* (1958) 92 ILTR 32 suggests that there is no need to give notice to the bank.

362 *Waterhouse* v *Barker* [1924] 2 KB 759.

363 White Book (1997) 38/13/2; *contra, Chemical Bank* v *McCormack* [1983] ILRM 350.

364 *Young* v *O'Neill* [1995] 3 BNIL 105 (Pringle J), following *Paterson* v *Chadwick* [1974] 1 WLR 890, which was doubted *obiter* in *Doone* v *McPartland* [1987] NI 119, at 123H.

documents in his possession, custody or power,[365] to disclose and produce them to the applicant (s.31). Obviously it is the potential plaintiff who applies under this section against the intended defendant. The defendant may resist inspection on any ground of privilege which he could claim as a party to existing proceedings (Ord.24 r.8(6)).

11.135 *Discovery against non-party (s.32(1)).* On application of a party to proceedings in which a claim in respect of personal injuries or death is made, the Court may order a non-party to those proceedings who is likely to have (had) relevant documents in his possession, custody or power, to disclose and produce them to the applicant (s.32(1)). *Semble*, it cannot be ordered against a non-party who is outside the jurisdiction, nor against a foreign State.[366] The applicant must adduce evidence which tends to show that the respondent has documents which are likely to contain material which may be relevant.[367] The usual application is by a defendant against a hospital authority for inspection of the plaintiff's records; in such case the Court orders disclosure to the defendant only after the documents have been first inspected by the plaintiff who may object to disclosure of such documents or parts thereof as would be privileged in the plaintiff's hands and to such as are irrelevant to the issues in the action.[368] In *Bell* v *NIHE*[367] Carswell J granted an order for the defendant to inspect the records to see if they reveal any inconsistency from the plaintiff's claim as to how the injury occurred. The respondent can resist inspection on any ground of privilege which he could raise if subpoenaed *duces tecum* as a witness (Ord.24 r.8(6)). In *Downey* v *Murray*[369] Carswell J refused an order to the defendant on the grounds of the plaintiff's objection that the document was subject to legal professional privilege in her hands and had been sent to the respondent in confidence (statement made to her solicitor for the action, copy sent to the police).

11.136 *Procedure.* Both sections 31 and 32 bind the Crown (s.35). An order cannot be made if injurious to the public interest (s.35). Application under section 31 is by originating summons (bearing a court fee of £35) served on the document-holder as defendant. Under section 32(1) it is by summons in Form 28A, to be served on the document-holder as respondent and on every party. It is supported by affidavit describing the documents sought, showing their relevance to a personal injury claim and their likely possession, and under section 31 stating why the parties are likely to be parties to a subsequent claim in the High Court for personal injuries; the order may be made conditional on security for costs; the documents may be inspected subject to any privilege which the defendant/respondent could claim (Ord.24 r.8). An order against a non-party should identify as clearly as possible the issue to which the

---

365 Including where the likelihood depends on what the documents reveal: *Dunning* v *United Liverpool Hospitals* [1973] 1 WLR 586.

366 *Fusco* v *O'Dea* [1994] 2 ILRM 389 (SC).

367 *Bell* v *NIHE* [1990] NI 119.

368 *Irwin* v *Donaghy*, QBD, NI, (Girvan J) 15 December 1995. A precedent of such an order, taken from the judgment in this case, appears in Appendix Two.

369 [1988] NI 600, at 602; and see *Lee* v *South West Thames HA* [1985] 1 WLR 845.

documents are relevant.[370] A section 32(1) order should be made if it is just to do so; the applicant need not show that sight of the documents is essential to preparing his case.[371] The Court may refuse or defer disclosure if satisfied that it is not necessary or not necessary for disposing fairly of proceedings or saving costs (Ord.24 r.9).[372] In the usual case, where the defendant seeks discovery of the plaintiff's medical records, disclosure of general health records unrelated to the injury claimed in the action or to a pre-existing medical condition that may be relevant to the prognosis is not necessary in the absence of some material suggesting another cause for his post-accident incapacity.[373] The respondent is entitled to his costs unless otherwise ordered (Ord.62 r.6(9)). An order under the 1970 Act must be for disclosure to the applicant and his solicitor; it cannot be confined to his medical adviser.[374] In exceptional circumstances, disclosure may be refused by the Court upon the respondent's undertaking to disclose the documents to a person other than the applicant.[374]

DISCLOSURE OF NAMES OF PARTNERS

11.137 Where partners sue or are sued, or an individual trader is sued, in the firm name, the Court may order the disclosure of the names of the partners, verified on oath or otherwise (Ord.81 r.2).

DISCLOSURE OF MEDICAL AND EXPERT EVIDENCE

11.138 Rules can be made under the Administration of Justice Act 1985 (s.64) for compelling a party who has been afforded a medical examination of another party to disclose its result; and for compelling a party to disclose the expert evidence on medical matters *and on other matters specified in rules* to be adduced at the trial; and for exclusion of undisclosed evidence. Unlike England, such rules have been confined to (a) medical matters, (b) maps, photographs, plans etc. and (c) from 9 January 1996, all expert evidence in actions in the Commercial List (see para. 18.29).

Medical examination

11.139 Under the inherent jurisdiction, the Court may stay an action involving a claim for personal injuries if the plaintiff refuses to allow himself to be medically examined by the defendant's medical expert. Presumably the defendant can later apply for dismissal for want of prosecution with costs if the plaintiff does not submit after a reasonable time (para. 11.197). The defendant must show that examination is necessary to prepare his case.[375] The usual conditions upon which the plaintiff can properly insist are: (a) that the

---

370 *Allied Irish Bank* v *Ernst & Whinney* [1993] 1 IR 375.

371 *O'Sullivan* v *Herdmans* [1987] 1 WLR 1047 (HL, NI), overruling NI case law.

372 It may still be that the applicant does not have to show that inspection is necessary under Ord.24 r.15, the predecessor of which was held not to apply in *O'Sullivan* v *Herdmans*; but McCollum J held, *obiter*, in *Neilly* v *Moypark Ltd*, QBD, NI, 20 October 1995, at p.6, that rule 15 does apply since the rules were amended in 1991.

373 *Neilly* v *Moypark Ltd*, QBD, NI, (McCollum J) 20 October 1995.

374 *McIvor* v *SHSSB* [1978] 1 WLR 757 (HL, NI). In England this has been overruled by statute (Supreme Court Act 1981, ss.33-4).

375 *Lane* v *Willis* [1972] 1 WLR 326; *Ross* v *Tower Upholstery* [1962] NI 3.

defendant pay his expenses in attending; (b) that the doctor should not give evidence of any statement by the plaintiff on issues of liability;[376] (c) that only the doctor be present. The defendant cannot be restricted in his choice of doctor.[377] Of course, in agreeing to a medical examination before proceedings commence, the plaintiff can impose such conditions as he wishes and can refuse outright. A defendant's counterclaim for personal injuries can be stayed pending medical examination.

11.140 The defendant must disclose any medical evidence resulting from the examination to the plaintiff within 10 weeks after close of pleadings or 21 days after receiving the report, and before the trial, or if received during the trial, immediately (Ord.25 rr.3, 5).

11.141 An action can be stayed until the plaintiff authorises a hospital authority to disclose to the defendant his treatment records and X-rays,[378] but this power is probably obsolete since the Administration of Justice Act 1970 (see para. 11.135).

11.142 The inherent jurisdiction has been invoked in other circumstances. In *Ross* v *Tower Upholstery*[379] there was a stay of contract action in which the plaintiff's health at a certain date was in issue. If the widow claiming in a fatal accidents action is on evidence thought to be suffering from an illness which may reduce her life expectancy, the action can be stayed till she is examined.[380] In *Herbinson* v *O'Neill*,[381] the defendant driver in a road accident claim pleaded that he had a "black-out"; he was debarred from defending until he submitted to a medical examination. In *Jackson* v *Mirror Group*,[382] where the plaintiff sued for defamatory words published about plastic surgery on his face, the action was stayed until he submitted to an examination.

Disclosure of medical reports

11.143 Order 25 applies to an action for damages for personal injuries or death, except a contested case of medical or surgical negligence (Ord.25 r.1). Medical evidence substantiating all the injuries alleged in the Statement of Claim must be served with it (Ord.25 r.2). A party must on demand give the names of the doctors and hospitals which gave treatment material to the action (Ord.25 r.7). A party must disclose any medical evidence resulting from a medical examination of another party (Ord.25 r.3). These provisions are regardless of whether such evidence is intended to be adduced at the trial; and non-compliance may result in the action being stayed or the defence being struck out (Ord.25 r.8). A party who proposes to adduce medical evidence at the trial must disclose it to the other parties within 10 weeks after close of pleadings or within 21 days of receiving it, and before the trial, or if received

---

376 The *McDowell* v *Strannix* condition: [1951] NI 57.

377 *Starr* v *NCB* [1977] 1 WLR 63. The plaintiff can object to the qualification or integrity of the doctor.

378 *Irvine* v *Freeland* [1967] NI 146; *O'Connor* v *McManus* [1969] NI 243, at 246.

379 [1962] NI 3.

380 *Lane* v *Willis* [1972] 1 WLR at 331-2, obiter.

381 [1985] 3 NIJB 84, and see *Lacey* v *Harrison* [1993] PIQR P10; [1993] CLY 3295.

382 'The Times', 29 March 1994 (CA).

during the trial, immediately (Ord.25 rr.4-5). Medical evidence cannot be adduced at the trial if its contents have not been thus disclosed, save by consent or by leave of court (Ord.25 r.6). In addition if Order 25 is not complied with, the defaulting party's action may be stayed or his defence struck out (Ord.25 r.8). Subject to the above rules, a party does not have to disclose a report which is not helpful to his case. If a party's evidence at the trial varies from that previously disclosed, the Court may adjourn the trial or make any order on terms as to costs or otherwise (Ord.25 r.10).

11.144 Under Order 25 disclosure of medical evidence means serving a copy of the signed doctor's report with any accompanying or supplemental documents from the doctor, including any surgical and radiological evidence and ancillary expert or technical evidence (Ord.25 rr.9(1),11). The whole report, including an accompanying note, must be served.[383] It must be drafted by the expert and its contents uninfluenced by the exigencies of the litigation.[384] Counsel must not draft the report but he may to a limited extent direct alterations to it, for example to exclude irrelevance.[385] On request the plaintiff must disclose the full medical history sent to the doctor on which his medical opinion was based.[386] *Quaere*, disclosure under Order 25 terminates the privilege in the report. *Quaere*, once a report has been served under Order 25 the opposing party is entitled to use it in evidence against the serving party.

11.145 A party obliged to disclose medical report may apply *ex parte* for leave to adduce the evidence without disclosure or to edit or amend the disclosed report (Ord.25 r.9(2)), as where the other party is suspected of fraud or misstatement of his injuries, or where disclosure might enable him deliberately to trim his evidence.[387] Note however the cases on disclosure of maps, films photographs etc. (para. 13.85), which state that non-disclosure should be exceptional.

REMITTAL TO COUNTY COURT

11.146 The transfer or 'remittal' of proceedings from the High Court to the county court is governed by the Judicature Act (s.31) and Order 78.[388] The county court jurisdiction was increased on 1st September 1993 and the ordinary jurisdiction in actions for debt or damages is now £15,000.

---

383 Cf. *Kenning* v *Eve Construction* [1989] 1 WLR 1189.

384 *Whitehouse* v *Jordan* [1981] 1 WLR 246.

385 Bar Handbook, 20.

386 *B* v *John Wyeth* [1992] 1 WLR 168.

387 *Naylor* v *Preston Area Health Authority* [1987] 1 WLR 958, at 968D, 976B.

388 This subject is dealt with in the author's *County Court Procedure in NI* (SLS 1985) Chap 3; and *Harper* v *Associated British Foods* [1991] NI 244.

REMOVAL FROM COUNTY COURT

11.147 The transfer or 'removal' of proceedings from the county court to the High Court is governed by the Judicature Act (s.31) and Order 78.[389] The Court cannot remove an action if its value is within the county court jurisdiction as it now is at the date of hearing the application.[390] On receipt of documents from the county court (under Order 22 rule 11 of the County Court Rules (NI) 1980) the proper officer files them, notes in the cause book and gives notice to all parties of the removal; the defendant must within 10 days enter an appearance under Order 12 and thereafter the proceedings continue as if begun by writ (Ord.78 r.9). Application for removal requires a new legal aid certificate.

PAYMENT INTO COURT

[References in this section to "CF Rules" are to the Court Funds Rules (NI) 1979]

'LODGMENTS'

11.148 'Lodgment' is the popular name for a payment into court under Order 22, by a defendant who wishes to offer settlement without admitting liability. It is not a defence and is kept secret until the judge considers it in ordering costs. It is not a contractual offer, but if accepted it effects a discontinuance of the action and a satisfaction of the claim without any finding of liability. Distinguish payment into court from a defence of tender before action (see para. 9.32) and payment into court by a defendant as condition of leave to defend (see para. 11.50). The defendant can treat the latter such payments as lodgments by a notice of appropriation, under the CF Rules, r.28.

11.149 At any time after appearance up to close of pleadings, the defendant may make payment into court (which contains an undertaking to pay costs to date) on a claim for debt or damages; thereafter only by leave or by consent (Ord.22 r.1(1)). He does so by presenting a request for lodgment at the Bank of Ireland, Belfast.[391] It is confined to a claim for debt or damages. It does not apply in an action for an account, nor a claim for return of goods;[392] nor an action for recovery of land;[393] nor an application under statutory jurisdiction.[394] In actions to which Order 25 applies (personal injury and death claims) the defendant, provided he has disclosed any medical evidence obtained by his examination of the plaintiff, may lodge up to 14 weeks after close of pleadings, or up to four weeks after the plaintiff has disclosed his medicals under Order 25 rule 4(a). A late lodgment, or increase, can be made only by consent or by

---

389 See further *County Court Procedure in NI* (SLS 1985) Chap 3; *McGuiness* v *Dunn* [1986] NI 81; *Crawford* v *James* [1988] 8 NIJB 19; *Dooley* v *Murdock Harwood*, QBD, NI (Girvan J) 4 June 1996.

390 *Brown* v *Hamilton* [1994] 1 BNIL 21.

391 CF Rules, r.18.

392 If the defendant returns the goods and the plaintiff proceeds for damages, a lodgment can be made: *Donnelly* v *Coyne* [1901] 2 IR 7.

393 *Lane* v *Lane* (1854) 4 ICLR 268.

394 *O'Neill* v *Ryanair* (No 2) [1992] 1 IR 160; *Director of Buildings* v *Shun Fung Ironworks* [1995] 2 AC 111 (PC).

leave.[395] A late lodgment for the purposes of a new trial was allowed in *Hanley* v *Randles (No 2)*.[396] The lodgment may be in respect of every or any cause of action on which the plaintiff claims.

11.150 The defendant must serve notice of it in Form 20 on the plaintiff and other defendants and the plaintiff must acknowledge receipt of the notice in three days (Ord.22 r.1(2)).[397] If there is more than one cause of action, the notice must specify that it is a total sum in respect of all the causes of action or state the causes in respect of which the lodgment is made; it should state how much money is lodged in respect of each and if not, the Court may order the notice to be amended to do so (Ord.22 r.1(4)(5)). In a death case, the claim for the estate and the claim for the dependants are treated as one cause of action (Ord.22 r.1(6)). Against co-plaintiffs, the defendant can make one payment in to cover both without apportionment, subject to the power of the Court to order a division if the plaintiffs are embarrassed.[398] Money paid in for a fatal accidents claim can be one sum without specifying the claimants' shares.[399] The money is deemed to be in satisfaction of the claims then pleaded, not of any added by later amendment.[400] If the defendant has counterclaimed for debt or damages, the lodgment is presumed to be in satisfaction of the plaintiff's claim alone, unless the notice states that the lodgment takes account of the value of his claim(s) (Ord.22 r.2). If the defendant has made an interim payment under Order 29 rules 11-20, the notice must state that the lodgment takes it into account (Ord.29 r.18).

11.151 The defendant may increase the amount paid in on notice, but only by leave if pleadings have closed;[401] and he may withdraw the lodgment by leave (Ord.22 r.1(3)). He may seek leave to withdraw the lodgment for good reason, for example in a fatal accident case when the widow dies.[402] In *Carey* v *Ryan*[403] the defendant's insurer got an order for repayment of a lodgment made on the mistaken assumption of liability to indemnify the defendant. Bankruptcy of the defendant is not a good ground.[404] Under Order 22 rule 3(4), the lodgment cannot be withdrawn once the plaintiff has accepted it. A defendant who has paid into court under Order 14 (see para. 11.50) may elect to appropriate it as a lodgment (Ord.22 r.8(2)), by notice of appropriation in Form 2 of the CF Rules (r.28 thereof).

---

395 *Ely* v *Dargan* [1967] IR 89 (where it was conditional on the defendant paying all costs to date).

396 [1960] Ir Jur R 67.

397 *Quaere* as to the effect of failure to give notice of the lodgment. In *Bettaney* v *Five Towns* (1971) 115 SJ 710, it was treated as valid because the plaintiff had actual knowledge of it.

398 *Walker* v *Turpin* [1994] 1 WLR 196.

399 Fatal Accidents (NI) Order 1977, Art.5(5).

400 *Tingay* v *Harris* [1967] 2 QB 327.

401 It seems that this rule requires leave to increase a lodgment already made even though in personal injury/death cases, the time limit for making an initial lodgment has not yet expired, thus apparently overruling *Gallagher* v *Young* [1939] NI 146.

402 *Goodman* v *Whyte* (1949) 83 ILTR 159.

403 [1982] IR 179.

404 *Sherratt* v *Bromley* [1985] QB 1038.

11.152 The lodgment is based on an educated guess as to the likely outcome of the trial and the various chances of the litigation. It should include an element for interest which may be awarded for the period up to the date of lodgment (Ord.22 r.1(7)). In a personal injuries case, the defendant may make a lodgment before he obtains a CRU certificate (see para. 14.66), in which case he must apply for the CRU certificate at once. If he has already received the CRU certificate he must deduct from the money lodged an amount equal to the CRU certificate and certify that he is deducting the amount of benefits paid to the plaintiff up to the date of lodgment, the deducted sum being treated as part of the lodgment (Ord. 22 r.1(2A)). In either case, he must pay the amount of the CRU certificate to the DHSS within 14 days after being notified that the money in court has been paid out to the plaintiff.[405] [*to be replaced by*: The effect of deductible CRU benefits on damages in a personal injury case will be provided for in regulations and rules of court under the Social Security (Recovery of Benefits) (NI) Order 1997 (Art.18).]

11.153 When faced with a lodgment the plaintiff's solicitor should consult with counsel and with the plaintiff and after advising him take written instructions from him as to whether to accept or refuse.

11.154 A plaintiff can make a lodgment against a counterclaim for debt and damages, and Order 22 applies, except that, it seems, the lodgment is taken to be in satisfaction of the counterclaim alone (Ord.22 r.6). *Semble*, a third party can make a lodgment against the defendant where the claim is for 'other relief' of a monetary nature, but it would be inappropriate where the defendant is seeking indemnity or contribution. As to investment of and interest in money in court, see Order 22 rule 12 and para. 11.171.

Acceptance of lodgment

11.155 Within 21 days of receipt of the notice (or the last notice) of the payment into court, and before the trial begins, the plaintiff may give notice of acceptance in Form 21 in satisfaction of the cause(s) on which the lodgment was made (Ord.22 r.3(1)), and if the action has been set down for trial, lodge a copy in the Listing Office (Ord.34 r.7(3)), and draw out the money from the Bank by producing a duly certified copy of the notice of acceptance in Form 6 (CF Rules, r.43(1)), or if legally aided, by request in Form 7 payable to his solicitor. If the plaintiff accepts, he is automatically entitled to his costs of the action up to the date of giving notice of acceptance (Ord.62 r.5(4)). Unless costs are agreed he may within six months lodge a bill of costs and sign judgment for the costs allowed on taxation (Ord.62 r.29(1)). The costs do not carry statutory interest from the date of acceptance.[406]

11.156 Save as follows, the plaintiff has an automatic right to take the money out (Ord.22 r.3(4)).[407] An order of the Court is always required where

---

405 Social Security Administration (NI) Act 1992, ss.79,89.

406 *Legal Aid Board* v *Russell* [1991] 2 AC 317 (a decision altered in England by a change in the Rules).

407 Unlike the old RSC where the Court could otherwise order: see Wylie Ord.22 r.6 and see *McCann* v *Belfast Corp* [1952] NI 49. *Semble*, where the plaintiff dies his personal

acceptance takes place after the start of the trial (Ord.22 r.4(3)). If the plaintiff is under disability, the acceptance must be approved by the Court (Ord.80 r.8), and no money can be paid out without an order (Ord.22 r.4(1); CF Rules, r.43(2)). The money must be dealt with under directions of the Court (Ord.80 r.10). In a death case, no money can be paid out without a court order unless there is only one person entitled to the damages (Ord.22 r.4(1), CF Rules, r.43(2)), and the order must apportion the money between the different causes of action and between the beneficiaries (Ord.80 r.12(1)). If any of the beneficiaries of the money is under disability, it must be approved by the Court and dealt with by directions under Order 80 rule 10.

11.157 The acceptance stays proceedings on that cause of action, against the lodging defendant, and against any co-defendant sued jointly or in the alternative (Ord.22 r.3(2)). If there is such a co-defendant the lodgment is paid out to the plaintiff only by order of the court, or on discontinuance against the co-defendant and with his consent (Ord.22 r.4(2), CF Rules, r.43(2).[408] The action can continue against a defendant who is liable on a different cause of action, though the plaintiff may get only judgment for costs if the money taken out of court has fully compensated him.[409] The action cannot continue against a defendant who is jointly, severally or alternatively liable on the same cause, save to seek judgment for costs against him.[409] Acceptance also stays any cause of action in which the same damage is alleged.[409] In a claim for interference with goods in which the plaintiff claims full title, acceptance effects an extinction of his title to the goods.[410] If the notice of payment in stated that the lodgment took account of the value of a counterclaim, the acceptance stays the counterclaim (Ord.22 r.3(3)),[411] and the defendant is automatically entitled to his costs of the counterclaim up to the date of receiving the notice of acceptance (Ord.62 r.5(6)). If on accepting the lodgment in satisfaction of one cause of action the plaintiff discontinues his other cause of action, he is entitled to his costs of the whole action (Ord.62 r.5(4)).[412] In a personal injury case, if accepted within 21 days the defendant must pay to the DHSS, within 14 days after being notified of the payment out to the plaintiff, a sum equal to the benefits paid to the plaintiff up to the date of the lodgment.[413] [*to be replaced by*: The effect of deductible CRU benefits on accepted lodgments in a personal injury case will be provided for in regulations and rules of court under the Social Security (Recovery of Benefits) (NI) Order 1997 (Art.18).] If acceptance is allowed after the trial has started, payment out must be by court order (CF Rules, r.43(2)(v)).

---

representative can accept the money lodged if the claim is one which survives to the estate: cf.*West* v *Morgan* (1988) 44 DLR 4th 381 (BC, CA).

[408] But see the special provisions as to defamation actions: para. 18.18.

[409] *Clark* v *Urquhart* [1930] AC 28; [1930] NI 4; especially *per* Lord Atkin.

[410] Tort (Interference with Goods) Act 1977, s.5.

[411] Where the defendant has pleaded a set-off (claim of defects in plaintiff's work), r. 3(3) does not apply and the acceptance of the lodgment does not satisfy the defendant's cause of action, so he can sue afresh for it: *Hoppe* v *Titman* [1996] 1 WLR 841 (CA). An amendment to the Rules is warranted to deal with this anomaly.

[412] *Hudson* v *Elmbridge BC* [1991] 1 WLR 880.

[413] Social Security Administration (NI) Act 1992, s.89.

11.158 The plaintiff may by leave make a late acceptance, applying under Order 3 rule 5 and Order 22 rule 5.[414] Leave should be refused if the chances of 'beating the lodgment' have reduced substantially since the time for acceptance.[415] If leave is given the plaintiff should pay costs since the lodgment.[416]

11.159 Leave to withdraw acceptance can be given, even after the money has been paid out.[417] The applicant must show good grounds.[418]

Lodgment not accepted

11.160 If not accepted under rule 3, the money remains in court. In the Queen's Bench Division, it is placed on deposit and interest on it goes to the Exchequer (CF Rules, r.54). It can be paid out in satisfaction of the plaintiff's claim, but only by order of the Court; during or after the trial the Court can order payment out as appropriate (Ord.22 r.5). The parties may of course settle upon a higher (or lower) award at any time, in which case the agreement will provide for an order that the money in court be paid out to the plaintiff in partial satisfaction, subject to approval where required. Otherwise the action will go to trial on all issues. The fact and amount of the lodgment must be kept secret from the trial judge (and jury) until the verdict on liability and quantum is given (Ord.22 r.7). If disclosed, the judge has a discretion to abort the trial and order the party responsible to pay costs thrown away, but only if substantial prejudice is shown, even in a jury trial.[419] The judge is then told of it and under Order 62 rule 9(b) he must take it into account in exercising his discretion as to costs. It is also kept secret at the hearing of an appeal, though no rule says so.

11.161 If the plaintiff wins and is awarded more than the lodgment he gets judgment with full costs and the money in court is paid out in partial satisfaction. The amount awarded is taken as that awarded by the Court regardless of the amount which the defendant will have to deduct and pay to the CRU (see para. 14.67). In deciding whether the plaintiff has 'beaten the lodgment' no account is taken of interest awarded for the period since the lodgment. If the plaintiff beats the lodgment by reason of an amendment to his pleadings raised after the lodgment, he should be ordered to pay costs since the lodgment.[420] If the plaintiff loses on liability, the defendant is awarded costs from the plaintiff and the money in court is paid out to him.

11.162 If the plaintiff wins but fails to beat the lodgment, the usual order is for the costs of the action to the date of lodgment to go to the plaintiff, the costs of

---

414 As in *Wilcox* v *McDonnell* (1913) 47 ILTR 169, where the plaintiff intended to accept within time but gave notice of discontinuance by mistake.

415 *Gaskins* v *British Aluminium* [1976] QB 524.

416 *Connolly* v *Crozier* (1924) 58 ILTR 171; *Wilcox* v *McDonnell*.

417 *Cohen* v *Downham* (1904) 5 NIJR 32.

418 *Kelly* v *Anglo-American Oil* (1907) 41 ILTR 243 (solicitor mistook client's wishes); *Doyle* v *Gaffney* (1923) 57 ILTR 156 (plaintiff discovered new evidence).

419 *Colgan* v *Rice* (1903) 37 ILTR 57.

420 *Cheeseman* v *Bowaters Ltd* [1971] 1 WLR 1773.

the action thereafter to go to the defendant.[421] Occasionally the judge might award costs after the lodgment solely referable to the issue of liability to the plaintiff.[422]

11.163 The Court may also order the costs to be set-off against each other; the balance of costs due to the defendant is paid out from the money in court, then the amount of the award less those costs is paid out to the plaintiff; the residue if any of money in court is paid to the defendant. Such a set-off might be ordered where the exact amount of the defendant's costs can be ascertained, as where the parties have agreed them. Such a set-off should always be ordered where the plaintiff is legally aided, because the LA Fund should bear the loss rather than the defendant (*Cook* v *Swinfen*).[423] Note that in the High Court, the onus is on the defendant to show why the money should remain in court until the costs are taxed.[424] Where a payment schedule directs that costs be taxed and paid out of funds in court the Taxing Master's certificate states the amount of the costs taxed, including the costs of the taxation proceedings, and the name and address of the payee, and is sent to the Accountant-General. (CF Rules, r.11).

11.164 A *Cook* v *Swinfen*-type order can be illustrated as follows (assuming no interest awarded and no CRU element)-

- Defendant lodged £30,000; plaintiff awarded £25,000
- Plaintiff's costs up to lodgment are £1,000; defendant's costs after lodgment are £5,000
- The order is: (£5,000-£1,000=) £4,000 paid out to the defendant; (£25,000-£4,000=) £21,000 paid out to plaintiff; residue of £5,000 paid out to defendant.

If the lodgment of £30,000 was in respect of one cause of action, and the plaintiff recovers at trial £30,000 on that and £10,000 on the other cause, he is awarded only such costs as the award of £10,000 carries.[425]

11.165 In a personal injury case, if the money is paid out to the plaintiff by order of court, by late acceptance or after judgment, or in any other way than after due acceptance within 21 days after notice of lodgment, the defendant must pay to the DHSS a sum equal to the benefits paid to the plaintiff up to the date on which the defendant is notified of the payment out to the plaintiff.[426] [*to be replaced by*: In personal injury cases, the situation as to deductible CRU benefits will be dealt with in regulations under the Social Security (Recovery of

---

421 *Hultquist* v *Universal Pattern* [1960] 2 QB 467.

422 As in *McMahon* v *Donaldson* [1969] NI 145 and *Harrison* v *Ennis* [1967] IR 286, cases where the award was brought below the lodgment by reason of deduction for contributory negligence.

423 [1967] 1 WLR 457.

424 White Book (1997) 22/5/5; *Maidment* v *Maxwell* [1938] NI 158.

425 *Myers* v *Phelan* (1890) 26 LR Ir 218. As to costs where the plaintiff succeeds on liability on appeal but fails to beat the lodgment: see *McDonnell* v *King* [1943] IR 1. Where one plaintiff beats his lodgment and the other plaintiff does not, see *Burns* v *Boland*, QBD, NI, 15 March 1968.

426 Social Security Administration (NI) Act 1992, s.89(5).

Benefits) (NI) Order 1997 (Art. 18).] If the award of the Court exceeds the lodgment the plainitff is entitled to full costs even if the amount actually received by him is less than the lodgment by reason of the deduction of those benefits.[427]

Special provisions for counterclaims

11.166 A defendant who has counterclaimed must state if it be the case that his lodgment is intended to satisfy his counterclaim (Ord.22 r.2), in which case acceptance by the plaintiff stays the counterclaim (Ord.22 r.3(3)), and the defendant is entitled to his costs incurred up to the date of the plaintiff's notice of acceptance (Ord.62 r.5(6)). A plaintiff may make a lodgment in respect of a counterclaim, and Order 22 rules 1-5 apply, save that the lodgment is deemed to be in satisfaction of the counterclaim alone and cannot take into account the value of the plaintiff's claim (Ord.22 r.6).

OFFERS ANALOGOUS TO LODGMENTS

11.167 In a claim for relief other than money such as injunction or specific performance, the defendant cannot lodge under Order 22, but he may make a '*Calderbank*' offer "without prejudice save as to costs" which can be brought to the trial judge's attention when he is considering costs.[428] If the judge awards an injunction or other remedy no greater than what was offered, he may order costs to the plaintiff up to the date of the offer, costs to the defendant from the date when the plaintiff could reasonably have accepted it. A *Calderbank* offer will not be taken into account against a monetary claim where the defendant could have made a lodgment.[429] In defamation an offer of amends can be made (see para. 18.20).

11.168 A third party or defendant liable for contribution may make a written offer to contribute to a specified extent to the plaintiff's damages (Ord.16 r.10), which the trial judge must take into account when deciding on costs between them (Ord.62 r.9(a)).

OTHER PROVISIONS FOR MONEY IN COURT

11.169 Various statutes and rules provide for payment of money into court, for example-

- As a lodgment under Ord.22 r.1 (see para. 11.148); for a minor under Ord.80 (see para. 3.08); under Ord.14 (see para. 11.50); as security for costs (see para. 11.56); to preserve subject-matter of dispute (see para. 11.81); in interpleader under Order 17; with a defence of tender (see para. 9.32); by a receiver under Ord.30 r.6; under the Libel Acts (see para. 18.19); the proceeds of sale of land under Ord.31 r.2(d); action to require trustee/personal representative to pay into court under Ord.85 r.2(3)(b).

---

[427] *McCaffery* v *Datta* [1997] 2 All ER 586 (CA); even though the sum lodged by the defendant was an exempt payment of £2,500. *Aliter,* where the award of the Court is £2,500 or less. See further para.14.67.

[428] *Cutts* v *Head* [1984] Ch 290.

[429] *Corby DC* v *Holst* [1985] 1 WLR 427. See further White Book (1997) 22 /1/6.

- Deasy's Act, s.64 (into High Ct); ss.63, 69 (into county court); Partition Act 1876, s.4; Judicature Act, s.94; Conveyancing Act 1881, s.69.
- Life Assurance Companies (Payment into Court) Act 1896, CF Rules, r.20; Banking Act 1987, s.26, Ord.92 rr.1,3A,4 (to Chancery Division).
- Tort (Interference with Goods) Act 1977, s.13 (bailee).
- Arbitration Act 1996, s.70(7) (payment in of award pending application to set it aside).
- Criminal Injuries (Compensation) (NI) Order 1988 and Criminal Damage (Compensation) (NI) Order 1977 (see para. 14.65).
- Trustees/personal representatives may pay money or securities into court (Trustee Act (NI) 1958, s.63; CF Rules, rr.20, 30; Ord.92 rr.2,4); applied to a debtor where the assignment of the chose in action is in dispute (Judicature Act, s.87). A liquidator is not a trustee for shareholders (*In re Belfast Empire* [1963] IR 41).

11.170 Under Chancery practice an accounting party can be ordered to pay money into court if he has been found liable to account and has admitted money in his hands;[430] and his solicitor can be ordered to pay in regardless of his lien for costs.[431]

Procedure

11.171 Payment into and out of court generally is governed by the Court Funds Rules (NI).[432] Lodgment under a court order is effected by the appropriate court officer making a Lodgment Schedule with a Payment Schedule directing the Accountant-General as to how to deal with the money (CF Rules, Pt I, rr.7-17). Except where paid in under Order 22, lodgment of funds is by direction of the Accountant-General (CF Rules, r.19). Lodgment in the Chancery Division (r.20) and in the Queen's Bench and Family Divisions (r.21) are by lodgment in the Court Funds Office or the Bank of Ireland (r.24). Effects and transferable securities are lodged by delivery to the Courts Funds Office (r.25). Any person claiming an interest in money in court may seek an account of it from the Accountant-General (CF Rules, rr.56-7). Cash in court may be invested (Ord.22 r.12) under the Judicature Act (ss.77-85). Subject to directions of the court, money is to be invested (Ord.22 r.12; CF Rules, rr.29-36). The Lord Chancellor may establish common investment funds for investing money in court (Administration of Justice Act 1982, s.42), and the dividend on shares so held is free of income tax (Income and Corporation Taxes Act 1988, s.328). For the purposes of the Taxation of Chargeable Gains Act 1992, funds invested in court are deemed to be vested in the person entitled to or interested in the funds (s.61 thereof). An order of a court vesting the right to Government stock in a person is binding on the bank.[433]

---

430 White Book (1997) 27/3/6.

431 *In re O'Kean* [1907] 1 IR 223.

432 SR 1979/105. Note that references therein to the Exhange Control Act 1947 are obsolete as it has been repealed. See Stop Press p.x.

433 Finance Act 1916, s.66.

Payment out

11.172 This is governed by the CF Rules, Part V (rr.37-50). Money paid into court under a court order can be paid out only by order (Ord.22 r.8(1)). If money is paid out by mistake or by a miscarriage, the Court can order repayment in.[434] Money paid into court under Order 22 rule 1 or under a court order is paid out to the party entitled or his solicitor, but only to his solicitor if he is or has been legally aided (Ord.22 r.9).

(Application for payment in the Chancery Division, see Order 92 rule 5. Where small sums of money in court are payable to the unrepresented estate of a deceased, not exceeding the sum currently prescribed under the Administration of Estates (Small Payments) Act (NI) 1967, the Court may order payment to the widow or closest relative (Ord.22 r.10). As to payment out to the personal representative where the person entitled has died, see CF Rules, r.41. Money can be ordered to be paid out to a personal representative under a grant abroad (*Smyth's Trusts* (1906) 40 ILTR 70); or the beneficiary (*McElhill* v *McElhill* (1938) 72 ILTR 14). Payment out where there has been a death, assignment etc., see CF r.42. And see *Ferguson* v *Ferguson* [1920] 1 IR 81, where an inquiry in chambers as to the persons entitled was ordered. Revenue duties due on money in court, see CF r.16. Payment of charity money to the Dept of Finance, see Charities Act (NI) 1964, s.8. Unclaimed funds, CF r.55.)

STAY OF PROCEEDINGS

11.173 "...A court, acting on equitable grounds, may stay any proceedings or the execution of any of its process subject to such conditions as it thinks fit." (Judicature Act, s.86(3)). The Court should impose a stay only if satisfied beyond reasonable doubt that the proceedings should not go on. Save as appears below the application must be brought in the court where the proceedings are pending. Part of an action, or a counterclaim may be stayed. Any person, whether or not a party, who before 1877 could apply to the Court of Chancery to restrain an action in another court can apply for a stay;[435] but only if the action amounts to a fraud on him by the plaintiff. In *Moore* v *Hughes*[436] a mortgagee intervened to stay the mortgagor's action. A stayed action is still a 'pending proceeding'.[437] The stay can be removed on good grounds.

Grounds for stay (not exhaustive)

11.174 An action, claim, counterclaim, proceeding or interlocutory proceeding, as the case may be, can be stayed. The grounds for such stay include -

(1) Any ground on which an action may be struck out as an abuse of process (see para. 11.181).

[434] *In re Persse* [1912] 1 IR 18.
[435] Supreme Court of Judicature (Ir) Act 1877, s.27(5) (repealed but the practice continues);
[436] (1906) 40 ILTR 139.
[437] *McCabe* v *Joynt* [1901] 2 IR 115, at 129.

(2) The action is bound to fail.[438]
(3) The defendant (domiciled in Great Britain or a Brussels Convention State) has not been served in time to defend.[439]
(4) The plaintiff is dead or defunct or non-existent or has not authorised the action.
(5) The solicitor named on the writ has not issued it (Ord.6 r.4(4)).
(6) The plaintiff is a nominal party put up to protect the real claimant from risk of costs.[440]
(7) *Semble*, the plaintiff is a vexatious litigant under section 32 of the Judicature Act who has not been given leave to sue.
(8) The costs of a previous discontinued action on the same cause have not been paid (Ord.21 r.5).
(9) The plaintiff has not paid the costs ordered against him on adjournment of the trial.[441]
(10) The plaintiff has not paid the costs of an action dismissed without prejudice in the county court.[442]
(11) The applicant has not paid the costs, or paid into court an estimate of the costs not yet taxed, of a previous application for the same interlocutory relief.[443]
(12) The plaintiff is in contempt of an order made in the same cause.[444]
(13) Pending trial of a 'test' action (Ord 4 r.5).
(14) The same point is substantially *res judicata* between the same parties.[445]
(15) There has been a compromise or release before proceedings commenced.[446]
(16) The action is in breach of good faith;[447] or in breach of an undertaking not to sue.[448]
(17) In defamation action, an offer of amends has been accepted (para. 18.20).
(18) By consent of the parties, on terms agreed (see para. 12.09).
(19) For medical examination (see para. 11.139).
(20) Where the defendant interpleads (Ord.17 r.4).

---

438 *Barry* v *Buckley* [1981] IR 306, e.g. where the Statement of Claim reveals a good cause of action and also an unbeatable defence, or the already agreed facts mean that it must fail. In *Sparks* v *Holland* [1997] 1 WLR 143, Sedley J stayed an action because of an unanswerable limitation defence; he did not dismiss the action altogether as there is a possibility that Parliament may change the law to remove the limitation defence retrospectively.

439 Civil Jurisdiction and Judgments Act 1982, Sch.1 Art.20; Sch.4 Art.20.

440 *Sheehy* v *Dorman* (1824) 2 Fox & Sm 238, stayed till the plaintiff gives security for costs.

441 *McCombe* v *Simmons* (1879) 4 LR Ir 527.

442 *Tormey* v *Tormey* (1894) 28 ILTR 48.

443 *Thames Investment* v *Benjamin* [1984] 1 WLR 1381.

444 *Bettinson* v *Bettinson* [1965] Ch 465.

445 *Blair* v *Crawford* [1906] 1 IR 578; *Gordon* v *Kirwan* (1889) 24 LR Ir 245.

446 *Braun* v *Johnston* (1901) 35 ILTR 55.

447 *Breen* v *Cooper* (1870) 4 ILT 65.

448 *Kelly* v *Falls* (1867) 1 ILT 702 (undertaking embodied in court order).

(21) The High Court may stay an action for a debt which is subject of an administration order by the EJ Office.[449]
(22) Stay under the Arbitration Act (see para. 7.16).

11.175 *Forum non conveniens.* Proceedings can be stayed if the defendant shows that justice can be done better in a foreign court, having regard to convenience expense and the interests of the parties;[450] or if the parties have contracted for the dispute to be heard in a foreign court;[451] or to be heard by any particular mode of resolution.[452] If two defendants have been sued on one cause of action and one only applies for a stay, the undesirability of separate actions in different countries is a strong factor against the stay.[453] This power is subject to the express provisions of the Brussels Convention, so that the doctrine cannot override the jurisdiction of a Convention State,[454] nor the jurisdiction of a state under any international convention,[455] but it can be used to override the jurisdiction of a part of the United Kingdom.[456]

11.176 *Lis alibi pendens.* An action may be stayed if there are pending proceedings elsewhere on the same issues and cause of action.[457] If a plaintiff sues both here and abroad, the court here can stay the action if (a) justice can be done abroad more conveniently, (b) the parties are amenable to its jurisdiction, and (c) the plaintiff will not lose any personal or juridical advantage.[458] Instead, the Court may restrain the foreign action on the same three criteria[459] or put the plaintiff to election between the two. If a prior related action is pending in a Brussels Convention State, the Court may stay or dismiss the action here.[460] If two persons have brought fatal accident actions relating to one deceased, the first commenced will be allowed to proceed unless irregular

---

449 Judgments Enforcement (NI) Order 1981, Art.84(4).

450 *Spiliada* v *Cansulex* [1987] AC 460; *Macrete* v *GRE* [1988] NI 332. Availability of legal aid is irrelevant: *Connelly* v *RTZ Corp* [1996] QB 361 (CA) (see Stop Press p.x).

451 *Buchanan* v *Brook Walker* [1988] NI 116.

452 *Channel Group* v *Balfour Beatty* [1993] AC 334.

453 *Turkington* v *St Oswald* [1996] 6 BNIL 79 (Carswell LJ).

454 Civil Jurisdiction and Judgments Act 1982, s.49.

455 *Milor S.r.l.* v *British Airways* [1996] QB 702 (CA).

456 Because Sch.4 to the 1982 Act is subject to the principles *forum non conveniens* and *lis alibi pendens: Walker* v *BMW* [1990] 6 NIJB 1; *Adair Smith Motors* v *Nissan Motor* [1993] 11 NIJB 18 (Carswell J, reversed on another point by the CA).

457 As to stay of a matrimonial cause: see Matrimonial Causes (NI) Order 1978, Sch.1 and FP Rules, r.2.29; of a probate action: *Montgomery* v *Bellew* (1903) 37 ILTR 241; of minor's custody proceedings: Child Abduction and Custody Act 1985, s.20; Sch.1 Art.16; Family Law Act 1986, s.22.

458 *Castanho* v *Brown & Root* [1981] AC 557, at 575B.

459 *Ibid,* at 574D.

460 In the Civil Jurisdiction and Judgments Act 1982, Sch.1 Arts.21-3. See *MV 'Turquoise Bleu'* [1995] 3 IR 437.

or *mala fide*.[461] There is no rule that an action, whether by or against the alleged offender, should be stayed because of a pending criminal prosecution.[462]

Staying proceedings in another court

11.177 A Division of the High Court cannot stay proceedings pending in any other Division or in the Court of Appeal (Judicature Act, s.86(4)). However it can by injunction restrain *commencement* of proceedings in any court, and can restrain *continuation* of pending proceedings in any inferior court or any court outside Northern Ireland. A county court action should not be stayed merely because the same issues between the same parties are the subject of a pending High Court action.[463] Proceedings in a foreign court may be stayed by injunction if they are vexatious or oppressive and if the stay will not unjustly deprive the person suing abroad of an advantage;[464] or if brought in breach of an agreement.[465]

STRIKING OUT PLEADINGS AND PROCEEDINGS

11.178 The High Court has inherent jurisdiction to remove from its records any material improperly placed thereon;[466] and to strike out proceedings as an abuse of process. The Court may at any stage strike out or amend any pleading or writ indorsement, originating summons or petition (or any passages therein) on any of these grounds -

(a) it discloses no reasonable cause of action/defence;
(b) it is scandalous, frivolous or vexatious;
(c) it may prejudice, embarrass or delay a fair trial;
(d) it is otherwise an abuse of process;

and may stay or dismiss or enter judgment accordingly (Ord.18 r.19).

11.179 Ground (a) must be determined on the face of the pleading without evidence (Ord.18 r.19(2)), and the cause pleaded must be unarguable or almost uncontestably bad.[467] Under the inherent jurisdiction and grounds (b)-(d), evidence by affidavit or otherwise is admissible; the Court can explore the facts fully, but should do so with caution.[468] A pleading will not be struck out merely for technical defect; nor on evidence that it is untrue.[469] In *Keefe* v *McCue*[470]

---

[461] *Merrigan* v *Clark* [1939] Ir Jur R 63.

[462] *Carroll* v *Masterson* (1905) 39 ILTR 211; *Dillon* v *Dunnes Stores* [1966] IR 397; *O'Keeffe* v *Ferris* [1993] 3 IR 165. Such rule does exist in South Africa: *Gwenzi* v *Cebekhula* 1996 (1) SA 525

[463] *Murphy* v *Hennessy* [1984] IR 378; *Wimpress* v *Scott* [1985] 6 BNIL 99.

[464] *Société Aerospatiale* v *Lee Kui Jak* [1987] AC 871. The principle applies whether it is alleged that the local courts or courts of some other state are the proper forum: *Airbus Industrie* v *Patel*, 'The Times', 12 August 1996 (CA).

[465] *Lett* v *Lett* [1906] 1 IR 618.

[466] *Nixon* v *Loundes* [1909] 2 IR 1.

[467] *Lonrho* v *Fayed* [1992] 1 AC 448; *Conlon* v *Times Newspapers* [1995] 2 ILRM 76 (Murphy J).

[468] *Mulgrew* v *O'Brien* [1953] NI 10, at 14.

[469] *Hildige* v *O'Farrell* (1881) 8 LR Ir 158 (where it was set aside for ambiguity of denial).

[470] (1840) 2 Cr & Dix CC 69.

Doherty CJ on an appeal struck out the civil bill for no cause of action but directed the order not to take effect if at the next assizes counsel showed a precedent. Claims and defences in the alternative are proper. Inconsistent claims are embarrassing, but inconsistent defences are not.

11.180 Examples of pleas struck out as scandalous, embarrassing are -

(1) defendant admits liability but has no means to pay (*Connor* v *Kelly* [1957] Ir Jur Rep 41),
(2) defendant alleging his own medical condition but refusing to allow examination by plaintiff's doctor (see para. 11.142),
(3) plea that the writ was irregularly served (*Maher* v *Hibernian Development* (1906) 36 ILTR 212),
(4) plea that the opposing party is of bad character (*Devonsher* v *Ryall* (1877) IR 11 Eq 460),
(5) unintelligible pleading (*Mulgrew* v *O'Brien* [1953] NI 10, at 22-3),
(6) amount claimed is too trivial (*Hannay* v *Graham* (1883) 12 LR Ir 413) where a general minimum of £2 was set for High Court actions, which would now be about £200,
(7) ambiguity (*Franklin* v *Walker* (1870) IR 4 CL 236),
(8) stating conclusions of law without facts (*Potts* v *Plunkett* (1858) 9 ICLR 290, at 300),
(9) mixing together separate claims (*Hoban* v *McPherson* (1905) 39 ILTR 15).

Rather than strike out a pleading the Court may cure it by amendment, or allowing the party to amend,[471] or by ordering further and better particulars.[472]

Striking out an action

11.181 An action may be struck out or stayed as an abuse of process if its real purpose is some other than satisfying the plaintiff's civil right;[473] or if commenced with no intention of bringing it to a conclusion;[474] or if it will relitigate an issue already decided substantially against the plaintiff in previous litigation.[475] It can be an abuse of process for a defendant to relitigate a finding of liability against him in an action by a different party;[476] and for a plaintiff to relitigate a finding of non-liability in an action against a different party.[477] In *Hunter* v *Chief Constable*[473] (the "Birmingham Six" civil action for assault by prison officers) it was said that the plaintiffs were trying to reopen and challenge the admissibility of the confessions and the findings of guilt against them in a criminal trial, and to mount a collateral attack on the final decision of a competent court in which they had full opportunity to make their case.[478] An

471 *Nicholson* v *Armstrong*, QBD, NI (Carswell LJ) 2 May 1996.
472 *Curran* v *Micheals* (1880) 14 ILTR 30; *Sun Fat Chan* v *Osseous* [1992] 1 IR 425, at 428.
473 *Hunter* v *Chief Constable* [1982] AC 529.
474 *Grovit* v *Doctor* [1997] 1 WLR 640, at 647G (HL).
475 *Stephenson* v *Garnett* [1898] 1 QB 677.
476 *North West Water* v *Binnie* [1990] 3 All ER 547.
477 *Palmer* v *Durnford* [1992] 1 QB 483.
478 At p.541B. See also *Pringle* v *Ireland* [1994] 1 ILRM 467.

action was stayed as being an attack on the decision to rule the plaintiff's confession admissible in a criminal trial, even though the jury had acquitted[479] or the Court of Appeal had quashed the conviction on other grounds,[480] and the action was thus not an collateral attack on a conviction. It is not necessarily an abuse of process to relitigate a finding made in favour of the accused in a criminal trial.[481] It is not an abuse where a plaintiff was a mere witness in the criminal trial whose evidence was not believed.[482]

In defamation actions, the claim can be dismissed summarily if it has no realistic prospect of success (para.18.22a).

11.182 If a previous action was dismissed for procedural default, a second action on the same cause can be struck out unless the plaintiff explains his fault.[483] If a claim relates to the operation of the implied equality clause in an employment contract, it may be struck out and/or referred to an industrial tribunal.[484] *Quaere*, whether an action can be struck out on the ground that it cannot succeed.[485]

11.183 If an action has been stayed, a new action on the same cause is an abuse of process: the proper course for the claimant is to make an application in the first action for a removal of the stay.[486]

DISMISSAL FOR WANT OF PROSECUTION

11.184 Both the inherent jurisdiction and the RSC provide for the court to deal with a cause or matter that has 'gone to sleep'. The defendant can apply to the Court for dismissal of an action for want of prosecution under the following rules-

(1) at least two years elapsed since the last proceeding (Ord.3 r.6(2));
(2) failure after notice to serve the writ (Ord.12 r.8A);
(3) failure to serve Statement of Claim on him (Ord.19 r.1);
(4) failing to comply with an order for discovery (Ord.24 r.19); or interrogatories (Ord.26 r.6);
(5) failing to set down for trial (Ord.34 r.2);
(6) failing to indicate readiness for trial (Ord.34 r.6);
(7) failure to appear at the trial (Ord.35 r.1).

Inherent jurisdiction

11.185 The Court has an inherent jurisdiction[487] to dismiss for want of prosecution: (a) where the delay is intentional and contumelious;[488] or (b) where

---

479 *Weeks* v *Chief Constable*, CA, NI, [1997] 3 BNIL 105.

480 *Mitchell* v *Chief Constable* [1992] NI 35 (CA). And see *Smith* v *Linskills* [1996] 1 WLR 763 (action for negligence against accused's solicitor struck out).

481 *Hunter* at p.543A; though such a plea was struck out in *Breathnach* v *Ireland (No 2)* [1993] 2 IR 448.

482 *Brady* v *Chief Constable* [1988] NI 32.

483 *Janov* v *Morris* [1981] 1 WLR 1389.

484 Equal Pay Act (NI)1970, s.2(3).

485 *Sun Fat Chan* v *Osseous* [1992] 1 IR 425, at 428.

486 *Buckland* v *Palmer* [1984] 1 WLR 1109.

the delay is inordinate, inexcusable and seriously prejudicial to the defendant.[489] The defendant bears the onus of proving the ground. The inherent jurisdiction can be exercised by the Court of its own motion. It can be invoked without recourse to any of the above rules.[490] In Northern Ireland, it is rarely invoked outside those rules.

Delay

11.186 Ground (b) requires proof of very lengthy delay since the issue of the writ for which the plaintiff or his lawyers are responsible; delay within the limitation period before issue of writ cannot be inordinate.[491] But the total delay from the accrual of the cause of action will be considered where the plaintiff has asked or will ask to disapply the limitation period. The plaintiff can be held responsible to defendant X for delay caused by failing to press defendant Y to enter an appearance or serve a Defence;[492] but of course defendant Y cannot rely on that. Post-writ delay is worse if the pre-writ delay is marked.[492] A comparatively short delay in taking a step is made more serious by previous delay in the action.[493] Even where the delay is not yet inordinate, the Court should readily consider making an 'unless order' requiring the plaintiff to proceed within a specified time.[494]

11.187 Inordinate delay is presumed to be inexcusable. Delay in awaiting an EC ruling in a similar case is excusable.[495] Difficulty is assembling a good case on liability is not an excuse.[496] Complexity of the action, priority given to unrelated litigation and internal disruption in the plaintiff corporation were rejected as excuses in *DHSS* v *Derry Construction*.[492] Delay by counsel is not an excuse, as the solicitor can dismiss him and retain another.[497]

Prejudice

11.188 Where there has been inordinate delay prejudice can be inferred, but not presumed,[498] and there must be specific evidence from which prejudice can be proved or inferred.[499] The defendant need not expressly aver it.[500] The overall delay[501] must be prejudicial to the defendant and the post-writ delay must have

---

487 White Book (1997) 25/1/4. See previous page.

488 *Wallersteiner* v *Moir* [1974] 1 WLR 991 ("gagging" libel writ). See previous page.

489 *Boyd* v *Sinnamon* [1974] June NIJB.

490 *NIHE* v *Wimpey* [1989] NI 395; *Braithwaite* v *Anley* [1990] NI 63; but see *Bannon* v *Craigavon DC* [1984] NI 387, at 391C.

491 *Birkett* v *James* [1978] AC 297.

492 *DHSS* v *Derry Construction* [1980] NI 187, at 194A.

493 *O'Reilly* v *CIE* [1973] IR 278, at 285.

494 *Grovit* v *Doctor* [1997] 1 WLR 640, at 644F (HL).

495 *Aero Zipp* v *YKK* [1978] 2 CMLR 88 (Ch D, Eng).

496 *Moore* v *Adair*, CA, NI, 9 February 1996.

497 *Sterling* v *Cohen* [1987] NI 409, at 413D; *Thorpe* v *Alexander Fork Lift* [1975] 1 WLR 1459.

498 *Houston* v *Corry* [1972] April NIJB at 5; *Boyd* v *Sinnamon* [1974] June NIJB.

499 *Shtun* v *Zaljejska* [1996] 3 All ER 411 (CA); *Purcell* v *Uprichard*, CA, NI, 6 March 1997.

500 *Allen* v *Redland Tile* [1973] NI 75.

501 I.e., the delay from the date of incident or transaction sued upon till the probable date of trial: *Moore* v *Adair*, CA, NI, 9 February 1996, at p.7.

caused more than minimal prejudice.[492] Prejudice in contesting the action can arise from the difficulty in recollection for witnesses even if the defendant has statements made by them at the time.[502] Obviously there is more prejudice if the action concerns oral transactions.[503] Death or disappearance of a witness is not prejudicial if he disappeared before the action might properly have come to trial;[504] nor if the plaintiff has traced him.[505] Prejudice may also consist in harm to the defendant's business, and in exceptional cases only the anxiety, of awaiting major litigation.[506] Prejudice can be that the defendant is not covered by insurance where he would have been if the plaintiff has shown reasonable expedition.[507] A defendant cannot complain of prejudice which he has brought on himself, for example, by failing to inspect or disposing of the machine or his records after being notified of the plaintiff's possible claim.[508]

11.189 *Delay during the limitation period.* Delay during the currency of the limitation period is not inordinate. The defendant must show more than minimal prejudice arising since the expiry of the limitation period;[509] but the former delay can be added to the consideration if there is delay thereafter.[510] If the limitation period has definitely not yet expired, the Court will regard dismissal of the action as pointless.[511] In *McCluskey* v *Colas*[512] the whole action was dismissed where one cause of action was statute-barred though other causes were not. Even if the limitation period is still alive, an action may be dismissed if it is alive only by reason of an extended limitation period, or if the plaintiff's delay is deliberate, or if a previous action by him on the same cause was dismissed for default in prosecuting it.

Discretion

11.190 Where all the necessary factors are present, inordinate inexcusable delay and prejudice to the defendant, the Court then exercises its discretion by assessing whether the balance of justice lies in dismissal or allowing the action to proceed.[513] Conduct by the defendant which induces the plaintiff to pursue the action and incur further costs.[514] is not a total bar to dismissal of the action:

---

[502] *Houston* v *Corry* [1972] April NIJB, at 4; but see *Morrisey* v *Kelly* (1972) 106 ILTR 9. A contemporaneous statement may not be detailed enough to obviate prejudice: *George* v *Camarthenshire CC* (1975) 119 SJ 407. In *Morrissey* v *Kelly* the dismissal was refused upon condition that the plaintiff undertake to allow the defendant to put in evidence all relevant witness statements.

[503] *NIHE* v *Wimpey* [1989] NI 395; *Braithwaite* v *Anley* [1990] NI 63.

[504] *NIHE* v *Wimpey* at 405; *O'Reilly* v *CIE* [1973] IR 278 at 282-3.

[505] *Dowd* v *Kerry CC* [1970] IR 27.

[506] *Dept of Transport* v *Chris Smaller* [1989] AC 1197, at 1209H.

[507] *Antcliffe* v *Gloucester Health Authority* [1992] 1 WLR 1044.

[508] *Sterling* v *Cohen* [1987] NI 409, at 413-4.

[509] *Neill* v *Corbett* [1992] NI 251, at 256c.

[510] *Rath* v *CS Lawrence* [1991] 1 WLR 399; *Braithwaite* v *Anley* [1990] NI 63.

[511] *Birkett* v *James* [1978] AC 297.

[512] [1994] 4 BNIL 69.

[513] *Rainsford* v *Limerick Corp* [1995] 2 ILRM 561 (Finlay P).

[514] Such as asking for discovery: *NIHE* v *Wimpey* [1989] NI 395.

it is a discretionary factor.[515] If there is subsequent further delay he can rely on the total delay.[516] He can rely on delay induced by a co-defendant.[516] Mere inaction by the defendant cannot amount to waiver or acquiescence in delay;[517] nor can his conduct in taking prudent steps to prepare a defence or maintaining the courtesy of replying to letters from the plaintiff's solicitor.[518] Where delay was inordinate and inexcusable, and the parties were at an impasse as to whether the plaintiff should reply to a Notice for Particulars before service of the Defence; in that situation, Pringle J held it unfair to dismiss the action because it would be sharp practice for the plaintiff to enter judgment in default of Defence.[519]

11.191 Dismissal will be given even though the delay is solely the fault of the plaintiff's solicitor or counsel;[520] whether or not there is a remedy against them. Dismissal may be refused where the plaintiff is wholly blameless, for example being a minor.[521] The plaintiff is to some extent vicariously liable for the fault of his lawyers, but the degree of his personal default is a factor in the discretion.[522] The Court will lean against dismissal if the trial is imminent, but will lean towards it if the plaintiff has emigrated, disappeared or shown no interest in his claim.[523] It is usually too late to dismiss if the action is now ready for trial.[524] Dismissal will be refused if there is another pending action between the parties on the same cause;[525] but the plaintiff must show that that action will not be dismissed for abuse or delay.[526]

11.192 If the limitation period has not yet expired or the delay is not yet inordinate or the defendant not yet seriously prejudiced, the Court may make an 'unless order', that is, order dismissal to take effect only if the plaintiff defaults on further steps in the action in time limits set by the Court. For instance in *Hughes* v *Hughes*[527] the master had ordered the plaintiff to serve the Statement of Claim by a set date; the plaintiff applied for an extension of time which Carswell J in his discretion refused.

---

515 *Roebuck* v *Mungovin* [1994] 2 AC 224.

516 *DHSS* v *Derry Construction* [1980] NI 187, at 203A.

517 *Allen* v *Sir Alfred McAlpine* [1968] 2 QB 229, at 260,272; *Moore* v *Adair*, CA, NI, 9 February 1996; but there is contrary Irish authority: *Hogan* v *Jones* [1994] 1 ILRM 512; *Rainsford* v *Limerick Corp* [1995] 2 ILRM 561. The defendant is in a better position if he has sent occasional reminders and warning letters.

518 *Moore* v *Adair*, CA, NI, 9 February 1996.

519 *Deery* v *Frazer*, QBD, NI, 6 December 1996.

520 *Boyd* v *Sinnamon* [1974] June NIJB.

521 *O'Reilly* v *CIE* [1973] IR 278. In any case, if the plaintiff is a minor the limitation period will not yet have expired.

522 *Hogan* v *Jones* [1994] 1 ILRM 512, at 516; *Rainsford* v *Limerick Corp* [1995] 2 ILRM 561.

523 *Houston* v *Corry* [1972] April NIJB at 6.

524 *NIHE* v *Wimpey* [1989] NI 395, at 407E.

525 *British Lighting* v *Simpritol Lighting* (1912) 46 ILTR 37.

526 *Joyce* v *Joyce* [1978] 1 WLR 1170.

527 [1990] NI 295.

Who may apply

11.193 One defendant can apply without giving notice to his co-defendant.[528] One defendant can apply under Order 3 rule 6(2) if there has been no proceeding relating to him for two years even though the action must continue against the other defendant because of a proceeding relating to him.[529] If two defendants apply the Court can exercise its discretion in favour of one and against the other.[530] In *Bannon* v *Craigavon DC*[531] Carswell J preferred the view that on application by one defendant the action can be dismissed against all. In many cases, on grounds of justice the action should continue against all.[532] A third party can have the claim against him dismissed for want of prosecution by the defendant, but not the plaintiff's claim. If a defendant succeeds in having the claim dismissed, his counterclaim continues;[533] though if it arises from the same incident or transaction, justice may require both to be dismissed. A plaintiff can seek dismissal of a counterclaim,[534] though he faces the difficulty that, in having control of the action, he may have acquiesced in the delay, except of course where his claim has already been disposed of.

The other grounds

11.194 The RSC provides other grounds on which an action can be dismissed arising out of failure to proceed, as noted above at para. 11.184. The principles and discretion under the inherent jurisdiction apply.

Failure to deliver Statement of Claim

If six weeks have elapsed since the appearance, the defendant can apply to dismiss for failure to deliver a Statement of Claim (Ord.19 r.1). Delivery of the Statement of Claim before the summons to dismiss is heard does not necessarily prevent this ground from being relied on.[535] If a late Statement of Claim is rejected by the defendant, the plaintiff should apply for an extension of time to serve it under Order 3 rule 5; and the Court may grant the extension and validate the Statement of Claim, or may dismiss the action.[536] If both the defendant's summons to dismiss and a plaintiff's summons for extension of time to deliver have been issued, the sensible course is to hear both together, and decide them on the same principle, namely whether the defendant has suffered prejudice not compensatable in costs.[537] In deciding whether to extend time the

---

[528] *Carlisle* v *Belfast Board of Guardians* (1881) 15 ILTR 49.

[529] *McMullan* v *Wallace* [1977] NI 1.

[530] *DHSS* v *Derry Construction* [1980] NI 187, at 203-4.

[531] [1984] NI 387.

[532] *Kelly* v *Marley Tile* (1977) 122 SJ 17.

[533] *Seddon's Pneumatic Tyre* v *Sweeny* (1895) 29 ILTR 96.

[534] *The Midhurst* v *The Lake Atlin* [1972] 2 Lloyds Rep 489; *Owen* v *Pugh* [1995] 3 All ER 345.

[535] *Neill* v *Corbett* [1992] NI 251, at 255d; White Book (1997) 19/1/1. This is because of the wording of Ord.19 r.1 which is different from the former RSC Ord.27 r.1. *McAllister* v *Wilson* [1955] NI 208, at 210 l.30, must be treated as overruled, and *Braithwaite* v *Anley* [1990] NI 63, at 66, as *per incuriam* on this point.

[536] *Neill* v *Corbett* [1992] NI 251, at 254j-255d.

[537] *Costellow* v *Somerset CC* [1993] 1 WLR 256.

Court looks at prejudice since the date when the Statement of Claim should have been delivered.[536] In cases where the plaintiff has obtained the draconian remedies of an *Anton Piller* order or *Mareva* or other interlocutory injunction, a comparatively short delay in serving the Statement of Claim may be unjustified and the action may be dismissed if the plaintiff makes no progress on the drafting of it before the hearing of the summons to dismiss.[538]

No proceeding had for two years

11.195 "Where two years or more have elapsed since the last proceeding in a cause or matter" the defendant may apply by summons to dismiss (Ord.3 r.6(2)). This additional and peculiarly Irish provision is exercised on the same principles as the inherent power.[539] "Proceeding" has a similar meaning to "step" under the Arbitration Act, but means a step by either party. It means an act of some formality and significance in furtherance of the action. A court document or something based on it (e.g. filing an affidavit in answer to a motion) is not necessarily a proceeding. A step less than a court application (e.g. serving a pleading) can be.[540]

A proceeding includes: defendant's application for particulars and the order thereon (*Donnelly* v *Gray* [1970] Oct NIJB), notice of trial (*McMullan* v *Wallace* [1977] NI 1).

The following are ***not*** a proceeding: notice of change of solicitor (*Allen* v *Redland Tile* [1973] NI 75), notice of intention to proceed under Order 3 rule 6(1) (*ibid.*); an application to dismiss for want of prosecution (*ibid*), a motion or summons on which no order is made (Ord.3 r.6(3)).

11.196 An irregular proceeding, such as a Statement of Claim served out of time, is a proceeding.[541] In *Boyd* v *Sinnamon*[539] delivery of a Statement of Claim pending appeal by the defendant from refusal to dismiss was apparently treated as not being a relevant proceeding, though it is a factor in the discretion (see *per* Lowry LCJ at p.3). In *McAllister* v *Wilson*[542] Lord MacDermott LCJ held that the crucial date was the date when the defendant issued his application, so that Order 3 rule 6(2) can be relied on even where the plaintiff then takes a proceeding before the hearing of the application. In *Braithwaite* v *Anley*[543] Carswell J seems to say that a proceeding taken at any time up to the issue or even up to the hearing of the summons to dismiss is a valid proceeding had. For the purposes of Order 3 rule 6(2), a proceeding had without the required notice of intention to proceed under Order 3 rule 6(1) can be ignored.[544]

---

538 *Group 4 Securitas* v *McIldowney*, Ch D, NI (Girvan J) 13 February 1997. The action was dismissed though the summons to dismiss was issued only two weeks after the due date for service of the Statement of Claim.

539 *Boyd* v *Sinnamon* [1974] June NIJB.

540 *Allen* v *Redland Tile* [1973] NI 75.

541 *Braithwaite* v *Anley* [1990] NI 63.

542 [1955] NI 208.

543 [1990] NI at 66H.

544 *McMullan* v *Wallace* [1977] NI 1.

Other instances

11.197 If the plaintiff takes out money in court paid under a defence of tender, the defendant can either set down for trial or apply to dismiss for want of prosecution with a view to obtaining an order for costs.[545]

If the action has been stayed till the plaintiff does a certain act, and the plaintiff does not do it, the defendant can apply for dismissal.[546]

The order of dismissal

11.198 If the Court orders the action to stand dismissed unless the plaintiff do a specified act within a stated time, the action stands dismissed in default, but the Court can thereafter extend the time limit[547] An order of dismissal is final for purposes of enforcing costs;[548] but is not on the merits and not *res judicata*. It is interlocutory for the purposes of appeal (para. 11.00). A second action can be brought, subject to limitation problems, and is not necessarily an abuse of process.[549]

Other provisions to prevent delay

11.199 Where at least a year has elapsed since the last proceeding, a party must give to every other party one month's notice of intention to proceed (Ord.3 r.6(1)), except a party who is in default of appearance or who has no address for service (Ord.65 r.9). The notice must be served on each separately represented defendant against whom it is intended to proceed.[544] The notice itself is invalid if given before the 12 months have elapsed. If no step is taken within a year after the notice, a new notice must be served.[550] Notice is unnecessary before issuing a summons to dismiss for want of prosecution.[551]

11.200 A solicitor or party guilty of delay can be penalised in costs (see para. 17.62). A complaint of delay by a solicitor can be made to the Law Society, which may take possession of his documents.[552]

---

545 *Grimes* v *Connell* [1920] 2 IR 61; and see para. 9.32.

546 *London Car Co* v *Kelly* (1886) 18 LR Ir 43.

547 *Samuels* v *Linzi Dresses* [1981] QB 115; *Hughes* v *Hughes* [1990] NI 295; not following *Feehan* v *Mandeville* (1890) 26 LR Ir 391.

548 *Tomkins* v *Greene* (1880) 6 LR Ir 474.

549 *Pople* v *Evans* [1969] 2 Ch 255.

550 *Sterling* v *Cohen* [1987] NI 409, at 413C.

551 *Warnock* v *Mann* [1896] 2 IR 630.

552 Solicitors (NI) Order 1976, Art.38.

CHAPTER TWELVE

WITHDRAWALS, COMPROMISES, AND FIXING THE TRIAL

DISCONTINUANCE

12.00 The plaintiff may discontinue the action or a claim in an action, against all or any defendants within 14 days after service of the Defence by notice on the defendant (Ord.21 r.2(1)). If there are two or more defendants the time runs from the date on which the last Defence was served or from the expiry if later of the time fixed for delivery of a Defence (Ord.21 r.2(3)). In an originating summons action the relevant event is the service of the defendant's affidavit evidence (Ord.21 r.2(3A)(3B). Leave or consent of the parties is required if an order for interim payment has been made (Ord.21 r.2(2A)). At any time, on production of a written consent signed by all parties, an action may be withdrawn (Ord.21 r.2(4)). A party may withdraw his appearance at any time by leave (Ord.21 r.1). In a writ action the defendant may withdraw his Defence at any time, and may discontinue his Counterclaim or any claim by him within 21 days after service of the Defence to Counterclaim, by notice to the plaintiff (Ord.21 r.2(2)). Where a party discontinues or withdraws a claim by notice without leave, the other party is automatically entitled to his costs of the action or withdrawn claim incurred up to the date of receiving the notice (Ord.62 r.5(3)). Withdrawing a claim means dropping a claim for relief on a set of acts which give rise to a cause of action. The plaintiff need not invoke Order 21 where he wishes to abandon a legal label such as trespass or nuisance, or a particular remedy such as injunction.

12.01 Save as stated above, leave is required to discontinue or withdraw a claim in an action; and the Court may refuse leave forcing the claimant to submit to trial, strike out the claim, or grant leave unconditionally or on conditions as to costs or as to the bringing of a new action (Ord.21 r.3). Leave may be granted on condition that no new action be brought.[1] Generally the defendant will be awarded all costs properly incurred to date, even if he has not entered an appearance.[2] In special cases the Court may award no costs to the defendant.[3] Costs of the action cannot be awarded to the plaintiff.[4]

12.02 In discontinuing against one defendant the Court can order that the costs payable by the plaintiff be part of the plaintiff's costs against the other

---

1 In *Suffolk Estate* v *McQuillan* (1932) 66 ILTR 78 (NI), leave was given even though the plaintiff intended to sue on a different cause of action based on the same facts.

2 *Moore* v *Southern Counties* [1889] WN 156.

3 As in *Garner* v *Foote* (1903) 3 NIJR 110, where the plaintiff discontinued after a plea of infancy; or where the defendant has now remedied the plaintiff's complaint.

4 *Lambton* v *Parkinson* (1887) 35 WR 545; save under Ord.62 r.10, where the defendant has been guilty of misconduct.

defendant.[5] One co-plaintiff who wishes to discontinue without the consent of the other must be added as a defendant unless his cause of action is separate or alternative. There is no special rule as to discontinuance by a plaintiff under disability, except that if it takes place as part of a compromise of a monetary claim, it must be approved by the Court under Order 80 rule 8.

12.03 Discontinuance or withdrawal of a claim under Order 21 puts an end to that claim in the present action, though a counterclaim or third-party notice already made can continue. An application to set aside an *ex parte* order made before discontinuance can continue.[6] A discontinuance made by mistake can be revoked by leave of the Court.[7] Discontinuance does not constitute a defence, or *res judicata* in any subsequent action (Ord.21 r.4). But if the discontinuing party is liable for costs, any subsequent action by him for (substantially) the same cause of action may be stayed till the costs are paid (Ord.21 r.5) even if commenced before the discontinuance,[8] even if there is a nominal change of parties.[9] The second action cannot be stayed if not substantially the same, even if the same transaction is sued upon.[10] The power to stay is discretionary. In *Bredin* v *Corcoran*[11] the defendant refused the costs tendered and applied for taxation; the plaintiff was allowed to continue the new action on payment into court of the costs claimed. The county court can stay an action till costs of a discontinued High Court action are paid;[12] and *semble*, *vice versa*.

12.04 Discontinuance often takes place in the context of a compromise between the parties. In that case the plaintiff can sue on the compromise as a contract, but he cannot sue successfully on the original cause of action, unless he can properly rescind or repudiate the contract of settlement.

SETTLEMENTS

12.05 The vast majority of civil claims are settled at some stage, whether before the writ is issued or at any time up to the day fixed for trial, or even after the trial has commenced. The solicitor for a party on the record has ostensible authority to effect a binding settlement in a pending action, but it is foolhardy to reach a settlement figure without the express written authority of the client. Solicitor and counsel cannot bind the client to a settlement of issues collateral to the litigation.[13] Counsel should negotiate only with opposing counsel if there is one, or with the opponent's solicitor; he should negotiate directly with the opposing party only by consent of his lawyers or if he is a

---

5 *Donegan* v *Fitzgerald* (1903) 37 ILTR 35.
6 *Lynch* v *Egan* (1901) 35 ILTR 74.
7 *Willcox* v *McDonnell* (1913) 47 ILTR 169 (intended to be a notice of acceptance of lodgment).
8 *Considine* v *Morony* (1842) 5 Ir LR 485.
9 *McCabe* v *Bank of Ireland* (1889) 14 App Cas 413(Ir); *Denis* v *Gorman* (1879) 4 LR Ir 356.
10 *Mulgrew* v *O'Brien* [1953] NI 10.
11 (1861) 12 ICLR App 9.
12 *Walsh* v *Fitzgerald* (1884) 18 ILTR 54.
13 *Gordon* v *Gordon* [1951] IR 301.

personal litigant.[14] In a case where the defendant is insured, as in road accident or factory accidents, the authority to settle is in effect that of the insurer's claims manager rather than the defendant personally, because of the terms of the policy. The parties to an action can compromise without consulting their lawyers, provided they act honestly;[15] and subject to the solicitor's charge for costs. Statements made in trying to negotiate a settlement are 'without prejudice' and inadmissible in litigation, except: (a) if both parties waive the privilege; (b) as evidence in a dispute as to what the terms of settlement are; or (c) if an offer is made "without prejudice save as to costs" the offering party reserves the right to mention the offer when the judge is exercising his discretion as to costs.

12.06 A settlement is a contract in which the parties may agree to any terms, including terms that the Court has no power to impose. It derives is binding effect under the law of contract (see further para.9.27). If the terms provide for an order or judgment of the Court, such will be made if announced to the Court, provided it is an order which the Court has power to make. Settlements take the form of a judgment by consent, or of a discontinuance/dismissal/general adjournment/stay, of the action on terms agreed, which terms may be announced in court or kept secret. Every settlement should specifically deal with costs and the disposal of any money in court. In a personal injuries case, it is advisable to deal specifically with the deductibility of CRU benefits from the amount agreed (see para.14.68e). A judgment by consent is evidence of the contract between the parties and also constitutes a *res judicata*.[16] Note that there is a difference between a judgment or order by consent and a judgment or order made without objection.

12.07 As soon as a settlement is reached in an action which has been set down, the parties should notify the appropriate Lists Officer as soon as possible; and must notify the Officer of the settlement or likely settlement (Ord.34 r.7(2)). If the settlement provides for an order or judgment, the Office lists it for announcement before a judge. If no order is required, the terms can be drawn up and lodged with the Office. If an action is settled on terms that the action be withdrawn, a written consent to the withdrawal signed by all parties can be lodged in the Office (Ord.21 r.2(4)). The courts try to facilitate settlement as far as possible, by granting an adjournment or passing a case to the end of the list. The judge will even rise for a limited time while negotiations are proceeding.

12.08 A meeting or 'joint consultation' between the relevant parties and their lawyers is a good way of facilitating agreement, where their minds are concentrated on looking for a compromise. A early settlement is good for a plaintiff as it gives him money in hand and ends the strain of waiting for the court case. For the defence it closes the file and reduces the workload. Attempts to settle can continue right up to the last moment. Most of the cases listed for trial on a particular day are settled on that morning. Indeed the administration

---

[14] Bar Handbook 6-10.
[15] *The Hope* (1883) 8 PD 144.
[16] White Book (1997) Vol.2 [4607-8].

of civil justice operates in present practice on that assumption. The pressure of doorstep negotiations can lead to injustice to the client, so counsel should ensure firstly that he discusses with the client beforehand what offer would be acceptable, and secondly, that either senior or junior counsel is available and prepared to run the case in court.

Methods of compromise

12.09 In a pending action a compromise may take one of the following forms-

(1) Acceptance of money lodged in court.

(2) The action may be discontinued or dismissed as one term of a contract between the parties. It puts an end to the action and cannot be embodied in any judgment or rule of court.

(3) The action may be adjourned or never set down for trial under a settlement. This is a fresh contract which supersedes any right to pursue any judgment in the present action.[17]

(4) The action can be "stayed on the terms scheduled hereto, save for the purpose of carrying the said terms into effect [with liberty to apply for that purpose]". This is a *Tomlin* order.[18] It is not a judgment and not registrable as such.[19] The terms are not enforceable by application in the present action. 'Liberty to apply' means that a party can apply to have the terms embodied in a court order and thereupon enforceable in the action; but a party cannot seek an inquiry into damages for breach of a term.[20] If the terms of the compromise are breached, the stay can be removed.[21] The Court has an inherent jurisdiction to rectify a *Tomlin* order if it does not accurately reflect the agreement;[22] or for greater clarity.[23]

(5) The action can be stayed, discontinued or dismissed "on terms indorsed in counsels' briefs"; which keeps them secret.

(6) If and only if the terms so provide, the agreement can be embodied as a court order or judgment or made a rule of court. A consent made a rule of court is enforceable by virtue of section 86(2) of the Judicature Act.[24] Therefore it must be one which the Court has jurisdiction to enforce, and within the scope of the issues raised in the action.[25] A judgment or order by consent is not a contract, but is documentary evidence of a contract and is governed by the rule against extrinsic evidence to vary it. Its force and effect derives from the contract, not the court order, except in Family

---

17 *Green* v *Rozen* [1955] 2 All ER 797.
18 See White Book (1997) Vol.2 [4616].
19 *Joynt* v *McCabe* [1899] 1 IR 104.
20 *Gallagher* v *Sloan [*1983] NI 78.
21 *Hollingsworth* v *Humphry*, 'The Independent', 21 December 1987; [1988] CLY 2931.
22 *Islam* v *Askar* 'The Times' 20 October 1994 (CA).
23 *Allied Irish Bank* v *Hughes*, 'The Times' 4 November 1994 (CA).
24 *Re Atkinson* (1908) 42 ILTR 226 (obiter).
25 *Hammond* v *Hammond* (1874) IR 8 Eq 322.

Division proceedings.[26] A judgment for £X,000 'with costs' means such costs as are allowed or prescribed by statute or rules of court.[27]

(As to settlements of defamation actions, see paras. 18.19-20. Orders by consent in the Chancery Division: Practice Direction, 23 August 1973.)

Effect of consent judgment

12.10 A consent judgment must be distinguished from a judgment made without objection;[28] a judgment made on admission of facts; and a judgment proposed by the judge and accepted by the parties.[29] A judgment by consent is final and cannot be set aside except as follows -

(1) Consent given by mistake can be withdrawn before it is embodied in a court order, on good grounds.[30]

(2) By fresh action it can be set aside on the same ground that any contract may be rescinded.

(3) Without need for fresh action it can be set aside for admitted fraud or mistake,[31] or altered by consent.[32]

(4) Provided notice of application is given before the order is perfected it can be set aside by the client showing that it was agreed by his lawyer contrary to his express instruction.[33]

(5) It can be amended under the 'slip rule' (see para. 15.12).

(6) A court may refuse to enforce a consent order if it is inequitable to do so.[34]

(7) A stay of execution embodied in the order can be varied later by the Court.[35]

(8) The Bankruptcy Court can re-open any compromise by a bankrupt.[36]

(9) It can be appealed to the Court of Appeal by leave of the High Court, or if made by a master, to a judge without leave.

12.11 A judgment or order by consent creates *res judicata* only insofar as it would do so without consent, so an agreed dismissal for want of prosecution is not a *res judicata*. A compromise intended by the parties not to be in full settlement does not bar a subsequent action.[37] In the case of a debt or liquidated demand, a settlement for less than the debt due, unless supported by

---

26 White Book (1997) Vol.2 [4608-9].
27 *Dennis* v *Best* (1878) 12 ILTR 152.
28 *Siebe Gorman* v *Pneupac* [1982] 1 WLR 185, at 189F.
29 *Aldam* v *Brown* [1890] WN 116.
30 *Dietz* v *Lennig Chemicals* [1969] 1 AC 170.
31 *Allsop* v *Allsop* (1980) 11 Fam Law 18; *Moss* v *Chin* (1994) 120 DLR 4th 406 (BC).
32 *Hill* v *Deakin* (1974) 118 SJ 389.
33 *Marsden* v *Marsden* [1972] Fam 280; and see *Crothers* v *Crothers* (1901) 35 ILTR 179.
34 *Thwaite* v *Thwaite* [1982] Fam 1.
35 *Northern Bank* v *Jeffers*, Ch D, NI (Girvan J) 5 December 1996 [1996] 10 BNIL 67.
36 White Book (1997) Vol 2 [4623].
37 *Buckland* v *Palmer* [1984] 1 WLR 1109, at 1117C.

consideration, does not bar a new action.[38] Where contributory fault has been pleaded, a settlement does not necessarily connote a finding of full liability.[39]

Restrictions on compromise

12.12 Compromise is restricted in the following circumstances-

(1) A co-plaintiff cannot compromise by himself and cannot drop out as of right.[40]

(2) A compromise on behalf of a plaintiff under disability must be approved by the Court (see para. 12.13).

(3) In proceedings concerning a deceased's estate, trust property or the construction of an instrument, any compromise which affects persons (including unknown or unborn) who are not parties must be approved by the Court (a judge, not a master) to be binding on them (Ord.15 r.13(4)).

(4) If a legally-aided plaintiff makes a settlement which makes any concession as to costs, then either he or his lawyers will lose out, because of the Legal Aid Fund's charge on any money recovered to pay the costs of the plaintiff's lawyers in so far as their costs are not paid by the defendant.[41] The parties should not agree any terms to defeat that charge. If a settlement involving a legally aided party (not under disability) is settled with agreed costs or an agreement to pay party-and-party costs, the assisted party's solicitor may apply to the Legal Aid Committee for it to assess his costs in lieu of taxation.[42]

(5) If the Chief Constable is sued for a tort committed by police, a compromise must be approved by the Police Authority to make it liable.[43]

(6) If the plaintiff's claim is illusory or *mala fide* (e.g. based on a betting transaction) a compromise is not binding as there is no consideration moving from him.[44]

(7) It is not binding if made by the parties under a common *bona fide* mistake as to a material fact or state of affairs on which they were induced to enter the agreement, unless one party has acted to his detriment.[45]

(8) It is not enforceable if it is champertous.

'MINOR SETTLEMENTS'

12.13 Under the general law of contract a minor or patient has very limited power to bind himself by any agreement.[46] "Where in any proceedings money is

---

[38] *In re Broderick* [1986] 6 NIJB 36. See para. 9.27. Contrast the effect of a judgment for less than the debt due: para. 3.30.
[39] *Trainor* v *McKee* [1988] NI 556.
[40] *Re Mathews* [1905] 2 Ch 460.
[41] See Legal Aid, Advice and Assistance (NI) Order 1981, Art.12(5).
[42] LA Gen Regs, reg.21(1)-(4).
[43] Police Act (NI) 1970, s.14(2)(b).
[44] *O'Donnell* v *O'Sullivan* (1913) 47 ILTR 253.
[45] *McEntire* v *Sun Fire Office* (1895) 29 ILTR 103.

claimed by or on behalf of a person under disability, no settlement, compromise or payment and no acceptance of money paid into court, whenever entered into or made, shall so far as it relates to that person's claim be valid without the approval of the Court" (Ord.80 r.8).[47] If a settlement or compromise is made before the action commences, it must be brought up for approval either by a "friendly action" by writ or, more appropriately, by an originating summons (to which no appearance need be entered) (Ord.80 r.9). The court fee on a writ is £150, whereas the court fee on such an originating summons is only £35. If a settlement is reached in a pending action, the plaintiff's solicitor will notify the Appeals and Lists Office, which will list the action for hearing by a judge to approve it. If the minor plaintiff has given notice of acceptance of a lodgment, that is brought up for approval by the judge in the same way. Settlement includes a stay or discontinuance on agreed terms, but not a unilateral discontinuance (which does not bar a fresh action). If the action is dismissed and the next friend fails to appeal because a settlement is made which is in his rather than the plaintiff's interests, it creates no estoppel.[48] Order 80 rule 9 applies to a claim for money, debt or damages, or for an account, but not an ejectment; *quaere* a claim for return of goods. Settlement of a monetary claim made by a defendant under disability, by counterclaim or third-party notice, also requires approval. A settlement with the Motor Insurers' Bureau cannot be approved.[49]

12.14 The purpose of the approval is to ensure that the next friend has made a settlement which is in the interests of the plaintiff, and to finalise it so that the defendant is discharged from further liability. A settlement made without approval, whether in pending proceedings or not, is subject to the law of contract and generally not binding on the minor. *Semble*, the Court should not allow or should strike out from its records any consent order or judgment which has not been approved under Order 80 rule 8. Of course the Court can only approve a settlement which has been agreed by both the next friend and the defence representatives. The Court can replace a next friend who refuses a beneficial settlement (see para. 3.09). Either party can repudiate the settlement at any time before approval.[50] If a minor comes of age between settlement and approval, he can either adopt or reject it so that approval ceases to be necessary in either event. If the minor dies between settlement and approval, it cannot be approved.[51]

12.15 Counsel has a particular duty both to the minor and to the Court. He must read his brief, consult with the minor, the next friend and solicitor, form his own view of the strength and value of the case and the advisability of the settlement and as to the investment etc. of the money. He must tell the judge of

---

46 The law as to minors is now contained partly in common law and partly in the Minors Contracts (NI) Order 1988. See previous page.

47 I.e. of a judge, not a master: Ord.32 r.11(1)(g).

48 *Blair* v *Crawford* [1906] 1 IR 578.

49 *Morrison* v *MIB* [1987] NI 204.

50 *Dietz* v *Lennig Chemicals* [1969] 1 AC 170; *Duffy* v *McLaron* [1985] NI 285.

51 *Clear* v *Thermal Ltd* [1969] IR 133, where the Judges differed as to whether the settlement binds his personal representative.

all relevant factors and give his opinion if asked.[52] At the approval hearing, usually in chambers in the absence of the defendant's lawyers, all the relevant factors as to the strength of the claim on liability and quantum are put before the judge by plaintiff's counsel. Oral evidence is not given. Counsel states the facts and hands up any relevant documents, and may give his opinion on the factors involved.

12.16 Taking as an example a personal injury road accident claim by a minor, he puts forward the following as appropriate: birth certificate; place and date of accident; occupation/schooling of the plaintiff then and now; facts alleged as to the accident; summary of evidence; whether the defendant admits full liability, and if not, any known frailties in the plaintiff's case; any information about the defence case; list of witnesses; the police report; coroner's depositions; details of criminal prosecutions; counsel's opinion on liability; whether the case is settled on full liability; all medical reports including those disclosed by the defence; up-to-date medicals on all aspects of the injuries; items and documentary proof of special damages; statement of statutory benefits (the up-to-date 'CRU' certificate); whether parties are legally aided; any lodgment and its amount; explanation for any delay in prosecuting the claim.

12.17 The plaintiff and his next friend should be present: the judge may want to inspect any visible injuries and ask them a few questions. Finally the judge is told of the agreed figure. If the judge thinks, considering only the minor's interest, that the figure is enough, he approves it and asks counsel's suggestion as to how the money should be dealt with. Normally he directs investment of the money as recommended by the Accountant-General's Office under the Judicature Act (s.81). Then he appoints a guardian of the settlement, normally the next friend. He may appoint a guardian of the child's estate (Ord.80 r.14). With the consent of the parties, the judge may order part of the damages to be paid out periodically for the plaintiff, under the Damages Act 1996 (s.2(1)). At any time the guardian can apply for the payment out of some money for a specific purpose for the minor's benefit. On reaching the age of 18 the plaintiff can take full control of the invested money. If not approved, the judge adjourns the hearing so that either the defendant will make a higher offer or the action will go to trial. The judge acts on his own judgement; the opinion of counsel is only a factor.[53]

12.18 When money is claimed or recovered or awarded or agreed to be paid for a minor plaintiff, unless the Court otherwise orders, the minor's costs to his own solicitor are taxed as between solicitor and client (Ord.62 r.16(2)); the costs payable by the defendant on the lesser 'standard basis'; and the master certifies the difference between the two (Ord.62 r.16(3)); which amount is payable to the plaintiff's solicitor out of the damages. However in most cases the solicitors for each party will agree costs so as to create no discrepancy. See further para. 17.79.

---

[52] *Matthews* v *Ulster Tin Box* [1970] Feb NIJB at 9-11.

[53] *Bourke* v *CIE* [1967] IR 319.

Patient's settlement

12.19 In relation to an action on behalf of a mental patient, the above passages (paras. 12.13 to 12.18) apply *mutatis mutandis.* The Master (Care and Protection) can approve a settlement on behalf of a patient in the exercise of his power over patients (Ord.32 r.11(2)).

Fatal accidents settlement

12.20 If a settlement is reached in a claim under the Fatal Accidents (NI) Order 1977, the Court must apportion the award among the beneficiaries (Ord.80 r.12(2)); and if any of them is a minor or patient, the amounts agreed insofar as they relate to him must be approved by the Court (Ord.80 r.8);[54] and dealt with by investment or otherwise under directions of the Court (Ord.80 r.10). If all the beneficiaries are adult and agree to the apportionment, presumably approval of the Court is unwarranted.

STRUCTURED SETTLEMENTS

12.21 In recent years in cases of severe injuries which would be settled for a very large figure of damages, the parties have been attracted to the idea of a structured settlement; that is, the payment of compensation by immediate lump sum and further instalments guaranteed for the rest of the plaintiff's life. The Inland Revenue conceded that the instalments are deferred payment of capital compensation, and therefore not taxable income of the plaintiff. (If the plaintiff receives only a lump sum award, any income from investment thereof is taxable). To attract the tax benefit, the plaintiff contracted with the defendant's insurer that part of his compensation be payable by regular instalments for life; the defendant's insurer contracted with a life insurer by purchasing an annuity for the plaintiff's life; the life insurer paid the annuity net of tax to the defendant's insurer, who paid the annuity gross to the plaintiff and set off the shortfall against its corporation tax liability at the end of the tax year. See further "Structured Settlements: a Practical Guide" ed. Goldrein and de Haas (Butterworths 1993). The need for structured settlements in this form has lessened since amendments made by the Finance Acts 1995 and 1996 which mean that any periodical payments of damages in a personal injury or death case are free from income tax (see para. 12.25). Thus it is now feasible for the annuity to be payable directly from the life insurer to the plaintiff. Under structured settlements set up in the old form before 1995 the annuity can now be assigned from the defence insurer to the plaintiff without attracting tax.

12.22 A typical structured settlement, in lieu of £1,000,000 lump sum settlement, consists of £200,000 lump sum compensation to be paid now; £100,000 contingency fund, to be used as needed; £700,000 dedicated to the structure. Defence insurers insist on a deduction of about 10 per cent of the structured sum,[55] so that £630,000 thereof is used to purchase the annuity. The compensator must deduct and pay to the DHSS the value of all 'CRU' benefits

---

[54] By originating summons under Ord.80 r.9 if settled before litigation.

[55] They justify this because of the tax advantage to the plaintiff and the tax shortfall and administration expenses caused to the defence insurer. The practice may be harder to justify now.

payable to the plaintiff up to the date of settlement but no further deductions are made from the annuity payments.[56] [*to be replaced by*: The deduction of CRU benefits will be provided for in regulations made under the Social Security (Recovery of Benefits) (NI) Order 1997 (Art.20(4)(5)(6)).] The type of annuity can vary. The normal and most prudent is to buy an annuity of, say, £1,000 per month, starting now or deferred for a fixed time, increasing in accordance with the Retail Price Index, for the rest of the plaintiff's life with a minimum period of years guaranteed in case the plaintiff dies sooner than expected. This is Model 4 of the structures which the Inland Revenue propose.

Under the Damages Act 1996, where a structured settlement has been reached (as defined by s.5)[57] with a defence insurance company, the Motor Insurers' Bureau or other body specified by the Lord Chancellor by Statutory Instrument, the beneficiary of the annuity (i.e. the plaintiff) is entitled to 100 per cent of the benefits under the annuity policy under the Policyholders Protection Act 1975 if the life insurer goes into liquidation (s.4). This applies whether the annuity is payable directly to the plaintiff under the settlement, or whether the annuity is assigned to the plaintiff after the settlement has been set up.

12.23 The role of the plaintiff's solicitor is to assess the value of the claim in lump sum terms, to negotiate a sum for immediate payment and contingency fund, to consider the most suitable type of annuity and to instruct an accountant. The accountant advises on the best type of structure for the plaintiff's needs and his present and future expenses, and gets a current quotation for an annuity from the life insurance market. The accountant is paid a commission or fixed fee, usually agreed to be paid by the defence insurer. The Court cannot order a structured settlement or dictate its terms, but if the plaintiff is a minor or patient, the settlement must be approved by a judge. In approving the judge requires a recommendation of a forensic accountant. The Court can now, under the Damages Act 1996, with consent order damages by way of periodical payments, and it seems to be envisaged by section 4(2) of the Act that the Court can embody the full terms of the structured settlement in an order of the court; indeed that has been said to be the primary purpose of the new provision.[58] Presumably, if the parties consent, the judge can decide what sum should be dedicated to the structure and the type of annuity.

12.24 If the defendant is a non-insured public body exempt from tax, such as a Government Department, Education and Library Board or the Police Authority, it has no tax liability against which to offset the shortfall on the annuity, so it would not consent to a structured settlement. This problem has been met by the changes in the Tax Acts,[60] which make the periodic payments tax free, and enable the public body to pay directly to the plaintiff out of its own resources. The Damages Act 1996 (s.6) deals with the risk that such a body might be dissolved by future legislation. A Minister of the Crown may

---

[56] Social Security Administration (NI) Act 1992, s.84.

[57] Including one embodied in an order of the court: s.4(2); and one where the periodic payments are agreed first and the annuity purchased or assigned to the plaintiff later: s.5(8).

[58] *Hansard* HL Vol.571 cols.1405-1412.

agree with the Treasury, and a NI Department may agree with the Department of Finance and Personnel, guidelines for a list of designated bodies; if such a body settles or is ordered by the court to pay a claim for damages against it in the form of a structured settlement without the purchase of an annuity, the Minister or NI Department may guarantee the payments.

12.25 Apart from the power to award provisional damages (see para. 14.75), the Court has no power to give damages by instalments; damages must be assessed once and for all.[59] However, in a personal injury/death case, with the consent of the parties the Court may order damages wholly or partly by way of periodical payments, under the Damages Act 1996 (s.2(1)). Periodical payments made under a settlement of a personal injury or death claim, or under a court order are not taxable as income.[60]

SETTING DOWN FOR TRIAL

12.26 In a writ action (Ord.34 r.1), within six weeks after close of pleadings or other period ordered by the Court, the plaintiff may set down the action for trial (Ord.34 r.2(1)). If he fails to do so, the defendant may set it down or apply to dismiss the action (Ord.34 r.2(2)). Any party who sets it down must notify the other parties within 24 hours in Form 35 (Ord.34 r.7(1)). The party lodges in the Appeals and Lists Office (or Chancery Office) a request to set down in Form 34, bearing a court fee of £80, along with two bundles bound and indexed containing copies of the writ, pleadings, notices for particulars and replies, any interlocutory orders, legal aid documents (Ord.34 rr.3,4); and the medical reports and documents served under Order 25 rule 2.[61] Any such documents which come into existence thereafter, such as replies to a notice for particulars, he must deliver (two copies) before the eve of the trial (Ord.34 r.4(6)). The Office will not accept the setting down if the bundle is not in order. The official stamps one bundle with the fee stamp and the names of the parties' solicitors, and keeps it in the Office, and keeps the other bundle for the trial judge. The bundle is the only information available to the judge when the trial starts. In setting down Chancery writ actions, affidavits need not be included unless ordered to stand as pleadings.[62]

12.27 The Form 34 request has on its face the words: "I/we further request that this action be tried with a jury/without a jury". In an action to which section 62 of the Judicature Act applies (see para. 14.04), the three penultimate or ultimate words must be deleted; in any other action the whole sentence must be deleted (see Ord.33 r.4(1)(3)).

---

[59] *Watkins* v *Olafson* (1989) 61 DLR 4th 577 (SC, Canada).

[60] Income and Corporation Taxes Act 1988, s.329AA, applying to payments made since 29 April 1996. It supercedes s.329A, which applied only to payments under a settlement made since 1 May 1995. These sections were inserted by the Finance Acts 1996 and 1995 respectively.

[61] Practice Direction [1992] 3 BNIL 112.

[62] Practice Direction [1994] 7 BNIL 84.

12.28 If there are third-party proceedings, the defendant must as soon as possible after the action has been set down, set down the third-party proceedings in the same way (Ord.34 r.4(3)).

Abatement, change of parties etc. See Order 34 rule 8 (para. 11.38).

FIXING A DATE

12.29 Near the end of each legal term, the Appeals and Lists Office prints a list of *Queen's Bench* actions which can be heard next term. So a party should notify the Office if the case will not be ready next term. Actions will be given priority in the order in which they were set down. If he wants for good reason to jump the queue and have the case tried early, he asks the Office to do so, enclosing the consent of the other party. If the other party has not consented, the Office will list the case for a judge to decide whether to try it early.

Unless notified that the action is not ready, the Office will next list it in the Provisional List indicating the week about seven weeks hence in which the action will be listed for hearing.

About three weeks later, the Clerk of Lists holds a Monday morning call-over to fix the day of that week in which the trials will be listed. The solicitors should attend or be represented to indicate any unsuitable day and to estimate the probable length of the case, or to apply for it to be taken out of that week's list.

12.30 The Office then issues the Weekly List showing the actions listed for each day (about 25 of them). If a party now finds that he is unable to proceed on that day, the action may be taken out of the list either by lodging a consent of the other party or by applying in court to the judge taking the daily call-over.[63] If an action is taken out it will be relisted as soon as practicable (about 2-3 months) or when a party asks for relisting.

12.31 In *Chancery* writ actions, the Chancery Office gives notice to the parties of the date when the judge or master will sit to fix dates. Solicitors and/or counsel for each party must attend. Writ action trials are heard on Tuesdays-Fridays. Initially the date of trial will be fixed provisionally and confirmed at a further hearing four weeks later, during which time counsel for each party must fully explore the possibility of settling the litigation. If counsel think it would assist, the Court will fix a hearing for a pre-trial review in the presence of the parties. If settled after the date of trial has been confirmed, counsel must so inform the Office at once. If it becomes clear that an action cannot proceed on the fixed date, the parties must inform the principal clerk for listing before the judge to fix a new date.[64]

12.32 If an action is settled or likely to be settled the Office should be notified as soon as possible (see para. 12.07). At any time after setting down the Court may require the parties to indicate to the Office their readiness for trial; if a party fails to respond the Court may of its own motion on seven days notice remove the action from the list (with power to re-list), or on application of a

---

63 Practice Direction [1990] 8 BNIL 47.

64 Practice Direction [1994] 7 BNIL 84; Practice Direction 1997 No 4 (Ch D) [1997] 5 BNIL.

party dismiss the action or strike out the defence (Ord.34 r.6). The system for listing is under the control of the LCJ, who may give directions as the date of hearing of specific actions (Ord.34 r.5).

CHAPTER THIRTEEN

EVIDENCE

PREPARING THE EVIDENCE FOR TRIAL

Senior counsel's directions

13.00 At the stage of setting down for trial, if the client (or the Legal Aid Certificate) authorises instruction of two counsel, senior counsel should be briefed. As solicitor for the plaintiff it is relevant to know whether the costs of senior counsel can be justified when costs are sought from the defendant, assuming that the plaintiff wins. The question is: will the defendant (or his insurance company) agree to pay for a senior, and if not, will the Taxing Master allow his fee? As a rule of thumb senior counsel can be justified if the case is worth at least £15,000 or if there is some other important feature in the case such as it being a test action.

13.01 (Senior) counsel should be asked to direct proofs as soon as possible after setting down for trial. For that purpose he should be sent a full brief containing: (a) an opening summary by the solicitor, referring to the main issues and difficulties and pointing to any important aspects of the case which are buried in the mass of papers; (b) the pleadings, notices and court orders, counsel's opinions; (c) documents on liability (engineer's report, photos, police report, notes from inquest or criminal proceedings, witness statements etc.); (d) documents on quantum (medicals, wages statements, photos of injuries, receipts for repairs etc.); (e) correspondence grouped by subject-matter and in chronological order, plus memoranda of telephone or oral communications.

13.02 In his direction of proofs (senior) counsel lists the witnesses to attend the trial and states which should be on *subpoena* to testify and/or to produce a document; the expert medical and other witnesses; and lists the documents to be available at the trial; any further notices and pre-trial steps to be taken, any necessary amendments or new parties to be added. He advises on what evidence has to be adduced to support the case and to rebut the opponent's case, advises on the prospect of success and on the monetary value of the claim, and on attempts to negotiate a settlement or to agree evidence with the opponent; further consultations with the client or witnesses; any further investigations to be carried out and reports to be made by the experts. Obviously the medical evidence at the trial must be up to date. He may give his opinion on a legal issue or direct that junior counsel be asked to do so.

PROCURING THE EVIDENCE

Subpoena

13.03 Having decided what witnesses and what documents must be brought to court, the solicitor must consider whether and how to secure their attendance by writ of *subpoena*. A *subpoena* in Form 24 can be issued on sealing from the appropriate Office (Ord.38 r.12). On sealing a court fee (new since 1996) of £5 per witness is payable. Leave must be obtained for a *subpoena* (in Form 25) to attend proceedings in chambers (Ord.32 r.9). A *subpoena* from the office can be served only in Northern Ireland. If issued and stated to be issued by order of a judge (obtained *ex parte* on affidavit), a writ of *subpoena* can be served anywhere in the United Kingdom[1] (Judicature Act, s.67). It is only enforceable if reasonable expenses of coming to, attending and returning from court are tendered at the time of service (s.67(6)). The affidavit must show that his attendance is necessary; but need not state that he has refused to come.[2] No *subpoena* can be served outside the United Kingdom, but the Court can order a witness abroad to be examined by deposition (see para. 13.10).

The High Court can issue a *subpoena* in aid of an inferior court or judicial tribunal,[3] or arbitral tribunal.[4]

13.04 A *subpoena* may be *ad testificandum* (to give oral evidence) and/or *duces tecum* (to produce a document). The former may include more than one witness (Ord.38 r.13). On the latter must be inserted the document(s) to be brought. It is sufficient to state "documents relating to the issue of ...".[5] Document includes pictures, tape-recordings, films etc., and the Court may order the witness to provide the apparatus for playing the film etc. Certain public documents cannot be subpoenaed; and a court order is necessary to produce an original judicial document.[6] Leave is necessary to compel production of original bankers' books,[7] and of documents kept by the Companies Registrar.[8] A mistake in the name or address can be corrected before service by re-sealing (Ord.38 r.14). A party should not, and probably cannot, be subpoenaed by his own solicitor, but can be subpoenaed by the other party. Close relatives and friends of the client can normally be trusted to attend without *subpoena*, but this cannot be assumed. Many apparent friends of the party, who have assured him that they will back his case all the way, get cold feet or go missing, or cannot get off work to attend the trial. A medical or other expert retained professionally in the case can be trusted to attend in response to an ordinary letter, providing he has been consulted about his availability. It may be necessary to subpoena a general practitioner or casualty officer. A police officer must be subpoenaed. It is essential to make sure that every witness knows exactly the date and time when he is required to appear, and how to get to the Court; and to make sure about a week before the trial that the witnesses are reminded of the case.

13.05 Save where leave is required, the Court has no power over the issue of a *subpoena*; and a judge cannot himself require the attendance of a witness save

---

1 But not the Republic of Ireland, Channel Islands or Isle of Man.

2 *Kingdom Yacht Co* v *Wilson* (1892) 26 ILTR 130.

3 *In re Sterritt* [1980] NI 234. It is issued out of the Crown Office with no court order needed: Ord.38 r.17.

4 Arbitration Act 1996, s.43.

5 *Greyhound Australia* v *Deluxe Coachlines* (1988) 14 Comm LB 106 (Fed Ct of Aus).

6 Phipson 8-08.

7 *Coleman* v *Coleman* (1898) 32 ILTR 66.

8 Companies (NI) Order 1986, Art.658(5).

in committal proceedings,[9] and *habeas corpus*. The Court can order a person to attend any proceedings and produce a document (Ord.38 r.11). The Court can compel production of a document at a date before the trial or hearing at which it is to be used, provided that advance inspection is clearly necessary by reason of the complexity of the document or otherwise.[10]

13.06 A *subpoena* requires the witness to attend on the date of trial (notice of which will be given later) and thereafter from day to day till the conclusion of the trial (Ord.38 r.16); and if it is adjourned for a longer period or to a date to be later fixed, the *subpoena* still operates if the witness is given notice of the new date. It must be served personally, even on a minor or patient (Ord.80 r.13(4)), within 12 weeks of issue and at least four days (or such period as the Court may fix) before attendance is required (Ord.38 r.15). Substituted service can be ordered.[11] Tender of expenses is not stipulated in the rules but is always made in practice (and see para. 16.68). A witness must obey a *subpoena*, and cannot claim any privilege until he is being asked questions in the witness box. On a *duces tecum* he must come with the document in his possession, and object to production in court, on the grounds (only): (a) that he has or is bound by a privilege in the document; or (b) that it is a public document held by him as public official, and his principal objects; or (c) that he holds as a mere servant or company secretary and his principal objects.[12] A witness *ad testifcandum* must be sworn if called by a party and can be compelled to produce any document brought by him. A witness *duces tecum* can produce the document without being sworn, though a party may call him to testify. There is an implied undertaking to use documents seen on *subpoena* only for the purposes of the action.[13]

13.07 Application can be made to a master to set aside a *subpoena* if it is oppressive or *mala fide*.[14] It may not be set aside if the witness can avoid prejudice by claiming privilege.[15]

13.08 If the witness fails to obey the *subpoena* he is liable for contempt (see para. 16.68), which is no consolation to the party who wishes to call him. However an application for an adjournment will be considered more sympathetically if the absent witness was under *subpoena*. If served in Great Britain under section 67, default may be punished by the Court of Session or English High Court.

13.09 *Witness in prison.* An application for a writ of *habeas corpus ad testificandum* under the Habeas Corpus Act 1804, or any other order to bring up a prisoner[16] to give evidence in any court or tribunal proceedings, must be

---

9 *Yianni* v *Yianni* [1966] 1 WLR 120 (Cross J).

10 *Greyhound Australia* v *Deluxe Coachlines* (1988) 14 Comm LB 106 (Fed Ct of Aus). It can be done by ordering production on a notional starting date for the trial: *Khanna* v *Lovell White* [1995] 1 WLR 121 (Ch D).

11 *Tower Tea* v *Doheny* (1908) 42 ILTR 22.

12 See Phipson 8-09.

13 *Sybron Corp* v *Barclays Bank* [1985] Ch 299.

14 White Book (1997) 38/14-19/11; *Morrison* v *AVX* [1990] 1 BNIL 81.

15 *In re Sterritt* [1980] NI 234, at 236B, *obiter*.

16 Detained under civil or criminal process: White Book (1997) 54/9/1.

made *ex parte* to a High Court Judge in chambers (Ord.54 r.9). A party can only be brought on *habeas corpus* if he is to give evidence.[17] The appropriate Secretary of State may, on application by informal letter, direct a prisoner detained in a prison, remand home, young offenders' centre etc. anywhere in the United Kingdom, Isle of Man or Channel Islands to be brought to court as a witness or as a party or to any place, in the interests of justice.[18] Under either procedure the applicant may be required to pay expenses of transport of the prisoner and an escort.[19] If a serving prisoner is to attend the High Court, the Appeals and Lists Office must be notified 48 hours before.[20]

13.10 *Examination by deposition.* If a witness cannot attend court or if otherwise necessary, an order can be sought for his deposition to be taken before an examiner (Ord.39 r.1) in a courtroom, at the witness's residence, a hospital or anywhere. Such procedure is often invoked where the witness is in the Republic of Ireland, Isle of Man, Channel Islands or anywhere outside the United Kingdom and does not agree to come to court. At the hearing counsel for the other party can attend and cross-examine. The examiner so appointed can administer an oath (Judicature Act, s.112((3)). A witness anywhere in the world can be so examined under Order 39 rules 2-3A. The rules can also be used to require a document to be produced in evidence.[21] An application for examination abroad must show that the evidence is probably material,[22] and that bringing the witness to Northern Ireland is impossible, or disproportionately expensive.[23] A plaintiff must show special grounds for having himself examined abroad.[24] Fear of arrest by the RUC is not enough.[25] See the White Book (1997) 39/2-3 for the ways in which the deposition can be taken in various countries. Order 39 rules 4-14 deal with the procedure for taking the examination and the examiner's report thereon. Relevance and admissibility of the evidence is for the trial judge to decide.[26] The deposition is admissible without proof of the examiner's signature, but is admissible only if the party against whom it is tendered consents or if the deponent is dead, beyond the jurisdiction, or unable to attend from illness; reasonable notice of intention to use the deposition must be given (Ord.38 r.7). Order 77 rule 13(2)[27] provides that the powers of the Court in regard to taking evidence are the same in proceedings by or against the Crown.

---

17 *In re Chambers* (1832) Alc & Nap 183.

18 Prisons Acts 1898, s.11 and (NI) 1953, s.16; Criminal Justice Act 1961, s.29 [*to be replaced by*: Crime (Sentences) Act 1997, Sch.1 para.3].

19 *R* v *Home Secretary ex parte Wynne* [1992] QB 406 (CA); *affd.* [1993] 1 WLR 115 (HL).

20 Practice Direction [1990] 8 BNIL 48.

21 *Panayiotou* v *Sony Music* [1994] Ch 142.

22 *Hardie Rubber* v *General Tire* (1973) 129 CLR 521 (order there made for witness whose names not yet known).

23 *Independent Newspapers* v *Irish Press* (1938) 72 ILTR 11.

24 *Neil* v *Silcock* (1904) 38 ILTR 5.

25 *Duffy* v *MOD* [1979] NI 120.

26 *Jocelyn* v *Webb* (1854) 6 Ir Jur OS 306.

27 Made under the Crown Proceedings Act, s.35(2)(f).

Other preparatory steps

13.11 If a party has a document which cannot be formally proved without calling a witness for that purpose alone, then he should serve a notice to admit authenticity under Order 27 rule 5. If he knows or believes that the opponent has an original document, the contents of which he wishes to adduce, he should serve a notice to produce under Order 27 rule 5(4). This enables him to adduce secondary evidence of its contents, such as a copy of it or oral evidence by someone who has read it. There is no need to serve such notice in relation to any document which the opponent has put in a list of discovered documents as being in his possession (Ord.27 r.4(3)).

Civil Evidence Act Notices. See para. 13.129.

Notices to Admit. See paras. 9.97 and 9.98.

Disclosure of medical reports. See para. 11.143.

Disclosure of map, photograph, plan etc. See para. 13.85.

Disclosure of expert evidence in commercial actions. See para. 18.29.

RECEIVABILITY OF EVIDENCE

13.12 Evidence is receivable if it is admissible, and relevant to the material facts. Material facts are those facts which appear to be in dispute between the parties having regard to the writ, pleadings, replies to notices for particulars and formal admissions. Evidence is relevant if, taken alone or in conjunction with other evidence, it is logically capable of being probative of a material fact. Evidence is admissible if it is not excluded by a rule of evidence such as the rule against hearsay. The admissibility of evidence is a matter for the trial judge to decide as it arises, not at an interlocutory stage in anticipation.[28]

13.13 In civil proceedings there is no general discretion to exclude receivable evidence, even in a jury trial, on the grounds that it was obtained unfairly,[29] or that its prejudicial effect outweighs its probative value.[30] Admissible evidence can only be excluded as follows-

(1) Some discretion is given under particular statutes or rules (e.g. the Civil Evidence Act, para. 13.129).

(2) The Court can strike out any material on its record or on the pleadings which is scandalous, etc. or an abuse of process, and thus by implication exclude evidence in respect of it.

(3) The Court can refuse to use its coercive power to compel a witness to give evidence or produce a document if he is unwilling to do so.

(4) In cases of expert evidence, the trial judge must have a discretion whether to admit evidence which is on the borderline of argumentative speculation on the issues to be decided by the court.[31]

---

28 *Dean* v *Gallagher* [1995] 4 BNIL 95 (CA), *per* MacDermott LJ.

29 *Harry Parker Ltd* v *Mason* [1940] 2 KB 590, at 599 (illicitly recorded interview of defendant).

30 *Re C* [1993] 4 All ER 690 (CA); *Crymble* v *Russell*, CA, NI, 23 May 1968, *per* Lowry J.

31 *AG* v *Equiticorp Industries* [1995] 2 NZLR 135.

(5) Under the privilege of public interest or the related 'administration of justice' privilege (see paras. 13.46-13.50).

Relevance

13.14 There are two types of relevant evidence-

(1) that which is directly probative (i.e. a primary fact), a fact which if believed conclusively establishes the fact to be proved; and
(2) that which is indirectly probative (i.e. a secondary or circumstantial fact), a fact which if believed may lead the jury to infer a fact to be proved.

In general circumstantial evidence is capable of proving any fact however crucial,[32] unless it is equally consistent with some other fact. Whether or not to draw the inference is a matter for the (judge as) jury.[33] A cumulation of circumstantial evidence, each item of which by itself is neutral, may lead to an inference because of the natural presumption against coincidence. The test of relevance is flexible. All sorts of facts are received which are incidental to the relevant facts, because the narrative of the event would be bare and disjointed without them. Facts divorced in time and space from the material event are not necessarily irrelevant for they may have some direct or circumstantial probative value. "Proofs ... must often be admitted, as it were, *de bene esse*, otherwise trials could scarcely be conducted."[34] The Court of Appeal in Northern Ireland has said *obiter* that evidence relevant only to a collateral issue can be excluded if it would lead to an investigation of facts of limited relevance prolonging the trial.[35] But the English Court of Appeal has held that, at least in the absence of an abuse of process, there is no discretion to exclude potentially relevant evidence or questions.[36] Facts relevant to admissibility of evidence are receivable for that purpose. Facts relevant of credibility of a witness are receivable in cross-examination and are said to be 'collaterally relevant'.

13.15 A party cannot call evidence to show that his witness is of good character.[37] The character, criminal record and unconnected conduct of a party are as a rule irrelevant, though with the following main exceptions-

(1) If he gives evidence his character is open to cross-examination on the collateral issue of credibility.
(2) His manners and temper may be relevant.[38]
(3) His habit of conduct may suggest how he behaved on a relevant occasion,[39] as where systematic fraud is pleaded.[40]

---

32 *Dowling* v *Dowling* (1860) 10 ICLR 236 (evidence of plaintiff's poverty to show that he did not lend money).
33 *Re Midland Rly Co* (1904) 38 ILTR 52.
34 *Per* Smith B, *Blackwood* v *Gregg* (1831) Hayes 277, at 313.
35 *Dean* v *Gallagher* [1995] 4 BNIL 95 (CA), *per* Carswell LJ.
36 *Vernon* v *Bosley* [1994] PIQR P337 (CA); *per* Ralph Gibson and Farquharson LJJ. Hoffman LJ thought that minimally relevant evidence could be balanced against the extra time and expense caused by it.
37 *Niedner Ltd* v *Lloyds Bank* (1990) 72 DLR 4th 147 (HC, Ont).
38 *AG* v *O'Leary* [1926] IR 445.
39 *Hales* v *Kerr* [1908] 2 KB 601 (negligence of barber causing diseases to customers).
40 *Edinburgh Life* v *Y* [1911] 1 IR 306.

(4) Previous conduct may show that he has or lacks knowledge or skill; but a bad driving record is not admissible to show that he drove negligently in the present accident.[41]
(5) Similar acts may be relevant to rebut a defence of mistaken identity, accident, innocent explanation; or to rebut coincidence;[42] or in any case where the acts may be logically probative of a relevant issue.[43]
(6) Conduct in preparation of the proceedings such as bribery or intimidation of witnesses may suggest that his case is false, but not *per se* delay in prosecuting the action.[44]
(7) In defamation actions, other publications may be relevant to show malice. The plaintiff's publicly known character, including criminal record, is relevant to his reputation; and of course the character of the plaintiff may be the very issue on which justification is pleaded.
(8) *Semble*, if a party claims a good character or blackens his opponent, it would be unjust to prevent contrary evidence.

13.16 Unconnected transactions and events are generally irrelevant, with the following main exceptions: (a) to show local or trade custom; (b) to show the common or recommended standard of conduct, or to show that the defendant should have known of the risk,[45] in actions for negligence ; (c) to prove valuation of property by comparable sales;[46] (d) other research and empirical findings on which an expert may base his opinion; (e) other acts in a conspiracy in which the defendant is alleged to be a participant;[47] (f) in mitigation of damages to show that the plaintiffs has been compensated for other publications of similar defamatory words.[48]

Opinion evidence

13.17 The opinion of any person, even a party or witness, is generally irrelevant, except-

(1) his state of mind or knowledge may itself be relevant;
(2) reputation (i.e. general opinion is admissible to prove a public right);
(3) family reputation to prove pedigree;
(4) local opinion to prove marriage;
(5) opinion of the plaintiff's character to show his reputation in a defamation action;
(6) by statute where the opinion or judgment of a governmental or public body is to be proved;[49]

---

41 *Brown* v *Eastern & Midland Rly* (1889) 22 QBD 391, at 393.
42 *Manchester Breweries* v *Coombs* (1901) 82 LT 347.
43 *McDermott* v *Derry Construction* [1976] 8 NIJB at 7; *McCartney* v *Sunday Newspapers* [1988] NI 565 (subject to a discretion to exclude).
44 *Mannix* v *Pluck* [1975] IR 169.
45 *Dean* v *Gallagher* [1995] 4 BNIL 95 (CA).
46 *Ulster Bank* v *Min of Finance* [1923] 2 IR 173 (NI).
47 *O'Keeffe* v *Walsh* [1903] 2 IR 681.
48 Defamation Act (NI) 1955, s.12.
49 To be proved by sealed certificate under the Ministries of Northern Ireland Act (NI) 1921, s.3; not by oral evidence of an official: *Belfast Corp* v *OD Cars* [1960] AC 490.

(7) a witness's prejudices and opinions may be probed in cross-examination;
(8) 'impression evidence': any witness can state the inferences and conclusions which he draws instinctively from things perceived by the senses and by common sense (e.g. to say that someone is old, or happy, or drunk, that a car was driving very fast);[50]
(9) opinion of an expert (see para. 13.88);
(10) where the state of opinion of the public or a class of the public is relevant to an issue, evidence of a properly conducted market research survey on a properly drafted questionnaire is admissible.[51]

BURDEN OF PROOF

13.18 In general a party bears the burden of proving any allegation of fact, positive or negative, which is a part of his case. The plaintiff must prove all matters which give a right to the relief claimed (i.e. all facts properly pleaded in the Statement of Claim). The defendant must prove all facts which disentitle or reduce the plaintiff's relief (i.e. all facts properly pleaded in the Defence other than bare traverses). The plaintiff must prove matters in rebuttal of the Defence other than bare traverses. A party is relieved of the burden: (a) on facts presumed in his favour by the law or by contract between the parties; (b) on matters of which the court takes judicial notice.

13.19 Though the legal burden of proof is fixed by the pleadings, there is an evidential burden which may shift to and fro. Though a party may not bear the legal burden he does have the evidential burden to raise an issue and to adduce some evidence against that of the opponent. For example the legal burden may lie on the plaintiff to prove a negative averment on a matter within the peculiar knowledge of the defendant (e.g. that the defendant failed to warn or instruct the plaintiff). Such an averment may be proved by its mere assertion by a plaintiff's witness unless the defendant gives some evidence that he did. Also the party on whom the legal burden of proof lies has an evidential burden to raise a prima facie case, that is, enough evidence for the issue to be left to the jury.

Standard of proof

13.20 The legal burden is discharged by proof on the balance of probabilities. To prove a contempt which renders a person liable to punitive sanction requires proof beyond reasonable doubt. Proof of a matrimonial offence may still require a higher standard, though the case law on this pre-dates the abolition of the matrimonial offence as such in 1978. Fraud, crime or professional incompetence is proved in the normal civil standard; but the more base the conduct, the clearer the proof ought to be.[52] The same applies to any issue on which the liberty of a person is at stake: the graver the intrusion the clearer the

---

[50] See *Sherrard* v *Jacob* [1965] NI 151, at 156-7.

[51] *Auckland RA* v *Mutual Rental Cars* [1987] 2 NZLR 647; *McCartan* v *Finnegan* [1994] 2 BNIL 67 (CA) (Chartered Institute of Marketing survey of local opinion as to adequacy of bookmaking services).

[52] *In re EB Tractors* [1986] NI 165, at 172G; *In re H (Minors) (Sexual Abuse: Standard of Proof)* [1996] AC 563. In the latter case the dissenting minority thought that it should be the balance of probabilities *simpliciter*.

proof.[53] There is a "heavy" onus to prove that a person abandoned his domicile of origin;[54] and on a legatee to prove a will or codicil.[55] "Convincing proof" is required for rectification of a contract.[56]

13.21 In a very few cases the claimant should corroborate evidence by other material evidence from an independent source: a charge of a matrimonial offence or impotence in matrimonial cases; a claim against the estate of a deceased;[57] and an allegation of perjury or subornation.

Judicial notice

13.22 The Court can take judicial notice of domestic law, of the law of England/Wales and the Republic of Ireland (but not of Scotland or any foreign State);[58] of matters of common sense and ordinary experience;[59] of a particular locus from personal knowledge of it; of specialised knowledge of the judge;[60] of matters of general knowledge or of knowledge available by general inquiry.[61] Notice was taken that the Sinn Fein party was associated with terrorism.[62] The Court may order a fact of common knowledge to be proved by a newspaper report (Ord.38 r.3).

Presumptions

Conclusive presumptions of law

13.23 Many statutes provide that a fact shall be presumed, by words such as X "shall be deemed" or "conclusively presumed" or "taken" to be true from fact Y. The Court may, interpreting in its context, treat it as a conclusive, irrebuttable presumption. Examples are: Land Registry Folio as evidence of title, rights and burdens on land;[63] criminal conviction as proof of guilt in defamation actions (see para. 13.25). On solemnisation of marriage, the pre-conditions as to residence, licence requirements etc. are conclusively presumed.[64] The words "Y shall be sufficient evidence of X" creates a conclusive presumption if X is a certificate or order or judicial decision of a person or tribunal acting under a duty; otherwise it is rebuttable.[65] A certificate is not conclusive if it is erroneous on its face.[66] A certificate of a Government Minister cannot be challenged by judicial review as unreasonable or *mala fide* unless the applicant can show extraneous evidence of bad faith.[67] The common

---

53 *R* v *Home Secretary ex p Khawaja* [1984] AC 74, at 113; which was applied to the case of a defence of lawful arrest in an action for false imprisonment: *Hanna* v *Chief Constable* [1986] NI 103, at 110.

54 *Holden* v *Holden* [1968] NI 7.

55 *Leahy* v *Corboy* [1969] IR 148.

56 *Irish Life* v *Dublin Land* [1989] IR 253.

57 But not mandatory: *Somers* v *Erskine (No 2)* [1944] IR 368.

58 Judicature Act, s.114.

59 *Byrne* v *Londonderry Tram Co* [1902] 2 IR 457, at 482.

60 *In re Stewart*, QBD, NI, 12 January 1996 (Carswell LJ), at p.13.

61 *Waters* v *Cruikshank* [1967] IR 378.

62 *In re McCartney* [1987] 11 NIJB 94, at 100-1.

63 Land Registration Act (NI) 1970, s.11.

64 Marriages (Ir) Act 1844, s.32.

65 *Muller Staub* v *McBride* (1922) [1925] NI 7.

66 *Dairy Disposal* v *Lixnaw Creamery* [1937] IR 592.

67 *In re Savage* [1991] NI 103.

law creates few instances of conclusive presumption, apart from issue estoppel (see para. 13.104). It is not conclusively presumed that a person knows his own private legal rights, in applying equitable doctrines of laches and acquiescence.[68]

Rebuttable presumptions of law

13.24 There are many presumptions of law, created by statute or common law, some general, some dependent on proof of an initial fact, which are rebuttable: they operate to shift the legal burden of proof. Common examples-

(1) of innocence of serious crime,[69] rebuttable on balance of probabilities;[70]
(2) of sanity;
(3) against suicide;
(4) of death of a person not heard of for seven years;
(5) of legitimacy, rebuttable on balance of probabilities;[71]
(6) of marriage from co-habitation;
(7) of validity of marriage ceremony;
(8) that an owner of land is its occupier, and that a person named in the rate book is the occupier;[72]
(9) *omnia rita acte esse praesumuntur,*[73] (e.g. a will in correct form is presumed duly executed);[74]
(10) *ex diurnitate temporis omnia rita acta esse praesumuntur*;[75]
(11) *omnia praesumuntur contra spoliatorem*;[76]
(12) a person on factory premises during work is presumed to be employed there;[77]
(13) a driver of motor vehicle is presumed to be agent of the owner in proceedings for damages for negligence against the latter;[78]
(14) as to disposal of car on hire-purchase (see Hire Purchase Act (NI) 1966, s.63).

Convictions

13.25 Under the Civil Evidence Act (NI) 1971 (s.7) the conviction of any person of an offence by a court in the United Kingdom or a court-martial anywhere is admissible to prove that he committed the offence, as revealed by the complaint, indictment, order of conviction etc.; and he is taken to be guilty of it unless the contrary is proved. In a defamation action such conviction *of a*

---

68 *Cooper* v *Phibbs* (1865) 17 Ir Ch R 73; varied (1867) LR 2 HL 149, at 170.
69 Phipson 4-28; possibly supported by *Quinn* v *Sec of State* [1977] 2 NIJB at 12.
70 *Cavendish* v *Dublin Corp* [1974] IR 171.
71 Family Law Reform (NI) Order 1977, Art.14.
72 *Kerry CC* v *Gun Browne* [1948] IR 399.
73 Formal acts presumed to have been performed under correct procedure: *Reid* v *Millar* [1928] NI 151.
74 *Goods of McLean* [1950] IR 180.
75 Formal acts of ancient origin presumed to have lawful basis: *Vandeleur* v *Glynn* [1905] 1 IR 483, at 526-7.
76 The most adverse presumptions are made against him who destroys or hides evidence: *Williamson* v *Rover Cycle* [1901] 2 IR 615; *Bowles* v *Stewart* (1803) 1 Sch & L 209.
77 Factories Act (NI) 1965, s.166.
78 Road Traffic (NI) Order 1981, Art.207.

plaintiff is conclusive evidence of his guilt insofar as it is relevant to an issue arising on his or any co-plaintiff's cause of action (s.9, as amended 1996). Section 8 provides a rebuttable presumption from any finding of adultery in a matrimonial High Court or divorce county court in the United Kingdom, and a finding of paternity in child care and other specified proceedings in the United Kingdom. The person convicted need not be a party but his guilt must be relevant to a material issue in dispute. The conviction for careless driving is proof of negligence but not of causation.[79] There are no fetters on a defendant in the civil case seeking to prove on balance of probabilities that his conviction is wrong, though it may be an uphill task if it was a fully contested trial; a plaintiff who sues to disprove his own conviction by fresh evidence will have his action struck out as abuse of process if the evidence could have been discovered for the criminal trial or if it is not such as to change entirely the aspect of the case (see para. 11.181). A 'spent' conviction under the Rehabilitation of Offenders (NI) Order 1978 is inadmissible unless the convicted person consents or the Court is satisfied that justice can be done only by admitting it (Arts.5(1), and 8). It normally will be in the interests of justice to admit it if the conviction is relevant under the 1971 Act.

13.26 A party must plead the conviction and particulars of it, and the issue to which it is relevant. In an action with pleadings, any party intending to rely on such a conviction or finding under section 7 or 8 of the 1971 Act must state in his pleading his intention to do so, with particulars of the conviction etc., the court and date, and the issue to which the conviction etc. is relevant in the present action (Ord.18 r.23(1)(2)).[80] Though not expressly required by the rule, it should also be pleaded in defamation actions (White Book (1997) 18/7A/4). The opponent must plead to it: (a) by denying it; (b) by alleging it to be erroneous (not available to plaintiff in defamation action); or (c) by denying its relevance (Ord.18 r.23(3)).[81] Only on plea (b) does the burden of proof lie on the party disputing the conviction. A United Kingdom conviction is proved by a certificate of conviction on indictment or certified copy of a summary conviction, under the Prevention of Crimes Act 1871 (s.18).

13.27 It remains the law that an acquittal, dismissal or withdrawal of a charge is not evidence of anything, nor is a foreign conviction. So a conviction in the Republic of Ireland is not admissible except as an admission by a party if he pleaded guilty.[82]

Presumptions of fact

13.28 The courts apply an inexhaustible number of presumptions or inferences of fact which aid a party to establish a fact regardless of where the legal burden of proof lies. Such presumption does not shift the legal burden but it may shift the evidential burden. It is a matter for the (judge as) jury what weight to attach to the inference, and the Court of Appeal can review it.

---

79 *Laffey* v *McCloskey* [1986] 1 NIJB 9, at 13.

80 *Semble*, if the finding was made after the close of pleadings, it must be raised by amendment of the pleading or by formal notice.

81 This appears to put the onus on a plaintiff to serve a Reply if a conviction etc. is alleged in the Defence.

82 *Securicor* v *Anglia Building Soc* [1992] 7 NIJB 34, at 51.

Common examples are presumptions: of continuance of life; of continuance of a state of affairs; of a document being executed on the date it bears;[83] that a person intends the natural and probable consequences of his acts; that a person knows what is apparent to a reasonable person. A failure to observe a provision of the Highway Code is relevant to liability,[84] but it is only a factor in assessing negligence.[85]

Where a person elects not to give evidence on a matter which implicated him (a co-respondent in a petition alleging adultery), McVeigh LJ said: "I am entitled to take this failure into account in considering his guilt".[86] Where a party declines to call an available witness, the Court may infer that the witness would not help his case.[87] But where a party calls or gives evidence of an alleged fact, the Court should not draw an inference against him merely because the evidence is not believed.[88]

13.29 *'Res ipsa loquitur'*. This maxim is the presumption that a person is guilty of negligence if damage has been caused by something in his exclusive control in such a way as would not have happened normally if proper care had been taken.[89] It is not applied where there is a latent defect,[90] but is applied where the defect cannot be explained by the defendant.[91] There has been much judicial conflict as to the effect of the presumption: whether it shifts the legal burden onto the defendant to disprove negligence, or merely puts an evidential burden on him.[92] In *Ng Chun Pui* v *Lee Chuen Tat*[93] the latter view was favoured by the Privy Council.

ADDUCTION OF EVIDENCE

13.30 Subject to rules, statutes and the laws of evidence, "any fact required to be proved at the trial of any action begun by writ by the evidence of witnesses shall be proved by the examination of witnesses orally and in open court" (Ord.38 r.1). But where a party causes a witness to be called, to give oral evidence which was unnecessary or could have been adduced in another manner, the Court may order him to pay the costs occasioned (Ord.62 r.10A). This rule can be invoked in particular to encourage the parties to abide by the

---

83 *Kenny* v *Kenealy* [1895] 2 IR 544.

84 Road Traffic (NI) Order 1995, Art.51(6).

85 *Dowie* v *Melvin* [1973] NI 60.

86 *Funston* v *Funston*, QB Mat, NI, 18 June 1965 at p.5, noted 16 NILQ 418.

87 *Lynch* v *MOD* [1983] NI 216, at 222H.

88 *Hutch* v *Dublin Corporation* [1993] 3 IR 551, at 558.

89 See for instance *Alexander* v *Anderson* [1933] NI 158 and *White* v *Garvin* (1933) 67 ILTR 105 (driving cases decided by the same three Appeal Judges in the same Term); *Palmer* v *Bateman* [1908] 2 IR 393 (gutter falling from house); *Lindsay* v *Mid Western Health Board* [1993] 2 IR 147 (medical negligence).

90 *McQueen* v *Glasgow Garden Festival* 1995 SLT 211.

91 *Merriman* v *Greenhills Foods* [1997] 1 ILRM 46 (SC).

92 See *McBride* v *Stitt* [1944] NI 7; *Millington* v *CIE* (1974) 108 ILTR 61; *Mullen* v *Quinnsworth* [1990] 1 IR 59; *Henderson* v *Henry Jenkins* [1970] AC 282; *Newell* v *Bowden* [1976] 4 NIJB at 8-9.

93 [1988] RTR 298; and by the Court of Session: *Binnie* v *Rederij Theodoro BV*, 1993 SC 71 (1st Div).

various rules which allow for evidence to be adduced by statements, reports etc. The powers over the taking of evidence apply to proceedings by or against the Crown (Ord.77 r.13(2)), without prejudice to the rule of law preventing disclosure of any matter injurious to the public interest.

13.31 The High Court has power to take evidence for the purpose of proceedings in a foreign court[94] under the Evidence (Proceedings in other Jurisdictions) Act 1975 by the procedure in Order 70. Evidence for the purpose of proceedings in our courts can be taken in the English High Court under the English RSC 1965 (Ord.70); in Scotland under the Rules of Court of Session 1994 (Chap.66); in the Republic of Ireland under the Rules of the Superior Courts 1986 (Ord.39 rr.39-44); and in courts of other foreign countries which have ratified the Hague Convention of 1970.

An action may be brought solely for perpetuation of testimony, that is, to take the evidence of a witness relevant to some future right to an honour, office, estate etc. (Ord.39 r.15). It can be brought against the Crown (Ord.77 r.13(1)).

13.32 The strict rules of evidence apply at the plenary hearing of proceedings in the High Court, whether at first instance or on appeal, save in the limited class of non-adversarial or administrative or child welfare proceedings.[95] In any proceedings, evidence in connection with the upbringing, maintenance and welfare of a child is admisssible notwithstanding the hearsay rule. [96]

Affidavit evidence

13.33 Affidavit evidence is more fully discussed in the context of interlocutory proceedings, at para.11.13. In a writ action the Court may order that the affidavit of a witness may be read at the trial if it is reasonable to do so, subject to any terms as to filing and serving the affidavit, or as to attendance of the deponent for cross-examination as the Court thinks fit (Ord.38 r.2(1)(2)). A request for cross-examination is the proper way to attack the deponent's credit, rather than a counter-affidavit.[97] Any such order can be revoked or varied (Ord.38 r.4). Once filed, the other party may rely on admissions contained in it.[98] Crucial facts should be proved by oral testimony.[99] An affidavit should not be allowed at the trial if oral evidence of the fact could be given.[100] In proceedings commenced by originating summons, motion or petition, or on any application by summons or motion, affidavit evidence can be given but any party may apply for the deponent to be ordered to attend for cross-examination (Ord.38 r.2(3)). A person cannot be compelled to make an

---

94 And the European Court: SI 1976/428.

95 *In re PB* [1986] NI 88. Rules of court may provide for hearsay in child care evidence: Children (NI) Order 1995, Art.169(5)(6).

96 Chidren (Admissibility of Hearsay Evidence) Order SR 1996/301, made under the Children (NI) Order 1995, Art.169(5)(6).

97 *Croft* v *Crofts* (1854) 6 Ir Jur OS 249.

98 White Book (1997) 38/2/6.

99 *Cronin* v *Paul* (1881) 15 ILTR 121.

100 *Hegarty* v *Henry* [1990] 7 BNIL 61 (Londonderry Rec Ct). And see *Phonographic Performance* v *Cody* [1994] 2 ILRM 241.

affidavit. In the Chancery Division, counsel should consider what facts can be proved by affidavit.[101]

Proof by other methods

13.34 The Court may order that evidence of any fact be given in any specified manner, for example by statement on oath of information or belief; by production of documents or entries in books or copies thereof; or of matters of common knowledge by newspaper report (Ord.38 r.3). This power is usually invoked to order proof by affidavit or statement of a formal obvious or peripheral fact. The Court has a wide discretion as to the fact to be proved and the mode of proof, but not, where crucial disputed facts are concerned, to obviate the proper rules of evidence.[102] In *Garcin* v *Amerindo Advisors*[103] it was used to allow the adduction of oral evidence through a live television link. Any such order may be later revoked or varied (Ord.38 r.4).

The Court may at any stage in any proceedings order a person to attend and produce a document, subject to his claim of privilege (Ord.38 r.11).

Evidence by deposition. See para. 13.10.

COMPETENCE AND COMPELLABILITY

13.35 Any human person may give evidence on oath in civil proceedings except-

(1) a person presently suffering from such lunacy or drunkenness etc., as prevents him from understanding the duty imposed by the oath.
(2) a child who does not understand the oath. There is no set age;[104] but a child who understands the duty to speak the truth can give unsworn testimony.[105]
(3) the judge in a case being heard by him (or the jury?).
(4) a witness cannot testify on a matter on which he is bound by a privilege vested in another.

Every competent witness is compellable to attend if subpoenaed, to be sworn if called and to answer any question, on pain of punishment for contempt. There is no property in a witness. A party can *subpoena* and call any person, including the opposite party. There is no rule of law that counsel/solicitor for one party may not consult with a person brought to court by the opponent. That person has the choice whether to speak or not. As a matter of etiquette the opposing party should be told in advance of the intention to do so. Any attempt to intimidate or persuade the person to change his evidence is contempt.[106] A barrister may freely consult with a witness in consultation arranged by his

---

101 Practice Direction 1997 No 4 (Ch D) [1997] 5 BNIL.

102 *Arab Monetary Fund* v *Hashim (No 7)* [1993] 1 WLR 1014.

103 [1991] 1 WLR 1140; and in *R* v *Horseferry Road Mag Ct ex p Bennett* [1995] COD 321 (DC), for a live TV link from South Africa.

104 *AG* v *O'Sullivan* [1930] IR 552.

105 Children (NI) Order 1995, Art.169(3)(4).

106 *Magrath* v *Browne* (1842) Arm Mac & Og 133.

solicitor, but cannot participate in the taking of a witness statement; in a road traffic case he may consult with a police witness only on the day of trial.[107]

13.36 The following are not compellable to testify: (a) persons who are incompetent; (b) the Queen or any foreign sovereign; (c) ambassadors and their suites, and diplomatic agents;[108] High Commissioners and their staff of the Commonwealth or Republic of Ireland; staff of United Nations and international organisations; (d) a consul, including an honorary consul, cannot be penalised for refusing to testify;[109] (e) a banker is not compellable without an order of a judge to produce his books or to prove transactions recorded therein, if he is not a party and the books can be proved by copies;[110] (f) the 'ombudsman' cannot be compelled to reveal matters disclosed by his investigations;[111] (g) a judge, barrister or juror cannot be compelled to testify as to matters known to them from the performance of their functions in court proceedings (para. 13.51).

PRIVILEGE

13.37 The general rule of compellability is that: (a) a party must on request under Order 24 disclose the contents of any relevant document in his possession; and (b) any witness on *subpoena* must attend to give evidence or produce any document, and must in the witness box answer any question and produce any document. Privilege is not a law of admissibility but is an exception to the law of compellability. It is a right vested in a particular person, as party or witness, and he may waive it. Except in so far as the right binds another person, evidence from any other source of the privileged fact or document is admissible. For example if a privileged document comes into the hands of a party fortuitously he may use it; and a person who overheard a privileged conversation can, and can be compelled to, give evidence of it (Phipson 20-06). However, the privileges without prejudice (para. 13.43) and public interest (para. 13.46) amount virtually to rules of admissibility.

The classes of privilege are as follows.

(i) Legal professional privilege

13.38 Privilege arises in relation to a client and his legal adviser, which means not only a solicitor but a full time salaried legal adviser;[112] a barrister and foreign lawyers; but not medical, spiritual or lay advisers, nor, *semble*, an MP. The privilege vests in the client and his successor in title only. No other person is bound by it except the legal adviser.

---

107 Bar Handbook 14-13 and 14-14.

108 Diplomatic Privileges Act 1964, Sch.1 Arts.31,37.

109 Consular Relations Act 1968, Sch.1 Arts.44, 58.

110 Bankers Books Evidence Act 1879, s.6. He is compellable if he refuses copies: *Coleman* v *Coleman* (1898) 32 ILTR 66.

111 Parliamentary Commissioner Act 1967, s.11; Ombudsman (NI) Order 1996, Art.19; Commissioner for Complaints (NI) Order 1996, Art.21.

112 *Geraghty* v *Min of Local Govt* [1975] IR 300.

Head A: ***communications privileged regardless of litigation***
confidential communications passing between client and solicitor or by, to or through an employee of either or counsel or the solicitor's partner or professional agent, made for the purpose of getting legal advice or assistance. It covers communications made through a non-legal person who is a mere conduit pipe. It covers only communications relating to legal advice or opinion;[113] and thus excludes communications relating to legal assistance.[114]

Head B: ***communications privileged only if in relation to any pending or contemplated litigation in any country***

B1 confidential communications between client and solicitor not for legal advice.

B2 confidential communications between solicitor and an agent or person not of the legal profession, made for the purpose either of preparing a case or of giving advice in the litigation; but not for deciding whether to sue at some future time.[115]

B3 confidential communications between the client and a non-legal person for the same purpose as B2 and made either at the solicitor's instigation or as agent for him, or for the purpose of giving it to the solicitor for legal advice on litigation. Communications for the purpose of deciding whether to go to a solicitor are not privileged.

13.39 B2 includes communications between solicitors representing parties with a common interest; and *semble*, it includes communications between solicitor and counsel, or between senior and junior counsel. Under Head B, a co-plaintiff or co-defendant is treated as a non-legal person. Heads B2 and B3 privilege only arise if the submission for legal advice was the dominant purpose.[116]

13.40 If a document was not privileged when created, privilege does not attach to it or to a copy of it used only in Head A circumstances.[117] A document obtained, or a copy made, for advice on litigation where the document was never yet in the possession of the client, is privileged; but where an unprivileged document which is or has been in the client's possession is furnished, or a copy made, for advice in litigation, it is not privileged unless it is put into a bundle of materials selected and organised for the purpose of the litigation.[118] Therefore a copy of treatment records[119] and a copy of the client's police statement[120] are

---

113 *Sankey* v *Alexander* (1874) IR 8 Eq 241.

114 *Smurfit Paribas* v *AAB* [1990] 1 IR 469.

115 *Rushbrooke* v *O'Sullivan* [1926] IR 500.

116 *Waugh* v *BRB* [1980] AC 521; *Mullen* v *Dublin United Tramways* (1907) 41 ILTR 236; *Hughes* v *Law* [1988] 12 NIJB 30 (routine post-accident report for Ulsterbus not privileged); *Mark* v *Flexibox* [1988] NI 58 (medical report on worker on reference from the factory doctor, not privileged); *Andrews* v *NIR* [1992] NI 1 (railway accident report made for transmission to defendant's insurer in the event of a claim, held privileged).

117 *Graham* v *Bogle* [1924] 1 IR 68 (NI).

118 Phipson 20-22; *Wilson* v *Liquid Packaging* [1979] NI 165; *O'Sullivan* v *Herdmans* [1986] NI 214 (CA); *Dubai Bank* v *Galadari* [1990] Ch 98 (CA).

119 *Watson* v *Cammell Laird* [1959] 2 All ER 757.

privileged if obtained for litigation. In *Ventouris* v *Mountain*[121] the English Court of Appeal has changed its mind and now says that a document obtained or a copy of it made for litigation, which document was never in the client's possession, is no more privileged than a document in the client's possession. This decision is in stark conflict with the cases quoted above, including the NI Court of Appeal in *O'Sullivan* v *Herdmans.* Since a petition for leave to appeal was refused by the House of Lords in *Ventouris,* it is hard to say what authority should be followed here.

13.41 The privilege can be claimed by the client or his successor in title in the litigation contemplated and in any subsequent litigation on any subject between any parties, ("once privileged, always privileged") certainly in relation to Head A communications. As to Head B communications, there is a conflict of authority. Some say that the same rule applies as in Head A;[122] some say that the privilege is confined to the litigation in contemplation of which the Head B communication was made or litigation on the same subject-matter.[123] The client can elect to waive the privilege, and his solicitor or counsel in pending proceedings has ostensible authority to do so.[124] Disclosing a privileged document to the other party for unrestricted use in the litigation is a waiver of privilege in that litigation;[125] unless the disclosure was procured by fraud or was by mistake.[126] Disclosure of a privileged report does not waive privilege in any source material which is neither contained in nor referred to in the report.[127] Where, on request by the defendant, the plaintiff discloses his medical history on which his doctor's report is based, documents identified therein do not cease to be privileged.[128] Using the document in open court waives privilege in the whole of it;[124] but using it before a judge in chambers in a minor settlement

---

120 *Osborne* v *Sullivan* [1965] NZLR 1095. See previous page.

121 [1991] 1 WLR 607 (CA), applied by Morritt J in *Dubai Bank* v *Galadari (No 7)* [1992] 1 WLR 106.

122 *Kerry CC* v *Liverpool Salvage* [1905] 2 IR 38, at 42-3, *per* Kenny J in the Divisional Court of the High Court, speaking of B3 communications; supported by the English CA in *The Aegis Blaze* [1986] 1 Lloyds R 203.

123 *Porter* v *Scott* [1979] NI 6, where Kelly J said that B2 communications, such as a medical report, are privileged only the litigation for which made and subsequent litigation on the same subject-matter. He cited the Court of Appeal in the previously noted case, *Kerry CC* v *Liverpool Salvage* (1904) 38 ILTR 7, where the Lord Justices said the same about B3 communications.

124 *Great Atlantic* v *Home Insurance* [1981] 1 WLR 529, at 539-40.

125 *Porter* v *Scott* [1979] NI 6.

126 *Derby & Co* v *Weldon (No 8)* [1991] 1 WLR 73; *National Insurance* v *Whirlybird Holdings* [1994] 2 NZLR 513. In *Carey* v *Cuthbert* (1872) IR 6 Eq 599, the defence solicitor sent a copy of his counsel's opinion to the plaintiff. The plaintiff applied for production of the original opinion and of the brief sent for the opinion, but these documents were held to be still privileged. Of course at the trial the plaintiff could adduce in evidence the copy of the opinion if the defendant refused to produce the original.

127 *A-G (Northern Territory)* v *Maurice* (1986) 161 CLR 475 (HC of Aus).

128 *B* v *John Wyeth* [1992] 1 WLR 168.

hearing does not.[129] Sending the document to another person for a purpose unconnected with the litigation does not waive privilege.[130]

13.42 In the following cases legal professional privilege is not upheld-

(1) a communication by, to or in the presence of the opposite party in the litigation (e.g. a statement taken by the solicitor from the opposite party for use in the litigation);[131]

(2) documents, the contents of which are *publici juris*, such as notes of proceedings and of orders made in court, though a selective collation of such documents for litigation is privileged;

(3) communications in furtherance of crime or fraud,[132] or of deliberate abuse of statutory power,[133] or of any underhand purpose or abuse of justice,[134] if a prima facie case thereof is shown;[135]

(4) against a party who has a proprietary right in the document, or to whom a fiduciary duty is owed;

(5) things, such as machines, which are real evidence;

(6) communications relating to execution of a judgment;[136]

(7) a solicitor can be compelled to use privileged documents to prove his client's handwriting;[137]

(8) where the privileged communications are a material issue, for example in determining the expiry of the limitation period; or the solicitor's authority to contract for the client is in dispute;[138] or where the privileged communication is relevant to show what the (deceased) client's true intention was;[139]

(9) Head B2 and B3 communications prepared for non-adversarial proceedings, such as wardship and child care, have no privilege in those proceedings or in any other proceedings.[140]

---

129 *Goldstone* v *Williams* [1899] 1 Ch 47, at 52-3.

130 *Wilson* v *Liquid Packaging* [1979] NI 165 (sent to client's MP); *Downey* v *Murray* [1988] NI 600 (sent to the police for use in possible police prosecution). And the privilege remains even though the prosecutor discloses the statement to the accused who is the opposing party in the civil litigation: *British Coal* v *Dennis Rye* [1988] 3 All ER 816.

131 *McKay* v *McKay* [1988] NI 611, but see the previous note. Statements taken from an employee of the opposing party are privileged: *Alberta* v *Stearns Catalytic* (1991) 81 DLR 4th 347 (CA, Alberta).

132 Including the criminal purpose of another person of which neither client nor solicitor are aware: *R* v *Central Crim Ct ex parte Francis* [1989] AC 346.

133 *A-G (Northern Territory)* v *Kearney* (1985) 158 CLR 500 (HC of Aus).

134 *Murphy* v *Kirwan* [1993] 3 IR 501; but not communications in furtherance of a civil tort: *Bula* v *Crowley* [1994] 1 ILRM 495 (SC).

135 *Matua Finance* v *Equiticorp Industries* [1993] 3 NZLR 650.

136 *Calbeck* v *Boon* (1873) IR 7 CL 32.

137 *Bowles* v *Stewart* (1803) 1 Sch & L 209, at 226.

138 *Century Insurance* v *Falloon* [1971] NI 234; *contra*, *Bula* v *Crowley* [1994] 1 ILRM 495.

139 *Geffen* v *Goodman Estate* (1991) 81 DLR 4th 211 (SC, Canada).

140 *In re L (Police Investigation: Privilege)* [1997] AC 16; *Vernon* v *Bosley (No 2)* [1997] 1 All ER 614, at 628c (CA, Evans LJ dissenting).

(ii) 'Without prejudice'

13.43 There is privilege for communications expressly or impliedly 'without prejudice', between the parties or their lawyers *bona fide* for the purpose of exploring or suggesting a compromise of matters in dispute in pending or contemplated litigation. The use or failure to use the words 'without prejudice' are not conclusive either way. An offer of settlement is admissible if it is expressed to be 'open'.[141] A gratuitous admission in pre-action correspondence not related to any offer of settlement and not marked 'without prejudice' is not privileged.[142] The privilege does not end if the dispute is settled, and can be claimed in any other litigation on the same subject-matter between the same or different parties.[143] However, without prejudice correspondence before settlement of an employee's action against his employer was not privileged in a later action by the employee against his solicitor for negligence.[144] An offer of compromise cannot be put to the Court in deciding costs unless it is 'without prejudice save as to costs'.[145] The privilege vests in the parties and can be waived only by the consent of both.[146] Secondary evidence cannot be given as the privilege binds all comers.[147] Thus communications between co-defendants with a view to negotiating a settlement are protected from disclosure to the plaintiff.[148] But without prejudice communications are admissible if relevant to a particular issue, such as delay in suing or proceeding, or the validity of a settlement agreement.

(iii) Self-incrimination

13.44 Any person is privileged from answering a question or producing a document or thing which would tend [i.e. materially increase the risk] to expose him or his spouse[149] to proceedings for a criminal offence or for recovery of a penalty under the law of any part of the United Kingdom,[150] unless liability has been extinguished by expiration of time limit, pardon or waiver, or by conviction or acquittal. This privilege is abrogated in proceedings in the High

---

141 *Dixon Stores* v *Thomas Television* [1993] 1 All ER 349, defamation case where the defendant offered to apologise and make a statement in open court. But the courts are reluctant to allow monetary offers to be mentioned to the jury, see para. 18.24.

142 *Gordon* v *East Kilbride Development Corp* 1995 SLT 62.

143 *Rush & Tomkins* v *GLC* [1989] AC 1280; *Greencore Group* v *Murphy* [1996] 1 ILRM 210 (Keane J).

144 *Muller* v *Linsley & Mortimer,* 'The Times' 8 December 1994 (CA).

145 *Cutts* v *Head* [1984] Ch 290.

146 *Computer Machinery* v *Drescher* [1983] 1 WLR 1379, at 1382H.

147 *Theodoropoulas* v *Theodoropoulas* [1964] P 311.

148 *Bula* v *Tara Mines (No 5)* [1994] 1 IR 487.

149 Of a subsisting marriage: s.14.

150 Civil Evidence Act (NI) 1971, s.10. Some Commonwealth and United States authorities hold that the privilege is appropriate only to human persons, not corporations: Cross p.458. There seemed to be no doubt that the privilege applied to a corporate body in *Rio Tinto Zinc* v *Westinghouse Electric* [1978] AC 547. Words in NI legislation importing persons include corporations and unincorporated bodies: Interpretation Act (NI) 1954, s.37. *Semble,* a director or member of a company as a party or witness in his own capacity has no privilege against incriminating the company.

Court relating to intellectual property (copyright, patent, trade mark, design, information etc.), and the evidence is not admissible in a prosecution.[151] There is no privilege for liability to debt or civil suit.[152] The privilege is removed in proceedings for care or protection of children under the Children (NI) Order 1995 (Art.171 thereof). Liability for an offence under the Theft Act (NI) 1969, Theft (NI) Order 1978 or Criminal Damage (NI) Order 1977 for him or his spouse does not protect him in proceedings for recovery or administration of property, execution of a trust or for an account.[153] In any case a court on ordering discovery can bar a claim of privilege by accepting the prosecuting authority's assurance that the information will not be used for criminal prosecution.[154]

13.45 A police witness who was part of an armed group who fired on a crowd can claim privilege for questions about the conduct of his colleagues and events around him, as inferences could be drawn against him on these matters on the issue of reasonable force.[155] The person must claim the privilege and state his *bona fide* belief of incrimination on oath.[156] Only he and his spouse can claim it. He can waive the privilege for himself. *Quaere,* can he waive it for his spouse? No adverse inference can be drawn against a person by reason of his claiming the privilege.[157]

(iv) Public interest

13.46 Privilege may be claimed for any document, evidence or communications, or class of such, which are confidential and of which disclosure would for any reason be injurious to the public interest, balanced against the public interest in the administration of justice.[158] The privilege covers such matters as: (a) national security; (b) communications between police officers, and prosecuting authorities;[159] and evidence of sources of information;[160] (c) the public administration of national government, except possibly in areas of business or commercial nature in which the State has engaged;[161] (d) functions of local government, and statutory, governmental or public bodies whose obligations are closely tied to government and public

---

[151] Judicature Act, s.94A.

[152] Witnesses Act 1806. This provision is not cited in *Comet Products* v *Hawkex Plastics* [1971] 2 QB 67, which held that the privilege covers liability for civil contempt.

[153] S.29, Art.7(2) and Art.11 thereof respectively.

[154] *AT & T Istel* v *Tully* [1993] AC 45; though, *quaere* how this will bind a criminal court to exclude the evidence. The civil court has no power to bind the prosecutor: *Reid* v *Howard* (1995) 69 ALJR 863.

[155] *Masokanye* v *Additional Magistrate* 1994 2 SA 308 (Cape Prov).

[156] *Kelly* v *Colhoun* (1899) 33 ILTR 33.

[157] *Dolan* v *AOTC* (1993) 19 Comm LB 1366 (Fed Ct Aus).

[158] *Conway* v *Rimmer* [1968] AC 910.

[159] *Monaghan* v *Chief Constable* [1988] NI 316; an action for malicious prosecution, where the judge inspected and then ordered partial disclosure.

[160] *R* v *Leipert* (1997) 143 DLR 4th 38 (SCC).

[161] *O'Leary* v *Min of Industry* [1966] IR 676, at 698.

service;[162] (e) information disclosed to a Member of Parliament on a public matter;[163] (f) judicial administration and jury deliberations.

13.47 Documents made under a statutory complaint against the police are not privileged,[164] but the report on the complaint is privileged.[165] A statement made for the purposes of an *informal* resolution of a police complaint is not admissible.[166]

13.48 The Crown, as a party, may refuse discovery on the ground of public interest (Crown Proceedings Act, s.28), and may refuse to disclose the existence of a document (Ord.77 r.11(2)). Any party or witness, including a Crown Servant or official, may claim the privilege and the judge may do so of his own motion. The Crown may intervene in proceedings at any stage, without having to be added as a party, claiming privilege by affidavit or certificate of a minister or departmental official and, through counsel, may object to privileged evidence during a trial. The judge need not treat a Crown claim of privilege as conclusive. He will often examine the document privately to decide the document's confidentiality and the competing interest of justice in the present litigation; and he may order disclosure of parts only or under certain conditions. Only where a Minister claims privilege for a single document on grounds of security, or the document is one of a class for which secrecy is recognised as essential, like Cabinet minutes, should the judge be wary of challenging the claim. A certificate is also an effective way for a Minister to claim immunity for the disclosure by oral evidence of a specified fact or type of information, such as facts about structures or operations of the Armed Forces, and the Court must pay full regard to it.[167] If the Crown seeks screening of a witness on grounds of national security, the Court will balance it against the interests of doing justice in public.[167]

13.49 No one, not even the Crown, can waive the privilege, at least in matters of the highest governmental level (Phipson 19-31), and only the judge can override it. In so deciding he will of course consider the strength of the objection of the persons who are privy to the communication. If the privilege is upheld no evidence of the document or matter can be given. In effect the privilege can be effectively overridden by any person who publishes the information to the public at large, since there is no longer a public interest against disclosure.

(v) 'Administration of justice privilege'

13.50 In *ITC* v *Video Exchange*[168] Warner J may have created a sub-head of public interest privilege imposed in the interests of justice itself: firstly, that any

---

162 *McCroary* v *McKendry* [1981] NI 71, at 75.

163 *Goodman International* v *Hamilton (No 3)* [1993] 3 IR 320.

164 *R* v *Chief Constable of West Midlands ex p Wiley* [1995] 1 AC 274; overruling a line of cases including *Lanigan* v *Chief Constable* [1991] NI 42.

165 *Taylor* v *Anderton* [1995] 1 WLR 447 (CA).

166 Police (NI) Order 1987, Art.22; *to be replaced by* Police (Amendment) (NI) Order 1995, Art.30.

167 *Doherty* v *MOD* [1991] 1 NIJB 68; *In re Ministry of Defence* [1994] 7 BNIL 9.

168 [1982] Ch 431.

document seen by a party by discovery in one action, with the implied undertaking to use the information only in that action, can be excluded from use by that party in another action by invoking privilege; secondly, that a document obtained by a party from his opponent in the court precincts by stealth or a trick tantamount of contempt can be excluded from use. Compare the exclusion of material disclosed to an accused person (para. 13.86).

(vi) Other privileges

13-51 Other recognised cases of privilege are-

(1) Under the Diplomatic Privileges Act 1964, Consular Relations Act 1968 and International Organisations Act 1968, diplomatic premises, archives and residence and private papers are inviolable.

(2) Judges[169] and barristers cannot be compelled to testify as to matters known to them arising from the performance of their functions in court proceedings, though they may speak unsworn from the bar of the court. Jurors cannot be asked about what was said in the jury room. An arbitrator cannot be compelled to state the reasons for his decision.

(3) Disclosure which would breach the Official Secrets Acts 1911-1989.

(4) Information obtained by the 'ombudsman' (Parliamentary Commissioner Act 1967, s.11; Ombudsman (NI) Order 1996, Art.19; Commissioner for Complaints (NI) Order 1996, Art.21).

(5) Information given to the Equal Opportunities Commission cannot be disclosed without a court order, save where it is a party to proceedings under the Sex Discrimination (NI) Order 1976 (Art.61 thereof); so also information about religion given to the Fair Employment Commission (Fair Employment (NI) Act 1989, s.19). As to restrictions on public interest privilege in proceedings under the Fair Employment (NI) Act 1976, see section 52 thereof.

(6) Information supplied to the Law Society in connection with a civil aid application is a privilege vested in the supplier.[170]

(7) A solicitor who has a lien on documents for unpaid costs can refuse to produce them on request of the former client.

(8) A banker in proceedings in which he is not a party cannot be compelled to produce any original books of which the contents can be proved by a copy, nor as a witness to prove matters recorded therein, unless the High Court so orders.[171]

(9) Communications with a patent agent,[172] or trade mark agent.[173]

(10) No evidence can be adduced and no cross-examination allowed which tends to suggest that a Crown official, post office or public telecommunications worker has intercepted a posted letter or

---

169 Including masters of the Supreme Court and judges of inferior courts: *Warren* v *Warren* [1996] 4 All ER 664 (CA).

170 Legal Aid, Advice and Assistance (NI) Order 1981, Art.24.

171 Bankers Books Evidence Act 1879, s.6.

172 Copyright Designs and Patents Act 1988, s.280.

173 Trade Marks Act 1994, s.87.

communication through the public (but not a private) telecommunications system either illegally or legally under a warrant (Interception of Communications Act 1985, s.9). This Act has been interpreted so as to render inadmissible the contents of such a letter or communication, whether intercepted by lawful authority or not,[174] unless the interception is by consent.[175]

(vii) Discretionary privilege

13.52 There is no general rule of privilege for information given in confidence, to doctors, priests,[176] bankers, etc., even though disclosure otherwise than in court litigation might amount to an 'equitable tort' of breach of confidence. But a party or witness can withstand disclosure until ordered by a court, and a court has a residual discretion to refuse discovery, and to refuse to force a witness to answer a question or produce a document, or it can order disclosure on condition that irrelevant parts are covered up, or that the information be used only in the action, or it can hear the evidence *in camera*. Disclosure of trade secrets will not be ordered as of course.[177]

13.53 By section 10 of the Contempt of Court Act 1981, a court cannot compel a publisher of information (usually a newspaper journalist) to reveal his source unless satisfied that it is necessary[178] in the interests of justice, national security or prevention of disorder or crime. Without the benefit of that provision, the Irish Supreme Court, in a libel action where the plaintiff was accused of IRA connections, upheld as a new ground of privilege that disclosure would expose informants to risk of death.[179] An order compelling a journalist to disclose his source may be a breach of the European Convention on Human Rights (Art.10).[180]

ORAL WITNESSES

13.54 Oral witnesses are called by counsel when presenting his case. A party can choose what witnesses to call and in what order, though it is sensible to do so in some logical order. Counsel may freely consult with a witness[181] before he gives evidence. He must not coach the witness,[182] and without leave of the parties and the Court, cannot consult during the witness's period of

---

[174] *R* v *Effik* [1995] 1 AC 309.

[175] *R* v *Rasool*, 'The Times' 17 February 1997 (CA).

[176] The Republic of Ireland recognises privilege for secret communications between a priest and parishioner, but such claim would not be recognised as of right in Northern Ireland, though there is authority for it before partition: *per* Palles CB *obiter*, *Tannian* v *Synnott* (1903) 37 ILT 275.

[177] *Hogan* v *Bayer Products* (1950) 84 ILTR 145.

[178] A preponderate or pressing need: *Haughey* v *Prendiville*, Ch D, NI (Sheil J) 17 December 96.

[179] *Burke* v *Central TV* [1994] 2 ILRM 161.

[180] *Goodwin* v *UK*, 'The Times,' 28 March 1996 (EHCR).

[181] Though only the solicitor may consult with a police witness: Lowry para. 9.

[182] Bar Handbook 8-20.

testimony.[183] Usually the party, if personally involved, is called first, then other witnesses as to fact in roughly chronological order, then experts. The convenience of a medical expert will be given priority. A witness may be called twice to deal with separate aspects.[184] After a party has closed his case he cannot call or re-call a witness unless in special circumstances.[185] Sedley J has claimed that the trial judge has power in the interests of justice to set prior time limits on the examination-in-chief, cross- and re-examination of witnesses, subject to necessary extensions.[186]

Anonymity for witnesses. See para. 14.03.

13.55 *Exclusion of witnesses.* At any stage the judge may, if a party so applies, direct all witnesses (of both parties) to stay out of court until they testify, then remain in court after testifying. Such order is usually made only in cases where honesty is at issue, in order to prevent witnesses from hearing other evidence, and it is very rare in civil cases. If grounds for exclusion are advanced, the Court will balance them against the fact that the issues in dispute can be more clearly and expeditiously resolved if the witnesses are able to hear the evidence. The exclusion does not apply to the parties, their solicitors and expert witnesses (White Book (1997) 38/1/6).

13.56 *The oath.* Every oral witness must take the oath or affirm[187] except the sovereign, a witness merely producing a document, or a judge or a barrister stating what happened in cases in which they took part. A child (up to 18 years) who does not understand the oath may be allowed to give evidence if he understands the duty to tell the truth and has sufficient understanding to justify being heard.[188] A child (up to 18 years) "promises" rather than "swears".[189] The oath or affirmation is administered by the court clerk in accordance with the Oaths Act 1978.

13.57 Any person lawfully sworn as witness or interpreter or who makes an affidavit is guilty of perjury if he wilfully makes a material statement of fact which he knows to be false or does not believe.[190] A witness must answer every question asked by any counsel unless he claims or is bound by privilege, or the judge disallows the question, or the judge in his discretion allows him not to answer. After testifying a witness must remain in court for the rest of the trial unless, through counsel, he asks the judge for permission to leave.

EXAMINATION-IN-CHIEF

13.58 Counsel for a party may call any person as a witness and may examine him in chief. Senior counsel, if present, examines most witnesses. Junior takes a

---

183 *Ibid.* 8-21.

184 *Good* v *Aherne* (1842) 2 Leg Rep 386.

185 *Murray* v *Sheriffs of Dublin* (1842) Arm Mac & Og 130.

186 *Vernon* v *Bosley* [1995] 2 FCR 78.

187 *Graham* v *Ulsterbus* [1993] 3 NIJB 102; *Mapp* v *Gilhooley* [1991] 2 IR 253. These cases concern children, who are now able to testify unsworn.

188 Children (NI) Order 1995, Art.169(3)(4).

189 *Ibid* Art.169(1).

190 Perjury (NI) Order 1979, Art.3.

careful note and records the use of exhibits. The solicitor takes a note and hands up documents and exhibits as required. After taking the oath the clerk asks and records the witness's full name. Though very rare in civil proceedings the witness can testify anonymously, as "Witness A" or "Soldier B". He may even be allowed to be screened from view of the parties and public (see further para. 14.03). Where a ministerial certificate seeks screening in the interests of national security, the Court does not treat it as conclusive.[191]

13.59 Counsel should put the witness at ease by conversational style, keep to a logical order and remember what he wants the witness to prove.[192] He must elicit the testimony by non-leading questions. A leading question is one which, in the way it is framed or worded, prompts or reminds the witness of the answer desired.[193] Whether a question is leading depends often on the context. Lawyers know intuitively when a witness is being led and prevented from giving the story in his own words. The most impressive witnesses are those who can narrate their experiences almost unaided. Leading questions are allowed: (a) on introductory and non-controversial matters, (e.g. to make a non-disputed identification); (b) on disputed matters if the other party consents (of which the judge should be told); (c) in reminding him of what he has already said; (d) to seek his response to what another witness or party has said or pleaded; (e) to help him in listing a series of facts, figures or items which are not easily remembered; (f) to direct his mind to a topic. To save time, some witnesses, especially experts, may simply hand in their written statement or report to stand as evidence-in-chief. In the Chancery Division, proper witness statements should be taken and counsel should try to agree such statements to be the evidence, or at least to be the evidence-in-chief of the witness.[194]

13.60 If the witness has to prove a document, map, etc., he identifies it as it is handed into court by himself or counsel, and the document is stamped by the court clerk and thereby becomes an exhibit.

Assisting memory

13.61 A witness in examination-in-chief and in cross-examination may 'refresh his memory' by looking at a note, document, diagram or recording made by him (or by someone else and checked by him) contemporaneously or later when his memory was fresh. Policemen, experts and persons involved in the disputed event in the course of their work are the type of people expected to rely on notes. Medical experts are by convention allowed to rely on notes and reports made by other doctors. It is not essential that the document stimulates his memory, provided he is sure that it is correct.[195] Some judges insist that the witness should first give as much as he can from recollection before referring to the document to aid him. The witness cannot refer to the document until he has stated orally that it is of a type which he can use. The witness may refer to a

---

[191] *Doherty* v *MOD* [1991] 1 NIJB 68.

[192] Lowry, para.8.

[193] Even worse than leading question is the question which assumes a fact that the witness has not already stated.

[194] Practice Direction 1997 No 4 (Ch D) [1997] 5 BNIL.

[195] *Northern Banking* v *Carpenter* [1931] IR 268, at 276.

copy or transcription of the document as follows: (a) if he claims an independent recollection; (b) if he made or checked the copy while the memory was fresh; (c) if he checked the copy with the original which is now lost; (d) if the transcription is an expanded version of the original sketchy note, both being brought to court; or (e) if the copy is in substance identical. A witness may read over a statement made non-contemporaneously before entering the witness box and the judge may in his discretion allow a witness to refer to such a statement to assist his memory whilst in the witness box.[196]

13.62 The document used to 'refresh memory' does not thereby become evidence of its truth,[197] nor an exhibit, and indeed the witness can use a document which is inadmissible in evidence. Of course the (judge as) jury may well find the testimony to be more reliable and accurate if they see that the witness made a note at the time. If the witness uses the document only to prove handwriting or if it fails to aid him to recall the event, opposing counsel has no right to see the contents. If it does help his recall, opposing counsel can demand to read it and can cross-examine out of it, and can be forced to put the document in evidence only if he cross-examines out of parts not used by the witness.[198] Opposing counsel should be allowed to see the document even if it is subject to a claim of public interest immunity.[199]

Attacking own witness

13.63 Counsel cannot question so as to dispute what his own witness has said, or failed to say, or attack his credibility unless called under a legal obligation. However: (a) he can ask a witness to reconsider an answer if the witness appears to have forgotten or is confused; (b) he can apply for leave to cross-examine his witness if he appears to be hostile (see below);[200] (c) he can adduce in evidence the statement of that witness if the conditions of section 1 of the Evidence Act (NI) 1939 are satisfied;[201] (d) he can call another witness who contradicts the first witness on some point, and may in his submission rely on the latter witness's version.

13.64 Counsel cannot adduce evidence of the bad character of his own witness; if the witness proves in the opinion of the judge to be "adverse" (i.e. hostile), counsel by leave may prove a previous statement (written or oral) inconsistent with his present evidence.[202] Counsel establishes hostility by showing the statement to the judge. If leave is given, he then puts the statement and its circumstances to the witness and asks him whether he admits making it.

---

196 *R* v *South Ribble Stip Mag, ex p Cochrane*, 'The Times' 24 June 1996 (DC).

197 It may be admissible under the Evidence Act (NI) 1939, s.1.

198 Phipson 12-46ff; Cross p.292. The same practice applies to documents read by the witness before entering the witness box: *In re McKerr* [1993] 5 NIJB 18 (read the previous day).

199 *McSorley* v *Chief Constable* [1993] 2 NIJB 73.

200 "Frequently at *Nisi Prius*, if a witness is or appears to be an unwilling witness, the judge allows leading questions to be put to him": Monahan CJ, *Lawder* v *Lawder* (1855) 5 ICLR 27, at 38.

201 *Harvey* v *Smith-Wood* [1964] 2 QB 171.

202 Criminal Procedure Act 1865, s.3. Belying its title, this Act applies to all courts.

If he says no, the statement must be proved formally.[203] Then counsel can cross-examine him by putting the statement, asking leading questions, and disputing his present testimony, but not attacking his character. Unless he admits it to be true or it can be adduced under the Evidence Act (NI) 1939, the previous statement is not evidence of its truth. The effect is usually to render the evidence worthless, unless the witness can persuade the jury that he is now telling the truth.

CROSS-EXAMINATION

13.65 Opposing counsel has a right to question a witness who is called and sworn, whether examined in chief or not and whether he gives any adverse evidence, unless sworn by mistake or stopped by the judge before giving any material answers. Counsel for each defendant, unless one appears for both, can separately question each plaintiff's witness and can cross-examine the co-defendant's witnesses. One plaintiff cannot cross examine a co-plaintiff's witness since they must be represented jointly. If the defendant calls a witness who has already testified for the plaintiff, the plaintiff can cross-examine him.[204]

13.66 Cross-examination need not be on matters raised in evidence in chief. Leading questions can be asked, but not to put words into his mouth, nor to intimidate or annoy. Trick questions may be proper but it is improper to deceive the witness as to the evidence which may be given; put fanciful hypotheses for which there is and can be no evidence; misrepresent what has been said by him or other witnesses; and prevent him from fully understanding and answering the question. Counsel must not cross-examine on a basis which he knows to be untrue.[205] The cross-examiner's function is to ask questions, not to make statements.[206] There is no distinction in the rules of admissibility of evidence in cross-examination. However a bad cross-examination may allow a witness to give inadmissible evidence adverse to the cross-examining party, precluding objection to it. By cross-examination one cannot put an inadmissible document to the witness and thus put it in evidence. Unless the witness is able to prove the document (e.g. where it is a statement made by him) it cannot be put in evidence unless it has been or will be proved. One must prove a document if one reads it to the witness or asks for a document which he has. One may hand a document to a witness without identifying it, and then question him without referring to it, and one does not then have to put it in, though counsel who called the witness can ask to see it.

Functions of cross-examination

13.67 Cross-examination typically has three strands: (a) to 'put one's own case' to the witness; (b) to explore and elicit from him facts favourable to one's case, such as admissions of his own fault; (c) to undermine his credibility. Of these (a) and (b) concern matters relevant to the facts in issue, whereas (c) may

---

203 *People* v *Taylor* [1974] IR 97.

204 *Malone* v *Spellessey* (1842) Ir Circ Rep 504.

205 Bar Handbook 8-02.

206 Some English cases suggest that argumentative cross-examination such as "I put it to you that.." or "Do you expect the court to believe that .." or "My client's evidence will be that .." are improper, but they are commonly used in our courts.

extend to matters not directly relevant to the facts in issue (which are said to be collaterally relevant).

Putting one's own case

13.68 The primary duty of the cross-examiner is to give a witness an opportunity to react to evidence which he may dispute. Since no defence evidence has yet been given, it is an imperative duty in cross-examining plaintiff's witnesses to put the defence case: (a) where he has alleged a fact which will be disputed by defence evidence; (b) where he was in a place at a time which may enable him to dispute or accept some fact to be alleged by defence evidence; and (c) where any allegation will be made against him by the defence. 'Putting the defence case' means more than asking if a fact is true: it means suggesting it so that there is no doubt that a denial of the fact is challenged by the defence; a party will not be allowed to gain unfair advantage by accidental or deliberate omissions in cross-examination.[207] Also cross-examining counsel must put to a witness any allegation which he intends to make against him in his closing submissions.[208] It is no excuse for failure to put a point to say that it is pleaded in the Defence. In *Crampsie* v *Unit Construction Company*,[209] the plaintiff's medical witness was, for his convenience, called first. Defence counsel cross-examined him suggesting that the plaintiff's injury, a slipped disc, could have been caused by an event other than the accident. The Court of Appeal held that it was desirable but not imperative that the suggestion should be repeated in cross-examination of the plaintiff; that plaintiff's counsel, being aware of the defence suggestion, could have raised it in examining the plaintiff in chief. However, Lord MacDermott (at p.6) said that any allegation that the plaintiff was dishonestly misrepresenting the cause of the injury would have to be put to him in cross-examination.

13.69 If any part of the defence case has not been put, the judge may (a) exclude evidence of it, especially where the defence has acted with deliberation; (b) recall the plaintiff's witness or allow the plaintiff to call evidence in rebuttal;[210] or (c) ignore it if it is trivial or peripheral or the defence evidence is not credible in any event. The plaintiff should object to the unput defence evidence at the time when it is adduced, and if he fails to do so he should not be allowed to challenge its admissibility in closing submissions;[211] nor on appeal.[212]

---

207 *McAvoy* v *Goodyear* [1972] NI 217, full report [1973] March-April NIJB.

208 Bar Handbook 8-14; as where he invites the court to infer dishonesty or fault, without necessarily having adduced positive evidence of it.

209 CA, NI, 29 June 1966.

210 It is for plaintiff's counsel, rather than the judge to decide whether to recall. The judge may offer the chance to do so but should not generally insist on recall. If plaintiff's counsel has not sought to recall, the judge may still place some credence on the defence evidence: *O'Doherty* v *Gallagher* [1995] 9 BNIL 44 (CA).

211 *Hanna* v *Chief Constable* [1986] NI 103, at 106-7.

212 *Moffat* v *RW Archer* (1962) 96 ILTR 21; *Bryce* v *British Railways*, 1996 SLT 1378 (2nd Div).

13.70 Plaintiff's counsel does not have to put his case to defence witnesses with the same degree of particularity, as the entire plaintiff's case should already have been heard. If a defence witness has given evidence which conflicts with the plaintiff's case on a crucial point, plaintiff's counsel must make clear that the divergent evidence is not accepted. If the defence witness has failed to contradict or explain the plaintiff's allegation, plaintiff's counsel has an option whether to raise the point.

Cross-examination as to credit

13.71 The secondary purpose of cross-examination is to undermine the credibility of the witness so as to suggest that his evidence on matters which are adverse to counsel's own case should be disbelieved. Counsel may impugn credit by suggesting dishonesty or crime if it is material to the issues, or if he has reasonable grounds for doing so;[213] but in the bulk of civil cases, it is bias, prejudice, observation, memory and reliability which are attacked rather than deliberate dishonesty. The judge has power to disallow questions which impugn the witness's credibility if they are of minimal relevance to his credibility or grossly disproportionate to the importance of his evidence.[214] His answers on credibility are final, and cannot be contradicted by evidence in chief, subject to the exceptions noted hereinafter.

13.72 *(i) Credibility on relevant issues.* He can be asked about his honesty or reliability in his evidence as to any facts relevant to the present case; and his answers can be contradicted by evidence in chief. Where a plaintiff claims to be completely deaf, she can be questioned to establish that she held a normal conversation with a defence witness, and her denial can be contradicted by evidence of that witness, but only because her action is for injuries including deafness as a result of the accident sued upon.[215] On the other hand where a witness claims to be able to speak only Irish, and denies in cross-examination that he knows any English, that denial is final because his bi-lingual capacity is irrelevant to the issues in the proceedings.[216]

13.73 *(ii) Reliability.* The reliability of a witness may be probed by questions as to his eye-sight, memory, distance from the event observed, and the answers are not final because they are relevant to the facts in issue.

13.74 *(iii) Character and honesty.* His character may be questioned to show that he is dishonest, by asking about instances where he has fantasised, lied or contradicted himself in the past, or about his reputation for dishonesty, or about bad or immoral behaviour, or about criminal convictions. A certificate listing the criminal convictions of any person can be obtained on payment of a fee on application by that person to the Secretary of State.[217] A witness cannot be asked or required to answer a question which reveals a 'spent' conviction,

---

[213] Bar Handbook 8-11

[214] *Eastwood* v *Channel 5* [1992] 2 NIJB 58.

[215] Cf. *Keyes* v *Sec of State* [1979] 4 NIJB.

[216] *R* v *Burke* (1859) 4 Ir Jur NS 11.

[217] Police Act 1997, s.112 *(not yet in force).*

unless he consents or justice cannot be done without it.[218] A previous conviction can be put to a witness without its having been pleaded (Ord.18 r.23(4)). It seems that Article 24 of the Legal Aid Advice and Assistance (NI) Order 1981 prevents a witness being asked about statements made in his application for legal aid.[219] The rule that answers are final is subject to the following exceptions: (a) medical evidence is admissible to show that the witness has a mental illness which hinders his capacity to distinguish fact from fiction; (b) evidence can be given that the witness has a reputation for dishonesty or is believed by the impeaching witness from personal experience to be likely to lie; (c) a criminal conviction, if it reflects on credibility, can be proved if the witness does not admit it.[220]

13.75 *(iv) Bias.* His honesty and reliability may questioned by asking about bias, prejudice, partiality. Evidence in chief can be given of partiality in relation to the present parties or the issues, being either behaviour showing bias or circumstances which show a motive to favour one party.

13.76 *(v) Consistency.* His consistency may be attacked, to show that he has fabricated or concocted his evidence or is now lying or confused or mistaken, by asking about previous statements he has made which are inconsistent with his present evidence. It must be a statement made, authorised or adopted by the witness. A soldier cannot be cross-examined from a statement issued by the Army Information Service.[221] Inconsistency can include failure to mention relevant facts which he mentioned in his previous statement, and *vice versa*. Credibility can also be attacked by showing that the witness failed to make statement or complaint at the time of or soon after the event. On cross-examination as to a previous oral or written statement relevant to the present proceedings, if he does not distinctly admit it, the cross-examiner may call evidence to prove the statement; but only if the witness has been told the occasion of the statement and asked directly whether he made it (Criminal Procedure Act 1865, s.4). If the previous statement is in writing he can be cross-examined about it without the document being shown to him; but his attention must be drawn to the passages which contradict him if the cross-examiner intends to prove the statement, and the judge can demand to see it (s.5). These sections of the 1865 Act only apply if the previous statement is relevant to an issue in the action.[222] They only relate to a document which is already in the hands of cross-examining counsel and it seems therefore that the

---

[218] Rehabilitation of Offenders (NI) Order 1978, Arts.5, 8. It is normally just to admit it if the witness's credit is at issue in the action (*per* Evans and Saville LJJ), but only (*per* Scott V-C) if the conviction reflects on his credibility: *Thomas* v *Commr. of Police* [1997] 1 All ER 747 (CA). A person cannot be asked about certain offences committed by him at least four years ago when he was under 14 years: Children and Young Persons Act (NI) 1968, s.71. This section probably applies only to criminal proceedings.

[219] Cf. *R* v *Stubbs* [1982] 1 WLR 509 (a criminal trial). In a civil case it is unlikely that the judge or opposing counsel could have sight of such documents.

[220] Criminal Procedure Act 1865, s.6, by certificate or certified copy under the Prevention of Crimes Act 1871, s.18.

[221] *R* v *McClafferty (No 2)* [1976] 6 NIJB.

[222] *R* v *McGrath* [1989] 4 BNIL 37.

sections are not in themselves a ground for treating the document as evidence admissible in the trial for the purposes of a statutory provision which allows a party to procure 'material evidence'.[223] The previous inconsistent statement tends to undermine the present testimony: it is not evidence of its truth unless the witness admits it to be true or it is admissible under the Evidence Act (NI) 1939.

RE-EXAMINATION

13.77 Counsel who called the witness has a right to re-examine in order to enable the witness to explain, qualify or amplify matters which arose in cross-examination, or to correct any false impression created by cross-examination; and for those purposes it is permissible to re-capitulate some of the evidence in chief. If he wishes to re-examine beyond that, as where by *bona fide* mistake a point was overlooked in examination-in-chief, he must say so and ask leave from the judge, which may be given subject to a right of re-cross-examination. It is easy to forget that re-examination is still in chief and not cross-examination, unless the judge gives leave to treat as hostile.[224]

13.78 If the bad character of the witness has been raised in cross-examination, evidence of his good character may be elicited.[225] If in cross-examination he was accused of inconsistency or fabrication, evidence may be given in chief of a previous consistent statement if it serves to explain or refute the inconsistency.[225] If accused of bias or malice, a previous consistent statement made before the bias or malice arose can be adduced.[225]

ROLE OF THE JUDGE AND JURY

13.79 The judge's role, sitting without a jury, is to hearken to the evidence, control the behaviour of counsel, exclude irrelevant and inadmissible evidence, discourage repetition and ensure by wise intervention that he can follow and assess the evidence and submissions of counsel, and at the end to decide the issues. He may ask elucidatory questions at any time but should not ask questions in the nature of cross-examination until the end of examination-in-chief. He should not question out of a document which is before the court otherwise than as evidence.[226]

13.80 In a jury trial the judge's function is the same, save that he does not make a final decision on the facts. He has to determine what evidence is prima facie admissible, what is material, and what capable of being relevant, and whether there is sufficient evidence of a material fact to warrant that issue being left for the consideration of the jury, and to direct the jury on the law and the burden of proof. He must not intervene so much as to hamper counsel in putting his case, and should not interrupt so as to encourage the witness and undermine the cross-examiner's case.[227] The jury can ask a question, which should be first approved by the judge. The jury's function is, at the end of the

---

223 *R* v *Derby Magistrates' Court, ex p B* [1996] 1 AC 487.

224 See *R* v *Foxford* [1974] NI 181, at 202-5.

225 *Flanagan* v *Fahy* [1918] 2 IR 361, at 382; *R* v *Coll* (1889) 24 LR Ir 522.

226 Cf. *R* v *Stubbs* [1982] 1 WLR 509.

227 *McAvoy* v *Goodyear* [1973] March-April NIJB, Lowry LCJ at p.11.

trial, to decide any factual issue which goes to admissibility, decide what is relevant, decide what weight to attach to the evidence according to its veracity and reliability, and thus to reach a verdict on the material facts in accordance with the judge's directions. Finally, the judge determines what judgment and other order to make upon the verdict.

13.81 The judge can direct a prosecution for perjury and commit for trial any witness if there is reasonable cause to believe that the witness has lied.[228] Usually he will simply send a report to the Director of Public Prosecutions.

13.82 After testifying a witness must remain in court for the rest of the trial unless, through counsel, he asks the judge for permission to leave.

Witness called by judge

13.83 The judge can call a witness, but only in contempt proceedings can he do so against the objection of either party. He can recall any witness already called. (See Phipson 11-31). A party who wants a witness recalled should apply for leave to do so and should not expect the judge to recall the witness of his own motion.[229]

ADMISSIBILITY OF EVIDENCE

13.84 Various grounds for exclusion of relevant evidence have grown up, some based on policy, some on fear of unreliability. The right time to object to admissibility of evidence is when it is offered.[230] If a party knows of major evidence to be tendered he should object as a preliminary point; if he accepts without reserve the admission of a type of evidence, and adduces some of that type in his own case, he cannot object to it on appeal.[231] If the judge rules evidence inadmissible and continues the trial on that basis, he cannot later act on the evidence; but he can later exclude evidence which he has admitted.[232]

Maps, photographs etc.

13.85 A map, diagram, photograph etc. is not admissible unless the other parties have been allowed to inspect it at least three weeks before the start of the trial, unless otherwise ordered (Ord.38 r.3A). It is then admissible without formal proof unless objected to (Ord.38 r.1A). An order under rule 3A may be later revoked or varied (Ord.38 r.4). Application for leave to adduce a map etc. without prior disclosure should be made on affidavit stating its relevance, and why it should not be disclosed.[233] In personal injuries cases leave is to be granted only in exceptional circumstances and even in fraud cases disclosure should be the norm.[234] Note that these rules are not confined to maps, photos

---

[228] Perjury (NI) Order 1979, Art.13.

[229] *O'Doherty* v *Gallagher* [1995] 9 BNIL 44 (CA).

[230] *Stoughton* v *Crosbie* (1843) 5 Ir Eq R 451; *Moffat* v *RW Archer* (1962) 96 ILTR 21; *Hanna* v *Chief Constable* [1986] NI 103, at 106-7.

[231] *Min of Development* v *Law* [1970] June NIJB, especially *per* Curran LJ.

[232] *Skeate* v *Slaters* [1914] 2 KB 429, at 438.

[233] *McGuiness* v *Kellogg Co* [1988] 1 WLR 913.

[234] *Khan* v *Armaguard Ltd* [1994] 1 WLR 1204.

etc. of an expert witness: the two cases noted above concerned disclosure of film taken surreptitiously by a private inquiry agent.

Miscellaneous

13.86 The rules of privilege for 'without prejudice' communications (para. 13.43); public interest (para. 13.46) and administration of justice (para. 13.50) are in effect rules of admissibility of evidence. Where an object or documentary information has been disclosed to an accused person in criminal proceedings under Part I of the Criminal Procedure and Investigations Act 1996 [*not yet in force*], the object or information is inadmissible in civil proceedings, unless it has been disclosed in open court or the criminal court has permitted its use (s.18(9)).

Answers or information given by a person in response to a requirement by a financial investigator may not be used in evidence against him.[235]

A 'lodgment' must be kept secret (see para. 11.160); so also an interim payment (para. 11.55). As to evidence in defamation, see paras. 18.20-18.24; defence evidence not 'put' to the plaintiff's witnesses, see para. 13.69; secondary evidence of documents, see para. 13.148.

OPINION EVIDENCE

13.87 As a general rule the opinion of any person is not evidence (see para. 13.17). The Court's job is to decide facts and form its own opinion. The opinion of any other court as expressed in its judgment or verdict is irrelevant, subject to the operation of *res judicata* (para. 13.100) and to the Civil Evidence Act (NI) 1971, ss.7-9 (para. 13.25).

Expert evidence

13.88 A party may call a witness qualified by experience or training to give an opinion which a layman is not allowed to give. The evidence can be by oral testimony or by written report. The witness must formally refer to his qualifications before giving any opinion.[236] He can base his opinion on matters outside his personal knowledge, such as the published research of others, and apply his opinion by commenting on the facts of the present case derived from his personal investigation, facts already stated in evidence and facts which have not yet been adduced in evidence but are put to him as a hypothesis.[237] He can testify as to observations and experiments done on the subject-matter of the present case, only if he performed or witnessed them.[238] An engineer should not comment on a machine if he has not seen it or one of similar description.[239] A psychiatrist cannot comment on a person whom he has never met.[240] In road accident cases, the investigating policeman is qualified to give his opinion on the causes of the accident, based on his observations of the scene and his

---

235 Proceeds of Crime (NI) Order 1996, Sch.2 para. 6.

236 The qualification need not be academic: *Clarke* v *Brown* [1986] 2 NIJB 1, at 16. Indeed in many areas practical experience is preferable.

237 *Clarke* v *Brown* [1986] 2 NIJB 1, at 14.

238 *R* v *Lanigan* [1987] NI 367, at 375F-376F.

239 *Morrow* v *McAdam* [1978] 3 NIJB at 2-3.

240 *RT* v v *P* [1990] 1 IR 545, at 551.

experience, and expert evidence may be warranted where there is an alleged defect on one of the vehicles. However the opinion of a professional expert on patterns of driving adduced to give an inference as to how the drivers drove in the particular case was treated with much scepticism by the Court of Appeal in *Clarke* v *Brown.*[241] Every expert witness has the following duties: to provide independent evidence by unbiased objective opinion in matters within his expertise; to state the facts and assumptions on which the opinion is based; to state facts which could detract from his opinion; to state so where the whole truth requires some qualification to his report; to state what matters are outside his expertise; to state that the opinion is provisional if it is based on incomplete research; and if on seeing the opponent's expert reports or for any other reason he changes his view on a material matter, to communicate his changed view through the legal representatives to the opponent.[242]

13.89 Unless the Court otherwise orders,[243] a party may call only two medical experts and one other expert of any other kind to give oral evidence at the trial (Ord.38 r.1B). If a court expert has been appointed a party may call only one expert witness on the same question, unless in exceptional circumstances leave is given to call more (Ord.40 r.6). Experts on each side should be called where they conflict.[244] Unless the Court otherwise orders, a medical report disclosed under Order 25 is admissible unless the other party requires his attendance; a map, drawing, photograph shown under Order 38 rule 3A is admissible unless the other party requires it to be proved (Ord.38 r.1A(1)(2)). If a court expert has been appointed a party calling an expert on the same issue must give reasonable notice (Ord.40 r.6). Even if his report is agreed the expert may have to be called to explain it or to be cross-examined on it.[245] Even if a medical report is agreed the judge is not bound by the doctor's opinion on causation.[246] A medical or other expert's report or his map, drawing or photograph may be admitted by the Court if he is unable to attend (Ord.38 r.1A(3)). Even apart from these rules the parties usually try to agree on exchange of reports and to agree on use of reports in evidence. Even if a report cannot be agreed, a party can seek to adduce it in evidence under the Evidence Act (NI) 1939. In *Smyth* v *Dempsey,*[247] Girvan J said: "The Court is faced with a dilemma when presented with written medical reports which conflict in material respects. It may be as a matter of strict theory that a medical report furnished on behalf of the plaintiff, insofar as not challenged by cross-examination by the defendant, will stand in preference to the medical evidence of the defendant."

13.90 The Taxing Master is not bound to allow the costs of an expert witness merely because he was called at the trial.[248] In an action on a road accident or other accident on land, the costs of a sketch map will be allowed on taxation,

---

241 [1986] 2 NIJB 1.
242 *Vernon* v *Bosley (No 1)* [1997] 1 All ER 577 (CA).
243 By application to a master in advance of the trial.
244 *Harrison* v *Liverpool Corp* [1943] 2 All ER 449.
245 *Proctor* v *Peebles* [1941] 2 All ER 80.
246 *Stevens* v *Simons*, 'The Times', 20 November 1987 (CA).
247 [1995] 9 BNIL 23.
248 White Book (1997) 62/A2/16.

but not the cost of a more elaborate plan unless the Taxing Master thinks it reasonable (Ord.62 App 2 Pt.I para.3).

13.91 A doctor's written report should be handed in before he starts to give oral evidence.[249] By convention, a medical witness in his report or oral evidence is allowed to give hearsay about the history of the accident and the treatment of the plaintiff by other doctors. It is extremely imprudent for a plaintiff to give evidence at the trial of a symptom or injury which is not referred to in any medical report or doctor's evidence.

13.92 The expert witness is in all other respects the same as any witness called by a party. He can be challenged on credibility and contradicted by other evidence. Often the court is faced with disagreement between distinguished experts on each side which the non-expert judge cannot and should not resolve: then the judge must apply common sense and logic, taking into account both schools of thought, to achieve the just result in the instant case.[250] Cross-examining an expert is a particularly difficult skill. Counsel should try to acquire some basic knowledge of the field of expertise and its terminology; he should consult specially with his own expert witness not only in relation to the latter's own evidence but also to discuss what lines to pursue in cross-examination.

13.93 Instead of or as well as hearing expert witnesses the Court can form its own view on some matters, take judicial notice, appoint an assessor (see para. 14.13), or refer to an arbitrator, court officer or referee (see para. 14.14). In any proceedings the Court may appoint an independent court expert to inquire and report on any question of fact or opinion,[251] other than one of law or construction; a party may apply to cross-examine the court expert, and may call one expert witness to give evidence on the same question (Ord.40). If a court expert is used, the parties will not be allowed in standard taxation the costs of expert witnesses on the same issue (Ord.62 App.1 para.4(2)).

FOREIGN LAW

13.94 Where under conflicts of law the law of any state outside Northern Ireland is relevant, that law is a matter of fact to be pleaded and proved, and determined by the judge (not the jury); a suitably qualified person may give expert evidence as to that law (Judicature Act, s.114(1)(3)). The canon law of the Roman Catholic Church is foreign law.[252] If no evidence of the foreign law is adduced, it is presumed to be the same as local law.[253] However judicial notice can be taken of the law of England/Wales and the Republic of Ireland (but not Scotland); and judicial notice may be taken of the findings as to foreign law in a reported decision of the superior courts in Northern Ireland or England/Wales or of the Privy Council (s.114(2)(4)). Notice of intention to

---

249 Practice Direction [1987] 8 BNIL 83.

250 *Best* v *Wellcome Foundation* [1993] 3 IR 421, at 462, *per* Finlay CJ.

251 Not confined to a scientific, technical or subsidiary issue: *Abbey National* v *Key Surveyors* [1996] 3 All ER 184 (CA).

252 *O'Callaghan* v *O'Sullivan* [1925] 1 IR 90.

253 *Emerald Stainless Steel* v *South Side Distribution* 1982 SC 61.

adduce such a finding should be given at least 21 days before the date of trial (Ord.38 r.5). In *Deighan* v *Sunday Newspapers*[254] the judge declined to take judicial notice under section 114 and called for expert evidence on a complex point of Irish law. Otherwise foreign law is a matter of fact which must be agree by the parties or proved by evidence of an expert qualified by practice or otherwise to give an opinion on the law. The Court may state the facts for a Superior Court in one of HM Dominions[255] to certify its opinion of the law of that State.[256] Copies of statutes of British Dominions are admissible.[257] The meaning and effect of the Treaties and instruments of the European Union are questions of law to be determined by the NI courts in accordance with decisions of the European Court.[258]

ESTOPPEL

13.95 Estoppel is a doctrine by which a party is barred from proving or denying a material fact. It removes a fact as an issue. If the party who may raise the estoppel fails to do so the case will be decided on the actual truth.[259]

Estoppel by conduct (*in pais*)

13.96 A party may be estopped from asserting the true fact if he "has by his conduct caused the other party on faith of the first party's action to change his position for the worse".[260] It operates only between the parties by whom and to whom the conduct was done, and their privies. It cannot be used to create a cause of action, nor to confer power or title on a person, nor make legal an illegality, nor evade mandatory statute, nor prevent the exercise of a statutory discretion or duty;[261] nor confer jurisdiction on a court; nor create a legal person out of a defunct company.[262] Instances of estoppel by conduct-

> by representation of existing fact;[263] by promise (an equitable estoppel);[264] by silence after a positive representation or where there is a duty to speak out;[265] proprietary estoppel'[264] where an owner permits or invites another to improve or repair land (this can create a cause of action);[266] by waiver of rights; by acquiescence or delay

---

254 [1987] NI 105, at 108.

255 Including the Republic of Ireland: Ireland Act 1949, s.3.

256 British Law Ascertainment Act 1859.

257 Evidence (Colonial Statutes) Act 1907.

258 European Communities Act 1972, s.3.

259 *Nowlan* v *Gibson* (1849) 12 Ir LR 5.

260 *Per* Lowry J, *Horner* v *Min of Development* [1971] March NIJB at 5.

261 *R.Bell & Co* v *DOE* [1982] NI 322, at 337.

262 *Dickson* v *Blackstaff Weaving* [1989] NI 197, at 204-5.

263 *Grainger Building* v *McCreedy* [1990] NI 126; e.g. by holding himself out as owner of a business: *Dunn* v *Shanks* [1932] NI 66.

264 *DOE* v *Leeburn* [1990] NI 135; *North Down Hotels* v *Province-wide Filling Stations* [1993] 10 NIJB 60.

265 *Doran* v *Thompson* [1978] IR 223 (no duty on defendant or his insurer to state before action that liability will be denied or that limitation defence will be pleaded).

266 *Devlin* v *NIHE* [1982] NI 377, at 390H.

(barring equitable and procedural rights and remedies). A defendant assuming a duty of care is estopped from denying it.[267]

Estoppel by deed

13.97 A party is estopped by an admission made clearly in a deed under seal (Cross p.99).

Estoppel by agreement

13.98 As between each other a landlord and tenant, a licensor and licensee, a bailor and bailee, a donor and donee, a seller and buyer, are estopped from denying the former's title. Parties who have dealt with each other on the basis that a fact is accepted as true are estopped from denying it.

Estoppel by election

13.99 If a plaintiff has alternative claims against one defendant or between two defendants, his pursuance to judgment of one is a binding election to drop the other.[268]

ESTOPPEL *PER REM JUDICATEM*

13.100 The final adjudication of an issue in dispute by a competent court of record in any country creates certain estoppels in litigation. There must be a final, not interlocutory judgment[269] which is valid and regular on point of jurisdiction, and not fraudulent or collusive. If there are two valid foreign judgments conflicting *inter se*, the first in time operates.[270] If given outside the United Kingdom it may not be recognised if contrary to public policy or made without jurisdiction, as determined by our law. A judgment in a non-Brussels Convention State is not recognised if obtained in breach of an agreement not to sue there (Civil Jurisdiction and Judgments Act 1982, s.32). A judgment of a Brussels Convention State is recognised except in special circumstances (1982 Act, Sch.1 Arts.26-30). All United Kingdom judgments are recognised without regard to private international law (1982 Act, s.19).[271]

13.101 Estoppel *per rem judicatem* is a procedural bar, not jurisdictional: it is effective only if pleaded and can be defeated by a plea of cross-estoppel or waiver.[272]

13.102 *In rem or in personam.* A judgment *in rem* binds all the world. A judgment *in personam* binds only the parties thereto and their privies. All judgments are *in rem* in so far as they make an order; all judgments are *in personam* in so far as they make findings on which the order is based. For example a judgment for damages binds all the world in making the plaintiff a

---

[267] *McGrory* v *DOE* [1977] 5 NIJB at 6.

[268] *Morel* v *Westmoreland* [1904] AC 11; *McConnell* v *Lombard & Ulster* [1982] NI 203.

[269] Though it may be subject to appeal: see *Deighan* v *Sunday Newspapers* [1987] NI 105.

[270] *Showlag* v *Mansour* [1995] 1 AC 431 (PC).

[271] Restriction on recognition of judgments given against a foreign state: 1982 Act, s.31. Recognition of judgments, monetary or not, of countries to which the Foreign Judgments (Reciprocal Enforcement) Act 1933 applies: s.8 thereof. Recognition of divorces, annulments and separations: Family Law Act 1986, ss.44-54.

[272] *Republic of India* v *India Steamship* [1993] AC 410, at 422A-423C.

judgment creditor of the defendant for the amount awarded, but only binds the parties in finding the defendant guilty of negligence. A decree of divorce binds all the word in dissolving the marriage but only the parties in declaring the respondent guilty of adultery, desertion etc. Judgments *in rem* include an order determining a person's domicile or nationality, a judgment admitting a will to probate, an order declaring a person insolvent, an order of custody of a minor.[273] A judgment *in personam* binds the parties in other proceedings between them, or their privies, in the same capacity.[274] So judgment for the mother for injuries caused by defects in the family house does not stop a separate action by her child;[275] judgment for X against Y does not prevent Y from giving contrary evidence in an action between Y and Z;[276] non-acceptance by a court in previous proceedings of the testimony of a mere witness does not estop him as a party now.[277] A privy is a person connected by blood, title or interest,[278] and a person jointly entitled or (subject to s.3 of the Civil Liability (Contribution) Act 1978) jointly liable.[279] The driver and the owner of a car are not *per se* privies.[278] Dependants suing under the Fatal Accidents (NI) Order 1977 are privies of the deceased.[280] The dependants of a deceased driver are not privy with the nominee of his insurance company.[281] Master and servant, and principal and agent are not privies.[282]

13.103 *Cause of action estoppel* arises *in personam* from the finding that the defendant is or is not liable and on any defence which was or could have been raised. It arises only on the precise cause of action adjudicated upon.[283] The right to sue on a debt merges into the rights under a judgment for that debt. If a plaintiff recovers judgment for only part of the debt due to him or for too small a sum, he cannot sue for the excess (see para. 3.30).

13.104 *Issue estoppel* arises *in personam* from any finding made on a single issue of material fact or law which is necessary to the judgment given.[284] The issues in dispute are those joined on the pleadings, the *facta probanda* not the *facta probantia*, and issues which a party could and should have raised.[285] Absence of pleadings does not prevent issue estoppel because the subsequent court can investigate the issues actually decided.[286] In special circumstances

---

273 *Registrar General* v *Chirwa* [1994] 1 LRC 146 (Zimbabwe SC).

274 *Shaw* v *Sloan* [1982] NI 393, *per* Gibson LJ at 408-10.

275 *C (a Minor)* v *Hackney LBC* [1996] 1 WLR 789 (CA).

276 *McConnell* v *Lombard & Ulster* [1982] NI 203, at 208-9.

277 *Brady* v *Chief Constable* [1988] NI 32.

278 *Shaw* v *Sloan*, at 396H.

279 *House of Spring* v *Waite* [1991] 1 QB 241.

280 *Mahon* v *Burke* [1991] 2 IR 495.

281 *Lawless* v *Bus Éireann* [1994] 1 IR 474.

282 *McConnell* v *Lombard & Ulster* [1982] NI 203, at 208-9.

283 *Joseph Lynch Land Co* v *Lynch* [1995] 1 NZLR 37.

284 *Mountcashel's Estate* [1920] 1 IR 1, at 5-6.

285 See *Deighan* v *Sunday Newspapers* [1987] NI 105, at 113-6.

286 See *Khan* v *Golleccha* [1980] 1 WLR 1482; e.g. by reading a solicitor's note of the oral judgment: *Gilroy* v *McLoughlin* [1988] IR 44, at 48; *sed contra, Irish Land Commission* v

issue estoppel can be defeated by newly discovered evidence, or by a change in the law.[287] Estoppel does not arise from a decision as to the interpretation of statute.[288]

13.105 A *judgment in default* raises estoppel only on liability and on what the judgment necessarily and with precision decides.[289] A judgment obtained on motion on the Statement of Claim creates estoppel on all issues pleaded,[290] and on any defence necessarily or precisely covered.[291]

13.106 A *judgment dismissing a claim* at a trial in a High Court action always creates estoppel, but a dismiss in the county court creates no estoppel if expressed to be 'without prejudice'. Even a county court dismiss 'on the merits' may not create estoppel.[292] A judgment dismissing a claim for procedural default, a discontinuance, and a strike out before trial cause no estoppel.[293] A dismissal for lack of jurisdiction raises an estoppel only on the issue of jurisdiction.[294]

13.107 Estoppel arises on a *settlement* of a case provided that a judgment is entered,[295] but only on the issue precisely decided by it. In the absence of an express indication, a judgment by consent does not decree that the defendant is 100 per cent liable if he has pleaded contributory negligence.[296] An admission of material fact made in court, or made the basis of the court judgment raises issue estoppel,[297] but not, *semble*, an admission made "for the purposes of this action only".

13.108 Cause of action estoppel applies if the defendant in the previous action failed to plead a claim which he could have raised by way of counterclaim or third-party notice and which relates to the same subject-matter as the action, save in special circumstances;[298] but there is case law to the contrary in respect

---

Ryan [1900] 2 IR 565. The *Irish Land Commission* case was doubted in *Kok Hoong* v *Leong Mines*, below, insofar as it says that only the judgment constitutes the record.

287 *Arnold* v *National Westminster* [1991] 2 AC 93.

288 *Kildare CC* v *Keogh* [1971] IR 330 (no authority quoted); *Clare CC* v *Mahon* [1995] 3 IR 193 (Carroll J).

289 *Kok Hoong* v *Leong Mines* [1964] AC 993, reading both the judgment and the 'plaint'.

290 *Cox* v *Dublin Distillery* [1917] 1 IR 203, at 223.

291 *McConnell* v *Lombard & Ulster* [1982] NI at 207.

292 See the author's *County Court Procedure in NI* (SLS 1985) 1st ed. para. 15.19.

293 *Royal Bank* v *O'Rourke* [1962] IR 159. See also *In re Land Registration Act 1970 and McNeill* [1996] 2 BNIL 58 (Higgins J) (dismissal by consent of application for registration is not *res judicata* if shown to be not on the merits).

294 *The Sennar* [1985] 1 WLR 490; *Hines* v *Birkbeck College (No 2)* [1992] Ch 33.

295 *Bradshaw* v *McMullan* [1920] 2 IR 412 (HL), only in so far as the judgment contains an adjudication.

296 *Trainor* v *McKee* [1988] NI 556.

297 *Khan* v *Golleccha* [1980] 1 WLR 1482.

298 *Talbot* v *Berkshire CC* [1994] QB 290. The defendant driver Talbot issued a third-party notice for contribution against the roads authority for negligent upkeep of the road; a later action by Talbot against the authority for his own injuries was held barred. *Semble,* no estoppel would arise if the road authority was not at any stage joined as a party to the first action.

of counterclaims and set-offs (see para. 9.51). In the case at least of a county court decree, the defendant is not estopped by his failure to raise an equitable right as a defence in an ordinary civil bill.[299]

13.109 An ejectment or judgment for the recovery of land on the title does not create an estoppel on the issue that the plaintiff has a better title to the land, because such actions concern possession, not title.[300] Nor does a dismissal of such an action. No estoppel arises from a judgment in rating[301] or water charges.[302]

13.110 *Convictions and acquittals.* The verdict of a criminal court creates estoppel *in rem* in convicting or acquitting the accused, but no estoppel arises in civil proceedings from the finding of guilt or innocence or any other issue,[303] except in defamation actions (see para. 13.25).

13.111 *Road accidents* create estoppel problems because one accident may give rise to different actions in different courts. The drivers may claim against each other, by claim and counterclaim or by cross-actions; a pedestrian or passenger may sue one or both drivers. One court may apportion blame between the two drivers in claims between them. Another court may apportion blame between them in fixing contribution *inter se* to the damages of the pedestrian. It is now settled in Northern Ireland, by *Shaw* v *Sloan*[304] that the drivers and their privies are bound by the apportionment of fault between them: but with the important qualification added by Lord Lowry LCJ (at p.396B) that the apportionment may differ if there is a material difference between the negligence of a driver as a tort contributing to another's injury, and the negligence in taking care of himself. For example, one driver after collision may by further negligent driving knock over the pedestrian. So also, a driver whose own damages are reduced by 20 per cent for his failure to wear a seat belt is not therefore 20 per cent to blame for the pedestrian's injuries. The same principles should apply to the claim and counterclaim between the two drivers.[305] Where an injured cyclist sues the car driver and the owner of the car sues the cyclist for car damage, and it is proved that the driver was not acting as servant or agent of the owner, *res judicata* does not apply, so that the courts trying the separate actions can reach conflicting decisions as to whether the cyclist was negligent.[306] The dependants of a deceased driver are not privy with

---

299 *Mulgrew* v *O'Brien* [1953] NI 10, at 21-2; not cited in the contrary decision of *McGucken* v *McGucken* [1990] NI 1.

300 *Lennon* v *Meegan* [1905] 2 IR 189, at 196ff; not cited in the contrary decision of *McGucken* v *McGucken* [1990] NI 1.

301 *Campbell College* v *Commrs of Valuation* [1964] NI 107 (HL).

302 *Clare CC* v *Mahon* [1995] 3 IR 193 (Carroll J).

303 *O'Donnell* v *Hegarty* [1941] IR 538 *In re McCotter* [1970] April NIJB; *Hunter* v *Chief Constable* [1982] AC 529, at 541A (contra: *Breathnach* v *Ireland (No 2)* [1993] 2 IR 448, where 'The People' were held to be privy with the State and the Attorney-General).

304 [1982] NI 393; and in England: *Wall* v *Radford* [1991] 2 All ER 741; but not in the Republic of Ireland: see *per* Blayney J in *Gilroy* v *McLoughlin* [1988] IR 44, at 49.

305 *Black* v *McCabe* [1964] NI 1. And see *Trainor* v *McKee supra* para. 13.107.

306 *Crawford* v *James* [1988] 8 NIJB 19, at 23.

the nominee of his insurance company who defended an action brought by the other driver.[307]

'BEST EVIDENCE' RULES

13.112 At one time the Courts attempted to formulate a general rule that only the best available evidence was admissible to prove a fact. This principle survives only in the specific rule against hearsay and the rule against secondary evidence of a written document.

HEARSAY

Definition of hearsay

13.113 The general rule is that a witness whose testimony is adduced by oral evidence, by affidavit or otherwise can only narrate matters which he saw and heard of his own personal knowledge. A statement made by a person out of court is admissible, original evidence if the fact of what he said or wrote is relevant to the case of the party adducing it. If the purpose in putting in evidence a statement made out of court is to prove thereby the truth of what that statement asserts, then one is adducing hearsay and must justify its admission under one of the exceptions to the rule against hearsay. Therefore a statement can be categorised as hearsay only in the context of the issues in dispute in the present action. A statement is hearsay if it is made by a human being, whether a party or not, whether called as a witness or not, whether alive or dead, whether known or untraced, whether made without any thought to the issue now disputed, whether made as part of a routine record however reliable, whether made by spoken or written word, by diagram, signal, or by conduct which asserts a message. A witness can testify that a policeman looked at his car tyres and let him drive on: that is original evidence if the issue is whether the witness knew that his tyres were bald; but it is hearsay by inference if the issue is whether the tyres were bald.[308] Where a police witness says: "As a result of a conversation with [the victim] I decided to interview [the defendant]"; that is clearly hearsay.[309] A photograph or tape-recording is original, not hearsay, evidence of what can be seen or heard on it, but it is hearsay evidence of the truth of any message contained in it. A 'statement' made by an animal, such as a tracker dog,[310] or a machine such as chemical test appara.tus, a clock or car speedometer is not hearsay. It is of course difficult to draw the line between statements made by a machine and a human being. The words "Produce of Morocco" stamped on a package were held hearsay in *Patel* v *Comptroller of Customs*,[311] but a postmark on a letter was held to be original evidence in *R* v *Leroy*.[312]

---

307 *Lawless* v *Bus Éireann* [1994] 1 IR 474.

308 See *R* v *Kearley* [1992] 2 AC 228 (charge of supplying drugs: orders of customers for drugs from the defendant are hearsay because their state of mind is not material).

309 *Hopson* v *R* [1994] 2 LRC 741 (PC).

310 A dog must be proved to be reliable: *R* v *Pieterson* [1995] 1 WLR 293.

311 [1966] AC 356.

312 (1987) 13 Comm LB 69 (CA, NSW).

EXCEPTIONS TO THE RULE AGAINST HEARSAY

Res gestae

13.114 Under this inclusionary rule of evidence are some statements admissible as exceptions to the hearsay rule, some as being outside the definition of hearsay. Words of threat, defamation, abuse may be relevant acts in themselves having regard to the issues.[313] A statement by a person of his state of mind, motive, mood, intention, health, symptoms, age, state of knowledge or belief, is admissible. An identifying witness or any person present at the identification can say that X was the person whom the witness picked out. A statement by a person of his name and address is evidence of identity.[314] Words spoken by a person at a time when he is performing or witnessing an event or so soon thereafter that he had little time to concoct a falsehood are admissible hearsay.[315]

13.115 Two old Irish cases illustrate the typical difficulties with hearsay and *res gestae* in civil cases. In *Gresham Hotel* v *Manning*[316] (action by hotel owner for obstruction of light) evidence of statements by guests that they refused to take rooms because of the darkness, though possibly admissible to prove the loss of custom due to lack of light, was held inadmissible to prove the lack of light. In *Hogan* v *Davis Estates*[317] (a claim for compensation for injury at work), the plaintiff's evidence as to what potential employers said as the reason for refusing him work was admitted as original evidence of his *bona fides* in seeking work, but not of the employers' motives. It is submitted that, as *res gestae*, the statements were admissible to prove the reason why he could not obtain work, but not to prove that that reason was justified. Similar problems arise as to repair bills, estimates and receipts in claims for damaged property. It is submitted that they are primary evidence of the actual cost of repair charged or to be charged by that repairer, but that they are not *per se* evidence of what is a normal or reasonable cost. If reasonableness of the costs is in dispute, the plaintiff should call an expert assessor to give his opinion that the cost is reasonable, or ask the judge to infer from his common sense and experience that it is reasonable.

Admissions by a party

13.116 A statement made by a party to the action is admissible *against* him, whether he testifies or not, whether it was an admission against his own interest or whether it is prejudicial to him in the context of the present action. A confession which was ruled involuntary in a criminal trial is admissible.[318] An admission can be oral or written, by indirect words or conduct, such as threatening the opposite party. Failure by a party to call an available witness may be construed as an implied admission that the witness does not corroborate

---

313 See e.g. *Fullam* v *Associated Newspapers* [1955-6] Ir Jur R 45.

314 *Creed* v *Scott* [1976] RTR 485.

315 *R* v *Andrews* [1987] AC 281.

316 (1867) IR 1 CL 125. Although the words accompanied an act of refusing to take the room, the act itself was hearsay by conduct.

317 [1942] IR 370, at 375.

318 *Bains* v *Yorkshire Insurance* (1963) 38 DLR 2d 417.

his case.[319] An offer to compensate may be an admission of guilt, unless it is motivated by charity or desire to make peace;[320] or in a *bona fide* attempt to settle pending or possible litigation (para. 13.43). An admission of matters outside his own personal knowledge is not probative, unless he had a special expertise or means of knowledge. Delay in prosecuting his claim is not an admission that the plaintiff thinks his case weak.[321] Failure by a party to respond to an allegation made in his presence is admissible, and capable of being evidence of an admission if the party and the speaker were on even terms.[322]

13.117 A party is affected not only by his own statements, but also statements of: (a) a predecessor in title of the right, defence, interest or property at issue in the action; (b) a person with a real interest where he is a nominal party; (c) a person with a joint right, or a co-conspirator,[323] but not a co-plaintiff or co-defendant *per se;*[324] (d) an agent within the scope of his authority;[325] (e) his solicitor if made with his authority, or made by the solicitor on record for him in pending proceedings. He adopts as his own any admission of another person in an affidavit or deposition which he elects to use, but not the oral testimony of a witness whom he calls. An admission by a partner concerning the firm business made in the course of business is evidence against the firm.[326]

13.118 An admission by a party is proved, if oral, by calling the person who heard it or by any other evidence admissible to prove what was said; if written, by proving the document in the same way as any documentary evidence is proved. If the party formally admits it or in the witness box agrees that he made the statement, no further proof is needed. *Semble*, the rule in criminal cases that the prosecutor must prove the defendant's admission as part of the prosecution case, does not apply in civil cases; so the plaintiff can keep the statement in reserve until cross-examination of the defendant. In civil, as in criminal cases, the whole of a party's statement of admission must be put before the court, including the parts favourable to him, and the court can give some weight to them.[327]

Statements in presence of party or witness

13.119 From the criminal case, *R* v *Christie*[328] and from the generally established practice in Northern Ireland courts, it can be said that one party or his witness may give in evidence what was said by the opposing party or his witness or what was said by someone in the presence of the opposing party or

---

319 *Lynch* v *MOD* [1983] NI 216, at 222F.

320 *Powell* v *McGlynn* [1902] 2 IR 154.

321 *Mannix* v *Pluck* [1975] IR 169.

322 *R* v *Murphy* [1993] 4 NIJB 42.

323 During the time when the conspiracy existed: *Blackwood* v *Gregg* (1831) Hayes 277, at 293, 312-3.

324 *Tait* v *Beggs* [1905] 2 IR 525.

325 *Securicor* v *Anglia Building Society* [1992] 7 NIJB 34, at 48*ff.*

326 Partnership Act 1890, s.15.

327 *McBride* v *Stitt* [1944] NI 7, at 11-12, 18.

328 [1914] AC 545.

his witness. In *Crymble* v *Russell*,[329] the plaintiff was a passenger in M's car and M was called by him as a witness. The defendant testified that an untraced observer said to the defendant in the presence of M that M was speeding and that M replied at once: "I was not". The Court (see Curran LJ at p.15) assumed without deciding that the testimony was admissible but that the judge should clearly direct the jury to attach no weight to it.

Self-corroboration

13.120 A party cannot adduce in evidence a previous statement made by himself or any witness called by him for the purpose of asserting the truth of what it asserted, except-

(1) if asked about it in cross-examination;
(2) if accused of fabrication, inconsistency or recent concoction;
(3) he can produce a sketch, map etc. made by him;
(4) he can use a contemporaneous note 'to refresh his memory';
(5) a written statement made by a disinterested person or *ante litem motam* is admissible under the Evidence Act (NI) 1939;
(6) information supplied by him and inserted in a duty record is admissible, but only by leave of the Court and after the end of his examination-in-chief (Civil Evidence Act (NI) 1971, s.1(2)), and it does not constitute corroboration in law of his evidence (s.3(4));
(7) if it is *res gestae*;
(8) if it was said in the presence of the opposite party or his witness;
(9) an identifying witness can state that he previously picked out a person as being the person who did a particular act.

Declarations by a deceased

13.121 At common law a statement, oral or written, by a person now deceased is admissible hearsay in the following circumstances.

(1) It was to his knowledge prima facie against his pecuniary or proprietary interest at the time to say what he did, about a matter within his personal knowledge.[330]
(2) He had a specific duty to another person to perform and record an act, with no motive to misrepresent the truth. It need not be a duty imposed by law. He must have done so contemporaneously and with personal knowledge.[331]
(3) Having competent knowledge, about ancient rights of public or general nature, he made the statement *ante litem motam.*[332]
(4) It was about pedigree (i.e. blood or marital ties in his own family) made *ante litem motam*, if the litigation involves a dispute between family

---

329 CA, NI, 23 May 1968, *per* Curran LJ at 12-15, Lowry J at 3-4.

330 E.g. a receipt for payment of a debt: *Richards* v *Gogarty* (1870) IR 4 CL 300.

331 *Ryan* v *Ring* (1890) 25 LR Ir 184; e.g. a dead solicitor's notes of interview with a client to prove what his instructions were: *Somers* v *Erskine (No 2)* [1944] IR 368.

332 E.g. a public right of way marked on an old ordnance survey map: *Giant's Causeway* v *AG* (1905) 5 NIJR 301, at 303.

members.[333] The witness who reports the statement need not be a member of the family.[334]

(5) It concerned the contents of his own will where it is not available.[335]

(6) in an application for provision out of his estate under the Inheritance (Provision for Family and Dependants) (NI) Order 1979 (Art.23 thereof).

13.122 In a Law Reform Act or fatal accidents action the plaintiff is a privy with the deceased so any statement by the deceased is admissible for the defendant, whether or not the deceased knew he was speaking against his own interest.[336] But if a personal representative or dependant is suing under a direct statutory right in respect of the death, such as a criminal injury application, there is no privity between the deceased and the applicant, so a statement by the deceased is admissible only if he was speaking consciously against his own interest, which he would not be if he knew he was dying.[337] In either case the plaintiff or applicant cannot adduce a self-serving statement by the deceased, except as *res gestae*, or under the Evidence Act (NI) 1939 if *ante litem motam*.

Testimony in previous proceedings

13.123 At common law, testimony given in previous legal proceedings between substantially the same parties or their privies involving the same issues is admissible if the party against whom the evidence is now given or his privy was able to cross-examine, and if the witness is now dead, insane, seriously ill, out of the jurisdiction, not found after diligent search or kept away by the opposing party.

13.124 The testimony given in an action to perpetuate testimony under Order 39 rule 15[338] is admissible in proceedings on the title, estate, office etc. for which the testimony related.

Documentary hearsay

13.125 The Evidence Act (NI) 1939 and the Civil Evidence Act (NI) 1971 provide for the admissibility of first-hand documentary hearsay and second-hand documentary hearsay compiled under a duty, respectively.[339]

1939 Act: personal knowledge documents

13.126 By section 1(1) of the Evidence Act (NI) 1939, where direct oral evidence of a fact would be admissible, a statement (including a representation of fact in words or otherwise) made by a person with personal knowledge of the matters in it, in a document (including a book, map, drawing figures etc.) tending to establish that fact is admissible as evidence of the fact (on production of the original), if: (a) the maker is called as a witness, or (b) he is

---

333 *Sec of State for War* v *Booth* [1901] 2 IR 692.

334 *In re Holmes* [1934] IR 693; *contra*: *Re Simpson* [1984] 1 NZLR 738 (CA).

335 *In re Gilliland* [1940] NI 125.

336 *Power* v *Dublin United Tramways* [1926] IR 302.

337 *Tucker* v *Oldbury UDC* [1912] 2 KB 317 (workmen's compensation).

338 Or under its predecessors RSC (NI) 1936 Ord.37 rr.36-9, RSC (Ir) 1905 (Wylie, Ord.37 rr.36-9) and previous RSC.

339 For the history of this peculiar dual system see Malcolm, 'Back to Base?' (1974) 25 NILQ 49.

dead, or unfit by bodily or mental condition[340] to attend as witness, or (c) he is beyond the seas[341] and it is not reasonably practicable to secure his attendance, or (d) reasonable efforts to find him have been made without success. It must be proved that the document was written or otherwise adopted by the maker (s.1(4)), and the rules for proving authenticity of a document apply (see para. 13.139). He is the maker of a tape recording only if he knew that he was being recorded.[342] A statement by an expert of his opinion can be a statement tending to establish a fact.[343] The party can seek to prove the statement by calling the maker to prove its authenticity,[344] and unless he is examined in chief he is protected from cross-examination.

13.127 The Court may draw inferences from the form and contents of the document, but only on the question of admissibility (s.1(5)), not authenticity.[345] Section 1(2) allows the court a discretion to admit the statement of a witness who is available but not called, if undue delay or expense would be caused. On the same ground the court can allow a certified copy in lieu of the original document, but not if the original is lost or destroyed.[346] There is a discretion to exclude the statement in a jury trial (s.1(5)). The authenticity of the document must be proved; it can be inferred from the circumstances.[347] In assessing the weight of the statement the Court must consider the circumstances, especially lapse of time from the facts described, and incentive to conceal or misrepresent (s.2(1)), and inability to cross-examine the maker.[348] A statement is not admissible under section 1 if made by an interested person when proceedings[349] on a dispute to which the statement is relevant were pending or anticipated at the time (s.1(3)). This probably excludes a statement by any driver or victim in a road accident.[350] There is no obligation to give advance notice of a statement

---

340 Proved by medical certificate: s.1(5).

341 The meaning of "beyond the seas" is discussed by Newark (1954) 11 NILQ 26. In *Rover International* v *Cannon Films* [1987] 1 WLR 1597, *affd.*[1989] 1 WLR 912, the English Court held that the Channel Islands and Isle of Man were beyond the seas of England, not because of sea but because an English *subpoena* cannot be served there. There are conflicting decisions from Australia on the meaning of the words as used in limitation statutes. A court in Canberra, ACT, decided that Sydney, NSW, is not beyond the seas because they are both subject to the overall control of the Federal Government: *Witten* v *Lombard Australia* [1969] Australian Law Digest, p.296. But in *Waung* v *Subbotovsky* (1969) 43 ALJR 372, the High Court of Australia held that in a NSW court, anywhere outside NSW was beyond the seas. It may be relevant to note that for the purposes of any law, the Republic of Ireland is not a "foreign" country: Ireland Act 1949, s.2.

342 *Ventouris* v *Mountain (No 2)* [1992] 1 WLR 887.

343 *Dass* v *Masih* [1968] 2 All ER 226.

344 *Hilton* v *Lancashire Dynamo* [1964] 2 All ER 769.

345 Newark, (1939) 3 NILQ 120, at 128 n.18.

346 *Bowskill* v *Dawson* [1954] 1 QB 288 (*sed quaere*).

347 *McKay* v *Hutchins* (1991) 17 Comm LB 845 (SC, Queensland).

348 *Rooney* v *Conway* [1982] 5 NIJB at 14.

349 Not necessarily the proceedings in which it is now sought to adduce the statement: it could be an anticipated criminal prosecution: *United Tobacco* v *Goncalves*, 1996 (1) SA 209.

350 See further Jackson p.105-113, and *Roberts* v *Burns Philp* (1987) 13 Comm LB 1310 (CA, NSW).

to be adduced under the 1939 Act, unless it is a medical report. The Act does render admissible a declaration as to pedigree which is not admissible at common law (s.7).

1971 Act: duty record documents

13.128 A statement of a fact of which direct oral evidence would be admissible is admissible if contained in a document which is or forms part of a record complied by a maker acting under a duty (official, trade, business etc.) from information supplied directly, or under a chain of duty, from a person (acting under a duty or not) reasonably supposed to have personal knowledge (Civil Evidence Act (NI) 1971, s.1(1)(3)). It does not include a note taken by a solicitor in the form of a witness statement dictated by a person with personal knowledge (*Johnson* v *Gilpins Ltd).*[351] In that case the majority of the Court went on to read onto the 1971 Act, to harmonise with the 1939 Act, a requirement that the supplier should not be a person interested in pending or anticipated proceedings (*per* Kelly LJ at 332C), or at least that the statement was recorded under a duty independent of the issues raised in the proceedings. For the purpose of determining its admissibility the Court may draw inferences from the circumstances of its creation and from its form and content (s.3(2)). 'Document' includes a map, drawing, photograph, film, audio recording etc.; 'statement' includes a representation of fact in words or otherwise (s.6).

13.129 At least 21 days before the date of trial a notice containing a copy of the document, particulars of its compilation and the identities of the supplier, the maker and any intermediaries, and of any reason why any of them cannot be called, must be served on the other party (Ord.38 rr.19, 20). The reasons why a person cannot be called are: that he is dead, beyond the seas, bodily or mentally unfit, that it is not possible to identify or find him, or that he cannot be expected to remember (Ord.38 r.22). The other party may serve a counter-notice within 21 days (Ord.38 r.23). An unreasonable counter-notice may be penalised in costs (Ord.38 r.29). Any party may apply to the Court for a pre-trial determination as to whether the person can be called (Ord.38 r.24). If the statement admissible under the Act comes from the record of oral evidence in other legal proceedings, a counter-notice cannot be served but any party may apply for directions (Ord.38 r.25). The Court has a discretion to admit the evidence even if the rules are not complied with (Ord.38 r.26). In fact the rules are often ignored, and the Court will admit the evidence unless it would cause real prejudice or there is a deliberate attempt to take the opponent by surprise.[352] Section 4 and Order 38 rules 27-8 regulate the right of the other party to impeach the credit of the maker, supplier etc. If the party adducing the statement is going to call the supplier as a witness, leave of the court is necessary to put the statement in evidence, and only after the supplier's examination-in-chief (s.1(2)). The statement cannot amount to corroboration in law of the supplier's evidence (s.3(4)). The document is proved by adducing the original or a copy, authenticated as the Court thinks fit (s.3(1)). In assessing its

---

[351] [1989] NI 294 (CA, Hutton LCJ dissenting).

[352] *Rover International* v *Cannon Films* [1987] 1 WLR 1597, at 1600B.

weight the Court may consider the contemporaneity of the supplier's report and any incentive of him or the maker to misrepresent (s.3(3)).

Computer records

13.130 Hearsay contents of computer records are admissible under the Civil Evidence Act (NI) 1971 (s.2) on proof by certificate that the computer was in regular use and proper order and that the information is of a type usually fed into the computer. Order 38 rules 18-19, 21-24, 26, 28-19 apply with broadly similar effect. There is no need to rely on section 2 where the computer was used merely to process or collate information proved by other evidence.

Medical reports and maps etc.

13.131 A medical report disclosed under Order 25, or a map, diagram, photograph etc. shown under Order 38 rule 3A may be given in evidence by the disclosing party unless another party gives sufficient notice that he requires the doctor to testify orally or the map etc. to be proved; the Court may allow the medical report, map etc. to be given in evidence without proof if the medical or other expert witness is unable to attend court (Ord.38 r.1A).

Public and official documents[353]

13.132 At common law, the following heads of documentary hearsay are admissible-

(1) Statements in British or foreign statutes, official journals, parliamentary journals, statutory reports, royal speeches etc..[354]

(2) Court Records and documents (see para. 13.153).

(3) Statements in official registers and records kept anywhere, if recorded under a duty and kept open for public inspection by proper officers who have satisfied themselves of the reliability of the information, for example a valuation certificate is evidence of the identity of the occupier of land.[355] It is not essential for the officer himself to know that the information is true, provided that his informant knows.[356]

(4) Assertions in reports and surveys by a public officer investigating matters of public concern. This does not cover findings of a coroner's court.[357]

(5) Entries by a proper officer in the public books of a public corporation.

None of those heads covers entries in a police occurrence book.[358]

Miscellaneous

13.133 Other heads of hearsay admissible under common law or statute.

(1) Matters of reputation, where admissible (see para. 13.17).

(2) Judicial notice (see para. 13.22).

---

[353] See Phipson, Chap.31; Cross pp.635-42.

[354] E.g. census records: *Dublin Corp* v *Bray Commrs* [1900] 2 IR 88.

[355] *In goods of Shellew* (1949) 83 ILTR 190.

[356] *R* v *Halpin* [1975] QB 907.

[357] *Bird* v *Keep* [1918] 2 KB 692.

[358] *Devenny* v *DOE* (Londonderry Rec Ct) 9 October 1985; reported on other points [1985] 9 BNIL 127; on appeal [1986] 5 BNIL 100.

(3) Examined copies of entries made in the course of business in the ordinary books of a bank or Building Society are prima facie evidence (Bankers Books Evidence Act 1879, ss.3-5).
(4) Under innumerable statutes dealing with documentary evidence (see para. 13.153).
(5) Affidavits (para. 13.33), reports (para. 13.93) and depositions (para. 13.10) taken under the RSC. A deposition taken outside the United Kingdom, taken by a justice in a colony or by a British consul anywhere, is admissible if the deponent cannot be found in the United Kingdom.[359]
(6) Hearsay in matrimonial causes (see FP Rules, rr.2.40-2.45).
(7) Hearsay relating to child care (see para. 13.32).

EXTRINSIC EVIDENCE OF A DOCUMENTED TRANSACTION

13.134 If a transaction has been reduced to writing, the general rule is that the document itself is the only admissible evidence of the terms of the transaction, whether or not the parties to the transaction are parties to the action, and whether or not the transaction is required by law to be in writing. No evidence from an external source is receivable to contradict, vary, add or subtract the terms.[360] The rule only applies to a document which appears to constitute the transaction, not merely evidence of it such as a receipt or invoice. A receipt is only prima facie evidence of what it says.[361]

13.135 *Restrictions and exceptions.* Extrinsic evidence is allowed-
(1) As to execution, authenticity, and as to whether the document was intended to represent an agreement.
(2) To show lack of consideration, illegality; fraud, duress, mistake, *non est factum*, incapacity to contract etc. which vitiate the contract.
(3) To show that an order of court is part of a contractual compromise, though not so stated on its face.[362]
(4) As to capacity of a party (e.g. that he acted as an agent).
(5) Of terms implied into the agreement by custom, usage, common law or statute.
(6) Of equitable interests where the document refers only to legal interests.
(7) Of subsequent variation, rescission or waiver of rights.
(8) As to the actual date of execution.[363]
(9) In a suit to rectify the document evidence is admissible to show the true terms agreed.
(10) Evidence can show in a contract for sale of lands that some material terms were agreed orally, so that the document is not enforceable under the Statute of Frauds.

---

[359] Merchant Shipping Act 1995, s.286.
[360] *Macklin* v *Graecen* [1983] IR 61.
[361] *R* v *Darcy* (1826) Batty 247.
[362] *Northern Bank* v *Jeffers*, Ch D, NI (Girvan J), 5 December 1996; [1996] 10 BNIL 67.
[363] *In re Maher* [1910] 1 IR 167.

(11) Evidence can show that the document was not intended to be a full record and if so, other evidence of agreed terms not inconsistent with the document are admissible, so also where the document appears on its face not to be a complete record.[364]

(12) A document referred to in the transactional document is admissible.

13.136 *Extrinsic evidence to interpret.* There is also a general rule that evidence is not admissible to interpret a document. Leaving aside the special powers of the Probate Court to cure mistakes and omissions in a will,[365] a court cannot interpret so as to contradict the clear meaning of the words or fill in total blanks. There are several instances in which a court can admit extrinsic evidence: to identify references ("my son", "this place"); to identify unclear, incorrectly or peculiarly described references; to resolve patent equivocations; to correct mistakes; to prevent absurdities; to give a special meaning of a word where the document or extrinsic facts show that the author cannot have intended the ordinary meaning;[366] to fill in partial blanks; in defamation cases on a plea of innuendo, to show facts which make the meaning defamatory. Evidence is admissible to show that there is a latent ambiguity (e.g. a gift to Joe Bloggs my cousin – evidence that there are two cousins of that name) and then by further evidence, including statements by the author as to what he meant, to resolve the ambiguity.

In all these exceptions, except the case of latent ambiguity, only circumstantial evidence is admissible, not direct evidence of what the author intended.[367] But circumstantial evidence extends to general statements by the author to show his habits of speech or his state of knowledge.

13.137 *Public documents.* Because of the importance of the public being able to rely on its terms, for a public document such as a grant of planning permission, the rule against extrinsic evidence is applied strictly.[368] However where a public document is put in evidence as admissible hearsay, to prove the truth of its contents, extrinsic evidence is admissible.[369]

PROVING A DOCUMENT

13.138 To prove a document, counsel simply asks the proper witness to identify it and hand it in to court He need not be sworn if that is all he does. If it is admissible without proof, counsel can hand it in through his attending solicitor. The court official receives it, stamps it and assigns an exhibit number. If a document is of any importance at least four copies of it, typed if the original is handwritten, should be in court for the judge, counsel and witnesses to refer to.

---

364 *Howden* v *Ulster Bank* [1924] 1 IR 117 (NI).

365 As to which see the Wills and Administration Proceedings (NI) Order 1994, Arts.25-9.

366 *In re Logan* [1975] 1 NIJB.

367 *In re Carlisle* [1950] NI 105.

368 *McClurg* v *DOE* [1990] NI 112.

369 *Re Peete* [1952] 2 All ER 599.

Proving a document: authenticity

13.139 Proving a document's authenticity means simply giving evidence that the document to be handed into court is what the tendering party claims it to be. This can be done by securing an admission of authenticity from the opponent; by calling its author; by calling someone who witnessed its execution; by calling someone who recognises the handwriting; by comparing the handwriting with genuine specimens; or by any evidence from which the court can infer its authenticity. In most cases there will be no problem because a party or someone who will be testifying at the trial anyway will be able to prove it. If not, one should have already obviated the need to prove it by securing agreement or formal admission by the opponent. In practice the parties should and do make every effort to agree documents and copies without formal proof. A Practice Direction, [1988] 7 BNIL 102, calls upon parties to agree the authenticity of inquest depositions without having to call the coroner to prove them. As a last resort one may ask the Court to infer that the document is genuine from its appearance and content.[370]

13.140 Handwriting can be proved by any lay person who is familiar with the alleged author's hand (including the author himself), without having to produce any specimens; but a lay person cannot base his opinion on observations made solely for the purpose of testifying. An expert witness can give his opinion based on his comparisons made for the purpose of the proceedings. If a witness denies that he is the writer, it can be compared with any document admitted by him to be genuine, or with a specimen which he writes in the witness box. Where the authenticity of a document written by any person is at issue, any writings proved[371] to be genuine can be received, and any witness may make a comparison with the writing in dispute (Criminal Procedure Act 1865, s.8). The Act applies whether the original or a copy of the disputed writing has been brought to court.[372] Authenticity of a document (including a copy of a lost document) can be proved by showing a comparison with genuine specimens of the way in which words are peculiarly spelt, punctuated or phrased.[373]

13.141 If a document has been attested, its authenticity can be proved by calling an attesting witness or proving his handwriting, without need to prove the author's writing, but there should be some prima facie evidence of the identity of the stated name of the author with the person alleged to be the author.[374]

13.142 A map, diagram, photograph, or model which has been disclosed under Order 38 rule 3A may be given in evidence at the trial (Ord.38 r.1A).[375]

13.143 A party, voluntarily in his pleadings or by notice under Order 27 rule 1, can admit the authenticity of a document. A party may, within 21 days after

---

370 *Aylward* v *Jones* (1884) 18 ILTR 111.

371 On balance of probabilities: *R* v *Ewing* [1983] QB 1039, at 1047A.

372 *Lockheed-Arabia* v *Owen* [1993] QB 806 (CA) (leave to appeal to HL refused); not following *McCullough* v *Munn* [1908] 2 IR 194.

373 *McCullough* v *Munn* at 205-6, 213.

374 *Keohane* v *Byrne* [1935] NI 63.

375 See para. 13.131. Costs of a sketch map in a land collision action, see para. 17.105.

setting down, serve a notice to admit, calling upon the opponent to admit the authenticity of a specified document; the opponent must serve a notice of non-admission within 21 days, otherwise it is admitted (Ord.27 r.5).[376] If a party has served a list of documents under Order 24, the opponent is deemed to admit the authenticity of those listed unless he serves a notice disputing authenticity (Ord.27 r.4).[376] An admission of authenticity admits only that the document is what it purports to be, not that it is relevant or admissible, nor that its contents are true. An admission of authenticity of a copy admits that the copy is genuine, but not that the original is authentic.[377]

13.144 *20 year-old documents.* If a document free from suspicion is proved or purports to have been executed at least 20 years ago, and is produced from proper custody, its authenticity and due execution and attestation are presumed by its mere production to the court.[378] Proper custody means any one of the places and persons where it would naturally and reasonably be expected to be found.

Proving a document: execution

13.145 Some documents, such as a contract, deed or will, are such that they have to be executed, that is, brought into operation. In most cases, if a document's authenticity is established, then its own words may prove its execution. However specific evidence of execution may have to be given: (a) where there is a dispute as to whether it was intended to be operative, as where it may have been written as a draft of a proposed agreement; (b) where some further act of execution was necessary (e.g. delivery); or (c) where parol evidence of the contents of a document lost or destroyed is admitted. If a document is attested (i.e. signed by persons as witnesses to its execution) then unless attested under an obligation of law, its execution may be proved as if there were no attesting witness.[379]

13.146 *Documents requiring attestation.* A will must be proved in the Probate Court by calling an attesting witness, and only if none is available and willing to prove the will can it be proved by other evidence. Any other document such as a power of attorney can be proved as if no attesting witness were alive.[380]

20 year-old documents. See above para. 13.144.

13.147 *Stamp.* A document is inadmissible if it does not bear an stamp which was required by law at the date of its execution; but if the law permits it to be stamped after execution, it is admissible on payment to the court officer of the duty and a penalty.[381] A copy of a lost deed must be stamped unless it is proved that the original was stamped.[382] The Court must take the objection of its own

---

376 In which case he will bear the costs of proving it (Ord.62 r.6(8).

377 *Rochfort* v *Sedley* (1861) 12 ICLR App.4.

378 Common law and the Evidence Act (NI) 1939, s.4.

379 Criminal Procedure Act 1865, s.7.

380 Evidence Act (NI) 1939, s.3.

381 Stamp Act 1891, s.14.

382 *Gardiner* v *Irish Land Comm* (1976) 110 ILTR 21.

motion and the parties cannot waive it. The judge's decision to admit an unstamped document cannot be a ground for new trial (Ord.59 r.11(5)).

Proving a document: the 'best evidence rule'

13.148 This ancient rule stipulates that the contents of a document must be proved by production of its original, and that secondary evidence (such as a copy of it or oral evidence of someone who has read it) of its contents is inadmissible.[383] An original includes a duplicate, including a memorial of a deed.[384] A document or copy executed by a party is an original against him. Failure to object to secondary evidence makes it admissible but it is still not sufficient proof of the transaction unless the opponent expressly or impliedly accepts it as such.[385]

13.149 If a party does not have the original document in his possession and wishes to adduce its contents in evidence by 'secondary evidence', that is admissible only in any of the following cases-

(1) The original is proved or inferred by admissible evidence to have been lost or destroyed. Loss or destruction of a useless or ephemeral document can be easily inferred.
(2) The original is in the hands of a non-party who refuses on grounds of privilege to obey a *subpoena* to produce it;[386] but not where he refuses without privilege.
(3) The original is proved or inferred to be in the possession of the other party and the latter has been called on to produce it.
(4) The original is in the opponent's possession and the nature of the litigation is such that its production is obviously necessary.
(5) The opponent has brought the document to court.
(6) The original is a notice served on the opponent.
(7) The original is included by the opponent in his list of discovery as a document in his possession (Ord.27 r.4(3)).
(8) The opponent has admitted that he had the document and has lost destroyed or parted with it.
(9) The opponent's admission of the contents or adduction of a document which recites the contents, is evidence thereof.[387]
(10) It cannot be easily transported (e.g. an inscription on a tombstone).
(11) Examined copies admissible of public documents.
(12) As provided by innumerable statutes and rules.

13.150 *Notice to produce.* A party may call upon the opponent to produce the document by a 'notice to produce' under Order 27 rule 5(4), served a reasonable time before the trial. It is operative for the trial and any new trial in

---

383 Production of a copy is generally admissible in criminal courts since 1989, but not as yet in civil courts.

384 *Staples* v *Young* [1908] 1 IR 135.

385 *McKay* v *McNally* (1879) 4 LR Ir 438, at 449-50; and see *Curry* v *Rea* [1937] NI 1.

386 *In re Hamilton* (1840) 1 Cr & D CC 624 (claim of lien).

387 *Martin* v *Doherty* (1880) 6 LR Ir 195; *Murphy d. Wray* v *Morrison* (1829) 2 Hud & Br 406.

the same action. Summary notice can be given if the opponent has the document in court. The notice must specify the document or class of documents. A notice to produce "all letters relating to the cause" is too vague. The notice is of no effect unless it is shown or inferred that the document is in the possession of the opponent or his agent, servant, or solicitor. Such notice does not mean that the opponent must produce the document.[388] Its effect is to allow one to adduce secondary evidence, comment on the failure to produce, and prevent the opponent from later adducing the original. The opponent, if he produces the document, cannot compel the serving party to put it in evidence unless he inspects or uses it.

13.151 *Types of secondary evidence:* (a) examined copies; (b) office copies of judicial documents (Ord.38 r.8); (c) certified copies, as prescribed by the particular statute; (d) an ordinary photographed, photostatted, facsimile, carbon or other copy; (e) a recital of the deed's contents in a subsequent deed; (f) abstracts and memorials of a deed; (g) a draft from which it was drawn up;[389] (h) oral testimony of someone who has read it; (j) admissible hearsay;[390] (k) circumstantial evidence from a person's conduct.[391]

13.152 Where secondary evidence is admissible all forms of it are generally equally admissible, save that public and judicial documents must be proved by a copy; and secondary evidence admissible under statute is always by some form of copy. When adducing an ordinary copy to prove a document, one must remember the need to prove or infer the authenticity of both the copy and the original (i.e. that the copy is the same as the original, and that the original is itself what it is alleged to be). A copy of a copy must be proved to be the same as copy and the original.[392]

STATUTORY PROVISIONS AS TO DOCUMENTARY EVIDENCE

13.153 Statute law provides numerous instances where a document is admissible without proof of authenticity and/or by production of a copy, and it may also deal with its admissibility as hearsay. For an extensive, if not complete, list of statutory provisions, see the *Index to the Statutes, Northern Ireland* (HMSO) (current edition to 31 December 1993) Heading "Evidence-5". A selection of the most important provisions is listed below.

General. Where statute makes a certificate, official or public document, public corporation document, certified copy, bye-law, entry in a book or register or other proceeding receivable, the seal, signature or stamp on it need not be proved (Evidence Act 1845, s.1). A document receivable without proof in England is receivable in Northern Ireland (Evidence Act 1851, s.9). A public document admissible on production from proper custody can be proved by examined or certified copy (1851 Act, s.14). If a copy is by

---

[388] Distinguish a Notice to Produce for Inspection under Ord.24.

[389] *Fury* v *Smith* (1822) 1 Hud & Br 735.

[390] E.g. family repute of the contents of a will: *In goods of Stuart* [1944] Ir Jur R 62.

[391] *Cummins* v *Hall* [1933] IR 419.

[392] *McCullough* v *Munn* [1908] 2 IR 194, at 205, 206-7.

statute made evidence of the contents of a document, it is not *per se* evidence of the truth of the contents (*O'Kane* v *Mullan* [1925] NI 1).

Judicial documents. Writs, orders, pleadings, sealed documents etc. of the Supreme Court (Judicature Act, s.115; Ord.38 r.8), English Supreme Court (Supreme Court Act 1981, s.132; Evidence Act 1845, s.2). County Court records and documents (County Courts (NI) Order 1980, Arts.57,59). Magistrates' courts orders (Magistrates Courts Rules (NI) 1984, r.20). Convictions and acquittals are proved by certificate (Evidence Act 1851, s.13; Prevention of Crimes Act 1871, s.18). Proof of care orders etc. (Children and Young Persons Act (NI) 1968, s.173). Proof of judgments of Brussels Convention states for purpose of the Convention, see Civil Jurisdiction and Judgments Act 1982, s.11.

Governmental documents. Proclamations, Orders, gazettes etc. are proved by HMSO copies (Documentary Evidence Acts 1868 to 1895), which apply to sealed or signed orders, certificates, licences etc. of a Ministry of Northern Ireland (Ministries of Northern Ireland Act (NI) 1921, s.3) (now Departments: Northern Ireland Act 1974, Sch.1 para. 2). A certificate is the only proper way to prove the opinion of a department (*Belfast Corp* v *OD Cars* [1960] NI 60 (HL)). Sealed copies of documents in the Public Record Office (Public Records Acts 1875, s.10 and (NI) 1923, s.6), including Supreme Court records (SR (NI) 1925/170, p.275). Bye-laws and council documents (Local Government Act (NI) 1972, ss.94,120,124). County boundaries etc. (County Boundaries (Ir) Act 1872; *Brown* v *Donegal CC* [1980] IR 132, at 143). State judicial and legal documents of foreign states[393] proved by examined or authenticated copies (Evidence Act 1851, s.7). Registers and certificates of foreign authorities are admissible as provided by Orders in Council (Oaths and Evidence (Overseas Authorities and Countries) Act 1963, s.5); see White Book (1997) 38/10/5, and Halsbury's *Statutes* Vol. 17 for a list of Orders.

Births, marriages, deaths. Old parochial records (Public Records (Ir) ... Amendment Act 1875, s.10; Parochial Records Act 1876. Births and Deaths Registration (NI) Order 1976, Arts.38-41, and SR (NI) 1973/373). Certified copies of marriages (Registration of Marriages (Ir) Act 1863, ss.17-19), are admissible under s.11 thereof (without prejudice to direct evidence of marriage, such as oral witnesses: *McCarthy* v *Hastings* [1933] NI 100). Non-catholic marriages (Marriages (Ir) Act 1844, ss.68-71). Foreign Marriage Act 1892, s.16-18. Registration of Births Deaths and Marriages (Army) Act 1879. Adopted children register (Adoption (NI) Order 1987, Art.63).

Property. Copy wills and certificates of grants (Administration of Estates (NI) Order 1979, Art.25). Copy to prove a lease (Deasy's Act, s.23). Recitals in 20 year old deeds are evidence of what they state in proceedings between parties to a contract for sale of land (Vendor and Purchaser Act

---

393 Including the Republic of Ireland: *R* v *McGlinchey* [1985] NI 435.

1874, s.2). Certificate on a deed as evidence of its registration (Registration of Deeds Act (NI) 1970, s.1(6)): certified copy of memorial (s.6). The Land Registry Folio is conclusive evidence of titles, rights and burdens on, but not except as provided of boundaries of, registered land (Land Registration Act (NI) 1970, ss.11,64). Judicial notice is taken of the Land Registry seal (Sch.1 para..11). The certificate is prima facie evidence of its contents (Land Registration Rules (NI) SR 1994/424, r.127). Certified copy of valuation list (Rates (NI) Order 1977, Art.48).

Evidence and Powers of Attorney Act 1940; Powers of Attorney Act 1971, s.3; Enduring Powers of Attorney Act 1985, s.7(3) (UK Acts).

Commercial matters. Bankers Books Evidence Act 1879 (para. 13.133). Evidence of tax due by certificate (Taxes Management Act 1970, s.70). Certified copies of documents kept by Companies Registrar (Companies (NI) Order 1986, Art.658)

Miscellaneous. Motor vehicle and driving licence records (Vehicles Excise and Registration Act 1994, s.52; Road Traffic (NI) Order 1981, Art. 190; to be replaced by the Road Traffic Offenders (NI) Order 1996, Art.16 (which may apply only to criminal proceedings); SR (NI) 1989/32). Evidence of unpaid social security contributions (Social Security Administration (NI) Act 1992, s.112). An entry in a factory register is evidence against the occupier; and non-entry is evidence of non-compliance (Factories (NI) 1965, s.166). Liquor licensing register and licences (Licensing (NI) Order 1990, Arts.42-3). Registers of newspaper proprietors (Newspaper Libel and Registration Act 1881, s.15).

REAL EVIDENCE

13.154 Real evidence is that which is perceived directly by the senses other than by the oral words of a witness or the assertions contained in documents. It includes an article, machine, the demeanour of a witness, the appearance of a document. An article or thing can be brought to court. A process or event can be demonstrated or reconstructed in court. The judge (and jury) may inspect any place or thing (Ord.35 r.5), anywhere in the world, without the consent of the parties. The Court can require a party to facilitate a reconstruction.[394] Some cases say that he can use the observation as an independent source of evidence;[395] others that he can only use it to assist comprehension of the evidence given in court.[396]

13.155 The Court can draw inferences as to the honesty and reliability of a witness from watching and listening to his testimony; and to some extent from the conduct of the witness in court when not in the witness box.[397]

---

394 *Ash* v *Buxted Poultry*, 'The Times' 29 November 1989, where it was to be recorded on video tape for the judge to see.

395 White Book (1997) 35/8/2.

396 *Hunter* v *Gray* [1970] NI 1; *Commr for Railways* v *Murphy* (1967) 41 ALJR 77 (HC of Aus); *Triple A Investments* v *Adams Bros* (1986) 23 DLR 4th 587 (Nfld CA).

397 *R* v *Meehan* [1981] 1 NIJB, 5-6.

13.156 In any proceedings in which paternity is at issue the Court can order blood tests under the Family Law Reform (NI) Order 1977 (Art.8), on notice by application at the hearing or by summons, and the Court can direct the person to be tested to be made a party; the proceedings stand adjourned for further consideration of a report of the test (Ord.112). A person (or his custodian if under 16 years) can refuse consent to the test (Art.9), in which case the Court may draw any proper inference (Art.11). The procedure for taking tests is set out in SR (NI) 1978/379, as amended by SR 1990/212 to take account of new "DNA" techniques,[398] under which paternity can be determined in all cases. The Court can also consider facial resemblances.[399]

13.157 A photograph is admissible if relevant and can be proved in the same way as a document, so it is not necessary to call the person who took it and/or developed it.[400] A tape-recording of a conversation, even if illicitly recorded, is admissible if relevant and if the identity of the voices can be proved; a typed transcript should be made for use in court. Where a transcript is made, it is for ease of reference by the judge/jury; the transcript is not a substitute for the tape which remains the only source of the evidence.[401] Films, audio and video recordings are not documents for the purpose of the 'best evidence' rule;[402] so a re-recording is admissible instead of the original. If the tape has been lost or erased a witness can say what he saw or heard on it.[403] The Court can derive evidence both from its own view of the film and from the testimony of persons who have viewed the film as to what they perceive in it.[404] Photographs and cine or video films are subject to the rules of Order 38 which require prior disclosure to the opposing party (paras. 13.85 and 13.131). *Quaere*, whether Order 38 applies to audio tape recordings.

EXHIBITS

13.158 Every document or thing put in evidence at a trial is handed to the official present in court who marks it P1, P2, D1, D2 etc. At the end of the trial he makes and keeps a list of all exhibits and returns them to the parties to be preserved in the event of appeal (Ord.35 rr.8-9). Junior counsel for each party should keep and agree a list of all documents put in evidence and at the end of the trial should sign and hand it to the official.[405] The Court has inherent jurisdiction to keep material documents in its custody in the interests of justice. Such impounded documents cannot be given to or inspected by any person unless a judge so orders (Ord.35 r.10).

---

398 See *JPD* v *MG* [1991] 1 IR 47.

399 *Bagot* v *Bagot* (1878) 1 LR Ir 308; reversed on appeal on other grounds (1880) 5 LR Ir 72.

400 *R* v *Dodson* [1984] 1 WLR 971.

401 *Butera* v *DPP* (1987) 164 CLR 181.

402 *Kajala* v *Noble* (1982) 75 Cr App R 149.

403 *Taylor* v *Chief Constable of Cheshire* [1986] 1 WLR 1479.

404 *R* v *Murphy* [1990] NI 306.

405 *Maguire* v *PJ Lagan* [1976] NI 49, at 51D.

CHAPTER FOURTEEN

THE TRIAL

14.00 A few weeks before the trial, the solicitor sends trial briefs to counsel. Junior counsel should check that action has been taken on the direction of proofs, look for necessary amendments of pleadings, check the documentary evidence, that interlocutory steps such as notices for particulars and discovery are completed, and arrange for a final consultation.

14.01 Most proceedings take place at the Royal Courts of Justice, Chichester Street, Belfast (Judicature Act, s.58; Ord.33 r.1), but on application of any party the Court may order trial at another place (s.58(3)).[1] A party may apply by summons for an action to be tried during vacation if there is urgent need (Ord.64 r.4(2)). The trial takes place before a judge sitting alone in open court; or a judge and jury; or a judge with assessors; or, under Orders 36 or 37, a master (Ord.33 r.2). The proceedings are recorded by audio-tape. All proceedings are in the English language.[2] If is an offence to take photographs or sketches in court,[3] and to make an audio recording.[4]

SITTING IN PRIVATE

14.02 All proceedings take place in open court to which any member of the public has access, unless statute or rules or rule of law authorise sitting *in camera* or in chambers. By a judgment or order made in court, the judge may direct proceedings in chambers (Ord.32 r.17). Any proceedings may, or must, be heard *in camera* if publicity may defeat justice; for example, if a secret document has to be read out; if witnesses are inhibited by the presence of the public; if the court is sitting in arbitration or in minor matters or administrative capacity; or if publicity may defeat justice. National security, including some anti-terrorist operations, is a ground for sitting in private in so far as open publicity might endanger the doing of justice (e.g. by deterring the Crown from presenting its case); the Court then balances the competing interests.[5] A court may exclude the public when a child (up to 18 years) is giving evidence of an indecent nature.[6] A non-judicial act need not be done in open court.[7] If proceedings are in chambers the Court can exclude all except the parties and

---

1 But only, where it is a party, with the consent of the Crown: Ord.77 r.12

2 Administration of Justice (Language) Act (Ir) 1737.

3 Criminal Justice Act (NI) 1945, s.29.

4 Unless the Court grants leave to bring and use a tape recorder in court: Contempt of Court Act 1981, s.9.

5 *In re Minister of Defence* [1994] 7 BNIL 9.

6 Children (NI) Order 1995, Art.168. Rules may provide for a court to sit in private in child care proceedings: Children (NI) Order 1995, Art.170(1).

7 *R (Hade)* v *Carlow JJ* [1912] 2 IR 382.

their lawyers, but a reporter is entitled to publish any information gleaned from someone present.[8]

14.03 On the same grounds the Court may adopt partial privacy, by directing a witness to be screened from public view, which is a matter for the trial judge to decide during the course of the trial. It is not unusual for a witness to be screened from the general public, but it is hard to envisage any circumstance in which an important witness should be screened from legal representatives.[9] Counsel who calls that witness should tell opposing counsel of any material about the witness which would help the opponent's case.[10] Where the testimony is not controversial, for example a witness called merely to prove a photograph or film, there is precedent for screening him from everyone except judge and counsel.[11] The Court also has a separate and distinct power, to be decided on the broad interests of justice, to allow a witness to testify without being named, as "Witness A", "Soldier B" etc., and his name and address should be handed on a note to the judge; for anonymity (and possibly even screening) is not a breach of the principle of open justice.[12] Where the Court lawfully allows a name or matter to be withheld, it may prohibit publication under the Contempt of Court Act 1981 (s.11). If necessary to avoid prejudice in the present or other proceedings, the Court may postpone publication (s.4(2)). The Matrimonial Causes (Reports) Act (NI) 1966 bans reports of evidence in divorce and other petitions, declarations of legitimacy, and financial provision applications. In child care proceedings, it is an offence to publish the identity of a child (up to 18 years) without leave of court.[13] By the Administration of Justice Act 1960 (s.12) publication of information about proceedings of a court sitting in private can be contempt only if the proceedings relate to care etc. of a minor or mental patient, national security or secret invention, or if the court expressly prohibits publication.

JURY TRIAL

14.04 If requested by any party, an action or issue of fact in an action in which a claim for libel, slander, malicious prosecution or false imprisonment is made, shall be tried with a jury; but the action or issue may be tried without a jury on application of any party if it (a) involves matters of accounts, (b) requires protracted examination of documents or accounts or technical, scientific or local investigation which cannot be conveniently made with a jury, (c) will be unduly prolonged, or (d) is for any special specified reason unsuitable for a jury (Judicature Act, s.62(1)(2)). A claim for false imprisonment gives a right to jury trial unless it is struck out as a total sham.[14] Request for trial by jury is made by the party on setting down or by any other

---

8 *In re Martin* [1990] NI 73, at 76B.

9 *Doherty* v *MOD* [1991] 1 NIJB 68, at 88-9; *In re Ministry of Defence* [1994] 7 BNIL 9.

10 *Doherty* v *MOD* at 91. The judge must satisfy himself that the party calling the witness has investigated and disclosed to the opponent the creditworthiness of the witness: *In re Murray* [1997] 3 BNIL 106 (Kerr J).

11 *Doherty* v *MOD* at 89-90.

12 *In re Jordan,* CA, NI, 28 June 1996, at pp.15-17; [1996] 7 BNIL 15.

13 Children (NI) Order 1995, Art.170(2).

14 *Hill* v *Chief Constable* [1990] 1 WLR 946.

party lodging a request within seven days after notice of setting down without a jury, or by any party applying by motion (Ord.33 r.4(1)(2)(5)). Where jury trial has been requested, any party may apply by motion on notice or at the trial for trial without a jury (Ord.33 r.4(4)), even on the eve of the trial;[15] which will be granted only in exceptional circumstances, as where the Court is satisfied that a jury is unlikely to be able to understand the evidence, and not merely because the evidence is difficult.[15] On such application the Court may order different modes of trial for different issues (Ord.33 r.4(6)). Under exception (b) a judge-only trial is usually ordered if in the overall interests of justice if inconvenience is clearly shown,[16] whereas the Northern Ireland pre-1987 cases adopt the stricter test that only if a jury is unlikely to be able to follow the issues.[17]

14.05 Any other action or issue of fact is tried without a jury, unless the Court orders trial with jury because of an allegation of actual fraud or undue influence or for some other reason (Judicature Act, s.62(3)(4)). Jury trial should not be ordered for a tort, such as misfeasance in public office, just because it is similar to the jury-trial torts.[18] In a personal injury case jury trial will be ordered only in exceptional circumstances.[19] Any party may apply for jury trial by motion (Ord.33 r.4(5)), and the Court may order different modes of trial for different issues (Ord.33 r.4(6)).

Empanelling a jury

14.06 Juries are chosen under the Juries (NI) Order 1996. A yearly Jurors' List is prepared and sent to the Juries Officer of each county court division (Art.4, SR 1996/269 reg.3). A jury panel is prepared by a Juries Officer, initially from the Divisional List (Art.5, SR 1996/269 reg.4). The list is kept for inspection as directed by the Lord Chancellor (Art.7). It contains the name, address and occupation (Art.6). All registered electors aged 18-70 are eligible for service save that some classes of person are disqualified, some ineligible, and some have a right to be excused (Art.3). The fact that a person is not on the panel or has been empanelled in breach of Article 5 is a ground of challenge (Art.16), but is not a ground for invalidating the trial (Art.16(4)). Want of qualification and failure to summon the juror properly are not grounds of challenge (Art.17). A verdict or finding cannot be impeached on the sole ground that a disqualified ineligible or misnamed person served in the jury (Art.29).

14.07 A juror is required to attend the Court by summons served[20] at least ten days before the day for attendance (Art.8). The court official calls over the panel and returns a copy of the panel marked with those who have attended to the Juries Officer (Art.9). Defaulting jurors may be fined up to £1,000 and the fine may be enforced in the same way as a fine by the Crown Court (Art.26). A judge has a general power to excuse a juror for good reason, such as hardship,

---

15 *Haughey* v *Sunday Newspapers* [1989] 5 NIJB 102

16 *Beta Construction* v *Channel 4* [1990] 2 All ER 1012; *Aitkin* v *Pressdram*, 'The Times' 21 May 1997 (CA).

17 In *Haughey* v *Sunday Newspapers* [1989] 5 NIJB 102, Carswell J did not find it necessary to decide which test should be applied now.

18 *Racz* v *Home Office* [1994] 2 AC 45.

19 White Book (1997) 33/5/2.

20 By registered or recorded delivery post: see para. 6.25.

ill health and if a juror appears to be excusable (Art.10). He must discharge the summons if satisfied that the person is unqualified, disqualified or ineligible (Art.11) or not properly appointed (Art.16(2)). Rules of court may enable these powers to be exercised by an officer.

14.08 The jurors for a particular action are selected by ballot in open court (Art.12(1)(2)), drawing out pieces of card from a container (SR 1996/269, reg.5). If the full jury cannot be sworn from those attending, talesmen may be sought (Art.18). Challenge to the whole panel can be allowed only for partiality fraud etc. of the Juries Officer (Art.13). Each party may challenge an unlimited number of jurors for cause shown.[21] Any challenge to the panel or to a juror for cause is tried by the judge (Art.14(1)). The plaintiff and defendant may each challenge up to six jurors without showing cause (Art.14(2)); if there is more than one plaintiff in the action, they can challenge only six in all, and so also more than one defendant (Art.14(3)). Those who are challenged before being sworn onto the jury stand down and do not serve on the jury. Each juror swears an oath in the form to be directed by the Lord Chancellor (Art.27). Rules may provide as to the empanelling, challenging and discharge of jurors (Judicature Act, s.65).

Trial by jury

14.09 The jury consists of seven persons (Judicature Act, s.64(1)). The judge may discharge the jury or a juror at any stage during the trial; the trial may continue without a jury by consent of the parties; if a juror dies or is discharged, the judge may continue with six, or by consent of the parties with as few as four jurors (Juries Order, Art.22). *Semble*, under Order 33 rule 4(4) the judge can discharge the jury during the trial and hear the rest of the case on his own.[22] With consent of the parties the Court may order a separate issue in the action to be tried by the same jury or by a jury consisting of the same members with some being challenged and replaced (Art.12(3)). The judge may order the jury to be detained during adjournments, but not overnight (Art.20(2)). Payments at prescribed rates are payable to jurors for travel, subsistence and financial loss (Art.28). Jurors may be allowed refreshments and meals free of charge (Art.23). Rules of Court may make provision for views by jurors (Art.19). At the end of an exceptionally exacting trial, the judge may excuse the jurors from further service (Art.24).

14.10 In a jury trial the judge's function is to determine what evidence is prima facie admissible, what is material, what capable of being relevant, and whether there is sufficient evidence of a material fact to warrant that issue being left for the consideration of the jury, and to direct the jury on the law and the burden of proof. He must not intervene so much as to hamper or undermine counsel in putting his case.[23] The jury's function is, at the end of the trial, to decide any factual issue which goes to admissibility, decide what is relevant, decide what weight to attach to the evidence according to its veracity and reliability, and thus to reach a verdict on the material facts in accordance with

---

[21] Huband p.654.

[22] Cf. *Gee* v *BBC*, 'The Times' 26 November 1984.

[23] *McAvoy* v *Goodyear* [1973] March-April NIJB, Lowry LCJ at p.11.

the judge's directions. Finally the judge determines what judgment and other order to make upon the verdict. As to the returning of a jury verdict, see para. 14.44.

Trial by judge alone, contrasted

14.11 A judge sitting without a jury exercises the functions of both. During the trial he wears his judicial hat; at its conclusion he becomes the jury, delivering a verdict which he then as judge uses as basis for the judgment.[24]

MODE OF TRIAL: SPLITTING INTO ISSUES

14.12 The Court may order different questions of fact in an action to be tried at different times or by different modes of trial (Judicature Act, s.62(5)), and may order an issue of fact and/or law to be tried before at or after the trial (Ord.33 r.3), by a statement of a special case or otherwise. The provisions as to evidence in Order 38 rules 1-5,18-29 apply (Ord.38 rr.6, 18(3)). If the decision on a preliminary issue substantially disposes of the proceedings or makes a trial unnecessary, the Court may give such judgment or dismissal as may be just (Ord.33 r.6). An issue of law should only be tried as a preliminary issue if the legal point is short and easily resolved, and the factual issues are complex, and should be designed to lead to judgment for one party or at least to a material shortening of the issues at the trial.[25] Though the issue be described as one of law, it may be necessary to hear some factual evidence.[26] The Court may decline to hear the preliminary issue of law if the determination of the facts may make the legal issue immaterial, especially if the resultant delay will prejudice the trial of the facts.[27] In *Curran* v *NICHA* [28] a preliminary issue as to whether on the facts alleged in the Statement of Claim a cause of action existed against one defendant, went on appeal to the Court of Appeal and the House of Lords; the issue was decided in the negative and that defendant dismissed from the action. The extension and/or disapplication of the limitation period, and the factual issues relevant thereto, may be tried by a judge as a preliminary issue.[29] Splitting issues is rare in personal injury cases, but it may be done if just and convenient, as where damages involves a complex issue.[30]

Trial with assessors

14.13 In any civil proceedings, the Court may call for the assistance of qualified assessor(s) (Judicature Act s.61; Ord.33 r.5). This is usually done in Admiralty actions.

---

[24] For an example of this split personality, see *Re Midland Rly Co* (1904) 38 ILTR 52.

[25] *Donaldson* v *Chief Constable* [1989] 7 NIJB 21, at 27-9. In that case the issue was whether there was an actionable duty of care. Murray J had previously, at [1989] 1 NIJB 63, at 74-5, stated his view that the issue should have been raised by applying to strike out the Statement of Claim under Ord.18 r.19, and he re-drafted the issue of law submitted by the defendant to make it clear that it was based on the assumption that the facts pleaded by the plaintiff must be taken as true.

[26] *Deighan* v *Sunday Newspapers* [1987] NI 105, at 107.

[27] *Cullen* v *Chief Constable* [1996] 6 BNIL 76 (CA).

[28] [1987] NI 80.

[29] White Book (1997) 33/4/6; *Moane* v *Reilly* [1984] NI 269. References in that case to jury trial are now obsolete.

[30] *Coenen* v *Payne* [1974] 1 WLR 984; *Millar* v *Peebles*, CA, NI, 23 October 1995.

Reference of issues

14.14 In any proceedings involving matters of account the Court may refer the whole proceedings or an issue therein to a master, referee or arbitrator agreed by the parties under Order 36 (made under the Judicature Act, s.55(2)(cc)). Order 38 rules 1-5,18-29 apply (Ord.38 rr.6,18(3)). The Court usually adjourns further consideration until after receipt of his report or directs proceedings after the report. Subject to the directions in the reference, the referee has all the powers of the judge except committal, in conducting the trial or proceedings before him. The referee consults with the parties and fixes a date for trial of the issue, and reports to the Court his decision on the facts or the question arising from his findings. The Court may adopt, vary, remit for further consideration, require explanation, or decide the issue on, his findings. The Court then fixes a hearing for further consideration of the report, at which a party may apply to vary or remit the report. A decision by a master on a reference is appealable to the Court of Appeal (Ord.58 rr.2-3).

14.15 The Court may make a reference to the Lands Tribunal in proceedings for establishment or enforcement of an impediment on land;[31] and to an industrial tribunal a question of the operation of an equality clause implied in a contract of employment.[32]

European law reference

14.16 Under Article 177 of the Treaty of Rome (as substituted by the Treaty on European Union) and similar provisions in other European Treaties and Conventions,[33] the European Court of Justice can give a preliminary ruling on the interpretation of the Treaty and interpretation and validity of acts of the European institutions and Central Bank. The European Court will refuse to interpret internal laws which are modelled on European legislation, such as Schedule 4 to the Civil Jurisdiction and Judgments Act 1982, if the internal law is not identical and the law does not make European Court rulings on the law to be binding.[34] If such a question is raised in a national court, that court may request a ruling if it considers the resolution of that question necessary for its judgment (Art 177(2)). "Question is raised" means raised in fact by any person at any stage or by the Court.[35] A court is obliged to refer if there is no judicial remedy here against its decision (Art.177(3)), and if the ruling is necessary for its judgment unless the European Court has already ruled on the point or the interpretation is obvious.[36] In other words the High Court or Court of Appeal has a discretion not to refer where an appeal lies from its decision; it may refuse a reference and interpret itself and should do so where the European

---

31 Property (NI) Order 1978, Art.6

32 Equal Pay Act (NI) 1970, s.2(3).

33 E.g. the Euratom, and European Coal and Steel Treaties, the Brussels Convention on Civil Jurisidiction and Judgments, and the Convention annexed to the Contracts (Applicable Law) Act 1990.

34 *Kleinwort Benson* v *Glasgow CC* [1996] QB 57 (ECJ).

35 *Pigs Marketing* v *Redmond* [1978] NI 73, at 80-1, *obiter*.

36 *CILFIT* v *Italian Minister of Health* [1982] ECR 3415.

Court has already ruled on the question.[37] The Court must refer where its decision is final, or where a certificate or granting of leave essential for an appeal is refused. The House of Lords has no discretion to refuse a reference.

14.17 Application may be made under Order 114 before the trial by motion or at the trial, or the Court may refer of its own motion. In the High Court only a judge in person can order the reference. The proceedings are then stayed and after waiting for any appeal, the master sends a copy of the order and the request for the ruling to the European Court in Luxembourg. An order of reference is appealable without leave to the Court of Appeal within 21 days (Ord.114 r.6). The Court of Justice has issued a 'Note for Guidance on References'.[38] It states that the reference must be drafted clearly asnd precisely for ease of translation into the other languages, with a statement of the essential facts and of the relevant national law, the reasons for the reference, and where appropriate the parties' arguments; and that the reference should be normally made after the proceedings are at a stage where the factual and legal context can be postulated and after both sides have been heard. The European Court merely instructs the national court on the meaning of the Community legislation; it does not rule on the effect on national law or the litigation.[39] A national court cannot declare an act of the European institutions to be invalid, but may refer that as an issue to the European Court,[40] and in exceptional cases may suspend it or grant other interim relief.

THE TRIAL OF AN ACTION

Failure to appear or proceed

14.18 If at the trial one party does not appear, the judge may proceed with the claim or counterclaim in his absence (Ord.35 r.1(2)). Thus if the plaintiff is not there, the defendant can ask for judgment dismissing the action, and call the evidence on his counterclaim. If the defendant is not there, the plaintiff may prove his claim and ask for dismissal of the counterclaim. If there is a solicitor on record for a non-appearing party, it is common courtesy to telephone the solicitor's office. If neither party appears the judge may strike out the action, with power to order its restoration (Ord.35 r.1(1)). Non-appearance by a party under these rules means that nobody at all, client, solicitor or counsel is present. Where a legal representative appears on the party's authority, even if he declares that he will take no part in the proceedings, the party is deemed to be present.[41] Judgment can be given against the Crown in its absence. Any judgment, verdict or order in the absence of a party at the trial may be set aside by the Court on application within seven days (Ord.35 r.2), usually with costs of the application and costs thrown away to be paid by the applicant. The time limit is of course extendable by the Court. The primary issue on such application is why the applicant did not appear at the trial; if he was absent

---

37 *CILFIT* v *Italian Minister of Health*; *Portion Foods* v *Min Of Agriculture* [1981] ILRM 161 (*obiter*).
38 Set out at [1996] 9 BNIL 43.
39 *Michel S* v *Fonds National des Handicapés* [1973] ECR 457.
40 *Foto-Frost* v *Hauptzollamt Lübeck-Ost* [1987] ECR 4199.
41 *Kirton* v *Augustus Ltd* [1996] 9 CLM 75 (CA).

deliberately he will normally be held bound by the judgment so that normally he must show that he was absent due to mistake or accident; strong reason must be shown for relitigation of a factual issue already investigated as there is a public interest in avoiding duplicated trials, and if the judgment was regularly obtained, the applicant must show a real prospect of success; an application may be refused if the applicant has delayed, especially, if persons have acted on faith of the judgment, if there is prejudice to the other party, or if the applicant has been guilty of previous default in the action.[42] An absent party can appeal to the Court of Appeal, but where appropriate it is better to invoke this rule.

14.19 In proving a claim against an absent opponent, counsel for the plaintiff (or counterclaiming defendant) must be careful to prepare the case for strict proof under the laws of evidence, as there is no-one with whom to agree any fact or document. Failure by the defendant to appear does not constitute a withdrawal or waiver of the Defence which he has served,[43] though of course the Court will not be persuaded to rule in his favour on any issue on which he bears the burden of proof. The plaintiff must prove all material facts alleged in the Statement of Claim which have been denied or not admitted in the Defence. He must deal with any plea, such as limitation or Statute of Frauds, which is raised in the Defence; but he need not rebut any fact alleged in the Defence on which the defendant has the burden of proof. He can only make the case pleaded in the Statement of Claim and recover the relief pleaded or relief consistent with it.[44] The judge, in giving damages in full against both jointly liable defendants, can apportion contribution *inter se* in the absence of one or both.

14.20 A judgment in the absence of a party, or on him failing to proceed with his claim, constitutes *res judicata.*[45] The power of the Superior Courts before 1877 to "non-suit" the plaintiff survives in the county court (in the form of "dismiss without prejudice") but does not exist in the High Court.[46] Even if the action is dismissed because the wrong form of procedure was used, it cannot be a non-suit.[47] There is only one case where judgment for the defendant at the trial is still a non-suit (so that the plaintiff can sue again on the same cause): that is an action for recovery of land on the title.[48]

Adjournment

14.21 The judge may adjourn a trial if expedient in the interests of justice upon any terms (Ord.35 r.3). An application to take a case out of the list should

---

42 *Shocked* v *Goldschmidt*, 'The Times' 4 November 1994. Contrast the more general approach of *Russell* v *Cox* [1983] NZLR 654.

43 *Banque Commerciale* v *Akhil Holdings* [1990] LRC (Comm) 702; 169 CLR 279 (HC of Aus).

44 White Book (1997) 35/1/1; Wylie p.540; *Banque Commerciale* v *Akhil Holdings.*

45 *Armour* v *Bate* [1891] 2 QB 233; *White* v *Spendlove* [1942] IR 224 (dismissal of counterclaim "the same not having been proceeded with").

46 *Fox* v *Star Newspaper* [1900] AC 19.

47 *Clanricarde* v *Ryder* [1898] 1 IR 98, where the CA held that the Chancery Division could not "dismiss without prejudice" an action commenced in the wrong Division; it must either hear the case or transfer it.

48 *Bywater* v *Dunne* (1883) 10 LR Ir 380; and see para. 13.109.

be made as soon as the need for it is known, so applications for adjournment on the morning of the trial should be very rare. A party may apply for an adjournment for some good reason such as the unexpected absence of a crucial witness. A *bona fide* adjournment should always be granted if refusal would cause injustice. If a party fails to appear, his counsel will normally wish to apply for an adjournment. It is desirable that the judge should investigate the reason before refusing an adjournment; but where a (legally aided) plaintiff failed to appear without explanation, it was held that refusal of her counsel's request to adjourn was not a breach of natural justice.[49] The applicant will usually be ordered to pay the costs thrown away, unless the need for adjournment arises from some act of the other party, such as a late amendment of pleadings.[50] Notice of intention to apply for an adjournment should be given to the other party as soon as possible. An adjournment can be granted only by the Court, and the order should state on whose application it was given.[51] It may be effected informally, as where the judge reserves judgment.[52] If a case cannot be reached in the list it will be adjourned by the Court, and given priority when relisted.

14.22 If the trial judge dies, falls ill, or retires during a trial, but not otherwise, the trial may be directed to start again with, by consent of the parties, the reading out of the evidence already given.[53]

CONTESTED TRIAL

14.23 A Practice Direction [1987] 8 BNIL 83 provides for the personal injury/fatal accident case lists which form the bulk of Queen's Bench trial business. The Court sits at 10.15am (usually in the *Nisi Prius* court) when the clerk in the presence of the judge calls over the day's list. The names of counsel in each case should be handed in. Counsel in each case should be there to announce whether the case is going on, or to announce a settlement, or to ask for an adjournment. After any other applications and approval of any minor settlements, the judge will arrange for the various 'going on' cases to be heard, either by himself or by another available judge in another court. Counsel should then go before that judge or tell other counsel whether he is ready to proceed. A trial should start at 11.00am. The court usually rises for lunch from 1pm to 2pm and rises for the day at about 4.15pm. Going proceedings should resume at 10.30am. Obviously these times are kept very flexible. In the Chancery Division, where counsel are expected to negotiate towards a compromise before the date of trial is finally fixed, the Court expects the trial to be ready to commence promptly at 10.30am.[54]

---

49 *In re Murphy* [1991] 7 NIJB 97. *Murphy* was a county court action in which the judge entered a dismiss without prejudice, so that the plaintiff could sue again or appeal by rehearing to the High Court: *quaere* therefore whether it applies to High Court actions where a dismissal is virtually final. Of course *Murphy* was not a case of dismissing in the absence of a party, as her counsel was present.

50 *Byers* v *Byers* [1927] IR 184.

51 *O'Leary* v *Clerke* (1893) 27 ILTR 123.

52 *Sloan* v *McGaffin* (1895) 29 ILTR 118.

53 *The Forest Lake* [1968] P 270.

54 Practice Direction 1997 No 4 (Ch D) [1997] 5 BNIL.

14.24 In all proceedings before a judge, a list of cases, texts and statutes to be relied on in argument should be handed to the judge's tipstaff 30 minutes before the start.[55] The official Law Report citation (AC, QBD, Ch, Fam, P, NI, IR, etc.) should be given, though the All England Reports (All ER) and Weekly Law Reports (WLR) Vol. 1 are also acceptable. For cases quoted in other reports, it is advisable to check whether the Court Library has the reports and if not to provide photocopies. The judge may notify the parties that he requires a skeleton argument. A copy of the list should be given to opposing counsel the previous day. In the Chancery Division counsel must furnish three copies of the list to the tipstaff (or the Chancery Office if for proceedings before the master) and to opposing counsel no later than 4.00pm on the previous day; the passages relied on in the case are to be specified; any supplemental list is to be furnished as soon as possible and at least 45 minutes before the hearing.[56]

14.24a In the Chancery Division, the Court may give directions relating to discovery, the time allowed for submissions and for questioning witnesses, the issues to be argued and the reading aloud of documents.[57] At least two clear days before the date of trial, the plaintiff must lodge in the Chancery Office two bundles: ring-bound, paginated and indexed-

Bundle A, the pleadings and orders to date, a summary of the issues, and summary of legal submissions and authorities, a chronology of events, and any proposed amendments to pleadings;

Bundle B, a list of documents relied on by the plaintiff and a list of documents which the other parties should have furnished to the plaintiff to be relied on; any documents not agreed must be in a separate file; any photographs must be put in an album or envelope.[58]

Order of speeches and evidence

14.25 Ord.35 r.4 directs the order of speeches and evidence. The usual order is-

(*P=plaintiff; D=defendant*)

(1) P opening speech
(2) P's evidence
(3) application for direction, if any
(4) D opening speech
(5) D's evidence
(6) P's evidence in rebuttal, if any
(7) D closing speech
(8) P closing speech
(9) verdict and judgment.

or, if the defendant adduces no evidence

---

55 Practice Direction [1981] 3 BNIL 79.
56 Practice Direction 1997 No 6 (Ch D) [1997] 5 BNIL.
57 Practice Direction 1997 No 4 (Ch D) [1997] 5 BNIL.
58 Practice Direction 1997 No 4 (Ch D) [1997] 5 BNIL.

(1) - (3) as above
(4) P closing speech
(5) D closing speech
(6) verdict and judgment.

A defendant adduces evidence if he calls any witness, or if he puts in a document in cross-examination or otherwise (Ord.35/4(8)).

If three defendants X, Y and Z (named in that order on the writ) are separately represented, and X and Z adduce evidence and Y does not, the order is-

(1) P opening speech
(2)P's evidence
(3) applications for direction, if any
(4) X opening speech
(5) Z opening speech
(6) X's evidence
(7) Z's evidence
(8) P's evidence in rebuttal, if any
(9) X closing speech
(10) Z closing speech
(11) P closing speech
(12) Y closing speech
(13) verdict and judgment.

If the burden of proof on all issues lies on the defendant (or on one separately represented defendant) the roles as between the plaintiff and that defendant are reversed. If a party making the closing speech raises a new point of law or cites a new authority, the opposing party may speak in reply to it. The judge may gives directions varying the order (Ord.35 r.4(1)).[59]

14.26 When the case is called for trial, counsel for each party announces his appearance ("I appear for the plaintiff with Mr X"). The name of instructing solicitor should not be mentioned as he is on the court record. The judge at this stage has before him the book of pleadings lodged on setting down. If senior counsel is present throughout he will speak and question the witnesses; junior should take a note of the evidence and make a list of the exhibits. Instructing solicitor, who must attend counsel, should also take notes. The taking of evidence is recorded on audio tape, so that a record can be transcribed in the event of an appeal.

Plaintiff's case

14.27 Except where on the issues pleaded the burden of proof lies on the defendant, the plaintiff's counsel opens his case first. He begins with a brief opening speech, stating briefly the alleged facts in a logical order, usually chronological, the main issues in dispute by reference to the pleadings, an outline of the damages claimed, any facts and documents which have been agreed, and an agreed bundle of correspondence. In jury cases, he will explain the fundamental legal points, the meaning of defamation, the burden of proof etc., and give the facts alleged in more detail. He should only open facts that can be proved and have been pleaded. If necessary he asks for an amendment of the pleadings. He cannot call evidence to prove a case inconsistent with the case made on opening.[60]

---

59 For directions for trial in a libel case where justification is pleaded, see *Eastwood* v *Channel 5* [1992] 2 NIJB 53.

60 *Grace* v *Finnucane* (1842) Arm Mac & Og 365.

14.28 Plaintiff's counsel then calls all his witnesses in an order which appears to make the case as clear as possible, usually the plaintiff first, then witnesses of fact, then expert witnesses. A medical witness may be called first to suit his convenience. As to examination and cross-examination of witnesses, see para. 13.54. After double-checking that no evidence has been overlooked, he announces that the plaintiff's case is closed and sits down.

Submission of no case to answer

14.29 Defence counsel may (in the absence of the jury) apply for a 'direction' that there is no case to answer. A ruling in favour of the defence at this stage will constitute a final dismissal (subject to appeal) of the claim. A defendant can seek a direction even though his cross-examination indicated that defence evidence would be called.[61] In a non-jury trial the judge may put the defendant upon his election, that is, he may refuse to make a ruling unless the defendant elects to call no evidence.[62] The reasons for this practice are that: (a) in the event of an appeal by the plaintiff it is desirable that the Court of Appeal can decide on the basis that all the evidence has been given; and (b) it would seem anomalous that a judge might rule for the plaintiff on the application and then at once, if no defence evidence is called, decide again as a jury.[63] When the right to jury trial was removed for personal injury and death cases in 1987, the Queen's Bench Judges indicated that they would continue to hear applications in such cases without putting the defendant upon election, but it was not given the status of a Practice Direction.

14.30 In *jury trials* the judge may grant a direction if there is no prima facie case or a vital proof has not been given, or no case in law is disclosed, or the evidence is so unsatisfactory or unreliable that it is not capable of discharging the burden of proof.[64] He should assume in favour of the plaintiff all primary facts of which there is some evidence capable of belief, and draw all inferences which tend to support the case.[65] In negligence cases the judge should not refuse a direction by picking out an isolated scrap of evidence which stands against all the other evidence.[66] On the other hand a direction should not be given merely because a plaintiff's witness states his belief of a fact which would defeat the claim.[67] In *O'Neill* v *DHSS (No 2)*[68] a *judge-only trial* (on appeal from county court), after refusing to put the defendant on his election, Carswell J applied the test whether a reasonable jury of people of ordinary reason and firmness properly directed could find for the plaintiff. Where a direction is sought on ground of neglect to adduce a material element of proof, the judge may recall the witness.[69]

---

61 *McIlveen* v *Charlesworth* [1973] NI 216, at 219.
62 See *Lowry* v *Buchanan* [1982] NI 243, at 244H.
63 *McCann* v *Kane* [1971] June NIJB at 2-3.
64 *Lowry* v *Buchanan,* at 244F; *Storey* v *Storey* [1961] P 63.
65 *McIlveen* v *Charlesworth* [1973] NI at 219; *Alexander* v *Anderson* [1933] NI 158, at 170-1.
66 *Graham* v *Hugh Burns* [1978] 3 NIJB at 8.
67 *Grierdon* v *Brereton* (1794) Ir Term R 281.
68 [1986] NI 290, at 292A.
69 *Mossman* v *Motherwell* (1842) Ir Cir R 668.

14.31 If there is no evidence on the plaintiff's case against one of several defendants sued *in the alternative*, a direction should not be given because the other defendant's evidence may disclose his liability.[70] In *O'Toole* v *Heavey*[71] it was said that the judge should not give a direction if there is any possibility that the remaining defendant could escape liability by placing blame on the dismissed defendant.

14.32 Failure to apply for a direction does not automatically bar the defence from arguing on appeal that there is no case to answer.[72]

Defence case

14.33 If no direction has been given and the defendant has preserved his right to call evidence, the next stage rests on the choice of the defendant. He may call no evidence and rely on the parts of the evidence for the plaintiff that support his case. Since the plaintiff's evidence is evidence for all purposes, the defendant can rely on it even to prove a positive defence or a counterclaim. By electing to call no evidence, the defendant takes two risks: (a) he puts nothing to weigh in the scales against the plaintiff's case; and (b) the failure of the defendant or a witness whom he could call to deny on oath the allegations made against him may lead the Court to draw an inference that strengthens the credibility of the allegation;[73] but the plaintiff cannot prove that the defendant knew of a defect merely from his refusal to testify.[74]

14.34 In most cases the defendant does call evidence, to discharge the evidential burden put on him by the plaintiff's evidence, and to prove any defence, set-off or counterclaim on which he bears the legal burden of proof. Defence counsel may open his case if he is calling evidence (Ord.35 r.4(4)). Defence counsel must be flexible: the choice of evidence and witnesses to be called is affected by the way the case has run so far.[75]

Evidence in rebuttal

14.35 The judge has a discretion to allow the plaintiff to call evidence in rebuttal at the end of the defence case, in the following circumstances -

(1) He may be allowed to rebut evidence given by the defendant on a matter on which the latter bears the burden of proof, even if the plaintiff became aware of the defence before his own case closed.

(2) If the defence evidence is contradictory or takes the plaintiff by surprise, as where a defence witness has said things which were not put to the plaintiff's witnesses.

---

[70] *Hummerstone* v *Leary* [1921] 2 KB 664. This does not apply if the plaintiff's evidence shows that one defendant cannot be blamed: *Higgins* v *Patterson* [1971] IR 111, which criticises the statement of this principle in the White Book (1997) 15/4/8.

[71] [1993] 2 IR 544.

[72] *Connolly* v *Morrow* [1979] 6 NIJB, at 3 ("technically"); *McKee* v *Alexander Greer* [1974] NI 60, at 65.

[73] *Funston* v *Funston*, QB, Mat, NI, 18 June 1965, noted 16 NILQ 418.

[74] *Hughes* v *Liverpool CC*, 'The Times', 30 March 1988.

[75] Lowry, para.18.

(3) If the defendant is called upon during the trial to produce an original document and does not do so, the plaintiff may call secondary evidence of it.[76]

(4) If there is a counterclaim or set-off, the plaintiff may rebut it, though not as of right if the counterclaim is on the same issues as the claim.

(5) If the defence witness has denied matters relevant only to his credit in cross-examination, then in so far as the denial is not final, the plaintiff may rebut it (see para. 13.71).

(6) The matters raised in the defence case may render relevant or admissible evidence which was irrelevant or inadmissible when the trial started. For example, the defence by calling a certain witness may render admissible a conversation at which that witness but not the defendant was present.

Further evidence by defendant

14.36 In the peculiar circumstances of *Wilson* v *Imrie Engineering*[77] Temporary Judge Coutts QC in the Court of Session allowed defender X to call further evidence after closing his case. After X had closed his case, the pursuer abandoned his claim against defender Y. X wanted to call an expert witness that Y would have called.

Closing submissions

14.37 At the end of the evidence each counsel may make closing submissions: defendant's first, then plaintiff's; but if the defence has called no evidence, plaintiff's first, then defendant's (Ord.35 r.4(3)(4)).

14.38 Though refused a direction *defence counsel* should renew his submission that there is no case to go to the jury.[78] Defence counsel can put forward inconsistent defences;[79] but not mutually exclusive or contradictory defences.[80] In *Crampsie* v *Unit Construction*[81] defence counsel was held to be entitled to suggest to the Court that the plaintiff's slipped disc might have a cause other than his accident, such suggestion having been put to the plaintiff's medical expert (who for convenience gave evidence first) though not to the plaintiff.

14.39 *Plaintiff's counsel* must base his submissions on an overall version of the facts which is not self-contradictory, though it may pose alternative propositions, and based on the evidence, or at least not inconsistent with it. The plaintiff must seek and recover judgment *secundum allegata et probata*, that is 'as alleged and proved' by the plaintiff. The judge should not base a finding of

---

[76] *Casson* v *O'Brien* (1842) Arm Mac & Og 263.

[77] 1993 SLT 235.

[78] *Christie* v *Odeon Ltd* (1957) 91 ILTR 25, at 28-9.

[79] *Kirkwood Hacket* v *Tierney* [1952] IR 185 (denial of slander and defence of privileged occasion).

[80] *O'Hanlon* v *ESB* [1969] IR 75, where in a factory accident claim, the employer sought to raise the defence that safety equipment was supplied, and a defence that the plaintiff took the risk upon himself by working when the equipment was not supplied.

[81] CA, NI, 29 June 1966.

negligence on a version suggested by defence counsel which the plaintiff rejected in cross-examination and of which no witness of either side has given any evidence.[82] However, there are four exceptions to that principle-

(1) Where the plaintiff has amnesia and cannot remember the accident, he does not have to produce a definite version of events;[82] so also, *semble*, in a fatal accident claim.

(2) The plaintiff can rely on facts stated by any witness which are merely a modification, variation or development of what he has pleaded.[82]

(3) If the defence has adduced positive evidence in chief of an alternative version, plaintiff's counsel might be allowed to argue negligence from that, subject to pleading points.[83]

(4) The Court is entitled to act on its own theory of the accident, provided it is derived from actual evidence of any witness or part of one witness and part of another, with any reasonable inferences.[84]

However, the plaintiff cannot recover judgment on the basis of a form of negligent conduct which has not been pleaded by him, unless the trial judge properly allows his Statement of Claim to be amended.[85]

14.40 In *Crampsie* v *Unit Construction*[81] Lord MacDermott LCJ thought that he might ask the jury to find alternatively that a lesser injury to the same part of the body was caused by the accident. By way of example, he suggested, a plaintiff who pleaded that he slipped and broke his wrist cannot ask the jury to find that he was injured otherwise than by slipping, but could ask them to find that he suffered only a sprained wrist as a result of the slipping. Curran and McVeigh LJJ seem to have preferred the view that the plaintiff must prove that the injury which he has pleaded was caused by the accident on which he sues.

14.41 Senior counsel decides who should make the closing speech, but whoever does so should have been present for a substantial part of the case.[86] In non-jury trials speeches should be succinct and functional rather than rhetorical. The following are rules for counsel to remember both in making submissions and generally in the conduct of a trial-

(1) Do not simply repeat the evidence: highlight the crucial evidence in your favour, urge the inference which you want the judge to draw, and refer to the relevant case or statute law. The judge is not so stupid that he needs to hear a good point repeated over and over. The importance of a point argued does not have to be marked by the length of time taken to say it.

(2) Do not say "I believe", " I think", "in my opinion". You are an advocate paid to urge views which favour your client; you are not a witness and not

---

82 *Graham* v *E & A Dunlop* [1977] 1 NIJB; *Gibson* v *British Rail* 1995 SLT 953.
83 *Graham* v *E & A Dunlop per* McGonigal LJ, said *arguendo*.
84 *Irvine* v *O'Hare* [1987] 2 NIJB 79, at 82; *Grimley* v *Henry* [1981] 1 NIJB at 6; *Thompson* v *Reynolds* [1926] NI 131, at 141.
85 *Potter* v *Carlisle* [1939] NI 114; *Walsh* v *Curry* [1955] NI 112. And see para. 9.00.
86 Bar Handbook 8-22.

the judge. Rather say "I submit", "I suggest" or "I urge your lordship to take the view that". Try however to *sound* as if you believe what you are saying. You can state your beliefs on matters of personal knowledge, (e.g. what has been said in court, and on matters of general knowledge).

(3) Do not suggest a figure for general damages unless the judge asks for it.

(4) Do not refer to evidence which has not been called.

(5) Do not impugn a witness by an allegation not put to the witness in cross-examination.

(6) You must not present and rely on evidence which you know to be perjured, or a case which you know to be fraudulent. If so the client must allow you to reveal it to the Court and if not you should withdraw from the case.[87] You and your client have a duty, not only to avoid mistating facts, but also to reveal a change of the state of affairs which was previously put forward *bona fide* (see para. 3.02).

(7) Do not misstate the facts or the law. You have a duty in civil proceedings to assist the judge with any relevant statute or case law authority of which you are aware.

(8) Do not make any reference whatsoever to negotiations which have taken place with a view to settlement. Do not mention a lodgment.

(9) Do not seek to obtain any document from the opponent by improper means, nor to use a document so obtained.[88]

(10) Be prepared for dialogue with and interruption from the judge in a non-jury case.

(11) Stand up when addressing the judge, jury or a witness and when being addressed by the judge.

(12) Speak loudly, clearly and convincingly, and, when examining your witness, slowly enough for the judge to take notes.

Verdict and judgment

14.42 After the submissions, the judge may sum up on the disputed issues of fact and/or law, and in a jury case he will address the jury in the same way as in a criminal trial. Counsel should take an accurate note of what he says. A judge should show the basis on which he decides, at least in decisions in the exercise of discretion, for the benefit of the parties and the Court of Appeal.[89] If in charging the jury (and, *semble*, in summing up to himself) the judge raises against a party an issue not mentioned during the trial, he should give that party an opportunity to call evidence on it.[90] Counsel may make objection or requisition to the judge on his charge to the jury or on the questions left to the

---

[87] Bar Handbook 8-12.
[88] Bar Handbook 8-15.
[89] *Eagil Trust* v *Pigott-Brown* [1985] 3 All ER 119, at 122.
[90] *Kennedy* v *Smith*, CA, NI, 9 February1968.

jury,[91] and should do so if he intends to rely on it on appeal, especially if the judge's error can be rectified at the time[92] The trial judge in summing up to himself does not have to mention every point that he would in charging a jury, and his omission of a relevant point of fact or law does not lead to the assumption that he has overlooked it.[93] The judge is not *functus officio* when he starts to deliver his judgment: he should allow any crucial new evidence which becomes available whilst he is delivering judgment.[94] In a non-jury case, the judge may reserve his decision and pronounce a written judgment on a date to be notified, especially where points of law are involved. In the Chancery Division the judge seeks to deliver a reserved judgment within four weeks or other specified period and if he cannot do so will re-list the case to tell the parties of a proposed date for judgment; on the day of judgment copies are available for collection at 9.30am and the judgment read out in synopsis at 10.00am, then counsel may be heard on consequential matters such as costs and as to the drafting of the order of the Court.[95]

14.43 Then the judge (in his capacity as a jury) gives a verdict, pronouncing on liability, and quantum of damages and other remedy. He may give a verdict that the defendant was negligent without specifying how.[96] In dismissing the claim he may, by consent of the parties, assess a figure for damages in the event of an appeal.[97]

14.44 In a jury trial, the foreman pronounces the verdict in the presence of all jurors, and if none dissent this must be accepted as the unanimous verdict.[98] It is highly desirable that the judge be present in court when the verdict is taken, but the verdict is not void if it is taken by the court official.[99] If the judge has left an issue to the jury he must accept their finding on it.[100] He can question them to clear up any ambiguity or doubt about the verdict.[101] The judge can draw inferences from the facts found by the jury.[102] There is no power to accept a majority verdict.[103] A verdict cannot be disturbed on evidence as to what happened during the jury's deliberations, but evidence is admissible from a juror that their intended verdict was not truly recorded by the Court.[104] A verdict or finding cannot be impeached on the sole ground that a non-qualified,

---

91 *Brennan* v *Minister of Finance* (1962) 96 ILTR 54.
92 *McKee* v *Alexander Greer* [1974] NI 60, at 65.
93 *Doherty* v *MOD* [1979] 6 NIJB at 9.
94 *Cheeseman* v *Bowaters Ltd* [1971] 1 WLR 1774.
95 Practice Direction 1997 No 5 (Ch D) [1997] 5 BNIL.
96 *Logan* v *O'Donnell* [1925] 2 IR 211 (jury verdict).
97 As in *Anderson* v *Belfast Corp* [1943] NI 34.
98 *Diven* v *Belfast Corp* [1969] NI 34.
99 *Hawkesley* v *Fewtrell* [1954] 1 QB 228.
100 *Power* v *Dublin United Tramway* [1926] IR 302, at 323; *Grimley* v *Henry* [1981] 1 NIJB at 6.
101 *Greene* v *Boyle* [1937] Ir Jur Rep 3 (NI).
102 *Schawel* v *Reade* [1913] 2 IR 64 (HL).
103 *McIntyre* v *Lewis* [1991] 1 IR 121, at 133.
104 *Ralston Purina* v *Thompson View Fur Farms* (1985) 12 DLR 4th 228 (Pr Edw Id, SC)

ineligible or misnamed person served on the jury, nor that a juror was not on the panel.[105]

14.45 Then winning counsel asks for judgment in accordance with the verdict. If the plaintiff wins on one cause of action and loses on another distinct claim, the defendant is entitled to judgment on the latter.[106] Judgment may be given notwithstanding the death of a party since the verdict or finding of fact, though the judge may elect to substitute his personal representative under Order 15 rule 7 (Ord.35 r.6). Judgment may be given against a trustee defendant as such in his absence if diligent search has been made and he cannot be found.[107] Where on one cause of action the plaintiff has claimed two alternative and mutually exclusive remedies, he is obliged to elect between them at the time when judgment is being given in his favour, and need not elect before that.[108] The judge then deals with other matters which may now arise: interest; costs,[109] including reserved costs of interlocutory proceedings, and whether any party is legally aided; payment out of money in court; investment of the award if the plaintiff is a minor, stay of enforcement (usually three weeks); and, especially in Chancery actions, directions as to proceedings under the judgment. The judge may direct that a matter be disposed of in chambers (Ord.32 r.17).

14.46 Since 1877 in any action in the High Court[110] the Court cannot 'non-suit' the plaintiff or 'dismiss without prejudice' his claim, and the plaintiff cannot elect to be non-suited without calling evidence. Every dismissal of a claim at the trial is a *res judicata* and he cannot sue again on the same cause.[111] The same is true of a claim made by way of counterclaim, so that where the Court dismisses a counterclaim "the same not having been proceeded with", it is *res judicata*.[112]

14.47 A losing party is under no obligation to tell the judge that he intends to appeal, but if he wishes to have a stay of execution pending appeal he should apply for that to the trial judge.

Claim and counterclaim

14.48 In the case of a true set-off the Court usually gives judgment for the balance. In the case of any counterclaim, it may give separate judgments on claim and counterclaim or may, under Order 15 rule 2(4), give one judgment for the balance, without prejudice to the discretion over costs. This is usually decided in the context of costs, and is fully discussed at paras. 17.41-17.45.

---

105 Juries (NI) Order 1996, Arts.29, 16(4).

106 *O'Kane* v *Higgins* (1901) 1 NIJR 276 (a case of alternative claims).

107 Trustee Act (NI) 1958, s.59. [107] *O'Kane* v *Higgins* (1901) 1 NIJR 276 (a case of alternative claims).

108 *Tang Man Sit* v *Capacious Investments* [1996] 1 All ER 593 (PC).

109 See further paras. 17.02, 17.15, 17.83.

110 Other than an appeal from a county court decree.

111 *Fox* v *Star Newspaper* [1900] AC 19.

112 *White* v *Spendlove* [1942] IR 224.

REMEDIES: DAMAGES

14.49 If a common law right or liability is established, the claimant has a right to the common law remedy, usually damages, which cannot be refused or withheld on discretionary equitable grounds. In a jury trial, unless damages are tried as a separate issue, they must be assessed by the jury. When a judge without a jury tries an action he usually assesses damages himself before entering judgment, but he can give judgment for damages to be assessed by a master (Ord.37 r.4(1)(a)). Where interlocutory judgment is entered for damages (e.g. in default of appearance or of defence, or under Order 14 summary judgment), the Court may direct that damages be assessed by trial before a judge with any appropriate directions (Ord.37 r.4(1)(b)(2)). If judgment in default of appearance or defence is given against one defendant, damages are to be assessed at the trial of the action against the other defendant (Ord.37 r.3).

14.50 Apart from that, and save as otherwise provided by the judgment, damages are assessed by a master (Ord.37 r.1). The claimant obtains an appointment and serves seven days' notice of it on the party liable under Order 65 rule 5 even if he is in default of appearance. The master tries the issue in accordance with Order 35 and witnesses can be compelled by *subpoena*. The provisions as to evidence in Order 38 rules 1-5,18-29 apply (Ord.38 rr.6,18(3)). Order 37 is subject to section 62 of the Judicature Act, so that where it so dictates, the assessment of damages must be by judge and jury.[113] Where damages are assessed by a master in the Queen's Bench Division he enters final judgment for the amount; in the Chancery Division he makes an order for payment (Ord.37 r.2). Order 37 rules 1-4 apply also to judgments for the value of goods to be assessed (Ord.37 r.5). An assessment of damages by the Queen's Bench master, under Order 37 or otherwise, is appealable to the Court of Appeal (Ord.58 r.2(b)).

How damages are assessed

14.51 Damages are assessed on the evidence presented, including events happening since the commencement of the action. However, a plaintiff cannot recover damages or any relief in respect of a cause of action arising since the issue of the writ. For example, if he has continued to be exposed to a danger at work after commencing his action, that is what may be called a recurring cause of action, and his damages in the present action are confined to that degree of injury which is attributable to the danger up to the issue of the writ.[114] Where the cause of action is complete before the issue of the writ with damage continuing, damages are assessed up to the date of the trial (see para. 3.29, para. 4.00). Where he sues on a continuing cause of action, damages are assessed up to the date of assessment (Ord.37 r.6). Apart from specific statutory powers, the Court has jurisdiction only to award a lump sum for damages; there is no power to order damages by periodic payments.[115] Such arrangements can be made by consent, as 'structured settlements' (para. 12.21)

---

113 *McParland* v *John Tinnelly* [1982] NI 110.

114 *Birch* v *Harland & Wolff* [1991] NI 90, at 100.

115 *Watkins* v *Olafson* (1989) 61 DLR 4th 577.

and in personal injury/death cases, the Court can order periodical payments (para. 14-73a) and can order provisional damages (para. 14.75).

14.52 *Damage to property.* If the plaintiff's car was a 'write-off', i.e. costs of repair exceeding its market value, he should be compensated on the basis that he should sell it for salvage and buy a comparable vehicle promptly, with interest on the cost from that date (*Murray* v *Doherty* [1986] NI 136). As to damages where the plaintiff repairs the vehicle himself: see *Ulsterbus* v *Donnelly* [1982] 13 NIJB.

Damages in false imprisonment cases. See *Harper* v *Associated British Foods* [1991] NI 244; *Thompson* v *Commr of Police* [1997] 2 All ER 762 (CA).

Exemplary and aggravated damages. Aggravated damages are compensatory, an element of general damages for injury to feelings and humiliation, distress, indignity, in so far as they aggravate the tortious injury or damage. Exemplary damages are a bonus to the plaintiff to punish and deter the defendant for his oppressive conduct in a public capacity or for the calculated profit derived from the tortious act. See *Scullion* v *Chief Constable* [1989] 6 NIJB 1; *Davey* v *Chief Constable* [1988] NI 139; *Walsh* v *MOD* [1985] NI 62; *Lavery* v *MOD* [1984] NI 99.

DAMAGES IN PERSONAL INJURY CASES

14.53 In a negligence case the test for damages is reasonable foreseeability. Damages are computed under the various common heads set out below; but having added up the figures assessed for each head, the judge should check again for overlaps and gaps and ensure that the total figure is fair and reasonable.[116] What follows in this section states the strictly correct practice as to assessment of damages. However the tendency of judges in Northern Ireland is to avoid excessive technicality in ordinary cases and to award damages as follows-

(1) 'general damages' for pain and suffering, loss of amenity and loss of future earnings, with interest at two per cent per annum from date of service of the writ

(2) 'special damages' for cost of property damaged or destroyed, expenses incurred to date, and loss of earnings to date, with interest at six per cent per annum from date of the accident.

The 'Ogden tables' (actuarial tables for peronal injury and fatal accident cases for assessing future pecuniary loss) are admissible in evidence.[117] Under the Damages Act 1996 the Court may by consent of the parties award all or part of the damages by way of periodical payments. This is dealt with at para. 14.73a.

Special damages

14.54 Each item and its amount must be pleaded and proved, though the parties should try to agree the special damages. Such items may include

---

116 *Clarke* v *Chief Constable* [1978] 3 NIJB at 13-14.

117 Civil Evidence Act 1995, s.10 (*not yet in force*).

expenses arising from treatment, the cost of repair of property damaged, the value of property destroyed or written off, the cost of hiring whilst property is repaired or replaced. If the plaintiff has been treated by the National Health Service, his free maintenance in hospital must be credited against his claim for loss of income.[118] If the plaintiff has been treated privately without recourse to the National Health Service, he can claim the cost;[119] and *semble,* the plaintiff's ordinary living expenses, if included in the private treatment, should be deducted. Article 18 of the Social Security (Recovery of Benefits) (NI) Order 1997 [*not yet in force*] requires the Court when assessing damages to state the amount that is awarded under the head of cost of care up to the date of payment of final compensation or five years after the accident, whichever is the earlier.

14.55 Any expenses paid by or the value of services given gratuitously by a friend or relative are recoverable, by assessing a reasonable compensation therefor. This includes the expenses of such persons in visiting the plaintiff in hospital, which may help his recovery. In the case of services the compensation should be assessed as the market value of the service.[120] This head of special damage must be regarded not as recovery by the plaintiff of loss occasioned to him but rather as money recovered by him on trust for the caring friend or relative. Therefore the identity of the carer may be relevant. The head of damage cannot be awarded where the carer is the defendant tortfeasor, such as the spouse or parent of the plaintiff who was the negligent driver.[121] This is so even though the damages ostensibly payable by the defendant are in fact paid by his insurer with no financial detriment to the defendant. Obviously, the plaintiff does not recover for the services given free by a state institution such as the Health Service.[122] No damages in tort are awarded to a plaintiff for the loss of the services of his/her spouse, child or servant.[123]

14.56 Damages for expenses and losses already incurred (or which should have been incurred under the duty to mitigate loss) will carry interest at the

---

118 Administration of Justice Act 1982, s.5. The defendant's insurer who knows that the plaintiff has been so treated is liable to pay up to £2,949 (current figure from 11 May 1995: SR (NI) 1995/139) to the Health and Social Services Board: Road Traffic (NI) Order 1981, Art.99.

119 Law Reform (Miscellaneous Provisions) Act (NI) 1948, s.3(4).

120 *Van Gervan* v *Fenton* (1992) 175 CLR 327 (HC of Aus). The value of such service may be greater if provided by a loving friend or relative, rather than a paid housekeeper, nurse or 'nanny': see *Official Solicitor and Briggs* v *Brett,* para. 14.71.

121 *Hunt* v *Severs* [1994] 2 AC 350. Legislative intervention would seem to be desirable in this area.

122 When the plaintiff receives free treatment under a private health insurance policy for which he has paid the premiums, can he recover the expense and value of the service and is it on trust for the 'carer'? There seems to be no authority on this point. Insurers such as "BUPA" have a clause in the policy that their expenses must be claimed against the tortfeasor and repaid to BUPA if recovered.

123 Administration of Justice Act 1982, s.2.

judgment rate (currently 8 per cent per annum) from the date of incurring till judgment.[124]

Financial cost of care etc.

14.57 The future cost of care and treatment due to the injuries can be claimed as general damages, based on an annual multiplicand and a multiplier. The value of future services to be provided by a friend or relative are recoverable on the principle stated above (para. 14.55). The multiplier must be a different number of years than that for loss of earnings, because it covers the rest of the plaintiff's natural life as expected with the injuries; the multiplier for loss of earnings is for the rest of his working life as it would have been but for the injuries taking into account contingencies such as redundancy etc., and taking into account a conventional figure of 4½ per cent as the likely investment return on the damages.[125]

Loss of earnings

14.58 In assessing the loss of earnings, past and future, the Court must deduct all tax, national insurance contributions etc. which are payable even if the plaintiff was illegally evading them.[126] Damages will be awarded for loss of earnings which were not declared for tax purposes, provided that the non-disclosure was innocent,[127] but earnings not disclosed when claiming social security benefits are irrecoverable.[128] Net earnings are after deduction for contributions to a pension scheme and for any expenses incurred in travelling to or executing the work,[129] but not expenses incurred by the plaintiff to make herself available for work.[130] Lawful earnings lost to the date of trial due to the accident are recoverable as special damages, usually with interest at half the judgment rate (i.e. 4 per cent) from the accident to date.[131] An army chaplain who under his vows paid all his earnings over to the Jesuits is still entitled to claim for the lost earnings.[132] Article 18 of the Social Security (Recovery of Benefits) (NI) Order 1997 [*not yet in force*] requires the Court when assessing damages to state the amount that is awarded under the head of loss of earnings up to the date payment of final compensation or five years after the accident, whichever is the earlier.

---

124 *Murray* v *Doherty* [1986] NI 136, at 144F. In practice this head is often lumped together with loss of earnings to date, and interest awarded at 6% from date of accident.

125 See *Stevenson* v *Sweeney* 1995 SLT 29 (Outer House); *Wells* v *Wells* [1997] 1 All ER 673 (CA).

126 *Donnelly* v *Hackett* [1988] 6 NIJB 6, at 8 (fatal accident action).

127 *Bush* v *Air Canada* (1992) 87 DLR 4th 248, at 254-7 (CA, NS).

128 *Hunter* v *Butler*, 'The Times', 28 December 1995 (CA).

129 *Dews* v *NCB* [1988] AC 1.

130 E.g. payments to a home help or child minder: *Wynn* v *NSW Insurance Corp* (1996) 70 ALJR 147, at 151-2 (HC of Aus).

131 In practice this head is often lumped together with expenses and losses incurred to date, and interest awarded at 6% from date of accident.

132 *Dowling* v *Great Southern Rly* [1943] Ir Jur R 7.

14.59 Earnings[133] which the plaintiff will lose in future due to the accident are recoverable as general damages. This is usually calculated by taking a multiplicand (net annual earnings which he would now be earning) and a multiplier. The multiplier is the estimation of the number of years that the plaintiff would live and work but for the accident from the date of trial, allowing for normal contingencies;[125] the normal maximum is 16. But if the accident is likely to cause early death, then in respect of the 'lost years' there will be deducted a sum for living expenses. The Court takes into account overtime, promotion, wage increases and pension rights;[134] which the plaintiff might have enjoyed. A deduction may be made for the possibility that he might have been made redundant.[135] No interest is awarded on loss of future earnings. Only in exceptional circumstances can the court take into account the effects of future taxation and inflation on a large lump sum award, and by the same token it should disregard the actual investment potential of the money awarded, but a reduction in the multiplier is made to take into account the fact that the money received now for a future loss can produce an investment rate of 4 or 5 per cent.[136] The Damages Act 1996 (s.1) now provides: "In determining the return to be expected from the investment of a sum awarded as damages for future pecuniary loss in an action for personal injury [or death] the court shall [subject to rules of court] take into account such rate of return (if any) as may be prescribed [by order of the Lord Chancellor]," though the court may take a different rate if a party shows that it is more appropriate in the case. The Lord Chancellor said when moving the legislation through Parliament[137] that 4 or 5 per cent is too high and thus makes too great a discount; he was consulting appropriate bodies and awaiting the decision of the English Court of Appeal in a pending case before prescribing the rate under the above provision. Since then the Court of Appeal has re-affirmed that 4½ per cent is the proper conventional figure until legislative intervention prescribes otherwise.[138] In Ontario, rules of court prescribe that the discount rate for future pecuniary damages to the extent that it reflects the difference between the estimated and price inflation rates is 2½ per cent and its Court of Appeal has upheld the decision of a judge, acting on expert evidence of the projected real value increase in average earnings, to reduce the discount to ½ per cent.[139]

---

133 And state benefits which would not have been deductible from his damages (para. 14.68).

134 *Clarke* v *Chief Constable* [1978] 3 NIJB at 10-11. On a head of damages for loss of occupational pension rights, there must be deducted any pension rights payable as a result of the accident: *West* v *Versil*, 'The Times' 31 August 1996 (CA).

135 *McGuigan* v *MOD* [1982] 19 NIJB at 19-20, bearing in mind the redundancy money which he would have received.

136 *Hodgson* v *Trapp* [1989] AC 807. In Malaysia it is the policy to use annuity tables based on a projected yield of 5%, to quantify future earning loss, so that the multiplier is reduced for contingencies but not subject to any further reduction for investment yield: *Tan Cheong Poh* v *Teo Ah Keow* [1995] 3 MLJ 89; (1995) 21 Comm LB 1131.

137 See *Hansard*, HL Vol.571 col.1412-3, Vol.572 col.1233.

138 *Wells* v *Wells* [1997] 1 All ER 673 (CA).

139 *Ligate* v *Abick* (1996) 134 DLR 4th 539.

Loss of earning capacity

14.60 Apart from provable future loss of earnings, the plaintiff can be awarded compensation for the effect of the accident (and of interruption of his career) on his prospects in the competitive labour market.[140] This is a present, not a future loss, and a head of general damages. It is particularly relevant where the plaintiff was a young child with no known career planned; or where the plaintiff has returned to the same or a similarly paid job. Interest is presumably not payable and the discount for investment return is made. Compensation can be awarded for the loss of congenial employment, that is inability to do work which the plaintiff enjoyed, but usually only as part of the general damages for loss of amenity.[141] In *Reekie* v *Messervey*[142] the Court allowed as a financial head of damages the loss of opportunity of a young unmarried woman to form a future dependency relationship by marriage or otherwise.

General damages

14.61 The Court assesses a sum for *pain and suffering* (including awareness of loss of expectation of life);[143] *loss of amenity* (i.e. loss of the enjoyments of living, social life and leisure, of bodily or mental functions, of particular hobbies);[144] *care and attention* (including a value for the voluntary assistance of relatives and friends).[145] "Pain and suffering" can be subdivided into pain and shock at the accident; medical treatment; recuperation; lasting symptoms;[146] and future prognosis. The judge usually awards a total sum for these heads, and awards interest at two per cent per annum from the date of service of the writ to judgment.[147] This sum is a wholly subjective figure based on the judge's experience of awards by himself and other judges, and pre-1987 juries. The English damages reports in *Kemp & Kemp* and *Current Law* can be consulted but are of limited value because Northern Ireland has its own range of damages.[148] The *Bulletin of Northern Ireland Law* enters all awards of damages made by a judge in the High Court.[149] In a case where personal injury

---

140 *Smith* v *Manchester Corporation* (1974) 17 KIR 1; a case where there was no forseeable loss of earnings as the plaintiff was able to continue in her existing job, but would be unfit for other types of job.

141 *Lenaghan* v *Ayrshire & Arran Health Board*, 1994 SC 365.

142 (1989) 59 DLR 4th 481, at 494-9 (CA, BC) *affd.* 66 DLR 4th 765 (SCC).

143 Damages are no longer awarded for loss of expectation of life *per se*: Administration of Justice Act 1982, s.1.

144 Article 18 of the Social Security (Recovery of Benefits) (NI) Order 1997 [*not yet in force*] requires the Court when assessing damages to state the amount that is awarded for loss of moblity up to the date payment of final compensation or five years after the accident, whichever is the earlier.

145 *Clarke* v *Chief Constable* [1978] 3 NIJB at 11-12. See above para.14.55.

146 See *Connolly* v *Morrow* [1979] 6 NIJB at 7-8

147 *Birch* v *Harland & Wolff* [1991] NI 90, at 101-2.

148 *Simpson* v *Harland & Wolff* [1988] NI 432.

149 The descriptions of the injuries and other losses are taken from the book of pleadings and then shown to at least one counsel in the case for checking; where possible the entry itemises the heads of damage; the figure stated is that given before interest is added.

damages are awarded by a jury (e.g. a claim for assault joined in an action for false imprisonment) the judge, after discussions with counsel, may give guidance, but not instruction, as to the normal range of awards for that type of injury.[150]

14.62 Damages for nervous shock are recoverable if they are the foreseeable result of the personal injury or if the proximate relationship of the plaintiff to the tort is such that there is a duty of care to prevent nervous shock.[151] Stress, distress and inconvenience are not heads of damage in general in tort and contract cases unless arising out of recoverable physical or nervous injury or disturbance.[152] Where damages for nervous shock are recoverable, they can take into account the increased stress and strain of conducting the litigation itself, in so far as it is prosecuted reasonably and with diligence.[153]

Deductions

14.63 Sick pay by the plaintiff's employer as of right is deductible from damages for loss of earnings unless the contract of employment makes it recoverable from damages paid by the tortfeasor.[154] Redundancy payments, unless related to inability to work,[155] charity payments,[156] occupational pensions and insurance money from a policy for which the plaintiff has paid premiums,[157] benefits paid under a collective agreement between the plaintiff's trade union and his employer,[158] are not deductible. Payments made as indemnity for loss of wages must be taken into account as they go to reduce the plaintiff's loss.[158] Gratuitous payments and the expenses and value of care are deductible if given by the tortfeasor.[159]

---

150 *Scotland* v *Commr of Metropolitan Police*, 'The Times', 30 January 1996 (CA).

151 See *Alcock* v *South Yorkshire Police* [1992] 1 AC 310; *Armstrong* v *Garrity* [1993] 10 NIJB 6; *Page* v *Smith* [1996] 1 AC 155; *Kelly* v *Hennessy* [1995] 3 IR 253 (SC).

152 See *Smith* v *Huey* [1993] 8 NIJB 49.

153 *McDonnell* v *Douglas*, QBD, NI (Girvan J) 30 January 1996

154 *Berriello* v *Felixstowe Dock & Rly* [1989] 1 WLR 695; *Logan* v *Cahoon*, QBD, NI, (Girvan J) 19 January 1996. And see *Ratych* v *Bloomer* (1990) 69 DLR 4th 25 (SC Canada).

155 *Colledge* v *Bass Mitchells* [1988] 1 All ER 536. If certified by the CRU to be related to the accident, the redundancy payments are not deductible in the award of the court but are recoupable under the CRU scheme (para. 14.66). Redundancy payments will not be recoupable under the new 1997 legislation (para. 14.68c)

156 *Redpath* v *Belfast and Co Down Rly* [1947] NI 167 (fund collected from public appeal).

157 *Parry* v *Cleaver* [1970] AC 1; *Smoker* v *London Fire Authority* [1991] 2 AC 502. *Quaere*, whether the plaintiff can claim the value of treatment and care provided free to him under a health insurance policy for which he has paid premiums.

158 *Cooper* v *Miller* (1994) 113 DLR 4th 1 (SC Canada).

159 *Hunt* v *Severs* [1994] 2 AC 350, at 358C. *Parry* v *Cleaver* and *Smoker* decided that ill-health pension or insurance payments are totally non-deductible even if the defendant tortfeasor was a contributor to the fund along with the plaintiff. They impliedly overruled *McCallum* v *G. Madill* [1965] NI 187 (CA) a case in which the defendant employer contributed two thirds of the contributions and the plaintiff one third, holding that two thirds of the money should be deducted from damages. However *McCallum* may be revived by *Hunt* v *Severs,* though the Lords there steered clear of the point.

14.64 *Criminal Court compensation.* Where a criminal or Armed Forces court has awarded compensation to the plaintiff for the personal injury, loss or damage on which he sues, damages are assessed without regard to it but the amount of the compensation actually paid is deducted from the award, and if compensation is unpaid, leave to enforce the judgment is required in respect of the amount equal to the unpaid compensation.[160]

14.65 *Northern Ireland Office compensation.* In awarding damages no deduction is made for any actual or prospective award of compensation by the Secretary of State under the Criminal Injuries (Compensation) (NI) Order 1988. In any civil action for damages against the offender, any compensation already paid by the Secretary of State must be re-imbursed to him out of the damages, and the court before which the award of damages is made or agreed may order the damages or part thereof to be paid into court and direct re-imbursement to the Secretary of State (Art.18). If damages have already been paid by or on behalf of the offender, they are deductible from the criminal injury award (Art.6(2)). The same principle applies in the case of compensation by the Secretary of State for damage to property under the Criminal Damage (Compensation) (NI) Order 1977 (see Arts.17 and 10(1)(c) respectively thereof).

State benefits

Paras.14.66-14.68 state the law as it now stands. This is followed by paras.14.68a-68g which state the law as it will be when the Social Security (Recovery of Benefits) (NI) Order 1997 comes into force, on a date yet to be appointed.

14.66 If the damages awarded (to one victim for one accident/disease) are not more than a prescribed sum [currently £2,500], one half of the value of relevant social security benefits[161] payable for five years are deductible from the damages as a whole.[162] The award of the Court is deemed to be the amount assessed after such deduction, for the purposes of the assessment of costs; and the net sum is that which the defendant must pay.

Otherwise the Social Security Administration (NI) Act 1992 (ss.77-99) apply, and its Regulations (SR 1990/85).[163] Before paying compensation

---

[160] Criminal Justice (NI) Order 1994, Art.17.

[161] As defined by the Regulations, SR 1990/85.

[162] Law Reform (Miscellaneous Provisions) Act (NI) 1948, s.3(1). The ceiling of £2,500 means the amount which the court would award before any deduction of relevant benefits but after any reduction for contributory negligence: s.3(1A)(3). If the accident happened or the disease was first claimed for before 1 January 1989, however large the damages, the old law applies and one half of the value of social security benefits specified payable for five years and the whole of other social security benefits (e.g. unemployment benefit, mobility allowance, income support) must be deducted, but only from the head of damages for loss of earnings and loss of earning capacity.

[163] For a treatise on this subject see Greer's pamphlet *Compensation Recovery: Substantive and Procedural Issues* (SLS 1996).

(whether by settlement or under a court judgment) the defendant[164] must send prescribed details of the claimant to the Department of Social Security and obtain the most up to date "CRU" certificate[165] from the DHSS stating the relevant benefits received by plaintiff to date as a result of the accident.[166] The relevant benefits are those listed in the 1990 Regulations (reg.2) which include nearly all the benefits, except child benefit, payable under the Social Security (Contributions and Benefits) (NI) Act 1992 which the plaintiff receives due to the injury or illness sued upon, including unemployment benefit, and income support. Statutory sick pay is no longer a relevant benefit since the Statutory Sick Pay (NI) Order 1994 now requires it to be paid by the employer with no contribution by the Department. The deductible benefits are those paid to the plaintiff up to the date of final compensation or up to five years after the accident, whichever is earlier.

14.67 The Court in its award makes no deduction for the relevant benefits (Social Security Administration Act, s.77(5)), but the defendant when paying the damages awarded must deduct and certify to the plaintiff the amount of the benefits and pay that amount within 14 days directly to the DHSS (ss.78-9). He does not have to make the deduction if he does not receive the certificate within four weeks of requesting it (ss.91-2). The deduction must be made from the damages as a whole, not merely from that part of the damages which is attributable to loss of earnings, but is not made from the plaintiff's legal costs (s.77(1)). If the sum left after deduction of benefits is not enough to satisfy the Legal Aid Fund's charge for unpaid costs on money recovered in the action, then the DHSS must make good the deficiency (s.86). In awarding interest on the damages, the Court must treat the award as reduced by the amount of the CRU benefits, first against special damages and then against general damages (s.98). For the purposes of the Court's discretion as to costs, where the damages are in excess of £2,500, the plaintiff is deemed to have been awarded the whole damages regardless of any deduction for relevant benefits.[167]

14.68 The CRU certificate is conclusive as to whether a benefit is due to the injury, subject to review by the DHSS (Social Security Administration Act, s.93), or a right of appeal by either party to a Commissioner within three months (s.94).[168] *Semble*, if at the time when the Court gives judgment there is a

---

[164] I.e. the compensator: the person making a compensation payment on behalf of the person liable. It also includes the Motor Insurers' Bureau. Fatal accident damages and criminal injury compensation are excluded. See s.77(1). 'Compensator' will include the Crown, by s.99, which however is not yet in force: see the Social Security (Consequential Provisions) (NI) Act 1992, Sch.4 para.11. The situation where there is more than one compensator contributing to the damages is dealt with in ss.82-3.

[165] CRU stands for "Compensation Recovery Unit", which is the section of the DHSS which administers the system.

[166] As to the recoupment provisions where the compensator or victim lives in Great Britain: see Social Security Administration Act 1992, s.101 (the GB Act).

[167] *McCaffery* v *Datta*, [1997] 2 All ER 586 (CA). As to the effect where the defendant lodges money in court under Ord.22, see paras. 11.152 and 11.164.

[168] See for instance *Commissioners Decision No 1/92(CRS)* [1993] 1 BNIL 95 (a claimant who got dermatitis when working with coolants and oils was sacked because he was unfit

pending review of the CRU certificate, the judge should order a stay of enforcement or direct that the damages be paid into court until the review is determined. If the plaintiff was working in stable employment at the date of the accident, he is awarded the loss of earnings to date and loss of future earnings as heads of damages, and the relevant benefits are deductible from the award and paid to the CRU. In *Hassall* v *Sec of State*[169] the victim was unemployed before his accident; after the accident he continued to receive roughly the same rate of state benefits. The Court upheld the Department's decision that the post accident benefits were attributable to the accident and must be recouped from his damages. The Court suggested *obiter* that the victim should avoid this injustice to him by claiming in his action against the tortfeasor a head of damages for loss of non-recoupable benefit.[169] This was applied in *Donnelly* v *McCoy*,[170] where Girvan J stressed that the *Hassall* head of damages is confined to the loss of benefits during the period when the plaintiff was objectively unable to work. In *Unsworth* v *Southern*,[171] the plaintiff would have retired in November 1994 but for the accident: the judge awarded damages for loss of earnings up to that date and for loss of non-recoupable benefits for the period thereafter. In *Morrison* v *Pankratz*[172] the plaintiff was in receipt of a means-tested income supplement benefit but by reason of the compensation paid to her she was now ineligible for it; she claimed the loss of entitlement for it as a head of damages; the Court refused on the ground that the loss was caused by the receipt of compensation not by the accident.

Paras.14.68a-14.68g state the law as it will be from a date to be appointed under the Social Security (Recovery of Benefits) (NI) Order 1997. The equivalent Act in Great Britain is planned to come into force in October 1997. [173] **It is described here as it applies in the context of a civil claim for damages.**

14.68a The Social Security (Recovery of Benefits (NI) Order 1997 applies to all compensation payments made on or after the appointed date, unless made in pursuance of a court order or an agreement made before then (Art.4 thereof). It applies regardless of when the accident happened.[174] The details are described below, but briefly the new system requires the defendant to pay the amount of all listed benefits received by the plaintiff over the relevant period to the "CRU"

for that work and no alternative work was available; after a period on sickness benefit he signed on as available for work and received income support: held, the income support was rightly on the CRU certificate being partly due to the dermatitis, as it was not shown that he would have lost his job in any event); and *No 2/92(CRS)* [1993] 4 BNIL 118 (income support has to be a deductible benefit if paid out on the claimant's claim to be unfit for work by reason of the injury on which he is suing).

169 [1995] 1 WLR 812 (CA).

170 [1995] 9 BNIL 20; not following the obiter view of Pringle J in *Mitchell* v *DOE* [1996] 3 BNIL 15. See further the comments of the sub-editor at [1995] 9 BNIL 20.

171 [1996] 2 CLM 222 (Cty Ct).

172 (1995) 122 DLR 4th 352 (CA, BC).

173 *Hansard*, HC Vol.292 col.751 (18 March 1997), Mr Evans, Under Secretary of State. The Act was passed before the General Election but it was broadly supported by the Labour Party.

174 *Hansard* HC Vol.291 col.291, Mr Evans.

(the Compensation Recovery Unit) of the DHSS; but the defendant must pay him the full damages agreed or awarded to the plaintiff, deducting from the payment the amount of the listed benefits only in so far as they can be deducted from the head of damages for a financial loss. For example, if the plaintiff has to date received £5,000 in incapacity benefit as stated in the CRU certificate, and the head of damages for loss of earnings to date is £4,000, the defendant must pay £5,000 to the CRU and can deduct from the damages only £4,000. Nothing can be deducted from the damages awarded under the head of pain and suffering, loss of amenity (except loss of mobility), loss of future earnings. loss of earning capacity, cost of future care, damages for damage to property (clothing etc.) and damages for any loss occurring more than five years after the accident.[175] If the damages are paid seven years after the accident the defendant must pay to the DHSS all the listed benefits during the seven years, and can deduct only the amount thereof paid for the first five years, and is out of pocket for the amount of benefits paid for the further two years. The intention of the legislation is to ensure that the defendant has an interest in the early disposal of the claim, because the sooner the compensation is paid, the smaller the amount he must pay to the DHSS.[176]

14.68b The 1997 Order (Art.3) applies the new regime to a person (in the context of a civil action, the defendant) who makes a payment who pays compensation for an accident, injury or disease on behalf of himself or another person liable for the damage, whether paid voluntarily, by court order, or by agreement, and whether made in the United Kingdom or elsewhere. It includes payments by the MIB. It applies to the Crown to the full extent authorised by the NI constitutional laws (Art.27). The situation where there is more than one compensator contributing to the compensation is to be dealt with in regulations under Article 21. If the injured person lives in Great Britain, the compensator applies for a certificate of deductible benefits under the provisions of the Social Security (Recovery of Benefits) Act 1997 (s.26 thereof). If the compensator lives in Great Britain the 1997 Order applies to him as if he lived in Northern Ireland (s.27). The 1997 Order (Sch.1) states the exemptions: it excludes, *inter alia*, payments in respect of costs, and any payment specified in regulations to be made under the Order. It excludes 'small payments' where the amount of compensation payment, or the aggregate of payments in respect of the same injured person in the same accident, does not exceed a prescribed sum in prescribed cases. The small payment limit is left to be set by regulations, and the Government's intention is to have no small payment limit; consideration may be given for setting a *de minimis* limit at a later stage if a good case is made for it.[177] Criminal injury compensation is not specifically excluded, but it

---

175 Though these general damages are protected from deduction, the problem will continue as before in that any state benefits which are means-tested may be reduced by the receipt by the plaintiff of investment income from the capital sum of compensation. This can be obviated by placing the compensation in a discretionary trust. See the comments of Lord Mackay of Ardbrecknish (Minister of State) *Hansard* HLVol.575 col.1202.

176 Mr. Evans, *Hansard* HC Vol.292 col.793.

177 Lord Mackay, *Hansard* HL Vol.575 cols.1203, 1220; Mr Lilley (Secretary of State) *Hansard* HC Vol.291 col.173.

is regarded as exempt by reason of the fact that such compensation paid by the Secretary of State is not a payment by a person liable for the injury.[178]

14.68c Before paying compensation (whether by settlement or under a court judgment) the defendant must send prescribed details of the claimant to the DHSS (Art.25(1)) and obtain the most up-to-date "certificate of recoverable benefits" from the CRU stating the listed benefits received or to be received by the plaintiff as a result of the accident; fresh certificates can be issued from time to time (Arts.6, 7). A plaintiff who claims or receives a listed benefit, or his personal representative, must give the DHSS prescribed information about the accident (Art.25(2)). On issue of the certificate the DHSS must send a copy of it to the plaintiff, who can request particulars of the manner in which it has been determined (Art.7(5)(6). The listed benefits are those in Schedule 2, with the heads of compensation against which deductible, as follows-

(1) *Benefit:* disability working allowance, disablement pension, incapacity benefit, income support, invalidity pension and allowance, jobseeker's allowance, reduced earnings allowance, severe disablement allowance, sickness benefit, unemployability supplement, unemployment benefit, and 80 per cent of statutory sick pay paid between 6 April 1991 and 5 April 1994.[179] *Head of compensation:* loss of earnings during the relevant period.

(2) *Benefit:* attendance allowance, care component of disability living allowance, disablement pension increase. *Head of compensation:* cost of care during the relevant period.

(3) *Benefit:* mobility allowance, mobility component of disability living allowance. *Head of compensation:* loss of mobility during the relevant period.

The 'relevant period' is five years from the day of the accident or the period from the date of accident to the date when payment in final discharge of the claim is made (Art.5).

14.68d The Court in its award makes no deduction on account of the listed benefits (Art.19)). When the Court makes an order for damages otherwise than by consent (i.e. when quantum is contested) the Court must specify on its order the amount of damages attributable to the heads of lost earnings, cost of care and loss of mobility during the relevant period (Art.17). If the trial ends within the five year period, this means that the Court must assess the loss under these heads up to the date when the defendant pays the damages, thus requiring the judge to foresee the date of an event which has not yet happened! The defendant must ascertain from the DHSS certificate the amount of listed benefits payable to the plaintiff up to the date when paying the damages, and that sum is a debt payable to the DHSS within 14 days (Arts.8,9). The defendant's liability insurance policy is deemed to cover this liability (Art.24). He deducts from the damages the amount of the listed benefits so paid from the appropriate head of

---

[178] Lord Mackay, *Hansard* HL Vol.576 col.140.

[179] Statutory sick pay paid since then is not relevant since the Statutory Sick Pay (NI) Order 1994 requires it to be paid by the employer with no contribution by the DHSS.

damages in so far as the amount of that head is enough to meet the deduction (Art.10). For the purposes of the Court's discretion as to costs, the plaintiff is deemed to have been awarded the whole damages ordered, regardless of any deduction for relevant benefits.[180] "We have no plans to take into account contributory negligence ... it will not be a relevant factor in the recovery of benefits."[181] Presumably, in cases where there is, say, a 50 per cent reduction in damages for contributory negligence, the head of damages from which the defendant can deduct benefits will be halved, but the defendant must still pay the benefits in full to the DHSS. The defendant is absolved from any obligation to pay the DHSS and cannot then deduct anything from the damages, if he has made and received written acknowledgement of an application for a certificate of recoverable benefits and the DHSS has not issued the certificate within four weeks (or other period prescribed by regulations) (Art.23).

14.68e There is no duty to specify the heads of damages when damages are agreed in an out-of-court settlement or an agreed judgment. "Under the reformed scheme the parties will negotiate a settlement on the basis that compensation for pain and suffering [and the other heads of general damages] is to be paid in full. This would apply regardless of the benefits which the compensator is to pay to the Department. ... A key advantage .... is that it will not complicate negotiation of out-of-court settlements. We will not be placing a bureaucratic requirement on the compensator to specify the elements of compensation that are payable in each individual case."[182] The DHSS has a right to recover the whole of the listed benefits up to the date of payment and has no concern over the settlement between the parties. The settlement should specify both the amount of the agreed damages and the amount, if any, to be deducted on account of the listed benefits. If the agreement merely states that damages of £20,000 are to be paid, with no apportionment for lost earnings, expense of care and loss of mobility, there might be a subsequent dispute as to whether the defendant can deduct any amount from the damages to be paid. It is submitted that in such a case it is implied that no part of the damages is attributable to any particular head of damages and therefore nothing can be deducted.

14.68f The CRU certificate is subject to review by the DHSS (Art.12), or a right of appeal (only after the disposal of the civil claim) by either party under regulations, on which any issue as to amount, rate and period of recoverable benefits or whether they are payable in respect of the accident must be referred to a medical appeal tribunal (Arts.13-14) with a further appeal on point of law from that tribunal to a Commissioner (Art.15). *Semble*, if at the time when the Court gives judgment there is a pending review of the CRU certificate, the judge should order a stay of enforcement or direct that the damages be paid into court until the review is determined. As envisaged by the government

---

180 *McCaffery* v *Datta* [1997] 2 All ER 586 (CA). As to the effect where the defendant lodges money in court under Ord.22, see para.11.152 and para.11.164.

181 Lord Mackay, *Hansard* HL Vol. 575 col.1220.

182 Lord Mackay, *Hansard,* HL Vol.575 col.1202.

minister[183] the appeal tribunal may decide that the period for which benefits are attributable to unfitness for work is not the same as the period for which the Court decided that the plaintiff suffered loss of earnings due to unfitness for work; there is deliberately no provision of the legislation for such difference to be reconciled. Regulations may provide for cases in which it transpires that the DHSS has been overpaid by the compensator (Art.22).

14.68g If the plaintiff was working in stable employment at the date of the accident, he is awarded the loss of earnings to date and loss of future earnings as heads of damages, and the relevant benefits are deductible from the head of lost earnings to date. It is expected that the new law will solve the problem highlighted in *Hassall* v *Sec of State* (para.14.68) where the victim was unemployed before his accident, because he will have little or nothing in the head of damages from which the deduction of benefits can be made. Thus a claim for loss of non-recoupable benefits will be unnecessary.

FATAL INJURIES

14.69 If the victim has died as a result of the accident, there are two causes of action: under the Law Reform (Miscellaneous Provisions) Act (NI) 1937, and the Fatal Accidents (NI) Order 1977. Both of these have been extensively amended by the Administration of Justice Act 1982. (See also para. 3.06).

14.70 *Law Reform Act damages* for his/her estate are recoverable by his personal representative, to be distributed as residuary estate under his will or intestacy, calculated without reference to any loss (other than funeral expenses) or gain to the estate consequent upon the death.[184] His estate is compensated for his funeral and other expenses and losses, pain and suffering, including awareness of loss of expectation of life, loss of amenity and loss of earnings up to his death. Where the injury and apprehension of the victim are all part of the death itself, no cause of action for pain and suffering etc. survives to the estate.[185] Exemplary damages cannot be awarded, nor compensation for loss of income in the lost years, to the estate.[184] 'CRU' benefits are recoupable from the award as shown in para. 14.68c.

14.71 *Fatal Accident damages* are recoverable on behalf of specified persons[186] in their own right for (a) loss of financial support;[187] and (b) funeral expenses incurred by a dependant (1977 Order, Art.5(4)); and (c) loss of the deceased's services to the family, a conventional yearly sum adding any special

---

183 Lord Mackay *Hansard* HL Vol.576 col.115.

184 Law Reform (Misc Provs) Act (NI) 1937, s.14, as amended by the 1982 Act, Sch.6 para. 9.

185 *Hicks* v *S Yorks Chief Constable* [1992] 2 All ER 65 (HL).

186 As defined by the Fatal Accidents (NI) Order 1977, Art.2, as amended. The "persons" are the following relatives of the deceased: the spouse, ex-spouse, person who co-habited as a spouse, parents or persons treated as such, children or persons treated as such, ascendants, brothers/sisters, uncles/aunts, nephews/nieces, and first cousins. An adopted child is deemed to be the child of the adopter: Adoption (NI) Order 1987, Art.40.

187 Not confined to support from earnings; it can be the support from the deceased's retirement pension: *Pidduck* v *Eastern Scottish Omnibuses* [1990] 1 WLR 993.

services pleaded and proved.[188] A fixed sum [currently £7,500] is payable for the spouse, or parent of an unmarried minor, for bereavement (Art.3A), which claim does not survive the death of the bereaved (1937 Act, s.14(1A)). Head (a) is based on a multiplicand, his net annual earnings[189] deducting money spent on himself, and a multiplier which is taken as the number of years he would have worked (allowing for normal contingencies) from the date of death up to a normal maximum of 16 or 18.[190] The Court should disregard both the actual investment potential of the damages award, and the future decline in the value of money, [191] but should reduce the multiplier on the basis that the claimants are receiving now money for a future loss in the same way as in assessing damages for future loss of a living victim (see para. 14.59). In assessing the loss of an unmarried co-habitee, the fact that he/she had no enforceable right to maintenance is relevant (1977 Order Art.5(3A)). If the deceased was not the 'breadwinner' the spouse can claim compensation for loss of his/her services, including the cost of a housekeeper or the spouse's loss if he/she has to give up work; and the children can claim for the loss of a parent's services.

A child of the deceased cannot receive a bereavement award, but can recover for the expense of future care, and if that expense is being incurred gratuitously by a friend or relative (e.g. the surviving parent or a grandparent) the sum is recoverable on trust on the same principle as stated in para. 14.55. The child can also recover a sum to reflect the loss of the personal comfort which the deceased parent would have provided, which sum is greater if the care is given by a paid nanny or housekeeper, and lesser if provided by a caring relative; the court also takes note of the fact that the cost of care of the child will decrease as the child reaches maturity.[192]

14.72 The bereavement award carries interest at the full rate (8% per annum) from the date of death. Dependency loss to the date of trial carries interest at half the full rate from the date of death, and future loss carries no interest. Some years' interest may be disallowed if there has been undue delay in pursuing the action to trial.[193] The judge directs each claimant's share as a proportion of the total award (apart from the bereavement award), and the money is distributed accordingly after deduction of costs not recovered from the defendant (1977 Order, Art.5(1)(1A)). The remarriage or prospects thereof of the wife (not the husband) are ignored if damages are assessed for her (Art.5(3)). A deduction from the damages can be made for fault of the deceased contributory to the death (Art.7), or of a dependant.[194] 'CRU' deductions are not made from Fatal Accidents compensation under the existing system; but

---

[188] *Donnelly* v *Hackett* [1988] 6 NIJB 6.

[189] I.e. legal earnings, which excludes earnings which the deceased did not disclose when claiming social security benefits: *Hunter* v *Butler*, 'The Times', 28 December 1995 (CA).

[190] *Graham* v *Dodds* [1983] NI 22 (HL); *Brennan* v *Gale* [1949] NI 178.

[191] *Mallett* v *McGonagle* [1969] NI 91 (HL) *per* Lord Diplock, approved in *Hodgson* v *Trapp* [1989] AC 807.

[192] *Official Solicitor and Briggs* v *Brett* [1996] 8 BNIL 22 (Girvan J).

[193] *Corbett* v *Barking Health Authority* [1991] 2 QB 408.

[194] *Mulholland* v *McCrea* [1961] NI 135, deductible from his own share only. The contributory fault of the personal representative as such is irrelevant.

under the new Social Security (Recovery of Benefits (NI) Order 1997 (*not yet in force)* CRU benefits may be deductible if the fatal accident claim is held to be within the definition of a "payment ... in respect of [the deceased] in consequence of any accident" under Article 3 thereof. It is possible that regulations under Schedule 1 may make fatal accident compensation an exempt payment. The Government has taken the view that there is no need to exempt fatal accident damages because the legislation does not permit deduction from compensation paid to a relative of the deceased.[195] Any benefit (past, future or potential) to any person from the estate or as a result of the death is to be disregarded (1977 Order, Art.6 as amended). Benefit includes any non-pecuniary benefit such as being absorbed into a new family.[196] A widow's pension as such, payable to the spouse, is a benefit to be disregarded because it is consequent upon the death.[197] However, a dependant cannot recover damages for the loss or reduction of a benefit or pension, where that loss or reduction is a consequence of the receipt of the fatal accident damages.[198]

14.73 The action is brought by and in the name of the personal representative; and no claimant should be joined as a plaintiff.[199] If there is no personal representative or he has not sued within six months of the death, a claimant may sue. Only one action can be brought in respect of one subject of complaint (1977 Order, Art.4(1)(2)(3)). The personal representative can join a claim on behalf of the estate with a claim for himself as dependant, but joinder of a claim for his own injury or loss arising from the same accident requires leave of the Court by *ex parte* application before the issue of the writ (Ord.15 r.1). The plaintiff must give full particulars of the claimants and the nature of the claim (Art.4(4)) (see para. 9.20). As to lodgments, see para. 11.150, para. 11.156; settlement, see para. 12.20.

DAMAGES BY PERIODICAL PAYMENTS

14.73a "A court awarding damages in an action for personal injury [including a claim for the estate or under the Fatal Accidents (NI) Order 1977] may, with the consent of the parties, make an order under which the damages are wholly or partly to take the form of periodical payments" (Damages Act 1996 s.2(1)). Such periodical payments are deemed not to be income and thus not taxable.[200] The primary purpose of this provision is to make clear that a structured settlement (para.12.21) agreed between the parties can be embodied in an order of the Court, but as Lord Meston remarked, it can be applied to an award of finite damages.[201] The Damages Act gives no instruction as to how the provision should be applied in practice. Presumably, once the consent in

---

195 Lord Mackay, *Hansard* HL Vol.576 col.141.

196 *Stanley* v *Saddique* [1992] QB 1. And no reduction is to be made from a child claimant who has been taken into the care of relatives who are wealthier than his deceased parents: *Sheppard* v *McAllister* (1988) 40 DLR 4th 233 (Ont CA).

197 *Pidduck* v *Eastern Scottish Omnibuses* [1990] 1 WLR 993.

198 *Maltby* v *MOD*, QBD, NI (Campbell J) 2 May 1997.

199 *Steele* v *GNR* (1890) 26 LR Ir 96.

200 Income and Corporation Taxes Act 1988, s.329AA.

201 *Hansard*, HL Vol.571, cols.1405-1417

principle is forthcoming, the judge is competent to decide how much of the damages should be set aside for periodical payments and how much and how often the payments should be. He may set aside that proportion of the damages which relates to future loss of earnings and future cost of care and treatment and assess the periodical payments as compensation for that loss. Or he may take a more general approach and set aside a part of the overall general damages for periodic payment in a way which meets the desires or convenience of the plaintiff. He will have to take into account the fact that damages so deferred are worth less financially than the same amount payable immediately; possibly this can be dealt with by making no discount under section 1 of the Act or by awarding interest on each periodical payment at the judgment rate from the date of judgment until each payment is received. It is not clear whether the judge must fix a total sum and then direct how it is to be paid over the future years, or whether he must simply assess the interval and amount of each payment. To put it another way, it is not clear whether the payments must extend over a fixed period or whether they are terminable on the death of the plaintiff. Possibly, he can direct payments to extend over a fixed period with a provision that the total remaining payments, if any, be made on the plaintiff's death. Presumably he can set the payments to increase by a set percentage to take into account future inflation, but it is doubtful if he can direct the payments to be increased by reference to some variable future factor such as the Retail Price Index. No special provision is made for deduction of CRU benefits; *semble,* section 84 of the Social Security Administration (NI) Act 1992 applies: the defendant must obtain a CRU certificate stating the amount of benefits received up to the date of the settlement (or up to five years from the accident if less) and deduct that amount from the sum payable initially and no further deductions are to be made from the periodical payments. [*to be replaced by*: Regulations under the Social Security (Recovery of Benefits) (NI) Order 1997 (Art.20) will provide for recovery of listed CRU benefits in cases of damages by periodical payments.]

CONTRIBUTORY NEGLIGENCE

14.74 The defence of contributory negligence (or 'contributory fault') is available against any claim based on breach of duty, including an intentional assault.[202] It is not a defence to conversion or intentional trespass to goods;[203] nor to a claim for breach of a strict contractual duty.[204] On a claim for intentional assault, unlawful conduct by the victim is also a defence in mitigation of damages.[205] The Court can consider the defence only if it is pleaded, and raised at the trial,[206] and proved. The judge (or jury) must find and record the total amount of damages net of any deductible benefits, and then make the "just and equitable" reduction for contributory fault to arrive at the figure to be awarded (Law Reform (Miscellaneous Provisions) Act (NI) 1948,

---

202 *Tumelty* v *MOD* [1988] 3 NIJB 51, at 65.

203 Tort (Interference with Goods) Act 1977, s.11(1).

204 *Barclays Bank* v *Fairclough Building* [1995] QB 214 (CA).

205 *Murphy* v *Culhane* [1977] QB 94.

206 *McMahon* v *Donaldson* [1969] NI 145, at 164; *Fookes* v *Slaytor* [1978] 1 WLR 1293

s.2).[207] Normally the fault is expressed as a fraction or percentage, in which case the reduction must be exact.[208] The 'last opportunity' rule can still play a part in assessing liability[209] and it is still the practice for plaintiffs to plead it in a Reply. The invocation of the 1948 Act logically presupposes that both sides are to blame: one person cannot be held 100 per cent contributorily negligent.[210] On a claim and counterclaim arising out of one incident, the apportionment of fault on each should be identical,[211] subject to the observations at para. 13.111. (As to deduction for failure to wear a seat belt, see *McAdoo* v *Wilson* [1981] 4 NIJB.) The Court should assess and deduct for the contributory fault of the plaintiff before apportioning damages between co-defendants.[212]

PROVISIONAL DAMAGES

14.75 At common law the Court must assess damages once and for all at the date of judgment, making forecasts as to the future of the plaintiff's injuries and prospects. If there is for instance a 30 per cent chance that he will go blind, the judge awards about 30 per cent of the damages that would be given for certain blindness.[213] By Order 37 rules 7-10, made under the Administration of Justice Act 1982 (Sch.6 para.10), the judge can award lump sum provisional damages now for the present injuries, giving the plaintiff the right to come back for a final award if the pessimistic forecast of deterioration comes about. The Act applies "to an action under Northern Ireland law for damages for personal injuries [including diseases or impairment of physical or mental condition] in which there is proved or admitted to be a chance that at some definite or indefinite time in the future the injured person will, as a result of the [accident] develop some serious disease or suffer some serious deterioration in his physical or mental condition". Provisional damages must have been pleaded. Judgment in default cannot be entered. The defendant can make a written secret offer of a specified sum of provisional damages, which if not accepted is kept secret from the trial judge until provisional damages are determined (Ord.37 r.9). The provisional award power is best exercised in cases where there is risk of serious deterioration, rather than where the deterioration is progressive. The order must specify the deterioration for which the provisional award is made; and should state the period within which the plaintiff may come back to the Court (a time limit which, by application before its expiry, the Court may extend) (Ord.37 r.8). The plaintiff must apply for his further damages within the time limit on three months' notice of intention; only one further application can be made in respect of each aspect of the injury for which the Court made a provisional award (Ord.37 r.10). As regards CRU benefits, it is submitted that section 82 of the Social Security Administration

---

[207] The Act binds the Crown: Crown Proceedings Act, s.4(2).

[208] *Kelly* v *Farrans* [1954] NI 41.

[209] *Sproule* v *Bogle* [1949] NI 134.

[210] *Pitts* v *Hunt* [1991] 1 QB 24.

[211] *Black* v *McCabe* [1964] NI 1.

[212] *Fitzgerald* v *Lane* [1989] AC 329.

[213] See *Malec* v *JC Hutton Ltd* (1990) 169 CLR 638; plus, *semble*, compensation for the plaintiff's worry and distress at the fear of blindness.

(NI) Act 1992 applies; the defendant must deduct the CRU benefits certified to date when making the payment under the provisional award, and on paying the damages finally awarded should deduct the CRU benefits certified to date (or up to five years after the accident, if less) minus the amount already deducted. [*to be replaced by*: Recovery of CRU benefits from provisional and final awards will be dealt with by regulations under the Social Security (Recovery of Benefits) (NI) Order 1997 (Art.20).]

14.76 If the plaintiff dies as a result of the accident after an award of provisional damages, a further award cannot include an amount for loss of income after the date of death; his death does not bar a fatal accident action but the court assessing the loss of the dependants must take into account any damages awarded before the death as compensation for loss which in the event falls after his death (Damages Act 1996, s.3).

INTERIM AWARD

14.77 Provisional damages should be distinguished from the power of the Court to order interim damages in advance of the trial of an action. This topic is dealt with at para. 11.55.

INTEREST

14.78 Section 33A of the Judicature Act provides that subject to rules, on any sum for which judgment is given for debt or damages, simple interest may be awarded on all or part of the debt/damages for which judgment is given or payment made before judgment, at such rate as the Court thinks fit or as rules provide, for all or part of the period from the date of the cause of action to the date of judgment or sooner payment.[214] "Debt or damages" means any monetary award payable in tort, contract, common law or equity, or under a statute such as the Frustrated Contracts Act (NI) 1947;[215] but not statutory compensation such as criminal injury award.[216] A claim for interest should be made in the writ (if a debt case) or Statement of Claim. In awarding judgment for a debt, or expense incurred, the Court normally awards interest from the date when the debt became payable or the expense was incurred, to the date of judgment at a rate not exceeding the judgment rate (currently 8% per annum),[217] though other rates, such as the "commercial rate" or the "investment rate" can be applied as stated in the White Book (1997) 6/2/12. As a result of *Thomas* v *Bunn*,[218] interest should be assessed up to the date when damages are assessed, not to the prior date when liability was found.

14.79 Interest under section 33A of the Judicature Act cannot be awarded if no money was due at the date of issue of the writ.[219] Subject to rules, in proceedings for a debt, if the debtor pays the whole debt before judgment, he is liable for simple interest as the Court thinks fit or as rules provide (s.33A(2)).

---

214 Including judgment for or against the Crown: Crown Proceedings Act, s.24(3).

215 *BP Exploration* v *Hunt (No 2)* [1983] 2 AC 352.

216 *McCaughey* v *Sec of State* [1975] NI 133.

217 *Watts* v *Morrow* [1991] 1 WLR 1421, at 1443, 1446.

218 [1991] 1 AC 362.

219 *Mathew* v *TM Sutton* [1994] 1 WLR 1455 (Ch D).

If the defendant has fully satisfied the plaintiff's claim for damages, the plaintiff may continue to seek judgment for the damages and interest thereon, crediting the money paid.[220] Interest on a debt is not available under section 33A in so far as interest is otherwise payable (s.33A(3)). Interest awarded on damages for personal injuries or in respect of death is not taxable income.[221] As the power is discretionary, interest may be withheld, for example if the Statement of Claim fails to plead it; if the plaintiff has delayed in bringing his claim; or if the plaintiff has failed to beat a lodgment.

14.80 At common law interest on money expended may be claimable as a part of the damages. The statutory power to award interest does not prevent the Court from awarding compensation for loss of use of money.[222] Presumably such a head of damages can be awarded even though the loss was made good before the issue of the writ.

Interest as of right

14.81 Interest is awardable as of right under an express or implied term of a contract or course of dealing or a trade custom; in an action on a negotiable instrument;[223] or under specific statute.[224]

Interest in equity

14.82 Courts of equity have always had power to award interest on a mortgage debt, on a surety's indemnity, or where a trustee, constructive trustee or fiduciary has failed to return or preserve money or assets.[225] Compound interest can be awarded if appropriate to reflect the benefit gained by the defendant.[226] Interest in equity can be awarded on its own, even where no money is due at the date of commencement of proceedings.[227]

OTHER REMEDIES

Restitution of goods

14.83 In an action for interference to goods, under the Tort (Interference with Goods) Act 1977 (s.3) the Court can grant -

(a) delivery of the goods and consequential damages;

(b) the above with an option to the defendant to give the value in lieu of delivery; or

---

[220] *Edmunds* v *Lloyds Italico* [1986] 1 WLR 492.

[221] Income and Corporation Taxes 1988, s.329.

[222] *Hungerfords* v *Walker* [1989] LRC (Comm) 397; 171 CLR 125.

[223] Bill of Exchange Act 1882, s.57.

[224] E.g. Arbitration Act 1996, s.49(4) (on arbitrator's award); Taxes Management Act 1970, ss.69, 86-92 (on arrears of tax). Any treasurer of taxes and public money who defaults in paying it for six months is liable for 12% interest per annum: Crown Debts (Ir) Act 1781, s.23.

[225] *McArdle* v *Gaughran* [1903] 1 IR 106; *Murphy* v *AIB* [1994] 2 ILRM 221 (mortgagee holding surplus proceeds of sale).

[226] *Equiticorp Industries* v *The Crown (No 3)* [1996] 3 NZLR 690 (H Ct).

[227] *Mathew* v *TM Sutton* [1994] 1 WLR 1455 (Ch D).

(c) damages, i.e. the value of the goods and consequential damages.

The plaintiff cannot insist on order (a). Order (c) can be substituted if (a) is not complied with. If order (b) is made the plaintiff can apply to the EJ Office to substitute an order for delivery.[228] If order (a) is made, or the claim dismissed, a valuation should be made in order to help the Taxing Master to assess the costs. Where the plaintiff does not represent all those with an interest in the goods, and does not have possessory title, he can be awarded damages only (Ord.42 r.6). The value of an article is its market value, or where it is not available on the open market, the cost of its replacement; the value of token documents, such as title deeds, is the cost of replacement or the cost of securing the proprietary right betokened.[229] Negotiable instruments are valued at their nominal value. Order 37 rules 1-4 (para.14.50) apply to the assessment of value as they apply to assessment of damages (Ord.37 r.5). Payment of damages which include an assessment of the plaintiff's full interest in the goods, operates as an extinction of his title (1977 Act, s.5). The 1977 Act also caters for the following situations: where the defendant has *bona fide* improved the goods; where there are two claimants against him; the defence of *jus tertii*; and co-ownership.

14.84 In an action for non-delivery of specific or ascertained goods, the court can order specific delivery and consequential damages under section 52 of the Sale of Goods Act 1979.

Injunction

14.85 An injunction is simply an order of court calling upon a person to do or not to do an act. It is infinitely variable in its form and application, and can be granted as interlocutory or interim or final relief. *Prohibitory* (negative) injunction is the more usual type of order: that a person do not do or stop doing something. *Mandatory* (positive) injunction, is an order to do an act or undo the damage of a past act. *Quia timet* injunction is an order to do or not to do an act in order to prevent damage which has not yet occurred. An injunction may be granted against a threatened or apprehended trespass or waste whether or not the defendant is in possession or claims title or right.[230]

14.86 As long as it relates to the protection of a legal right, the injunction is not confined to restraining unlawful acts; it can restrain a lawful act if necessary, for example to order a defendant who is harassing or molesting the plaintiff to stay out of an area.[231] Harassment is now a tort and where an injunction is granted against it, a breach thereof may lead to a warrant of arrest.[232] Normally the plaintiff or defendant who has made a claim in the action applies for an injunction as a final substantive remedy. It can be granted as a part of the judgment at the trial or thereafter by motion, as where the

---

[228] Judgments Enforcement (NI) Order 1981, Art.57(2).

[229] *McQuaid* v *Sec of State* [1976] 9 NIJB.

[230] Judicature Act, s.91(3).

[231] *Burris* v *Azadani* [1995] 1 WLR 1372.

[232] Protection from Harassment (NI) Order 1997, Art.5 (*not yet in force*) (See Stop Press p.x).

defendant renewed his trespass after damages were awarded.[233] An injunction can be granted or refused with liberty to apply in respect of it.[234] Any remedy sought by application after judgment must be based on the original cause of action, so that a new injunction is not on a new cause of action; it is rather a new remedy given on the original cause in the light of further wrongful acts after the trial. Against the Crown the Court can give only a declaration in lieu (see para.14.97). Injunction cannot be given against a foreign state or sovereign.[235] On application by a person affected, the High Court can restrain unlawful industrial action,[236] and on application of a trade union member, the High Court can restrain industrial action without a ballot.[237] A court cannot by specific performance or injunction compel an employee to perform his contract of employment.[238] The High Court can by injunction restrain a person from acting in a public office.[239]

14.87 The plaintiff must show that the claim relates to a legal or equitable right vested in him, unless he is the Attorney-General enforcing the law (on his own or in a 'relator' action). Among the grounds on which the Court may in its discretion refuse an injunction are -

(1) the harm is slight;

(2) damages an adequate remedy;

(3) performance difficult or disproportionately costly;

(4) the obligation too uncertain to specify in words;

(5) it would force the defendant to breach local or foreign law;

(6) no prospect that the damage will continue to be repeated;

(7) the defendant's act would be lawful but for a technical defect;

(8) delay or 'laches', amounting to fraud in equity or expiry of limitation period;

(9) acquiescence or waiver;

(10) plaintiff at fault;

(11) the conduct is beyond the jurisdiction of the court to control;

(12) other remedies available (e.g. criminal prosecution);

(13) lack of mutuality;

(14) not in the public interest.

14.88 The Irish courts have said that an injunction or declaration should not be withheld merely because it has to be enforced abroad; it is for the plaintiff to

---

233 *Agnew* v *McDowell* (1884) 14 LR Ir 445.

234 *Gilmurray* v *Corr* [1978] NI 99.

235 State Immunity Act 1978, s.13.

236 Trade Union and Labour Relations (NI) Order 1995, Art.120.

237 *Ibid*, Art.29.

238 *Ibid*, Art.123.

239 Judicature Act, s.24.

seek such enforcement as the foreign court will grant him.[240] An injunction will not be granted to restrain a company from exercising its power to alter its memorandum or articles of association.[241] An injunction should not be granted against a person too mentally ill to understand it, nor against a minor who cannot be effectively punished.[242] If the judge decides that an injunction should be given he should do so; he should not declare a right to an injunction and then call upon the party to give an undertaking in lieu, because that is in effect making an order which is unappealable.[243]

14.89 The order must be precise and clear as to what must be done or not done and conform to the substance of what must be done or not done, though it need not specify the manner of achieving it.[244] If it requires the defendant to do a positive act it must set a time limit. A prohibitory injunction can be suspended for a period, as where the defendant cannot easily stop the conduct at once.

Specific performance

14.90 This is a discretionary equitable remedy ordering the defendant to perform an obligation other than payment of money assumed under contract. The order, to be enforceable by committal, must set a time limit. The Court can make only a declaration in lieu of specific performance against the Crown (see para. 14.97).

Damages in lieu

14.91 A court may award damages in addition to or in lieu of an injunction or specific performance under section 92 of the Judicature Act.[245] This power is necessary where the plaintiff is suing on an equitable right, such as breach of trust or breach of confidence, or where common law damages would be nominal. Damages in equity are assessed usually as compensation for not getting the injunction. They cannot be awarded if the injunction is refused because the plaintiff has no title or *locus standi*[246] or refused as unnecessary.[247] If the injunction would be oppressive, and the injury is small and capable of compensation in money, damages in lieu should be given. Even then the Court may grant the injunction if the defendant has acted in a high-handed manner.[248]

14.92 Some Commonwealth cases have held that pure compensatory damages can be awarded for an equitable wrong such as breach of confidence.[249]

---

240 *Kutchera* v *Buckingham Holdings* [1988] IR 61.

241 *Russsell* v *Northern Bank Development Corporation* [1989] 5 NIJB 1, at 67-74.

242 *Wookey* v *Wookey* [1991] Fam 121.

243 *McConnell* v *McConnell* (1980) 10 Fam Law 214.

244 *Concrete Constructions* v *Plumbers and Gasfitters* (1988) 14 Comm LB 1266 (Fed Ct of Aus).

245 The descendant of "Lord Cairns' Act".

246 *Beaumont* v *Figgis* [1945] IR 78; *Wentworth* v *Woollahra Council* (1982) 149 CLR 672.

247 *O'Neill* v *DHSS (No 2)* [1986] NI 290, at 296.

248 *McGrath* v *Munster & Leinster* [1959] IR 313, at 328; *Jaggard* v *Sawyer* [1995] 2 All ER 189; *National Trust* v *Shields*, Ch D, NI (Campbell J) 6 June 1995.

249 *Aquaculture* v *NZ Green Mussel Co* [1992] LRC (Comm) 692; [1990] 3 NZLR 299 (CA).

Rectification

14.93 This is an equitable remedy to correct a mistake in a contract or other document,[250] whether a mistake shared by the parties or a mistake of one party of which the other is aware.[251]

Rescission

14.94 Generally in equity, and in certain circumstances at common law, a contract or deed can be rescinded by the Court, with restitution of money paid under it.

Declaration

14.95 Section 23(1)(2) of the Judicature Act provides that in any action or proceeding the High Court may make a binding declaration of right whether or not consequential relief is claimed; and a merely declaratory judgment or order can be sought on its own.[252] A declaration can be made as to rights depending on events which have not yet occurred (s.23(3)). The declaration must relate to the legally enforceable rights or liabilities of the plaintiff, subsisting or future.[253] Declaration is a statutory not an equitable remedy, but it is discretionary and can be refused if the plaintiff does not come with 'clean hands'.[254] The High Court will not grant, at least in a writ action, a declaration that an inferior court should make a particular decision under a statute which confers exclusive jurisdiction on that court,[255] nor should it grant an injunction to stop a court from exercising its jurisdiction.[256] Declarations as to matters of public law rights should be sought in judicial review applications and not in actions. The Courts are reluctant to grant declaratory relief without a full contested hearing. There is little point in giving a declaration by consent, as that can be achieved by agreement between the parties themselves.

Accounts

14.96 A claim can be made for the taking of an account (see para. 18-25). On a claim for breach of trust, the plaintiff can be awarded an account of the defendant's profits or damages for the plaintiff's loss, but not both.[257]

Sale

14.97 The Court has a general power to order sale of property at an interlocutory stage (para. 11.82), and in proceedings under a judgment (paras. 15.18-15.20), and there is a specific power of sale of land in the Chancery Division (para. 18.55).

---

[250] See *Rooney and McParland* v *Carlin* [1981] NI 138.

[251] *Commission for New Towns* v *Cooper (GB)* [1995] Ch 259 (CA).

[252] See White Book (1997) 15/16; and *Kingston* v *Irish Dunlop* [1969] IR 233.

[253] *In re S (Hospital Patient: Court's Jurisdiction)* [1996] Fam 1 (CA).

[254] *Hongkong Bank* v *Wheeler Holdings* (1993) 100 DLR 4th 40, at 53-5 (SC Canada).

[255] *McDermott* v *Dept of Agriculture* [1984] 2 NIJB; White Book (1997) 15/16/4.

[256] *Colmey* v *Pinewood Developments* [1995] 1 ILRM 331 (Carroll J).

[257] *Tang Man Sit* v *Capacious Investments* [1996] 1 AC 514 (PC).

Receiver

14.98 The Court can appoint a receiver at an interlocutory stage, in or after judgment to preserve property or a business as a going concern. See paras. 11.83, 15.21.

REMEDIES AGAINST THE CROWN

14.99 The Crown Proceedings Act (s.21) applies to civil proceedings by or against the Crown, except judicial review proceedings (s.38), relator actions, and proceedings relating to Northern Ireland charities or Land Registry (s.23(3)). By section 21 a court can make any order as would be made between citizens, but (a) cannot grant an injunction or specific performance against the Crown (or indirectly against the Crown by order against an official), only a declaration of rights; and (b) cannot order recovery of land or other property against the Crown, only a declaration of the claimant's right to the same. However an injunction (and presumably specific performance and the other remedies) can be given against a minister or government official personally liable, even where he was acting in the course of his duties.[258] It cannot be given where the official acts as a representative of the Crown, a Department or the Attorney-General.[259]

---

[258] *M* v *Home Office* [1994] 1 AC 377.

[259] *Ibid.* at 412. See also *MacDonald* v *Sec of State*, 1994 SC 234.

CHAPTER FIFTEEN

THE JUDGMENT

15.00 A 'judgment' is a decision determining liabilities obtained in an action, and every other decision is an 'order'.[1] A decision upon a case stated is an 'order'.[2] In the Judicature Act and RSC, 'judgment' includes order, but not *vice versa*. If given at a trial, the official present in court enters particulars of the judgment in the register, as well as the record and title of the action, the judge's name, the date(s) and length of the trial, the solicitors, counsel and witnesses (Ord.35 r.7). He also keeps a list of all exhibits which is attached to the pleadings and forms part of the court record, and of which any party may receive an office copy (Ord.35 r.8). At the conclusion of the trial the parties must take back their original exhibits and preserve them in the event of an appeal (Ord.35 r.9).

15.01 In Order 42 'judgment' includes order, decision and direction (Ord.42 r.1). A note of the judgment of a judge is made by the officer present; and every judgment, except a judgment in default,[3] is drawn up and signed by the proper officer and sealed and filed in the appropriate office and a note entered in the cause book and the judgments book (Ord.42 r.2). The recent introduction of computer-recorded orders, being entered onto the hard disc record by the court official as soon as the judge or master pronounces the order, has caused some difficulties. However it should be noted that such an order is no more final and unchangeable than an order recorded in writing before the officer signs the order book (see para.15.10). The document or computer entry constitutes the judgment, not the oral pronouncement by the judge, but the former dates back to the latter.[4] A judge can suspend an order before it is signed, in which case it does not take effect.[5] Where a form of judgment is set out in Appendix A of the RSC it should be adopted. Only forms of judgment in default and under Order 113 are prescribed there (Forms 29-33).[6] Note that under the new RSC all judgments are expressed in the form of a command to the defendant: "the defendant do give possession of the land" rather than "the plaintiff do recover

---

1 White Book (1997) 42/1/7. Synonymous with 'judgment' is a "decree", which is the term used in matrimonial causes and in the county court.

2 *Onslow* v *Inland Revenue* (1890) 25 QBD 465; but see *JG McGregor* v *Grampian RC*, para. 20.88.

3 See Chap.8.

4 *Pennefather* v *Tobin* (1884) 18 ILTR 54; White Book (1997) 35/10/3; cf. *Donnan* v *Creaney* [1995] 10 BNIL 26 (CA). An appeal can be brought before it is drawn up but the order on appeal will not be drawn up until the lower court order is: *Maple Ridge District* v *BC Assessors* (1991) 84 DLR 4th 512 (CA, BC).

5 *In re Cullen* [1987] 5 NIJB 102, at 104-5 (in that case an *ex parte* order giving leave to bring judicial review).

6 For forms of judgment at trial see the White Book (1997) Vol. 2, Pt 2.

possession of the land". Such phrasing means, if a time limit is set, that the defendant is in contempt if he does not obey it.[7] In the Chancery Division, where court orders are often complex matters giving directions for further proceedings, the Court may give directions as to the drafting of the order and may direct counsel to draft, agree or comment upon the draft court order.[8]

15.02 All judgments must be drawn up unless otherwise ordered. Some *orders* do not have to be drawn up (Ord.42 r.3) -

(1) an order extending a time limit;[9]

(2) an order containing no special terms or directions;

(3) an order giving leave to issue a writ, to amend a writ or pleading, to file a document, or to a court officer to do any act. An order of leave to issue a writ for service outside the jurisdiction must be drawn up.

15.03 If the plaintiff succeeds on two causes of action, the judgment should make it clear whether the damages awarded are in satisfaction of both causes.[10] If he succeeds on only one cause the defendant is entitled to judgment on the other.[11] 'Cause of action' is used here in the sense of a set of facts giving a right to relief, rather than the legal label such as trespass, nuisance, negligence etc. If there are two defendants, and they are jointly or jointly and severally liable for the damage, the judgment must be for full damages against both jointly with contribution *inter se* to a specified proportion.[12] If the plaintiff recovers against only one defendant sued jointly, the other is entitled to judgment for him.[13]

15.04 Judgment may be expressed in any foreign currency or its present sterling equivalent, where that best expresses the plaintiff's loss. If the plaintiff, being registered for VAT, recovers judgment for remuneration for goods or services given by him to the defendant in his business, VAT must be included in the award; but where the plaintiff recovers damages for expenses incurred by him in the course of business (e.g. the repair cost of his business vehicle) he should *not* be awarded VAT on his expenses because that VAT can be set off by him against his VAT liability. If the plaintiff is not registered for VAT or the action does not concern his business, the converse propositions are true.

15.05 A judgment or order requiring a person to do an act must state a specified time within which the act is to be done, though an order for payment of money or delivery of possession of land or goods need not state a time (Ord.42 r.4). Where a judgment does not state a time, on application by summons, the Court may by order fix a time (Ord.42 r.5(2)). Where a judgment or order fixes a time, the Court may extend or abridge the time limit (Ord.3 r.5), or, on summons, make an order fixing a new time limit (Ord.42 r.5(1)). A summons to fix a new time must always be served on the person ordered, even

---

[7] See White Book (up to 1988 ed.) 42/1/2.
[8] Practice Direction 1997 No 5 (Ch D) [1997] 5 BNIL.
[9] But see Ord.45 r.5, para. 16.49.
[10] *B.O.Morris* v *Perrott* [1945] 1 All ER 567.
[11] *O'Kane* v *Higgins* (1901) 1 NIJR 276 (where the claims were in the alternative).
[12] *Clarke* v *McLaughlin & Harvey* [1978] 2 NIJB.
[13] *Kennedy* v *Merchant Warehousing* [1924] 2 IR 85.

if in default of appearance (Ord.42 r.5(3)). The original order and any order fixing or altering the time limit must be served personally on the person to be enforceable by committal (see Ord.45 r.5(5)).

15.06 A copy of a judgment, sealed and stamped "copy" can be issued (Ord.42 r.10). If the original has been lost the Court can by *ex parte* order issue a duplicate.[14] A judgment takes effect on the day of its date, which is unless otherwise ordered the date on which it is given (Ord.42 r.8).[15] It is deemed to be made at the earliest moment of the day (see para.1.31).

Stay of enforcement

15.07 It is normal for the losing party to ask for a short stay of enforcement, usually three weeks, or longer for good reason (see para. 16.03). If an appeal is contemplated, counsel may ask for a stay pending appeal (para. 20.33). The effect of such stay is to defer the right of the winning party to apply to the Enforcement of Judgments Office to enforce the judgment.

Judgment for person under disability

15.08 Where money is awarded or agreed to be paid to or for a person under disability, the money must be dealt with under the directions of the Court, by investment, transfer to the county court[16] or otherwise; nothing is to be paid out except by order of the Court (Ord.80 rr.10-11). Usually it is invested as recommended by the Accountant-General's Office. An adult, usually the next friend, is appointed guardian of the settlement. He may apply for payment of a sum out for a good reason for the minor (e.g. for educational or medical expense).[17] When a minor reaches his eighteenth birthday the Accountant-General's Office releases the money if satisfied that the claimant is still alive, unless otherwise ordered (Court Funds Rules, r.39). Where the plaintiff is a mental patient, the proper order is for the money "to be lodged in court and dealt with in accordance with Part VIII of the Mental Health (NI) Order 1986". The Office of Care and Protection may then agree to a request to set up a form of discretionary trust so as to ensure that his right to social security benefits and to free care and maintenance in a Health Service or other institution is not affected by the receipt in his own name of a large capital sum.[18] A patient who recovers his health should apply for payment out under Order 80 rule 10 on affidavit exhibiting a medical report.

FINALITY OF JUDGMENT

15.09 Subject to rules and to statute, a judgment and order is final in the proceedings in which it is made and in proceedings to enforce it. The binding nature of the order in other proceedings, by estoppel *per rem judicatem*, is another matter (see para. 13.100). Finality for the purposes of restricting a

---

[14] *Hibernian Bank* v *McArdle* (1932) 66 ILTR 28.

[15] I.e. that date on which it is pronounced in court: *Holtby* v *Hodgson* (1889) 24 QBD 103.

[16] County Courts (NI) Order 1980, Art.21.

[17] In *Official Solicitor and Briggs* v *Brett* [1996] 8 BNIL 22, the minors in a fatal accident action applied for payment out of that amount of their damages attributable to the expenses of care by their relatives.

[18] A precedent of such a court order and discretionary trust is given in Appendix Two, no. 9.

right of appeal under the Judicature Act (s.35) is yet another matter (see para. 11.00). A formally correct order made within jurisdiction cannot be challenged in other proceedings.[19] Where a plaintiff proceeds to obtain a decree in breach of a contractual agreement to stay the action, he can be sued for breach of contract.[20] The decisions of the High Court and of any superior court are not subject to judicial review or *habeas corpus*, and in the absence of a statutory right of appeal or review, its errors, even jurisdictional, cannot be corrected.[21]

15.10 There is no general power to vary a judgment or order (including an interlocutory order) once it is entered or drawn up.[22] The judge can change his mind before the judgment is drawn up if satisfied that it is wrong and that it is just and fair to the parties to do so;[23] but thereafter it can only be altered by consent.[24]

15.11 Exceptions to the rule of finality are as follows -

(1) Rights of appeal or of review under statute or rules.

(2) Judicial review of the decision of an inferior court.

(3) An order which is a nullity will be set aside.

(4) An irregular order may be set aside under Order 2 rule 1.

(5) An *ex parte* order is liable to be set aside.

(6) A judgment in default of appearance or defence can be set aside. A judgment at the trial in a party's absence can be set aside.

(7) Some interlocutory orders (e.g. of discovery, judgment in default, summary judgment) can be varied or set aside under specific rules.

(8) The High Court has inherent discretion to review orders and proceedings of a master or other officer under a power delegated from the Court.[25]

(9) A financial order in the matrimonial jurisdiction can be set aside for non-disclosure.[26] A maintenance order can be varied.[27]

(10) An injunction can be varied or discharged by reason of subsequent events, by application made in the action in which it was given.[28]

(11) A supplemental order can be made where the first has not been complied with (e.g. specific performance).

(12) A time limit set can be altered (see para. 15.05).

---

[19] *Moore* v *O'Donnell* (1856) 6 ICLR 46; *Govern* v *Rowland* (1858) 7 ICLR 619.
[20] *Burke* v *O'Callaghan* (1865) 17 ICLR 42.
[21] *Re Racal* [1981] AC 374; *In re Beggs* [1944] NI 121.
[22] See White Book (1997) 20/11/6.
[23] *Pittalis* v *Sherefettin* [1986] QB 868; and see para. 15.01.
[24] *Irving* v *Askew* (1870) LR 5 QB 208.
[25] *In re Weir* [1988] NI 338, at 351F-352G.
[26] *Jenkins* v *Livesey* [1985] AC 424.
[27] *Magowan* v *Magowan* [1921] 2 IR 314.
[28] *Howard* v *Commrs of Public Works* [1994] 2 ILRM 301.

(13) A judgment obtained by fraud can be set aside by a fresh action, but not merely on discovery of new evidence.[29]

(14) The High Court in Insolvency can go behind a judgment against the bankrupt.[30]

(15) The High Court in Insolvency can vary or rescind its own orders (Insolvency (NI) Order 1989, Art.371).

(16) In proceedings under a judgment for administration or execution, a noticed party can apply to set it aside.

(17) A partition order can be amended before sale.[31]

(18) The Court can refuse to invoke its coercive powers where it would be unjust.[32]

(19) If a court has made an order in relation to registered land, the registrar of titles (only) can apply summarily and the court may vary it or give directions or make a new order (Land Registration Act (NI) 1970, s.9), but the court cannot make an alteration of substance.[33]

(20) After a decree in ejectment (including on forfeiture) for non-payment of rent, the Court may restore the tenant to possession if he pays or lodges in court the rent due and costs (Judicature Act, s.94).

(21) Errors and mistakes in judgments can be corrected, as stated in the next paragraph.

Correction of judgments and orders

15.12 Clerical mistakes and errors arising from accidental slip or omission in a judgment or order may be corrected at any time by the Court on motion or summons under the 'slip rule' (Ord.20 r.11). Beyond the terms of that rule, the Court has inherent jurisdiction to vary its own order to carry out or clarify its manifest intention; and to correct errors on the court record.[34] It must be a mistake, whether induced by the judge, the parties or the court official, in expressing the manifest intention of the court.[35] It can be an error in an order induced by a mistake in the notice of motion;[36] an arithmetical miscalculation;[36] misnaming of a party;[37] and omission of a provision which the judge would have put in the order but forgot and was not reminded by the parties.[38] It does not allow a change of mind; nor a correction of a misapprehension of law or

---

[29] *Tassan Din* v *Banco Ambrosiano* [1991] 1 IR 569.

[30] *In re Pedlow,* QBD (Bankruptcy) NI (Lowry J) 4 October 1965; (1965) 17 NILQ 163; Hunter *Northern Ireland Bankruptcy Law and Practice* (SLS 1984), para.7.25.

[31] *In re Martin* (1879) 3 LR Ir 255.

[32] *Thwaite* v *Thwaite* [1982] Fam 1.

[33] *O'Leary* v *O'Dea* [1922] 1 IR 8.

[34] *In re Creeney* [1988] NI 167; *Belville Holdings* v *Revenue Commrs* [1994] 1 ILRM 29.

[35] *Ibid.*

[36] *McCaughey* v *Stringer* [1914] 1 IR 73, where the court made no mistake, the error being that of the applicant.

[37] *Loughery* v *Swan* (1889) 23 ILTR 54.

[38] *McNicholl* v *Neely* [1983] NI 43.

fact or of an error induced by misrepresentation or fraud; nor where the order made has unforeseen effects;[39] nor can it cure an excess of jurisdiction.

15.13 If the rule is applicable it should be invoked because appeal is inappropriate.[40] Usually the correction is made by the individual judge, but the power can be exercised by any judge of the Court.[41] If the order is that of an appellate court, that court should make the correction.[42] A correction can be refused if it is inequitable to correct it or if persons have acted on it, but not *per se* because of undue delay.

'Judgment by consent'

15.14 A judgment or order of a judge expressed to be by consent, is not appealable to the Court of Appeal without leave of the judge (see para. 20.08). An order is by consent only if it is part of a contractual agreement, not if it is in reality only an order conceded or made without objection.[43] If by consent it should be expressed as such.[44] A judgment by consent can be set aside by a new action on the same grounds as any contract can be set aside or varied. See further para. 12.10.

INTEREST ON JUDGMENTS

15.15 Every monetary judgment of the Court over £200 carries interest automatically, subject to any contrary provision in the judgment or direction of the judge, from the date it was given until application to the Enforcement of Judgments Office or sooner payment (Judgments Enforcement (NI) Order 1981, Art.127).[45] The interest is at the 'judgment rate', currently 8 per cent per annum, unless a different rate is specified (Ord.42 r.9).[46] The appropriate rate is that current at the date of judgment.[47] "Judgment" means an award made by court order or obtained from a court office. It does not mean the right to payment of money arising under the rules, such as costs payable to a plaintiff on accepting a lodgment,[48] nor an award agreed under a settlement which is not embodied in a court judgment. The plaintiff can claim a higher rate only if the contract on which he sued specifically gave a right to interest at the higher rate after judgment.[49]

15.16 Interest under Article 127 runs from the date when damages are assessed, not the date when judgment on liability was given.[50] Interest runs on costs from the date of the judgment awarding costs, not from the date when

---

39 *Baillie* v *Inglis* [1926] NI 53, at 56.
40 *Hatton* v *Harris* [1892] AC 547 (Ir).
41 *R* v *Cripps, ex p Muldoon* [1984] QB 686, at 695B.
42 Cf. *Ryan* v *Shee* (1845) 8 Ir LR 268; *L.Shaddock Pty* v *Parramatta CC* (1983) 151 CLR 590.
43 *Siebe Gorman* v *Pneupac* [1982] 1 WLR 185.
44 *Chandless* v *Nicholson* [1942] 2 KB 321.
45 Article 127 applies to judgments for or against the Crown: Crown Proceedings Act, s.24(1).
46 On judgments dated from 2 September 1985 and before 19 April 1993, the rate is 15% per annum.
47 *Rocco* v *Tradex* [1984] 1 WLR 742.
48 *Legal Aid Board* v *Russell* [1991] 2 AC 317.
49 *Ealing LBC* v *El Isaac* [1980] 1 WLR 932.
50 *Thomas* v *Bunn* [1991] 1 AC 362.

they are taxed.[51] Interest runs during such time as enforcement has been delayed by the appeal unless the Court of Appeal otherwise orders (Ord.59 r.13(2)). *Quaere,* whether this is confined to delay due to a stay of enforcement ordered pending appeal. In any case, where there has been no stay ordered the Court of Appeal has inherent jurisdiction to order interest to run on an affirmed judgment from its original date.[52] Arrears of interest are statute-barred six years after the interest became due.[53] Interest under Article 127 is not taxable (White Book (1997) 42/1/13).

PROCEEDINGS UNDER OR AFTER JUDGMENT

15.17 Further proceedings after judgment, apart from enforcement, are rare in Queen's Bench actions, but most Chancery Division judgments provide for accounts, inquiries or other proceedings (see para. 18.56). Any evidence at the trial of proceedings is admissible in subsequent proceedings (Ord.38 r.10).

15.18 *Sale of land.* Apart from specific powers in the Chancery Division, the High Court has a general power, unique to the Judicature Act in Northern Ireland, to order sale of any property including land, where it is just and convenient for the purposes of proceedings before it (s.91(1)(a)). To enforce the right of sale the Court has inherent jurisdiction to order possession for the purpose of carrying it out.[54] If it is difficult to procure a release from incumbrancers, the Court may order the proceeds to be paid into court under section 5 of the Conveyancing Act 1881.[55] It is wrong to order sale subject to the encumbrances of those who object.[56] Procedure for sale in the Chancery Division is dealt with in Order 31. Conduct is usually given to the legal owner. The Court may for the purposes of any civil cause or matter appoint conveyancing counsel under section 113 of the Judicature Act (Ord.31 r.5). All persons with a legal interest, whether parties to the action or not, should join in the conveyance. The Court has power to convey property on behalf of an owner who refuses to do so (see para. 16.59). Where any court orders the sale or mortgage of land, every interested person who is a party to the action or is bound by the order is deemed to be a trustee.[57]

15.19 A judgment affecting registered land can be inserted as a burden under the Land Registration Rules (NI) 1994 (r.85).

15.20 *Sale of property.* Section 91 gives power to order sale of any property. In any proceedings between spouses concerning property, the Court can order sale.[58]

---

51 *Hunt* v *RM Douglas* [1990] 1 AC 398.
52 *Central Electricity* v *Bata Shoe* [1983] 1 AC 105.
53 Limitation (NI) Order 1989, Art.16(2).
54 Cf. *In re O'Neill* [1967] NI 129.
55 *Archdale* v *Anderson* (1888) 21 LR Ir 527.
56 *Kelly* v *Rice* (1904) 38 ILTR 193.
57 Trustee Act (NI) 1958, s.47.
58 *Ward* v *Ward* [1980] 1 WLR 4. See also the Law Reform (Husband and Wife) Act (NI) 1964, s.3(7).

15.21 *Receiver*. A receiver may be appointed to preserve, maintain and keep going any property such as a business concern which needs active care. See Order 30 (para. 11.83).

'Liberty to apply'

15.22 Some judgments, particularly interlocutory orders, or judgments in the Chancery Division, give the parties liberty to apply. This implies a right to apply only for the purpose of working out, putting into effect or enforcing the judgment.[59] It does not allow application to vary or set aside the judgment,[60] nor amendment of pleadings,[61] nor an inquiry as to damages from breach of the terms.[62] Liberty to apply is implied in any non-final order or a primary judgment.

---

[59] *Ulster Bank* v *Chambers* [1979] NI 1.
[60] *Thwaite* v *Thwaite* [1982] Fam 1.
[61] *Cox* v *Electricity Board (No 2)* [1943] IR 231.
[62] *Gallagher* v *Sloan* [1983] NI 78.

CHAPTER SIXTEEN

ENFORCEMENT AND PENAL PROVISIONS

ENFORCEMENT OF JUDGMENTS

16.00 Before judgment a plaintiff cannot do anything to ensure that money awarded to him can be effectively recovered, except as follows: (a) notice to Road Traffic insurer (para. 2.04); (b) application for *Mareva* injunction (para. 11.74); (c) application under Order 29 for preservation of the subject-matter of the dispute (para. 11.78); (d) application for appointment of a receiver to manage the business or fund in dispute (Ord.30 r.1); (e) in an action relating to land, registration of *lis pendens*;[1] (f) secure an order for payment into court as a condition for leave to defend on an Order 14 application.

16.01 After judgment there are several methods by which a judgment can be enforced, most of which are achieved through the Enforcement of Judgments Office (in this Chapter referred to as the "EJ Office"). The High Court has only a peripheral role in relation to proceedings in the EJ Office. Also in this Chapter "the JE Order" means the Judgments Enforcement (NI) Order 1981 and "the JE Rules" means the Judgments Enforcement Rules (NI) 1981.[2]

16.02 There is no need to serve the judgment or notice of it on the person liable,[3] save to enforce by committal or sequestration. It is his duty as a debtor to pay the creditor. The judgment creditor's solicitor has implied and ostensible authority to receive the money unless the creditor is under disability.[4] In paying the money awarded the defendant must deduct and pay directly to the DHSS the amount of the benefits in the 'CRU' certificate (see para. 14.66). Where a judgment or order grants relief subject to a condition, the party entitled is deemed to waive the benefit of the order if he fails to fulfil the condition (Ord.45 r.8), and the judgment cannot be enforced by the EJ Office (JE Rules, r.5(1)(c)). An order made in favour of, or against a person who is not a party to proceedings, may be enforced as if he were a party (Ord.45 r.7). A judgment affecting registered land can be inserted as a burden under the Land Registration Rules (NI) 1994 (r.85).

Stay of enforcement

16.03 A judgment takes effect on the day on which it is given (para. 15.06), but the judge can, on request of the defendant or by agreement, stay enforcement or postpone the date of the judgment. In the case of a money judgment it is normal to stay for three weeks, even if the judgment debtor is a

---

[1] JE Order 1981, Art.117. For unregistered land the Registration of Deeds Act (NI) 1970, s.3; SR 1971/86; and for registered land the Land Registration Rules (NI) 1994, r.91.

[2] SR 1981/147.

[3] *Ely* v *Moule* (1851) 5 Exch 918 (155 ER 401).

[4] White Book (1997) Vol. 2 [3881]; *Leather* v *Kirby* [1965] 1 WLR 1489.

large corporation or covered by insurance, to give time for a cheque to be delivered and cleared. If the judgment debtor cannot pay at once but will be able to gather up the money, he may ask for a longer stay. A stay can be given pending trial of a counterclaim, though rarely where judgment has been given at the trial.[5] It is doubtful if the Court can stay enforcement conditional upon payment of instalments.[6] Enforcement can be stayed by reason of matters occurring after judgment (Ord.45 r.9) even if the stay was part of a contractually agreed judgment; and the matter occurring must be something that would have justified a stay at the time of judgment.[7] If the Court stays enforcement on grounds of inability to pay forthwith, the court officer transmits a copy of the judgment to the EJ Office (JE Order, Art.116(3)). The EJ Office can stay enforcement under Articles 13(1)(f) and 14 of the JE Order and rules 27 and 103-5 of the JE Rules.

Restrictions

16.04 Leave of the Court is necessary to enforce a judgment -

(1) against a non-party bound by the judgment in a representative action (Ord.15 r.12);

(2) against a third party for contribution or indemnity by a defendant who has not yet satisfied the plaintiff's award (Ord.16 r.7(2));

(3) against a partner or individual trader's personal property when judgment is given against a firm (Ord.81 r.5; JE Order, Art.17(4));

(4) where judgment is given against a person in a name or style other than his own (Art.17(5));

(5) where the person's property is held in a name or style other than his own;[8]

(6) between a firm and its members or firms with common membership (JE Rules, r.5(1)(f)); and the Court may direct accounts and inquiries (Ord.81 r.6);

(7) on certain judgments against a defendant performing relevant service;[9]

(8) if there has been a change of parties entitled or liable since the judgment (JE Rules, r.5(1)(b)); there is no change of parties where one co-plaintiff jointly entitled dies;[10]

(9) against a personal representative on assets *quando acciderint*, against such assets (JE Rules, r.5(1)(g)).

Application for leave of the Court is made *ex parte* on affidavit unless the Court directs a summons (Ord.46 r.1).

---

5 *Schofield* v *Church Army* [1986] 1 WLR 1328, at 1335G.

6 *Brien* v *Sullivan* (1884) 14 LR Ir 391.

7 *Northern Bank* v *Jeffers*, Ch D, NI (Girvan J) 5 December 1996; [1996] 10 BNIL 67.

8 White Book (1997) 45/1/18.

9 Reserve and Auxiliary Forces (Protection of Civil Interests) Act 1951, s.2, as modifed for NI by SI 1979/291.

10 *Baird* v *Thomson* (1884) 14 LR Ir 497.

16.05 An amendment as to parties can be made by the Court after judgment under Order 15 rule 6(2). Where parties change by reason of death, bankruptcy etc., an order can be made under Order 15 rule 7 (see para. 11.36). The death of a party does not affect the right to enforce a judgment, even a judgment on a cause of action which abates on death such as defamation. Thus where an applicant for family provision dies, the claim abates on her death, but not her rights under an interim judgment already given.[11]

Matrimonial orders

16.06 Orders in the matrimonial jurisdiction can be enforced by the special provisions of the Family Proceedings Rules (NI) 1996 (r.8). Periodic payments can be enforced by the Court by committal under Article 107, or by attachment of earnings under Article 98 of the JE Order (and see Art.96A).

The Crown

16.07 The Crown can enforce a judgment (Crown Proceedings Act, s.26(1)); and the JE Order and Rules apply in its favour (s.26(2)). It is not liable for any process to execute a judgment against it; a person who obtains a judgment against the Crown, or Crown officer or Government Department, obtains a certificate from the proper officer of the Court within 21 days, which is served on the Crown's solicitor (s.25). A separate certificate for costs may be sought *ex parte* (Ord.77 r.14(2)). Nothing in Orders 45-52 applies to an order against the Crown (Ord.77 r.14(1)). Enactments and rules relating to stay of enforcement apply in Crown proceedings (s.22). Crown debts have priority against other judgment debts subsequently enforced.[12]

Other bodies

16.08 As to enforcement of judgments against the police, see the Police Act (NI) 1970 (s.14); against a member of the Armed Forces by deduction from pay, Army Act 1955 (s.151A); Air Force Act 1955 (s.151A); Naval Discipline Act 1957 (s.128E). Non-commercial property of a foreign state is immune from enforcement (State Immunity Act 1978, s.13). Property of a diplomat or on diplomatic premises is immune (see para. 3.20). As to enforcement against a corporation, see *Kearon* v *Dublin Port and Docks Board* (1906) 40 ILTR 74. Some property of a Trade Union or Employers' Association is immune from execution (Industrial Relations (NI) Order 1992, Art.23).

16.09 *Firms.* Judgment against a firm in the firm's name can only be enforced against the firm property (Partnership Act 1890, s.23(1)), except that, by leave of the Court obtained *ex parte*, it may be enforced against the property of a partner who has appeared as, admitted or been adjudged to be a partner or who was served as a partner and failed to appear (JE Order, Art.17(4); Ord.81 rr.5-6). (See also para. 3.15). On a judgment against a partner, the EJ Office can make an order charging his interest in the firm property and may appoint a receiver and direct accounts (1890 Act, s.23(2)).

---

[11] *In re O'Reilly* [1995] 6 BNIL 97.
[12] Crown Debts (Ir) Act 1781, s.4.

Against trustee/personal representative

16.10 A judgment against a personal representative is enforceable only against the assets of the estate. If in the action he has pleaded and proved '*plene administravit*' (that the estate does not have sufficient assets to meet the claim) judgment will be entered for enforcement against assets proved to be in his possession (i.e. '*de bonis testatoris*'). If there are uncollected assets or there is a possibility of assets to come in, the Court gives judgment against assets '*in futuro*' or '*quando acciderint*',[13] which cannot be enforced without leave of the Court (JE Rules, r.5(1)(g)). In reply to a defence of *plene administravit*, the plaintiff may allege and prove *devastavit* (i.e. that the personal representative had assets but has wasted or converted them), and judgment will be against his own property, '*de bonis testatoris et sinon de bonis propriis*'.[14] If the plaintiff alleges that the personal representative has improperly failed to collect in the assets, he must plead and prove it, whether in an ordinary action or an administration action, and the court will then give judgment for an account to be taken on the footing of wilful default.[15]

16.11 A judgment against an executor *de son tort* (one who has dealt with the deceased's estate as if a personal representative without having taken a grant) is liable to the value if assets shown to have been received by him; and against assets *quando acciderint*, without need for leave under rule 5(1)(g) of the JE Rules because an executor *de son tort* is not a legal personal representative.[16]

A trustee is chargeable only for the assets shown to have been received by him unless guilty of wilful default.[17]

Against defendant's insurer

16.12 Save as provided by statute, the plaintiff has no right to enforce his judgment against the defendant's insurer if for some reason the defendant does not claim or enforce his indemnity under his policy. The insurer's or any indemnifier's liability to indemnify is not a debt which can be attached under Article 69 of the JE Order,[18] though possibly a debt under a judgment against the insurer on the indemnity might be attached. Unfortunately, there is no power to order discovery of the identity of his insurer or other person liable to indemnify him, and the defendant cannot be compelled to disclose that information even if the plaintiff has a direct right against the insurer by statute.[19]

16.13 If the insured defendant goes bankrupt, or his estate is administered as insolvent, or he makes a composition with his creditors or a winding-up or receiver order is made, the plaintiff, having established the defendant's liability,[20] can enforce the defendant's right of indemnity against the insurer.

---

13 *Findlater* v *Tuohy* (1885) 16 LR Ir 474.
14 And if he has died, against his estate: Administration of Estates (NI) Order 1979, Art.40.
15 *Blount* v *O'Connor* (1886) 17 LR Ir 620.
16 *Westmeath* v *Coyne* [1896] 2 IR 436.
17 Trustee Act (NI) 1958, s.31(1).
18 *Israelson* v *Dawson* [1933] 1 KB 301.
19 *McKenna* v *Best Travel* [1995] 1 IR 577 (Murphy J).
20 By judgment or agreement: *Bradley* v *Eagle Star* [1989] AC 957.

This is because upon his bankruptcy etc., an insured person's right of indemnity against his insurer, whether incurred before or after the bankruptcy, vests in the party claiming against him, and is not affected by any settlement between the insured and the insurer made after the liability to the claimant was incurred.[21] The insured, his trustee in bankruptcy etc., have a duty to give information about the insurance to the claimant.[21] The claimant is subject to any defence that the insurer might have against the defendant.[22] The insurer's liability ceases if the defendant company is defunct.[23]

16.14 Liability for oil pollution by a ship under the Merchant Shipping Act 1995[24] can be enforced against the insurer under section 165 thereof, or against the International Oil Pollution Fund under section 175.

Road traffic insurer

16.15 The Road Traffic (NI) Order 1981[25] requires a person who uses or permits use of a motor vehicle on a public road to be insured for liability to any person who suffers personal injury or[25] damage to property (see para. 10.07). If due notice of the action has been given by the plaintiff to the insurer (see para. 2.04), any judgment against the owner or driver in respect of that liability can be enforced against the insurer unless enforcement is stayed pending appeal (Arts.98-98A). An insurer who has been served with notice is entitled to be added as a party (Art.98A(4)). An application for an order for an insurer to satisfy a judgment must be brought by motion on notice within six months of the date of judgment against the owner/driver (Ord.16 r.13(2)); but under the new Articles 98-98A as amended it seems that the insurer's liability to satisfy the judgment arises automatically without need for application to the Court.

16.16 Any liability for which it is not compulsory to insure, even if it is in the same insurance policy, cannot be claimed.[26] A person liable to the victim who pays his damages cannot enforce contribution from a joint tortfeasor's insurer.[27] The insurer can be liable even on a judgment against a person not covered by the insurance. The insurer cannot escape by reason of a term excluding liability for persons driving without a licence, nor by reason of having avoided or cancelled the policy or of a right to avoid or cancel the policy unless he has sued and obtained a declaration to that effect and given notice to the plaintiff (Art.98A(2)(3)). He cannot escape where he repudiates the policy for breach of condition.[28] He can escape if the policy was cancelled before the accident and the certificate surrendered within 14 days after cancellation (Art.98A(1)(c). The burden of proof lies on the claimant to show that the liability is within the scope of the insurance policy,[29] but lies on the insurer to escape liability.[30]

---

[21] Third Parties (Rights against Insurers) Act (NI) 1930.
[22] *Pioneer Concrete* v *NEMGIA* [1985] 2 All ER 395.
[23] *Dickson* v *Blackstaff Weaving* [1989] NI 197, at 205.
[24] See Sch.4 thereto for transitional provision.
[25] As amended by SR 1989/84.
[26] *McPherson* v *Fox* [1941] NI 163.
[27] *Campbell* v *McFarland* [1972] NI 31.
[28] *Motor & General* v *Pavy* [1994] 1 WLR 462 (PC).
[29] *Whelan* v *Dixon* [1963) 97 ILTR 195.
[30] *Bruce* v *Pascoe* (1940) 74 ILTR 14 (NI).

16.17 If a plaintiff cannot recover on the liability for which the Road Traffic Order requires insurance, he can sue the owner for breach of statutory duty to insure. If judgment against the tortfeasor is unsatisfied, the victim can claim on the undertaking of the Motor Insurer's Bureau to the Government.[31] As the MIB is under no legal obligation to the claimant, the rights under the undertakings are not justiciable in court,[32] though possibly its refusal to compensate may be subject to judicial review if wholly unreasonable.[33] However it is the common practice of the MIB to apply or consent to be added as a defendant, and waive its plea of no legal liability. It might do so for two reasons: (a) to ensure that the liability in negligence of the tortfeasor is contested; or (b) to obtain an opinion of the Court as to whether, under the terms of its undertaking, it should satisfy a judgment against the tortfeasor.[34]

RECIPROCAL ENFORCEMENT OF JUDGMENTS

Enforcement of Northern Ireland judgments abroad

16.18 It is a matter of the internal law of another state whether and how a judgment obtained in Northern Ireland can be sued upon in that state. Specific provision has been made by some states for enforcement by registration. A monetary judgment of the High Court can be enforced in certain Commonwealth and other countries under section 10 of the Administration of Justice Act 1920 and section 10 of the Foreign Judgments (Reciprocal Enforcement) Act 1933.[35] Application for a certified copy of the High Court judgment is made *ex parte* on affidavit to a master (Ord.71 r.11).

16.19 A monetary judgment can be enforced in countries which have enacted the Brussels Convention (see para. 1.14) under the Civil Jurisdiction and Judgments Act 1982;[36] application for a certified copy of the judgment is made *ex parte* on affidavit to the Court (Ord.71 r.32).[37] In the Republic of Ireland, the procedure for registering such judgment is set out in the Rules of the Superior Courts 1986,[38] Order 42A. A judgment (including a non-monetary judgment) may be enforced in England/Wales and Scotland under section 18 and Schedules 6 and 7; application is made for a certified copy of a monetary judgment (Sch.6 para..2 and Ord.71 r.33(3)), or non-monetary judgment (Sch.7 para. 2 and Ord.71 r.34(5)), and it can be registered in the English High Court under the English RSC Order 71 rules 37-8; or in the Scottish Court of Session under the Rules of the Court of Session[39] Chapter 62 rules 37, 38.

---

31 The Uninsured Drivers Agreement, 20 December 1989. The MIB has also undertaken to compensate victims of untraced drivers.

32 *Morrison* v *MIB* [1987] NI 204.

33 *Bowes* v *MIB* [1989] IR 225.

34 See *Bell* v *Bell* [1995] 9 BNIL 58 (Girvan J); and also *Doyle* v *Doris* [1993] 6 NIJB 1; *Wood* v *Cousins* [1993] 6 NIJB 41.

35 See the White Book (1997) 71/1/2-6.

36 Sch.1 Arts. 31- 49. The 1991 Act of the same name enacts the Lugano Convention which incorporates the Brussels text.

37 Rule made under s.12.

38 As amended by SI 1989/14.

39 SI 1994/1443.

16.20 Where a judgment has been or is to be enforced in the United Kingdom or in a Brussels Convention State, the courts of that part of the United Kingdom or of that State have exclusive jurisdiction over proceedings concerned with the enforcement of the judgment.[40]

Enforcement of foreign judgments in Northern Ireland

By action

16.21 At common law a foreign monetary judgment can be sued upon as a debt, if it is: (a) final, (b) within the territorial, procedural and substantive jurisdiction of the foreign court, (c) not a penal or revenue claim, (d) not repugnant to our law, and (e) not obtained by fraud or breach of natural justice. It cannot be enforced if in breach of an agreement to settle the dispute by other means (Civil Jurisdiction and Judgments Act 1982, s.32). A writ to enforce a judgment or arbitral award can by leave be issued for service outside Northern Ireland (Ord.11 r.1(1)(m)). No proceedings may be brought on a cause of action where judgment, enforceable here, has been given thereon between the parties or their privies in any court outside Northern Ireland (1982 Act, s.34).[41] Judgment is final though subject to appeal or liable to be set aside.[42] If an action is brought to enforce a judgment registrable under the 1920 Act, no costs are recoverable (s.9(5) thereof). An action cannot be brought to enforce a judgment registrable under the 1933 Act (s.6 thereof). There seems to be no ban on suing on a judgment registrable under the 1982 Act, save that a registrable judgment of England/Wales or Scotland cannot be enforced otherwise than by registration (s.18(8)).

By registration

16.22 Monetary judgments of specified Commonwealth and other countries can be registered under the Administration of Justice Act 1920 (s.9) or the Foreign Judgments (Reciprocal Enforcement) Act 1933 (s.2). Proceedings to enforce a judgment under the 1920 Act or the 1933 Act are set out in Order 71 rules 1-10. European Community judgments can be registered (SI 1972/1590, Ord.71 rr.13-21). Enforcement of monetary judgments in Brussels/Lugano Convention territories is by registration under the Civil Jurisdiction and Judgments Act 1982 (s.4; Sch.1 Arts.31-2); with appeal against the grant or refusal of registration to the High Court (Arts.36-7,40), with further appeal on point of law (Arts.37,41), to the Court of Appeal, or by 'leap-frog' to the House of Lords (s.6). For procedure see Order 71 rules 22-31. Application to enforce it by the EJ Office is accepted only after expiry of the time limit for appeal or after disposal of an appeal (JE Rules, r.5A). The 1982 Act is applied to "authentic instruments" and court settlements in courts outside the United Kingdom which are agreements between persons not drawn up as court orders.[43] See the notes to Order 71 in the White Book. The Brussels Convention does not apply to the recognition and enforcement of judgments

---

[40] Civil Jurisdiction and Judgments Act 1982, Sch.1 Art.16, Sch.4 Art.16.

[41] This is a procedural bar, not an extinction of the cause of action: *Republic of India* v *India Steamship* [1993] AC 410.

[42] *Sunday Newspapers* v *Deighan* [1989] 3 NIJB 51(CA).

[43] SI 1993/604.

obtained in non-Convention States.[44] Enforcement of judgments (monetary or non-monetary) of England/Wales and Scotland is by application to a 'proper officer' for registration, (1982 Act s.18; Schs.6 or 7; and Ord.71 rr.33-5, and the JE Order applies to such judgments for recovery of land or goods and to sequestratable judgments.[45]

16.23 *Enforcement of Foreign Arbitration Awards.* See the Arbitration Act 1950, sections 35-42; Arbitration (International Investment Disputes) Act 1966; Arbitration Act 1996, sections 99-104.[46]

Action to enforce domestic judgment

16.24 When a judgment is recovered on a cause of action, the cause merges into the judgment ('*transit in rem judicatem*') and is supplanted by it,[47] except in the case of an action for recovery of land.[48] An action can be brought in a court to enforce a judgment of the same or another court in Northern Ireland, subject to it being struck out if shown to be an abuse of process if the processes for enforcement of the judgment are fully available.[49] A judgment of any other court in Northern Ireland cannot be sued upon in the county court.[50] Irish cases have held that a county court decree can be sued upon in the High Court, unless expressly or impliedly removed by statute,[51] but it may be that the right to enforce any judgment under the JE Order constitutes implied removal. It is submitted that it is proper and fair that a defendant who is sued on a monetary claim should plead as a *counterclaim or set-off* an unsatisfied judgment debt due from the plaintiff. Where a fine or penalty has been imposed on a person now dead, the Crown can sue his personal representative for the sum as a debt.[52] If after obtaining a decree *de bonis testatoris* against a personal representative there are found to be no assets of the estate on which to execute it, the plaintiff can sue the personal representative alleging *devastavit.*[53]

APPLICATION TO THE EJ OFFICE

16.25 Before 1969 proceedings to enforce a judgment were in the hands of the creditor. Since then, though the methods of enforcement are the same, all enforcement proceedings to enforce civil judgments for payment of money, possession of land, recovery of goods, and foreign money judgments (JE Order, Art.4), except committal and sequestration, are taken through the Enforcement of Judgments Office, under the Judgments Enforcement (NI) Order 1981 and

---

44 *Owens Bank* v *Bracco* [1994] QB 509 (ECJ).
45 SR 1986/360.
46 Replacing, in respect of arbitrations commenced on or after 31 January 1997, the Arbitration Act 1975, ss.3-6.
47 *Jones* v *Horne* (1852) 4 Ir Jur OS 203.
48 *Derham* v *Doyle* [1914] 2 IR 135.
49 *Gerrard* v *Beggan* (1857) 2 Ir Jur NS 311; *E.D. & F. Man (Sugar)* v *Haryanto*, 'The Times' 9 August 1996 (CA).
50 County Courts (NI) Order 1980, Art.37.
51 *Carey* v *Grispi* (1858) 9 ICLR 25; but see *English* v *Murphy* (1941) 75 ILTR 128 (no action lies in High Court on a District Court decree).
52 *AG* v *Mines* [1943] NI 66.
53 *Barron* v *Ryan* (1907) 41 ILTR 39, because the personal representative did not raise *plene administravit.*

Rules (NI) 1981 (the 'JE Order' and 'JE Rules').[54] Fees are payable for applications to the EJ Office.[55] Subject to the JE Order, the old jurisdiction of the courts in relation to the enforcement of judgments is vested in the EJ Office (JE Order, Art.11).[56] A party seeking to enforce a judgment can seek a copy of it under Order 42 rule 10. There is no need to serve the judgment or notice of it on the defendant, unless enforcing by committal or sequestration.

16.26 Application is made by a person entitled to enforce the judgment under Article 22 and rules 6-11, on payment of the appropriate fee. It cannot be accepted if the restrictions stated in Article 17 and rule 5 operate; for example, that necessary leave of court to enforce has not been obtained; that a stay of enforcement is in force; that the judgment is subject to a condition not yet fulfilled. After being enforceable for six years, leave of the EJ Office is necessary; and notice of the application to the debtor is usually required.[57] After 12 years, it cannot be enforced at all. The EJ Office cannot refuse to enforce a judgment on the ground that it contains "liberty to apply".[58] It seems that refusal by the EJ Office to enforce can be appealed only to the Court of Appeal on point of law under Article 140. *Semble*, it can be challenged by judicial review.

16.27 *Powers of the EJ Office*. Under Article 16 of the JE Order the EJ Office can enforce a judgment by instalment order; seizure and sale of goods; charge on land;[59] order to deliver possession of land (on a judgment for same); order for delivery of goods (on a judgment for same); charging order on and vesting and disposal of funds, shares etc.;[60] debenture order; stop order on funds in court; restraining order on shares; partnership order; appointment of receiver; attachment of debts owed to the debtor by a "garnishee", including a bank account;[61] attachment of earnings.

16.28 The mode of enforcing a money judgment is the choice of the EJ Office. It has procedural powers to issue a warrant taking custody of goods; require information and examine the debtor and others as to his means; make an administration order where the debtor cannot pay his debts; execute documents in the name of the debtor; give and set side a certificate of unenforceability; keep a registry of judgments. A certificate of unenforceability is conclusive evidence of inability to pay, on which a winding-up petition or bankruptcy

---

54 See para. 16.01.

55 See SR 1996/101. On a judgment over £10,000 it is £645 + £1.80 per £100 over £10,000.

56 Enforcement of matrimonial orders is a separa.te matter governed by Articles 96A-105 and 107 of the JE Order and the FP Rules r.8; and the Maintenance and Affiliation Orders Act (NI) 1966, ss.9-16.

57 Cf. *National Bank* v *Cullen* [1894] 2 IR 683. In respect of a judgment against a 'squatter' under Ord.113, leave of the Court is necessary to enforce it after three months: JE Rules, r.5(1)(h).

58 *Ulster Bank* v *Chambers* [1979] NI 1.

59 Statutory interest runs from the date of the registration of the order: Ord.42 r.9(3).

60 Statutory interest runs from the date of the charging order: Ord.42 r.9(3).

61 It does not include a debt on which the judgment debtor's right is held jointly with another person: *Belfast Telegraph* v *Blunden* [1995] 10 BNIL 48 (CA).

petition can be founded.[62] The EJ Office seeks to recover: (a) the money payable under the judgment, (b) interest at 8 per cent per annum from the date of judgment, (c) the creditor's costs of enforcement and (d) its own expenses (JE Order, Art.126). The EJ Office can set off cross-judgments (Art.128). Interpleader proceedings may be taken in the EJ Office where there is doubt as to whom the judgment debt should be paid (para. 16.36).

16.29 A judgment for possession of land is enforceable by the EJ Office making an order for possession (JE Order, Art.53). The EJ Office gives notice of intention to make such an order to the parties and to any person in actual possession (JE Rules, r.35). A judgment for delivery of goods is enforceable by order for delivery (JE Order, Art.57; JE Rules, r.39). Such judgments are enforceable even if they do not command the defendant to deliver up within a stated time, that being essential only to enforcement by committal or sequestration. A judgment for possession of land entitles the EJ Office to eject any person in possession, whether the defendant or not.[63] If the EJ Office delivers possession of land a person claiming an interest may apply to the EJ Office for possession, and the EJ Office may refer it to the High Court (Art.56).

16.30 A summons or order to attend before the EJ Office can be enforced by warrant of arrest (Arts.27-9). Any contumelious behaviour and any failure to answer or produce documents may be referred to the High Court and treated like contempt of the High Court (Art.114). Any order of the EJ Office has like effect as a High Court order (Art.15). If the debtor fails to execute a document ordered by the EJ Office, the EJ Office may direct someone else to do so for him (Art.139).

16.31 Appeal lies to the High Court from some decisions of the EJ Office[64] and otherwise on point of law to the Court of Appeal[65] (Art.140). Presumably its decisions are subject to judicial review.

Admitted debt procedure for public debts

16.32 If a creditor claims a "sum certain" not exceeding £3,000, he may, without court action, apply directly to the EJ Office and the EJ Office may summon the debtor; if the debtor admits the debt or does not respond, the EJ Office may enforce the debt as if it were a judgment (JE Order, Arts. 95-6). If the debtor attends and disputes the debt, or gives written notice of dispute, or claims a set-off or counterclaim, no enforcement can be had. Procedure is governed by the Judgments Enforcement (Recovery of Admitted Debts) Rules (NI) 1985.[66] Rule 7 restricts the procedure to debts due to the Crown, a Government Department, or local or public authority, excluding rates. The procedure cannot be used against a minor, patient, or person outside Northern Ireland, nor if the debtor is dead.

---

62 Insolvency (NI) Order 1989, Art.103(1)(b) and Art.242(1)(b). It used to be called 'an act of bankruptcy': see *In re Crossey* [1975] NI 1.

63 *R* v *Wandsworth County Court ex p Wandsworth LBC* [1975] 1 WLR 1314.

64 As in *Ulster Bank* v *Chambers* [1979] NI 1.

65 As in *Belfast Telegraph* v *Blunden* [1995] 10 BNIL 48.

66 SR 1985/78.

Court proceedings relating to EJ Office enforcement

16.33 The Chancery Division can enforce by sale or possession a charge on land made by the EJ Office under Article 46 to enforce a judgment debt (JE Order, Art.52). Application is by originating summons with an affidavit stating the matters listed in Order 88 rule 5A. The Court will give a primary judgment and direct enquiries as to prior encumbrances. Under Article 52 the Court will be able to order partition or sale in lieu thereof, so that if the debtor's interest in the property is owned along with an undivided share with another, such as his wife, the creditor can sue for partition against the wife.[67] The charge imposed by the EJ Office is subject to any prior equitable interest unless the creditor shows that after some investigation he has no actual or constructive notice.[68] It is also subject to statutory provisions such as the Administration of Justice Acts 1970 and 1973 relating to dwelling houses (see para.18.73). Having some of the powers of a mortgagee, the creditor can also sue by ordinary action for recovery of land, but relief may be refused if there are prior encumbrances (see para.18.75).

16.34 Articles 62-5 of the JE Order provide for enforcement of a monetary judgment by the EJ Office making a 'stop order' freezing funds, money or stocks in Court in which the judgment debtor has an interest. The Court may on application apply the funds in satisfaction of the judgment, or discharge the order (Art.65). Indeed Order 50 allows any person who has a mortgage or charge on another person's interest in court funds to apply to the Court to make a stop order. An Order 50 summons must be served on the Accountant-General.

16.35 Money due to the debtor by the Crown can be attached by order of the EJ Office (Crown Proceedings Act, s.27) or, in matrimonial proceedings only,[69] by the Court by summons under Order 77 rule 15. One NI or UK Government Department cannot attach a debt due by another NI or UK Department because in law the Crown is one person.[69]

16.36 If another person claims an interest in property taken from the debtor, the debtor may apply by 'interpleader' to the EJ Office, which may refer the claim for hearing by the High Court or a county court, or lodge proceeds in court (Art.44).[70] If the EJ Office delivers possession of land a person claiming an interest may apply to the EJ Office for possession, and the EJ Office may refer it to the High Court (Art.56).

OTHER METHODS OF ENFORCING A MONEY JUDGMENT

16.37 An order to pay money is not enforceable by committal for contempt, but a party in default is nonetheless a party in contempt,[71] if a time for payment is specified.

---

[67] Property (NI) Order 1997, Art.48 (*not yet in force*); overruling *Northern Bank* v *Haggarty* [1995] 5 BNIL 64.

[68] *Allied Irish* v *McWilliams* [1982] NI 156.

[69] *McAllister* v *NI Office* [1988] NI 606.

[70] The Crown may interplead: Crown Proceedings Act, s.16.

[71] *Leavis* v *Leavis* [1921] P 299.

16.38 A judgment debt, like any due debt can found a 'statutory demand' which replaces the former debtor's summons.[72] Failure of the debtor to pay the debt is conclusive evidence of inability to pay on which a bankruptcy petition can be founded.[73] It is improper to use this device as a means of extorting a debt, and it should only be used *bona fide* where it is believed that the debtor may be insolvent. The demand should be for the balance of the debt now due if the debtor has paid part of the judgment.[74] It may induce the defendant to pay up quickly, but if not it may mean that the plaintiff ends up as one of several unsecured creditors chasing the assets. In the case of a company, a creditor can make a statutory demand, failure to pay being grounds for winding up under the Insolvency (NI) Order 1989 (Art.103(1)(a)), or grounds for a petition for administration (Art.21(1)).

Order to pay money into court

16.39 A judgment or order to pay money into court within a limited time can be enforced by sequestration (JE Order, Art.111); by appointment of a receiver, or if the order specifies a time limit for paying, by committal (Ord.45 r.2). Failure to pay into court is proved by certificate of the Accountant-General.[75]

COMMITTAL POWERS ON MONEY JUDGMENT

Where debtor has means

16.40 Save under Article 107 and Article 115 or by other statute, a person cannot be arrested or imprisoned for default in payment of a money judgment or an instalment thereof (JE Order Art.106).[76] The High Court can commit to prison until payment but not exceeding six weeks, any person who makes default: (a) in payment of the amount due or recoverable on foot of a judgment of any court; or (b) in payment of any one or more instalments due under an instalment order made by the EJ Office or by a court under Article 107(3); or (c) in payment of an amount due under a matrimonial periodic payment order of the High Court or divorce county court (Art.107(1)).[77] It includes money due under a judgment for costs.[78] If the amount due is on judgment enforceable through the EJ Office, the Court cannot act unless application has been first made to the EJ Office (Art.107(2)(c)). There is no time limit for applying, except possibly the six years for an action to enforce a judgment under Article 16(1) of the Limitation (NI) Order 1989.[79] *Quaere*, the person is not in default of payment unless the judgment has stated a time for payment.

---

[72] See Hunter's *Personal Insolvency*, Chap.6.
[73] Insolvency (NI) Order 1989, Art.242(1)(a); which used to be called an 'act of bankruptcy'.
[74] *In re Miller* [1912] 3 KB 1.
[75] White Book (1997) 45/1/4.
[76] Arts.106 and 107 apply to money payable to the Crown: Crown Proceedings Act, s.26(2A).
[77] In respect of a non-matrimonial judgment of the High Court, where not more than £15,000 is due, a county court may do so: Art.107(2), amended SR 1993/282.
[78] *Gillespie* v *Reid* (1894) 28 ILTR 140.
[79] Art.16(1) applies to an 'action ... upon a judgment', action being defined to include any proceeding (other than criminal proceedings) in a court established by law (*ibid.* Art.2(2)). The identical English equivalent of Art.16 does not apply to proceedings such as a warrant of possession to enforce a judgment: *National Westminster* v *Powney* [1991] Ch 339, at

16.41 In the High Court applications under Articles 107-110 of the JE Order are assigned to the Queen's Bench Division, or if on foot of a matrimonial order, to the Family Division. The procedure is for the person entitled to enforce the judgment to apply for a 'judgment summons', by filing an affidavit of the amount due (Ord.111 r.2). The summons is then issued and served personally on the debtor with a sum for his travel expenses, at least 10 days before the return day (Ord.111 r.3), which he must obey. No order can be made under Article 107 unless it is proved that the debtor has or has had (or would have but for his own act or default) since the date of the judgment/instalment order, the means to pay the judgment debt or part of it or the instalment due, and that he has neglected or refused to pay (Art.107(4)). The evidence may be oral or on affidavit (Ord.111 r.4). Means may be proved in such manner as the Court thinks fit;[80] for that purpose, the debtor and any witness may be summoned and examined on oath (Art.108(2)). Means to pay money due under an instalment order made by the EJ Office or the Court is presumed unless rebutted (Art.108(1)). As it involves the liberty of the subject the hearing must be by a judge, not a master. There is a discretion to refuse an order.[81] An Article 107 order cannot be made in respect of an amount due on a judgment on which an attachment of earnings order has been made (Art.107(5)). The expenses paid to the debtor to attend may be allowed as witness expenses (of the applicant); but if no committal order is made, the judge may allow the debtor his costs of attendance (Ord.111 r.5). If the summons is dismissed the judge may award the debtor his legal costs, but only in exceptional circumstances.[82]

16.42 At the hearing the judge may make one of the following types of order-

(1) He may make an immediate order of committal. This is rare as it will hardly assist the purpose of the proceedings.

(2) An order of committal may be stayed on terms that the debtor pay the debt or instalment(s) due, and costs, within a stated time or by instalments (Art.107(3(c); Ord.111 r.6). The debtor may apply for a further stay (Ord.111 r.8). If the creditor files an affidavit that the debtor has defaulted, the order of committal can then be issued (Ord.111 r.7).

(3) He may direct payment by instalments and thereupon dismiss the summons (Art.107(3)(a)), and in default of payment the applicant may issue a new judgment summons.

(4) He may direct instalments and adjourn the hearing (Art.107(3)(b)), and in default the applicant can ask for committal when the hearing is resumed.

(5) He may make an attachment of earnings order (Art.98(b)), and before doing so may require the debtor and his employer to give details of his employment (Art.103).

353-7 (CA); but does apply to a statutory demand commencing bankruptcy or winding-up proceedings: *In re a Debtor* [1997] 2 WLR 57 (Ch D, Judge Baker QC).

80 Including hearsay: *Johnson* v *Sandiford* (1897) 31 ILT 392.

81 *Kennedy* v *Connick* (1912) 46 ILTR 67 (greater debt owed by applicant to the debtor).

82 *McLaughlan* v *Brown* (1878) 12 ILT 89.

16.43 An order of committal is directed to a police officer or other person (Ord.111 r.11). Any order made by the Court must be personally served by the creditor on the debtor (Ord.111 r.10). A copy of any order under Articles 107 or 98 must be transmitted to the EJ Office (Art.116(3)). Any order may be stayed, varied or rescinded by a subsequent order (Ord.111 r.9). Appeal lies (only) by a person committed to prison, from the High Court to the Court of Appeal (Art.110). The debtor is released in accordance with Article 109 and Order 111 rule 12 when he has paid the debt or instalment for which he was committed, and costs. If he does not pay, he must be released at the end of the term set by the Court, which must not exceed six weeks. Imprisonment does not extinguish any debt or the rights under the JE Order (Art.125). *Quaere* whether this means that he can be committed again in respect of the same amount for which he has already served imprisonment. He can be committed separately for each unpaid instalment.[83]

Trustees and solicitors

16.44 In the following cases, under the Article 115 of the JE Order,[84] it is contempt of the High Court to default in payment under an order of the Court to pay money, and the Court may commit to prison for a period or periods not exceeding one year in all, or until payment (whichever happens first) -[85]

(1) To pay a non-contractual penalty or sum in nature of a penalty.

(2) To pay money held by a trustee or fiduciary in his possession or control. This includes a solicitor, agent, receiver, but not a director or partner. The order to pay must be to the person to whom the fiduciary duty is owed.[86] It means actual, not notional money,[87] which he has or did have.

(3) By a solicitor to pay costs of misconduct in his professional capacity[88] or to pay money in his capacity as officer of the court.

(4) To pay money due in respect of estate duties.[89]

16.45 He is only liable if the order commanded him to pay and stated a time limit.[90] His ability to pay is only a factor in the Court's discretion. The procedure for enforcement is exactly the same as for any order to do a positive act (see paras. 16.49-16.53). The order must be personally served with a penal notice: it must specify the money due but not necessarily the grounds on which Article 115 applies. The notice of motion to commit is served personally and at the hearing the evidence must show how Article 115 applies, unless it is obvious from previous proceedings in the action.[91] The order of committal must show how Article 115 applies; and must specify a term not exceeding 12 months. Committal does not extinguish the debt or the right to make any

---

83 *Faley* v *O'Mahony* [1929] IR 1.
84 Art.115 applies to an order to pay to the Crown: Crown Proceedings Act, s.26(2B).
85 See White Book (1997) 45/1/24.
86 *Taaffe* v *Fitzsimmons* [1894] 1 IR 63.
87 *Hickey* v *Kelly* [1929] IR 628.
88 Acting on behalf of a client: *Re M* (1878) 1 LR Ir 188.
89 Crown Proceedings Act, s.26(2B)(b).
90 *Gilbert* v *Endean* (1878) 9 Ch D 259, at 266.
91 *Kelly* v *Kelly* (1874) IR 8 Eq 497.

application under the JE Order (Art.125 thereof), but, *semble*, the debtor cannot be committed again for default of the same order for payment.[92] Once the debtor has been dealt with for his default and still does not pay, the creditor should apply for a new order to pay. Appeal lies under section 44 of the Judicature Act.

NON-MONETARY JUDGMENTS

16.46 A judgment or order in the nature of an injunction, whether final or interlocutory, is enforceable by committal for civil contempt if it is so worded that the person against whom it is made is expressly commanded to do, or not to do something. A judgment that "X shall recover possession of land from Y" is declaratory not coercive, but a judgment that "Y shall deliver possession of lands to X" is coercive.[93] Forms of judgment in the High Court now adopt the latter. A finding of contempt cannot be made against the Crown directly, but can be made against a Government Department or minister in his official capacity.[94] The procedures for enforcing an order of a civil court are unwieldy and easily flouted. There is no summary power for the police or any court official or other person to force compliance or arrest for non-compliance: the only way to induce compliance is the threat of being summoned to the Court and punished for disobedience. Some statutory exceptions are made to this, for example the Protection from Harassment (NI) Order 1997 (the anti-stalking statute, *not yet in force*) which provides in Article 5 thereof that the court which grants such injunction may issue a warrant of arrest if the plaintiff shows that there are reasonable grounds for believing that the defendant has breached the injunction. Certain acts can be directly enforced by being done by some one else on the defaulter's behalf (see para.16.59).

16.47 A person, including a party, who deliberately acts so as to set at naught any order of a court is guilty of criminal contempt.[95] Any person who contumaciously disregards or helps or incites another to disregard a declaratory order is liable in contempt.[96] Though an order is not normally enforceable against a party unless a copy of the order has been served under the rules, contempt proceedings lie against a party who is shown to be actually aware of a prohibitive injunction, or against any person who with actual notice of the injunction steps into his shoes and does the prohibited act,[97] or who aids and abets the party to do the act.[98] An order made in favour of, or against a person who is not a party to proceedings, may be enforced as if he were a party (Ord.45 r.7), so that, *semble,* such a person is liable in civil contempt. A non-party to whom the court order is not addressed can only be guilty of criminal

---

92 *Church's Trustee* v *Hibbard* [1902] 2 Ch 784.
93 See White Book (up to 1988 ed.) 42/1/2.
94 *M* v *Home Office* [1994] 1 AC 377, at 424-5.
95 *Smith* v *Molloy* [1905) 39 ILTR 221. In effect, therefore, an injunctive order is enforceable against a non-party: *MacMillan Bloedel* v *Simpson* (1996) 137 DLR 4th 633 (SC Canada).
96 *Webster* v *Southwark LBC* [1983] QB 698.
97 White Book (1997) 45/7/8.
98 *Johnston* v *Moore* [1965] NI 128, where it was treated as civil contempt.

contempt.[99] In *In re Cook (No 2)*,[100] Hutton J said that when councillors voted for and passed a resolution to disobey an order against the City Council, they are in contempt themselves, but he did not say whether their contempt is civil or criminal. In so far as the contempt is criminal it is an arrestable offence and under the Police and Criminal Evidence (NI) Order 1989 (Art.26) a police officer and any citizen can arrest a person committing such contempt.[101]

16.48 A '*prohibitive*' order requiring a person to abstain from doing an act is enforceable by committal if he disobeys it (Ord.45 r.4(1)(b)). No time limit need be stated.[102] A '*mandatory*' order requiring a person to do an act within a time specified under Order 42 rules 4 or 5, is enforceable by sequestration (JE Order, Art.111), or by committal, if he refuses or neglects to so do it (Ord.45 r.4). A mandatory order is valid but unenforceable by committal unless and until a time limit is fixed by the order itself (Ord.42 r.4(1)(a)), or by a supplemental order (Ord.42 rr.4(2), 5).[103] The time limit may be a certain day, or X days/weeks after service of the order. "Forthwith" is a sufficiently certain expression of time and means as soon as reasonably possible after service of the order.[104]

16.49 Enforcement can be had only if a copy of the order (and any supplementary order altering or fixing a time) is served on him personally. The copy order must be indorsed with a 'penal notice' warning him that he is liable to process to compel obedience (Ord.45 r.5). The penal notice should be worded in the form set out in the White Book (1997) 45/7/6. Failure to serve the copy order and the penal notice together is fatal to committal.[105] There is no contempt of a mandatory order if it is not served before the time limit for compliance.[106] An order against a party under disability must be personally served on him, unless the Court otherwise orders (Ord.80 r.13(4)). An order can be served outside Northern Ireland on the same conditions as a writ can (Ord.11 r.9(4)). The Court may dispense with service of the copy order "if it thinks it just to do so" (Ord.45 r.5(7)), or order substituted service (Ord.65 r.4). Where an order is made against a husband and wife or two co-habitees, there being a risk that one will intercept mail, the Court should order

---

99 *Moore* v *AG (No 2)* [1930] IR 471, at 486-7; *AG* v *Times Newspapers* [1992] 1 AC 191, at 217-8.

100 [1986] NI 283, at 285H-286D.

101 *MacMillan Bloedel* v *Simpson* (1996) 137 DLR 4th 633 (SC Canada) held that the police can arrest for any contempt of a court order if the order so provides.

102 *Murphy* v *Willcocks* [1911] 1 IR 402.

103 On a strictly literal interpretation of Ord.45 r.4, it does not apply if an order requiring an act to be done did not state a time and the time is fixed subsequently under Ord.42 r.5. The jurisdiction to fix a time limit subsequently where none was fixed is also inherent: *Needham* v *Needham* (1842) 1 Hare 633 (66 ER 1183), *affd.* 12 LJ Ch 378.

104 *In re Hogan (No 2)* [1986] 9 NIJB 45, at 51.

105 *Iberian Trust* v *Founders Trust* [1932] 2 KB 87; *Prior* v *Johnston* (1893) 27 ILTR 108. Orders of discovery or interrogatories need only be served on the party's solicitor: see paras.11.120 and 11.127.

106 Ord.45 r.5(2)(b); *Century Insurance* v *Larkin* [1910] 1 IR 91; *McClure* v *McClure* [1951] IR 137.

substituted service by post only if personal service is impossible and if absolutely certain that the form of service will ensure notification to both parties.[107] Service can be dispensed with only in exceptional circumstances, as where the respondent is aware of the order and is evading service;[108] but otherwise a mandatory order must always be served even if the respondent was personally in court when it was pronounced.[106] A direction to dispense with service of a mandatory order under Order 45 rule 5(7) can be made at any time whether before or after the alleged breach.[109] A prohibitive order may be enforced before service if the Court is satisfied that the person was present when the order was made or was notified of its terms by telephone or otherwise (Ord.45 r.5(6)). Service of a prohibitory order may be dispensed with if the respondent has knowingly breached it before it was served.[110] A prohibitory order is effective and falls to be obeyed when it is pronounced in court though not yet drawn up and signed.[111]

16.50 To be guilty of civil contempt, the breach of an order does not have to be contumacious, but the party's conduct must be more than casual or accidental.[112] It is no defence that the order is irregular: it must be obeyed unless set aside.[113]

16.51 A person liable on a non-monetary judgment can be ordered to attend to be examined on oath in aid of enforcement (Ord.48).[114] If the order to attend is served personally and 'conduct money' tendered to him, he is in contempt if he does not appear.

16.52 An order for possession of land is enforceable by the EJ Office under Article 53 of the JE Order, or if the order commands the giving of possession within a specified time, by committal (Ord.45 r.3). So also an order for delivery of goods.

Committal and other punishment

16.53 Where an order of the Supreme Court is enforceable by committal, the person liable, the 'contemnor', may be punished under Order 52 by a single judge, *by application for which no prior leave is necessary*[115] (Ord.52 rr.1(3),2(1)). The Court of Appeal has no jurisdiction to enforce its appellate orders by committal; application is made to the Court appealed from.[116] It is made by notice of motion stating the grounds supported by affidavit, to be

---

107 *Abbey National* v *Grugan*, Ch D, NI (Girvan J) 7 March 1997.

108 *In re Hogan (No 2)* [1986] 9 NIJB 45, at 52-3.

109 *Davy International* v *Tazzyman*, 'The Times' 9 May 1997 (CA), treating *Lewis* v *Lewis* [1991] 1 WLR 235 as *per incuriam*.

110 *United Telephone* v *Dale* (1884) 25 Ch D 778.

111 Cf. *Baxter Laboratories* v *Cutter Ltd* (1984) 2 DLR 4th 621.

112 *Heaton's Transport* v *TGWU* [1973] AC 15, at 109.

113 *Isaacs* v *Robertson* [1985] AC 97; *Re Battersby* (1892) 31 LR Ir 73.

114 As in *Butterly* v *Cuming* [1898] 1 IR 196 (for the defendant to identify the property ordered to be sold).

115 Practitioners please note.

116 *In re Cook (No 2)* [1986] NI 283, at 285G.

served personally on the respondent;[117] the judge may order substituted service or dispense with service (Ord.52 r.4). The motion should be issued out of the Crown Office if the order was made in a Queen's Bench case, *or out of the appropriate Office if the order was made in Chancery or Family Division proceedings*. The notice is served on the person sought to be committed, that is, the party in default or the non-party who has breached the order,[118] or the director or officer liable for contempt by a corporation.[119] The notice must give a sufficient description of the contempt.[120] A notice of motion for committal can be brought *ex parte* under Order 8 rule 2, but only in the most exceptional circumstances, as where any delay would cause irreparable prejudice.[121]

16.54 The Court must sit in open court unless the application arises out of proceedings relating to a minor or patient, or secret process or invention, or if necessary in the interests of justice or national security; if heard in chambers, any order of committal must be stated in open court (Ord.52 r.8(1)(2)). The respondent may give evidence if he expresses a wish to do so (Ord.52 r.8(4)). He is not compellable as a witness, save that if he has filed an affidavit he can be compelled to be cross-examined on it.[122] If the respondent fails to appear, the Court may commit him if it thinks just (Ord.52 r.5). Urgent applications can be heard during vacation (Ord.64 r.4). The applicant's affidavit must prove: (a) service of the copy order and penal notice, unless that is dispensed with; (b) service of the notice of motion to commit, if the contemnor does not appear; and (c) the act or omission which constitutes breach of the order. The contempt must be proved beyond reasonable doubt,[123] but that "does not mean that the extent of the breach need be great".[124] The judge can summons and call witnesses of his own motion.[125] If the contempt is civil, the statutes relating to civil evidence apply, and, at least if the order breached is an interlocutory order, the committal application is interlocutory and hearsay is admissible in affidavits.[126] The rule against double jeopardy applies: the respondent cannot be punished if he has already been adjudicated upon on the merits for the same contempt.[127] If he has been punished for failing to perform a mandatory order within the time limit stated, the contempt has been dealt with, and he cannot be committed again on the same order.[128] See further para. 16.82.

---

[117] Even if he is under disability, unless the Court otherwise orders: Ord.80 r.13(4).

[118] *O'Neill* v *McErlean* (1896) 30 ILTR 162.

[119] *Iberian Trust* v *Founders Trust* [1932] 2 KB 87.

[120] *Chiltern DC* v *Keane* [1985] 1 WLR 619.

[121] *Doyle* v *Commonwealth* (1985) 156 CLR 510.

[122] *Comet Products* v *Hawkex Plastics* [1971] 2 QB 67.

[123] *Dean* v *Dean* [1987] 1 FLR 517, which says that civil contempt was a common law misdemeanour.

[124] *Per* Lowry J, *Irish Bonding* v *Belfast Securities*, Ch D, NI, 23 December 1965; (1966) 17 NILQ 288.

[125] *Yianni* v *Yianni* [1966] 1 WLR 120.

[126] *Savings Bank* v *Gasco BV* [1988] Ch 423.

[127] *El Capistrano* v *ATO* [1989] 1 WLR 471.

[128] *Kumari* v *Jalal* [1996] 4 All ER 65 (CA). The proper course is for the Court to make a new order requiring the act to be done within a new time limit.

16.55 The judge can commit to prison, which must be for a fixed period not exceeding two years,[129] or impose an unlimited monetary fine (see para. 16.83). The Court can suspend committal on stated terms, or order consecutive or concurrent periods for separate contempts.[130] As the primary purpose in civil contempt is to induce compliance rather than to punish, committal should be refused if the court order can be enforced in other ways.[131] Since the Contempt of Court Act 1981, committal for an indefinite period, or "till further order" is unlawful; but presumably the Court can order committal for a fixed period or until further order within that period.[132] An order of committal must recite service or waiver of service of the notice of motion,[133] and state particulars of the contempt.[134] It must identify the contemnor sufficiently, by name or otherwise.[135] At the end of the period the contemnor is automatically released. Before that he may be released on his own application or by application of the Official Solicitor, if he has purged his contempt or if further detention is useless, as where he is exploiting his imprisonment as a martyr.[136]

16.56 Instead of committing to prison, the Court may impose a fine, or accept an undertaking from the contemnor, or grant a further injunction; or if he is likely to comply in future, it may make no order and award costs to the applicant.[137] A fine can be suspended.[138] A fine against a council should bear some relation to the number of councillors.[139] If the contemnor is not complying with an order because it would in effect put him out of business, which is no defence, the best course is to impose a committal suspended for a period so that he can cease his operations; a fine would be inappropriate because the contemnor will either pay it and carry on, or comply with the order in which case the fine will be an extra penalty.[140] A fine is enforceable under the Fines (Ir) Act 1851. In punishing for a contempt, the Court can impose a daily fine for each further day on which it continues.[141]

Orders against corporate bodies

16.57 A company or corporation cannot be committed to prison for disobedience of a court order. By Article 113 of the JE Order an order, prohibitive or mandatory, against a corporate body, including for payment of money, can be enforced by sequestration if Order 45 rule 5 is complied with by serving a copy of the order on its officer (Ord.45 r.5(3)). The same

---

[129] Or one year if committing for non-payment of money under the JE Order, Art.115.

[130] *Lee* v *Walker* [1985] QB 1191.

[131] *Danchevsky* v *Danchevsky* [1975] Fam 17.

[132] Cf. *Delaney* v *Delaney*, para. 16.83.

[133] *Wright* v *Jess* [1987] 1 WLR 1076.

[134] *Chiltern DC* v *Keane* [1985] 1 WLR 619.

[135] *Doyle* v *Commonwealth* (1985) 156 CLR 510.

[136] *Enfield LBC* v *Mahoney* [1983] 1 WLR 749.

[137] *Gore-Booth* v *Gore-Booth* (1962) 96 ILTR 32.

[138] *In re Cook (No 2)* [1986] NI 283, at 288H.

[139] *In re Morrow* [1987] 3 NIJB 16, at 20.

[140] *PJ Holdings* v *Gilroy* [1985] 12 NIJB 39, at 62-3, *affd.*[1986] 3 NIJB 100.

[141] So held in *Australasian Meat Employees* v *Mudginberri Station Pty* [1987] LRC (Crim) 587; (1986) 161 CLR 98 (HC of Aus).

requirements as to service of the copy order and penal notice apply as for committal of a human party.[142] Under an Article 113 order against a company, the Court may also prohibit the debtor from receiving money due by the Crown.[143] Also a corporate body can be summoned to answer for its contempt,[144] and can be fined.[145] If the order is of a type for which a human person could be committed, application can be made to commit a director or officer on whom the copy order has been served.[146] A company is vicariously liable for acts of contempt by its employees even if the directors have tried to stop them.[147]

Sequestration

16.58 This is an order whereby a sequestrator enters the lands and premises of the person in contempt and seizes the rents, profits and personal property until the person complies with the court order. It is available for any judgment against a company (see above). Against a human person it lies for contempt in failing to comply with any judgment to pay money into court, or to do an act (other than payment of money) within a limited time (JE Order, Art.111). As with enforcement by committal, there are the same requirements for service of the order and penal notice before the expiry of the time limit. There is no power to sequestrate against a human for breach of a prohibitory order.[148] The application for sequestration is by notice of motion to a judge on affidavit, served personally on the person whose property is to be seized: service may be dispensed with if it is just to do so, or substituted service may be ordered (Ord.47 r.1). The hearing is in open court in so far as would a hearing of a committal application (Ord.47 r.1(4)).

Direct enforcement

16.59 In general there is no direct method of enforcing a judgment (see para.16.46). If a person does not comply with a *mandamus*, mandatory order, injunction or order of specific performance, then apart from its punitive powers, the Court may order it to be done by someone else at his expense (Ord.45 r.6). If a person fails to execute a conveyance, contract or other document or endorse a negotiable instrument, the Court may order it to be done by a nominee (Judicature Act, s.33). There is no limit on the class of document or on the purpose for which it is to be executed, in which an order may be put into effect under these provisions, nor is it confined to a document to be executed by a party.[149] If a trustee fails to convey land within 28 days of being asked to do so,[150] the Court may vest the land in any person, or appoint a

---

142 *In re Hogan (No 2)* [1986] 9 NIJB 45, at 49.
143 Crown Proceedings Act, s.27(3).
144 *R* v *Freeman's Journal* [1902] 2 IR 82.
145 *In re Cook (No 2)* [1986] NI 283, at 286D.
146 *Iberian Trust* v *Founders Trust* [1932] 2 KB 87; *In re Cook (No 2)* at 286.
147 *Re Supply of Ready Mixed Concrete (No 2)* [1995] 1 AC 456.
148 *PJ Holdings* v *Gilroy* [1985] 12 NIJB 39, at 60-1; *affd.* [1986] 3 NIJB 100.
149 *Astro Exito* v *Southland Enterprise* (No 2) [1983] 2 AC 787.
150 Having been tendered the deed: *Kehoe* v *Agar* (1930) 64 ILTR 86.

person to convey.[151] The EJ Office can also enforce its own order to execute a document by directing someone else to do so (JE Order, Art.139).

EFFECT OF PARTY BEING IN CONTEMPT

16.60 A party who has breached an order of the Court (including an order to pay money) is in contempt. The Court has a discretion, to be exercised with flexibility, to refuse to entertain any application by him in the proceedings,[152] but will not bar an application to purge his contempt, or to appeal against or set aside the order of which he is in contempt. A party in contempt is liable to have his claim stayed; but not struck out,[153] nor his defence struck out.[154] Where a rule empowers the Court on making an order to make such other order as may be just, that confers power to order that the action will be dismissed or the Defence struck out in default of compliance within a stated time.[155]

OTHER FORMS OF CIVIL CONTEMPT

By a solicitor

16.61 A solicitor for a party who fails to give notice to his client of an order for discovery or inspection of documents, or interrogatories, is guilty of civil contempt (see paras. 11.120 and 11.127). Posing as a solicitor is criminal contempt (see para. 16.70). The High Court has inherent jurisdiction to order a solicitor to deliver up money or documents, subject to his lien.[156]

16.62 Since he is an officer of the High Court, the Court has inherent jurisdiction to punish, as civil contempt, the breach of an undertaking given by a solicitor personally in his professional business, to the court or to his client or to another party. It need not be given in court and need not be embodied in a court order.[157] It must be clear and capable of performance, but it is no defence that the performance is useless.[158] In *Young* v *Power*,[159] an attorney was held bound by an undertaking given by his clerk. The Court will always give the solicitor a chance to perform his undertaking. It can relieve him of the undertaking. He should only be punished if the default is culpable and inexcusable, and even if performance is impossible or useless, the Court can exercise its inherent jurisdiction to order the solicitor to compensate any person who is at a loss.[160] Application should be made by summons or notice of motion "In the Matter of A.B. a Solicitor", supported by affidavit, in the Division or Court of Appeal in which the undertaking was given. As to penalties, see para. 16.55.

---

[151] Trustee Act (NI) 1958, s.43(1)(f); s.50. There are similar powers where a trustee fails to transfer stock: s.51.

[152] *X Ltd* v *Morgan-Grampian* [1991] 1 AC 1.

[153] *Pyke* v *Nat West*, 'The Times' 10 December 1977; [1977] CLY 2310.

[154] *Annesley* v *Annesley* (1913) 47 ILTR 207.

[155] *Church and General* v *Moore* [1996] 1 ILRM 202 (SC).

[156] White Book (1997) Vol. 2 [3878].

[157] See White Book (1997) Vol. 2 [3876].

[158] *Re a Solicitor* (1919) 53 ILTR 51.

[159] (1862) 7 Ir Jur NS 388 (ostensible authority).

[160] *Udall* v *Capri Lighting* [1988] QB 907.

Undertaking by a party

16.63 It is civil contempt by a party to proceedings to breach an undertaking given by him to the Court or by his advocate on his behalf in open court.[161] Undertakings are usually given as part of a settlement between parties, or as an alternative to an injunctive order which the court might otherwise make, or as a condition upon which a party is granted relief. There is an implied undertaking not to use documents seen on discovery or *subpoena* for purposes other than the litigation. A party should not be forced to give an undertaking. If the judge decides that an injunction should be given he should do so: he should not declare a right to an injunction and then call upon the party to give an undertaking in lieu, because that is in effect making an order which is unappealable.[162]

16.64 The undertaking is enforceable by committal proceedings. It is not necessary to show that a copy of the order containing the undertaking was served on the party, if he gave it personally in court.[163] Even if the undertaking was given on behalf of a party it is not essential that a copy of the court order reciting the undertaking be served on him, but is desirable.[164] However service may be necessary to enforce against a director a positive undertaking given on behalf of a company.[165] A person who knowingly aids and abets a party to breach his undertaking is guilty.[166] The Court can relieve a party of an undertaking, or discharge or modify it on good grounds. An undertaking cannot be varied unless it was expressed to be "till further order" or "with liberty to apply".[167] An undertaking to pay money is enforceable by committal only in so far as a court order to pay would be.[168] As to penalties, see para. 16.55.

CONTEMPT GENERALLY

(In the remainder of this Chapter, the Contempt of Court Act 1981 is referred to as "the Contempt Act". Note that some provisions of the Act are modified for Northern Ireland by Schedule 4 thereto.)

16.65 Contempt is either civil or criminal. The significance of the classification is that: (a) there is privilege from arrest on civil contempt for Members of Parliament, and lawyers going to and from court; (b) the Court may remit the sentence for either but only in criminal contempt can the Crown remit the sentence; (c) civil contempt is an issue between parties, so that a party can waive his right to have the contempt punished, but criminal contempt is between the court and the contemnor;[169] (d) civil contempt is not a criminal

---

161 *R* v *Devereux* (1838) Cr & D ANC 157.
162 *McConnell* v *McConnell* (1980) 10 Fam Law 214.
163 *In re H (a bankrupt)* (1936) 70 ILTR 199.
164 *Hussain* v *Hussain* [1986] Fam 134.
165 *Ronson Products* v *Ronson Furniture* [1966] Ch 603, at 615.
166 *Malevez* v *Knox* [1977] 1 NZLR 463.
167 *Lonrho* v *Fayed (No 4)* [1994] QB 775, at 791.
168 *Buckley* v *Crawford* [1893] 1 QB 105.
169 White Book (1997) 52/1/2.

offence.[170] (e) most importantly, civil contempt in connection with High Court proceedings is dealt with by application to a single judge, whereas criminal contempt not committed in the presence of a sitting judge is dealt with by a Divisional Court of two or three Queen's Bench judges.

CIVIL CONTEMPT

16.66 Categories of civil contempt -

(1) Non-compliance with a court order (see para. 16.46).

(2) Non-compliance with a court order to pay money into court (see para. 16.39).

(3) Non-compliance with a court order to pay money as trustee, solicitor (see para. 16.44).

(4) Breach of undertaking by a party (see para. 16.63).

(5) Breach of undertaking by a solicitor (see para. 16.61).

CRIMINAL CONTEMPT

Contempt in the face of a court

16.67 The High Court has jurisdiction to punish contempt committed in the face of the High Court or any other court. This includes assaulting or insulting the judge/magistrate etc.,[171] seizing a document in court, presenting or being a party to a fraudulent case, assaulting a lawyer in court precincts, or any interference with proceedings by acts in or near the court,[172] insolence to a court officer who was trying to quell a riot in court.[173] Words may be contempt though the judge did not hear them.[174] A barrister or solicitor may be guilty of such contempts, as where he uses insulting words of the judge,[175] adopts an insolent manner,[176] or absents himself from court with the intent and effect of hindering the hearing of a case.[177] Mere lateness if not wilful is not contempt.[178] If committed in the High Court, such contempt may, if necessary, be dealt with summarily by the presiding judge, who acts as prosecutor and judge; the contempt does not have to be proved by evidence. There is no need to allow the

---

[170] Miller *Contempt of Court* (Clarendon Press 2nd ed 1989) pp.26-9; *Australian Consolidated* v *Morgan* (1965) 112 CLR 483, at 497-8; *contra: Dean* v *Dean* [1987] 1 FLR 517. In so far as contempt is a criminal offence it is an indictable offence carrying an unlimited imprisonment and/or fine, and a person committing it can be arrested by a constable or by any citizen under Art.26 of the Police and Criminal Evidence (NI) Order 1989.

[171] *R* v *McNeill* [1987] 10 NIJB 41.

[172] *Balogh* v *St Albans Crown Ct* [1975] QB 73.

[173] *R* v *Gardner* (1794) Ir Term Rep 285.

[174] *Mitchell* v *Smyth* [1894] 2 IR 351, at 356.

[175] *Lewis* v *Ogden* (1984) 153 CLR 682.

[176] *R* v *Shumiatcher* (1967) 64 DLR 2d 24.

[177] *Weston* v *Central Criminal Court Administrator* [1977] QB 32, at 43G.

[178] *Cameron* v *Orr*, 1995 SLT 589; *Murdanaigum* v *Henderson*, 1996 SLT 1297.

offender to show cause against committal,[179] but the judge may do so (Ord.52 r.7). The judge may grant legal aid if it is desirable and the offender has insufficient means, and may assign any counsel or solicitor who is in the precincts (Contempt Act, s.13, as set out in Sch. 4).

By a witness

16.68 Failure to obey a *subpoena* is contempt if due service thereof is proved and if the witness was tendered reasonable expenses at that time.[180] He can even refuse to testify if expenses have not been paid.[180] He cannot refuse to attend on grounds that expenses are insufficient if he accepted them.[181] A witness who obeys a *subpoena* but leaves the court that day without leave is in contempt.[182] Non-attendance is established by the name being called in court and the absence being noted by a court official.[183] A witness, whether subpoenaed or not, who is in court and refuses to enter the witness box when called, or to produce a document or to be sworn or to answer any proper question is in contempt, subject to the law of privilege.

16.69 *Witness in custody.* If a witness is in custody, the failure of a person on whom a writ of *habeas corpus ad testificandum* is served to produce him is contempt.

Acting as solicitor

16.70 Save as provided by an enactment, an unqualified person cannot act as a solicitor and is guilty of contempt of the court in relation to which he so acts.[184]

Interfering with justice

16.71 The High Court can punish contempts committed outside a court. The contempt should be proved by evidence. There are three types.

(i) Scandalising a court

16. 71a Words scandalising a court by abusing or intimidating a judge, accusing him of bias or corruption etc.[185] This is discussed in the White Book (1997) 52/1/8.

(ii) Interfering directly with justice

16.72 Interfering with particular proceedings, for example: bribing, victimising or intimidating parties, lawyers, witnesses or jurors; interfering with court officers, impeding service of process, forging or destroying court documents, abusing process of court; deliberately defying or helping a party to disobey a court order, or frustrating rights declared by a court; preventing a

---

179 *In re Rea (No 2)* (1879) 4 LR Ir 345.

180 *Re Working Men's Mutual* (1882) 21 Ch D 831; even if not wilful: White Book (1997) 52/1/11.

181 *Hempston* v *Humphreys* (1867) IR 1 CL 271.

182 *Chute* v *McGillicuddy* (1833) Hay & Jon 172.

183 *O'Donnell* v *O'Donnell* (1852) 3 ICLR 29.

184 Solicitors (NI) Order 1976, Art.19; White Book (1997) 52/1/11.

185 *State(DPP)* v *Walsh* [1981] IR 412, at 421.

citizen from access to the courts; neglect of duty by a court officer; violating jury-room confidentiality (Contempt Act, s.8);[186] bringing a tape recorder into court (s.9). This is dealt with in the White Book (1997) 52/1/10.

(iii) Conduct likely to prejudice justice (strict liability contempt)

16.73 See further the White Book (1997) 52/1/9. Words or conduct which are calculated to interfere with justice in particular proceedings with or without intent to do so ('strict liability rule'), for example: publishing facts and opinions on a matter on which there will be a trial; publishing facts or names of which a court has ordered postponement (Contempt Act, s.4), or publishing a fact or name which a court has properly prohibited from publication (s.11). Section 2 limits punishment for this to public communications which create a substantial risk that the proceedings will be impeded or prejudiced, and only if the proceedings are 'active', as defined by Schedule 1. There is obviously a particular danger of this in relation to jury cases. A judge is unlikely to be prejudiced by publication of matter which is clearly at variance with the evidence before him.[187]

16.74 Section 6 of the Contempt Act makes clear that the Act does not operate to extend the law of contempt to conduct which is not contempt at common law, nor to remove any common law defence, nor does it remove liability for conduct of types (i) and (ii) above. Sections 3-5 provide the following defences: to a publisher, that he did not reasonably suspect proceedings to be active; to a distributor, that he did not reasonably suspect the publication to contain improper matter; that the publication is a fair report of public legal proceedings; that it is part of *bona fide* discussion of matters of public interest. At common law a mere printing employee is not liable,[188] and there is a defence that the party prejudiced has condoned the publication by delay or otherwise.[189] Unless by motion of the Court, an application to punish strict liability contempt requires consent of the Attorney-General (s.7). Publication of information about proceedings of a court sitting in private can be contempt only if the proceedings relate to care etc. of a minor or mental patient, national security or secret invention, or the court expressly prohibits publication.[190]

16.75 A party to litigation, or the Attorney-General, can apply for an injunction to restrain any threatened or continuing conduct or publication which may prejudice proceedings. The Court hearing the contempt proceedings may do so.

---

[186] See *A-G* v *Associated Newspapers* [1994] 2 AC 238.

[187] *Wong* v *Minister of Justice* [1994] 1 IR 223.

[188] *Sheehy* v *Freeman's Journal* (1892) 26 ILTR 47.

[189] *Hastings* v *Henry* (1912) 46 ILTR 308, where the condonation by inactivity was nullified by renewal of the contemptuous words.

[190] Administration of Justice Act 1960, s.12.

DEALING WITH CONTEMPT

The appropriate court

16.76 The Crown cannot be punished for contempt, but a minister or official of the Crown acting in a personal capacity can.[191] With a few exceptions all contempts are punishable by committal to prison, and in some cases by sequestration. The power of the Supreme Court to punish contempt is exercisable by committal (Ord.52 r.1(1)). All contempts can be punished by a Divisional Court of two or more judges of the High Court.[192] Where civil contempt in connection with High Court proceedings, the power may be exercised by a single judge on application made without prior leave (Ord.52 r.1(3) (see para. 16.53). If the contempt was in the face of or a disobedience of an order of a criminal court, it may be dealt with by that court. The Crown Court has the powers of the High Court to commit for contempt, and inferior courts, such as county courts and magistrates' courts have certain statutory powers. If the contempt was in relation to the Court of Appeal or proceedings therein, it may be punished by that Court or the Divisional Court (Ord.52 r.1(4)).

16.77 Any Division of the High Court and the Court of Appeal have power to commit a person for contempt of court, of their own motion (Ord.52 r.6), where committed in relation to proceedings before them. In particular the Court may deal with a person who commits contempt in the presence of a sitting judge, by calling upon him to show cause why he should not be committed, or may order him (on recognisance and sureties or not) to appear before it at a future date to show cause (Ord.52 r.7).

16.78 Save as aforesaid, the jurisdiction to punish contempt committed in connection with proceedings in the High Court, any criminal court or inferior court, or not in connection with any proceedings at all, is exclusively vested in the Divisional Court (Ord.52 r.1(2)(6)). The Divisional Court can punish contempts of an inferior court even if that inferior court has power to do so.[193] The procedure is as follows.

Procedure

16.79 Where the application is to be made to the Divisional Court (or Court of Appeal) it must first be made *ex parte* to a judge in chambers supported by a statement verified on affidavit of the identity of the applicant and respondent and the grounds of committal, these having been lodged in the Crown Office the previous day; if leave is refused the application may be renewed to the full Court within eight days (Ord.52 r.2). If leave is granted, the applicant has 14 days to enter a motion for committal; he serves personally on the respondent a notice of motion, with the Order 52 rule 2 documents, for hearing at least eight clear days after service; the judge giving leave may direct a different period of notice, may order substituted service or may dispense with service if he thinks it

---

191 *M* v *Home Office* [1994] 1 AC 377, at 424-7.

192 Contempt of the Judicial Committee of the House of Lords can be dealt with only by the House: *In re Lonrho* [1990] 2 AC 154.

193 *A-G* v *Connolly* [1947] IR 213, at 224.

just to do so (Ord.52 r.3). The Court must sit in open court unless the application arises out of proceedings relating to a minor or patient, or secret process or invention, or if necessary in the interests of justice or national security; if so, any order of committal must be stated in open court (Ord.52 r.8(1)(2)). Save by leave or by amendment, the applicant can rely only on the grounds stated in his Order 52 rule 2 statement (Ord.52 r.8(3)). The respondent may give evidence if he expresses a wish to do so (Ord.52 r.8(4)). If the respondent fails to appear, the Court may commit him if it thinks just (Ord.52 r.5). Urgent applications can be heard during vacation (Ord.64 r.4).

16.80 It is settled law that proceedings to commit must comply strictly with the procedures of the Rules.[194] The notice of motion to commit and the order of committal must state the particulars of the contempt.[195] The acts of contempt must be proved beyond reasonable doubt.[196] The Court has power to summon and call witnesses. The Court should make a finding of guilty or not guilty of the contempt, and it has a discretion as to ordering costs between the parties. If "no rule" is made on the application, that is equivalent to an acquittal.[197] The Court has a discretion to refuse to commit, for example for delay in applying,[198] or that the contemnor has purged or will purge his contempt.

16.81 The Court may suspend execution of the committal order for a specified period and conditions: in which case the applicant must serve on the respondent a notice of the order (Ord.52 r.9). A committal order is addressed to a policeman or other person (Ord.52 r.1(5)). "The Court may, on application of [a contemnor] committed to prison *until further order* ..., discharge him", especially if his property has also been sequestrated (Ord.52 r.10). The words in italics should be omitted (as has been done in the English rule) because, since the Contempt Act, any committal to prison must be for a fixed period. At the end of the period the contemnor must be released. Alternatively a Court acting under Order 52 has power to deal with, or hear an application to deal with, the contempt by ordering the respondent to pay a fine or give security for good behaviour (Ord.52 r.11). In *R* v *Montgomery*[199] the Court of Appeal gave sentencing guidelines for criminal contempt by a witness. An order of committal cannot be executed on a Sunday.[200]

16.82 The rule against double jeopardy applies to both civil and criminal contempt: a contemnor cannot be punished twice for the same contempt; and if contempt proceedings are dismissed on the merits (as opposed to a procedural defect), further proceedings for the same contempt cannot be had.[201]

---

194 *O'Donnell* v *O'Donnell* (1937) 71 ILTR 148; but see *M* v *P* below.

195 *Chiltern DC* v *Keane* [1985] 1 WLR 619.

196 *National Irish Bank* v *Graham* [1994] 1 IR 215.

197 *In re MM* [1933] IR 299.

198 *Hastings* v *Henry* (1912) 46 ILTR 308.

199 [1995] 2 All ER 28.

200 Sunday Observance Act (Ir) 1695, s.7. The Act excepts orders in relation to an indictable offence, and criminal contempt is an indictable offence.

201 *Jelson Estates* v *Harvey* [1983] 1 WLR 1401.

Punishment powers

16.83 Where there is no specified maximum, a superior court has power to commit for civil or criminal contempt to prison for a fixed term not exceeding two years (without prejudice to power of early discharge); or to impose an unlimited fine; or to make a hospital or guardianship order under Article 44 of the Mental Health (NI) Order 1986, or an interim hospital order under Article 45, or to remand to the care of the DHSS for a mental report (Contempt Act, s.14). It seems that a court cannot order *both* committal (or suspended committal) *and* a fine for one contempt. It may require the contemnor to give security for his good behaviour. A fine may be enforced like a fine imposed by a Crown Court (s.16). There is a limited power sequestration for civil contempt (see paras. 16.57 and 16.58). There is no power to 'defer sentence' pending consideration of the penalty at a later date, but the Court can impose an immediate fixed sentence and direct that an application for early discharge will be entertained after a certain period.[202] A committal order can be suspended; and there is no obligation to activate it on further breach.[203] For separate contempts imprisonments can be consecutive or concurrent; but consecutive sentences passed on one occasion cannot exceed two years.[203] A child up to 14 years cannot be imprisoned for contempt, and a young person aged up to 17 cannot be committed to prison or Young Offenders' Centre unless certified unruly or depraved.[204] A person committed for contempt is treated separa.tely from persons sentenced on conviction by a criminal court and has the same rights of access to lawyers and visitors as a remanded prisoner and has a right of remission on a sentence over five days.[205]

Effect of a party being in contempt

16.83a See para. 16.60.

APPEAL

16.84 Appeal lies from the exercise of the civil or criminal jurisdiction in contempt, only as follows (by virtue of section 44 of the Judicature Act)-

- FROM any inferior court or a single judge of the High Court - TO the Court of Appeal, the notice of appeal to be served on the proper officer of the lower court as well as the parties affected (Ord.59 r.18).
- FROM a decision of the Divisional High Court and the Court of Appeal (original or appellate) - TO the House of Lords, with leave of the Court or the Lords.

For an appeal from the Divisional Court/Court of Appeal to the House of Lords, leave of the former or of the Lords is necessary, and if the appeal is from an appellate decision of the Court of Appeal that Court must certify a point of law of public importance (s.44(4)). Either the contemnor or the applicant, if any, may appeal.

---

[202] *Delaney* v *Delaney* [1996] QB 387 (CA).

[203] *Villiers* v *Villiers* [1994] 2 All ER 149, at 153h.

[204] Children and Young Persons Act (NI) 1968, s.72.

[205] Prison and Young Offenders' Centre Rules (NI) 1995, rr.107-9.

16.85 The Court hearing an appeal may reverse or vary the decision and make any other just order (s.44(3)). This provision enables the appellate court to validate a committal order in defective proceedings, in exceptional circumstances and if no injustice was caused.[206] Rules may authorise release on bail (s.44(3)). Where a committal has been ordered by a court of competent jurisdiction, appeal under section 44 rather than *habeas corpus* is the appropriate course. The appellate court can vary the sentence or substitute a proper sentence in cases of irregularity on the face of the order, but is less likely to cure a defect in the application.[207] On appeal against a finding of contempt, it can hear new evidence in the interests of justice.[208]

---

[206] *M* v *P* [1993] Fam 167(CA).
[207] White Book (1997) 52/1/16.
[208] *Irtelli* v *Squatriti* [1993] QB 83.

CHAPTER SEVENTEEN

COSTS

GENERAL PRINCIPLES

17.00 All legal proceedings inevitably entail costs, expenses and fees being expended by each party. Unless the case is worth a great deal of money, the costs usually amount to a sizeable proportion of the amount at stake in the proceedings. This Chapter concerns the two major issues in relation to costs: firstly, who pays them? and secondly, how are they quantified? The answer to the first question in most civil courts is that the policy is generally to make the losing party responsible for all costs, his own and his opponent's. To the second, the policy in the Supreme Court is to have the costs assessed for the work done in each individual case; whereas in the county court, it is the policy to assess costs under scales dependent on the size of the claim. In certain circumstances a party may be required to give security to ensure that his opponent's costs will be met if the latter wins (see para. 11.56). *Legal Costs in Northern Ireland* (SLS 1993) by the late Master Anderson, is a treatise on costs in all courts and in non-litigious matters.

17.01 Costs of Supreme Court proceedings are dealt with under Order 62, which was completely revised in 1988. "Costs" is defined[1] to include fees, charges, disbursements, expenses and remuneration and, in relation to proceedings, includes costs of and incidental to the proceedings (Ord.62 r.1(4)), such as the letter before action; pre-action reports etc. "Party" includes a party to an action ordered to be tried together (Ord.62 r.1(2)). "Costs of an action" includes costs of a counterclaim.[2] Order 62 applies to all civil and criminal proceedings in the High Court and Court of Appeal (but not the Crown Court); and to costs of any arbitrator, umpire, tribunal or other body which are by statute taxable in the High Court (Ord.62 r.2). It is subject to any statutory limitation on costs recoverable (Ord.62 r.2(3)).

DISCRETION OVER COSTS

17.02 Costs of and incidental to[3] all proceedings in the High Court or Court of Appeal[4] are in the discretion of the Court and as to by whom payable and to what extent, subject to the Judicature Act, rules of court and express provision of statute, and subject to the practice in a criminal cause or matter (Judicature

---

1 Repeating the words of the Judicature Act, s.120, and the Interpretation Act (NI) 1954, s.46(2).

2 *Craig* v *Boyd* [1901] 2 IR 645.

3 A court hearing one action cannot deal with the costs of a proceeding in another court which is not ancillary to the action: *Zanussi* v *Anglo-Venezuelan Development*, 'The Times', 18 April 1996.

4 Costs on appeals to the House of Lords are dealt with by the House of Lords Costs Taxation Act 1849.

Act, s.59(1)(4)). Costs are 'taxed' (i.e. assessed as to amount) by the Master (Taxing Office) (s.60(1)). Costs are payable notwithstanding the death of a party (s.60(2)). Subject to specific rules, costs are not payable by one party to another unless so ordered by the Court; and if the court decides to order costs it orders that costs should follow the event unless it appears that some other order should be made (Ord.62 r.3(1)(2)(3)).[5] So normally, if the plaintiff wins judgment or an order, the judge/master orders that the defendant pay the costs of the plaintiff's solicitor to the plaintiff, and the defence solicitor is left to seek his costs from the defendant.

Costs against non-party

17.03 The general rule is that only a party to proceedings should be awarded or ordered to pay costs thereof. Costs can be awarded against a non-party,[6] but with very great caution, especially if the applicant could have joined him as a party.[7] Costs can be ordered against a trade union, insurer or other person who has agreed to indemnify the losing party for liability for costs.[8] If costs are awarded against a party under disability, no order for costs is to be drawn up until it is ascertained whether he or his next friend or guardian *ad litem* is to pay the costs.[9]

Whether costs follow the event

17.04 The basic principle is that costs follow the event. 'The event' is not necessarily the judgment for one party. For instance, if the plaintiff recovers a judgment but does not exceed the amount lodged in court under Order 22, the event is, in respect of costs after the date of lodgment, in favour of the defendant. In *Alltrans Express* v *CVA*[10] the plaintiff in a contract action claimed £80,000, and was awarded only £2; the Court held that in substance the action had failed and awarded costs to the defendant. In its discretion the Court may withhold all or some costs from a successful party or, exceptionally, award costs against him, where it is just to do so[11] on grounds such as the following-

(1) The claim is prosecuted for inflated costs rather than the relief due,[12] or resulted in only nominal relief.[13]

(2) The plaintiff was enticed into a losing action by the acts or promises of the defendant,[14] for example by hinting that he accepted liability[15] or by concealing an old case which related to the subject-matter.[16]

---

5 Costs do not necessarily follow the event in matrimonial proceedings: White Book (1997) 62/B/40.

6 *Aiden Shipping* v *Interbulk* [1986] AC 965.

7 *Symphony Group* v *Hodgson* [1994] QB 179. See the White Book (1997) 62/2/7.

8 *Murphy* v *Young & Co* [1997] 1 All ER 518 (CA).

9 Practice Direction (LCJ) [1982] 9 BNIL 90.

10 [1984] 1 WLR 394.

11 See White Book (1997) 62/2/9.

12 *Hobbs* v *Marlowe* [1978] AC 16.

13 *Alltrans Express* v *CVA Holdings* [1984] 1 WLR 394.

14 *McGrory* v *DOE* [1977] 5 NIJB (in without prejudice correspondence); *McCarthy* v *ATGW*, Ch D, NI, 31 January 1966.

(3) The defendant defeats the claim by reliance on his own wrong.[17]

(4) The defendant, though found liable, succeeds because equitable relief is refused on discretionary grounds.[19]

(5) The claim or defence succeeds due to a late amendment.[18]

(6) The plaintiff sued after failing to meet a request for full details of his complaint.[19]

(7) The defendant offered a compromise which substantially met all that the plaintiff was awarded by the court, but not where he could have made a lodgment.[20]

(8) The losing party lost on the facts but won on a separate issue of law.[21]

(9) The case was decided on an important issue which the losing party was justified in contesting.

(10) The winning party presented a false or oppressive case.

17.05 There must be material relevant to the litigation on which to depart from the rule of costs following the event.[22] Foolishness or exaggeration, reliance on unappealing case are not grounds for withholding costs from the winner, and misfortune, poverty or sympathy of the court are not grounds for waiving costs against the loser. The judge must decide judicially, and cannot delegate the discretion. Normally he should not hear evidence solely for the purpose of deciding costs, but can do so, whether after a trial or settlement,[23] and in every case he must be fully informed about material matters as to costs, such as legal aid, a lodgment under Order 22, or a '*Calderbank*' offer. Costs are normally dealt with at the conclusion of the proceeding in which they are incurred; but the Court can make an order as to costs not yet incurred.[24]

Provisions as to the incidence of costs

17.06 Order 62 rule 5 states that costs are payable automatically without an order: (a) by a party whose summons to set aside a proceeding for irregularity is dismissed; (b) by a party who discontinues an action or withdraws a claim without leave; (c) to a party who accepts a lodgment; (d) costs of a

---

15 *Buckley* v *Irish Industrial Benefit Society* (1888) 22 LR Ir 579; as in *JC Campbell* v *Davidson*, Ch D, NI, 27 September 1967, 18 NILQ 461, were a co-defendant responded to the letter of claim by stating justification for the tort, then after the action was brought raised successfully the defence that he was not vicariously liable. See previous page.

16 *Brankenbank Lodge* v *Peart*, 'The Times' 26 July 1996 (HL). See previous page.

17 *Morelli* v *DOE* [1976] NI 159 (costs there awarded against him).

18 *City of Glasgow Friendly Society* v *Gilpin* [1970] Dec NIJB.

19 *Valentine* v *Valentine* (1893) 31 LR Ir 488.

20 *Revere Trust* v *Wellington Handkerchief* [1931] NI 55.

21 *Ledwith* v *Ross* [1910] 1 IR 151.

22 *Scherer* v *Counting Instruments* [1986] 1 WLR 615.

23 *Computer Machinery* v *Drescher* [1983] 1 WLR 1379, at 1385.

24 E.g. to direct in a representative or 'test' action that any order for costs against the plaintiff be spread over all the claimants represented (see para. 17.47); to direct that a trustee etc. should recover costs from the property in dispute whatever the result of the case (see para. 17.56).

counterclaim to a defendant whose lodgment, expressed to take into account the value of his counterclaim, is accepted.

17.07 Order 62 rule 6 specifically provides that costs are payable unless otherwise ordered: (a) to a trustee etc. out of the trust fund; (b) to a claimant who proves his claim in proceedings under a judgment; (c) by a party amending without leave; (d) by a party who makes an application to extend time; (e) costs of proof by a party who fails or refuses on notice to admit a fact; (f) costs of proof by a party who gives notice of non-admission of a document; (g) to a person against whom pre-action or non-party disclosure of documents is sought. Costs wasted by a party's neglect may be ordered against him (Ord.62 r.10), or by a solicitor's neglect against him (Ord.62 r.11).

17.08 *Offers of settlement.* As a general rule the negotiations and offers of settlement or compromise made between the parties before the trial do not affect the incidence of costs, save as follows. Order 62 rule 9 requires the Court to take into account: (a) an offer of contribution between persons liable under Order 16 rule 10 (see para. 10.13); and (b) a payment into court by a defendant in satisfaction of a monetary claim under Order 22 (see para. 11.160). If the claim is of a type for which the defendant cannot make a lodgment, as in an action for an injunction or specific performance, the defendant may make a '*Calderbank*' offer either by open letter[20] or by letter headed "without prejudice save as to costs", which may be considered by the trial judge in exercising his discretion as to costs.[25] There is no rule penalising a defendant who rejects a reasonable compromise offered by the plaintiff, but Waterhouse J has held that the Court can direct payment of the plaintiff's costs on the indemnity basis where the award of damages is greater than the sum for which he offered to settle.[26]

17.09 *Crown proceedings.* Costs in proceedings by or against the Crown are the same as between citizens, but in proceedings in which the Attorney-General, Government Department or officer of the Crown is authorised to be a party by reason of an enactment or otherwise, the Court must have regard to the circumstances of his appearance and has a discretion to order his costs to be paid by another party whatever the result.[27] This section does not apply to judicial review applications, relator actions or proceedings relating to Northern Ireland charities or Land Registry.

Statutory restrictions on costs

17.10 Certain statutes place limits on the right to or the amount of costs-

(1) Where the relief obtained is within the county court jurisdiction (see para. 17.23).

---

[25] *Cutts* v *Head* [1984] Ch 290. Under the English Rules since 1986 the judge is expressly enjoined to take it into account.

[26] *McDonnell* v *Woodhouse*, 'The Times', 25 May 1995. In some Canadian states, rules of court provide that if a plaintiff is awarded a form of judgment no less favourable to him than that which he sought before the trial, then the plaintiff's costs should be taxed on a more generous basis: see *Fletcher* v *Manitoba Insurance* (1990) 74 DLR 4th 637, at 662.

[27] Crown Proceedings Act, s.21A.

(2) Where a party is legally aided (see para. 17.88).

(3) By the Civil Liability (Contribution) Act 1978 (s.4), if more than one action for unliquidated damages is brought by the sufferer against persons liable (jointly or otherwise) for that damage, the plaintiff is entitled to no costs other than in that in which judgment is first given, unless the court thinks it was reasonable.

(4) By the Solicitors (NI) Order 1976 (Arts.19, 25), a person who acts as a solicitor when not qualified cannot recover his costs, and his client can recover costs from another party only insofar as he has paid the 'solicitor'.

(5) Costs of suing on foreign judgment (see para. 16.21).

(6) By the Rent (NI) Order 1978, Art.69(3) (private dwelling tenancies); Housing (NI) Order 1983, Art.46(3) (NIHE tenancies), no costs are allowed of proceedings which could have been commenced in the county court under those Orders.

(7) In a claim for slander imputing unchastity to a female where no special damage is shown, the plaintiff recovers no more costs than the damages, unless the judge certifies reasonable ground for suing.[28]

An enactment or rule relating to costs of a High Court action which could have been brought in an inferior court does not apply to proceedings by the Crown.[29]

Quantification of a party's costs

17.11 It must be noted that a party is only entitled to costs if and to the extent that he is liable (in theory at least) to his own solicitor for those costs.[30] He is presumed to be liable to his own solicitor unless it is clearly agreed that he will not be liable in any circumstances.[31] If the party entitled to costs has made a "business agreement" with his solicitor in relation to those costs, his rights and liabilities as to costs *inter partes* are not affected, but he cannot recover from the other party more than the amount payable under the agreement; and the solicitor can claim only those costs plus any costs which are expressly excepted from the agreement.[32] A solicitor who has made a champertous agreement for his costs, or an agreement for costs conditional upon success, cannot recover any costs from the other party.[33]

In the following cases a party can recover full costs for which he is not liable to his solicitor: (a) a corporate or public body whose solicitor is a salaried employee;[34] (b) the Attorney-General; (c) a legally aided party; (d) a Trade Union member on whose behalf the Union has employed the solicitor;[35] (e) a

---

28 Slander of Women Act 1891.
29 Crown Proceedings Act, s.20(2)(c).
30 *Gundry* v *Sainsbury* [1910] 1 KB 645.
31 *R* v *Miller* [1983] 1 WLR 1056.
32 Solicitors (NI) Order 1976, Arts.65(3)(4),71A(5).
33 Solicitors Order, Art.64(2); *British Waterways* v *Norman*, 'The Times', 11 November 1993.
34 *Bank of Ireland* v *Lyons* [1981] IR 295.
35 *Adams* v *London Coach* [1921] 1 KB 495.

litigant in person; (f) a party who has a right of indemnity for his costs (e.g. under a policy of insurance).[36]

17.12 Unless otherwise ordered, where costs are payable by one party to another, payable out of any fund or payable without an order, those costs are of an amount allowed on taxation, subject to Order 62 rule 7; and they are to be taxed on the 'standard basis' unless it appears appropriate to the Court to order 'indemnity basis' (Ord.62 r.3(4)). If the Court orders costs without specifically stipulating the indemnity basis, or if it uses any other form of taxation,[37] the standard basis applies (Ord.62 r.12(3)). In awarding costs the Court may order, in lieu of taxed costs: (a) a specified proportion of the costs from or to a specified stage in the proceedings; or (b) a specified gross sum (Ord.62 r.7(4)). An order for a specified proportion is likely to be invoked where there are multiple parties or issues which have been decided different ways; it saves the Taxing Master from having to divide costs among the issues. The power to award a gross sum is to avoid a complex and costly taxation process, and the judge should fix the figure by broad assessment without embarking on a taxation exercise.[38] The Court can also refer assessment of costs to a master other than the Taxing Master, under the general power to refer issues and questions: the master must apply the same bases for assessing costs as on a taxation (Ord.62 r.13).

17.13 Costs are not to be taxed until the conclusion of the cause or matter, unless the Court directs costs (against a non legally-aided party) to be taxed earlier (Ord.62 r.8(1)(2)(3)). If it appears that the proceedings will not progress further, the Taxing Master may on application tax forthwith the costs of interlocutory proceedings (Ord.62 r.8(8)).

Appeal as to costs. The decision of the judge as to costs only is appealable to the Court of Appeal only by his leave (see para. 20.08).

Meaning of terms in an order for costs

17.14 In relation to the proceeding in which it is made, an order for costs has the following meaning by virtue of Order 62 rule 3(5)-

"costs to X"	X to get those costs in any event. Such an order made at the conclusion of the cause or matter means that X can tax his costs forthwith
"costs to X in any event"	The same (save that, obviously, such order is not made at the conclusion)
"costs in the cause"	Costs to go to the party who eventually gets an order for costs at the conclusion

---

36 *Davies* v *Taylor (No 2)* [1974] AC 225. For applications under the Trade Union and Labour Relations (NI) Order 1995, the NI Commissioner for the Rights of Trade Union Members, if he assists an application, indemnifies the applicant for costs and has a statutory charge on costs or agreed compensation recovered: Arts.93(5), 122(3).

37 Such as the old 'common fund' or 'solicitor and client' bases which were abolished in 1988.

38 White Book (1997) 62/7/7.

"costs in application"	The same
"costs reserved"	The same, unless the Court otherwise orders (except in the Family Division)
"X's costs in the cause"	X to get those costs if he eventually wins judgment at the conclusion, and does not have to pay costs if he loses
"costs here and below to X"	X to get the costs of the proceeding and the costs of the same proceeding in a lower court (e.g. on an appeal from a lower court)
"costs thrown away awarded to X"	X to get costs of a proceeding or part thereof which has been ineffective or has been set aside

"No order as to costs" means that each party pays its own costs, colloquially called 'back-to-back costs'.

"Costs of the day to X" means that X gets his costs of the proceedings today.

Asking for costs

17.15 Save where costs are payable automatically under the RSC, no costs are payable between party and party unless so ordered by the Court, so that the party entitled should always ask for his costs. The judge should be told of any material matter affecting costs, such as a lodgment, or that a party is legally aided. If he is not told, or forgets about it, in making his order, the order can be amended under the slip rule.[39]

When does plaintiff's right to costs arise?

17.16 The decisive point is the issue of the writ.

In a claim for a *debt or liquidated demand*, if the defendant pays the amount claimed by the plaintiff at any time (including earlier the same day) before the writ is issued, the plaintiff cannot sue for his costs, even though he has incurred costs, for example his solicitor's pre-action letter. Once a writ has been issued, whether or not served, the plaintiff has a right to costs.[40] If the defendant pays the debt claimed and the sum claimed on the endorsement for '14-day costs' before service or within 14 days of service of the writ, the plaintiff must accept those costs subject to the defendant's right to have them taxed under Order 62 rule 7(3). If the defendant pays the debt claimed after issue of writ and before or after service, but pays nothing for costs and does not enter an appearance, the plaintiff may enter judgment for the 14-day costs endorsed on the writ (Ord.62 r.7(3)), or he may enter judgment in default for the debt, crediting the payment of it, with scale costs on a default judgment under Order 62 Appendix 3 Part I column (b).[41]

17.17 The same applies where a defendant sued for *recovery of land* gives up possession, the scale costs being fixed by Order 62 Appendix 3 Part II.

---

39 *Gregan* v *Rafter* [1940] Ir Jur R 80; *McNicholl* v *Neely* [1983] NI 43 (both cases where the Court forgot to order costs to be paid by a next friend).

40 *Simonds* v *Cronin* (1910) 44 ILTR 47; *Murphy* v *Kearns* (1924) 58 ILTR 29.

41 Ord.62 r.17(3); White Book (1997) 62/7/4-5. The Court can 'otherwise order', i.e. award costs to be taxed.

17.18 If on an *unliquidated claim* the defendant offers a satisfactory sum for damages but no costs before the issue of the writ, the plaintiff may choose to commence the action, and proceed. If the defendant offers a satisfactory sum without costs after the issue of the writ, the plaintiff should not accept it and should proceed for judgment and costs.[42] If the plaintiff accepts the damages offered, the position as to costs is not so clear; in principle the plaintiff should be able to accept the money as being not in full settlement, and to seek judgment for his damages, crediting the amount paid, and costs.

17.19 If in a *non-monetary claim* the defendant, before issue of the writ, performs or concedes the relief sought without offer of costs, *semble*, the plaintiff should not sue to get his costs unless there is an ancillary right to damages for the wrong suffered. If the defendant performs or concedes the relief without costs after issue of the writ, the Court on application of the plaintiff may in its discretion give judgment for costs only.[43]

17.20 If the plaintiff settles collusively after commencement of the action so as to deprive his solicitor of costs, the solicitor may by leave continue the action for his costs (see para. 17.76).

PARTICULAR CASES WHERE ISSUES AS TO COSTS ARISE

COSTS OF DEFAULT OR SUMMARY JUDGMENT

17.21 *Summary judgment (Order 14).* If judgment is given either absolutely or in default of payment into court, it will carry costs. If the summons is dismissed, then costs are awarded to the defendant and may be ordered to be paid forthwith unless the plaintiff is legally aided. Otherwise the normal order will be for costs in the cause. Unless the Court otherwise orders, summary judgment for a debt carries scale costs under Order 62 Appendix 3 Part I column (c), if at least £600 is awarded; summary judgment for recovery of land carries scale costs under Order 62 Appendix 3 Part II; and the plaintiff will recover full High Court costs under Appendix 3 even if the judgment is within the county court limit (Ord.62 r.17(3)). In a large or complex case, the Court may order the plaintiff's costs to be taxed.

When judgment in default has been given in an action for debt or recovery of land, costs are automatically added to the judgment at the fixed scale in Appendix 3, but the Court has a discretion to order the plaintiff's costs to be taxed (Ord.62 r.17(3)). On any other judgment in default or summary judgment, the costs are to be taxed.

If summary judgment or judgment in default is given in an action in which a party is legally-aided, the judgment must direct his costs to be taxed under Schedule 2 to the LA Order.[44]

---

42 *Smith* v *Springer* [1987] 3 All ER 252. And see *Laing* v *Channel Reprographics* etc. [1989] CLY 2942-2945.

43 *Upmann* v *Forester* (1883) 24 Ch D 231; *American Tobacco* v *Guest* [1892] 1 Ch 630.

44 LA Gen Regs, reg. 21(5).

Costs of setting aside judgment in default

17.22 If the judgment is set aside *ex debito justitiae* for irregularity, the defendant should be given the costs of setting aside.[45] If the defendant's application to set aside for irregularity is dismissed he is automatically liable for costs (Ord.62 r.5(2)). If the judgment was obtained regularly and properly, the Court on setting it aside will order the defendant to pay costs thrown away, unless the plaintiff refused an offer of costs for consent to set aside[46] or neither party was at fault.[47]

COSTS WHERE RELIEF WITHIN COUNTY COURT JURISDICTION

17.23 Section 59(2) of the Judicature Act and Order 62 rule 17(4) provide that, subject to any post-1978 statute and to the rules, "if damages or other relief awarded could have been obtained in proceedings commenced in the county court, the plaintiff shall not, except for special cause shown and mentioned in the judgment making the award, recover more costs than would have been recoverable had the same relief been awarded by the county court". If the amount quantified by the Court as the full amount of the claim exceeds the county court limit but the amount awarded is within rule 17(4) by reason only of a deduction for the claimant's own fault, the rule is, unless the judge otherwise directs, that the plaintiff recover one-half of High Court costs (Ord.62 r.17(5)(6)).[48]

17.24 The costs penalty does not apply: (a) if the judge otherwise orders for special cause shown; (b) if any defendant successfully opposed an application, by or supported by the plaintiff, to remit to the county court (Ord.62 r.17(8)); (d) on an appeal from the county court; (e) in judgment in default for a debt or recovery of land, or in summary judgment under Order 14, where the scale costs in Order 62 Appendix 3 apply. It does not apply to any proceedings by the Crown.[49] It could be argued that the costs penalty does not apply to an action removed from the county court, on the basis that proceedings which were in fact commenced in the county court are not "proceedings which could have been commenced in the county court"; but Girvan J has said *obiter* in a judgment about removal: "If the plaintiff fails to recover the sum in excess of the county court jurisdiction, then normally he will only recover costs on the county court scale".[50] The costs penalty applies only to costs between party and party,[51] not between solicitor and own client.[52] The costs penalty applies

---

45 *Hughes* v *Justin* [1894] 1 QB 667.

46 *Joynt* v *Mecredy* (1899) 33 ILTR 175.

47 *Peter Cox* v *Thirwell* (1981) 125 SJ 481 (writ served by ordinary post when defendant on holiday).

48 In r 17(5) there is a mistaken reference to para.(7), which should be to para.(6).

49 Crown Proceedings Act, s.20(2)(c).

50 In *Dooley* v *Murdock Harwood*, QBD, NI, 4 June 1996, at p.10.

51 *Guardians of Sligo* v *Miller* (1903) 3 NIJR 203.

52 *Carroll* v *Tighe* (1906) 40 ILTR 150.

where the award is reduced below the county court limit by the Court of Appeal, at least in relation to the costs in the High Court.[53]

17.25 Section 59(2) does not apply to restrict costs awarded to a defendant, nor to a counterclaiming defendant,[54] because he has not chosen the forum;[55] nor to a defendant counterclaiming against a person added as defendant to a counterclaim;[56] nor does it apply to restrict costs of a counterclaim awarded to the plaintiff;[57] nor to costs awarded to the plaintiff on an unsuccessful application to set aside judgment in default.[58] In a case where the plaintiff recovers against the defendant and the defendant recovers against the third party, Girvan J gave county court scale costs against the defendant, to be re-imbursed by the third party, with the defendant's costs on full High Court taxation to be paid by the third party.[59]

"Damages or other relief awarded"

17.26 The Taxing Master considers only the damages or relief actually awarded, not what the judge might have given; if the plaintiff is dissatisfied with the form or amount of the relief he should appeal.[60] The amount claimed in the writ or Statement of Claim is irrelevant.[61] He should consider only the relief which the court of trial granted or would have granted if not conceded as a result of the litigation.[62]

17.27 In the unfortunate absence of any reported decision interpreting the words in section 59(2), one must resort to the many decisions under its ancestors in the RSC(Ir) 1905,[63] which use the words: "having regard to the amount recovered or paid in settlement or the relief awarded". The different wording may be significant. Where the Court awarded £15 for assault and £15 for false imprisonment, being two separate causes of action, the plaintiff was held to have recovered £30 in the action.[64] If the plaintiff's award was reduced below the county court limit by reason of a set-off proper,[65] he suffered the costs penalty; but not where the award was so reduced by reason of a full counterclaim.[66] The penalty did not apply where the award was reduced by reason of a payment after action commenced,[67] even if the defendant paid in

---

[53] *Reynolds* v *Enfield Cycle Co* (1903) 3 NIJR 205; decided under old Rules (Wylie Ord.65 r.65(41)). Fitzgibbon LJ held that the penalty would also apply to costs in the Court of Appeal but the other judges left that point open.

[54] Judicature Act, s.120.

[55] *Blake* v *Appleyard* (1878) 3 Ex D 195.

[56] *Lewin* v *Trimming* (1888) 21 QBD 230.

[57] *Colton* v *McCaughey* [1969] 3 All ER 1460; *Griffith* v *Patterson* (1888) 22 LR Ir 656; *Amon* v *Bobbett* (1889) 22 QBD 543.

[58] *Spencer* v *Hayes* [1894] 2 IR 14.

[59] *Morris* v *Wallis*, QBD, NI, 4 February 1997.

[60] *Nicolls* v *Corr* [1909] 2 IR 655, at 667-73.

[61] *Hudson* v *Dublin Corp* [1931] IR 264.

[62] *Buckley* v *Healy* [1965] IR 618 (SC), where the majority held that the plaintiff was adjudged not to be entitled to an injunction.

[63] Wylie, Ord.65 r.4 and r.65(41)(42).

[64] *Donnelly* v *Verschoyle* [1919] 2 IR 101 (distinguishing *Myers* v *Phelan* below).

[65] *Ryan* v *Fraser* (1884) 16 LR Ir 253.

[66] *Griffiths* v *Patterson* (1888) 22 LR Ir 656; Wylie p.882.

[67] *Quinn* v *McKinlay* [1902] 2 IR 315; *Murray* v *O'Riordan* (1915) 49 ILTR 186.

ignorance of the issue of the writ.[68] Where a solicitor suing on a bill of costs included an item for a fee payable to an expert, and the defendant after action brought paid the sum directly to the expert, the sum was held to be part of the money recovered.[69] The penalty did not apply where the defendant proved a tender before action of part of the debt awarded, unless the tender was in respect of a severable debt.[70]

17.28 Money was held to be "recovered in the action" if it was paid under a compromise,[71] or accepted by the plaintiff as a lodgment.[72] If the plaintiff refuses the lodgment and at the trial is awarded £14 on the first cause and £10 on the second, he was deemed to have recovered in the action only £10.[73] If the plaintiff is awarded less than the county court limit against one co-defendant, he is entitled only to the reduced costs against that defendant, even if he is awarded more than the county court limit on a separate cause of action against the other defendant.[74] If the plaintiff is given Order 14 summary judgment for £10 and proceeds at the trial to recover an award of £10 then *semble*, he has recovered £20 in the action.[75]

17.29 If defendants are sued in the alternative and the plaintiff recovers less than the county court limit from the defendant liable, he gets the reduced costs against him and the Court should make a *Sanderson* order, that the losing defendant to pay the winning defendant's full costs;[76] or it can make a *Bullock* order for payment by the losing defendant to the plaintiff of such of the winning defendant's costs as would be recoverable on a county court decree.[77]

17.30 Where the statute restricting costs applied "in case the jury shall find the damages to be under 40 shillings", it was held not to apply where the plaintiff accepted 6 pence lodged in court.[78] Under the same statute, where the action joins two separate causes, and the defendant makes a lodgment of £1 in respect of the first cause, and the plaintiff accepts it and proceeds to trial and is awarded £2 on the second cause, he is deemed for costs purposes to have been awarded only £2.[79] These cases are probably not authoritative under the

---

68 *Lamb* v *Keeping* (1914) 111 LT 527.
69 *Scott* v *McDade* (1898) 32 ILTR 89.
70 *Scott's Tyre* v *Northern Wheeleries* [1899] 2 IR 34; *Bradshaw* v *McMullan* (1922) 56 ILTR 93.
71 *Colton* v *McCaughey* [1969] 3 All ER 1460.
72 *Donnelly* v *Coyne* [1901] 2 IR 7. The defendant having delivered up the goods claimed, the action became one for damages only.
73 *Myers* v *Phelan* (1890) 26 LR Ir 218; overruling *Arkins* v *Armstrong* (1869) IR 3 CL 373.
74 *Duxbury* v *Barlow* [1901] 2 KB 23.
75 Though in *Barker* v *Hempstead* (1889) 23 QBD 8, that was held to be the case only because the statute said so.
76 *Parkes* v *Knowles* [1957] 3 All ER 600.
77 Cf. *Rice* v *Toombes* [1971] IR 38.
78 *McSheffrey* v *Lanagan* (1887) 20 LR Ir 528.
79 *Walsh* v *Walsh* (1866) 17 ICLR 195. The judges in this case based their decision on two grounds: (a) that on acceptance of the lodgment the action became an action on the second cause only; and (b) that where an action joins two causes they are two separate actions for the purposes of costs. The second ground is definitely overruled by *Donnelly* v *Vershoyle*, above. *Walsh* was treated as wrong by the dissenting minority in *Myers* v *Phelan*.

"recovered in the action" test, but may be more relevant to the "damages or other relief awarded" test in section 59(2) of the Judicature Act.

"Could have been obtained in proceedings commenced in the county court"

17.31 The jurisdiction of the county court is set out in Chapter 2 of the author's *County Court Procedure in NI* (see in particular Chap.2.29). The financial limits are those set by the County Courts (NI) Order 1980.[80] If an equitable remedy, such as injunction, declaration or specific performance, or damages in lieu thereof, is awarded in a High Court action, the plaintiff is entitled to full High Court costs, unless (a) the action is within the equity or title jurisdiction of the county court; or (b) the plaintiff has claimed and/or been awarded common law damages not exceeding £15,000, even nominal damages.[81] If the High Court awards £15,000 plus interest thereon under section 33A of the Judicature Act the costs penalty applies because the county court could have done so under Article 45A of the County Courts Order. If the plaintiff claims in his writ an injunction or other equitable remedy alone, then he is entitled to High Court costs if he is awarded that injunction, or even if he is awarded damages in lieu of that injunction.[82] If the action is framed as one over which the county court has no jurisdiction, such as Admiralty, the plaintiff is entitled to full costs.[83]

17.32 With the two recent increases in the county court jurisdiction, (in debt and damages claims, from £5,000 to £10,000 in November 1992; to £15,000 in September 1993) High Court Judges have had to decide on several occasions whether these provisions apply if the judgment now given is for a sum within the present county court jurisdictional limit but beyond that limit as it was when the writ was issued. There has never been any reported judgment on this point, except *Cretazzo* v *Lombardi.*[84] There Hogarth J, in the South Australian Supreme Court, held that if the plaintiff in a High Court action failed to recover more than the limit of a local court as it stood at the time when he could last have applied for remittal of the action to that court, the costs penalty should apply.

17.33 The general impression amongst practitioners in previous years when the county court jurisdiction was increased, was that the plaintiff should get full High Court costs if he beat the limit as it was when he issued his writ.[85] After November 1992 there were a few cases in which Judges treated the costs penalty as applicable if the plaintiff failed to beat the current county court limit, thus following unconsciously *Cretazzo* v *Lombardi*. However in March 1993 the High Court Judges conferred and let it be known through Carswell J that

---

80 As amended by SR 1993/282 from 1 September 1993.

81 See the cases cited in the author's *County Court Procedure in NI*. *Keates* v *Woodward* [1902] 1 KB 532 and *Buckley* v *Healy* [1965] IR 618 are not authoritative because of the wording of the statutes under which they were decided.

82 *Beaumont* v *Figgis* [1945] IR 78.

83 *Grimes* v *Owners of SS Bangor Bay* [1948] IR 350.

84 (1975) 13 SASR 4; [1976] Australian Law Digest p.91.

85 Jones LJ implied so in *Bell* v *Quinn* [1982] 8 NIJB, though he said he was acting under the general discretion.

they would adopt the traditional view. Thus if a plaintiff who issued his writ in 1991 recovers more than £5,000, he will receive full High Court costs as of right. However a Court before which the issue is fully argued might take a different view.[86]

Half costs: contributory negligence cases

17.34 If the amount quantified by the Court as the full amount of the claim exceeds the county court limit but the amount awarded is within rule 17(4) by reason only of a deduction for the claimant's own fault, the rule is, unless the judge otherwise directs, that the plaintiff recover one-half of High Court costs (Ord.62 r.17(5)(6)). The Judges in March 1993 further decided that the half costs rule for a plaintiff whose award fell within the county court limit due to contributory negligence was often unjust because half High Court costs would be rather less than full county court costs. Therefore, when a plaintiff's award of £20,000 is reduced by contributory negligence to a sum within the county court limit at the time of issue of the writ, he should be awarded half High Court costs or full county court costs, whichever is the greater. In doing so the Court would be refusing to give effect to a rule of the Supreme Court, and it would be preferable if the rule itself were amended by the Rules Committee. 'Half costs' means half of disbursements as well as half of profit costs.[87]

What costs are recoverable

17.35 Subject to the directions of the Court, it is for the Taxing Master to decide whether and how to apply section 59(2) and Order 62 rule 17. If he holds that section 59(2) applies, he taxes the costs allowing those items which would have been incurred in a county court action, and allows such sum as would have been allowable under the county court costs rules, exercising any discretion to allow costs which the county judge would have had (Ord.62 r.17(7)). He may also have to apply Order 55 rule 19 of the County Court Rules (NI) 1980, which restricts costs where the award is within the district judge's defended jurisdiction or could have been brought in the small claims court. When judgment is given for damages assessed by a master or judge after interlocutory judgment in default of appearance, the Taxing Master must apply Order 55 rule 14(3)(4) of the County Court Rules.[88] Often when actions are settled for a sum within the county court limit, the parties agree that the plaintiff recover "costs on the county court scale plus High Court outlay". In *Hesketh* v *Ford Motor Co*,[89] Taxing Master Napier, in taxing such agreed costs, held that 'High Court outlay' does not include the fees of counsel.

---

[86] Especially in view of the decision of Kerr J in *Brown* v *Hamilton* [1994] 1 BNIL 21, that the increase in the county court jurisdiction is retrospective in effect, in that a civil bill claim can be amended up to £15,000 even where the action was commenced before September 1993. Note also *Warnock* v *Harland & Wolff* [1976] NI 156.

[87] *Kennedy* v *Healy* [1897] 2 IR 258 (defendant's argument accepted, judgment being reserved on another point).

[88] *Black* v *Baxter*, QBD, NI (Master Wilson) January 1996.

[89] Taxing Office, NI, 11 May 1995.

Disapplication of section 59(2)

17.36 "For special cause shown and mentioned in the judgment making the award", the judge may direct that the plaintiff be awarded full High Court costs. The fact that a party is legally aided is irrelevant.[90] In *Lavelle* v *Robinson*[91] Lord MacDermott LCJ suggested *obiter* that an order for full costs might be given where the plaintiff reasonably assessed the case as worth more than the county court limit. In *Kavanagh* v *Kilmurray*[92] Davitt J made a special order for full costs where he thought that a jury award above the circuit court limit would not have been excessive. However in *Lavelle* v *Robinson,*[91] Sheil J thought that it would be wrong to make a special order merely because the award might have been higher. In *Finch* v *Telegraph Construction*[93] the fact that the injuries appeared more serious when the writ was issued was held by Devlin J not to be a special ground. In *Lavelle* v *Robinson*, the Court of Appeal held that complex issues of factory safety legislation were within the competence of any county court judge and thus did not justify a special order. That case was not cited in *Birch* v *Harland & Wolff*[94] where the special complexity of Health and Safety legislation was treated as a special cause.

17.37 A special order is a decision as to costs, and thus only appealable to the Court of Appeal by leave of the trial judge, but a special order made where no special cause exists is not a mere order as to costs and is appealable without leave.[95] In *Birch* v *Harland & Wolff*[94] the trial judge failed to state the special cause in his judgment, but the Court of Appeal, in agreeing with his decision, held that it had power to decide and insert in its judgment the special cause.

17.38 Whether or not section 59(2) applies, it is without prejudice to the general discretion of the judge to withhold costs altogether from the plaintiff and even to award costs against him. In *Whitmore* v *O'Reilly*[96] in a very small claim, the judge properly awarded general costs to the defendant, setting off and deducting the damages and county court scale costs awarded to the plaintiff. In a case where section 59(2) does not apply strictly but which is substantially a county court matter, the judge may award costs on county court scales, or no costs at all.[97] Where section 59(2) does apply, the judge may award the plaintiff a proportion of, or a gross sum in lieu of,[98] his county court scale costs, and if he finds and states a special cause he may award full High Court costs or a proportionate sum or a gross sum in lieu thereof. In *Birch* v *Harland & Wolff*[94] the Court awarded the plaintiff four-fifths of his full costs.

---

90 Cf. *Starkey* v *Railway Executive* [1951] 2 All ER 902.

91 [1964] NI 17; where the statute allowed a special certificate of the action was "fit to be tried in the High Court".

92 [1945] Ir Jur R 61; where the statute allowed a certificate "if it was reasonable ... that the action should have been commenced in the High Court".

93 [1949] 1 All ER 452.

94 [1991] NI 90, at 102.

95 *Lavelle* v *Robinson* [1964] NI 17.

96 [1906] 2 IR 357.

97 *Thornton* v *McTaggart* (1910) 44 ILTR 119.

98 *Black* v *Baxter*, QBD, NI (Master Wilson) January 1996.

COSTS WHERE SEPARATE ISSUES DISPUTED

17.39 If the losing party has won on one issue it is generally proper to divide the costs of that issue, rather than order a proportion of the whole costs to the winning party; and in general the winning party should not have to pay any costs unless he was unreasonable in disputing that issue.[99] The Court may order that the overall winner be given a fraction or percentage of his full costs, the loser to bear all his own costs. In dividing the costs of an issue the Taxing Master should determine what items, or what increase in the amount of an item is caused by the presence of that issue.[100] Where the plaintiff wins on the issue of liability he should not be deprived of any costs merely because he has lost on the issue of one head of damages, the defendant having failed to avail of the opportunity to make a sufficient lodgment.[101] Where the plaintiff wins on one cause of action and loses on another distinct cause of action, the costs should be apportioned/divided,[102] but the general costs of the action should be given to the plaintiff.[103] 'Apportioning' costs is a process which the Taxing Master performs where the Court order directs it: it involves making a proportionate split of costs of a common item. Unfortunately some judges tend to use the word 'apportion' without being aware of the distinction, as is explained in the *Medway Oil* case below.

COSTS WHERE CONTRIBUTORY NEGLIGENCE

17.40 In cases where the plaintiff proves his case on liability and the defendant also succeeds on the issue of contributory negligence, thus reducing the award to a specified proportion of the total damage, the authorities do not give satisfactory guidance on how costs should be dealt with. In the days when contributory negligence was a complete defence, costs of the whole action were to be awarded to the defendant.[104] The Court may make an order for costs to the plaintiff but costs referable to the issue of contributory negligence awarded to the defendant and the two sets of costs to be set off. If so, the Taxing Master should assess costs on the basis of the full value of the damage being at stake.[105] Alternatively the judge may award all the costs to the plaintiff, in which case the Master should apply the principle of *Carr* v *Poots* (para. 17.98) and assess costs taking into account the 'real' value. A more sensible course might be to

---

99 *Re Eglindata (No 2)* [1992] 1 WLR 1207.

100 *Smith* v *Campbell* (1895) 29 ILTR 97 (Andrews J); *Crean* v *McMillan* [1922] 2 IR 105 (High CA); *Millican* v *Tucker* [1980] 1 WLR 640.

101 *William Nimmo & Co* v *Russell Construction (No 2)*, 1997 SLT 122 (2nd Div).

102 *Kennedy* v *Healy* [1897] 2 IR 258. In *Bickerstaff* v *ATGWU*. QBD NI, 15 January 1965, Sheil J said that where there are two disjunctive causes of action they are two events, and that all items of costs should be apportioned and the general costs should not be given to the plaintiff unless so ordered by the judge. *Bickerstaff* is probably not to be followed because there is authority that separate causes of action are not separate events: see *Donnelly* v *Verschoyle* [1919] 2 IR 101, and *Medway Oil* v *Continental Contractors*, *infra*.

103 White Book (1997) 62/7/8; *Smith* v *Campbell* (1895) 29 ILTR 97. Note that there appears to be a mistake in line 6 of the report of the judgment: "defendant" should read "plaintiff".

104 *Jackson* v *Anglo-American Oil* [1923] 2 KB 601.

105 *McMahon* v *Donaldson* [1969] NI 145, at 165 (Lowry J) speaking in the context of costs after lodgment awarded to the defendant; but see *Carr* v *Poots* at para. 17.98.

award to the plaintiff a proportion of his full taxed costs, the proportion being commensurate with the proportionate reduction in damages.

Costs of claim and counterclaim

One party wins

17.41 If the plaintiff wins on both claim and counterclaim, then obviously he will be awarded all the costs of the action. If he has failed to beat the county court limit on his claim, he is restricted in the costs of the claim but he still gets full costs referable to the counterclaim.[106] If the defendant wins on both claim and counterclaim, he will also get the full costs of the action; but if the counterclaim was unnecessary in that it related only to matters in reduction of the claim, the Court may award no costs on the counterclaim.[107]

Both claims win

17.42 If the claim and counterclaim both succeed, the usual order is to direct the Taxing Master to award the general costs of the action to the plaintiff, but to award those costs which are solely attributable to the counterclaim to the defendant.[108] For example the costs of the writ and of a witness who testified as to the plaintiff's claim only are costs payable to the plaintiff; the costs of items and witnesses relating solely to the counterclaim are payable to the defendant; items such as counsel's brief fees or the expenses of a witness whose testimony touches on all issues are divided by estimating how much that cost is increased by the presence of the counterclaim.[109] Only by special order can the judge direct the Master to apportion costs, (i.e. to make a proportionate split of the cost of common items).[109]

17.43 If the counterclaim is in substance a set-off, the judge may give judgment for the balance and direct costs to be taxed on the basis that the plaintiff has recovered only the excess of claim over counterclaim. If the counterclaim is equal to the claim, he may dismiss the action and give all costs to the defendant. If the counterclaim exceeds the claim he may dismiss the claim with costs and give the defendant costs of the counterclaim to be taxed on the basis that he has recovered the excess.[110] However justice may require that even if the counterclaim is in substance an equitable set-off, the judge should give separate judgments for the claim with costs and the counterclaim with

---

[106] *Griffiths* v *Patterson* (1888) 22 LR Ir 656.

[107] *Curtis* v *Armstrong* [1897] 2 IR 327.

[108] *Medway Oil* v *Continental Contractors* [1929] AC 88; *Crean* v *McMillan* [1922] 2 IR 105; the same order being made where both claims are reduced by contributory negligence: *Connolly* v *Huddleston* [1952] NI 21. In relation to items which are common to both (e.g. counsel's brief fees, expenses of witnesses who give evidence relevant to both) the position is: (a) if the counterclaim is in substance a set-off, they are treated as costs of the claim; (b) if the counterclaim is in substance a separate cause of action, they are "apportioned" between claim and counterclaim: *Crean* v *McMillan*. In *Medway Oil*, this was approved, save that the Lords said that the word "divided" rather than "apportioned " should be used.

[109] *Millican* v *Tucker*[1980] 1 WLR 640.

[110] See *Hanak* v *Green* [1958] 2 QB 9 (equitable set-off).

costs, and can then order the two judgments to be set off against each other.[111] The Court can make any order which best reflects the justice of the outcome of the proceedings.[112] If the defendant makes a formal admission of the claim and wins at the trial on his counterclaim, the general practice is to award costs up to the date of admission and costs of setting down to the plaintiff, and all other costs to the defendant.[113]

Both claims lose

17.44 If the claim and counterclaim both fail, the above principles apply *mutatis mutandis*.[114] In other words the costs of the claim go to the defendant and the costs referable to the counterclaim go to the plaintiff, subject to the same principle of division or apportionment.

17.45 The above principles are subject, in the case (only) of the costs of an award on the plaintiff's claim, to the restriction on costs in section 59(2) where the award is within the county court jurisdiction (see para. 17.23).

Costs where defendant has lodged money in court

17.46 In a case where the plaintiff has recovered judgment for a sum not exceeding that lodged by the defendant under Order 22, the normal order is for the plaintiff to be awarded costs up to the date of lodgment and the defendant to be awarded costs thereafter. (See para. 11.162, and White Book (1997) 62/5/4).

COSTS WHERE MULTIPLE PARTIES

Two plaintiffs

17-47 Plaintiffs must be represented by the same solicitor, even if one is legally aided, and they receive only one set of costs if both win. Where one plaintiff X wins and the other Y loses, or where X beats his lodgment and Y does not, the normal alternative orders which can be made are-

- (A) The costs of each to be apportioned and the defendant to pay only those costs payable by X to the plaintiffs' solicitor, which on an item common to both plaintiffs is prima facie a half; and (B) (*i*) the defendant

---

[111] *Chell Engineering* v *Unit Tool* [1950] 1 All ER 378, where a judgment for the balance only would have meant that the plaintiff would recover only county court scale costs.

[112] For example in *Public Works* v *AF Hastings* [1972] June NIJB (Pt. I) at 20: the plaintiff won substantially on his damages claim for breach of contract and the defendant proved a small counterclaim for money due under it; Lord MacDermott simply gave judgment for the balance and awarded the plaintiff three quarters of his taxed costs. In *Forrest* v *Carte* [1897] 2 IR 314, an action for £150, the price of goods sold and delivered, where the defendant pleaded and counterclaimed that the goods were inferior, the jury awarded £120, deducting £30 for inferior quality, and one shilling on the counterclaim; the Divisional Court ordered general costs to the plaintiff, costs referable to the issues of defence to the defendant, and no order as to costs of the counterclaim.

[113] *NV Amsterdamsche Lucifersfabrieken* v *H & H* [1940] 1 All ER 587, the "Dutch Match case".

[114] *Crean* v *McMillan*; and *Medway Oil* v *Continental Contractors*.

to get his costs from Y solely attributable to Y's joinder;[115] or (*ii*) alternatively the defendant to get his full costs from Y.[116]
or

- (A) X to get full costs from the defendant; and (B) (*i*) the defendant to get his costs from Y solely attributable to Y's joinder; or (*ii*) alternatively no order as to costs between defendant and Y.[117]

17.47a *Representative or test action.* Where there are numerous claims arising out of the same or an identical transaction, and one plaintiff is selected to sue as a representative of all claimants, the Court may direct before the trial that, in the event of the action failing, all claimants be liable for a proportion of the costs payable by the selected plaintiff.[118]

Two defendants

17.48 Defendants A and B who are represented by one solicitor are in the same position as co-plaintiffs.[119] If A wins and B loses, A gets from the plaintiff only those costs which he is liable to pay to the defence solicitor, prima facie one-half of the general costs plus the whole of any costs incurred solely by him.[120] Defendants separately represented who both win will be allowed both sets of costs in full, only in so far as the separate representation was reasonable.[121]

17.49 If the plaintiff wins against defendants A and B on a joint or several liability on one cause of action, the plaintiff recovers one set of costs for which A and B are jointly liable with a right of contribution between A and B in the same proportion as their contribution to the damages.[122] If A allowed judgment in default against him or paid money in settlement and B lost after a trial, *semble*, the proper order should be that they are jointly liable for costs incurred up to judgment in default or settlement, and B solely liable for costs thereafter.[123]

17.50 If the plaintiff wins against defendant L but loses against W, then in the absence of a special order, the plaintiff will get his full costs against L, if L and W are represented by the same solicitor.[124] If L and W are separately represented and properly so, W will be entitled to his full costs from the plaintiff.

---

115 *Keen* v *Towler* (1924) 41 TLR 86; *Burns* v *Boland*, QBD, NI (Jones J) 15 March 1968; possibly ordered to be set off against costs payable to X: *Umfreville* v *Johnson* (1875) LR 10 Ch App 580.

116 *Terry* v *Gould (No 2)* (1924) 69 SJ 212.

117 See *Gort* v *Rowney* (1886) 17 QBD 625; doubted in *Keen* v *Towler*.

118 *Ward* v *Guiness Mahon & Co* [1996] 4 All ER 112 (CA).

119 See *Beaumont* v *Senior* [1903] 1 KB 282.

120 *McGowan* v *Hamilton* [1903] 2 IR 311; *Smithwick* v *Boland* (1905) 5 NIJR 269.

121 *Tobin* v *Hourihane* (1946) 80 ILTR 60; *Spalding* v *Gamage* [1914] 2 Ch 405 (where separate counsel were allowed though one solicitor was retained).

122 *Clarke* v *McLaughlin & Harvey* [1978] 2 NIJB.

123 See also *Banque Keyser* v *Skandia (No 2)* [1988] 2 All ER 880.

124 *O'Connell* v *Peckin* (1913) 47 ILTR 80; but see White Book (1997) 62/B/120.

'Bullock' order: defendants sued in the alternative

17.51 A situation often arises in which the judge, adjudging L liable, believes that the plaintiff has reasonably sued defendants L and W as being liable in the alternative on one cause of action, as in the case of drivers who have both denied fault and blamed each other for the accident,[125] or where L claims that he contracted as agent for W and W denies it. The two claims must be interdependent or in a real sense alternative.[126] The judge is then concerned to ensure that L should pay all the costs and that the plaintiff does not suffer in costs by having joined W. Whilst awarding the plaintiff costs against L, he may make either a *Sanderson* order, that L pay W's costs, or a *Bullock* order, that the plaintiff pay W's costs and add them to the bill of costs against L. A *Bullock* order was made in *McGucken* v *Kennedy*[127] where the judge thought that the plaintiff was persuaded to join W because of L's false allegations. A *Sanderson* order is proper where the plaintiff is insolvent.[128] It may also be made where L is insolvent.[129] It is generally more popular because it makes taxation proceedings easier. Confusingly, practitioners tend to call both types a *Bullock* order. An order should only be made if the conduct of L in relation to the plaintiff's claim makes it just that he should bear the costs.[130]

Third party joined

17.52 The Court has a discretion as to who should pay the costs of all parties. If the plaintiff loses the general practice is to award costs of the third party against the defendant. If the third party's joinder was a proper response to the plaintiff's claim, the Court may order the plaintiff to pay to the defendant his own costs and the costs payable to the third (and fourth etc.) party. In a proper case the plaintiff may be ordered to pay costs directly to the third (and fourth etc.) party. If the plaintiff wins, the costs of the third-party proceedings usually follow the event. If the defendant wins against the third party he will get not only his own costs but also the costs payable to the plaintiff. A third party who is substantially the real defendant may be ordered to pay costs directly to the plaintiff. See further para. 10.26.

COSTS IN PARTICULAR CASES

Costs out of a fund

17.53 Where litigation concerns the disposal or administration of property or a fund, such as probate actions, partition, administration of an estate, and partnership dissolution, it is common to award all parties, except a losing appellant, their costs out of the common fund if they have litigated reasonably.[131] 'Fund' includes any estate or real or personal property held for the benefit of persons or a class by a trustee/personal representative, whether in

---

125 *Mulligan* v *Mulligan* [1934] NI 9.
126 *Norwest Refrigeration* v *Bain Davies* (1984) 157 CLR 149, at 163.
127 [1928] NI 54.
128 *Mayer* v *Harte* [1960] 1 WLR 770, at 778-9,783.
129 *Bankamerica* v *Nock* [1988] AC 1002.
130 *Gould* v *Vaggelas* (1984) 157 CLR 215, at 229-30, 260.
131 See *Cummins* v *Murray* [1906] 2 IR 509; *In re Morelli* [1968] IR 11.

his possession or not (Ord.62 r.1(3)). The Taxing Master may restrict the costs of attendance at taxation proceedings to necessary parties; he may direct a copy of the bill of costs to be sent to a person interested in the fund informing him of the taxation proceedings (Ord.62 r.26). If no other party is interested in the fund, the applicant for taxation of his costs must apply for a nominee solicitor to represent the estate.[132]

Costs of trustee, mortgagee

17.54 A party to proceedings as a trustee, personal representative or mortgagee is entitled to his costs, insofar as not paid by another person, from the fund, estate or property represented by him, unless the Court otherwise orders on the ground that he has acted unreasonably (or as trustee/personal representative for his own benefit) (Ord.62 r.6(2)). Costs payable to a trustee/personal representative are to be taxed on the indemnity basis, but costs incurred contrary to his duty are presumed to be unreasonable (Ord.62 r.14). See the Practice Direction 1990 No.2 [1990] 6 BNIL 63.

17.55 A trustee/personal representative is entitled to all expenses of execution of the trust from the estate,[133] unless he is guilty of misconduct. [134] A trustee who acts also as solicitor is not generally entitled to profit costs;[135] but a solicitor who is a mortgagee is entitled to the same solicitor's fees and charges as if he were not his own solicitor.[136] If a trustee/personal representative has not obeyed an order to pay money owed by him to the estate, he will not be allowed his costs out of the estate.[137] A trustee who appeals unsuccessfully should not be allowed his costs from the estate.[138] A trustee in bankruptcy is entitled to costs out of the estate if he has consent or ratification for bringing or defending the action from the creditors' committee.[139] A trustee in bankruptcy, liquidator, receiver or personal representative who takes up the prosecution or defence of an action already commenced by or against the bankrupt, company or deceased, is entitled or personally liable for all the costs of the action, without prejudice to his right to costs from the estate. [140]

17.56 The case of *Re Beddoe*[141] approves the principle that a trustee is entitled to his costs out of the fund, but then says that he sues or defends an action without leave of the Court at his own peril; that in view of the

---

132 Practice Direction [1990] 6 BNIL 63.
133 Trustee Act (NI) 1958, s.31(2).
134 *Martin* v *Wilson* [1913] 1 IR 470.
135 White Book (1997) 62/14/8.
136 Mortgagees Legal Costs Act 1895.
137 *Ferris* v *O'Kean* [1907] 1 IR 223.
138 *Fogarty* v *O'Donoghue* [1926] IR 531.
139 Hunter's *Personal Insolvency*, para..28.24.
140 *Watson* v *Holliday* (1882) 20 Ch D 780; *Pembroke* v *Warren* [1896] 1 IR 76, at 103, 142; even if, as a receiver, he is not a party: *Anderson* v *Hyde* [1996] 3 BNIL 6; 'The Times', 2 May 1996 (CA). A liquidator is, for policy reasons, only to be made liable if impropriety and exceptional circumstances are shown: *Metalloy Supplies* v *MA (UK)*, 'The Times', 12 December 1996 (CA).
141 [1893] 1 Ch 547, at 557-8.

comparative ease and small expense in obtaining the opinion of the Chancery Court on whether to litigate at the expense of the trust, if he loses in the litigation it is for him to show that the costs were properly incurred. *Re Beddoe* was a case in which the trustee unsuccessfully defended a Queen's Bench action against the trust and subsequently applied to the Chancery Court by originating summons for an order that the costs of the action be paid out of the trust estate. A *Beddoe* application need only be made where the trustee wished to ensure *in advance of* the disposal of the litigation that he will recover his costs; it must be made by separate proceeding, not by summons in the litigation itself, and such an order will only be made if the trustee shows that it is just to do so, that he has a good cause for suing or defending, that the court hearing the litigation would probably grant his costs and that there are special circumstances to justify making the order in advance.[142]

17.57 Most mortgage deeds provide that the mortgagee's full legal costs be added to the mortgage debt. A mortgagee has a contractual right to his costs out of the property, but not if he is guilty of misconduct, [143] nor if he has incurred costs improperly or unreasonably (Ord.62 r.10),[144] nor if he proceeds after his debt has been satisfied,[145] nor if the issue in the litigation is his title to the mortgage or rights thereunder.[146]

Party under disability

17.58 The next friend of a minor or mental patient plaintiff is personally liable for costs, with a right of re-imbursement from the plaintiff's property if he acted *bona fide* and reasonably.[147] Where a settlement is not approved by the Court, the costs of the application should be allowed unless there is evidence that there were not reasonably incurred.[148] The guardian *ad litem* of a defendant is not personally liable unless so ordered because of his misconduct.[149] If costs are awarded against a party under disability, no order for costs is to be drawn up until it is ascertained whether he or his next friend/guardian is to pay the costs.[150] As to taxation of costs, see para. 17.79.

Personal litigant

17.59 In taxing costs of a litigant in person[151] (other than a practising solicitor) the Taxing Master may allow a sum not exceeding two-thirds of what

---

142 *Alsop Wilkinson* v *Neary* [1996] 1 WLR 1221 (Ch D).

143 *McDonnell* v *McMahon* (1889) 23 LR Ir 283 (successful redemption suit).

144 E.g. the costs of a proceeding which is useless or mistaken: *National and Provincial Building Soc* v *Chambers* [1996] 6 BNIL 76 (Girvan J); *National and Provincial Building Soc* v *Graham* [1997] 2 BNIL 76 (Master Ellison).

145 *Cassidy* v *Sullivan* (1878) 1 LR Ir 313.

146 *Parker-Tweedale* v *Dunbar Bank* [1991] Ch 26.

147 *McNicholl* v *Neely* [1983] NI 43; *McHugh* v *Phoenix Laundry* [1966] IR 60; White Book (1997) 62/16/4.

148 *Shanley* v *Casey* [1967] IR 338.

149 White Book (1997) 62/B/123.

150 Practice Direction (LCJ) [1982] 9 BNIL 90.

151 Which means the party himself; it does not include the director of a company, which must appear by a solicitor: *Jonathan Alexander* v *Proctor* [1996] 1 WLR 518 (CA).

would have been allowed for work done by a solicitor and all of his disbursements; he can allow a reasonable sum up to £8 per hour (from 1 November 1992) and £9.25 per hour (from 1 September 1996) for time spent on an item involving no pecuniary loss;[152] the litigant cannot recover witness expenses for himself if he is allowed costs for attending as advocate (Ord.62 r.18).[153] He is allowed two-thirds of a notional solicitor's profit charges, but nothing for a notional counsel's fee. The costs provisions for 14-day costs, summary judgment and judgment in default in a debt or recovery of land case do not apply. The rule does not apply to a solicitor litigant in person, who is entitled to full costs which he would have claimed if acting for a lay client including any scale fees, save those charges and disbursements which are rendered unnecessary by reason of him being his own client.[154]

Costs in Crown Proceedings

17.59a See para. 17.09.

COSTS OF MISCONDUCT, NEGLECT

17.60 If it appears to the Court that anything has been done or omitted improperly or unreasonably by a party, it may order that party's costs in respect thereof to be disallowed and/or order him to pay costs occasioned by it to another party, or it may refer the matter to the Taxing Master (Ord.62 r.10). For example where defendants employ separate solicitors unnecessarily; or a party adopts an inappropriate mode of procedure or needlessly multiplies proceedings which could be brought in one action; or a party fails to agree facts or documents for no good reason. The same principle is reflected in various rules, such as Order 62 rule 5 (para. 17.06) and rule 6 (para. 17.07). The Court may order costs of an unnecessary oral evidence to be borne by the party who caused it (Ord.62 r.10A).

COSTS AGAINST A SOLICITOR

17.61 A party's solicitor who has received costs under an order which is set aside or reversed on appeal[155] is not personally liable to repay. Generally there is no power to order costs against a party's solicitor or barrister as such,[156] except against a solicitor: (a) on application of the Official Solicitor the Court can make him personally liable for unpaid court fees (Ord.62 r.11(7)); (b) on his undertaking to do so; or (c) under the following rule.

17.62 Where it appears that costs have been improperly or unreasonably incurred, or wasted by lack of competence or expedition, by a solicitor or his agent, the Court may order the solicitor to re-imburse his client for costs payable to another party; re-imburse another party for his own costs; and

---

152 I.e. time spent outside working hours: *Mainwaring* v *Goldbeck Investments* [1997] 1 All ER 467 (Ch D).

153 Made under the Litigants in Person (Costs and Expenses) Act 1975.

154 *Morgan* v *Kelly* (1897) 31 ILT 546; *McHale* v *Johnston* (1935) 69 ILTR 256; White Book (1997) 62/B/134.

155 *Newman* v *Caffelle* (1900) 34 ILTR 108n*; *Burke* v *Beatty* [1928] IR 91.

156 *Tolstoy-Miloslavsky* v *Aldington* [1996] 1 WLR 736 (CA).

disallow his costs against his own client (Ord.62 r.11). It can order him to repay costs to the Legal Aid Fund. The Court may make such order forthwith, or after directing a report from the Taxing Master, or may refer the matter to him. The solicitor must always be given an opportunity to appear and show cause against the order, except where the solicitor's absence or failure to proceed has caused a court proceeding to be abortive. Because of a change by statute in England in 1991, the principles applicable in Northern Ireland remain as stated in *Gupta* v *Comer*.[157] There is no need to show gross dereliction or misconduct; the purpose is compensatory rather than punitive. Apart from rule 11 the Supreme Court has inherent power to order restitution, compensation or costs against solicitor, but only in a case of serious misconduct or gross negligence,[158] or breach of undertaking (para. 16.62). The solicitor can appeal against the order without leave (see para. 20.08).

17.63 Where the Solicitors' Disciplinary Tribunal finds that a solicitor has not provided good service to his client, it may limit his costs (Solicitors (NI) Order 1976, Art.51A), and for the purposes of taxation or payment of costs by his client (and therefore also of taxation of costs payable by another party to the client) the amount so limited shall be deemed to be the proper charges (Art.51A(5)).

17.64 *Counsel.* Costs cannot be awarded against counsel.[159] English counsel are, since 1991, not so fortunate. Of course, counsel, and solicitor, may be liable in an action for negligence in the conduct of proceedings outside the area of advocacy.

COSTS OF INTERLOCUTORY PROCEEDINGS AND ADJOURNMENTS

17.65 Normally, where X brings a successful application against Y, the order is "X's costs in the cause"; and if Y successfully resists it "Y's costs in the cause". Where X's application has been made necessary by his own default, (e.g. application for adjournment or to extend time) the normal order would be "costs to Y". Unless otherwise ordered, costs are not to be taxed until the conclusion of the cause or matter, but if on application it appears to the Taxing Master that the case is unlikely to progress further, he may tax forthwith the costs of interlocutory proceedings (Ord.62 r.8(1)(2)(8)). If an interlocutory order is silent as to costs, they are treated as costs in the cause unless otherwise ordered,[160] or the successful party's costs in the cause.[161] But note that "No order as to costs" is an order dealing with costs, ordering each party to bear his

---

157 [1991] 1 QB 629. See the White Book (up to 1991 ed.) 62/11. See also *O'Neill* v *Nicholson* [1996] 4 BNIL 77 (M.Higgins J), where costs were awarded against the plaintiff's solicitor because adjournment of the trial was caused by his failure to send a two-week-old medical report to the defence until the last working day before the trial and to his own counsel until the morning of the trial.

158 White Book (up to 1991 ed.) Vol. 2 [3873].

159 *Davy-Chiesman* v *Davy-Chiesman* [1984] Fam 48, where the solicitor was held liable for following the glaringly wrong advice of counsel. In *Reid* v *Edinburgh Accoustics,* 1995 SLT 982, the solicitor was held not liable for following counsel's wrong advice.

160 *Dawson* v *Thomson* (1837) 5 Law Rec NS 199.

161 *Friis* v *Para.mount Bagwash (No 2)* [1940] 2 KB 654; White Book (1997) 62/B/79.

own.[160] Where by consent an interlocutory hearing is treated as the hearing of the action, the Court may direct that the full costs of action be taxed.[162]

17.66 If a trial or other proceeding is adjourned, the "costs of the day" (rather than "costs thrown away") should be ordered to be borne by the party who applied for the adjournment, or by the other party if his conduct has justified the application.[163] If the plaintiff has been given an adjournment of the trial with costs against him, the action can be stayed until he pays the costs.[164] If the trial is adjourned because a judge is not available, that is regarded as one of the hazards of litigation and the costs of the day should be costs in the cause.[165]

17.67 Interlocutory costs can be ordered to be paid forthwith, but not against a legally aided party. There is no rule that an action should be stayed because costs of a previous interlocutory proceeding have not been paid,[166] but a renewed motion may be stayed pending payment of costs of a previous abandoned motion.[167]

17.68 *Proceedings under judgment.* Costs of proceedings under a Chancery judgment are costs of the suit unless further consideration is reserved.[168]

COSTS OF APPEALS AND REMOVED PROCEEDINGS

17.69 *Appeal to Court of Appeal.* The Court of Appeal can deal with costs incurred both in the appeal and in the lower court (Judicature Act, s.38(1)(g); Ord.62 r.8(4)), as to which see para. 20.73.

17.70 *Appeal to High Court.* The High Court on an appeal has the same powers as the court/tribunal appealed from and may make such order as it thinks fit as to costs and expenses.[169] In such cases, and where a judge is hearing an appeal from a master, the appellate court may deal with the costs 'here and below', and may specify the costs to be allowed for the proceedings before the master or direct their taxation by the lower court or its officer (Ord.62 r.8(4)(6)). On an appeal from the county court, it may direct the costs of the proceedings in the county court to be taxed by the Taxing Master (Ord.62 r.8(6)(c)).

17.71 *Removed proceedings.* If proceedings are transferred or removed from another court to the High Court, it may deal with the whole costs, subject to order of removal, and may specify the pre-removal costs or order them to be taxed by the previous court or its officer (Ord.62 r.8(5)(6)). Where proceedings have been transferred or removed from the county court to the High Court, the High Court will, subject to the order of removal, deal with all the costs (Ord.62 r.8(5)(7)).

---

162 *Byrne* v *Fox* [1938] IR 683, at 693-4.

163 *O'Driscoll* v *Irish Shell* [1968] IR 215. *Sed quaere*, now that "costs of the day" is not defined in Ord.62 r.3(5).

164 *McCombe* v *Simmons* (1879) 4 LR Ir 527.

165 Practice Note 21 April 1986 (by Taxing Master addressed to the LCJ).

166 *Foley* v *Daly* [1938] Ir Jur R 5.

167 White Book (1997) 62/B/89.

168 Daniel's *Chancery Practice* (8th ed., Stevens 1914) p.1016.

169 Interpretation Act (NI), s.22.

SOLICITOR AND OWN CLIENT COSTS

17.72 It should not be forgotten that the primary liability for all costs incurred by a solicitor lies with his client (or if legally-aided, the Legal Aid Fund). Where the opposing party in the litigation is ordered to pay the client's costs, they are payable to the client, not to his solicitor. (In practice the opposing party pays the costs directly to the solicitor, who credits them against the liability of the client, but the client could insist on the costs being paid to him.) The liability of the client for his solicitor's costs rests on the relationship of contract between them, but they rarely agree terms as to the amount of remuneration. The courts have an important role in that respect, and also a supervisory role.

17.73 In the Solicitors (NI) Order 1976, "contentious business" means business done in or for the purposes of proceedings begun before a court or arbitrator; "non-contentious business" is any other business done as a solicitor, including non-contentious probate (Art.3). Thus work done in preparation for an action which is never commenced is non-contentious. "Client" includes any person as principal or agent retaining a solicitor and any person liable to pay his costs (Art.3). An "employee" of a solicitor includes an apprentice or clerk (Art.3). An unqualified person who purports to act as a solicitor cannot sue for his costs, nor are his costs recoverable in any proceedings by him (Arts.19(2)(b); 25(1)), but a solicitor who has no practising certificate can (Art.25(3)). An Irish solicitor can contract with an English solicitor for the costs of suing in Ireland for the English solicitor's client.[170]

Solicitor's methods of enforcing costs

17.74 A solicitor in contentious business may take security from the client for his costs; and has good cause to withdraw on reasonable notice if the client does not comply with a request for a reasonable sum on account; and on application for an order declaring that the solicitor has ceased to act, the court may determine the reasonableness (Solicitors Order, Art.69). At common law he has a 'passive lien', a right to retain documents or money in his possession as against his client for unpaid costs.[171]

17.75 The solicitor has an active or charging lien at common law, without any court order, for the costs of proceedings over any property (including money or costs, but excluding land) recovered or preserved in those proceedings.[172] Also, any court in which he has conducted proceedings may at any time declare for him a charge for his costs on the property (including land) recovered or preserved in the proceedings and may make orders for taxation and payment of the costs (Art.71H), on application to a judge in chambers (Ord.106 r.2). The charge can cover costs paid to a party under a court order,[173]

---

170 *Porter* v *Kirtlan* [1917] 2 IR 138.

171 See *Curry* v *Rea* [1937] NI 1; *Rath* v *McMullan* [1916] 1 IR 349; White Book (1997) Vol. 2 [3885].

172 White Book (1997) Vol. 2 [3886-9].

173 *Garbett* v *Cooper (No 2)* [1936] NI 64, even if not yet taxed: *Fairfold Properties* v *Exmouth Docks (No 2)* [1993] Ch 196.

property or money preserved or recovered under a compromise,[174] but not the amount by which a claim is reduced by a set-off of costs due to the client.[175] Where a plaintiff's claim to land is disputed, a compromise whereby he abandons his claim to the land in return for money does not make the land 'recovered or preserved'.[176] Where a defendant vendor is persuaded by his solicitor not to contest an action for specific performance, the charge cannot attach to the proceeds of sale.[177] Only costs incurred by the solicitor after he is retained are protected.[178] If the client sacks his solicitor during the action, the solicitor can still apply.[179] The court has a discretion to refuse to enforce the charge, as where the solicitor has delayed in applying and a third person has acquired *bona fide* rights in the property.[180] If the court has ordered costs due between the parties to be set off against each other, the charge attaches only to the balance, if any (para. 17.110).

17.76 *Collusive compromise.* If the plaintiff settles his action without reference to his solicitor with the intent and likely effect of depriving the latter of his costs, the latter may apply for leave to continue the action to recover his costs from the defendant,[181] if the defendant had notice of the lien and colluded with the plaintiff.[182] It may be that if the plaintiff buys off the defendant collusively with the object of preventing the defendant's solicitor from having a lien on the costs of a possible dismiss, the solicitor can apply for an order for his costs against the plaintiff.[183]

17.77 A solicitor cannot bring an action for his costs unless a signed bill of costs (describing the services done with a lump sum charge and itemising the disbursements) has been delivered before action is commenced to the person to be charged (Arts.71D-71E).[184] Unless and until the court orders taxation, the solicitor is free to sue on his untaxed bill of costs as a debt.[185] The High Court (and in relation to county court business, the county court) has jurisdiction to order delivery by a solicitor of a bill of costs and of any documents in his

---

174 *McLarnon* v *Carrickfergus UDC* [1904] 2 IR 44.

175 *Barry* v *Griffin* (1906) 40 ILTR 10.

176 *Cole* v *Dawson* (1882) 16 ILTR 96 (so held on appeal, the Exchequer Division being divided).

177 *Re Flynn & McMorrow* [1951] Ir Jur Rep 1.

178 *Kearney* v *AG* (1916) 50 ILTR 85.

179 *Steel* v *Slocock* (1926) 60 ILTR 100.

180 *Roche* v *Roche* (1892) 29 LR Ir 339.

181 *In re Cosgrave* [1937] IR 292.

182 *Manley* v *Law Society* [1981] 1 WLR 335, at 347B.

183 *Colville* v *Hall* (1865) 10 Ir Jur NS 261; not collusive in that case because the defendant's attorney was aware of it.

184 A defect in the bill is not fatal to the action; the Court can allow a new bill to be delivered: *Zuliani* v *Veira* [1994] 3 LRC 705 (PC). This requirement only applies to a Northern Ireland solicitor, not to an English or foreign solicitor suing here for his costs: *Wilson* v *Casey* (1952) 86 ILTR 34. A solicitor can issue a statutory demand without prior delivery of a bill of costs, under the Insolvency (NI) Order 1989 (see para. 5.13): *Re a Debtor* [1993] Ch 286.

185 *Gilsenan* v *McGovern* (1892) 30 LR Ir 300.

possession (Art.71C). The Chancery Division on originating summons may order the solicitor to deliver a cash account or pay to the client or the court any money or securities or give a list thereof, and the Court may thereon order security for and taxation of any costs claimed by the solicitor (Ord.106 rr.3-5). Either solicitor or client (or person liable to pay the costs) may apply to the Taxing Master[186] for (delivery and) taxation of a bill of costs (Art.71F). Save in exceptional circumstances, the client cannot apply more than three months after delivery, nor after he has paid or suffered judgment on the bill;[187] the client cannot apply at all after six months (Art.71F(3)). This latter time limit is absolute.[188] If solicitor and client dispute the existence of a retainer, the High Court may determine it and if found may order the bill of costs to be taxed (Art.71F(1)), and the taxation proceedings must be commenced within two months (Ord.62 r.29(2)). Where the solicitor has delivered a bill and then been ordered to deliver a bill for taxation, he cannot make a higher claim for costs in the new bill.[189] Applications to the Court under Articles 71C-71H are to a judge in chambers (Ord.106 r.2). Procedure on taxation is outlined in Article 71F-71G, with an appeal from the Taxing Master to the High Court. Order 62 rules 12-35 apply, and the Practice Directions Consolidation 11 April 1988 Part 1 (set out in Anderson p.163), especially paragraphs 8-9.

Assessing amount of solicitor's costs

17.78 Except where the client is legally-aided, taxation is on the indemnity basis; costs are presumed reasonably incurred and reasonable in amount if they are expressly or impliedly approved by the client; unusual costs are presumed unreasonably incurred unless the solicitor shows that he forewarned the client that they might not be awarded *inter partes* (Ord.62 r.15). Any interest received on a judgment for costs belongs to the client, unless expressly agreed otherwise.[190] The Master applies Order 62 Appendix 2 in the taxation, but where any of the business is of like kind to non-contentious business, he must tax in accordance with any general regulatory order of the Non-contentious Costs Committee (Ord.62 r.17(2)).[191] A disbursement claimed in the bill will be disallowed if the client shows that it has not yet been paid by the solicitor; and in any case payment of all disbursements must be vouched before the taxation certificate is issued.[192] Subject to any rules, the Master may allow interest on money disbursed, or improperly retained by the solicitor, and assess remuneration in the light of the skill, labour and responsibility involved (Solicitors (NI) Order 1976, Art.70). The Master may issue an interim certificate as to any amount due from the solicitor to the client, which amount the Court may order to be paid to the client or into court (Ord.62 r.22(2)(3)).

---

186 By originating summons with an appeal to a judge: Ord.106 r.2A.

187 See *In re Horan* [1964] IR 263.

188 Cf. *Harrison* v *Tew* [1990] 2 AC 523.

189 *Agitrex* v *O'Driscoll* [1995] 2 ILRM 23 (Lynch J).

190 White Book (1997) 62/35/9.

191 They are the Solicitors Remuneration Order SR 1977/252; and Solicitors Remuneration (Land Registry) Order SR 1977/253: see Anderson Chap.2.

192 Anderson p.45.

The Court may disallow costs where the solicitor has been at fault (Ord.62 r.11, para. 17.62).

17.79 When money is claimed or recovered or awarded or agreed to be paid for a minor plaintiff (or counterclaiming defendant), unless the Court otherwise orders, the costs of the minor and of any adult co-plaintiff to his own solicitor are taxed on the 'indemnity basis' (Ord.62 r.16(2)), the costs payable by the defendant on the lesser 'standard basis'. The Master has to certify the difference between the two (Ord.62 r.16(3)), that difference is the amount payable to the plaintiff's solicitor out of the damages. However in most cases the solicitors for each party will agree costs so as to create no discrepancy, either by the defence agreeing to pay indemnity costs and/or the plaintiff's solicitor waiving any further costs. The rule applies equally to a 'patient'.

Agreement as to costs between solicitor and client

17.80 A solicitor may make a written agreement for remuneration in contentious business[193] at a gross sum or salary or otherwise (1976 Order, Art.64). The costs thereunder are not subject to taxation and the solicitor need not deliver a bill of costs (Art.65), but either solicitor or client may apply to a judge in chambers (Ord.106 r.2) who may enforce it if it is fair and reasonable, set it aside or determine its validity or effect (Art.66). To be enforceable by the solicitor the agreement must be fully evidenced in writing.[194] The client may enforce an oral agreement.[195] If the agreed costs have already been paid the person who has paid may apply within 12 months (time extendable) in special circumstances for the agreement to be reopened (Art.66(5)). If the business covered by the agreement is in an action, the client may apply to the Taxing Master to examine it (Art.66(3)(4); Ord.106 r.2B). If the client is a guardian/trustee/controller etc. of a minor/beneficiary/patient whose property is to be charged with the costs, the agreement must be examined by the Taxing Master before payment and if not the client and solicitor are liable to re-imburse (Art.67; Ord.106 r.2B). If the solicitor dies, is dismissed or withdraws before completing the agreed work, the Court may enforce it or set it aside and may direct the taxation of the work already done (Art.68). The powers under Articles 66-9 are exercised by the High Court Judge (in chambers: Ord.106 r.2) and Taxing Master in all business done in the High Court and Lands Tribunal and in any other court where more than £5,000[196] is payable; otherwise the powers are vested in the county court and district judge respectively (Art.66(6)(7)).

Non-contentious costs

17.81 Under Article 71 of the 1976 Order, a "Non-contentious Costs Committee" makes orders regulating the remuneration of solicitors in non-contentious business, to which any taxation is subject. But the solicitor and

---

193 Which must have no "champertous" provision for the solicitor to purchase an interest of the client in the proceedings or stipulate for payment on success.

194 *Chamberlain* v *Boodle* [1982] 1 WLR 1443.

195 *O'Brien* v *Fleming* [1946] IR 236 (where its existence was disputed and the Master was directed to decide on full evidence).

196 A figure not increased in SR 1993/282 dealing with county court limits.

client can make a written agreement which is not subject to taxation, does not require delivery of a bill of costs, and is enforceable by the High Court (a judge in chambers: Ord.106 r.2) if it is fair and reasonable (Art.71A).

LEGAL AID

17.82 In this section references to the 'LA Order' are to the Legal Aid, Advice and Assistance (NI) Order 1981. The 'LA Gen Regs' are the Legal Aid (General) Regulations (NI) 1965.[197] The 'LA Fund' is the Legal Aid Fund. In this section, let us assume that a party to proceedings called '*Hardup*' has been granted a legal aid certificate in an action between him and '*Rockefeller*'.

17.83 Whether Hardup wins or loses, all remuneration for his solicitor and counsel comes only from the LA Fund (LA Order Arts.11(1)(b);13(1)), and does not exceed the amounts prescribed under Schedule 2 (Art.13(2)). For proceedings in the Supreme Court and House of Lords, costs are taxed on the standard basis and counsel is allowed 95 per cent of his taxed fees; the solicitor 100 per cent of his other disbursements and 95 per cent of his profit costs. Counsel's fees are taxable as if already paid by the solicitor (Sch.2 para.3). Where judgment is given by the Court or judgment in default entered by or against Hardup, the judgment must direct Hardup's costs to be taxed under Schedule 2 (LA Gen Reg.21(5)). As to taxation, see Anderson Chapter 7. The solicitor may seek interim payment on account of his costs from the LA Fund (reg.19). The taxation must confine itself to costs of work done within the limits of the certificate.[198] In respect of work done in proceedings not covered by the certificate, the solicitor can charge Hardup direct,[199] but cannot charge for work done in the proceedings during the currency of the certificate even if outside the scope of the certificate (reg.15(16)). In certain cases (e.g. where the case is settled with costs agreed against Rockefeller, or the certificate is revoked, or the case has concluded without an order to tax the legal aid costs) Hardup's solicitor may apply to the LA Committee, lodging a bill of costs, for his costs to be assessed by the Committee in lieu of taxation (reg.21(1)(3)). On a complaint of professional misconduct etc., the Solicitors' Disciplinary Tribunal may exclude a solicitor from legal aid work or may reduce or cancel his legal aid costs.[200]

17.84 Save as provided by the LA Order and regulations thereunder the fact that a party is legally-aided does not affect the rights and liabilities of Rockefeller, nor the principles on which the Court exercises its discretion (LA Order, Art.10(6)). In particular, Hardup as a winning party should not be refused costs from Rockefeller merely because Hardup is legally-aided.[201]

---

197 SR 1965/217 as extensively amended, especially by SR 1974/126.

198 *Donnelly* v *Northern HSSB* [1993] 10 NIJB 31. There in taxation of costs under a certificate limited to applying for 'pre-action discovery' Pringle J held it to include the full costs of some work which also happens to relate to the issue of liability in the intended action. No apportionment or division of items in this case.

199 *Littauer* v *Steggles Palmer* [1986] 1 WLR 287.

200 Solicitors (NI) Order 1976, Art.51B.

201 *Knight* v *Lambeth LBC* [1995] CLY 3969 (CA).

Costs recoverable by the LA Fund

17.85 If Hardup wins, the judge must direct his costs to be taxed under Schedule 2 against the LA Fund (reg.21(5)), and should order taxation on the standard basis,[202] both as to payment by the losing party and as to payment by the LA Fund to Hardup's solicitor (LA Order, Art.13; Sch.2 para.4; LA Gen reg.23). The Court can disallow any costs incurred by the solicitor's unreasonable conduct (Ord.62 r.11). In presenting the bill of costs for taxation (para. 17.107), the LA certificate should be annexed.[203] The solicitor should present one bill for both taxations, delineating any items payable by the LA Fund only and any payable by the losing party only. Of course some items of costs may be within the scope of the LA certificate and outside the scope of the costs of the litigation, or *vice versa*. Solicitor and counsel must contemporaneously date a document made by them or place the date of receipt of any undated document received by them, and the Taxing Master has resolved that, if not so dated, the document will be presumed to have been created or received before the issue of the LA certificate.[204] Drafting and serving notice of the issue, discharge etc. of a LA certificate are costs in the cause (LA Gen reg.21(7)). Fees of counsel are recoverable from the other party as if already paid by the solicitor (Art.13(3)(b)). In taxing items which appear in both taxations, the Taxing Master should apply the same criteria of reasonableness and the amounts allowed for such item on each taxation should normally be the same.[205] If prior authorisation for an item has been given by the LA Committee, it must be allowed on LA taxation or assessment, but in the absence of such authority it is payable only if expressly allowed on taxation or assessment (reg.15(8))[206] and on an *inter partes* taxation such an item may be allowed if the Master finds it reasonable.[207] It is the duty of Hardup's solicitor to safeguard the interests of the LA Fund in recovering as much as possible from taxation of the costs payable by Rockefeller; and the costs of the taxation are payable from the LA Fund (reg.23(2)(3); the solicitor, with the authority of the LA Committee, can object to the taxations both against the LA Fund and against Rockefeller, and apply for a review by the Master and then by a judge (reg.23(4)(5)), and where available[208] to appeal from the decision of the judge (reg.25(1)). Costs will be given if the assessment is significantly increased on taxation, and costs of a review by the Master will be allowed if the review is authorised by the Legal Aid authority,[209] but only if the issue arises out of work

---

[202] Never on the indemnity basis: see para. 17.95.

[203] Practice Order [1988] 4 BNIL 89.

[204] Practice Direction [1996] 4 BNIL 76.

[205] *Carr* v *Poots* [1995] 6 BNIL 80 (Carswell LJ).

[206] *McGarvey* v *McGarvey*, Taxing Master NI, June 1992, held that that such item cannot be allowed against the LA Fund if not authorised, but this decision seems to be *per incuriam* reg.15(8).

[207] *Caruth* v *Caruth*, Taxing Master NI, 7 November 1995.

[208] As to when an appeal lies from a judge's decision as to costs to the Court of Appeal, see para. 20.08.

[209] *O'Connor* v *O'Connor*, Taxing Master NI, undated 1995.

done under Hardup's LA certificate.[210] A review or appeal by the solicitor cannot be heard if the LA Committee has not authorised it.[211] In taxation proceedings the LA Fund is not represented, so that the Master must scrutinise the bill so as to protect the LA Fund (Anderson p.53). In *Donaldson* v *EHSSB*,[212] a test case, the Master ordered that the Lord Chancellor and the Legal Aid authority could attend the taxation proceedings before him. On a review by the judge, the LA Fund can be represented by an appointee of the Lord Chancellor (reg.24(1)).[213] The Lord Chancellor can appeal directly from the judge[208] (reg.25(2)).

17.86 All costs from Rockefeller must be paid to the LA Fund (Art.11(1)(d)). Because of the 95 per cent rule this means that the LA Fund may receive more in costs than it has to pay over to Hardup's solicitor. If the LA Fund receives from Rockefeller an amount which, when added to any contribution from Hardup, exceeds the solicitor's remuneration, the excess must be paid to Hardup (Art.12(4)). The practice of the Court is to avoid that result by directing that the *inter partes* costs be "taxed under the Second Schedule [to the LA Order]".

17.87 The LA Fund has various methods of mitigating its liability for the solicitor costs.

(1) It can impose and enforce a contribution to costs from Hardup, depending in his disposable income and capital.

(2) If Hardup has a right of indemnity for his costs (e.g. as insured car driver), the LA Fund is subrogated to his rights against the insurer or other indemnitor (LA Order, Art.26).

(3) All costs from Rockefeller must be paid to the LA Fund (Art.11(1)(d)).

(4) Where by order or agreement any property is recovered or preserved for Hardup or costs awarded to him, the Law Society may take proceedings necessary to enforce it in its own name, or allow Hardup to do so (LA Gen reg.17(3)(4)(5)). Any money payable from Rockefeller, other than costs, is paid to Hardup's solicitor, but he must pay to or deal with that money as the Law Society directs (reg.17(1)(2)).

(5) If any property (wherever situate) is recovered or preserved for Hardup in the proceedings the LA Fund has first charge on it, vested in the Law Society, for any shortfall of the costs payable to his solicitor from the costs received from Rockefeller and for any unpaid contribution due from Hardup (Art.12(5); LA Gen reg. 26), and so money awarded to him should not be paid out until the LA Fund has received the costs. The charge also attaches to rights under a compromise and costs recovered in the proceedings from Rockefeller not payable to the LA Fund

---

210 *Donaldson* v *EHSSB*, Taxing Master NI, 17 December 1996.

211 *Storer* v *Wright* [1981] QB 336.

212 Taxing Master NI, undated 1996.

213 As in *In re Mitchell* [1992] 8 NIJB 10, where he appointed the Crown Solicitor.

(Art.12(6)). Property recovered or preserved means any property at issue in the proceedings (and not only where ownership is in dispute) and any property included in the compromise, whether at issue in the proceedings or not. Property includes money.[214] The charge is comparable to the charge of a solicitor (see para. 17.75).[215] It is imperative and is a first charge, subject to the rights of Rockefeller and any costs due to Rockefeller,[216] and subject to any set-off of damages[217] or costs ordered by the Court (Art.12(7)). The Law Society can enforce the charge like a charge between parties (reg.26(2)). The Law Society has a public duty to enforce the charge.[218] If the Law Society applies to enforce it, the Court is bound to grant it.[219] If the charge is on property in the form of money, it cannot be waived or postponed, because of regulation 17(2).[220] Any act done to defeat the charge is void against the Law Society except a conveyance to a *bona fide* purchaser for value without notice (reg.26(3)). The charge survives though the certificate has been revoked or discharged (reg.13(4)). The solicitor's pre-certificate costs are shared proportionately with the costs of the LA Fund out of the property charged (reg.14(3)). Where money recovered is kept in court or invested, the LA Fund's charge attaches only to a sufficient part (reg.17(8)). Certain money recovered in matrimonial or affiliation proceedings is exempt (reg.17(9)).[221]

Costs against legally-aided party

17.88 If Hardup loses, his own solicitor's costs and disbursements must be ordered by the Court to be taxed under Schedule 2 to the LA Order and paid by the LA Fund (reg.21(5). If Rockefeller fails to have the judgment drawn up or entered, Hardup's solicitor must apply to the appropriate officer for an order to have his costs taxed under Schedule 2 (reg.21(6)). Rockefeller's costs[222] can be awarded against Hardup but his liability to pay does not exceed such amount (if any) as is reasonable for him to pay having regard to the means of the parties and their conduct (Art.11(1)(e)). This protection extends to a next friend or guardian *ad litem* etc. (LA Gen reg.4(7)), and a representative, official or fiduciary party (reg.18(6)). *Semble,* it does not protect Hardup if his certificate has been revoked (as opposed to discharged) because a person whose certificate is revoked is deemed never to have been legally aided (reg.13(1)). This protection only covers the costs of proceedings or part of the proceedings during the currency of the LA certificate (reg.14(1)). The usual order is for

---

214 See White Book (1997) Vol. 2 [4017].

215 *Hanlon* v *Law Society* [1981] AC 124, *per* Lord Lowry.

216 *Cooke* v *Head (No 2)* [1974] 1 WLR 972.

217 Including any money payable under a court order: *Brookes* v *Harris* [1995] 1 WLR 918 (Ch D).

218 *Blatcher* v *Heaysman* [1960] 1 WLR 663, at 666.

219 *R* v *Judge Fraser Harrison, ex p Law Society* [1955] 1 QB 287.

220 *Simpson* v *Law Society* [1987] AC 861.

221 The references to legislation in the regulation need to be updated.

222 Including disbursements and expenses: Interpretation Act (NI) 1954, s.46(2).

costs against him, not to be enforced without further order. Rockefeller will have to show that Hardup has the means to pay some or all of the costs. Hardup is not liable for the costs until the Court has made a full determination under Article 11 of both the means (capital and income) of the parties and the nature of Hardup's conduct.[223] The trial judge may do so at the trial or may adjourn the determination, or refer to an officer for a report on the facts; he may limit the amount or postpone payment, or postpone payment until Hardup has paid his LA contribution; the determination is final, save for Rockefeller's right to apply for variation within six years (reg.18). Rockefeller may at any stage before judgment at the trial file an affidavit of his means in the court and serve a copy on Hardup's solicitor (reg.16(6)(7)). If Hardup subsequently acquires substantial assets or money, the Court in its discretion may vary the original order to make him pay all or part of the costs.[224]

17.89 Hardup's means exclude his home[225] and furniture and tools of trade (reg.18(2)), but the Court can take into account other income and capital, including that which the Legal Aid authority must ignore when assessing eligibility and contribution.[226] If Hardup recovers money in the proceedings, the Court can order any costs due to Rockefeller to be set off against the money recovered;[227] but the Court must first ascertain Hardup's total financial position.[223] Costs of interlocutory proceedings or an adjournment can be ordered against Hardup as plaintiff, to be enforced by set-off against his eventual award at the trial court's discretion.[228] The Court can take into account money recovered by Hardup in another action.[229] In considering the conduct of the parties, the Court can look at without prejudice offers of compromise.[230] If Hardup has discontinued his action, or suffered judgment in default or summary judgment, he is fully liable for costs unless he applies to the Court for a determination (reg.18(5)).

Costs against LA Fund

17.90 If Hardup loses, Rockefeller may apply to the Court to make an order for payment of his costs against the LA Fund under Article 16. Procedure is laid down in the Legal Aid (Costs of Successful Unassisted Parties) Regulations (NI) (SR 1965/235). The conditions are as follows-

---

[223] *In re Murphy* [1991] 7 NIJB 97, at 103-6; *Danvers* v *Danvers* (1974) 118 SJ 168.

[224] *Wraith* v *Wraith* [1997] 2 All ER 526 (CA).

[225] His disposable means includes the proceeds of sale of his home but generally the Court should not order costs therefrom if the money is needed to buy a new home: *Chaggar* v *Chaggar* [1997] 1 All ER 104.

[226] *McGucken* v *McGucken* [1991] NI 33.

[227] E.g. if Hardup as plaintiff fails to beat the lodgment: *Burns* v *Boland*, QB, NI, 15 March 1968. And see *McInally* v *Clackmannan DC*, 1993 SC 314 (1st Div).

[228] *Lockley* v *National Blood* [1992] 1 WLR 492; followed with some hesitation by Girvan J in *McWatters* v *Belfast Educ and Lib Board*, QBD, NI, 1 February 1996.

[229] *In re Murphy* [1991] 7 NIJB 97, at 104-5; *Wraith* v *Wraith* [1997] 2 All ER 526 (CA).

[230] *McCallum* v *Westbridge* [1971] CLY 9360.

(1) The LA Fund can only be ordered to pay costs if and to the amount that Hardup would be ordered to pay, though the costs of applying under Article 16 can be added (Art.16(4)(6)).

(2) The order can be made only by the Court in which the proceedings have been finally determined (substantially) in favour of Rockefeller, or discontinued, and no appeal is pending and the time for appeal has expired (Art.16(1), Art.17(4)). 'Proceedings' means all the claims included in the originating process.[231] The proceedings are substantially determined against Hardup where he loses on the main issue even if he recovers judgment.[232] An interlocutory appeal to the Court of Appeal is a separate proceeding so determined.[233] Any proceedings for which a separate certificate could be issued are separate proceedings (Unassisted Party Regs, reg.2).

(3) In respect of a proceeding or part of a proceeding outside the scope of the LA certificate, Hardup, not the LA Fund, is liable for the costs (Art.17(6)).

(4) The Court must first consider the extent to which Hardup should be personally liable under Article 11(1)(e): (Art.16(2)).

(5) It is just and equitable to make an order out of public funds (Art.16(2)). There must be, for example, an element of perjury, vexation, deception by Hardup, or irresponsibility by the LA Committee, or hopelessness in the claim or appeal.[234]

(6) Costs cannot be awarded from the LA Fund to Rockefeller if he is himself legally assisted; but he may seek an order in respect of costs incurred by him at a time when he was not assisted.[235]

In respect of costs incurred at first instance, the proceedings must have been instituted by Hardup; and the Court must be satisfied that Rockefeller will suffer severe financial hardship if an order is not made (Art.16(3)). If Rockefeller was a party in a representative, fiduciary or official capacity, this can be judged only upon the resources of the fund and its beneficiaries (Unassisted Party Regs, reg.3). These conditions do not apply to the costs incurred on an appeal. 'Appeal' means proceedings before the House of Lords and Court of Appeal, and the High Court on a statutory appeal from an inferior court or tribunal. The High Court in judicial review of the decision of a non-judicial body is a court of first instance.[236] A judge hearing an appeal from a master's order granting judgment or dismissing an action is an appellate court; a judge hearing an appeal from an ordinary interlocutory order is probably a court of first instance.[237] Rockefeller can apply for payment of the

---

231 *R* v *Greenwich LBC ex p Lovelace* (No 2) [1992] QB 155, at 164B.

232 E.g. where he fails to beat the lodgment: *Kelly* v *London Transport* [1982] 1 WLR 1055.

233 *Megarity* v *Ryan* [1982] AC 81; *Herd* v *Clyde Helicopters*, 1997 SLT 672 (HL).

234 *Thompson* v *YMCA* [1986] NI 183.

235 *In re H* (No 2) [1992] 2 AC 303.

236 *R* v *Greenwich LBC ex p Lovelace* (No 2) [1992] QB 155.

237 *Megarrity* v *Ryan* [1982] AC 87.

costs of an appeal even if he is covered by insurance, and indeed his insurance company can, by virtue of subrogation, apply itself. In respect of appeal costs an order is more likely to be made where Hardup is the appellant, but note that the order can be made on an appeal by Rockefeller.

17.91 Under the Unassisted Party Regulations application is made in the same way as for any order for costs (reg.4). The Court may determine the application itself forthwith or after adjournment or refer it to the Taxing Master for determination (with an appeal to the Court) or for report; if the Court grants an order forthwith, it must be served on the secretary of the LA Committee who may apply to vary or discharge the order (regs.11-14). The secretary may appear at the hearing or make written submissions (reg.5). The money payable by the LA Fund under Article 16 cannot be charged against Hardup under Article 12.[238] Appeal lies from the Court's decision only on a point of law (Art.16(5)).

"Green Form" assistance

17.92 If Hardup's solicitor has claimed a fee for advising about litigation under the "Green Form" scheme in Articles 3-8 of the LA Order, his costs come from any contribution by Hardup (paid direct to the solicitor), then from costs recovered from Rockefeller, on which there is a charge for costs, then from any property recovered or preserved, on which there is a charge which the Committee can waive, and then from the LA Fund. Green Form assistance is of course of very little importance in the context of costs of a High Court action.

TAXATION OF COSTS

17.93 The jurisdiction of the Supreme Court in relation to taxation of costs is vested in the Master (Taxing Office), by the Judicature Act (s.60(1)) and Order 62 rule 19. The Taxing Office transacts the taxation of all costs in civil proceedings in the Supreme Court; in criminal proceedings in the Crown Court and Court of Appeal; in proceedings before an arbitrator, umpire or tribunal under statute which provides for taxation in the High Court; costs under an order by the Taxing Master under Article 71F(2)(a) of the Solicitors (NI) Order 1976; any costs to be taxed by the Taxing Master under any statute;[239] and the measurement of insolvency remuneration (Ord.1 r.18). When the Taxing Master is assessing costs of an appellant out of the Legal Aid Fund under section 28 of the Criminal Appeal (NI) Act 1980 (appeals from Crown Court),[240] that is not a taxation under Order 62, and his assessment was unchallengeable, but in respect of costs assessed by the Master from 2 February 1995, the Act is amended by the Criminal Justice and Public Order Act 1994 (s.53) so as to allow an appeal to the High Court.[241]

17.94 All costs must be taxed (in default of agreement): (a) if ordered to one party from another; (b) if ordered out of any fund or from the Legal Aid Fund;

---

[238] *O'Sullivan* v *Herdmans (No 2)* [1988] 1 WLR 1373.
[239] E.g. Notice of Accidents Act 1894, s.3(4); Charities Act (NI) 1964, s.9.
[240] A Practice Direction [1991] 10 BNIL 54 applies to the assessment by the Master.
[241] Assigned to the QBD: Ord.1 r.11(h).

or (c) if payable automatically without an order (Ord.62 r.3(4)). This is subject to Order 62 rule 7 which allows costs without taxation: to a receiver appointed by the Court; on judgment in default on a writ for a debt or ejectment claim; or where the Court orders a gross sum in lieu of taxed costs. Costs are not to be taxed until the conclusion of the cause or matter,[242] unless the Court directs costs (against a non legally-aided party) to be taxed earlier (Ord.62 r.8(1)(2)(3)). If it appears that the proceedings will not progress further, the Taxing Master may on application tax forthwith the costs of interlocutory proceedings (Ord.62 r.8(8)). As to taxation of costs payable out of money in court, see the Court Funds Rules, r.11 (para. 11.163).

17.95 *Basis of taxation.* When awarding costs to a represented party the Court can direct the basis of taxation, that is the degree of generosity which the Taxing Master should apply when assessing the costs. The bases are: "standard" (Ord.62 r.12(1)), and "indemnity" (Ord.62 r.12(2)). Unless expressly directed as indemnity, the costs between party and party are to be taxed on standard basis (Ord.62 r.12(3)). The Court should direct indemnity basis only in exceptional cases, for example, where the losing party's case is without merit; the action is a major test case; or in proceedings for committal for contempt; but never where the winning party is legally aided.[243] In taxing a mortgagee's costs the Master must take into account the contractual right to all expenses.[244] He must also apply any statute or rule which restricts the amount of costs; so that a judgment for costs does not necessarily mean that some costs must be allowed (White Book (1997) 62/12/2). He must remember that a party cannot recover more for costs than the amount which he is liable to pay to his own solicitor,[245]save in legal aid and certain other cases (para. 17.11).

17.96 *Agreed costs.* Unless the claimant is under disability, the parties can agree the costs payable by one to the other. If the total bill is agreed, there can be no taxation; but if only parts of the costs are agreed the Master taxes the whole bill and is not bound to accept the agreed items.[246] However, where only items of disbursement are in dispute, the 'short form taxation' can be used under Order 62 rule 32A (see para. 17.107). In most cases, where costs are to be taxed between party and party in proceedings, whether settled or contested, the solicitors do their utmost to agree costs so as to avoid the delay and expense of taxation. As well as the scale fees published by the Taxing Master for interlocutory proceedings, pleadings etc., they normally use the professional scales recommended by the professions: (a) the Belfast Solicitors' Scale;[247] and (b) the Bar Council's recommended scale fees (in personal injury actions only)

---

242 It is concluded in the High Court when the proceedings under judgment are concluded, even if an appeal is pending: White Book (1997) 62/8/1.

243 *Willis* v *Redbridge HA* [1996] 3 All ER 114 (CA).

244 *Gomba Holdings* v *Minories Finance* [1993] Ch 171.

245 Solicitors (NI) Order 1976, Art.65(3)

246 Anderson p.92; *Black* v *Harland & Wolff* [1977] 2 NIJB.

247 The current scale, for settlements since 1 May 1996, is printed in the Law Society (NI) magazine *The Writ*, No 69 (May 1996) p.14.The figure varies according to the amount of the settlement and the stage after issue of writ at which settled.

for senior counsel, or junior acting alone.[248] In cases for which there is a scale fee provided by the County Court Rules, they may agree by reference to it. The scales represent rough justice in that, being tied purely to the monetary value of the case, they may over- or under-pay for the work done by the lawyers in the instant case. They have no official status, though the Bar Council's fees are accepted as reasonable (see para. 17.103).

HOW COSTS ARE TAXED

17.97 When taxing costs the Master decides three questions in relation to each item claimed: (a) was it in fact incurred? (b) was it reasonable to incur it? (c) is the sum claimed for it reasonable? In a standard taxation he must be satisfied of all three: any doubt is in favour of the person paying. On an indemnity taxation he must be satisfied of (a) and presumes (b) and (c) in favour of the person receiving. The criterion for reasonableness in questions (b) and (c) is the same irrespective of the basis of taxation and irrespective of whether the costs are payable by a party, a fund or the Legal Aid Fund.[249] In taxing all costs in contentious business, he applies Order 62 Appendix 2, or in judgment in default for debt or recovery of land Appendix 3 (Ord.62 r.17(1)(3)). Each item of disbursement (fees to counsel and to experts, expenses to witnesses, court fees etc.) is scrutinised. For himself the solicitor claims remuneration in preparation (interviewing witnesses, obtaining reports, perusing documents, negotiating etc.), attending at interlocutory hearings, attending consultation with counsel, attending the trial, appeal etc., preparing and attending taxation proceedings. All items of preparation are scrutinised as to need, time spent and amount claimed. The Master should disallow the costs of proving an issue incurred after the opponent has conceded it.[250] In exercising his discretion as to the amount of costs, the Master has regard in particular to the factors set out in Order 62 Appendix 2 (Pt.I para. 1(2)), which under the identical Irish provision were summarised by Barron J[251] as (a) special expertise of the solicitor, (b) amount of work done, and (c) degree of responsibility borne.

Solicitor's fees

17.98 The assessment of the solicitor's own fees for: (a) attending interlocutory proceedings, (b) consultations with counsel, (c) attendance at trial, reading of judgment or appeal hearing, (d) preparatory work (e.g. taking instructions, gathering and perusing evidence, negotiating, drafting notices),

---

248 New scale from 1 February 1996 [1996]1 BNIL 69.

249 *Carr* v *Poots* [1995] 6 BNIL 80 (Carswell LJ). So the Taxing Master was wrong to consider the full liability value for the legal aid taxation and the settlement value for the *inter partes* taxation.

250 *Maguire* v *Duffy* (1938) 72 ILTR 132. In *Murphy* v *Duffy* [1996] 10 BNIL 73, the Taxing Master disallowed the cost of proving a fact where the plaintiff's solicitor had failed to obey counsel's direction to serve a notice calling for a withdrawal of a defence, but Pringle J on review allowed the costs because the solicitor rightly believed that it would not induce such withdrawal.

251 In *Best* v *Wellcome Foundation* [1996] 1 ILRM 34, at 43. At p.45, he disapproved the practice of assessing a percentage increase for special factors: such should be reflected in the amount of work properly done.

and (e) taxation of costs (Ord.62 App.2 Pt.II). Each of these is made up of three elements-

- *the A factor*: a rate per hour for work done by the solicitor covering his rate of earnings/salary and a share of office overheads at the rates current when the work was done;[252]
- *the B mark-up (or uplift)*: a figure added on as a percentage of the A figure to reflect care and conduct, influenced amongst other things by the monetary value of the case, and special skill;
- *the C factor* at the same rate as A, for time spent in travelling and waiting, with no B mark-up. (The cost of travel is a disbursement, being the cost of petrol or, where the solicitor uses his own car the current civil service mileage rate).

The law as it was until the recent change in policy by the Taxing Master (para. 17.98a) is as follows.

The A figure is based on a notional salary appropriate for a Northern Ireland solicitor.[253] The current rate (from 1 April 1996) is £47 per hour for A,[254] with a 'run of the mill' case mark-up for B of 50 per cent[255] for prepara.tion and court attendance and 33 per cent for attending consultations with counsel.[256] Only in indemnity taxation, and not in a standard or LA taxation, should the hourly rate be varied to take into account the grade of fee-earning solicitor engaged. No fee is allowed for administrative steps such as attending call-overs, issuing, lodging or stamping documents, unless it was necessary for a fee-earning solicitor to act personally, in which case it is allowable at 'legal executive' rates only.[257] Legal executive work is work appropriate for performance by pupil/apprentice solicitors, clerks and unqualified fee-earning staff. The B mark up may be increased in a 'test' action.[258] The B mark up can be increased to 75 per cent or more for proceedings (such as bankruptcy) where the solicitor acts as advocate.[259] It is not increased merely because he instructs only one counsel, though authorised by the LA certificate to instruct two.[256] A higher mark-up may be allowed if the solicitor has worked more quickly than the average.[257] In *Gallaher* v *Brand*[260] Murray J decided to calculate the B figure by aggregating 100 per cent of the A figure and one per cent of the value of the case. Routine telephone calls and letters by the solicitor are paid at one-tenth the hourly rate. The Master should

---

252 *Johnson* v *Reed* [1992] 1 All ER 169.

253 *Thompson* v *DOE* [1986] NI 196, at 206G-209D.

254 This rate is raised each year. Rates for work done in previous years are: 1993-4 £40; 1994-5 £42.50; 1995-6 £45.

255 *D* v *NHSSB* [1993] 5 BNIL 92 (Taxing Master).

256 *Williamson* v *DOE*, Taxing Master NI, undated 1995.

257 *Boyd* v *Ellison*, Taxing Master NI, 22 February 1995.

258 *Loveday* v *Renton (No 2)* [1992] 3 All ER 184.

259 *Re Mitchell* [1992] 8 NIJB 10, at 14-5 (there 150% because of complex documents).

260 [1987] 2 NIJB 54, at 70; approved in *In re Selective Trimming*, Taxing Master NI, 2 February 1994.

ensure that the overall remuneration is not too far out of line with the county court scale and the (unofficial) Belfast Solicitor's' Scale.[261] The value of the case and the nature of the work are potent factors in assessing the B factor.[262] In *Carr* v *Poots*[263] Carswell LJ considered the case where a damages claim has a very high value on full liability but the actual award is much reduced on a compromise settlement or because of deduction for contributory fault: the profit costs should take into account the 'real' value of the case, which derives from the full value and the reduced award value and from the responsibility involved in dealing with the problem of reduction. However in *McMahon* v *Donaldson*[264] Lowry J said that where a deduction has been made for contributory fault, the Taxing Master should have regard to the value on full liability. The Master should assess a 'spot figure' for the value element of the profit costs, which can be treated, by way of cross-check, as either a 1 per cent value charge (1 per cent of the 'real value') or an enhanced B uplift; he should not give both a value charge and a enhancement on B uplift.[263] In cases of very large value, complexity, skill or responsibility, the Master should assess remuneration without reference to the hourly rate criterion.[265] If one solicitor appears in several actions the Master may give a reduced fee for each case after the first if the work done is the same.[266] In taxing costs of a hearing in the Court of Appeal, the solicitor will generally be allowed for the A factor only the work in obtaining, considering and sending a copy of the transcript to counsel and keeping counsel up-to-date, with a 'run of the mill' B mark-up of 75 per cent.[267]

17.98a In 1996, in a test case on a taxation between solicitor and client against the LA Fund,[268] the Master decided on the review to increase the hourly rate figure by introducing a new Composite Hourly Rate for cases which warrant the use of a solicitor of average competence and experience: 1994-5 £57.50; 1995-6 £59; 1996-7 £61.50; and the hourly rate for legal executive work: 1994-5 £43.12; 1995-6 £44.25; 1996-7 £46.12. In view of this increase he has announced that the B mark-up will be adjusted: mark-ups of over 100 per cent will no longer be allowed and they should be aligned with the more modest mark-ups given in England: 30-35 per cent, up to 50 per cent in large personal injury cases, and higher mark-ups only in cases outside the 'run-of-the mill'. There will no longer be allowed any additional 'spot figure'. He re-affirmed that there should be only one hourly rate for solicitors in standard and LA taxations, without regard to the grade of fee-earning solicitor involved (though on an indemnity taxation the hourly rate will vary according to which level of

---

261 *Thompson* v *DOE* at 210-2.

262 *Ibid.* at 209E.

263 [1995] 6 BNIL 80.

264 [1969] NI 145, at 165; speaking in the context of taxation of defence counsel's fee, in a case where post-lodgment costs were awarded to the defendant.

265 *Thompson* v *DOE* at 203H. This may no longer be good law in relation to solicitors' remuneration.

266 *Ormond* v *Ireland* [1988] ILRM 490.

267 *Power* v *Lorimer*, Taxing Master NI, 4 March 1993.

268 *Donaldson* v *EHSSB*, Taxing Master NI, taxation undated 1996, review 4 September 1996; and a 'Memorandum to the Profession' (Taxing Office) 4 September 1996.

fee-earner is engaged). However, it is important to consider whether the costs were incurred by the appropriate level of fee-earner. The existing practice as to mileage expenses and travel time will be discontinued and travel time will be allowed only in exceptional cases. The case is currently subject to review by a judge, and it remains to be seen to what extent this change in policy will be upheld.

17.99 Unless the Court otherwise orders, on a claim for a liquidated sum of at least £600, the plaintiff's solicitor recovers costs fixed under Order 62 Appendix 3 Part I: under column (a) if the defendant pays the sum within the time stated on the writ, under column (b) if judgment in default of appearance or Defence is entered, or under column (c) if judgment is granted under Order 14. The same costs system applies to a judgment in default for recovery of land (Ord.62 App.3 Pt.II). Of course, if a debt or recovery of land claim is defended, Order 62 Appendix 2 applies as in any other action.

17.100 *Value Added Tax.* The winning party claims the VAT on his costs charged to him by his own solicitor, and the losing party must pay it, and cannot set it off against the VAT which he pays to Customs and Excise; but if the winning party is registered for VAT and the litigation related to his business, the losing party does not pay the VAT: the winning party pays it and sets it off against the VAT which he pays to Customs & Excise, under the Value Added Tax Act 1994 (s.25).[269]

Disbursements

17.101 Expenditure by the solicitor (e.g. court fees, fees of counsel, travel costs, fees and expenses of witnesses) are claimed as disbursements. Expenditure in research into the law is not a disbursement, even where an outside specialist (other than counsel instructed) is paid to report on the law.[270] The Master can reduce or disallow an item of disbursement or counsel's fees if satisfied that no reasonably careful and prudent solicitor would have agreed it.[271]

Counsel

17.102 The fees of counsel are claimed by the solicitor as a disbursement (see Anderson Chap.10). Costs of two counsel are generally allowed in Supreme Court litigation, and of three counsel in cases of magnitude, importance or difficulty.[272] If the case justifies two counsel, the fee of a junior counsel should not be disallowed merely because he is instructed at a late stage when it is clear

---

[269] See O'Hare & Hill p.565; Anderson p.93, and an English Practice Direction [1994] 1 WLR 431. See also the Practice Directions Consolidation, 11 April 1988, Pt.4 (Anderson p.168). As to drawing up a bill of costs for work done before and after the rate of VAT went up on 1 January 1991, see Practice Direction [1991] 3 BNIL 96.

[270] Cf. *R* v *Legal Aid Board, ex p Bruce* [1992] 1 WLR 694 (HL).

[271] *State (Gallagher Shatter)* v *de Valera* [1991] 2 IR 198; *Best* v *Wellcome Foundation* [1996] 1 ILRM 34, at 48-50. And see para. 17.97.

[272] Anderson p.80. See *McMahon* v *Donaldson* [1969] NI 145, at 163 (two seniors justified in cases worth, in 1968 values, more than £2,000-3,000). In practice, two seniors are very rarely retained for one party in a case. As to the English approach, see White Book (1997) 62/A2/9.

that the senior needs cover.[273] For the trial, counsel is assessed for a brief fee for the case as a whole, which fees include and reflect the necessary work in preparing for trial,[274] and refreshers for each day after the first day of trial. The brief fee should be taxed as the fee which a hypothetical counsel of average ability and experience would properly agree with the solicitor at the time of delivery of the brief (even though in practice counsel does not mark a brief fee until the end of the case).[276] The fee which opposing counsel has agreed with his client is irrelevant.[275] Value of the case is one important factor; it is less important in cases where the claim was settled or reduced by the Court to an amount much lower than the value on full liability, where the value is to be taken as the broad 'real value' of the case, which takes account of the full value and the reduced award value and the responsibility involved in dealing with the problem of reduction (*per* Carswell LJ in *Carr* v *Poots*).[276] But in *McMahon* v *Donaldson,*[277] Lowry J said that where a deduction has been made for contributory fault, the Taxing Master should have regard to the value on full liability. Refreshers are assessed at an amount in the Master's discretion either for each five-hour period or part thereof after the first five hours, or for any day after the first (Ord.62 App.2 Pt.I, para.2(2)(b)). Junior counsel is no longer entitled to two-thirds of senior's fee, but an experienced junior can properly be allowed that or more.[278] The usual current practice as between the Bar and defence insurers, is for the junior to mark two-thirds of the senior's fee if the trial of the action commences, whether concluded by settlement or judgment, but only 60 per cent if the case is settled on the day of trial without being opened.[279] In *Carr* v *Poots,*[276] a minor plaintiff's action for damages settled and approved by the Court on reduced value compromise, Carswell LJ decided on two-thirds. In assessing the brief fee for counsel at a hearing in the Court of Appeal, the starting point is the brief fee for the trial plus an amount for the extra work on prepara.tion and length of time in argument.[282] Except in a LA taxation,[280] no fee to counsel is allowed unless a receipt signed by counsel is produced before the taxation certificate is issued (Ord.62 App.2 Pt.I, para.2(1)). Costs of counsel appearing before a High Court master in chambers are not allowable[281] unless that master certifies the attendance as being proper; and costs of a second counsel appearing before a judge in chambers are not allowable[281] unless the judge certifies the attendance as being proper; in both cases such certificate is to be produced at taxation (Ord.62 App.2 Pt.I,

---

273 *McCance* v *Newall Installations*, 1996 SLT 1133 (Temp Judge Coutts QC).

274 *Loveday* v *Renton (No 2)* [1992] 3 All ER 184.

275 *Boyd* v *Ellsion*, Taxing Master NI (preliminary ruling), undated 1994.

276 *Carr* v *Poots* [1995] 6 BNIL 80.

277 [1969] NI 145, at 165; speaking in the context of taxation of defence counsel's fee, in a case where post-lodgment costs were awarded to the defendant.

278 *Wallace* v *Mulhall* [1979] 7 NIJB.

279 This practice was noted without approval or disapproval by Carswell LJ in *Boyd* v *Ellison*, QBD, NI, 29 June 1995, at p.4.

280 Where the solicitor should lodge a copy of a note to counsel stating that the bill is to be taxed: Practice Directions Consolidation, 11 April 1988 (Anderson p.163) para.5.

281 Except in a taxation of costs of a trustee/personal representative out of a fund, or between solicitor and client.

para.2(2)(a)). As a general rule the costs of one consultation between witnesses and counsel should be allowed and a second consultation only for good reason.[282]

17.103 The Master must have regard in fixing the 'market rate' to any scale fees laid down by the Bar Council.[283] The Bar Council issues from time to time a list of 'going rate' fees for counsel in Queen's Bench personal injury actions, known as the "Comerton Scale". The most recent is from 1 February 1996, set out in [1996] 1 BNIL 69, and said by the Taxing Master to be reasonable in a letter to the Bar dated 16 January 1996. Its predecessor was said by Carswell LJ[284] to be fair and reasonable in all aspects except one which has been deleted in the new Scale. Also in response to his observations, the new scale gives a small discount for cases in which liability is admitted.[285] The fees are reduced if the case is disposed of before being listed in the four-week warning list. The Bar scale does not apply to professional negligence, respiratory claims, claims against security forces, employers or occupiers, nor to cases of exceptional complexity or substantial compromise. The brief fee is for work done, excluding consultations, pleadings and interlocutory work, in preparing for trial and for the first day of trial if the action proceeds. Refreshers must be agreed or taxed. The fee is for senior counsel acting with a junior; a junior acting alone should mark five-sixths of the scale. Counsel should not agree to a fee based on any other scale which the Bar Council does not recognise, and agreement to accept a lower fee may constitute touting for business. In taxing work to which a scale is not applied, the Taxing Master decides what is a reasonable time for the work properly done and allows about £80 per hour for a junior counsel of substantial experience,[286] and £115 to £200 per hour for an experienced senior counsel,[287] but in assessing counsel's fees a strict mathematical approach is avoided.[288] In a large or complex case, a senior's fees will be taxed by the present Taxing Master at around £5,000 brief and £500 per day refreshers (on 1995 values). If not all issues are in dispute the fees will be less; discount will be imposed if liability is admitted, unless the issues of quantum are very complex.[289] The Taxing Master publishes from time to time to time a list of approved fees for counsel for pleadings, consultations, direction of proofs, opinions and interlocutory work.[290]

---

282 *Power* v *Lorimer*, Taxing Master NI, 4 March 1993.

283 *Matthews* v *Ulster Tin Box* [1970] Feb NIJB.

284 *Boyd* v *Ellison*, QBD, NI, 29 June 1995, on appeal from the Taxing Master 22 February 1995.

285 Under the Bar scale, a case where contributory fault is pleaded (other than failure to wear a seat belt) is a non-admitted case; and it should be so treated on taxation if it is a genuine plea, however minimal: *Murphy* v *Duffy* [1996] 10 BNIL 73 (Pringle J).

286 *Hurst Ltd* v *Brown*, Taxing Master NI, 1 April 1993.

287 *Cresswell* v *Ministry of Defence*, Taxing Master NI, 28 September 1993.

288 *Oscar* v *Chief Constable*, Taxing Master NI, 21 June 1995.

289 *Boyd* v *Ellison*, Taxing Master NI, 22 February 1995.

290 The current scale at [1996] 1 BNIL 70, is operative from 1 February 1996. As in the Bar scale there is a smaller fee for some items where liability is admitted.

Witnesses

17.104 See Anderson Chapter 11. Expenses (travel and loss of earnings) are allowed for any person reasonably required to attend the trial as a witness, whether or not on *subpoena*;[291] even if not actually called.[292] A stand-by fee (i.e. a smaller fee paid to a witness to be available to come to court) is recoverable where the case does not proceed on the day of trial.[293] The Taxing Master can disallow the costs of a witness whose evidence he considers to have been unnecessary.[294] A witness includes the party himself,[295] or his solicitor, if attending for the purpose of giving material evidence.[296] A party cannot claim the expenses of attending his legal or other expert advisers,[297] but the cost of a party in attending throughout the trial to be available to give instructions to counsel may be allowed if it was necessary.[298] A witness is allowed the expenses of attending on every day of a trial,[299] unless he has been excused by the Court or would have been excused if he asked.[300] If a witness gives evidence in relation to two different causes or in two actions heard together, on which different orders as to costs are made, his expenses should be apportioned.[301] Where a civil servant gave expert evidence during his work hours without loss of pay, his fee was allowed on taxation; the proper test is not whether the witness was at a loss, rather whether a prudent solicitor would have paid the fee which he claimed, and it is reasonable to do so where the witness is an expert.[302] It is irregular to allow a gross sum for a witness,[303] except for the professional fees of an expert.

17.105 *Experts*. An expert will be allowed his expenses, loss of time and a professional fee (for which there may be informally agreed scales), if he is properly retained to give evidence (orally or by affidavit) or to make a written report to be used in evidence,[304] including a fee for investigating the facts and preparing his report. In an ordinary High Court action, where experts on each side are called to give oral evidence, the costs of the expert attending throughout the trial to assist counsel is reasonable; but in cases heard on affidavit evidence where leave is needed for oral evidence, such as judicial review, the cost of his attendance at consultation is reasonable, but attendance

---

291 *Craig* v *Boyd* [1901] 2 IR 645; so says the headnote.
292 *Colhoun* v *McNamee* (1901) 1 NIJR 275.
293 *Aspell* v *O'Brien* [1993] 3 IR 516.
294 *McLaughlin* v *NIHE* [1986] NI 379, at 387B.
295 *Colhoun* v *McNamee* (1901) 1 NIJR 275; Copinger p.135.
296 *Hamilton* v *Colhoun* [1906] 2 IR 104.
297 White Book (1997) 62/B/149.
298 *Petrunic* v *Barnes* (1990) 16 Comm LB 764 (Vic, SC) (in that case a doctor sued for medical negligence).
299 *O'Meara* v *Barry* [1895] 2 IR 454.
300 *McAnuff* v *Taylor*, QBD, NI (Sheil J) 5 June 1964.
301 *Kennedy* v *Healy* [1897] 2 IR 258; *Conroy* v *Connolly* (1943) 77 ILTR 15.
302 *Staunton* v *Durkan* [1996] 2 ILRM 509 (SC).
303 *Stewart* v *Kilkenny* (1911) 45 ILTR 154.
304 *Reen* v *Jeffers* (1939) 73 ILTR 100 (Circuit Ct).

at the court hearing is not.[305] The fee of an expert retained merely to advise is not allowed.[306] The solicitor is often justified in following speculative lines of inquiry, and an expert's report should be allowed on taxation if it was reasonable at the time to commission the report because it appeared then that a report was capable of helping the party's case; the fact that the report is inadmissible in evidence or is a duplication of other evidence is a factor which might justify disallowance of the costs of the report.[307] The costs of advices or reports of an expert should be disallowed if they are properly part of the plaintiff's special damages.[308] In an action about an accident on land, the costs of a plan of the scene (other than a sketch) are not allowed unless the Taxing Master is satisfied that it was reasonable (Ord.62 App.2 Pt.I para..3). The Master regards the attendance of an expert to give oral evidence as reasonable only if a reasonable effort has been made to agree his report.[309] The Master should assess the fee of an engineer expert witness for the whole day: he should not assume that the engineer can go back to other work if the trial finishes before lunch.[310] The costs of an engineer in preparing up to four copies of photographs and plans is allowed,[311] but not generally if the photographs, plans etc. have not been disclosed to the other party before the trial under Order 38 rule 3A.[312] Where, however, counsel has directed the attendance of the expert to give oral evidence, the costs of his attendance and his undisclosed photographs etc. will be allowed.[312] A party is to be granted reasonable scope in choosing an expert from any part of the province.[311] The scale of recommended fees emanating from a responsible professional body is presumed to be reasonable,[313] but a professional scale based on value of subject-matter should be ignored.[314] If an expert is retained for a legally aided party, being aware of that, he is presumed to accept the fees payable at rates laid down by the Legal Aid authority.[315] It is implied that the solicitor is personally liable to

---

305 *In re Bangor Flagship Developments*, Taxing Master NI, 4 March 1993.

306 *Mulholland* v *McParland* (1908) 42 ILTR 2.

307 *Carr* v *Poots* [1995] 6 BNIL 80. In *Murphy* v *Duffy*, 1995, the Taxing Master said of 'para.-medical' experts (physiotherapists, chiropodists etc.) that the costs will usually be allowed only of advised in the medical expert's report or directed in writing by counsel; but on review (*ibid.* [1996] 10 BNIL 73) Pringle J ruled that a direction by counsel need not be in writing; and that the solicitor should normally be entitled to rely on the directions of senior or experienced junior counsel.

308 *Best* v *Wellcome Foundation* [1996] 1 ILRM 34, at 50-51; *Clark* v *Stow*, Taxing Master NI 14 June 1995.

309 *Caruth* v *Caruth*, Taxing Master NI, 7 November 1995.

310 *Black* v *Harland & Wolff* [1977] 2 NIJB.

311 *McClements* v *Larkin* [1991] 1 BNIL 82 (Master Napier).

312 *Brown* v *Pollen*, Taxing Master NI, 20 March 1991. The decision in this case does not apply to medical experts in cases where Order 25 applies, nor to experts of any kind in Commercial List actions; there the costs of the attendance of the expert will not be allowed if his report is undisclosed.

313 *Electronic Sales* v *Sec of State* [1979] NI 151.

314 Anderson p.86.

315 *Ellis* v *Ballycassidy Sawmills*, Taxing Master NI, 18 September 1991.

pay a proper fee to the expert before it is paid by the client or Legal Aid Fund.[316]

Taxing powers and procedure

17.106 The Taxing Master has various powers: to examine witness, order documents, require separate representation, specify or extend time limits, grant interim certificates of costs so far taxed, set off costs between parties, or delay a certificate for costs to a party who has not yet paid costs due by him; restrict costs of unnecessary attendance of parties at taxation of costs payable from a fund, direct the bill of costs to be shown to a beneficiary of the fund, penalise a party or solicitor for misconduct or neglect (Ord.62 rr.19-28). He may administer the oath (Ord.41 r.12). Master Napier has held[317] that a party can *subpoena* a relevant witness, and that he has the powers of other masters to order discovery etc., but note that the Taxing Master is not within the definition of "the Court" or "a master" under the RSC (see para. 1.08). Of his own motion the Master will disallow costs which should not under the rules have been incurred.[318] If it is intended to apply under Order 62 rule 28 for a solicitor to be personally liable for costs, 14 days notice must be given.[319]

17.107 The procedure is described in Anderson Chapter 6. See the detailed Practice Notes and Directions of the Taxing Office at [1988] 3 BNIL 110-113 (as amended [1989] 4 BNIL 78; [1990] 3 BNIL 101; [1990] 6 BNIL 64). Taxation proceedings should be brought within six months or such longer time as the Master allows,[320] by producing to the Taxing Office the judgment or other document showing a right to costs, a statement of the parties, a bill of costs and other relevant documents; a date is fixed and other parties notified (Ord.62 rr.29-30). The Practice Directions Consolidation 11 April 1988,[321] Part 1 lays down the requirements as to form and content of the bill of costs; Part 4 deals with VAT. The Practice Notes [1988] 3 BNIL 112 (amended [1988] 4 BNIL 90) give guidance on the drafting of the bill of costs and on supporting documentation. Unless by leave, the bill must conform to office specimens.[322] All documents created or received by solicitor or counsel for the litigation must have been contemporaneously dated.[323] Practice Direction [1990] 3 BNIL 101 sets out a reasonable sum which the solicitor should

---

316 Anderson p.85.

317 *Boyd* v *Ellison*, Taxing Master NI (preliminary ruling) undated 1994.

318 Anderson p.34 n.17.

319 Practice Direction [1990] 7 BNIL 95.

320 If the Master extends time he usually does so on condition that no interest will be allowed on the costs during the period of delay: *Drayne* v *Chiko Foods Ltd*, Taxing Master NI, 31 January 1991. He may also disallow costs: Ord.62 r.28(4).

321 Cited at [1988] 3 BNIL 111, set out in Anderson p.163; amended [1990] 6 BNIL 64 (Anderson p.183) (date of travel to be stated in travel certificate) and corrected by Directions [1989] 4 BNIL 78; [1989] 7 BNIL 133. The Direction [1988] 3 BNIL 110 deals with objections to items by the paying party; [1988] 3 BNIL 113 sets out Forms of Statements of Parties and Objections.

322 Practice Direction [1988] 9 BNIL 70; this does not apply to matrimonial causes: Practice Direction [1989] 1 BNIL 119.

323 Practice Direction [1996] 4 BNIL 76.

normally claim as the allowance for taxation. Order 62 rule 31 deals with provisional taxation where only the applicant for costs is entitled to be heard. Order 62 rule 32 deals with short urgent taxations. Order 62 rule 32A (in force 1 September 1996) provides for 'short form taxation' in inter-party taxations, save where Schedule 2 to the LA Order applies; if the professional charges are agreed and only item(s) of disbursement remain in dispute, the Master may conduct a short form taxation under Order 62 rule 29 where only documents relevant to the disputed item are lodged; rules 27(3), 30(1(2)(3), 31 and 32 do not apply.

The party seeking costs draws up a bill of costs, a specialist art often done by a professional costs drawer.[324] After a bill has been lodged it can be amended only by the Master.[325] The party claiming costs must waive privilege in relevant documents charged in the bill of costs, for use in taxation proceedings only.[326] Evidence is usually by affidavit. As he does not sit as a court, the Master can allow non-legal representation, such as a costs accountant.[327] Counsel can appear to justify the solicitor's costs or his own fee. An expert can appear to argue for his own fee; and evidence of the market rates for experts is admissible.[328] No interest can be awarded on an item of costs from the date of the work done until the date of the taxation, unless the client has agreed to pay interest to the solicitor.[329] Costs of the taxation are given to the party whose costs are being taxed, unless the Master makes a different order, and he may take into account a written offer by the party liable to pay a specified sum (Ord.62 r.27). If the taxing party recovers less costs on taxation that the amount offered to him by the paying party which should have been accepted, the taxing party may be disallowed his costs incurred after the offer.[330] The Master may order or disallow costs where a party or solicitor has been guilty of misconduct, neglect or delay (Ord.62 r.28).[331] On a taxation against the Legal Aid Fund, costs will be given if the assessment is significantly increased on taxation, and costs of a review under rule 33 (below) will be allowed if the review is authorised by the Legal Aid authority.[332] Costs include an hourly rate for preparation and attendance with a B uplift. At the conclusion of the taxation the Master issues a certificate of the costs allowed by him (Ord.62 r.22).

---

[324] Ord.62 App.2 Pt.II para.5 allows a reasonable fee for preparing the bill for taxation. This fee is assessed without reference to whether the solicitor drafts it himself or employs a costs drawer, nor to the amount of the costs drawer's fee: *Best* v *Wellcome Foundation* [1996] 1 ILRM at 53-4; *Donaldson* v *EHSSB*, Taxing Master NI, 17 December 1996. No allowance is made for preparing the bill presented to the client: *McCreedy Ltd* v *SE & LB*., Taxing Master NI, June 1991; but allowance is made for perusing the bill for submission for taxation: *Williamson* v *DOE*, Taxing Master NI, undated 1995.

[325] Practice Direction [1989] 1 BNIL 119.

[326] *Goldman* v *Hesper* [1988] 1 WLR 1238. But see *Giannarelli* v *Wraith* (1991) 171 CLR 592.

[327] *Magauran* v *Dargan* [1983] ILRM 7.

[328] *Clarke* v *Stow*, Taxing Master NI, 14 June 1995.

[329] *A-G (McGarry)* v *Sligo CC* [1991] 1 IR 99, at 118-20.

[330] *Chrulew* v *Borm-Reed* [1992] 1 WLR 176.

[331] On application on 14-day notice: Practice Direction [1990] 7 BNIL 95.

[332] *O'Connor* v *O'Connor*, Taxing Master NI, undated 1995.

17.108 The Master can be asked within 21 days to review his taxation (Ord.62 r.33),[333] with a review by summons within 14 days to a judge in chambers (Ord.62 r.35).[334] Rule 35(1) requires that for the purposes of a review by the judge the Master be requested to state his reasons; but failure to request is a waivable irregularity.[335] The judge has all the powers and discretion of the Master, but new evidence or objections are received only if he so directs. He can freely review all aspects of the Master's taxation, including both incidence and amount of each costs item.[336] He can amend the certificate; he can remit a disputed item for taxation by the Master.[337] The judge should alter the B uplift figure only if it is outside a reasonable range or if the Master made an error in arriving at it.[335]

17.109 Costs may be taxed and recovered in any action notwithstanding the death of the party to or against whom they were awarded (Judicature Act, s.60(2)).

PAYMENT OF COSTS

17.110 An order for costs, when payable, is enforceable like any monetary judgment of the Court.[338] A subsequent action on the same cause can be stayed pending payment of costs of a previous action. The Court can order that money or costs due between the same parties in the same or different actions can be set off against each other,[339] and it operates to override a solicitor's charge for costs, which then attaches to the balance if any.[340] It also overrides the Legal Aid Fund's charge.[341] The Taxing Master can also set off costs payable by the taxing party or postpone taxation of his costs until costs payable by him are paid (Ord.62 r.23).

Interest

17.111 Interest at the judgment rate runs on costs from the date of the order for costs, not from the date of final assessment.[342] Any order for costs to be taxed and paid (e.g. as a term of an agreed stay of an action) is a judgment carrying interest,[342] but costs payable automatically under a rule (e.g. costs payable on

---

[333] Time extendable, usually on condition that no interest be given during the period of default: *In re Benburb Meats*, 29 June 1995.

[334] Not a master: Ord.32 r.11(1)(c).

[335] *McCurry* v *DOE* [1988] 6 NIJB 1.

[336] *Re Mitchell* [1992] 8 NIJB 10; *Donnelly* v *NHSSB* [1993] 10 NIJB 31, at 33-4; having due regard to the Master's special expertise: *Carr* v *Poots* [1995] 6 BNIL 80.

[337] If so, the party should apply to the Master for the review within 21 days: *In re Benburb Meats,* Taxing Master NI, 29 June 1995, reversed on appeal on another point, by Campbell J (undated, 1996).

[338] An order for costs by the High Court or Court of Appeal in a criminal cause or matter is enforceable like a civil order: Costs in Criminal Cases Act (NI) 1968, s.4A.

[339] *Ogle* v *Mills* [1931] NI 26; *Larkin* v *Groeger* [1990] 1 IR 461.

[340] *Young* v *Mead* [1917] 2 IR 258.

[341] Legal Aid, Advice and Assistance (NI) Order 1981, Art.12(7).

[342] *Hunt* v *RM Douglas* [1990] 1 AC 398, but see *Drayne* v *Chiko Foods Ltd,* noted in para. 17.107.

acceptance of a lodgment) do not carry interest.[343] Where the Court of Appeal overturns a judgment of the High Court and it is clear that the appellant should have won at first instance, the Court should normally back-date its order for costs of the High Court so that it carries interest from the date of the High Court judgment.[344]

---

343 *Legal Aid Board* v *Russell* [1991] 2 AC 317.

344 *Kuwait Airways* v *Iraqi Airways (No 2)* [1994] 1 WLR 985.

CHAPTER EIGHTEEN

SPECIAL TYPES OF PROCEEDINGS

EXTENT OF HIGH COURT JURISDICTION UNDER STATUTE

EXCLUSIONS OF JURISDICTION

18.00 It is a matter of interpreting a statute whether the laying down of a statutory mode of enforcing rights ousts the general civil jurisdiction,[1] bearing in mind the maxim *'ubi ius, ibi remedium'*. If a statute creates a civil right not existing at common law and provides a summary method to enforce it, an action does not lie,[2] and the High Court has no power to grant an ancillary remedy such as a *Mareva* injunction.[3] Where a statute provides that a dispute shall be referred to an arbitral tribunal, then Part I of the Arbitration Act 1996 is applied by section 94 thereof, and a claim in court (whether by way of claim or counterclaim) on the dispute must be stayed unless the statutory provision is null and void, inoperative or incapable of being performed, if the application for a stay is made after taking the appropriate procedural step (if any) to acknowledge the proceedings and before taking any step to answer the substantive claim (see para. 7.27). Where a statute provides that any question arising under it "shall, in default of agreement, be referred to the Lands Tribunal", an action should be stayed ('sisted') rather than dismissed.[4] If a statute provides a summary method for enforcing an existing right at common law, the claimant may choose either, unless the statute expressly or by necessary implication excludes the common law remedy.[5] On the other hand, some statutes merely embody or modify an existing cause of action, in which case an action remains the only method of enforcement.[6] Some statutes, such as the Carriage by Air Act 1961 (enacting the international convention on liability to passengers injured on international flights), substitute for a common law cause of action a remedy under the statute which is itself enforceable by ordinary action. As to ouster of the High Court's power of review, see para. 19.16.

APPLICATIONS AND APPEALS TO THE HIGH COURT

18.01 Many statutes confer jurisdiction on the High Court, by action, appeal, application, reference or otherwise. For a list of some of these, see the *Index to Statutes in Force in Northern Ireland*; and for rules of procedure the *Index to*

---

1 *McGrath* v *Taylor* [1936] NI 158.
2 *Fermanagh CC* v *Parker* [1932] NI 153.
3 *Dept of Social Security* v *Butler* [1995] 1 WLR 1528 (CA).
4 *Osborne* v *British Coal*, 1996 SLT 736 (2nd Div).
5 *Fermanagh CC* v *Parker*, per Wilson J. See also *Waterford Corp* v *Newport* (1846) 11 Ir LR 359.
6 *Murphy* v *O'Shea* (1944) 78 ILTR 151 (Circuit Ct).

Statutory Rules and Orders in Northern Ireland. A fairly full list of statutes conferring jurisdiction on the High Court (and Court of Appeal) is given in Appendix One of this work. If a statute confers jurisdiction on a court and lays down an unqualified time limit for application, the court has no jurisdiction to hear a late application (see para. 1.33). Any statutory provision which confers jurisdiction on the High Court or a judge thereof includes a power to exercise a discretion over costs (Judicature Act, s.59(3)).

Appeals

18.02 The High Court has original inherent jurisdiction, inherited from the pre-1877 Courts, but there is no such thing as inherent appellate jurisdiction. Jurisdiction to hear the appeal depends upon strict compliance with the procedure for appealing laid down by statute, save in so far as the statute contains a dispensing power. If the statute gives a right to appeal to the Court within X weeks, it is to be interpreted that the lodgement of the notice of appeal in the court, rather than its service under rules, must be done in that time.[7] If a statute gives a right of appeal to a party to proceedings, the appeal is available to a party on record, not to a person, such as a child in child care or wardship, whose interests are at issue.[8] If an appeal can be by a party "dissatisfied with" a decision, it does not necessarily connote a legal grievance or prejudicial effect on that person, but extends to a person or body whose own determination has been rejected on a point of law.[9] Some statutes give an appeal only to a person "aggrieved with" an order or decision; these words are narrower - he must show that he feels and is fairly to be considered aggrieved.[9] He must have a genuine grievance because the order under appeal affects his interests prejudicially.[10] He cannot be aggrieved by a decision of a tribunal which could not in law have decided otherwise.[11] Where a public body contests proceedings under a statutory function with no other interest in the result, it is not aggrieved unless costs are awarded against it.[12] A party aggrieved includes a person with an economic interest.[13]

An appeal to the High Court under statute is governed by Order 55 rules 13-18,[14] subject to the statute or rules. Evidence may be given by affidavit (Ord.38 r.2(3)). If leave to appeal is necessary it is sought *ex parte* from a judge (Ord.55 r.17). The appeal is by originating motion entitled in the matter of the relevant statute, and specifying grounds relied on; the appellant must issue it, enter the appeal in the Division to which the appeal is assigned and serve it personally or by post on every person affected, within 21 days of

---

7 *In re Secretary of State* [1991] NI 64; *Morris* v *Power Supermarkets* [1990] 1 IR 296.

8 *S* v *Special Needs Tribunal* [1996] 1 All ER 171.

9 *Min. of Development* v *Law* [1970] June NIJB, *per* Lord MacDermott LCJ.

10 *Antrim Newtown* v *DOE* [1989] NI 26, at 32F (CA).

11 *Tansey* v *Sec. of State* [1981] NI 193, at 198 (CA). In effect, this means that he cannot appeal on the basis of facts not available to the tribunal.

12 *In re M* [1976] 8 NIJB (HC) *per* Lowry LCJ *obiter*.

13 *Re Macton* (1988) 43 DLR 4th 391 (BC, CA).

14 Except appeals from the civil jurisdiction of the county court, Ord.55 rr.1-12A (see the author's *County Court Procedure in NI,* Chap.19), and appeals by case stated, Order 56 (see para. 18.06).

receiving notice of the decision to be challenged, and lodge an appeal book within a further seven days (Ord.55 rr.14-16). Of course all these time limits are extendable by the High Court. The appeal carries a court fee of £45. In a tax appeal the respondent may apply for a stay until the appellant gives security (Ord.55 r.18).

18.03 Since the 1980 Revision, the RSC do not stipulate that the appeal is by way of rehearing. However, it is a rehearing in the same sense as an appeal from High Court to Court of Appeal, so it is neither a full oral rehearing nor an appeal on point of law; the Court can freely review the findings of fact and law whilst giving great weight to the lower body's findings especially of primary fact.[15] Where an appeal from any court, tribunal, person or body may be brought under NI legislation, the appellate court has all the powers of the original body and may confirm reverse or vary its decision, remit the appeal or a matter arising therein with declarations or directions which the original body must obey, and may make any proper order as to costs and expenses; and any order has the like effect and is enforceable as an order of the original court or body.[16] By Order 55 rule 22, the High Court also has the same appellate powers as the Court of Appeal under Order 59 rule 10 (see para. 20.53). The proper officer sends a copy of the final order made on the appeal to the body concerned (Ord.55 r.21).

References

18.04 Where a statute provides for a matter or question of law or fact to be referred or submitted to the High Court, the above procedure for appeals applies (Ord.55 r.19(1)). By Order 55 rule 22 the High Court has the same powers on a reference as the Court of Appeal under Order 59 rule 10 (see para. 20.53).

Applications

18.05 Save as otherwise provided for, on an application to the High Court under a statutory provision, the above procedure for appeals may be applied (Ord.55 r.20). However Order 5 rule 3 says that an application to the High Court or a judge thereof must be begun by originating summons, save where the RSC or a statutory provision expressly require or authorise some other means. There would seem to be a conflict between these two rules. If the statute gives a right to apply to the Court within X weeks, it is the issue of the notice of application, rather than its service under rules, which must be done in that time.[17]

Appeals by case stated

18.06 In Northern Ireland, only a few statutes provide for a case stated to the High Court; most are to the Court of Appeal. Where a pre-1978 statute confers final jurisdiction on an appeal on a case stated or point of law to the High Court or a judge of the Supreme Court, the appellate jurisdiction is transferred

---

[15] *Re Baird* [1989] NI 57, at 60-2.

[16] Interpretation Act (NI) 1954, s.22.

[17] *Morris* v *Power Supermarkets* [1990] 1 IR 296.

to the Court of Appeal.[18] An appeal by case stated lies only on a point of law actually decided by the lower court/tribunal. A procedural error or breach of natural justice must be challenged by judicial review.

18.07 Procedure for a case stated to the High Court is governed by Order 56. Save as otherwise provided by the statute, the requisition to the court, tribunal or person for a case stated must be made within six weeks and settled and signed by the judge/tribunal chairman etc. within six weeks (Ord.56 rr.1(2),3). The appellant must lodge and serve it within 14 days after receiving it (Ord.56 r.1(1)), and lodge an appeal book within a further 14 days (Ord.56 r.2). It carries a court fee of £40. The applicant or party having carriage of the appeal may apply by motion for leave to withdraw, at which any other party may apply to proceed with it (Ord.56 r.4). A copy of the final order made on the appeal is sent to the court/tribunal concerned (Ord.56 r.5).

18.08 Appeals from VAT and other tribunals under section 11 of the Tribunals and Inquiries Act 1992 are by case stated under Order 56 (Ord.94 r.1). Those tribunals which are listed in Schedule 1 to the Act[19] and in Order 94 rule 3, may state a special case on a point of law in the course of their proceedings, and some of them may be directed to do so (Ord.94 r.3).

MODE OF PROCEEDING

18.09 Apart from some types of appeal and appeals by case stated, and originating *ex parte* applications, virtually all proceedings in the High Court are commenced by writ, originating summons, originating motion or petition. Only the first two are within the definition of an action. The last two are “matters”. All are within the definition of proceedings. In originating summons, motion or petition proceedings, service is under Order 10 rule 5. Service of an originating summons or motion or petition may be effected outside Northern Ireland by leave in the same way as a writ (Ord.11 r.9). All evidence may be given by affidavit unless otherwise provided by rules or Court direction; on application of a party, the Court may order attendance of a deponent for cross-examination (Ord.38 r.2(3)). The most significant feature of proceeding by an originating summons, rather than motion or petition, is that the defendant may plead a counterclaim and issue a third-party notice.

ORIGINATING SUMMONS

18.10 An action may be begun by originating summons, which is appropriate if it concerns interpretation of a statute, contract or other document, or a question of law, or if there is no likely dispute of fact (Ord.5 r.4(2);[20] or where a statute specifically provides. Order 7 provides for its form and issue: it must state the question for determination by the Court, *or* a concise statement of the remedy sought with particulars to identify the cause of action. The parties are called ‘plaintiff’ and ‘defendant’. Order 28 applies to all classes of originating

---

[18] Judicature Act, s.35(6). In England, appeals by case stated go to the Divisional Court of the High Court.

[19] As modified by Statutory Instrument under s.13.

[20] But see Ord.85 r.4 (para. 18.65).

summons subject to any special provisions (Ord.28 r.1). There are three types of originating summons -

(1) The ordinary form in Form 6, which is used where the rules or statute do not specify another form: the summons is served on the defendant and he enters an appearance.

(2) The expedited form in Form 7, where the summons is served but the defendant can appear at the date of hearing without having entered an appearance. An Order 113 summons (in Form 9) against squatters is an altered form of this (see para. 18.43).

(3) The *ex parte* form in Form 8, where the summons is not served and there is no defendant.

18.11 Save as otherwise provided, the summons is issued out of the Central Office, or if assigned to the Chancery Division, out of the Chancery Office or, where Order 1 rule 15 applies, the Bankruptcy and Companies Office (Ord.7 r.5). The summons in ordinary or expedited form is served like a writ (Ord.10 r.5). If the defendant is under disability and no guardian *ad litem* enters an appearance for him, the plaintiff must apply for one to be appointed under Order 80 rule 4 before proceeding; if the summons is of a type that does not require an appearance, the Court may appoint a guardian at the hearing (Ord.80 r.4(3)). In a mortgagee's action for possession and/or payment of the secured debt, if the defendant does not appear, the plaintiff must serve the notice of appointment for hearing and his affidavit on the defendant (Ord.88 r.4). Order 13 does not apply, so that judgment cannot be entered in default of appearance. In the ordinary form, after service on and appearance by the defendant under Order 12 rule 9, the parties file and exchange affidavit evidence (Ord.28 r.1A) and the plaintiff then obtains an appointment for hearing, 14-day notice of which in Form 10 is served on every defendant who has entered an appearance (Ord.28 rr.2(1),3(1)(5)). If the plaintiff fails to obtain an appointment, a defendant who has entered an appearance may do so by leave of the Court (Ord.28 r.2(4)). The Form 10 notice must specify the order sought and the party served who seeks a different order must so specify by notice served seven days before the hearing (Ord.28 r.3(3)). If the defendant does not enter an appearance, he cannot lodge an affidavit without leave, and the plaintiff proceeds to obtain an appointment for hearing, without having to serve the Form 10 notice (Ord.65 r.9). The Court may require to be satisfied that the defendant is in default of appearance (Ord.28 r.6). In the expedited form, the plaintiff obtains a date for hearing from the Office before or after issue of the summons, then lodges his affidavits under Order 28 rules 1A, 2(2), and serves the summons on the defendant at least four clear days before the date of hearing (Ord.28 rr.2(2)(3),3(2)). In the *ex parte* form the plaintiff lodges his affidavits four clear days before the date of hearing or obtains a date for hearing and lodges his affidavits at least a day before the date of hearing (Ord.28 rr.1A(2), 2(2)).

18.12 This initial hearing is by a judge or master in chambers. At the hearing the Court may make an order for the plaintiff or give directions as to further hearing, for example for disposal in chambers or for further hearing in open court, for oral evidence, cross-examination of deponents, for the action to continue as if begun by writ, or for remittal to the county court; at any stage the Court may order affidavits to stand as pleadings (Ord.28 r.4). If any party does not appear the Court may proceed in his absence (Ord.32 r.7). The hearing of the summons may be adjourned generally or to a date (Ord.28 r.5). A summons dismissed in the absence of the plaintiff may be restored to the list (Ord.32 r.7(4)). An order made in the absence of the defendant can be varied or revoked (Ord. 28 r.4(1)). An order made against a defendant who is in default of appearance need not be served on him (Ord.65 r.9) but the Court may first require to be satisfied that he is in default (Ord.28 r.6). A master cannot determine the issue if the summons raises a question of construction of a document or a point of law (Ord.32 r.11(3)). The hearing may be adjourned from time to time, either generally or to a specific date (Ord.28 r.5). If an ordinary or expedited form summons is adjourned, any party who wishes an order not previously asked for must so specify by notice issued seven days before the resumed hearing (Ord 28 r.3(4)). The summons is heard in chambers unless a judge in chambers directs it to be in open court (Ord.32 rr.2,13). If further hearing in court is ordered, the Court determines the mode of trial (Ord.28 r.9). If such order for further hearing is made in a Queen's Bench action, Order 34 (setting down for trial) applies (Ord.28 rr.9(4),11).[21] At any stage the Court may order the action to continue as if begun by writ (Ord.28 r.8) which involves pleadings (or affidavits etc. standing as pleadings) and a plenary trial on oral evidence. Such order may be made if there are contested issues of fact.[22] The defendant can make any form of counterclaim[23] but he must inform the Court as soon as possible and the Court may give directions as to how it should be heard (Ord.28 r.7). The action can be dismissed if the plaintiff defaults on any direction of the court or does not prosecute it with due dispatch (Ord.28 r.10).

18.13 Originating summons actions in the Chancery Division should usually be listed before the master, unless directed in exceptional circumstances to be listed before the judge; and those outside his jurisdiction or reserved to the judge must be listed for the judge (see para. 18.54). [Where a question arises as to the construction of a will or trust, the trustee/personal representative may apply to the High Court for an order authorising reliance on the written opinion of a barrister of ten years, if appropriate to do so without hearing argument.][24]

ORIGINATING MOTION

18.14 An originating motion is in Form 11, containing "a concise statement of the nature of the claim made *or* the relief or remedy required" and an address

---

21 Ord.28 r.9(4) makes reference to Ord.33 r.4(2) being applicable. This is a mistake. If the rule is intended to be modelled on the equivalent Ord.28 r.9 in the English RSC, then the reference should be to s.62(5) of the Judicature Act (which allows the Court to order different issues to be tried separately).

22 As in *Johnston* v *Cliftonville FAC* [1984] NI 9 (Murray J: "quite unsuited to the originating summons procedure").

23 Even if the originating summons does not claim substantive relief: *Balkanbank* v *Taher (No 2)* [1995] 1 WLR 1067 (CA).

24 Wills and Administration Proceedings (NI) Order 1994, Art.33 - *not yet in force*.

for service (Ord.8 r.3). It is issued, upon sealing, out of the Central Office, Chancery Office or Bankruptcy and Companies Office as appropriate. Like any motion (para. 11.05) it must be served at least two days before the hearing unless leave is given for short notice or it needs to be done *ex parte* (Ord.8 r.2). Proceedings are to be begun by originating motion only if required or authorised by statute or rule (Ord.5 r.5) (but see para. 18-05). If the respondent is under disability, and no guardian appears for him the Court may appoint one at the hearing (Ord.80 r.4(3)). The hearing may be adjourned (Ord.8 r.5).

PETITIONS

18.15 Order 9 applies to petitions subject to any specific provisions. A petition is to be presented to the Chancery Office unless otherwise provided (Ord.9 r.3). Many petitions are assigned to the Family Division and issued in the Probate and Matrimonial Office. Proceedings are begun by petition only if so required or authorised by statute or rules (Ord.5 r.5). No interlocutory application can be brought by petition (Ord.9 r.5). A petition must include "a concise statement of the nature of the claim made *and* the relief or remedy required"; at its foot it states the persons, if any, to be served, and an address for service (Ord.9 r.2). It must be served at least seven days before the date stated on it for hearing (Ord.9 r.4). If the respondent is under disability, and no guardian appears for him the Court may appoint one at the hearing (Ord.80 r.4(3)).

QUEEN'S BENCH DIVISION

18.16 Order 1 rule 11 list those matters which are assigned to the Queen's Bench Division-

(a) all proceedings, civil or criminal, within its jurisdiction at the coming into force of the 1980 Rules

(b) Admiralty jurisdiction

(c) Judgment Enforcement (NI) Order 1981, Articles 107-110, save in respect of orders made in matrimonial proceedings

(d) *habeas corpus*

(e) judicial review

(f) proceedings assigned by statute

(g) appeals re legal aid costs in criminal proceedings in the Crown Court

(h) appeals re legal aid costs in criminal appeals in the Court of Appeal arising out of Crown Court proceedings

Broadly speaking causes of action based on common law, seeking the common law remedies of damages, ejectment or rescission, are brought in this Division, often coupled with a claim for an equitable remedy. In this section some special types of proceedings normally brought in the Division are considered. Judicial review, bail applications and *habeas corpus* are dealt with in Chapter 19.

ADMIRALTY

18.17 Apart from the Crown Court's criminal jurisdiction, exclusive jurisdiction in admiralty is vested in the High Court (Judicature Act, s.30) and is assigned to the Queen's Bench.

The jurisdiction is set out in the Administration of Justice Act 1956 (Sch.1); Merchant Shipping Act 1995 (ss.166,177); Naval Prize Act 1864 (ss.3-4); Prize Courts Act 1915; Naval Prize (Procedure) Act 1916; Prize Act 1939 (extending to aircraft); Aircraft (Wreck and Salvage) Order 1938.[25] Jurisdiction over collisions at sea: see *Doran* v *Power* [1995] 2 IR 402. Procedure is dealt with in Order 75 and Order 18 rule 22. And see the Crown Proceedings Act, sections.29-30; Order 77 rule 17(2). Stay of proceedings, see Civil Jurisdiction and Judgments Act 1982, section 26. Stay for arbitration: Arbitration Act 1996, section 11. Appeal lies without leave from interlocutory judgment on liability (Judicature Act, s.35(2)(g) (iv)).

DEFAMATION ACTIONS

18.18 Order 82 applies to actions for libel or slander. A writ for libel must be indorsed with particulars of the publication (Ord.82 r.2). In the pleadings the plaintiff must give particulars of defamatory innuendo; the defendant on a 'rolled-up plea' of justification of fact and fair comment opinion must plead particulars of the justification element; the plaintiff need not give particulars of facts showing malice, but if the defendant pleads fair comment or privilege the plaintiff must do so by a Reply (Ord.82 r.3). See further as to pleadings, para. 9.79. If the plaintiff accepts a lodgment under Order 22 rule 3 made by one of several defendants sued jointly, he is automatically entitled to his costs against that defendant up to the date of giving notice of acceptance (Ord.62 r.5(5)). The plaintiff may still proceed against the other defendant to recover the amount by which the Court's assessment of his damage exceeds the lodgment; if the Court awards no more he is entitled to no costs since the lodgment unless the judge thinks it was reasonable to proceed (Ord.82 r.4(1)).

18.19 In a libel action against a newspaper or periodical, the defendant may plead that he had no malice, no gross negligence, that he had published an apology and has paid money into court (Libel Acts, 1843 s.2, 1845, s.2). Such payment need not be kept secret (Ord.82 r.4(2)), overruling case law. Apart from that the defendant can make an ordinary lodgment under Order 22 which is kept secret; or he can make a payment under the Libel Acts and state it by notice to be also a lodgment under Order 22, in which case it can be raised on the question of costs even if the Libel Acts defence fails.[26] Where the plaintiff accepts a lodgment or the action is settled before trial, either party may apply to a judge for leave to make a statement in open court in terms approved by the judge (Ord.82 r.5).

18.20 If the defendant made or offered an apology, he may give evidence thereof in mitigation of damages after giving written notice of that intention

---

[25] SRO (UK) 1938/136 amended SI 1964/489; made under the Civil Aviation Act 1982, s.91. See Halsbury's *SIs* Vol.3.

[26] *Bell* v *Northern Constitution* [1943] NI 108.

(Libel Act 1843 s.1), without having to pay into court. If the defendant wants to give evidence in mitigation of damages of the circumstances of the publication or the character of the plaintiff, he must give particulars thereof at least seven days before the trial (Ord.82 r.7).

Where defamatory words have been published innocently, the publisher may make an offer of amends, that is to publish a correction and apology, with an affidavit of facts (Defamation Act (NI) 1955, s.4). If accepted, no action for defamation may be commenced or continued, and application may be made to the High Court for directions as to steps to fulfil the offer and/or for payment of costs by the publisher (s.4). The application for directions as to the steps in offer of amends can be by originating summons (expedited form, no appearance required) to a Queen's Bench judge in chambers (Ord.82 r.8). If the action has already been commenced, it should be by way of summons to stay the action. If not accepted, the offer of amends may be raised as a defence, confined to the facts stated in the affidavit (s.4). [*to be replaced by*: A publisher of an alleged defamatory statement may make a written 'offer to make amends' (i.e. to make and publish a correction and apology and to pay compensation and costs); such offer cannot be made after serving a Defence (Defamation Act 1996, s.2).[27] If the offer is accepted the claimant cannot commence or continue any action on that cause of action, but may apply to the Court to enforce the offer; in default of agreement the publisher may take such steps as he thinks appropriate to make a correction and apology; in default of agreement, the amount of compensation and/or costs are determined by the Court in the same way as in a contested action, taking account of the correction and apology made, but no jury is used (1996 Act, s.3). If the offer is not accepted, the publisher may choose to rely on it as a defence in the action,[28] which is a full defence[27] unless it is proved that he knew or had reason to believe that the statement would be taken as referring to the plaintiff and was defamatory and false; if raised as a defence the publisher cannot rely on any other defence; in any case he may raise the offer in mitigation of damages (1996 Act, s.4).]

18.21 Other substantive defences are provided by [the Defamation Act (NI) 1955 (ss.5-10), Defamation Act 1996 (ss.1, 13) and the Law of Libel Amendment Act 1888 (s.3)] *to be replaced by* the Defamation Act (NI) 1955 (ss.5, 6, 9(1), 10) and the Defamation Act 1996 (ss.1, 13-15). Evidence can be given in mitigation of damages of other compensation for similar publications (1955 Act, s.12). An indemnity agreement is lawful if the defamer published innocently or had reasonable belief in a defence (1955 Act, s.11). Consolidation of actions for defamation, malicious falsehood is dealt with by section 5 of the 1888 Act and section 13 of the 1955 Act (see para. 3.36).

18.22 An interlocutory injunction *quia timet* to restrain publication of an alleged libel can be granted, but only if there is substantial risk of grave injustice.[29] As to interrogatories, see *Cleland* v *Neill* [1951] NI 61; *Eastwood* v

---

[27] Under s.2 the publisher can make a 'qualified offer' of amends in relation to a specific defamatory meaning. If accepted, s.3 applies. If not, the offer is a defence in respect of that specific meaning under s.4.

[28] *Semble,* he must plead it in his Defence.

[29] *Finucane* v *Yorkshire TV* [1997] 2 BNIL 105 (MacDermott LJ).

Channel 5 [1992] 2 NIJB 45; discovery, see *Hermon* v *Yorkshire TV* [1992] NI 27. The defendant can be asked as to the sources of information which he published,[30] but if the defendant pleads fair comment or privilege, interrogatories are not allowed as to his source or grounds of belief (Ord.82 r.6). The defendant must give discovery of the names of the printer, publisher etc. of the newspaper in which the libel appeared.[31]

18.22a In defamation proceedings in the High Court, the court (without a jury) may dispose of the action summarily under section 8 of the Defamation Act 1996 (*not yet in force).* If it appears "that the plaintiff's claim has no realistic prospect of success and there is no reason why it should be tried", the Court may dismiss it. If it appears "that there is no defence to the claim which has a realistic prospect of success and that there is no other reason why the claim should be tried", the Court may grant summary relief under section 9 if it will be adequate compensation, being any of the following: a declaration, an order to publish a correction and apology; damages up to £10,000; an injunction. Rules of procedure may be made under section 10.

18.23 An action containing a claim for defamation may be tried by judge and jury at the option of either party (see para. 14.04), and is invariably chosen by the plaintiff. Actions are often fiercely contested, and huge costs are incurred on both sides. Legal aid is not available. If the plaintiff does not have a deep pocket, or if he does not think that his case will impress a jury, he might be well advised to sue for the modest damages (up to £3,000) available in the county court, where his case is heard by a judge alone with appeal by rehearing to the High Court without a jury, and there is some reasonable limit on the costs.

18.24 In *McCartney* v *Sunday Newspapers*[32] Carswell J ruled that the defendant should not be allowed to put in evidence an offer in an "open" letter to pay a specified sum to charity.[33] The judge may give directions as to the order of proceedings at the trial.[34] The Court cannot rule as to whether a statement is arguably capable, as opposed to capable, of bearing a particular meaning (Defamation Act 1996, s.7- *not yet in force*). It is for the judge to rule whether a publication is privileged, but it is for the jury to rule whether a privileged report is fair and accurate.[35] In a defamation action, a criminal conviction by a United Kingdom court or British court-martial of a plaintiff is conclusive evidence of his guilt, in so far as his guilt is relevant to the cause of action of him or any co-plaintiff.[36] Although Order 18 rule 23 does not expressly apply, intention to rely on the conviction should be pleaded.[37] As to

---

30 *Marriott* v *Chamberlain* (1886) 17 QBD 154.

31 Newspapers Printers and Reading Room Repeals Act 1869, Sch.2.

32 [1988] NI 565, at 566; but see *Dixon Stores* v *Thomas Television*, para. 13.43.

33 His remark, made *obiter*, that a payment into court under s.1 [*sic*] of the 1843 Act should be kept from the jury seems to be erroneous, having regard to Ord.82 r.4(2).

34 As in *Eastwood* v *News Group* [1992] 2 NIJB 1; *Eastwood* v *Channel 5* [1992] 2 NIJB 53; cases where the main disputed issues were quantum of damages and a plea of justification.

35 *Turkington* v *The Telegraph* [1996] 6 BNIL 105 (Carswell LJ).

36 Civil Evidence Act (NI) 1971, s.9 (as amended for trials commencing after 4 September 1996; previously it applied to the conviction of any person). As to the effect of "spent" convictions see the Rehabilitation of Offenders (NI) Order 1978, Art.9.

37 *Levene* v *Roxhan* [1970] 1 WLR 1322.

exemplary damages, see *McCartney* v *Sunday Newspapers.*[38] The cases of huge damages in recent years have led the English Court of Appeal to rule that the judge may tell the jury the quantum of defamation awards made or affirmed by the Court of Appeal but not of other juries.[39] He may also indicate the normal level of awards for serious personal injuries and ask them to consider whether the damage to reputation is any worse than that; and the judge and counsel for each party may suggest figures.[40] If a verdict or judgment in default is given for a blasphemous or seditious libel the court may order seizure of copies of the libel from the defendant.[41]

COMMERCIAL AND ACCOUNTING ACTIONS

Accounts and inquiries

18.25 A cause of action can lie for the taking of an account, this being usually an equitable rather than a common law remedy. Such a claim arises often in Chancery actions, but it can also be in Queen's Bench actions. In a claim for a general account where no specific sum is claimed, the claimant does not have to give particulars of the money.[42] Where a writ or counterclaim involves the taking of an account, the plaintiff (after the time for entry of appearance) or counterclaiming defendant may apply by summons on affidavit for an order for an account to be taken (Ord.43 r.1), and may do so where he is the accounting party.[43] In any other proceedings the Court may direct any necessary accounts or inquiries (Ord.43 r.2). Inquiries may concern such matters as members of a class,[44] dates of birth and death, value of a chattel or land, assessment of damages. The Court may direct the manner in which the account or inquiry is to be done, and may direct that books of account be evidence (Ord.43 r.3). All just allowances are to be made (Ord.43 r.6). If there is undue delay in the prosecution of accounts or inquiries, the Court may call upon the parties to explain and give orders to deal with it, and may give conduct of the proceedings to the Official Solicitor (Ord.43 r.7). The accounting party must lodge his account exhibited by affidavit and notify the other parties, save as otherwise directed (Ord.43 r.4). A party who alleges omissions or errors in the account must give notice stating the ground of objection (Ord.43 r.5). If there is difficulty in ascertaining all the persons entitled to a share in a fund, the Court may authorise payment of the shares of those who have been found (Ord.43 r.8). If an account to be taken includes a bill of costs, the Court may direct the Taxing Master to tax and report on the costs (Ord.62 r.24). The judge can adopt, vary or disregard the report.[45] The judge must consider any party's objections,[46] but the findings are not to be set

---

38 [1988] 13 NIJB 48, at 50.

39 *Rantzen* v *Mirror Group* [1994] QB 670, at 694-5.

40 *John* v *Mirror Group*, [1996] 2 All ER 35 (CA).

41 Criminal Libel Act 1819, s.1. There is nothing in the Act to say that this section excludes civil actions.

42 *In re Wells* [1962] 1 WLR 397, 874; *Short* v *Lamb* [1925] 1 IR 135.

43 *Molony* v *Molony* (1888) 21 LR Ir 91.

44 E.g. the cousins of the testator.

45 *Wenlock* v *River Dee* (1887) 19 QBD 155, at 158.

46 *Adamson* v *Connaughton* (1893) 27 ILTR 114.

aside except for gross mistake.[47] Once the report is confirmed no application to vary it can be heard.[48]

18.26 The Crown may apply summarily for information and accounts relating to Inheritance Tax, excise duties, VAT, stamp duties or taxes under NI statute.[49]

18.27 In any proceedings involving matters of account the Court may refer the whole proceedings or an issue therein to a master, referee or arbitrator agreed by the parties under section 55(2)(cc) of the Judicature Act, and Order 36. Order 38 rules 1-5,18-29 apply. The Court usually adjourns further consideration until after receipt of his report or directs proceedings after the report. Subject to the directions in the reference, the referee has all the powers of the judge except committal, in conducting the trial or proceedings before him. The referee consults with the parties and fixes a date for trial of the issue, and reports to the Court his decision on the facts or the question arising from his findings. The Court may adopt, vary, remit for further consideration, require explanation of, or decide the issue on, his findings. The Court then fixes a hearing for further consideration of the report, at which a party may apply to vary or remit the report. A decision by a master on a reference is appealable to the Court of Appeal (Ord.58 rr.2-3).

Actions for debt

18.27a An action upon a debt or liquidated demand can be brought by writ, usually in the Queen's Bench Division, as described at para. 5.13 and para. 9.12.

Commercial List actions

18.28 A cause in the Queen's Bench Division relating to a "business or commercial transaction",[50] such as building contracts, sale of goods, insurance, banking, agency, bailment, carriage of goods, may be listed in the Commercial List if so directed by the Commercial Judge (at present Pringle J) (Ord.72 rr.1,2(1)). The Judge (or another judge at the request of the Chief Justice) supervises the listing, interlocutory applications and disposal of those actions by the Registrar of the Commercial List (Ord.72 rr.2(3),8(3)). Upon commencement of a commercial action the plaintiff's solicitor, and thereafter any party, may request the Registrar to ask the Judge to take the action into his list; the Judge decides having regard to the amounts involved or the issues in the action; he may later remove the action from the List (Ord.72 r.3). The decision to enter the action in the List can be appealed against on the ground that it is not a commercial action.[51] All pleadings, particulars, lists of discovered documents must be given to the Registrar as soon as they are served on the

---

[47] *Re Ryan* (1916) 50 ILTR 11.

[48] *In re Kane* [1943] Ir Jur R 30.

[49] Crown Proceedings Act, s.14, by originating motion or summons (Ord.77 r.6).

[50] Under a statute which allows an action relating to "an ordinary transaction of persons engaged in commerce or trade" to be put into the Commercial List, it includes an action concerning a lease of commercial premises: *Pavilion Restaurant* v *Dominion Breweries* [1987] 2 NZLR 644 (CA).

[51] *Sea Insurance* v *Carr* [1901] 1 QB 7, leave to appeal being required (para. 20.10).

other party (Ord.72 r.4). After close of pleadings the Registrar refers the action to the Judge for directions[52] as to its conduct and the Judge may at any stage entertain the proposals of any party (Ord.72 r.6). He will want to know in particular counsels' estimate of the length of the trial. All interlocutory applications are to be made to the Judge unless he otherwise directs and requests another judge or a master to hear it (Ord.72 rr.5,8(1)). A date for hearing is fixed in advance by the Registrar and Judge and the parties may apply at any stage in relation to the fixing of a date (Ord.72 r.7). The action is heard by the Judge unless he requests another judge to hear it (Ord.72 r.8(2)).

Expert evidence

18.29 By a highly significant amendment introduced in 1996, expert evidence must be disclosed in actions in the Commercial List. The new rule 9 in Order 72 is the rough equivalent of the English RSC Order 38 rules 35-44.[53] A party who proposes to adduce expert evidence at the trial must disclose it to the other party(ies) in such time and manner as the judge directs and give a copy thereof to the registrar within two days (Ord.72 r.9(1)(2)). An expert includes any person whether an independent expert, an 'in-house' or employed expert of the party or even the party himself.[54] The English rule imposes an obligation on the party to apply for the judge's directions, and if he fails to do so in good time the judge has power to refuse a direction and to prohibit the use of the evidence.[55] Under the new rule in Northern Ireland, no such obligation is expressly imposed: the Commercial Judge looks at each case and issues directions as appropriate. It is anticipated that a general practice direction will be issued only if the volume of cases becomes so great that the Judge cannot consider each individually.

18.30 Subject to the judge's directions, disclosure is made by furnishing a copy of the report, signed and dated and stating the author's qualifications and of any documents emanating from its author which are intended by him to accompany or supplement the report (Ord. 72 r.9(4)). 'Expert evidence' means evidence contained in a report and accompanying or supplemental documents and includes ancillary technical evidence (r.9(7)). If the direction is not complied with, the judge may stay the action or strike out the Defence or make such other order as seems meet (r.9(3)). The whole report, including an accompanying note, must be served,[56] but the Court cannot compel disclosure of the report of the expert on a matter on which the party does not intend to adduce evidence from him at the trial.[57] It must be drafted by the expert and its contents should be uninfluenced by the exigencies of the litigation.[58] Counsel must not draft the report but he may to a limited extent direct alterations to it,

---

52 For a standard set of directions see Appendix Two.
53 The English rules are not confined to commercial actions.
54 *Shell Pensions* v *Pell Frischmann* [1986] 2 All ER 911.
55 *Winchester Cigarette Machinery* v *Payne*, 'The Times', 19 October 1993.
56 *Kenning* v *Eve Construction* [1989] 1 WLR 1189.
57 *Derby & Co* v *Weldon (No 9)*, 'The Times', 9 November 1990 (CA); disapproving *Kenning* v *Eve Construction* on this point.
58 *Whitehouse* v *Jordan* [1981] 1 WLR 246.

(e.g. to exclude irrelevance).[59] *Quaere*, disclosure under rule 9 terminates the privilege in the report. *Quaere*, once a report has been served under rule 9 the opposing party is entitled to use it in evidence against the serving party.

18.31 However the party bound by a direction to disclose may apply *ex parte* for leave to adduce the evidence without disclosure or to omit or amend any part of the evidence on disclosure (r.9(5)). However English courts strongly favour the "cards on the table" approach in civil litigation, because disclosure of expert evidence helps in the fair and expeditious resolution of the dispute by trial or by settlement; even in fraud cases disclosure should be the norm.[60]

18.32 In relation to the adduction of expert evidence at the trial, the general principles stated at para. 13.88 apply as in any ordinary action. Unless the Court otherwise orders, a party may call only one non-medical expert to give oral evidence at the trial (Ord.38 r.1B). Unless the Court otherwise orders, a map, drawing, photograph shown under Order 38 rule 3A is admissible unless the other party requires it to be proved (Ord.38 r.1A(1)(2)). An expert's report or his map, drawing or photograph may be admitted by the Court if he is unable to attend (Ord.38 r.1A(3)). Unless the Court otherwise orders a party adducing expert evidence at the trial cannot, save by leave or consent, lead evidence from the expert of which the substance has been undisclosed, save as to new matters arising during the trial (Ord.72 r.9(6)(a)). The 'substance of the evidence' means both the factual observations and findings of the expert and the opinion which he has formed.[61] The Court may direct that the disclosed evidence or part of it shall stand as the expert's evidence-in-chief (r.9(6)(b)). The opposing party may refer in cross-examination to any part of the disclosed evidence whether or not it has been adduced in chief (r.9(6)(c)).

ACTIONS RELATING TO GOODS AND CHATTELS

18.33 In an action for wrongful interference with goods, the plaintiff must indorse the writ with a statement of the value of the goods (Ord.6 r.2(d)). If he does not have their written authority to sue, he must indorse on the writ his interest in the goods and the identities of all persons interested in the goods (Ord.15 r.17(1)). A defendant can contend that someone else has a better right to the goods than the plaintiff (Tort (Interference with Goods) Act 1977, s.8). He may apply at any time between appearance and judgment (by summons to be personally served) for directions as to whether a person with a competing right to the goods should be joined (Ord.15 r.17(2)). (As to delivery up of the goods pending trial, see s.4 and Ord.29 r.3 (para. 11.78)). (Forms of judgment, see para. 14.83).

ACTIONS RELATING TO LAND

18.34 Actions for the recovery of land can be brought in the High Court:[62] (a) in any case where the plaintiff claims such title as gives him right to possession

---

[59] Bar Handbook 20.

[60] *Khan* v *Armaguard Ltd* [1994] 1 WLR 1204.

[61] *Ollett* v *Bristol Aerojet* [1979] 1 WLR 1197.

[62] Most actions for possession of land are brought by way of ejectment civil bill in the county court. The county court can hear an ejectment on the title if the net annual value does not

against the tenant; (b) by a landlord against an overholding tenant whose tenancy has expired by efflux of time, forfeiture for breach of covenant or notice to quit; (c) by a landlord for non-payment of one year's rent under the Law of Landlord and Tenant (Ir) Act 1860 (s.52). That Act is universally known as 'Deasy's Act'. The High Court also has jurisdiction to hear an action for a declaration as to title to land.[63] (As to indorsement of the writ, see Ord.6 r.2(c); service, see Ord.10 r.4). Only a person in possession need be sued; but a person named as defendant has a right to defend whether or not in possession.[64] In an action for a declaration of title as to land the plaintiff must sue any person claiming rights inconsistent to his.[65] As to judgment in default (Ord.13 r.4, Ord.19 r.5), see paras. 8.00-8.01 and para. 9.63; pleading the Defence (Ord.18 r.8(2)) see para. 9.29; intervention as defendant by person in possession (Ord.15 r.10), see para. 11.27.

18.35 If an application is made to the High Court or county court for sale, conveyance or declaration of title to land which includes the shore or sea bed or land abutting thereto, the Court must give notice to the Board of Trade and the Commissioners of Crown Lands.[66]

18.36 The right of a mortgagor with right to possession or rents and profits to sue for recovery of land, rent or profits, or for trespass is not defeated by the vesting of legal title in the mortgagee (Judicature Act, Art.93(2)).

18.37 No order for recovery of land can be given against the Crown, only a declaration of right,[67] and in the RSC references to action for recovery of land include action for such declaration (Ord.1 r.5).

18.38 *Further provisions in Deasy's Act.* Against an overholding tenant the plaintiff may require security (s.75). He may claim double payment of rent for wilful overholding (s.76). In an ejectment for non-payment of rent or overholding the plaintiff can claim rent and *mesne* profits up to the date of judgment in his 'plaint' (s.77). In an ejectment for non-payment of rent the landlord's affidavit is evidence of the rent due and if one year's rent is due he may get judgment in default (s.58). If the amount due is paid or tendered at any time before execution of the judgment and the sum lodged in court, the judge may stay the action on payment of taxed costs (s.64). The judgment must state the amount of rent due and if the defendant pays it the EJ Office stays execution (s.65). An ejectment judgment does not prejudice the right to the rent due (s.66). On obtaining judgment for recovery of land on determination of the

---

exceed £500, and can hear other types of ejectment action set out in the County Courts (NI) Order 1980, Art.12.

63 These actions are always brought in the Queen's Bench Division, save as follows. An action for delivery of possession of real or leasehold property by a mortgagee/chargee against the mortgagor or person in possession is assigned to the Chancery Division (Ord.88 r.2), but not an action between either of them and a stranger. An action for declaration as to the *equitable* title to land should be brought in the Chancery Division.

64 *(Marquis of) Ormond* v *Burke* (1854) 6 Ir Jur OS 112. See also White Book (1997) Vol. 2 [4699], and Harrison *Law of Ejectments in Ireland.*

65 *Howard* v *Howard* (1892) 30 LR Ir 340, at 349-50.

66 Northern Ireland (Miscellaneous Provisions) Act 1932, s.9(3).

67 Crown Proceedings Act, s.21(1)(b).

tenancy for non-payment of rent, the plaintiff is entitled to damages for loss of rent.[68]

18.39 An action for rent or *mesne* profits may be brought in the High Court (Deasy's Act, ss.45-6), usually the Queen's Bench Division.

18.40 Where a lessor is proceeding by action or otherwise to enforce a right of re-entry or forfeiture for breach of covenant or condition, the lessee may seek relief in that action or by suing himself (Conveyancing Act 1881, s.14(2)). Proceedings under that Act are assigned to the Chancery Division (s.69). An action for relief from forfeiture for non-payment of rent or unlawful assignment should be in the Queen's Bench Division.[69] After judgment[70] of ejectment for (forfeiture for) non-payment of rent, the lessee may apply for restoration of the tenancy on payment of the rent (Judicature Act, s.94).

18.41 *Defences.* Some statutory protection is given to tenants from eviction or ejectment by the [Land Law (Ir) Acts 1887 s.30, 1896 s.16 (agricultural or pastoral)];[71] Business Tenancies (NI) Order 1996 (business premises); Rent (NI) Order 1978 Arts.13-14 (private dwellings); Housing (NI) Order 1983 Arts.24-47 (where the NIHE or a Housing Association is landlord); and Family Law (Miscellaneous Provisions) (NI) Order 1984 Art.4 (for spouse in matrimonial home).

18.42 *Enforcement.* A judgment for possession of land is enforceable by the Enforcement of Judgments Office making an order for possession. Such judgments are enforceable even if they do not command the defendant to deliver up within a stated time, that being essential only to enforcement by committal or sequestration. A judgment for possession of land entitles the EJ Office to eject any person in possession, whether the defendant or not.[72] (See further para. 16.29).

Proceedings against 'squatters'

18.43 Without prejudice to the option of suing for an injunction and/or damages for trespass,[73] Order 113 provides a summary procedure by originating summons (in Form 9) for possession of land against a person who is not a tenant or overholder and who entered into or remained in occupation without the consent of the plaintiff or his predecessor in title (Ord.113 rr.1,2), usually a squatter who enters without any permission or a mere licensee who stays when asked to leave. Action may be in the Queen's Bench or Chancery Division. The plaintiff must prove a possessory title to the land.[74] The summons names as defendant the person known to be occupying and if the name is not known "the occupier". A date for hearing is obtained from the Office when the

---

[68] *Rainey Bros* v *Kearney* [1990] NI 18.

[69] *Duncan* v *Mackin* [1985] 10 NIJB 1, at 7; where Lord Lowry LCJ pointed out that suing in the wrong Division is never fatal.

[70] Including summary judgment: Ord.14 r.10.

[71] The 1887 and 1896 Acts are repealed from a date to be appointed, save in relation to tenancies existing on that day: Property (NI) Order 1997, Art.38.

[72] *R* v *Wandsworth County Court ex p Wandsworth LBC* [1975] 1 WLR 1314.

[73] *NIHE* v *Fox* [1981] 9 NIJB at 8-9.

[74] *DOE* v *Leeburn* [1990] NI 135.

summons is issued and that date is entered on the summons. With the summons the plaintiff files an affidavit stating his interest, the circumstances of the "squatting" and that no person other than the defendant is known to be in occupation (Ord.113 r.3). The affidavit may contain statements of hearsay and belief if the source and grounds thereof are stated. The summons and affidavit are served on the named defendant like a writ or by leaving copies or sending them to the premises or otherwise as the Court directs; and also by affixing copies to the door and putting copies through the letter box in an envelope addressed to "the occupiers" (Ord.113 r.4). The defendant need not enter an appearance (Ord.113 r.2). Since the date for hearing is obtained and the summons served *ab initio*, Order 28 rule 3 does not apply. Any occupier may apply to be joined as a defendant (Ord.113 r.5).

18.44 A final order can be made only by a judge in person; this means that the substantive hearing takes place before a judge in chambers unless he adjourns into open court under Order 32 rule 13. Save by leave in case of urgency, the hearing must be at least five clear days after the date of service (Ord.113 r.6). Possession should be granted unless the defendant raises a substantial defence, in which case the judge should direct a full trial, usually by ordering the action to continue as if by writ. In an action by a local or housing authority, the Court may adjourn the hearing if there is an arguable case for judicial review of the decision to evict.[75] Any order may be set aside or varied by the judge (Ord.113 r.7).

18.45 By Order 113 rule 6(3) as amended, the Court can direct that possession be given on a specific date in the same way as it can in a writ action. Despite this amendment the White Book (1997) 113/1-8/9, continues to adhere to the previous case law,[76] that the Court has no power to suspend an order of possession against a trespasser unless the plaintiff consents. The order in Form 33 allows for the optional insertion of the words: "the defendant do give possession of the said lands on [date]". Where inserted this may mean, if the White Book is correct, that the plaintiff can have the order enforced by the EJ Office at any time, but that proceedings to commit for contempt can only be brought after that date, the court order having been served personally with penal notice before that date. Therefore it is advisable for the plaintiff to ensure that these words are inserted in the Court order, or added later under Order 113 rule 7, in any case where there is a named person as squatter.[77] In relation to a judgment under Order 113, application to the EJ Office to enforce must be made within three months, or later by leave of the High Court.[78] An order for possession of land can be enforced against any person found in possession whether the defendant or not.[79] A stay of enforcement cannot be granted under rule 103 of the JE Rules (r.103(6) thereof).

---

[75] *South Hams DC* v *Shough*, 'The Times' 8 December 1992 (CA).
[76] See *NIHE* v *McAuley* [1974] NI 233.
[77] *NIHE* v *Magee*, Ch D, NI (Girvan J), 9 November 1995.
[78] Judgments Enforcement Rules (NI) 1981, r.5(1)(h).
[79] *R* v *Wandsworth CC ex p Wandsworth LBC* [1975] 1 WLR 1314.

FAMILY DIVISION

18.46 Order 1 rule 12[80] assigns to the Family Division -

a(i)	grant or revocation of representation of estate of a deceased
a(ii)	matrimonial causes (dissolution of marriage, judicial separation and related matters)
a(iii) *	inherent jurisdiction relating to children (i.e. wardship)
b(i)(ii)	enforcement of maintenance orders
b(iii)	Family Law (Miscellaneous Provisions)(NI) Order 1984, Pt.II (spouse's right of residence)
b(iv)(v) *	international child abduction and custody disputes under Child Abduction and Custody Act 1985 and Family Law Act 1986
b(vi)(vii) *	affairs of patients under Mental Health (NI) Order 1986 and Enduring Powers of Attorney (NI) Order 1987
b(viii) *	adoption of children
b(ix)	declarations under the Matrimonial and Family Proceedings (NI) Order 1989, Pts.IV and V
b(ix) *	declarations under Art.33 of the Matrimonial and Family Proceedings (NI) Order 1989
b(x) *	proceedings under the Parental Orders (Human Fertilisation and Embryology) Regs SI 1994/2767
b(xi) *	proceedings under the Children (NI) Order 1995, not in a pending matrimonial cause
b(xi)	proceedings under the Children (NI) Order 1995, in a pending matrimonial cause
(c)	proceedings assigned by statute

Proceedings are served by the Probate and Matrimonial Office, except categories marked * which are served by the Office of Care and Protection (Ord.1 rr.16,17).

Appendix One of this book includes proceedings under statute assigned to the Family Division: see in particular para. 14 thereof .

MATRIMONIAL CAUSES

18.47 Petitions for divorce, annulment of marriage etc. are dealt with under the Matrimonial Causes (NI) Order 1978 and the Family Proceedings Rules (NI) 1996.[81] The High Court shares the jurisdiction under these provisions with divorce county courts. Jurisdiction of High Court: Art.48. Parties: Art.53 and FP Rules, r.2.8. A matrimonial cause is by petition issued in the Probate and Matrimonial Office (r.2). Costs SR 1996/105; White Book (1997) 62/B/40; Anderson p.22; *Beggs* v *Beggs*, Taxing Office, NI (Master Napier) 11 May 1994. Fees SR 1996/105, amended 1997/177. Affidavit of service of petition: Practice Direction [1992] 3 BNIL 111. Appeal from a decree *nisi* lies without leave to the Court of Appeal (Judicature Act, s.35(2)(g)(iv)). The RSC do not

---

80 As substituted by SR 1996/212.

81 SR 1996/322, in force 4 November 1996. The Matrimonial Causes Rules (SR 1981/184 amended 1989/246) apply to proceedings commenced before that date.

generally apply to matrimonial causes (Ord.1 r.2), but rule 1.4 of the FP Rules applies the RSC to proceedings in the High Court.

- Alteration of maintenance agreements: Art.38.
- Registration of Commonwealth maintenance orders: Maintenance Orders (Facilities for Enforcement) Act 1920; Ord.105 r.2 (applies only to countries which are not yet designated under the 1972 Act).
- Enforcement of orders of designated countries: Maintenance Orders (Reciprocal Enforcement) Act 1972 (as amended 1992): Ord.105 rr.16-23
- Enforcement of UK maintenance orders: Maintenance Orders Acts 1950 , Pt.II (ss.16-25), and 1958, ss.2, 2A and 5: Ord.105 rr.3-9.
- Enforcement between High Court and magistrates' courts: Maintenance and Affiliation Orders Act (NI) 1966, ss.9-16; Ord.105 rr.10-15.
- Attachment of earnings orders to enforce maintenance orders: Judgments Enforcement (NI) Order 1981, Arts. 99, 102, 105; Ord.105 rr.24-34.
- Matrimonial and Family Proceedings (NI) Order 1989: application for financial relief after overseas divorce: Pt.IV (Arts.16-30). Declarations as to marital status, as to legitimacy, adoption: Pt.V (Arts 31-40); transfer to spouse of Rent Order tenancy (Sch.1).
- Proceedings under the Married Women's Property Act 1882 are assigned to Chancery Division.

PROBATE

Contentious

18.48 A probate action must be begun by writ, issued out of the Probate and Matrimonial Office (Ord.76 r.2), in Form 3. It may be issued for service outside Northern Ireland by leave (Ord.11 r.1(1)(*l*)). The plaintiff does not have to join a person jointly entitled with him (Ord.15 r.4(2)). Order 76 deals with parties, disclosure of testamentary scripts, required counterclaims, pleadings etc. Orders 13, 19 and 21 do not apply. In default of appearance or pleading, the Court may dismiss the action or proceed to trial. An action can be discontinued or dismissed only by order to the Court. If the defendant makes a probate counterclaim in another type of action then it must be struck out or the whole action transferred to the Family Division (Ord.76 r.15). If the defendant in his Defence merely puts the plaintiff to proof in solemn form of the will, no order for costs is made against him unless he had no reasonable grounds (Ord.62 r.4(3)).

18.49 The High Court may appoint an administrator *pendente lite* under the Administration of Estates (NI) Order 1979 (Art.6) and Ord.76 r.14. [The High Court may pronounce for one will without a hearing if all potential beneficiaries consent (Wills and Administration (NI) Order 1994, Art.34)- *not yet in force*]. Costs see White Book (1997) 62/B/92; *Ormsby* v *Good* [1895] 1 IR 103; *Craig* v *Boyd* [1901] 2 IR 645. The High Court may issue a *subpoena* for service in the United Kingdom to testify about or produce testamentary documents (Judicature Act, s.67(2)).

Non-contentious

18.50 The High Court can grant probate or administration for an estate under the Administration of Estates (NI) Order 1979 (Arts.3-11).

Applications are made and business is conducted at the Probate and Matrimonial Office by the Master (Probate and Matrimonial) or at a branch office by a district judge (1979 Order, Art.18; Order 97). Appeal lies to a judge in chambers (Ord.58 r.1). Fees, see SR 1996/104, amended SR 1997/176. Costs see Anderson p.15. The Court may also grant administration limited as the Court thinks fit (1979 Order, Art.5) on application to the judge or master (Ord.97 r.51). It may grant administration limited to real estate or personal estate (Administration of Estates Act (NI) 1955, s.1(2)), by application to the judge or master (Ord.97 r.50). It may grant special administration while the personal representative is abroad (1979 Order, Art.8) by motion to the judge (Ord.97 r.54). As to interpretation and rectification of wills see the Wills and Administration Proceedings (NI) Order 1994, Articles 25-9. The Probate and Matrimonial Office can receive a deposit of the will of a living person under the Administration of Justice Act 1982, section 23.

See further Appendix One, para.1.12b.

JURISDICTION OVER MINORS

18.51 The Court of Chancery had jurisdiction to take custody of any minor for any reason by making him a ward of court, and the wardship jurisdiction is now exercised by the Family Division under section 26 of the Judicature Act; and Order 90 rules 3-5. See also the Children (NI) Order 1995 (Pt.III (Arts.8-16) and Art.173). The Judicature Act (s.29) and Order 89 deal with the co-ordination of jurisdiction where proceedings pending in another Division concern a minor. Practice Direction for wardship, see [1982] 7 BNIL 87. The Children (Allocation of Proceedings) Order (SR 1996/300) provides for the allocation of proceedings between the High Court, county court, family proceedings court and family care centre, and transfer between them, but commencement or transfer of proceedings in breach of the Order does not render the proceedings invalid and is not a ground of appeal (r.16). Procedure is governed by the FP Rules, r.4. Hearsay evidence is admissible (see para. 13.32). Where money awarded to a child is paid into court, or money awarded to a child by a foreign court, or in any other case where desirable, the High Court may appoint a guardian of his estate (Ord.80 r.14).

Adoption

18.51a See the Adoption (NI) Order 1987 (Arts.12-27,28-32,50-6,57) and Order 84 (SR 1989/343) (not included in the loose leaf *Red Book*).

JURISDICTION OVER MENTAL PATIENTS

18.52 The High Court has inherited the ancient jurisdiction, now exercised under the Mental Health (NI) Order 1986 (Arts.97-118) and Order 109 by the Family Judge or the Master (Care and Protection) to manage and administer the property and affairs of a person who is incapable by reason of mental disorder (a 'patient'), which powers it may delegate to a controller. Only a judge or the Master (Care and Protection) can approve a compromise on behalf of a 'patient' (Ord.32 r.11(2)). The Queen has custody of the lands of natural fools.[82] The Judicature Act (s.29) and Order 89 deal with the co-ordination of jurisdiction where proceedings pending in another Division concern a patient. As to registration of power of attorney over property of a person who is mentally incapable: Enduring Powers of Attorney (NI) Order 1987; Order 109A.

See further Appendix One, para.1.13b.

CHANCERY DIVISION

18.53 The following are assigned to the Chancery Division, by Order 1 rule 10 -

(1) all proceedings assigned to Chancery Judge/Division when the 1980 Rules came into force

(2) all proceedings assigned to Chancery Judge/Division by statute

(3) administration of estates; partnership dissolution and accounts; redemption and foreclosure of mortgages; raising portions or charges on land; sale and distribution of proceeds of property subject to lien or charge; actions for payment of money secured by mortgage or charge on real or leasehold property, or for possession by the mortgagee/chargee (Ord.88 r.2); execution of trusts; rectification, setting aside or cancellation of deeds and instruments; specific performance/forfeiture of deposit, of agreements for sale, exchange, mortgage or assignment of lease of, any property; partition or sale of land; copyright

(4) Bankruptcy, Insolvency and Companies Acts proceedings; injunctions to restrain a winding-up petition;[83] proceedings under JE Order 1981, Arts 88(3A), 90(3A).

These are served by the Chancery Office, except category (4) and applications under the Financial Services Act 1986, which are served by the Bankruptcy and Companies Office. (As to the jurisdiction of the Chancery Master, see Ord.32 r.11, para. 11.04.)

18.54 Originating summons actions in the Chancery Division are listed before and heard by the master, save proceedings which are heard by the judge.[84] The proceedings to be heard by the judge are: (a) excepted proceedings under Order 32 rule 11(1);[85] (b) summons raising the construction of a document or a question of law (Ord.32 r.11(3); and (c) applications under the Solicitors (NI)

---

82 Prerogative of the Crown, c.11 & 12 (statute of the English Parliament passed in the 1320s).

83 By originating motion: Ord.29 r.1A.

84 The Practice Direction [1990] 3 BNIL 98, in so far as it provides that all cases be listed initially before the master, is not now operated in practice and is about to be revoked.

85 Matters relating to criminal proceedings or liberty of the subject; review of taxation of costs; leave to a vexatious litigant to sue; approval of transactions under inherent jurisdiction; granting of an injunction save on terms agreed; approval of settlements for minors and patients; charities; applications under ss.40,56,57,61 of the Trustee Act (NI) 1958, or Art.133(2) of the Mental Health (NI) Order 1986.

Order 1976; Inheritance (Provisions for Family and Dependants) (NI) Order 1979; Married Women's Property Act 1882; (d) proceedings begun by (or ordered to continue as if by) writ, and originating motions and petitions; and (e) any individual case specially directed to be listed before the judge.[86] [Where a question arises as to the construction of a will or trust, the trustee/personal representative may apply to the High Court for an order authorising reliance on the written opinion of a barrister of ten years, if appropriate to do so without hearing argument.][87]

Originating and interlocutory summons for hearing by the master are listed under a "block listing" appointment arrangement for hearings on each morning and afternoon on weekdays throughout term. The master's 11am list on each day starts with short applications lasting not more than five minutes (e.g. settlements, *Tomlin* orders, agreed adjournments listed for that day, and unopposed applications listed for that 11am sitting) if notice is given in writing before 10.50am; such applications should be issued for or switched to the 11am list when settlement or agreement to adjourn is effected.[88] In the case of a 'matter' before a judge or master (*semble*, excluding the trial of an action) a first adjournment by consent may be applied for by hand delivery or by 'FAX' not later than mid-day on the day before the hearing.[89]

As to listing of summonses before the judge, see the Practice Direction [1987] 9 BNIL 70. For a list of Chancery Practice Directions see [1994] 7 BNIL 84. Three new Directions in 1997, dealing with fixing dates, lodging documents for trial and delivery of judgments, are dealt with at the appropriate places in previous chapters.

Sale of land

18.55 In any cause or matter relating to land in the Chancery Division, the Court may order sale of the land or an interest in it (Ord.31 r.1). See further para. 15.18. The Court may allow the party having conduct to arrange the sale or may give directions as to the party or person to have conduct of the sale and as to the mode of sale, the reserve price etc. (Ord.31 r.2). If so directed or if the proceeds are to be paid into court, the result of the sale is certified to the Court (Ord.31 r.3). Rules 2 and 3 apply also to a mortgage, exchange or partition of land under an order (Ord.31 r.4). In administration and execution of trust actions, conduct of the sale is normally given to the trustee/personal representatives (Ord.85 r.6); in other cases to the plaintiff or party who has carriage of the litigation unless he wishes to bid (Daniell p.942). Where the Court orders the sale of land it may declare that a party hold his interest as trustee for the purposes of the Trustee Act (NI) 1958 (para. 15.18).

Proceedings under judgment or order

18.56 In a Chancery action an order or primary judgment is often given with directions for further proceedings before the master, for example for accounts

[86] Subject to Ord 32 r.11(1), the master can hear interlocutory summonses in such cases.
[87] Wills and Administration Proceedings (NI) Order 1994, Art.33 - *not yet in force*.
[88] Practice Note [1995] 3 BNIL 106.
[89] Practice Direction [1995] 4 BNIL 91.

and inquiries, for settling deeds and instruments, for sale and distribution of proceeds, for advertising for and adjudicating on claims against the estate or property. The Court may give conduct of proceedings to any person (Ord.15 r.18). This rule includes proceedings not yet commenced but which are directed in the course of existing proceedings.[90] Generally conduct is given to a plaintiff; or in proceedings for the sale of property, to the holder of the legal title. Conduct may be refused or removed from a party who has delayed unreasonably. Accounts and inquiries, whether before or after judgment, are taken under Order 43 rules 3-9 (see para. 18.25). The judgment may direct no further proceedings to be taken without leave, so as to give time to collect and value the estate.

18.57 In an action for the administration of an estate, execution of a trust or sale of property, the Court on giving primary judgment or order or in proceedings thereunder may direct service of notice of the judgment on non-parties who are affected by it, and who are thereby bound by the judgment unless they have service discharged, and can appear in proceedings under it (Ord.44 rr.1-2). The direction should state the capacity or right in which the person to be served is interested.[91] *Semble*, it may be served outside Northern Ireland.[92] If the noticed party is under disability, and no guardian appears for him the Court may appoint one at the hearing (Ord.80 r.4(4)). A minor with a guardian *ad litem* is bound like an adult.[93] A person improperly served need not appear and is not bound by the proceedings.[94] If the person served has no interest he may apply for the service on him to be discharged and for costs.[95] A person interested who is not served may still be bound by the proceedings if he was fully aware of them and took no steps to intervene.[96] A person not served may appear by leave and be bound as if a noticed party.[97]

18.58 The Court may give directions as to the manner of taking accounts, the evidence, the preparation and service of a deed or instrument, parties and legal representation (Ord.44 r.3). In administration of estate or execution of trust actions (to which Order 85 also applies), or any proceedings in which an account of debts and liabilities or inquiry for claimants is directed, procedure is under Order 44 rules 4-8. The Court may direct advertisements for creditors and claimants to claim within a stated time. The personal representative or party directed to examine the claims must make an affidavit of his findings at least a week before the date for adjudication. The Court may allow claims without proof or direct proof or investigation; and notice of the adjudication must be given to those creditors who do not attend. On adjudication of the

---

90 *McKinlay* v *Mackey* [1895] 1 IR 302, at 306.

91 *Swan* v *Doak* (1856) 6 Ir Ch R 55.

92 *Spence* v *Parkes* [1900] 2 IR 619, at 626-7. An order may be served outside NI with leave of the Court, or without leave in proceedings where the originating process could have been so served without leave: Ord.11 r.9(4).

93 *Fry* v *Johnson* (1856) 6 Ir Ch R 56.

94 *Bristow* v *Millar* (1854) 6 Ir Jur OS 285.

95 *Re Symons* (1886) 54 LT 501.

96 *Re Lart* [1896] 2 Ch 788.

97 *McDonnell* v *McDonnell* (1886) 17 LR Ir 582.

claims, the claimant's business books are admissible.[98] There is a rule of practice that claims should be corroborated (see para. 13.21). The costs of a claim by a creditor/claimant follow the event unless otherwise ordered (Ord.62 r.6(3)(4)), and the Court may assess the claimant's costs in lieu of taxation (Ord.62 r.7(5)). Unless he directs further consideration, the master then states his findings in the form of a final order, subject to appeal to a judge in chambers (Ord.44 rr.11-12). This means that in most cases there will be no further consideration nor confirmation by the judge unless a party or claimant is dissatisfied. There is no power to reverse the primary judgment.[99] The master's findings should be varied only if clear mistake or abuse is shown.[98]

18.59 Order 44 applies to a mortgage suit in which sale is ordered, so that a prior incumbrancer may be served,[100] thus preventing him from exercising his power of sale under section 19 of the Conveyancing Act 1881.[101]

PROCEEDINGS RE SALE OF PROPERTY

18.60 In a Chancery writ action for specific performance, rescission or forfeiture of a deposit, on an agreement for the sale, exchange or mortgage of land or any property, the Court may hear a summons for summary judgment under Order 86. It cannot be given against the Crown (Ord.77 r.5(1)). *Semble,* Order 86 only applies to an action between parties to the agreement.[102] It is similar to Order 14 procedure (para. 11-45), except that it can be applied for before the defendant enters an appearance and before Statement of Claim, and that a counterclaiming defendant cannot apply for it. The summons, and affidavit of facts stating the belief that there is no defence, with minutes of the judgment desired, must be served on the defendant at least four days before the date of hearing. Judgment may be given for the plaintiff unless there is an issue which ought to be tried or some other reason for a trial, in which case the defendant may be given leave to defend unconditionally or on terms. The Court may declare a party or unborn person to be a trustee of his interest in land and may vest the interest (Trustee Act (NI) 1958, s.48).

18.61 If an action for specific performance relates to registered land, the Court may cause a person who has a registrable interest or who has entered a caution or inhibition to appear and he is bound by order of the court.[103] If an application is made to the High Court or county court for sale, conveyance or declaration of title to land which includes the shore or sea bed or land abutting thereto, the Court must give notice to the Board of Trade and the Commissioners of Crown Lands.[104]

Other land proceedings

18.61a See Appendix One, para.1.12a.

---

98 *Re Ryan* (1916) 50 ILTR 11.
99 *Mullen* v *Smith* (1933) 67 ILTR 103.
100 *Armstrong* v *Dickson* [1911] 1 IR 435.
101 *Duff* v *Devlin* [1924] 1 IR 56 (NI).
102 Cf. *Miller* v *Hatrick* [1907] 1 IR 82.
103 Land Registration Act (NI) 1970, s.5.
104 Northern Ireland (Miscellaneous Provisions) Act 1932, s.9(3).

ADMINISTRATION OF ESTATES; EXECUTION OF TRUSTS

18.62 Order 85 applies to actions for the administration of a deceased's estate or for execution of a trust, including a constructive trust,[105] a claim for a declaration of trust,[106] or a claim for declaration as to equitable title.[107] The action is titled "In the matter of the estate of AB deceased [or] of the ... Trust, and between X plaintiff and Y defendant". When an order is made for administration of an estate, the Chancery Judge may transfer to his Division any pending proceedings in another Division by or against the personal representative, after hearing all the parties (Ord.4 r.2). Practitioners must remember that proceedings relating to grants and revocation of representation are assigned to the Family Division, whilst proceedings relating to administration of the estate are assigned to the Chancery Division. If the estate is known to be insolvent, proceedings for administration should be brought in the Chancery Division in its insolvency jurisdiction, served out of the Bankruptcy and Companies Office.[108]

18.63 *Limited proceedings.* The RSC tend to discourage full administration/execution actions where the issues can be resolved by more limited proceedings. A judgment for administration or execution need not be granted if the issues can be resolved otherwise (Ord.85 r.5(1)). An action can be brought for the determination of a question such as the class or interests of claimants, the rights of creditors and claimants,[109] or for any specific relief such as directing the trustee/personal representative to do an act or approving a sale, without having to bring full administration/execution proceedings (Ord.85 r.2).[110] An action can be brought to interpret a will or instrument. Application can be made under a provision of the Administration of Estates Act (NI) 1955 (s.43 thereof), or the Administration of Estates (NI) Order 1979 (e.g. to order transfer of land to the beneficiary after one year) (1955 Act, s.34); to exhibit an inventory, render accounts or deliver up the grant (1979 Order, Art.35)). Money can be paid into court under section 63 of the Trustee Act (NI) 1958; and other proceedings can be brought under that Act.

18.64 *Full proceedings.* A full administration/execution order may be necessary: (a) if the estate is insolvent; (b) if the trustee/personal representatives have failed to perform their duties; (c) to prevent beneficiaries or claimants from bringing separate actions; or (d) if fraud or wilful default is alleged. A creditor can claim against the estate for a debt incurred by the deceased during his lifetime. In respect of a debt incurred by the personal representative in administering the estate, the creditor is subrogated to the

---

[105] *Clayton* v *Renton* (1867) LR 4 Eq 158.

[106] *McConnell* v *McConnell* (1880) 5 LR Ir 474.

[107] *Sullivan* v *Orpen* [1909] 1 IR 47.

[108] Insolvency (NI) Order 1989, Art.245, as modified by the Administration of Insolvent Estates of Deceased Persons Order (NI) 1991. See Hunter *Northern Ireland Personal Insolvency* Chap. 25.

[109] Presumably overruling *In re McQuillan* [1939] NI 164 on this point.

[110] See Wylie Ord.55 r.4; *Farrell* v *Reilly* (1955) 89 ILTR 7.

personal representative's right of indemnity from the estate and thus can claim the debt against the estate.[111]

18.65 Any proceedings under Order 85 should be brought by originating summons, even if breach of trust, wilful default or misconduct is alleged (Ord.85 r.4). If there is a substantial dispute of fact the action should begin or be continued as if begun by writ. All trustee/personal representatives must be parties; and, apart of course from the beneficiary or creditor who initiates the action, beneficiaries and claimants need not be parties generally (Ord.85 r.3). An action can be brought by a trustee/personal representative against a beneficiary; or by a beneficiary[112] or creditor against the trustee/personal representative and any beneficiary who has participated in a breach of trust. If in the course of administration proceedings the Court is satisfied that the estate is insolvent, it may transfer the proceedings to the Chancery Division in its insolvency jurisdiction[113] and the beneficiaries have no further interest save as to their costs.[114] Where the unrepresented estate of a deceased is interested in proceedings, the Court may proceed in the absence of or may appoint a person to represent the estate for the proceedings (Ord.15 r.15). An administration suit is not properly constituted unless a personal representative representing the estate to be administered is a party.[115] If the trustee/personal representative defendant has not been served because he cannot be found, judgment may be given in his absence under the Trustee Act (NI) 1958 (s.59). The Court can appoint a new trustee under section 40 thereof. If pending proceedings concern the property of a deceased and no personal representative is appointed or available, the Probate Court may appoint a limited administrator to represent the estate in the proceedings under the Administration of Estates (NI) Order 1979 (Art.5); the application may be made to the Probate Master (Ord.97 r.51). The trustee/personal representatives represent the beneficiaries unless otherwise ordered (Ord.15 r.14). The Court can allow or direct a beneficiary to be a party. The Court can appoint a person to represent unascertained, untraced or unborn persons (Ord.15 r.13). A compromise affecting persons who are not parties must be approved by the Court (Ord.15 r.13(4)); that is, by a judge (Ord.32 r.11(1)(e)).

18.66 Conduct of an administration action is usually given to the personal representative if his conduct is unimpeached.[116] If there is a charitable bequest in an administration/execution action, the DHSS can apply for conduct in cases of delay.[117] If several actions are pending, the practice is to stay all but one and give conduct to the plaintiff who first sued.[118] In an action by a creditor or beneficiary, the Court may stay proceedings and order the trustee/personal

---

[111] *In re Geary* [1939] NI 152.

[112] I.e. a beneficiary or legatee or his personal representative or assignee of his interest.

[113] Insolvency (NI) Order 1989, Art.245, as modified by the Administration of Insolvent Estates of Deceased Persons Order (NI) 1991.

[114] *In re van Oppen* [1953] WN 51.

[115] *Julian* v *Goodbody* (1943) 77 ILTR 160.

[116] *McKinlay* v *Mackey* [1895] 1 IR 302.

[117] Charities Act (NI) 1964, s.6.

[118] *In re Dunne* [1907] 1 IR 202.

representatives to furnish accounts, or give primary judgment and restrict the bringing of claims by other claimants under the judgment (Ord.85 r.5(2)).

18.67 To obtain a primary decree the claimant must give prima facie evidence of his beneficial interest or claim and prove the title of the defendant as trustee/personal representative. If the trustee/personal representative is suing he must prove his title, the interest of the beneficiary named as defendant and the grounds on which administration of the estate is necessary. If an order for administration or execution is made, the Court then directs proceedings under Order 44 and accounts and inquiries under Order 43. Accounts will be directed on the footing of wilful default only if the plaintiff has pleaded and proved wilful default in collecting the assets (para. 16.10). In proceedings under a judgment for administration, only the personal representatives need appear in proceedings on a claim against the estate (Ord.85 r.3(3)). Defences available to the trustee/personal representative include *plene administravit* (para. 16.10), expiry of limitation period (para. 4.03). As to costs see White Book (1997) 62/B/61. If the estate of the deceased is solvent, interest is allowed on expenses and debts at 8 per cent per annum (Ord.44 r.9), and on legacies at 6 per cent after one year (Ord.44 r.10), unless otherwise ordered.

18.68 In High Court actions relating to estates or trusts (or otherwise as specified by rules) the RSC may provide for judgment to be binding on persons who have notice of the action, who are affected by the judgment but would not otherwise be bound by it.[119] On an application relating to an estate made by a personal representative or beneficiary the High Court may substitute a personal representative .[120]

Inheritance (Provision for Family and Dependants)(NI) Order 1979

18.69 This important statute (the 'Family Provision Order') empowers a dependant of a deceased to apply for reasonable provision out of his estate where by his will or intestacy he has failed to do so. It is brought by originating summons, with no appearance needed (Ord.99). On issue the plaintiff should lodge with the affidavit a copy of the grant of probate and will, or grant of letters of administration, and a certificate of his solicitor that he thinks the case to be beyond the county court jurisdiction.[121] The first appointment is for hearing by the judge. If contested a hearing by the judge is arranged and it is usually directed to be resolved by full trial with attendance of witnesses.

Trustee Act (NI) 1958 and Charities Act (NI) 1964

18.69a See Appendix One, para.1.12a/c.

---

[119] Wills and Administration Proceedings (NI) Order 1994, Art.32 - *not yet in force.*

[120] *Ibid.* Art.35 - *not yet in force.*

[121] Practice Direction [1990] 3 BNIL 98.

MARRIED WOMEN'S PROPERTY ACT 1882

18.70 Section 17 of this Act[122] provides a procedure for determining the property rights between husband and wife (even of void, annulled or dissolved marriages) or engaged couples, over money and property in Northern Ireland which is or has been in their possession. Either of them, or the bank etc. in whose books the property is standing, may apply. The Court can only declare existing legal and equitable rights and order a division or sale and division of proceeds.[123] It can restrain one spouse from interfering with property but it cannot restrain a spouse from entering premises.[124] The Court cannot declare the rights of a third party unless the latter is a party or is served with the summons.[125] Proceedings are assigned to the Chancery Division (Ord.93 r.1), and cannot be remitted to/removed from the county court. They are reserved for hearing by the judge. Section 17 proceedings are less important than they used to be because of the powers of the Family Division on divorce or judicial separation to order adjustment of property rights between the spouses.

MORTGAGES AND CHARGES

18.71 Order 88 deals with 'mortgage actions', that is, actions by mortgagee/chargee or mortgagor/chargor or by any person having a right to redeem or foreclose, claiming the payment of money, sale, foreclosure, possession, or redemption, re-conveyance in relation to legal or equitable mortgages and charges (Ord.88 r.1). This highly important part of the Chancery master's business is dealt with in the standard English textbooks, in Wylie's *Irish Land* Law (2nd ed. 1986) Chapters 12-13; Wallace 'Mortgagees and Possession' (1986) 37 NILQ 336; and the *Second Annual Review of Property Law* (ed. Harkness) (SLS 1995) p.35. The writ or originating summons (which bears a court fee of £130) must state the location of the property and, if possession is sought, whether it includes a dwelling-house and whether it is subject to the Rent Order (Ord.88 r.3). In any mortgage action by writ, the plaintiff must apply by summons for leave to enter judgment in default of appearance or of Defence, and the summons must be served on the defendant, and rules 4 and 5 then apply (Ord.88 r.6).

In a mortgagee's action by originating summons for possession and/or payment of the secured money, if the defendant does not enter an appearance, the plaintiff must serve copies of the notice of appointment for hearing and of any adjournment and his affidavits on the defendant (Ord.88 r.4); the affidavit, which may contain hearsay unless otherwise directed, must exhibit the original or copy mortgage or certificate of charge, depose to the right of possession and the state of accounts and other matters in strict compliance with Order 88 rule 5 and the original mortgage or certificate of charge must be produced at the hearing. The affidavit in an action seeking possession to enforce an order

---

122 As extended by the Law Reform (Husband and Wife) Act (NI) 1964, s.3, the Matrimonial Causes (NI) Order 1978, Art.55 and the Family Law (Misc Provs) (NI) Order 1984, Art.16.

123 *McFarlane* v *McFarlane* [1972] NI 59.

124 *Gaynor* v *Gaynor* [1901] 1 IR 217.

125 *Allied Irish Bank* v *McWilliams* [1982] NI 156, at 162.

charging land by sale must comply with Order 88 rule 5A. See also the Practice Direction [1994] 10 BNIL 83. At the hearing of an application under rule 5 or 5A, the plaintiff's legal representative should inform the Court of all payments since the affidavit was sworn, the current monthly payments and the arrears, the total debt secured, and any relevant communication from the defendant. In a dwelling-house case the parties should have available to the Court the residue of the mortgage term, a valuation of the security, the current payments and recent payment history, and the excess periodic payments that would be required to pay off the arrears over the entire residue. It may be necessary to have a detailed budget of the mortgagor's income and outgoings, and a valuation of the security.

Mortgagee's action

18.72 In the vast majority of cases the mortgagee is a financial institution which is interested only in securing its financial investment and has no desire to take over the property in itself. In general, the mortgagee need not join any other incumbrancer on the lands who is not in possession, but all incumbrancers should be served with notice of the decree.[126] However where the mortgagor's interest is held in an undivided share with another person, the remedies of sale or possession against the mortgagee only are virtually worthless,[127] and the mortgagee should claim for partition or sale in lieu, instead of or as well as a mortgagee's claim for sale, joining both co-owners as defendant.[128] The Property (NI) Order 1997 (Art.50, *not yet in force*) says that the creation of a charge on the estate of a joint tenant is deemed always to have effected a severance of the joint tenancy, so that the mortgage or charge continues against the chargee's estate on his death as the estate does not merge in the estate of the surviving joint tenant. The remedies chiefly sought are-

(1) *Sale.* A legal mortgagee, an equitable mortgagee and a chargee where the transaction was by deed has a right of sale without recourse to the Court once the debt is due.[129] Usually however application is made to the Court, traditionally in Ireland by way of an action for a declaration that the land is well charged with the debt and an order of sale unless the mortgagor pays the debt within three months. The Court has general power to order sale under section 91 of the Judicature Act (para.15.18), as well as Order 31 (para.18.55). In an action claiming sale, no other mortgagee need be a party

---

[126] Osborne p.106.

[127] Because the Court will decline to enforce the ejection of one whilst the other remains entitled to possession: *Albany Home Loans* v *Massey* [1997] 2 All ER 609 (a case where both husband and wife co-owners were co-mortgagors but the wife had a defence).

[128] *Hill* v *Maunsell-Eyre* [1944] IR 499, at 504-5. This situation often arises where the wife of the mortgagor has an equitable interest in the house by virtue of agreement or direct contribution to the purchase, and the Bank or Building Society mortgagee may have actual or constructive notice: the "eternal triangle". See also *Northern Bank* v *Adams*, Ch D, NI (Master Ellison) 1 February 1996. A chargee cannot yet claim under the Partition Acts: see para.18.78.

[129] Conveyancing Act 1881, s.19. This power is also available to a judgment chargee under the Judgments Enforcement (NI) Order 1981, Art.52(1).

unless he is in possession or in receipt of profits (Ord.88 r.7(2)). Conduct of the sale is usually given to the mortgagee as the person having carriage of the litigation. An order for sale may direct an enquiry as to all prior, contemporaneous and subsequent mortgages and charges, but the Court may exclude subsequent incumbrances from the enquiry in order to avoid delay (Ord.88 r.7(6)(7)). An order for sale is for the benefit of all incumbrancers, and anyone whose debt was not statute-barred when the action was commenced can claim.[130] Order 44 applies to a mortgage suit in which sale is ordered, so that a prior incumbrancer may be served,[131] thus preventing him from exercising his power of sale.[132] After sale and satisfaction of the debt and costs of the plaintiff and all prior and contemporaneous mortgagees, the Court may order distribution of any surplus money in court to other mortgagees (Ord.88 r.7(4)), and a subsequent mortgagee may apply for an order for sale of an unsold part of the property (Ord.88 r.7(5)).

(2) *Appointment of a receiver.* Where the charged property is farm or business property or rented out to tenants, the mortgagee or chargee may seek appointment of a receiver to preserve its profit yield. The right to appoint a receiver is available in the same way as the right of sale, under the Conveyancing Act 1881 (s.19)

(3) *Foreclosure*, under which the whole equity of redemption is extinguished, is a remedy used in Ireland only in exceptional circumstances.[133]

(4) *Possession.* As noted above, the mortgagee very rarely has any desires over the property as such and would only want possession either because it yields rent or profits or because vacant possession is necessary in order to get a good sale price. A legal mortgagee has a right to possession against the mortgagor,[134] but in the case of a chargee of registered land and of an equitable mortgagee it seems that possession is at the discretion of the Court to be granted only if sought *bona fide* to enforce the debt.[135] Possession for purposes of sale is granted in a proper case[136] under the Court's inherent jurisdiction.[137] An order for possession of land can be enforced against any person found in possession whether he is the defendant or not.[138]

---

130 *Harpur* v *Buchanan* [1919] 1 IR 1.

131 *Armstrong* v *Dickson* [1911] 1 IR 435.

132 *Duff* v *Devlin* [1924] 1 IR 56 (NI).

133 *Bruce* v *Brophy* [1906] 1 IR 611.

134 But not necessarily against a tenant of the mortgagee: *Quennell* v *Maltby* [1979] 1 All ER 568.

135 Wylie's *Irish Land Law* (2nd ed. 1986) paras.13.042 to 13.044.

136 *Bunyan* v *Bunyan* [1916] 1 IR 70.

137 *In re O'Neill* [1967] NI 129, where it was done by the High Court in Bankruptcy.

138 *R* v *Wandsworth CC ex p Wandsworth LBC* [1975] 1 WLR 1314.

(5) *Common law remedies.* The mortgagee also has his common law right to sue for the debt. If the creditor, such as a bank suing on an overdraft, chooses to sue for the debt without seeking to invoke the mortgage or charge, he can do so by ordinary writ and Order 88 does not apply.[139] He can sue for recovery of the land on the title, even if the legal estate is outstanding in a prior incumbrancer,[140] and should do so in the Chancery Division (Ord.88 r.2) and Order 88 applies.

18.73 *Postponing possession.* Where the property comprises or includes a dwelling-house, the Court may adjourn, stay or suspend enforcement, or postpone the date for possession, if it appears that the mortgagor will be able to pay the sums due within a reasonable period under the powers given by the Administration of Justice Acts 1970 (s.36), and 1973 (s.8). Under the general law, the mortgagee can waive his right to immediate possession and the Court may accept without inquiry any stay or adjournment agreed by him. However, where the parties have made an agreement which constitutes in substance an exercise of the power under the Acts, in *National and Provincial* v *Slane*,[141] Master Ellison held that it is a matter of jurisdiction and thus cannot be done merely on consent of the parties. By the same token, the Court's jurisdiction under the Acts cannot be ousted by agreement between the parties.[142] There must be material of weight to show the likelihood that the defendant will be able to pay within the period which the Court adjudges to be reasonable.[143] There is conflicting authority as to whether the Court can take into account the fact that the mortgagee has a counterclaim against the mortgagee (e.g. for negligent valuation).[144] Where the mortgagor proposes to pay by instalments, a reasonable period may be as long as the remaining term of the mortgage.[145] Where he proposes to pay by selling the property, the stay can be granted only if the the sale proceeds together with money from other sources will suffice to discharge the mortgage debt[146] and a reasonable period may be a matter of a few months or years.[147] Further Girvan J has held that *Norgan*[145] should be followed, if at all, only when the mortgagee's security is not at risk; and that where the outstanding debt is close to or greater than the value of the premises there is no presumption in favour of the remaining term: the proper approach is to assess how much the mortgagor can pay and decide whether that would clear the arrears in a reasonable time.[148] Where a court order has been made for

---

139 *National Westminster* v *Kitch* [1996] 1 WLR 1316 (CA).

140 *Antrim Land* v *Stewart* [1904] 2 IR 357.

141 Ch D, NI, 28 July 1995. In that case he also held that a judgment for possession can be stayed pending the resolution of an unrelated claim for damages by the mortgagor if there is evidence of a likelihood that it will secure damages sufficient to clear the sums due.

142 *Northern Bank* v *Jeffers*, Ch D, NI (Girvan J) 5 December 1996; [1996] 10 BNIL 67.

143 *National and Provincial* v *Williamson* [1996] 9 BNIL 79 (Girvan J) (decision given 17 November 1995, not 1996).

144 See Wallace *Second Annual Review of Property Law* (SLS 1995) p.44.

145 *Cheltenham & Gloucester* v *Norgan* [1996] 1 All ER 449 (CA).

146 *Cheltenham & Gloucester* v *Krausz* [1997] 1 All ER 104 (CA).

147 *Bristol & West* v *Ellis*, 'The Times', 2 May 1996 (CA).

148 *National & Provincial* v *Lynd* [1996] 9 BNIL 69.

possession, even one by contractual compromise, application can be made at a later time under the Acts by reason of a subsequent change of circumstances.[142]

Paradoxically, where the property does not comprise a dwelling-house, there is a wider discretion in the EJ Office under Article 13(1)(f) of the Judgments Enforcement (NI) Order 1981 to refuse to enforce possession if it is not fair and reasonable.[149] In an action by a legal mortgagee in relation to property which does not comprise a dwelling-house, the Court may adjourn for a short period for procedural reasons (e.g. party absent through illness) or if there is a reasonable prospect of the mortgagor paying the debt in full or otherwise satisfying the mortgagee.[150] There is inherent jurisdiction to stay enforcement of an order for possession for a short time to enable either the mortgagor or mortgagee to sell the property.[151]

18.74 A mortgage may be affected by the charge for occupation of a spouse, who may be entitled to be added as a party; if such charge is registered, notice of the mortgagee's action must be given to the spouse,[152] and the supporting affidavit must deal with this aspect (Ord.88 r.5(4)(b); r.5A(2)(f)).

Chargee's action

18.75 A chargee can sue under Order 88. Note that there can only be a charge not a mortgage on registered land. A chargee of registered land applies for possession under the Land Registration Act (NI) 1970 (Sch.7 Pt.I para.5), and there is a discretion to refuse possession to him.[153] A chargee of a charge to enforce a monetary judgment is in the same position. A vendor can invoke Order 88 to enforce his lien for unpaid purchase money.[154] A chargee and a judgment chargee of a co-owner of land will be able, from a date to be appointed, to seek partition or sale in lieu thereof (see para.18.78). A chargee has the same right of sale as a mortgagee (para.18.72).

Mortgagor's action

18.76 A mortgagor has a legal right to redeem the property free of the mortgage on or before the legal date for redemption (usually six months after its creation), and an equitable right to redeem thereafter on payment of the outstanding money due and on six months' notice or paying interest in lieu. A subsequent mortgagee can redeem a prior mortgage,[155] making all subsequent mortgagees parties.[156] An action for redemption may join an alternative claim

---

149 In dwelling-house cases, Art.13(1)(f) cannot prevail over the Act because it is expressed to be "subject to any statutory provision": *Allied Irish Bank* v *McAllister* [1993] 5 NIJB 82.

150 *Birmingham Citizens* v *Caunt* [1962] Ch 883.

151 *Cheltenham & Gloucester* v *Booker*, 'The Times', 20 November 1996 (CA); *contra*: *Cheltenham & Gloucester* v *Krausz* [1997] 1 All ER 104 (CA).

152 Family Law (Misc Provs) (NI) Order 1984, Art.12.

153 *Northern Banking* v *Devlin* [1924] 1 IR 90 (NI); *Hughes* v *Hughes* [1997] 1 BNIL 47 (Girvan J); Wallace (1986) 37 NILQ 336, at 356.

154 *Anderson* v *Londonderry & Enniskillen Rly* (1855) 4 Ir Ch R 254.

155 Clandestine Mortgages Act (Ir) 1697.

156 Osborne p.130.

for a declaration that the mortgage is void.[157] The right of redemption may be lost if the mortgagor has not disclosed a prior incumbrance.[155] There is no power in Northern Ireland equivalent to the power in England to grant a mortgagor's application for sale in lieu of redemption.

PARTITION

18.77 The Partition Acts 1868 and 1876 provide for the physical partition or sale and division of proceeds of the sale of land which is owned by joint tenants or tenants in common. Business is transacted in the Chancery Office, except a suit by a trustee in bankruptcy under Article 309 of Insolvency (NI) Order 1989, which is in the Bankruptcy and Companies Office. Suit may be brought against one interested party without making the others defendant (1868 Act, s.9). A mortgagee of a co-owner should be a party or served with notice of judgment, but a mortgagee of the entire interest is not affected by partition and need not be served (Daniell p.198; Osborne p.196). The plaintiff may claim sale alone (1876 Act, s.7). Primary judgment should be served on all interested persons, unless the Court directs advertisements in lieu under section 3 of 1876 Act. The Court may order sale in lieu of partition on grounds that it is more beneficial (1868 Act, s.3) and should do so if persons owning at least half of the interest[158] asks for it (1868 Act, s.4). Where sections 3 and 4 do not apply, it may order sale if any interested party so applies, unless another party undertakes to purchase the former's share as valued by order of the Court (1868 Act, s.5). The affidavit in support should include the following matters: (a) which section of the Acts the plaintiff wishes to invoke; (b) where applicable, an averment as to why sale is more beneficial than physical partition;[159] (c) the standing and interest in the property which gives the plaintiff a right to apply under the Acts; (d) where section 4 is invoked, that the Court has power to order sale thereunder, and in particular that person or persons with at least one-half of the interest request sale. In *Gingles* v *Magill*[160] the judgment directed service on persons interested and sale in lieu of partition if those owning at least one-half of the interest desired it. If the plaintiff proves a right to judgment under the Acts, the Court must order either partition or sale;[161] but from a date to be appointed, it can, on making the order or pending enforcement, stay or suspend the order or impose conditions as it

157 *Hunt* v *Worsfold* [1896] 2 Ch 224.

158 I.e. at least one-half of the realisable monetary value of the land: *Northern Bank* v *Adams*, Ch D, NI (Master Ellison) 1 February 1996.

159 *Evans* v *Evans* (1883) LJ Ch 304; *Northern Bank* v *Adams*.

160 [1926] NI 234.

161 *Per* Murray J, *Northern Bank* v *Beattie* [1982] 18 NIJB at 20-5; approved in *Glass* v *McManus*, High Ct, NI (Girvan J) 7 June 1996; and see *Fleming* v *Hargreaves* [1976] 1 NZLR 123. But in *Northern Bank* v *Adams*, Ch D, NI (Master Ellison) 1 February 1996, the Master took the view that under the 1868 Act s.3 the Court, though ruling that sale is more beneficial than partition, has a discretion to stay or even refuse sale on equitable grounds. If, as is said in Irish cases, such as *FF* v *CF* [1987] ILRM 1 (Barr J), partition is an equitable remedy, then surely Master Ellison is correct is saying that both partition and sale in lieu are discretionary remedies.

thinks fit.[162] If partition is ordered, proceedings before the master are directed involving valuation and survey evidence and mutual conveyances between the co-owners (Daniell pp.1173-4). If vacant possession is necessary to effect the sale, the Court can so order.[163] If one co-owner has wrongly ousted the other from the lands, the Court can order an inquiry as to *mesne* profits and direct them to be deducted from the ousting party's share of the proceeds of sale.[164] In ordering partition or sale, the Court may declare any co-owner to be a trustee,[165] thus enabling the vesting of his interest (para.16.59). Costs properly incurred in the realisation and division of the property are usually borne out of the sale proceeds.[166]

18.78 A legal or equitable mortgagee of the interest of a co-owner should bring a partition suit, but a chargee under a charge by the EJ Office to enforce a monetary judgment cannot claim under the Partition Acts.[167] Wallace[168] argues on the principle of *Northern Bank* v *Haggerty,*[167] that a chargee of registered land cannot bring a partition suit, because the Land Registration Act (NI) 1970 (Sch.7 Pt.I para.1(2)) says that a charge to secure a debt does not operate to vest any freehold or leasehold estate in the chargee. Even if the chargee has separate charges against all of the co-owners, he does not have an estate in the land entitling him to partition and possession of the lands.[169] However under the Property (NI) Order 1997, Art.48 (*not yet in force*), the owner of a charge (including a judgment chargee) on land held in co-ownership will be able to request partition or sale in lieu under the Partition Acts. The creation of a charge on the estate of a joint tenant causes a severance of the joint tenancy (see para.18.72).

PARTNERSHIPS

18.79 A partnership is an unincorporated business firm with two or more members (see para. 3.15).

Grounds for dissolution, see Partnerships Act 1890, section 35. Costs, White Book (1997) 62/B/93. As to the application of the insolvency legislation to partnerships, see the Insolvent Partnerships Order (NI) 1995/255.

PERSONAL INSOLVENCY

18.80 The law of bankruptcy of human individuals has been completely revised by the Insolvency (NI) Order 1989 and Rules 1991, modelled on the equivalent English legislation. See Hunter *Northern Ireland Personal Insolvency* (SLS 1992 with Supplement 1995) and the leading English texts:

---

162 Property (NI) Order 1997, Art.49 (*not yet in force*).

163 *Northern Bank* v *Beattie*, at 25. This is under the Court's inherent jurisdiction: *In re O'Neill* [1967] NI 129.

164 *Glass* v *McManus*, High Ct, NI (Girvan J) 7 June 1996, at pp.13-14 [1996] 5 BNIL 75.

165 Trustee Act (NI) 1958, s.48.

166 *In re Mahony* [1909] 1 IR 133.

167 *Northern Bank* v *Haggerty* [1995] 5 BNIL 64 (Campbell J), not following the *obiter* remarks of Murray J in *Tubman* v *Johnston* [1981] NI 53.

168 In *The Second Annual Review of Property Law* (SLS 1995) p.38

169 *Rainey* v *Weatherup* [1997] 2 BNIL 50 (Master Ellison).

Muir Hunter *Personal Insolvency* (Sweet & Maxwell); Sealy and Milman *Annotated Guide to the Insolvency Legislation* (CCH, 4th ed. 1994). Costs, Anderson p.24. See Appendix One, para. 1.9b.

COMPANIES

18.81 See Appendix One, para.1.9a/b. The legislation is substantially the same as in England. Procedure Order 102; costs of creditor's claim, see Ord.62 r.6(3). See Palmer's *Company* Law (Sweet & Maxwell 25th ed. 1992) Company insolvency, see Boyd (1992) 43 NILQ 357. Taxation of winding-up costs, see *In re Selective Trimming* [1992] 3 BNIL 113. Disqualification of director, see Mithani and Wheeler *The Disqualification of Company Directors* (Butterworths 1996); *In re Topglass* [1996] 2 BNIL 8 (Pringle J). In a debenture holder's action, the receiver appointed by the Court keeps a register of debenture transactions (Ord.87). Costs, White Book (1997) 62/B/65-66. If proceedings concern the constitution, nullity or dissolution of a company or other association of persons, or the decisions of their organs, where its seat is in a part of the United Kingdom or a Brussels Convention State, the courts thereof have exclusive jurisdiction (Civil Jurisdiction and Judgments Act 1982, Sch.1 Art.16, Sch.4 Art.16).

CHAPTER NINETEEN

CROWN SIDE

19.00 Crown side proceedings, which are assigned to the Queen's Bench Division, include judicial review, *habeas corpus*, applications to punish for contempt (para. 16.76), and bail. The expression 'Crown side' arose from the fact that historically, such proceedings were brought in the name of the King or Queen, based upon the theory that Government and public authority could do no wrong and the Crown itself should correct any errors. It has no real practical significance today, save that the remedies are not available against the Crown, but the remedies are available against Government ministers and officials exercising statutory or prerogative powers: see para. 19.12. All writs are issued out of and filed in the Crown Office, which is part of the Judgments Office of the Central Office (Ord.57 r.4). The records are held by the Master (Queen's Bench and Appeals) (Ord.57 r.1). Proceedings are intitled "Queen's Bench Division, Crown Side" (Ord.57 r.2)). A motion is issued out of the Crown Office; a party entering a motion must lodge copy documents in the Crown Office for the use of the Court at least seven days before the hearing (Ord.57 r.5). An application to estreat a recognisance is by summons before a judge in chambers (Ord.57 r.3). In the Crown Proceedings Act (s.38) and Order 77, "civil proceedings by or against the Crown" includes any civil proceeding (including for recovery of a fine or penalty) in which the Attorney-General or a Government Department or Crown official is a party. The definition expressly excludes applications for judicial review, but does not (unlike the English version of the Act) exclude other Crown side proceedings.

BAIL

19.01 The jurisdiction of the High Court to grant bail to a person detained under a civil or criminal power, other than under sentence of a competent criminal court, is inherent not statutory.[1] In the case of a person charged with a scheduled offence, the power is restricted by the Northern Ireland (Emergency Provisions) Act 1996 (s.3). The High Court also has statutory jurisdiction to grant bail to a person under sentence.[2] The Court of Appeal can grant bail pending appeal from the Crown Court.[3] See the author's *Criminal Procedure in NI* (SLS 1988), Chapter 5. Procedure is set out in Order 79.

---

[1] White Book (1997) Vol. 2 [5142].

[2] Magistrates' Courts (NI) Order 1981, Art.148 (pending appeal to county court or to Court of Appeal); Judicature Act, s.25(4) (pending judicial review); Criminal Appeal Act 1995, s.12(7) (pending referral by Criminal Cases Review Commission from magistrates' court to county court).

[3] Criminal Appeal (NI) Act 1980, s.17.

JUDICIAL REVIEW

19.02 Judicial review concerns the challenge to the conduct of bodies which exercise powers and duties under an official and public function. The present system, which was introduced in 1978, brings together the old prerogative remedies of *certiorari*, *mandamus* and prohibition, and incorporates some relief (damages, final injunction or declaration) which previously could be had only in an action; but it does not extend the substantive remedies available.[4] "Judicial review is the appropriate remedy where a person seeks to establish that the decision of a person or authority infringes rights protected by public law."[5] *Semble*, there is a right protected by public law where a statute or rule of law imposes a duty justiciable in the courts and there is no cause of action or civil or criminal procedure available to enforce it.

19.03 Sections 18 to 25 of the Judicature Act and Order 53 are regarded as a new code for judicial review. See generally Graham 'Judicial Review: the New Procedure' (1980) 31 NILQ 317; Hadfield 'Judicial Review in Northern Ireland: a Primer' (1991) 42 NILQ 332; *Judicial Review: a Thematic Approach* (ed. Hadfield) (Gill and Macmillan, Dublin 1995); Hadfield 'Introduction to JR in Northern Ireland' [1996] JR 170. For statistical data up to 1992, see Hadfield and Weaver 'Judicial Review in Perspective' (1995) 46 NILQ 113.

THE SCOPE OF JUDICIAL REVIEW

Its target area

19.04 Judicial review is available to challenge: (a) the exercise or non-exercise of a power which is derived from primary or delegated legislation or from Royal prerogative; (b) decisions under non-contractual public law power of a body which is an emanation of the State or has power devolved from governmental power; (c) a decision which is in its nature a public decision in which the Government has a potential interest; and (d) decisions under judicial, administrative or executive powers, including any inferior court or tribunal. It generally excludes decisions made by a person or body which derives its binding effect from contract or from the consent of its members.[6] It seems now that it is the nature of the power being exercised, not only the source, which determines whether it is reviewable;[7] and it is the public nature of the decision, rather than the public nature of the rights and liabilities of the applicant, which is important. Indeed, in most cases, it is the private interests of the applicant

---

4 *R* v *Belfast Recorder ex p McNally* [1992] NI 217, at 230j-231a.

5 *Per* Hutton LCJ, *R* v *Chief Constable ex p McKenna* [1992] NI 116, at 123a.

6 In Scotland, judicial review is not confined to public law decisions, and the Court of Session can review decisions of any body which derives its authority from any statute, agreement or instrument: see *West* v *Sec of State for Scotland* 1992 SC 385; *Brown* v *Executive Committee of Edinburgh District Labour Party* 1995 SLT 985.

7 *R* v *Panel on Take-overs ex p Datafin* [1987] QB 815 (CA); *In re Phillips*, QBD, NI (Carswell LJ) 18 January 1995.

which give him *locus standi* to apply. Carswell LJ[8] suggested that the primary test is whether the issue on which the challenge is founded is one which involves public law. He took as his starting point the words of Woolf LJ[9] that an employee of the Crown or a public body cannot challenge his employer's treatment of him by judicial review unless it involves a ruling by a disciplinary body established under statute or prerogative powers or is a treatment applied to employees generally, or[10] it involves public policy or the interpretation of legal powers. Another test was proposed by the Divisional Court,[11] that a decision is private law if made under an obligation which is imposed on a class of persons generally (e.g. employer's duty to consult regarding redundancies) but is public law if the obligation is imposed on the challenged body directly by special statutory provision.

Instances where review is *not* available

19.05 Under the case law, judicial review has been held not to be available, and the decision classified as not in the public law domain, in the following situations-

In re Lyle [1987] 7 NIJB 24	Unionist Party not a public body
Murphy v *Turf Club* [1989] IR 171 *R* v *Disciplinary Committee of the Jockey Club, ex p Aga Khan* [1993] 2 All ER 853	Jockey's rights against the Jockey Club are contractual, not public law[12]
In re Wislang [1984] NI 63, at 85 *In re Malone* [1986] 9 NIJB 74 *In re Deman*, QBD, NI, (Carswell LJ) 19 Jan.1996[13]	University exercising contractual not public power in employment
In re Phillips, CA, NI, 12 Feb.1996	Dismissal of civil servant employed under royal prerogative
O'Neill v *Iarnrod Eireann* [1991] ILRM 129	Employment by privatised transport enterprise, though leave was granted for the point to be argued
Blair v *Lochaber DC*, 1995 SLT 407	Suspension of chief executive by local council
Rajah v *Royal College of Surgeons* [1994] 1 IR 384	College under royal charter is private in its rules for student progress committee

8 *In re Phillips*, QBD, NI, 18 January 1995. On appeal (*ibid*, CA, NI, 12 February 1996) Pringle J giving the judgment of the Court was "in complete agreement with what he has said", but found that the contractual relationship between the applicant and the challenged body was enough to bar judicial review.

9 In *McClaren* v *Home Office* [1990] ICR 824.

10 *R* v *Lord Chancellor's Dept, ex p Nangle* [1992] 1 All ER 897, at 908C.

11 In *R* v *British Coal Corp, ex p Vardy* [1993] ICR 720.

12 But in *Quirke* v *Bord Luthchleas na h'Eireann* [1988] IR 83, Barr J gave review against the Irish athletics body.

13 Affirmed on appeal on other grounds without deciding whether the decision was subject to review: *Deman* v *QUB* [1997] 1 BNIL 34; 'The Times', 16 December 1996 (CA). Review lies against University visitors, but not for error of law within jurisdiction: *R* v *Hull University Visitors, ex p Page* [1993] AC 682; *In re Perry* [1996] 5 BNIL 37 (Carswell LJ).

Buckley v *Daly* [1990] 8 NIJB 28	Rules of Roman Catholic Church
State (Colquhoun) v *D'Arcy* [1936] IR 641	Court of General Synod of Church of Ireland is contractual not public[14]
R(Butler) v *Navan UDC* [1926] IR 466	Local authority as neighbour causing nuisance, private law
R v *NCB, ex p NUM* [1986] ICR 791; doubted in *R* v *British Coal, ex p Vardy* [1993] ICR 720	Decision to close a pit is a business, executive or management decision
R(Kelly) v *Maguire* [1923] 2 IR 58	No review against a self-styled court or public body which has no legal source of authority - the Dail Eireann system set up in opposition to, and not recognised by, the UK Government.

Instances where judicial review is available

19.06 In the following cases, judicial review was entertained-

R v *Employment Sec, ex p EOC* [1995] 1 AC 1	UK statute challenged as incompatible with EC law
In re Police Association [1990] NI 258	Subordinate legislation made under statute
Mercury Ltd v *Electricity Corp* [1994] 1 WLR 521 (PC, NZ)	State enterprise whose shares are owned by the Government
In re Dallas [1997] 3 BNIL 76	District Council decision to regulate non-statutory functions of mayor
R v *Legal Aid Board, ex p Donn & Co* [1996] 3 All ER 1	Board's selection of solicitor in awarding contract to conduct multi-party action
R v *Panel on Take-overs ex p Datafin* [1987] QB 815 (CA)	Non-statutory non-governmental body exercising functions which are public in nature and have legal consequences
R v *BBC ex p Referendum Party* 'The Times' 29 April 1997	Allocation by BBC and ITV of election broadcast time may be reviewable
In re Morris, QBD, NI (Kerr J) 29 Nov 1996	Privatised electricity supply licensee exercising power to discontinue its statutory duty to supply to consumer.[15]
In re Meekatharra Ltd [1995] 6 BNIL 105	Planning Appeals Commission inquiry

---

[14] Private law rights may involve concepts similar to those of public law, like natural justice, as implied terms of a contract. A member of a private club may seek damages by writ action for breach of contract where he has been disciplined without a fair hearing: see *Singapore Amateur Athletics Assoc.*v *Haron bin Mundir* [1994] 3 LRC 563 (Singapore CA). If a contract of employment provides procedure for dismissal for misconduct it is implied that the procedure will be fair: *Glover* v *BLN Ltd* [1973] IR 388. But there is no implied term that an insurer will give reasons for cancelling an insurance policy: *Carna Foods* v *Eagle Star* [1995] 1 IR 526. A disciplinary rule of the International Tennis Federation may be void for restraint of trade if it is unfair or unreasonable: *Wilander* v *Tobin*, 'The Times', 8 April 1996.

[15] And see Lidbetter 'Privatised Utilities and Judicial Review' [1996] JR 249.

Minister of Education v *Letterkenny Technical College* [1995] 1 ILRM 438	Appointments of staff to statutory body under statutory procedures
Eogan v *University College Dublin* [1996] 1 IR 390	Dismissal of professor who was appointed pursuant to statutory power
Wells v *NI Office* [1993] 5 NIJB 61	Sacking of prison officer under statutory-based procedures
Beirne v *Commissioner of Garda Siochána* [1993] ILRM 1	Dismissal of gard, reviewable unless wholly private power derived from contract
R (McPherson) v *Min of Education* (1973)[1980] NI 115	Review of dismissal of statutory appeal to Ministry of sacking of State School teacher
In re Gribbon [1990] 6 NIJB 15	Board of Governors of Grammar School, selection of pupils
Murtagh v *St Emer's* [1991] 1 IR 482	Board of national school, suspension of pupil
R (Doris) v *Min of Health* [1954] NI 79	Review of sacking of dentist under regulations
In re Locke [1988] 4 NIJB 18	Review of decision of Secretary of State on appeal from police disciplinary hearing
In re Maher [1986] 16 NIJB 1 *In re Haughey* [1986] 16 NIJB 17	Law Society and its education committee, admission of apprentices
In re Carroll [1988] NI 152	Alteration under statutory power of employee's terms: discretion to hear complaint by judicial review where power involves both public and contractual power
Gestion Complexe v *Canada* (1995) 125 DLR 4th 559 *Webster* v *Auckland Harbour* [1987] 2 NZLR 129 *Tata Cellular* v *Union of India* [1996] 1 LRC 342	Power under statute to enter contracts; decision whether to do so is reviewable

What conduct is reviewable

19.07 It is sometimes said[16] that judicial review relates only to the challenge of a decision or refusal to decide, but cases show that it lies against any conscious act, omission or course of conduct. Review has also been given against findings of a coroner or 'ombudsman', bye-laws, subordinate legislation under an Act of Parliament,[17] schemes set up under the prerogative, public or official recommendations, policy pronouncements, reports, guidelines and advices, where they have or lead to some legal consequence.[18] Thus a recommendation to a minister is reviewable, where by statute it is a necessary

---

[16] E.g. by Lord Diplock in *CCSU* v *Min for Civil Service* [1985] AC 374.

[17] See further paras. 19.12-19.13.

[18] See Supperstone & Goudie p.304; *Gillick* v *West Norfolk Health Authority* [1986] AC 112; *R* v *Environment Sec ex p Tower Hamlets LBC* [1993] QB 632; *Ainsworth* v *Criminal Justice Commission* (1992) 175 CLR 564.

factor in the process by which the minister reaches a decision.[19] *Mandamus* lies only against a refusal to act when called upon to do so, unless failure to act was inadvertent and the time limit set to perform the duty has expired.[20] Certain remedies, such as prohibition and declaration, can be given where no decision has yet been made. A statement by a Department or minister that he regards a statute as valid under EC law is not a decision and not reviewable, though the statute itself can be so challenged.[21] Where a body gives an opinion on the law relevant to its area of decision, the opinion is subject to judicial review if it is outside the statutory powers, and declaration, rather than *certiorari*, is the appropriate remedy.[22] A statement of law by a court which is not necessary to its decision which it has made in the case before it is not a decision and cannot be reviewed.[23]

Choosing judicial review or private action: the hard choice

19.08 An action for a declaration or other remedy will be struck out if it concerns public rights and should have been brought by judicial review,[24] but only if proceedings otherwise than by judicial review are an abuse of process.[25] This principle is prompted by three main reasons for objection to allowing procedure by action: (a) an action is not subject to any prior leave to initiate the proceedings; (b) the pleadings system in actions does not put on the parties a duty of candour and good faith; (c) it is undesirable that public law issues, reviewing the decisions of administrative bodies and inferior courts, should be entertained in an inferior court such as the county court.[26] Possibly the action may be allowed to continue if the public law issues are collateral or if the parties do not object.[27] If the aggrieved person is in doubt as to whether he should proceed by judicial review, the prudent course is to do so and also issue a precautionary writ. An action (or defence in an action) to enforce a private right will not be struck out merely on the ground that it involves a challenge to the jurisdictional validity of a public law decision or subordinate legislation.[28] Where a public body repudiates a contract for public law policy reasons, the contractor may choose to quash the repudiation by judicial review rather than sue in private law.[29] The decisions of a state body about entering or terminating

---

19 *Hot Holdings* v *Creasy* (1996) 70 ALJR 286 (HC of Aus). But see *Southern HSSB* v *Lemon*, para. 19.31.

20 *R* v *Henley Revising Barrister* [1912] 3 KB 518.

21 *R* v *Employment Sec ex p EOC* [1995] 1 AC 1.

22 *Petaling Tin* v *Lee Kian Chan* [1994] 4 LRC 180 (Malaysia SC); *B and B* v *An Bord Uchtála* [1997] 1 ILRM 15 (SC).

23 *R* v *West London Licensing JJ ex p Davis*, 'The Times' 16 March 1994 (DC).

24 *O'Reilly* v *Mackman* [1983] 2 AC 237; probably overruling *Geo Whaley* v *DOE* [1983] 3 NIJB, where the good faith and natural justice of a compulsory purchase order was challenged by originating summons action.

25 *Mercury Communications* v *DG of Tele-communications* [1996] 1 WLR 48 (HL).

26 *Cf. Brown* v *Hamilton DC*, 1983 SC (HL) 1; *Gupta* v *Gupta's Trustee*, 1994 SC 74.

27 *O'Reilly* v *Mackman* at 285. Ord.53 r.9 gives the Court power to order the judicial review proceedings to continue as if begun by writ (see para.19.79) but not *vice versa*.

28 *Roy* v *Kensington FPC* [1992] 1 AC 624.

29 *Browne* v *Dundalk UDC* [1993] 2 IR 512 (Barr J).

without breach a commercial contract are challengeable only by judicial review and probably only on grounds of fraud, corruption or bad faith.[30]

19.09 Invalidity of regulations, decisions and notices under statute can be litigated in proceedings to enforce them.[31] In *Mawhinney* v *NIHE*[32] an action for trespass by demolition of the plaintiff's home, the defendant pleaded statutory consent of the DOE as a defence: Hutton J held the consent to be invalid on *Wednesbury* and *Anisminic* grounds. However the Court of Session has held that a prisoner cannot sue by private action for damages for a search which is alleged to be unlawful by reason of the invalidity of the standing order of the Secretary of State under which it was authorised.[33] *Wednesbury* unreasonableness is the issue in a writ action for negligence in the policy area, as opposed to operational activity, by a public authority.[34] Validity of a statutory decision or notice can be raised in proceedings to enforce it,[35] unless the statute states that it is not open to challenge in a court.[36] On a prosecution for breach of a planning enforcement notice which is formally valid, it is not a defence that decision to issue the notice is *ultra vires*; the defendant's must seek judicial review.[37] A challenge to the procedural validity of a bye-law cannot be entertained unless it is quashed by judicial review.[38] In *Co. Meath Education Committee* v *Joyce*[39] itinerants sued for squatting on a road side near a school were allowed to claim on a third-party notice against the local authority for indemnity or contribution for its breach of duty to provide for the homeless; Flood J described the objection as a mere procedural point.

19.10 One can discern echoes of the familiar *dictum* about promissory estoppel, being a "shield not a sword". It could be argued as follows: if the only issue to be litigated is the reviewability of a public law act or decision, then judicial review is the only recourse of the aggrieved citizen; but if the review of the act or decision would enable the citizen to build a private cause of action or rebut a defence to it, or would be a defence to civil or criminal proceedings taken against him, then the reviewability of the public law act or decision can be raised in those proceedings.

Persons and decisions immune from review

19.11 No judicial review lies against the decision of any part of the Supreme Court (including in Northern Ireland, the Crown Court) and any court expressed to be a superior court, nor of any judge, master or officer exercising its jurisdiction,[40] but it does lie against the officer's exercise of a power

---

30 *Mercury Ltd* v *Electricity Corp* [1994] 1 WLR 521 (PC).

31 *Chief Adjudication Officer* v *Foster* [1993] AC 754, at 766; *R* v *Reading Crown Ct ex p Hutchinson* [1988] QB 384; *DPP* v *Hutchinson* [1990] 2 AC 783; *Forde* v *McEldowney* [1970] NI 11(HL); *Belfast Corp* v *Daly* [1963] NI 78 (bye-law challenged for irrationality).

32 [1982] NI 302.

33 *MacDonald* v *Sec of State for Scotland (No 2)*, 1996 SLT 575 (Extra Div).

34 See *Chambers* v *DOE* [1985] NI 181; *X* v *Bedfordshire CC* [1995] 2 AC 353.

35 *DOE* v *George* [1982] NI 357.

36 *DOE* v *Thompson* [1991] 11 NIJB 56.

37 *R* v *Wicks* [1997] 2 All ER 801 (HL).

38 *Boddington* v *British Transport Police*, 'The Times', 23 July 1996 (DC).

39 [1994] 2 ILRM 210.

40 *Contra: Elwyn Ltd* v *Master of High Court* [1989] IR 14.

designated independently of his Supreme Court duties.[41] It lies against any inferior court, such as a magistrates' court, county court, coroner's court, or industrial tribunal. The decision of the High Court affirming a decree by a lower court is not reviewable on the ground that the lower court had no jurisdiction.[42]

19.12 Lewis (pp.150,162,169) and Wade & Forsyth (p.637) say that no judicial review remedy can be given against the Crown itself, or against a servant performing a function of the Crown[43] (functions such as the dissolution of Parliament, declaration of war, which are almost certainly non-justiciable in any case); but that it does lie against bodies, officials and ministers exercising statutory or prerogative powers.[44] Even the decision of the cabinet is reviewable if made under a statutory power.[45] A UK statute (i.e. an Act of the Westminster Parliament), is accepted by all courts without question, save that it can be challenged where it is incompatible with EC law.[46] Review lies against any subordinate legislation, such as bye-laws, Statutory Rules and Orders and Statutory Instruments, even those subject to affirmative resolution of both Houses of Parliament, on virtually the same grounds as any administrative decision.[47] One point which does not appear yet to have arisen in any case law is whether the Orders in Council made for Northern Ireland as Statutory Instruments which rank as NI statutes, are as freely reviewable as any subordinate legislation: in theory they should be. The validity of an EC Directive cannot be challenged in any proceedings in the High Court on any ground.[48] A national court cannot declare an act of European institutions to be invalid, but may refer that as an issue to the European Court,[49] and the national court may suspend the act and grant interim relief pending the reference.[50]

19.13 Courts will not review certain types of decision regarded as non-justiciable, for example: certain prerogative powers of the Government or ministers;[51] the Royal prerogative of mercy;[52] decisions of national security; decisions of the Attorney-General or his deputy as to whether to bring court proceedings;[53] and operational decisions of the police. There is no enforceable duty on the Government to introduce legislation to ratify a treaty,[54] nor against the Dail to vote in a particular way.[55] The Court cannot force a minister to

---

41 *In re Weir* [1988] NI 338, at 353-5; *In re Rice* [1994] 4 BNIL 67.

42 *Blackall* v *Grehan* [1995] 3 IR 208 (appeal from Circuit Court).

43 Declarations can be given against the Crown in actions but not in judicial review, because the definition of "civil proceedings" in s.38(2) of the Crown Proceedings Act excludes judicial review.

44 See also *M* v *Home Office* [1994] 1 AC 377, at 415-7.

45 *C.O.Williams* v *Blackman* [1995] 1 WLR 102 (PC).

46 *R* v *Sec of State for Transport ex p Factortame* (No 2) [1991] 1 AC 603.

47 Wade & Forsyth, pp.874-897.

48 *Young* v *Pharmaceutical Society* [1994] 2 ILRM 262.

49 *Foto-Frost* v *Hauptzollamt Lübeck-Ost* [1987] ECR 4199.

50 *Atlanta* v *Bundesamt* [1996] All ER (EC) 31 (ECJ).

51 Supperstone & Goudie pp.41,126.

52 *Burt* v *Governor-General* [1992] 3 NZLR 672 (CA).

53 *R* v *Solicitor-General ex p Taylor*, 'The Times' 14 August 1995 (DC).

54 *Hutchinson* v *Min of Justice* [1993] ILRM 602.

55 *Dudley* v *An Taoiseach* [1994] 2 ILRM 321.

bring a statute into force but can require him to consider doing so, and cannot force a minister to draw up and enact a scheme under a statutory power, but can prohibit him from using prerogative powers to bring in a different scheme.[56]

19.14 The decisions of the police as to enforcement of the law or protection of the public can be reviewed, on grounds only of *Wednesbury* unreasonableness.[57] In the Republic of Ireland, a decision of the Director of Public Prosecutions as to whether to prosecute in a particular case is reviewable only for *mala fides* or improper motive or policy.[58] But Kerr J has reviewed the decision of the Independent Commission for Police Complaints to bring a disciplinary charge against a policeman on the issue of whether there was any evidence to support the charge.[59] In *In re Madden*[60] the refusal of the police and DPP to disclose information to an accused before his trial was reviewed. Decisions of the police under a statutory power are freely reviewable, such as banning marches,[61] or deferring access of an arrested suspect to a solicitor.[62] The decision of an Appeal Committee hearing applications for release by an internee under the old Special Powers Act was reviewed in *In re Mackey*.[63] An arrest is reviewable.[64] The issue of a warrant for arrest is reviewable,[65] but not for want of evidence.[66] An arrest can be reviewed for *Wednesbury* unreasonableness,[64] but not for breach of natural justice.[67]

19.15 The Court will not review purely administrative and ministerial decisions of a prison governor,[68] but his disciplinary decisions are, like the decision of a board of visitors, judicial and reviewable.[69] Even his administrative decisions are reviewable if they breach the duty of fairness.[70] In *In re Quinn*[71] and *In re O'Hare*[72] it was held that the governor's award in a disciplinary hearing was reviewable as an administrative decision.[73]

---

56 *R* v *Home Sec ex p Fire Brigades Union* [1995] 2 AC 513; *Aletesmesh Rein* v *Union of India* (1989) 15 Comm LB 1178 (SC, India). See also *New Zealand Maori Council* v *AG* [1996] 3 NZLR 140.

57 See *In re Gillen* [1990] 2 NIJB 47.

58 *H* v *DPP* [1994] 2 ILRM 285 (SC). As to review of the decision to issue a certificate that an offence must be tried in a special non-jury court, see *Kavanagh* v *Government of Ireland* [1996] 1 ILRM 133.

59 *In re Marshall* [1996] 10 BNIL 72.

60 [1991] NI 14.

61 *In re Murphy* [1991] 5 NIJB 88, at 103-4.

62 *R* v *Chief Constable ex p McKenna* [1992] NI 116.

63 [1971] Nov-Dec NIJB.

64 *Holgate-Mohammed* v *Duke* [1984] AC 437; *R* v *Chief Constable ex p McKenna* [1992] NI 116, at 124a.

65 *In re Burns* [1985] NI 279.

66 *State (Batchelor)* v *DJ Ó Floinn* [1958] IR 155.

67 *Grech* v *Min of Immigration* (1993) 19 Comm LB 39 (Aus Fed Ct).

68 *Re Russell* [1990] NI 188 ("the running of the prison").

69 *In re McKieran* [1985] NI 385, approved in *Leech* v *Gov. of Parkhurst* [1988] AC 533.

70 *In re Maguire* [1993] 9 NIJB 60, at 65.

71 [1988] 2 NIJB 10, at 20-21.

72 [1989] NI 77, at 98F-.

73 Restrictions on visits to prisoners were reviewed in *In re Mulvenna* [1985] 13 NIJB 76 and *In re McCartney* [1986] 13 NIJB 46, *affd.* [1987] 11 NIJB 94; and refusal of Christmas home leave in *In re McFarlane* [1991] 6 NIJB 42.

Ouster clause

19.16 Where a decision is stated by statute to be final and not subject to appeal or review by any court,[74] or where its purported orders are deemed to be made within jurisdiction, the Court can review it as a nullity if it is without or in excess of jurisdiction: so held in the landmark case *Anisminic* v *Foreign Compensation Commission*.[75] An error of law, whether on the face of the record or not, if made within jurisdiction, is rendered non-reviewable by the ouster clause.[76] However, according to *Anisminic* (at p.171), an error of law by an administrative body in interpreting its statutory provision, bad faith, breach of natural justice and mistake as to what is relevant, is an excess of jurisdiction. Thus the Court will ignore the ouster clause where it finds that the decision was reached in breach of the duty of fairness.[77] Note that there are instances where the common law has created a partial ouster clause.[78] A provision that a decision shall be "final and conclusive" does not oust the power to review for excess of jurisdiction or error on face of the record.[79]

19.17 A 'conclusive evidence provision' (i.e. statute stating that a statement, certificate or determination of an official is conclusively deemed true) makes the determination unreviewable by judicial review, however unreasonable, unless it is is legally invalid (*ultra vires* the statutory power) or shown by extraneous evidence to be *mala fide*.[80] The statute itself prevents the applicant from adducing evidence to show that the determination is wrong. Indeed the very purpose of the statute is to make the true facts irrelevant.

19.18 A statutory provision made before 1 August 1958 "to the effect that any order or determination shall not be called into question in any court or which by similar words excludes any of the powers of the High Court" cannot operate so as to prevent the High Court from granting *certiorari* or *mandamus*, save by setting a time limit (Judicature Act, s.22).[81] 'Conclusive evidence provisions' are not rendered inoperative by section 22 (Lewis p.323-4).

---

74 For an example of a recent 'ouster clause' see the Intelligence Services Act 1994, s.9, which says that "the decisions of [a complaints tribunal etc.] (including decisions as to their jurisdiction) shall not be subject to appeal or liable to be questioned in any court". See also, the Criminal Justice (Serious Fraud) (NI) Order 1988, Art.3(3) and the Children's Evidence (NI) Order 1995, Art.4(4), which say the same about the prosecutor's decision to transfer for trial without committal.

75 [1969] 2 AC 147; and *State (O'Duffy)* v *Bennett* [1935] IR 70.

76 So held in *SE Asia Fire* v *Non-metallic Union* [1981] AC 363 (industrial court award); *R v Belfast Recorder ex p McNally* [1992] NI 217, at 233d; *sed contra*, *R (SBC)* v *Belfast SB Appeal Trib* [1980] 6 NIJB at 12.

77 *R* v *Sec of State for Home Dept ex p Fayed* [1997] 1 All ER 228 (CA, Kennedy LJ dissenting).

78 E.g. in respect of inferior courts, and in respect of decisions of University Visitors: *R* v *Hull University Visitors, ex p Page* [1993] AC 682 (3-2 majority).

79 *R (Flanigan)* v *Armagh* JJ (1922) 56 ILTR 46 (NI); *Hockey* v *Yelland* (1984) 157 CLR 124 (HC of Aus).

80 *Re Savage* [1991] NI 103.

81 Any such clause in a NI statute made before 28 May 1975 was repealed by the (now repealed) Administration of Justice (NI) Order 1975, Art.6. Unlike that Article and the equivalent English provision (Tribunals and Inquiries Act 1992, s.12), s.22 of the Judicature Act does not make an exception for orders by courts of law.

Territorial jurisdiction

19.19 One point on which there is a dearth of express authority is the territorial extent of the High Court's power of review. Supperstone & Goudie (at p.300) suggests that the English High Court can order *certiorari* against all inferior courts and statutory tribunals within England and Wales and possibly the Isle of Man, but not courts in Crown territories overseas. It seems obvious that the decisions of a foreign authority or made under foreign law cannot be reviewed by the Northern Ireland High Court;[82] but there have been instances of the High Court reviewing, without objection, a decision by an English authority made in England.[83] The Civil Jurisdiction and Judgments Act 1982, Schedules 1 and 4[84] (which regulate the bringing of proceedings against persons domiciled in EC Countries and Great Britain respectively) do not apply to "administrative matters"; and Schedule 4 does not apply to "review of decisions of tribunals" (Sch.5 para. 4).[85]

19.20 In *R* v *Commr of Police ex p Bennett*[86] the English High Court held that it could not review the execution in England of a Scottish warrant of arrest. In *In re McGlinchey*,[87] the Court refused review on the ground that its only effect would be on the course of a criminal trial outside the jurisdiction. In *Lord Advocate* v *RW Forsyth*[88] it was held that where a tax assessment was made in Scotland, judicial review of the appeal, though heard in England, was within the jurisdiction of the Court of Session, not the English High Court.

19.21 In *Sokha* v *Sec of State for Home Dept*[89] the Court of Session heard a petition for judicial review against the Home Secretary's decision to detain an Indian under the Immigration Act. He had at all times lived and worked in England and was arrested and detained in England. The only Scottish connection was that his relatives in Scotland had instructed a Scottish solicitor on his behalf. The Home Secretary accepted that the Court had jurisdiction on the ground that as a Government minister he was domiciled throughout the

---

82 See for instance *A-G (UK)* v *Heinemann* [1988] LRC (Const) 1007; 165 CLR 30, an action for an injunction (the "Spycatcher" case) where the High Court of Australia said that claims to enforce the public law of a foreign state were unmaintainable; and *Buttes Gas* v *Hammer Gas (No 3)* [1982] AC 888, at 933: the courts of one country will not judge the acts of the government of another done within its own territory. See also *A-G for UK* v *Wellington Newspapers* [1988] 1 NZLR 129.

83 *In re Chan* [1987] NI 13 (review of English Home Secretary's decision to deport an immigrant who has lived intermittently in England and Northern Ireland); *In re McLaughlin* [1990] 6 NIJB 41 (review of Home Secretary's ban on broadcasting Sinn Fein members on UK television and radio, a judicial review application having been already dismissed in the English High Court); *In re Grogan* [1993] 10 NIJB 18 (decision of Home Secretary not to transfer prisoner from English to Northern Ireland prison).

84 S.16(1)(a) of the Act states that Sch.4 covers the same type of proceedings as Sch.1

85 Sch.8, which modifies Sch.4 in relation to the jurisdiction of Scottish Courts, does not exclude administrative matters, and therefore Sch.8 applies to judicial review by the Scottish Court of a decision made in the UK: *Bank of Scotland* v *IMRO* 1989 SLT 432

86 [1995] QB 313 (DC).

87 [1987] 3 NIJB 1.

88 1990 SLT 458.

89 1992 SLT 1049.

United Kingdom,[90] but argued that the Scottish court was *forum non conveniens* (para. 11.175). Lord Prosser dismissed the petition on that principle, holding that Scotland was a wholly inappropriate forum and England was the natural and proper forum, and it was not shown that justice could not be done in England. It is submitted that the Home Secretary's concession was correct only under the law of Scotland,[85] but that the Scottish Court's jurisdiction also rested on the fact that the source of the reviewed decision (the Immigration Act 1971) was a law of Scotland as well as England; and that a decision by him under a purely English Act, for example to approve a ban on a march in London under the Public Order Act 1986, would not be within the Scottish or Northern Ireland Court's jurisdiction in judicial review. In short, the author's view is that the challenged decision can be reviewed in the Northern Ireland High Court only where the source of the authority for it is a law applicable to the whole of the United Kingdom in general or of Northern Ireland in particular, subject to the discretion to refuse review. The identity of the particular Secretary of State who makes the decision is of no legal significance, as the power of any Secretary of State can be exercised by all; statutes which refer to "the Secretary of State" never define the expression (see para. 1.10).

GROUNDS FOR JUDICIAL REVIEW

19.22 The onus of proving a ground is on the applicant. The applicant can challenge by judicial review not the merits or wisdom of the decision of a court, tribunal, body or official, but the lawfulness of it and the manner of reaching it, on any of the following grounds. The classic statement by Lord Diplock in *CCSU* v *Min of Civil Service*[91] summarises them as illegality, irrationality, and procedural impropriety.

(i) Error of fact precedent to jurisdiction

19.23 It made an error as to the existence of a fact which is a condition precedent to the exercise of the power;[92] or a collateral fact relevant to the existence of its jurisdiction.[93] If a statute says that a Minister may deport an illegal immigrant, the fact that the person is an illegal immigrant is a fact precedent to the power to deport, and the decision to deport will be quashed unless the fact is proved on balance of probabilities,[94] though the Court can consider any evidence available to the decider without regard to judicial rules of

---

90 At p.1051 col.1D.

91 [1985] AC 374, at 410D.

92 *R (Magee)* v *Down JJ* [1935] NI 51 (harbouring cattle illegally imported); *Sec for Education* v *Tameside MBC* [1977] AC 1014 (power to act "where satisfied that ..."); *R (Baines)* v *Industrial Ct* [1970] NI 197; *In re Duffy* [1991] 7 NIJB 62; *R* v *Chief Constable ex p McKenna* [1992] NI 116; *State (Holland)* v *Kelly* [1977] IR 193 *Greene* v *Governor of Mountjoy* [1995] 3 IR 541 (juvenile certified unruly); *R(AG)* v *Co Ct Judge for Co Down* [1967] NI 171; *In re Doherty* [1988] NI 14 (facts which must exist before liquor licence can be renewed).

93 *R (Greenaway)* v *Armagh JJ* [1924] 2 IR 55 (the net annual value of the land in a county court title action).

94 *R* v *Home Sec ex p Khawaja* [1984] AC 74. At least it must be shown that the factual conclusion is justified on the evidence.

evidence.[95] If the statute says: "If X has reasonable grounds for believing that ...", the Court reviews the reasonableness by objective test.[97] If the statute says: "If X believes/is satisfied/is of the opinion that ...", then the Court reviews the decision for misdirection of law, misapprehension of relevant factors;[96] for *Wednesbury* unreasonableness,[97] or on the ground of absence of any evidence[98]or on the ground that the facts relevant to forming the opinion were not put before X.[99] Of course a mistake of law in applying the test for the condition precedent is freely reviewable.[100]

(ii) Error or excess of jurisdiction

19.24 It acted without or exceeded its jurisdiction, for example by making a decision which it has no jurisdiction to make, by making a decision after a matter has arisen which ousts its jurisdiction, by misinterpreting the provisions of the regulatory statute or European Law measure,[101] exercising the power predominantly for a purpose for which the power was not granted,[102] misdirecting itself in law,[103] exercising a power without any grounds; failing to comply with a mandatory procedural provision of statute or rules.[104] Provided that its decision is authorised by some legal source, an administrative body does not have to specify, or even be aware of, the correct authority under which it acted.[105] Review will be refused where it made the right decision for the wrong reason.[106]

---

95 *In re Rahman* [1997] 1 All ER 796 (CA), a *habeas corpus* case.

96 *Buck* v *Bawone* (1976) 135 CLR 110, at 118-9.

97 *R* v *Chief Constable ex p McKenna* [1992] NI 116, at 132-3, 143j-147; Supperstone & Goudie p.76, interpreting the obscure remarks of Lord Wilberforce in *Tameside* at 1047.

98 *Bowes* v *Judge Devally* [1995] 1 IR 315 (Geoghegan J).

99 *State (Nevin)* v *Tormey* [1976] IR 1.

100 *R* v *Newham LBC ex p Dada* [1996] QB 507 (misinterpreting the word "homeless").

101 Regulations, and decisions made under the EC Treaty, the Euratom Treaty and the ECSC Treaty are directly applicable and have the force of statute. Directives, which require the Member States to introduce national laws from a certain date, are not directly part of the national law, but they do bind the Government and bodies performing a public function under the control of the State, so that failure of such bodies to observe a Directive is a ground for judicial review. See Supperstone & Goudie Chap.12; and *Re Norbrook Laboratories* [1992] 10 NIJB 36.

102 *Padfield* v *Min of Agriculture* [1968] AC 997; *Re Curran* [1985] NI 261; *In re McCann* [1992] 9 NIJB 1, at 21.

103 *R* v *Barnet LBC ex p Shah* [1983] 2 AC 309 (misinterpreting the wording of the precedent fact "ordinarily resident").

104 *R* v *Governor of Crumlin Road ex p Jordan* [1992] NI 148.

105 *British Columbia (Milk Board)* v *Grisnich* (1995) 126 DLR 4th 191 (SC Canada).

106 *Andrew* v *City of Glasgow DC*, 1996 SLT 814 (OH); *Southern HSSB* v *Lemon* [1995] 6 BNIL 60 (CA); *In re Devine* [1990] 9 NIJB 96, at 110 (evidence rightly admitted by coroner under wrong rule of evidence). On appeal the Lords held the coroner's ground of admission to be correct: *R* v *HM Attorney-General, ex p Devine* [1992] 1 WLR 262.

(iii) Under-use of jurisdiction

19.25 It under-assessed the extent of its powers,[107] or wrongly decided that it had no jurisdiction.[108]

(iv) Under-use of discretion

19.26 It failed to exercise its power, for example by following a pre-determined path,[109] failing to exercise its discretion in the individual case,[110] sub-delegating its decisions.[111] Delegation of administrative decisions to an official is proper,[112] and the act of delegation can be presumed without specific proof.[113]

Where a body is required by statute to publish criteria for making its decisions, it must follow them.[114] A body may adopt and apply a policy or guideline, provided that the policy is not improper and that it considers each case.[115] It must in every case take into account its own guideline or policy and will generally be protected from judicial review if it applies the policy in a way which is not wholly unreasonable.[116] If it changes its policy that will ground a review only if the change is *Wednesbury* unreasonable.[117] Misinterpretation of its own guidelines makes its decision reviewable.[118]

(v) Misuse of discretion

19.27 It did not act within the boundaries of its discretion, for example taking into account irrelevant matters, or failing to take into account relevant matters. The Court decides, being a matter of law, what is or is not a relevant factor, but not the assessment and weight to be attached to those factors.[119] A body must take into account its own declared policy (see para. 19.26). An administrative body must take into account relevant Government policy,[120] but *semble,* a judicial body should not do so. A decision maker is obliged to take into account

---

[107] *Re Cooper* [1991] NI 257.

[108] *R(McGrath)* v *Clare JJ* [1905] 2 IR 510; *In re Perry* [1996] 5 BNIL 37 (Carswell LJ); *Devrajan* v *DJ Ballagh* [1993] 3 IR 377 (Brussels Convention on civil jurisdiction).

[109] *Re O'Connor* [1991] NI 77.

[110] *In re Grogan* [1993] 10 NIJB 18.

[111] *CR* v *An Bord Uchtala* [1993] 3 IR 535.

[112] *Carltona* v *Works Commrs* [1943] 2 All ER 560, at 563. Some enactments specifically authorise delegation, e.g. Deregulation and Contracting Out Act 1994, ss.69-79 and (NI) Order 1996, Arts.11-16; Civil Service (Management Functions) Act 1992 and (NI) Order 1994.

[113] *McM* v *Manager of Trinity House* [1995] 1 IR 595, at 609 (Laffoy J).

[114] *In re Farren* [1990] 6 NIJB 72.

[115] *British Oxygen* v *Min of Technology* [1971] AC 610.

[116] *Casey* v *Dept of Education*, QBD, NI, 16 October 1996 (Girvan J).

[117] *R* v *Sec of State for Home Dept, ex p Hargreaves* [1997] 1 All ER 397 (CA).

[118] *Chui* v *Min of Immigration* [1994] 2 NZLR 541 (CA); [1994] 1 LRC 433.

[119] *Re Murphy* [1991] 5 NIJB 88, at 103-4; *In re FW Wellworth (No 2)* [1996] 8 BNIL 131 (CA); 'The Times', 16 December 1996.

[120] *In re Meekatharra* [1995] 6 BNIL 105 (Kerr J); *R* v *Islington LBC ex p Rixon*, 'The Times', 17 April 1996 (Sedley J).

only those factors which are known to him at the time of making the decision,[121] and need not search out matters which the party affected could bring to his attention;[122] but Kerr J has held that a discretionary decision can be reviewed because of material factors which were not put before the decider through inadvertence on his part or on the part of the parties.[123] Normally where an under- or mis-use of discretion is found the Court quashes the decision and leaves the body to decide anew; but where the proper exercise of the discretion must surely have led to only one decision, the Court will by *mandamus* compel that decision to be made.[124]

(vi) Decision without evidence

19.28 It reached a conclusion for which there was no or insufficient evidence,[125] that being an error of law.

(vii) Misapprehension of fact?

19.29 Wade & Forsyth (pp.316-8) contend that there are enough stray *dicta* to be able to say that a decision is reviewable if reached on a basis of a clear misapprehension of fact. (See also Aldous & Alder pp.15-9). If this ground exists it must be stressed that it does not allow a review of the findings of fact, but is confined to cases where the body has fundamentally mistaken one of the clear basic facts. Review cannot be based on a fact which was unknown and unavailable to the knowledge of the decision-maker at the time of making the decision.[126]

(viii) Error of law on face of record

19.30 It made an error in law which appears on the face of the record, an issue discussed in detail at para. 19.45. The Tribunal and Inquiries Act 1992 (s.10) requires a large number of specified tribunals, and a minister after a statutory inquiry has been or could have been held, if so requested, to state its/his reasons; and any statement of reasons, oral or written, is deemed to be part of the record.

(ix) Breach of natural justice

19.31 It breached the rules of fairness or natural justice as they apply to the subject-matter, for example, the deciding authority having an interest or showing bias so as to cause reasonable suspicion that a fair decision is not possible,[127] deciding without consulting or allowing representations from persons with a legitimate interest,[128] not meeting the legitimate expectation of a

---

[121] *R* v *Immigration Appeal Tribunal, ex p Hassesin* [1987] 1 All ER 74; *In re Quigley*, [1997] 3 BNIL 40 (DC) (*per* Sheil J only). The former decision is misconstrued in Wade & Forsyth.

[122] *R* v *Horseferry Road Mag Ct, ex p Pearson* [1976] 2 All ER 264, at 266-7.

[123] *In re Murray* [1997] 3 BNIL 106.

[124] *Commr of State Revenue* v *Royal Insurance* [1994] 4 LRC 511, at 532, 537-8 (HC of Aus).

[125] *Neill* v *North Antrim Mag Ct* [1992] 1 WLR 1220 (HL, NI).

[126] *Shetland Line* v *Sec of State for Scotland*, 1996 SLT 653 (OH).

[127] *In re Grogan* [1988] 8 NIJB 87.

[128] *In re NUPE* [1988] NI 255. The duty to consult is cast upon the decision-maker, not the person who makes recommendations to the decider: *Southern HSSB* v *Lemon* [1995] 6

person to present his case in a particular way,[129] not letting the person know the case against him, not letting him call a witness,[130] court convicting defendant on an alleged admission made in court without allowing him to present his case any further;[131] not allowing him to present his case;[132] refusing an adjournment of an oral hearing so that he is unable to make his case.[133] Natural justice may extend in some cases to requiring a right to prior discovery of documents.[134] A prima facie breach of natural justice is not significant if there is no actual injustice capable of remedy.[135] Judicial review does not lie automatically against all procedural flaws; 'routine mishaps' such as the unexpected unavailability of a witness are better remedied by the appropriate avenue of appeal.[136]

19.32 In the case of an investigative body, natural justice requires: (a) that its findings be based on evidence of some logically probative value; and (b) that it must listen to any evidence or argument which a person would wish to put forward if aware of the risk of a finding being made which affects his interests or reputation.[137] Natural justice may be excluded or restricted in certain cases, for example: of national security; of urgency; of impracticability because of volume of cases; in preliminary or provisional determinations or decisions to investigate; in decisions to introduce regulations; by express statutory provision as to procedure; by agreement or fault of the applicant (Supperstone & Goudie pp.179-88). A decision to arrest does not require observance of natural justice.[138]

(x) Failure to give reasons

19.33 There is conflict as to whether a court or body is required to give reasons for its decision where not so required by statute or rules. In *State (Creedon)* v *Criminal Injuries Compensation Tribunal*[139] Finlay CJ said that it was unacceptable and improper for that tribunal to reject a claim in full without giving any reason (but the judicial review was given only on *Wednesbury* grounds). A court in an appellate jurisdiction from which no appeal lies on facts has a duty to give reasons for its decision.[140] There is no general rule that

---

BNIL 60 (CA). Natural justice does not in all cases require the decider to make known all relevant factors to those who are consulted: *ibid.*

129 *In re Chan* [1987] NI 13.

130 *In re Stephenson* [1987] 4 NIJB 79; *In re Rowntree* [1991] 11 NIJB 67.

131 *R (Cahill)* v *Dublin JJ* [1920] 2 IR 230.

132 *In re North Down BC* [1986] NI 304; including where the error is no fault of the tribunal: see para.19.36.

133 *In re Jamison,* QBD, NI (Kerr J) 14 October 1996.

134 *Nolan* v *Irish Land Commission* [1981] IR 23.

135 *In re Gribben* [1987] NI 129, a very odd decision on its facts.

136 *Maher* v *Judge O'Donnell* [1995] 3 IR 530, at 539-40.

137 *Re Erebus Royal Commission* [1983] NZLR 663, at 671 (PC, *per* Lord Diplock).

138 *Grech* v *Min for Immigration* (1993) 19 Comm LB 40 (Aus Fed Ct).

139 [1988] IR 51.

140 *R* v *Harrow Crown Ct ex p Dave* [1994] 1 WLR 98. In *Manning* v *Shackleton* [1994] 2 IR 397, Barron J said that failure to state reasons by a judicial body vitiates its decision only if justice is not done and seen to be done.

an administrative body should give reasons,[141] unless there is some special factor, as where its decision appears inexplicable,[142] or its reasons are not discernible.[143] No duty to give reasons can be implied where the statute expressly states that reasons need not be given.[144] The failure of the challenged party to state its reasons, where there is no duty to do so, does not by itself lead to an inference of irrationality unless the facts point overwhelmingly towards a different decision.[145] The failure of the body to keep a minuted record of the material on which it made its decision is a ground for review only if that material is not otherwise available.[146] If an inadequate statement of reasons is cured by fuller statement in the respondent's affidavit, not being suspected to be *ex post facto* reasoning, review should be refused.[147] Even though reasons for the decision are not required, the duty of fairness may still require the body to make known to the party affected, before the decision is made, the factors weighing on its mind against him.[144] See also para. 19.30.

(xi) Legitimate expectation

19.34 It failed to meet the applicant's legitimate expectation. Judicial review can protect his legitimate expectation of a right not enforceable in private law, arising from an express promise (made to the applicant or to the public at large) or regular practice of the public body.[148] He can claim a legitimate expectation that he will be consulted, or his rights and interests considered.[149] An applicant cannot complain of failure to consult persons other than himself where the duty to consult is not imposed by statute or rules.[150] In *In Re Police Association*[151] Carswell J held that the expectation can relate only to procedure, the manner of deciding, and cannot bind the body as to the content of its decision.[152] English cases are ambiguous on this point.[153] Irish courts have held that legitimate

---

141 *In re Thompson* [1993] 10 NIJB 25; *Public Service Board* v *Osmond* [1987] LRC (Const) 681; (1986) 159 CLR 656 (HC of Aus); even where the body changes its mind: *R* v *Aylesbury Vale DC, ex p Chaplin*, 'The Times', 23 July 1996 (Keene J).

142 *R* v *Higher Education Council* [1994] 1 WLR 242. In *Rajah* v *College of Surgeons* [1994] 1 IR 384, at 395, Keane J went so far as to say that judicial and quasi-judicial bodies, and administrative bodies affecting legal rights, should give reasons.

143 *In re Oliver* [1995] 6 BNIL 69 (Carswell LJ) (refusal of legal aid).

144 *R* v *Sec of State for Home Dept ex p Fayed* [1997] 1 All ER 228 (CA).

145 *R* v *Secretary of State for Trade and Industry, ex p Lonrho* [1989] 1 WLR 525 (HL).

146 *O'Keeffe* v *An Bord Pleanala* [1993] 1 IR 39, at 77 (SC).

147 *In re O'Dwyer*, CA, NI, 19 December 1996.

148 *CCSU* v *Min of Civil Service* [1985] AC 374, *per* Lord Fraser at 401.

149 *In re NUPE* [1988] NI 255, at 264; *In re Donnelly* [1988] 8 NIJB 26. Conversely, over-consultation, where the body considers the views of persons whom it is not empowered to consult, may make a decision reviewable: *In re O'Connor* [1991] NI 77.

150 *In re Shearer* [1993] 2 NIJB 12, at 28-9 (*sed quaere*).

151 [1990] NI at 271-6.

152 See also *Haoucher* v *Min for Immigration* (1990) 169 CLR 648; [1991] LRC (Const) 819 (HC of Aus); *Furey* v *Conception Bay RC School* (1993) 104 DLR 4th 455 (Nfld CA).

153 See *CCSU* v *Minister for Civil Service* [1985] AC 374, at 408-9; *R* v *IRC ex p Preston* [1985] AC 835, at 866-7; *R* v *Health Sec ex p US Tobacco* [1992] QB 353, at 368-9; Singh & Steyn 'Legitimate Expectation in 1996: What Now?' [1996] JR 17. The latest, *R* v *Sec of State for Home Dept, ex p Hargreaves* [1997] 1 All ER 397 (CA) (change of policy on

expectation of a favourable decision can arise from a virtually unqualified assurance,[154] but not so as to bind a Minister in the exercise of a discretion.[155] O'Hanlon J has equated the principle with equitable or promissory estoppel, that is, that the challenged body should be allowed to resile on its promise on reasonable notice unless the applicant has acted on faith of it irrevocably.[156] In *In re McKee*[157] the Court of Appeal appears to have accepted that the Secretary of State would be bound by his undertaking to the Irish extraditing court that the prisoner's time in custody there would be credited to his sentence. There is a legitimate expectation that a government body will act in accord with a treaty obligation and will depart from it only after allowing affected persons to make representations.[158]

(xii) Rules of procedure

19.35 It breached the rules of procedure expressly laid down by statute or rules,[159] as where it failed to give reasons for the decision as required by statute.[160] If the Court interprets the procedure as mandatory, it will normally quash the decision, but if the procedure is regarded as directory only, breach of it is not usually a ground for quashing *per se*.

Where required by statute to give reasons, the body must deal with the substantial issues in an intelligible way, showing the real reasons and the principal material issues but need not mention every material consideration; the amount of detail required depends on the circumstances (e.g. that the body is reversing a decision of a lower authority).[161] Only in rare cases will the Court allow the reviewed body to respond to the judicial review by relying on reasons other than those stated by it under the statutory procedure.[162] Failure to give reasons with its decision does not automatically lead to quashing of the decision. The duty to give reasons can be enforced by *mandamus*. If the body gives its reasons belatedly, for example in a replying affidavit in a motion for judicial review, the failure to state reasons is not in itself a ground of review unless the reasons stated are suspected to be in the nature of *ex post facto*

---

when home leave for sentenced prisoner will be considered) favours the Carswell view. Carswell LCJ, as he has since become, is now less firmly attached to his previous view: see *In re Croft*, QBD, NI, 29 January 1997.

154 *Kenny* v *Kelly* [1988] IR 457; *Devitt* v *Min of Education* [1989] ILRM 639; *Abrahamson* v *Law Society* [1996] 1 IR 403.

155 *Dempsey* v *Min of Justice* [1994] 1 ILRM 401; and see *R* v *IRC ex p Preston* [1985] AC 835, at 866-7; *R* v *Health Sec ex p US Tobacco* [1992] QB 353, at 368-9.

156 *Association of General Practitioners* v *Minister of Health* [1995] 1 IR 382, and *In re FW Wellworth* (No 2), QBD, NI, 28 June 1996 (Carswell LJ).

157 [1993] 8 NIJB 88. The point was left open in *In re McFarlane* [1991] 6 NIJB 42.

158 *Minister of Immigration* v *Teoh* [1995] 3 LRC 1 (HC Aus).

159 *R (Smyth)* v *Co Antrim Coroner* [1980] NI 123; *In re Morrison* [1991] NI 70.

160 *In re Fair Employment Commission* [1990] 10 NIJB 38.

161 *R* v *Criminal Injuries Compensation Board, ex p Cook* 1996] 1 WLR 1037; *Safeway Stores* v *National Appeal Panel*, 1996 SLT 235 (2nd Div).

162 *R* v *Westminster CC, ex p Ermakov* [1996] 2 All ER 302 (CA).

reasoning,[163] or the applicant has been prejudiced in mounting a challenge to the decision.[164]

(xiii) Fault of other party or person

19.36 Its decision was procured by the fraud of a party or perjury of his witness,[165] or by a serious mistake or negligence which renders the decision-making process unfair;[166] but not where the fault is of the applicant's own lawyer.[167] In these cases the decision is reviewed without there being any fault by the challenged body.

(xiv) 'Wednesbury' unreasonableness

19.37 It made a decision so absurd that no reasonable person acting honestly and *bona fide* and directing himself properly on the law could have made it. This ground was classically stated by Lord Greene MR in *Associated Provincial Picture Houses* v *Wednesbury Corp.*[168] It might arise in cases where the decision cannot be held to be consistent with the policy of the empowering statute,[169] or where the benefit from the decision is disproportionately small compared to the harm, cost or inconvenience involved.[170] The 'irrationality' or *Wednesbury* test as it is usually called, has been defined by Lord Diplock in *CCSU* v *Min of Civil Service*[171] as "so outrageous in its defiance of logic or of accepted moral standards that no sensible person who had applied his mind to the question to be decided could have arrived at it". The Irish Supreme Court thought that logic and morality might not be the sole considerations in all instances and preferred to state it as "whether the impugned decision plainly and unambiguously flies in the face of fundamental reason and common sense".[172] In *R* v *Ministry of Defence, ex p Smith*[173] the Court of Appeal has subtly widened the scope of 'irrationality' to mean "beyond the range of responses open to the reasonable decision-maker". The onus of establishing irrationality is on the applicant.[174] The Court can look at the justification for the decision given both in the reasons given in the decision itself and the other

---

163 *In re Anglin,* QBD, NI, 29 August 1996; [1996] 9 BNIL 63 (Kerr J).

164 *In re Tucker*, QBD, NI, 25 August 1995 (Girvan J).

165 *R (Burns)* v *Tyrone CC Judge* [1961] NI 167.

166 *In re Allen* [1987] 6 NIJB 94, at 103 (induced by opposite party); *R* v *Harrow Crown Ct ex p Dave* [1994] 1 WLR 98 (failure of prosecutor to disclose matters helpful to defendant); *R* v *Bolton JJ ex p Scally* [1991] 1 QB 537 (mistake by prosecuting authority or police in assembling evidence, rendering applicant's trial unfair); *R(AG)* v *Belfast JJ* [1981] NI 208 (innocent person convicted of offence without his knowledge because the offender gave a false name).

167 *R* v *Home Sec ex p Al-Mehdawi* [1990] 1 AC 876.

168 [1948] 1 KB 223; *In re Blair* [1985] NI 68.

169 *In re McCann* [1992] 7 NIJB 60, at 83.

170 The European 'proportionality doctrine' not yet treated as a separate head in UK law: *R* v *Home Sec ex p Brind* [1991] 1 AC 696; *In re Crawford* [1995] 2 BNIL 60 (Div Ct).

171 [1985] AC 374, at 410G.

172 *State (Keegan)* v *Stardust Compensation Tribunal* [1986] IR 642. at 657-8.

173 [1996] QB 517 (review of Armed Forces' ban on homosexuals).

174 *P & F Sharpe* v *Dublin City Manager* [1989] IR 701.

reasons stated by the challenged party in its affidavits.[175] The more the decision infringes fundamental human rights, the more the Court will require justification of the reasonableness.[173]

(xv) Substantial unfairness?

19.38 Its decision is "substantially unfair". Unfairness in the *content* of the decision may have achieved recognition as a ground of review which is independent of, though influenced by, the other grounds of procedural impropriety, abuse of power, legitimate expectation, irrationality.[176] 'Injustice' is not a ground *per se*.[177] Unfair and inconsistent treatment of like persons is a ground of review only if it is an abuse of power by failing to exercise the discretion lawfully.[178]

(vxi) Discrimination

19.39 Any legislation applying to Northern Ireland, except a UK Act, is void if it discriminates against people on grounds of religious belief or political opinion (Northern Ireland Constitution Act 1973, s.17). If the Secretary of State so decides, the legislation can be referred to the Privy Council (s.18). If he does not, *semble,* the High Court can declare it void on judicial review. It is unlawful for a Minister or NI Department or any body subject to investigation by an ombudsman to discriminate or aid discrimination in its Northern Ireland functions against people on the grounds of religious belief or political opinion; any person adversely affected may sue for damages and/or an injunction (s.19). Such unlawfulness is also a ground for judicial review. This provision was raised in judicial review in *In re Lavery*[179] where the refusal of the Secretary of State to allow free security protection to a Sinn Fein councillor was challenged: Kerr J held that the refusal was legitimate because its effect on persons of a particular political opinion was incidental. And in *In re O'Neill*[180] he held the closure of leisure facilities on a Sunday not to be discriminatory because it affected persons of all beliefs and opinions; he also said *obiter* that a decision can be discriminatory where it is influenced by the beliefs or opinions of the decider or of those affected by the decision. In *In re Thompson*[181] Carswell J would have given leave for judicial review if the prison authority had acted in such a way as to prevent a prisoner of a particular religion from attending worship. In *In re Spence*,[182] McCollum J said that discrimination on grounds of sex or religious or political opinion is not a ground of review *per se* under the *Wednesbury* test unless it was positively unfair or unjust. Where an Irish

---

[175] *In re McKee* [1993] 8 NIJB 88, at 108-9.

[176] See *R* v *IRC ex p Preston* [1985] AC 835; *Wheeler* v *Leicester CC* [1985] AC 1054, at 1078-9; *Thames Valley Electricity* v *NZFP* [1994] 2 NZLR 641 (CA). This ground was doubted in *In re Croft*, QBD, NI, 29 January 1997 (Carswell LCJ), at p.18, and rejected in *Shetland Line* v *Sec of State for Scotland*, 1996 SLT 653 (OH).

[177] *In re Doherty* [1996] 2 BNIL 77 (CA).

[178] *In re Croft*, QBD, NI (Carswell LCJ) 29 January 1997.

[179] [1994] 6 BNIL 2.

[180] QBD, NI, 20 March 1995.

[181] [1993] 10 NIJB 25.

[182] [1993] 4 NIJB 97.

national was barred from applying for a position in a branch of the Civil Service, Girvan J declared it to be a breach of Article 48 of the EC Treaty as being discriminatory between nationals of member states;[183] but the Court of Appeal, in the case of a spouse of an Irish national, confined it to the context of an applicant moving from one member state to another.[184]

THE 'JUDICIAL OR ADMINISTRATIVE' DICHOTOMY

19.40 The historical view, now well and truly buried, was that no review lay against an administrative decision, only against a judicial or quasi-judicial decision. A decision to acquire land by compulsory purchase, being a power for the public good, is administrative.[185] A judicial tribunal acts on principles of law; an administrative tribunal acts on policy and expediency.[186] A judicial tribunal is one which makes decisions which impose liability or affect rights; a tribunal investigating a complaint against the police was held not to be judicial in *In re Sterritt*.[187] The decision to release a life-sentenced prisoner on licence is not judicial, being a decision taken in the public interest,[188] nor is the decision by a Minister whether to remit a sentence under the prerogative of mercy.[189] In *In re Mailey*[190] it was held that a coroner's inquest was an investigative proceeding to which the rules of natural justice do not apply, but that case was not cited in *In re Price*[191] where it was held that natural justice requires notice of the inquest to be given to the next of kin. At least, although the full force of natural justice may not apply to inquests, there is an obligation to act fairly.[192]

Administrative decision

19.41 An administrative decision (or refusal to decide) is reviewable if it affects a person by altering his private law rights or obligations or by depriving him of a benefit or advantage which he legitimately expected or was assured would be taken away only on good ground and after consultation.[193] It is reviewable on the grounds of error of law; *Wednesbury* unreasonableness; or failure to act fairly.[194] An administrative body is in excess of jurisdiction if its decision is founded on an error of law in interpreting the statute conferring the power on it,[195] so that its error of law is in effect an error of jurisdiction.[196] A

---

183 *In re Colgan*, QBD, NI, undated 1996.

184 *In re Bignell*, CA, NI, 21 March 1997, affirming Higgins J, 29 October 1996.

185 *O'Brien* v *Bord na Mona* [1983] IR 255, *per* O'Higgins CJ at 282-3.

186 *Giese* v *Williston* (1963) 37 DLR 2d 447.

187 [1980] NI 234. A tribunal of inquiry into the conduct of a Revenue Officer is quasi-judicial: *Gallagher* v *Revenue Commissioners (No 2)* [1995] 1 IR 55 (SC).

188 *In re Whelan* [1990] NI 348, at 360-1.

189 *Brennan* v *Minister of Justice* [1995] 1 IR 612.

190 [1980] NI 102.

191 [1986] NI 390.

192 *In re McKerr* [1993] 5 NIJB 18, at 32 (CA).

193 *CCSU* v *Min of Civil Service* [1985] AC 374, at 408E-G.

194 *Ibid* at 414E.

195 *Anisminic* v *Foreign Compensation Commission* [1969] 2 AC 147; *Re Racal* [1981] AC 374, at 383.

provision that a decision shall be "final and conclusive" does not oust the power to review for excess of jurisdiction or error on face of the record.[197] It can be reviewed for unlawful decision; unreasonable exercise of discretion, by misconstruing the relevance of factors or reaching a decision which no reasonable body properly directing itself could make; or deciding contrary to the policy of the enabling statute.[198] Though it must act fairly, it is not necessarily bound to apply the rules of natural justice, unless there is a legitimate expectation thereof. The standards of fairness vary from time to time and in the context of the decision, the wording of the statute and the administrative system; fairness may require an opportunity for the person adversely affected to make representations and notice of the case against him,[199] and notice of the matters bearing against him in the decision-maker's mind.[200] Fairness may in the circumstances require a right to cross-examine[201] or not.[202] A quasi-judicial tribunal must adopt a fair hearing of both sides; it may allow hearsay evidence but in some circumstances it must allow a party to challenge by cross-examination.[203] A judicial or quasi-judicial tribunal must be free from suspicion of bias ('justice must be seen to be done'), but to challenge an administrative decision for bias, actual bias must be proved.[204] The Canadian Supreme Court has said that administrative decisions of an adjudicative nature must be subject to the 'suspicion of bias' test, but that for decisions of a policy nature by elected representatives, actual bias must be shown.[205]

Judicial decision

Grounds for review

19.42 The five conditions for *certiorari* stated by Gibson J in *R (Martin)* v *Mahony*[206] are: (a) want or excess of jurisdiction in beginning or during the inquiry; (b) error on the face of the record; (c) abuse of jurisdiction (e.g. by mis-stating the complaint or disregard of essentials of justice and regulatory conditions); (d) court disqualified by likelihood of bias or by interest; (e) fraud.

19.43 Against a judicial body, the courts in Ireland have not yet claimed expressly the power to review a judicial decision made within its jurisdiction,

---

196 *In re Quinn* [1988] 2 NIJB 10, at 20. The problem that can arise from the *Anisminic* doctrine is that it makes a decision void if founded on an error of law, with the unfortunate consequence that no such decision can be enforced or relied on; and it turns statutory 'ouster clauses' into meaningless verbiage. See further Narain 'Jurisdictional Error in Administrative Law' (1983) 34 NILQ 315; and *Pollock* v *Sec of State for Scotland* 1993 SLT 1173. See previous page.

197 *Hockey* v *Yelland* (1984) 157 CLR 124 (HC of Aus).

198 *In re Finlay* [1983] 9 NIJB at 9-12.

199 *In re Crawford* [1995] 2 BNIL 60. See further para. 19-31/32.

200 *R* v *Sec of State for Home Dept ex p Fayed* [1997] 1 All ER 228 (CA).

201 *Errington* v *Wilson* 1995 SLT 1193 (1st Div).

202 *O'Rourke* v *Miller* (1985) 156 CLR 342.

203 *Gallagher* v *Revenue Commissioners (No 2)* [1995] 1 IR 55 (SC).

204 *In re Moore* (1994) [1996] 6 BNIL 40 (CA); *contra*: *R* v *Sec of State for Environment, ex p Kirkstall Valley Ltd* [1996] 3 All ER 304 (Sedley J), and *Huerto* v *College of Physicians* (1996) 133 DLR 4th 100, at 156-7 (Sask CA).

205 *Newfoundland Telephone Co* v *Board of Public Utilities* (1992) 89 DLR 4th 289.

206 [1910] 2 IR 695, at 731; approved in *In Re Doherty* [1988] NI 14, at 26D.

on grounds of error of law off the face of the record;[207] nor on grounds of *Wednesbury* unreasonableness or perversity.[208] It was traditionally held that a judicial body can be reviewed for an error of law as to its jurisdiction, but *cannot* be reviewed for an error of law within its jurisdiction[209] on which its decision is based, unless the error appears on the face of the court record.[210] This principle has been under siege for some years in England, and the text book writers (Lewis p.158, and Supperstone & Goudie p.54) claim that it is now obsolete; but the traditional view has been emphatically re-affirmed by the High Court of Australia.[211] The House of Lords discussed it in *R* v *Hull University Visitors ex p Page.*[212] Lord Griffiths said at 693C that *certiorari* is available to correct any error of law made by an inferior court whether or not on the face of the record; but that review of such error is excluded if by statute the inferior court's decision is declared to be final.[213] Lord Browne-Wilkinson at 701F, 703E (Lord Keith agreeing), said that all errors of law are presumed to be reviewable but that where a power of decision has been conferred on a court of law there is no such presumption; and that where Parliament has declared the court's decision to be final and conclusive, there is a contrary presumption that its error of law is not reviewable.[213] Lord Slynn, at 706B-E (Lord Mustill agreeing) appeared to take the view that all errors of law are reviewable. Since then the test propounded by Lord Griffiths has been repeated by Lord Cooke giving judgment agreed by all five presiding members in *R* v *Bedwellty JJ, ex p Williams,*[214] whilst emphasising the discretion to refuse relief if the error has caused no injustice.

19.44 Error of law includes a finding contrary to the evidence or to reasonable inferences from the evidence, and is distinguished from *Wednesbury* unreasonableness which is required for administrative decisions.[215] A decision

---

[207] *In re McColgan* [1986] NI 370, at 377; *Lennon* v *Clifford* [1993] ILRM 77.

[208] *In re Weatherall* [1984] 19 NIJB; *In re J McL* [1986] NI 397; *R* v *Belfast Recorder ex p McNally* [1992] NI 217, where, at p232c, Lord Lowry LCJ went so far as to say that the same applies to the decision of a tribunal other than a court; but he must surely be taken as meaning a judicial, not an administrative, tribunal.

[209] An error of law within jurisdiction is an error on a point of law arising on an issue which the court has jurisdiction to decide; it includes a dismissal of a complaint on the ground that the wrong person was prosecutor: *State (Cronin)* v *Western Circuit Judge* [1937] IR 34.

[210] *Re Racal* [1981] AC 374, at 383E; *In re Gribben* [1987] NI 129; *In re Quinn* [1987] NI 325; *In re Doherty* [1988] NI 14.

[211] *Craig* v *South Australia* (1995) 69 ALJR 873.

[212] [1993] AC 683, where the Lords disagreed on the issue of whether University visitors are in an anomalous position and also discussed the general position about review of errors of law.

[213] Every decree (including an order, decision or determination made in civil proceedings instituted under statutory provision) and any appeal from an order of a magistrates' court and the decision on any appeal from or application in respect of an order of a tribunal, body etc. brought under statute, of a *county court* is final and conclusive: County Courts (NI) Order 1980, Arts.2(2), 28(1) and 45(1). There appear to be no such finality provisions for orders of magistrates' courts, coroners' courts and industrial tribunals.

[214] [1997] AC 225; a review of a committal for trial by magistrates on insufficient evidence.

[215] *In re Allen* [1987] 6 NIJB 94, at 100-3.

of fact as part of a decision made within jurisdiction is not reviewable, but a decision of fact on a preliminary or incidental point is reviewable.[216] A judicial decision is void if it does not show on its face that the court had jurisdiction,[217] and can be quashed if it is not clear which of two alternative jurisdictions it acted under,[218] but if such a defect is technical the order can be validated under section 18(5) of the Judicature Act.

19.45 "*The record*" consists of the originating process, the pleadings if any, and the formal order or adjudication of the court or tribunal. The written or oral judgment stating findings and reasons is not part of the record unless, as is the case in many tribunals, a formal order is not drawn up.[219] It was common in the 1950s to 1970s for a court to agree at the request of the parties to incorporate in its formal judgment a 'speaking order' stating the findings of fact and law, so that a party could apply for *certiorari* on the legal point decided: this enabled a ruling by the High Court instead of by the Court of Appeal by case stated.[220] In *In re Morrison*[221] the Court quashed a prison governor's adjudication of a disciplinary offence because of an error of law disclosed in the transcript of the oral hearing;[222] and in *R* v *Knightsbridge Crown Court ex p ISC*[223] the transcript of the oral reasons for judgment was treated as the record. In *In re Allen*[224] Lord Lowry LCJ discussed without deciding whether the transcript of evidence could be part of the record. The High Court of Australia holds the transcript of proceedings and reasons to be outside the record unless incorporated by reference in the court's order.[225] In *R (DHSS)* v *Armagh Supplementary Benefit Appeal Tribunal*[226] Kelly J, citing Halsbury's *Laws*, said that the record cannot be supplemented by affidavit or other evidence.[227] In *In re Stevenson*[228] Carswell J held that the record includes any affidavit treated as such by the consent of the parties; any affidavit by the court/tribunal; and (*sed quaere*) any affidavit used by the "notice party" (i.e. the adversary party).

---

216 *State (Davidson)* v *Farrell* [1960] IR 438; *R (Bryson)* v *Lisnaskea Guardians* [1918] 2 IR 258, 274-5.

217 *R (McSwiggan)* v *Co Londonderry JJ* [1905] 2 IR 318; *Clarke* v *Judge Hogan* [1995] 1 IR 310 (Barron J); *Taylor* v *Clemson* (1842) 2 QB 978 (114 ER 378).

218 *State (Browne)* v *Feran* [1967] IR 147; *aliter*, an administrative decision (see para. 19.24).

219 *R* v *Belfast Recorder ex p McNally* [1992] NI 217, at 236.

220 See *R(King)* v *Judge Hanna*, CA, NI, 29 June 1962 *per* Black LJ at 2; and *R(Campbell College)* v *Judge Hanna*, CA, NI, 29 March 1963, *per* Black LJ at 1-2. In *R (McCreesh)* v *Armagh CC Judge* [1978] NI 164, it was done because no right of appeal was available.

221 [1991] NI 70.

222 The transcript is part of the record having been put in by the challenged party: *In re Quinn* [1988] 2 NIJB 10, at 21. Of course it must be remembered that a disciplinary decision by a prison governor may be an administrative, not a judicial proceeding (see para. 19.15).

223 [1982] QB 304.

224 [1987] 6 NIJB 94, at 100-1.

225 *Craig* v *South Australia* (1995) 69 ALJR 873.

226 [1980] 9 NIJB at 4.

227 It was said in *R v Belfast Recorder ex p McNally* [1992] NI 217, at 236e, that only an affidavit from the challenged body can supplement the record.

228 [1984] NI 373, at 386.

In *R* v *Department of Environment ex p Scullion*[229] a *verbatim* note of the judge's judgment was treated as part of the record by agreement of the parties. The record includes any other document referred to or quoted in the formal order.[230] Possibly, if the court record is incomplete, the High Court may direct it to be completed.[231]

19.46 *Lack of evidence.* The traditional view has been, especially in Ireland, that a decision of a competent court within jurisdiction cannot be quashed on ground of no or insufficient evidence for it,[232] unless it is evident on the face of the record: the classic authority is *R (Martin)* v *Mahony.*[233] So also an acquittal or dismiss cannot be reviewed for no evidence of a defence or exception to liability.[234] However in *Neill* v *North Antrim Magistrates' Court*[235] the House of Lords seems to have moved towards the position that such a decision, though not perhaps a nullity, is voidable and quashable on *certiorari* if it has caused an injustice for which there is no other remedy.

19.47 The *collateral decision* of a court can be challenged as a review of the exercise of discretion or on *Wednesbury* grounds. This covers decisions as to granting legal aid;[236] or adjournment;[237] or as to waiving non-compliance with a rule of procedure;[238] or as to an interlocutory decision.[239] The decision as to whether a question has been raised which can be referred to the European Court under Article 177 of the Treaty of Rome is reviewable.[240] Traditionally a mere error by the court as to the admissibility of evidence on the issue which it has to decide, is not amenable to judicial review, and that was not disputed in *Neill* v *North Antrim Magistrates' Ct.*[235]

VOID OR VOIDABLE

19.48 It is only in the case of excess or want of jurisdiction (which includes an error of law) that a judicial decision is void; otherwise it is voidable only. The High Court has a discretion to refuse *certiorari,*[241] or validate the decision

---

229 [1992] NI 278, at 281a.

230 *In re Doherty* [1988] NI 14, at 31A. And see *Hockes* v *Yelland* (1984) 157 CLR 124.

231 *In re Stevenson* [1984] NI 373, at 385C.

232 Except in extradition cases.

233 [1910] 2 IR 695, at 707. See *R(Hanna)* v *Min of Health* [1966] NI 52; *R(Proctor)* v *Hutton* [1978] NI 139, at 142; *Roche* v *DJ Martin* [1993] ILRM 651; but see *R (Bobbett)* v *Meath JJ* (1917) 51 ILTR 182.

234 *R (Darcy)* v *Co Carlow JJ* [1916] 2 IR 313.

235 [1992] 1 WLR 1220, at 1233; re-affirmed in *R* v *Bedwellty JJ ex p Williams* [1997] AC 225. See Osborne 'The Floodgates of Judicial Review' (1993) 44 NILQ 233.

236 *In re McCauley* [1992] 4 NIJB 1, at 6; *R* v *Belfast Magistrate ex p McKinney* [1992] NI 63 (where the challenge was to the deferral of decision on legal aid).

237 *In re Murphy* [1991] 7 NIJB 97; *In re Black* [1993] 2 NIJB 63, at 70; *In re Wilson* [1983] 10 NIJB.

238 *In re O'Loughlin* [1985] NI 421.

239 *In re Oaklee Housing Assoc* [1994] 6 BNIL 46.

240 *In re Chief Constable* [1983] 3 NIJB. A decision to refer to the European Court is not a decision on which a case stated can be founded: *Pigs Marketing* v *Redmond* [1978] NI 73 (*obiter*).

241 *R (McSwiggan)* v *Co Londonderry JJ* [1905] 2 IR 318.

under section 18(5) of the Judicature Act, even if it is void. The authorities tend to show that a breach of natural justice and *Wednesbury* unreasonableness makes a decision void,[242] at least where it amounts to a failure to deal with the matter on the merits. The distinction is important in the following ways-

(1) a void decision is a nullity and therefore any enforcement or other proceeding taken on it is also void and unlawful;[243]

(2) a voidable decision may be protected from review if there is a statutory ouster clause, but a void decision is not;

(3) an acquittal by a court of summary jurisdiction cannot be quashed unless it is void;[244]

(4) if a conviction is quashed as void, the accused can be prosecuted again, but if it is quashed as voidable, the quashing operates as an acquittal.[245]

Courts have found great difficulty in distinguishing four categories: (a) errors made in the proper discharge of a decision-making power which are correctable only by such right of appeal as may exist; (b) errors which amount to a misuse of the power and make the decision voidable on *certiorari*; (c) errors which are so fundamental as to constitute a want or excess of jurisdiction and make the decision void if so declared by a court; and (d) errors which make a decision patently void on its face and thus of no effect. The courts, especially in England, in recent times tend to blur the differences and seem to make the distinction on an *ad hoc* basis, allowing the diagnosis to be coloured by the desired end result. The difficulties are well illustrated by the judgments of the House of Lords[246] where it was necessary to put a stop to the prospect that a defendant in a criminal prosecution might call upon the magistrates to act as a court of judicial review of the decision to issue the planning notice of which he was allegedly in breach.

---

242 Supperstone & Goudie p.206; *R* v *Hendon JJ ex p DPP* [1994] QB 167.

243 *In re Doherty* [1988] NI 14 (liquor licence renewed without jurisdiction is not valid). So a void decision can be challenged in ordinary litigation. Where an order varying a tithe rent charge was made by justices without jurisdiction, the tithe owner, even though he had appeared without objecting and had made no application for *certiorari*, was held able to sue on the original tithe: *Blackburne* v *Gernon* (1899) 33 ILTR 119. In theory a void decision can be treated by a person as non-existent, but the courts are reluctant to say so because of the confusion that would ensue if ostensibly valid orders and decisions are prone to be so treated. In almost all cases, the courts say that a void order cannot be treated as a nullity until it is declared void.

244 See the author's *Criminal Procedure in NI*, Chap.17.23; *McMenamin* v *A-G* [1985] 2 NZLR 274 (justices dismissing charge because there were too many cases in the day's list). In *R* v *Hendon JJ ex p DPP* [1994] QB 167, the justices unreasonably refused to wait till the prosecutor arrived in court and entered an acquittal of the defendant, there being no hearing on the merits. The High Court now has statutory power to quash an acquittal where it has been certified by a criminal court, convicting a person of interference with a juror or witness, that such interference may have caused the acquittal: Criminal Procedure and Investigations Act 1996, s.54.

245 *Sweeney* v *DJ Brophy* [1993] 2 IR 202(SC); *Grennan* v *DJ Kirby* [1994] 2 ILRM 199.

246 *R* v *Wicks* [1997] 2 All ER 801.

19.49 It should be remembered that the excess of jurisdiction which is enough to have a body's decision quashed on judicial review is not the same as the excess of jurisdiction which makes the body liable to an action for damages, for example for false imprisonment. The latter requires some exceptional breach of proper procedure.[247] Against a resident magistrate or a county court judge on appeal therefrom, no action lies for damages for an act done in the execution of his duties within his jurisdiction and no action lies for an act done in purported execution of his duties outside his jurisdiction unless in bad faith.[248]

DISCRETION TO REFUSE JUDICIAL REVIEW

19.50 The Court has a discretion to refuse review, for example in the following cases-

(1) The applicant's negligence or behaviour,[249] or lack of candour in the application.

(2) Delay in applying, especially if other persons have acted in reliance on the challenged decision.[250]

(3) Overturning the decision would affect the rights and expectations of other persons who rely on its validity or who have acted on faith of it.[251]

(4) Overturning the decision would cause great administrative inconvenience to the challenged body; but if the reviewability of the decision causes difficulties, it is for Parliament to change the law.[252]

(5) The applicant may be estopped by having accepted the jurisdiction of the challenged body,[253] or failed to object to the irregularity or to the unfairness or bias.[254]

(6) The technicality or triviality of the breach of duty.[255]

(7) The application is premature, being against a preliminary or incidental decision in the course of a proceeding or decision process.

(8) Overturning the decision would create injustice. Where sample cases were brought to challenge the decision of a Minster to remit fines, the Court made a declaration that the remittal of the fines was unlawful, but did not

---

247 *McCann* v *Mullan* [1984] NI 186, at 218-222 (sub nom *In re McC* [1985] AC 528, at 543-7); a point overlooked in *R v Belfast Recorder ex p McNally* [1992] NI 217, at 235d. See also *McGrillen* v *Cullen* [1991] NI 54; and *Harvey* v *Derrick* [1995] 1 NZLR 314.

248 Magistrates Courts (NI) Order 1981, Arts.5-6, 145A. (as amended 1990).

249 *In re O'Neill* [1990] 3 NIJB 1, at 32-4.

250 *State (Cussen)* v *Brennan* [1981] IR 181.

251 *Min of Education* v *Letterkenny Technical College* [1995] 1 ILRM 438(SC).

252 *R* v *Chief Constable ex p McKenna* [1992] NI 116, at 123f.

253 E.g. by appealing against it on the merits: *R (Kildare CC)* v *Commr of Valuation* [1901] 2 IR 215; but not necessarily by litigating on the merits before the challenged body: *Browne* v *An Bord Pleanala* [1991] 2 IR 209.

254 *Auckland Casino* v *Casino Control* [1995] 1 NZLR 142 (CA).

255 *In re Police Association* [1990] NI 258; and see para. 19.80.

quash the remittal because it would be unfair to restore fines only on those persons whose cases had been selected for the test case.[256]

(9) The applicant has suffered no injustice or prejudice (e.g. where the applicant has been wrongly barred from applying for a job for which there was no evidence of any real prospect of being appointed).[257] This aspect is less important where the applicant is a public body seeking to enforce the law.

(10) The review can confer no benefit,[258] such as where the challenged authority would inevitably reach the same decision apart from its error,[259] even if there was a breach of natural justice,[260] and even if the decision is void.[261]

(11) The effect of implementing the decision which should have been made would be trivial.

(12) Where the only effect would be on the course of a criminal trial outside Northern Ireland.[262]

(13) The matter is spent,[263] though the Court may still grant *certiorari* or a declaration if the point is of general importance and no person's interests would be prejudiced.[264]

(14) The Court will give some deference to the decisions of fact and even of law of a specialist administrative body or tribunal in areas of special expertise, on the basis that the body itself is best able to interpret and apply its statutory framework.[265]

(15) Statute confers full and exclusive jurisdiction to review on another body.[266]

(16) The applicant has not fully pursued other remedies.[267]

Alternative remedy

19.51 Review is not barred by the existence of a right of appeal, unless it is more effective and convenient;[268] but may be refused if an effective appeal is pending.[269] English case law tends to treat the existence of an alternative

---

256 *Brennan* v *Minister of Justice* [1995] 1 IR 612.

257 *In re Ó Cathain*, QBD, NI (Girvan J) undated 1996.

258 *In re Hunter* [1989] 1 NIJB 86.

259 *R (Campbell College)* v *Dept of Education* [1982] NI 125.

260 *In re Quinn* [1988] 2 NIJB 10, at 21-4.

261 *R(McPherson)* v *Min of Education* (1973)[1980] NI 115, at 121; *R(McSwiggan)* v *Co Londonderry JJ* [1905] 2 IR 318.

262 *In re McGlinchey* [1987] 3 NIJB 1.

263 *In re Stafford* [1990] 5 BNIL 1; *Barry* v *Fitzpatrick* [1996] 1 ILRM 513.

264 *R (DHSS)* v *Nat Ins Commrs* [1980] 8 NIJB at 10-13.

265 *Canada (AG)* v *Mossop* (1993) 100 DLR 4th 658; [1994] 2 LRC 436 (SC, Canada).

266 *In re Wislang* [1984] NI 63.

267 *R* v *Chief Constable ex p McKenna* [1992] NI 116.

268 *In re McFarland* [1987] NI 246, at 254; *CR* v *An Bord Uchtála* [1993] 3 IR 535.

269 *R(Miller)* v *Monaghan JJ* (1906) 40 ILTR 51; *State (Roche)* v *Delap* [1980] IR 170.

remedy as a bar in all but exceptional cases.[270] A right of appeal is no less effective by reason of the need for leave to appeal, as it is there only to sift out hopeless cases.[271] Even where the applicant was denied natural justice, his right of appeal will be regarded as a sufficient remedy unless the circumstances and purpose of the statutory context is such that the applicant is entitled to a fair hearing at both the original and the appellate stage;[272]a person tried for a criminal offence before a magistrates' court is so entitled, so that his right of appeal by re-hearing to the county court is no bar to judicial review if there is a good arguable case that the magistrate breached natural justice or procedural propriety.[273] But where the only ground of judicial review is a breach of natural justice or procedural irregularity, judicial review may be allowed to proceed as the Court is as least as well able to deal with that complaint as any appellate tribunal.[274] In an application for *certiorari*, the Court may defer the decision to grant leave until the expiry of the time limit for any right of appeal against the judgment or order sought to be quashed (Ord.53 r.3(7)). Review of refusal of access to a solicitor by a detained suspect will not be refused on the ground that the prejudice can be raised in the event of a confession at a possible future criminal trial.[275] Where a person complains to the 'ombudsman' about maladministration by specified local public bodies, a report finding injustice entitles the complainant to damages and/or an injunction in the county court under the Commissioner for Complaints (NI) Order 1996 (Art.16). There is no such right in cases of maladministration by UK or NI Government Departments under the Parliamentary Commissioner Act 1967 and Ombudsman (NI) Order 1996.

Discretion where review refused

19.51a On the other hand, in cases where the Court dismisses the application for review it may direct that no action be taken to enforce the challenged decision if there is no substantial purpose to be served.[276]

PROCEDURE IN CIVIL CAUSES

19.52 In ordinary circumstances, an intending applicant should complain in writing to the challenged body and await its reply before commencing judicial review.[277] Such a step is probably inappropriate in the case of a judicial decision, where the court is *functus officio* and there may be a set procedure for reviewing or appealing the decision. A party to a court proceeding who intends *bona fide* to apply for judicial review of its decision can apply to that court for

---

270 Supperstone & Goudie pp.341-6; *Harley Development* v *Commr of Inland Revenue* [1996] 1 WLR 727 (PC).

271 *Delmas* v *Vancouver Stock Exchange* (1996) 130 DLR 4th 461 (BC, CA).

272 *Calvin* v *Carr* [1980] AC 574, at 592-3.

273 *R* v *Hereford Mag Ct ex p Rowlands* [1997] 2 WLR 854 (DC).

274 *In re Jamison*, QDB, NI (Kerr J) 14 October 1996.

275 *R* v *Chief Constable ex p McKenna* [1992] NI 116.

276 *In re Tarr* [1995] 2 BNIL 59, where it would have required the applicant to go back to prison for ten days.

277 *R* v *Horsham DC ex p Wenman* [1995] 1 WLR 680, at 709; a case of reviewing a decision of a local council.

a stay of enforcement of its decision, and where the immediate enforcement would hamper the reversal of the decision, the court should grant it.[278]

19.53 Under the old procedure, the application was brought in the name of the Queen on the part of X, the aggrieved applicant, against the court, body or official whose decision is to be reviewed. Under the new Northern Ireland procedure the matter is entitled "In re an application by X for judicial review". The applicant should be a person with a legal grievance against the challenged decision, which in the case of a decision made in some form of proceedings means a party to those proceedings, not a person whose welfare is at issue.[279] If leave *ex parte* is given, X then serves notice of the motion for judicial review on persons directly affected, that is in most cases: (a) the official, body or court whose decision is challenged; and (b) the other party, if any, in favour of whom the challenged decision was made. The latter is sometimes called "the respondent", sometimes, and more properly, the "notice party". Throughout these notes X will be described as the "applicant", the decision-maker as the "challenged party", and the other party as the "adversary party". Normally it is the adversary party who appears in court to resist the application. The challenged body usually does so only if there was no-one else involved in the decision against the applicant (which is more likely to be the case in review of an administrative decision) in which case the challenged party and the adversary party are the same person. A challenged judicial body has a right to contest the review by affidavit and by appearing though counsel,[280] but where there were two contesting parties before it, it should not resist the application unless its *bona fides* is questioned or there are other exceptional circumstances.[281] Especially in the case of a judicial body, in the absence of an adversary party with a desire in interest in resisting review, the Attorney-General, Official Solicitor, Lord Chancellor, NI Court Service or other public body may take on the role of adversary party.

Application for leave

19.54 Save where the Attorney-General is seeking *certiorari*, leave for judicial review must be sought by *ex parte* application, lodging in the Central Office a statement of the applicant's identity, the relief sought and the grounds (which can be amended by leave of the Court), verified by affidavit in which the facts and points of complaint are stated (Ord.53 r.3(1)(2)(4)). It carries a court fee of £40, which is credited against the fee for the originating motion. The power to grant leave may be exercised in chambers (Ord.53 r.3(3)): this means that a master may hear it if it is a civil cause or matter unless it relates to the liberty of the subject or an injunction is sought (Ord.32 r.11). An urgent application may be heard by the judge during vacation (Ord.64 r.4(1)). In accordance with advices given by Lord Lowry LCJ in the 1980s, a master

---

278 *In re J McL* [1986] NI 397, at 416 (county court order of custody with leave to remove child from Northern Ireland).

279 So thought Girvan J in *In re Kerr,* QDB, NI, 31 July 1996, but he declined to rule because the objection was taken too late in the judicial review proceedings.

280 *In re Darley,* QBD, NI (Girvan J) 16 June 1997.

281 *R* v *Newcastle-under-Lyme JJ ex p Massey* [1994] 1 WLR 1684, at 1692C.

either grants leave or if he is doubtful or minded to refuse refers it to a judge under Order 32 rule 12; a master never refuses leave himself.[282] An *ex parte* application is made by motion on '*ex parte* docket' and usually is determined by the master on the papers with no hearing, but if the application is referred to a judge there may be an oral hearing of applicant's counsel. The affidavit should be sworn personally by the applicant, unless he is in custody and his solicitor has been denied access to him.[283] The applicant has a duty of *uberrimae fides*.[284] The application should deal with the question whether there are alternative remedies available, and if there are, then why judicial review is justified. Legal aid is available (see para. 3.58).

19.55 The Judicature Act (s.18(2)(a)) and Order 53 rule 3(1) expressly state that the Attorney-General seeking *certiorari* on behalf of the Crown can apply directly without having to obtain leave of the Court. There is no equivalent in the English provisions. It is significant in several ways. The Attorney-General does not have to show sufficient interest in the matter; obviously as custodian of public law his interest is presumed. Also he is not subject to the time limit in Order 53 rule 4.[285]

19.56 Leave will be granted -

(1) if there is a serious issue which ought to be determined; that is, prima facie an arguable case,[286] a case fit for further investigation on *inter partes* hearing;[287] and

(2) if the Court considers that there is a prima facie case that the applicant has *locus standi* (a "sufficient interest").[288] The test is: does the statute give an express or implied right to a person in the position of the applicant to complain?[288] or does the decision affect the financial or non-material interests or the right to be consulted of the applicant or of the persons whom, as representative, spokesman, pressure group or public authority, the applicant represents?[289] or does it affect the interests which a body is empowered by statute to promote?[290] At this stage leave will be refused only if the applicant's claimed interest is entirely specious (the 'busybody' test).[291] In seeking *mandamus* to review refusal to release a prisoner who

---

282 Ironically this policy of never exercising the power to refuse leave would be challengeable by judicial review if the master were an inferior court.

283 *In re Cullen* [1987] 5 NIJB 102, at 106.

284 *R(Cross)* v *Co Tyrone JJ* (1908) 42 ILTR 112.

285 This confirms the position under the old law as stated in *In re an Application by the A-G* [1965] NI 67.

286 *Ho Ming-sai* v *Director of Immigration* [1994] 1 LRC 409 (Hong Kong CA).

287 *In re Jones* [1996] 9 BNIL 84 (Campbell J).

288 S.18(4); Ord.53 r.3(5); *In re Hogan* [1986] 5 NIJB 81, at 91-102.

289 *R* v *Secretary of State for Foreign Affairs, ex p World Development Movement* [1995] 1 WLR 386 (DC).

290 *R* v *Employment Sec ex p EOC* [1995] 1 AC 1.

291 *R* v *IRC ex p Nat Fed of Self-employed* [1982] AC 617. See also *G* v *DPP* [1994] 1 IR 374(SC). See Graham, 'Judicial Review: From the Frog to Mickey Mouse' (1981) 32 NILQ 284.

was ill, it was held that his MP and his sister did not have *locus standi.*[292] Geoghegan J has held that in challenging a government decision to remit a sentence of a court, the trial judge has *locus* standi to apply, and he even said that no-one else has, not the victim, not the DPP or police.[293] An application for judicial review in respect of the decision or failure to act of a council on a matter affecting accounts can be brought by the Local Government Auditor.[294]

19.57 *Delay.* The application for leave must be made promptly and within three months from the date when the grounds arose (or within any specific statutory time limit), unless there is good reason to extend the time (Ord.53 r.4(1)(3)).[295] In *certiorari* against a judgment, order, conviction or other proceeding, the ground arises on the date of the judgment etc. (Ord.53 r.4(2)). 'The date of the proceedings' is the date when the challenged court pronounced its order or decision, not the later date when that decision was drawn up as a speaking order.[296] Review can be refused for lack of promptness even if made within three months.[297] Even if the application is promptly brought, it is a good idea to make that clear in the affidavit. Notice must be given to the adversary party of application to extend time. The applicant must show an explanation for the delay by his affidavit.[298] The explanation for delay must be disclosed in the application for leave.[303] To extend time the applicant should usually show a basis in evidence to account for all periods of delay, balanced against the prejudice to the adversary party; the liberty of the subject, and the issue of public rights are to be taken into account; and the extension can be reconsidered at the full hearing.[299] The applicant may put forward the default of his own previous solicitor as a ground for extending time, provided that he can account for all periods of delay.[300] Pursuit of legal aid for the application can be an excuse.[301] The Legal Aid authority often requires counsel's opinion or other information before granting legal aid and a short delay for that reason is regarded with sympathy. Delay caused by the pursuit of an alternative remedy

---

[292] *R (Diamond and Fleming)* v *Warnock* [1946] NI 171.

[293] *Brennan* v *Minister of Justice* [1995] 1 IR 612.

[294] Local Government Act (NI) 1972, s.82D.

[295] Since 1989 the Rules no longer require absence of hardship or prejudice to other persons. We have no express equivalent of the section of the English Act which permits the Court to refuse leave or refuse review where the application was unduly delayed and review is likely to cause substantial hardship or substantial prejudice to any person or harm to good administration. However the hardship or prejudice issue is still regarded as an important factor: *In re McCabe* , QBD, NI (Kerr J) 20 September 1994.

[296] *Re Min of Home Affairs* [1972] May NIJB. In that case Jones J refused to extend time, but his refusal must have been overturned in some way because the application was subsequently heard on the merits: see *R (Sec of State)* v *Recorder of Belfast* [1973] NI 112.

[297] *In re Shearer* [1993] 2 NIJB 12, at 27; *In re McCabe,* QBD, NI (Kerr J) 20 September 1994.

[298] *O'Flynn* v *Mid-Western Health Board* [1991] 2 IR 223.

[299] *In re Wilson* [1989] NI 415.

[300] *In re McCabe*, QBD, NI (Kerr J) 20 September 1994.

[301] *R* v *Wareham Mag Ct ex p Seldon* [1988] 1 WLR 825, at 827C.

is excusable.[302] The importance of the issue is no excuse for delay, rather the reverse.[303] Where a council's decision to close its facilities on a Sunday was challenged well out of time, the delay was waived in the unusual circumstances that the council was awaiting the disposal of the current judicial review and would then debate the issue again and certainly reach the decision to maintain closure upon which a new application could be brought.[304]

19.58 Leave is refused if the Court is satisfied that the challenged party is a person or body of such nature that *certiorari*, *mandamus*, or prohibition cannot be granted against it (Judicature Act, s.18(2)(b); Ord.53 r.3(6)). If reviewability of the decision is an arguable issue, the benefit of any doubt should be given to the applicant at this stage and leave should be given.[305]

19.59 In an application for *certiorari*, the Court may defer its decision until the expiry of the time limit for any right of appeal against the judgment or order sought to be quashed (Ord.53 r.3(7)).

19.60 In practice the master who is minded to refuse leave always refers the application directly to a judge under Order 32 rule 12. If the master were to refuse leave, the applicant would have an automatic right of appeal within five days to a judge (Ord.58 r.1). The Court may direct the applicant to appear and must allow the applicant a chance to be heard before refusing leave (Ord.53 r.3(10)). If in doubt, the judge may invite the proposed adversary party to appear before deciding whether to grant leave,[306] by fixing a day and time for an oral hearing and instructing the court officer to contact the solicitors for the applicant and adversary party by telephone. If the adversary party attends he is within the definition of 'party' under the Judicature Act (s.120).[307] Apart from the obligatory oral hearing when the judge is minded to refuse leave, the judge will direct an oral hearing if there has been delay in applying; if the grounds of relief are not clearly specified; if the proposed adversary party may be able to contribute to the airing of issues at this stage; or if the judge wishes to arrange a timetable for the progress of the application. Leave may be subject to terms as to costs or security (Ord.53 r.3(8)). The Court may direct or allow the statement to be amended by altering or adding grounds or otherwise (Ord.53 r.3(4)). If the applicant is not present he must be informed of the result of the application (Ord.53 r.3(12)). Granting leave for *mandamus*, declaration or injunction allows the Court to grant interim relief such as is available in an action; and leave to apply for *certiorari* or prohibition operates, if the Court so directs, as a stay of the reviewed proceedings (para. 19.69).

---

302 *In re Trainor* [1997] 1 BNIL 33 (Kerr J) ; *In re Bailie* [1995] 7 BNIL 82 (Kerr J).

303 *In re Black* [1993] 2 NIJB 63, at 66-7.

304 *In re O'Neill*, QBD, NI (Kerr J) 20 March 1995.

305 *O'Neill* v *Iarnrod Eireann* [1991] ILRM 129.

306 *R* v *Sec of State for Home Dept ex p Begum* [1990] COD 107.

307 Contrast *R* v *Camden LBC ex p Martin*, [1997] 1 All ER 307, decided under a different definition of 'party'.

19.61 The Court may grant *mandamus*, *certiorari* or prohibition forthwith if special circumstances warrant it (Ord.53 r.3(9)).[308] Having been granted *ex parte*, any person affected may apply to set the order aside.

Challenging the decision as to leave

19.62 In a civil cause or matter, the applicant can "appeal" [*sic*] to the Court of Appeal against refusal of leave, without leave (Ord.53 r.10(a)). The 'appeal' is not an appeal from the refusal of the High Court because the refusal of a court to give leave to apply to itself is not appealable,[309] rather it is a renewal of the *ex parte* application for leave under Order 59 rule 14(3).[310] The distinction is important, because if it is an appeal the time limit for appeal is 21 days, but if it is a renewal the time limit is seven days. No appeal lies to the House of Lords from the refusal of the Court of Appeal to grant leave.[311]

19.63 In a civil cause the Court of Appeal, if it grants leave on 'appeal' from refusal, may allow the substantive application *inter partes* to be heard by the High Court, or may itself hear it (Ord.53 r.5(8)). It has even been held that the Court of Appeal has a quasi-original jurisdiction to grant judicial review in the course of a pending statutory appeal before it,[312] and on appeal in *habeas corpus*.[313] The Court of Appeal in *In re Bignell*[314] regarded the procedure of appeal and renewal as alternative routes to challenge the refusal of leave; the applicant having challenged the refusal of leave by way of renewal of the application, the Court invited her to do so by way of an appeal, so that the Court could then grant leave and hear the full application (which it in fact dismissed).

19.64 The concept of the Court of Appeal having an 'original' jurisdiction to grant leave for judicial review or hear the application itself seems to be repugnant to the principle that its substantive jurisdiction is wholly statutory. In *In re Racal*[315] it was said that the Court of Appeal has no original jurisdiction in judicial review. In *WEA Records* v *Visions Channel 4*[316] Donaldson MR said: "The Court of Appeal hears appeals from orders and judgments. It does not hear original applications ... save in respect of an entirely anomalous form of

---

308 As in *In re Wilson* [1983] 10 NIJB (a criminal cause where the Divisional Court had to be convened to do so).

309 *R* v *Home Secretary ex p Turkoglu* [1988] QB 398; *R* v *Monopolies Commission ex p Argyll Group* [1986] 1 WLR 763, at 774A (*obiter*); cf. *Lane* v *Esdaile* [1891] AC 210; *In re Poh* [1983] 1 WLR 2 (HL). In *In re Poh*, the applicant refused leave in the Divisional Court of the High Court, then appealed *ex parte* for leave to the Court of Appeal which refused; Lord Diplock said, at 3D: " Their Lordships are not concerned with the procedure whereby this application moved from the Divisional Court to the Court of Appeal."

310 See Lewis p.242 n.12; Superstone & Goudie pp.389-90; *O'Neill* v *Iarnrod Eireann* [1991] ILRM 129 (*per* Finlay CJ; the other two judges called it an appeal).

311 *In re Poh* [1983] 1 WLR 2.

312 *Chief Adjudication Officer* v *Foster* [1992] QB 31; affirmed without comment on this point [1993] AC 754.

313 *R* v *Home Sec ex p Muboyayi* [1992] QB 244.

314 CA, NI, 21 March 1997.

315 [1981] AC 374, at 381H and 388E.

316 [1983] 1 WLR 721, at 727.

proceeding in relation to the grant of leave to apply ... for judicial review". But how can this anomaly arise? Possibly from the inherited jurisdiction[317] of the old Court of Appeal which could grant a rule *nisi* for a writ of *certiorari* refused by the High Court and then hear the application for a rule absolute.[318]

19.65 Leave having been granted *ex parte*, the adversary party can apply to the High Court to set aside the leave. For obvious reasons, the Court does not encourage a re-opening of the decision to grant leave. He bears a heavy burden in seeking to show that there is no arguable case for review; unless the issue he raises is one of pure law, in which case the Court should fully investigate it.[319] Leave can be set aside if it is shown that the applicant did not disclose a material fact. On the principle of *Lane* v *Esdaile*,[320] the adversary party should not be able to appeal against the High Court's granting of leave; but in *R* v *Special Educational Need Tribunal ex p South Glamorgan CC*[321] the Court of Appeal allowed an appeal against the judge's refusal to set aside leave. Case law suggests that if leave is set aside, the application for leave can be renewed to the Court of Appeal, rather than by appeal against the order setting aside.[322]

The originating motion

19.66 Leave having been granted, the applicant proceeds, within 14 days of the leave (Ord 53 r.5(5)), to issue an originating motion. The motion carries a Court fee of £150, less the £40 paid on the application for leave. If before doing so the challenged party satisfies the grievance, the applicant should apply by motion on notice for his costs (White Book (1997) 53/1-14/53). The notice of motion recites who gave leave and the date thereof, and specifies the relief and refers to the previous statement and affidavit on which leave was sought; the notice and the statement are served on all persons directly affected, and if seeking *certiorari* or *mandamus* arising from court/tribunal proceedings, on the clerk and judge of the reviewed court; it must be for hearing not less than ten days after service (Ord.53 r.5). Although the 14-day time limit is extendable, it should be strictly adhered to as it may be the first intimation to the other parties of the existence of the challenge.[323] Generally the notice is to be served on the challenged party, and on the adversary party (i.e. the person, if any, who was the opposite party in the challenged proceedings). 'Directly affected' means affected without intervention of any intermediate agency, so a Government minister is not directly affected merely because he will have to subsidise the liability of the challenged body.[324] In *In re Breslin*[325] where review was sought

---

317 Under s.34(2)(a) of the Judicature Act.

318 See *R* v *Industrial Injuries Commr ex p AEU* [1966] 2 QB 21. See also the speeches of Lord Hailsham LC and Lord Denning in *Hansard* HL Debs (1985) Vol. 459 col.943; Vol. 461 cols.443-64.

319 *Re Savage* [1991] NI 103, at 106-7.

320 [1891] AC 210.

321 'The Times', 12 December 1995.

322 White Book (1997) 53/1-14/34; Supperstone & Goudie pp.360-1, & 393.

323 *R* v *Institute of Chartered Accountants ex p Andreou* (1996) 8 Admin LR 557; [1997] 1 CLM 13 (CA).

324 *R* v *Rent Officer, ex p Muldoon* [1996] 3 All ER 498; sub nom *R* v *Liverpool CC, ex p Muldoon* [1996] 1 WLR 1103 (HL).

of a decision vested by statute in the Lord Chancellor, notice was served on the Northern Ireland Court Service. The applicant serves the notice of motion, the statement and affidavit on which leave was granted (see Ord.53 r.6(1)), and in practice also any further affidavits intended for use at the hearing. The adversary party can apply to strike out the motion as an abuse of process (Ord.18 r.19), but he has a difficult task here as leave has already been granted.

Matters arising pending the hearing

19.67 *Semble*, judicial review does not abate on the death of a party.[326] In *Wells* v *NI Office* [327] the application continued after the death of the applicant, who died before judgment as respondent on appeal.

19.68 The applicant is confined to any one or more of the reliefs and grounds specified in the statement and the application (Ord.53 r.5(1)), unless the Court directs or allows an amendment (Judicature Act, s.18(2)(c)(d)). Then before it is entered for hearing, he files an affidavit stating where, when and on whom the notice of motion has been served, and why any proper person has not been served (Ord.53 r.5(6)). No adversary party need enter an appearance, defence or return to the motion (s.18(6)); but every party must supply on demand copies of any affidavit intended to be used at the hearing (Ord.53 r.6(4)). In practice, each party files and serves his affidavits automatically. There is some onus on the challenged party to give full and fair disclosure of what it did and why, so far as necessary to meet the challenge.[328] Having received the opposing affidavits, it is the duty of the applicant's legal advisers to reconsider the merits of the application.[329]

19.69 The Court may grant a stay of proceedings or of enforcement of an order, or interim relief pending determination of the judicial review (s.19), and may suspend a disqualification from driving pending *certiorari* of the conviction or sentence.[330] Interim orders are often done when leave is granted (Ord.53 r.3(13)), but can be done at any time before leave has been granted (if urgent) or thereafter, but not after leave has been refused.[331] If the application for leave is renewed to the Court of Appeal, that Court may grant interim relief.[331] If interim relief is refused on the *ex parte* application for leave, the application for interim relief can be renewed in the Court of Appeal.[332] In *In re Cullen*[333] the High Court on a prisoner's application granted leave to review a governor's adjudication which meant loss of remission which would otherwise entitle the applicant to immediate release; it was held that in giving leave the Court should also grant interim relief by suspending the adjudication and thus effecting the prisoner's immediate release pending the decision on judicial

325 [1987] NI 1. See previous page.
326 *R* v *Roberts* (1732) 2 Str 937 (93 ER 953).
327 [1993] 5 NIJB 61.
328 *R* v *Lancashire CC ex p Huddleston* [1986] 2 All ER 941.
329 *R* v *Horsham DC ex p Wenman* [1995] 1 WLR 680, at 701.
330 Road Traffic Offenders (NI) Order 1996, Art.45(5).
331 *M* v *Home Office* [1994] 1 AC 377, at 423.
332 *R* v *Chief Constable ex p McKenna* [1992] NI 116.
333 [1987] 5 NIJB 102(CA).

review. In *In re Black*[334] the Court suspended disqualification from driving pending review of the magistrate's order. In *Minister of Foreign Affairs* v *Vehicles and Supplies Ltd*[335] the Privy Council held that the Court cannot grant a stay of a non-judicial order; but the English Court of Appeal has refused to follow that decision: see *R* v *Home Sec ex p Muboyayi.*[336] If the stay of an administrative order will affect the operations of a third party, the Court should apply the principles on which interlocutory injunctions are granted.[337] Only on compelling grounds will the Court restrain publication of the challenged body's decision.[338]

19.70 The Court can grant an interlocutory injunction but for a mandatory injunction the applicant must show a strong prima facie case.[339] An injunction cannot be given directly against the Crown,[340] but it seems now that it can be given against a minister or officer of the Crown.[341] The Court cannot grant an interim declaration against anyone.[342] It seems that, in a case where the applicant is likely to recover damages (para. 19.88), he can apply for interim damages under Order 29 rule 12 (see Ord.29 r.20).

19.71 The Court can grant discovery under Order 24 rule 3, there being no automatic discovery. The principles are the same as in writ actions, but in ordinary judicial review cases discovery will be shown to be unnecessary, and the applicant has an evidential burden before the adversary party has to prove it to be unnecessary.[343] Discovery is not necessary to challenge an assertion in the adversary party's affidavits unless the applicant can show from some other source that the affidavits may be insufficient, inadequate or inaccurate.[343] Discovery is unnecessary on the issue whether the challenged party's decision is unreasonable, unless there is a case for arguing that its decision is founded on inaccurate evidence; nor is discovery necessary on the issue of fairness, breach

---

334 [1993] 2 NIJB 63, at 66.

335 [1991] 1 WLR 551, at 556H.

336 [1992] QB 244, at 269.

337 *R* v *Pollution Inspectorate ex p Greenpeace* [1994] 1 WLR 570.

338 *R* v *Advertising Standards Authority ex p Vernons* [1992] 1 WLR 1289.

339 *R* v *Kensington & Chelsea LBC ex p Hammell* [1989] QB 518, at 528A, 531E.

340 Save to protect EC law rights pending a ruling by the European Court of Justice: *R* v *Transport Sec ex p Factortame (no 2)* [1991] 1 AC 603 (case where the validity of a UK statute was at issue).

341 *M* v *Home Office* [1994] 1 AC 377, at 405-23.

342 White Book (1997) 15/16/7; but see *R* v *Sec of State for Environment, ex p Royal Society for Protection of Birds* [1995] CLY 2162 (HL), discussed by Houseman [1996] JR 34.

343 *In re McGuigan*, [1994] 6 BNIL 1 (CA); *In re Rooney,* CA, NI, 12 September 1995. Even where the decision was based on facts which the applicant asserts from his own knowledge to be incorrect, discovery is not necessary because the correctness of the decision is not *per se* at issue in judicial review. The fact that the adversary party will be able to claim public interest immunity if discovery is ordered is no reason for ordering discovery (*per* Hutton LCJ at p.16). "An assertion, albeit on oath by the person with the best knowledge of the matter that the material before the [challenged party] was incorrect or incomplete [is not] enough to ground an order discovery" (*per* Carswell LJ at p.9).

of procedure or natural justice,[344] nor on an issue of failure to state reasons or failure to consult: these points are obviously known to the applicant without discovery.[345] Nor is it necessary as to factual material where the complaint is that the challenged party has failed to take that material into account.[346] If inspection is sought and resisted on a claim of public interest immunity, the Court must first decide that the documents are likely to help the applicant's case and then balance the competing interests of justice against public interest.[347] The restrictions placed on discovery in judicial review have arisen only in the last few years in the English and NI Courts of Appeal, and some view them as unduly cautious. Whilst appreciating that the merits of a decision are not at issue in judicial review and that issues of fact are rarely at issue, it could be argued that discovery is useful in disclosing what the challenged body perceived to be relevant factors in making its decision, and there may arise cases where there is a factual dispute as to what procedures were adopted.

19.72 *Semble*, the Court has inherent jurisdiction to grant bail, save where the applicant is imprisoned under a criminal conviction, where the power to grant bail is given by section 25(4) of the Judicature Act.

19.73 Where the applicant is under detention in a civil matter (e.g. immigration) the High Court can grant bail at any time while the application for leave is pending, or on granting leave, or whilst the motion for judicial review is pending; and if he refuses bail there is an appeal to the Court of Appeal under section 35(1) of the Judicature Act. If the High Court refuses leave it is *functus officio* and cannot grant bail, but if the application for leave is renewed to the Court of Appeal that Court can grant bail.[348]

19.74 An interlocutory application may (i.e. should) be made directly to a judge in chambers, unless a judge or master otherwise directs (Ord.53 r.8(1)). An interlocutory order made by a master can be appealed under Order 58, not to a judge in chambers, but to the Court, that is, in a civil cause, to a judge in open court (Ord.53 r.8(2)). From the judge appeal lies by leave of the judge or the Court of Appeal, to the Court of Appeal. Urgent applications during vacation may be heard by the vacation judge (Ord.64 r.4(1)).

The hearing of the motion

19.75 The motion, in a civil cause, is heard by a single judge.[349] Where the Court of Appeal has granted leave, that Court may decide to hear the motion (Ord.53 r.5(8)). Any party may apply by summons for the hearing to take place

---

[344] *In re Glor Na nGael* [1991] NI 117, at 132-3; but note that the challenged body's duty to gave fair disclosure of its actions may be assisted by orders for discovery or interrogatories: *R* v *Lancashire CC ex p Huddleston* [1986] 2 All ER 941, at 947d.

[345] *In re Rooney, per* Carswell LJ at p.10.

[346] *In re FW Wellworth* [1996] 6 BNIL 1 (CA). In that case the question was raised but not decided, whether discovery could be ordered against an adversary party.

[347] *In re McKee* [1990] 11 NIJB 1.

[348] *R* v *Home Secretary ex p Turkoglu* [1988] QB 398.

[349] In *Re Coleman* [1988] NI 205, at 209, the Court of Appeal held that the hearing of a civil cause or matter by a Divisional Court of two judges was an irregularity but not such as to render the Divisional Court's decision a nullity.

on urgent need during vacation (Ord.64 r.4(2)). The Court may direct or allow the grounds and/or relief in the statement to be amended, and may allow him to use further affidavits;[350] if the applicant wishes to so apply he must give prior notice to every party (Ord.53 r.6(2)(3)).[351] At the hearing the Court may adjourn for the notice to be served on any person whom the Court thinks should be served (Ord.53 r.5(7)).[352] Any person who appears to be a proper person to be heard, though not served, may intervene at the hearing (Ord.53 r.9(1)). Apart from those rules, there is inherent jurisdiction to ensure that any person who might be affected can intervene.[353]

19.76 Except presumably in very urgent cases where the Court may hear oral evidence, all evidence is adduced by affidavit. A clear statement of fact in a party's affidavit should be believed unless shown by other evidence or inferred from other facts to be unreliable.[354] The Court can order a deponent to attend for cross-examination (Ord.38 r.2(3), which order may be made on interlocutory application in chambers (Ord.53 r.8(1)). Cross-examination should be allowed in the Court's discretion and only if necessary in the interests of justice.[355] Generally, since judicial review is not an appeal by rehearing, evidence of facts occurring since the challenged decision is not relevant.[356] In reviewing an error of law as to jurisdiction or on the face of the record, no evidence is admissible;[357] but is admissible as to an error of jurisdiction as to a condition precedent fact.[358] A decision in excess of jurisdiction or in breach of natural justice or procured by fraud, can be reviewed by affidavit or other evidence exploring fully the facts.[359]

19.77 The burden of proof is on the applicant but if a prima facie case of illegality is shown, the adversary party must prove justification for any infringement of rights or property.[360] Any burden of proof must be discharged on the balance of probabilities.[361]

19.78 There is no issue estoppel *per rem judicatem* in judicial review, even if the parties are the same as in a previous application.[362] There are three reasons for this: (a) the application is technically brought in the name of the Crown; (b) there is no *lis* between the applicant and the respondent and no pleading of

---

350 An unrestricted power since the 1993 amendment.

351 See *In re Stevenson* [1984] NI 373, at 378-9 (decision before amendment of the rules).

352 As in *In re NIES* [1987] NI 271, at 274.

353 *R* v *Minister of Agriculture ex p Anastasiou* [1994] COD 329 (Popplewell J).

354 *In re Russell* [1990] NI 188, at 193G.

355 *Roussell Uclaf* v *Pharmaceutical Management* [1997] 1 NZLR 650 (CA).

356 *Meng Ching Hai* v *AG* [1992] LRC (Const) 840 (CA Hong Kong).

357 *R (Lee)* v *Fermanagh JJ* (1936) 70 ILTR 132 (NI).

358 Wade & Forsyth p.319.

359 *R (Burns)* v *Tyrone CC Judge* [1961] NI 167.

360 *R* v *Home Sec, ex p Khawaja* [1984] AC 74, especially *per* Lord Scarman.

361 *Khawaja* at 112.

362 *R* v *Environment Secretary ex p Hackney LBC* [1983] 1 WLR 524, *affd.*[1984] 1 WLR 592; *O'Grady* v *Synan* [1900] 2 IR 602. But in *Abrahamson* v *Law Society* [1996] 1 IR 403, McCracken J held that an estoppel *in rem* (binding all the world) arises from the the decision as to the validity of legislation.

issues; and (c) the decision on the application is not a final judgment.[362] As judicial review is not based on any cause of action, presumably there is also no cause of action estoppel, save possibly where the Court awards damages. Where judicial review is sought on grounds X and Y, and the Court granting leave on ground X specifically refused leave on ground Y, the applicant can technically rely on ground Y at the hearing of the substantive motion, but will probably be disallowed as an abuse of process.[363]

19.79 Relief can be granted only if the applicant has sufficient interest in the matter (Judicature Act, s.18(4)). This issue can be reconsidered even though a prima facie interest was shown to justify leave.[364] The Court may grant: (a) *mandamus*; (b) *certiorari*; (c) prohibition; (d) a declaration; (e) an injunction (s.18(1); Ord.53 r.1). Instead or as well, it may grant damages (Ord.53 r.7). The Court may grant any of the above remedies (a) to (e) if claimed and proved whether or not any other appears appropriate (s.18(3)). If the applicant seeks a declaration, injunction or damages, and the Court thinks that the relief might have been granted in a writ action and should not be on judicial review, it may refuse the motion, or may order the proceedings to continue as if begun by writ (Ord.53 r.9(5)).[365] It enables the application to continue as if by writ where the Court finds that the decision affects rights in the private rather than the public law area.[366] Continuance as if by writ means that the parties will have to exchange pleadings, unless the Court directs the affidavits already filed to stand as pleadings, and *semble*, it means that the judicial review remedies cease to be available. Where the Court decides that the grievance involves both public law and private law rights, it can grant judicial review relief, injunction, declaration and/or damages; but it cannot grant other private law remedies, such as ejectment, restitution of goods, rescission or rectification of a contract, payment of money due as a debt. To grant both judicial review and the latter types of remedy, the Court might invite the applicant to issue a writ or originating summons and order it to be tried together with the hearing of the judicial review motion.

19.80 The Court may refuse relief and validate the order of the reviewed authority if (a) the sole ground of relief is a defect in form or technical irregularity and (b) no substantial wrong and no substantial miscarriage of justice has occurred or no remedial advantage could accrue to the applicant (s.18(5)). If the order or conviction of a magistrates' court has a mistake or omission of an obvious or clerical nature which the court should not have made, the High Court on an application to quash it may amend the order and review it

---

[363] *R* v *Staffordshire CC, ex p Ashworth*, 'The Times' 18 October 1996 (Turner J).

[364] *In re Hogan* [1986] 5 NIJB 81, at 91.

[365] As amended in 1989 to overrule *In re Malone* [1988] NI 67, at 84.

[366] *O'Reilly* v *Mackman* [1983] 2 AC 237, at 283H; but see *R* v *Home Secretary ex p Dew* [1987] 1 WLR 881, which held that the power cannot be exercised where the application is wholly outside the scope of judicial review (*sed quaere*). In *In re Phillips*, QBD, NI (Carswell LJ) 18 January 1995, the judge declined to do so because the claim as cast by the applicant was in substance for the quashing of the decision to dismiss him, not for compensation for it.

as if the mistake or omission had not been made.[367] As to further powers on *certiorari*, see below.

Remedies

Certiorari

19.81 *Certiorari* is an order bringing up and quashing a decision. An applicant must lodge in the Central Office a copy of the reviewed order, warrant, record etc., verified by affidavit, or account for failure to do so (Ord.53 r.9(2)), a requirement which the Court can waive.[368] The Court may defer its decision until the expiry of the time limit for any right of appeal against the judgment or order sought to be quashed (Ord.53 r.3(7)). *Certiorari* will not be used to quash a decision of a lower court affirmed on appeal, unless the appellate order is also quashed.[369] The Court can quash a severable part of the challenged decision without touching the rest, but only if excising or altering specific words of the challenged decision (or regulation) leaves a sensible and effective residue in accord with its purpose.[370] If the Court is satisfied of grounds for *certiorari*, it may: (a) remove and quash the reviewed order; (b) reverse or vary it, making the order which the challenged party should have made;[371] or (c) remit the matter to the challenged party with a direction to reconsider its decision in accordance with the Court's ruling (Judicature Act, s.21; Ord.53 r.9(3)(4)).[372] The power to give directions can only be exercised if there are grounds established for quashing the decision.[373] The Court may in its discretion decline to remit and quash the challenged decision outright, as where long delay has supervened.[374] On the other hand, if *certiorari* is refused the Court may direct that no action be taken to enforce the challenged decision if there is no substantial purpose to be served.[375]

Mandamus

19.82 *Mandamus* is an order to perform a duty. *Mandamus* lies against a refusal to act; in such case it must be shown that the challenged party was called upon to do so, unless failure to act was inadvertent and the time limit set

---

367 Magistrates' Courts (NI) Order 1981, Art.159.

368 *State (Wood)* v *West Cork Board* [1936] IR 401.

369 *R (Fleming)* v *Londonderry JJ* (1908) 42 ILTR 205; *State (Quinn)* v *Mangan* [1945] IR 532. But in *Byrne* v *McDonnell* [1996] 1 ILRM 543, Keane J reviewed the District Court order where the Circuit Court judge on appeal had struck out the appeal merely because of the pending judicial review. And in *In re Trainor* [1997] 1 BNIL 33 (Kerr J), the decision of a School Board on admission of a pupil was quashed but the order affirming it by an Appeal Tribunal was upheld. This meant that the School Board had to decide the matter afresh and there was a new appeal to the Tribunal.

370 *R(DHSS)* v *NI Commrs* [1980] 8 NIJB at 9; *DPP* v *Hutchinson* [1990] 2 AC 783.

371 As in *In re McCauley* [1992] 4 NIJB 1, at 9.

372 As in *In re Murphy* [1991] 7 NIJB 97, at 106; and *R (AG)* v *Belfast JJ* [1981] NI 208.

373 *R* v *Belfast Magistrate ex p McKinney* [1992] NI 63, at 65e.

374 *Dawson* v *DJ Hamill (No 2)* [1991] 1 IR 213.

375 *In re Tarr* [1995] 2 BNIL 59, where it would have required the applicant to go back to prison for ten days.

to perform the duty has expired.[376] If a court has wrongly ruled that it has no jurisdiction, *mandamus* lies together with *certiorari* to quash the dismissal,[377] but not where the dismissal is a decision made upon acceptance of jurisdiction to decide.[378] It lies to compel an adjournment only if the challenged party declined to consider an adjournment, that is, declined to exercise its jurisdiction.[379] It lies to stop a court from ordering unreasonable adjournments;[380] against a local authority persistently failing to enforce the law;[381] to a highway authority to repair a road.[382] It does not lie against the Crown,[383] but lies against an officer of the Crown to do an administrative statutory duty.[384] *Mandamus* can be granted after the time limit for performance has expired or after the challenged party has left office, addressed to him or his successor.[376] Failure to comply is contempt;[385] but *semble*, only if the order of *mandamus*, or a subsequent order sets a time limit for compliance (Ord.42 rr.4,5; Ord.45 r.4(1)(a)(2)). Also, if not complied with, the Court may direct the act to be done by someone else at the expense of the disobedient party (Ord.45 r.6).

Prohibition

19.83 Prohibition is an order restraining an intended act or decision outside jurisdiction and is used to challenge the decision of a court that it has jurisdiction;[386] to stop it commencing an inquiry without, or proceeding beyond, jurisdiction;[387] or to stop further prosecution of unfair proceedings.[388] *Semble*, it is enforceable like any prohibitory order under Order 45 rule 4(1)(b). Prohibition does not lie where the challenged body has done its work.[389]

Other remedies

19.84 An *injunction* cannot be granted against the Crown save as interim relief to enforce European Community law.[390] But the Law Lords have now held that an injunction can be given against a minister or official of the Crown in any case where a prerogative order or declaration can be given against him.[391]

---

376 *R* v *Henley Revising Barrister* [1912] 3 KB 518.
377 *State (AG)* v *Judge Connelly* [1948] IR 176.
378 Cf. *Clinton* v *Kell* [1993] 10 NIJB 52, at 58 (a case stated).
379 *In re Wilson* [1983] 10 NIJB at 5; *sed quaere* now.
380 *In re McAleenan* [1985] NI 496, at 506-7.
381 *R (IUDWC)* v *Rathmines UDC* [1928] IR 260.
382 *R (Westropp)* v *Clare RDC* [1904] 2 IR 569.
383 Supperstone & Goudie p.311.
384 The remedies given against the Crown by the Crown Proceedings Act do not prejudice any right of *mandamus*: Crown Proceedings Act, s.40(5).
385 *In re Cook (No 2)* [1986] NI 283.
386 As in *In re Secretary of State* [1991] NI 64.
387 *Devonshire* v *Foot* [1900] 2 IR 211, at 217-8.
388 *KM* v *DPP* [1994] 1 IR 514.
389 *In re Clifford* [1921] 2 AC 570, at 584 (Ir). In so far as that case also said that prohibition lies only against a judicial body, it is no longer law; see Wade & Forsyth pp.627-30.
390 *R* v *Sec of State for Transport ex p Factortame (No 2)* [1991] 1 AC 603.
391 *M* v *Home Office* [1994] 1 AC 377, at 405-23.

19.85 *'Quo warranto'*. The High Court may grant an injunction to restrain a person from purporting to act in a public office (s.24). Order 53 applies (Ord.53 r.11). This replaces the old order of *quo warranto*.[392]

19.86 A *declaration* can be given instead of or as well as one of the other orders, for example to quash a decision and declare the true position, or to show the challenged body how to act in future, or in lieu of quashing where the decision is *fait accompli* and the body has changed its policy since.[393] Where a body gives an opinion on the legal effect of its previous decision, the opinion is subject to judicial review if it is outside the statutory powers: a declaration is the appropriate remedy.[394] The Court has a discretion.[395] A declaration cannot, in judicial review, be given against the Crown or a servant exercising its powers,[396] but can be given against an officer or minister exercising statutory or prerogative powers. See further the Judicature Act (s. 23) and para. 14.95.

19.87 The power under section 18 of the Judicature Act to grant an injunction or declaration does not extend the powers of the High Court to enforce private law rights in judicial review proceedings;[397] though since 1989, the Court may do so by ordering continuance as if by writ.

19.88 *Damages* can be given instead of or as well as other relief if a claim for damages, giving particulars under Order 18 rule 12 of the fault and the damage alleged, was included in the applicant's statement seeking leave, and if he would have been entitled to damages in an action commenced at the same time (s.20; Ord.53 r.7). This can be done if the challenged decision operates as a breach of statutory duty which gives rise to a cause of action to the applicant, or the tort of (malicious) misfeasance by a public officer, or where the conduct of the challenged body is tortious unless justified by the challenged decision;[398] or where *Francovich*[399] damages are payable by the State for harm caused by failure to implement European law. The claim can be met by a defence of the statute of limitations.[400] Damages only arise if the right to judicial review is shown.[401] Damages are not available for failure to perform a purely public law duty.[402] An administrative act which is held to be without jurisdiction does not

---

392 See *Republic* v *High Court* [1988] LRC (Const) 610 (Ghana SC); White Book (1997) 53/1-14/56.

393 *In re Colgan*, QBD, NI (Girvan J) undated 1996.

394 *Petaling Tin* v *Lee Kian Chan* [1994] 4 LRC 180 (Malaysia SC).

395 *In re Russell* [1990] NI 188, at 198.

396 Because judicial review is excluded from the definition of "civil proceedings" in s.38(2) of the Crown Proceedings Act.

397 *In re Malone* [1988] NI 67, at 84H.

398 Graham (1980) 31 NILQ 317, at 331.

399 *Francovich* v *Italian Republic* [1993] 2 CMLR 66(ECJ); *Brasserie du Pêcheur* v *Germany* [1996] QB 404 (ECJ).

400 *Tate* v *Minister of Social Welfare* [1995] 1 IR 421. There Carroll J gave *Francovich* damages for failure to implement equal treatment in state benefits, but confined to a period of six years before commencement of the proceedings.

401 *Davy* v *Spelthorne BC* [1984] AC 262, at 277-8.

402 E.g. deciding that the applicant is not eligible for public housing: *R* v *Northavon DC, ex p Palmer*, 'The Times' 1 August 1995 (CA).

give a right to damages unless: (a) it constitutes a tort, (b) it was done with malice, or (c) it was done knowingly in excess of power.[403] The Court cannot make an order for payment of money due as a debt,[404] but a public duty to pay money can be enforce by *mandamus*.[405] Against a resident magistrate or a county court judge on appeal therefrom, no action lies for damages for an act done in the execution of his duties within his jurisdiction and no action lies for an act done in purported execution of his duties outside his jurisdiction unless in bad faith.[406]

The Crown is not liable to any execution of an order against it (see para. 16.07).

Costs

19.89 Costs are in the discretion of the Court as in any High Court proceedings. As a general rule costs should follow the event. If relief is refused in the court's discretion even though the grounds for judicial review are established, costs should be awarded to the adversary party[407] or at least not awarded against him.[408] But it is always in the judge's discretion to make the unusual order of costs against the successful party if a good ground exists.[409] If the applicant has discontinued, the incidence of costs should be influenced by whether he did so because of likelihood of failure (costs against him), or because the challenged party has changed his decision to pre-empt loss of the case (costs to applicant), or because the challenged party has changed his policy for other reasons (no order as to costs).[410] Normally only one set of costs is awarded against the unsuccessful applicant even where there is more than one adversary party.[411] In the case of a judicial decision, costs should be awarded against the challenged court/tribunal only if the judge etc. acted *mala fide* or if he/it chose to put in argument against judicial review,[412] and not if he/it merely filed an affidavit.[413] Costs should not be awarded against the person who was the opposing party in the lower court who neither caused the court's error nor sought to oppose the judicial review.[414]

Appeal

19.90 Subject to appeal the order of judicial review is final (s.18(6)). In a civil cause or matter, appeal lies from the decision on the judicial review

---

403 *Pine Valley* v *Minister of Environment* [1987] IR 23.

404 *Roy* v *Kensington FPC* [1992] 1 AC 624.

405 *Commissioners of State Revenue* v *Royal Insurance* [1994] 4 LRC 511.

406 Magistrates' Courts (NI) Order 1981, Arts.5-6, 145A.

407 *R* v *Trafford BC, ex p Colonel Food* [1990] COD 351 (refused because of alternative remedy).

408 *In re Quigley* [1997] 3 BNIL 40 (DC, *per* Nicholson LJ) (relief refused where the consideration wrongly ignored would not have altered the decision).

409 *In re Morris*, CA, NI, 30 April 1997 (oral judgment).

410 See Mulcahy 'Costs where the Respondent changes its Policy' [1996] JR 208.

411 White Book 53/1-14/53.

412 *McIlwraith* v *Judge Fawsitt* [1990] 1 IR 343.

413 *R* v *Newcastle-under-Lyme JJ ex p Massey* [1994] 1 WLR 1684 (DC).

414 White Book (1997) 62/B/64.

hearing to the Court of Appeal (or by leap frog straight from the High Court to the House of Lords, see para. 20.85). A decision to grant or refuse *certiorari* is interlocutory in nature, [415] therefore the time limit for appeal to the Court of Appeal is 21 days, but Order 53 rule 10(b) says that leave to appeal is not necessary.[416] Appeals are governed by Order 59 like appeals in High Court actions. New evidence is admitted subject to the restrictions of the *Ladd* v *Marshall*[417] principles, but there is a discretion to waive those principles in the wider public interest.[418] Thence appeal lies to the House of Lords. Because of this, decisions of county courts and magistrates' courts on points of law (where a case stated to the Court of Appeal is final in a civil cause) are sometimes challenged by *certiorari* by having the decision of law put on the court record. This is not necessarily an improper tactic.[419]

IN A CRIMINAL CAUSE OR MATTER

What is a criminal cause?

19.91 A criminal cause or matter is any application arising from a proceeding which may result in the trial and punishment for an offence: bail on a criminal charge;[420] applications under 'PACE'[421] and similar legislation relating to the securing of search and obtaining of evidence; review of witness summons for a criminal case; applications made before the start or after the conclusion of the criminal proceeding.[422] A criminal cause includes: the binding over of a witness by a summary criminal court;[423] disqualification from driving on conviction;[424] legal aid on a criminal charge;[425] committal for trial on indictment;[426] extradition;[427] questioning by the Serious Fraud Office;[428] extension of detention by the Secretary of State after arrest under the terrorism provisions.[429] Though confiscation orders by a convicting court of the proceeds of crime may be a criminal matter, a restraint order by the High Court pending and in aid of such confiscation is civil.[430] Application to a juvenile court to send a juvenile to a

---

[415] *R(Curry)* v *National Insurance Commr* [1974] NI 102; *R* v *Environment Secretary ex p Hackney LBC* [1983] 1 WLR 524, at 539A, *affd.* [1984] 1 WLR 592. *Semble*, any order on judicial review is interlocutory except a decision whether to award damages.

[416] A rule made under s.35(2)(g)(vi) of the Judicature Act

[417] See para. 20.42.

[418] *R* v *Sec of State for Home Dept ex p Momin Ali* [1984] 1 WLR 663.

[419] *Per* Black LJ, *R (King)* v *Judge Hanna*, CA, NI, 29 June 1962 at p.2. *Jennings* v *Kelly* [1940] NI 47 reached the Lords in this way.

[420] *R* v *Clarke* [1985] 2 NZLR 212.

[421] Police and Criminal Evidence (NI) Order 1989.

[422] See White Book (1997) 59/1/24; and the author's *Criminal Procedure in NI,* Chap.1.01.

[423] *In re Hughes* [1986] NI 13.

[424] *In re Black* [1993] 2 NIJB 63.

[425] *AG* v *Alick* [1993] 3 LRC 535 (CA, Hong Kong).

[426] *Spratt* v *Doherty* [1983] NI 136.

[427] *In re McGlinchey* [1987] 3 NIJB 1; *US Govt* v *Bowe* [1990] 1 AC 501.

[428] *R* v *Director of SFO, ex p Smith* [1993] AC 1.

[429] *In re Quigley* [1997] 3 BNIL 40 (DC); heard by two judges, one of whom had granted leave.

[430] *In re O* [1991] 2 QB 520.

training school for non-attendance at school is civil against him but criminal against his parent.[431] Assessment of fees to be paid to a solicitor and counsel out of the Legal Aid Fund for work done in a criminal case is a civil matter.[432]

19.92 The distinction between civil and criminal cause is hard to discern, partly because in most of these cases there is no indication from the judgment that the Court considered the issue. In *In re Madden*[433] review of the DPP's decision to refuse disclosure of interview notes to a suspect now awaiting trial would seem to be in a criminal cause, but the application was renewed to the Court of Appeal (but see *R* v *Bolton JJ ex p Graeme*, below para. 19.95). In *In re Hone*[434] proceedings against a prisoner for offences against prison discipline were treated as civil, judicial review being heard by a single judge, the Court of Appeal, and the House of Lords. In *R* v *Chief Constable ex p McKenna*[435] and *In re Duffy*[436] reviews of a Superintendent's order to defer access of a suspect to his solicitor under the Northern Ireland (Emergency Provisions) Act 1996 (s.47) were treated as criminal and heard by the Divisional Court, but in the *McKenna* case (p.122c) an interim order, originally given *ex parte* then revoked, was appealed to the Court of Appeal. The decision of a Secretary of State regarding the release of a convicted prisoner on licence is a civil matter,[437] but the Secretary of State's decision to revoke a licence of a prisoner detained for life or during Her Majesty's pleasure, was treated as criminal and heard by a Divisional Court in *In re Crawford.*[438] The implementation of a sentence of imprisonment for default of paying fines, and its effect on the release date for another sentence was treated as criminal in *In re Tarr.*[439] But the question whether a direction under section 38 of the Prison Act (NI) 1953 as to disallowance of time when the prisoner had escaped from custody was affected by the Government's undertaking to an extraditing court was treated as civil in *In re McKee.*[440] Review of a decision as to time to be served on a sentence of a foreign court under the Repatriation of Prisoners Act 1984 was treated as criminal.[441] Conviction and sentence by a special military court during time of war, as opposed to a statutory court-martial, are a civil matter.[442]

Procedure

19.93 The procedures and powers in civil matters (paras. 19.52-19.89) apply to judicial review in a criminal cause or matter, and Order 1 rule 2(3) states

---

431 *In re Coleman* [1988] NI 205, at 208-9.
432 *In re Weir* [1988] NI 338.
433 [1991] NI 14.
434 [1987] NI 160.
435 [1992] NI 116.
436 [1991] 7 NIJB 62.
437 *In re Whelan* [1990] NI 348; *In re Hardy* [1989] 2 NIJB 81, at 88; *In re Doherty* [1996] 2 BNIL 77 (CA).
438 [1995] 2 BNIL 60.
439 [1995] 2 BNIL 59.
440 [1993] 8 NIJB 88.
441 *R* v *Home Secretary, ex p Read* [1989] AC 1014.
442 *In re Clifford* [1921] 2 AC 570.

that the RSC apply in relation to any criminal proceedings to which Order 53 applies, but subject to the following differences. The main difference is that the substantive jurisdiction is exercised by a Divisional Court of two or three judges unless the parties consent to a single judge.

Application for leave

19.94 A master cannot hear any application in judicial review relating to criminal proceedings (Ord.32 r.11(1)(a)). A single judge in chambers may grant leave (Ord.53 r.3(3), and may hear any interlocutory proceeding (Ord.53 r.8(1)). An order by a vacation judge cannot be appealed, but a motion to set it aside can be made within ten days to the Divisional Court. Save during vacation, or by consent, the judge cannot grant full relief forthwith, nor can he refuse leave himself; only a full Divisional Court can do so (Ord.53 r.3(11)). In practice the single judge who is minded to refuse leave or grant review forthwith refers the case to the Divisional Court and sits as one of the judges.[443] The adversary party often intervenes and the hearing may be treated as the full application on notice.

Challenging decision as to leave

19.95 Refusal of leave cannot be appealed to the Court of Appeal in a criminal cause or matter (Judicature Act s.35(2)(a)); nor, on the principle of *Lane* v *Esdaile*[444] to the House of Lords.[445] Order 53 envisages that if leave is refused by the High Court, the *ex parte* application can be 'renewed' in the Court of Appeal under Order 59 rule 14(3) (as in *In re Madden*, above para. 19.92), and if the Court of Appeal grants leave it must allow the substantive application to be heard in the High Court (Ord.53 r.5(8)). But in *R* v *Bolton JJ ex p Graeme*[446] Donaldson MR said that although a renewal was not a purported appeal, the Court should apply section 35(2)(a) by analogy "because it would be very peculiar indeed if this Court was to exercise an original jurisdiction to give leave to proceed by judicial review in circumstances in which any consequent decision was unappealable to this Court". The adversary party cannot appeal against the granting of leave.

Matters arising pending hearing

19.96 Any interlocutory application is made to a judge in chambers (Ord.53 r.8(1)), and not to a master. Pending *certiorari* of a conviction or sentence of a magistrates' court or county court on appeal, the Court may grant bail (Judicature Act, s.25(4)). If the person is in custody otherwise than under a conviction, the High Court has inherent power to grant bail.[447] No appeal lies from an order on interlocutory application made by a judge in chambers; but it

---

443 As in *In re Wilson* [1983] 10 NIJB at 3-4; and *In re Weatherall* [1984] 19 NIJB at 2.

444 [1891] AC 210.

445 Lewis p.243 n.18; Supperstone & Goudie pp.390-1. Note however that under s. 41 of the Judicature Act appeal lies from the High Court to the House of Lords in a criminal matter from any 'decision', not merely from a 'judgment or order'. This distinction of wording was held to make no difference in *Durity* v *JLSC* [1996] 2 LRC 451 (Trinidad CA).

446 (1986) 150 JP 190.

447 As to bail where the applicant is detained in a civil cause, see para. 19.73.

can be set aside or substituted by motion to the Divisional Court within five days (Ord.53 r.8(3)) with an appeal to the House of Lords.

Hearing the motion

19.97 The motion for judicial review is heard by a Divisional Court of three judges, or of two judges if the Lord Chief Justice so directs; if two disagree it must be re-heard before three (Ord.53 r.2(1)(2)(5)(7)). On points of law the Court is strictly bound by decisions of the Court of Appeal.[448] A single judge sitting in court may hear the motion on consent (Ord.53 r.2(6)) or where necessary during vacation (Ord.53 r.2(3)).[449] Appeal lies from a single judge hearing by consent under rule 2(6), to the House of Lords under section 41 *infra*. No appeal lies from a single judge hearing a motion during vacation under rule 2(3), but on application within ten days the Divisional Court may set aside, discharge or vary it (Ord.53 r.2(4)). Instead of quashing an invalid sentence or other order made on conviction the Court may substitute a proper sentence without quashing the conviction (s.25).[450]

Appeal

19.98 No appeal lies from any decision in judicial review in a criminal cause to the Court of Appeal (s.35(2)(a)), but lies from the Divisional Court to the House of Lords under the Judicature Act (s.41), by leave of either, provided that the Divisional Court certifies a point of law of public importance.

HABEAS CORPUS

HABEAS CORPUS AD SUBJICIENDUM

Where it lies

19.99 This is assigned to the Queen's Bench Division. '*Habeas corpus ad subjiciendum*' is a remedy for any person suffering the tort of false imprisonment.[451] Whereas judicial review lies only against a body or person who has some form of public and legal authority, *habeas corpus* can be ordered against a 'kangaroo court' or any person whether or not the detention is under any pretence of legal authority. It is the remedy available to enforce a court order for release on bail.[452] In *Phillip* v *DPP*[453] it was used to challenge arrest and detention on a charge where a pardon had been granted. The remedy is refused if the detention is lawful. In *R(O'Hanlon)* v *Governor of Belfast Prison*[454] the issue was whether internment regulations were *intra vires* the

448 *In re Russell* [1996] 9 BNIL 33 (DC).

449 Alternatively on urgent need, any party may apply by summons for a hearing by the Divisional Court during vacation (Ord.64 r.4(2)).

450 Overruling *Conlin* v *Patterson* [1915] 1 IR 169. See further *R(McCann)* v *Belfast JJ* [1978] NI 153, at 158.

451 *Quigley* v *Chief Constable* [1983] NI 238, at 239-40.

452 *In re Close* [1972] NI 27. See also *In re Lange,* QBD, NI (Lowry J) 17 May 1965 (deportation case).

453 [1992] 1 AC 545.

454 (1922) 56 ILTR 170.

statute. Detention is not rendered unlawful by poor conditions,[455] but is made unlawful by reason of an unlawful purpose such as assaulting the detainee.[456]

19.100 *Habeas corpus* lies against the Crown.[457] A decision of an inferior court made within jurisdiction (e.g. a remand) cannot be challenged on the ground of no evidence for it,[458] except in extradition cases.[459] No *habeas corpus* lies against a sentence on imprisonment by a competent court within its legal powers, however unreasonable[460] or procedurally unfair,[461] nor against any extant order of detention or imprisonment, unless it is set aside by appeal or judicial review;[462] but it lies against detention which is without or in excess of jurisdiction.[463] It never lies against a sentence of a superior court.[464] It does not lie against any custody authorised by an extant order or decision of a governmental body, until the order is set aside by judicial review.[465] During a state of war or rebellion, *habeas corpus* does not lie against governmental authority;[466] but it is for the Court to decide whether such a state exists.[467] The Court has no jurisdiction to consider *habeas corpus* in respect of a person detained in a state outside Northern Ireland.[468] If a person is about to be arrested and taken abroad before *habeas corpus* can be applied for, the Court can grant an injunction to restrain the arrest,[469] or some form of '*quia timet*' order of *habeas corpus*.[470]

Procedure

19.101 All applications relating to *habeas corpus* must be heard by a judge not a master (Ord.32 r.11(1)(b)). An application for a writ of *habeas corpus ad subjiciendum* may be made *ex parte* or by originating motion, supported by affidavit of the detainee, or if he cannot, by someone on his behalf (Ord.54 r.1). In practice it is always commenced *ex parte*. A civil application relating to the custody, care and control of a minor is heard *ex parte* or by originating

---

455 *R* v *Deputy Governor of Parkhurst ex p Hague* (orse. *Weldon* v *Home Office*) [1992] 1 AC 58.

456 *In re Gillen* [1988] NI 40.

457 *R* v *Home Secretary, ex p Muboyayi* [1992] QB 244, at 254.

458 *In re McAleenan* [1985] NI 496, at 502.

459 Wade & Forsythe p.622.

460 *In re Weatherall* [1984] 19 NIJB at 4-6.

461 *McSorley* v *Governor of Mountjoy* [1996] 2 ILRM 331.

462 *Linnett* v *Coles* [1987] QB 555, at 561.

463 E.g. where a precedent fact to the exercise of jurisdiction does not exist: *Re S-C (Mental Patient: Habeas Corpus)* [1996] QB 599 (CA).

464 *In re Beggs* [1944] NI 121; but see *R* v *Gov. of Spring Hill ex p Sohi* [1988] 1 WLR 596.

465 *R* v *Home Secretary ex p Muboyayi* [1992] QB 244.

466 *R (Childers)* v *Adjutant-General* [1923] 1 IR 5; *R (Johnstone)* v *O'Sullivan* [1923] 2 IR 13.

467 *R(O'Brien)* v *Governor of Military Camp* [1924] 1 IR 32 (CA).

468 *In re Keenan* [1972] 1 QB 533, cited without comment in *In re McElduff* [1972] NI 1, at 6; and see *White* v *Warnock* (1947) 81 ILTR 35 (HL); and *In re Lange*, QBD, NI (Lowry J) 17 May 1965 (deportation case).

469 *O'Boyle* v *AG* [1929] IR 558.

470 *R* v *Home Sec ex p Muboyayi*, at 258F.

summons (in chambers).[471] The motion may claim interim relief such as an injunction.[472] The applicant should swear the affidavit personally, so as to make him bound by the law of perjury.[473] If made *ex parte* the Court may in its discretion: (a) order immediate release (Ord.54 r.4(1));[475] (b) at once issue the writ; or (c) direct application by originating motion (in open court) or originating summons (in chambers), to be served on the respondent and any other person directed at least eight clear days before the hearing (Ord.54 r.2). If reasonable cause is shown (i.e. prima facie evidence of detention and of its unlawfulness) the writ must be issued.[474]

19.102 In a criminal cause or matter (which includes detention under Mental Health legislation) a single judge must either release the detainee or direct an originating motion before a Divisional Court of two or more judges (Ord.54 rr.4(2), 11; Administration of Justice Act 1960 s.14(1)).

19.103 Note that in Northern Ireland *habeas corpus* in a civil matter is not excluded from the operation of the Crown Proceedings Act (s.38(2) thereof).

19.104 Each party to the application must supply on demand copies of any affidavit to be used at the hearing (Ord.54 r.3). The Court hearing the application: (a) may order the release of the detainee (Ord.54 r.4(1);[475] (b) may refuse the application; or (c) may issue the writ. The purpose of the writ is to bring the 'body' of the detainee to the court. On issuing a writ (in Form 59), the Court directs the court and date for which the writ is returnable (Ord.54 r.5). Where the person is detained other than under a civil or criminal suit, the Court may issue a writ during vacation returnable immediately (Habeas Corpus Act 1816, s.1). The writ must be served on each respondent, personally if possible, or left with a servant where the respondent is a prison governor or public official, with a notice in Form 60 stating the date and place to bring the detainee (Ord.54 r.6). When a writ of *habeas corpus* is directed to a gaoler, minister etc. and served on him or left at the prison, he must (unless the prisoner has been committed for an arrestable offence) make return of the writ and bring the prisoner before the court and certify the cause of the detention, within three days (or ten days if more than 20 miles away) after service (Habeas Corpus Act (Ir) 1781, s.1). The return must be indorsed on or annexed to the writ and state all the causes of detention (Ord.54 r.7(1)). If the gaoler fails to do so, or fails to deliver on demand a true copy of the warrant of commitment, he is liable to a penalty (1781 Act, s.4). If a person on whom a writ is served does not obey it, he is guilty of contempt and the Court may issue a warrant to bring the person to court and commit him (1816 Act, s.2). A return stating that the alleged detainee is not being held against her will is a valid return and the respondent is not then obliged to produce the body to the

---

471 As in *In re B* [1946] NI 1; *In re EEL* [1938] NI 56; now called 'residence' under the Children's (NI) Order 1995.

472 *In re Gillen* [1988] NI 40, at 55G.

473 *In re Copeland* [1990] NI 301.

474 *Quigley* v *Chief Constable* [1983] NI 238.

475 As in *R(McCann)* v *Belfast JJ* [1978] NI 153 (where the detention was held to be invalid on a pure point of law).

Court; but the veracity of the return can be investigated under section 3 of the 1816 Act.[476] The respondent can answer that the applicant is no longer in his custody.[477]

19.105 The return of the writ is first read out, then counsel for the detainee moves for the discharge of the detainee or the quashing of the return, then counsel for the respondent speaks, then the first counsel replies (Ord.54 r.8). The return can be amended or substituted by leave of the Court (Ord.54 r.7(2)). If the applicant has already been released the Court may in its discretion rule on the validity of the detention on grounds of an issue of public importance, or to decide as to costs.[478] If the return states a valid ground of detention, the applicant must show a prima facie case of illegality.[479] The Court can investigate the truth of the facts stated in the return by affidavit, and if doubtful may release the detainee on bail until a day fixed in the next term (1816 Act, s.3); and the Court can call witnesses of its own motion without consent of the parties.[480] If the return claims that the body is under voluntary protection, the Court should require his attendance (directing the respondent to serve a *subpoena* on him), and can direct the examination to be in chambers so as to preserve the alleged protection.[481]

19.106 A decision that detention is lawful is conclusive only as to the grounds of detention raised in the application.[482] A new application for *habeas corpus* cannot be made on the same grounds without fresh evidence (Administration of Justice Act 1960, s.14(2)). A prisoner released on *habeas corpus* cannot be re-committed for the same offence, save by due process of a court having jurisdiction (1781 Act, s.5).[483] A prisoner committed under a warrant by a judge or justice charged with an arrestable offence stated in the warrant cannot be removed to a court under the Act (1781 Act, s.15).

19.107 *Appeal.* Appeal lies against the grant or refusal of *habeas corpus*, whether civil or criminal, as follows (Judicature Act, s.45)-

- in a civil cause to the Court of Appeal under section 35(1), then to the House of Lords under section 42;
- in a criminal cause no appeal lies from a single judge, but lies from the Divisional Court to the House of Lords under section 41 with leave of either and with no need for the Court to certify a point of law of public importance.

---

476 *In re Quigley* [1983] NI 245, at 246-52.

477 *White* v *Warnock* (1947) 81 ILTR 35 (HL). But in child custody cases, the Court can inquire into a return that the respondent has parted with the child, in order to find out where the child now is: *Barnardo* v *Ford* [1892] AC 326.

478 *In re Fox* [1987] 1 NIJB 12 (DC).

479 White Book (1997) 54/7/3.

480 *In re Quigley* [1983] NI 245, at 256B.

481 *In re Quigley*, at 252-6.

482 *Application of Woods* [1970] IR 154.

483 See *State (McFadden)* v *Governor of Mountjoy (No 2)* [1981] ILRM 120.

In an appeal from an order of release, the intending appellant may apply to the Court for continuing detention or release on bail pending appeal. In a criminal case the detainee cannot otherwise be returned to custody if the appeal succeeds (s.45(4), and Sch.1 para.4).

19.108 Arrest under the Prevention of Terrorism Act is a criminal matter.[484] Conviction and sentence by a special military court during time of war, as opposed to a statutory court-martial, are a civil matter, so that appeal lies to the Court of Appeal.[485] So also detention under the 'sentence' of a 'kangaroo' or illegal self-styled punishment court. As to what is a criminal cause or matter in the context of judicial review, see further para. 19.91.

OTHER FORMS OF *HABEAS CORPUS*

19.109 An application for *habeas corpus ad testificandum* (in Form 61) under the Habeas Corpus Act 1804, or *ad respondendum* (in Form 62) must be made *ex parte* to a judge in chambers (Ord.54 r.9). The former is for a prisoner to be brought to any court as a witness (see para. 13.09); the latter to a court to answer a charge. They are little used now.

---

[484] *In re Fox* [1987] 1 NIJB 12 (DC).

[485] *R(Johnstone)* v *O'Sullivan* [1923] 2 IR 13; cf. *In re Clifford* [1921] 2 AC 570.

CHAPTER TWENTY

APPEALS

20.00 This Chapter concerns appeals *from* the High Court to the Court of Appeal and to the House of Lords, and also appeals from other courts and tribunals to the Court of Appeal. Appeals *to* the High Court are dealt with at para. 18.01. An appeal from any judgment, order or decision of a master lies in accordance with Order 58 to a High Court judge. From the decision of a master in Queen's Bench on a reference under Order 36 or on assessment of damages, and from a Chancery master on Order 36 reference, it lies directly to the Court of Appeal (see paras. 14.14 and 14.50). All enactments relating to appeals and stay of execution apply to civil proceedings by or against the Crown (Crown Proceedings Act, s.22).

APPEALS TO COURT OF APPEAL

20.01 The substantive jurisdiction of the Court of Appeal is statutory and it has no inherent jurisdiction to hear an appeal where no statute confers it.[1] It has no original jurisdiction, except on certain ancillary and procedural matters, such as amendment, enforcement, contempt of its proceedings.[2] In *In re Racal*[3] it was said that the Court of Appeal has no original jurisdiction in judicial review, but see para. 19.64. In *WEA Records* v *Visions Channel 4*[4] Donaldson MR said: "The Court of Appeal hears appeals from orders and judgments. It does not hear original applications". A right of appeal cannot be conferred by rules.[5]

Who may appeal

20.02 A party in the lower court can appeal, including a person served with notice of judgment under Order 44. One of two plaintiffs can appeal alone,[6] and one of two co-defendants.[7] The High Court can add a party for the purposes of appeal, if the time limit for appeal subsists or if an appeal is pending.[8] A non-party can apply on motion on notice to the Court of Appeal for leave to appeal[9] if he has *locus standi* in the dispute,[10] upon undertaking to be bound by the proceedings so far and by the result of the appeal as if he were a party. Where

---

1 *Cf.Scottish Widows* v *Blennerhassett* [1912] AC 281 (Ir).

2 *Ocean Software* v *Kay* [1992] QB 583.

3 [1981] AC 374, at 381H and 388E.

4 [1983] 1 WLR 721, at 727.

5 *McGimpsey* v *O'Hare* [1959] NI 98, at 104.

6 *Beckett* v *Attwood* (1881) 18 Ch D 54; *Sutherland* v *Gustar* [1994] Ch 305.

7 *Moore* v *A-G* [1929] IR 544.

8 *Millen* v *Brown* [1984] NI 328, at 338F.

9 *Guardians of Belfast Union* v *Belfast Corp* (1909) 43 ILTR 247.

10 *In re Dunne* (1880) 5 LR Ir 76.

available, application should be made initially to the High Court.[11] The test for *locus standi* is whether the intending appellant could have been made a party in the lower court.[12]

What may be appealed

20.03 Subject to statutory provision, the Court of Appeal can hear an appeal from any judgment or order of the High Court or a judge (Judicature Act, s.35(1)); including a judge in chambers (Ord.58 r.4) and from the decision of the Queen's Bench Master in a reference under Order 36 rule 1 or an assessment of damages; and from the Chancery Master on a reference under Order 36 rule 1 (Ord.58 rr.2-3). "Judgment includes order, decision and decree" (s.120).

20.04 Where a pre-1978 statute confers final jurisdiction on an appeal on a case stated or point of law to the High Court or a judge of the Supreme Court, the appellate jurisdiction is transferred to the Court of Appeal (s.35(6)).

Appeal always lies to the Court of Appeal from a decision involving the validity of provisions made by or under a NI statute, unless there is a right of appeal to the Lords (s.35(5)); and Order 59 applies (Ord.59 r.16).

RESTRICTIONS ON APPEAL

No appeal

20.05 No appeal lies -

(1) if the parties have agreed not to appeal and that is recorded in the order of the High Court;[13]

(2) if the point on the appeal is academic or hypothetical;

(3) if the judge sat as an arbitrator;

(4) if by consent of the parties the judge decided a matter outside his judicial capacity or jurisdiction;[14]

(5) from a purely administrative decision (e.g. as to place and time of sitting, or that a case be listed before a particular judge);[15]

(6) from the rulings of fact or law on which the judge based his decision;[16]

(7) by a party against an undertaking given by him embodied in a court order;[17]

(8) by a party who has forfeited his right of appeal by his conduct after judgment (see para. 20.39).

---

[11] *Millen* v *Brown* at 334B. Under English practice he applies *ex parte* to the Court of Appeal for leave: White Book (1997) 59/3/2.

[12] *The Millwall* [1905] P 155.

[13] *In re Hull & County Bank* (1880) 13 Ch D 262.

[14] *Lawler* v *Kelly* (1899) 33 ILTR 38.

[15] *Yorkshire Electricity* v *West Yorkshire CC* [1980] CLY 2193 (CA).

[16] *Lake* v *Lake* [1955] P 336.

[17] *McConnell* v *McConnell* (1980) 10 Fam Law 214.

20.06 The Court of Appeal has inherent jurisdiction to strike out an appeal which is hopeless.[18] Section 35 of the Judicature Act provides restrictions on the right of appeal from the High Court to the Court of Appeal, which restrictions apply also to a respondent's cross-notice of appeal or notice to vary under Order 59 rule 6.

20.07 Appeal does not lie from the High Court to the Court of Appeal at all-

(1) from the judgment in a criminal cause or matter (s.35(2)(a)).[19] Appeal lies from the High Court to the House of Lords.

(2) from an order *allowing* extension of time for appeal from a judgment/order (s.35(2)(b)). It seems now that appeal does lie from an order *refusing* an extension of time.[20]

(3) from a judge's order granting unconditional leave to defend an action (s.35(2)(c))

(4) from a judgment/order declared by statutory provision [i.e. a UK or NI statute or subordinate legislation under either] to be final (s.35(2)(d)).

(5) from a decree absolute in divorce/nullity of marriage if the appellant could have appealed against the decree *nisi* (s.35(2)(e))

(6) from a decision of the High Court under the Arbitration Act 1996, subject to the provisions thereof (s.35(2)(fa)). Most of its provisions allow an appeal by leave of the High Court

(7) from a decision of law under sections 120-156 of the Representation of the People Act 1983 (s.35(2)(h)).

(8) from a decision to grant or refuse a certificate under section 12 of the Administration of Justice Act 1969 ('leap-frog' appeal to House of Lords) (s.35(2)(i)).

Appeal by leave of High Court

20.08 Under the Judicature Act, appeal lies only with leave of the High Court or judge thereof-

- from an *order made by consent* of the parties (s.35(2)(f)). It is a consent order if so recorded in a court order.[21] An order made on acceptance or non-objection by the party against whom it is made is not an order by consent

---

[18] *Burgess* v *Stafford Hotel* [1990] 1 WLR 1215.

[19] See White Book (1997) 59/1/24. The Court of Appeal hears appeals in criminal causes, from the Crown Court and, by case stated, from the magistrates' court and county court.

[20] *Rickards* v *Rickards* [1990] Fam 194; *Regalbourne* v *East Lindsey DC*, 'The Times', 16 March 1993. These cases say that there is a conceptual distinction between a provision which states that a court may extend the time limit for appeal, and a provision which says that a court may give leave to appeal after a time limit has expired. In *Geogas SA* v *Trammo Gas* [1991] 1 WLR 776, at 779, the House of Lords re-iterated that a court's decision whether to give leave to appeal is unappealable.

[21] Cf. *In re Hull & County Bank* (1880) 13 Ch D 261.

(see para. 15.14). A consent order can be set aside on appeal if it was imposed on the appellant without his full and free consent.[22]

- from an *order "as to costs only"* (s.35(2)(f)).[23] Where a court makes an adjudication against a party and makes no order save as to costs, that is not an order as to costs only (Wylie p.115), nor is an order for costs against a non-party.[24] Where a trustee who has fought unsuccessfully a Queen's Bench action applies by originating summons in the Chancery Division for an order that the costs be paid out of the estate, the decision of the Chancery judge is not an order for costs only, and is appealable without leave.[25] An order against a solicitor of a party to pay costs personally *is not* an order as to costs only, but an order as to the costs of an application for that purpose *is* an order as to costs only.[26] Appeal lies without leave of the High Court if the judge failed to exercise his discretion or exercised it without grounds or on extraneous grounds non-judicially,[27] such as a mortgagee deprived of his costs without evidence of his misconduct.[28] If the appeal genuinely relates to matters other than costs, the Court of Appeal can review any order of costs connected with those matters.[29] If the High Court judge does give leave then the Court of Appeal will hear the appeal in the same way as an appeal from any discretionary order.[30] Against the High Court's decision as to ordering costs against the Legal Aid Fund, appeal is further restricted to a point of law (para. 17.91).

20.09 Where appeal lies from the High Court only by leave of the High Court, the refusal of leave is unappealable.[31] If an appellant contends that an order by consent or as to costs is outside the need for leave, he should issue a

---

22 *In re R* [1995] 1 WLR 184 (CA). In that case the lower court judge gave leave to appeal: the Court did not decide whether in those circumstances an appeal would lie without his leave.

23 Beware the particular wording of the Judicature Act. The English Supreme Court Act 1981, s.18 (before it was amended) and the Supreme Court of Judicature (Ir) Act 1877, s.52 refer to an order "relating only to costs which are by law left to the discretion of the court". The cases cited here were all decided under that phrase.

24 *Re Land and Property* [1991] 1 WLR 601.

25 *Re Beddoe* [1893] 1 Ch 547.

26 *Wilkinson* v *Kenny* [1993] 1 WLR 963.

27 *Scherer* v *Counting Systems* [1986] 1 WLR 615; *Donald Campbell* v *Pollak* [1927] AC 732; *Lavelle* v *Robinson* [1964] NI 17; *Cockle* v *Treacy* [1896] 2 IR 267; *Bankamerica* v *Nock* [1988] AC 1002, at 1009. These are now called the '*Scherer* principles'. In *Smith Ltd* v *Middleton* [1986] 1 WLR 598, the CA put it a different way: appeal lies without leave if the matter wrongly taken into account was the sole or overriding factor in the way the judge exercised his discretion.

28 *McDonnell* v *McMahon* (1889) 23 LR Ir 283.

29 As in *Fahy* v *Pullen* (1968) 102 ILTR 81; *Wheeler* v *Somerfield* [1966] 2 QB 94.

30 *Alltrans Express* v *CVA* [1984] 1 WLR 394.

31 *Min of Justice* v *Wang Zhu Jie* [1993] 1 IR 426; *Seamar Holdings* v *Kupe Group* [1995] 2 NZLR 274 (CA); cf. *Cambridge Street Properties* v *City of Glasgow Licensing Board* 1995 SLT 913.

notice of appeal and the need for leave can be tried as a preliminary point by the Court of Appeal.[32] No appeal lies against the granting of leave to appeal.[33]

Interlocutory orders

20.10 Leave of either the High Court judge or the Court of Appeal is necessary to appeal from an interlocutory order of a judge. The following types of orders are appealable without leave: orders relating to liberty, residence and contacts of a minor, liability decision in Admiralty, injunction or appointment of receiver, claims and liabilities under the Companies Order, orders of decree nisi, and such orders prescribed by the Rules Committee as appear to be final in nature[34] (Judicature Act, s.35(2)(g)). Thus an order granting or refusing an injunction or an order on application to continue, vary or discharge it can be appealed without leave.[35] An order refusing unconditional leave to defend is not interlocutory under this section (s.35(3)). The Court of Appeal determines whether or not an order is interlocutory or final (s.35(4)). An order is final only if it is made at a proceeding on an application which must determine the rights of the parties.[36] Where the trial of an action is split, for example into issues of liability and quantum, the decision made at each is final.[36] If an interlocutory order provides, either by its own terms or by provision of the rules, that it can be revoked or varied by the High Court, application should be made to the High Court rather than an appeal. The use of the word 'final' in this context should be distinguished from the use of that word in section 35(2)(d), which says that no appeal at at all lies from a judgment or order of the High Court *which is expressed by a statutory provision* to be final.

20.11 *Ex parte decisions.* The Court of Appeal can hear a renewed *ex parte* application after the refusal by the High Court of an order sought *ex parte*[37] which should be applied for within seven days of the refusal (Ord.59 r.14(3)), but the Court of Appeal will not usually hear an appeal from the granting of an *ex parte* order.[38] If an *ex parte* order is made, even by the Court of Appeal on appeal, an application to set aside the order should be brought to the High Court.[39]

---

[32] *Bankamerica* v *Nock* [1988] AC 1002. *Semble,* the appellant should first ask the judge for leave timeously.

[33] *Lobb* v *Phoenix Assurance* [1988] 1 NZLR 285 (CA).

[34] E.g. Ord.53 r.10 (which provides, in a civil cause or matter, that leave is not necessary to appeal against an order refusing leave to apply for judicial review, and an order granting or refusing judicial review) and Ord.114 r.6 (which says that an order referring a question to the European Court is not interlocutory though the time limit is still 21 days).

[35] *Atlas Maritime* v *Avalon* (No 2) [1991] 1 WLR 633.

[36] *White* v *Brunton* [1984] QB 570. As to the distinction between interlocutory and final orders, see further the White Book (up to 1979 ed.) 59/4, (up to 1988 ed.) 59/1/25, and see para. 11.00.

[37] E.g. for leave to issue and serve outside the jurisdiction, for leave to bring judicial review. Where the High Court's decison on an *ex parte* application is stated by a statutory provision to be final, neither appeal nor renewal lies to the Court of Appeal: *Ex parte Austintel* [1997] 1 WLR 616 (CA).

[38] *WEA Records* v *Visions Channel 4* [1983] 1 WLR 721.

[39] *Ocean Software* v *Kay* [1992] QB 583.

20.12 Where a court has power to give leave to appeal to itself, the decision to grant or refuse leave is unappealable.[40] A petition for leave to appeal to the Lords against a refusal of leave to appeal to the Court of Appeal is inadmissible (see para. 20.90).

PROCEDURE FOR APPEAL TO COURT OF APPEAL

20.13 Order 59 applies to every type of appeal to the Court of Appeal from a judge, court, master or tribunal which is not otherwise provided for by statute or rules; and to an application for a new trial or to set aside a trial judgment (Ord.59 rr.1-2). All business of the Court of Appeal, from whatever Division or body the appeal is brought, is transacted in the Appeals and Lists Office of the Central Office (Ord.1 r.13(b)).

Obtaining leave

20.14 Where the Act requires leave to appeal, it is a matter of jurisdiction and the Court and its officer must raise the point of its own motion.[41] In the case of an order by consent or as to costs only, leave to appeal must be sought from the High Court only. In the case of an interlocutory order, where leave to appeal can be granted by the High Court or the Court of Appeal, the applicant should, unless special circumstances make it impossible or impracticable, apply to the High Court in the first instance (Ord.59 r.14(4));[42] but if the time for appeal has expired it is better to ignore this rule and make one application to the Court of Appeal for both leave to appeal and extension of time.[43] Any High Court judge can grant leave,[43] but it is obviously desirable to ask for leave at the time when the judgment or order is given (when the other party will be present) or failing that to apply *ex parte* to the judge who gave it. An application to the Court of Appeal for leave to appeal must be brought *ex parte* in the first instance and the Court may (a) refuse leave; (b) grant leave if delay would cause undue hardship; or (c) adjourn for service of notice on the parties affected (Ord.59 r.14(2)). An application made outside the time limit for appeal must be on notice (*ibid*). If the lower court has refused an application made *ex parte*,[44] it may be renewed by *ex parte* motion within seven days of the refusal (Ord.59 r.14(3)).[45] The lower court as well as the Court of Appeal can

---

40 *Lane* v *Esdaile* [1891] AC 210; *Geogas SA* v *Trammo Gas* [1991] 1 WLR 776. The contrary decision of *Ipswich BC* v *Fisons* [1990] Ch 709 is *per incuriam*.

41 *White* v *Brunton* [1984] QB 570.

42 Note that Ord.59 r.14(4), which is descended from the old Rules (Wylie Ord.58 r.18) applies to any application, not merely an application for leave to appeal.

43 *Warren* v *T Kilroe* [1988] 1 WLR 516.

44 Whether it is an application for an emergency injunction, leave to apply for judicial review (see para.19.62) etc., or for leave to appeal to the Court of Appeal: White Book (1997) 59/14/13. Where the High Court's decison on an *ex parte* application is stated by a statutory provision to be final, neither appeal nor renewal lies to the Court of Appeal: *Ex parte Austintel* [1997] 1 WLR 616 (CA). In that case, at p.619F, Mustill LJ went further and said that "the applications envisaged by [Ord.59 r.14] are those incidental to a substantive appeal whether past, pending or prospective".

45 Descended from the old Rules, Wylie Ord.58 r.10

extend that time limit (Ord.59 r.15). A copy of the order appealed from must be lodged.[46]

20.15 Leave to appeal will be granted if there is a prima facie case of error; or a question of general principle not already decided; or a point of importance on which consideration by the Court of Appeal is of public advantage.[47] Leave may be limited to a particular issue, or may be made conditional upon the appellant agreeing terms as to costs or otherwise. The respondent can apply to set aside an *ex parte* grant of leave to appeal but will have to show some decisive factor or point of law not considered originally.[48] The grant or refusal by the Court of Appeal of leave to appeal to itself is unappealable to the House of Lords.[49]

20.16 Application for leave is heard by a full Court of Appeal of two or three judges. A single judge of the Court of Appeal can grant leave to appeal during vacation, without review by the full Court (Judicature Act, s.37(2)). Since leave to appeal is a statutory requirement, it seems that a notice of appeal served before any necessary leave has been granted is void,[50] though of course the time limits for both steps can be extended.

20.17 The English RSC (Ord.59 r.4(3)) says that if leave to appeal is granted on an application made within the time limit for appeal, the time for service of the notice of appeal is automatically extended for one week after the date of granting leave. In Northern Ireland the Court in granting leave should expressly direct an extension of time if necessary.

Notice of appeal

The notice

20.18 Appeal is by way of motion, instigated by a notice of appeal, and it may relate to all or any specified part of the lower court decision (Ord.59 r.3(1)(2)). It may contain appeals from several orders made at the trial of one action.[51] The notice must specify the order or part thereof appealed against, the grounds of appeal and the precise order sought on the appeal (Ord.59 r.3(2)). An informal notice of appeal is sufficient, but not a mere communication of intention to appeal.[52] The grounds of appeal must specify the precise finding, decision or ruling that is challenged and the reason why it is wrong.[53] The form of notice of appeal in the White Book (1997) 59/3/9 can be adopted, with the addition of a (notional) date for hearing.

---

[46] *Hudson* v *Lindsay* (1880) 6 LR Ir 420 n.1.

[47] White Book (1997) 59/14/7.

[48] *The Iran Navubat* [1990] 1 WLR 1115. This decision might apply with even greater force because leave to appeal is considered by the full Court. In England leave to appeal is considered by a single CA Judge.

[49] *Lane* v *Esdaile* [1891] AC 210; *Geogas SA* v *Trammo Gas* [1991] 1 WLR 776 (HL).

[50] White Book (1997) 59/1/4; 59/1/56.

[51] *Hawes* v *Chief Constable of Avon*, 'The Times' 20 May 1993.

[52] White Book (1997) 59/3/3.

[53] White Book (1997) 59/3/6.

20.19 Appeal may be in respect of all or part of the judgment.[54] For instance a defendant may appeal against the amount of damages and not liability, or *vice versa*; or he may appeal against the judgment on the claim or counterclaim only. The parties should note that any unchallenged part of the judgment of the trial court creates estoppel *per rem judicatem*.[55] But note the powers under section 38 of the Judicature Act and Order 59 rule 10(4) to review parts of the decision not put in issue by the parties to the appeal, and to go beyond the grounds of appeal. The Court of Appeal has power to affirm or vary a decision on grounds not stated in the notice, and to review the parts of the decision of the lower court even though no notice of appeal or respondent's notice refers to it and though a party has not appealed against it (s.38(2)(b)). On the other hand a notice of appeal drafted too widely may increase liability for costs.

Service

20.20 An appeal is initiated by serving notice on the other party, without need to issue it out of any Office or lodge it until setting down the appeal.[56] It must be served on all those parties to the lower proceedings who are directly affected by the appeal (Ord.59 r.3(4)). The time limit for doing so is set by Order 59 rule 4(1), namely within-

- 21 days (interlocutory order)[57]
- 21 days (order in Order 14 or Order 86 summary judgment proceedings)
- 28 days (insolvency)
- six weeks (any other final order)

of the date when the order of the lower court was filed. "Where a summons to vary or discharge a certificate and the further *consideration of the action are heard together, and an order is made on both,*[58] notice of appeal in respect of the order made on the summons may be served at any time before the expiration of the period within which notice of appeal could be served in respect of the order made on further consideration" (Ord.59 r.4(2)). The period for appeal is postponed where the High Court has given a certificate of suitability for 'leap-frog' appeal to the House of Lords (Ord.59 r.4(3)). As notice of appeal is not a pleading, the time limit runs during vacation. Order 3 rule 4 does not extend the time because service is not an act required to be done at a court office.

20.21 The time limit is extendable, prospectively by the lower court (Ord.59 r.15), or at any time by the Court of Appeal, or by written consent of the

---

54 *Keenahan* v *Gannon* [1894] 1 IR 412.

55 See *Scarson* v *Maguire* (1953) 87 ILTR 200; *Belfast CC* v *Valuation Commr* [1915] 2 IR 319. In *Scarson* there was a claim and counterclaim between a car driver and a cow owner for a road collision. The driver's claim was successful and the cow owner's counterclaim was dismissed. The cow owner appealed only against the dismissal of his counterclaim. On appeal he was estopped from alleging any liability on the driver because of the unappealed decree against him.

56 White Book (1997) 59/3/3.

57 For the purposes of r.4, an order on a summary application by the Crown re revenue duties under s.14 of the Crown Proceedings Act is deemed to be interlocutory: Ord.77 r.6(7).

58 The words in italics have been omitted in error from the rule as published in the current *Red Book*.

respondent (Ord.3 r.5). An application to the Court of Appeal, after the time limit has expired, for leave to appeal must be made by motion on notice (Ord.59 r.14(2)). Order 3 rule 5 also gives power to abridge the time limit for appeal, on application presumably of the appellant who wants a hearing within a few hours or days.

20.22 Since the time limits for appeal are set by the RSC, a notice of appeal served out of time is a mere irregularity under Order 2 rule 1,[59] which the respondent may not be able to have set aside if he takes a step to contest the appeal on the merits.

Urgent appeals

20.23 In very urgent cases the appeal can be listed for hearing in a few hours or days by telephoning or going to the Appeals and Lists Office, without a written notice of appeal being served but giving as much notice as possible to the respondent.[60]

Extension of time

20.24 Extension of time is a matter of discretion.[61] The applicant and his lawyers do not have to be blameless, and it is not essential to show that the appeal is meritorious; the merits of the appeal can be considered but if the delay is short and excusable, extension will be refused only if the appeal is hopeless.[62] Efforts to obtain legal aid for the appeal can be a good excuse.[63] In *Philpot* v *Philpot*[64] extension was granted for appeal four years late where the applicant had just come of age. In *Johnson* v *Gilpins Ltd*,[65] the Court of Appeal gave leave nine months late where the issue was an important point of evidence on which the case law was unclear and a new English decision had just been given which counsel advised was relevant to the issue on appeal. Extension is not granted as of course merely because there is no irreparable prejudice to the respondent.[66] On the other hand, prejudice to the respondent and others is a potential ground of refusal.[67]

---

59 *Whitehouse Hotels* v *Lido Savoy* (1974) 48 ALJR 406.

60 White Book (1997) 59/1/12 n.'Very Urgent Appeals'.

61 See para. 1.33. In case law under the old Rules, where "special leave" of the Court of Appeal was required for late appeals, the applicant had to show a *bona fide* intention to appeal formed within the time limit.

62 White Book (1997) 59/4/4.

63 *Norwich Building Society* v *Steed* [1991] 1 WLR 449. But note the words of Hodson LJ in *Addison* v *Addison* [1960] 1 WLR 1088: " I cannot understand why parties are not prepared, if they seek to appeal, to incur the very small expense of giving notice of appeal and filing it in the proper place, without waiting to see whether the public purse will bear the cost of their litigation."

64 (1908) 42 ILTR 165, the subject-matter, funds in court, being still intact.

65 [1989] NI 294, at 298.

66 *Davis* v *Northern Ireland Carriers* [1979] NI 19, at 20D-H. This case sets out the principles for extending time limits, discussed at para. 1.35.

67 *Esdaile* v *Paine* (1889) 40 Ch D 520, *affd.* [1891] AC 210.

Mode of service

20.25 Service is effected under Order 65 rule 5 (para. 6.20), and the solicitor on record for the respondent can be served.[68] Substituted service can be ordered.[69] Notice may be served outside Northern Ireland in so far as a writ could (Ord.11 r.9(4)). Notice of appeal must be served (only) on the parties directly affected by the appeal, even those who did not appear. An appealing plaintiff need not serve a third party, though the defendant may then want to seek leave to do so. An appealing defendant should serve any defendant who is alleged to be liable in the alternative or jointly and/or severally for the same damage. A party unnecessarily served may be disallowed the costs of appearing.[70]

Setting down

20.26 The appellant then enters the appeal within seven days after service, or longer if the Master (Queen's Bench and Appeals) allows, by lodging in the Central Office (Appeals and Lists Office)[71] two copies of the notice, one stamped and endorsed with particulars of service, and a copy of the order appealed against (Ord.59 r.5(1)). A Court Fee of £150 is payable. The seven days excludes weekends and public holidays (Ord.3 r.2(5)). The Court or a single judge thereof can extend or abridge the time under Order 3 rule 5. Order 59 rule 5(2) says that "upon an appeal being entered it shall be listed for hearing not earlier than the date named in the notice of appeal". Presumably this means that, unlike England, the setting down implies that the appellant is ready for the hearing. Therefore, presumably, an extension of time will be granted more readily than in England, and more readily than extension of time for notice of appeal.

20.27 A court official should not enter an appeal for hearing if the notice of appeal is improper or improperly served, but the acceptance by the Office of an appeal does not connote that the Court has jurisdiction to hear the appeal.[72] If the appellant fails to set down, the respondent may bring a motion on notice for the notice to be struck out,[73] or dismissed for want of prosecution.[74]

20.28 The appellant must lodge a copy of the judgment or order appealed against. This means the operative court order, not the written verdict or judgment which must be lodged at a later stage. If the order has not been drawn up it must be drawn up by the lower court before the appeal can be set down,[75] unless leave is given to proceed without lodging the order.[76] Except in cases of

---

[68] White Book (1997) 65/5/7. See para. 6.20.
[69] *Ibid.* 59/3/13.
[70] *Ibid.*59/3/11.
[71] Even if the appeal is from the Chancery or Family Division.
[72] *Dalton* v *Ringwood* (1906) 40 ILTR 52.
[73] White Book (1997) 59/5/11.
[74] *Dhand* v *McCrabbe* (1962) 96 ILTR 196.
[75] *Hudson* v *Lindsay* (1880) 6 LR Ir 420.
[76] *Mahon* v *Mahon* (1903) 3 NIJR 253, where the judge had refused to draw up his order refusing an *ex parte* application.

genuine urgency, the Office will not set down the appeal unless all the requisite documents are lodged and the revenue fee paid.

Respondent's case

20.29 The respondent may serve a 'respondent's notice' if he contends that: (a) the judgment should be varied, or varied in the event of the appeal being allowed; (b) it should be affirmed on different grounds from those given by the lower court; or (c) by way of cross-appeal, that the lower court decision is wrong (Ord. 59 r.6(1)). According to the White Book (1997) 59/1/52, section 35(2) of the Judicature Act applies where appropriate to require leave to serve a cross-notice or notice to vary. The notice must state the grounds and the precise order which he seeks on the appeal. The respondent's notice must be served on the appellant and all parties directly affected by it within seven days (interlocutory order), 21 days (final order), after service of the notice of appeal; and within a further two days, two copies must be presented by the respondent in the Central Office (Ord.59 r.6(3)(4)). A Court fee of £40 is payable. The time can be extended by the Court of Appeal or a single judge thereof under Order 3 rule 5.

20.30 After a notice of appeal has been served on him, the respondent should not serve a 'notice of appeal' unless he is appealing against an order which is not the subject of the appellant's notice (Ord.59 r.3(5)). He should always serve a notice of appeal, applying for any necessary leave or extension of time, if he wishes to challenge the order on a distinct claim or counterclaim which is not included in the appellant's notice, or the order made between himself and another party not served with the appeal. He should serve a cross-appeal if he wishes to dispute the lower court's jurisdiction. He can serve a respondent's notice on a party who is co-respondent to the notice of appeal. He may without leave serve notice and a copy of the notice of appeal on a third party against whom he claims a remedy in the event of the appeal succeeding.[77]

INTERLOCUTORY POWERS

20.31 The power to make interlocutory orders in a pending appeal is exercised by the full Court of Appeal. A single judge may at any time give incidental directions in a pending appeal not involving a decision of the appeal, and during vacation may grant leave to appeal or make an interim order; any such order, other than granting of leave, may be reviewed by the full Court (Judicature Act, s.37). An application to the Court of Appeal is by motion under Order 8 (Ord.59 r.14(1)). Where under the rules an application may be made either to the court below or the Court of Appeal, it should not be made initially to the Court of Appeal unless it is impracticable to apply to the court below (Ord.59 r.14(4)). For the purposes of a pending appeal, the Court of Appeal can grant discovery but the applicant must show either exceptional circumstances or that new evidence will be admitted under the *Ladd* v *Marshall* principles.[78]

---

[77] *British Road Services* v *Crutchley* [1967] 1 WLR 835.

[78] *R* v *Sec of State for Home Dept, ex p Gardian*, 'The Times' 1 April 1996 (CA).

20.32 *Striking out.* The Court has inherent power to strike out summarily any appeal which is plainly incompetent, or frivolous, vexatious or an abuse of process,[79] and the respondent is entitled to his costs.[80] An appeal can be struck out not only for non-compliance with the rules, but also for want of prosecution.[81] Then the order of the lower court stands.

20.33 *Stay of enforcement.* The proceedings of the lower court remain effective unless the lower court or Court of Appeal stays enforcement pending appeal (Ord.59 r.13(1)). Application should be made initially to the trial judge or other judge of the lower court. A stay is granted only for good reason, for example where the plaintiff/respondent is a foreigner or there is little prospect of recovering the money if the judgment is reversed.[82] Stay should be granted where the appeal has some prospect and the appellant would be ruined without a stay.[83] In *Redmond* v *Ireland* [84] the Irish Supreme Court set out the main considerations in a personal injury action where the defendant (being insured) appeals against an award; they are: (a) whether there is arguable case for appeal on liability; (b) whether the money will be recoverable from the plaintiff if the appeal succeeds; (c) prejudice to the plaintiff in being kept out of the money pending appeal; (d) the length of time before the appeal may be heard; and (e) whether the defendant applied for a stay to the trial court. Where the appeal is against a non-monetary order, such as an order for discovery, a stay of enforcement should be given where the appeal would be rendered academic.[85] In order to ensure that an appeal is not rendered nugatory, the lower court or the Court of Appeal has power, by stay of enforcement, injunction or otherwise, to preserve the *status quo,*[86]and grant to an appellant a *Mareva* injunction if there is a good arguable appeal.[87] Interest on the judgment of the High Court runs while enforcement is delayed pending the appeal, unless the Court of Appeal otherwise orders (Ord.59 r.13(2)). In practice, respondents rarely seek to enforce a judgment pending appeal.

20.34 *Withdrawal of appeal.* There is no provision in the rules for abandonment of an appeal. An appeal can be withdrawn only by leave of the Court of Appeal,[88] but that constitutes a withdrawal of the notice of appeal, and the Court can later give leave to lodge a new notice of appeal if the respondent is not prejudiced. Leave to withdraw will be given only in exceptional circumstances.[89] The appellant who wishes to give up, or who has reached a compromise whereby the appeal is to be dropped, should lodge a request for the

---

[79] White Book (1997) 59/3/4.
[80] *Gilson* v *Bennett* [1920] 1 IR 75, where the appeal was struck out by the registrar for being out of time.
[81] *Dhand* v *McCrabbe* (1962) 96 ILTR 196; *Treacy* v *Ryan* (1878) 2 LR Ir 130 (where the appeal was ordered to stand dismissed unless the appellant set it down within one week).
[82] *Commr of Taxation* v *Myer Emporium* (1986) 160 CLR 220.
[83] *Linotype-Hell* v *Baker* [1992] 4 All ER 887.
[84] [1992] 2 IR 362.
[85] *Megaleasing* v *Barrett* [1992] 1 IR 219.
[86] *Orion Properties* v *du Cane* [1962] 1 WLR 1085.
[87] *Ketchum* v *Group Public Relations* [1996] 4 All ER 314 (CA).
[88] *Tod-Heatley* v *Barnard* [1890] WN 130.
[89] *Re Samuel* [1945] Ch 364.

appeal to be dismissed with costs, or a consent of all parties to dismissal of the appeal.[90] Such a course is final once the dismissal order has been perfected and there is no jurisdiction for the appeal to be revived or a new notice of appeal to be allowed;[91] but until the dismissal order is perfected, the original notice of appeal is still alive and can still be proceeded with unless the Court strikes it out as an abuse of process by reason of prejudice to the respondent.[92] If a consensual dismissal order has not yet been perfected, it is binding if the respondent has given consideration (e.g. by waiving costs or dropping his cross-appeal) or has acted on it to his detriment.[93] Dismissal or withdrawal of the appeal does not stop the cross-appeal or respondent's notice seeking variation of the lower court order, unless the respondent has agreed to do so.

Compromise of appeal. See para. 20.45.

20.35 *Security for costs.* In special circumstances, the respondent may apply to the Court of Appeal for an order that the appellant give security for costs of appeal (Judicature Act, s.38(1)(h); Ord.59 r.10(5)). The application may be on any ground, for example that the appellant is impecunious, or that the appeal appears vexatious. The grounds for security at first instance (para. 11.56) provide some guidance.[94] Under Irish practice, poverty is not *per se* a special circumstance,[95] if there is a substantial point of appeal.[96] The NI Court of Appeal[97] has recently considered the question: it treated insolvency or impecuniosity as a special circumstance; the Court has a discretion to do what is just and equitable looking generally at all the relevant circumstances, including the merits of the appeal or lack thereof, the respondent's delay in applying for security, the balance of hardship (e.g. that the appellant cannot afford security and will thus be barred from appeal, that the result of the appeal will save or ruin him), and the extent to which the appellants' impecuniosity is a result of the respondent's alleged wrongdoing. Security should rarely be more than one third of the probable costs.[98] It should not normally be ordered against a legally aided appellant.

20.36 *Amendment.* The appellant is confined to the grounds and the relief stated on the notice of appeal, save by leave of the Court (Ord.59 r.3(3)). So also the respondent is bound by his notice (Ord.59 r.6(2)). Either notice may be amended by or with leave of the Court of Appeal at any time (Ord.59 r.7).

---

90 See White Book (1997) 59/1/15.

91 *Ogwr BC* v *Knight*, 'The Times' 13 January 1994.

92 *Re Samuel* [1945] Ch 364. *Portrush UDC* v *Mairs* [1937] NI 52 says that a notice of withdrawal cannot be set aside unless given by mistake, but the decision is based on authority which was treated as obsolete in *Re Samuel.*

93 *National Benzole* v *Gooch* [1961] 1 WLR 1489.

94 White Book (1997) 59/10/19.

95 Wylie p.798; *Richardson* v *Richardson* (1910) 44 ILTR 196. It is a ground if he is an undischarged bankrupt: *Hennessy* v *Keating* (1907) 41 ILTR 203.

96 *Moore* v *AG* [1929] IR 544. And see *Malone* v *Brown Thomas* [1995] 1 ILRM 369 (SC).

97 *Humberclyde Finance* v *McFarland* [1997] 3 BNIL 108. The Irish cases are not cited in the judgment.

98 *Fallon* v *An Bord Pleanala* [1992] 2 IR 380, *sed contra*: White Book (1997) 59/10/26, which says that the security should be such as to cover the respondent's full costs on standard taxation.

There are no particular fetters on the discretion to allow amendment, though the Court may be reluctant to allow an issue to be raised which is not at issue on the pleadings in the High Court. In *McAvoy* v *Goodyear*[99] the Court of Appeal allowed the appellant to amend the notice to insert a ground of appeal that the trial judge intervened unfairly against him, but commented that appellant's counsel had not thought of that as a ground of appeal before seeing the trial transcript. The Court also has power to amend the pleadings (see below para. 20.41).

20.37 *Amendment as to parties to the appeal.* The Court may direct that the notice of appeal or respondent's notice be served on any person, whether a party to the lower proceedings or not, and may postpone the hearing on doing so (Ord.59 r.8). It may then give any judgment or order as if the person were an original party (Ord.59 r.8(2)(b)). Only a person with a legal or proprietary interest should be added. The Court can also exercise the lower court's powers of amendment, or of adding or striking out of parties. It is not the practice to add a party to enable relief to be claimed against him that was not sought in the lower court.[100] The Court may make any order to ensure that it determines the real question in controversy between the parties (Judicature Act, s.38(2)).

20.38 *Change of parties by death etc.* If either party dies or becomes bankrupt pending appeal after service of notice, the Court of Appeal can exercise the powers of the High Court to continue in the name of the personal representative, trustee in bankruptcy etc., under Order 15 rule 7. If the death etc. occurs before service of a notice of appeal, then the intending appellant can apply under that rule to the High Court. If the intending appellant dies, his personal representative can apply to the Court of Appeal for leave to appeal. It may be that if the intended respondent dies, the appellant can serve notice of appeal on his solicitor and apply to the Court of Appeal under Order 15 rule 7.

PRESENTING THE CASE FOR APPEAL

Loss of right of appeal

20.39 A party may lose his right of appeal or his right to appeal on a particular ground by conduct which renders it inequitable,[101] for example, acting towards the subject-matter of the action so that justice cannot now de done;[102] acting on and accepting the benefit of the lower court's ruling or judgment;[103] accepting the practice of the lower court without reserve;[104] contesting the merits without objecting to the plaintiff's mode of procedure[105] or

---

99 [1973] March-April NIJB, at 11-12.

100 *Edison & Swan* v *Holland* (1889) 41 Ch D 28.

101 *Lissenden* v *Bosch* [1940] AC 412, at 420.

102 *Re Naish* [1895] 1 IR 266 (mother, appealing against custody order, abducted child and failed to obey order to bring child to appeal hearing).

103 *Per* Curran LJ, *Min of Development* v *Law* [1970] June NIJB (appeal against admission of evidence unchallenged at trial); *Pirrie* v *York Street Flax Spinning* [1894] 1 IR 417 (appeal against rejection of evidence, having not sought to justify its admission at the trial).

104 *Per* Lord MacDermott LCJ, *Min of Development* v *Law*.

105 *McCooey* v *Breen* [1980] 2 NIJB at 2.

the constitution of the court;[106] or acting upon an 'unless order'.[107] Demand and acceptance of money under the judgment is not *per se* a bar, provided that restitution is possible,[108] unless it amounts to an election to waive an alternative remedy.[109]

New case on appeal

20.40 The parties may raise a new point or argument on appeal not raised at the trial, but only if after careful scrutiny the Court of Appeal is satisfied beyond reasonable doubt that it can be dealt with on the evidence given at the trial; and a new point of pure law will usually be allowed unless the other party is prejudiced.[110] The Court of Appeal itself may raise a new point, and in doing so must ensure that both parties are allowed to present argument on it.[111] In *McKee* v *Alexander Greer*[112] Lowry LCJ stated the following guidelines (in the context of jury trials)-

(1) It is for the Court's discretion whether to allow a point to be raised on appeal which was not made by requisition or objection to the judge.

(2) The Court may allow an argument that there was no evidence of an issue where that argument was not made to the trial judge, but it will rarely allow an argument that an issue should have been left to the jury when that was not argued before the trial judge.

(3) If the failure to object at the trial is calculated to secure an advantage the point will rarely be entertained on appeal. A party has a duty to object at the trial to any defect which can be remedied there.

(4) The dominant principle is that justice must be done.

(5) The discretion as to costs will be influenced by the fact that an appeal has succeeded on a point which if made at the trial would have obviated the appeal.

20.41 A party may also be restricted in his case on appeal by an estoppel or election arising from his conduct of the trial, or in the case of a procedural matter by his failure to object. A party should not be heard to make for the first time on appeal an objection to evidence of facts not pleaded if the trial judge could have dealt with the objection by amendment without any prejudice to the objecting party.[113] He cannot make a new case inconsistent with that

---

[106] *QUB* v *McLaughlin* [1982] 9 NIJB at 10.

[107] *McHugh* v *McGoldrick* [1921] 2 IR 163 (order remitting to county court unless plaintiff gives security).

[108] *Sterling Realty* v *Manning* [1964] NZLR 1017; *Horner* v *Min of Development* [1971] March NIJB.

[109] *Meng Leong* v *Jip Hong Trading* [1985] AC 511 (PC).

[110] *Pittalis* v *Grant* [1989] QB 605, at 611.

[111] *Hoecheong Products* v *Cargill Ltd* [1995] 1 WLR 404 (PC).

[112] [1974] NI 60, at 65-6.

[113] *Petticrew* v *Chief Constable* [1988] NI 192, at 199H-200A.

made at the trial.[114] The Court can find that there was no case to answer on the plaintiff's evidence even though the defendant did not so apply at the trial.[115] An objection can always be made for the first time on appeal to the jurisdiction of the lower court;[116] to the legality of a contract;[117] or to the plaintiff's competency to sue.[118] It is usually too late to apply at the appeal hearing for a substantial amendment of pleadings to raise an issue not considered by the trial judge.[119] In *Ards BC* v *Northern Bank*[120] the defendant had in its Defence admitted legal liability for part of the amount claimed; it sought at the appeal hearing leave to amend the Defence to withdraw that admission and argue that there was no legal liability on the cause of action as pleaded by the plaintiff; the Court of Appeal refused leave as prejudicial to the plaintiff because it would lead to the claim being dismissed with the plaintiff unable to bring a new action correctly pleaded. Apparently the option of directing a new trial with liberty for both parties to amend their pleadings was not considered.

Amendment of the notice of appeal. See above, para. 20.36.

New evidence

20.42 If a party wishes to adduce fresh evidence he should apply to the Court of Appeal for leave before the hearing. The Court may receive further evidence, by oral examination, affidavit or deposition (Ord.59 r.10(2)). If there has been "a trial or hearing on the merits" in the High Court, rule 10(2) demands special grounds to be shown. The case of *Ladd* v *Marshall*[121] laid down three conditions: (a) that the evidence could not with reasonable diligence have been obtained for the trial; (b) that it will probably have important influence on the result; and (c) that it appears credible. Where the new evidence is that of a trial witness who now has changed his story, it will fail the third condition unless it appears that he was bribed or coerced or made a mistake.[121] These conditions have been applied rigidly in the English and Irish courts.[122] A grant of judgment under Order 14 or Order 86, or, *semble*, Order 113, is a hearing on the merits, but the refusal thereof is not.[123]

20.43 The three *Ladd* v *Marshall* conditions can be waived in at least eight cases-

(1) Judicial review, if in the wider public interest (para. 19.90).

(2) Orders of committal to prison (where the practice on appeals from conviction on indictment is adopted).

---

114 *McKnight* v *Armagh CC* [1922] 2 IR 137 (High CA), *per* Andrews LJ at 149-50.
115 *Connolly* v *Morrow* [1979] 6 NIJB; *Devine* v *Carson* [1929] NI 26.
116 *Kirkpatrick* v *Watson* [1943] Ir Jur R 4 (NI); *Keenan* v *Shield Insurance* [1988] IR 89.
117 *Snell* v *Unity Finance* [1964] 2 QB 203.
118 Cf. *Revenue Commrs* v *Bradley* [1943] IR 16 (case stated).
119 *Livingstone* v *MOD* [1984] NI 356, at 363-4 (where the amendment was allowed for the purposes of a new trial).
120 [1994] 10 BNIL 34.
121 [1954] 1 WLR 1489. See White Book (1997) 59/10/7.
122 See *Murphy* v *MOD* [1991] 2 IR 161; *Linton* v *MOD* [1983] NI 51(HL).
123 *Langdale* v *Danby* [1982] 1 WLR 1123 (HL).

(3) Welfare of minors.

(4) By the terms of Order 59 rule 10 itself there is no need for special grounds where it is evidence of matters which have occurred (as opposed to being discovered) after the date of trial. Such evidence will be admitted at the Court's discretion if it is relevant and substantial. This often arises in personal injury cases where the plaintiff's injuries have taken an unexpected turn or the prognosis has significantly altered. Indeed the Court is bound to decide on the facts as they exist at the date of appeal,[124] so evidence of subsequent events is received if it substantially changes a basic assumption made at the trial or if justice or common sense demand it.[125]

(5) The other party was guilty of deception or impropriety.[126]

(6) The principles can be relaxed if the trial was on affidavit.[127]

(7) The principles can be relaxed on an appeal in interlocutory proceedings.[128]

(8) Where the appellant applies for a new trial under the inherited jurisdiction (para. 20.56), the injustice or irregularity on which the appeal is based may warrant new evidence of matters occurring before or during the trial.

THE HEARING OF THE APPEAL

20.44 The appellant's solicitor should 'bespeak' all relevant court records, the transcript or note of the evidence relevant to the appeal, and the trial judge's written judgment or the transcript of his oral judgment; then offer copies of the same to the respondent's solicitor on payment of half the cost. The Court of Appeal sits near the end of each term for the purpose of fixing dates for hearing of appeals during the next term. Counsel should attend to give an indication of the nature of the appeal, whether witnesses will be required, and the likely length of the hearing. Not less than seven days before it is likely to be listed for hearing, the appellant must lodge three copies of: the notice of appeal, respondent's notice, lower court order, pleadings and particulars, a transcript of the judge's judgment or his note of his reasons, a transcript or judge's note of such parts of the evidence in the lower court as are relevant, a list of exhibits or schedule of evidence, and any relevant affidavits and exhibits used in the lower court (Ord.59 r.9). The appeal is listed for hearing on a date not sooner than the date stated on the notice of appeal, though it can be listed for early hearing on written consent of the parties (Ord.59 r.5(2)). Applications to postpone the date fixed for hearing are not favourably received, and a good reason must invariably be shown.

---

124 *Blumberg* v *McCormick* [1915] 2 IR 402, at 408; *Dowd* v *Kerry CC* [1970] IR 27.

125 *Mulholland* v *Mitchell* [1971] AC 666; *Fitzgerald* v *Kenny* [1994] 2 ILRM 8; cf. *Irwin* v *Brown* [1993] 6 NIJB 18.

126 *Linton* v *MOD* [1983] NI 51, at 77A.

127 *McKernan* v *HM Prison Governor* [1983] NI 83, at 95D.

128 *Forward* v *West Sussex CC* [1995] 4 All ER 207, at 212b (CA).

Compromise

20.45 Though the parties can come to their own private contractual arrangement after a judgment in the lower court, it is only by appellate proceedings that they can have the judgment of the lower court changed. Where the claimant at first instance is under disability any compromise after judgment must be approved and only the Court of Appeal can do so, so that a 'friendly' notice of appeal must be lodged to have it approved.[129] The main methods of compromise are-

(1) By written consent of the parties lodged in the Appeals Office, an appeal may be marked dismissed by consent, but the respondent's notice or cross appeal may continue.

(2) A dismissal by consent may be part of a contractual agreement between the parties. The Court will not accept such a dismissal where the terms of the agreement involve a variation of the lower court's order.[130]

(3) The parties may ask for the appellate court to make an order by consent, though the Court may be reluctant to reverse or vary a lower court judgment without a hearing.[131]

(4) Where a simple dismissal by consent is not practicable, the parties may agree to a '*Tomlin* order' to stay the appeal on terms agreed, with liberty to apply to the lower court.

Any settlement of an appeal must be announced in court, even if no order of the Court is required.

The hearing

20.46 An appeal is heard by two or three judges (excluding the judge appealed from) in the Royal Courts of Justice (Judicature Act, s.36). If, due to its difficulty or importance, a party wishes to have the appeal heard by three judges, application should be made as soon as possible after notice of appeal. If a two-judge court disagrees, the appeal may on application (shall, in a criminal cause or matter) be re-heard before three judges (s.36), and if it is not reheard the judgment of the lower court stands affirmed.[132]

20.47 In all cases except ordinary personal injury appeals grounded on weight of evidence, appellant's counsel should lodge a skeleton legal argument and give a copy to opposing counsel at least two days before the hearing; and respondent's counsel may lodge and serve an argument at his option.[133] A list of authorities should be lodged and exchanged before the hearing (para. 14.24). On points of law, the Court is bound by precedents of the Northern Ireland

---

[129] *Walsh* v *George Kemp* [1938] 2 All ER 266.

[130] White Book (1997) 59/1/19.

[131] *Ibid.* 59/1/21.

[132] *In re McConnell* [1956] NI 151.

[133] Practice Direction [1987] 9 BNIL 73.

Court of Appeal, except where the Court's decision is final.[134] Decisions of the House of Lords are binding, though strictly speaking only such decisions on appeal from Northern Ireland.[135]

20.48 The Court may call for an assessor to assist (s.61). It has the same powers as the court appealed from, for example to order discovery and production of documents, to refer a matter to an officer under Order 36, to sit *in camera,*[136] to amend the pleadings or add or strike out parties. It is vitally important, as in the lower court, to ensure that the pleadings and the record of the trial conform to the issues actually in dispute so that the Court can adjudicate on those issues.[137] Pleadings can be amended for the purpose of the appeal hearing or a new trial.[138]

20.49 *Non-appearance.* If the appellant does not appear the appeal should be dismissed.[139] If the respondent does not appear the Court may hear the argument of the appellant and determine the appeal. As to re-opening an appeal determined in the absence of a party, see para. 20.77.

Nature of the hearing

20.50 Except where the appeal is based solely on an application for a new trial on grounds of an error or irregularity in the lower court (Ord.59 r.2) every appeal under Order 59 "shall be by way of rehearing" (Ord.59 r.3(1)). It is a rehearing on the record of the evidence at the trial without the trial testimony being re-heard. In most appeals the hearing consists entirely of speeches and dialogue by counsel with the judges. Not only can the Court hear new evidence, and evidence of events happening since the trial, but it can consider points not raised in the notice of appeal, and can make any order which now appears proper.[140] It applies the common (i.e. non-statutory) law as it now stands.[141] It applies the statute law as at the time of the cause of action arising, save in so far as a new statute is to be interpreted retrospectively. Order 59 rule 11(1) allows the Court to order a new trial on such an appeal. The Court must have a record of relevant oral evidence, by *verbatim* transcript or, where the trial judge deems it sufficient, his note, or by other means; and office copies of every affidavit used as evidence must be before the Court (Ord.59 r.12). Where by reason of a breakdown in the recording apparatus, there is a gap in the transcript, counsel for each side should try to agree a record of the missing evidence.[142] Though not expressly stated in the RSC, the existence and amount

---

[134] *Leppington* v *Belfast Corp*, CA, NI 18 March 1969, discussed by Miers (1969) 20 NILQ 308.

[135] See further White Book (1997) 59/1/61, Vol 2 [4629].

[136] Though that is generally undesirable as appeals are more likely to be of general concern.

[137] See *Farrell* v *Sec of State for Defence* [1980] NI 55 (HL).

[138] *Livingstone* v *MOD* [1984] NI 356.

[139] *Spanier* v *Marchant* [1878] WN 214.

[140] White Book (1997) 59/3/1.

[141] *Ferguson* v *Rapid Metal* [1972] June (Pt II) NIJB.

[142] *James P. Corry* v *Clarke* [1967] NI 62, at 67.

of any lodgment under Order 22 should be kept secret from the Court until liability and quantum are decided.

20.51 The appellant's counsel always begins. If there is a cross-appeal the cross-appellant may begin if the burden on all issues lies on him.[143] The Court will be slow to differ from the trial judge, especially if there was a full oral hearing, on his conclusions of fact, but will freely review his inferences of fact or his failure to draw such inference. It will only review his discretionary decisions if he wrongly exercised it or failed to exercise it. It will alter his decision on quantum of damages only if it is wrong in principle or out of the proper range. It will freely review his decision on a point of law. The parties may adduce new evidence, by oral testimony, affidavit or deposition; but if there was a trial on the merits in the lower court, evidence of events which occurred up to the date of trial can be heard only on special grounds (para. 20.42).

Powers of the Court of Appeal

20.52 The Court of Appeal has for the purposes of and incidental to an appeal and the amendment or enforcement of any judgment made thereon[144] all the jurisdiction of the lower court, and under section 38(1) of the Judicature Act may-

(a) confirm reverse or vary its decision;

(b) remit to the lower court with directions;

(c) on appeal from the High Court, order a new trial or make any order as could be made on an application for a new trial;

(d) adjourn;

(e) draw any inference of fact or make any order which the lower court might have made;

(f) in an appeal by case stated, amend or remit for amendment;

(g) make any order as to costs and expenses in both courts;

(h) in special circumstances order security for costs;

(i) make other necessary orders.

The Court of Appeal itself may raise a new point, and in doing so must ensure that both parties are allowed to present argument on it.[145] In *Cunningham* v *Milk Marketing Board*[146] the Court of Appeal held that an issue not raised before the trial judge was material: it remitted to the judge to rule on the law on that issue. In *Cullen* v *Chief Constable*[147] on an appeal against the judge's

---

[143] White Book (1997) 59/6/3.

[144] But otherwise has no original jurisdiction: *Ocean Software* v *Kay* [1992] QB 583.

[145] *Hoecheong* v *Cargill Ltd* [1995] 1 WLR 404 (PC).

[146] [1990] 11 NIJB 33, at 54-8.

[147] [1996] 6 BNIL 76

ruling on a preliminary issue of law, it remitted to the trial judge to have the facts decided first.

20.53 It may make any order to ensure that the real question in dispute is determined on the merits and its powers are not restricted by any unappealed interlocutory order (s.38(2)(a); Ord.59 r.10(6)).[148] Its power to review all parts of the lower court's decision is exercisable without any notice of appeal or respondent's notice on that part, or without an appeal by any particular party, or it may affirm or vary the decision on a ground not stated in the notices (s.38(2)(b)). Thus it may quash a finding made against a party who has not appealed.[149] It has all the powers and duties of the lower court, for example as to amendment and as to reference of a question of fact under Order 36 (Ord.59 r.10(1)), but this means only those powers which the lower court could have exercised on the particular application out of which the appeal arises.[150] It can amend the pleadings and the record of the trial.[151] If the Court has directed service on a person under Order 59 rule 8 it may give any judgment or order as if that person were a party (Ord.59 r.8(2)(b)). Documents impounded by the Court can be inspected or removed only by order of the Court, or on request by the Attorney-General or Director of Public Prosecutions (Ord.59 r.10(7)(8)).

Form of appeal

20.54 Appeals operate under a dual system, both of which are governed by the same rules of procedure: (a) the jurisdiction of appeal by rehearing; and (b) the inherited jurisdiction to hear an application for a new trial or to set aside judgment. The Court's powers are cumulative. The appeal can be treated as brought under either or both forms. This is because upon either form of appeal the Court can order a new trial or can alter or substitute the proper judgment (Judicature Act, s.38(1); Ord.59 rr.2, 11).

(i) Appeal by rehearing

20.55 The Court here considers freely the lower court's findings of fact and law and makes its decision on the basis of the record of the evidence given below, and the documentary and real evidence exhibited, and of any new evidence which it admits. It is concerned with the resolution of the issues of fact and law joined between the parties. It applies the common (i.e. non-statutory) law as it now stands.[152] It applies the statute law as at the time of the cause of action arising, save in so far as a new statute is to be interpreted retrospectively. Order 59 rule 11(1) allows the Court to order a new trial on such an appeal.

---

148 The purpose of the rule is that the parties be not prejudiced by omission to appeal against an interlocutory order which incidentally involves a decision on the point of the appeal, and that the whole thing is open on the merits on the appeal: Wylie, Ord.58 r.14. But it cannot override an interlocutory order which is unappealable: *Hannays* v *Baldeosingh* [1992] 1 WLR 395, at 401E (PC).

149 White Book (1997) 59/10/18.

150 *Hannays* v *Baldeosingh* [1992] 1 WLR 395 (PC).

151 White Book (1997) 20/5-8/15; but see para. 20.40 as to making a new case on appeal.

152 *Ferguson* v *Rapid Metal* [1972] June (Pt II) NIJB.

(ii) Application for new trial

20.56 The Court has been given the jurisdiction formerly vested in Divisional Courts of the High Court[153] to hear an application for a new trial, and the procedure is the same as for any appeal, except that the appeal is not by way of rehearing (Ord.59 r.2). Under this jurisdiction the Court considers the trial record and if necessary hears evidence of matters relating to the conduct of the trial in the lower court. On any appeal the Court may make any order which could be made on an application for a new trial or to set aside a verdict (Ord.59 r.11(1)). On an application for a new trial, the Court can direct judgment for the appellant,[154] unless there is a prospect of further material evidence.[155]

20.57 Among the grounds for ordering a new trial-

(1) Misdirection or non-direction by the judge of himself or the jury on a factual or legal issue causing a substantial wrong or miscarriage.[156]

(2) Wrongly leaving or withdrawing an issue from the jury. The refusal (as well as the granting) of a direction of no case to answer on the plaintiff's evidence can be challenged on appeal, even if the defendant then elects to give evidence; but the Court of Appeal can then invoke the defence evidence to cure the alleged defect in the plaintiff's case.[157]

(3) Wrongly admitting or excluding evidence causing a substantial wrong or miscarriage.[158]

(4) Reaching a verdict which no reasonable jury properly directed could have reached on the evidence. If a new trial has been ordered on this ground and the second jury reach the same finding, the Court should hesitate to order a third trial.[159]

(5) Misconduct, bias shown, irregular or inconsistent verdict by the jury.[160]

(6) Surprise which put the appellant at a substantial disadvantage which he could not reasonably have prepared for,[161] including an unexpected legal argument[162] and procedural surprise,[163] but not an unexpected witness.[164]

---

153 See Wylie, Ord.39.
154 *Steele* v *Gilliland* [1928] NI 19; *Maguire* v *PJ Lagan* [1976] NI 49.
155 *McEvoy* v *James Calder* (1921) 55 ILTR 121 (HL).
156 *Neill* v *Short Bros* [1971] NI 73.
157 *Payne* v *Harrison* [1961] 2 QB 403.
158 *Mercer* v *Mercer* [1924] 2 IR 50(NI); *Colgan* v *Rice* (1903) 37 ILTR 57 (jury hearing of lodgment, not automatically leading to new trial).
159 *McGreene* v *Hibernian Taxi* [1931] IR 377.
160 *Crawford* v *Vance* [1908] 2 IR 521.
161 *Magrath* v *Moffett* (1901) 1 NIJR 176; *McCarthy* v *Fitzgerald* [1909] 2 IR 445 (pleading amended at trial without offering adjournment).
162 *Douglas* v *Ewing* (1856) 6 ICLR 395; affd. 3 Ir Jur NS 174..
163 *Graham* v *Dublin, Wicklow & Wexford Rly* (1895) 29 ILTR 134 (party not notified of date of trial until the morning through error by Post Office).
164 *Christie's Curator* v *Kirkwood* 1996 SLT 1299 (1st Div).

(7) New evidence not available at the trial.

(8) Fraud in obtaining judgment, though this is better dealt with by a fresh action.

(9) Irregularity or error or mistake in the proceedings; or trial generally unsatisfactory.[165]

20.58 Even where the appellant has asked only for a new trial, the Court can allow the appeal and give judgment in his favour if a new trial would serve no purpose other than to give the respondent another chance to present his case.[166] Judgment can be set aside between parties even though only one of them is party to the appeal. For instance, where the plaintiff has been awarded judgment against defendant L and not against defendant W, on appeal by defendant L the Court can set side the plaintiff's judgment against him and also set aside the dismissal against the plaintiff in favour of defendant W. [167] The Court does not have to order a new trial merely because of misdirection, improper admission or rejection of evidence, failure to take jury verdict on an issue where not sought by the parties, unless some substantial wrong or miscarriage resulted (Ord.59 r.11(2)),[168] and it has an overall discretionary power. Thus a new trial may be refused where the appellant's counsel did not make objection or requisition to the judge on his charge to the jury,[169] especially where the error could have been rectified at the trial.[170] The trial judge in summing up to himself does not have to mention every point that he would in charging a jury, and his omission of a relevant point of fact or law does not lead to the assumption that he has overlooked it.[171] Failure to object that there is no evidence on an issue to be left to the jury does not preclude such objection on appeal; but failure to ask the judge to leave an issue to the jury makes such complaint difficult on appeal. It is harder to object to a question left to the jury where the appellant's counsel actually agreed it.[172]

20.59 If the Court orders a new trial it usually avoids any detailed discussion of the factual issues.[173] The Court may order a new trial on one question without disturbing the finding on another question; and if it appears that the substantial wrong or miscarriage affects only part of the matter or some only of the parties, it may confine a new trial to that part or those parties and give final judgment on the rest (Ord.59 r.11(3)). The action is set down for trial by lodging the appropriate documents plus the order for the new trial, bespoken from the office (Ord.34 r.4(4)). The new trial takes place *de novo*, usually before a different judge, on the issues limited by the pleadings and by the order

---

165 *O'Reilly* v *McCall* [1910] 2 IR 42 (HL). See Wylie pp.586-592.
166 *Maguire* v *PJ Lagan* [1976] NI 49.
167 *Sandford* v *Porter* [1912] 2 IR 551.
168 See *Judge* v *McBrien* [1971] March NIJB; White Book (1997) 59/11/8.
169 *Colville* v *Bowman* (1904) 38 ILTR 75.
170 *McKee* v *Greer* [1974] NI 60.
171 *Doherty* v *MOD* [1979] 6 NIJB at 9.
172 *Wightman* v *Mullan* [1977] 3 NIJB, per Jones LJ at 8.
173 *McIlveen* v *Charlesworth* [1973] NI 216, at 224.

of new trial. No estoppel arises from the findings made at the first trial, save insofar as they are outside the scope of the issues ordered to be retried. In a case where the plaintiff appealed against a dismissal on the basis of new evidence and the Court of Appeal ordered a new trial, and the new trial judge awarded damages with a reduction for contributory fault, saying that he did not find the new evidence to be credible, the Court of Appeal then declined to set aside its order for a new trial in the absence of clear evidence that the plaintiff's appeal amounted to a fraud on the Court of Appeal.[174]

Issues on appeal

20.60 *Jurisdictional points.* A decision by the High Court that it has or has not jurisdiction to hear a proceedings is presumably appealable.[175] The Court of Appeal must of its own motion take any point as to its own appellate jurisdiction or as to the lower court's jurisdiction,[176] even if the respondent refuses to argue the point.[177] A point as to the appellate court's jurisdiction should be argued as a preliminary point. Of its own motion the Court can strike out summarily an appeal which is plainly incompetent.[178] The entry and listing of an appeal is a ministerial act and does not affect the issue of jurisdiction.[179] If the Court finds that the lower court had no jurisdiction, it allows the appeal and substitutes the order that the lower court should have made.[180]

20.61 *Evidential ruling.* The admission or exclusion of evidence by the lower court is a matter on which an appeal can be grounded.[181] The decision of a court to admit in evidence an unstamped or insufficiently stamped document cannot found an appeal,[182] and a new trial cannot be ordered on that ground (Ord.59 r.11(5)).[183] The Court of Appeal should take the point about non-compliance with the Stamp Act of its own motion.[184]

20.62 *Discretionary decisions.* The Court of Appeal will hear an appeal from a judgment or order made by a judge wholly within the scope of his discretion, but will not review the decision unless he erred in law or principle, misunderstood the facts, considered irrelevant matters, had no material for the exercise of the discretion, failed to consider his discretion, came to a decision which no reasonable tribunal could make, or made an order which might result

---

[174] *Wood* v *Gahlings*, 'The Times', 29 November 1996 (CA).

[175] Cf. *Ballyjamesduff Loan Society* v *Tierney* (1907) 41 ILTR 187.

[176] *Benson* v *NIRTB* [1942] AC 520 (NI); *Simpson* v *Crowle* [1921] 3 KB 243.

[177] *Re Rowan Hamilton* [1927] NI 132.

[178] *Aviagents* v *Balstravest* [1966] 1 WLR 150.

[179] *Dalton* v *Ringwood* (1906) 40 ILTR 52, at 54.

[180] *Benson* v *NIRTB* [1942] AC 520.

[181] *Vernon* v *Bosley* [1994] PIQR P337, where the appeal was brought, by leave as an interlocutory matter, before the end of the trial.

[182] Phipson 35-35.

[183] But the validity of an unstamped document was the issue heard on appeal in *A-G* v *Ross* [1909] 2 IR 246.

[184] *Routledge* v *McKay* [1954] 1 WLR 615.

in injustice.[185] Discretionary decisions include the granting or refusal of equitable or interlocutory relief such as injunctions, whether to strike out or stay an action or dismiss for want of prosecution, whether to remit an action to the county court, whether to punish for contempt, whether to order security for costs;[186] to whether to stay an action pending medical examination of the plaintiff.[187] As to appeal from a decision in an Order 14 summons, see para. 11.54.

20.63 *Adjournment decision. Semble*, a decision of the High Court to grant or refuse an adjournment is a discretionary decision or order which can be appealed.[188]

Interlocutory orders. See para. 20.10.

Appeal from order as to costs. See para. 20.08.

20.64 *Appeal from judgment in default.* Appeal lies (subject to leave, as it is interlocutory) from a judgment in default. If the defendant alleges that the judgment was obtained irregularly he should apply to the High Court to set it aside; but if he elects to waive that irregularity, he may appeal on the merits to the Court of Appeal. However such appeals should be very rare: it would be hard to find a ground of appeal arising from a judgment in default regularly obtained, and the better course would be to apply to set the judgment aside on an affidavit showing a defence on the merits. If application is made to the High Court to set it aside, the decision on that application is appealable with leave. If a party suffers judgment in default of appearance at the trial, he should apply to the High Court to set it aside under Order 35 rule 2, but if instead he appeals directly to the Court of Appeal, that Court in its discretion may entertain an application for a new trial.[189] *Semble*, leave to appeal is not necessary against a judgment in default obtained at the trial.

Issues of fact

20.65 Unless limited by statute, any appeal is presumed to allow the Court of Appeal freely to review findings of fact as well as of law.[190] The burden of proof is on the party to show that the trial judge's decision of fact is wrong; the Court must examine and weigh the evidence. As a matter of common sense it is reluctant to review a finding of primary fact of which there is any evidence, because the trial judge was able to hear and see the witnesses and assess their

---

185 *Customs and Excise* v *JH Corbitt* [1981] AC 22; *Millar* v *Peebles*, CA, NI, 23 October 1995; White Book (1997) 59/1/59; e.g. where he gave no reasons for exercising the discretion as he did: *Anderson* v *Hyde*, CA, NI, 23 February 1996, at pp.7-8.

186 *Munchie Foods* v *Eagle Star* [1993] 9 NIJB 69.

187 *Ross* v *Tower Upholstery* [1962] NI 3.

188 *Yates* v *Yates* [1954] 1 WLR 564; *de Freyne* v *Fitzgibbon* (1904) 4 NIJR 253. There are several such cases on appeal from the county court to the High Court; but see *Co-operative Retail* v *Sec of State* [1980] 1 WLR 271, where it was held that adjournment is not "a decision on appeal".

189 *In re Edwards* [1982] Ch 30, at 39.

190 Cf. *Ulster Chemists* v *Hemsborough* [1957] NI 185, at 186-7.

credibility.[191] However the Court has express power to draw inferences of fact (Judicature Act, s.38(1)(e); Ord.59 r.10(3)), and will freely review the inferences drawn by the judge from the primary facts and from documentary and real evidence, or draw inferences which he failed or refused to draw, though the view of the trial judge is still given weight.[192] In *McIlveen* v *Charlesworth*[193] the Court itself examined the real evidence. Even where the primary facts are undisputed, the Court will not overturn the judge's conclusions of fact merely because it might have decided differently.[194] The Court should hesitate to review an inference made by the trial judge which depends on oral evidence or recollection of fact.[195] The trial judge's findings are more readily overturned if he has misdirected himself or misunderstood or misused the facts; but the Court of Appeal should not use conjecture and assessment of probabilities in a balanced situation to overturn his conclusions.[196] A negative finding (i.e. a verdict on an issue against the party who bears the burden of proof) is harder to upset.[197]

20.66 The refusal (as well as the granting) of a direction of no case to answer on the plaintiff's evidence can be challenged on appeal, even if the defendant elected to give evidence; but the Court of Appeal can then invoke the defence evidence to cure the alleged defect in the plaintiff's case.[198] A ruling as to whether there is sufficient evidence of the claim to amount to a case to answer, or of a defence or any material issue, is a matter of law.

20.67 The principles as to reviewing findings of fact apply to the verdict of a jury, though it is rare that the Court will be able to know what findings of primary fact the jury made.[199] The Court can draw inferences from the facts found by the jury.[200] An appellate court can review a finding of pure fact of a jury only if it is based on no evidence or if it is a finding which no reasonable person properly directed could have reached.[201]

Damages and apportionment of liability

20.68 The decision of a *judge* as to quantum of damages can be reviewed on appeal but will only be varied if he acted on a wrong principle, erred in law or

---

[191] *Northern Bank* v *Charlton* [1979] IR 149, at 177-81; *Kitson* v *Black* [1976] 1 NIJB at 5-7; White Book (1997) 59/1/58; even expert witnesses: *Ward* v *Macdonald's Restaurants* (1987) 39 DLR 4th 469 (SC Canada). Since most High Court trials are recorded on audio tape in order to enable a transcript to be typed for an appeal, the Court could actually give itself the advantage of hearing the witnesses. So far as the author is aware it has never done so.

[192] *SS Gairloch* [1899] 2 IR 1, at 18.

[193] [1973] NI 216, at 223.

[194] *White* v *DOE* [1988] 5 NIJB 1.

[195] *Hay* v *O'Grady* [1992] 1 IR 210.

[196] *Northern Ireland Rlys* v *Tweed* [1982] 15 NIJB at 10-11.

[197] *Irvine* v *O'Hare* [1987] 2 NIJB 79, at 81.

[198] *Payne* v *Harrison* [1961] 2 QB 403.

[199] *Moan* v *Moan* [1984] 3 NIJB at 6-7.

[200] *Schawel* v *Reade* [1913] 2 IR 64 (HL).

[201] *Mechanical & General* v *Austin* [1935] AC 346.

fact, made a significant miscalculation or awarded a sum so extremely high or low that it amounts to an erroneous assessment.[202] The same criteria are generally used in reviewing the apportionment of contributory fault.[203] The verdict of a *jury* on quantum of damages will be set aside only if it is one which no reasonable jury, applying the right measures and considering all and only the proper matters, could have arrived at.[204] The Court may overturn the award either by subjective approach (if the amount is out of all proportion to the Court's *de novo* assessment of an appropriate amount) or objectively (if the award is materially higher or lower than the Court's assessment arrived at by making all reasonable inferences in favour of the respondent).[205] An award which is not over-excessive may still be overturned if some unfairness in the trial is established.[206] The Northern Ireland cases cited here relate to jury awards in personal injury actions before 1987. Such cases are now heard by judge alone. In defamation cases, still heard by jury, the proper test to be applied when asked to reduce the award is: could a reasonable jury have thought that this award was necessary to compensate the plaintiff and to re-establish his reputation?[207]

20.69 In appeals from judge-only trials the Court has always been able to substitute a proper figure instead of ordering a new trial. It could not formerly substitute a different figure for the award of a jury, but in appeals set down since 1 November 1992, the Court is now free to alter the amount of damages, if excessive or inadequate, without a new trial (Ord.59 r.11(4)).[208] In allowing an appeal by the plaintiff against a dismissal, the Court may remit to the High Court to assess damages,[209] or it may assess damages itself.[210] If there is a very small amount at stake on the appeal, or if the Court finds that the proper judgment bears only an insignificant amount of difference from the judgment appealed against, it may simply dismiss the appeal without variation.[211]

The order on appeal

20.70 If a two-judge court disagrees, the appeal may on application (shall, in a criminal cause or matter) be re-heard before three judges (Judicature Act, s.36). If not reheard the judgment of the lower court stands affirmed.[212] Any settlement of an appeal must be announced in court, even if no order of the

---

202 White Book (1997) 59/10/16; *Davies* v *Powell Duffryn* [1942] AC 601, at 617.

203 *Donoghue* v *Burke* [1960] IR 314.

204 Wylie p.590; White Book (1997) 59/11/3; *Blanchfield* v *Murphy* (1913) 47 ILTR 24; *Mallett* v *McGonagle* [1970] AC 166; [1969] NI 91 (HL); *McKee* v *Alexander Greer* [1974] NI 60, at 67.

205 *McKee* v *Greer* [1974] NI 60, at 68-9.

206 *McAvoy* v *Goodyear* [1973] March-April NIJB, *per* Curran LJ at p.3.

207 *Rantzen v Mirror Group* [1994] QB 670, at 692H (CA).

208 Power given by the Courts and Legal Services Act 1990, s.8.

209 *Hanrahan* v *Merck, Sharp* [1988] ILRM 629.

210 *Bakht* v *Medical Council* [1990] 1 IR 515, at 524.

211 *Scott* v *Pollock* [1976] NI 1 (where the judge's errors in calculation more or less cancelled each other out).

212 *In re McConnell* [1956] NI 151.

Court is required. Any declaration or direction must be obeyed by the lower court; any order of the Court of Appeal is enforceable as if made by the lower court (s.38(3)(4)).

20.71 If on appeal from the High Court, a monetary award is affirmed (in whole or in part) interest is allowed during the delay in enforcement pending appeal unless otherwise ordered (Ord.59 r.13(2)), and *semble*, interest runs on the lower court's judgment if it has not been paid whether or not a stay of enforcement was granted. If the monetary award of the lower court is affirmed in part, interest should be ordered to run on that part from the date of the lower judgment.[213] If on appeal the appellant is awarded a monetary judgment which was refused by the lower court, statutory interest runs on the judgment from the date of the appeal judgment, but the Court can order it to run from the date of the lower court judgment.[214] If the Court makes an order which reverses the order of the lower court as to costs, it is normally proper to order that those costs of the appellant should carry interest from the date of the lower court's judgment, when the costs should have been awarded to him.[215]

20.72 If an appeal succeeds, the respondent has an automatic duty of restitution of money and costs received under the lower court judgment. The Court of Appeal can order repayment with interest,[216] or the appellant can sue for the money and any profit made on it.[217] The respondent's solicitor is not personally liable for repayment of any costs received by him, unless he is guilty of misconduct or has undertaken to repay.[218]

Costs

20.73 *Of successful appeal.* See the White Book (1997) 62/B/13. Generally a successful appellant gets costs of the appeal and, unless winning on a new point or new evidence, costs of the proceedings in the lower court. If the appeal succeeds in part only, as where a defendant appeals on liability and quantum and has quantum reduced, the Court may make a special order for division of the costs of the issues, or proportionate costs. If the defendant appeals on quantum and damages are reduced to a figure still in excess of the amount of a lodgment by him, he is entitled to his costs of the appeal.[219] An appellant may be disallowed all or part of his costs-

(1) if he succeeds only in part or wins on a technicality;

(2) if guilty of objectionable conduct;

---

213 *O'Sullivan* v *Dwyer* (No 2) [1973] IR 81.

214 *Central Electricity* v *Bata Shoe* [1983] 1 AC 105, at 107F (inherent jurisdiction).

215 *Kuwait Airways v Iraqi Airways* [1994] 1 WLR 985.

216 *Central Electricity* v *Bata Shoe* [1983] 1 AC 105, at 107G (inherent jurisdiction).

217 *East Cork Foods* v *O'Dwyer Steel* [1978] IR 103, on the basis that the respondent is constructive trustee of the money from the service of a notice of appeal on him.

218 *Burke* v *Beatty* [1928] IR 91; *Hood-Barrs* v *Crossman* [1897] AC 172; White Book (1997) 59/13/7.

219 *Morrison* v *Barton*, 1994 SC 100.

(3) if the lower court's wrong order was made of its own motion and not asked for or induced by the respondent;[220]

(4) if the respondent does not contest the appeal;[221]

(5) if the appeal succeeds on an objection which could have been but was not made at the trial;[222] or

(6) if the appeal succeeds on a case not made below,[223] on authority not cited below,[224] on a change of law or new development, or on new evidence.[225]

20.74 *Of unsuccessful appeal.* If the respondent wins and the lower court order is affirmed, he should get the costs of appeal and the lower court's order as to costs left intact; respondents with the same interest should get only one set of costs.[226] Costs can be awarded against the appellant if an appeal is dismissed for lack of jurisdiction.[227] The costs incurred by a respondent's notice or cross-appeal can be dealt with and taxed as a separate proceeding if it raises issues substantially separate from the appeal, but documents prepared for the appeal though also used in the cross-appeal are treated as costs of the appeal.[228] A respondent may be disallowed all or part of his costs-

(1) if his case is discreditable;

(2) if he has deceived the appellant or his conduct justified the appeal;

(3) if an important point of law was involved; or

(4) if the appeal is a test case.[229]

20.75 An unsuccessful trustee/personal representative appellant is normally ordered to bear the costs without reimbursement from the estate.[230]

20.75a *Costs on appeal against the Legal Aid Fund.* Costs can be awarded against the Legal Aid Fund where the losing party on the appeal is legally aided where it is just and equitable to do so (para. 17.90).

20.76 *New trial.* If a new trial is ordered the Court usually orders costs of the appeal to the appellant and the costs of the first trial to follow the event of costs of the second trial;[231] but if the error was caused or induced by the respondent the costs of the first trial should normally be appellant's costs in the cause.[232] Where the plaintiff appeals against a direction of no case to answer granted on

---

220 *Thompson* v *Kennedy* (1794) Ir Term R 253.

221 *Rosse* v *Sylvester* (1893) 27 ILTR 109.

222 *McKee* v *Alexander Greer* [1974] NI 60, at 66.

223 *Dempsey* v *Scribbans* [1944] Ir Jur R 17 (amendments made to the Defence).

224 *Boyd* v *Antrim CC* [1941] NI 127, at 132.

225 *Swanzy* v *Southwell* (1878) 12 ILTR 25.

226 *Cornwall* v *Saurin* (1886) 17 LR Ir 595.

227 *Guardians of South Dublin* v *Jones* (1883) 12 LR Ir 358.

228 White Book (1997) 59/6/3.

229 *Warnock* v *Harland & Wolff* [1976] NI 156 (ordered as respondent's costs in the cause).

230 *Fogarty* v *O'Donoghue* [1926] IR 531, at 569, 579-80; White Book (1997) 62/B/20.

231 White Book (1997) 62/8/7; Wylie p.591; *O'Reilly* v *McCall* [1910] 2 IR 42.

232 *Morrow* v *McAdam* [1978] NI 82; full report [1978] 3 NIJB.

application of the defendant, the Court of Appeal on directing a new trial should normally order costs of the appeal and costs of the first trial to the plaintiff.[233]

Finality

20.77 The judgment of the Court of Appeal creates an estoppel *per rem judicatem* in substitution for the judgment of the lower court, save for any unaltered part of the lower court judgment. If an appeal is withdrawn or struck out by consent the lower court's judgment stands as *res judicata*. A judgment of the Court of Appeal has the like effect as a judgment of the court appealed from (Judicature Act, s.38(4)). That means that its judgment is final in the present litigation, subject to its own terms, and to statutory right of appeal. The Court can alter its decision before it is perfected.[234] Thereafter its order can be challenged only by a fresh action to set it aside in the same way as a High Court judgment can;[235] or in special circumstances where it is clear that the appeal judgment was obtained by fraud, the Court of Appeal can set aside its judgment to save extra litigation.[236] Dismissal of an appeal, once the order is perfected, is final.[237] An appeal dismissed or struck out on non-appearance of the appellant can be re-instated on application to the full Court,[238] but an appeal granted where the respondent does not appear cannot be re-opened after perfection of the order, because it has been determined on the merits.[239]

PARTICULAR TYPES OF APPEAL

20.78 Save as otherwise provided for, the Judicature Act (ss.36-8) and Order 59 apply to all appeals to the Court of Appeal, from the High Court or a master and from any court or tribunal (Ord.59 r.1), including appeals on a point of law. For examples of such appeals see Appendix One. Most appeals on a point of law are prescribed by statute or by rules to be by way of case stated, in which case a special procedure applies. Where the appeal is conferred by NI legislation, the Court of Appeal has all the powers of the body appealed from and may remit the appeal etc. (see para. 18.03).

Appeals by case stated

20.79 An appeal by case stated is an appeal on a point of law whereby the court or tribunal appealed from is required to state its findings of fact and the

---

233 *McIlveen* v *Charlesworth* [1973] NI 216. But in the identical situation different orders have been made. In *McCarthy* v *Hastings* [1933] NI 100 the order was: costs of the appeal to be plaintiff's costs in the cause and costs of the first trial to be costs in the cause. In *Dillon* v *Lynch* (No 2) (1961) 95 ILTR 189, the usual practice of the Irish Supreme Court was said to be: costs of the appeal to the appellant and costs of the first trial to be costs in the cause.

234 As in *Vernon* v *Bosley (No 2)* [1997] 1 All ER 614 (CA), where new evidence was unearthed that showed that the plaintiff had substantially recovered from the injuries.

235 White Book (1997) 59/1/60. See *Autodesk* v *Dyason* (No 2) (1993) 173 CLR 330.

236 *Wood* v *Gahlings*, 'The Times', 29 November 1996 (CA).

237 *Ogwr BC* v *Knight*, 'The Times', 13 January 1994.

238 *Brooksbank* v *Rawsthorne* [1951] 2 All ER 413.

239 *Hession* v *Jones* [1914] 2 KB 421; a decision criticised by the White Book (1997) 59/1/63.

issue of law concluding with a question of law which the Court of Appeal is to answer. Subject to the specific provisions of the statute, Order 61 applies. The application to the lower court/tribunal must be made within six weeks, and the latter must settle the case and sign it within six weeks; the applicant must enter the appeal and serve the case stated on the other parties within 14 days after receiving it from the lower court/tribunal, and within a further 14 days lodge three appeal books (Ord.61 rr.1,2,7). These time limits can be extended on the established principles for extension of time for an appeal (para. 1.35); a good excuse must be show and mere absence of irreparable prejudice to the respondent is not enough unless the appellant is a public authority appealing on an issue of general legal principle.[240] The lodging of the case stated carries a court fee of £150. Where a statutory provision provides for the Court of Appeal to compel a case stated, application is by motion within 14 days of the refusal or failure to state the case (Ord.61 r.4). That rule only applies where the statute provides for an order directing a case stated; otherwise the appellant compels a case stated by applying to the High Court for *mandamus*.[241]

20.80 In stating a case the court/tribunal can state facts and conclusions not given in its judgment, provided that they do not materially change the reasons for the decision.[242] The appellant or party having carriage may apply by motion to the Court of Appeal to withdraw the appeal, at which any other party may apply to proceed (Ord.61 r.3). The Court has the powers in the Judicature Act (s.38) and in particular may amend the case stated or remit it for rehearing, amendment or restatement (s.38(1)(f)). After the disposal of the appeal the proper officer sends a copy of the Court's order to the lower court/tribunal (Ord.61 r.8).

20.81 Order 94 rule 2 lists various appeals to be brought by case stated, for example under the Social Security Acts and Orders, Fair Employment Acts, and Industrial Training (NI) Order 1984. Order 94 rule 3 specifies some tribunals which may state a special 'consultative' case on a point of law arising in the course of proceedings, and which the Court of Appeal may direct to do so.[243]

20.82 A fuller discussion on the principles of appeal by case stated appears in the author's *County Court Procedure in NI* as to appeals from the county court, and the author's *Criminal Court Procedure in NI* as to appeals in summary criminal proceedings. Various instances of appeal by case stated are contained in Appendix One of this work.

APPEAL TO HOUSE OF LORDS

20.83 The sole jurisdiction of the House of Lords is contained in the Acts mentioned below, apart from jurisdiction in contempt cases (para. 16.84). The

---

240 *Graffin* v *Famac Network*, CA, NI, 24 January 1997.

241 *In re Western HSSB* [1988] 5 NIJB 20; *In re Limavady BC* [1993] 5 NIJB 43.

242 *Hughes* v *European Components* [1990] 2 NIJB 29, at 40-2.

243 In accordance with Ord.61 r.4: *In re Western HSSB* [1988] 5 NIJB 20.

substantive jurisdiction of the House is entirely statutory and it has no inherent jurisdiction.[244]

From the High Court

20.84 In a *criminal* cause or matter, appeal lies from any decision of the High Court with leave of the High Court or of the Lords, provided that the High Court has certified that a point of law of general public importance is involved in the decision[245] (Judicature Act, s.41; Sch.1).

20.85 In a *civil* cause or matter (other than contempt), 'leap frog' appeal may lie from a "decision" of the High Court direct to the House of Lords under Part II (ss.12-16) of the Administration of Justice Act 1969. On application made at the time of his judgment or at his discretion within a further 14 days, the judge certifies that: (a) the parties consent, (b) the decision involves a point of law of public importance, relating to interpretation of statute or rules, or the subject of a binding decision of the Court of Appeal or House of Lords, and (c) a sufficient case for appeal has been made out (s.12).[246] A certificate can only be given if the order is such as could be appealed to the Court of Appeal and thence to the House of Lords. The judge has a discretion to refuse a certificate even if all the conditions are met.[247] If such a certificate is granted, the Lords may grant leave to appeal under section 13 within one month (time extendable). After the certificate has been granted no appeal lies from the decision so certified to the Court of Appeal, until the application for leave of the Lords has lapsed or been refused (s.13(5)); in which case the time limit for appeal to the Court of Appeal starts to run (Ord.59 r.4(3)).

20.86 Where there is doubt as to whether the decision of the High Court relates to a civil or criminal matter, the High Court might grant a 'leap frog' certificate so that the House of Lords has jurisdiction in either case.[248]

From the Court of Appeal

20.87 In a *criminal* cause or matter, appeal lies only from any decision of the Court of Appeal from the Crown Court or on a case stated from a magistrates' court or county court, if the Court or the Lords give leave and provided that the Court has certified a point of law of general public importance (Judicature Act, s.41; Sch.1).

20.88 In a *civil* cause or matter, appeal lies from any "order or judgment" of the Court of Appeal, with leave of the Court or of the Lords (s.42). Section 35 restrictions on appeal to the Court of Appeal do not apply so that the House of Lords can grant leave to bring an appeal as to costs only.[249] Leave should be

---

244 *Scottish Widows* v *Blennerhassett* [1912] AC 281 (Ir).

245 No such certificate is needed in habeas corpus.

246 No appeal lies from the Judge's decision as to whether to grant the certificate: Judicature Act, s.35(2)(i).

247 *Inland Revenue* v *Church Commrs* [1975] 1 WLR 251.

248 *Re Smalley* [1985] AC 622, at 632H-633B.

249 *Jennings* v *Kelly* [1940] NI 47, at 63-4 (HL).

sought orally at the hearing, or in writing thereafter.[250] In *Strathclyde RC* v *Gallagher*[251] leave to appeal was refused when based on a point not argued in the Court of Session. Where the decision of the Court of Appeal is expressed to be final (as it is on cases stated by a magistrates' court, county court or the High Court) appeal lies only if it involves the validity of a provision made by or under a NI statute (s.42(6)). The decision of the Court of Appeal on a case stated by an arbitrator is not an "order or judgment".[252] Where the Court of Appeal has reversed the trial judge on a finding of fact, the Lords should reverse the appellate court only if clearly satisfied that the latter was wrong.[253]

Procedure

20.89 Procedure is governed by the House of Lords Practice Directions set out in the White Book (1997) Volume 2 Part 16. All appeals and applications for leave to appeal are made to the Lords by petition, and are subject to such conditions as to value, security for costs, costs, time limits, as may be imposed by orders of the Lords (Appellate Jurisdiction Act 1876). Leave of the Court appealed from must be sought first. The Directions for Civil Appeals (para. 2.1) set a time limit of one month for lodging the petition for leave, which is held in abeyance pending the decision of the Law Society on a legal aid application (para. 25.3). Paragraph 8.1 sets a time limit of three months for the appeal petition. Security for costs is automatically required from the appellant, save where he is legally aided or is a Minister or Government Department or the respondent waives it in writing (para. 11). Leap frog appeals from the High Court are dealt with in paragraph 6. The orders made by the House of Lords should be made an order of the High Court by *ex parte* application (RSC, Ord.32 r.10). Costs are taxed by the House's own taxing master.[254]

20.90 Note that the House of Lords cannot hear an appeal as such from the grant or refusal of leave to appeal to the Court of Appeal, but *semble,* it can hear an appeal from the grant or refusal of extension of time to appeal to the Court of Appeal. The Directions for Civil Appeals (para. 1.6) expressly state that a petition is inadmissible and will be dismissed if it is against the refusal of the Court of Appeal to give leave to appeal to itself, or against the refusal of the Divisional Court or Court of Appeal to grant leave to seek judicial review. A petition by a vexatious litigant is inadmissible unless the High Court gives leave.

20.91 A stay of execution pending appeal can be granted in exceptional circumstances.[255] It should be sought from the court appealed from, not from the House of Lords.[256]

---

250 White Book (1997) 59/1/64.

251 1995 SLT 747.

252 So held in *John G.McGregor* v *Grampian RC* 1991 SC (HL) 1; *contra*: *Onslow* v *Inland Revenue*, para. 15.01.

253 Cf. *Scotsburn Co-op* v *WT Goodwin* (1985) 16 DLR 4th 161, at 167 (SC Canada).

254 House of Lords Costs Taxation Act 1849, and Directions for the Taxation of Bills of Costs 1993.

255 White Book (1997) 59/13/7.

20.92 The White Book also sets out the Directions as to Criminal Appeals, which apply to all criminal matters, including appeals from the Court of Appeal in Crown Court trials, and from the High Court in bail, *habeas corpus* and judicial review in a criminal cause or matter. Leave of the lower court must be sought within 14 days and if refused, leave of the Lords within 14 days.

REFERENCE TO EUROPEAN COURT OF JUSTICE

20.93 The Court of Appeal may in its discretion refer to the European Court of Justice any question raised as to the Interpretation of the Treaty of Rome and other European Treaties if its resolution is necessary for its judgment. If the Court of Appeal's decision is declared by statute to be final, or if in a criminal cause it refuses to certify a point of law of public importance, it must refer such a question. If such a question is raised in an appeal in the House of Lords, the House must refer. See further para. 14.16.

[256] Practice Direction (HL) [1996] 10 CLM 58. See previous page.

APPENDIX ONE

STATUTORY JURISDICTIONS OF THE HIGH COURT AND COURT OF APPEAL

- *Readers should note s.17 of the Interpretation Act 1978 and s.29 of the Interpretation Act (NI) 1954, which provide in effect that where Rules of Court refer to procedure under an enactment which has been repealed and replaced, the rules continue to apply as if made under the new enactment.*
- *Jurisdiction is of the High Court unless otherwise stated.*
- *References to* Ord.X *or to* Ord.X r.Y *are to* Order X *or* Order X rule Y *of the Rules of the Supreme Court (NI) unless otherwise stated*

1-a GOVERNMENT AND PUBLIC AUTHORITIES

Judicature (NI) Act 1978
Judicial Review s.18 (see para.19.02)
Parliamentary Commissioner Act 1967; Ombudsman (NI) Order 1996
High Ct may deal with contempt in his investigations 1967 Act, s.9; 1996 Order, Art.15
Commissioner for Complaints (NI) Order 1996
injunction against maladministration Art.17
High Ct may deal with contempt of investigations Art.14
Local Government Act (NI) 1972
declaration that councillor is reprehensible ss.31-33
auditing ss.81-82D
powers of judge s.130
quashing vesting order Sch.6 para.5
Elected Authorities (NI) Act 1989
determination that person has breached anti-terrorist declaration s.7: by originating motion within two months, assigned to QB Div: Ord.103
Elections (NI) Order SI 1996/1220
declaration of disqualification in negotiating body/forum elections Art.7

1-b ELECTIONS

Representation of the People Act 1983
election petition ss.120-57 (appeal on law to CA with leave); Election Petition Rules SR 1964/28 (in *Red Book*)
application for relief from failure to make return ss.86-7
application for relief from illegal practices etc. s.167
application for mitigation of incapacity s.174
appeal from county court re registration of elector to CA s.56; costs Ord.62 r.4(2)
Electoral Law Act (NI) 1962
election expenses ss.43,44,49
election courts s.72, s.81
case stated to CA s.83
European Parliamentary Elections Act 1978
application for disqualification Sch.1 para.6
petition under 1983 Act (as applied by SI 1984/198), see SR 1984/162 amended 1985/347

1-c DISCRIMINATION

Fair Employment (NI) Acts 1976 and 1989
certifying contempt of tribunal 1989 Act, s.17
appeal on law to CA 1989 Act, ss.18, 35, 40; 1976 Act, s.27 (subst. 1989); by case stated: Ord.94 r.2, or by cases stated during proceedings Ord.94 r.3
revision of contract 1976 Act, s.32 (amended 1989)
injunction against adverts 1976 Act, s.36

1-d JUSTICE AND COURTS

Judicature (NI) Act 1978
order restricting vexatious litigant s.32 (heard by judge not master: Ord.32 r.11)
leave to serve *subpoena* in GB s.67
Supreme Court Act 1981
punishment for disobedience of *subpoena* of English High Ct s.36
County Courts (NI) Order 1980
subpoena or examination of witness in aid of county ct proceedings Art.43
injunctions in interval between county ct sittings Art.35
appeal from county court to High Ct Art.60,Ord.55 rr.1-12A
case stated from small claims arbitration to High Ct Art.30(4)(b), under Ord.56 (see Ord.94 r.1)
case stated from county ct to CA Art.61, Ord.61
case stated from High Ct to CA Art.62, Ord.61 rr.5-6

Magistrates' Courts (NI) Order 1981
case stated to CA Art.146
application to High Ct for bail pending appeal or case stated Art.148(2)
Habeas Corpus Act (Ir) 1781
action for penalty against officer not obeying writ of *habeas corpus* s.4
Judgments Enforcement (NI) Order 1981
enforcing charge on land Art.52, Ord.88 r.5A
reference of wrongful delivery of land Art.56
discharging stop order Art.65, Ord.50
reference of garnishee issue Art.70
setting aside rights of receiver, etc. Arts.88(3A), 90(3A) (assigned to Chancery Div, out of Bankruptcy and Companies Office: Ord.1 rr.10,15)
attachment of earnings order Art.98
committal for default on money judgment Art.107, Ord.111, (assigned to QB Div or Family Div)
appeal against committal order by county ct (under Art.107) Art.110
referral of contempt of EJ Office Art.114
appeal from some orders of EJ Office to High Ct Art.140(1)
appeal from other orders on law to CA Art.140(2)

2-a TRIBUNALS, VARIOUS
Tribunals and Inquiries (Evidence) Act 1921
reference of contempt by witness s.1
Tribunals and Inquiries Act 1992:
appeals from VAT and other tribunals: s.11; by case stated to High Ct: Ord.94 r.1, or by case stated during proceedings: Ord.94 r.3

2-b ARBITRATION
Arbitration Act (NI) 1937; (UK) 1975; Consumer Arbitration Agreements Act 1988.
(An application under these Acts (under Ord.73 Pt II (rr.23-27) is only in respect of applications or arbitral proceedings commmenced before 31 Jan 1997)
Arbitration Acts 1950 and 1996
(An application under the Acts, unless made in proceedings assigned to the Chancery Div, is assigned to the QB Div)
jurisdiction is allocated to High Ct by order of Lord Chancellor under 1996 Act, s.105 (see para.7.22)
enforcement of foreign awards 1950 Act, s.37; 1996 Act, ss.99-104; Ord.73 Pt III (rr.28-32)

Proceedings under 1996 Act
procedure Ord.73 Pt.I (rr.1-22)
extending time to start arbitration s.12, Ord.73 r.22
setting aside appointment of sole arbitrator s.17
appointment of arbitral tribunal s.18
umpire to replace arbitrators s.21
removal of arbitrator s.24
resigning arbitrator seeking relief and fees s.25
adjustment of arbitrator's fees s.28
determination of arbitrator's jurisdiction s.32, Ord.73 r.19
order to comply with peremptory order s.42
attendance of witness s.43, Ord.73 r.16
injunctions etc. s.44, Ord.73 r.18
preliminary point of law s.45, Ord.73 rr.15,19
extending time for award s.50
order to tribunal to deliver award s.56
assessment of costs s.63
assessment of arbitrator's fees s.64
leave to enforce award s.66
challenge award for lack of jurisdiction s.67, Ord.73 r.22
challenge award for irregularity s.68, Ord.73 r.22
appeal on point of law s.69, Ord.73 rr.15,22
challenge by non-participant s.72
service of documents s.77
extending general time limits s.79
Arbitration (International Investment Disputes) Act 1966 Ord.73 r.32

2-c TORT
Defamation Act 1996 (*not yet in force*)
steps and compensation in amends s.3
Newspapers, Printers and Reading Rooms Act 1869
"bill" for discovery of printer, publisher for action for defamation Sch.

3-a JUSTICE ABROAD
Evidence (Proceedings in other Jurisdictions) Act 1975 Ord.70
Administration of Justice Act 1920, s.9; **Foreign Judgments (Reciprocal Enforcement) Act 1933,** s.2
enforcement of foreign judgments Ord.71
Civil Jurisdiction and Judgments Act 1982:
appeal on law to CA re registration of Convention judgment s.6
interim relief in aid of proceedings in a Convention territory s.25
application to enforce judgment Sch.1 Art 31, Sch.6, Sch.7

3-b IMMIGRATION
Asylum and Immigration Appeals Act 1993:
appeal from Tribunal on law to CA, by leave of either s.9; SI 1984/2041, amended 1993/1662; SI 1993/1661; SI 1996/2070; Ord.61 rr.11-12

4-a CRIME
bail see para.18.01
Criminal Procedure and Investigations Act 1996
quashing acquittal secured by interference with justice ss.54-55 (See Stop Press p.x)
Law of Libel Amendment Act 1888
leave of judge in chambers to prosecute criminal libel s.8
Legal Aid in Criminal Proceedings (Costs) Rules (NI) 1992, SR 1992/319, amended 1994/209
appeal to High Ct (assigned to QB Div: Ord.1 r.11(g))
Criminal Appeal (NI) Act 1980
appeal from Crown Court to CA, see *Criminal Procedure in NI* Chap.15
appeal to the High Ct from the Taxing Master's assessment of legal costs of a legally aided appellant s.28; assigned to QB Div: Ord.1 r.11(h) procedure Ord.117
Criminal Appeal Act 1995
reference by Review Commission s.10
Criminal Justice Act 1988
reference of lenient sentence s.36
Chemical Weapons Act 1996
compensation for destruction by Sec of Sate ss.8,16
Extradition Act 1989
discharge ss.6,14,16
statement of case to High Ct (appeal to House of Lords) s.10
habeas corpus s.11
judicial review s.13
Sch.1 to the 1989 Act applies to extradition under pre-1989 treaties
Republic of Ireland (Backing of Warrants) Act 1965
statement of case to High Ct (appeal to House of Lords) s.2A
discharge s.6

4-b PUBLIC ORDER
Public Order Amendment Act (NI) 1970
restraint on property and search warrant re quasi-military organisation s.7 (Chancery Div Ord.93 r.1, by originating summons r.4)
Incitement to Disaffection Act 1934
search warrant s.2

4-c PROCEEDS OF CRIME
Applications in the nature of a "*Mareva*" order to preserve the proceeds of crime, under the **Prevention of Terrorism (Temporary Provisions) Act 1989**, Sch.4 Pt.III; **Proceeds of Crime (NI) Order 1996**, Arts.21-43, 54 are initiated by *ex parte* originating summons to a QB Div judge in chambers: Ord.116
Prevention of Terrorism (Temporary Provisions) Act 1989 (Enforcement of External Orders) Order SI 1995/760 rr.20-26
Criminal Justice (International Co-operation) Act 1990 (Enforcement of Overseas Forfeiture Orders) (NI) Order SI 1991/1464, r.5

5-a REVENUE, CUSTOMS AND TAX
(*assigned to Chancery Div*)
writ may be served outside NI by leave if defendant not domiciled in GB: Ord.11 r.1(1)(n)
Inland Revenue Regulation Act 1890
fine or penalty (other than income or corporation tax) under the Revenue Acts may be sued for in the High Ct s.22
Taxes Management Act 1970
appeal against penalty by Commrs s.53 (to Chancery Div: Ord.91 r.1, by originating summons r.4)
case stated by Commrs for CA ss.56,58
tax may sued for as debt in High Ct s.68
appeal against penalty s.100B
penalty for fraud s.100D
[*NB s.100 of the Taxes Management Act has been amended to remove High Ct jurisdiction so reference in the RSC to that section is redundant*].
Inheritance Tax Act (formerly **Capital Gains Tax Act**) **1984**
appeal to High Ct s.222; by originating summons, assigned to Chancery Div: Ord.91 rr.1,.2
case stated from Special Commrs to CA s.225
application or appeal to High Ct re recovery of penalties s.249; Ord.91 r.4
appeal against summary penalty s.251: Ord.91 r.4
[*NB, the rules in Ord.91 refer to the 1975 Finance Act which was repealed and replaced by the 1984 Act*].
General Commissioners (Jurisdiction and Procedure) Regulations 1994 SI 1812
case stated to CA reg.23
Crown Proceedings Act 1947
summary application in revenue matters s.14; by originating summons or motion, 21

days to appeal to CA Ord.77 r.6
Stamp Act 1891:
case stated to the High Ct s.13 (to Chancery Div: see Ord.91 rr.1,3)
Stamp Duties Management Act 1891
IRC may sue in High Ct for account of duties received s.2
Value Added Tax Act 1994
appeal from VAT (and Duties) Tribunal to CA (Ord.61 rr.9-10) or in prescribed cases by case stated to High Ct (Ord.94 r.1): s. 86; SI 1994/1978,, amended1994/2617

5-b SOCIAL SECURITY AND PENSIONS

(writ for contributions may be served outside NI by leave Ord.11 r.1(1)(o))
Social Security Administration (NI) Act 1992
appeal from DHSS on law to CA s.16
from Commr ss.22 and 32 (also under the GB Act s.24)
appeal on law to CA under Social Security Regs s.56(8)
All appeals to CA under these provisions are by case stated (Ord.94 r.2) or, under s.16 by case stated in course of proceedings (Ord.94 r.3)
Pneumoconiosis etc. (Workers Compensation) (NI) Order 1979
appeal on law to CA Art.8
Social Security Pensions (NI) Order 1975
appeal from Occupational Pensions Board to CA on law Art.63, by case stated: Ord.94 r.2; or by case stated during proceedings: Ord.94 r.3
Pension Appeals Tribunals Act 1943
case stated (in NI to CA) s.6, rules SR 1981/231, Ord.101; no costs Ord.62 r.4(1)
Pensions (NI) Order 1995
applications re occupational schemes Arts.13,14,24
reference or appeal on question of law Art.95
Pension Schemes (NI) Act 1993
appeal on point of law s.50
appeal from Board on law to CA s.168 (to be repealed)
Superannuation (NI) Order 1972
appeal on law to CA from Ministry in civil service scheme Art.4

6-a EMPLOYMENT

Industrial Training (NI) Order 1984
appeal from industrial tribunal to CA Art.31; by case stated: Ord.94 r.2; or by case stated during proceedings: Ord.94 r.3
Industrial Relations (NI) Order 1992
orders protecting trade union property Arts.8,9
application for declaration that convicted persons are union officers Art.13C
allowing member to inspect records Art.37
appeal from Certification Officer re listing of trade union Arts.5,6,70
dispensing with distribution of retiring auditor's representations Sch.1 para.15
High Ct jurisdiction under the Order is assigned to the Chancery Div: Ord.93 r.1 (*which refers to the repealed Trade Union Act 1913*)
Trade Union and Labour Relations (Consolidation) Act 1992
application re political ballot s.81
Trade Union and Labour Relations (NI) Order 1995
application for direction that register of members is not kept or not kept secret Art.6
application for declaration that election of officers not properly conducted Art.23
application by union member to restrain industrial action without a ballot Art.29
application for declaration that political resolution ballot not properly held Art.56
application for direction that union cease to collect political contributions Art.64
appeal to CA from Certification Office re amalgamations Art.85
application by customer for order to stop unlawful inducement of industrial action Art.120
High Ct jurisdiction under the Order is assigned to the Chancery Div: Ord.93 r.1 (*which refers to the repealed Trade Union Act 1913*)

6-b PROFESSIONS

Architects Registration Act 1931
appeal from removal from register s.9 [*to be replaced by*]
Architects Act 1997
appeal from non-entry or removal from Register s.27
Estate Agents Act 1979
appeal on point of law from Sec of State to judge of High Ct, then by leave to CA s.7
Insurance Brokers (Registration) Act 1977
Osteopaths Act 1993
appeal from Council s.29
Pharmacy (NI) Order 1976
appeal from Standing Committee Art.22
Chiropractors Act 1994
appeal to High Ct re registration ss.24,29
Hearing Aid Council Act 1968 (amended 1975) appeal to judge of Sup Ct s.9
Nurses Midwives and Health Visitors Act 1997 s.12

6-c SOLICITORS

Solicitors (NI) Order 1976

appeal to judge from some orders of Disciplinary Tribunal Art.53, by originating motion: Ord.106 rr.10-15

restraint on money, documents etc. held by solicitor Sch.1

appointment of Law Society as attorney for solicitor Sch.1 para.22A

incorporated practices Sch.1A

applications under Schs. 1,1A to judge in chambers: Ord.106 r.2, by originating summons in Chancery Div: Ord.106 rr.5-9

applications to LCJ (under various provisions of Solicitors' Order) Ord.106 r.16

solicitor's costs: jurisdiction of High Ct in contentious and non-contentious business agreements Arts.66(6),71A(3)

order to deliver bill of costs Art.71C

taxation of costs Arts.71F-G (see para.17.77) originating summons, no appearance Ord.106

7-a FINANCE

Banking Act 1987

(extended to European Institutions by SI 1992/3218)

(assigned to Chancery Div)

appeal from tribunal by case stated to High Ct, and appeal to CA with leave of either s.31

sale of shares and payment into court s.26, Ord.92 r.3A

unauthorised deposits ss.48-9

appeal by institution re name ss.71, 77

injunctions s.93; see Ord.93 r.8

process may be served outside NI by leave: Ord.11 r.1(1)(q)

Banking Appeal Tribunal Regulations SI 1987/1299

taxation and enforcement of costs reg.17

Banks (Administration Proceedings) Order (NI) SR 1991/295

Building Societies Act 1986

ss. 49, 84, 86-92 (winding up), Sch.14, assigned to Chancery Div: Ord.93 r.1

Building Societies Appeal Tribunal Regulations SI 1987/891

taxation and enforcement of costs reg.16

Industrial and Provident Societies Act (NI) 1969

appeal by Society from decisions of registrar s.17

extending time to register charge s.29, Ord.95 r.7 (to master in QB Div)

winding up s.64 (Chancery Div Ord.93 r.1)

appeal by case stated from arbitration to CA s.69

Industrial Assurance (NI) Order 1979

appeal from Commissioner Art.18 (to Chancery Div Ord.93 r.1,5)

Friendly Societies Acts 1974 (applied to NI 1992)

appeal to High Ct from registrar ss.16,20,92

statement of case to High Ct s.78, to county ct s.79

Friendly Societies Act 1992

(assigned to Chancery Div Ord.93 r.1)

winding up ss.19-26,52

injunction to protect assets s.52A

appeal on law from tribunal to High Ct, then with leave to CA s.61

other jurisdiction in county ct s.119

Friendly Societies Appeal Tribunal Regulations SI 1993/2002

taxation and enforcement of costs reg.16

Credit Unions (NI) Order 1985

appeal against refusal to register Art.62

winding up and dissolution Arts.63,68

case stated to CA Art.72(8)

Financial Services Act 1986

winding up of authorised investor s.73

other applications re investors ss.5, 6, 93, 188 (assigned to Chancery Div, out of Bankruptcy and Companies Office) Ord.93 r.7

(Process may be served outside NI by leave Ord.11 r.1(1)(q))

National Debt Act 1870

petition to Chancery Div for unclaimed dividends s.55; Ord.93 r.1,2

Government Annuities Act 1929 s.35

Insurance Companies Act 1982

injunction against disposing assets s.40A

sanction for transfer of business s.49

winding up ss.53-9; rules SR 1992/307

Life Assurance Companies (Payment into Court) Act 1896 Ord.92 r.1

7-b COMMERCIAL AND TRADE

Consumer Credit Act 1974

enforcement, relief and re-opening of consumer credit transactions and hire-purchase ss.127-144: see Ord.83

Unfair Terms in Contract Regulations SI 1994/3159

injunction against unfair term reg. 8

Control of Misleading Advertisements Regulations SI 1988

injunction against misleading advertisement reg.5

Bills of Sale (Ir) Act 1879

registration by QB Master: s.13; Ord.95

Restrictive Practices Court Act 1976

appeal to CA s.10 and Ord.60

Fair Trading Act 1973

enforcement of orders of Monopolies and Mergers Commission ss.85,93

Public Service Contracts Regulations SI 1993/3228 regs.28,32
Public Supply Contracts Regulations SI 1995/201 regs. 26, 29
Public Works Contracts Regulations SI 1991/2680 reg. 31
Utilities Supply and Works Contracts Regulations SI 1992/3279 regs. 27,30

7-c AGRICULTURE AND FOOD
Agricultural Marketing Act 1958
appeal re registration of marketing contracts: to county ct or, by removal or by consent, to High Ct s.18
Dairy Produce Quota Regulations SI 1993/927
application for *habeas corpus ad test.* reg.20
Products of Animal Origins (Import and Export) Regulations SI 1992/3298
enforcement of directions by *mandamus* reg.4
Food Safety (NI) Order 1991
declaration that Crown has breached the Order Art.49

7-d ENERGY
Electricity (NI) Order 1992
appeal by supplier against Director's order to comply with duty Art.30
order to give document or information to Director Art.31
Gas (NI) Order 1996
appeal by licensee against Director's order to comply with duty Art.21
order to give document or information to Director Art.30
Nuclear Installations Act 1965
jurisdiction of High Ct: ss.16-17 (writ may be served outside NI by leave: Ord.11 r.1(1)(o))

8-a COMMUNICATIONS
Post Office Act 1969
leave to sue Post Office for loss of postal packet, by person other than sender or addressee s.30(5); by originating summons in QB Div Ord.77 r.16
Telecommunications Act 1984
application to quash order of Dept to enforce broadcasting licence s.18

8-b ROAD TRAFFIC
Road Traffic (NI) Order 1981 (*to be repealed*)
application for permission to drive pending appeal from conviction by magistrates' ct: Art.194(3)

8-c TRANSPORT
Airports (NI) Order 1994
leave to sell aircraft for unpaid charges Art.23(4)
challenging order by CAA Art.40
challenging direction re airport land Sch.2
Civil Aviation (Investigation of Air Accidents) Regulations SI 1989/2062
taxation of costs reg.15
Civil Aviation (Navigation Services Charges) Regulations SI 1995/497
Access for Community Air Carriers to Intra-Community Air Routes Regulations SI 1992/2993
action for breach of duty by Sec of State reg.13
Transfrontier Shipment of Radioactive Waste Regulations SI 1993/3031 regs. 14,18
Petroleum Production Act (NI) 1964
tribunal compensation may be entered as judgment by leave of High Ct s.8

8-d SHIPPING
Admiralty jurisdiction, (QB Div) see para.18.17
Merchant Shipping Act 1894
removal of master s.472
Merchant Shipping Act 1995
forfeiture of ship s.7
time limit for claims for injury etc. s.190
sale of registered ship Sch.1
Ports (NI) Order 1994
proceedings for penalty Art.17
appeal from assessment Art.17A

9-a COMPANIES AND FIRMS
Companies (NI) Orders 1986-90
(*assigned to Chancery Div, business transacted in Bankruptcy and Companies Office*)
Procedure Ord.102; costs of creditor Ord.62 r.6(3)
Applications are made to the Court having jurisdiction to wind up Art.2
Enforcement of orders 1986 Order, Art.676
Examples of jurisdiction
cancelling alteration of company objects 1986 Order, Art.16
cancelling change of name 1986 Order, Art.42
cancellation of variation of class rights 1986 Order, Art.137
confirming reduction in capital 1986 Order, Art.146
order to revise accounts 1986 Order, Art.253B
rectification of members' register 1986 Order, Art.367
order to call meeting 1986 Order, Art.379
sanction for compromise with creditors or members 1986 Order, Art.418

petition to prevent unfair prejudice 1986 Order, Art.454; rules SR 1991/74
declaring dissolution void 1986 Order, Art.602
inspection of books by police or DPP 1986 Order, Art.670
relief to officer or auditor for negligence, default etc. 1986 Order, Art.675
disqualification from being director, liquidator etc. 1989 Order, Arts.4-21; rules SR 1991/367; SR 1991/368; (assigned to Chancery Div: Ord.1 r.10)*
company auditors 1990 Order, Art.41
order to stop dissipation of assets in financial markets contract 1990 Order (No 2) Art.84
* *RSC does not generally apply: Ord.1 r.2.*
Debenture holders' actions Ord.87
Partnerships Act 1890
dissolution ss.35,39,40 (assigned to Chancery Div)
Insolvent Partnerships Order (NI) SR 1995/225

9-b INSOLVENCY
(assigned to Chancery Div)
Insolvency (NI) Order 1989
Companies
winding up Arts.14-208
disqualification of unfit directors SR 1991/367
reports on conduct of directors SR 1991/368, r.5
unregistered companies Arts.184-193
application to restrain winding up is by originating motion in Chancery Div: Ord.29 r.1A; issued out of Bankruptcy and Companies Office: Ord.1 r.15.
banks SR 1991/295
Humans
deeds of arrangement Arts.209-225
voluntary arrangements Arts.226-237
bankruptcy Arts.238-345
partnerships Art.364; SR 1995/225
insolvent estates Art.365; SR 1995/225
nullifying effect of transactions at undervalue Art.367
review of orders Art.371
Procedure
Insolvency Rules SR 1991/364 (amended 1994/26; 1995/295 (*RSC apply so far as consistent: r.7.45)*
Insolvency Regulations SR 1996/574
deposit for presentation of petition SR 1991/384
Fees SR 1991/385, amended1992/398.
Costs 1991 Rules rr.7.29-7.37
assessment of remuneration transacted in Taxing Office: Ord.1 r.18
appeal to CA only by leave: Judicature Act s.35(2)(j); time for appeal 28 days: Ord.59 r.4
Insolvency Act 1986
evidence for GB winding up s.197
reciprocal assistance and enforcement s.426

10-a INTELLECTUAL PROPERTY
(assigned to Chancery Div)
Copyright, Designs and Patents Act 1988
(assigned to Chancery Div Ord.93 rr.1,6)
copyright infringement ss.99, 114-5
appeal on law from Copyright Tribunal to High Ct s.152; SI 1989/1129
illicit recording of performances ss.195, 204-5
design right ss.231-2, 251-2; SI 1989/1130
Patents Act 1949
amendment, revocation of patents ss.30-2, reference of disputes s.48: assigned to Chancery Div Ord.104
action of infringement (by writ: Ord.104 r.5) and counterclaim for revocation ss.59-62
costs Ord.62 App 1 r.4(3)
Patents Act 1977
compensation to employee s.40
reference of disputes s.58
infringement ss.61-71
revocation s.72
amendment s.75
Ord.104 (Chancery Div); SI 1995/2093
appeal from comptroller to High Ct, then to CA s.97 and Ord.59 r.17
Costs Ord.62 App 1 r.4(3)
Trade Marks Act 1994
ss.75-6 (replacing 1938 Act s.66); by originating motion; Ord.100 (assigned to Chancery Div); SI 1994/2583 rr.58-9
Community Trade Marks Regulations SI 1996/1908
Olympic Symbols etc. Protection Act 1995
and Regs SI 1995/3325: Ord.100
Scotch Whisky (NI) Order 1988
injunction against passing off as Scotch whisky Art.3
Registered Designs Act 1949
s.27; Sch.1 para.3: Ord.104 r.15; SI 1995/2912
Defence Contracts Act 1958
reference of disputes s.4; Ord.104 r.15

11-a HOUSING AND BUILDING
Building Regulations (NI)Order 1979
appeal from Dept to CA by case stated Art.17
Housing (NI)Order 1992
appeal by Housing Association: Arts.17, 25

12-a LAND, TRUSTS AND PROPERTY
ejectment: see para.18.34

Partition Acts (Chancery Div), see para.18.77
Married Women's Property Act see para.18.70

Land Registration Act (NI) 1970
(assigned to Chancery Div: Ord.93 r.1)
appeal from registrar s.6, with appeal to CA s.7
enforcement of orders ss.8-9
reference of adverse possession s.53
time limit six weeks: Ord.55 r.19(2)
appointment of representative for person under disability ss.60-1
directions to trustee s.57
entry of inhibition s.67
rectification of register s.69
possession to owner of registered charge Sch.7 para.5

Registration of Deeds Act (NI) 1970
damages over £15,000 for breach of duty s.17

Property (NI) Order 1997 (*not yet in force*)
Art.4 cancellation of certificate of redemption (Chancery Div)

Vendor and Purchaser Act 1874
(assigned Chancery Div: Ord.93 r.1)

Conveyancing Acts 1881, 1911
(assigned to Chancery Div: 1881 s.69; Ord.93 r.1)
High Ct has the jurisdiction under the **Settled Estates Act 1877**, **Settled Land Act 1882** (ss.46,65), *Re Tuthill and Wayne* [1907] 1 IR 305; **Landed Estates Court (Ir) Act 1858**; [**Landlord and Tenant (Ir) Act 1870**, **Land Law (Ir) Acts 1881**-- *to be repealed*]), **1887, 1896**, **Irish Land Acts 1903,1909**, **Northern Ireland Land Acts 1925, 1929** (1929 appeal to CA s.4) **Purchase of Land (Ir) Act 1891** (application by Dept of Finance for possession s.25)
Rules see *Index to SROs in NI* 'Landlord and Tenant: Supreme Court--4(c)'
Proceedings in High Ct under the Land Purchase Acts and Settled Land Acts are assigned to the Chancery Div: Ord.93 r.1

Landlord and Tenant (War Damage) Act (NI) 1941
appeal from county ct s.33

Fines and Recoveries (Ir) Act 1834
High Ct jurisdiction over entails ss.11,31,46-7

Renewable Leasehold Conversion Act 1849 petition to effect grant s.22 (*to be repealed)*

Property (NI) Order 1978
reference of impediment on land application by lands tribunal to CA Art.4

Enduring Powers of Attorney (NI) Order 1987
registration where donor becomes incapable Ord.109A, assigned to Family Div out of Office of Care and Protection

Public Trustee Act 1906
s.10 (Chancery Div)

Trustee Act (NI) 1958
s.66 (assigned to Chancery Div Ord.93 r.1); cannot be remitted to/removed from county ct
leave to replace trustee of unsound mind s.35(9): Ord.109 r.12,31
appointment of new trustee s.40; Ord.109 r.31
authorising remuneration s.41
vesting land s.43
releasing land from contingent rights of unborn s.44
vesting land, shares etc. ss.45-55
authorising transactions s.56
varying trusts and settlements s.57; Ord.93 r.3
relieving trustee from liability s.61
ordering beneficiary to indemnify trustee s.62
payment into court s.63; Ord.92 r.2
applications under ss.40,56,57,61 cannot be heard by a master: Ord.32 r.11(1)
costs out of property s.60

Tort (Interference with Goods) Act 1977
court may authorise sale of goods held by bailee s.13

Lands Tribunal and Compensation Act (NI) 1964: s.8; **Mineral Development Act (NI) 1969** s.45; **Property (NI) Order 1978** Art.4
appeals from Lands Tribunal on law to CA. Ord.94 r.3

Enterprise Zones (NI) Order 1981
application to challenge enterprise zone scheme Art.6

12-b ESTATES

grants of Probate and Letters of Administration assigned to Family Div out of Probate and Matrimonial Office: see para.18.48~50
Administration proceedings assigned to Chancery Div

Wills and Administration (NI) Order 1994
authorisation to trustee/PR to rely on opinion of counsel Art.33 [*not in force*]
substitution, removal of PR Art.35 [*not in force*]

Colonial Probates Acts 1892 and 1927, Administration of Estates Act (NI) 1971
sealing of Commonwealth grants, under Ord.97 r.39

Administration of Estates Acts (NI) 1955 and 1971; (NI) Order 1979
(assigned to Chancery Div)
1955 Act, s.43
grant of representation 1979 Order, Art.4
revocation 1979 Order, Art.11
limited administration 1979 Order, Art.5
administration *pendente lite* 1979 Order, Art.6
during minority 1979 Order, Art.7
personal representative abroad 1979 Order, Art.8
trust corporation 1979 Order, Art.10
ancillary powers 1979 Order, Arts.13-28
transfer of land to beneficiary 1979 Order, Art.34
giving inventory and accounts and delivery up of grant 1979 Order, Art.35
leave to sue surety of administrator 1979 Order, Art.17; 1971 Act s.4(5); Ord.97 r.40
Inheritance (Provision for Family and Dependants) (NI) Order 1979
application by relative or spouse for provision out of estate; assigned to Chancery Div: Ord.99; by originating summons, no appearance required; remittal to county ct: Ord.99 r.10
Forfeiture (NI) Order 1982
Court declaring that forfeiture rule applies may modify its effect where beneficiary guilty of killing other than murder Art.4

12-c CHARITIES
Charities Act (NI) 1964
(assigned to Chancery Div: Ord.93 r.1)
(applications cannot be heard by a master: Ord.32 r.11(1)(h))
ss.8,12,13,24,25,29
taxation of costs s.9

12-d HERITAGE
Historical Monuments and Archaeological Objects (NI) Order 1995
challenging DOE's decision re monument Art.12
Return of Cultural Objects Regulations 1994 SI 501

12-e POLLUTION AND PUBLIC HEALTH
Litter (NI) Order 1994
declaration that Crown is in breach Art.24

13-a PERSONAL DATA
Access to Health Records (NI) Order 1993
(pre-application steps see SR 1994/158; control of access SR 1994/159)
order to give access Art.10; by originating summons in QB Div: Ord.96
Data Protection Act 1984
appeal to High Ct from Tribunal on law re registration of data users s.14
access and correction of data s.25
contempt of tribunal Sch.3 para.5

13-b MEDICAL AND HEALTH
Mental Health (NI) Order 1986
(assigned to Family Div out of Office of Care and Protection)
management of property and affairs of patient Arts.97-118, Ord.109, see para.3.11 and para.18.52
leave to sue for acts done under Order Art.133 (not to be heard by a master: Ord.32 r.11(1)(m))
direction to refer hospital order case to Review Tribunal Art.72
Registered Homes (NI) Order 1992
appeal by case stated to High Ct Art.34, Ord.94 r.1
Genetically Modified Organisms (NI) Order 1991
declaration that Crown has breached Order Art.23
Human Embryology and Fertilisation Act 1990
appeal on point of law from refusal of licence s.21
parental order s.30
Parental Orders (Human Fertilisation and Embryology) Regulations SI 1994/2767
Ord.84A, assigned to Family Div out of Office of Care and Protection
Medicines (Monitoring of Advertising) Regulations SI 1994/1933

14-a FAMILY
(Matrimonial causes (assigned to Family Div out of Probate and Matrimonial Office) see para.18.47)
Inheritance (Provision for Family and Dependants) (NI) Order 1979
matrimonial court on divorce etc. may bar family provision claims Arts.17, 17A
Married Women's Property Act 1882
disputes between spouses etc. as to title to property (assigned to Chancery Div): s.17; Ord.93 r.1; cannot be remitted to/removed from, county ct
Family Law (Misc Provs) (NI) Order 1984
spouse's registrable right of residence in matrimonial home Part II Arts.3-14; by originating summons in Family Div, out of Probate and Matrimonial Office, Ord.115; or in Chancery Div out of Bankruptcy and Companies Office if taken by virtue of Arts.309-10 of Insolvency (NI) Order 1989

Maintenance and Affiliation Orders Act (NI) 1966
ss.9-16 (assigned to Family Div out of Probate and Matrimonial Office) Ord.105 rr.1-23
Domestic Proceedings (NI) Order 1980
revocation of magistrates' ct maintenance order Art.30
Matrimonial and Family Proceedings (NI) Order 1989
(assigned to Family Div, by petition out of Probate and Matrimonial Office: Ord.98)
ancillary relief after overseas divorce etc. Part IV (Arts.16-30); FP Rules r.3.12
declaration as to marriageability of related persons Art.31A
declaration as to legitimacy Art.32
transfer of tenancy Art.41, Sch.1; FP Rules r.3.9
Judicature Act
Wardship ss.26, 29; assigned to the Family Div, out of the Office of Care and Protection. Procedure by originating summons Ord.90 rr.1-5
Family Law Reform (NI) Order 1977
application for blood or DNA tests to determine paternity: Ord.112
Child Abduction and Custody Act 1985
jurisdiction under Hague Convention: s.4; (assigned to Family Div out of Office of Care and Protection), by originating summons Ord.90 rr.10-25
Family Law Act 1986
jurisdiction and recognition of child custody orders; (assigned to Family Div out of Office of Care and Protection) Ord.90 rr.26-35
Children (NI) Order 1995
Arts.159-163 (assigned to Family Div out of Office of Care and Protection, or Probate and Matrimonial Office if in pending matrimonial cause); FP Rules r.4
jurisdiction under Order Art.164
appeal from county ct Art.166
care and supervision Arts.49-59
child assessment order Arts.62-3
appointment and removal of guardian Arts.159,163
alteration of maintenance agreement after death Sch.1 para.13
guardian's accounts: Ord.43 r.9.
Infants Property Act 1830
Child Support (NI) Order 1991
appeal on law from Commr to CA Art.26.
Adoption (NI) Order 1987
Art.2(2) (assigned to Family Div out of Office of Care and Protection) and Ord.84 (SR 1989/343, not printed in *Red Book*); applications cannot be remitted to county ct; removal from county ct Art.64
Matrimonial and Family Proceedings (NI) Order 1989
declaration as to foreign adoption (assigned to Family Div): Art.33; by petition out of Office of Care and Protection: Ord.98
Adoption (Hague Convention) Act (NI) 1969
recognition of foreign orders re adoption ss.5-10

INDEX OF TITLES OF STATUTES AND RULES

Access for Community Air Carriers 8-c
Access to Health Records 13-a
Administration of Estates 12-b
Administration of Justice (1920) 3-a
Adoption 14-a
Adoption (Hague Convention) 14-a
Agricultural Marketing 7-c
Airports 8-c
Arbitration 2-b
Arbitration (International Investment Disputes) 2-b
Architects Registration 6-b
Asylum and Immigration Appeals 3-b
Banking 7-a
Banks (Administration Proceedings) 7-a
Bills of Sale 7-b
Building Regulations 11-a
Building Societies 7-a
Capital Gains Tax 5-a
Charities 12-c
Chemical Weapons Act 1996 .... 4-a
Child Abduction and Custody 14-a
Child Support 14-a
Children 14-a
Chiropractors 6-b
Civil Aviation 8-c
Civil Jurisdiction and Judgments 3-a
Colonial Probates 12-b
Companies 9-a
Consumer Arbitration Agreements 2-b
Consumer Credit 7-b
Control of Misleading Advertisements 7-b
Conveyancing 12-a
Copyright, Designs and Patents 10-a
County Courts 1-d
Credit Unions 7-a
Criminal Appeal 4-a
Criminal Justice (1988) 4-a
Criminal Justice (Confiscation) 4-c
Criminal Procedure and Investigations 4-a
Crown Proceedings 5-a
Custody of Children 14-a
Dairy Produce Quota 7-c
Data Protection 13-a
Defamation 2-c
Defence Contracts 10-a
Domestic Proceedings 14-a
Elected Authorities 1-a
Election Petition 1-b
Electoral Law 1-b
Electricity 7-d
Enduring Powers of Attorney 12-a
Enterprise Zones 12-a
Estate Agents 6-b
European Parliamentary Elections 1-b
Evidence (Proceedings in other Jurisdictions) 3-a
Extradition 4-a

Fair Employment (NI) 1-c
Fair Trading 7-b
Family Law 14-a
Family Law (Misc Provs) 14-a
Family Law Reform 14-a
Family Proceedings 14-a
Finance .... 5-a.
Financial Services 7-a
Fines and Recoveries 12-a
Food Safety 7-c
Foreign Judgments (Reciprocal Enforcement) 3-a
Forfeiture 12-b
Friendly Societies 7-a
Gas 7-d
General Commissioners (Jurisdiction and Procedure) 5-a
Genetically Modified Organisms 13-b
Government Annuities 7-a
Guardianship of Infants 14-a
Habeas Corpus 1-d
Hearing Aid Council 6-b
Historical Monuments and Archaeological Objects 12-d
Housing 11-a
Human Embryology and Fertilisation 13-b
Incitement to Disaffection 4-b
Industrial and Provident Societies 7-a
Industrial Assurance 7-a
Industrial Relations 6-a
Industrial Training 6-a
Infants Property 14-a
Inheritance (Provision for Family and Dependants) 12-b, 14-a
Inheritance Tax 5-a
Inland Revenue Regulation 5-a
Insolvency 9-b, 14-a
Insolvent Partnerships 9-a
Insurance Brokers (Registration) 6-b
Insurance Companies 7-a
Irish Land 12-a
Judgments Enforcement 1-d
Judicature (Northern Ireland) 1-a, 1-d, 9-b, 14-a
Land Law (Ireland) 12-a
Land Registration 12-a
Landed Estates Court 12-a
Landlord and Tenant 12-a
Landlord and Tenant (War Damage) 12-a
Lands Tribunal and Compensation 12-a
Law of Libel Amendment 4-a
Legal Aid in Criminal Proceedings (Costs) 4-a
Life Assurance Companies (Payment into Court) 7-a
Litter 12-e
Local Government 1-a
Magistrates' Courts 1-d
Maintenance and Affiliation 14-a
Married Women's Property 12-a, 14-a
Matrimonial and Family Proceedings 14-a
Matrimonial Causes 14-a
Medicines (Monitoring of Advertising) 13-b
Mental Health 13-b
Merchant Shipping 8-d
Mineral Development 12-a

National Debt 7-a
Newspapers, Printers and Reading Rooms 2-c
Northern Ireland Land 12-a
Nuclear Installations 7-d
Nurses Midwives and Health Visitors 6-b
Ombudsman 1-a
Osteopaths 6-b
Parental Orders (Human Fertilisation and Embryology).......... 13-b
Parliamentary Commissioner 1-a
Partition 12-a
Partnerships 9-a
Patents 10-a
Pension Appeals Tribunals 5-b
Pension Schemes 5-b
Pensions 5-b
Petroleum Production 8-c
Pharmacy 6-b
Pneumoconiosis etc. (Workers Compensation) 5-b
Ports 8-d
Post Office 8-a
Prevention of Terrorism (Temporary Provisions) 4-c
Proceeds of Crime 4-c
Products of Animal Origins (Import and Export) 7-c
Property 12-a
Public Order Amendment 4-b
Public Service Contracts 7-b
Public Supply Contracts 12-b
Public Trustee 12-a
Public Works Contracts 7-b
Purchase of Land 12-a
Registered Designs 10-a
Registered Homes 13-b
Registration of Deeds 12-a
Renewable Leasehold Conversion 12-a
Representation of the People 1-b
Republic of Ireland (Backing of Warrants) 4-a
Restrictive Practices Court 7-b
Return of Cultural Objects 12-d
Road Traffic 8-b
Scotch Whisky 10-a
Settled Estates 12-a
Settled Land 12-a
Social Security Administration 5-b
Social Security Pensions 5-b
Solicitors 6-c
Stamp 5-a
Stamp Duties Management 5-a
Superannuation 5-b
Supreme Court [England/Wales] 1-d
Taxes Management 5-a
Telecommunications 8-a
Tort (Interference with Goods) 12-a
Trade Marks 10-a
Trade Union and Labour Relations 6-a
Trade Union and Labour Relations (Consolidation).......... 6-a
Transfrontier Shipment of Radioactive Waste 8-c
Tribunals and Inquiries 2-a
Tribunals and Inquiries (Evidence) 2-a
Trustee Act 12-a
Unfair Terms in Contract 7-b

RSC, Ord.93 rr.1,6 .... 10-a
RSC, Ord.93 r.3 .... 12-a
RSC, Ord.93 r.7 .... 7-a
RSC, Ord.93 r.8 .... 7-a
RSC, Ord.94 r.1 .... 2-a, 5-a, 13-b
RSC, Ord.94 rr.2, 3 .... 1-c, 5-b, 6-a
RSC, Ord.94 r.3 .... 2-a, 12-a
RSC, Ord.95 .... 7-b
RSC, Ord.95 r.7 .... 7-a
RSC, Ord.96 .... 13-a
RSC, Ord.97 r.39 .... 12-b
RSC, Ord.97 r.40 .... 12-b
RSC, Ord.98 .... 14-a
RSC, Ord.99 .... 12-b
RSC, Ord.100 .... 10-a
RSC, Ord.101 .... 5-b
RSC, Ord.102 .... 9-a
RSC, Ord.103 .... 1-a
RSC, Ord.104 .... 10-a
RSC, Ord.104 r.15 .... 10-a
RSC, Ord.105 rr.1-23 .... 14-a
RSC, Ord.106 .... 6-c
RSC, Ord.106 rr.2, 5-9,16 .... 6-c
RSC, Ord.106 rr.10-15 .... 6-c
RSC, Ord.109 .... 13-b
RSC, Ord.109 rr.12,31 .... 12-a
RSC, Ord.109A 12-a
RSC, Ord.111 .... 1-d
RSC, Ord.112 .... 14-a
RSC, Ord.115 .... 14-a
RSC, Ord.116 .... 4-c
RSC, Ord.117 .... 4-a

APPENDIX TWO

HIGH COURT PLEADINGS AND OTHER PRECEDENTS

1. Ordinary road accident
2. Road accident occurring outside Northern Ireland
3. Occupier's liability
4. Factory accident
5. Highway tripping accident
6. Death case
7. Contract action (Commercial list)
8. Other precedents (legal aid notice; minor; appeal from master; medical records disclosure order)
9. Application to approve settlement on behalf of mental patient plaintiff and discretionary trust.
10. Judicial review (a) Motor Insurers' Bureau; (b) State benefits; (c) Prison adjudication; (d) Criminal trial))

These precedents are confined to proceedings commonly brought in the Queen's Bench Division: actions and judicial review applications. They are based on or adapted from actual cases, and state the established practice as it is in Northern Ireland. Some of the practices, particularly the habit of traversing all allegations in the Defence are possibly undesirable, but have not been criticised in the Courts. All names and dates are fictitious.

1. ORDINARY ROAD ACCIDENT

Two cars involved - driver and owner of one sued
[Heading]

Between JK plaintiff

and NP and
OP defendants

Writ of Summons
The plaintiff's claim is for damages for personal injury loss and damage sustained by reason of the negligence of the defendants in and about the driving management and control of a motor car.

Notice to Road Traffic Insurer

NOTICE TO INSURER
ROAD TRAFFIC (NI) ORDER 1981 ARTICLE 98
ORDER 52 RULE 1

[Heading as for Writ]
TAKE NOTICE that the above-named plaintiff on the 4th day of February 1996 caused a Writ of Summons to be issued against the above-named defendants claiming against the above-named defendants damages for personal injuries loss and damage sustained by reason of the negligence of the first defendant in and about the driving management control and repair of a motor vehicle.

The accident in respect of which the proceedings are brought occurred on the 20th January 1995.

A motor vehicle numbered AAA 0000 in respect of which the second defendant holds a Policy of Insurance issued by you was involved in the accident.

Dated this 4th day of February 1996.

Signed ....
Solicitor for the plaintiff
To: .... Insurance Company.

Statement of Claim
[Heading as in Writ]

STATEMENT OF CLAIM

Delivered this 20th day of April 1996 , by ...., solicitors for the plaintiff

Writ issued on 4th February 1996 .

1. The plaintiff, who was born on 24th November 1950 , is a civil servant .
2. On or about the 20th January 1995, the plaintiff was driving her motor vehicle on R Road T Town, when the first-named defendant so negligently drove managed and controlled a motor car that it collided with the plaintiff's vehicle thereby occasioning her serious personal injuries, loss and damage, as hereinafter appear. The first named defendant was driving the said motor car as servant and agent of the second-named defendant, who was owner of the said motor car.

PARTICULARS OF NEGLIGENCE OF FIRST DEFENDANT

(a) driving too fast
(b) failing to keep a proper or any look out
(c) failing to notice the plaintiff's car in time or at all
(d) driving on a part of the road which was dangerous in the circumstances
(e) failing to sound his horn, flash his headlights, or give the plaintiff any or adequate warning of his presence, movements or approach in time or at all
(f) driving on the wrong side of the road

(g) overtaking the plaintiff at an unsafe location
(h) failing to see or have regard to the plaintiff's right-side light indicator
(i) failing to permit the plaintiff to execute her right-hand turn before attempting to pass her car
(j) driving into and colliding with the plaintiff
(k) failing to brake, halt, swerve, decelerate, steer or otherwise manage and manoeuvre his car so as to avoid the collision

The plaintiff will rely in proof of the negligence alleged upon the conviction of the first-named defendant at T Magistrates' Court on the 4th September 1995 for the offence of careless driving contrary to Article 153 of the Road Traffic (NI) Order 1981, which arose out of and is relevant to the issues between the parties in this action.

The plaintiff will further rely on such facts as are within the knowledge of the defendants and their witnesses but not of the plaintiff, and on such facts as may appear from the evidence for the defence at the trial of this action.

3. By reason of the aforesaid wrongful acts and omissions, the plaintiff has sustained serious personal injuries, loss and damage, has suffered and will suffer pain and discomfort, loss of amenity, loss of enjoyment of life, she has lost and will lose earnings and her future employment prospects have been diminished, and she has suffered damage to property and other loss and damage

PARTICULARS OF INJURIES

Shock and upset. In hospital for two days. Nose deviated to right. Nasal septum dislocated. Nasal air passage badly blocked. Bi-lateral hearing loss. Lacerations on forehead, left upper eyelid, left temple, upper lip. Glass fragments from the windscreen and from his own spectacles had to be removed from his face. Multiple stitching. Numbness and muscle paralysis on left forehead. Two teeth had to be removed. Soreness in back and neck. Cuts and bruises to left arm and pain in left elbow and wrist. Abrasion on right thigh and abrasion and pain in left knee. Pain in chest wall. The plaintiff continues to suffer dizziness; frequent headaches; visible disfiguring permanent scars on the face, one 8cm long, one 12cm long; all remaining upper teeth extracted and four lower teeth extracted, permanent paralysis of frontal muscle in face; permanent deformity of nose.

The following medical reports substantiating the injuries alleged are served herewith
report of Mr .... FRCS, orthopaedic surgeon, dated ...
report of Mr ...., BDS dental surgeon, dated ...
report of Mr ...., FRCS, neurological surgeon, dated ...
letter of Dr .... , medical practitioner, dated ...

PARTICULARS OF LOSS OF EARNINGS

Loss of earnings from 20th January 1995 to date, being 15 months at £607 per month net = £9105. This loss continues and may increase and the plaintiff will claim the benefit of any relevant salary increases

PARTICULARS OF SPECIAL DAMAGE

Insurance excess £250
Vehicle hire £469
Vehicle depreciation £1,500
Replacement of jacket, blouse £130
Cost of replacement of spectacles .... £ 65
Expenses of visits to hospital for treatment £260

And the plaintiff claims damages and interest thereon under section 33A of the Judicature (NI) Act 1978.

Defence

[*Heading as in Writ*]

DEFENCE

Delivered this .. th day of etc.

1. The defendants deny that at any time material to this action the first-named defendant drove, managed or controlled a motor car and deny that any motor car collided with the plaintiff's vehicle as alleged in paragraph 2 of the Statement of Claim or at all.

2. The defendants deny that at any time material to this action, the first defendant or any other person drove a motor car as servant or agent of the second-named defendant or drove any car owned by the second defendant.
3. The defendants deny that they were guilty of any negligence or wrongful acts or omissions as alleged or at all and further deny each and every allegation in paragraph 2 of the Statement of Claim as if the same were herein set out and specifically denied.
4. The defendants do not admit that the first-named defendant was convicted as alleged in paragraph 2 of the Statement of Claim. If (which is denied) the first defendant was so convicted, the defendants deny that the said conviction is relevant to any issues in the action. The defendants also say that the said conviction was erroneous.
5. The defendants deny that the plaintiff suffered any personal injury loss or damage as a result of any wrongful acts or omissions of the defendants or at all, and further deny each and every allegation in paragraph 3 of the Statement of Claim as if the same were set out herein and each specifically denied.
6. If (which is denied) the defendants were guilty of any negligence, the plaintiff was guilty of contributory negligence

PARTICULARS OF CONTRIBUTORY NEGLIGENCE

(a) driving too fast
(b) driving on a part of the road which was dangerous
(c) driving into the path of the defendant's car
(d) failing to give way to the defendant's vehicle
(e) failing to see the defendants' vehicle in time or at all
(f) failing to keep a proper look out
(g) failing to stop, slow, swerve, steer, brake, manage or manoeuvre her vehicle so as to avoid the collision
(h) failing to give any or adequate warning
(i) failing to indicate her intention to turn right by signal in time or at all
(j) commencing a right-hand turn when the first defendant was established in an overtaking position
(k) failing to make any or adequate check behind her before commencing a right-hand turn.

The defendants will rely in proof of the contributory negligence alleged on such facts as are within the knowledge of the plaintiff but not of the defendants and as may appear from the evidence of the plaintiff and her witnesses at the trial of this action.

2. ROAD ACCIDENT

Passenger suing driver; accident occurred in Republic of Ireland

Between	AB	plaintiff
and	CD	defendant

Writ of Summons

The plaintiff's claim is for damages for personal injury, loss and damage sustained by reason of the negligence of the defendant in and about the driving management control and repair of a motor vehicle.

Statement of Claim

1. The plaintiff was born on .. th .... 19.. ; and is an unemployed labourer.
2. On ...th .... 19.. the plaintiff was a passenger in a motor vehicle owned and driven by the defendant at S Street, Buncrana, County Donegal, Republic of Ireland, when the defendant so negligently drove and controlled the vehicle that it swerved onto the wrong side of the road and collided with an oncoming vehicle driven by one EF. The law of the Republic of Ireland, so far as material to the issues in this action, is identical to that of Northern Ireland.
3. The said collision was caused by the negligence of the defendant in and about the driving and control of his vehicle, and further and in the alternative in and about the maintenance and repair of the said vehicle.

PARTICULARS OF NEGLIGENCE

(a) colliding with an oncoming vehicle
(b) failing to control the steering
(c) driving on the wrong side of the road
(d) failing to avoid a collision
(e) failing to control the vehicle
(f) failing to control the brakes
(g) failing to maintain and repair the steering system
(h) failing to maintain and repair the braking system

In proof of the negligence alleged the plaintiff will rely on the doctrine of *res ipsa loquitur* and will rely on such facts as are within the knowledge of the defendant and his witnesses but not of the plaintiff, and on such facts as may appear from the evidence for the defence at the trial of this action.

4. By reason of the said negligence, the plaintiff has suffered and will suffer personal injury loss and damage as hereinafter appears, and he has suffered loss of amenity, loss of enjoyment of life and loss of earning capacity.

PARTICULARS OF INJURIES

[complete as appropriate] ....

SPECIAL DAMAGES

At the date of the said accident the plaintiff was in receipt of unemployment benefit of £41 per week and the period for which he was incapable of work due to the accident was two years. The plaintiff therefore claims £41 x 104 for loss of such benefit, being a benefit which would not have been deductible from his damages under the Social Security Administration (Northern Ireland) Act 1992. Total £4,264

And the plaintiff claims the benefit of any increase in the said benefit

5. And the plaintiff claims damages and interest thereon under section 33A of the Judicature NI) Act 1978.

Signed .... BL

Defence

1. For the purposes of this action only, the defendant admits that he was guilty of negligence, and that the plaintiff was a passenger in the vehicle owned and driven by the defendant, in the circumstances as alleged in paragraphs 2 and 3 of the Statement of Claim.
2. The defendant denies that the plaintiff has suffered or will suffer any personal injury loss or damage or any consequences thereof as alleged in paragraph 4 of the Statement of Claim or at all.
3. If (which is denied) the plaintiff suffered any personal injury loss or damage, the same was not caused or occasioned by the negligence of the defendant as alleged in paragraph 4 of the Statement of Claim or at all.
4. The plaintiff was guilty of contributory negligence

PARTICULARS OF CONTRIBUTORY NEGLIGENCE

(a) failing to use the seat belt provided in the vehicle
(b) failing to secure properly or at all the said seat belt

Signed .... BL

3. OCCUPIER'S LIABILITY

Between	AB	Plaintiff
and	CD District Council	Defendant

Writ of Summons

The plaintiff's claim is for damages for personal injury, loss and damage sustained by reason of the negligence, nuisance and breach of statutory duty of the defendant its servants and agents in and about the maintenance, care and occupation of a football pitch and its environs

Statement of Claim

1. The plaintiff was born on ..th .... 19...
2. At all material times the defendant was owner and occupier of a football pitch at P Park, T Town, C County.
3. The defendant arranged and controlled a series of physical activities for young persons at the said place, and on ...th .... 19.. the plaintiff was lawfully participating in a game of football there with permission of the defendant.
4. During the said game the plaintiff had occasion to run at speed towards the goal line with the intent of keeping the ball in play and his momentum carried him forward onto a grassy slope behind the goal line. He slipped and fell and his right knee landed on a broken piece of glass concealed in the grass and thereby sustained personal injury loss and damage as hereinafter appears.
5. The said injury loss and damage was caused by the negligence nuisance and breach of statutory duty of the defendant, its servants and agents.

PARTICULARS OF NEGLIGENCE

(a) failing to keep the grass cut short
(b) failing to keep the grass clear of harmful objects
(c) failing to inspect the grass
(d) failing to warn the plaintiff
(e) failing to prevent the plaintiff from going onto and falling on the grass
(f) failing to institute and maintain a system for inspecting and clearing the grass and keeping it safe

PARTICULARS OF NUISANCE

Paragraphs (a) to (f) above are repeated as particulars of nuisance

PARTICULARS OF BREACH OF STATUTORY DUTY

Paragraphs (a) to (f) above are repeated as breaches of the duty to take reasonable care for the safety of the plaintiff as a visitor under section 2 of the Occupiers' Liability Act (NI) 1957.

The plaintiff will further rely in proof of the negligence, nuisance and breach of statutory duty alleged, on such facts as are within the knowledge of the defendant. its servants and agents but not of the plaintiff, and as may appear from the evidence of the defendant and its witnesses upon the trial of this action

6. By reason of the above the plaintiff has suffered and will suffer pain and suffering, loss of amenity, loss of earning capacity and diminution of his enjoyment of life.

PARTICULARS OF INJURIES

Major laceration to right knee contaminated with dirt and glass; stitching required for eight weeks; long U-shaped scar at right knee, poor circulation and reduced sensation; increased vulnerability to injury in right (dominant) leg

By reason of the injury the plaintiff was hampered in his performance of his O-levels in June 19... , and passed only three out of eight. His chances of a career as a professional footballer have been diminished or destroyed because he was not able to play at his best at subsequent representative and trial football matches and trial sessions for professional clubs. His proneness to injury at the area of the right knee, which cannot be properly protected have made substantially reduced his chances of a professional football career. The injury has interfered with his hobbies of squash, keep fit, jogging and weight training.

The plaintiff relies on all the injuries mentioned in the following reports served herewith:
Mr XY, FRCS dated ...... 19..
Dr YZ, dated .... 19..
And the plaintiff claims damages with interest thereon pursuant to section 33A of the Judicature (NI) Act 1978.

Defence

1. The defendant does not admit that at any time material to this action it was the owner or occupier of any football pitch at any place whether as alleged in the Statement of Claim or at all.
2. The defendant denies that at any time material to this action it arranged or controlled any physical activity at any place or that the plaintiff participated in football with the permission of the defendant whether as alleged in paragraph 3 of the Statement of Claim or at all
3. The defendant denies that at any time material to this action, whether in the course of a football match or at all the plaintiff slipped or fell or came into contact with broken pieces of glass, whether as alleged in paragraph 4 of the Statement of Claim or at all.
4. The defendant denies that it or any of its servants or agents was guilty of the alleged or any negligence, nuisance or breach of statutory duty and it denies each and every allegation in paragraphs 4 and 5 of the Statement of Claim as if the same were herein set out and each denied *seriatim*.
5. The defendant denies that the plaintiff has sustained the alleged or any personal injuries loss and damage and it denies each and every allegation of fact contained in paragraph 6 of the Statement of Claim as if the same were herein set out and each specifically denied.
6. If (which is denied) the plaintiff has sustained the alleged or any personal injuries loss or damage, none of the same was caused by or contributed to by any wrongful act, neglect, nuisance or breach of statutory duty on the part of the defendant or of any of its servants or agents.
7. If (which is denied) the defendant or any servant or agent was guilty of the alleged or any negligence, nuisance or breach of statutory duty, the plaintiff was guilty of contributory negligence.

PARTICULARS OF CONTRIBUTORY NEGLIGENCE

(a) running onto an area off the football pitch
(b) failing to prevent himself from slipping or falling over
(c) failing to observe the glass
(d) failing to complain about the presence of the glass
(e) failing to avoid the glass

The defendant will further rely in proof of the contributory negligence alleged herein on such facts as are within the knowledge of the plaintiff but not of the defendant, and as may appear from the evidence of the plaintiff and his witnesses upon the trial of this action.

Reply

1. Save insofar as the same consists of or contains admissions, the plaintiff joins issue with the defendant upon its Defence.
2. The plaintiff denies that he was guilty of contributory negligence as alleged or at all.

4. FACTORY ACCIDENT

Illness contracted at work. Limitation issue.

Between	XY	plaintiff
and	Z Company plc	defendant

Writ of Summons (issued 5 September 1994)

The plaintiff's claim is for damages for personal injuries, loss and damage sustained by reason of the negligence and breach of statutory duty of the defendant in and about the employment of the plaintiff.

Statement of Claim

1. The plaintiff was born on 12 th May 1940.
2. At all times material to this action and in particular from on or about April 1973 to July 1993 the plaintiff was employed by the defendant as a sprayer and as a cleaner at the defendant's factory premises to which the Factories Act (NI) 1965 applies.
3. During the course of his employment the plaintiff was obliged to come into contact with and handle injurious substances, namely nickel salt and leather, and by reason thereof contracted dermatitis and thereby sustained severe personal injury loss and damage as hereinafter appear.
4. The said contact was caused by reason of the negligence and breach of statutory duty of the defendant, its servants and agents.

PARTICULARS OF BREACH OF STATUTORY DUTY

(a) failing to provide and maintain a safe place of work, contrary to Factories Act (NI) 1965, section 30
(b) failing to provide adequate washing and drying facilities, contrary to section 57 thereof
(c) failing to take reasonable care for the safety of the plaintiff as a visitor in the manner stated as particulars of negligence below, contrary to section 2 of the Occupiers Liability Act (NI) 1957.

PARTICULARS OF NEGLIGENCE

(a) the acts and omissions constituting breach of statutory duty, above
(b) causing or permitting the plaintiff to come into contact with the said substances
(c) causing or permitting the plaintiff to have repeated contact with the substances
(d) failing to provide any or adequate warnings, instructions or training to the plaintiff
(e) failing to provide any or adequate protection
(f) failing to provide any or adequate or suitable gloves
(g) failing to provide any or adequate barrier creams, emollient or bland creams
(h) failing to arrange medical examinations of the plaintiff before and during his employment
(i) failing to remove the plaintiff to other safe employment after having knowledge or means of knowledge that the plaintiff was contracting dermatitis
(j) failing to supervise or monitor the plaintiff's work and conditions
(k) failing to provide and maintain suitable washing and drying facilities
(l) failing to have regard to the complaints and requests of the plaintiff from 1985 onwards
(m) failing by reason of the above to provide and maintain safe plant and equipment, a safe place of work and a safe system of work.

The plaintiff will say that a safe system of work would have included the precautions expressly or impliedly alleged to have been omitted in the foregoing particulars.

The plaintiff will further rely in proof of the negligence, nuisance and breach of statutory duty alleged , on such facts as are within the knowledge of the defendant, its servants and agents but not of the plaintiff, and as may appear from the evidence of the defendant and its witnesses upon the trial of this action.

5. By reason of the aforesaid wrongful acts and omissions, the plaintiff has sustained serious personal injuries, loss and damage, has suffered and will suffer pain and discomfort, loss of amenity, loss of enjoyment of life, he has lost and will lose earnings and his future employment prospects have been diminished, and he has suffered damage to property and other loss and damage.

PARTICULARS OF INJURIES

Contact dermatitis due to nickel sensitivity

PARTICULARS OF LOSS OF EARNINGS

From July 20th 1993 to date, X weeks at £108 per week net = £

And the plaintiff claims damages and interest thereon under section 33A of the Judicature (NI) Act 1978.

Defence

1. The defendant does not admit that the plaintiff was at any material time employed by it as alleged or at all and denies that any premises owned or occupied by it or any operations carried out thereon were such as to which the Factories Act (NI 1965 applies.
2. The defendant denies that the plaintiff was obliged to come into contact with or handle the alleged or any injurious substances.
3. The defendant denies that the plaintiff contracted dermatitis from any such alleged substances or at all.
4. The defendant denies that it or its servants or agents were guilty of any negligence or breach of statutory duty.
5. The defendant denies that the plaintiff has sustained the alleged or any personal injury loss or damage, and if so (which is denied) says that the same was not caused or occasioned by any wrongful act or omission of the defendant or its servants or agents.
6. If (which is denied) the plaintiff has suffered any personal injury, loss or damage, the plaintiff was guilty of contributory negligence.
7. The defendant denies each and every allegation in paragraphs 2 to 4 of the Statement of Claim as if the same were set out herein and traversed *seriatim*.
8. The defendant says that the plaintiff's causes of action, if any, are barred by the operation of the Limitation (NI) Order 1989, Article 7, and by previous enactments repealed by that Order.

Reply

1. The plaintiff joins issue with the defendant upon its defence save in so far as the same consists of admissions.
2. If (which is denied) the plaintiff was guilty of contributory negligence, the defendant nevertheless could have avoided the personal injury loss and damage sustained by the plaintiff by the exercise of reasonable care and skill and compliance with its statutory duties.
3. The date when the plaintiff first had knowledge
   (a) that the injuries alleged were significant;
   (b) that the said injuries were attributable in whole or in part to the acts and omissions constituting negligence or breach of statutory duty;
   (c) of the identity of the defendant and of such other persons as were guilty of such acts and omissions and of the additional facts supporting the bringing of the action against the defendant;

   was not earlier than three years before the date on which this action was brought. The plaintiff will object in point of law that Article 7 of the Limitation (NI) Order 1989 does not afford any bar or defence to this action, nor does any enactment repealed by that Order.
4. Further and in the alternative, the plaintiff will rely on the discretion of the Court under Article 50 of the said Order.

5. HIGHWAY TRIPPING CASE

Plaintiff tripped on public footpath on 'adopted' road

(Defendant: Department of the Environment for Northern Ireland)

Statement of Claim

1. The plaintiff is an unemployed labourer born on the 12th October 1927.
2. At all times relevant to this action the defendant was the Roads Authority responsible for maintenance of roads, footpaths and pavements at C Road, Belfast.
3. On or about the 10th June 1995 the plaintiff was lawfully walking along the C Road, Belfast, when he tripped and fell at the edge of the footpath and thereby sustained severe personal injuries loss and damage as hereinafter appears. The said road and location were at all material times a public road within the meaning of the Roads (NI) Order 1993.
4. The said personal injury loss and damage was caused and occasioned by reason of the negligence, nuisance and breach of statutory duty of the defendant, its servants and agents.

PARTICULARS OF BREACH OF STATUTORY DUTY
failing to comply with Article 8(1) of the Roads (NI) Order 1993

PARTICULARS OF NEGLIGENCE

(a) breach of the statutory duty outlined above
(b) failing to inspect the said footpath regularly or at all to ensure that the same was free from defects
(c) failing to maintain the said footpath in a reasonably safe condition
(d) failing to repair the footpath adequately or at all
(e) with knowledge or means thereof that defects existed in the said footpath, failing to take any or adequate steps to remedy the same
(f) causing or permitting the footpath to be irregular, uneven and broken
(g) failing to remove or make safe a drainage channel when the rest of the footpath was resurfaced
(h) failing to ensure that the drainage channel was properly maintained, if it was to remain on the public highway
(i) causing or permitting large defects to be and to remain on the said public footpath
(j) failing to fill in holes and level off the footpath
(k) failing to provide any or adequate lighting
(l) causing and permitting concrete around the said drainage channel to be and remain in broken condition
(m) failing to cordon off the area of the said defect
(n) failing to place warning signs at the area of the said defect, or otherwise to give any or adequate warning to the plaintiff
(o) causing and permitting the plaintiff to fall and be injured

The plaintiff will further rely in proof of the negligence, nuisance and breach of statutory duty alleged , on such facts as are within the knowledge of the defendant, its servants and agents but not of the plaintiff, and as may appear from the evidence of the defendant and its witnesses upon the trial of this action.

5. Further and in the alternative, the plaintiff says that the condition of the said public roadway constituted a public nuisance actionable at his suit in that it was rendered dangerous. The plaintiff repeats the allegations in paragraph 4 above and says that the defendant caused or continued or adopted the said nuisance at all material times.
6. By reason of the aforesaid wrongful acts and omissions the plaintiff has sustained serious personal injuries, loss and damage, has suffered and will suffer pain and discomfort, loss of amenity, loss of enjoyment of life, he has lost and will lose earnings and his future employment prospects have been diminished.

PARTICULARS OF PERSONAL INJURY

Severe injury to right ankle with displaced fracture; admitted to theatre for open reduction and internal fixation of trimalleolar fracture, using a seven hold plate with six screws. The medial fracture line extended to involve the tibial plafond which was reduced and stabilised with two screws. Initial difficulty in healing of wound, plaster cast applied and he remained in hospital for three weeks. Likely discomfort and stiffness in long term, unlikely to resume availability for employment. Long term possibility of osteo-arthritis.

PARTICULARS OF LOSS OF NON-RECOUPABLE BENEFITS

Loss of social security benefit of £.. per week payable to the plaintiff at the time of the accident by reason of his unemployment, which would not be recoupable from damages, from .. th .... 19.. to date, xx weeks (total £x,xxx). Since the accident the plaintiff has been and continues to be paid relevant social security benefits within the meaning of the Social Security Administration (NI) Act 1992 by reason of his unfitness for work attributable to the accident. This loss continues and the plaintiff will claim the benefit of any relevant increases in benefit. [*Valentine version*]

OR

Loss of social security benefits of £.. per week payable to the plaintiff at the date of the accident by reason of unemployment (which would not be recoupable by the DHSS under the Social Security Administration (NI) Act 1992) which but for the accident would continue to have been paid by reason of unemployment from ..th .... 19.. to date , being xx weeks (total £x,xxx). This loss continues and the plaintiff will claim the benefit of any relevant increases in benefit. [*Greer version*][1]

And the plaintiff claims damages and interest thereon pursuant to section 33A of the Judicature (NI) Act 1978.

Defence

1. The defendant admits that at times material to this action it was the Roads Authority responsible for maintenance of public roads, footpaths and pavements within the meaning of the Roads (NI) Order 1993 in Northern Ireland.
2. The defendant denies that on or about the 10th June 1995 the plaintiff was walking along the C Road, Belfast and denies that he tripped and fell in the circumstances or for the reasons or with the consequences as alleged or at all.
3. The defendant denies that the location at which the plaintiff allegedly fell or the C Road or any part thereof is a public road within the meaning of the Roads (NI) Order 1993 or that the defendant is responsible for its maintenance.
4. The defendant denies that it or any of its servants or agents was guilty of the alleged or any negligence, nuisance or breach of statutory duty, denies that the said footpath was in a condition which constituted a nuisance or that the defendant, its servants and agents caused, continued or adopted such nuisance, and denies each and every allegation contained in paragraphs 4 and 5 of the Statement of Claim as if the same were herein set out *seriatim* and each specifically denied.
5. If (which is denied) the defendant failed to comply with Article 8(1) of the Roads (N) Order 1993, the defendant says that the alleged defect did not create an unevenness exceeding 20mm and that in all the circumstances, the defendant took such care as was in all the circumstances reasonable required to secure that the said location was not dangerous, under Article 8(2) of the said Order.
6. The defendant denies that the plaintiff has sustained the alleged or any personal injuries, loss or damage and further denies each and every allegation contained in paragraph 6 of the Statement of Claim as if the same were herein set out *seriatim* and each specifically denied.

---

1 Suggested by Prof. D S Greer, author of *Compensation Recovery: Substantive and Procedural Issues* (SLS, 1996)

7. If (which is denied) the plaintiff has sustained or will sustained any personal injury, loss or damage, none of the same was caused or occasioned by reason of any wrongful act, neglect, default, omission or breach of any statutory or other duty on the part of the defendant or any of its servants or agents.
8. If (which is denied) the plaintiff has suffered any personal injury, loss or damage as alleged, as a result of tripping or falling on any alleged defect in the footpath, the plaintiff was guilty of contributory negligence.

PARTICULARS OF CONTRIBUTORY NEGLIGENCE

(a) failing to look where he was going
(b) failing to look where he was placing his feet
(c) failing to keep any or adequate look-out when walking
(d) failing to see the defect in time or at all
(e) failing to walk round or otherwise avoid the defect
(f) causing or permitting himself to walk in the vicinity of the defect is such a way as to come into contact with it
(g) failing to adjust his speed of movement on approaching and negotiating the defective area
(h) causing or permitting himself to fall
(i) failing to prevent himself from falling
(j) failing to keep an adequate foothold
(k) failing to have any or adequate or proper regard for his own safety in all the circumstances

The defendant will further rely in proof of the contributory negligence alleged on such facts as are within the knowledge of the plaintiff but not of the defendant, and as may appear from the evidence of the plaintiff and his witnesses upon the trial of this action.

6. FATAL INJURY CASE

Writ

The plaintiff's claim is for damages as widow and personal representative of the estate of CK deceased:

(a) under the Law Reform (Miscellaneous Provisions) (NI) Act 1937 for loss and damage sustained by the said estate by reason of his death caused by reason of the negligence of the defendant in and about the driving of a motor vehicle; and

(b) under the Fatal Accidents (NI) Order 1977 for loss and damage sustained by the plaintiff and dependants of the deceased by reason of the death caused as aforesaid.

Statement of Claim

1. The plaintiff is the widow and administratix of the estate of CK deceased (hereinafter called "the deceased") and as such sues under and by virtue of the Fatal Accidents (NI) Order 1977 on her own behalf and on behalf of the other dependants of the deceased for loss and damages sustained by her and other dependants of the deceased by reason of his death caused as hereinafter appears, and under and by virtue of the Law Reform (Miscellaneous Provisions) At (NI) 1937 on behalf of the said estate by reason of the death of the deceased.
2. On or about the 4th January 1996 in the course of his duties as a police officer the deceased was participating in a vehicle control check point at Road, town, when the defendant so negligently drove, managed and controlled his motor vehicle that he drove into and collided with the deceased whereby the deceased sustained severe personal injuries and died a week later on 12th January 1996 in hospital.
3. The said injuries and death were caused by the negligence of the defendant, as follows

PARTICULARS OF NEGLIGENCE

(a) driving into and colliding with the deceased
(b) failing to keep a proper look out
(c) failing to pay any or adequate attention to the road ahead
(d) failing to notice a stop signal given by a police officer on the road ahead
(e) failing to slow down and stop immediately, in time or at all
(f) failing to brake in time, adequately or at all
(g) failing to provide any or adequate warning
(h) failing to take any or adequate evasive action
(i) failing to have regard for the safety of the deceased

The plaintiff will further rely in proof of the negligence alleged, on such facts as are within the knowledge of the defendant but not of the plaintiff, and as may appear from the evidence of the defendant and his witnesses upon the trial of this action

4. By reason of the aforesaid acts and omissions the deceased suffered personal injuries, pain and suffering, loss of amenity, loss of earnings, loss and damage and caused his death; and his estate has suffered loss and damage

PARTICULARS OF INJURIES

[complete as appropriate] ....

PARTICULARS OF SPECIAL DAMAGE TO ESTATE

Loss of overtime for one week at £.. per week net
Funeral expenses £............
Damage to clothing £ ....

5. By reason of the said acts and omissions the plaintiff, as wife of the deceased has suffered bereavement and she and the other persons named below have suffered and will suffer loss and damage.

PARTICULARS PURSUANT OT FATAL ACCIDENTS ORDER

A. Persons on whose behalf the action is brought

APK, the plaintiff, widow of the deceased, born on ......

JHK, daughter of the deceased born on ....
FLK, daughter of the deceased born on ....
PMK, son of the deceased born on ....

B. Particulars of nature of claim
The deceased was a robust healthy man aged 38 years at the date of death, employed as a police constable earning approximately £ per month including overtime net, of which the deceased spent not more than £ per month on himself. His earnings were likely to increase. The deceased contributed generously to the support and upkeep of the aforesaid persons and by reason of his death they have been deprived of and will be deprived of such support and further and increased support in the future. The deceased assisted in the running and maintenance of the family home at which the above-named persons reside and they have been deprived of such assistance in the future.

And the plaintiff claims damages and interest thereon pursuant to section 33A of the Judicature (NI) Act 1978

(a) under the Law Reform (Miscellaneous Provisions) Act (NI) 1937
(b) under the Fatal Accidents (NI) Order 1977

7. CONTRACT ACTION

Sale of car; Commercial List action.

Between	LM	plaintiff
and	OP	defendant

Writ of Summons

The plaintiff's claim is for rescission of an agreement entered into between the plaintiff and the defendant for the sale to the plaintiff of a Mercedes motor car, the property of the defendant, on grounds of breach of condition and misrepresentation;
and for repayment of the sum of £21,000 and damages;
and damages for misrepresentation, negligent misstatement and breach of contract in and about the sale of the said car.

Statement of Claim

1. On or about the ...th ..... 19.., the plaintiff agreed to purchase from the defendant a Mercedes motor car registration no AAA 0000 ("the car") for the sum of £21,000.
2. In order to induce the plaintiff to enter into the said agreement, the defendant represented to him by oral statement on or about the ..th .... 19.. at the defendant's home at 21 S Street Antrim, as follows-
   (a) that the car had only one previous owner
   (b) that it was in good working order
   (c) that it had been serviced regularly
   (d) that the brakes had been recently repadded and were in good working order
3. Acting in reliance upon the said representations, and induced thereby and not otherwise, the plaintiff entered into the said agreement and bought the car from the defendant for £21,000.
4. (a) The plaintiff thereafter discovered the said representations to be untrue and the said representations are untrue, in so far that-
   (b) the car had two previous owners
   (c) it is not in good working order and has required a new engine and extensive repairs to the barrels and pistons, clutch assembly and brakes
   (d) it has not been serviced regularly and properly
   (e) the brakes were faulty and required replacement
5. The defendant was guilty of negligence in making the said representations.

PARTICULARS OF NEGLIGENCE

   (a) failing to inspect the said car adequately or at all
   (b) making representations which he did not know to be true
   (c) failing to warn the plaintiff that he could not vouch for each representation
6. The said representations were untrue and negligently made and the plaintiff is entitled to relief under section 2 of the Misrepresentation Act (NI) 1967.
7. Further and in the alternative, the express and implied terms of the said agreement were as follows-
   (a) that the car was of satisfactory quality
   (b) that it was fit for the purpose for which it was purchased
   (c) the plaintiff repeats each and every representation referred to in paragraph 2 herein as terms of the said agreement
8. The defendant breached the said contract in the following manner-
   (a) the car was not of satisfactory quality
   (b) it was not fit for its purpose
   (c) the plaintiff repeats each and every allegation in paragraph 4 herein as breaches of the said agreement

   In proof of the negligence, misrepresentation and breach of contract alleged, the plaintiff will rely on such facts as may be known to the defendant but not to the plaintiff, and as may appear from the evidence of the defendant and his witnesses at the trial.

9. By reason of the above-mentioned statements, acts and omissions, the plaintiff has suffered and will suffer loss and damage.

PARTICULARS OF DAMAGE

Repairs carried out to date £3,947
Estimated cost of future repairs £4,585

And the plaintiff claims:
(a) rescission of the said contract
(b) repayment of the sum of £21,000
(c) damages for misrepresentation and for negligent misstatement
(d) damages for breach of contract

And the plaintiff claims interest at 8 per cent per annum under section 33A of the Judicature (NI) Act 1978 on such sums as shall be found due to the plaintiff until judgment or sooner payment.

Defence

1. The defendant denies that in order to induce the plaintiff to enter into the agreement referred to in paragraph 1 of the Statement of Claim he made any of the representations alleged in paragraph 2.
2. The defendant denies that any of the representations alleged in paragraph 2 were made by him orally or at all
3. The defendant does not admit that the plaintiff relied on any representations in entering the agreement alleged in paragraph 1.
4. The defendant denies-
   (a) that the car had two previous owners
   (b) that the car was not in good working order and that it required a new engine and any extensive repairs
   (c) that it had not been serviced regularly and properly
   (d) that the brakes were faulty and required replacement
5. The defendant denies that he was guilty of the negligence alleged in paragraphs 5 and 6 or at all.
6. The defendant denies that any of the representations allegedly made were untrue.
7. The defendant denies that the representations referred to in paragraph 7(c) were express or implied terms of the agreement.
8. The defendant says that the car was of satisfactory quality and fit for the purpose for which it was bought.
9. The defendant denies that he breached the said agreement and each and every breach alleged in paragraph 8 is denied as if the same were set out *seriatim* and each specifically traversed.
10. The defendant says that it was an express term of the agreement alleged in paragraph 1 that no warranty or promise was given by the defendant as to the condition or performance of the car and that the car was sold "as seen", and that liability for any representation, or negligence and any express or implied terms as to the condition, satisfactory quality or fitness for purpose of the car was excluded.
11. The defendant denies that the plaintiff has sustained any loss or damage as alleged or at all and denies that any loss or damage were caused by any misrepresentation, breach of contract or negligence of the defendant.
12. If (which is denied) the defendant has been guilty of any misrepresentation, or breach of contract, the plaintiff has waived any right to rescission and repayment of the sum paid by reason of his having accepted the car and continued to accept the car after knowledge of the alleged misrepresentations and breaches of contract.

Standard directions from the Registrar of the Commercial List
[Matters to be answered in writing by the solicitors for each party before a specified date]

The above action has been transferred to the Commercial List. It is accordingly withdrawn from the ordinary list and all matters concerning it will be dealt with in the Office of the Registrar of the Commercial List.

If any pleadings, notices, replies, interrogatories, affidavits of discovery or similar documents have been served which are not included in the setting down bundle, two copies must be filed with me forthwith.

All interlocutory applications are to be made to the Commercial Judge and dates for hearing will be fixed by the Commercial Judge or by me in consultation with him, as soon as possible after setting down.

This action has been included in the call-over of the Commercial List to be held on ......th ...... 19... at ...am/pm.

The Judge will require attendance at the call-over of the person in your firm who is dealing with the action and who will be able personally to deal with any matters which may be raised. If you wish to instruct counsel to attend, the Judge would welcome that. Any counsel attending should be fully instructed about the state of the action.

At the call-over the matters with which the Court will wish to deal include the following-

(a) whether the action is ready to proceed to trial and if not the reasons for inability to proceed, and the date when it will be ready for trial

(b) the day or days on which it can be heard

(c) an accurate estimate of the duration, preferably made or confirmed by counsel

(d) (*i*) whether the pleadings lodged include copies of all notices and replies, interrogatories and replies, affidavits, lists of documents, interlocutory orders etc.;

(*ii*) whether the books of pleadings are properly legible, indexed and bound in correct order

(e) whether any interlocutory application may still require to be brought

(f) whether discovery has been completed

(g) (*i*) the number of expert witnesses who may be required

(*ii*) whether their evidence has been exchanged

(*iii*) whether any expert evidence can be agreed

(*iv*) whether any meetings of experts can be held which may reduce areas of disagreement and identify the issues over which the parties are in difference

(*v*) at what time and in what matter the expert evidence must be disclosed

(h) (*i*) whether any legal aid application is outstanding

(*ii*) whether all legal aid certificates have been lodged in Court

(j) whether any bundles of correspondence and documents have been prepared and agreed

(k) whether skeleton arguments, opening statements, chronologies, lists of *dramatis personae* in the action or similar documents would be of assistance to the Court.

8. OTHER PRECEDENTS

NOTICE THAT CLIENT IS LEGALLY AIDED

The Incorporated Law Society of Northern Ireland
Legal Aid Advice Assistance (Northern Ireland) Order 1981
NOTICE OF ISSUE OF EMERGENCY OR CIVIL AID CERTIFICATE

No. ....

Title as for writ
TAKE NOTICE that a civil aid certificate dated ..th .... 19.. has been issued to A in connection with the following proceedings: **As plaintiff to prosecute an action against B in the High Court for damages arising out of an accident occurring at (place) on (date)** [These words follow exactly the words used in the Civil Aid certificate issued by the Law Society to the party's solicitor]
AND TAKE FURTHER NOTICE that in consequence thereof the plaintiff in these proceedings is and has been from that date an assisted person.
AND TAKE FURTHER NOTICE that Regulation 16(6) of the Legal Aid Regulations provides that any person, not being himself an assisted person, who is a party to proceedings to which an assisted person is a party, may at any time before the judgment file in the appropriate court office or registry an affidavit exhibiting thereto a statement setting out the rate of his own income and amount of his own capital and any other facts relevant to the determination of his means in accordance with the provisions of Article 11(1)(e) of the Order

Dated
To the defendant and his solicitor Signed ....

NOTICE TO PRODUCE

[*Title as in action*]
TAKE NOTICE that you are hereby required to produce and show to the Court on the trial of this action, all books, papers, letters, copies of letters and all writings and other documents in your custody, possession or power, containing any entry, memorandum or minute relating to the matters in question in this action.

AND FURTHER TAKE NOTICE that should you fail or neglect to produce the above documents or any of them, secondary evidence will be given as to the nature and contents thereof.

CONSENT OF NEXT FRIEND FOR ACTION BY MINOR

BETWEEN
ABB (a minor) by BB his father and next friend Plaintiff
and
XY Defendant

I, BB, the father and next friend of ABB of [address] hereby consent to act as next friend in the above entitled action in which ABB is plaintiff and XY is defendant

Dated this th day of 19
Signed
Address
Occupation

Witness
Address
Occupation

Certificate of solicitor
[Title as above]
I, JS, of JS and Company, [address], a solicitor of the Supreme Court hereby certify that-
1. I know that ABB of [address] is a minor.
2. of [address] has no interest in the cause in question adverse to that of the minor

Dated this ...th day of 19...
Signed ....
of..

ORDER ON MINOR COMING OF AGE

[Date]
Before Master ....

BETWEEN
ABB (a minor) by BB his father and next friend — Plaintiff
and
XY — Defendant

AND BY THIS ORDER

BETWEEN
ABB — Plaintiff
and
XY — Defendant

UPON APPLICATION of the solicitor for the above-named plaintiff and upon reading the Writ of Summons and the Certificate of Birth of the above-named plaintiff from which it appears that he was born on .....day .. th .... 19..,

IT IS ORDERED that the plaintiff, lately a minor, be at liberty to proceed in his own name, he having attained full age, and that the title hereof be amended accordingly

---

NOTICE OF APPEAL FROM INTERLOCUTORY ORDER OF MASTER TO JUDGE IN CHAMBERS UNDER ORDER 58 RULE 1

TAKE NOTICE that the above named plaintiff intends to appeal against the decision of Master X on the 10th October 1996 ordering that this action be remitted to the County Court for the Division of Belfast.
AND FURTHER TAKE NOTICE THAT you are required to attend before the Judge in chambers at the Royal Courts of Justice, Chichester Street, Belfast on 30th October 1996 at 10.30 in the forenoon on the hearing of an application by the said plaintiff that the order of remittal be quashed.

Dated this 15th day of October 1996

Signed ....
To ....

ORDER UNDER ADMINISTRATION OF JUSTICE ACT 1970, SECTION 32 (1), FOR DISCLOSURE OF PLAINTIFF'S MEDICAL RECORDS TO THE DEFENDANT

[*This precedent is adapted from the form of order recited by Mr Justice Girvan in* Irwin *v* Donaghy *(QBD, NI) 15 December 1995; but the author has indicated by means of deletion and bold type his suggestion as to an alternative wording. In particular it is submitted that the plaintiff has no privilege in documents which are in the possession of a hospital authority or doctor, who are not his privy or agent, and therefore that the order must specify the privilege which could be claimed if the documents were in the plaintiff's possession.*]

IT IS ORDERED that the ...... Health and Social Services Board and Doctor ..... do, within 14 days of service of this order, disclose on oath whether they have in their possession, custody or power any medical notes, records or X-rays relating to the plaintiff
AND IT IS ORDERED that the said Board and Doctor do serve on the plaintiff and the defendant a list of the documents so disclosed together with a notice stating a time within 10 days after the service thereof at which the said documents may be inspected by the plaintiff at a place specified in the notice
~~AND the plaintiff shall be entitled to inspect the said documents and object on the grounds of privilege or irrelevancy to the production to the defendant of the said documents or part or parts thereof~~
AND the plaintiff shall be entitled to inspect the said documents and object to the production to the defendant of the said documents or part or parts thereof on the grounds that (a) they are irrelevant to the issues in the action, or (b) that they would be privileged it they were in the possession custody or power of the plaintiff; and to cover or seal up such documents or parts
AND IT IS ORDERED that, in the event that the plaintiff does not object to the production of the said documents or any parts thereof, the Board and Doctor do produce to the defendant all the document so disclosed and permit the defendant to take copies thereof. or to provide the defendant following such production with copies thereof at **the latter's** expense
AND IT IS ORDERED that in the event that the plaintiff does object to the production of the said documents or any parts thereof, the plaintiff or his solicitor shall by affidavit verify that the said documents have been examined and explain the plaintiff's objection to production of the said documents or to the objection to production of parts thereof and shall verify that no relevant and unprivileged parts have been sealed up and shall furnish to the defendant a copy of the said affidavit
AND in that event IT IS ORDERED that the Board and Doctor do produce to the defendant all the documents disclosed with those **documents or** parts **thereof** to which objection is taken covered or sealed up and shall permit the defendant to take copies thereof so covered or sealed up or provide the defendant following such production with copies thereof at the defendant's expense
PROVIDED ALWAYS that in the event of the defendant objecting to such covering or sealing up nothing herein shall prejudice the right of the defendant to apply to the Court to inspect any covered or sealed up **documents or** parts and to direct their production.

---

9. SETTLEMENT OF CLAIM FOR MENTAL PATIENT

Application in action by mental patient for approval of settlement, annexing copy of discretionary trust

[*When a judgment is given for a mental patient in a personal injury action (whether or not the mental disorder is associated with the cause of action) a problem may arise in that the acquisition of the damages for his benefit may prejudice his rights to state benefits or his free maintenance and care in a Heath Service institution. To obviate this risk the judge approving the settlement may be asked to approve the payment of the damages into court to be dealt with by the Office of Care and Protection under the Mental Health (NI) Order 1986 (Part VIII) which may vest the money in a trustee (e.g. the Official Solicitor) under a discretionary trust, so that the plaintiff never has during his lifetime any proprietary interest in the damages awarded*]

Summons

Let all parties attend before the judge in chambers at [time] in the fore/after noon on the ... th day of .... 199. on the hearing of an application by the plaintiff for an order that the parties have agreed terms of settlement or compromise in this action in the form of the draft set out in the Schedule hereto, the same to be approved by the Court, and that all further proceedings herein be stayed except for the purpose of carrying the said terms into effect and that there be liberty to apply for such purpose and generally

SCHEDULE

1. That the plaintiff be at liberty to accept that the sum of £60,000 be paid in satisfaction of the claim herein in the manner hereinafter provided.
2. That the said sum be satisfied as follows- that the defendant do pay £60,000 within ... days together with any interest thereon (subject to the first charge under the Legal Aid, Advice and Assistance (NI) Order 1981) into court to be dealt with in accordance with Part VIII of the Mental Health (NI) Order 1986.
3. That the defendant do pay to the plaintiff his costs of this action and his costs incidental to the claim herein and consequent thereon and of this summons, to be taxed on the standard basis, the plaintiff waiving any claim to any further costs.
4. That the plaintiff's costs be taxed in accordance with Schedule 2 to the Legal aid, Advice and Assistance (NI) Order 1981.
5. That upon payment by the defendant of the several sums and costs afore-mentioned, the defendant be discharged from any further liability in respect of the plaintiff's claim herein

TRUST DEED DRAFTED BY OFFICE OF CARE AND PROTECTION

THIS TRUST DEED is made on ... th day of .... 19..

Whereas .... of [address] (hereinafter called 'the beneficiary') is a patient as defined by the Mental Health (NI) Order 1986,
There has been paid to the Official Solicitor of the Supreme Court [or] ..... controller of the estate of the beneficiary appointed by the Office of Care and Protection on ..th .... 19... (hereinafter called 'the Trustee')
the sum of £60,000 being a payment in consequence of a personal injury to the plaintiff pursuant to a judgment granted in favour of the beneficiary by the High Court of Justice in Northern Ireland on ..th .... 19..
to be held on trust hereinafter declared:
AND the Trustee declares that he holds the said sum of £60,000 upon trust to invest it in any manner authorised by law by the Investment Trust Funds and to hold such investment upon the trust hereinafter declared:-

1. He will apply the income of the Trust Fund in such manner as he may in his uncontrolled discretion think fit for the benefit of the beneficiary and also at his uncontrolled discretion apply the whole or any part of the capital of the Trust Fund for the benefit of the beneficiary.
2. After the death of the beneficiary this Trust shall determine and the Trustee shall transfer any of the Trust Fund remaining to any executor or executors of the Will of the beneficiary

which has been duly admitted to probate, or if no such Will be admitted to probate, to any administrator of the beneficiary to whom letters of administration have been granted by the Family Division of the High Court of Justice in Northern Ireland

3. Notwithstanding anything hereinafter contained the Trustee may:-
   (a) out of the said sum of £60,000 defray the costs and expenses of and incidental to the preparation and execution of this Deed and to his acceptance and continued administration of the trusteeship thereof; and
   (b) at his uncontrolled discretion withhold and accumulate the whole or any part of the income of the Trust Fund and shall hold any such accumulations as an accretion of capital
4. In the execution and administration of this trust, the Trustee shall not be liable for any loss to the Trust Fund arising by reason of any improper investment made in good faith or by reason of any mistake or omission made in good faith or by reason of any mistake or omission made in good faith by the Trustee.
5. In this Deed the expression 'Trust Fund' means any investments from time to time representing the unexpended residue of the said sum of £60,000 and includes any accumulation of income hereby authorised.

Signed sealed and delivered by the said Trustee
[Trustee's signature] ....
in the presence of ....
[signatures of witnesses] ....

---

10. JUDICIAL REVIEW

(a) Review of Motor Insurers' Bureau Decision (civil matter)

DOCKET FOR *EX PARTE* MOTION

1997 No 106

IN THE HIGH COURT OF JUSTICE IN NORTHERN IRELAND
QUEEN'S BENCH DIVISION (CROWN SIDE)

IN THE MATTER OF an application by Joseph Smith to apply for judicial review

Mr [solicitor] to move on Monday the 10th day of February 1998 on behalf of Joseph Smith for leave to apply for judicial review

Readings Statement of Joseph Smith dated 30th January 1998
Affidavit of Joseph Smith filed 10th February 1998

Signed ....
Solicitor for ....
Address ....

1997 No 106

IN THE HIGH COURT OF JUSTICE IN NORTHERN IRELAND
QUEEN'S BENCH DIVISION (CROWN SIDE)

IN THE MATTER of an application by Joseph Smith for Leave to apply for Judicial Review
AND IN THE MATTER of an Agreement dated 1st March 1973 between the Ministry of Home Affairs (NI) and the Motor Insurers' Bureau

STATEMENT PURSUANT TO THE RULES OF THE SUPREME COURT (NI) 1980 ORDER 53 RULE 3(2)(A)

1. The applicant is Joseph Smith of [address]
2. The relief sought is-
   (a) a declaration that the applicant is entitled to have a decision of the Fire and Automobile Insurance Company Ltd, acting as agent for the Motor Insurers' Bureau, on his application dated 10th August 1997 made under the terms of the above-named 1973 Agreement
   (b) an order that the Fire and Automobile Insurance Company Ltd, acting as agent for the Motor Insurers' Bureau, do make a decision on his application dated 10th August 1997 made under the terms of the above-named 1973 Agreement
   (c) such further and other relief as may be just
   (d) costs
   (e) all necessary and consequential directions.
3. The grounds on which the said relief is sought are as follows-
   (a) The Motor Insurers' Bureau and its agent the Fire and Automobile Insurance Company Ltd have acted contrary to natural justice and have not discharged their duty of acting fairly by their failure to deliver a decision on the applicant's application pursuant to the above-named Agreement.
   (b) The Motor Insurers' Bureau and its agent the Fire and Automobile Insurance Company Ltd have acted unlawfully in failing to give any or proper consideration to the applicant's application and to exercise their power and discharge their responsibilities and duties under the above-named Agreement.
   (c) The Motor Insurers' Bureau and its agent the Fire and Automobile Insurance Company Ltd have filed to respond to a request made by the applicant dated 10th January 1998 to reach a decision on his application within seven days.
   (d) The Motor Insurers' Bureau and its agent the Fire and Automobile Insurance Company Ltd have acted unlawfully in failing to consider according to proper criteria whether to reach a decision on the applicant's application.

(e) The Motor Insurers' Bureau and its agent the Fire and Automobile Insurance Company Ltd have filed to invite representations from the applicant as to why a decision on his application should not be made

(f) The Motor Insurers' Bureau and its agent the Fire and Automobile Insurance Company Ltd have failed to give to the applicant any reasons why a decision should not be made.

Dated this 30th day of January 1998
Signed ....
solicitor for the applicant

To-
The first respondent
The Motor Insurers' Bureau
[address]
To-
The second respondent
The Fire and Automobile Insurance Company Ltd
[address]

AFFIDAVIT
I, Joseph Smith, [address] aged 21 and upward, make oath and say as follows-

1. I am the applicant herein.
2. I was born on .... 19..
3. [State full facts of accident, date and place, exhibit police report as 'JS1'.] I believe that the other driver, who has not been identified or traced was guilty of negligent driving and solely to blame for the accident.
4. As a result of the said accident I received the following injuries: ...... I beg leave to refer to the medical reports of Doctor ...., dated 8th June 1996 and 29th March 1997, on which marked "JS2" I have appended my initials at the time of swearing hereof.
5. I beg leave to refer to a bundle of correspondence between my solicitor and Motor Insurers' Bureau and between my solicitor and the Fire and Automobile Insurance Company Ltd, on which marked "JS3" I have appended my initials at the time of swearing hereof.
6. [Following paragraphs describe the history of correspondence and other steps]
7. On 10th January 1998 my solicitor again wrote to the Insurance Company calling upon it to issue a decision under the 1973 Agreement within seven days and stating that in default an application would be brought for judicial review. I beg leave to refer to this letter, on which marked "JS4" I have appended my initials at the time of swearing hereof. There has been no reply to this letter.
8. On 28th January 1998 my solicitor applied for legal aid in respect of these proceedings, and legal aid was granted on 8th February 1998.
9. I believe from the foregoing facts that I have no other way of requiring the Insurance Company or the Motor Insurers' Bureau to reach a decision, save by applying for an order of *mandamus* from this Honourable Court. I therefore ask for the relief stated in the application herein.
10. Save as otherwise appears I depose to the foregoing facts of my own personal knowledge.

ORIGINATING MOTION

1997 No 106

IN THE HIGH COURT OF JUSTICE IN NORTHERN IRELAND
QUEEN'S BENCH DIVISION (CROWN SIDE)

IN THE MATTER of an application by Joseph Smith for Leave to apply for Judicial Review
AND IN THE MATTER of an Agreement dated .... between the Department of the Environment for NI and the Motor Insurers' Bureau

Take notice that pursuant to leave of Master Z granted on the 14th day of February 1998 an application will be made by counsel on behalf of the above-named applicant on a date to be fixed for hearing of an application at the Royal Courts of Justice Chichester Street Belfast for the following orders-

(a) a declaration that the applicant is entitled to have a decision of the Fire and Automobile Insurance Company Ltd, acting as agent for the Motor Insurers' Bureau, on his application dated 10th August 1997 made under the terms of the above-named 1973 Agreement

(b) an order that the Fire and Automobile Insurance Company Ltd, acting as agent for the Motor Insurers' Bureau, do make a decision on his application dated 10th August 1997 made under the terms of the above-named 1973 Agreement

(c) such further and other relief as may be just

(d) costs

(e) all necessary and consequential directions.

The application will be grounded on the applicant's statement, his affidavit and the reasons to be offered.

Dated this 18th day of February 1998
Signed .... [solicitor]

(b) Review of state benefits decision (civil matter)

DOCKET FOR *EX PARTE* MOTION

1997 No 106

IN THE HIGH COURT OF JUSTICE IN NORTHERN IRELAND
QUEEN'S BENCH DIVISION (CROWN SIDE)

IN THE MATTER OF an application by James Brown to apply for judicial review

Mr [solicitor] to move on 7th January 1996 on behalf of James Brown for leave to apply for judicial review

Readings   Statement of James Brown dated 20th December 1995
Affidavit of James Brown filed 20th December 1995
Affidavit of Frank Sugg filed 20th December 1995

Signed ....
Solicitor for ....
Address ....

1997 No 106

IN THE HIGH COURT OF JUSTICE IN NORTHERN IRELAND
QUEEN'S BENCH DIVISION (CROWN SIDE)

IN THE MATTER of an application by James Brown for Leave to apply for Judicial Review
AND IN THE MATTER of a decision dated 20th September 1995 by a Housing Benefit Review Board (Ballymena District)

STATEMENT PURSUANT TO THE RULES OF THE SUPREME COURT (NI) 1980 ORDER 53 RULE 3(2)(A)

1. The applicant is James Brown of [address].
2. The relief sought is-
   (a) an order of *certiorari* to bring up and quash a decision of the Housing Benefit Review Board dated 20th September 1995 whereby the said Board decided that the applicant was disentitled to housing benefit
   (b) a declaration that the said decision was unlawful, *ultra vires* and void
   (c) an order that the matter be remitted to a differently constituted Board to be considered in accordance with the ruling of this Court
   (d) such further and other relief as may be just
   (e) costs
   (f) all necessary and consequential directions.
3. The grounds on which the said relief is sought are as follows-
   (a) The decision was reached following a hearing which was conducted in breach of the rules of natural justice in that-
   (i) there was a procedural impropriety in that the Board adjourned the hearing before the applicant had an opportunity fully to state his case, depriving him of his right to put questions to the attending officer of the NI Housing Executive, in breach of regulation 82(2)(c) of the Housing Benefit (General) Regulations (NI) 1987, as amended.
   (ii) in consequence of (i) above, the Board attached weight to the evidence of the attending officer without that evidence being fully explored or challenged.
   (b) The Board reached its decision without affording the applicant an opportunity to present his case and evidence.
   (c) The Board acted in contravention of the legitimate expectation of the applicant that it would resume the hearing on 14th September 1995, by subsequently notifying the applicant that it no longer intended to resume the hearing at all as a decision had already been reached.
   (d) The Board misconstrued the law that regulated its decision-making power, and misinterpreted the above Regulations.

(e) The Board's decision is unreasonable and irrational
(f) The Board failed to apply its mind to the question to be decided , in that having stated the evidence to be inconclusive, it still upheld the decision of the Housing Executive
(g) The Board failed to give any or sufficient reasons for its decision in breach of reg. 83(4)(b) of the above Regulations.
(h) The Board's decision was *ultra vires* by reason of its failure to apply the statutory scheme.

Dated this 20th December 1995
Signed ....
Solicitor for the applicant

To-
the Crown Solicitor's Office
[address]

AFFIDAVIT

I, James Brown, [address] aged 21 and upward, make oath and say as follows-

1. I am the applicant herein.
2. I was born on .
3. [States background facts as to applicant's financial situation at time of the application for benefit, stating that his savings of £129,000 had been stolen from him when in England].
4. On returning to Northern Ireland, I received unemployment benefit which was my only source of income. I was awarded housing benefit on 14 March 1994. On 24th January 1995 I received notification from the Northern Ireland Housing Executive Ballymena District Office, which marked 'JB1' I have appended hereto, that I would have to pay full rent and rates from that date because I was not entitled to housing benefit; that I had been re-assessed on the basis that I possessed £29,000 in capital. Under the Regulations, capital in excess of £16,000 disqualifies an applicant from receiving housing benefit.
5. The said notification informed me of a right of appeal to the Office within six weeks, and I appealed on 6th February 1995.
6. By letter dated 6th March 1995, which marked 'JB2' I have appended hereto, Mr.Smith, Assistant Manager, stated that he had reviewed and affirmed the decision to withdraw housing benefit, relying on regulation 43 of the Housing Benefit (General Regulations (NI) 1987: "A claimant shall be treated as possessing capital of which he has deprived himself for the purpose of gaining entitlement to housing benefit..."
7. On 10th April 1995 I exercised my right to apply to an independent review Board. A hearing was fixed for 10th July 1995 at the Town Hall.
8. At the hearing my legal representative Mrs LM, barrister, give a brief statement of my case. The three members of the Board indicated that the procedure was informal. Mrs Jones, the attending Housing Executive Officer, gave her account of the reasons for withdrawal of the benefit.
9. My representative began to question Mrs Jones about her interpretation of the Regulations. She appeared to be uncertain about that matter. The Board then requested a short adjournment, and on its return the Board indicated that it was uncertain about the meaning of reg. 43 and pronounced an adjournment to 14th September 1995 to allow inquiries to be made and guidance sought.
10. Before that date I received notification that the Board had reached a decision and that the hearing would not be resumed.
11. Save as otherwise appears I depose to the foregoing facts of my own personal knowledge. I assumed that this signified a favourable result to my appeal, as the Board had not heard enough evidence on my part to reach a decision. I assumed that the Housing Executive had failed to make out a case. I was stunned when I received a letter from the Review Board dated 20th September 1995 enclosing a copy of Board's decision not to amend the Housing Executive decision. I append a copy of the said decision marked 'JB3'.
12. I believe that the Board did not have sufficient information to justify its decision. I believe that the Board reached its decision when the case had been only partially heard, and before the attending officer's statement had been fully challenged and explored. I feel that it was

inappropriate for the Board to attach any weight to the attending officer's statements. I claim that the Board reached its decision without a proper understanding of the relevant legal provisions, or without making it apparent that it had a proper understanding of the relevant legal provisions. At no time did the Board state any reason for reaching its decision.

13. As a result of the Board's decision I have suffered and continue to suffer financial hardship. I ask this Honourable Court to quash the decision of the Board on 20th September 1995 and to remit the case for consideration by a differently constituted Board to reconsider and decide the case in accordance with the law and evidence and the directions of this Court
14. Save as otherwise appears I depose to the foregoing of my own personal knowledge.

Sworn ....

This affidavit is filed on behalf of the applicant James Brown by F Sugg and Co, solicitors , [address].

AFFIDAVIT

I, Frank Sugg, solicitor of [address] aged 18 years and upwards, make oath and say as follows-

1. I am the solicitor acting for the applicant James Brown in these proceedings and am authorised to make this affidavit on his behalf.
2. Delay in making application for leave to apply for judicial review of the decision of the Housing Benefit Review Board dated 20th September 1995 has been caused by the matters hereinafter stated.
3. I took instructions from the applicant and completed legal aid forms which were submitted to the Legal Aid Department on 23rd October 1995.
4. On 30th October 1995 I received a letter requesting copies of correspondence and Opinion of counsel. I beg leave to refer to the said letter, marked 'FS1', attached hereto.
5. On 6th November 1995 I wrote to counsel, Mrs LM, requesting an opinion. I beg leave to refer to the letter marked 'FS2' attached hereto.
6. On 16th November 1995 I received counsel's opinion and on the same day I sent a letter enclosing counsel's opinion and copies of all correspondence to the Legal Aid department. I beg leave to refer to the said letter marked 'FS3' attached hereto. [Note that counsel's opinion itself is not exhibited.]
7. A legal aid certificate dated 25th November 1995 was received by me on 12th December 1995. I beg leave to refer to the certificate marked 'FS4', attached hereto,
8. On 25th November 1995 I sent a copy of the certificate to counsel, by letter which marked 'FS 5' I have attached hereto.
9. I request this Honourable Court to grant leave to apply for judicial review notwithstanding the delay which is explained in this affidavit.
10. Save as otherwise appears I depose to the foregoing of my own personal knowledge.

ORIGINATING MOTION

1997 No 106

IN THE HIGH COURT OF JUSTICE IN NORTHERN IRELAND
QUEEN'S BENCH DIVISION (CROWN SIDE)

IN THE MATTER of an application by James Brown for Leave to apply for Judicial Review
AND IN THE MATTER of a decision dated 20th September 1995 by a Housing Benefit Review Board (Ballymena District)

TAKE NOTICE that pursuant to leave of Master Y granted on the 22nd day of December 1995 an application will be made by counsel on behalf of the above-named applicant on the 2nd February 1996 at 10.30 am at the Royal Courts of Justice Chichester Street Belfast, for the following orders-

(a) an order of *certiorari* to bring up and quash a decision of the Housing Benefit Review Board dated 20th September 1995 whereby the said Board decided that the applicant was disentitled to housing benefit
(b) a declaration that the said decision was unlawful, *ultra vires* and void
(c) an order that the matter be remitted to a differently constituted Board to be considered in accordance with the ruling of this Court
(d) such further and other relief as may be just

(e) costs
(f) all necessary and consequential directions.

The application will be grounded on the applicant's statement and the applicant's affidavit dated 20th December 1995 and on the reasons to be offered.

Dated this

Signed F Sugg & Co
[address]

To-
Crown Solicitor's Office.

(c) Against Prison Governor's adjudication (civil matter)

IN THE HIGH COURT OF JUSTICE IN NORTHERN IRELAND
QUEEN'S BENCH DIVISION (CROWN SIDE)

IN THE MATTER OF an application by Peter Potts for leave to apply for judicial review of a decision of a prison governor of Her Majesty's Prison, Maghaberry, made on 28th July 1996

STATEMENT
PURSUANT TO THE RULES OF THE SUPREME COURT (NI) 1980 ORDER 53 RULE 3(2)

1. The applicant is Peter Potts, a prisoner serving a sentence at Maghaberry Prison.
2. The applicant seeks the following relief, namely
   (a) an order of *certiorari* to remove into this Honourable Court and quash a decision of a Governor of HM Prison Maghaberry made on 28th July 1996
   (b) a declaration that the said decision was *ultra vires*, unlawful and of no force and effect.
   (c) an order by way of interim relief suspending the operation of the award of loss of association and loss of privileges imposed by the Governor
   (d) such other relief as may seem appropriate
   (e) costs
3. The grounds on which the said relief is sought are-
   (a) that the applicant was convicted of the charges of causing damage to prison property without there being any evidence to connect him to the charges
   (b) that the Governor did not apply the correct burden and standard of proof.
   (c) that it was unfair of the Governor not to allow the applicant to call his cell-mate as a witness in his defence.
   (d) that the decision of the Governor was one which no reasonable tribunal properly directing itself in law could have reached on the evidence presented
   (e) that the Governor's decision was arbitrary, irrational, unfair and contrary to the rules of natural justice
   (f) that the Governor failed to hold the inquiry within 24 hours after the laying of the charge, contrary to rule 36(2) of the Prison and Young Offenders' Centre Rules (NI) 1995
   (g) that the Governor did not ensure a full and fair trial and an opportunity to the applicant to present his case properly, contrary to the Prison Act (NI) 1953 section 13(2) and the 1995 Rules rule 36(4).

AFFIDAVIT

I, Peter Potts , make oath and say as follows-

1. I am the applicant in this application.
2. I was born on .... and am presently a prisoner serving a sentence in HM Prison, Maghaberry.
3. On 26th August 1996 a cell search was carried out at my cell in the said prison which I shared at that time with a fellow prisoner called Thomas Timpkins. The officers who conducted the search discovered in an excavated hole behind a cupboard unit a substance which they alleged to be a bottle containing alcohol. This hole was covered over and was not visible without a thorough search of the cell.
4. Thomas Timpkins and I were both charged with the causing damage to prison property and possession of a prohibited substance. The charges were laid on 28th August 1996.
5. The hearing of the charges against me before the Governor took place on 30th August 1996. I pleaded not guilty to both and applied to call Thomas Timpkins as a witness in my defence.
6. I argued that there was no evidence to show that I, rather than Thomas Timpkins was guilty of the charges and that in the absence of any evidence connecting either or both of us with responsibility, neither of us could be found guilty.
7. The governor found both of us guilty. I was awarded the following punishments-
   (a) 40 days loss of association
   (b) 2 days cellular confinement
   (c) 14 days loss of privileges
   (d) 14 days loss of parcels and tuckshop privileges.
8. I wish to challenge the above adjudication and punishment on the ground that there was no evidence before the Governor on which he could find me guilty of the charges; and that I was

deprived of the right to call a witness. I also seek by way of interim relief a suspension of the above awards pending a full hearing of this application.

9. Save as otherwise appears I depose to the foregoing facts of my own personal knowledge and belief.

IN THE HIGH COURT OF JUSTICE IN NORTHERN IRELAND
QUEEN'S BENCH DIVISION (CROWN SIDE)

IN THE MATTER OF an application by Peter Potts for leave to apply for judicial review of a decision of a prison governor of Her Majesty's Prison, Maghaberry, made on 28th July 1996

TAKE NOTICE that pursuant to leave of the Honourable Mr Justice X granted on the 22nd August 1996 an application will be made by counsel on behalf of the above-named applicant on the 2nd October 1996 at 10.30 am at the Royal Courts of Justice Chichester Street Belfast, for the following orders-

(a) an order of *certiorari* to remove into this Honourable Court and quash a decision of a Governor of HM Prison Maghaberry made on 28th July 1996
(b) a declaration that the said decision was *ultra vires*, unlawful and of no force and effect.
(c) an order by way of interim relief suspending the operation of the award of loss of association and loss of privileges imposed by the Governor
(d) such other relief as may seem appropriate
(e) costs.

The application will be grounded on the applicant's statement, his affidavit and on the reasons to be offered.

(d) Admission of evidence in criminal trial in magistrates' court (criminal cause)

IN THE HIGH COURT OF JUSTICE IN NORTHERN IRELAND
QUEEN'S BENCH DIVISION (CROWN SIDE)

IN THE MATTER OF an application by James Jones for leave to apply for judicial review of a decision of Belfast Magistrates' Court, made on the 30th September 1996

STATEMENT
PURSUANT TO THE RULES OF THE SUPREME COURT (NI) 1980 ORDER 53 RULE 3(2)

1. The applicant is James Jones, of [address], who was convicted by Belfast Magistrates' Court on 30th September 1996 of the offences of intimidation and criminal damage and was sentenced to six months' imprisonment.
2. The applicant seeks the following reliefs, namely -
   (a) an order of *certiorari* to remove into this Honourable Court and quash the decision of the court to admit evidence and to convict the applicant
   (b) a declaration that the said decision was *ultra vires*, unlawful and of no force and effect.
   (c) an order by way of interim relief suspending the operation of the conviction and sentence and to grant bail to the applicant
   (d) such other relief as may seem appropriate
   (e) costs
3. The grounds on which the said relief is sought are-
   (a) that the applicant was convicted of the charge without there being any evidence or any sufficient evidence
   (b) that there was a breach of natural justice in that the applicant was deprived of the right to cross-examine crucial prosecution witnesses
   (c) that the conviction was one which no reasonable tribunal properly directing itself in law could have reached on the evidence presented
   (d) that the court was biased against the applicant on the charge of the offence by reason of the prejudicial allegations put before the court to justify the admission of Arthur Adams statement
   (e) that the court erred in law in deciding that the statements of prosecution witnesses were admissible under Article 3 of the Criminal Justice (Evidence etc.) (NI) Order 1988
   (f) that the court failed to exercise its discretion under Articles 5 and 6 of the Criminal Justice (Evidence etc.) (NI) Order 1988
   (g) that the court failed to exercise its discretion to exclude evidence under Art 76 of the Police and Criminal Evidence (NI) Order 1989
   (h) the court failed to exercise its discretion to grant applicant's counsel's application for an adjournment of the trial
   (i) that the conviction was arbitrary, irrational, unfair and contrary to the rules of natural justice and deprived the applicant of a fair trial by reason of the decisions of the court referred to in grounds (e) to (h) and by reason of the absence of any advance notice to the applicant's legal representatives as to the nature of the case which was to be presented against him
   (j) that the court failed to give any reason for its decision to admit evidence against the applicant, and failed to give any reason for finding him guilty, and failed to express any caution as to the dangers of relying on evidence of identification which was crucial to the case against him.

AFFIDAVIT

I, James Jones , make oath and say as follows-

1. On 11th July 1996 I was arrested by police and taken to Musgrave Street police station and charged with the offences of intimidation against Arthur Adams contrary to section 1 of the Protection of Persons and Property Act (NI) 1969, and criminal damage to a window contrary to Article 3(1) of the Criminal Damage (NI) Order 1977. The complainant on the charge sheet was Superintendent JS Smith. I was released on recognisance conditioned for appearance at Belfast Magistrates' Court. I beg leave to refer to a copy of the charge sheet on which a complaint of the above charges was made, marked 'JJ 1' at the time of swearing hereof.

2. The date for the trial of the prosecution against me was fixed for 30th September 1996. Neither I nor my solicitor and counsel were given any advance notice of the evidence which would be presented against me on behalf of the prosecutor.
3. On that date Constable Brown gave evidence that he had spoken to Arthur Adams on 27th September 1996 and that the latter had said that he did not wish to proceed with his complaint against me. When questioned by my counsel Constable Brown said that Arthur Adams declined to give any reason for his decision.
4. Constable Brown then gave evidence that he spoke to Mrs Angela Adams, the wife of the afore-mentioned Arthur Adams, and that she said that she and her husband were both afraid that either of them might be attacked or their home attacked by reason of the proceedings against me; and that she was afraid to come to court.
5. After hearing the evidence of Constable Brown and after hearing a submission from my counsel the court decided under Article 3 of the Criminal Justice (Evidence etc.) (NI) 1988 Order to admit two written statements to the police made Arthur Smith and his wife in which they claimed to see a person identified as me shouting intimidatory and threatening remarks about him and throwing a stone through their front window. No reason was given for the admission of the evidence.
6. As soon as he had become aware of the nature of the evidence which Constable Brown was going to give, my counsel applied for an adjournment to consider the allegations made and the statements of Mr and Mrs Adams and to prepare the defence in the light thereof, but the court refused the application without stating any reason.
7. The only other evidence against me was a statement by a NI Housing Executive Member of the cost of replacement of the window allegedly broken. At the end of the prosecution evidence, I elected not to give or call any evidence and the Court convicted me of the offences charged without stating any reasons. I beg leave to refer to a copy certificate of the said conviction, marked 'JJ 2' at the time of swearing hereof.
8. Thus I was convicted by the court without my counsel having had an opportunity to cross-examine Mr and Mrs Adams as to the facts alleged by them and as to the reasons why he was unwilling to come to court, and of the opportunity to cross-examine his wife as to the facts alleged by her.
9. I was in no way involved in the offences alleged by Mr and Mrs Adams and I have no knowledge of any reason why they should be unwilling to testify in court.
10. I wish to challenge the above conviction and punishment on the ground that there was no evidence before the court on which it could find me guilty of the charges; and that I was deprived of the right to challenge the evidence. I also seek by way of interim relief a suspension of the above sentence and bail pending a full hearing of this application.
11. Save as otherwise appears I depose to the foregoing facts of my own personal knowledge and belief.

IN THE HIGH COURT OF JUSTICE IN NORTHERN IRELAND
QUEEN'S BENCH DIVISION (CROWN SIDE)

IN THE MATTER OF an application by James Jones for leave to apply for judicial review of a decision of Belfast Magistrates' Court, made on the 30th September 1996

TAKE NOTICE that pursuant to leave of the Honourable Mr Justice X granted on the 2nd October 1996 an application will be made by counsel on behalf of the above-named applicant on the 23rd October 1996 to a Divisional Court of the High Court at 10.30 am at the Royal Courts of Justice Chichester Street Belfast, for the following orders-

(a) an order of *certiorari* to remove into this Honourable Court and quash the decision of the court to admit evidence and to convict the applicant
(b) a declaration that the said decision was *ultra vires*, unlawful and of no force and effect.
(c) an order by way of interim relief suspending the operation of the conviction and sentence and to grant bail to the applicant
(d) such other relief as may seem appropriate
(e) costs

The application will be grounded on the applicant's statement, his affidavit and on the reasons to be offered.

To-

The Clerk of Petty Sessions,
Magistrates Court
Chichester St Belfast

To-
Superintendent JS Smith
Musgrave St Station
Royal Ulster Constabulary

To-
The Director of Public Prosecutions
Royal Courts of Justice
Chichester St Belfast

APPENDIX THREE

TABLE OF BASIC STEPS IN A HIGH COURT ACTION (QUEEN'S BENCH DIVISION)

This is only a general guide to the type of steps which may be taken in an ordinary action. It is not to be assumed that all listed steps must be taken, nor that these are the only necessary steps in a particular case, nor that the time limits are all strictly observed, nor that all steps must be taken in the order given.

BY PLAINTIFF'S SOLICITOR	BY BOTH	BY DEFENCE SOLICITOR
(1) Green Form legal advice (2) Apply to Law Society for legal aid (3) Solicitor's letter to defendant (4) Notice to road traffic insurer		
		(5) Secure authority to accept service of writ and notify plaintiff's solicitor thereof
(6) Instruct counsel (7) Originating summons for disclosure of documents or inspection of property (8) Issue writ within limitation period (9) Serve writ within 12 months after step (8)		
		(10) Enter appearance within 14 days after step (9), or apply to set aside service of writ (11) Instruct counsel
(12) Enter judgment in default in absence of step (10) [for the debt] or [for damages to be assessed]		(13) Apply to set aside step (12)
	(14) In commercial action, consider whether to request Registrar to enter action in Commercial List	
(15) Serve Statement of Claim up to six weeks after step (10) [with supporting medical reports]		
		(16) Serve Defence (and Counterclaim) up to 21 days after step (15)

(17) Serve reply and/or Defence to Counterclaim up to 21 days after step (16)		(18) Issue third-party notice -- leave necessary unless done before step (16)
	(19) Amend pleadings once without leave up to date of step (20)	
(21) Apply for summary judgment at any time after step (15)	(20) Pleadings deemed to be closed 21 days after steps (16) or (17)	
	(22) Serve notice for further and better particulars	
	(23) Reply to step (22)	
	(24) Automatic discovery (not in road traffic cases): exchange list of documents within 14 days after step (20)	(25) Apply for security for costs
	(26) Apply for injunction, inspection, or other interlocutory relief	(27) If plaintiff in default of required steps, or if no proceeding had for two years, apply to dismiss for want of prosecution
		(28) Apply to stay action if plaintiff does not agree to be medically examined
	(29) Apply for discovery on oath	(30) Demand names of doctors and hospitals which treated plaintiff
	(31) Disclose medical evidence within 10 weeks after step (20)	
	(32) Write to CRU for certificate of plaintiff's state benefits	(33) Make lodgment before step (20) or within 4 weeks after step (29)
(34) Accept lodgment within 21 days after step (33).		
	(35) Serve interrogatories	(36) Make offer of contribution to co-defendant
(37) Set down for trial within 6 weeks after step (20), and notify other party		

	(38) Arrange preliminary consultation, possibly informing opponent so as to explore negotiation possibilities or agree facts (39) Obtain direction of proofs from senior counsel (40) Serve notices:- to admit facts; to admit documents; to produce documents (41) Look at provisional list (42) Check availability of witnesses and counsel (43) Attend call-over to fix date (44) Check availability of witnesses and serve subpoenas. Check pleadings for any necessary amendments. Disclose recent medical reports (45) Apply to take case out of list if necessary (46) Watch for case in weekly list (47) Attend High Court on day of trial (48) Settle case or run it in court (49) If successful, ask for judgment and costs (50) If unsuccessful, ask for stay of execution for 3 weeks or pending appeal (51) Agree amount of costs or apply for taxation within 6 months of step (49) (52) Apply to EJ Office to enforce (53) Appeal to Court of Appeal within 6 weeks after step (49)	

APPENDIX FOUR

In the course of writing this book, the author has noticed a number of mistakes in the Rules of the Supreme Court. Some of the errors occur solely in the reprinted page of the loose-leaf *Red Book*. Some are errors in the Rules themselves. The text of this Appendix (plus one item on which action has since been taken) was submitted to the Supreme Court Rules Committee in May 1995. The assertion that these errors exist is made by the author and its justification is his responsibility alone. Of course it is not warranted that the author has discovered all errors.

ERRORS IN RED BOOK

These are mistakes in the reprinting of pages of the Rules as published for subscribers of the up-dating service. The errors require no action to change the Rules themselves, but the Red Book pages should be re-published in correct form.

Order 1

Paras.(d) and (e) of rule 12 and paras.(1) and (2) of rule 12A were left out, making it look as if (3) is part of rule 12. SR 1996/212 has substituted a new rule 12 and as this is translated into the *Red Book* the opportunity has been taken to correct this omission. The complete rule 12A reads as follows:-

[1] **12A.** *Choice of Division by plaintiff*

(1) Without prejudice to the power of transfer under Order 4, rules 1 or 2, the person by whom any cause or matter is commenced in the High Court shall allocate it to whatever Division he thinks fit by marking the document by which the cause or matter is commenced with the name of that Division.

(2) All interlocutory or other steps or proceedings taken in a cause or matter shall be taken in the Division to which the cause or matter is for the time being allocated or transferred.

(3) The fact that a cause or matter falls within a class of business assigned by these Rules to a particular Division does not make it obligatory for it to be allocated to that Division.

In **Order 7 rule 2(2)**, the text as printed omits the words here underlined.

(2) The party taking out an originating summons (other than a summons under Part II of Order 90 or an *ex parte* summons) shall be described as a plaintiff and the other parties shall be described as defendants.

Order 18 rule 8(4) should read

A party must plead specifically any claim for interest under section 33A of the Act or otherwise.

Order 44 rule 2(4) was amended by SR 1992 no 399 and should read:

A person served with notice of a judgment may, within one month after service of the notice on him and after entering an appearance apply to the Court to discharge, vary or add to the judgment.

---

[1] Inserted by SR 1983 no 407.

In **Order 59 rule 2**, for "by way of rehearsing" substitute by way of rehearing

In **Order 59 rule 4(2)** the text as printed omits the words underlined:

Where a summons to vary or discharge a certificate and the further consideration of an action are heard together, and an order is made on both, notice of appeal in respect of the order made on the summons may be served at any time before the expiration of the period within which notice of appeal could be served in respect of the order made on further consideration.

In **Order 59** the heading before rule 16 should read
SPECIAL PROVISIONS AS TO PARTICULAR APPEALS
not "PRACTICAL"

ERRORS IN THE RULES THEMSELVES

These are errors in the Rules as passed by the Rules Committee and require amendment by SR & O.

Order 5 rule 3(1) is rendered meaningless by **Order 55 rule 20**, or *vice versa*. The former says that save as otherwise provided by statute or rules, all original applications under statute to the High Court MUST be begun by originating summons. The latter says that applications under statute not otherwise provided for MAY be begun by originating motion.

Order 7 rule 7(2): "apply in writing to" should read "apply in relation to".

In **Order 11 rule 1(1)** (grounds for leave to serve writ outside jurisdiction) para.(o) should read:

(o) the claim is brought under the Nuclear Installations Act 1965 or in respect of contributions under the Social Security Contributions and Benefits (NI) Act 1992

In **Order 14 rule 7(1)**, the reference to rule 4(1) of Order 62 is a reference to the original Order 62 before its revision in 1988. The rule should now read:
without prejudice to Order 62 and in particular to rule 8(2) and (3) thereof

In **Order 15 rule 6(5)**, the references to "section 9A or 9B of the Statute of Limitations Act (NI) 1958" and "the Limitation Acts (NI) 1958 to 1982" should be, respectively
Article 7 or 9 of the Limitation (NI) Order 1989
and the Limitation (NI) Order 1989

Order 16 rule 8(6) (no need for third party notice for contribution between co-defendants sued as joint tortfeasors) should be revised to take into account the extension of contribution effected by the Civil Liability (Contribution) Act 1978 to all persons liable for the same damage whether in tort, breach of contract, breach of trust or otherwise.

In **Order 28 rule 9(4)** (order for trial of originating summons action) the text is copied from the equivalent in the English RSC. But Order 33 rule 4(2) of the English RSC is not the same as in our RSC. Our equivalent provision is section 62(5) of the Judicature (NI) Act 1978 Therefore, for "Order 33 rule 4(2)" and "the said rule 4" there should be substituted, respectively:

Section 62(5) of the Act
and the said section

Order 32 rule 12A should read:

The jurisdiction to direct, under Article 50 of the Limitation (NI) Order 1989, that Article 7 or 9 of that Order should not apply to an action or any specified cause of action to which the cause of action relates shall be exercisable by the Court.

In **Order 39**, the title should be EVIDENCE BY DEPOSITION not DESPOSITION

In **Order 42**, the Lunacy Regulation (Ireland) Act 1871, should be amended to the Mental Health (Northern Ireland) Order 1986

In **Order 45 rule 4,** it is arguable on a strict interpretation of para.(2) thereof, that where a judgment or order requires a person to do an act without specifying a time, and an order is subsequently made under Order 42 rule 5 requiring the act to be done within a newly specified time, paragraph (1) does not apply and the judgment or order is not enforceable by committal. If this is a mistake, the same error exists in the English RSC.

In **Order 52 rule 1(2)** the reference to rule 5 should be to rule 7.

In **Order 52, rule 8(1)(b)**, and in **Order 74 rule 1**, for "Mental Health Act (NI) 1961" substitute
Mental Health (NI) Order 1986

The first paragraph of **Order 52 rule 8(3)** should read, as does the equivalent English rule:-

Except with leave of the Court hearing an application for an order of committal, no grounds shall be relied upon at the hearing except the grounds set out in the statement under rule 2 or as the case may be, the notice of motion under rule 4.

In **Order 52 rule 10(1)**, the underlined words should be revoked:

The Court may, on the application of any person committed to prison until further order for any contempt of court, discharge him.

These words have been taken out of the English rule. The reason is that under the Contempt of Court Act 1981 all committals for contempt must be for a fixed term.

In **Order 55 rule 2** (regarding appeals from the county court) paragraph (4) has been rendered redundant and should be revoked, because of the amendment to paragraph (3)

In **Order 62 rule 6(9)** the text omits some of the statutory provisions. To be consistent with the English RSC, and also with the duty placed on the Rules Committee by section 33(2) of the Administration of Justice Act 1970, rule 6(9) should read:

Where an application is made in accordance with Order 24 rule 8 or Order 29 rule 9 for an order under section 21 of the Administration of Justice Act 1969 or under section 31, 32(1) or 32(2) of the Administration of Justice Act 1970 the person against whom the order is sought shall be entitled to his costs of the application, and of complying with any order made thereon.

In **Order 62 rule 17(5)**, (half costs where award reduced to county court limit by deduction for contributory fault) there is a mistaken reference to paragraph (7). It should read:
In cases to which paragraph (6) applies ....

In **Order 62 Appendix 3**, Part III, para.1 needs to be amended to read in accordance with the 1988 revision of Order 62. It should read:
1. Where the plaintiff or defendant is entitled to costs by virtue of rule 5 there shall be allowed .....

In **Order 77 rule 16(1)** (Proceedings re postal packets), section 9(3) of the Crown Proceedings Act has been repealed. The rule should read:
An application by any person under section 30(5) of the Post Office Act 1969 for leave to bring proceedings ...

In **Order 91 rules 1, 2 and 4**, the references to section 100 of the Taxes Management Act 1970 should be revoked, as the High Court jurisdiction under that section has been removed; and references to Sch.4 of the Finance Act 1975 should be replaced by, in rule 2, s.222, and, in rule 4, ss.249 and 251, of the Inheritance Tax Act (originally called the Capital Transfer Tax Act) 1984.

Order 92 rule 3 is redundant as the War Damage Act 1943 has been repealed

Order 93 rule 1(2), three paragraphs should be amended to read:
(g) Industrial Relations (NI) Order 1992
(j) Building Societies Act 1986
(n) Friendly Societies Acts 1974 and 1992

In **Order 94 rule 2(1)**,
(ii) should be amended to
sections 22 and 32 of the Social Security Administration (NI) Act 1992
(ii) should be amended to
sections 16 and 56(8) of the Social Security Administration (NI) Act 1992
and rule 3(1)(iii) should be amended accordingly

Order 97 (Non-contentious Probate) should be amended to take into account the Wills and Administration Proceedings (NI) Order 1994

In **Order 102, rule 2(3)(e)** note that Article 465 of the 1986 Order was repealed by the Insolvency Order 1989

INDEX

12.08- means: from para.12.08 onwards
12.08-12 means: from para.12.08 to para.12.12
12.08n means: para.12.08 in the footnote thereto

ABANDONMENT
appeal, of 20.34
claim, of 11.17, 12.00
relief, of 11.17

ABATEMENT
11.36

ABROAD
enforcement of NI judgment 16.18-
examination of witness 13.10
judicial review of decision made 19.19
residence 11.58
service, mode of 6.18

ABSENT PARTY
3.04
administration of estate, in 3.38, 18.65
trustee 14.44

ABUSE OF PROCESS
11.181-183
action on public law issue 19.08
service outside NI 6.17

ACCEPTANCE
accord and satisfaction 9.27
lodgment, of 11.155
.. defamation action, in 18.18
.. within county court limit 17.28
offer of amends, of 18.20

ACCORD AND SATISFACTION
5.00, 9.27

ACCOUNT
action for 18.25
.. limitation period 4.03
.. particulars 9.87
.. personal representative, against
16.10
.. pleadings 9.82
directions for taking 18.25, 18.58
matters of
.. jury trial 14.04
.. reference to officer 14.14, 18.27
party liable to 11.170

ACCOUNT STATED
5.14

ACCOUNTANT-GENERAL
1.05, 11.171, 12.17, 15.08

ACQUITTAL
estoppel from 13.110
evidence, as 13.27
judicial review of 19.48

ACTION(s)
abuse of process 11.181, 19.08
commencement of 5.03
.. costs before 5.00, 17.16-20
.. minor's claim settled before 12.13
concurrent 11.176
conduct of 3.03, 18.56
consolidation of 3.35
contribution or indemnity, for 10.17
costs, for 17.77
cross- 9.51
definition 1.07, 18.09
discontinuance of 12.00-04
discovery before 11.134
discovery, for 11.130-131
enforce judgment, to 16.21, 16.24
evidence at trial of 13.30-
injunction before 11.73
judgment in 15.00
pleadings, without 9.05
probate 18.48
public rights, based on 19.08
representative 3.37
setting down for trial 12.26
stay of 11.173
steps before 2.01, 5.00
summary judgment 11.45-
'test' 3.39

ADDING PARTY see NON-PARTY

ADDRESS
outside NI 11.58
parties', on writ 5.05
.. misstatement of 11.56
service, for 3.51, 5.05, 6.24-27, 7.03

ADJOURNMENT
amendment due to 11.20
appeal as to decision relating to
20.63
appeal hearing, of 11.08, 20.44

compromise, under 12.09
costs of 14.21, 17.66, 17.89
judicial review hearing, of 19.75
judicial review of 19.47, 19.82
mortgagee's action 18.73
originating summons, of 18.12
summons, of 11.06
trial, of 12.30, 14.21
witness absent, due to 13.08

ADMINISTRATION OF ESTATE
action for 18.62-69
.. avoidance of need for 18.63
.. parties 3.43
.. proceedings under judgment 18.57
.. representation of persons 3.38, 18.65
.. service outside NI 6.16
proceedings concerning 18.50, 18.62-69

'ADMINISTRATION OF JUSTICE ACT'
discovery 11.133-136
inspection 11.87-89

ADMINISTRATION ORDER
Enforcement of Judgments Office, by 11.174, 16.28

ADMINISTRATIVE DECISIONS
High Court, of 14.02, 20.05
judicial review of 19.40-41
.. stay pending 19.69

ADMIRALTY
18.17

ADMISSIBILITY OF EVIDENCE
13.12-
appeal as to 20.61
cross-examination, in 13.66
deposition, of 13.10
document not disclosed 11.119
document not stamped 13.147
expert report 18.32
intercepted letters and 'phone-calls 13.51
interim award, of 11.55
lodgment, of 11.160
map, photo etc. 13.85, 13.131
medical report 11.143, 13.131
new trial on grounds of 20.57
objection to 13.84, 20.41

ADMISSION
failure to traverse as 9.24
formal 9.95-98, 13.107
.. by counterclaiming defendant 17.43
.. withdrawal of on appeal 20.41
interrogatories, in 11.128
minor, by 3.08, 9.95
party, by 13.116-118
'without prejudice' 13.43

ADOPTION
18.51a

ADVERTISEMENT
claimants and creditors, for 18.58
substituted service by 6.22

AFFIDAVIT
11.13-15, 13.33
accounts verified by 18.25
'Administration of Justice Act' discovery, for 11.136
amendment of 11.18
committal application, in 16.54, 16.79
discovery, of 11.95
.. conclusiveness of 11.107
documents referred to in 11.112
habeas corpus, for 19.101, 19.104
inspection of lodged 1.25
interrogatories on 11.126
judicial review, in 19.54, 19.66, 19.68, 19.75-76
leave to serve writ outside NI, for 6.17
mortgage action 18.71
motion, with 11.05
originating summons, on 18.11-12
service, of 6.28
.. in judicial review 19.68
summary judgment, for 11.46
summons, with 11.06

AGENT
admission by 13.117
discovery by 11.98
foreign defendant, of 6.14
indemnity 10.03, 10.12

AGREEMENT
accord and satisfaction 5.00, 9.27
appeal, not to 20.05
arbitration, for 7.14, 7.21
costs between party and party 17.96
costs between solicitor and client 17.80
estoppel by 13.98
service under 6.03, 6.14

ALTERNATIVE
counterclaim or set-off in the 9.40
defences 9.26, 14.38
liability 3.33, 8.10, 9.52, 11.157
.. costs 17.51
.. direction of no case to answer 14.31
.. election between 13.99
pleading in the 9.06, 9.14
remedies 9.14, 14.45

AMENDMENT
11.16-35
answers to interrogatories, of 11.128
appearance, of 7.11
bill of costs, of 17.107
costs occasioned by 11.23, 17.07
judgment, of 15.10-13
.. in default 8.08, 8.14
judicial review statement, of 19.68, 19.75
limitation problems on 11.31-35
lodgment, after 11.150, 11.161
motion, of 11.05
notice of appeal, of 20.36
order, of 15.10-13
parties, as to 11.24-29
.. on appeal 20.37
pleadings, of 9.02, 11.16-18
.. on appeal 20.41, 20.48
replies to notice for particulars, of 9.94
summons, of 11.05
time problems on 11.30-35
writ, of 11.16-18

AMENITY, LOSS OF
damages for 14.61
pleading 9.19

ANISMINIC REVIEW
19.16, 19.41

ANTON PILLER ORDER
11.86

APPEAL
20.00
arbitrator, from 7.22
contempt proceedings, in 16.84-85
costs on 17.69-70, 20-73-76
.. against Legal Aid Fund on 17.90
Enforcement of Judgments Office, from
16.31
ex parte order, from 11.12, 20.11
interlocutory 11.08-10, 20.10
irregular proceeding, from 1.30, 20.64
judicial review refused or deferred
because of 19.51, 19.59
jurisdictional point on 20.60
legal aid for 3.62
loss of right of 20.39
master to judge, from 11.08
notice of 20.18
.. amendment of 20.36
order on 11.03, 20.70
.. correction of errors in 15.13
procedure in absence of rules 1.12
restitution of costs after 17.61
restrictions on 20.05
summary judgment proceedings, in
11.54
taxation of costs, from 17.85
time for 18.02, 20.20
.. extension of 1.35, 20.24

APPEAL TO COURT OF APPEAL
20.01-82
and see APPEAL
case stated, by 20.79-82
committal of judgment debtor, from 16.43
consent judgment, from 20.08
contempt proceedings, in 16.84
costs on 20.73-76
.. counsel's 17.102
.. solicitor's 17.98
costs, appeal as to 17.37, 20.08
Enforcement of Judgments Office, from
16.31
entry of 20.26
form of 20.54
habeas corpus, in 19.107
hearing of 20.44-51
interest on costs 17.111
interest on affirmed judgment 15.16
interlocutory order, from 20.10, 20.43
issues on 20.60-69
judicial review, in 19.62, 19.90
non-appearance on 20.49, 20.77
order on 20.70
part of judgment, against 20.19, 20.30
powers 20.52-53
procedure 20.13-30
right of 20.01-12
summary judgment proceedings, from
11.54
third-party proceedings, in 10.25
time for 20.20-24

APPEAL TO HIGH COURT
18.02-03
case stated, by 18.06-08
costs of 17.70
Court of Appeal, from 20.87-88
Enforcement of Judgments Office, from
16.31

APPEAL TO HOUSE OF LORDS
20.83-92
contempt proceedings, in 16.84
from refusal of leave to appeal
20.12, 20.15
habeas corpus, in 19.107
High Court, from 20.84-86
judicial review, in 19.62, 19.90, 19.98

APPEARANCE
7.00-11
added defendant, by 11.29
amendment of 11.18
counterclaim, to 9.54
originating summons action, in 18.11
party in default of

.. judgment in default against 8.00-12
.. service on 6.20
removed action, in 11.147
setting aside service before 6.10
third-party notice, after 10.19
third-party notice, to 10.20
trial, at 14.18
unserved writ, to 6.00, 7.07
writ, to 7.00-11
.. conditional 7.09
.. unconditional 7.07
.. withdrawal of 12.00
APPELLANT
20.02, 20.51
costs of 20.73, 20.76
non-appearance by 20.49, 20.77

APPLICANT
judicial review, for 19.53
.. death of 19.67
.. sufficient interest 19.56, 19.79

APPLICATION
amendment, for 11.20
costs, for 17.15
direction, for 14.29
discovery, for 11.95
Enforcement of Judgments Office, to
16.26
evidence on 11.13-15
ex parte 11.11
High Court, to 18.05
interlocutory 11.01-6, 11.62
judgment in default, for 8.02, 8.12, 9.63
.. to set aside 8.16-18
judicial review, for 19.54
leave to appeal, for 20.14
procedure in absence of rules 1.12
take out of list, to 12.29-32

APPOINTMENT FOR HEARING
assessment of damages 14.50
interlocutory summons 11.06
originating summons 18.11-13

APPORTIONMENT
fatal accident damages 14.72
lodgment, of 11.150

APPROPRIATION
money in court as lodgment, of 11.151

APPROVAL
settlement, of 11.156, 12.13-20, 12.23
.. on appeal 20.45
.. use of privileged documents in 13.41

ARBITRATION
7.14-24
award 7.22, 14.81n, 16.23
interpleader, on 10.33
payment into court 11.169
reference to 14.14

ARREST
committal order, under 16.81
Enforcement of Judgments Office, by
16.30
habeas corpus against 19.99
judicial review of 19.14
ne exeat regno 11.76

ARTICLE OR THING
13.154
inspection of 11.78-89

ASSESSMENT
costs, of 17.11, 17.93
damages, of 4.00, 14.49-52
.. appeal to Court of Appeal 20.03, 20.68
.. in default 8.11

ASSESSORS
appeal with 20.48
trial with 14.13

ASSETS
discovery of 11.131
Mareva injunction over 11.74

ATTACHMENT
debt, of 16.27, 16.35
earnings, of 16.27, 16.42

ATTESTATION
proving document by 13.141, 13.147

ATTORNEY-GENERAL
3.22, 9.44, 11.27, 11.28, 11.43
certiorari sought by 19.55
consent to committal motion 16.74
costs against 17.09
injunction sought by 14.87, 16.75
relator action 3.23

AUDIENCE, RIGHT OF
3.54

AUTHENTICITY OF DOCUMENT
13.139-141
admission of 9.98, 11.105, 13.143
handwriting to prove 13.42, 13.140

AUTHORITY
counsel for party, of 3.55
Legal Aid Committee, by 3.57, 3.62,
17.85
solicitor for party, of 3.48, 6.00
writ issued without 5.04, 7.00

AUTOMATIC DISCOVERY
11.92-94

BAIL
habeas corpus to enforce 19.99
judicial review, pending 19.72-73, 19.96
jurisdiction of High Court 19.01
.. venue 1.03

BANK
compellability as witness 13.36, 13.51
lodgment in 11.149, 11.155, 11.171

BANKERS' BOOKS
evidence of transactions, as 13.133
inspection of 11.132
privilege for 13.51
subpoena for 13.04

BANKRUPT(CY)
18.80
appeal, pending 20.38
compromise by 12.10
enforcement against insurer of 16.13
estate 18.62, 18.64, 18.65
petition 16.38
proceedings by or against 3.05, 11.42
security for costs against 11.57, 11.59

BANKRUPTCY AND COMPANIES OFFICE
1.05, 18.53

BAR COUNCIL
3.55
recommended fees 17.96, 17.103

BARRISTER see COUNSEL

'BELFAST SOLICITORS' SCALE' COSTS
17.96

BENEFICIARIES
action by 3.40
indemnity by 10.04
representation of 3.19, 3.40
.. administration action, in 18.64-65

BENEFITS, COLLATERAL
14.63, 14.72

BEREAVEMENT
damages for 14.71

BIAS
court or tribunal, of 19.31
jury, of 20.57
witness, of 13.75, 13.78

BILL OF COSTS 17.77, 17.107
included in accounts 18.25
legal aid 17.85

BIRTHS, MARRIAGES AND DEATHS
records 13.153

BLOOD AND 'DNA' TESTS
11.26, 13.156

BONDS
1.26, 11.56

BRITISH ISLANDS
defined 1.10

BRUSSELS CONVENTION see CONVENTIONS AND TREATIES

'BULLOCK'
costs order 17.51
.. award within county court limit 17.29
letter 2.01

BUSINESS NAME
3.15

'*CALDERBANK*' OFFER
9.27, 11.167, 17.08

CALL-OVER
12.29-30, 20.44

CAMERA
court sitting in 14.02

CARE AND ATTENTION see MEDICAL

CARE AND PROTECTION, OFFICE OF
1.05, 3.10, 3.11, 3.12
approval of settlement 12.19, 18.52
proceedings issued in 18.46, 18.52

CASE STATED
appeal to Court of Appeal by 20.04, 20.79-82
appeal to High Court by 18.06-08, 20.04
decision on 15.00, 20.88

CAUSE
definition 1.07

CAUSE BOOK
1.07, 15.01

CAUSE(S) OF ACTION
absence of 11.178
accrual of 4.00, 11.19, 11.30, 14.51
.. date of 9.09, 11.31
adding 4.09, 11.22, 11.32-34
amendment to 11.31

costs of 17.39
damages for, in judicial review 19.88
estoppel 13.103
indorsement on writ of 5.07
joinder of 3.25
.. judgment on 14.45, 15.03
.. lodgment against 11.150, 11.157
merges in judgment 16.21, 16.24
pleading 9.10
set-off, in 9.37
splitting 3.27, 3.30
surviving death 11.39
title to 3.42
withdrawal of 12.00

CENTRAL OFFICE
1.05
Appeals and Lists Office 20.13, 20.26
Crown Office 16.53, 16.79, 19.00

CERTIFICATE
conviction, of 13.26

'CRU' deductible benefits, of 14.66, 14.68c
government minister or official, by 13.153
judgment against Crown, of 16.07
legal aid 3.58-62, 17.85
.. emergency 3.59
point of law of public importance 20.84-85
presumptions from 13.23
public interest immunity 13.48
taxation, of 17.107
unenforceability, of 16.28

CERTIORARI
19.81
Attorney-General seeking 19.55
bail pending 19.72-73, 19.96
deferred pending appeal 19.60
time for applying for 19.57

CHALLENGE
juror, to 14.06, 14.08

CHAMBERS
committal application in 16.54, 16.79
interlocutory application in 11.02
originating summons in 18.12
proceedings in 11.02, 14.02

CHAMPERTY AND MAINTENANCE
3.19, 12.12, 17.11

CHANCERY DIVISION
leave to trustee to litigate 17.56, 20.08
proceedings assigned to 18.53

CHANCERY PROCEEDINGS
accounting party 11.170
charge on land, enforcing 16.33
citation of authorities in 14.24
evidence in 13.59
joinder of parties 3.31, 3.33
judgment in 14.42, 15.01
listing of 12.31
originating summons in 18.13
.. delivery up by solicitor, for 17.77
proceedings under judgment 18.56-59
.. costs of 17.68
relief from forfeiture 18.40
setting down for trial 12.26
summary judgment in 18.60
summons in 11.06
trial in 14.23

CHANCERY OFFICE
1.05, 12.26
petition out of 18.15
proceedings issued in 18.53

CHANGE OF PARTIES
11.36-44
appeal, on 20.38
judgment, after 16.05

CHARACTER
cross-examination of witness as to 13.74
defamation action, in 18.20
evidence of 13.15
re-examination of witness as to 13.78

CHARGE ON PROPERTY
action concerning 18.71-76
Legal Aid Fund's 17.87
limitation period 4.03
partition suit 18.78
service outside NI 6.16
solicitor's 17.75

CHARITY PAYMENTS
deduction from damages 14.63

CHEQUE AND BILL OF EXCHANGE
counterclaims 9.43
interest on 5.09, 8.09, 14.81
notice of dishonour 5.01
order to endorse 16.59

CHILD
contempt by 16.83
evidence in camera of 14.02
legitimacy of 13.24
paternity of 11.26, 13.25, 13.156
unsworn testimony by 13.35, 13.36

CHILD CARE PROCEEDINGS
evidence in 13.32, 13.44
habeas corpus 19.101, 19.104
legal aid 3.57, 3.58
publicity in 14.03
wardship 18.51

CHOSE IN ACTION, ASSIGNMENT OF
3.19, 5.01, 9.36, 9.50,10.34,11.44,11.169

CIRCUMSTANTIAL EVIDENCE see FACTS

CIVIL CAUSE OR MATTER
appeal to House of Lords in 20.85, 20.88
judicial review in 19.52-90
meaning of 19.91-92, 19.108

CIVIL EVIDENCE ACT 1971
criminal conviction 13.25
duty record hearsay 13.128-

CLAIM
and see CAUSE OF ACTION
account, for 18.25
Chancery judgment, under 18.58
discontinuance of 12.00-04
new, in pending action 4.09
particulars of 9.83
writ stating 5.07

CLERICAL ERROR, MISTAKE etc.
15.12

CLIENT
costs payable to solicitor 17.72-81
.. agreement for 17.11, 17.80
dealing with 2.01
.. privilege for communications 13.38
legal aid for 3.57-

CLOSE OF PLEADINGS
9.66
lodgment before 11.149

CLUB
proceedings by or against 3.18
representation of 3.45

'COMERTON SCALE' COSTS
17.96, 17.103

COMMENCEMENT
appeal, of 18.02
claim added by amendment, of
11.32-34
cross-claim, of 9.46, 9.53
proceedings, of 5.03-
.. compromise before 12.13, 17.16-19
.. costs before 5.00, 17.16-19
.. delay before 11.186
.. injunction against 11.177
.. injunction before 11.62
third-party proceedings, of 10.18, 10.23

COMMERCIAL ACTION
5.03, 18.28-32
expert evidence in 18.29-32
interlocutory proceedings in 11.03
List 18.28

COMMITTAL
contempt, for 16.81-83
disobedience of judgment, for 16.53-56
.. money judgment, on 16.40
discovery, for failure to give 11.120
order to pay money, on 16.40-45
proceedings for 16.53-66, 16.81-83
.. judge calling witness in 13.05

COMMITTEE
legal aid 3.58

COMMONWEALTH COUNTRIES
affidavit sworn in 11.13
enforcement of NI judgment in 16.18
judgment in 16.22
law of, proving 13.94

COMPANY
added as plaintiff 11.34
committal of director or officer of 16.57
contempt by 16.57
defunct 3.13, 11.43
documents of 13.04, 13.153
jurisdiction over 18.81
liquidation 5.02, 11.43, 16.13, 16.38, 18.81
party, as 3.13
representation of 3.45, 7.03, 17.59n
.. by director 3.45, 17.59
security for costs against 11.60
service on 6.01

COMPELLABILITY
document, to produce 13.06, 13.37
witness, of 13.06, 13.37, 13.57

COMPENSATION
deduction from damages of 14.64-65
defamation, on offer of amends 18.20
interest on 14.78

COMPROMISE
12.05-25
appeal, of 20.45
approval of 12.12, 12.13-20
.. absent persons, for 18.65
.. appeal, on 20.45
.. patient, for 12.19, 18.52

authority of solicitor in 3.48, 12.05
collusive against solicitor 17.76
costs, effect on 17.08
county court limit, within 17.28
deduction of social security benefits 14.68e
defamation claim, of 18.19, 18.20
defendant seeking contribution after 10.11
discontinuance under 12.04
estoppel 13.107
methods of 12.09
offer of 11.167
pre-action 2.08, 9.27, 11.174
structured settlement 12.21-25
taxation of costs 17.98

COMPUTER
court records on 1.08, 15.01
records 13.130

CONDITIONAL
appearance 7.09
judgment 16.02
leave to defend 11.50

CONDITION PRECEDENT
jurisdictional 19.23
pleading 9.06

CONDUCT
accounts, taking of 18.25
administration action, of 18.66
proceedings, of 3.03, 18.56
sale of land, of 18.55

CONFESSION AND AVOIDANCE 9.26

CONSENT
amendment by 11.17
discontinuance by 12.00
dismissal of appeal by 20.34, 20.45
expert evidence admitted by 13.89
judgment by 12.10, 15.14
.. appeal to Court of Appeal from 20.08
periodical payment of damages, by 12.25, 14.73a
plaintiff, added, of 11.25, 11.36
taking out of list, by 12.29-30

CONSOLIDATION 3.35

CONSULTATION
legitimate expectation of 19.34

CONSTRUCTION OF DOCUMENTS
actions relating to
.. compromise 12.12
.. representation of persons in 3.38
.. originating summons 5.03, 18.10, 18.13

CONSUMER
arbitration agreement 7.19
credit 5.13, 7.12, 8.04, 9.29
indemnity against 10.02

CONTEMPT
civil or criminal 16.65
civil 16.66
criminal 16.67-75
.. defiance of court order as 16.47
.. interference with justice 16.71-75
.. procedure and punishment 16.78-83
habeas corpus 19.104
non-compliance with order 16.46-59
.. of Enforcement of Judgments Office 16.30
party in 16.60
proof of 13.20
publication of private proceedings 14.03, 16.73
solicitor, by 16.61-62
.. entering appearance without authority 7.05
undertaking by party 16.63

CONTENTIOUS BUSINESS COSTS 17.74-80
agreement 17.80

CONTRACT
accord and satisfaction 9.27
arbitration, of 7.14
chain of 10.32
compromise as 12.06
evidence of terms 13.134
execution of 13.145, 16.59
illegality 9.28, 20.41
indemnity under 10.02
interest under 5.09, 8.09, 14.81
interpretation of 13.136, 18.10
judicial review of decision under 19.04-05
limitation period 4.03
money due under as debt 5.11
.. as penalty 5.12, 8.06
rectification of 14.93
rescission of 14.94
resolution of disputes, for 7.14, 7.21, 11.175
service outside NI 6.14, 6.16
set-off of cross-claims 9.36
specific performance of 14.90
structured settlement 12.21
third-party notice 10.15
writ action 5.03

CONTRIBUTION
appeal relating to 20.68

assessment of 10.12
defendants, between 3.33, 10.28
enforcement against insurer 16.16
joint debtors, between 10.14
joint wrongdoers, between 10.07, 10.09
.. costs 17.49
.. 'CRU' deduction by 14.66
.. estoppel 13.111
.. negligent medical treatment 10.09n
limitation period 4.03
offer of 11.168
third-party notice for 10.09-13

CONTRIBUTORY NEGLIGENCE
appeal relating to 20.68
costs 17.40, 17.98
damages reduced for 14.74
.. below county court limit 17.23, 17.34
.. fatal accident 14.72
deduction of social security benefits 14.68d
estoppel 13.107, 13.111
judgment by consent 12.11, 13.107
judgment in default 8.11
pleading 9.75

CONTROLLER
of patient 3.11

CONVENTIONS AND TREATIES
Civil Jurisdiction and Judgments (Brussels) 1.14, 11.01, 11.70, 11.175 11.176
European Union (Treaty of Rome) 13.22, 14.16, 20.93
Human Rights 1.16
part of internal law, as 1.16, 19.34
service of documents 6.18

CONVEYANCE
execution of 13.145-146, 16.59
reference to counsel of 11.84

CONVICTION
cross-examination on 13.74
estoppel from 13.110
judicial review of 19.48
presumption of guilt from 13.25
.. defamation action, in 18.24
.. pleading 13.26, 9.24
sentence under
.. *habeas corpus* 19.100
.. judicial review 19.97
'spent' 13.25, 13.74

COPY
affidavit 11.15
concurrent writ 5.06
discoverable documents, of 11.114
document, proof by 13.149
.. hearsay 13.127, 13.129
exhibited to affidavit 11.14
judgment 8.10, 15.06, 16.18-19
privileged document, of 13.40

CORONER'S COURT
evidence from 13.132, 13.139
judicial review of 19.40

CORPORATION
3.13, 3.20-24
committal of officer of 16.57
contempt by 16.57
discovery against 11.98
enforcement against 16.08, 16.57
interrogatories against 11.126
public records of 13.132
representation of 3.45
service on 6.01, 6.21

CORROBORATION
13.21

COSTS
17.00-111
acceptance of lodgment, on 11.155-157
action for 17.77
adjournment, of 14.21, 17.66
agreed 17.96
amendment, of 11.23, 17.07
appeal as to 11.08, 17.37, 20.08
appeal, of 17.69-70, 20.73-76
application, of
.. to extend time 1.33
.. to set aside proceedings 1.28
apportionment of 17.39, 17.42
bill of
.. action on 5.12, 17.77
Chancery judgment proceedings, of 18.58
change of parties, after 11.37
claimed on writ for debt 5.08
common fund, out of 17.53
compromise, on 12.09
defamation action, in 18.18
defined 17.01
discontinuance, on 12.00-01
discretion as to 17.02-08, 18.01
division of 17.39-45
ex parte application, of 11.12
fourth-party proceedings 10.32
gross sum 17.12
interest on 15.16, 17.111
interlocutory 17.67
judgment for costs only 8.02, 9.63, 19.66
judicial review, in 19.66, 19.89
jury, of 14.09
legal aid 17.82-92
lodgment not beaten 11.162-164, 17.46
meaning of orders as to 17.14

minor settlement, on 12.18
misconduct, of 17.60, 17.62
neglect, of 17.60, 17.62
non-contentious 17.81
non-party, against 17.03
.. appeal 20.08
offer "without prejudice save as to ..." 11.167, 17.08
official solicitor, of 3.53
partition suit, of 18.77
payment of 17.110
pre-action 5.00, 17.16-20
proportionate order for 17.12
quantification of 17.11
security for 11.56-61, 20.35
.. solicitor from client 3.52
set-off of 11.163, 17.43, 17.110
solicitor and client 17.72-81
stay of action till payment of 11.174
summary judgment application, in 11.51
taxation of 17.12, 17.93-108
tender proved, where 9.35
third-party proceedings 10.26-27, 17.52
unadmitted document, proof of 9.98
unadmitted fact, proof of 9.97
unnecessary 1.30, 9.24, 17.60, 17.62
when right arises 17.16-20
witness, of 17.104
.. expert 13.90, 17.105

COUNSEL
appearance of party by 14.18
audience, right of 3.54
authority of 9.95, 12.05
brief to 2.01, 2.09-, 14.00
compromise by 12.05
contempt of court by 16.67
conveyancing 11.84, 15.18
costs against 17.64
cross-examining 13.65-
direction of proofs by 13.01-02
disclosure, duties of 3.02
discovery, duties relating to 11.106, 11.117
examines witness 13.58-
legal aid for 3.62
minor settlement, duties in 12.15
opinion on will or trust 18.13
pleadings drafted by 9.04
practising barrister 3.55
privileged communications 13.38
senior (QC) 3.55, 13.00, 17.102-103
speeches by 14.41
taxation of fees 17.102
trial functions of 14.23-41
"watching brief" 3.45

COUNTERCLAIM
9.35-51
adding party for 9.52-56
appeal 20.19
contribution or indemnity, for 10.28
co-plaintiff, against 10.28
costs of 17.25
costs of claim and 17.41-45
discontinuance of 12.00
effect of 9.47
judgment on claim and 14.48, 17.41-45
limitation period 4.09, 11.34
lodgment, where 11.150, 11.154, 11.157, 11.166
mortgagor, by 18.73n
originating summons, against 18.12
rebuttal of 14.35
Reply to 9.57
security for costs of 11.56
stay pending trial of 16.03
summary judgment on 11.45
want of prosecution of 11.193

COUNTY COURT
action could be brought in 6.17, 17.23
action removed from 9.51, 11.147
.. appearance in 11.147
.. costs in 17.71
appeal from 17.70
cross-action in 9.51
defamation action, in 18.23
dismissal without prejudice in 11.174, 13.106, 14.20
estoppel 13.106, 13.108
judgment, action on 16.24
judicial review of 19.43n
jurisdiction 17.31
.. increase in 17.32-33
records of 13.153
remittal to 11.146, 18.12
removal from 7.03, 9.51, 11.147
stay of action in 11.177, 12.03

COURT
audience in 3.54
choice of 3.00
constitution of 1.06, 1.08
contempt in face of 16.67
contempt of 16.71-75
expert 13.93
inferior see INFERIOR COURT
records 13.132, 13.153
reports case of misconduct by solicitor 3.49
sittings of 1.03, 1.06
subpoena by 13.05
trial, of 14.01

COURT (OPEN)
committal application in 16.54, 16.79
motion in 11.02
originating summons in 18.12
proceedings in 14.02

COURT FUNDS OFFICE
1.05, 11.171

COURT OF APPEAL
appeal from 20.87-88
business in 20.13
committal for contempt by 16.53, 16.76
contempt of 16.76-77
costs in 17.01, 17.69, 17.90, 20.73-76
full Court
.. leave to appeal by 20.16
.. hearing by 20.46
judgment of 20.70
.. finality of 20.77
judicial review
.. appeal 19.90
.. original jurisdiction in 19.62-65, 19.95
jurisdiction 1.02, 20.01
.. issue as to 20.60
.. original 19.64, 20.01
office serving 1.05
powers of 20.48, 20.52
reference to European Court by 14.16, 20.93
single judge
.. incidental direction by 20.31
.. leave to appeal by 20.16

COURT SERVICE
1.04

CREDIBILITY
witness, of 13.71-76

CREDIT see DEBT

CRIMINAL CAUSE OR MATTER
appeal in 20.07, 20.84, 20.87
judicial review in 19.91-98
meaning of 19.91-92, 19.108

CRIMINAL OFFENCE
burden of proving 13.20, 13.24
compensation to plaintiff for 14.64-65
contempt as 16.65
incrimination for 13.44
presumption from conviction for 13.25
privilege defeated by purpose of 13.42
witness's record of 13.74

CRIMINAL PROCEEDINGS
civil action as challenge to 11.181
confession in 13.116
defence in 19.09
evidence of material disclosed in 13.86
judicial review relating to 19.14, 19.91-92
stay pending 11.176

CROSS-APPEAL
20.29

CROSS-CLAIM
9.36-51
limitation period 9.46, 11.34
separate action, by 9.51

CROSS-EXAMINATION
13.65-76
affidavit, on 13.33, 18.09
.. judicial review 19.76
commercial action, expert in 18.32
memory refreshing document, from 13.62
own witness, of 13.63

CROWN
'Administration of Justice Act' inspection against 11.87, 11.89
contempt by 16.46, 16.76
costs against 17.09
counterclaim against 9.44
'CRU' deduction of benefits by 14.66
debt due to 5.13, 14.81n, 16.32, 16.35
defined 3.22
discovery 11.92, 11.104, 11.136
enforcement against 16.07
habeas corpus against 19.100
interlocutory injunction against 11.66, 19.84
interlocutory injunction for 11.69
interpleader 10.33
interrogatories against 11.122, 11.126
judgment in default against 8.04, 10.23
judicial review against 19.12, 19.82, 19.84
land action against 18.37
particulars on writ against 5.10
public interest immunity claim by 13.48
remedies against 14.99
service on 6.01, 6.20, 6.21
summary judgment 11.45, 11.46, 18.60
summary recovery of debts 5.13
third-party notice against 10.19

CROWN COURT
contempt of 16.76

CROWN PROCEEDINGS
3.21-22, 14.97
appeals 20.00
contribution and indemnity 10.00n
costs in 17.09, 17.10
Crown Side proceedings 19.00
discovery in 11.92
enforcement of judgments 16.07
evidence in 13.10, 13.30
service outside NI 6.12

CROWN SIDE
19.00
Crown Office 1.05

CROWN SOLICITOR
3.21

'C R U' see SOCIAL SECURITY BENEFITS

DAMAGES
14.49-52
accord and satisfaction 9.27
appeal as to 20.68-69
assessed once and for all 12.25, 14.75
assessment to date of trial 4.00
contributory negligence reducing 14.74
costs in action for 17.18
deductions from 9.36, 14.63-68
defamation, in 18.23-24
.. mitigation of 18.20, 18.21
equity, in 14.91
exemplary and aggravated 14.52
expenses and services of relatives etc. 14.55
goods, for conversion of 14.83
heads of, to be specified 14.68d
incurred in NI 6.16
instalments, by 12.25
interest on 14.78-
interest on judgment for 15.16
interim 11.54
joint liability 3.33, 10.09, 17.10
judge or magistrate, against 19.49, 19.88
judgment in default for 8.00, 8.11, 9.63
.. within county court limit 17.35
judicial review, in 19.88
lodgment 11.149
loss of non-recoupable benefits, for 14.68
payment in satisfaction 9.27
periodical 11.55, 12.25, 14.73a
pleading 9.06, 9.19, 9.69, 9.76
provisional 14.75
recurring 3.29
set-off 9.36
summary judgment 11.49, 11.50
undertaking as to 11.69
VAT on 15.04

DEATH see also FATAL ACCIDENT; ESTATE
action after 3.06
action in respect of 3.06
.. defined 1.08
between verdict and judgment 14.45
cause of action surviving 11.39
judicial review surviving 19.67
pending appeal 20.38
presumption of 13.24
process server, of 6.28
proof of 13.153
provisional damages award, after 14.76
taxation of costs after 17.109

DEBT OR LIQUIDATED DEMAND
accord and satisfaction 9.27
'admitted debt procedure' 16.32
attachment of 16.27, 16.35
claim under Chancery judgment for 18.58
consumer see CONSUMER CREDIT
contribution 10.14
costs 17.16, 17.21, 17.99
deceased's estate, against 9.36, 18.64
defined 5.11
demand before suing 4.00, 5.00
interest awarded on 8.09, 14.78
interest claimed on 5.09
interim payment 11.55
interpleader 10.34
judgment in default for 8.00-01, 8.07-08, 9.63
.. costs 17.99
.. interest included 8.09
judicial review to enforce 19.88
legal aid for 3.58
limitation period 4.03, 4.04
lodgment 11.149
methods of pursuing 5.13
mortgage 18.72
payment before action 9.27
penalty 5.12, 8.06, 11.92
public debt 16.32
secured see CHARGE
separate items 3.27
set-off 9.36
splitting 3.30
Statement of Claim 9.12
stay of action 11.174
writ for 5.08
VAT on 15.04

DECEASED
action purportedly by or against 3.44
action involving 3.06
appearance for 7.05
declarations by 13.121
set-off of debts 9.36

DECISION
discretionary, appeal against 20.62
judicial or administrative 19.40
judicial review of 19.07, 19.86

DECLARATION
14.95
appeal from lower court, on 18.03
Crown, against 14.99
defamation action 18.22a

equitable title, of 18.62
judgment in default for 8.02
judicial review, in 19.86
public rights, of 19.08
trust, of 18.62

DECREE
judgment, as 15.00

DEFAMATION
18.18-24
abatement on death 11.39
amendment 11.34
consolidation of actions 3.36
counterclaim for 9.42
damages appeal 20.68
discovery of printer, publisher 11.130
indemnity for 10.02
interrogatories 11.123
jury trial of 14.04
legal aid 3.58
limitation period 4.03, 4.04
particulars of defence 9.86
pleadings 9.79
presumption from conviction 13.25
Reply 9.57
slander of women, costs 17.10
stay of 11.142
summary disposal of 18.22a
writ for 5.10

DEFAULT
and see DELAY
judgment in 8.00-12, 9.63
.. appeal from 20.64
.. costs 17.21, 17.35
.. counterclaim, on 9.54
.. legally aided party, against 17.89
.. setting aside 8.13-18, 17.22, 20.64
replying to notice for particulars, in 9.92
third-party proceedings, in 10.23
"unless" order, under 1.37

DEFECT
affidavit, in 11.15
name of party, in 11.28
pleadings, in 11.17, 11.18
proceedings, in 1.28
striking out for 11.178

DEFENCE
accord and satisfaction 9.27
affidavit of 8.13, 11.48
costs of 17.25
defamation action 18.19-21
ejectment, to 18.41
estoppel from failure to raise 13.105, 13.108
evidence of 14.33, 14.36
judgment in default, not considered in 8.06
judgment in default, showing on application to set aside 8.13
jus tertii 18.33
particulars of 9.83-
payment 9.27
performance 9.27
pleading of 9.25- , 9.74
putting to plaintiff's witnesses 13.68
rebuttal of 9.01, 9.11, 14.35
set-off 9.36
special 9.31
tender 9.32
third party raising 10.22
withdrawal of 12.00

DEFENCE (the PLEADING)
9.21-31
defamation action 18.18-21
judgment in default of 9.63
particulars of claim before 9.84
service on co-defendant 10.31
withdrawal of 12.00

DEFENDANT(s)
abroad 1.14, 6.11
adding 11.26, 11.29, 11.32-35
alternative liability 3.33, 8.10, 14.31
.. costs 17.29, 17.51
appeal by 20.02, 20.25
applying for 'direction' 14.29
bankruptcy of 11.42
burden of proof on 13.18
case for, preparing 2.11
case for, presenting 14.33
change of, on death etc. 11.36
cross-examination of 13.65, 13.70
death of 11.41
default of appearance 8.00-12
.. at trial 14.19, 20.64
default of Defence 9.63
defined 1.07
delay contributed to by 11.190
discontinuance against one 12.02
dismissal for want of prosecution, applying for 11.193
discovery between 11.95
domicile of 1.14
expenses and services to plaintiff, by 14.55
evidence for 14.33, 14.36
joinder of 3.31, 3.33
.. costs 17.48-51
joint liability 3.33, 8.10
.. costs 17.49
.. judgment on 15.03
land, in action relating to 18.34
medical examination of 11.142
preparing case for 2.11

response to writ by 7.00-03
security for costs against 11.56
set aside judgment, applying to 8.16
striking out 11.26
third-party proceedings between 10.28

DEFENDANT TO COUNTERCLAIM
9.52-55

DEFINITIONS
statutes and rules, in 1.07-

DELAY
accounts, in taking of 18.25
amending, in 11.20
appeal, in 20.24
ex parte application, in 11.12
injunction, in applying for 11.64, 14.87
judicial review, in applying for 19.50, 19.57
no proceeding had for one year 11.199
no proceeding had for two years 11.195
originating summons action, in 18.12
pleading, in 9.61-
prosecution of action, in 11.184
.. contributed to by defendant 11.190
setting aside judgment, in applying for 8.17

DENIAL see TRAVERSE

DEPARTMENTS OF GOVERNMENT and see GOVERNMENT
3.21, 9.44, 11.28
costs against 17.09
debts due to 16.32, 16.35
Department of Economic Development 3.13

DEPARTMENTS OF SUPREME COURT
1.04

DEPARTURE
commercial action expert evidence, in 18.32
medical evidence, in 11.143
pleadings 9.10, 9.58, 9.91, 20.41

DEPOSITION
evidence by 13.10, 13.133

DEPUTY
judge 1.01
officer 1.04

DETENTION
11.78-
seizure, *ex parte* order of 11.86

DIPLOMAT
3.20
affidavit sworn before 11.13
counterclaim against 9.45
judgment in default against 8.06
privileges of 13.51
witness, as 13.36

DIRECTION OF NO CASE TO ANSWER
14.29-32
appeal relating to 20.41, 20.57, 20.66
.. costs 20.76

DIRECTIONS
accounts and inquiries, for 18.25
appeal, pending 20.31
appeal from lower court, on 18.03
certiorari, on 19.81
Chancery proceedings, in 14.24a
commercial action 18.28
interlocutory order, on 11.69, 11.85
leave to defend, on 11.50
originating summons, on 18.12
proceedings under judgment, for 18.57
sale of land, as to 18.55
third-party 10.20

DISABILITY, PARTY UNDER
acceptance of lodgment by 11.156
admission by 9.95
compromise for 12.13-19, 17.58
costs against 17.58
costs of, taxation 17.79
defendant to counterclaim 9.54
discontinuance by 12.02
discovery against 11.90
injunction against 14.88, 16.49
judgment in default against 8.02, 8.05, 9.63
money awarded to 15.08
originating motion against 18.14
originating summons against 18.11
petition against 18.15
proceedings by or against 3.07-12
representation of 3.45, 7.03
third party 10.23
writ, named on 5.05

DISBURSEMENTS
17.101-105
interest on 17.78
'outlay' as 17.35

DISCLOSURE
11.90-145
commercial action expert evidence, of 18.32
general duty of 3.02
maps, photos etc., of 13.85

medical evidence, of 11.138-145
mistake, by 11.117
objection to 11.104, 11.115

DISCONTINUANCE
12.00-04
acceptance of lodgment, on 11.157
compromise, under 12.04, 12.09, 12.13
costs of 11.174, 12.00.01
legally aided party, by 17.89
third-party proceedings, of 10.23

DISCOVERY
11.91-120
appeal to Court of Appeal, pending 20.31
application for 11.95-
automatic 11.92-94
before replies to notice for particulars
9.90
defamation, in 18.22
defendant's insurer, identity of 16.12
documents listed in, admission of
authenticity 9.98
enforcement of 11.120
further 11.93, 11.106-111
judicial review, in 19.71
non-party, against 11.135-136
pre-action 11.134, 11.136
specific document, of 11.110
substantive remedy, as 11.130-131
third-party proceedings 10.22, 10.23

DISCRETION
appeal, extension of time for 20.24
appeal from decision within 20.62
costs, at to 17.02, 20.08
discovery, to refuse 11.97, 11.136
dismiss for want of prosecution, to 11.190
exclude evidence, to 13.13
injunction, for 11.63, 14.87
interest at 14.79
interrogatories, for 11.124
judicial review, to refuse 19.50, 19.80
legal aid, effect of 3.61, 11.175n, 17.84
misuse of 19.26-27
privilege at 13.52
review of 19.25-27, 20.62
security for costs 11.57
service outside NI, leave for 6.17
stay for arbitration 7.18

DISCRIMINATION
equality clausc 11.182, 14.15
judicial review 19.39
privilege for investigation of 13.51

DISMISSAL
appeal, of 20.34, 20.77
.. consent to 20.45
compromise under 12.09

defamation action 18.22a
estoppel from 13.106, 14.20
failure to indicate readiness, for 12.32
"non-suit" 14.20, 14.46
procedural default, for 11.182, 13.106,
16.60
summary judgment application, of
11.50

DISTRESS AND INCONVENIENCE
damages for 14.62

DIVISIONAL COURT
contempt jurisdiction of 16.76
former jurisdiction of 20.56
habeas corpus 19.102
judicial review 19.93-97

DIVISIONS (HIGH COURT)
consolidation of actions in 3.35
interlocutory proceedings in 11.03
jurisdiction 1.01, 1.18
transfer between 1.21

DOCUMENTS
admission in 13.118
amendment of 11.22
attested 13.141, 13.146
authenticity 13.139-144
.. admission of 9.98, 13.11
cross-examination out of 13.66, 13.76
definition of 11.99
discovery of 11.92-111
exhibits 11.14
.. impounding of 13.158, 20.53
execution of 13.145
.. order for 16.59
hearsay 13.125
inspection of 11.78, 11.88, 11.112-116
interrogatories as to 11.124
lodging in court 1.25
.. judgment in default, for 8.00, 9.63
.. setting down for trial, on 12.26
memory refreshing 13.61-62
notice to produce 13.11, 13.150
original 13.148
privileged 13.37-53
production to court 11.115, 13.05
proving in court 13.60, 13.138
rectification of 14.93
secondary evidence of 11.105, 13.149
service of 6.20-28
stamping of 13.147, 20.61
subpoena to produce 13.04, 13.06
twenty year old 13.144

DOMICILE
burden of proving 13.20
defined 1.14
defendant's 1.14, 6.16

DOUBLE JEOPARDY
committal application, in 16.54, 16.82

DRAFTING
9.03, 9.06

EARNINGS, LOSS OF
damages for 14.58-59
.. deductions from 14.63, 14.68c
.. earning capacity 14.60
particulars 9.88
pleading 9.19

EJECTMENT see LAND, RECOVERY OF

ELECTION,PUTTING DEFENDANT ON
14.29

ELECTION
13.99, 14.45

ELECTIONS
appeal to Court of Appeal 20.07
legal aid 3.58

EMPLOYERS' LIABILITY
action on 2.02
contempt, for 16.57
insurance 10.06n, 10.08
pleadings 9.73

EMPLOYMENT LAW
equality clause in 11.182, 14.15
judicial review 19.05-06

ENFORCEMENT OF JUDGMENTS
16.00-59
action for 16.21-24
.. service outside NI 6.16
charge on land, by 16.27, 16.39, 18.75, 18.78
costs, for 17.110
executor *de son tort*, against 3.41
injunction in aid of 11.74
leave for 14.64, 16.04
mandamus 19.82
matrimonial 18.47
prohibition 19.83
reciprocal 16.18-22
recovery of land, for 18.42, 18.45
setting aside 8.18
third-party judgment 10.24

ENFORCEMENT OF JUDGMENTS OFFICE
16.25-
direct enforcement by 16.59
goods, order for restitution of 14.83
stay by 8.18, 16.03

ENGLAND AND WALES see GREAT BRITAIN

EQUITY
damages in 14.91-92
estate or interest in 11.34, 18.62
interest on money awarded in 14.82
remedies of 14.85-95, 17.31
rules of 1.17, 11.173

ERROR
judgment or order, in 15.12
.. costs 17.15

ESTATE
and see ADMINISTRATION
action against 3.44
.. limitation period 4.03, 4.04
action concerning 3.38, 18.62
.. compromise 2.12
.. costs 17.53
.. service outside NI 6.16
action on behalf of 3.06, 11.39
claim against 13.21
damages for 11.39, 14.70
enforcement against 16.10
insolvent 16.13, 18.62, 18.64, 18.65
judgment in default against 8.05
representation of 3.40
unrepresented 3.43, 11.172

ESTOPPEL
13.95-99
promissory 9.27

ESTOPPEL *PER REM JUDICATEM*
13.100-111
appeal, on 20.19, 20.77
cause of action 3.30, 13.103
.. substantially decided against plaintiff 11.181
consent order, from 12.11
contribution proceedings 10.11
discontinuance not 12.03
failure to appear or proceed, on 14.20
habeas corpus, in 19.106
interlocutory order, from 11.08
issue 13.104
judicial review, in 19.78

EUROPEAN UNION
civil jurisdiction and judgments 1.14
discrimination between nationals 11.58, 19.39
domicile in 1.14, 9.39
enforcement of NI judgment in 16.19-
interlocutory proceedings relating to 11.01, 11.70
judgment in 16.22
judicial review, in 19.12, 19.84

law of 13.94, 14.16
lawyer from 3.54
residence in 11.58

EVENT
costs follow 17.02-10
.. exceptions 17.04

EVIDENCE
13.00-158
accounts, books of 18.25
adduction of 13.30
affidavit 11.13-15
amendment of 11.18
appeal as to 20.61
appeal, on 20.50, 20.65-67
assembling before action 2.01
assembling before trial 13.00-11
'best evidence rules' 13.112
closing speeches, after 14.42
contempt, of 16.54, 16.80
costs, relevant to 17.05
defamation actions, in 18.20-24
defamatory meaning, of 18.24
delay prejudicing 11.188
discovery of 11.97
exclusion of 13.13, 13.50, 20.57
expert 13.88
.. commercial action 18.29
habeas corpus, on 19.104-105
insufficient 19.28, 19.46, 20.66
interlocutory appeal, on 11.08
judicial review, in 19.76
jurisdiction, of 1.14
lack of 19.28, 19.46
order of 14.25
originating summons, on 18.11-12
particulars of 9.85
pleading 9.06
real 13.154
summons, on 11.06

EVIDENCE ACTS
13.126, 13.153

EXAMINATION
deposition, by 13.10
enforcement, in aid of 16.28, 16.51
in chief 13.58-64
.. commercial action expert witness 18.32

EXCLUSION
evidence, of 13.13, 13.50
.. new trial on grounds of 20.57
judicial review, of 19.16-18
jurisdiction of court, of 18.00
witnesses, of 13.55

EXECUTION OF DOCUMENT
13.145
order for 16.30, 16.59

EXECUTION OF JUDGMENT see ENFORCEMENT

EXECUTION OF TRUST see TRUST

EXECUTOR see PERSONAL REPRESENTATIVE

EXECUTOR DE SON TORT
3.41, 16.11

EXHIBIT
13.158, 15.00
affidavit, to 11.14

EX PARTE (ORDER)
appeal from 11.12, 20.11
application 11.05, 11.11-12
change of parties on death etc. 11.36
committal motion 16.53
extension of time for service of writ
6.07
habeas corpus, application for
19.101
injunction 11.73
judicial review, leave for 19.54
.. renewal of 19.62-65
leave to appeal 20.14
leave to enforce judgment 16.04
leave to move for committal 16.79
originating summons 18.10
seizure 11.86, 11.109
service outside NI, leave for 6.17
subpoena to serve in GB 13.03

EXPECTATION OF LIFE, LOSS OF
damages for 14.61, 14.70

EXPENSES
funeral 14.70-71
future 14.57, 14.61
hospital 2.12, 14.54
interest on 14.80
jury 14.09
legal 17.101-105
plaintiff's friend or relative, incurred by
14.55, 14.61
witness 17.104
.. expert 13.90, 17.105
.. tender of 13.03, 13.06, 16.68
VAT on 15.04

EXPERIMENTS AND SAMPLES
11.78, 11.87, 11.89

EXPERT
commercial action, in 18.29-32
court appointing 13.93
evidence by 13.88-93
.. appeal on credibility of 20.65
.. costs of 17.105
.. disclosure of 18.29
handwriting 13.140
legal aid authority for 3.57, 3.62
limitation on oral witnesses 13.89, 18.32
report by
.. admissibility of 13.89
.. amendment of 11.18
.. costs of 17.105
subpoena to 13.04
summons hearing, at 11.06

EXTRINSIC EVIDENCE
interpret document, to 13.136
terms of transaction, of 13.134-135

FACT
appeal on issue of 20.65, 20.88
circumstantial or secondary 13.14, 20.65
error of 19.29
interrogatories as to 11.123
jurisdictional 19.23
jury trial of 14.04
no dispute as to 18.10
presumptions of 13.28
primary 13.14
proof of 13.30
trial of 13.30- , 14.12
and see MATERIAL FACTS; RELEVANCE

FACTORY ACCIDENT
action, steps before 2.02
evidence 13.24, 13.153

FAIRNESS
duty of 19.31, 19.41
substantial 19.38

FALSE IMPRISONMENT
amendment of claim 11.34
damages 14.52
.. related assault, for 14.61
habeas corpus 19.99
jury trial 14.04
particulars of defence 9.86
pleadings 9.11, 9.80

FAMILY DIVISION
consent order in 12.09
proceedings assigned to 18.46
transfer to 9.42

FAMILY PROVISION
18.69

FATAL ACCIDENT ACTION
3.06, 14.71-73
acceptance of lodgment 11.156
adding plaintiff 11.25
bereavement claim 11.39, 14.71
commenced by writ 5.03
concurrent actions 11.176
damages for 14.71-
disclosure of medical evidence
11.143-
limitation period 4.03-06, 11.34
lodgment in 11.150
periodical payments in 12.25, 14.73a
pleadings 9.20
privity between claimants and deceased
13.102, 13.122
provisional award to deceased, after
14.76
settlement, approval of 12.20
stay pending medical examination
11.142

'FAX'
service by 6.20

FEES (COURT)
affidavit, on filing 11.15
appeal to Court of Appeal 20.26,
20.29, 20.79
appeal to High Court 18.02, 18.07
appeal from master to judge 11.08
case stated, on 20.79
Enforcement of Judgments Office, in16.25
ex parte application 11.12
interlocutory motion or summons 11.03
judgment in default, application for 8.02
judicial review 19.54, 19.66
minor settlement 12.13
mortgage action 18.71
originating process 5.03
pre-action discovery 11.136
pre-action inspection 11.87
setting down action 12.26
subpoena 13.03
Supreme Court proceedings 1.24

FILING see LODGING

FINAL ORDER
appeal from 20.07
appeal, on 20.34, 20.77
Chancery judgment proceedings, on
18.58
defined 11.00
judgment as 15.09
judgment in default 8.01-12, 9.63
judicial review of 19.16
provisional damages, after 14.75

FINE
contempt, for 16.55, 16.57, 16.81-83
deceased, on 16.24
juror, on 14.07

FIRM
appearance by 7.04
disclosure of partners in 11.137
enforcement against 16.09
proceedings by or against 3.16
representation of 3.45
service on 6.01, 6.14
sole trader 3.17, 6.01, 16.04

FORECLOSURE
18.72

FOREIGN
affidavit 11.13
arbitration agreement 7.15, 16.23
company 3.13
conviction 13.27
court
.. evidence for 13.31
.. more convenient 11.175
.. proceedings pending in 11.176
currency, judgment in 15.04
decision, judicial review of 19.19
defendant 6.11
government 3.20
.. counterclaim against 9.45
.. injunction against 14.86
.. judgment in default against 8.04
.. records of 13.153
grant of representation 3.42
limitation period 4.08
plaintiff 11.58
trust 3.40
witness 13.10

FOREIGN JUDGMENT
enforcement of 16.21-22
estoppel from 13.100

FOREIGN LAW
contribution proceedings, in 10.11
judicial notice of 13.22, 13.94
proof of 13.94

FORMS
discovery, of 11.95, 11.102
notice of appeal 20.18
use of prescribed 1.27

FORUM NON CONVENIENS
11.175
judicial review 19.21

'FOURTEEN DAY COSTS'
on writ for debt 5.08, 17.16, 17.99

FOURTH-PARTY NOTICE
10.32

FRAUD
amendment alleging 11.19
arbitration dispute, in 7.18
burden of proving 13.20
judgment obtained by 8.15
jury trial of 14.05
limitation period 4.03, 4.04
new trial on grounds of 20.57
pleading 9.06
privilege defeated by 13.42
writ action 5.03

FRIENDLY SOCIETY
3.14

FRIVOLOUS see VEXATIOUS
FUNDS IN COURT
11.171-172
change of party entitled to 11.38
party under disability, for 15.08
stop order on 16.34

FURTHER AND BETTER PARTICULARS
9.83-94
order for 9.92
replies 9.90
third-party proceedings 10.22

FURTHER CONSIDERATION
Chancery judgment proceedings, in
18.58
referee's report, of 14.14, 18.27

GAMBLING TRANSACTION
9.28

GENERAL DAMAGES
loss of earning capacity 14.60
loss of future earnings 14.59
pain and suffering etc. 14.61
particulars 9.89
personal injury, for 14.53-
pleading 9.19

GOODS
defective
.. limitation period 4.03, 11.34
interpleader 10.33
repair costs, proving 13.115
sale of 9.82, 14.84
tortious interference with 18.33
.. damages 14.83
.. delivery up where lien claimed 11.81
.. enforcement of judgment 16.29, 16.52
.. interim delivery of 11.78
.. judgment in default for 8.01, 9.63

.. *jus tertii* defence 9.29
.. limitation period 4.03
.. lodgment in 11.149, 11.157
.. particulars on writ 5.10
.. restitution 14.83
.. summary judgment 11.50

GOVERNMENT
costs against 17.09
documents 13.153
foreign 3.20
minister, orders against 11.66, 14.99
.. contempt 16.46, 16.76
.. judicial review against 19.12, 19.82, 19.84
public interest immunity 13.46-49
Secretary of State 1.10, 1.11
UK and NI 3.21

GRANT OF REPRESENTATION
3.42

GREAT BRITAIN
affidavit sworn in 11.13
domicile in 1.15, 9.39
enforcement of NI judgment in 16.19-20
evidence taken in 13.31
interlocutory proceedings relating to 11.01, 11.70
judgment in 16.22
law of, proving 13.94
residence in 11.58
service in 6.17
witness *subpoena*ed in 13.03

GUARDIAN *AD LITEM*
3.09, 8.05
costs against 17.58
originating motion, in 18.14
originating summons action, in 18.11
petition, in 18.15

HABEAS CORPUS
ad subjiciendum 19.99-108
.. writ of 19.104
ad testificandum 13.09, 16.69, 19.109
other forms of 19.109

HANDWRITING
13.42, 13.140

HARASSMENT
action for 9.16
injunction against 14.86, 16.46
limitation period 4.03

HEARING
action, of 14.18-48
appeal, of 20.46-51
originating motion, of 18.14
originating summons, of 18.12
petition, of 18.15

HEARING TOGETHER
3.35

HEARSAY
13.113-133
admissible categories of 13.114-
affidavit, in 11.14
documentary 13.125
expert opinion based on 13.88
medical expert giving 13.91

HIGH COURT
appeal from 20.03, 20.05-12
.. leave granted by 20.14
.. to House of Lords 20.84-86
appeal to 18.02-03, 18.06-07
application to 18.05
arbitration, powers over 7.22
costs in 17.01, 17.77, 17.80
Divisions of 1.18
finality of orders of 15.09
jurisdiction 1.00, 1.02, 1.14, 11.09, 18.01
.. exclusion of 18.00
.. in contempt 16.76-78
reference to 18.04
reference to European Court by 14.16
stay of proceedings in 11.173, 11.177
venue 14.01

"HIGH COURT OUTLAY"
17.35

HOSTILE WITNESS
13.64

HOUSE OF LORDS
20.83-92
reference to European Court by 20.93

HUSBAND AND WIFE see SPOUSE

ILLEGALITY
judicial review of 19.22
pleading 9.28

IMPRISONMENT
contempt, for 16.55, 16.81-83
habeas corpus against 19.100

INCOME
funds in court, from 11.81

INCRIMINATION see PRIVILEGE

INDEMNITY
10.01-08

contribution amounting to 10.12
costs 10.26
defamation, for 18.21
limitation period 4.03
subrogation 3.19

INDEMNITY BASIS OF TAXATION
17.08, 17.12, 17.95, 17.97
solicitor and client 17.78

INDORSEMENT
acceptance of service, of 6.00
writ, on 5.07

INDUSTRIAL DISPUTE
11.64, 11.67, 14.86

INFERENCE
13.28
Court of Appeal drawing 20.65
failure to call witness, from 13.28, 13.116, 14.33
failure to testify, from 13.28

INFERIOR COURTS
appeal from 18.02-03, 20.78
.. case stated by 18.07, 20.79
.. costs 17.70
collateral decisions of 19.47
contempt in face of 16.67
contempt of 16.71-75
declaration or injunction to 14.95
habeas corpus against 19.100
judicial decisions of 19.43
.. reasons for 19.33
judicial review of 19.40, 19.52-53
service of motion on 19.66
subpoena in aid of 13.03

INFERIOR TRIBUNALS
appeal from 18.02-03, 20.78
case stated by 18.07, 20.79
judicial or administrative 19.40
reasons, duty to give 19.33
subpoena in aid of 13.03

INJUNCTION
appeal, pending 20.33
Calderbank offer 11.167
contempt of 16.46
Crown, against 14.99
defamation action, in 18.22, 18.22a
defendant outside NI 6.16
discretion to refuse 14.87
enforcement of 16.46-52
final 14.85-89
interlocutory 11.62-77
.. appeal to Court of Appeal 20.10
.. defamation action, in 18.22, 18.22a
.. judicial review, in 19.70, 19.84
.. receiver order, in aid of 11.83
.. setting aside 11.07
.. types of 11.67
judgment in default for 8.02, 9.63
judicial review, in 19.84
limitation period 4.03
staying proceedings in another court 11.177
summary judgment for 11.45

INQUIRIES
18.25
and see ACCOUNT

INSOLVENCY
18.80-81
and see BANKRUPT
actions involving insolvent 3.05
appeal, time limit 20.20
estate 18.62, 18.64, 18.65
High Court jurisdiction in 12.10, 18.80

INSPECTION
bankers' books, of 11.132
documents, of 11.112-116
.. enforcement of 11.120
.. in court office 1.25
place or thing, of 13.154
property, of 11.78-89
.. 'Administration of Justice Act' 11.87-89

INSTALMENT ORDER
16.41-42

INSURANCE
excess, action for 3.28
indemnity 10.06
money due under is unliquidated 5.12
payments, deduction from damages 14.63

INSURER
action in name of insured 3.28
control over conduct of action 2.11, 12.05
discovery of name of 11.101, 16.12
enforcement against 16.12-17
indemnity 10.06
intervention by 11.27
Legal Aid Fund's right against 17.87
lodgment by 11.151
motor vehicle 2.04, 2.12, 16.15
solicitor for defendant instructed by 3.50
structured settlement 21.21
substituted service on 6.22

INTEREST
appellate judgment, on 20.71
contractual 14.81
.. claim for 5.09
costs, on 11.155, 17.107, 17.111, 20.71
discretionary (s.33A) 14.78-79

.. in judgment in default 8.09
equity, in 14.82
exceeding county court limit 17.31
fatal accident damages, on 14.72
judgment, on 15.15-16, 17.78
legacies and debts from estate, on 18.67
lodgment containing element for 11.152
periodical payments, on 14.73a
personal injury damages, on 14.53, 14.67
pleading claim for 9.13
special damages, on 14.56, 14.58
statutory 14.81

INTERIM ORDER
injunction 11.69
judicial review, pending 19.69

INTERIM PAYMENT
11.55
discontinuance after 12.00

INTERLOCUTORY (ORDER)
11.07
ancillary to judgment in default 8.03
appeal from 11.08-10, 20.10
.. new evidence 20.43
.. time for 20.20
application 11.01-
commercial action, in 18.28
costs of 17.65-68, 17.89
defined 11.00
dismissed, costs of 11.174, 17.67
judgment in default 8.01, 8.11, 9.63
judicial review 19.70-74, 19.96
pending appeal to Court of Appeal 20.31
service of writ outside NI for 6.16
setting aside, varying 11.07

INTERPLEADER
10.33-34
Enforcement of Judgments Office, in
16.28, 16.36

INTERPRETATION
documents, of 13.136
statutory provisions and enactments
1.07-11

INTERROGATORIES
11.121-129
answers 11.126-129
.. amendment of 11.18
defamation, in 18.22
substantive remedy, as 11.130-131

INTERVENTION see NON-PARTY

INVESTMENT
funds in court, of 11.171
money awarded to minor, of 12.17, 15.08

return on damages 14.59

IRELAND (REPUBLIC OF)
affidavit sworn in 11.13
evidence taken in 13.31
law of, proving 13.94
registration of judgment in 16.19-20

IRRATIONALITY see *WEDNESBURY*

IRREGULARITY
affidavit, in 11.15
appearance, in 7.05-06
application to set aside for 1.28, 17.06,
17.22
contempt proceedings, in 16.81, 16.85
forms, in 1.27
judgment in default, in 8.08, 8.14
judicial review on grounds of 19.80
misjoinder of causes 3.25
misjoinder of parties 3.34
new trial on grounds of 20.57
proceedings, in 1.28, 11.17, 11.18
Reply, late 9.59
service, in 6.05
valid unless set aside 1.28, 11.196, 16.50
writ issued without authority 5.04

ISSUE
costs of 17.39
counterclaim against added party, of 9.54
estoppel 13.104
notice of motion, of 11.05
objection to 20.58
pleading an 9.00
raised on appeal 20.40
reference of 14.14
split trials of 14.12
summons, of 11.06
third-party notice, of 10.19, 10.28
third-party notice on 10.16
triable 11.48
writ, of 5.06

JOINDER
causes of action, of 3.25
parties, of 3.31
.. discovery, for 11.131

JOINDER OF ISSUE
9.57

JOINT LIABILITY
3.33, 8.10, 9.36, 11.26, 11.34, 11.157
contribution 10.09, 10.14, 10.30
.. medical negligence after accident 10.09
costs 17.10
partners 3.15

JOINT RIGHT
3.32, 11.34, 11.40, 13.117

JUDGE OF COURT OF APPEAL
directions by 20.31
leave to appeal by 20.16
Lord Justice 1.01

JUDGE OF HIGH COURT
abusing 16.67, 16.71a
appeal from 20.03, 20.05
.. assessment of damages 20.68
.. findings of fact 20.65
appeal to 11.08, 18.02-08
approves compromise 12.12, 12.13, 12.17
chambers, in 11.02, 11.08
changing mind 15.10
Chancery 1.01
Commercial 18.28
contempt jurisdiction of 16.53, 16.67
Court, sitting as 1.06
death or retirement of 14.22
Family 1.01
habeas corpus jurisdiction 19.101
inspection of place by 13.154
judicial review jurisdiction 19.75,19.94, 19.97
.. interlocutory relief 19.74, 19.94
.. leave by 19.54, 19.60, 19.94
oath of 1.16
privilege for 13.51
public interest immunity, deciding 13.48-49
Queen's Bench 1.01
squatter's summons heard by 18.44
subpoena by 13.05
summing up by 14.42, 20.58
taxation of costs 17.108
temporary 1.01
trial function of 13.69, 13.79-80, 14.10-11
unavailable 17.66
verdict by 14.43
withdrawal of case by 14.29-32
witness called by 13.83

JUDGMENT
action on 16.21
.. limitation period 4.03
.. service outside NI 6.16
admissions, on 9.96
amendment as to parties after 11.24
amendment of 8.14, 15.10-13
amendment of pleadings after 11.20
appeal from 20.03
.. lodging 20.28
appeal, on 20.70
arbitration award, on 7.22
change of parties after 11.38
compromise providing for 12.06, 12.09
conditional 16.02
consent, by 12.10, 15.14
.. appeal to Court of Appeal 20.08
costs only, for 8.02, 9.63, 11.155-157, 17.16-20
.. appeal to Court of Appeal 20.08
counterclaim 9.47
cross- 16.28, 17.43
death after 11.40
death before 14.49
default, in 8.00-12, 9.63, 10.23
.. appeal from 20.64
.. application for 8.12
.. costs 17.21, 17.35, 17.99
.. counterclaim, on 9.54
.. estoppel from 13.105
.. legally aided party, against 17.89
.. mortgage action, in 18.71
.. setting aside 8.13-18, 17.22, 20.64
defined 15.00
duplicate or copy 15.06
enforcement of 16.00-
.. outside NI 16.18-20
estate, against 3.44
estoppel from 13.100
final 11.00
finality of 15.09, 20.77
foreign 16.21-22
injunction on or after 14.86
interest on 15.15-16
interlocutory 11.00
monetary 16.28, 16.37-43
non-monetary 16.46-59
non-party, against 16.02
notice of 18.57
proceedings under 15.17-22, 18.56-
.. costs of 17.68
record of 1.23
reversal on appeal 20.72
service of 15.05, 16.02, 16.49
set-off 9.48
setting aside 3.30
summary 11.50
tender proved, where 9.35
third party, against 10.22
time limit in 15.05
time of 1.31
variation of 15.10-13
verdict, upon 14.45

JUDICIAL DECISION
19.40, 19.42-47

JUDICIAL NOTICE
13.22
foreign law, of 13.94

JUDICIAL REVIEW
19.02-98
appeal 19.90

applicant 19.52
.. sufficient interest 19.56, 19.79
bail pending 19.72-73, 19.96
costs 19.89
.. of evidence in 17.105
Court of Appeal jurisdiction 19.62-65
discretion 19.50-51, 19.80
Enforcement of Judgments Office, against 16.26
exclusion of 19.16-18
extent of 19.02-15, 19.58
grounds of 19.22-39
.. statement of 19.54
hearing of motion 19.75
interim relief pending 19.69
interlocutory relief 19.70-74
leave for 19.54-65, 19.94
.. refusal of 19.62, 19.95
legal aid for 3.58
legal aid, refusal of, challenging 3.58
master's decision, of 11.09
motion for 19.66
order for 19.81-88
.. granted *ex parte* 19.61
procedure in civil cause 19.52-90
procedure in criminal cause 19.91-98
remedies of 19.79
stay of proceedings pending 19.60, 19.69
time for applying 19.57
void or voidable 19.48-49

JURISDICTION
Court of Appeal 20.01
decision without 19.24
dismissal for lack of 13.106
enforcement of judgments, in 16.25
error or excess of 19.24
evidence as to 1.14
exclusion of 18.00, 19.16
fact precedent to 19.23
High Court 1.00, 1.17, 18.01
.. inherent 11.09, 11.173, 11.178, 11.185, 15.12
.. solicitors, over 3.47, 16.61-62
issue as to 7.07, 7.09
.. taken on appeal 20.41, 20.60
refusal of 19.25
service outside 6.11-19
submission to 7.07, 7.09
territorial 1.13, 6.11-19
.. judicial review, in 19.19-21

JURY
14.04-10, 14.44
damages award
.. appeal from 20.68-69
.. false imprisonment and assault case, in 14.61
.. defamation case, in 18.23
interference with 16.72
misconduct or bias of 20.57
new trial 20.57
privilege for 13.46, 13.51
setting down for trial by 12.27
third-party proceedings 10.24
trial functions of 13.80, 14.10
verdict by 14.44
.. appeal from 20.67
withdrawal of case from 14.30, 20.66

KNOWLEDGE
general 13.22
particulars of 9.86

LADD v *MARSHALL* CONDITIONS 20.42

LAND
charge on 18.75
coast or shore 18.35, 18.61
contract for sale of 18.60-61
conveyancing and title of 11.84, 13.23
impediment on 14.15
inside NI, jurisdiction 6.16
judgment charge on 16.33
legal and equitable rights 1.17
lis pendens 16.00
mortgage action 18.71-76
order vesting 16.59
outside NI, jurisdiction 1.13
partition of 18.77-78
registered
.. charge on 18.75
.. order affecting 15.11, 15.19, 16.02, 18.61
relief for breach of covenant 18.40
sale in lieu of partition 18.77
sale of 15.18, 18.55
title to
.. declaration as to 18.34
.. proof of 13.153
transmission of interest in 11.44

LAND, RECOVERY OF 18.34-45
costs 17.17, 17.21, 17.99
counterclaim 9.43
Crown, against 14.99
enforcement of judgment 16.29, 16.52
estoppel 13.109, 14.20, 16.24
intervention by non-party 11.27
judgment in default 8.00-01,9.63
limitation period 4.03, 4.04, 4.07
mortgagee, by 18.72
particulars on writ 5.10
pleadings 9.29, 9.82
security for costs in 11.56
service of writ 6.00, 6.04
squatter, against 18.43-45
summary judgment 11.50, 11.56
writ action 5.03

LAW
action on question of 18.10
appeal on 18.06, 20.79, 20.84-85
change of 20.50
citation of 14.24, 20.47
common law 1.17
.. remedies 14.49
error of 19.16, 19.24, 19.41
.. on face of record 19.30, 19.45
.. sufficiency of evidence 20.66
EC compatibility 11.66
European 14.16
.. overrides national law 11.66
foreign 13.94
judicial notice of 13.22
new point on appeal 20.40
particulars of 9.85
pleading 9.06, 9.30
presumptions of 13.23-24
separate trial of issue of 14.12
skeleton argument 14.24, 20.47

'LAW REFORM ACT' ACTION
3.06, 11.39, 14.70

LAW SOCIETY
indemnity to solicitor 10.04
legal aid charge 17.87
supervision of solicitors 3.47, 3.49, 11.200, 17.63

'LEAP FROG' APPEAL
20.85

LEAVE FOR
acceptance of lodgment out of time 11.158
amendment 11.18
amendment of summons 11.06
appearance, withdrawal of 7.11
commercial action expert evidence undisclosed 18.31
committal application 16.79
conditional appearance 7.09
Crown counterclaim 9.44
discontinuance, for 12.01
enforcement of judgment 16.04
expert evidence undisclosed 18.31
fourth party notice 10.32
hostile witness, treating as 13.64
interrogatories 11.122
joinder of causes 3.25
judgment in default 8.04
judicial review 19.54, 19.94
.. renewal of application for 19.62-64, 19.94
.. setting aside 19.65
lodgment out of time 11.149
medical evidence undisclosed 11.145
re-examination 13.77
service outside NI 6.13-17
subpoena 11.06
supplementary particulars 9.91
third-party notice 10.19

LEAVE TO APPEAL
appeal against grant or refusal of 20.09, 20.90
Court of Appeal, to 20.08-12
.. application for 20.14-
High Court, to 18.02
House of Lords, to 20.89
summary judgment 11.54

LEAVE TO DEFEND
11.49-50, 18.60, 20.07

LEAVE TO SUE
5.02
company in liquidation 3.13
unnecessary 1.30

LEGAL ADVICE AND ASSISTANCE
3.57, 17.92

LEGAL AID
3.56-62, 17.82-91
amendment of 3.60
application for 2.01, 2.11
certificate 3.59
.. emergency 3.59, 11.11
.. proceedings covered by 3.61
charge on property recovered 17.87
Committee 3.57
contempt in face of court, for 16.67
discharge of 3.51, 3.60
discretion of court, effect on 3.61, 17.84
.. stay for arbitration 7.18
.. *forum conveniens* 11.175
Fund
.. charge on property recovered or preserved 14.67, 17.87
.. costs against 17.90-91
'green form' see LEGAL ADVICE AND ASSISTANCE
judicial review 19.47
party in receipt of
.. acceptance of lodgment by 11.155
.. compromise by 12.12
.. failing to beat lodgment 11.163
.. liability for costs 17.88-89
.. non-appearance by 14.21
.. security for costs against 11.57
privileged communications 13.51
revocation of 3.51, 3.60, 17.88

LEGAL REPRESENTATION
3.45-55
defendants, costs of separate 17.48
plaintiffs, of 3.32

LEGISLATION
interpretation 1.09
judicial review of 19.06-07, 19.12

LEGITIMACY
13.24, 18.47

LEGITIMATE EXPECTATION
19.34

LETTER
amendment, giving notice of 11.17
before action 2.01, 5.00
requiring discovery 11.94
requiring particulars 9.83
service of writ by 6.00, 6.02

LETTER BOX
service by insertion in 6.00, 6.02

LIBEL AND SLANDER see DEFAMATION

LIBERTY TO APPLY
compromise, under 12.09
judgment, under 15.22

LIEN
defence of 11.81
solicitor's 3.50, 13.51, 17.74

LIMITATION PERIOD
4.02-09
amendment after expiry of 11.31-35
arbitration 7.22
change of party after expiry of 11.36
contribution, for 10.10
counterclaim or set-off 9.41, 9.46, 9.55
delay before expiry of 11.189
disapplication of 4.04, 11.00, 11.123
extension of 4.04, 11.123
extension of time for service of writ 6.07
extinguishing cause of action 4.07
fourth party proceedings 10.32
joint debtors 10.14
pleading of 9.11, 9.31
.. defeated by 'relation back' 11.35
third-party proceedings 10.18, 10.29

LIQUIDATED DEMAND see DEBT

LIQUIDATOR
action by 5.02
costs against 17.53

LIS ALIBI PENDENS
11.176

LIST
authorities, of 14.24
Commercial 18.28
Daily 14.23
discovery by 11.92, 11.102
Jurors' 14.06
Provisional 12.29
Term 12.29
Weekly 12.30

LISTING
action for trial 12.29-31
appeal 20.44
approval of settlement, for 12.13
interlocutory appeals, of 11.08

LITIGANT IN PERSON see PERSONAL LITIGANT

LOCAL AUTHORITY
3.24
access to records of 11.130
contempt by 16.47, 16.56
injunction for 11.69
public interest immunity 13.46
records of 13.153

LOCUS IN QUO
inspection by judge/jury 13.154
.. by 'view jury' 14.09

LOCUS STANDI
appeal, for 20.02
injunction, for 11.63
judicial review, for 19.56, 19.79

LODGING
affidavit 11.15
documents on appeal to Court of Appeal
20.26, 20.44
documents on setting down 12.26
money in court 11.171

'LODGMENT'
11.148-166
acceptance 11.155
.. within county court limit 17.28
appeal, effect on 20.50
costs 11.161-165, 17.46
defamation action, in 18.19

LORD CHANCELLOR
investment return prescribed by 14.59
judges appointed by 1.01
legal aid taxation 17.85
remittal of court fees by 1.24

LORD CHIEF JUSTICE
1.01
control over lists 12.32
jurisdiction over solicitors 3.47

LORD JUSTICE
1.01

'LOST YEARS'
damages for 14.59, 14.70

MAGISTRATES' COURT
judicial review of 19.43n, 19.80
records of 13.153

MANDAMUS
19.82
direct enforcement of 16.59
money obligation enforceable by 19.88

MANDATORY ORDER
contempt of 16.48, 16.58
direct enforcement 16.59
injunction 11.67, 14.85
time limit on 15.05, 16.48

MAPS, DIAGRAM, PHOTOS etc.
13.85, 13.89, 13.131, 13.142
costs of 17.105

MAREVA INJUNCTION
11.74-77
with judgment in default 8.03

MARRIAGE
damages for loss of opportunity of
14.60
proof of 13.23, 13.24, 13.153

MASTER
1.04
affidavit sworn before 11.13
appeal from 11.08
.. costs 17.70
audience before 3.54
Court, sitting as 1.06
damages assessed by 8.11, 14.50
defined in RSC 1.08
jurisdiction of 1.30, 11.04, 18.12-13
.. in judicial review 19.54, 19.60, 19.74
limitation period disapplied by 4.06
originating summons before 18.12
reference of accounts to 14.14
.. appeal from 20.03
reference of costs to 17.12
review of 11.09
setting aside *subpoena* 13.07
summons before 11.04
trial by 11.52

MASTER (CHANCERY)
18.54, 18.58

MASTER (TAXING OFFICE)
jurisdiction 17.93
reference of accounts to 18.25

MATERIAL FACTS
9.03, 9.85, 13.12, 13.104

MATRIMONIAL CAUSES
18.47
adultery, finding of 13.25
appeal in 20.07
attachment of debts 16.35
court fees 1.24
enforcement of orders 16.25, 18.47
publicity of 14.03
security for costs 11.61

MATRIMONIAL PROPERTY
18.70

MATTER
18.01-08
defined 1.07, 18.09

MEANS TO PAY
16.41, 17.89

MEDICAL
disclosure of doctor and hospital treating plaintiff 11.143
examination 11.139-142
expenses, damages for 14.54, 14.57, 14.61
.. deductions from 14.63, 14.68c
hospital
.. action against 3.24
.. expenses 2.12, 14.54, 14.57, 14.61
negligence 10.09n, 11.143
records
.. copies of 13.40
.. disclosure of 11.141
.. discovery 11.135
.. patient's access to 11.130
report
.. accompanying note to 11.144
.. admissibility of 13.89, 13.131
.. defendant's 11.140
.. hearsay in 13.91
.. Statement of Claim supported by 9.17
witnesses, oral 13.89

MEMORANDUM
appearance, of 7.03

MENTAL DISORDER
liability for acts done under Mental Health Order 5.02
patient suffering 3.11

MINISTER see GOVERNMENT

MINISTRY see DEPARTMENT

MINOR
and see DISABILITY, PARTY UNDER
action by or against 3.07
custody/residence of 19.101, 20.10
injunction against 14.88, 16.49
money awarded to 15.08
service on 3.08, 6.01, 6.21
settlement 12.13-18
.. structured 12.23
wardship 18.51

MISDIRECTION
new trial on grounds of 20.57

MISJOINDER
3.34, 11.24

MISTAKE
consent judgment by 12.10, 12.12
disclosure by 11.117
discontinuance by 12.03, 11.158n
judgment or order, in 15.12

MIXED CLAIMS
judgment in default for 8.02, 9.63

MOBILITY, LOSS OF
deductions from damages for 14.68c

MONEY
claimed by party under disability
12.13
interim award of 11.55
judgment for 14.49
.. committal on 16.40-45
.. enforcement of 16.28, 16.37-45
.. restitution on appeal 20.72
liability to account for 11.170

MORTGAGE
action concerning 18.71-76
.. sale of land 18.55, 18.59
costs of mortgagee 17.54, 17.57
limitation period 4.03, 4.04, 4.07
mortgagee
.. action by 18.72-74
.. partition suit by 18.78
mortgagor's action 18.76
service outside NI 6.16

MOTION
11.03
committal for contempt, for 16.53, 16.79
Crown Side 19.00
Court of Appeal, in 20.18, 20.31
evidence on 11.13
notice of 11.05
road traffic insurer, against 16.15
sequestration, for 16.58
trial with or without jury, for 14.04-05

MOTOR INSURERS' BUREAU
16.17
'CRU' deduction of benefits by
14.66, 14.68b
intervention by 11.27
minor settlement with 12.13
structured settlement by 12.21

MULTIPLIER AND MULTIPLICAND
cost of future care 14.57
fatal accident dependency 14.71
loss of future earnings 14.59

NAME
amendment as to 11.28, 11.31
change of 11.36, 11.43
mistake as to 11.34
writ, on 5.05

NATURAL JUSTICE
19.31

NE EXEAT REGNO
11.76

NEGLIGENCE
contributory 14.74
limitation period 4.03
pleading 9.08, 9.15-20, 9.70
proof of 14.39
res ipsa loquitur 13.29

NEGOTIATIONS
pre-action 2.08
pre-trial 12.08
'without prejudice' 12.05, 13.43

NERVOUS SHOCK
damages for 14.62

NEW CASE
raised on appeal 20.40-41, 20.52

NEW EVIDENCE
appeal, on 20.42-43
interlocutory appeal, on 11.08
issue estoppel affected by 13.104
summary judgment application, on 11.54

NEW FACTS
evidence on appeal 20.43

NEW TRIAL
20.59
application to Court of Appeal for
20.56-59
costs 20.76

NEXT FRIEND
3.09

compromise by 12.14
costs against 17.58
named on writ 5.05

NOMINAL PARTY
security for costs against 11.59

NON-CONTENTIOUS COSTS
17.81

NON-JUDICIAL DECISION see
ADMINISTRATIVE DECISION

NON-MONETARY CLAIM
costs 17.19
judgment on 16.46-59
performance of 9.27

NON-PARTY
adding by amendment 11.24-29, 11.32-34
appeal by 20.02
contempt by 16.47
costs against 17.03, 20.08
counterclaim against 9.52-55
counterclaim by 9.56
discovery against 11.135
inspection of property of 11.89
intervention by 8.16, 11.27
.. Crown, to claim privilege 13.48
.. in judicial review 19.75
notice of judgment to 18.57
third-party notice against 10.00

NORTHERN IRELAND
judicial review of decision outside
19.19
legislation
.. interpretation of 1.11
.. service under 6.25-26
.. validity of 19.12, 20.04
residence outside 11.58
service outside 6.11-19
subpoena, service of 13.03

NOTICE and see KNOWLEDGE
admit, to 9.97
admit document, to 9.98, 11.105, 13.11, 13.143
amendment, of 11.17
appeal, of 11.08, 20.18
application to extend time, of 1.35
appointment for hearing, of 18.11
Civil Evidence Act hearsay, of 13.129
consumer credit 7.12
discontinuance, of 12.04
further and better particulars, for 9.83
how given under RSC 1.08
intention to proceed, of 9.63, 11.199
judicial notice 13.22
legal aid, of 3.60
Libel Act 18.20
lodging in court 1.25
lodgment, of 11.150
motion, of 11.05
.. and see MOTION
produce document, to 13.11, 13.150
respondent's 20.29
service of 6.20
service of writ, requiring 6.08, 7.00
short 1.34
solicitor, appointment or discharge of 3.50
third-party 10.00, 10.28
writ served by post, of 6.02

NOTICED PARTY
judgment, under 18.57, 20.02
judicial review, in 19.53

NULLITY
appearance for dead person 7.05
judicial review of 19.16, 19.48-49

OATH(S)
Commissioner for 11.13
discovery on 11.94, 11.95
examination on 13.10
judicial 1.16
testimony on 13.56
testimony without 13.35

OFFER
'*Calderbank*' 9.27, 11.167, 17.08
contribution, of 10.13, 11.168, 17.08
defamation action, in 18.20, 18.24
'without prejudice' 13.43

OFFICERS
affidavit sworn before 11.13
Crown 3.22
.. contempt by 16.76
.. costs against 17.09
.. judicial review against 19.12, 19.82, 19.84
review of 11.09
statutory 1.04
Supreme Court 1.04
.. judgments recorded by 15.00
.. judicial review of 19.11

OFFICES (SUPREME COURT)
1.04
closed 1.31
issue of *subpoena* in 13.03
issue of writ in 5.06
judgment in default in 8.00-01, 8.06, 9.63
opening times 1.06
serving documents in 1.25

OFFICIAL SOLICITOR
1.04, 3.53

unpaid fees, recovery by 1.24, 17.61

'OMBUDSMAN'
investigation by 1.04, 19.51
privilege of 13.36 13.51

OMNIA RITA ACTA ESSE PRAESUMUNTUR
13.24

OPINION EVIDENCE
and see EXPERT
13.17, 13.87-

ORAL EVIDENCE
13.30-
contents of document, of 13.151
order of witnesses 13.54
subpoena for 13.04

ORDER
account, for taking of 18.25
amendment of 15.10-13
appeal from 20.03
appeal, on 20.70
appeal to High Court, on 18.03, 18.07
case stated, on 18.07
Chancery judgment, under 18.58
committal for contempt, of 16.55, 16.81
compromise providing for 12.09
conditional 16.02
consent, by 12.10, 15.14, 20.08
costs, as to 17.02, 17.14, 20.08
defined 15.00
discovery, of 11.95-98
.. against non-party 11.135
drawing up of 15.02
interlocutory 11.07
interlocutory or final 11.00
interest on 15.15-16
non-party, against 16.02
particulars, for 9.92
payment into/out of court 11.171-172
subpoena, for 13.03
time limit on 15.05
"unless" 1.37, 11.198

ORDERS IN COUNCIL
1.11
judicial review of 19.12

ORIGINATING MOTION
18.14
amendment of 11.18
appeal to High Court by 18.02
application to High Court by 18.05
habeas corpus, for 19.101
judicial review for 9.66
service of 6.09, 6.19

ORIGINATING SUMMONS
18.10-13
actions commenced by 5.03
administration of estate, for 18.65
amendment of 11.18
approval of settlement, for 12.13
defamation amends offer, for 18.20
defined 1.08
discovery, for 11.136
enforcement of charge on land, for 16.33
execution of trust, for 18.65
family provision 18.69
habeas corpus, for 19.101
inspection of property, for 11.87
interpleader 10.33
service of 6.09, 6.19
'squatter', against 18.43-45
statutory application by 18.05
striking out 11.178

OVERTOPPING SET-OFF
9.49

PAIN AND SUFFERING
damages for 14.61
pleading 9.18

PARTICULARS
conviction, of 13.26
debt, of 9.12
defamation action, in 18.18-20
fatal accident claim 9.20
notice for 9.83-89
pleading 9.07
waiver of 9.93

PARTITION
costs 17.53
land subject to judgment charge 16.33
land subject to mortgage 18.72, 18.78
order of 18.77
.. amendment 15.11

PARTNER(s)
actions by or against 3.16
admission by 13.117
appearance by 7.04
discovery of names of 11.137
enforcement, against 16.09

PARTNERSHIP
18.79
and see FIRM
actions by or against 3.15
dissolution of 18.79
.. costs 17.53

PARTY (-ies)
3.02-3.44
adding 11.24-29

.. counterclaim, on 9.52-56
.. limitation period 4.09, 11.32-34
administration action, in 18.65
admission by 13.116
.. formal 9.95-98, 13.107
appeal by 20.02
appeal, on 20.20
.. amendment as to 20.37
capacity of 3.25, 5.10, 7.08, 11.24, 11.34
change of 11.36-44
character of 13.15
contempt, in 16.60
costs between party and party 17.02
.. quantification of 17.11
costs unnecessarily caused by 17.60, 17.107
defined 1.07
discovery between 11.95
.. before action 11.134
discovery by 11.98
duty of good faith 3.02
habeas corpus, in 19.101
identity of 11.34
joinder of 3.31
judicial review, in 19.53
legal aid, effect of 3.61, 7.18
necessary 6.16, 11.34
notice of motion, to 11.05
privity between 13.102
representation of 3.45
representative 3.37
statement in presence of 13.119
striking out 11.24-29
subpoena to 13.04
substituting 11.24-29, 11.34
summons, to 11.05
trust action, in 18.65
undertaking by 16.63-64
witness expenses of 17.104
writ, named on 5.05

'PATIENT' (MENTAL)
and see DISABILITY, PARTY UNDER
action by or against 3.11
care and protection of 18.52
injunction against 14.88
money awarded to 15.08
service on 6.01, 6.21
settlement for 12.19
writ, statement on 5.05

PAYMENT
9.27
periodical 14.73a

PAYMENT INTO COURT
11.148-171
damages, of 14.65
defamation action, in 18.19
fund in dispute 11.81
leave to defend, on 11.50
Mareva injunction, on 11.75
minor, to 12.17
order for 16.39, 16.58
proceeds of sale of land 15.18
security for costs, as 11.56
tender, with defence of 9.32
under statute or rules 11.169

PAYMENT OUT OF COURT
11.172
acceptance of lodgment, on 11.156
order for 11.160, 16.39, 16.58
party under disability, to 15.08

PEDIGREE DECLARATIONS
13.121

PENALTY see CONTRACT; STATUTE

PENSION
deduction from damages 14.63

PERIODICAL PAYMENTS
11.55, 12.25, 14.73a

PERJURY
11.13, 13.21, 13.57, 13.81

PERPETUATION OF TESTIMONY
13.31, 13.124

PERSON
corporate see CORPORATION
human 3.04-12
.. unknown or untraced 3.04, 12.12, 18.65

PERSONAL INJURIES (ACTION FOR)
appeal 20.68
.. stay of enforcement 20.33
commenced by writ 5.03
daily listing of 14.23
damages 14.53-68
.. deductible benefits 11.152, 11.165, 14.66
defined in RSC 1.08
DHSS, information to 2.01a, 2.13
disclosure of medical evidence in 11.143-
discovery against non-party 11.135
discovery before action 11.134
extension of time for service 6.07
evidence of 3.91
interim payment in 11.55
limitation period 4.03-06, 11.34
legal aid authority in 3.57, 3.62
lodgment, time for 11.149
minor settlement 12.16
particulars of 9.89

periodical damages in 12.25, 14.73a
pleading 9.77
proof of 14.40
provisional damages 14.75
split trial 14.12
Statement of Claim 9.17-20
stay of 11.139

PERSONAL LITIGANT
3.46
appointing or discharging solicitor 3.50
costs of 17.59
service on 3.51, 6.20

PERSONAL DATA
access to 11.130

PERSONAL REPRESENTATIVE
absence of 3.43, 3.44, 18.65
action against 3.40-44
.. limitation period 4.03
action by 3.06, 14.70
.. fatal accident 14.73
.. joinder of personal claim 3.25, 14.73
administration action, in 18.65
appointment by Probate Court 18.48-50
continuing action or defence 11.41
costs of 17.54-55
.. on appeal 20.75
enforcement against 16.10
indemnity for 10.03
judgment in default against 8.05
limitation period against 4.03
payment into court by 11.169
privity with deceased 13.102, 13.122
represents estate 3.40, 18.65
set-off of debts 9.36
summary judgment against 11.50
title of 3.42

PERSONAL SERVICE
6.21

PETITION
18.15
amendment of 11.18
House of Lords, to 20.89
service of 6.09, 6.19
striking out 11.178

PHOTOGRAPHS, FILM etc.
and see MAPS, DIAGRAMS etc..
hearsay, as 13.113
proof of 13.157

PLAINTIFF(s)
adding 11.25
appeal by 20.02, 20.25
bankrupt 11.42
burden of proof on 13.18
case for, preparing 2.01
case for, presenting 14.27, 14.39
change of, on death etc. 11.36
compromise by one 12.12
conduct of action by 3.03
counterclaim against 9.38, 10.28
cross-examination of 13.65, 13.68
death of 11.41
defamation action, conviction of 18.24
defined 1.07
delay in prosecution by 11.184
disability, under 12.13-19
discontinuance by 12.02
evidence for 14.28
joinder of 3.32
.. costs 17.47
.. lodgment against 11.150
legally aided 11.155, 11.163
medical examination of 11.139
rebuttal evidence by 14.35
resident outside NI 11.58
security for costs against 11.56
service on 5.05
striking out 11.25
third party and 10.22, 11.95
title to sue of 4.00, 11.19, 20.41

PLEADINGS
9.00-08
amendment of 11.16, 11.18, 11.21
.. on appeal 20.41, 20.48
close of 9.66
commercial action, in 18.28
conviction 13.26
counterclaim or set-off 9.40
defamation 18.18-19
defined 1.07, 1.08
discovery before 11.96
documents referred to in 11.112
drafting 9.03, 9.06, 9.68
estoppel 13.95, 13.101
inspection of 1.25
issues defined by 13.104
originating summons action, in 18.12
striking out 11.178
subsequent to Reply 9.60
third-party 10.21
trial without 9.05

POLICE
actions against 3.24, 12.12
enforcement against 16.08
judicial review of 19.13-14
privilege 13.46, 13.47
report by 2.06
road traffic accident report by 2.05
statement to 13.40
witness 2.07

'POSSESSION, CUSTODY AND POWER'
11.100

POST, SERVICE BY
documents 6.20
writ 6.00, 6.02, 6.24-27

POST AND TELE-COMMUNICATIONS
interception of letters and 'phone calls 13.51
leave to sue Post Office 5.02

POVERTY
security for costs on grounds of 11.57, 20.35

POWER OF ATTORNEY
3.04, 13.153

PRACTICE AND PROCEDURE
breach of rules of 1.28, 19.35
Chancery 18.54
duty of good faith 3.02
House of Lords 20.89-92
Supreme Court 1.12
third-party 10.17-
time limits, observance of 1.36

PREJUDICE
amendment causing 11.20
delay causing 11.188
delay in appeal causing 20.24
judicial review, in 19.50

PRELIMINARY ISSUE
discovery, before 11.96
limitation period 4.06
order on, deemed final 11.00
trial of 14.12

PREROGATIVE POWERS
19.13

PRESERVATION OF PROPERTY
11.78

PRESUMPTION
13.23-29
conclusive 13.23, 19.17
foreign law 13.94
res ipsa loquitur 9.06
service by post 6.02, 6.24-27

PREVIOUS PROCEEDINGS
estoppel from 13.100
evidence in 13.123

PREVIOUS STATEMENT
consistent 13.78
cross-examination on 13.64, 13.76
proving 13.76

PRIMA FACIE CASE
14.30

PRIMARY EVIDENCE see FACTS

PRISON
habeas corpus 19.104
inspection of 11.80
judicial review 19.15, 19.40, 19.69, 19.92
witness in 13.09, 16.69

PRIVATE see SECRECY; PUBLICITY

PRIVILEGE
13.37-53
'administration of justice' 13.50
discovery, in 11.102, 11.104, 11.113, 11.115
incrimination 11.85, 11.86, 11.124, 13.44-45
interrogatories, in 11.127
journalist's sources 13.53
legal aid communications 3.61
legal professional 13.38-42
.. legal aid 3.61
public interest see PUBLIC INTEREST
reply to notice of particulars, in 9.91
secondary evidence 13.149
waiver of 11.117, 13.41
.. in taxation proceedings 17.107
'without prejudice' 12.05, 13.43
.. legal aid 3.61

PRIVITY
13.102, 13.117

PROBATE AND MATRIMONIAL OFFICE
1.05
petition out of 18.15
proceedings issued in 18.46-49

PROBATE AND LETTERS OF ADMINISTRATION
contentious proceedings 18.48
.. administrator *pendente lite* 3.43, 18.49
.. costs 17.53
.. counterclaim 9.42
.. security for costs 11.56
.. service outside NI 6.16
limited administration 3. 43, 18.50, 18.65
non-contentious 18.50
.. court fees 1.24

PROCEEDINGS
commencement 5.03, 18.09
conduct of 3.03

elsewhere 11.176-177
interference with, direct 16.72
interference with, indirect 16.73
irregular 1.28
judgment, under 15.17-22, 18.56
.. administration action 18.67
.. costs of 17.68
.. trust action 18.67
legal aid for 3.62
.. costs against Legal Aid Fund in 17.90
mode of 18.09
none for one year 11.199
none for two years 11.195
reference of 14.14
stay of 11.173
venue of 14.01

PRODUCTION
documents, of 11.112
.. to court 11.115

PROHIBITION
19.83

PROHIBITORY ORDER
11.67, 14.85
contempt of 16.47-48

PROOF
burden of 13.18-21
.. discovery for 11.97
.. evidential 13.19
.. inspection, for 11.116
.. interim payment, for 11.55
.. interlocutory injunction, for 11.63
.. judicial review, for 19.58, 19.77
.. *Mareva* injunction, for 11.75
.. summary judgment, for 11.49
claims under Chancery judgment, of 18.58
contempt, of 16.54, 16.80
conviction, of 13.26, 13.153
documents, of 13.138
facts, of 13.34
service, of 6.20, 6.28
standard of 13.20

PROPERTY
contract for sale of 18.60
costs out of common 17.53
damage to
.. repair costs 13.115, 14.52, 14.54
.. limitation period 4.03, 4.04, 4.07
.. writ action 5.03
inspection of 11.78
legal and equitable rights 1.17
perishable 11.82
preservation, detention of 11.78
sale of 15.18-21

PROVISIONAL DAMAGES
14.75

PUBLIC BODIES
judicial review against 19.04-06, 19.12
.. respondent 19.53
public interest immunity 13.46

PUBLIC DEBT
admitted debt recovery 5.13, 16.32
judicial review to enforce 19.88

PUBLIC DOCUMENTS
evidence, as 13.132
extrinsic evidence 13.137
privilege for 13.42
production of 13.04
proof of 13.153

PUBLIC INTEREST IMMUNITY
13.46-49
administration of justice and 13.46, 13.50
discovery 11.102, 11.115, 11.116
inspection of property 11.87, 11.89

PUBLIC OPINION
13.17

PUBLIC RIGHTS
hearsay evidence of 13.121
judicial review 19.02
relator action 3.23

PUBLICITY
prohibition of 14.02-03, 16.73-74

PUISNE JUDGE
1.01

PUNISHMENT
contempt, for 16.55-56, 16.81-83
.. corporation, of 16.57

PUTTING ONE'S CASE
13.68

QUASI-JUDICIAL DECISION
19.41

QUEEN'S BENCH DIVISION
Commercial List 18.28
Crown Side 19.00
listing of actions in 12.29-30
Office serving 1.05
originating summons in 18.12
proceedings assigned to 1.19, 18.16
proceedings under judgment 15.17
summons in 11.06

QUESTIONING
judge or jury, by 13.79
leading 13.59, 13.66

QUIA TIMET
injunction 11.67, 14.85

QUO WARRANTO
19.85

REAL EVIDENCE
13.154-157

REASONS
decision or judgment, for 19.33

REBUTTAL
evidence in 14.35
particulars of 9.87
pleading 9.01, 9.11, 9.57
'unput' evidence, of 13.69

RECEIVABILITY OF EVIDENCE
13.12-17

RECEIVER
costs against 17.55
indemnity for 10.03
order appointing 11.82-83, 15.21
.. mortgages cases 18.72

RECOGNISANCE
19.00

RECORD
duty record hearsay 13.128
error on face of 19.30, 19.45
Supreme Court proceedings, of 1.23
.. striking out from 11.178
.. trial 20.50

RECTIFICATION
14.93
burden of proof 13.20

"RED BOOK"
1.12

RE-CROSS-EXAMINATION
13.77

RE-EXAMINATION
13.77-78

REFERENCE
Enforcement of Judgments Office, by
16.29, 16.36
European Court, to 14.16, 20.93
High Court, to 18.04
Legal Aid Fund, costs against 17.91
legally aided party's means 17.88
master to judge, from 11.06
matters of account, of 14.14
.. appeal to Court of Appeal 20.03
procedure in absence of rules 1.12

REFRESHING MEMORY
13.61-62

REGISTRAR OF COMMERCIAL LIST
18.28

REGISTRATION
judgments, of 16.22

RE-HEARING
appeal to Court of Appeal by 20.50, 20.55

REJOINDER etc.
9.60

'RELATION BACK'
11.31-35

RELATIVES
damages for expenses and services of
14.55, 14.61
deceased's, fatal accident claim for 14.71

RELATOR ACTION
3.23, 11.34
legal aid 3.58

RELEVANCE
13.12-17
discovery, in 11.96, 11.101
interrogatories, of 11.123
res inter alios acta 11.97, 13.16
similar fact evidence 11.97, 13.15

RELIEF AND REMEDIES
14.49-96
affidavit claiming 11.14
alternative 14.45
counterclaim for 9.39
discovery 11.130-131
interlocutory 11.01
judgment in default, on 8.02
judicial review, in 19.02, 19.79-88
legal and equitable 1.17
pleading 9.14
secundum allegata et probata 14.39
third-party notice for 10.15

REMITTAL
appeal in Court of Appeal to lower court
20.52
appeal in High Court to lower court
18.03
certiorari, by High Court on 19.81

county court, to 11.146, 18.12

REMOVAL
costs 17.71
county court, from 9.51, 11.147

RENEWAL
application for leave for judicial review, of 19.62-65
.. in criminal cause 19.95
application for leave to appeal, of 20.14

RENT
action for 18.39
.. counterclaims 9.43
.. limitation period 4.03
non-payment of 18.38

REPLIES
9.90-94

REPLY (Pleading)
9.57-59
counterclaim in 9.41

REPORT
and see MEDICAL and EXPERT
accounts and inquiries, of 18.25
referee, by 14.14, 18.27

REPRESENTATION
beneficiary, of 3.19, 3.40
estate, of 3.40
legal 3.45

REPRESENTATIVE ACTION
costs 17.47a
enforcement against non-party 16.04
party 3.37
.. intervention by member of class 11.27
.. legal aid 3.58

REPUTATION EVIDENCE
13.17

RES GESTAE
13.114-115

RES IPSA LOQUITUR
13.29

RES JUDICATA see ESTOPPEL *PER REM JUDICATEM*

RESIDENCE
outside NI 11.58

RESPONDENT
appeal to Court of Appeal, in 20.20
.. costs of 20.74
.. cross-appeal by 20.30
.. non-appearance by 20.49, 20.77
.. notice by 20.29
.. .. amendment of 20.36
habeas corpus, in 19.104-105
judicial review, in 19.53
.. affidavits by 19.68
.. objecting to leave 19.60, 19.65
.. service on 19.66

RETAINER
solicitor and client, between 3.48

REVENUE, TAXES etc.
appeal to High Court 18.02
Commissioners as party 11.26
counterclaim 9.44
damages for loss of earnings 14.58
funds in court, on 11.171
interest on 14.81n
plaintiff evading 14.58
structured settlement 12.21
summary application for accounts of 18.26, 20.20n
summary recovery 5.13
service outside NI 6.16

REVIEW
and see JUDICIAL REVIEW
arbitration, of 7.22
CRU certificate, of 14.68f
master's or officer's order, of 11.09
pre-trial, in Chancery Division 12.31
taxation of costs, of 17.108
.. legal aid 17.85

ROAD TRAFFIC
consolidation of actions 3.36
cross-claims 9.36, 9.47
damage to vehicle 14.51
discovery 11.92, 11.97
disqualification, *certiorari* against 19.69
driver presumed agent of owner 13.24
estoppel *per rem judicatem* 13.102, 13.111
expert evidence in 13.88
Highway Code 13.28
hospital expenses 2.12
insurance 10.07
.. enforcement against insurer 16.15-17
.. notice to insurer 2.04
interrogatories 11.125
legal aid authority in 3.57
map, plan etc., costs of 13.90, 17.105
pleadings 9.72
steps before action 2.03
third-party notice 10.15

ROYAL COURTS OF JUSTICE
1.03

RULES
breach of 1.28-, 19.35
judicial review of 19.06-07, 19.12
law and equity, of 1.17
.. indemnity under 10.03
originating motion under 18.14
times in 1.33
validity of 19.09

RULES OF THE SUPREME COURT
1.12
definitions in 1.07, 1.08
breach of 1.28-
forms in 1.27
times in 1.31-

SALE
interlocutory order of 11.82
judgment, under 15.18
Mareva order of 11.77
perishable property, of 11.82
property, of 15.18-20
.. mortgagee's action 18.72
.. proceedings under judgment 18.55-59

SANDERSON ORDER
17.29, 17.51

SCOTLAND see GREAT BRITAIN

SECONDARY EVIDENCE
facts 13.14, 20.65
document, of 11.105, 13.149-152, 14.35
privileged communication, of 13.37, 13.43, 13.49

SECRECY
interim payment 11.55
lodgment 11.160, 20.50
need for trial in 14.02
privileged communication 13.37-53
terms of compromise for 12.09

SECRETARY OF STATE
powers of 1.10, 3.21
prisoner brought to court by 13.09

SECURITY FOR COSTS
11.56-61
appeal to Court of Appeal 20.35
solicitor from own client 3.52, 17.74

SEIZURE
11.86, 11.109

SELF-CORROBORATION
13.78, 13.120

SEPARATE TRIAL
3.26, 3.31, 14.12
counterclaim 9.42
jury case, in 14.05, 14.09
third-party proceedings 10.20

SEQUESTRATION
16.57-58

SERVICE
6.00-28
added party, on 11.29
address for 5.05, 7.03
affidavit, of 11.15
change of party, on 11.36
Court office, on 1.25
committal motion, notice of 16.54, 16.79
defendant to counterclaim, on 9.53
judgment, of 16.02, 16.49
judicial review motion, of 19.66, 19.75
minor, on 3.08
notice by defendant requiring 6.08
notice of appeal, of 20.20, 20.25, 20.37
notice of judgment, of 18.57
notice of motion, of 11.05
orders, of 16.49
originating process, of 6.09
outside jurisdiction 6.11-19
.. interlocutory relief for 11.01
patient, on 3.11
pending proceedings, in 6.20-
personal 6.21
petition, of 6.09, 18.15
post, by 6.02
proof of 6.28
setting aside 6.10
solicitor, on 3.48
statutory provision, under 6.24-27
'squatter's summons', of 18.43
subpoena, of 13.03, 13.06
substituted 6.04, 6.22
summons, of 11.05
third-party notice, of 10.19
time limit for 6.07
waived by appearance 7.07
writ, of 6.00-18
.. amended 11.16, 11.26

SET-OFF
9.36-37
costs, of 11.163, 17.43, 17.110
cross-judgments, of 16.28
effect of 9.48
judgment on 14.48
limitation period 4.09, 11.34
pleading 9.40
Reply to 9.57
restrictions on 9.43

SETTING ASIDE
appearance 7.05
certiorari, by 19.81

discovery/inspection order 11.118
enforcement 8.18
ex parte order 11.12
interlocutory order 11.07
interrogatories order 11.129
judgment by consent 12.10
judgment, by Court of Appeal 20.58
judgment in default 8.13-18, 9.65, 14.18
.. costs 17.22
.. leave for judicial review 19.65
order by consent 12.10
proceedings 1.28
service of writ 6.10
summary judgment 11.53
subpoena 13.07
third-party proceedings 10.23
undertaking by party 16.64
writ 7.09-10

SETTING DOWN ACTION FOR TRIAL
12.26-28
abatement after 11.38
acceptance of lodgment after 11.155
compromise after 12.07
jury, by 14.04
originating summons action 18.12

SETTING DOWN APPEAL
20.26-28

SETTLEMENT
dispute or proceedings, of: see COMPROMISE

'SLIP RULE'
15.12, 17.15

SOCIAL SECURITY BENEFITS
deductible 'CRU' 14.66-68g
.. duty to report claim 2.10a, 2.13
.. fatal accident claim, in 14.72
.. lodgment, on 11.152, 11.165
.. periodical payment of damages, on 14.73a
.. settlement, on 12.06
.. structured settlement, on 12.22
plaintiff claiming when working 14.58
recovery of contributions 6.16

SOLICITOR
accounting party, for 11.170
action for costs by 17.77
admission by 13.117
affidavit sworn before 11.13
appearance entered by 7.05
audience of 3.54
authority of 3.48, 6.00, 7.00, 9.95, 12.05, 13.117, 16.02
change of 3.50, 3.61
compromise by 12.05
contempt by 16.61, 16.70
costs against 17.61-63, 17.107
.. appeal from 20.08
costs from client 17.72-81
.. agreed 17.11, 17.80
.. charge and lien for 17.75
costs of 17.98
costs of misconduct by 16.44 17.62, 20.08
court fees, liability for 1.24
Crown, for 3.21
delay caused by 11.191, 11.200, 17.62
discharge of 3.50
discovery by 11.98
discovery, duty to ensure 11.120
indemnity for 10.04
lien for costs 3.50, 13.51
minor, appearing for 3.07
misconduct by 3.49
negligence action against 2.11, 11.133, 17.64
order to pay money 16.44
personal litigant 17.59
privileged communications 13.38-42
produce documents to court, order to 11.115
service on 6.00, 6.20, 6.22
.. notice of appeal 20.25
steps before action by 2.01, 5.00
supervision of 3.47, 3.49, 17.63
trustee, costs of 17.55
undertaking by 16.62
unqualified 16.70, 17.10, 17.73
withdrawal of 3.50, 3.52

'SPECIAL CAUSE'
full High Court costs 17.36

SPECIAL DAMAGES
damage to property 13.115, 14.52, 14.54
loss of earnings 14.58
particulars of 9.88
personal injury case, in 14.54-56
pleading 9.19, 9.78

SPECIFIC PERFORMANCE
14.90
contempt of 16.48
Crown, against 14.99
direct enforcement of 16.58
judgment in default for 8.02, 9.63
limitation period 4.03
pleadings 9.82
summary judgment 18.60

SPEECHES
closing 14.37-41
order of 14.25

SPOUSE
charge on dwelling house for 18.74
fatal accident damages 14.71
incrimination of 13.44
proceedings for benefit of 3.19

'SQUATTER'S SUMMONS'
18.43-46

STAMP
13.147, 20.61

STANDARD BASIS OF TAXATION
17.12, 17.95, 17.97

STATEMENT
admission, of 13.118
in presence of opposing party or witness 13.119
judicial review, for 19.54
witness, by 13.64, 13.76, 13.78
written 13.125-131

STATEMENT OF CLAIM
9.09-20
dismissal in default of 9.62, 11.194
judgment in default on 8.02, 8.12, 9.63
writ, indorsed on 5.07
.. amendment of 11.16

STATUS QUO
11.63, 20.33

STATUTE
appeal under 18.02, 18.06
application under 18.05
.. survives death 11.39n
costs restricted by 17.10
documentary evidence under 13.153
EC compatibility of 11.66
exclusion of jurisdiction by 18.00
indemnity under 10.04
interest due under 8.09, 14.81
interpretation of 1.09
.. action relating to 5.03, 18.10
judicial review of 19.06, 19.12
jurisdiction under 18.01
notice or decision under, validity of 19.08-10
originating motion under 18.14
penalty under
.. enforcement of 16.44
.. incrimination for 13.44
pleading 9.06
presumptions under 13.23
reference under 18.04
rules under 1.12
times in 1.32, 1.33
validity of 19.06, 19.12, 20.04

STATUTE OF FRAUDS
9.31

STATUTORY DEMAND
5.13, 16.38

STATUTORY DUTY, BREACH OF
pleading 9.16

STATUTORY OFFICERS
1.04

STATUTORY RULES (NI)
RSC as 1.12

STAY OF ENFORCEMENT
15.07, 16.03
appeal, pending 20.33, 20.91
judicial review, pending 19.52, 19.69
set aside judgment, on application to 8.18
summary judgment, of 11.50

STAY OF PROCEEDINGS
11.173-177
acceptance of lodgment, on 11.157
administration action 18.66
bankruptcy, on 11.42
compromise, on 12.09, 20.45
costs of discontinued action paid, till 12.03
cross-action 9.51
defamation 18.20
dismissal after 11.197
ejectment 18.38
mortgagee's action 18.73
partition order, of 18.77
pending arbitration 7.16, 7.21
pending interlocutory appeal 11.08
pending judicial review 19.60, 19.69
pending medical examination 11.139-142
pending probate grant 3.42
pending 'test' action 3.39
winding up, on 11.43
writ issued without authority 5.04, 7.00
writ served outside NI 6.17

STEP
action, in 7.16

STOP ORDER
16.34

STRICT LIABILITY
criminal contempt 16.73-75

STRIKING OUT
action or defence 11.120, 12.32, 14.18, 16.60
affidavit 11.14
amendment 11.16

appeal to Court of Appeal 20.27, 20.32
counterclaim 9.42
discontinuance 12.03
minor settlement, unapproved 12.14
party 11.24-29
pleading 9.92, 11.178
third-party notice 10.20

STRUCTURED SETTLEMENT
12.21-24

SUBMISSION OF NO CASE TO ANSWER
14.29-32
appeal relating to 20.41, 20.57, 20.66
.. costs 20.76

SUBPOENA
13.03-08, 16.68
chambers, for 11.06

SUBROGATION
3.19, 10.05, 18.64
legal aid 17.87

SUBSTITUTED SERVICE
6.22
notice of appeal, of 20.25
subpoena, of 13.06

SUBSTITUTION
party, of 11.24-29, 11.34
.. on death, assignment etc. 11.36-44

SUMMARY JUDGMENT
11.45-54
appeal to Court of Appeal 20.20, 20.42
costs 17.21, 17.99
defamation 18.22a
legally aided party, against 17.89
specific performance etc., for 18.60
'squatter', against 18.43

SUMMONS
application by 11.03, 11.06
committal of judgment debtor, for 16.41
directed on *ex parte* application 11.12
discovery, for 11.94, 11.136
evidence on 11.13
interpleader 10.33
interrogatories, for 11.122
juror, to 14.07
service of 6.20
summary judgment, for 11.46, 18.60

SUNDAY
arrest on 16.81
proceedings on 1.31
service on 6.21

SUPREME COURT
1.01
audience in 3.54
costs in 17.01, 17.93
finality of orders 15.09
judicial review against 19.11
records of 1.23, 13.153
seal of 1.23
sittings of 1.03, 1.06
solicitor officer of 3.47

SURPRISE
judgment set aside for 8.15, 20.57

SURVEY
public opinion 13.17

TAX see REVENUE

TAXATION OF COSTS
17.12, 17.93-108
acceptance of lodgment, on 11.155
agreed costs 17.80, 17.96
bases of 17.12, 17.95
bill of costs, of 17.77-78
common fund, out of 17.53
costs of 17.107
disbursements 17.101
gross sum in lieu of 17.12
"High Court outlay" 17.35
legal aid 17.83
.. review and appeal 17.85
minor settlement, on 12.18
personal litigant's 17.59
powers and procedures 17.106-109
relief within county court limit 17.26, 17.35
review and appeal 17.108
short form 17.96, 17.107
summary judgment, on 11.51, 17.21
Taxing Office 1.05
third-party proceedings 10.27
time for 17.13

TENDER
9.32-35, 11.197

TERMS OF LEGAL YEAR
1.06

TERRITORIAL JURISDICTION
1.13, 19.19, 19.100

'TEST' ACTION
3.39, 17.47

THIRD-PARTY PROCEEDINGS
10.00-31
appeal 20.25
contribution 10.09

costs 10.26-27, 17.52
discovery in 11.92, 11.95
estoppel from failure to plead in 13.106n
existing party, against 10.28
indemnity 10.01
limitation period 4.09, 11.35
lodgment in 11.154
other relief 10.15-16
procedure 10.17-
service outside NI 6.19
setting down for trial 12.28
want of prosecution of 11.193

TIME
abridgement of 1.34
acceptance of lodgment, for 11.155
action on bill of costs, for 17.77
alteration of 1.33
amendment, for 11.20
amendment as to parties, for 11.24
appeal, for 11.08, 18.02
appeal to Court of Appeal, for 20.20, 20.17
.. setting down 20.26
appeal to House of Lords, for 20.89
appearance, for 7.03
case stated, for 18.07, 20.79
Counterclaim, for 9.40, 9.54
Defence, for 9.21
disclosure of medical evidence, for 11.143
discontinuance, for 12.00
discovery, of 11.92
Enforcement of Judgments Office, for application to 16.26
extension of 1.33, 15.02
.. for appeal 20.07, 20.24
.. limitation period 4.04
.. Statement of Claim 11.194
final order after provisional damages, for 14.75
fourth party notice, for 10.32
interim award- for 11.55
judgment, for taking effect of 1.31, 15.01, 15.06
judicial review, for applying for 19.57
lodgment, for 11.149
mandatory order, on 15.05, 16.48
objection to evidence, for 13.84
one year, no proceeding had in 11.199
Reply, for 9.57
respondent's notice, for 20.29
rules and judgments, in 1.31-
service, of 6.21, 6.23
service of petition, for 18.15
service of writ, for 6.07
setting down for trial, for 12.26
Statement of Claim, for 9.09
.. extension of 11.194
statute 1.32, 1.33
subpoena, for 13.06
suing, for 4.00
summary judgment application, for 11.46
taxation of costs, for 17.13, 17.107
.. solicitor and client 17.77, 17.80
third-party notice, for 10.19
two years, no proceeding had in 11.195
urgent appeals 20.23
urgent applications 11.11, 11.73
.. judicial review 19.61, 19.94
year, no proceeding had in 9.63, 11.199

TITLE
change of parties, on 11.37
injunction, for 14.87
pleading, of 9.04
Statement of Claim, of 9.09
writ, of 5.05

TOMLIN ORDER
12.09, 20.45

TORT
contributory negligence 14.74
exemplary damages 14.52
joint liability 10.30
jury trial of 14.05
limitation period 4.03-06
pleadings 9.79-81
service outside NI 6.16
writ action 5.03

TRADE UNION
3.18, 16.08
illness benefits negotiated by 14.63

TRANSFER BETWEEN DIVISIONS
1.21, 9.42
Chancery Division, to 18.62
Family Judge, to 3.10, 3.12

TRAVERSE
particulars of 9.23-24
pleading 9.87

TRESPASS
assault
.. damages for 14.61, 14.74
limitation period 4.06
pleadings 9.26, 9.81

TRIAL
14.00-48
affidavit evidence at 13.33
amendment at 11.17, 11.20
Chancery Division, in 14.24a
commencement of 14.23
date for 12.29
.. Commercial List 18.28
defamation action 18.24
early 11.65, 11.85, 12.29

evidence at 13.30
exhibits at 13.158
interpleader issue 10.33
judgment at 15.00
jury, by 14.09-10, 14.44
new, see NEW TRIAL
non-appearance at 14.18-20, 20.64
originating summons, of 18.12
pleadings, without 9.05
preparing for 13.00-11
readiness for 12.32
record of 14.01, 20.50
.. unauthorised 16.72
secrecy for lodgment at 11.160
separate see SEPARATE TRIAL
setting down for 12.26-28
third party 10.24
venue of 14.01

TRIBUNAL see INFERIOR TRIBUNAL

TRUST
breach of 18.65
.. damages for 14.96
.. limitation period 4.03
construction of 18.13, 18.54
damages on trust for relative, friend 14.55
declaration of 18.62
execution action 3.43, 17.53, 18.57, 18.62-68
proceedings concerning 18.62
.. compromise 12.12
.. costs 17.53
.. pleadings 9.82
.. representation of persons 3.38
.. service outside NI 6.16
representation of 3.40

TRUSTEE
bankruptcy, in 3.05, 11.42, 17.55
costs of 17.54-56, 20.08, 20.75
discovery against 11.130
enforcement against 16.11, 18.67
indemnity for 10.04
judgment against absent 14.44, 18.65
limitation period against 4.03
owner of land to be sold is 18.55
order to convey land 16.59
order to pay money 16.44
payment into court by 11.169
represents estate 3.40, 18.65
service outside NI 6.16
wilful default of 16.11

UBERIMAE FIDES
3.02, 11.17, 11.75

UNDERTAKING
appeal from 20.05
damages,by applicant for injunction 11.69
implied, for use of documents 11.117, 13.06, 13.50
injunction, in lieu of 11.72
next friend, by 3.09
party, by 16.63-64
solicitor, by 16.62

UNITED KINGDOM
civil jurisdiction and judgments 1.15
defined 1.10
legislation, interpretation of 1.10
.. service under 6.24

'UNLESS' ORDER
1.37, 11.192, 11.198

VACATION
1.06
interlocutory proceedings in 11.01
judicial review in criminal cause 19.94, 19.97
time limits during 1.31
trial in 14.01

VALUE ADDED TAX
accounts of 18.26
costs, on 17.100
judgment including 15.04

VARIATION see SETTING ASIDE

VERDICT
14.43-44
death after 11.40
inconsistent 20.57

VEXATIOUS, SCANDALOUS, FRIVOLOUS
affidavit, contents of 11.14
appeal 20.32
pleadings 11.178-
proceedings 11.178-
subpoena 13.07

VEXATIOUS LITIGANT
5.02

WAIVER
appearance constituting 7.07
civil contempt, of 16.65
delay, of 11.190
election, by 13.99
irregularity, of 1.28, 8.17
particulars, right to 9.93
privilege, of 11.117, 13.41, 13.43, 13.45, 13.49
right of appeal, of 20.39
service, of 6.10, 6.23, 6.27

WANT OF PROSECUTION
11.184-199
accounts, in taking of 18.25
appeal to Court of Appeal, in 20.27, 20.32
dismissal for 11.184
.. as interlocutory order 11.00
.. originating summons 18.12

WARD OF COURT
18.51
action by or against 3.07, 3.10
writ, statement on 5.05

'WASTED COSTS ORDER'
17.60, 17.62

WEDNESBURY UNREASONABLENESS
19.37, 19.41, 19.47, 19.48

WILL
burden of proving 13.20
construction of 18.10, 18.13, 18.54
declarations by maker 13.121
proof of 13.146, 18.48

WINDING UP see COMPANY

WITHDRAWAL
acceptance of lodgment, of 11.159
action, of 12.00-04
admission, of 9.96
appeal, of 20.34
appearance, of 7.11
case stated, of 18.07, 20.80
claim, of 12.00-
lodgment, of 11.151
summons, of 11.06

'WITHOUT PREJUDICE'
13.43

WITNESS
abroad 13.10
affidavit 11.14
anonymous 14.03
attacked by own counsel 13.63
committal motion, on 16.54
compellability of 13.35-36, 16.68
competence of 13.35
consultation with 13.35
contempt by 16.68
credibility of 13.71-76, 20.65
cross-examination of 13.65-
demeanour of 13.155
deposition 13.10
exclusion of 13.55
expenses of 13.06, 16.68, 17.104-105
expert 13.88, 18.29
failure to call 13.28, 13.116, 14.33
hostile 13.64
judge calling 13.83
police 2.07, 13.04
prisoner 13.09, 16.69
procuring attendance of 13.03-09
putting case to 13.68
recalling 13.54, 13.83
remains in court 13.82
screening of 14.03
statement in presence of 13.119
subpoena to 13.03
supplier of duty record hearsay 13.129
unavailable 13.126

WRIT
action commenced by 5.03
amendment of 11.16, 11.18, 11.24
concurrent 5.06
delay before issue of 11.186
departure, from 9.10
form and contents of 5.05-5.10
habeas corpus, of 19.101-105
interference with goods, for 18.33
interlocutory relief claimed with 11.01
joinder of causes 3.25
judgment follows 8.07
judicial review as if begun by 19.79
libel, for 18.18
originating summons as if begun by 18.12
probate 18.48
public rights claimed in 19.08
service of 6.00-08
.. outside NI 6.15-18
.. time limit for 6.07
striking out indorsement on 11.178
subpoena, of 13.03